Linux®
Administration
Handbook

SECOND EDITION

Evi Nemeth
Garth Snyder
Trent R. Hein

*with Lynda McGinley, Ben Whaley,
Adam Boggs, Jeffrey S. Haemer, Tobi Oetiker,
Fritz Zaucker, Scott Seidel, Bryan Buus,
Ned McClain, and David Schweikert*

PRENTICE
HALL

Upper Saddle River, NJ • Boston • Indianapolis • San Francisco
New York • Toronto • Montreal • London • Munich • Paris • Madrid
Capetown • Sydney • Tokyo • Singapore • Mexico City

Many of the designations used by manufacturers and sellers to distinguish their products are claimed as trademarks. Where those designations appear in this book, and the publisher was aware of a trademark claim, the designations have been printed with initial capital letters or in all capitals.

Red Hat Enterprise Linux and the Red Hat SHADOWMAN logo are registered trademarks of Red Hat Inc., and such trademarks are used with permission.

Ubuntu is a registered trademark of Canonical Limited, and is used with permission.

Fedora is a trademark of Red Hat Inc., and is used with permission.

Novell, the Novell logo, the N logo, and SUSE are registered trademarks of Novell Inc. in the United States and other countries.

The authors and publisher have taken care in the preparation of this book, but make no expressed or implied warranty of any kind and assume no responsibility for errors or omissions. No liability is assumed for incidental or consequential damages in connection with or arising out of the use of the information or programs contained herein.

The publisher offers excellent discounts on this book when ordered in quantity for bulk purchases or special sales, which may include custom covers and content particular to your business, training goals, marketing focus, and branding interests. For more information, please contact:

> U.S. Corporate and Government Sales
> (800) 382-3419
> corpsales@pearsontechgroup.com

For sales outside the United States, please contact:

> International Sales
> international@pearsoned.com

Visit us on the Web: www.prenhallprofessional.com

Library of Congress Cataloging-in-Publication Data

Nemeth, Evi.
    Linux administration handbook / Evi Nemeth, Garth Snyder, Trent R. Hein.—2nd ed.
        p. cm.
    Includes index.
    ISBN 0-13-148004-9 (pbk. : alk. paper)
    1. Linux. 2. Operating systems (Computers) I. Snyder, Garth. II. Hein, Trent R. III. Title.
    QA76.76.O63N448 2006
    005.4'32—dc22

                                                                                    2006030150

ISBN 0-13-148004-9
Text printed in the United States on recycled paper at Courier in Stoughton, Massachusetts.
First printing, October 2006

Contents

FOREWORD TO THE FIRST EDITION   xxxiii

PREFACE   xxxiv

ACKNOWLEDGMENTS   xxxvii

SECTION ONE: BASIC ADMINISTRATION

CHAPTER 1 WHERE TO START   3

Suggested background 4
Linux's relationship to UNIX 4
Linux in historical context. 5
Linux distributions. 6
    So what's the best distribution? 8
    Distribution-specific administration tools. 9
Notation and typographical conventions 9
    System-specific information. 10
Where to go for information. 11
    Organization of the man pages. 12
    man: read manual pages 13
    Other sources of Linux information 13
How to find and install software. 14

Essential tasks of the system administrator 16
    Adding, removing, and managing user accounts 16
    Adding and removing hardware.................................... 16
    Performing backups 17
    Installing and upgrading software 17
    Monitoring the system.. 17
    Troubleshooting 17
    Maintaining local documentation 17
    Vigilantly monitoring security 17
    Helping users... 18
System administration under duress................................... 18
    System Administration Personality Syndrome 18
Recommended reading 19
Exercises.. 20

CHAPTER 2   BOOTING AND SHUTTING DOWN   21

Bootstrapping 21
    Automatic and manual booting 22
    Steps in the boot process 22
    Kernel initialization 23
    Hardware configuration 23
    Kernel threads 23
    Operator intervention (manual boot only).......................... 24
    Execution of startup scripts...................................... 25
    Multiuser operation 25
Booting PCs 25
Using boot loaders: LILO and GRUB................................. 26
    GRUB: The GRand Unified Boot loader 26
    LILO: The traditional Linux boot loader........................... 28
    Kernel options.. 29
    Multibooting on PCs 30
    GRUB multiboot configuration 30
    LILO multiboot configuration 31
Booting single-user mode 31
    Single-user mode with GRUB.................................... 32
    Single-user mode with LILO 32
Working with startup scripts 32
    init and run levels.. 33
    Red Hat and Fedora startup scripts 36
    SUSE startup scripts... 38
    Debian and Ubuntu startup scripts 40

Rebooting and shutting down 40
    Turning off the power 41
    shutdown: the genteel way to halt the system 41
    halt: a simpler way to shut down 42
    reboot: quick and dirty restart 42
    telinit: change **init**'s run level 42
    poweroff: ask Linux to turn off the power 42
Exercises 43

CHAPTER 3 ROOTLY POWERS   **44**

Ownership of files and processes 44
The superuser 46
Choosing a root password 47
Becoming root 48
    su: substitute user identity 48
    sudo: a limited **su** 48
Other pseudo-users 51
    bin: legacy owner of system commands 51
    daemon: owner of unprivileged system software 51
    nobody: the generic NFS user 51
Exercises 52

CHAPTER 4 CONTROLLING PROCESSES   **53**

Components of a process 53
    PID: process ID number 54
    PPID: parent PID 54
    UID and EUID: real and effective user ID 54
    GID and EGID: real and effective group ID 55
    Niceness 55
    Control terminal 56
The life cycle of a process 56
Signals 57
kill and **killall**: send signals 60
Process states 60
nice and **renice**: influence scheduling priority 61
ps: monitor processes 62
top: monitor processes even better 65
The **/proc** filesystem 65
strace: trace signals and system calls 66
Runaway processes 67
Recommended reading 69
Exercises 69

CHAPTER 5   THE FILESYSTEM   70

Pathnames 72
Filesystem mounting and unmounting 73
The organization of the file tree 75
File types 76
    Regular files 78
    Directories 78
    Character and block device files 79
    Local domain sockets 80
    Named pipes 80
    Symbolic links 80
File attributes 81
    The permission bits 81
    The setuid and setgid bits 82
    The sticky bit 82
    Viewing file attributes 82
    chmod: change permissions 84
    chown: change ownership and group 86
    umask: assign default permissions 86
    Bonus flags 87
Access control lists 88
    ACL overview 88
    Default entries 91
Exercises 92

CHAPTER 6   ADDING NEW USERS   93

The **/etc/passwd** file 93
    Login name 94
    Encrypted password 96
    UID (user ID) number 96
    Default GID number 97
    GECOS field 98
    Home directory 98
    Login shell 98
The **/etc/shadow** file 99
The **/etc/group** file 101
Adding users 102
    Editing the **passwd** and **shadow** files 103
    Editing the **/etc/group** file 104
    Setting an initial password 104

Creating the user's home directory 105
Copying in the default startup files 105
Setting the user's mail home 106
Verifying the new login 106
Recording the user's status and contact information 107
Removing users 107
Disabling logins 108
Managing accounts 108
Exercises 110

CHAPTER 7 ADDING A DISK **111**

Disk interfaces 111
The PATA interface 112
The SATA interface 114
The SCSI interface 114
Which is better, SCSI or IDE? 118
Disk geometry 119
Linux filesystems 120
Ext2fs and ext3fs 120
ReiserFS 121
XFS and JFS 122
An overview of the disk installation procedure 122
Connecting the disk 122
Formatting the disk 123
Labeling and partitioning the disk 124
Creating filesystems within disk partitions 125
Mounting the filesystems 126
Setting up automatic mounting 127
Enabling swapping 129
hdparm: set IDE interface parameters 129
fsck: check and repair filesystems 131
Adding a disk: a step-by-step guide 133
Advanced disk management: RAID and LVM 138
Linux software RAID 139
Logical volume management 139
An example configuration with LVM and RAID 140
Dealing with a failed disk 144
Reallocating storage space 146
Mounting USB drives 147
Exercises 148

CHAPTER 8   PERIODIC PROCESSES   **150**

cron: schedule commands. 150
The format of crontab files 151
Crontab management. 153
Some common uses for **cron** 154
    Cleaning the filesystem 154
    Network distribution of configuration files 155
    Rotating log files 156
Other schedulers: **anacron** and **fcron**. 156
Exercises. 157

CHAPTER 9   BACKUPS   **158**

Motherhood and apple pie 159
    Perform all dumps from one machine. 159
    Label your media 159
    Pick a reasonable backup interval 159
    Choose filesystems carefully 160
    Make daily dumps fit on one piece of media 160
    Make filesystems smaller than your dump device. 161
    Keep media off-site. 161
    Protect your backups 161
    Limit activity during dumps 162
    Verify your media. 162
    Develop a media life cycle 163
    Design your data for backups 163
    Prepare for the worst 163
Backup devices and media. 163
    Optical media: CD-R/RW, DVD±R/RW, and DVD-RAM. 164
    Removable hard disks (USB and FireWire) 165
    Small tape drives: 8mm and DDS/DAT. 166
    DLT/S-DLT 166
    AIT and SAIT. 166
    VXA/VXA-X 167
    LTO. 167
    Jukeboxes, stackers, and tape libraries 167
    Hard disks 168
    Summary of media types 168
    What to buy 168
Setting up an incremental backup regime with **dump** 169
    Dumping filesystems 169
    Dump sequences. 171

Restoring from dumps with **restore** 173
    Restoring individual files. 173
    Restoring entire filesystems 175
Dumping and restoring for upgrades 176
Using other archiving programs. 177
    tar: package files 177
    cpio: archiving utility from ancient times 178
    dd: twiddle bits 178
Using multiple files on a single tape 178
Bacula 179
    The Bacula model 180
    Setting up Bacula 181
    Installing the database and Bacula daemons 181
    Configuring the Bacula daemons. 182
    bacula-dir.conf: director configuration. 183
    bacula-sd.conf: storage daemon configuration 187
    bconsole.conf: console configuration 188
    Installing and configuring the client file daemon 188
    Starting the Bacula daemons. 189
    Adding media to pools. 190
    Running a manual backup 190
    Running a restore job. 192
    Monitoring and debugging Bacula configurations 195
    Alternatives to Bacula 197
Commercial backup products 197
    ADSM/TSM 197
    Veritas 198
    Other alternatives 198
Recommended reading 198
Exercises. 198

CHAPTER 10   SYSLOG AND LOG FILES   **201**

Logging policies 201
    Throwing away log files. 201
    Rotating log files. 202
    Archiving log files. 204
Linux log files 204
    Special log files 206
    Kernel and boot-time logging. 206
logrotate: manage log files 208

Syslog: the system event logger..209
    Alternatives to syslog...209
    Syslog architecture..210
    Configuring **syslogd**..210
    Designing a logging scheme for your site.............................214
    Config file examples...214
    Sample syslog output...216
    Software that uses syslog..217
    Debugging syslog...217
    Using syslog from programs...218
Condensing log files to useful information...............................220
Exercises..222

CHAPTER 11   SOFTWARE AND CONFIGURATION MANAGEMENT   223

Basic Linux installation...223
    Netbooting PCs...224
    Setting up PXE for Linux...225
    Netbooting non-PCs...226
    Kickstart: the automated installer for Enterprise Linux and Fedora...226
    AutoYaST: SUSE's automated installation tool.........................230
    The Debian and Ubuntu installer......................................231
    Installing from a master system......................................232
Diskless clients...232
Package management...234
    Available package management systems................................235
    rpm: manage RPM packages...235
    dpkg: manage Debian-style packages...............................237
High-level package management systems....................................237
    Package repositories...239
    RHN: the Red Hat Network...240
    APT: the Advanced Package Tool.......................................241
    Configuring **apt-get**..242
    An example **/etc/apt/sources.list** file............................243
    Using proxies to make **apt-get** scale.............................244
    Setting up an internal APT server...................................244
    Automating **apt-get**...245
    yum: release management for RPM..................................246
Revision control...247
    Backup file creation...247
    Formal revision control systems.....................................248
    RCS: the Revision Control System.....................................249
    CVS: the Concurrent Versions System..................................251
    Subversion: CVS done right...253

Localization and configuration. 255
    Organizing your localization 256
    Testing 257
    Local compilation. 258
    Distributing localizations 259
    Resolving scheduling issues 260
Configuration management tools 260
    cfengine: computer immune system 260
    LCFG: a large-scale configuration system. 261
    The Arusha Project (ARK) 261
    Template Tree 2: **cfengine** helper 262
    DMTF/CIM: the Common Information Model 262
Sharing software over NFS 263
    Package namespaces 264
    Dependency management. 265
    Wrapper scripts 265
    Implementation tools. 266
Recommended software 266
Recommended reading 268
Exercises. 268

SECTION TWO: NETWORKING

CHAPTER 12 **TCP/IP NETWORKING**   **271**

TCP/IP and the Internet 272
    A brief history lesson 272
    How the Internet is managed today. 273
    Network standards and documentation 274
Networking road map 275
Packets and encapsulation 276
    The link layer. 277
    Packet addressing. 279
    Ports 281
    Address types 281
IP addresses: the gory details 282
    IP address classes 282
    Subnetting and netmasks 282
    The IP address crisis. 285
    CIDR: Classless Inter-Domain Routing 287
    Address allocation 288
    Private addresses and NAT 289
    IPv6 addressing. 291

Routing 293
    Routing tables 294
    ICMP redirects 295
ARP: the address resolution protocol 296
Addition of a machine to a network 297
    Hostname and IP address assignment 298
    ifconfig: configure network interfaces 299
    mii-tool: configure autonegotiation and other media-specific options 302
    route: configure static routes 303
    Default routes 305
    DNS configuration 306
    The Linux networking stack 307
Distribution-specific network configuration 307
    Network configuration for Red Hat and Fedora 308
    Network configuration for SUSE 309
    Network configuration for Debian and Ubuntu 310
DHCP: the Dynamic Host Configuration Protocol 311
    DHCP software 312
    How DHCP works 312
    ISC's DHCP server 313
Dynamic reconfiguration and tuning 314
Security issues 316
    IP forwarding 316
    ICMP redirects 317
    Source routing 317
    Broadcast pings and other forms of directed broadcast 317
    IP spoofing 317
    Host-based firewalls 318
    Virtual private networks 318
    Security-related kernel variables 319
Linux NAT 319
PPP: the Point-to-Point Protocol 320
    Addressing PPP performance issues 321
    Connecting to a network with PPP 321
    Making your host speak PPP 321
    Controlling PPP links 321
    Assigning an address 322
    Routing 322
    Ensuring security 323
    Using chat scripts 323
    Configuring Linux PPP 323
Linux networking quirks 330
Recommended reading 331
Exercises 332

CHAPTER 13 ROUTING   **334**

Packet forwarding: a closer look 335
Routing daemons and routing protocols 337
     Distance-vector protocols 338
     Link-state protocols 339
     Cost metrics 340
     Interior and exterior protocols 340
Protocols on parade 341
     RIP: Routing Information Protocol 341
     RIP-2: Routing Information Protocol, version 2 341
     OSPF: Open Shortest Path First 342
     IGRP and EIGRP: Interior Gateway Routing Protocol 342
     IS-IS: the ISO "standard" 343
     MOSPF, DVMRP, and PIM: multicast routing protocols 343
     Router Discovery Protocol 343
routed: RIP yourself a new hole 343
gated: gone to the dark side 344
Routing strategy selection criteria 344
Cisco routers 346
Recommended reading 348
Exercises 349

CHAPTER 14 NETWORK HARDWARE   **350**

LAN, WAN, or MAN? 351
Ethernet: the common LAN 351
     How Ethernet works 351
     Ethernet topology 352
     Unshielded twisted pair 353
     Connecting and expanding Ethernets 355
Wireless: nomad's LAN 359
     Wireless security 360
     Wireless switches 360
FDDI: the disappointing, expensive, and outdated LAN 361
ATM: the promised (but sorely defeated) LAN 362
Frame relay: the sacrificial WAN 363
ISDN: the indigenous WAN 364
DSL and cable modems: the people's WAN 364
Where is the network going? 365
Network testing and debugging 366
Building wiring 366
     UTP cabling options 366
     Connections to offices 367
     Wiring standards 367

Network design issues 368
    Network architecture vs. building architecture 368
    Existing networks 369
    Expansion. 369
    Congestion. 369
    Maintenance and documentation 370
Management issues. 370
Recommended vendors 371
    Cables and connectors 371
    Test equipment 371
    Routers/switches. 372
Recommended reading 372
Exercises 372

CHAPTER 15   DNS: THE DOMAIN NAME SYSTEM   **373**

DNS for the impatient: adding a new machine. 374
The history of DNS 375
    BIND implementations 376
    Other implementations of DNS 376
Who needs DNS?. 377
The DNS namespace. 378
    Masters of their domains 381
    Selecting a domain name 382
    Domain bloat. 382
    Registering a second-level domain name 383
    Creating your own subdomains 383
How DNS works 383
    Delegation 383
    Caching and efficiency. 384
    The extended DNS protocol 386
What's new in DNS. 386
The DNS database. 389
    Resource records. 389
    The SOA record. 392
    NS records 395
    A records 396
    PTR records. 396
    MX records 397
    CNAME records 399
    The CNAME hack. 400
    LOC records. 401
    SRV records 402
    TXT records. 403
    IPv6 resource records. 404

IPv6 forward records 404
IPv6 reverse records. 405
Security-related records 405
Commands in zone files 405
Glue records: links between zones 407
The BIND software 409
Versions of BIND 410
Finding out what version you have 410
Components of BIND 411
named: the BIND name server. 412
Authoritative and caching-only servers 412
Recursive and nonrecursive servers 413
The resolver library 414
Shell interfaces to DNS. 415
Designing your DNS environment. 415
Namespace management. 415
Authoritative servers 416
Caching servers. 417
Security. 417
Summing up 418
A taxonomy of DNS/BIND chores 418
BIND client issues. 418
Resolver configuration. 418
Resolver testing. 420
Impact on the rest of the system. 420
BIND server configuration 420
Hardware requirements. 421
Configuration files 421
The include statement. 423
The options statement. 423
The acl statement 429
The key statement 430
The trusted-keys statement. 430
The server statement 431
The masters statement 432
The logging statement. 432
The zone statement 432
The controls statement. 436
Split DNS and the view statement 438
BIND configuration examples 439
The localhost zone 439
A small security company. 441
The Internet Systems Consortium, isc.org. 444
Starting **named** 446

Updating zone files 447
  Zone transfers 447
  Dynamic updates 448
Security issues 451
  Access control lists revisited 451
  Confining **named** 453
  Secure server-to-server communication with TSIG and TKEY 453
  DNSSEC 456
  Negative answers 463
  Microsoft and DNS 464
Testing and debugging 466
  Logging 466
  Sample logging configuration 470
  Debug levels 471
  Debugging with **rndc** 471
  BIND statistics 473
  Debugging with **dig** 473
  Lame delegations 475
  doc: domain obscenity control 476
  Other DNS sanity checking tools 478
  Performance issues 478
Distribution specifics 478
Recommended reading 481
  Mailing lists and newsgroups 481
  Books and other documentation 481
  On-line resources 482
  The RFCs 482
Exercises 482

CHAPTER 16   THE NETWORK FILE SYSTEM   484

General information about NFS 484
  NFS protocol versions 484
  Choice of transport 485
  File locking 486
  Disk quotas 486
  Cookies and stateless mounting 486
  Naming conventions for shared filesystems 487
  Security and NFS 487
  Root access and the nobody account 488

Server-side NFS... 489
    The **exports** file... 490
    nfsd: serve files 492
Client-side NFS 492
    Mounting remote filesystems at boot time............................ 495
    Restricting exports to insecure ports................................... 495
nfsstat: dump NFS statistics... 495
Dedicated NFS file servers 496
Automatic mounting 497
    automount: mount filesystems on demand 497
    The master file.. 498
    Map files... 499
    Executable maps.. 499
Recommended reading 500
Exercises... 501

CHAPTER 17   SHARING SYSTEM FILES   **502**

What to share 503
nscd: cache the results of lookups 504
Copying files around 505
    rdist: push files 505
    rsync: transfer files more securely................................... 508
    Pulling files 510
NIS: the Network Information Service 511
    Understanding how NIS works 512
    Weighing advantages and disadvantages of NIS...................... 514
    Prioritizing sources of administrative information 515
    Using netgroups 517
    Setting up an NIS domain 517
    Setting access control options in **/etc/ypserv.conf**................ 519
    Configuring NIS clients 519
    NIS details by distribution 520
LDAP: the Lightweight Directory Access Protocol 520
    The structure of LDAP data 521
    The point of LDAP 522
    LDAP documentation and specifications............................. 523
    OpenLDAP: LDAP for Linux 523
    NIS replacement by LDAP 525
    LDAP and security 526
Recommended reading 526
Exercises... 527

CHAPTER 18 ELECTRONIC MAIL   **528**

Mail systems. 530
    User agents. 531
    Transport agents. 532
    Delivery agents 532
    Message stores. 533
    Access agents. 533
    Mail submission agents 533
The anatomy of a mail message 534
    Mail addressing. 535
    Mail header interpretation 535
Mail philosophy. 539
    Using mail servers. 540
    Using mail homes 542
    Using IMAP or POP 542
Mail aliases. 544
    Getting mailing lists from files 546
    Mailing to files. 547
    Mailing to programs. 547
    Aliasing by example 548
    Forwarding mail 549
    The hashed alias database 551
Mailing lists and list wrangling software. 551
    Software packages for maintaining mailing lists .551
    LDAP: the Lightweight Directory Access Protocol 555
sendmail: ringmaster of the electronic mail circus. 557
    Versions of **sendmail**. 557
    sendmail installation from sendmail.org. 559
    sendmail installation on Debian and Ubuntu systems 561
    The switch file 562
    Modes of operation. 562
    The mail queue 563
sendmail configuration. 565
    Using the **m4** preprocessor 566
    The **sendmail** configuration pieces. 567
    Building a configuration file from a sample **.mc** file 568
    Changing the **sendmail** configuration 569
Basic **sendmail** configuration primitives 570
    The VERSIONID macro 570
    The OSTYPE macro 570
    The DOMAIN macro 572
    The MAILER macro 573

Fancier **sendmail** configuration primitives 574
    The FEATURE macro 574
    The use_cw_file feature 574
    The redirect feature 575
    The always_add_domain feature 575
    The nocanonify feature 576
    Tables and databases 576
    The mailertable feature 578
    The genericstable feature 579
    The virtusertable feature 579
    The ldap_routing feature 580
    Masquerading and the MASQUERADE_AS macro 581
    The MAIL_HUB and SMART_HOST macros 583
    Masquerading and routing 583
    The nullclient feature 584
    The local_lmtp and smrsh features 585
    The local_procmail feature 585
    The LOCAL_* macros 586
    Configuration options 586
Spam-related features in **sendmail** 588
    Relaying 589
    The access database 591
    User or site blacklisting 594
    Header checking 595
    Rate and connection limits 596
    Slamming 597
    Miltering: mail filtering 597
    Spam handling 598
    SpamAssassin 598
    SPF and Sender ID 599
Configuration file case study 599
    Client machines at sendmail.com 599
    Master machine at sendmail.com 600
Security and **sendmail** 603
    Ownerships 603
    Permissions 604
    Safer mail to files and programs 605
    Privacy options 606
    Running a **chroot**ed **sendmail** (for the truly paranoid) 607
    Denial of service attacks 608
    Forgeries 608
    Message privacy 610
    SASL: the Simple Authentication and Security Layer 610

sendmail performance 611
   Delivery modes 611
   Queue groups and envelope splitting 611
   Queue runners. 613
   Load average controls 613
   Undeliverable messages in the queue 613
   Kernel tuning. 614
sendmail statistics, testing, and debugging 615
   Testing and debugging. 616
   Verbose delivery 617
   Talking in SMTP 618
   Queue monitoring 619
   Logging. 619
The Exim Mail System 621
   History 621
   Exim on Linux. 621
   Exim configuration. 622
   Exim/**sendmail** similarities. 622
Postfix. 623
   Postfix architecture. 623
   Receiving mail. 624
   The queue manager 624
   Sending mail 625
   Security. 625
   Postfix commands and documentation 625
   Configuring Postfix 626
   What to put in **main.cf** 626
   Basic settings 626
   Using **postconf**. 627
   Lookup tables 627
   Local delivery. 629
   Virtual domains 630
   Virtual alias domains 630
   Virtual mailbox domains. 631
   Access control 632
   Access tables 633
   Authentication of clients 634
   Fighting spam and viruses. 634
   Black hole lists. 635
   SpamAssassin and **procmail** 636
   Policy daemons 636
   Content filtering 636
   Debugging 637
   Looking at the queue 638

Soft-bouncing 638
Testing access control 638
Recommended reading 639
Exercises. 640

CHAPTER 19   NETWORK MANAGEMENT AND DEBUGGING   643

Network troubleshooting 644
ping: check to see if a host is alive 645
traceroute: trace IP packets 647
netstat: get network statistics. 649
Inspecting interface configuration information 649
Monitoring the status of network connections 651
Identifying listening network services. 652
Examining the routing table 652
Viewing operational statistics for network protocols 653
sar: inspect live interface activity. 654
Packet sniffers 655
tcpdump: king of sniffers 656
Wireshark: visual sniffer 657
Network management protocols 657
SNMP: the Simple Network Management Protocol 659
SNMP organization 659
SNMP protocol operations 660
RMON: remote monitoring MIB 661
The NET-SMNP agent 661
Network management applications. 662
The NET-SNMP tools 663
SNMP data collection and graphing 664
Nagios: event-based SNMP and service monitoring. 665
Commercial management platforms. 666
Recommended reading 667
Exercises. 668

CHAPTER 20   SECURITY   669

Is Linux secure?. 670
How security is compromised 671
Social engineering. 671
Software vulnerabilities. 672
Configuration errors 673
Certifications and standards. 673
Certifications. 674
Standards 675

Security tips and philosophy...676
    Packet filtering 677
    Unnecessary services 677
    Software patches 677
    Backups 677
    Passwords...677
    Vigilance..677
    General philosophy..678
Security problems in **/etc/passwd** and **/etc/shadow** 678
    Password checking and selection....................................679
    Password aging 680
    Group logins and shared logins 680
    User shells 680
    Rootly entries...681
    PAM: cooking spray or authentication wonder? 681
POSIX capabilities...683
Setuid programs 683
Important file permissions 684
Miscellaneous security issues 685
    Remote event logging..685
    Secure terminals 685
    /etc/hosts.equiv and **~/.rhosts** 685
    Security and NIS 685
    Security and NFS...686
    Security and **sendmail**...686
    Security and backups 686
    Viruses and worms...686
    Trojan horses..687
    Rootkits 688
Security power tools 688
    Nmap: scan network ports 688
    Nessus: next generation network scanner...........................690
    John the Ripper: find insecure passwords...........................690
    hosts_access: host access control 691
    Samhain: host-based intrusion detection 692
    Security-Enhanced Linux (SELinux)..................................693
Cryptographic security tools..694
    Kerberos: a unified approach to network security...................695
    PGP: Pretty Good Privacy 696
    SSH: the secure shell..697
    One-time passwords..698
    Stunnel 699
Firewalls 701
    Packet-filtering firewalls 701
    How services are filtered 702

Service proxy firewalls 703
Stateful inspection firewalls 703
Firewalls: how safe are they? 704
Linux firewall features: IP tables 704
Virtual private networks (VPNs) 708
IPsec tunnels 709
All I need is a VPN, right? 710
Hardened Linux distributions 710
What to do when your site has been attacked 710
Sources of security information 712
CERT: a registered service mark of Carnegie Mellon University 712
SecurityFocus.com and the BugTraq mailing list 713
Crypto-Gram newsletter 713
SANS: the System Administration, Networking, and Security Institute 713
Distribution-specific security resources 713
Other mailing lists and web sites 714
Recommended reading 715
Exercises 716

CHAPTER 21 WEB HOSTING AND INTERNET SERVERS   719

Web hosting basics 720
Uniform resource locators 720
How HTTP works 720
Content generation on the fly 722
Load balancing 722
HTTP server installation 724
Choosing a server 724
Installing Apache 724
Configuring Apache 726
Running Apache 726
Analyzing log files 727
Optimizing for high-performance hosting of static content 727
Virtual interfaces 727
Using name-based virtual hosts 728
Configuring virtual interfaces 728
Telling Apache about virtual interfaces 729
The Secure Sockets Layer (SSL) 730
Generating a certificate signing request 731
Configuring Apache to use SSL 732
Caching and proxy servers 733
The Squid cache and proxy server 733
Setting up Squid 734
Anonymous FTP server setup 734
Exercises 736

SECTION THREE: BUNCH O' STUFF

CHAPTER 22   THE X WINDOW SYSTEM   **741**

The X display manager. 743
Running an X application 744
    The DISPLAY environment variable 744
    Client authentication 745
    X connection forwarding with SSH 747
X server configuration 748
    Device sections 750
    Monitor sections. 750
    Screen sections 751
    InputDevice sections. 752
    ServerLayout sections. 753
Troubleshooting and debugging 754
    Special keyboard combinations for X 754
    When good X servers go bad. 755
A brief note on desktop environments 757
    KDE. 758
    GNOME 758
    Which is better, GNOME or KDE? 759
Recommended Reading. 759
Exercises 759

CHAPTER 23   PRINTING   **761**

Printers are complicated 762
Printer languages 763
    PostScript. 763
    PCL 763
    PDF 764
    XHTML 764
    PJL. 765
    Printer drivers and their handling of PDLs. 765
CUPS architecture. 767
    Document printing. 767
    Print queue viewing and manipulation 767
    Multiple printers. 768
    Printer instances 768
    Network printing 768
    The CUPS underlying protocol: HTTP 769
    PPD files 770
    Filters 771

CUPS server administration 772
 Network print server setup 773
 Printer autoconfiguration 774
 Network printer configuration....................................... 774
 Printer configuration examples 775
 Printer class setup.. 775
 Service shutoff... 776
 Other configuration tasks 777
 Paper sizes 777
 Compatibility commands 778
 Common printing software... 779
 CUPS documentation 780
Troubleshooting tips 780
 CUPS logging.. 781
 Problems with direct printing....................................... 781
 Network printing problems 781
 Distribution-specific problems 782
Printer practicalities.. 782
 Printer selection 782
 GDI printers 783
 Double-sided printing 783
 Other printer accessories... 783
 Serial and parallel printers 784
 Network printers 784
Other printer advice.. 784
 Use banner pages only if you have to 784
 Provide recycling bins 785
 Use previewers 785
 Buy cheap printers 785
 Keep extra toner cartridges on hand 786
 Pay attention to the cost per page 786
 Consider printer accounting... 787
 Secure your printers.. 787
Printing under KDE 788
 kprinter: printing documents 789
 Konqueror and printing 789
Recommended reading 790
Exercises.. 790

CHAPTER 24   MAINTENANCE AND ENVIRONMENT   791

Hardware maintenance basics 791
Maintenance contracts.. 792
 On-site maintenance 792
 Board swap maintenance 792
 Warranties.. 793

Electronics-handling lore 793
    Static electricity 793
    Reseating boards 794
Monitors 794
Memory modules 794
Preventive maintenance 795
Environment 796
    Temperature 796
    Humidity 796
    Office cooling 796
    Machine room cooling 797
    Temperature monitoring 798
Power 798
Racks 799
Data center standards 800
Tools 800
Recommended reading 800
Exercises 802

CHAPTER 25   PERFORMANCE ANALYSIS   **803**

What you can do to improve performance 804
Factors that affect performance 806
System performance checkup 807
    Analyzing CPU usage 807
    How Linux manages memory 809
    Analyzing memory usage 811
    Analyzing disk I/O 813
    Choosing an I/O scheduler 815
    sar: Collect and report statistics over time 816
    oprofile: Comprehensive profiler 817
Help! My system just got really slow! 817
Recommended reading 819
Exercises 819

CHAPTER 26   COOPERATING WITH WINDOWS   **821**

Logging in to a Linux system from Windows 821
Accessing remote desktops 822
    Running an X server on a Windows computer 823
    VNC: Virtual Network Computing 824
    Windows RDP: Remote Desktop Protocol 824
Running Windows and Windows-like applications 825
    Dual booting, or why you shouldn't 826
    The OpenOffice.org alternative 826

Using command-line tools with Windows 826
Windows compliance with email and web standards 827
Sharing files with Samba and CIFS 828
    Samba: CIFS server for UNIX 828
    Samba installation 829
    Filename encoding 830
    Network Neighborhood browsing 831
    User authentication 832
    Basic file sharing 833
    Group shares 833
    Transparent redirection with MS DFS 834
    smbclient: a simple CIFS client 835
    The smbfs filesystem 835
Sharing printers with Samba 836
    Installing a printer driver from Windows 838
    Installing a printer driver from the command line 839
Debugging Samba 840
Recommended reading 841
Exercises 842

CHAPTER 27 SERIAL DEVICES   843

The RS-232C standard 844
Alternative connectors 847
    The mini DIN-8 variant 847
    The DB-9 variant 848
    The RJ-45 variant 849
    The Yost standard for RJ-45 wiring 850
Hard and soft carrier 852
Hardware flow control 852
Cable length 853
Serial device files 853
setserial: set serial port parameters 854
Software configuration for serial devices 855
Configuration of hardwired terminals 855
    The login process 855
    The **/etc/inittab** file 856
    Terminal support: the **termcap** and **terminfo** databases 858
Special characters and the terminal driver 859
stty: set terminal options 860
tset: set options automatically 861
Terminal unwedging 862
Modems 862
    Modulation, error correction, and data compression protocols 863
    minicom: dial out 864
    Bidirectional modems 864

Debugging a serial line 864
Other common I/O ports 865
    USB: the Universal Serial Bus 865
Exercises 866

CHAPTER 28 DRIVERS AND THE KERNEL   868

Kernel adaptation 869
Drivers and device files 870
    Device files and device numbers. 870
    Creating device files 871
    sysfs: a window into the souls of devices 872
    Naming conventions for devices 872
Why and how to configure the kernel 873
Tuning Linux kernel parameters 874
Building a Linux kernel 876
    If it ain't broke, don't fix it 876
    Configuring kernel options. 876
    Building the kernel binary. 878
Adding a Linux device driver 878
    Device awareness 880
Loadable kernel modules. 880
Hot-plugging 882
Setting bootstrap options. 883
Recommended reading 884
Exercises 884

CHAPTER 29 DAEMONS   885

init: the primordial process. 886
cron and atd: schedule commands 887
xinetd and inetd: manage daemons 887
    Configuring xinetd. 888
    Configuring inetd. 890
    The services file 892
    portmap: map RPC services to TCP and UDP ports 893
Kernel daemons. 893
    klogd: read kernel messages 894
Printing daemons 894
    cupsd: scheduler for the Common UNIX Printing System 894
    lpd: manage printing 894
File service daemons. 895
    rpc.nfsd: serve files 895
    rpc.mountd: respond to mount requests. 895

amd and **automount**: mount filesystems on demand 895

rpc.lockd and **rpc.statd**: manage NFS locks 895

rpciod: cache NFS blocks 896

rpc.rquotad: serve remote quotas 896

smbd: provide file and printing service to Windows clients 896

nmbd: NetBIOS name server 896

Administrative database daemons 896

ypbind: locate NIS servers 896

ypserv: NIS server 896

rpc.ypxfrd: transfer NIS databases 896

lwresd: lightweight resolver library server 897

nscd: name service cache daemon 897

Electronic mail daemons 897

sendmail: transport electronic mail 897

smtpd: Simple Mail Transport Protocol daemon 897

popd: basic mailbox server 897

imapd: deluxe mailbox server 897

Remote login and command execution daemons 898

sshd: secure remote login server 898

in.rlogind: obsolete remote login server 898

in.telnetd: yet another remote login server 898

in.rshd: remote command execution server 898

Booting and configuration daemons 898

dhcpd: dynamic address assignment 899

in.tftpd: trivial file transfer server 899

rpc.bootparamd: advanced diskless life support 899

hald: hardware abstraction layer (HAL) daemon 899

udevd: serialize device connection notices 899

Other network daemons 900

talkd: network chat service 900

snmpd: provide remote network management service 900

ftpd: file transfer server 900

rsyncd: synchronize files among multiple hosts 900

routed: maintain routing tables 900

gated: maintain complicated routing tables 901

named: DNS server 901

syslogd: process log messages 901

in.fingerd: look up users 901

httpd: World Wide Web server 901

ntpd: time synchronization daemon 902

Exercises 903

CHAPTER 30   MANAGEMENT, POLICY, AND POLITICS   **904**

Make everyone happy. 904
Components of a functional IT organization 906
The role of management 907
    Leadership 907
    Hiring, firing, and personnel management 908
    Assigning and tracking tasks. 911
    Managing upper management 913
    Conflict resolution 913
The role of administration. 915
    Sales. 915
    Purchasing 916
    Accounting. 917
    Personnel 917
    Marketing. 918
    Miscellaneous administrative chores. 919
The role of development 919
    Architectural principles. 920
    Anatomy of a management system 922
    The system administrator's tool box 922
    Software engineering principles 923
The role of operations 924
    Aim for minimal downtime 925
    Document dependencies 925
    Repurpose or eliminate older hardware 926
The work of support 927
    Availability. 927
    Scope of service 927
    Skill sets 929
    Time management 930
Documentation 930
    Standardized documentation 931
    Hardware labeling. 933
    User documentation. 934
Request-tracking and trouble-reporting systems 934
    Common functions of trouble ticket systems. 935
    User acceptance of ticketing systems. 935
    Ticketing systems 936
    Ticket dispatching 937
Disaster recovery. 938
    Backups and off-line information 939
    Staffing your disaster 939
    Power and HVAC 940
    Network redundancy 941

Security incidents 941
Second-hand stories from the World Trade Center 942
Written policy 943
Security policies 945
User policy agreements 946
Sysadmin policy agreements. 948
Legal Issues 949
Encryption. 949
Copyright. 950
Privacy 951
Click-through EULAs. 953
Policy enforcement. 953
Control = liability 954
Software licenses. 955
Regulatory compliance 956
Software patents 957
Standards 958
LSB: the Linux Standard Base. 959
POSIX 959
ITIL: the Information Technology Interface Library 960
COBIT: Control Objectives for Information and related Technology 960
Linux culture 961
Mainstream Linux 962
Organizations, conferences, and other resources 964
Conferences and trade shows 965
LPI: the Linux Professional Institute. 967
Mailing lists and web resources 967
Sysadmin surveys 968
Recommended Reading. 968
Infrastructure 968
Management 969
Policy and security 969
Legal issues, patents, and privacy 969
General industry news 970
Exercises. 970

INDEX   973
ABOUT THE CONTRIBUTORS   999
ABOUT THE AUTHORS   1001

Foreword to the First Edition

I was quite excited to preview this Linux-only edition of the *UNIX® System Adminis-tration Handbook*. The third edition of *USAH* included coverage of Red Hat Linux, but it was only one of four very different variants of UNIX. This version of the book covers several major Linux distributions and omits most of the material that's not relevant to Linux. I was curious to see how much of a difference it would make.

A lot, it turns out. Linux distributions draw from a common pool of open-source software, so they're far more similar to one another than are other versions of UNIX. As a result, the text seems to have become considerably more specific. Instead of suggesting various ways your system *might* behave, the authors can now tell you ex-actly how it *does* behave.

At the same time, it's clear that all the richness and variety of UNIX software are still represented here. Just about all of the world's popular software runs on Linux these days, and Linux sites are finding themselves faced with fewer and fewer compro-mises. As big-iron vendors like IBM, Oracle, and Silicon Graphics embrace Linux, it is rapidly becoming the universal standard to which other versions of UNIX are compared (and not always favorably!).

As this book shows, Linux systems are just as functional, secure, and reliable as their proprietary counterparts. Thanks to the ongoing efforts of its thousands of develop-ers, Linux is more ready than ever for deployment at the frontlines of the real world. The authors of this book know that terrain well, and I am happy to leave you in their most capable hands. Enjoy!

Linus Torvalds
April 2002

Preface

When we wrote the first edition of this book (about five years ago), Linux was just beginning to prove itself in the corporate world. We hoped that *Linux Administration Handbook* would help spread the news that Linux was a first-tier operating system capable of matching off against offerings from Sun, HP, and IBM.

Now Linux *is* IBM. For anyone awaiting an unambiguous signal that the Linux waters were safe for corporate swimmers, IBM's 2004 announcement of Linux support across its entire server line must have been quite comforting. No one was ever fired for buying IBM; these days, Linux in general is an equally safe proposition.[1]

We set out to write a book that would be the professional Linux system administrator's best friend. Where appropriate, we've adapted the proven concepts and materials from our popular book, *UNIX System Administration Handbook*. We've added a truckload of Linux-specific material and updated the rest, but much of the coverage remains similar. We hope you agree that the result is a high-quality guide to Linux administration that benefits from its experience in a past life.

None of the other books on Linux system administration supply the breadth and depth of material necessary to effectively use Linux in real-world business environments. Here are the features that distinguish our book:

- We take a practical approach. Our purpose is not to restate the contents of your manuals but rather to summarize our collective experience in system administration. This book contains numerous war stories and a wealth of pragmatic advice.

---

1. At least on servers. Today's battleground is the desktop, a domain over which Microsoft Windows still maintains a near-lock. The outcome of that struggle remains difficult to predict. As of this writing, Windows still provides a more polished user interface. But it's hard to argue with "free."

- This is not a book about how to run Linux at home, in your garage, or on your PDA. We describe the use of Linux in production environments such as businesses, government offices, and universities.

- We cover Linux networking in detail. It is the most difficult aspect of system administration and the area in which we think we can be of most help.

- We do not oversimplify the material. Our examples reflect true-life situations with all their warts and unsightly complications. In most cases, the examples have been taken directly from production systems.

- We cover five major Linux distributions.

OUR EXAMPLE DISTRIBUTIONS

Like so many operating systems, Linux has grown and branched in several different directions. Although development of the kernel has remained surprisingly centralized, packaging and distribution of complete Linux operating systems is overseen by a variety of groups, each with its own agenda.

We cover five Linux distributions in detail:

- Red Hat® Enterprise Linux® 4.3 ES
- Fedora™ Core 5
- SUSE® Linux Enterprise 10.2
- Debian® GNU/Linux 3.2 "Etch" (testing release of 9/06)
- Ubuntu® 6.06 "Dapper Drake"

We chose these distributions because they are among the most popular and because they represent the Linux community as a whole. However, much of the material in this book applies to other mainstream distributions as well.

We provide detailed information about each of these example distributions for every topic that we discuss. Comments specific to a particular operating system are marked with the distribution's logo.

THE ORGANIZATION OF THIS BOOK

This book is divided into three large chunks: Basic Administration, Networking, and Bunch o' Stuff.

Basic Administration presents a broad overview of Linux from a system administrator's perspective. The chapters in this section cover most of the facts and techniques needed to run a stand-alone Linux system.

The Networking section describes the protocols used on Linux systems and the techniques used to set up, extend, and maintain networks. High-level network software is also covered here. Among the featured topics are the Domain Name System, the Network File System, routing, **sendmail**, and network management.

Bunch o' Stuff includes a variety of supplemental information. Some chapters discuss optional software packages such as the Linux printing system. Others give advice on topics ranging from hardware maintenance to the politics of running a Linux installation.

Each chapter is followed by a set of practice exercises. Items are marked with our estimate of the effort required to complete them, where "effort" is an indicator of both the difficulty of the task and the time required.

There are four levels:

no stars	Easy, should be straightforward
★	Harder or longer, may require lab work
★★	Hardest or longest, requires lab work and digging
★★★★★	Semester-long projects (only in a few chapters)

Some of the exercises require root or **sudo** access to the system; others require the permission of the local sysadmin group. Both requirements are mentioned in the text of the exercise.

OUR CONTRIBUTORS

We're delighted that Adam Boggs, Bryan Buus, and Ned McClain were able to join us once again as contributing authors. With this edition, we also welcome Ben Whaley, Tobi Oetiker, Fritz Zaucker, Jeffrey S. Haemer, David Schweikert, and Scott Seidel as contributors and friends. Their deep knowledge of a variety of areas has greatly enriched the content of this book. Above all, we thank and acknowledge Lynda McGinley, who in addition to taking ownership of a substantial amount of text also worked tirelessly to organize and facilitate our contributors' work.

CONTACT INFORMATION

Please send suggestions, comments, and bug reports to linux@book.admin.com. We answer most mail, but please be patient; it is sometimes a few days before one of us is able to respond. Because of the volume of email that this alias receives, we regret that we are unable to answer technical questions. To get a copy of our current bug list and other late-breaking information, visit our web site, www.admin.com.

We hope you enjoy this book, and we wish you the best of luck with your adventures in system administration!

Evi Nemeth
Garth Snyder
Trent R. Hein

October 2006

Acknowledgments

Many folks have helped with this book in one way or another, assisting with everything from technical reviews or suggested exercises to overall moral support. These people deserve special thanks for hanging in there with us:

Bo Connell	Jon Corbet	Jim Lane
Sam Leffler	Cricket Liu	Derek Martin
Laszlo Nemeth	Eric Robinson	Sam Stoller
Paul Vixie	Aaron Weber	Greg Woods

Our editors at Prentice Hall, Catherine Nolan and Mary Franz, deserve not only our thanks but also an award for successfully dealing with flaky authors and a supporting cast that sometimes seemed to run to thousands of contributors.

Mary Lou Nohr once again did an exceptional job as copy editor. She is a car crushing plant and botanical garden all rolled into one. We'd like to say that we'll gladly work with her again in the future, but future tense is not permitted.

Mark G. Sobell's thoughtful and patient indexing work paid off in spades. We're very happy with the result, and the help is much appreciated.

Finally, Evi thanks and apologizes to the myriad beachside bars and cafes of the Caribbean whose free wireless connections she hijacked by anchoring her boat at the point of maximum signal strength. As she sat oblivious to the paradise around her and wrestled with book chapters, she swore this would be her last edition. But who's she kidding?

SECTION ONE

BASIC ADMINISTRATION

1 *Where to Start*

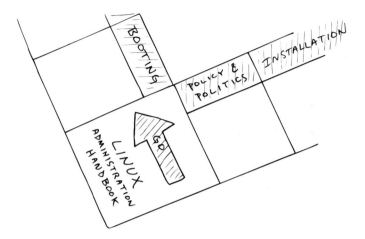

We set out to write a book that could be a system administrator's trusty companion, affording the practical advice and basic system administration theory that you can't get from reading manual pages. As a result, this book is designed to complement—not replace—the existing body of Linux documentation.

This book helps you in five ways:

- It reviews the major administrative systems, identifying the different pieces of each and explaining how they work together.

- It introduces general administrative techniques that we have found, through experience, to be efficient and beneficial.

- It helps you choose solutions that continue to work well as your site grows in size and complexity.

- It helps you sort good ideas from bad and educates you about assorted atrocities of taste committed by distributors.

- It summarizes common procedures so that you don't have to dig through the excessive detail of the manuals to accomplish simple tasks.

It's impossible to perform these functions with perfect objectivity, but we think we've made our biases fairly clear throughout the text. One of the interesting things about system administration is that reasonable people can have dramatically different notions of what constitute the most appropriate policies and procedures. We offer our subjective opinions to you as raw data. You'll have to decide for yourself how much to accept and to what extent our comments apply to your environment.

1.1 SUGGESTED BACKGROUND

We assume in this book that you have a certain amount of Linux or UNIX experience. In particular, you should have a general concept of how Linux looks and feels from the user's perspective before jumping into administration. Several good books can get you up to speed; see the reading list on page 19.

You perform most administrative tasks by editing configuration files and writing scripts, so you must be familiar with a text editor. To the dismay of many, using Microsoft Word as one's only text editor is a significant impediment to effective system administration.

We strongly recommend that you learn **vi** (which is seen most commonly on Linux systems in its rewritten form, **vim**). It is standard on all UNIX and Linux systems, and though it may appear a bit pallid when compared with glitzier offerings such as **emacs**, it is powerful and complete. We also like **pico**, which is a simple and low-impact "starter editor" that's good for new sysadmins. It's included in many distributions. Be wary of nonstandard editors; if you become addicted to one, you may soon tire of dragging it along with you to install on every new system.

One of the mainstays of administration (and a theme that runs throughout this book) is the use of scripts to automate administrative tasks. To be an effective administrator, you must be able to read and modify Perl and **sh** scripts (which in the Linux world are really **bash** scripts). Scripts that you write from scratch can be written in the shell or scripting language of your choice.

See cpan.org for a complete selection of useful Perl software. For new scripting projects, we recommend Perl or Python. As a programming language, Perl is a little strange (OK, more than a little). However, it does include many features that are indispensable for administrators. The O'Reilly book *Programming Perl* by Larry Wall et al. is the standard text; it's also a model of good technical writing. A full citation is given on page 20.

Many administrators prefer Python to Perl, and we know of sites that are making a concerted effort to convert from Perl to Python. Python is a more elegant language than Perl, and Python scripts are generally more readable and easier to maintain. A useful set of links that compare Python to other scripting languages (including Perl) can be found at

> www.python.org/doc/Comparisons.html

We also recommend that you learn **expect**, which is not a programming language so much as a front end for driving interactive programs. You will most likely pick up **expect** quite rapidly.

1.2 LINUX'S RELATIONSHIP TO UNIX

Using the names Linux and UNIX together in one sentence is like stepping into a political minefield, or perhaps like blundering into a large patch of quicksand. Here is our short version of the facts, stated as clearly and objectively as we can make them.

Linux is a reimplementation and elaboration of UNIX. It conforms to the POSIX standard, runs on several hardware platforms, and is compatible with most existing UNIX software. It differs from most other variants of UNIX in that it is free, open source, and cooperatively developed, with contributions having come from thousands of different individuals and organizations. Linux incorporates technical refinements that did not exist in the original versions of UNIX, so it is more than just a UNIX clone. It is also a legally distinct entity and cannot be properly be referred to as "UNIX."

It's worth noting that Linux is not the only free UNIX-like operating system in the world. FreeBSD, NetBSD, and OpenBSD, all offshoots of the Berkeley Software Distribution from UC Berkeley, have ardent followers of their own. These OSes are generally comparable to Linux in their features and reliability, although they enjoy somewhat less support from third-party software vendors.

Linux software is UNIX software. Thanks largely to the GNU Project, most of the important software that gives UNIX systems their value has been developed under some form of open source model. The same code runs on Linux and non-Linux systems. The Apache web server, for example, doesn't really care whether it's running on Linux or HP-UX. From the standpoint of applications, Linux is simply one of the best-supported varieties of UNIX.

UNIX and Linux systems have been used in production environments for many years. This book, unlike most others on Linux administration, focuses on the effective use of Linux in a production environment—not just as a single-user desktop.[1]

1.3 LINUX IN HISTORICAL CONTEXT

Linux originated in 1991 as a personal project of Linus Torvalds, a Finnish graduate student. He originally conceived the project as a modest offshoot of Minix, a model operating system written by Andrew S. Tanenbaum. However, Linux generated substantial interest in the world at large, and the kernel soon took on a life of its own. By exploiting the power of cooperative development, Linus was able to tackle a much more ambitious agenda. Kernel version 1.0 was released in 1994; as of this writing (September 2006), the most recent stable version of the Linux kernel is 2.6.17.

Because Linux owes much to its UNIX ancestors, it's not quite fair to locate the dawn of the Linux era in 1991. The history of UNIX goes back several decades to 1969, when UNIX originated as a research project at AT&T Bell Labs. In 1976, UNIX was made available at no charge to universities and thus became the basis of many operating systems classes and academic research projects.

Berkeley UNIX began in 1977 when the Computer Systems Research Group (CSRG) at the University of California, Berkeley, licensed code from AT&T. Berkeley's releases

---

1. A "production" environment is one that an organization relies on to accomplish real work (as opposed to testing, research, or development).

(called BSD, for Berkeley Software Distribution) started with 1BSD for the PDP-11 and culminated in 1993 with 4.4BSD.

As UNIX gained commercial acceptance, the price of source licenses rose rapidly. Eventually, Berkeley set the long-term goal of removing AT&T's code from BSD, a tedious and time-consuming process. Before the work could be completed, Berkeley lost funding for operating systems research and the CSRG was disbanded.

Before disbanding, the CSRG released its final collection of AT&T-free code, known as 4.4BSD-Lite. Most current versions of BSD UNIX (including FreeBSD, NetBSD, Mac OS X,[2] and OpenBSD) claim the 4.4BSD-Lite package as their grandparent.

Most other major versions of UNIX (including HP-UX and Solaris) are descendants of the original AT&T lineage. Linux doesn't share code with the AT&T or BSD flavors of UNIX, but from a functional perspective it falls somewhere between the two.

1.4 LINUX DISTRIBUTIONS

See the section starting on page 962 for additional comments on distributions.

Linux differs from other variants of UNIX in that the core kernel project defines only an OS kernel. The kernel must be packaged together with commands, daemons, and other software to form a usable and complete operating system—in Linux terms, a "distribution." All Linux distributions share the same kernel lineage, but the ancillary materials that go along with that kernel can vary quite a bit among distributions.

Those "ancillary materials" consist of a vast collection of software developed over the last 30 years by thousands of individuals. It has been argued, with some justification, that the act of referring to the completed operating system simply as "Linux" fails to acknowledge the contributions of those developers and the historical context in which they worked. Unfortunately, the most commonly suggested alternative, "GNU/Linux," has its own political baggage and has been officially endorsed only by the Debian distribution. The Wikipedia entry for "GNU/Linux naming controversy" outlines the arguments on both sides.

Distributions vary in their focus, support, and popularity. Table 1.1 lists the most popular general-purpose distributions. Distributions are listed in alphabetic order, not in order of preference or popularity.

Many smaller distributions are not listed in Table 1.1, and many unlisted special-purpose distributions are targeted at groups with specialized needs (such as embedded system developers).

One useful distribution not found in Table 1.1 is Knoppix (www.knoppix.com), a version of Linux that lives on a bootable CD-ROM. Its primary value lies in its utility as a recovery CD for a Linux system rendered unbootable by a security compromise or technical problem. The bootable CD concept has proved so popular that most major distributions are moving in that direction. Now that Ubuntu can boot from

---

2. Strictly speaking, the Mac OS X kernel is a variant of Mach, a hybrid system that includes both BSD sections and parts that are rather non-UNIX in flavor.

Where to Start

Table 1.1 Most popular general-purpose Linux distributions

Distribution	Web site	Comments
CentOS	www.centos.org	Free analog of Red Hat Enterprise Linux
Debian	www.debian.org	A popular noncommercial distribution
Fedora	fedora.redhat.com	De-corporatized Red Hat Linux
Gentoo	www.gentoo.org	Source-code based distribution
Mandriva[a]	www.mandriva.com	One of the most user-friendly distros
openSUSE	www.opensuse.org	Free analog of SUSE Linux Enterprise
Red Hat Enterprise	www.redhat.com	Super-corporatized Red Hat Linux
Slackware	www.slackware.com	Stable, basic, bare-bones distribution
SUSE Linux Enterprise	www.novell.com/linux	Strong in Europe, multilingual
TurboLinux	www.turbolinux.com	Strong in Asia, multilingual
Ubuntu	www.ubuntu.com	Cleaned-up version of Debian

a. Formerly Mandrakelinux

the distribution CD, Knoppix is becoming less important. An updated list of bootable Linux distributions can be found at www.frozentech.com/content/livecd.php.

 Red Hat has been a dominant force in the Linux world for most of the last decade, and its distributions are predominant in North America. In 2003, the original Red Hat Linux distribution was split into a production-centered line called Red Hat Enterprise Linux (which we sometimes refer to as RHEL in this book) and a community-based development project called Fedora. The split was motivated by a variety of technical, economic, logistic, and legal reasons, but so far the distributions have remained similar. RHEL offers great support and stability but is effectively impossible to use without paying licensing fees to Red Hat.

The CentOS Project (www.centos.org) collects source code that Red Hat is obliged to release under various licensing agreements (most notably, the GNU public license) and assembles it into a complete distribution that is eerily similar to Red Hat Enterprise Linux, but free of charge. The distribution lacks Red Hat's branding and a few proprietary tools, but is in other respects equivalent. CentOS aspires to full binary and bug-for-bug compatibility with RHEL.

CentOS is an excellent choice for sites that want to deploy a production-oriented distribution without paying tithes to Red Hat. A hybrid approach is also feasible: front-line servers can run Red Hat Enterprise Linux and avail themselves of Red Hat's excellent support, while desktops run CentOS. This arrangement covers the important bases in terms of risk and support while also minimizing cost and administrative complexity.

 SUSE, now part of Novell, has recently taken the path of Red Hat and forked into two related distributions: one (openSUSE) that contains only free software; and another (SUSE Linux Enterprise) that costs money, includes a formal support path, and offers a few extra trinkets. In the past there seemed to be an effort to hide the existence of the free version of SUSE, but Novell has been more up front about this edition than SUSE's previous owners. Now, you can go right to www.opensuse.org for the latest information. Nothing in this book is specific to one SUSE distribution or the other, so we simply refer to them collectively as "SUSE."

The Debian and Ubuntu distributions maintain an ideological commitment to community development and open access, so there's never any question about which parts of the distribution are free or redistributable. Debian survives on the zeal and goodwill of the GNU community, while Ubuntu currently enjoys philanthropic funding from South African entrepreneur Mark Shuttleworth. Ubuntu will even send you free CDs in the mail, no postage required.

So what's the best distribution?

A quick search on the net will reveal that this is one of the most frequently asked— and least frequently answered—Linux questions. The right answer for you depends on how you intend to use the system, the varieties of UNIX that you're familiar with, your political sympathies, and your support needs.

Most Linux distributions can do everything you might ever want to do with a Linux system. Some of them may require the installation of additional software to be fully functional, and some may facilitate certain tasks; however, the differences among them are not cosmically significant. In fact, it is something of a mystery why there are so many different distributions, each claiming "easy installation" and "a massive software library" as its distinguishing feature. It's hard to avoid the conclusion that people just like to make new Linux distributions.

On the other hand, since our focus in this book is the management of large-scale Linux installations, we're partial to distributions such as Red Hat Enterprise Linux that take into account the management of networks of machines. Some distributions are designed with production environments in mind, and others are not. The extra crumbs of assistance that the production-oriented systems toss out can make a significant difference in ease of administration.

When you adopt a distribution, you are making an investment in a particular vendor's way of doing things. Instead of looking only at the features of the installed software, it's wise to consider how your organization and that vendor are going to work with each other in the years to come. Some important questions to ask are:

- Is this distribution going to be around in five years?
- Is this distribution going to stay on top of the latest security patches?
- Is this distribution going to release updated software promptly?
- If I have problems, will the vendor talk to me?

Viewed in this light, some of the more interesting, offbeat little distributions don't sound quite so appealing. On the other hand, the most viable distributions are not necessarily the most corporate. For example, we expect Debian (OK, OK, Debian GNU/Linux!) to remain viable for quite a while despite the fact that Debian is not a company, doesn't sell anything, and offers no formal, on-demand support.

A comprehensive list of distributions, including many non-English distributions, can be found at www.linux.org/dist, lwn.net/Distributions, or distrowatch.com.

In this book, we use five popular distributions as our examples: Red Hat Enterprise Linux 4.3 ES, Fedora Core 5, SUSE Linux Enterprise 10.2, Ubuntu 6.06 ("Dapper Drake"), and the current (as of September 2006) testing release of Debian GNU/Linux 3.2 ("Etch"). These systems represent a cross-section of the enterprise Linux market and account collectively for a majority of the installations in use at large sites today.

Distribution-specific administration tools

Many distributions include visually oriented tools (such as the Red Hat Network Administration Tool or SUSE's YaST2) that help you configure or administer selected aspects of the system. These tools can be very useful, especially for novice administrators, but they do tend to obscure the details of what's actually going on when you make changes. In this book, we cover the underlying mechanisms that the visual tools refer to rather than the tools themselves, for several reasons.

For one, the visual tools tend to be proprietary, or at least distribution-specific— they introduce variation into processes that may actually be quite consistent among distributions at a lower level. Second, we believe that it's important for administrators to have an accurate understanding of how their systems work. When the system breaks, the visual tools are usually not helpful in tracking down and fixing problems. Finally, manual configuration is often just plain better: it's faster, more flexible, more reliable, and easier to script.

1.5 NOTATION AND TYPOGRAPHICAL CONVENTIONS

In this book, filenames, commands, and literal arguments to commands are shown in boldface. Placeholders (e.g., command arguments that should not be taken literally) are in italics. For example, in the command

> **cp** *file directory*

you're supposed to replace *file* and *directory* with the names of an actual file and an actual directory.

Excerpts from configuration files and terminal sessions are shown in a fixed-width font.[3] Sometimes, we annotate interactive sessions with italic text. For example:

```
$ grep Bob /pub/phonelist        /* Look up Bob's phone # */
Bob Knowles 555-2834
Bob Smith 555-2311
```

Outside of these specific cases, we have tried to keep special fonts and formatting conventions to a minimum as long as we could do so without compromising intelligibility. For example, we often talk about entities such as the Linux group named daemon and the printer anchor-lw with no special formatting at all.

---

3. Actually, it's not really a fixed-width font, but it looks like one. We liked it better than the real fixed-width fonts that we tried. That's why the columns in some examples may not all line up perfectly.

In general, we use the same conventions as the manual pages for indicating the syntax of commands:

- Anything between square brackets ("[" and "]") is optional.
- Anything followed by an ellipsis ("…") can be repeated.
- Curly braces ("{" and "}") mean that you should select one of the items separated by vertical bars ("|").

For example, the specification

bork [**-x**] {**on**|**off**} *filename* …

would match any of the following commands:

```
bork on /etc/passwd
bork -x off /etc/passwd /etc/termcap
bork off /usr/lib/tmac
```

We use shell-style globbing characters for pattern matching:

- A star (*) matches zero or more characters.
- A question mark (?) matches one character.
- A tilde or "twiddle" (~) means the home directory of the current user.
- ~*user* means the home directory of *user*.

For example, we might refer to the Debian startup script directories **/etc/rc0.d**, **/etc/rc1.d**, and so on with the shorthand pattern **/etc/rc*.d**.

Text within quotation marks often has a precise technical meaning. In these cases, we ignore the normal rules of English and put punctuation outside the quotation marks so that there can be no confusion about what's included and what's not.

System-specific information

Information in this book generally applies to all of our example distributions unless a specific attribution is given. Details particular to one distribution are marked with the vendor's logo:

 Red Hat® Enterprise Linux® 4.3 ES

 Fedora™ Core 5

 SUSE® Linux Enterprise 10.2

 Ubuntu® 6.06 "Dapper Drake"

 Debian® GNU/Linux 3.2 "Etch" (testing release of 9/06)

These logos are used with the kind permission of their respective owners. However, the distributors have neither reviewed nor endorsed the contents of this book.

1.6 WHERE TO GO FOR INFORMATION

Linux documentation is spread over a number of sources, some of which you will find installed on your system and some of which live out on the net. The biggies are

- Manual pages (man pages), read with the **man** command
- Texinfo documents, read with the **info** command
- HOWTOs, short notes on various subjects (www.tdlp.org)
- Guides, longer treatises on various subjects (www.tdlp.org)
- Distribution-specific documentation
- Web pages associated with specific software projects

The man pages and Texinfo documents constitute the traditional "on-line" documentation (though, of course, all the documentation is on-line in some form or another). These docs are typically installed with the system; program-specific man pages usually come along for the ride whenever you install a new package.

Man pages are concise descriptions of individual commands, drivers, file formats, or library routines. They do not address more general topics such as "How do I install a new device?" or "Why is my system so slow?" For those questions, consult the HOWTOs.

Texinfo documents were invented long ago by the GNU folks in reaction to the fact that the **nroff** command to format man pages was proprietary to AT&T. These days we have GNU's own **groff** to do this job for us, and the **nroff** issue is no longer important. Unfortunately, many GNU packages persist in documenting themselves with Texinfo files rather than man pages. In addition to defining an unnecessary second standard for documentation, Texinfo proves to be a rather labyrinthine little hypertext system in its own right.

To escape from Texinfo hell, pipe **info**'s output through the **less** command to evade **info**'s built-in navigation system. As a side effect, this procedure also lets you take advantage of the searching features built into **less**.

Fortunately, packages that are documented with Texinfo usually install man page stubs that tell you to use the **info** command to read about those particular packages. You can safely stick to the **man** command for doing manual searches and delve into **info** land only when instructed to do so. **info info** initiates you into the dark mysteries of Texinfo.

HOWTOs and guides are maintained by The Linux Documentation Project, reachable on-line at www.tldp.org. The LDP is a central repository for all sorts of useful Linux information. It also centralizes efforts to translate Linux-related documents into additional languages.

Some free, on-line LDP guides of particular relevance to system administrators are *The Linux System Administrators' Guide* by Lars Wirzenius, Joanna Oja, Stephen Stafford, and Alex Weeks; the *Advanced Bash-Scripting Guide* by Mendel Cooper;

The Linux Network Administrator's Guide, Second Edition, by Olaf Kirch and Terry Dawson; and *Linux System Administration Made Easy* by Steve Frampton.

Unfortunately, many of the LDP documents are not assiduously maintained. Since Linux-years are a lot like dog-years in their relation to real time, untended documents are apt to quickly go out of date. Always check the time stamp on a HOWTO or guide and weigh its credibility accordingly.

Many of the most important parts of the Linux software base are maintained by neutral third parties such as the Internet Systems Consortium and the Apache Software Foundation. These groups typically generate adequate documentation for the packages they distribute. Distributions sometimes package up the software but skimp on the documentation, so it's often useful to check back with the original source to see if additional materials are available.

Another useful source of information about the design of many Linux software packages is the "Request for Comments" document series, which describes the protocols and procedures used on the Internet. See page 274 for more information.

Organization of the man pages

The Linux man pages are typically divided into nine sections as shown in Table 1.2.

Table 1.2   Sections of the Linux man pages

Section	Contents
1	User-level commands and applications
2	System calls and kernel error codes
3	Library calls
4	Device drivers and network protocols
5	Standard file formats
6	Games and demonstrations
7	Miscellaneous files and documents
8	System administration commands
9	Obscure kernel specs and interfaces

Some sections are further subdivided. For example, section 3M contains man pages for the system's math library. Sections 6 and 9 are typically empty. Many systems have a section of the manuals called "l" for local man pages. Another common convention is section "n" for software-specific subcommands (such as **bash** built-ins).

nroff input for man pages is usually kept in the directories **/usr/share/man/man**X, where X is a digit **1** through **9**, or **l** or **n**. The pages are normally compressed with **gzip** to save space. (The **man** command knows how to uncompress them on the fly.) Formatted versions of the manuals are kept in **/var/cache/man/cat**X. The **man** command formats man pages as they are needed; if the **cat** directories are writable,

man also deposits the formatted pages as they are created, generating a cache of commonly read man pages.

The **man** command actually searches a number of different directories to find the manual pages you request. You can determine the search path with the **manpath** command. This path (from Fedora) is typical:

```
$ manpath
/usr/kerberos/man:/usr/local/share/man:/usr/share/man/en:/usr/share/man
```

If necessary, you can set your MANPATH environment variable to override the default path. You can also set the system-wide default in **/etc/man.config** (RHEL and Fedora) or **/etc/manpath.config** (SUSE, Debian, and Ubuntu).

man: read manual pages

man *title* formats a specific manual page and sends it to your terminal with **less** (or whatever program is specified in your PAGER environment variable). *title* is usually a command, device, or filename. The sections of the manual are searched in roughly numeric order, although sections that describe commands (sections 1, 8, and 6) are usually searched first.

The form **man** *section title* gets you a man page from a particular section. Thus, **man tty** gets you the man page for the **tty** command, and **man 4 tty** gets you the man page for the controlling terminal driver.

man -k *keyword* prints a list of man pages that have *keyword* in their one-line synopses. For example:

```
$ man -k translate
objcopy (1)          - copy and translate object files
dcgettext (3)        - translate message
tr (1)               - translate or delete characters
snmptranslate (1)    - translate SNMP OID values into more useful information
tr (1p)              - translate characters
gettext (1)          - translate message
ngettext (1)         - translate message and choose plural form
...
```

Other sources of Linux information

There's a great big Linux-lovin' world out there. We couldn't possibly mention every useful collection of Linux information, or even just the major ones, but a few significant sources of information are shown in Table 1.3 on the next page.

Don't be shy about accessing general UNIX resources, either—most information is directly applicable to Linux. A wealth of information about system administration is available on the net, in many forms. For example, you can type sysadmin questions into any of the popular search engines, such as Google, Yahoo!, or Ask. A list of other "starter" resources can be found in Chapter 30, *Management, Policy, and Politics.*

Table 1.3   Linux resources on the web

Web site	Description
linux.slashdot.org	Linux-specific arm of tech news giant Slashdot
lwn.net	Linux and open source news aggregator
www.freshmeat.net	Large index of Linux and UNIX software
www.kernel.org	Official Linux kernel site
www.linux.com	Linux information clearing house (unofficial)
www.linux.org	Another Linux information clearing house (unofficial)
www.linuxhq.com	Compilation of kernel-related info and patches
www.linuxworld.com	On-line magazine from the Computerworld folks
www.tldp.org	The Linux Documentation Project
www.tucows.com	Multiplatform software archive with Linux content

Many sites cater directly to the needs of system administrators. Here are a few that we especially like:

- www.ugu.com – the UNIX Guru Universe; lots of stuff for sysadmins
- www.stokely.com – a good collection of links to sysadmin resources
- www.tucows.com – Windows and Mac software, filtered for quality
- slashdot.org – "the place" for geek news
- www.cpan.org – a central source for Perl scripts and libraries
- securityfocus.com – security info; huge, searchable vulnerability database

Another fun and useful resource is Bruce Hamilton's "Rosetta Stone" page at

bhami.com/rosetta.html

It contains pointers to the commands and tools used for various system administration tasks on many different operating systems.

1.7 HOW TO FIND AND INSTALL SOFTWARE

Linux distributions divide their software into packages that can be installed independently of one another. When you install Linux on a new computer, you typically select a range of "starter" packages to be copied onto the new system.

This architecture simplifies many aspects of system configuration and is one of Linux's key advantages over traditional versions of UNIX. Unfortunately, this design also complicates the task of writing about these distributions because it's never really clear which packages are "part of" a given distribution. Is a package "included" if it's on the installation CDs but isn't part of the default installation? Only if it's on every computer running that distribution? If it's on the "bonus" CDs that come only with the supersize version of the distribution?

In this book, we generally describe the default installation of each of our example distributions. When we say that a particular package isn't included in the default installation, it doesn't necessarily mean that the package won't be on *your* system or that it isn't supported by your distribution. Here's how to find out if you've got it, and if not, how to get it.

First, use the shell's **which** command to find out if a relevant command is already in your search path. For example, the following command reveals that the GNU C compiler has already been installed on this machine in **/usr/bin**:

```
$ which gcc
/usr/bin/gcc
```

If **which** can't find the command you're looking for, try **whereis**; it searches a broader range of system directories and is independent of your shell's search path. Be aware also that some systems' **which** command does not show you files that you do not have permission to execute. For example:

```
$ which ipppd
/usr/bin/which: no ipppd in (/bin:/usr/bin:/sbin:/usr/sbin)
$ whereis ipppd
ipppd: /usr/sbin/ipppd
$ ls -l /usr/sbin/ipppd
-rwx------    1 root     root       124924 Aug  3 2000 /usr/sbin/ipppd
```

Another alternative is the incredibly useful **locate** command, which consults a precompiled index of the filesystem to locate filenames that match a particular pattern. It is not specific to commands or packages but can find any type of file. For example, if you weren't sure where to find the **signal.h** include file (which is the authoritative source for Linux signal definitions), you could try

```
$ locate signal.h
/usr/include/asm/signal.h
/usr/include/linux/signal.h
/usr/include/signal.h
/usr/include/sys/signal.h
```

locate's database is usually regenerated every night by the **updatedb** command, which runs out of **cron**. Therefore, the results of a **locate** don't always reflect recent changes to the filesystem.

If you know the name of a package you're looking for, you can also use your system's packaging utilities to check directly for the package's presence. For example, on a Red Hat, Fedora, or SUSE system, the following command checks for the presence of the Python scripting language:

```
$ rpm -q python
python-1.5.2-27
```

See Chapter 11, *Software and Configuration Management*, for more information about our example distributions' packaging commands.

If the package you're interested in doesn't seem to be installed, the first place to look for it is your distribution's automatic package management system. Every distribution supports some form of Internet-based system for updating old packages and finding new ones. The most common systems are **yum** and APT, both of which are described in the section *High-level package management systems*, which starts on page 237.

For example, on a Debian system, which uses APT, the following command could be used to obtain and install the most recent version of Python:

```
# apt-get install python
```

Most Linux software is developed by independent groups that release the software in the form of source code. Linux distributors then pick up the source code, compile it appropriately for the conventions in use on their particular system, and package the resulting binaries. It's usually easier to install a distribution-specific binary package than to fetch and compile the original source code. However, distributors are sometimes a release or two behind the current version.

The fact that two distributions use the same packaging system doesn't necessarily mean that packages for the two systems are interchangeable. Red Hat and SUSE both use RPM, for example, but their filesystem layouts are somewhat different. It's always best to use packages designed for your particular distribution if they are available.

If all else fails, try looking for the package at a download site such as freshmeat.net or doing a Google search on the name of the package.

1.8   ESSENTIAL TASKS OF THE SYSTEM ADMINISTRATOR

The sections below briefly summarize some tasks that system administrators are typically expected to perform. These duties need not necessarily be performed by one person, and at many sites the work is distributed among several people. However, at least one person must understand all the chores and make sure that someone is doing them.

Adding, removing, and managing user accounts

See Chapter 6 for more information about adding new users.

The system administrator adds accounts for new users and removes the accounts of users that are no longer active. The process of adding and removing users can be automated, but certain administrative decisions (where to put the user's home directory, on which machines to create the account, etc.) must still be made before a new user can be added.

When a user should no longer have access to the system, the user's account must be disabled. All the files owned by the account should be backed up to tape and disposed of so that the system does not accumulate unwanted baggage over time.

Adding and removing hardware

See Chapters 7, 28, and 23 for more information about these topics.

When new hardware is purchased or when hardware is moved from one machine to another, the system must be configured to recognize and use that hardware. Hardware-support chores can range from the simple task of adding a printer to the more complex job of adding a disk array.

Performing backups

See Chapter 9 for more information about backups.

Performing backups is perhaps the most important job of the system administrator, and it is also the job that is most often ignored or sloppily done. Backups are time consuming and boring, but they are absolutely necessary. Backups can be automated and delegated to an underling, but it is still the system administrator's job to make sure that backups are executed correctly and on schedule (and that the resulting media can actually be used to restore files).

Installing and upgrading software

See Chapter 11 for more information about software management.

When new software is acquired, it must be installed and tested, often under several operating systems and on several types of hardware. Once the software is working correctly, users must be informed of its availability and location. As patches and security updates are released, they must be incorporated smoothly into the local environment.

Local software should be installed in a place that makes it easy to differentiate local from system software. This organization simplifies the task of upgrading the operating system since the local software won't be overwritten by the upgrade procedure.

Monitoring the system

Large installations require vigilant supervision. Daily activities include making sure that email and web service are working correctly, watching log files for early signs of trouble, ensuring that local networks are all properly connected, and keeping an eye on the availability of system resources such as disk space.

Troubleshooting

Linux systems and the hardware they run on occasionally break down. It is the administrator's job to play mechanic by diagnosing problems and calling in experts if needed. Finding the problem is often harder than fixing it.

Maintaining local documentation

See page 930 for suggestions regarding documentation.

As the system is changed to suit an organization's needs, it begins to differ from the plain-vanilla system described by the documentation. It is the system administrator's duty to document aspects of the system that are specific to the local environment. This chore includes documenting any software that is installed but did not come with the operating system, documenting where cables are run and how they are constructed, keeping maintenance records for all hardware, recording the status of backups, and documenting local procedures and policies.

Vigilantly monitoring security

See Chapter 20 for more information about security.

The system administrator must implement a security policy and periodically check to be sure that the security of the system has not been violated. On low-security systems, this chore might involve only a few cursory checks for unauthorized access. On a high-security system, it can include an elaborate network of traps and auditing programs.

Helping users

Although helping users with their various problems is rarely included in a system administrator's job description, it claims a significant portion of most administrators' workdays. System administrators are bombarded with problems ranging from "My program worked yesterday and now it doesn't! What did you change?" to "I spilled coffee on my keyboard! Should I pour water on it to wash it out?"

1.9 SYSTEM ADMINISTRATION UNDER DURESS

System administrators wear many hats. In the real world, they are often people with other jobs who have been asked to look after a few computers on the side. If you are in this situation, you may want to think a bit about where it might eventually lead.

The more you learn about your system, the more the user community will come to depend on you. Networks invariably grow, and you may be pressured to spend an increasing portion of your time on administration. You will soon find that you are the only person in your organization who knows how to perform a variety of important tasks.

Once coworkers come to think of you as the local system administrator, it is difficult to extricate yourself from this role. We know several people who have changed jobs to escape it. Since many administrative tasks are intangible, you may also find that you're expected to be both a full-time administrator and a full-time engineer, writer, or secretary.

Some unwilling administrators try to fend off requests by adopting an ornery attitude and providing poor service. We do not recommend this approach; it makes you look bad and creates additional problems.

Instead, we suggest that you document the time you spend on system administration. Your goal should be to keep the work at a manageable level and to assemble evidence that you can use when you ask to be relieved of administrative duties. In most organizations, you will need to lobby the management from six months to a year to get yourself replaced, so plan ahead.

On the other hand, you may find that you enjoy system administration and that you yearn to be a full-time administrator. Your prospects for employment are good. Unfortunately, your political problems will probably intensify. Refer to Chapter 30, *Management, Policy, and Politics*, for a preview of the political aspects of system administration.

System Administration Personality Syndrome

One unfortunate but common clinical condition resulting from working as a system administrator is System Administration Personality Syndrome. The onset of this condition usually begins early in the third year of a system administrator's career and the syndrome can last well into retirement. Characteristic symptoms include but are not limited to

- Acute phantom pagerphobia: the disturbing feeling that your pager has gone off (when it really hasn't) and that your peaceful evening with your significant other is about to abruptly end, resulting in a 72-hour work marathon without food

- User voodoographia: the compulsive creation of voodoo-doll representations of the subset of your user population that doesn't seem to understand that their persistent lack of planning doesn't constitute an emergency in your world

- Idiopathic anal tapereadaplexia: the sudden, late-night urge to mount backup tapes to see if they're actually readable and labeled correctly

- Scientifica inapplicia: the strong desire to violently shake fellow system administrators who seem never to have encountered the scientific method

Many curative therapies can be used to treat this unfortunate condition. The most effective are a well-developed sense of humor and the construction of a small but well-endowed office wine cellar. You might also consider the more meditative approach of silently staring off into space and clicking your heels together whenever the words "Is the server down again?" are spoken in your vicinity. If all else fails, take a vacation.

1.10 RECOMMENDED READING

The best resources for system administrators in the printed realm (aside from this book :-) are the O'Reilly series of books. The series began with *UNIX in a Nutshell* over 20 years ago and now includes a separate volume on just about every important UNIX and Linux subsystem and command. The series also includes books on the Internet, Windows, and other non-UNIX topics. All the books are reasonably priced, timely, and focused. Tim O'Reilly has become quite interested in the open source movement and runs a conference, OSCON, on this topic as well as conferences on other trendy techie topics. OSCON occurs twice yearly, once in the United States and once in Europe. See www.oreilly.com for more information.

Although a variety of introductory Linux books are on the market, we have not yet found one that we could recommend without reservation. In general, you're better off looking for the UNIX "classics." Almost everything you read will apply equally well to Linux.

SIEVER, ELLEN, AARON WEBER, AND STEPHEN FIGGINS. *Linux in a Nutshell (5th Edition)*. Sebastopol, CA: O'Reilly Media, 2006.

LAMB, LINDA, AND ARNOLD ROBBINS. *Learning the vi Editor (6th Edition)*. Sebastopol, CA: O'Reilly & Associates, 1998.

POWERS, SHELLY, JERRY PEEK, TIM O'REILLY, AND MIKE LOUKIDES. *UNIX Power Tools (3rd Edition)*. Sebastopol, CA: O'Reilly Media, 2003.

WALL, LARRY, TOM CHRISTIANSEN, AND JON ORWANT. *Programming Perl (3rd Edition)*. Cambridge, MA: O'Reilly Media, 2000.

CHRISTIANSEN, TOM, AND NATHAN TORKINGTON. *Perl Cookbook (2nd Edition)*. Sebastopol, CA: O'Reilly Media, 2003.

GANCARZ, MIKE. *Linux and the Unix Philosophy*. Boston: Digital Press, 2003.

SALUS, PETER. *The Daemon, the GNU & the Penguin*. Groklaw. 2006.

This fascinating history of the open source movement by UNIX's best-known historian is being serialized at groklaw.com under the Creative Commons license. It's currently about 75% complete. The URL for the book itself is quite long; look for a currently link at groklaw.com or try this compressed equivalent: tinyurl.com/d6u7j.

1.11 EXERCISES

E1.1 What command would you use to read about the **sync** system call (*not* the **sync** command)? How would you read **sync**'s local man page that was kept in **/usr/local/share/man**?

E1.2 Does a system-wide config file control the behavior of the **man** command at your site? What lines would you add to this file if you wanted to store local material in **/doc/man**? What directory structure would you have to use in **/doc/man** to make it a full citizen of the man page hierarchy?

E1.3 What are the main differences between **man** and **info**? What are some advantages of each?

E1.4 What is the current status of Linux kernel development? What are the hot issues? Who are some of the key players? How is the project managed?

E1.5 Research several Linux distributions (see page 7 for a starter list) and recommend a distribution for each of the following applications. Explain your choices.

a) A single user working in a home office
b) A university computer science lab
c) A corporate web server

E1.6 Suppose you discover that a certain feature of Apache **httpd** does not appear to work as documented on Fedora Core 5.

a) What should you do before reporting the bug?
b) If you decide that the bug is real, whom should you notify and how?
c) What information must be included to make the bug report useful?

2 *Booting and Shutting Down*

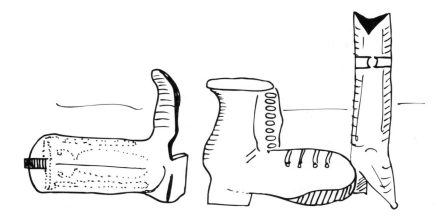

Linux is a complex operating system, and turning Linux systems on and off is more complicated than just flipping the power switch. Both operations must be performed correctly if the system is to stay healthy.

Although the bootstrapping process has always been somewhat mysterious, it was simpler in the days when manufacturers controlled every aspect of the system's hardware and software. Now that we have Linux running on PC hardware, the boot procedure has to play by PC rules and deal with a large variety of potential configurations.

This chapter appears early in the book, but it refers to material that is not discussed in detail until many hundreds of pages later. In particular, familiarity with the material in Chapter 5, *The Filesystem*, Chapter 28, *Drivers and the Kernel*, and Chapter 29, *Daemons*, will prove helpful. If your system already boots without any problem, you may want to skip this chapter and come back to it later.

2.1 BOOTSTRAPPING

Bootstrapping is the standard term for "starting up a computer." The operating system's normal facilities are not available during the startup process, so the computer must "pull itself up by its own bootstraps." During bootstrapping, the kernel is loaded into memory and begins to execute. A variety of initialization tasks are performed, and the system is then made available to users.

Boot time is a period of special vulnerability. Errors in configuration files, missing or unreliable equipment, and damaged filesystems can all prevent a computer from coming up. Boot configuration is often one of the first tasks an administrator must perform on a new system. Unfortunately, it is also one of the most difficult, and it requires some familiarity with many other aspects of Linux.

When a computer is turned on, it executes boot code that is stored in ROM. That code in turn attempts to figure out how to load and start the kernel. The kernel probes the system's hardware and then spawns the system's **init** process, which is always process number 1.

Several things must happen before a login prompt can appear. Filesystems must be checked and mounted, and system daemons started. These procedures are managed by a series of shell scripts that are run in sequence by **init**. The startup scripts are often referred to as "rc files" because of the way they are named; the "rc" stands for "runcom" or "run command," a historical remnant of the CTSS operating system circa 1965. The exact layout of the startup scripts and the manner in which they are executed vary among systems. We cover the details later in this chapter.

Automatic and manual booting

Linux systems can boot in either automatic mode or manual mode. In automatic mode, the system performs the complete boot procedure on its own, without any external assistance. In manual mode, the system follows the automatic procedure up to a point but then turns control over to an operator before most initialization scripts have been run. At this point, the computer is in "single-user mode." Most system processes are not running, and other users cannot log in.

In day-to-day operation, automatic booting is used almost exclusively. A typical boot procedure for a modern machine is for a user to turn on the power and wait for the system to come on-line. Nevertheless, it's important to understand the automatic boot procedure and to know how to perform a manual boot. You'll usually have to boot manually when some problem breaks automatic booting, for example, a corrupted filesystem or an improperly configured network interface.

Steps in the boot process

A typical Linux bootstrapping process consists of six distinct phases:

- Loading and initialization of the kernel
- Device detection and configuration
- Creation of kernel threads
- Operator intervention (manual boot only)
- Execution of system startup scripts
- Multiuser operation

Administrators have little control over most of these steps. We effect most bootstrap configuration by editing the system startup scripts.

Kernel initialization

*See Chapter 28 for
more information
about the kernel.*

The Linux kernel is itself a program, and the first bootstrapping task is to get this program into memory so that it can be executed. The pathname of the kernel is usually **/vmlinuz** or **/boot/vmlinuz**.

Linux implements a two-stage loading process. During the first stage, the system ROM loads a small boot program into memory from disk. This program then arranges for the kernel to be loaded.

The kernel performs memory tests to find out how much RAM is available. Some of the kernel's internal data structures are statically sized, so the kernel sets aside a fixed amount of real memory for itself when it starts. This memory is reserved for the kernel and cannot be used by user-level processes. The kernel prints on the console a message that reports the total amount of physical memory and the amount available to user processes.

Hardware configuration

One of the kernel's first chores is to check out the machine's environment to see what hardware is present. When you construct a kernel for your system, you tell it what hardware devices it should expect to find; when the kernel begins to execute, it tries to locate and initialize each device that you have told it about. The kernel prints out a line of cryptic information about each device it finds. These days, distributions include kernels that work on most machine configurations, requiring minimal (if any) customization.

The device information given at kernel configuration time is often underspecified. In these cases, the kernel tries to determine the other information it needs by probing the bus for devices and asking the appropriate drivers for information. The drivers for devices that are missing or that do not respond to a probe will be disabled. If a device is later connected to the system, it is also possible to load or enable a driver for it on the fly. See Chapter 28, *Drivers and the Kernel*, for details.

Kernel threads

Once basic initialization is complete, the kernel creates several "spontaneous" processes in user space. They're called spontaneous processes because they are not created through the normal system **fork** mechanism; see page 56 for more details.

*See page 62 for more
information about ps.*

The number and nature of the spontaneous processes vary from system to system. Under Linux, there is no visible PID 0. **init** (always process 1) is accompanied by several memory and kernel handler processes, including those shown in Table 2.1 on the next page. These processes all have low-numbered PIDs and can be identified by the brackets around their names in **ps** listings (e.g., [kacpid]). Sometimes the process names have a slash and a digit at the end, such as [kblockd/0]. The number indicates the processor on which the thread is running, which may be of interest on a multiprocessor system.

Table 2.1   Some common Linux kernel processes

Thread	Purpose
kjournald	Commits ext3 journal updates to disk[a]
kswapd	Swaps processes when physical memory is low
kreclaimd	Reclaims memory pages that haven't been used recently
ksoftirqd	Handles multiple layers of soft interrupts
khubd	Configures USB devices

a. There is one **kjournald** for each mounted ext3 filesystem.

Among these processes, only **init** is really a full-fledged user process. The others are actually portions of the kernel that have been dressed up to look like processes for scheduling or architectural reasons.

Once the spontaneous processes have been created, the kernel's role in bootstrapping is complete. However, none of the processes that handle basic operations (such as accepting logins) have been created, nor have most of the Linux daemons been started. All of these tasks are taken care of (indirectly, in some cases) by **init**.

Operator intervention (manual boot only)

See Chapter 3 for more information about the root account.

If the system is to be brought up in single-user mode, a command-line flag (the word "single") passed in by the kernel notifies **init** of this fact as it starts up. **init** eventually turns control over to **sulogin**, a special neutered-but-rabid version of **login** that prompts for the root password.[1] If you enter the right password, the system spawns a root shell. You can type <Control-D> instead of a password to bypass single-user mode and continue to multiuser mode. See page 31 for more details.

See Chapter 5 for more information about file-systems and mounting.

From the single-user shell, you can execute commands in much the same way as when logged in on a fully booted system. However, on SUSE, Debian, and Ubuntu systems, only the root partition is usually mounted; you must mount other filesystems by hand to use programs that don't live in **/bin**, **/sbin**, or **/etc**.

In many single-user environments, the filesystem root directory starts off being mounted read-only. If **/tmp** is part of the root filesystem, a lot of commands that use temporary files (such as **vi**) will refuse to run. To fix this problem, you'll have to begin your single-user session by remounting **/** in read/write mode. The command

```
# mount -o rw,remount /
```

usually does the trick.

Red Hat and Fedora's single-user mode is a bit more aggressive than normal. By the time you reach the shell prompt, these distributions have tried to mount all local filesystems. Although this seems helpful at first, it can prove problematic if you have a sick filesystem.

1. See the man pages for **inittab** and **sulogin** for more information. Sadly, even modern versions of Red Hat and Fedora do not by default require a password to enter single-user mode.

The **fsck** command is normally run during an automatic boot to check and repair filesystems. When you bring the system up in single-user mode, you may need to run **fsck** by hand. See page 131 for more information about **fsck**.

When the single-user shell exits, the system attempts to continue booting into multiuser mode.

Execution of startup scripts

By the time the system is ready to run its startup scripts, it is recognizably Linux. Even though it doesn't quite look like a fully booted system yet, no more "magic" steps are left in the boot process. The startup scripts are just normal shell scripts, and they're selected and run by **init** according to an algorithm that, though sometimes tortuous, is relatively comprehensible.

The care, feeding, and taxonomy of startup scripts merits a major section of its own. It's taken up in more detail starting on page 32.

Multiuser operation

See page 855 for more information about the login process.

After the initialization scripts have run, the system is fully operational, except that no one can log in. For logins to be accepted on a particular terminal (including the console), a **getty** process must be listening on it. **init** spawns these **getty** processes directly, completing the boot process. **init** is also responsible for spawning graphical login systems such as **xdm** or **gdm** if the system is set up to use them.

Keep in mind that **init** continues to perform an important role even after bootstrapping is complete. **init** has one single-user and several multiuser "run levels" that determine which of the system's resources are enabled. Run levels are described later in this chapter, starting on page 33.

2.2 BOOTING PCS

At this point we've seen the general outline of the boot process. We now revisit several of the more important (and complicated) steps.

PC booting is a lengthy ordeal that requires quite a bit of background information to explain. When a machine boots, it begins by executing code stored in ROMs. The exact location and nature of this code varies, depending on the type of machine you have. On a machine designed explicitly for UNIX or another proprietary operating system, the code is typically firmware that knows how to use the devices connected to the machine, how to talk to the network on a basic level, and how to understand disk-based filesystems. Such intelligent firmware is convenient for system administrators. For example, you can just type in the filename of a new kernel, and the firmware will know how to locate and read that file.

On PCs, this initial boot code is generally called a BIOS (Basic Input/Output System), and it is extremely simplistic compared to the firmware of a proprietary machine. Actually, a PC has several levels of BIOS: one for the machine itself, one for the video card, one for the SCSI card if the system has one, and sometimes for other peripherals such as network cards.

The built-in BIOS knows about some of the devices that live on the motherboard, typically the IDE controller (and disks), network interface, keyboard, serial ports, and parallel ports. SCSI cards are usually only aware of the devices that are connected to them. Thankfully, the complex interactions required for these devices to work together has been standardized in the past few years, and little manual intervention is required.

Modern BIOSes are a little smarter than they used to be. They usually allow you to enter a configuration mode at boot time by holding down one or two special keys; most BIOSes tell you what those special keys are at boot time so that you don't have to look them up in the manual.

The BIOS normally lets you select which devices you want to try to boot from, which sounds more promising than it actually is. You can usually specify something like "Try to boot off the floppy, then try to boot off the CD-ROM, then try to boot off the hard disk." Unfortunately, some BIOSes are limited to booting from the first IDE CD-ROM drive or the first IDE hard disk. If you have been very, very good over the previous year, Santa might even bring you a BIOS that acknowledges the existence of SCSI cards.

Once your machine has figured out what device to boot from, it will try to load the first 512 bytes of the disk. This 512-byte segment is known as the master boot record or MBR. The MBR contains a program that tells the computer from which disk partition to load a secondary boot program (the "boot loader"). For more information on PC-style disk partitions and the MBR, refer to Chapter 7, *Adding a Disk*.

The default MBR contains a simple program that tells the computer to get its boot loader from the first partition on the disk. Linux offers a more sophisticated MBR that knows how to deal with multiple operating systems and kernels.

Once the MBR has chosen a partition to boot from, it tries to load the boot loader specific to that partition. The boot loader is then responsible for loading the kernel.

2.3 USING BOOT LOADERS: LILO AND GRUB

What would life be like without choices? Two boot loaders are used in the Linux world: LILO and GRUB. LILO is the traditional boot loader. It is very stable and well documented but is rapidly being eclipsed by GRUB, which has become the default boot loader on Red Hat, SUSE, and Fedora systems. In fact, current Red Hat and Fedora distributions do not include LILO at all. On the other hand, Debian still uses LILO as its boot loader of choice.

GRUB: The GRand Unified Boot loader

GRUB is particularly popular among users who run a variety of operating systems (such as Windows, OpenBSD, FreeBSD, etc.) on the same machine or who are actively working on kernel development. GRUB is also useful for folks who change their system configuration frequently. Unlike LILO, which must be reinstalled into the boot record or MBR every time it is reconfigured, GRUB reads its configuration file at boot time, eliminating an easy-to-forget administrative step.

You install GRUB on your boot drive by running **grub-install**. This command takes the name of the device from which you'll be booting as an argument. The way GRUB names the physical disk devices differs from the standard Linux convention (although GRUB can use standard Linux names as well). A GRUB device name looks like this:

```
(hd0,0)
```

The first numeric value indicates the physical drive number (starting from zero), and the second numeric value represents the partition number (again, starting from zero). In this example, (hd0,0) is equivalent to the Linux device **/dev/hda1**. Ergo, if you wanted to install GRUB on your primary drive, you would use the command

```
# grub-install '(hd0,0)'
```

The quotes are necessary to prevent the shell from trying to interpret the parentheses in its own special way.

By default, GRUB reads its default boot configuration from **/boot/grub/grub.conf**. Here's a sample **grub.conf** file:

```
default=0
timeout=10
splashimage=(hd0,0)/boot/grub/splash.xpm.gz
title Red Hat Linux (2.6.9-5)
        root (hd0,0)
        kernel /boot/vmlinuz-2.6.9-5 ro root=/dev/hda1
```

This example configures only a single operating system, which GRUB boots automatically (default=0) if it doesn't receive any keyboard input within 10 seconds (timeout=10). The root filesystem for the "Red Hat Linux" configuration is the GRUB device (hd0,0). GRUB loads the kernel from **/boot/vmlinuz-2.6.9-5** and displays a splash screen from the file **/boot/grub/splash.xpm.gz** when it is loaded.

GRUB supports a powerful command-line interface as well as facilities for editing configuration file entries on the fly. To enter command-line mode, type **c** from the GRUB boot image. From the command line you can boot operating systems that aren't in **grub.conf**, display system information, and perform rudimentary filesystem testing. You can also enjoy the command line's shell-like features, including command completion and cursor movement. Anything that can be done through the **grub.conf** file can be done through the GRUB command line as well.

Press the <Tab> key to obtain a quick list of possible commands. Table 2.2 on the next page lists some of the more useful commands.

Table 2.2   GRUB command-line options

Command	Meaning
reboot	Soft-reboot the system
find	Find a file on all mountable partitions
root	Specify the root device (a partition)
kernel	Load a kernel from the root device
help	Get interactive help for a command
boot	Boot the system from the specified kernel image

For detailed information about GRUB and its command line-options, refer to the official manual:

> www.gnu.org/software/grub/manual/

LILO: The traditional Linux boot loader

LILO is configured and installed with the **lilo** command. **lilo** bases the installed configuration on the contents of the **/etc/lilo.conf** file. To change your boot configuration, you simply update **/etc/lilo.conf** and rerun **lilo**. You must reconfigure LILO every time the boot process changes—in particular, every time you want to add a new boot partition, and every time you have a new kernel to boot.

You can install LILO either into the MBR of the disk or into the boot record of the Linux root partition.

Here's a basic **lilo.conf** file for a Linux system that has both a production kernel and a backup kernel:

```
boot=/dev/hda            # Put boot loader on MBR
root=/dev/hda1           # Specify root partition
install=/boot/boot.b
map=/boot/map
delay=20                 # 2 sec for user interrupt
image=/vmlinuz           # Kernel to boot
    label=linux          # Label to refer to this entry
    read-only
image=/vmlinuz-backup # Backup entry
    label=backup
    read-only
```

Each possible boot scenario has a label. At boot time, you can tell LILO which one to use by entering the appropriate label. The first label to appear in **lilo.conf** becomes the default.

The default scenario (named linux) boots the file **/vmlinuz**. The read-only tag specifies that the kernel should mount its root filesystem read-only. This option should always be present; the startup scripts will take care of remounting the partition read-write at the appropriate time. This system is also configured to boot a backup kernel,

/vmlinuz-backup. It's always a good idea to have such an alternative; a broken kernel configuration can lead to an unbootable system.

Running **lilo** without any arguments generates and installs the boot loader and tells you which entries are available. It puts a star next to the default image. However, if you have made an error in the **lilo.conf** file, **lilo** usually won't discover the problem until halfway through the installation of the boot loader. When this happens, the boot loader is in a confused state. *Do not reboot* until you've run **lilo** successfully.

To avoid getting into this situation, you can run **lilo -t** to test the configuration without really installing it. If everything looks kosher, you can then run **lilo** for real. It is something of a mystery why **lilo** does not run this pretest for you by default.

lilo's output when run with the config file above is:

```
# lilo
Added linux*
Added backup
```

When the system boots, LILO prints the following prompt:

```
LILO:
```

It then waits 2 seconds (20 tenths of a second, set with the delay tag), boots the kernel **/vmlinuz**, and mounts the first partition of the first IDE disk as the root partition. You can see a list of defined boot scenarios by pressing the <Tab> key:

```
LILO: <Tab>
linux   backup
LILO:
```

To boot using an alternate scenario, just enter its label at the prompt.

Kernel options

LILO and GRUB allow command-line options to be passed to the kernel. These options typically modify the values of kernel parameters, instruct the kernel to probe for particular devices, specify the path to **init**, or designate a specific root device. Table 2.3 shows a few examples.

Table 2.3 Examples of kernel boot-time options

Option	Meaning
init=/sbin/init	Tells the kernel to use **/sbin/init** as its **init** program
init=/bin/bash	Starts only the **bash** shell; useful for emergency recovery
root=/dev/foo	Tells the kernel to use **/dev/foo** as the root device
single	Boots to single-user mode

Multibooting on PCs

Since many operating systems run on PCs, it is fairly common practice to set up a machine to be able to boot several different systems. To make this work, you need to configure a boot loader to recognize all the different operating systems on your disks. In the next few sections, we cover some common multiboot stumbling blocks and then review some example configurations.

Each disk partition can have its own second-stage boot loader. However, there is only one MBR. When setting up a multiboot configuration, you must decide which boot loader is going to be the "master." For better or worse, your choice will often be dictated by the vagaries of the operating systems involved. LILO and GRUB are the best options for a system that has a Linux partition. GRUB is superior to LILO in a multibooting situation.

GRUB multiboot configuration

A multiboot GRUB system is much like its single-boot counterpart. Install all the desired operating systems before making changes to **/boot/grub/grub.conf**.

A **grub.conf** configuration for booting Windows looks different from one for booting a UNIX or Linux system:

```
title Windows XP
     rootnoverify (hd0,0)
     chainloader +1
```

The chainloader option loads the boot loader from a the specified location (in this case, sector 1 on the first partition of the primary IDE drive). The rootnoverify option guarantees that GRUB will not try to mount the specified partition. This option keeps GRUB from messing with partitions it can't understand, such as NTFS partitions or partitions outside the area that GRUB can read.

The **grub.conf** file below can boot Windows XP from partition 1, Red Hat Enterprise Linux from partition 2, and Fedora from partition 3:

```
default=0
timeout=5
splashimage=(hd0,2)/boot/grub/splash.xpm.gz
hiddenmenu
title Windows XP
     rootnoverify (hd0,0)
     chainloader +1
title Red Hat
     root (hd0,1)
     kernel /boot/vmlinuz
title Fedora
     root (hd0,2)
     kernel /boot/vmlinuz
```

LILO multiboot configuration

To configure a multiboot system that uses LILO in the MBR (e.g., Linux with Windows XP), begin with the standard LILO configuration as outlined on page 28. You can then go back and add entries for the other operating systems to **/etc/lilo.conf**.

Here's the **lilo.conf** entry you need to boot Windows from the first partition of your first IDE disk:

```
other = /dev/hda1
label = windows
table = /dev/hda
```

A complete **lilo.conf** file that boots Windows from partition 1, Linux from partition 2, and FreeBSD from partition 3 would look something like this:

```
boot = /dev/hda            # install on the MBR of 1st IDE drive
delay = 20                 # Wait 2 sec. for user's boot choice
default = linux            # If no input, boot linux from 2nd partition
image = /boot/vmlinuz-2.6.9
    root = /dev/hda2
    label = linux
    read-only
other = /dev/hda1          # boot from 1st partition
    label = windows
    table = /dev/hda
other = /dev/hda3          # boot from 3rd partition
    label = freebsd
    table = /dev/hda
```

You'll need to rerun **lilo** after putting these entries into **lilo.conf**. Remember to run **lilo -t** first to test the config file. See page 124 for more partitioning information.

Vendors (or volunteers) often release patches for Linux distributions, and the kernel is no exception. Security vulnerabilities, bugs, and features are added on a regular basis. Unlike other software packages, however, kernel patches are not updated, but rather are installed side-by-side with the existing kernel. This helps administrators back out of an upgrade easily if a kernel patch breaks their system. As time goes by, the LILO and GRUB boot menus fill up with all the different versions kernel. It's usually safe to use the default selection, but be aware of this potentially simple fix if your system doesn't boot after patching.

2.4 BOOTING SINGLE-USER MODE

Single-user mode is a great way to change the system configuration or perform maintenance tasks without worrying about affecting (or being troubled by) other users. It's also a lifesaver when you're working on a broken system.

*See page 33 for
more information
about run levels.*

It's most common to enter single-user mode by passing arguments to the boot loader. However, you can usually enter single-user mode from another run level by running the command **telinit 1**. It isn't necessary to reboot unless you're debugging a boot-dependent problem.

As a precautionary measure against a possibly unstable system, the filesystem root directory starts off being mounted read-only. This may be counterproductive to your mission if you're trying to fix a problem with a configuration file or command that lives in the root filesystem or if you need to execute a command that modifies files. To fix this problem, remount the root filesystem in read/write mode with

```
# mount -o remount -w /
```

The exact procedure for invoking single-user mode at boot time differs between GRUB and LILO.

Single-user mode with GRUB

You don't need to use the command line to boot single-user mode under GRUB. The GRUB authors realized that boot options should be easily modifiable and decided on the 'a' key as the appropriate tool. At the GRUB splash screen, highlight the desired kernel and press 'a' to append to the boot options. To boot single-user mode, add the **single** flag to the end of the existing kernel options. An example for a typical configuration might be

```
grub append> ro root=LABEL=/ rhgb quiet single
```

Single-user mode with LILO

Distributions provide different ways of getting to the LILO command prompt. If you've installed LILO in favor of GRUB on Red Hat, Fedora, or SUSE, choose the command-line menu option from the fancy graphic user interface. Debian and Ubuntu users should press and hold the shift key just after the BIOS has performed its memory checks and other system self-tests.

At the LILO prompt, enter the label of the configuration you want to boot (as specified in **lilo.conf**) followed by **-s** or **single**. For example, the default configuration shipped with Debian is called "linux", so to boot that configuration into single-user mode, you'd use

```
LILO: linux single
```

2.5 WORKING WITH STARTUP SCRIPTS

After you exit from single-user mode (or, in the automated boot sequence, at the point at which the single-user shell would have run), **init** executes the system startup scripts. These scripts are really just garden-variety shell scripts that are interpreted by **sh** (well, **bash**, really). The exact location, content, and organization of the scripts vary considerably from system to system.

Some tasks that are often performed in the startup scripts are

- Setting the name of the computer
- Setting the time zone
- Checking the disks with **fsck** (only in automatic mode)
- Mounting the system's disks
- Removing old files from the **/tmp** directory
- Configuring network interfaces
- Starting up daemons and network services

Most startup scripts are quite verbose and print a description of everything they are doing. This loquacity can be a tremendous help if the system hangs midway through booting or if you are trying to locate an error in one of the scripts.

On systems of yore, it was common practice for administrators to modify startup scripts to make them do the right thing for a particular environment. However, fine-grained packaging of software and frequent Internet updates have forced the adoption of a more robust approach. These days, systems accommodate numerous small startup scripts installed by individual pieces of software, and the scripts read their local configuration information from separate files. The local configuration files usually take the form of mini **sh** scripts that set the values of shell variables; these variables are then consulted by the scripts.

init and run levels

Traditionally, **init** defines seven run levels, each of which represents a particular complement of services that the system should be running:

- Level 0 is the level in which the system is completely shut down.
- Level 1 or S represents single-user mode.
- Levels 2 through 5 are multiuser levels.
- Level 6 is a "reboot" level.

Levels 0 and 6 are special in that the system can't actually remain in them; it shuts down or reboots as a side effect of entering them. The general multiuser run level is 2 or 3. Run level 5 is often used for X Windows login processes such as **xdm**. Run level 4 is rarely used, and run levels 1 and S are defined differently on each system.

Single-user mode was traditionally **init** level 1. It brought down all multiuser and remote login processes and made sure the system was running a minimal complement of software. Since single-user mode permits root access to the system, however, administrators wanted the system to prompt for the root password whenever it was booted into single-user mode. The S run level was created to address this need: it spawns a process that prompts for the root password. On Linux, the S level serves only this purpose and is not a destination in itself.

There seem to be more run levels defined than are strictly necessary or useful. The usual explanation for this is that a phone switch had 7 run levels, so it was thought that a UNIX system should have at least that many. Linux actually supports up to 10 run levels, but levels 7 through 9 are undefined.

The **/etc/inittab** file tells **init** what to do at each of its run levels. Its format varies from system to system, but the basic idea is that **inittab** defines commands that are to be run (or kept running) when the system enters each level.

As the machine boots, **init** ratchets its way up from run level 0 to the default run level, which is also set in **/etc/inittab**. To accomplish the transition between each pair of adjacent run levels, **init** runs the actions spelled out for that transition in **/etc/inittab**. The same progression is made in reverse order when the machine is shut down.

Unfortunately, the semantics of the **inittab** file are somewhat rudimentary. To map the facilities of the **inittab** file into something a bit more flexible, Linux systems implement an additional layer of abstraction in the form of a "change run levels" script (usually **/etc/init.d/rc**) that's called from **inittab**. This script in turn executes other scripts from a run-level-dependent directory to bring the system to its new state.

These days, most Linux distributions boot to run level 5 by default, which may not be appropriate for servers that don't need to run X. The default run level is easy to change. This excerpt from a SUSE machine's **inittab** defaults to run level 5:

```
id:5:initdefault:
```

System administrators usually don't have to deal directly with **/etc/inittab** because the script-based interface is adequate for most applications. In the remainder of this chapter, we tacitly ignore the **inittab** file and the other glue that attaches **init** to the execution of startup scripts. Just keep in mind that when we say that **init** runs such-and-such a script, the connection may not be quite so direct.

The master copies of the startup scripts live in the **/etc/init.d** directory. Each script is responsible for one daemon or one particular aspect of the system. The scripts understand the arguments **start** and **stop** to mean that the service they deal with should be initialized or halted. Most also understand **restart**, which is typically the same as a **stop** followed by a **start**. As a system administrator, you can manually start and stop individual services by running their associated **init.d** scripts by hand.

For example, here's a simple startup script that can start, stop, or restart **sshd**:

```
#! /bin/sh
test -f /usr/bin/sshd || exit 0
case "$1" in
    start)
        echo -n "Starting sshd: sshd"
        /usr/sbin/sshd
        echo "."
        ;;
    stop)
        echo -n "Stopping sshd: sshd"
        kill `cat /var/run/sshd.pid`
        echo "."
        ;;
```

```
        restart)
            echo -n "Stopping sshd: sshd"
            kill `cat /var/run/sshd.pid`
            echo "."
            echo -n "Starting sshd: sshd"
            /usr/sbin/sshd
            echo "."
            ;;
    *)
            echo "Usage: /etc/init.d/sshd start|stop|restart"
            exit 1
            ;;
esac
```

Although the scripts in **/etc/init.d** can start and stop individual services, the master control script run by **init** needs additional information about which scripts to run (and with what arguments) to enter any given run level. Instead of looking directly at the **init.d** directory when it takes the system to a new run level, the master script looks at a directory called **rc***level***.d**, where *level* is the run level to be entered (e.g., **rc0.d**, **rc1.d**, and so on).

These **rc***level***.d** directories typically contain symbolic links that point back to the scripts in the **init.d** directory. The names of these symbolic links all start with **S** or **K** followed by a number and the name of the service that the script controls (e.g., **S34named**). When **init** transitions from a lower run level to a higher one, it runs all the scripts that start with **S** in ascending numerical order with the argument **start**. When **init** transitions from a higher run level to a lower one, it runs all the scripts that start with **K** (for "kill") in descending numerical order with the argument **stop**.

This scheme gives administrators fine-grained control of the order in which services are started. For example, it doesn't make sense to start SSH before the network interfaces are up. Although the network and **sshd** are both configured to start at run level 2 on a Fedora system, the **network** script gets sequence number 10 and the **sshd** script gets sequence number 55, so **network** is certain to be run first. Be sure to consider this type of dependency when you add a new service.

To tell the system when to start a daemon, you must place symbolic links into the appropriate directory. For example, to tell the system to start CUPS at run level 2 and to stop it nicely before shutting down, the following pair of links would suffice:

```
# ln -s /etc/init.d/cups /etc/rc2.d/S80cups
# ln -s /etc/init.d/cups /etc/rc0.d/K80cups
```

The first line tells the system to run the **/etc/init.d/cups** startup script as one of the last things to do when entering run level 2 and to run the script with the **start** argument. The second line tells the system to run **/etc/init.d/cups** relatively soon when shutting down the system and to run the script with the **stop** argument. Some systems treat shutdown and reboot differently, so we have to put a symbolic link in the **/etc/rc6.d** directory as well to make sure the daemon shuts down properly when the system is rebooted.

Red Hat and Fedora startup scripts

 Red Hat and Fedora's startup scripts have historically been on the messy side. Embedded in the code, you might see a variety of comments like this one:

```
# Yes, this is an ugly, but necessary hack
```

At each run level, **init** invokes the script **/etc/rc.d/rc** with the new run level as an argument. **/etc/rc.d/rc** usually runs in "normal" mode, in which it just does its thing, but it can also run in "confirmation" mode, in which it asks you before it runs each individual startup script.

Red Hat and Fedora have a **chkconfig** command to help you manage services. This command adds or removes startup scripts from the system, manages the run levels at which they operate, and lists the run levels for which a script is currently configured. See **man chkconfig** for usage information on this simple and handy tool.

Red Hat also has an **rc.local** script much like that found on BSD systems. **rc.local** is the last script run as part of the startup process. Historically, **rc.local** was overwritten by the **initscripts** package. This has changed, however, and it is now safe to add your own startup customizations here.

Here's an example of a Red Hat startup session:

```
[kernel information]
INIT: version 2.85 booting
Setting default font (latarcyrhev-sun16):              [  OK  ]
            Welcome to Red Hat Linux
         Press 'I' to enter interactive startup.
Starting udev:                                         [  OK  ]
Initializing hardware... storage network audio done
Configuring kernel parameters:                         [  OK  ]
Setting clock  (localtime): Tue Mar 29 20:50:41 MST 2005: [  OK  ]
...
```

Once you see the "Welcome to Red Hat Enterprise Linux" message, you can press the 'i' key to enter confirmation mode. Unfortunately, Red Hat gives you no confirmation that you have pressed the right key. It blithely continues to mount local filesystems, activate swap partitions, load keymaps, and locate its kernel modules. Only after it switches to run level 3 does it actually start to prompt you for confirmation:

```
      Welcome to Red Hat Enterprise Linux WS
         Press 'I' to enter interactive startup.
Starting udev:                                         [  OK  ]
Initializing hardware... storage network audio done
Configuring kernel parameters:                         [  OK  ]
setting clock  (localtime): tue mar 29 20:50:41 mst 2005:  [  OK  ]
Setting hostname rhel4:                                [  OK  ]
Checking root filesystem
/dev/hda1: clean, 73355/191616 files, 214536/383032 blocks
                                                       [  OK  ]
Remounting root filesystem in read-write mode:         [  OK  ]
```

```
Setting up Logical Volume Management:            [  OK  ]
Checking filesystems
Mounting local filesystems:                      [  OK  ]
Enabling local filesystem quotas:                [  OK  ]
Enabling swap space:                             [  OK  ]
INIT: Entering runlevel: 3
Entering interactive startup
Start service kudzu (Y)es/(N)o/(C)ontinue? [Y]
```

Interactive startup and single-user mode both begin at the same spot in the booting process. When the startup process is so broken that you cannot reach this point
safely, you can use a rescue floppy or CD-ROM to boot.

You can also pass the argument **init=/bin/sh** to the kernel to trick it into running a
single-user shell before **init** even starts.[2] If you take this tack, you will have to do all
the startup housekeeping by hand, including manually **fsck**ing and mounting the
local filesystems.

Much configuration of Red Hat's boot process can be achieved through manipulation of the config files in **/etc/sysconfig**. Table 2.4 summarizes the function of some
popular items in the **/etc/sysconfig** directory.

Table 2.4   Files and subdirectories of Red Hat's /etc/sysconfig directory

File/Dir	Function or contents
clock	Specifies the type of clock that the system has (almost always UTC)[a]
console	A mysterious directory that is always empty
httpd	Determines which Apache processing model to use
hwconf	Contains all of the system's hardware info. Used by Kudzu.
i18n	Contains the system's local settings (date formats, languages, etc.)
init	Configures the way messages from the startup scripts are displayed
keyboard	Sets keyboard type (use "us" for the standard 101-key U.S. keyboard)
mouse	Sets the mouse type. Used by X and **gpm**.
network	Sets global network options (hostname, gateway, forwarding, etc.)
network-scripts	Contains accessory scripts and network config files
sendmail	Sets options for **sendmail**

a. If you multiboot your PC, all bets are off as to how the clock's time zone should be set.

Several of the items in Table 2.4 merit additional comments:

- The **hwconf** file contains all of your hardware information. The Kudzu service checks it to see if you have added or removed any hardware and asks
  you what to do about changes. You may want to disable this service on a

2. We once had a corrupted keymap file, and since the keymap file is loaded even in single-user mode,
   single-user was useless. Setting **init=/bin/sh** was the only way to boot the system to a usable single-
   user state to fix the problem. This can also be a useful trick in other situations.

production system because it delays the boot process whenever it detects a change to the hardware configuration, resulting in an extra 30 seconds of downtime for every hardware change made.

- The **network-scripts** directory contains additional material related to network configuration. The only things you should ever need to change are the files named **ifcfg-***interface*. For example, **network-scripts/ifcfg-eth0** contains the configuration parameters for the interface eth0. It sets the interface's IP address and networking options. See page 299 for more information about configuring network interfaces.

- The **sendmail** file contains two variables: DAEMON and QUEUE. If the DAEMON variable is set to yes, the system starts **sendmail** in daemon mode (**-bd**) when the system boots. QUEUE tells **sendmail** how long to wait between queue runs (**-q**); the default is one hour.

SUSE startup scripts

 Although SUSE's startup system resembles that of RHEL and Fedora, SUSE's startup scripts are one area in which it really outshines other Linux variants. SUSE's scripts are well organized, robust, and well documented. The folks that maintain this part of the operating system deserve a gold star.

As in Red Hat and Fedora, **init** invokes the script **/etc/init.d/rc** at each run level, providing the new run level as an argument. Package-specific scripts live in the **/etc/init.d** directory, and their configuration files live in **/etc/sysconfig**. An excellent introduction to the SUSE startup process can be found in **/etc/init.d/README**.

Although both SUSE and RHEL/Fedora concentrate their boot configuration files in **/etc/sysconfig**, the specific files within this directory are quite different. (For one thing, SUSE's files are generally well commented.) Options are invoked by setting shell environment variables, and these variables are then referenced by the scripts within **/etc/init.d**. Some subsystems require more configuration that others, and those needing multiple configuration files have private subdirectories, such as the **sysconfig/network** directory.

The **windowmanager** file is a typical example from the **sysconfig** directory:

```
## Path:          Desktop/Window manager
## Description:
## Type:          string(kde,fvwm,gnome,windowmaker)
## Default:       kde
## Config:        profiles,kde,susewm
#
# Here you can set the default window manager (kde, fvwm, ...)
# changes here require at least a re-login
DEFAULT_WM="kde"

## Type:          yesno
## Default:       yes
#
```

```
# install the SUSE extension for new users
# (theme and additional functions)
#
INSTALL_DESKTOP_EXTENSIONS="yes"
```

Each variable is preceded by YaST-readable[3] configuration information and a verbose description of the variable's purpose. For example, in the **windowmanager** file, the variable DEFAULT_WM sets the desktop window manager used by X.

SUSE did a particularly nice job with the network configuration files found in the subdirectory **/etc/sysconfig/network**. This directory contains both global configuration files (which set options pertinent to all network interfaces) and network-specific files. For example, the **network/routes** file contains global routing information. On a typical SUSE installation, its contents might look like this:

```
# Destination    Dummy/Gateway    Netmask        Device
default          192.168.10.254   0.0.0.0        eth0
```

Routes that should be present only when a particular interface is up and running can be specified in a file called **ifroute-*ifname***. For example, on an interface called eth1, the file would be named **ifroute-eth1** and its contents might be

```
# Destination    Dummy/Gateway    Netmask        Device
10.10.0.0/24     10.10.0.254
```

The netmask and device can be specified if you wish, but the startup scripts will infer the correct values.

SUSE also includes a **chkconfig** command for managing startup scripts. It's entirely different from the version provided by Red Hat, but it's an effective tool nonetheless and should be used in favor of manual script management.

Whether you choose to use YaST or **chkconfig** or maintain your startup scripts by hand, it's a good idea to look through **/etc/sysconfig** and ponder its contents.

A typical SUSE boot session looks like this:

```
[kernel information]
INIT: version 2.85 booting
System Boot Control: Running /etc/init.d/boot
Mounting /proc filesystem                                    done
Mounting sysfs on /sys                                       done
Mounting /dev/pts                                            done
Boot logging started on /dev/tty1(/dev/console) at Tue Mar 29 14:04:12 2005
Mounting shared memory FS on /dev/sh                         done
Activating swap-devices in /etc/fstab...
Adding 1052248k swap on /dev/hda2. Priority:42 extents:1     done
Checking root file system...
    ...
```

3. YaST is a SUSE-specific graphical configuration utility that maintains many aspects of a SUSE system. See page 230 for more information.

Debian and Ubuntu startup scripts

 If SUSE is the ultimate example of a well-designed and well-executed plan for managing startup scripts, Debian is the exact opposite. The Debian scripts are fragile, undocumented, and outrageously inconsistent. Sadly, it appears that the lack of a standard way of setting up scripts has resulted in chaos in this case. Bad Debian!

At each run level, **init** invokes the script **/etc/init.d/rc** with the new run level as an argument. Each script is responsible for finding its own configuration information, which may be in the form of other files in **/etc**, **/etc/default**, another subdirectory of **/etc**, or somewhere in the script itself.

If you're looking for the hostname of the system, it's stored in **/etc/hostname**, which is read by the **/etc/init.d/hostname.sh** script. Network interface and default gateway parameters are stored in **/etc/network/interfaces**, which is read by the **ifup** command called from **/etc/init.d/networking**. Some network options can also be set in **/etc/network/options**.

Debian and Ubuntu have a sort of clandestine startup script management program in the form of **update-rc.d**. Although its man page cautions against interactive use, we have found it to be a useful, if less friendly, substitute for **chkconfig**. For example, to start **sshd** in run levels 2, 3, 4, and 5, and to stop it in levels 0, 1, and 6, use:

```
$ sudo /usr/sbin/update-rc.d sshd start 0123 stop 456
```

2.6 REBOOTING AND SHUTTING DOWN

Linux filesystems buffer changes in memory and write them back to disk only sporadically. This scheme makes disk I/O faster, but it also makes the filesystem more susceptible to data loss when the system is rudely halted.

Traditional UNIX and Linux machines were very touchy about how they were shut down. Modern systems have become less sensitive (especially when using a robust filesystem such as ext3fs), but it's always a good idea to shut down the machine nicely when possible. Improper shutdown can result in anything from subtle, insidious problems to a major catastrophe.

On consumer-oriented operating systems, rebooting the operating system is an appropriate first course of treatment for almost any problem. On a Linux system, it's better to think first and reboot second. Linux problems tend to be subtler and more complex, so blindly rebooting is effective in a smaller percentage of cases. Linux systems also take a long time to boot, and multiple users may be inconvenienced.

You may need to reboot when you add a new piece of hardware or when an existing piece of hardware becomes so confused that it cannot be reset. If you modify a configuration file that's used only at boot time, you must reboot to make your changes take effect. If the system is so wedged that you cannot log in to make a proper diagnosis of the problem, you obviously have no alternative but to reboot.

Whenever you modify a startup script, you should reboot just to make sure that the system comes up successfully. If you don't discover a problem until several weeks later, you're unlikely to remember the details of your most recent changes.

Unlike bootstrapping, which can be done in essentially only one way, shutting down or rebooting can be done in a number of ways:

- Turning off the power
- Using the **shutdown** command
- Using the **halt** and **reboot** commands
- Using **telinit** to change **init**'s run level
- Using the **poweroff** command to tell the system to turn off the power

Turning off the power

Even on a desktop system, turning off the power is not a good way to shut down. You can potentially lose data and corrupt the filesystems.

Many machines feature "soft power," which means that when you press the power button, the machine actually runs some commands to perform a proper shutdown sequence. If you're not sure whether a machine has this feature, don't poke the power button to find out! It's better to run the shutdown sequence yourself.

That said, however, powering off is not the end of the world. It's OK to turn off the power in an emergency if you can't afford the time to bring machines down gracefully. Old-style machine rooms often had a panic button that turned everything off at once. Our sysadmins once triggered it with a poorly aimed Nerf football.

shutdown: the genteel way to halt the system

shutdown is the safest, most considerate, and most thorough way to initiate a halt or reboot or to return to single-user mode.

You can ask **shutdown** to wait awhile before bringing down the system. During the waiting period, **shutdown** sends messages to logged-in users at progressively shorter intervals, warning them of the impending downtime. By default, the warnings simply say that the system is being shut down and give the time remaining until the event; you can also supply a short message of your own. Your message should tell why the system is being brought down and should estimate how long it will be before users can log in again (e.g., "back at 11:00 a.m."). Users cannot log in when a **shutdown** is imminent, but they will see your message if you specified one.

shutdown lets you specify whether the machine should halt (**-h**) or reboot (**-r**) after the shutdown is complete. You can also specify whether you want to forcibly **fsck** the disks after a reboot (**-F**) or not (**-f**). By default, Linux automatically skips the **fsck** checks whenever the filesystems were properly unmounted.

For example, a **shutdown** command that reminds users of scheduled maintenance and halts the system at 9:30 a.m. would look something like this:

```
# shutdown -h 09:30 "Going down for scheduled maintenance. Expected
    downtime is 1 hour"
```

It's also possible to specify a relative shutdown time. For example, the following command will effect a shutdown 15 minutes from when it is run:

```
# shutdown -h +15 "Going down for emergency disk repair."
```

halt: a simpler way to shut down

The **halt** command performs the essential duties required to bring the system down. It is called by **shutdown -h** but can also be used by itself. **halt** logs the shutdown, kills nonessential processes, executes the **sync** system call (called by and equivalent to the **sync** command), waits for filesystem writes to complete, and then halts the kernel.

halt -n prevents the **sync** call. It's used by **fsck** after it repairs the root partition. If **fsck** did not use **-n**, the kernel might overwrite **fsck**'s repairs with old versions of the superblock that were cached in memory.

reboot: quick and dirty restart

reboot is almost identical to **halt**, but it causes the machine to reboot instead of halting. **reboot** is called by **shutdown -r**. Like **halt**, it supports the **-n** flag.

telinit: change init's run level

You can use **telinit** to direct **init** to go to a specific run level. For example,

```
# telinit 1
```

takes the system to single-user mode.

When you use **telinit**, you do not get the nice warning messages or grace period that you get with **shutdown**, so most of the time you'll probably want to avoid it. **telinit** is most useful for testing changes to the **inittab** file.

poweroff: ask Linux to turn off the power

The **poweroff** command is identical to **halt**, except that after Linux has been shut down, **poweroff** sends a request to the power management system (on systems that have one) to turn off the system's main power. This feature makes it easy to turn off machines remotely (for example, during an electrical storm).

Unfortunately, there is no corresponding **poweron** command. The reason for this apparent oversight is left as an exercise for the reader.

2.7 EXERCISES

E2.1 Why is it important to run **lilo -t** before installing the LILO boot loader? How do you boot a kernel named something other than **vmlinuz**?

E2.2 Why shouldn't a Linux system be turned off with the power button on the computer case? What are some of the alternatives?

E2.3 Use the GRUB command line to boot a kernel that isn't in **grub.conf**.

★ **E2.4** Explain the concept of run levels. List the run levels defined in Linux, and briefly describe each. What is the relationship between run level 1 and run level S?

★ **E2.5** Write a startup script to start the "foo" daemon (**/usr/local/sbin/foo**), a network service. Show how you would glue it into the system to start automatically at boot time.

★ **E2.6** Obtain and install the **mactime** program by Dan Farmer and Wietse Venema (it's part of the TCT toolkit). Run **mactime** to create an initial database of the time stamps associated with your system files. Reboot the machine. Run **mactime** again and determine which files have been modified by your booting the machine. Which files were accessed but not modified? (Requires root access.)

★★ **E2.7** If a system is at run level 4 and you run the command **telinit 1**, what steps will be taken by **init**? What will be the final result of the command?

★★ **E2.8** Draw a dependency graph that shows which daemons must be started before other daemons on your Linux system.

★★ **E2.9** List in order the steps used to create a working multi-OS system that includes Linux and Windows. Use GRUB and the Windows boot loader.

3 *Rootly Powers*

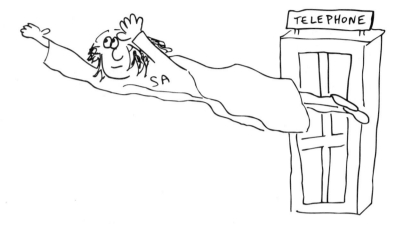

Every file and process on a Linux system is owned by a particular user account. Other users can't access these objects without the owner's permission, so this convention helps protect users against one another's misdeeds, both intentional and accidental.

System files and processes are most commonly owned by a fictitious user called "root," also known as the superuser. As with any account, root's property is protected against interference from other users. To make administrative changes, you'll need to use one of the methods of accessing the root account described in this chapter.

The root account has several "magic" properties. Root can act as the owner of any file or process. Root can also perform several special operations that are off-limits to other users. The account is both powerful and, in careless or malicious hands, potentially dangerous.

This chapter introduces the basics of superuser access for administrators. Chapter 20, *Security*, describes how to avoid unwanted and embarrassing superuser access by others. Chapter 30, *Management, Policy, and Politics* covers the relevant political and administrative aspects.

3.1 OWNERSHIP OF FILES AND PROCESSES

Every file has both an owner and a "group owner." The owner of the file enjoys one special privilege that is not shared with everyone on the system: the ability to modify the permissions of the file. In particular, the owner can set the permissions on a file so restrictively that no one else can access it.[1] We talk more about file permissions in Chapter 5, *The Filesystem*.

See page 97 for more information about groups.

Although the owner of a file is always a single person, many people can be group owners of the file, as long as they are all part of a single Linux group. Groups are traditionally defined in the **/etc/group** file, but these days group information is more commonly stored on an NIS or LDAP server on the network; see Chapter 17, *Sharing System Files*, for details.

The owner of a file gets to specify what the group owners can do with it. This scheme allows files to be shared among members of the same project. For example, we use a group to control access to the source files for the www.admin.com web site.

Both ownerships of a file can be determined with **ls -l** *filename*. For example:

```
$ ls -l /staff/scott/todo
-rw-------   1  scott  staff  1258 Jun 4 18:15 /staff/scott/todo
```

This file is owned by the user "scott" and the group "staff."

Linux actually keeps track of owners and groups as numbers rather than as text names. In the most basic case, identification numbers (UIDs for short) are mapped to user names in the **/etc/passwd** file, and group identification numbers (GIDs) are mapped to group names in **/etc/group**. The text names that correspond to UIDs and GIDs are defined only for the convenience of the system's human users. When commands such as **ls** want to display ownership information in a human-readable format, they must look up each name in the appropriate file or database.

The owner of a process can send the process signals (see page 57) and can also reduce (degrade) the process's scheduling priority. Processes actually have at least seven identities associated with them: a real, effective, and saved UID; a real, effective, and saved GID; and under Linux, a "filesystem UID" that is used only to determine file access permissions. Broadly speaking, the real numbers are used for accounting and the effective numbers are used for the determination of access permissions. The real and effective numbers are normally the same.

Saved IDs have no direct effect. They allow programs to "park" an inactive ID for later use, thus facilitating the parsimonious use of enhanced privileges. The filesystem UID is generally explained as an implementation detail of NFS and is usually the same as the effective UID.

See page 81 for more information about permission bits.

Although it is not normally possible for a process to alter its ownership credentials, there is a special situation in which the effective user and group IDs can be changed. When the kernel runs an executable file that has its "setuid" or "setgid" permission bits set, it changes the effective UID or GID of the resulting process to the UID or GID of the file containing the program image rather than the UID and GID of the user that ran the command. The user's privileges are thus "promoted" for the execution of that specific command only.

---

1. In fact, the permissions can be set so restrictively that even the owner of a file cannot access it.

Linux's setuid facility allows programs run by ordinary users to make use of the root account in a limited and tightly controlled way. For example, the **passwd** command that users run to change their login password is a setuid program. It modifies the **/etc/shadow** (or **/etc/passwd**) file in a well-defined way and then terminates. Of course, even this limited task has potential for abuse, so **passwd** requires users to prove that they know the current account password before it agrees to make the requested change.

3.2 THE SUPERUSER

The defining characteristic of the root account is its UID of 0. Linux does not prevent you from changing the username on this account or from creating additional accounts whose UIDs are 0, but both are bad ideas. Such changes have a tendency to create inadvertent breaches of system security. They also engender confusion when other people have to deal with the strange way you've configured your system.

Traditional UNIX allows the superuser (that is, any process whose effective UID is 0) to perform any valid operation on any file or process.[2] In addition, some system calls (requests to the kernel) can be executed only by the superuser. Some examples of such restricted operations are

- Changing the root directory of a process with **chroot**
- Creating device files
- Setting the system clock
- Raising resource usage limits and process priorities[3]
- Setting the system's hostname
- Configuring network interfaces
- Opening privileged network ports (those numbered below 1,024)
- Shutting down the system

An example of superuser powers is the ability of a process owned by root to change its UID and GID. The **login** program and its window system equivalents are a case in point; the process that prompts you for your password when you log in to the system initially runs as root. If the password and username that you enter are legitimate, the login program changes its UID and GID to your UID and GID and starts up your user environment. Once a root process has changed its ownerships to become a normal user process, it can't recover its former privileged state.

Linux systems are theoretically capable of subdividing the privileges of the root account according to the POSIX standard for "capabilities." For various reasons, including problems with the current implementation, this facility is not as helpful or as relevant to system administrators as it might initially appear. For more comments on capabilities, see the discussion on page 683.

2. "Valid" is an important weasel word here. Certain operations (such as executing a file on which the execute permission bit is not set) are forbidden even to the superuser.

3. As of kernel version 2.6.12, a new resource limit allows users other than the superuser to raise process priorities if the system administrator allows this.

3.3 CHOOSING A ROOT PASSWORD

See page 690 for more information about password cracking.

The root password should be at least eight characters in length; seven-character passwords are substantially easier to crack. On systems that use DES passwords, it doesn't help to use a password longer than eight characters because only the first eight are significant. See the section *Encrypted password* starting on page 96 for information about how to enable MD5 passwords, which can be longer than eight characters.

It's important that the root password be selected so as not to be easily guessed or discovered by trial and error. In theory, the most secure type of password consists of a random sequence of letters, punctuation, and digits. But because this type of password is hard to remember and usually difficult to type, it may not be optimally secure if administrators write it down or type it slowly.

Until recently, a password consisting of two randomly selected words separated by a punctuation mark was a pretty good compromise between security and memorability. Unfortunately, such passwords can now be cracked fairly quickly; we now advise against this scheme.

These days, we suggest that you form a root password by boiling down a phrase of "shocking nonsense," defined by Grady Ward in an earlier version of the PGP Passphrase FAQ:

> *"Shocking nonsense" means to make up a short phrase or sentence that is both nonsensical and shocking in the culture of the user. That is, it contains grossly obscene, racist, impossible or otherwise extreme juxtapositions of ideas. This technique is permissible because the passphrase, by its nature, is never revealed to anyone with sensibilities to offend.*

> *Shocking nonsense is unlikely to be duplicated anywhere because it does not describe a matter of fact that could be accidentally rediscovered by someone else. The emotional evocation makes it difficult for the creator to forget. A mild example of such shocking nonsense might be, "Mollusks peck my galloping genitals." The reader can undoubtedly make up many far more shocking or entertaining examples for him or herself.*

You can reduce such a phrase to a password by recording only the first letter of each word or by some similar transformation. Password security will be increased enormously if you include numbers, punctuation marks, and capital letters.

You should change the root password

- At least every three months or so
- Every time someone who knows the password leaves your site
- Whenever you think security may have been compromised
- On a day you're not planning to party so hard in the evening that you will have forgotten the password the next morning

Rootly Powers

3.4 BECOMING ROOT

Since root is just another user, you can log in directly to the root account. However, this turns out to be a bad idea. To begin with, it leaves no record of what operations were performed as root. That's bad enough when you realize that you broke something last night at 3:00 a.m. and can't remember what you changed; it's even worse when an access was unauthorized and you are trying to figure out what an intruder has done to your system. Another disadvantage is that the log-in-as-root scenario leaves no record of who was really doing the work. If several people have access to the root account, you won't be able to tell who used it when.

For these reasons, most systems allow root logins to be disabled on terminals and across the network—everywhere but on the system console.[4] We suggest that you use these features. See *Secure terminals* on page 685 to find out what file you need to edit on your particular system.

su: substitute user identity

A slightly better way to access the root account is to use the **su** command. If invoked without any arguments, **su** will prompt for the root password and then start up a root shell. The privileges of this shell remain in effect until the shell terminates (by <Control-D> or the **exit** command). **su** doesn't record the commands executed as root, but it does create a log entry that states who became root and when.

The **su** command can also substitute identities other than root. Sometimes, the only way to reproduce or debug a user's problem is to **su** to their account so that you reproduce the environment in which the problem occurs.

If you know someone's password, you can access that person's account directly by executing **su** *username*. As with an **su** to root, you will be prompted for the password for *username*. You can also first **su** to root and then **su** to another account; root can **su** to any account without providing a password.

It's a good idea to get in the habit of typing the full pathname to the **su** command (e.g., **/bin/su**) rather than relying on the shell to find the command for you. This will give you some protection against programs called **su** that may have been slipped into your search path with the intention of harvesting passwords.[5]

sudo: a limited su

Since the privileges of the superuser account cannot be subdivided (at least, not arbitrarily), it's hard to give someone the ability to do one task (backups, for example) without giving that person free run of the system. And if the root account is used by

---

4. Ubuntu Linux goes even further. By default, the system has no valid root password and requires the use of **sudo**, detailed later in this section.

5. For the same reason, we highly recommend that you *not* include "." (the current directory) in your shell's search path. Although convenient, this configuration makes it easy to inadvertently run "special" versions of system commands that a user or intruder has left lying around as a trap. Naturally, this advice goes double for root.

Rootly Powers

several administrators, you really have only a vague idea of who's using it or what they've done.

The most widely used solution to these problems is a program called **sudo** that is currently maintained by Todd Miller. It's included by default on all our example distributions but is also available in source code form from www.courtesan.com.

sudo takes as its argument a command line to be executed as root (or as another restricted user). **sudo** consults the file **/etc/sudoers**, which lists the people who are authorized to use **sudo** and the commands they are allowed to run on each host. If the proposed command is permitted, **sudo** prompts for the *user's own* password and executes the command.

Additional **sudo** commands can be executed without the "sudoer" having to type a password until a five-minute period (configurable) has elapsed with no further **sudo** activity. This timeout serves as a modest protection against users with **sudo** privileges who leave terminals unattended.

sudo keeps a log of the command lines that were executed, the hosts on which they were run, the people who requested them, the directory from which they were run, and the times at which they were invoked. This information can be logged by syslog or placed in the file of your choice. We recommend using syslog to forward the log entries to a secure central host.

A log entry for randy executing **sudo /bin/cat /etc/sudoers** might look like this:

```
Dec 7 10:57:19 tigger sudo: randy: TTY=ttyp0 ; PWD=/tigger/users/randy;
    USER=root ; COMMAND=/bin/cat /etc/sudoers
```

The **sudoers** file is designed so that a single version can be used on many different hosts at once. Here's a typical example:

```
# Define aliases for machines in CS & Physics departments
Host_Alias    CS = tigger, anchor, piper, moet, sigi
Host_Alias    PHYSICS = eprince, pprince, icarus

# Define collections of commands
Cmnd_Alias  DUMP = /sbin/dump, /sbin/restore
Cmnd_Alias  PRINTING = /usr/sbin/lpc, /usr/bin/lprm
Cmnd_Alias  SHELLS = /bin/sh, /bin/tcsh, /bin/bash, /bin/ash, /bin/bsh

# Permissions
mark, ed     PHYSICS = ALL
herb         CS = /usr/sbin/tcpdump : PHYSICS = (operator) DUMP
lynda        ALL = (ALL) ALL, !SHELLS
%wheel       ALL, !PHYSICS = NOPASSWD: PRINTING
```

The first five noncomment lines define groups of hosts and commands that are referred to in the permission specifications later in the file. The lists could be included literally in the specs, but the use of aliases makes the **sudoers** file easier to read and understand; it also makes the file easier to update in the future. It's also possible to define aliases for sets of users and for sets of users as whom commands may be run.

Each permission specification line includes information about

- The users to whom the line applies
- The hosts on which the line should be heeded
- The commands that the specified users can run
- The users as whom the commands can be executed

The first permission line applies to the users mark and ed on the machines in the PHYSICS group (eprince, pprince, and icarus). The built-in command alias ALL allows them to run any command. Since no list of users is specified in parentheses, **sudo** will only run commands as root.

The second permission line allows herb to run **tcpdump** on CS machines and dump-related commands on PHYSICS machines. However, the dump commands can only be run as operator, not as root. The actual command line that herb would type would be something like

```
$ sudo -u operator /sbin/dump 0u /dev/hda2
```

The user lynda can run commands as any user on any machine, except that she can't run several common shells. Does this mean that lynda really can't get a root shell? Of course not:

```
$ cp -p /bin/bash /tmp/bash
$ sudo /tmp/bash
```

Generally speaking, any attempt to allow "all commands except…" is doomed to failure, at least in a technical sense. However, it may still be worthwhile to set up the **sudoers** file this way as a reminder that root shells are frowned upon. It may discourage casual use.

The final line allows users in group wheel to run **lpc** and **lprm** as root on all machines except eprince, pprince, and icarus. Furthermore, no password is required to run the commands.

Note that commands in **/etc/sudoers** are specified with full pathnames to prevent people from executing their own programs and scripts as root. Though no examples are shown above, it is possible to specify the arguments that are permissible for each command as well. In fact, this simple configuration only scratches the surface of the beauty and splendor that is the **sudoers** file.

To modify **/etc/sudoers**, you use the **visudo** command, which checks to be sure no one else is editing the file, invokes an editor on it, and then verifies the syntax of the edited file before installing it. This last step is particularly important because an invalid **sudoers** file might prevent you from **sudo**ing again to fix it.

The use of **sudo** has the following advantages:

- Accountability is much improved because of command logging.
- Operators can do chores without unlimited root privileges.
- The real root password can be known to only one or two people.

- It's faster to use **sudo** to run a single command than to **su** or log in as root.
- Privileges can be revoked without the need to change the root password.
- A canonical list of all users with root privileges is maintained.
- There is less chance of a root shell being left unattended.
- A single file can be used to control access for an entire network.

See page 690 for more information about John the Ripper.

There are a couple of disadvantages as well. The worst of these is that any breach in the security of a sudoer's personal account can be equivalent to breaching the root account itself. There is not much you can do to counter this threat other than to caution your sudoers to protect their own accounts as they would the root account. You can also run John the Ripper regularly on sudoers' passwords to ensure that they are making good password selections.

sudo's command logging can be subverted by tricks such as shell escapes from within an allowed program or by **sudo sh** and **sudo su** if you allow them.

3.5   OTHER PSEUDO-USERS

Root is the only user that has special status in the eyes of the kernel, but several other pseudo-users are defined by the system. It's customary to replace the encrypted password field of these special users in **/etc/shadow** with a star so that their accounts cannot be logged in to.

bin: legacy owner of system commands

On some older UNIX systems, the bin user owned the directories that contained the system's commands and most of the commands themselves as well. This account is often regarded as superfluous these days (or perhaps even slightly insecure), so modern systems (including Linux) generally just use the root account. On the other hand, now that the bin account is "standard," it can't really be done away with either.

daemon: owner of unprivileged system software

Files and processes that are part of the operating system but that need not be owned by root are sometimes given to daemon. The theory was that this convention would help avoid the security hazards associated with ownership by root. A group called "daemon" also exists for similar reasons. Like the bin account, the daemon account is not used much by most Linux distributions.

nobody: the generic NFS user

See page 488 for more information about the nobody account.

The Network File System (NFS) uses the nobody account to represent root users on other systems for purposes of file sharing. For remote roots to be stripped of their rootly powers, the remote UID 0 has to be mapped to something other than the local UID 0. The nobody account acts as the generic alter ego for these remote roots.

Since the nobody account is supposed to represent a generic and relatively powerless user, it shouldn't own any files. If nobody does own files, remote roots will be able to take control of them. Nobody shouldn't own no files!

A UID of -1 or -2 was traditional for nobody, and the Linux kernel still defaults to using UID 65534 (the 16-bit twos-complement version of -2). Some distributions assign a low-numbered UID to nobody (for example, Red Hat and Fedora use 99), which makes more sense than 65534 now that we have 32-bit UIDs. The only snag is that **exportfs** does not seem to pay attention to the **passwd** file, so you must explicitly tell it with the **anonuid** option to use a different UID for nobody.

3.6 EXERCISES

★ **E3.1**   Use the **find** command with the **-perm** option to locate five setuid files on your system. For each file, explain why the setuid mechanism is necessary for the command to function properly.

★ **E3.2**   Create three "shocking nonsense" passphrases but keep them to yourself. Run your three passphrases through **md5sum** and report these results. Why is it safe to share the MD5 results?

★ **E3.3**   Enumerate a sequence of commands that modify someone's password entry and show how you could cover your tracks. Assume you had only **sudo** power (all commands allowed, but no shells or **su**).

★ **E3.4**   Create two entries for the **sudoers** configuration file:

   a) One entry that allows users matt, adam, and drew to service the printer, unjam it, and restart printer daemons on the machine printserver

   b) One entry that allows drew, smithgr, and jimlane to kill jobs and re-boot the machines in the student lab

★ **E3.5**   Install **sudo** configured to send its mail tattling about misuse to you. Use it to test the **sudo** entries of the previous question with local usernames and machine names; verify that **sudo** is logging to syslog properly. Look at the syslog entries produced by your testing. (Requires root access; you'll most likely have to tweak **/etc/syslog.conf**, too.)

4 Controlling Processes

A process is the abstraction used by Linux to represent a running program. It's the object through which a program's use of memory, processor time, and I/O resources can be managed and monitored.

It is part of the Linux and UNIX philosophy that as much work as possible be done within the context of processes, rather than handled specially by the kernel. System and user processes all follow the same rules, so you can use a single set of tools to control them both.

4.1 COMPONENTS OF A PROCESS

A process consists of an address space and a set of data structures within the kernel. The address space is a set of memory pages[1] that the kernel has marked for the process's use. It contains the code and libraries that the process is executing, the process's variables, its stacks, and various extra information needed by the kernel while the process is running. Because Linux is a virtual memory system, there is no correlation between a page's location within an address space and its location inside the machine's physical memory or swap space.

The kernel's internal data structures record various pieces of information about each process. Some of the more important of these are:

- The process's address space map
- The current status of the process (sleeping, stopped, runnable, etc.)

---

1. Pages are the units in which memory is managed, usually 4K on PCs.

- The execution priority of the process
- Information about the resources the process has used
- Information about the files and network ports that the process has opened
- The process's signal mask (a record of which signals are blocked)
- The owner of the process

Some of these attributes may be shared among several processes to create a "thread group," which is the Linux analog of a multithreaded process in traditional UNIX. Though they may share an address space, the members of a thread group have their own execution priorities and execution states. In practice, few processes of interest to system administrators use multiple threads of execution, and even those that do (such as BIND 9's **named**) don't generally require administrative attention at this level of granularity.

Many of the parameters associated with a process directly affect its execution: the amount of processor time it gets, the files it can access, and so on. In the following sections, we discuss the meaning and significance of the parameters that are most interesting from a system administrator's point of view. These attributes are common to all versions of UNIX and Linux.

PID: process ID number

The kernel assigns a unique ID number to every process. Most commands and system calls that manipulate processes require you to specify a PID to identify the target of the operation. PIDs are assigned in order as processes are created.

PPID: parent PID

Linux does not supply a system call that creates a new process running a particular program. Instead, an existing process must clone itself to create a new process. The clone can then exchange the program it is running for a different one.

When a process is cloned, the original process is referred to as the parent, and the copy is called the child. The PPID attribute of a process is the PID of the parent from which it was cloned.[2]

The parent PID is a useful piece of information when you're confronted with an unrecognized (and possibly misbehaving) process. Tracing the process back to its origin (whether a shell or another program) may give you a better idea of its purpose and significance.

UID and EUID: real and effective user ID

See page 96 for more information about UIDs.

A process's UID is the user identification number of the person who created it, or more accurately, it is a copy of the UID value of the parent process. Usually, only the creator (aka the "owner") and the superuser are permitted to manipulate a process.

---

2. At least initially. If the original parent dies, **init** (process 1) becomes the new parent. See page 56.

The EUID is the "effective" user ID, an extra UID used to determine what resources and files a process has permission to access at any given moment. For most processes, the UID and EUID are the same, the usual exception being programs that are setuid.

Why have both a UID and an EUID? Simply because it's useful to maintain a distinction between identity and permission, and because a setuid program may not wish to operate with expanded permissions all the time. The effective UID can be set and reset to enable or restrict the additional permissions it grants.

Linux also keeps track of a "saved UID," which is a copy of the process's EUID at the point at which the process first begins to execute. Unless the process takes steps to obliterate this saved UID, it remains available for use as the real or effective UID. A conservatively written setuid program can therefore renounce its special privileges for the majority of its execution, accessing them only at the specific points that extra privileges are needed.

Linux also defines a nonstandard FSUID process parameter that controls the determination of filesystem permissions. It is infrequently used outside the kernel.

The implications of this multi-UID system can be quite subtle. If you need to delve into the details, David A. Wheeler's free on-line book *Secure Programming for Linux and Unix HOWTO* is an excellent resource. It's available from www.dwheeler.com.

GID and EGID: real and effective group ID

See page 97 for more information about groups.

The GID is the group identification number of a process. The EGID is related to the GID in the same way that the EUID is related to the UID in that it can be "upgraded" by the execution of a setgid program. The kernel maintains a saved GID similar in intent to the saved UID.

The GID attribute of a process is largely vestigial. For purposes of access determination, a process can be a member of many groups at once. The complete group list is stored separately from the distinguished GID and EGID. Determinations of access permissions normally take account of the EGID and the supplemental group list, but not the GID.

The only time at which the GID gets to come out and play is when a process creates new files. Depending on how the filesystem permissions have been set, new files may adopt the GID of the creating process. See page 82 for more information.

Niceness

A process's scheduling priority determines how much CPU time it receives. The kernel uses a dynamic algorithm to compute priorities, taking into account the amount of CPU time that a process has recently consumed and the length of time it has been waiting to run. The kernel also pays attention to an administratively set value that's usually called the "nice value" or "niceness," so called because it tells how nice you are planning to be to other users of the system. We take up the subject of niceness in detail on page 61.

In an effort to provide better support for low-latency applications, Linux has added "scheduling classes" to the traditional UNIX scheduling model. There are currently three scheduling classes, and each process is assigned to one class. Unfortunately, the real-time classes are neither widely used nor well supported from the command line. System process all use the traditional niceness-based scheduler. In this book we discuss only the standard scheduler. See www.realtimelinuxfoundation.org for more discussion of issues related to real-time scheduling.

Control terminal

Most nondaemon processes have an associated control terminal. The control terminal determines default linkages for the standard input, standard output, and standard error channels. When you start a command from the shell, your terminal normally becomes the process's control terminal. The concept of a control terminal also affects the distribution of signals, which are discussed starting on page 57.

4.2 THE LIFE CYCLE OF A PROCESS

To create a new process, a process typically copies itself with the **fork** system call. **fork** creates a copy of the original process that is largely identical to the parent. The new process has a distinct PID and has its own accounting information.

fork has the unique property of returning two different values. From the child's point of view, it returns zero. The parent receives the PID of the newly created child. Since the two processes are otherwise identical, they must both examine the return value to figure out which role they are supposed to play.

After a **fork**, the child process will often use one of the **exec** family of system calls to begin execution of a new program.[3] These calls change the program text that the process is executing and reset the data and stack segments to a predefined initial state. The various forms of **exec** differ only in the ways in which they specify the command-line arguments and environment to be given to the new program.

Linux defines an alternative to **fork** called **clone**. This call creates sets of processes that share memory, I/O spaces, or both. The feature is analogous to the multithreading facility found on most versions of UNIX, but each thread of execution is represented as a full-fledged process rather than a specialized "thread" object.

*See Chapter 2 for more information about booting and the **init** daemon.*

When the system boots, the kernel autonomously creates and installs several processes. The most notable of these is **init**, which is always process number 1. **init** is responsible for executing the system's startup scripts. All processes other than the ones the kernel creates are descendants of **init**.

init also plays another important role in process management. When a process completes, it calls a routine named **_exit** to notify the kernel that it is ready to die. It supplies an exit code (an integer) that tells why it's exiting. By convention, 0 is used to indicate a normal or "successful" termination.

3. Actually, all but one are library routines, not system calls.

Before a process can be allowed to disappear completely, Linux requires that its death be acknowledged by the process's parent, which the parent does with a call to **wait**. The parent receives a copy of the child's exit code (or an indication of why the child was killed if the child did not exit voluntarily) and can also obtain a summary of the child's use of resources if it wishes.

This scheme works fine if parents outlive their children and are conscientious about calling **wait** so that dead processes can be disposed of. If the parent dies first, however, the kernel recognizes that no **wait** will be forthcoming and adjusts the process to make the orphan a child of **init**. **init** accepts these orphaned processes and performs the **wait** needed to get rid of them when they die.

4.3 SIGNALS

Signals are process-level interrupt requests. About thirty different kinds are defined, and they're used in a variety of ways:

- They can be sent among processes as a means of communication.

- They can be sent by the terminal driver to kill, interrupt, or suspend processes when special keys such as <Control-C> and <Control-Z> are typed.[4]

- They can be sent by the administrator (with **kill**) to achieve various results.

- They can be sent by the kernel when a process commits an infraction such as division by zero.

- They can be sent by the kernel to notify a process of an "interesting" condition such as the death of a child process or the availability of data on an I/O channel.

A core dump is a process's memory image. It can be used for debugging.

When a signal is received, one of two things can happen. If the receiving process has designated a handler routine for that particular signal, the handler is called with information about the context in which the signal was delivered. Otherwise, the kernel takes some default action on behalf of the process. The default action varies from signal to signal. Many signals terminate the process; some also generate a core dump.

Specifying a handler routine for a signal within a program is referred to as "catching" the signal. When the handler completes, execution restarts from the point at which the signal was received.

To prevent signals from arriving, programs can request that they be either ignored or blocked. A signal that is ignored is simply discarded and has no effect on the process. A blocked signal is queued for delivery, but the kernel doesn't require the process to act on it until the signal has been explicitly unblocked. The handler for a newly unblocked signal is called only once, even if the signal was received several times while reception was blocked.

---

4. The functions of <Control-Z> and <Control-C> can be reassigned to other keys with the **stty** command, but this is rare in practice. In this chapter we refer to them by their conventional bindings.

Table 4.1 lists some signals with which all administrators should be familiar. The uppercase convention for signal names derives from C language tradition. You might also sometimes see signal names written with a SIG prefix (e.g., SIGHUP) for similar reasons.

Table 4.1   Signals every administrator should know

#	Name	Description	Default	Can catch?	Can block?	Dump core?
1	HUP	Hangup	Terminate	Yes	Yes	No
2	INT	Interrupt	Terminate	Yes	Yes	No
3	QUIT	Quit	Terminate	Yes	Yes	Yes
9	KILL	Kill	Terminate	No	No	No
a	BUS	Bus error	Terminate	Yes	Yes	Yes
11	SEGV	Segmentation fault	Terminate	Yes	Yes	Yes
15	TERM	Software termination	Terminate	Yes	Yes	No
a	STOP	Stop	Stop	No	No	No
a	TSTP	Keyboard stop	Stop	Yes	Yes	No
a	CONT	Continue after stop	Ignore	Yes	No	No
a	WINCH	Window changed	Ignore	Yes	Yes	No
a	USR1	User-defined	Terminate	Yes	Yes	No
a	USR2	User-defined	Terminate	Yes	Yes	No

a. Varies depending on the hardware architecture; see **man 7 signal**.

There are other signals not shown in Table 4.1, most of which are used to report obscure errors such as "illegal instruction." The default handling for signals like that is to terminate with a core dump. Catching and blocking are generally allowed because some programs may be smart enough to try to clean up whatever problem caused the error before continuing.

The BUS and SEGV signals are also error signals. We've included them in the table because they're so common: ninety-nine percent of the time that a program crashes, it's ultimately one of these two signals that finally brings it down. By themselves, the signals are of no specific diagnostic value. Both of them indicate an attempt to use or access memory improperly.[5]

The signals named KILL and STOP cannot be caught, blocked, or ignored. The KILL signal destroys the receiving process, and STOP suspends its execution until a CONT signal is received. CONT may be caught or ignored, but not blocked.

TSTP is a "soft" version of STOP that might be best described as a request to stop. It's the signal generated by the terminal driver when <Control-Z> is typed on the

5. More specifically, bus errors result from violations of alignment requirements or the use of nonsensical addresses. Segmentation violations represent protection violations such as attempts to write to read-only portions of the address space.

keyboard. Programs that catch this signal usually clean up their state, then send themselves a STOP signal to complete the stop operation. Alternatively, programs can ignore TSTP to prevent themselves from being stopped from the keyboard.

Terminal emulators send a WINCH signal when their configuration parameters (such as the number of lines in the virtual terminal) change. This convention allows emulator-savvy programs such as text editors to reconfigure themselves automatically in response to changes. If you can't get windows to resize properly, make sure that WINCH is being generated and propagated correctly.[6]

The signals KILL, INT, TERM, HUP, and QUIT all sound as if they mean approximately the same thing, but their uses are actually quite different. It's unfortunate that such vague terminology was selected for them. Here's a decoding guide:

- KILL is unblockable and terminates a process at the kernel level. A process can never actually "receive" this signal.

- INT is the signal sent by the terminal driver when you type <Control-C>. It's a request to terminate the current operation. Simple programs should quit (if they catch the signal) or simply allow themselves to be killed, which is the default if the signal is not caught. Programs that have a command-line should stop what they're doing, clean up, and wait for user input again.

- TERM is a request to terminate execution completely. It's expected that the receiving process will clean up its state and exit.

- HUP has two common interpretations. First, it's understood as a reset request by many daemons. If a daemon is capable of rereading its configuration file and adjusting to changes without restarting, a HUP can generally be used to trigger this behavior.

  Second, HUP signals are sometimes generated by the terminal driver in an attempt to "clean up" (i.e., kill) the processes attached to a particular terminal. This behavior is largely a holdover from the days of wired terminals and modem connections, hence the name "hangup".

  Shells in the C shell family (**tcsh** et al.) usually make background processes immune to HUP signals so that they can continue to run after the user logs out. Users of Bourne-ish shells (**ksh**, **bash**, etc.) can emulate this behavior with the **nohup** command.

- QUIT is similar to TERM, except that it defaults to producing a core dump if not caught. A few programs cannibalize this signal and interpret it to mean something else.

6. Which may be easier said than done. The terminal emulator (e.g., **xterm**), terminal driver, and user-level commands may all have a role in propagating SIGWINCH. Common problems include sending the signal to a terminal's foreground process only (rather than to all processes associated with the terminal) and failing to propagate notification of a size change across the network to a remote computer. Protocols such as TELNET and SSH explicitly recognize local terminal size changes and communicate this information to the remote host. Simpler protocols (e.g., direct serial lines) cannot do this.

The signals USR1 and USR2 have no set meaning. They're available for programs to use in whatever way they'd like. For example, the Apache web server interprets the USR1 signal as a request to gracefully restart.

4.4 KILL AND KILLALL: SEND SIGNALS

As its name implies, the **kill** command is most often used to terminate a process. **kill** can send any signal, but by default it sends a TERM. **kill** can be used by normal users on their own processes or by the superuser on any process. The syntax is

> **kill** [-*signal*] *pid*

where *signal* is the number or symbolic name of the signal to be sent (as shown in Table 4.1) and *pid* is the process identification number of the target process. A *pid* of **–1** broadcasts the signal to all processes except **init**.

A **kill** without a signal number does not guarantee that the process will die, because the TERM signal can be caught, blocked, or ignored. The command

> **kill -KILL** *pid*

will "guarantee" that the process will die because signal 9, KILL, cannot be caught. We put quotes around "guarantee" because processes can occasionally become so wedged that even KILL does not affect them (usually because of some degenerate I/O vapor lock such as waiting for a disk that has stopped spinning). Rebooting is usually the only way to get rid of these processes.

Most shells have their own built-in implementation of **kill** that obeys the syntax described above. According to the man page for the stand-alone **kill** command, the signal name or number should actually be prefaced with the **-s** flag (e.g., **kill -s HUP** *pid*). But since some shells don't understand this version of the syntax, we suggest sticking with the **-HUP** form, which the stand-alone **kill** also understands. That way you needn't worry about which version of **kill** you're actually using.

If you don't know the PID of the process you want to signal, you'd normally look it up with the **ps** command, which is described starting on page 62. Another option is to use the **killall** command, which performs this lookup for you. For example, to make the **xinetd** daemon refresh its configuration, you could run

> $ **sudo killall -USR1 xinetd**

Note that if multiple processes match the string you supply, **killall** will send signals to all of them.

The vanilla **kill** command actually has a similar feature, but it does not seem to be as smart as **killall** at matching command names. Stick with **killall**.

4.5 PROCESS STATES

A process is not automatically eligible to receive CPU time just because it exists. You need to be aware of the four execution states listed in Table 4.2.

Table 4.2 Process states

State	Meaning
Runnable	The process can be executed.
Sleeping	The process is waiting for some resource.
Zombie	The process is trying to die.
Stopped	The process is suspended (not allowed to execute).

A runnable process is ready to execute whenever CPU time is available. It has acquired all the resources it needs and is just waiting for CPU time to process its data. As soon as the process makes a system call that cannot be immediately completed (such as a request to read part of a file), Linux will put it to sleep.

Sleeping processes are waiting for a specific event to occur. Interactive shells and system daemons spend most of their time sleeping, waiting for terminal input or network connections. Since a sleeping process is effectively blocked until its request has been satisfied, it will get no CPU time unless it receives a signal.

Some operations cause processes to enter an uninterruptible sleep state. This state is usually transient and not observed in **ps** output (indicated by a D in the STAT column; see page 62). However, a few degenerate situations can cause it to persist. The most common cause involves server problems on an NFS filesystem mounted with the "hard" option. Since processes in the uninterruptible sleep state cannot be roused even to service a signal, they cannot be killed. To get rid of them, you must fix the underlying problem or reboot.

Zombies are processes that have finished execution but not yet had their status collected. If you see zombies hanging around, check their PPIDs with **ps** to find out where they're coming from.

Stopped processes are administratively forbidden to run. Processes are stopped on receipt of a STOP or TSTP signal and are restarted with CONT. Being stopped is similar to sleeping, but there's no way to get out of the stopped state other than having some other process wake you up (or kill you).

4.6 NICE AND RENICE: INFLUENCE SCHEDULING PRIORITY

The "niceness" of a process is a numeric hint to the kernel about how the process should be treated in relationship to other processes contending for the CPU. The strange name is derived from the fact that it determines how nice you are going to be to other users of the system. A high nice value means a low priority for your process: you are going to be nice. A low or negative value means high priority: you are not very nice. The range of allowable niceness values is -20 to +19.

Unless the user takes special action, a newly created process inherits the nice value of its parent process. The owner of the process can increase its nice value but cannot lower it, even to return the process to the default niceness. This restriction prevents processes with low priority from bearing high-priority children. The superuser may set nice values arbitrarily.

It's rare to have occasion to set priorities by hand these days. On the puny systems of the 1970s and 80s, performance was significantly affected by which process was on the CPU. Today, with more than adequate CPU power on most desktops, the scheduler usually does a good job of servicing all processes. The addition of scheduling classes gives developers additional control in cases where low response latency is essential.

I/O performance has not kept up with increasingly fast CPUs, and the major bottleneck on most systems has become the disk drives. Unfortunately, a process's nice value has no effect on the kernel's management of its memory or I/O; high-nice processes can still monopolize a disproportionate share of these resources.

A process's nice value can be set at the time of creation with the **nice** command and adjusted later with the **renice** command. **nice** takes a command line as an argument, and **renice** takes a PID or a username. Confusingly, **renice** requires an absolute priority, but **nice** wants a priority *increment* that it then adds to or subtracts from the shell's current priority.

Some examples:

```
$ nice -n 5 ~/bin/longtask      // Lowers priority (raise nice) by 5
$ sudo renice -5 8829           // Sets nice value to -5
$ sudo renice 5 -u boggs        // Sets nice value of boggs's procs to 5
```

To complicate things, a version of **nice** is built into the C shell and some other common shells (but not **bash**). If you don't type the full path to the **nice** command, you'll get the shell's version rather than the operating system's. This duplication can be confusing because shell-**nice** and command-**nice** use different syntax: the shell wants its priority increment expressed as +*incr* or -*incr*, but the stand-alone command wants an **-n** flag followed by the priority increment.[7]

The most commonly **nice**d process in the modern world is **xntpd**, the clock synchronization daemon. Since CPU promptness is critical to its mission, it usually runs at a nice value about 12 below the default (that is, at a higher priority than normal).

If a process goes berserk and drives the system's load average to 65, you may need to use **nice** to start a high-priority shell before you can run commands to investigate the problem. Otherwise, you may have difficulty running even simple commands.

4.7 PS: MONITOR PROCESSES

ps is the system administrator's main tool for monitoring processes. You can use it to show the PID, UID, priority, and control terminal of processes. It also gives information about how much memory a process is using, how much CPU time it has

---

7. Actually, it's even worse than this: the stand-alone **nice** will interpret **nice -5** to mean a *positive* increment of 5, whereas the shell built-in **nice** will interpret this same form to mean a *negative* increment of 5.

consumed, and its current status (running, stopped, sleeping, etc.). Zombies show up in a **ps** listing as <defunct>.

The behavior of **ps** tends to vary widely among UNIX variants, and many implementations have become quite complex over the last few years. In an effort to accommodate people who are used to other systems' **ps** commands, Linux provides a trisexual and hermaphroditic version that understands many other implementations' option sets and uses an environment variable to tell it what personality to assume.

Do not be alarmed by all this complexity: it's there mainly for kernel developers, not for system administrators. Although you will use **ps** frequently, you only need to know a few specific incantations.

You can obtain a general overview of all the processes running on the system with **ps aux**. Here's an example (we removed the START column to make the example fit the page and selected only a sampling of the output lines):

```
$ ps aux
  USER      PID  %CPU %MEM   VSZ   RSS  TTY  STAT  TIME  COMMAND
  root        1   0.1  0.2  3356   560   ?   S     0:00  init [5]
  root        2   0    0       0     0   ?   SN    0:00  [ksoftirqd/0]
  root        3   0    0       0     0   ?   S<    0:00  [events/0]
  root        4   0    0       0     0   ?   S<    0:00  [khelper]
  root        5   0    0       0     0   ?   S<    0:00  [kacpid]
  root       18   0    0       0     0   ?   S<    0:00  [kblockd/0]
  root       28   0    0       0     0   ?   S     0:00  [pdflush]
  ...
  root      196   0    0       0     0   ?   S     0:00  [kjournald]
  root     1050   0    0.1  2652   448   ?   S<s   0:00  udevd
  root     1472   0    0.3  3048  1008   ?   S<s   0:00  /sbin/dhclient -1
  root     1646   0    0.3  3012  1012   ?   S<s   0:00  /sbin/dhclient -1
  root     1733   0    0       0     0   ?   S     0:00  [kjournald]
  root     2124   0    0.3  3004  1008   ?   Ss    0:00  /sbin/dhclient -1
  root     2182   0    0.2  2264   596   ?   Ss    0:00  syslogd -m 0
  root     2186   0    0.1  2952   484   ?   Ss    0:00  klogd -x
   rpc     2207   0    0.2  2824   580   ?   Ss    0:00  portmap
rpcuser    2227   0    0.2  2100   760   ?   Ss    0:00  rpc.statd
  root     2260   0    0.4  5668  1084   ?   Ss    0:00  rpc.idmapd
  root     2336   0    0.2  3268   556   ?   Ss    0:00  /usr/sbin/acpid
  root     2348   0    0.8  9100  2108   ?   Ss    0:00  cupsd
  root     2384   0    0.6  4080  1660   ?   Ss    0:00  /usr/sbin/sshd
  root     2399   0    0.3  2780   828   ?   Ss    0:00  xinetd -stayalive
  root     2419   0    1.1  7776  3004   ?   Ss    0:00  sendmail: accepi
  ...
```

Command names in brackets are not really commands at all but rather kernel threads scheduled as processes. The meaning of each field is explained in Table 4.3 on the next page.

Another useful set of arguments is **lax**, which provides more technical information. It is also slightly faster to run because it doesn't have to translate every UID to a

Table 4.3   **Explanation of ps aux output**

Field	Contents
USER	Username of the process's owner
PID	Process ID
%CPU	Percentage of the CPU this process is using
%MEM	Percentage of real memory this process is using
VSZ	Virtual size of the process
RSS	Resident set size (number of pages in memory)
TTY	Control terminal ID
STAT	Current process status:

Current process status:

R = Runnable	D = In uninterruptible sleep
S = Sleeping (< 20 sec)	T = Traced or stopped
Z = Zombie	

Additional flags:

W = Process is swapped out
< = Process has higher than normal priority
N = Process has lower than normal priority
L = Some pages are locked in core
s = Process is a session leader

Field	Contents
START	Time the process was started
TIME	CPU time the process has consumed
COMMAND	Command name and arguments[a]

a. Programs can modify this info, so it's not necessarily an accurate representation of the actual command line.

username—efficiency can be important if the system is already bogged down by some other process.

Shown here in an abbreviated example, **ps lax** includes fields such as the parent process ID (PPID), nice value (NI), and resource the process is waiting for (WCHAN).

```
$ ps lax
  F   UID   PID   PPID PRI NI  VSZ   RSS   WCHAN  STAT TIME  COMMAND
  4     0     1      0  16  0  3356   560  select  S    0:00  init [5]
  1     0     2      1  34 19     0     0  ksofti  SN   0:00  [ksoftirqd/0
  1     0     3      1  5-10       0     0  worker  S<   0:00  [events/0]
  1     0     4      3  5-10       0     0  worker  S<   0:00  [khelper]
  5     0  2186      1  16  0  2952   484  syslog  Ss   0:00  klogd -x
  5    32  2207      1  15  0  2824   580  -       Ss   0:00  portmap
  5    29  2227      1  18  0  2100   760  select  Ss   0:00  rpc.statd
  1     0  2260      1  16  0  5668  1084  -       Ss   0:00  rpc.idmapd
  1     0  2336      1  21  0  3268   556  select  Ss   0:00  acpid
  5     0  2384      1  17  0  4080  1660  select  Ss   0:00  sshd
  1     0  2399      1  15  0  2780   828  select  Ss   0:00  xinetd -sta
  5     0  2419      1  16  0  7776  3004  select  Ss   0:00  sendmail: a
...
```

4.8 TOP: MONITOR PROCESSES EVEN BETTER

Since commands like **ps** offer only a one-time snapshot of your system, it is often difficult to grasp the "big picture" of what's really happening. The **top** command provides a regularly updated summary of active processes and their use of resources.

For example:

```
top - 16:37:08 up  1:42,  2 users,  load average: 0.01, 0.02, 0.06
Tasks: 76 total,   1 running, 74 sleeping,   1 stopped,   0 zombie
Cpu(s):  1.1% us,  6.3% sy,  0.6% ni, 88.6% id,  2.1% wa,  0.1% hi,  1.3% si
Mem:   256044k total, 254980k used,    1064k free,   15944k buffers
Swap:  524280k total,      0k used, 524280k free,  153192k cached

  PID USER  PR  NI  VIRT  RES  SHR  S %CPU %MEM TIME+   COMMAND
 3175 root  15   0 35436  12m 4896  S  4.0  5.2 01:41.9 X
 3421 root  25  10 29916  15m 9808  S  2.0  6.2 01:10.5 rhn-applet-gui
    1 root  16   0  3356  560  480  S  0.0  0.2 00:00.9 init
    2 root  34  19     0    0    0  S  0.0    0 00:00.0 ksoftirqd/0
    3 root   5 -10     0    0    0  S  0.0    0 00:00.7 events/0
    4 root   5 -10     0    0    0  S  0.0    0 00:00.0 khelper
    5 root  15 -10     0    0    0  S  0.0    0 00:00.0 kacpid
   18 root   5 -10     0    0    0  S  0.0    0 00:00.0 kblockd/0
   28 root  15   0     0    0    0  S  0.0    0 00:00.0 pdflush
   29 root  15   0     0    0    0  S  0.0    0 00:00.3 pdflush
   31 root  13 -10     0    0    0  S  0.0    0 00:00.0 aio/0
   19 root  15   0     0    0    0  S  0.0    0 00:00.0 khubd
   30 root  15   0     0    0    0  S  0.0    0 00:00.2 kswapd0
  187 root   6 -10     0    0    0  S    0    0 00:00.0 kmirrord/0
  196 root  15   0     0    0    0  S    0    0 00:01.3 kjournald
...
```

By default, the display is updated every 10 seconds. The most active processes appear at the top. **top** also accepts input from the keyboard and allows you to send signals and **renice** processes, so you can observe how your actions affect the overall condition of the machine.

Root can run **top** with the **q** option to goose it up to the highest possible priority. This can be very useful when you are trying to track down a process that has already brought the system to its knees.

4.9 THE /PROC FILESYSTEM

The Linux versions of **ps** and **top** read their process status information from the **/proc** directory, a pseudo-filesystem in which the kernel exposes a variety of interesting information about the system's state. Despite the name **/proc** (and the name of the underlying filesystem type, "proc"), the information is not limited to process information—all the status information and statistics generated by the kernel are represented here. You can even modify some parameters by writing to the appropriate **/proc** file—see page 874 for some examples.

Controlling Processes

Although some of the information is easiest to access through front-end commands such as **vmstat** and **ps**, some of the less popular information must be read directly from **/proc**. It's worth poking around in this directory to familiarize yourself with everything that's there. **man proc** also lists some useful tips and tricks.

Because the kernel creates the contents of **/proc** files on the fly (as they are read), most appear to be empty when listed with **ls -l**. You'll have to **cat** or **more** the contents to see what they actually contain. But be cautious—a few files contain or link to binary data that can confuse your terminal emulator if viewed directly.

Process-specific information is divided into subdirectories named by PID. For example, **/proc/1** is always the directory that contains information about **init**. Table 4.4 lists the most useful per-process files.

Table 4.4   Process information files in /proc (numbered subdirectories)

File	Contents
cmd	Command or program the process is executing
cmdline[a]	Complete command line of the process (null-separated)
cwd	Symbolic link to the process's current directory
environ	The process's environment variables (null-separated)
exe	Symbolic link to the file being executed
fd	Subdirectory containing links for each open file descriptor
maps	Memory mapping information (shared segments, libraries, etc.)
root	Symbolic link to the process's root directory (set with **chroot**)
stat	General process status information (best decoded with **ps**)
statm	Memory usage information

a. May be unavailable if the process is swapped out of memory.

The individual components contained within the **cmdline** and **environ** files are separated by null characters rather than newlines. You can filter their contents through **tr "\000" "\n"** to make them more readable.

The **fd** subdirectory represents open files in the form of symbolic links. File descriptors that are connected to pipes or network sockets don't have an associated filename. The kernel supplies a generic description as the link target instead.

The **maps** file can be useful for determining what libraries a program is linked to or depends on.

4.10 STRACE: TRACE SIGNALS AND SYSTEM CALLS

On a traditional UNIX system, it can be hard to figure out what a process is actually doing. You may have to make educated guesses based on indirect data from the filesystem and from tools such as **ps**. By contrast, Linux lets you directly observe a process with the **strace** command, which shows every system call the process makes and

Controlling Processes

every signal it receives. You can even attach **strace** to a running process, snoop for a while, and then detach from the process without disturbing it.[8]

Although system calls occur at a relatively low level of abstraction, you can usually tell quite a bit about a process's activity from **strace**'s output. For example, the following log was produced by **strace** run against an active copy of **top**:

```
$ sudo strace -p 5810
gettimeofday({1116193814, 213881}, {300, 0})              = 0
open("/proc", O_RDONLY|O_NONBLOCK|O_LARGEFILE|O_DIRECTORY) = 7
fstat64(7, {st_mode=S_IFDIR|0555, st_size=0, ...})        = 0
fcntl64(7, F_SETFD, FD_CLOEXEC)                           = 0
getdents64(7, /* 36 entries */, 1024)                    = 1016
getdents64(7, /* 39 entries */, 1024)                    = 1016
stat64("/proc/1", {st_mode=S_IFDIR|0555, st_size=0, ...}) = 0
open("/proc/1/stat", O_RDONLY)                           = 8
read(8, "1 (init) S 0 0 0 0 -1 4194560 73"..., 1023)     = 191
close(8)                                                  = 0
...
```

Not only does **strace** show you the name of every system call made by the process, but it also decodes the arguments and shows the result code returned by the kernel.

In this example, **top** starts by checking the current time. It then opens and stats the **/proc** directory and reads the directory's contents, thereby obtaining a list of processes that are currently running. **top** goes on to stat the directory representing the **init** process and then opens **/proc/1/stat** to read the **init**'s status information.

4.11 RUNAWAY PROCESSES

See page 817 for more information about runaway processes.

Runaway processes come in two flavors: user processes that consume excessive amounts of a system resource, such as CPU time or disk space, and system processes that suddenly go berserk and exhibit wild behavior. The first type of runaway is not necessarily malfunctioning; it might simply be a resource hog. System processes are always supposed to behave reasonably.

You can identify processes that use excessive CPU time by looking at the output of **ps** or **top**. If it is obvious that a user process is consuming more CPU than can reasonably be expected, investigate the process. Step one on a server or shared system is to contact the process's owner and ask what's going on. If the owner can't be found, you will have to do some poking around on your own. Although you should normally avoid looking into users' home directories, it is acceptable when you are trying to track down the source code of a runaway process to find out what it's doing.

There are two reasons to find out what a process is trying to do before tampering with it. First, the process may be both legitimate and important to the user. It's unreasonable to kill processes at random just because they happen to use a lot of CPU.

8. Well, usually. In some cases, **strace** can interrupt system calls. The monitored process must then be prepared to restart them. This is a standard rule of UNIX software hygiene, but it's not always observed.

Second, the process may be malicious or destructive. In this case, you've got to know what the process was doing (e.g., cracking passwords) so you can fix the damage.

If the reason for a runaway process's existence can't be determined, suspend it with a STOP signal and send email to the owner explaining what has happened. The process can be restarted later with a CONT signal. Be aware that some processes can be ruined by a long sleep, so this procedure is not always entirely benign. For example, a process may wake to find that some of its network connections have been broken.

If a process is using an excessive amount of CPU but appears to be doing something reasonable and working correctly, you should **renice** it to a higher nice value (lower priority) and ask the owner to use **nice** in the future.

Processes that make excessive use of memory relative to the system's physical RAM can cause serious performance problems. You can check the memory size of processes by using **top**. The VIRT column shows the total amount of virtual memory allocated by each process, and the RES column shows the portion of that memory that is currently mapped to specific memory pages (the "resident set").

Both of these numbers can include shared resources such as libraries, and that makes them potentially misleading. A more direct measure of process-specific memory consumption is found in the DATA column, which is not shown by default. To add this column to **top**'s display, type the **f** key once **top** is running and select DATA from the list. The DATA value indicates the amount of memory in each process's data and stack segments, so it's relatively specific to individual processes (modulo shared memory segments). Look for growth over time as well as absolute size.

Runaway processes that produce output can fill up an entire filesystem, causing numerous problems. When a filesystem fills up, lots of messages will be logged to the console and attempts to write to the filesystem will produce error messages.

The first thing to do in this situation is to stop the process that was filling up the disk. If you have been keeping a reasonable amount of breathing room on the disk, you can be fairly sure that something is amiss when it suddenly fills up. There's no command analogous to **ps** that will tell you who's consuming disk space at the fastest rate, but several tools can identify files that are currently open and the processes that are using them. See the info on **fuser** and **lsof** that starts on page 74 for more information.

You may want to suspend all suspicious-looking processes until you find the one that's causing the problem, but remember to restart the innocents when you are done. When you find the offending process, remove the files it was creating.

An old and well-known prank is to start an infinite loop from the shell that does:

```
while 1
    mkdir adir
    cd adir
    touch afile
end
```

This program occasionally shows up running from a publicly accessible system that was inadvertently left logged in. It does not consume much actual disk space, but it fills up the filesystem's inode table and prevents other users from creating new files. There is not much you can do except clean up the aftermath and warn users to protect their accounts. Because the directory tree that is left behind by this little jewel is usually too large for **rm -r** to handle, you may have to write a script that descends to the bottom of the tree and then removes directories as it backs out.

If the problem occurs in **/tmp** and you have set up **/tmp** as a separate filesystem, you can reinitialize **/tmp** with **mkfs** instead of attempting to delete individual files. See Chapter 7 for more information about the management of filesystems.

4.12 RECOMMENDED READING

BOVET, DANIEL P. AND MARCO CESATI. *Understanding the Linux Kernel (3rd Edition)*. Sebastopol, CA: O'Reilly Media, 2006.

4.13 EXERCISES

E4.1 Explain the relationship between a file's UID and a running process's real UID and effective UID. Besides file access control, what is the purpose of a process's effective UID?

E4.2 Suppose that a user at your site has started a long-running process that is consuming a significant fraction of a machine's resources.

   a) How would you recognize a process that is hogging resources?

   b) Assume that the misbehaving process might be legitimate and doesn't deserve to die. Show the commands you would use to put it "on ice" (stop it temporarily while you investigate).

   c) Later, you discover that the process belongs to your boss and must continue running. Show the commands you would use to resume the task.

   d) Alternatively, assume that the process needs to be killed. What signal would you send, and why? What if you needed to guarantee that the process died?

E4.3 Find a process with a memory leak (write your own program if you don't have one handy). Use **ps** or **top** to monitor the program's memory use as it runs.

★ **E4.4** Write a simple Perl script that processes the output of **ps** to determine the total VSZ and RSS of the processes running on the system. How do these numbers relate to the system's actual amount of physical memory and swap space?

5 *The Filesystem*

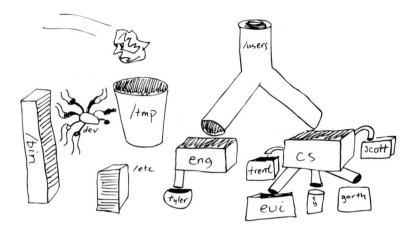

Quick: which of the following would you expect to find in a "filesystem"?

- Processes
- Serial ports
- Kernel data structures and tuning parameters
- Interprocess communication channels

If the system is Linux, the answer is "all of the above." And yes, you might find some files in there, too.[1]

Although the basic purpose of a filesystem is to represent and organize the system's storage resources, programmers have been eager to avoid reinventing the wheel when it comes to managing other types of objects. Frequently, it has proved to be natural and convenient to map these objects into the filesystem namespace. This unification has some advantages (consistent programming interface, easy access from the shell) and some disadvantages (filesystem implementations akin to Frankenstein's monster), but like it or not, this is the UNIX (and hence, the Linux) way.

The filesystem can be thought of as comprising four main components:

- A namespace – a way of naming things and organizing them in a hierarchy
- An API[2] – a set of system calls for navigating and manipulating objects

---

1. It's perhaps more accurate to say that these entities are *represented* within the filesystem. In most cases, the filesystem is used as a rendezvous point to connect clients with the drivers and servers they are seeking.

2. Application Programming Interface, a generic term for the set of routines that a library, operating system, or software package provides for programmers to call.

- A security model – a scheme for protecting, hiding, and sharing things
- An implementation – software that ties the logical model to actual hardware

NFS, the Network File System, is described in Chapter 16.

Linux defines an abstract kernel-level interface that accommodates many different back-end filesystems. Some portions of the file tree are handled by traditional disk-based implementations; others are fielded by separate drivers within the kernel. For example, NFS filesystems are handled by a driver that forwards the requested operations to a server on another computer.

Unfortunately, the architectural boundaries are not clearly drawn, and there are quite a few special cases. For example, device files provide a way for programs to communicate with drivers inside the kernel. They are not really data files, but they're handled by the basic filesystem driver and their characteristics are stored on disk. Perhaps the details would be somewhat different if the filesystem were reimplemented in light of the last few decades' experience.

See www.namesys.com for more information about ReiserFS.

Another complicating (but ultimately beneficial) factor is that Linux supports more than one type of disk-based filesystem. In the modern best-of-breed category are the ext3fs filesystem that serves as most distributions' default, along with ReiserFS, JFS from IBM, and XFS from SGI. The older ext2fs, precursor to ext3fs, is still supported by all distributions and will remain supported for a long time.

There are also many implementations of foreign filesystems, such as the FAT and NTFS filesystems used by Microsoft Windows and the ISO 9660 filesystem used on CD-ROMs. Linux supports more types of filesystem than any other variant of UNIX. Its extensive menu of choices gives you lots of flexibility and makes it easy to share files with other systems.

The filesystem is a rich topic that we approach from several different angles. This chapter tells where to find things on your system and describes the characteristics of files, the meanings of permission bits, and the use of some basic commands that view and set attributes. Chapter 7, *Adding a Disk*, is where you'll find the more technical filesystem topics such as disk partitioning. Chapter 16, *The Network File System*, describes the file sharing systems that are commonly used with Linux. You may also want to refer to Chapter 26, *Cooperating with Windows*, which discusses the software Linux systems use to share filesystems with computers running Microsoft Windows.

With so many different filesystem implementations available for Linux, it may seem strange that this chapter reads as if there were only a single Linux filesystem. We can be vague about the implementations because most modern filesystems either try to provide the traditional filesystem functionality in a faster and more reliable manner or they add extra features as a layer on top of the standard filesystem semantics. (Some filesystems do both.) For better or worse, too much existing software depends on the model described in this chapter for that model to be discarded.

5.1 PATHNAMES

The filesystem is presented as a single unified hierarchy[3] that starts at the directory **/** and continues downward through an arbitrary number of subdirectories. **/** is also called the root directory.

The list of directories that must be traversed to locate a particular file, together with its filename, form a pathname. Pathnames can be either absolute (**/tmp/foo**) or relative (**book4/filesystem**). Relative pathnames are interpreted starting at the current directory. You might be accustomed to thinking of the current directory as a feature of the shell, but every process has one.

The terms *file*, *filename*, *pathname*, and *path* are more or less interchangeable (or at least, we use them interchangeably in this book). *Filename* and *path* can be used for both absolute and relative paths; *pathname* generally suggests an absolute path.

The filesystem can be arbitrarily deep. However, each component of a pathname must have a name no more than 255 characters long, and a single path may not contain more than 4,095 characters. To access a file with a pathname longer than this, you must **cd** to an intermediate directory and use a relative pathname.[4]

The naming of files and directories is essentially unrestricted, except that names are limited in length and must not contain the slash character or nulls. In particular, spaces are permitted. Unfortunately, UNIX has a long tradition of separating command-line arguments at whitespace, so legacy software tends to break when spaces appear within filenames.

Spaces in filenames were once found primarily on filesystems shared with Macs and PCs, but they have now metastasized into Linux culture and are found in some standard software packages as well. No two ways about it: administrative scripts must be prepared to deal with spaces.

In the shell and in scripts, spaceful filenames can be quoted to keep their pieces together. For example, the command

```
$ less "My excellent file.txt"
```

preserves **My excellent file.txt** as a single argument to **less**. You can also escape individual spaces with a backslash. The filename completion feature of the common shells (usually bound to the <Tab> key) does this for you.

When you are writing scripts, a useful weapon to know about is **find**'s **-print0** option. In combination with **xargs -0**, this option makes the **find/xargs** combination work correctly regardless of the whitespace contained within filenames. For example, the command

---

3. The single-hierarchy system differs from that used by Windows, which retains the concept of disk-specific namespaces.

4. In case this isn't clear: most filesystem disk formats do not themselves impose a limit on the total length of pathnames. However, the system calls that access the filesystem do not allow their string arguments to be longer than 4,095 characters.

```
$ find /home -size +1M -print0 | xargs -0 ls -l
```

prints a long **ls** listing of every file in the **/home** partition over one megabyte in size.

5.2 FILESYSTEM MOUNTING AND UNMOUNTING

The filesystem is composed of smaller chunks—also called filesystems—each of which consists of one directory and its subdirectories and files. It's normally apparent from the context which type of "filesystem" is being discussed, but for clarity, we use the term "file tree" to refer to the overall layout of the filesystem and reserve the word "filesystem" for the chunks attached to the tree.

Most filesystems are disk partitions, but as we mentioned earlier, they can be anything that obeys the proper API: network file servers, kernel components, memory-based disk emulators, etc. Linux even has a nifty "loopback" filesystem that lets you mount individual files as if they were distinct devices.

Filesystems are attached to the tree with the **mount** command. **mount** maps a directory within the existing file tree, called the mount point, to the root of the newly attached filesystem. The previous contents of the mount point become inaccessible as long as another filesystem is mounted there. Mount points are usually empty directories, however.

For example,

```
# mount /dev/hda4 /users
```

installs the filesystem stored on the disk partition represented by **/dev/hda4** under the path **/users**. You could then use **ls /users** to see that filesystem's contents.

A list of the filesystems that are customarily mounted on a particular system is kept in the **/etc/fstab** file. The information contained in this file allows filesystems to be checked (**fsck -A**) and mounted (**mount -a**) automatically at boot time. It also serves as documentation for the layout of the filesystems on disk and enables short commands such as **mount /usr** (the location of the filesystem to mount is looked up in **fstab**). See page 127 for a complete discussion of the **fstab** file.

Filesystems are detached with the **umount** command. You cannot unmount a filesystem that is "busy"; there must not be any open files or processes whose current directories are located there, and if the filesystem contains executable programs, they cannot be running.

Linux kernels 2.4.11 and above define a "lazy" unmount option (invoked with **umount -l**) that removes the filesystem from the naming hierarchy but does not truly unmount it until all existing file references have been closed. It's debatable whether this a useful option. To begin with, there's no guarantee that existing references will ever close on their own. In addition, the "semi-unmounted" state can present inconsistent filesystem semantics to the programs that are using it; they can read and write through existing file handles but cannot open new files or perform other filesystem operations.

If the kernel complains that a filesystem you are trying to unmount is busy, you can run **fuser** to find out why. When invoked with the **-mv** flags and a mount point, **fuser** displays every process that's using a file or directory on that filesystem:

```
$ fuser -mv /usr
          USER  PID   ACCESS  COMMAND
/usr      root  444   ....m   atd
          root  499   ....m   sshd
          root  520   ....m   lpd
          . . .
```

The letter codes in the ACCESS column show what each process is doing to interfere with your unmounting attempt. Table 5.1 describes the meaning of each code.

Table 5.1   Activity codes shown by fuser

Code	Meaning
f	The process has a file open for reading or writing.
c	The process's current directory is on the filesystem.
e	The process is currently executing a file.
r	The process's root directory (set with **chroot**) is on the filesystem.
m	The process has mapped a file or shared library (usually an inactive executable).

To determine exactly what the offending processes are, just run **ps** with the list of PIDs returned by **fuser**. For example,

```
$ ps -fp "444 499 520"
          UID   PID   PPID  C  STIME  TTY  TIME      CMD
daemon    444   1     0  Apr11  ?     00:00:00  /usr/sbin/atd
          root  499   1     0  Apr11  ?     00:00:23  /usr/sbin/sshd
          lp    520   1     0  Apr11  ?     00:00:00  [lpd]
```

The quotation marks force the shell to pass the list of PIDs to **ps** as a single argument.

fuser can also report on the use of specific files (as opposed to entire filesystems); the syntax is **fuser -v** *filename*. **fuser** also accepts the **-k** option to kill (or send a signal to) each of the offending processes. Dangerous—and you must be root (or use **sudo**; see page 48).

An alternative to **fuser** is the **lsof** utility by Vic Abell of Purdue University. It runs on many different UNIX and Linux variants, making it especially useful to call from scripts that must run on a variety of systems. **lsof** is a more complex and sophisticated program than **fuser**, and its output is correspondingly verbose.

Scripts in search of specific pieces of information also have the option to read files in **/proc** directly. However, **lsof -F**, which formats **lsof**'s output for easy parsing, is an easier and more portable solution. Use additional command-line flags to request just the information you need.

5.3 THE ORGANIZATION OF THE FILE TREE

Filesystems in the UNIX family have never been very well organized. Various incompatible naming conventions are used simultaneously, and different types of files are scattered randomly around the namespace. In many cases, files are divided by function and not by how likely they are to change, making it difficult to upgrade the operating system. The **/etc** directory, for example, contains some files that are never customized and some that are entirely local. How do you know which files to preserve during the upgrade? Well, you just have to know...

Innovations such as **/var** have helped solve a few problems, but most systems are still a disorganized mess. Nevertheless, there's a culturally correct place for everything. It's particularly important not to mess with the default structure of the file tree under Linux because software packages and their installation tools often make broad assumptions about the locations of files (as do other sysadmins!).

See Chapter 28 for more information about configuring the kernel.

The root filesystem includes the root directory and a minimal set of files and subdirectories. The file containing the kernel lives within the root filesystem in the **/boot** directory; its name normally starts with **vmlinuz**.[5] Also part of the root filesystem are **/dev** for device files (except **/dev/pts**, which is mounted separately), **/etc** for critical system files, **/sbin** and **/bin** for important utilities, and sometimes **/tmp** for temporary files.

See page 124 for some reasons why partitioning might be desirable and some rules of thumb to guide it.

The directories **/usr** and **/var** are also of great importance. **/usr** is where most standard programs are kept, along with various other booty such as on-line manuals and most libraries. It is not strictly necessary that **/usr** be a separate filesystem, but for convenience in administration it often is. Both **/usr** and **/var** must be available to enable the system to come up all the way to multiuser mode.

/var houses spool directories, log files, accounting information, and various other items that grow or change rapidly and vary on each host. Since **/var** contains log files, which are apt to grow in times of trouble, it's a good idea to put **/var** on its own filesystem if that is practical.

Home directories of users are often kept on a separate filesystem, usually mounted in the root directory. Separate filesystems can also be used to store bulky items such as source code libraries and databases.

Some of the more important standard directories are listed in Table 5.2 on the next page (alternate rows are shaded to improve readability).

The evolving Filesystem Hierarchy Standard (www.pathname.com/fhs) attempts to codify, rationalize, and explain the standard directories. It's an excellent resource to consult when you're trying to figure out where to put something. We discuss some additional rules and suggestions for the design of local hierarchies on page 258.

---

5. It was once common for **/boot** to be a separate filesystem, mostly because the kernel had to be located near the beginning of the boot disk to be accessible to the BIOS. Modern PCs no longer have this problem, and **/boot** is more typically part of the root filesystem.

The Filesystem

Table 5.2   Standard directories and their contents

Pathname	Contents
/bin	Commands needed for minimal system operability
/boot	Kernel and files needed to load the kernel
/dev	Device entries for disks, printers, pseudo-terminals, etc.
/etc	Critical startup and configuration files
/home	Home directories for users
/lib	Libraries and parts of the C compiler
/media	Mount points for filesystems on removable media
/opt	Optional application software packages (not yet widely used)
/proc	Information about all running processes
/root	Home directory of the superuser (often just /)
/sbin	Commands for booting, repairing, and recovering the system
/tmp	Temporary files that may disappear between reboots
/usr	Hierarchy of secondary files and commands
/usr/bin	Most commands and executable files
/usr/include	Header files for compiling C programs
/usr/lib	Libraries; also, support files for standard programs
/usr/local	Local software (software you write or install)
/usr/local/bin	Local executables
/usr/local/etc	Local system configuration files and commands
/usr/local/lib	Local support files
/usr/local/sbin	Statically linked local system maintenance commands
/usr/local/src	Source code for **/usr/local/***
/usr/man	On-line manual pages
/usr/sbin	Less essential commands for system administration and repair
/usr/share	Items that might be common to multiple systems (read-only)
/usr/share/man	On-line manual pages
/usr/src	Source code for nonlocal software packages (not widely used)
/var	System-specific data and configuration files
/var/adm	Varies: logs, system setup records, strange administrative bits
/var/log	Various system log files
/var/spool	Spooling directories for printers, mail, etc.
/var/tmp	More temporary space (preserved between reboots)

5.4 FILE TYPES

Linux defines seven types of files. Even when developers add something new and wonderful to the file tree (such as the process information listed under **/proc**), it must still be made to look like one of these seven types:

- Regular files
- Directories
- Character device files

- Block device files
- Local domain sockets
- Named pipes (FIFOs)
- Symbolic links

You can determine the type of an existing file with **ls -ld**. The first character of the **ls** output encodes the type. The following example demonstrates that **/usr/include** is a directory:

```
$ ls -ld /usr/include
drwxr-xr-x  27 root     root        4096  Jul 15 20:57  /usr/include
```

ls uses the codes shown in Table 5.3 to represent the various types of files.

Table 5.3   File-type encoding used by ls

File type	Symbol	Created by	Removed by
Regular file	-	editors, **cp**, etc.	**rm**
Directory	d	**mkdir**	**rmdir, rm -r**
Character device file	c	**mknod**	**rm**
Block device file	b	**mknod**	**rm**
Local domain socket	s	**socket**(2)	**rm**
Named pipe	p	**mknod**	**rm**
Symbolic link	l	**ln -s**	**rm**

As you can see from Table 5.3, **rm** is the universal tool for deleting files you don't want anymore. But how would you delete a file named, say, **-f**? It's a perfectly legitimate filename under most filesystems, but **rm -f** doesn't work because the **-f** is interpreted as an **rm** flag. The answer is either to refer to the file by a more complete pathname (such as **./-f**) or to use **rm**'s -- argument to tell it that everything that follows is a filename and not an option (i.e., **rm -- -f**).

Filenames that contain control characters present a similar problem since reproducing these names from the keyboard can be difficult or impossible. In this situation, you can use shell globbing (pattern matching) to identify the files to delete. When you use pattern matching, it's a good idea to get in the habit of using the **-i** option to **rm** to make **rm** confirm the deletion of each file. This feature protects you against deleting any "good" files that your pattern inadvertently matches. For example, to delete a file named **foo**<Control-D>**bar**, you could use

```
$ ls
foo?bar      foose      kde-root

$ rm -i foo*
rm: remove `foo\004bar'? y
rm: remove `foose'? n
```

Note that **ls** shows the control character as a question mark, which can be a bit deceptive.[6] If you don't remember that **?** is a shell pattern-matching character and try to **rm foo?bar**, you might potentially remove more than one file (although not in this example). **-i** is your friend!

To delete the most horribly named files, you may need to resort to **rm -i ***.

Another option for removing files with squirrely names is to use an alternative interface to the filesystem such as **emacs**'s dired mode or a visual tool such as Nautilus.

Regular files

A regular file is just a bag o' bytes; Linux imposes no structure on its contents. Text files, data files, executable programs, and shared libraries are all stored as regular files. Both sequential and random access are allowed.

Directories

A directory contains named references to other files. You can create directories with **mkdir** and delete them with **rmdir** if they are empty. You can delete nonempty directories with **rm -r**.

The special entries "." and ".." refer to the directory itself and to its parent directory; they may not be removed. Since the root directory has no parent directory, the path "/.." is equivalent to the path "/." (and both are equivalent to /).

A file's name is stored within its parent directory, not with the file itself. In fact, more than one directory (or more than one entry in a single directory) can refer to a file at one time, and the references can have different names. Such an arrangement creates the illusion that a file exists in more than one place at the same time.

These additional references ("links") are indistinguishable from the original file; as far as Linux is concerned, they are equivalent. Linux maintains a count of the number of links that point to each file and does not release the file's data blocks until its last link has been deleted. Links cannot cross filesystem boundaries.

References of this sort are usually called "hard links" these days to distinguish them from symbolic links, which are described below. You create hard links with **ln** and remove them with **rm**.

It's easy to remember the syntax of **ln** if you keep in mind that it mirrors that of **cp**. The command **cp oldfile newfile** creates a copy of **oldfile** called **newfile**, and **ln oldfile newfile** makes the name **newfile** an additional reference to **oldfile**.

It is important to understand that hard links are not a distinct type of file. Instead of defining a separate "thing" called a hard link, the filesystem simply allows more than one directory entry to point to a file. In addition to the file's contents, the underlying attributes of the file (such as ownerships and permissions) are also shared.

---

6. **ls -b** shows the special characters as octal numbers, which can be helpful if you need to identify them specifically. <Control-A> is 1 (\001 in octal), <Control-B> is 2, and so on.

Character and block device files

See Chapter 28 for more information about devices and drivers.

Device files allow programs to communicate with the system's hardware and peripherals. When the kernel is configured, modules that know how to communicate with each of the system's devices are linked in.[7] The module for a particular device, called a device driver, takes care of the messy details of managing the device.

Device drivers present a standard communication interface that looks like a regular file. When the kernel is given a request that refers to a character or block device file, it simply passes the request to the appropriate device driver. It's important to distinguish device *files* from device *drivers*, however. The files are just rendezvous points that are used to communicate with the drivers. They are not the drivers themselves.

Character device files allow their associated drivers to do their own input and output buffering. Block device files are used by drivers that handle I/O in large chunks and want the kernel to perform buffering for them. In the past, a few types of hardware were represented by both block and character device files, but that configuration is rare today.

Device files are characterized by two numbers, called the major and minor device numbers. The major device number tells the kernel which driver the file refers to, and the minor device number typically tells the driver which physical unit to address. For example, major device number 6 on a Linux system indicates the parallel port driver. The first parallel port (**/dev/lp0**) would have major device number 6 and minor device number 0.

Drivers can interpret the minor device numbers that are passed to them in whatever way they please. For example, tape drivers use the minor device number to determine whether the tape should be rewound when the device file is closed.

You can create device files with **mknod** and remove them with **rm**. However, it's rarely necessary to create device files by hand. Most distributions use **udev** to automatically create and remove device files as hardware is detected by the kernel. **udev** keeps **/dev** tidy by limiting the number of spurious device files and by ensuring that the device numbers assigned to files are consistent with those expected by the kernel. See Chapter 28, *Drivers and the Kernel*, for more information.

An older script called **MAKEDEV** makes a good backup for **udev** in case you ever do need to create device files by hand. The script encodes the conventional names and device numbers for various classes of device so that you need not look up these values yourself. For example, **MAKEDEV pty** creates the device files for pseudo-terminals.

If you ever need to determine what major and minor device numbers are used by a driver, you can find this information in the driver's man page in section 4 of the manuals (e.g, **man 4 tty**).

---

7. These modules can also be loaded dynamically by the kernel.

The Filesystem

Local domain sockets

Sockets are connections between processes that allow them to communicate hygienically. Linux provides several different kinds of sockets, most of which involve the use of a network. Local domain sockets are accessible only from the local host and are referred to through a filesystem object rather than a network port. They are sometimes known as "UNIX domain sockets."

See Chapter 10 for more information about syslog.

Although socket files are visible to other processes as directory entries, they cannot be read from or written to by processes not involved in the connection. Some standard facilities that use local domain sockets are the printing system, the X Window System, and syslog.

Local domain sockets are created with the **socket** system call and can be removed with the **rm** command or the **unlink** system call once they have no more users.

Named pipes

Like local domain sockets, named pipes allow communication between two processes running on the same host. They're also known as "FIFO files" (FIFO is short for the phrase "first in, first out"). You can create named pipes with **mknod** and remove them with **rm**.

Symbolic links

A symbolic or "soft" link points to a file by name. When the kernel comes upon a symbolic link in the course of looking up a pathname, it redirects its attention to the pathname stored as the contents of the link. The difference between hard links and symbolic links is that a hard link is a direct reference, whereas a symbolic link is a reference by name; symbolic links are distinct from the files they point to.

You create symbolic links with **ln -s** and remove them with **rm**. Since they can contain arbitrary paths, they can refer to files on other filesystems or to nonexistent files. Multiple symbolic links can also form a loop.

A symbolic link can contain either an absolute or a relative path. For example,

```
# ln -s archived/secure /var/log/secure
```

links **/var/log/secure** to **/var/log/archived/secure** with a relative path. It creates the symbolic link **/var/log/secure** with a target of "**archived/secure**", as demonstrated by this output from **ls**:

```
$ ls -l /var/log/secure
lrwxrwxrwx 1 root root 18 2005-07-05 12:54 /var/log/secure -> archived/secure[8]
```

The entire **/var/log** directory could be moved somewhere else without causing the symbolic link to stop working (not that moving this directory is advisable).

8. The file permissions that **ls** shows for a symbolic link, lrwxrwxrwx, are dummy values. Permission to create, remove, or follow the link is controlled by the containing directory, whereas read, write, and execute permission on the link target are granted by the target's own permissions. Therefore, symbolic links do not need (and do not have) any permission information of their own.

It is a common mistake to think that the first argument to **ln -s** has something to do with your current working directory. It is *not* resolved as a filename by **ln**; it's simply used verbatim as the target of the symbolic link.

5.5 FILE ATTRIBUTES

Under the traditional UNIX and Linux filesystem model, every file has a set of nine permission bits that control who can read, write, and execute the contents of the file. Together with three other bits that primarily affect the operation of executable programs, these bits constitute the file's "mode."

The twelve mode bits are stored together with four bits of file-type information. The four file-type bits are set when the file is first created and cannot be changed, but the file's owner and the superuser can modify the twelve mode bits with the **chmod** (change mode) command. Use **ls -l** (or **ls -ld** for a directory) to inspect the values of these bits. An example is given on page 82.

The permission bits

Nine permission bits determine what operations may be performed on a file and by whom. Traditional UNIX does not allow permissions to be set per-user (although Linux now supports access control lists in all major filesystems; see page 88). Instead, three sets of permissions define access for the owner of the file, the group owners of the file, and everyone else. Each set has three bits: a read bit, a write bit, and an execute bit.

It's convenient to discuss file permissions in terms of octal (base 8) numbers because each digit of an octal number represents three bits and each group of permission bits consists of three bits. The topmost three bits (with octal values of 400, 200, and 100) control access for the owner. The second three (40, 20, and 10) control access for the group. The last three (4, 2, and 1) control access for everyone else ("the world"). In each triplet, the high bit is the read bit, the middle bit is the write bit, and the low bit is the execute bit.

Each user fits into only one of the three permission sets. The permissions used are those that are most specific. For example, the owner of a file always has access determined by the owner permission bits and never the group permission bits. It is possible for the "other" and "group" categories to have more access than the owner, although this configuration is rarely used.

On a regular file, the read bit allows the file to be opened and read. The write bit allows the contents of the file to be modified or truncated; however, the ability to delete or rename (or delete and then recreate!) the file is controlled by the permissions on its parent directory, because that is where the name-to-dataspace mapping is actually stored.

The execute bit allows the file to be executed. There are two types of executable files: binaries, which the CPU runs directly, and scripts, which must be interpreted by a shell or some other program. By convention, scripts begin with a line similar to

```
#!/usr/bin/perl
```

that specifies an appropriate interpreter. Nonbinary executable files that do not specify an interpreter are assumed (by your shell) to be **bash** or **sh** scripts.[9]

For a directory, the execute bit (often called the "search" or "scan" bit in this context) allows the directory to be entered or passed through while a pathname is evaluated, but not to have its contents listed. The combination of read and execute bits allows the contents of the directory to be listed. The combination of write and execute bits allows files to be created, deleted, and renamed within the directory.

The setuid and setgid bits

The bits with octal values 4000 and 2000 are the setuid and setgid bits. When set on executable files, these bits allow programs to access files and processes that would otherwise be off-limits to the user that runs them. The setuid/setgid mechanism for executables is described on page 45.

When set on a directory, the setgid bit causes newly created files within the directory to take on the group ownership of the directory rather than the default group of the user that created the file. This convention makes it easier to share a directory of files among several users, as long as they all belong to a common group. This interpretation of the setgid bit is unrelated to its meaning when set on an executable file, but there is never any ambiguity as to which meaning is appropriate.

You can also set the setgid bit on nonexecutable plain files to request special locking behavior when the file is opened. However, we've never seen this feature used.

The sticky bit

The bit with octal value 1000 is called the sticky bit. It was of historical importance as a modifier for executable files on early UNIX systems. However, that meaning of the sticky bit is now obsolete and modern systems silently ignore it.

If the sticky bit is set on a directory, the filesystem won't allow you to delete or rename a file unless you are the owner of the directory, the owner of the file, or the superuser. Having write permission on the directory is not enough. This convention helps make directories like **/tmp** a little more private and secure.

Viewing file attributes

The filesystem maintains about forty separate pieces of information for each file, but most of them are useful only to the filesystem itself. As a system administrator, you

9. The kernel understands the #! ("shebang") syntax and acts on it directly. However, if the interpreter is not specified completely and correctly, the kernel will refuse to execute the file. The shell then makes a second attempt to execute the script by calling **sh**.

will be concerned mostly with the link count, owner, group, mode, size, last access time, last modification time, and type. You can inspect all of these with **ls -l** (or **ls -ld** for a directory).

An attribute change time is also maintained for each file. The conventional name for this time (the "ctime," short for "change time") leads some people to believe that it is the file's creation time. Unfortunately, it is not; it just records the time that the attributes of the file (owner, mode, etc.) were last changed (as opposed to the time at which the file's contents were modified).

Consider the following example:

```
$ ls -l /bin/gzip
-rwxr-xr-x    3 root     root         57136 Jun 15  2004 /bin/gzip
```

The first field specifies the file's type and mode. The first character is a dash, so the file is a regular file. (See Table 5.3 on page 77 for other codes.)

The next nine characters in this field are the three sets of permission bits. The order is owner-group-other, and the order of bits within each set is read-write-execute. Although these bits have only binary values, ls shows them symbolically with the letters r, w, and x for read, write, and execute. In this case, the owner has all permissions on the file and everyone else has only read and execute permission.

If the setuid bit had been set, the x representing the owner's execute permission would have been replaced with an s, and if the setgid bit had been set, the x for the group would also have been replaced with an s. The last character of the permissions (execute permission for "other") is shown as t if the sticky bit of the file is turned on. If either the setuid/setgid bit or the sticky bit is set but the corresponding execute bit is not, these bits appear as S or T.

The next field in the listing is the link count for the file. In this case it is 3, indicating that **/bin/gzip** is just one of three names for this file (the others are **/bin/gunzip** and **/bin/zcat**). Every time a hard link is made to a file, the count is incremented by 1.

All directories will have at least two hard links: the link from the parent directory and the link from the special file "." inside the directory itself. Symbolic links do not affect the link count.

The next two fields in the **ls** output are the owner and group owner of the file. In this example, the file's owner is root, and the file also belongs to the group named root. The filesystem actually stores these as the user and group ID numbers rather than as names. If the text versions (names) can't be determined, then these fields contain numbers. This might happen if the user or group that owns the file has been deleted from the **/etc/passwd** or **/etc/group** file. It could also indicate a problem with your NIS or LDAP database (if you use one); see Chapter 17.

The next field is the size of the file in bytes. This file is 57,136 bytes long, or about 56K.[10] Next comes the date of last modification: June 15, 2004. The last field in the listing is the name of the file, **/bin/gzip**.

ls output is slightly different for a device file. For example:

```
$ ls -l /dev/tty0
crw-rw----  1 root root    4, 0 Jun 11 20:41 /dev/tty0
```

Most fields are the same, but instead of a size in bytes, **ls** shows the major and minor device numbers. **/dev/tty0** is the first virtual console, controlled by device driver 4 (the terminal driver).

One **ls** option that's useful for scoping out hard links is **-i**, which makes **ls** show each file's "inode number." Without going into too much detail about filesystem implementations, we'll just say that the inode number is an index into a table that enumerates all the files in the filesystem. Inodes are the "things" that are pointed to by directory entries; entries that are hard links to the same file have the same inode number. To figure out a complex web of links, you need **ls -li** to show link counts and inode numbers along with **find** to search for matches.[11]

The system automatically keeps track of modification time stamps, link counts, and file size information. Conversely, permission bits, ownership, and group ownership change only when they are specifically altered.

Some other **ls** options that are important to know are **-a** to show all entries in a directory (even files whose names start with a dot), **-t** to sort files by modification time (or **-tr** to sort in reverse chronological order), **-F** to show the names of files in a way that distinguishes directories and executable files, **-R** to list recursively, and **-h** to show file sizes in a human-readable form (e.g., 8K or 53M).

chmod: change permissions

The **chmod** command changes the permissions on a file. Only the owner of the file and the superuser can change its permissions. To use the command on early UNIX systems, you had to learn a bit of octal notation, but current versions accept either octal notation or a mnemonic syntax. The octal syntax is generally more convenient for administrators, but it can only be used to specify an absolute value for the permission bits. The mnemonic syntax can modify some bits while leaving others alone.

The first argument to **chmod** is a specification of the permissions to be assigned, and the second and subsequent arguments are names of files on which permissions

---

10. K stands for kilo, a metric prefix meaning 1,000; however, computer types have bastardized it into meaning 2^{10} or 1,024. Similarly, a computer megabyte is not really a million bytes but rather 2^{20} or 1,048,576 bytes. The International Electrotechnical Commission is promoting a new set of numeric prefixes (such as kibi- and mebi-) that are based explicitly on powers of 2. At this point, it seems unlikely that common usage will change. To add to the confusion, even the power-of-2 units are not used consistently. RAM is denominated in powers of 2, but network bandwidth is always a power of 10. Storage space is quoted in power-of-10 units by manufacturers and power-of-2 units by everyone else.

11. Try **find** *mountpoint* **-xdev -inum** *inode* **-print**.

should be changed. In the octal case, the first octal digit of the specification is for the owner, the second is for the group, and the third is for everyone else. If you want to turn on the setuid, setgid, or sticky bits, you use four octal digits rather than three, with the three special bits forming the first digit.

Table 5.4 illustrates the eight possible combinations for each set of three bits, where r, w, and x stand for read, write, and execute.

Table 5.4   Permission encoding for chmod

Octal	Binary	Perms	Octal	Binary	Perms
0	000	– – –	4	100	r – –
1	001	– – x	5	101	r–x
2	010	–w–	6	110	rw–
3	011	–wx	7	111	rwx

For example, **chmod 711 myprog** gives all permissions to the owner and execute-only permission to everyone else.[12]

The full details of **chmod**'s mnemonic syntax can be found in the **chmod** man page. Some examples of mnemonic specifications are shown in Table 5.5.

Table 5.5   Examples of chmod's mnemonic syntax

Spec	Meaning
u+w	Adds write permission for the owner of the file
ug=rw,o=r	Gives r/w permission to owner and group, and read permission to others
a-x	Removes execute permission for all categories (owner/group/other)
ug=srx,o=	Makes the file setuid and setgid and gives r/x permission to the owner and group only
g=u	Makes the group permissions be the same as the owner permissions

The hard part about using the mnemonic syntax is remembering whether **o** stands for "owner" or "other"; "other" is correct. Just remember **u** and **g** by analogy to UID and GID; only one possibility will be left.

You can also specify the modes to be assigned by analogy with an existing file. For example, **chmod --reference=filea fileb** makes **fileb**'s mode the same as **filea**'s.

chmod can update the file permissions within a directory recursively with the **-R** option. However, this is trickier than it looks, since the enclosed files and directories may not all share the same attributes (for example, some might be executable files

12. If **myprog** were a shell script, it would need both read and execute permission turned on. For the script to be run by an interpreter, it must be opened and read like a text file. Binary files are executed directly by the kernel and therefore do not need read permission turned on.

while others are text files). The mnemonic syntax is particularly useful with **-R** because any bits whose values you don't set explicitly are left alone. For example,

```
$ chmod -R g+w mydir
```

adds group write permission to **mydir** and all its contents without messing up the execute bits of directories and programs.

chown: change ownership and group

The **chown** command changes a file's ownership and group ownership. Its syntax mirrors that of **chmod**, except that the first argument specifies the new owner and group in the form *user:group*. You can omit either *user* or *group*. If there is no group, you don't need the colon either, although you can include it to make **chown** set the group to *user*'s default group. The form *user.group* is also accepted, for historical reasons, although it's a bit degenerate since usernames can include dots.

To change a file's group, you must either be the owner of the file and belong to the group you're changing to or be the superuser. You must be the superuser to change a file's owner.

Like **chmod**, **chown** offers the recursive **-R** flag to change the settings of a directory and all the files underneath it. For example, the sequence

```
# chmod 755 ~matt
# chown -R matt:staff ~matt
```

might be used to set up the home directory of a new user after you had copied in the default startup files. Make sure that you don't try to **chown** the new user's dot files with a command such as

```
# chown -R matt:staff ~matt/.*
```

The pattern will match **~matt/..** and will therefore end up changing the ownerships of the parent directory and probably the home directories of other users.

Traditional UNIX uses a separate command, **chgrp**, to change the group owner of a file. Linux has **chgrp** too. It works just like **chown**; feel free to use it if you find it easier to remember.

umask: assign default permissions

You can use the built-in shell command **umask** to influence the default permissions given to the files you create. The **umask** is specified as a three-digit octal value that represents the permissions to take away. When a file is created, its permissions are set to whatever the creating program requests minus whatever the **umask** forbids. Thus, the individual digits of the **umask** allow the permissions shown in Table 5.6.

For example, **umask 027** allows all permissions for the owner but forbids write permission to the group and allows no permissions for anyone else. The default **umask** value is often 022, which denies write permission to the group and world but allows read permission.

Table 5.6 Permission encoding for umask

Octal	Binary	Perms	Octal	Binary	Perms
0	000	rwx	4	100	-wx
1	001	rw-	5	101	-w-
2	010	r-x	6	110	--x
3	011	r--	7	111	---

See Chapter 6 for more information about startup files.

You cannot force users to have a particular **umask** value because they can always reset it to whatever they want. However, you can put a suitable default in the sample **.profile** and **.cshrc** files that you give to new users.

Bonus flags

Linux's ext2fs and ext3fs filesystems define some supplemental attributes you can turn on to request special filesystem semantics ("request" being the operative word, since many of the flags haven't actually been implemented). For example, one flag makes a file append-only and another makes it immutable and undeletable.

Since these flags don't apply to filesystems other than the ext* series, Linux uses special commands, **lsattr** and **chattr**, to view and change them. Table 5.7 lists the flags that actually work (currently only about 50% of those mentioned in the man page).

Table 5.7 Ext2fs and ext3fs bonus flags

Flag	Meaning
A	Never update access time (st_atime; for performance)
a	Allow writing only in append mode (only root can set)
D	Force directory updates to be written synchronously
d	No backup—make **dump** ignore this file
i	Make file immutable and undeletable (only root can set)
j	Keep a journal for data changes as well as metadata
S	Force changes to be written synchronously (no buffering)

With the possible exception of the "no backup" flag, it's not clear that any of these features offer much day-to-day value. The immutable and append-only flags were largely conceived as ways to make the system more resistant to tampering by hackers or hostile code. Unfortunately, they can confuse software and protect only against hackers that don't know enough to use **chattr -ia**.[13] Real-world experience has shown that these flags are more often used *by* hackers than *against* them.

The **S** and **D** options for synchronous writes also merit a special caution. Since they force all filesystem pages associated with a file or directory to be written out imme-

---

13. The capability mechanism described on page 683 can make it harder to turn off these bits, but the feature is not widely used.

diately on changes, they might seem to offer additional protection against data loss in the event of a crash. However, the order of operations for synchronous updates is unusual and has been known to confuse **fsck**; recovery of a damaged filesystem might therefore be made more difficult rather than more reliable. Filesystem journaling, as supported by ext3fs, is usually a better option. The **j** option can force data journaling for specific files, albeit at some performance cost.

5.6 ACCESS CONTROL LISTS

The 9-bit owner/group/other access control system has proved to be powerful enough to accommodate most administrative needs. Although the system has clear limitations, it's very much in keeping with the UNIX traditions (some might say, "former traditions") of simplicity and predictability.

Virtually all non-UNIX operating systems use a substantially more complicated way of regulating access to files: access control lists, or ACLs. ACLs have no set length and can include permission specifications for multiple users or groups. The more sophisticated systems allow administrators to specify partial sets of permissions or negative permissions; some also have inheritance features that allow access to depend on more than one ACL at a time. These systems are clearly more powerful than the traditional UNIX model, but they are also an order of magnitude more complex, both for administrators and for software developers.

See page 126 for more information about the **mount** command and filesystem mounting.

As a result of efforts to include ACLs in the POSIX specification, many variants of UNIX have come to support a relatively standard ACL mechanism that operates in parallel with the traditional UNIX 9-bit model. Under Linux, ACLs are supported by ext2, ext3, ReiserFS, XFS, and JFS. They are usually disabled by default; use the **-o acl** option to **mount** to turn them on.

For completeness, we describe the Linux ACL model here. But don't be seduced by the pretty colors—ACLs are not necessarily "better" than traditional file permissions, and knowledgeable administrators should use them with a degree of trepidation. Not only are they complicated and tiresome to use, but they can also cause problems in conjunction with NFS, backup systems, and programs such as text editors. ACLs tend toward entropy and so become unmaintainable over time.

See page 828 for more information about Samba.

Perhaps the most plausible reason for using ACLs is to increase compatibility with other operating systems. In particular, the Samba suite used for file sharing with Windows systems is ACL-aware and makes a good-faith effort to translate between the ACLs of Linux and Windows.

ACL overview

Linux ACLs are a mostly straightforward extension of the standard 9-bit model. Read, write, and execute permission are the only capabilities the system deals with. Embellishments such as the setuid and sticky bits are handled exclusively through the traditional mode bits.

ACLs allow the rwx bits to be set independently for any combination of users and groups. Table 5.8 shows what the individual entries in an ACL can look like.

Table 5.8   Entries that can appear in an access control list

Format	Example	Sets permissions for
user::*perms*	user::rw-	The file's owner
user:*username:perms*	user:trent:rw-	A specific user
group::*perms*	group::r-x	The group that owns the file
group:*groupname:perms*	group:staff:rw-	A specific group
other::*perms*	other::---	All others
mask::*perms*	mask::rwx	All but owner and other[a]

a. Masks are somewhat tricky and are explained later in this section.

Users and groups can be identified by name or by UID/GID. The exact number of entries that an ACL can contain varies with the filesystem implementation and ranges from a low of 25 with XFS to a virtually unlimited number with ReiserFS and JFS. The ext2 and ext3 filesystems allow 32 entries, which is probably a reasonable limit for manageability in any case.

The **getfacl** command displays a file's current ACL, and the **setfacl** command modifies or sets it. Use **setfacl -b** *file* to clear the ACL, **setfacl -m** *aclspec file* to modify or extend it, and **setfacl -x** *aclspec file* to delete specific entries in the list. (Omit the permission specification portion of the *aclspec* when using **-x**.) The *aclspec* can contain more than one list entry as long as the entries are separated with a comma.

Files with ACLs retain their original mode bits, but consistency is automatically enforced and the two sets of permissions can never conflict. The following example demonstrates that the ACL entries update automatically in response to changes made with **chmod**:

```
$ touch /tmp/example
$ ls -l /tmp/example
-rw-rw-r-- 1 garth  garth    0 Jun 14 15:57 /tmp/example
$ getfacl /tmp/example
getfacl: Removing leading '/' from absolute path names
# file: tmp/example
# owner: garth
# group: garth
user::rw-
group::rw-
other::r--
$ chmod 640 /tmp/example
$ getfacl --omit-header /tmp/example
user::rw-
group::r--
other::---
```

This enforced consistency allows older software with no awareness of ACLs to play reasonably well in the ACL world. However, there's a twist. Even though the group:: ACL entry in the example above appears to be tracking the middle set of traditional mode bits, this will not always be the case.

To understand why, suppose that a legacy program clears the write bits within all three permission sets of the traditional mode (e.g., **chmod ugo-w** *file*). The intention is clearly to make the file unwritable by anyone. But what if the resulting ACL were to look like this?

```
user::r--
group::r--
group:staff:rw-
other::r--
```

From the perspective of legacy programs, the file appears to be unmodifiable, yet it is actually writable by anyone in group staff. Not good. To reduce the chance of ambiguity and misunderstandings, Linux has adopted the following rules:

- The user:: and other:: ACL entries are by definition identical to the "owner" and "other" permission bits from the traditional file mode. Changing the mode changes the corresponding ACL entries, and vice versa.

- In all cases, the effective access permission afforded to the file's owner and to users not mentioned in another way are those specified in the user:: and other:: ACL entries, respectively.

- If a file has no explicitly defined ACL or has an ACL that consists only of one user::, one group::, and one other:: entry, these ACL entries are identical to the three sets of traditional permission bits. This is the case illustrated in the **getfacl** example above. (Such an ACL is termed "minimal" and need not actually be implemented as a logically separate ACL.)

- In more complex ACLs, the traditional group permission bits correspond to a special ACL entry called "mask" rather than the group:: ACL entry. The mask limits the access that the ACL can confer upon *all* named users, *all* named groups, *and* the default group.

In other words, the mask specifies an upper bound on the access that the ACL can assign to individual groups and users. It is conceptually similar to the **umask**, except that the ACL mask is always in effect and specifies the allowed permissions rather than the permissions to be denied. ACL entries for named users, named groups, and the default group can include permissions bits that are not present in the mask, but the kernel simply ignores them.

As a result, the traditional mode bits can never understate the access allowed by the ACL as a whole. Furthermore, clearing a bit from the group portion of the traditional mode clears the corresponding bit in the ACL mask and thereby forbids this permission to everyone but the file's owner and those who fall in the category of "other."

When the ACL shown in the previous example is expanded to include entries for a specific user and group, **setfacl** automatically supplies an appropriate mask:

```
$ setfacl -m user::r,user:trent:rw,group:admin:rw /tmp/example
$ ls -l /tmp/example
-r--rw----+ 1 garth  staff    0 Jun 14 15:57 /tmp/example
$ getfacl --omit-header /tmp/example
user::r--
user:trent:rw-
group::r--
group:admin:rw-
mask::rw-
other::---
```

As seen here, **setfacl** generates a mask that allows all the permissions granted in the ACL to take effect. If you want to set the mask by hand, include it in the ACL entry list given to **setfacl** or use the **-n** option to prevent **setfacl** from regenerating it.

When access is attempted, the effective UID is compared to the UID that owns the file. If they are the same, access is determined by the user:: permissions in the ACL. Otherwise, if there is a matching user-specific ACL entry, permissions are determined by that entry in combination with the ACL mask. If no user-specific entry is available, the filesystem tries to locate a valid group-related entry that provides the requested access; such entries are also processed in conjunction with the ACL mask. If no matching entry can be found, the other:: entry prevails.

If you use the traditional **chmod** command to manipulate the group permissions on an ACL-bearing file, be aware that your changes affect only the mask. To continue the previous example:

```
$ chmod 770 /tmp/example
$ ls -l /tmp/example
-rwxrwx---+ 1 garth  staff    0 Jun 14 15:57 /tmp/example
$ getfacl --omit-header /tmp/example
user::rwx
user:trent:rw-
group::r--
group:admin:rw-
mask::rwx
other::---
```

The **ls** output in this case is misleading. Despite the apparently generous group permissions, no one actually has permission to execute the file by reason of group membership. To grant such permission, you must edit the ACL itself.

Default entries

In addition to the ACL entry types listed in Table 5.8, the ACLs for directories can include "default" entries that are propagated to the ACLs of newly created files and subdirectories created within them. Subdirectories receive these entries both in the form of active ACL entries and in the form of defaults. Therefore, the original defaults may eventually propagate down through several layers of the directory hierarchy.

The connection between the parent and child ACLs does not continue once the default entries have been copied. If the parent's default entries change, the changes are not reflected in the ACLs of existing subdirectories.

5.7 EXERCISES

E5.1 What is a **umask**? Create a **umask** that would give no permissions to the group or the world.

E5.2 What is the difference between hard links and symbolic (soft) links? When is it appropriate to use one or the other?

★ **E5.3** Read the man page for the **/etc/fstab** file. Write an entry that automatically mounts a Windows NTFS partition, **/dev/hda1**, at startup. Use the mount point **/mnt/win_c**.

★ **E5.4** When installing a Linux system, it's important to partition the hard drive such that each filesystem (**/var**, **/usr**, etc.) has adequate space for both current and future needs. The "Foobar Linux" distribution uses the following defaults:

/	100MB
/var	50MB
/boot	10MB
<swap>	128MB
/usr	remaining space

What are some potential problems with this arrangement on a busy server box?

★ **E5.5** Why is it a good idea to put some partitions (such as **/var**, **/home**, and swap) on a separate drive from other data files and programs? What about **/tmp**? Give specific reasons for each of the filesystems listed.

★ **E5.6** Write a script that finds all the hard links on a filesystem.

★ **E5.7** Give commands to accomplish the following tasks.

   a) Set the permissions on the file **README** to read/write for the owner and read for everyone else.

   b) Turn on a file's setuid bit without changing (or knowing) the current permissions.

   c) List the contents of the current directory, sorting by modification time and listing the most recently modified file last.

   d) Change the group of a file called **shared** from "user" to "friends".

6 *Adding New Users*

Adding and removing users is a routine chore on most systems. These tasks are simple, but they are also boring; most administrators build tools to automate the process and then delegate the actual work to an assistant or operator.

These days we are seeing a resurgence of centralized servers with logon accounts for hundreds of people in addition to the distributed server with as few as two users. Administrators need a thorough understanding of the account system in order to manage network services and configure accounts appropriately for the local computing environment.

Account hygiene is also a key determinant of system security. Infrequently used accounts are prime targets for attackers, as are accounts with easily guessed passwords. Even if you use your system's automated tools to add and remove users, it's important to understand the changes the tools are making.

In this chapter we'll first examine the underlying model that the automated tools implement, then describe the tools themselves (**useradd**, **userdel**, etc.). The default **useradd** tool is actually quite good and should be sufficient for most sites' needs. Unfortunately, **userdel** is not quite as thorough as we would like.

6.1 THE /ETC/PASSWD FILE

The **/etc/passwd** file is a list of users recognized by the system. The system consults the file at login time to determine a user's UID and home directory, among other things. Each line in the file represents one user and contains seven fields separated by colons:

- Login name
- Encrypted password or password placeholder (see page 96)
- UID (user ID) number
- Default GID (group ID) number
- "GECOS" information: full name, office, extension, home phone
- Home directory
- Login shell

For example, the following lines are all syntactically valid **/etc/passwd** entries:

```
root:lga5FjuGpZ2so:0:0:The System,,x6096,:/:/bin/sh
jl:x:100:0:Jim Lane,ECT8-3,,:/staff/jl:/bin/sh
dotty:$1$Ce8QpAQI$L.DvJEWiHlWetKTMLXFZO/:101:20::/home/dotty:/bin/tcsh
```

These days it is not acceptable to leave encrypted passwords in plain view. With fast hardware, they can be "cracked" in minutes. All versions of UNIX and Linux allow you to hide the encrypted passwords by placing them in a separate file that is not world-readable. This is known as a shadow password mechanism, and it is (appropriately) the default on most systems.

The shadow password system makes more sense when explained as an extension of the traditional **/etc/passwd** (as it historically was), so we defer our discussion of this feature until page 99. A more general discussion of the security implications of shadow passwords can be found on page 678.

The contents of **/etc/passwd** are often shared among systems with a database such as NIS or LDAP. See Chapter 17, *Sharing System Files*, for more information.

The following sections discuss the **/etc/passwd** fields in more detail.

Login name

See page 511 for more information about NIS.

Login names (also known as usernames) must be unique and no more than 32 characters long. They may contain any characters except colons and newlines. If you use NIS, login names are limited to 8 characters, regardless of the operating system.

Some older versions of UNIX limit the permissible characters to alphanumerics and impose an 8-character length limit. At heterogeneous sites, it's a good idea to heed the most restrictive limits. Such a policy will avert potential conflicts with older software and will guarantee that users can have the same login name on every machine. Remember, just because you have a homogeneous environment today doesn't mean that this will be the case tomorrow.

Login names are case sensitive; however, RFC822 calls for case to be ignored in email addresses. We are not aware of any problems caused by mixed-case login names, but lowercase names are traditional and also easier to type.

Login names should be easy to remember, so random sequences of letters do not make good login names. We suggest that you avoid nicknames, even if your organization is relatively informal. They're really not that much fun, and they tend to draw scorn; names like DarkLord and QTPie belong in front of @hotmail.com. Even if your users have no self-respect, at least have some thought for your site's overall credibility.

Since login names are often used as email addresses, it's useful to establish a standard way of forming them. It should be possible for users to make educated guesses about each other's login names. First names, last names, initials, or some combination of these all make reasonable naming schemes.

See page 544 for more information about mail aliases.

Any fixed scheme for choosing login names eventually results in duplicate names or names that are too long, so you will sometimes have to make exceptions. In the case of a long name, you can use your mail system's aliasing features to equate two versions of the name, at least as far as mail is concerned.

For example, suppose you use an employee's first initial and last name as a paradigm. Brent Browning would therefore be bbrowning, which is 9 characters and therefore potentially incompatible with some systems. Instead, you could assign the user the login brentb, leaving bbrowning as an **aliases** file entry:

    bbrowning: brentb

If your site has a global mail alias file, each new login name must be distinct from any alias in this file. If it is not, mail will be delivered to the alias rather than the new user.

It's common for large sites to implement a full-name email addressing scheme (e.g., John.Q.Public@mysite.com) that hides login names from the outside world. This is a fine idea, but it really doesn't obviate any of the naming advice given above. If for no other reason than the sanity of administrators, it's best if login names have a clear and predictable correspondence to users' actual names.

Login names should be unique in two senses. First, a user should have the same login name on every machine. This rule is mostly for convenience, both yours and the user's.

See page 685 for a discussion of login equivalence issues.

Second, a particular login name should always refer to the same person. Some commands (e.g., **ssh**) can be set up to validate remote users according to their login names. Even if scott@boulder and scott@refuge were two different people, one might be able to log in to the other's account without providing a password if the accounts were not set up properly.

Experience also shows that duplicate names can lead to email confusion. The mail system might be perfectly clear about which scott is which, but users will often send mail to the wrong address.

Adding New Users

Encrypted password

A quick reminder before we jump into the details of passwords: most systems now keep encrypted passwords in **/etc/shadow** rather than **/etc/passwd**. However, the comments in this section apply regardless of where passwords are actually kept.

Passwords are stored in an encrypted form. Unless you can execute encryption algorithms in your head (we want to meet you), you must either set passwords by using the **passwd** command (**yppasswd** if you use NIS) or by copying an encrypted password string from another account.

If you edit **/etc/passwd** by hand to create a new account, put a star or an x in the encrypted password field. The star prevents unauthorized use of the account until you have set a real password. Never leave this field empty—that introduces a jumbo-sized security hole because no password is required to access the account. Even if you are using shadow passwords, it's wise to be a bit anal retentive about password hygiene in the **/etc/passwd** file. You never know when some obsolete program or script is going to peek at it in order to make some kind of security decision.[1]

Major Linux distributions recognize multiple methods of password encryption, and they can determine the encryption method used for each password by examining the encrypted data. It isn't necessary for all passwords on the system to use the same form of encryption.

Most Linux distributions default to using MD5 encryption. MD5 is slightly cryptographically better than the former DES standard, and the MD5 scheme allows passwords of arbitrary length. Longer passwords are more secure—if you actually use them. Since the use of MD5 won't hurt and might help, we recommend it for all systems that support it.

Encrypted passwords are of constant length (34 characters long for MD5, 13 for DES) regardless of the length of the unencrypted password. Passwords are encrypted in combination with a random "salt" so that a given password can correspond to many different encrypted forms. If two users happen to select the same password, this fact usually cannot be discovered by inspection of the encrypted passwords. MD5 passwords are easy to spot because they always start with 1.

 SUSE defaults to Blowfish encryption for new passwords. Like MD5, this is a strong algorithm and a very reasonable default. However, you can't copy SUSE's Blowfish passwords to non-SUSE systems since only SUSE understands them. You can identify Blowfish passwords by their prefix of $2a$.

UID (user ID) number

UIDs are unsigned 32-bit integers. However, because of interoperability issues with older systems, we suggest limiting the largest UID at your site to 32,767 (the largest signed 16-bit integer) if possible.

---

1. Jon Corbet, one of our technical reviewers, commented, "If you don't know when security decisions are being made, you're already in trouble. Administrators should not be surprised by such things."

By definition, root has UID 0. Most systems also define pseudo-users bin, daemon, and lots of others. It is customary to put such fake logins at the beginning of the **/etc/passwd** file and to give them low UIDs; never assign these logins a real shell. To allow plenty of room for any nonhuman users you might want to add in the future, we recommend that you assign UIDs to real users starting at 500 (or higher).

*See page 48 for more information about **sudo**.*

It is never a good idea to have multiple accounts with UID 0. While it might seem convenient to have multiple root logins with different shells or passwords, this setup just creates more potential security holes and gives you multiple logins to secure. If people need to have alternate ways to log in as root, you are better off if they use a program such as **sudo**.

Avoid recycling UIDs for as long as possible, even the UIDs of people that have left your organization and had their accounts permanently removed. This precaution prevents confusion if files are later restored from backups, where users may be identified by UID rather than by login name.

See Chapter 16 for more information about NFS.

UIDs should be kept unique across your entire organization. That is, a particular UID should refer to the same login name and the same person on every machine. Failure to maintain distinct UIDs can result in security problems with systems such as NFS and can also result in confusion when a user moves from one workgroup to another.[2]

It can be hard to maintain unique UIDs when groups of machines are administered by different people or organizations. The problems are both technical and political. The best solution is to have a central database that contains a record for each user and enforces uniqueness. (We use a home-grown database to address this problem.) A simpler scheme is to assign each group within an organization a range of UIDs and let each group manage its own set. This solution keeps the UID spaces separate (a requirement if you are going to use NFS to share filesystems) but does not address the parallel issue of unique login names. LDAP is becoming a popular management tool for UIDs as well.

Default GID number

Like a UID, a group ID number is 32-bit integer. GID 0 is reserved for the group called "root". GID 1 is the group "bin" and GID 2 is the group "daemon".

See page 82 for more information about setgid directories.

Groups are defined in **/etc/group**, with the GID field in **/etc/passwd** providing the default (or "effective") GID at login time. The default GID is not treated specially when access is determined;[3] it is relevant only to the creation of new files and directories. New files are normally owned by the user's effective group. However, in directories on which the setgid bit (02000) has been set and on filesystems mounted with the **grpid** option, new files default to the group of their parent directory.

---

2. Another NFS-related issue is the "nobody" UID that is traditionally used to hamper access by remote root users. See page 488 for details.

3. Linux considers all group memberships when performing access calculations. Kernels before 2.6.4 allow a maximum of 32 group memberships, but more recent kernels impose no limit.

Adding New Users

GECOS field[4]

The GECOS field is commonly used to record personal information about each user. It has no well-defined syntax. The GECOS field originally held the login information needed to transfer batch jobs from UNIX systems at Bell Labs to a mainframe running GECOS (the General Electric Comprehensive Operating System); these days, only the name remains. A few programs will expand an '&' in the GECOS field to the user's login name, which saves a bit of typing. Both **finger** and **sendmail** perform this expansion, but many programs do not. It's best not to rely on this feature.

Although you can use any formatting conventions you like, **finger** interprets comma-separated GECOS entries in the following order:

- Full name (often the only field used)
- Office number and building
- Office telephone extension
- Home phone number

See page 520 for more information about LDAP.

The **chfn** command lets users change their own GECOS information. **chfn** is useful for keeping things like phone numbers up to date, but it can be misused: a user can change the information to be either obscene or incorrect. Most college campuses disable **chfn**. GECOS information is the perfect candidate for LDAPification.

Home directory

Users' shells are **cd**'ed to their home directories when they log in. If a user's home directory is missing at login time, the system prints a message such as "no home directory."[5] If DEFAULT_HOME is set to no in **/etc/login.defs**, the login will not be allowed to continue; otherwise, the user will be placed in the root directory.

Be aware that if home directories are mounted over a network filesystem, they may be unavailable in the event of server or network problems.

Login shell

The login shell is normally a command interpreter such as the Bourne shell or the C shell (**/bin/sh** or **/bin/csh**), but it can be any program. **bash** is the default and is used if **/etc/passwd** does not specify a login shell. On Linux systems, **sh** and **csh** are really just links to **bash** (the GNU "Bourne again" shell) and **tcsh** (a superset of the C shell), respectively. Many distributions also provide a public-domain version of the Korn shell, **ksh**.

Users can change their shells with the **chsh** command. The file **/etc/shells** contains a list of "valid" shells that **chsh** will permit users to select; SUSE enforces this list, but

---

4. When Honeywell took over the computer division of GE, GECOS was changed to GCOS; both spellings survive today

5. This message appears when you log in on the console or on a terminal, but not when you log in through a display manager such as **xdm**, **gdm**, or **kdm**. Not only will you not see the message, but you will generally be logged out immediately because of the display manager's inability to write to the proper directory (e.g., ~/.gnome).

Red Hat just warns you if the selected shell is not on the list. If you add entries to the **shells** file, be sure to use absolute paths since **chsh** and other programs expect them.

6.2 THE /ETC/SHADOW FILE

The **/etc/shadow** file is readable only by the superuser and serves to keep encrypted passwords safe from prying eyes. It also provides account information that's not available from **/etc/passwd**. The use of shadow passwords is standard on some distributions and configured as an optional package on others. Even when shadow passwords are optional, it's a good idea to treat them as if they were standard.

When shadow passwords are in use, the old-style password fields in **/etc/passwd** should always contain an x.

The **shadow** file is not a superset of the **passwd** file, and the **passwd** file is not generated from it; you must maintain both files (or use tools such as **useradd** that maintain them both on your behalf). Like **/etc/passwd**, /etc/shadow contains one line for each user. Each line contains nine fields, separated by colons:

- Login name
- Encrypted password
- Date of last password change
- Minimum number of days between password changes
- Maximum number of days between password changes
- Number of days in advance to warn users about password expiration
- Number of days after password expiration that account is disabled
- Account expiration date
- A reserved field that is currently always empty

*See page 109 for more information about **usermod**.*

The only fields that are required to be nonempty are the username and password. Absolute date fields in **/etc/shadow** are specified in terms of days (*not* seconds) since Jan 1, 1970, which is not a standard way of reckoning time on UNIX systems. Fortunately, you can use the **usermod** program to set the expiration field.

A typical **shadow** entry looks like this:

```
millert:$1$buJ6v3Ch$BwLIoF5eaCh9Nv.OEzD3T0:13348:0:180:14::14974:
```

Here is a more complete description of each field:

- The login name is the same as in **/etc/passwd**. This field connects a user's **passwd** and **shadow** entries.

- The encrypted password is identical in concept and execution to the one previously stored in **/etc/passwd**.

- The last change field records the time at which the user's password was last changed. This field is generally filled in by **passwd**.

Adding New Users

- The fourth field sets the number of days that must elapse between password changes. The idea is to force authentic changes by preventing users from immediately reverting to a familiar password after a required change. However, we think this feature could be somewhat dangerous when a security intrusion has occurred. We recommend setting this field to 0.

- The fifth field sets the maximum number of days allowed between password changes. This feature allows the administrator to enforce password aging; see page 680 for more information. The actual enforced maximum number of days is the sum of this field and the seventh (grace period) field.

- The sixth field sets the number of days before password expiration that the **login** program should begin to warn the user of the impending expiration.

- The seventh field specifies how many days after the maximum password age has been reached to wait before treating the login as expired. The exact purpose of this feature is not clear.

- The eighth field specifies the day (in days since Jan 1, 1970) on which the user's account will expire. The user may not log in after this date until the field has been reset by an administrator. If the field is left blank, the account will never expire.

- The ninth field is reserved for future use.

Now that we know what each of the fields means, let's look at our example line again:

```
millert:$1$buJ6v3Ch$BwLIoF5eaCh9Nv.OEzD3T0:13348:0:180:14::14974:
```

In this example, the user millert last changed his password on July 18, 2006. The password must be changed again within 180 days, and millert will receive warnings that the password needs to be changed for the last two weeks of this period. The account expires on December 31, 2010.

You can use the **pwconv** utility to reconcile the contents of the **shadow** file to those of the **passwd** file, picking up any new additions and deleting users that are no longer listed in **passwd**. **pwconv** fills in most of the shadow parameters from defaults specified in **/etc/login.defs**.

The following example illustrates the format of the **login.defs** file. The comments do a good job of explaining the various parameters. This particular example is from a Fedora system; the default contents vary quite substantially among distributions, as do the parameters that can be specified.

```
# *REQUIRED*
#   Directory where mailboxes reside, _or_ name of file, relative to the
#   home directory.  If you _do_ define both, MAIL_DIR takes precedence.
#   QMAIL_DIR is for Qmail

# QMAIL_DIR      Maildir
MAIL_DIR        /var/spool/mail
```

```
# MAIL_FILE          .mail

# Password aging controls:
# PASS_MAX_DAYS Maximum # of days a password may be used.
# PASS_MIN_DAYS Minimum # of days allowed between password changes.
# PASS_MIN_LEN  Minimum acceptable password length.
# PASS_WARN_AGE Number of days warning given before a password expires.

PASS_MAX_DAYS      99999
PASS_MIN_DAYS      0
PASS_MIN_LEN       5
PASS_WARN_AGE      7

# Min/max values for automatic uid selection in useradd

UID_MIN            500
UID_MAX            60000

# Min/max values for automatic gid selection in groupadd

GID_MIN            500
GID_MAX            60000

# If defined, this command is run when removing a user.
# It should remove any at/cron/print jobs etc. owned by
# the user to be removed (passed as the first argument).

# USERDEL_CMD       /usr/sbin/userdel_local

# If useradd should create home directories for users by default
# On RH systems, we do. This option is ORed with the -m flag on
# useradd command line.

CREATE_HOME        yes
```

6.3 THE /ETC/GROUP FILE

The **/etc/group** file contains the names of UNIX groups and a list of each group's members. For example:

```
wheel:x:10:trent,ned,evi,garth,lynda,boggs,millert
csstaff:*:100:lloyd,evi
student:*:200:dotty
```

Each line represents one group and contains four fields:

- Group name
- Encrypted password or contains an x, indicating a **gshadow** file
- GID number
- List of members, separated by commas (be careful not to add spaces)

As in **/etc/passwd**, fields are separated by colons. Group names should be limited to 8 characters for compatibility, although Linux does not actually require this. While it is possible to enter a group password (to allow users not belonging to a group to change to it by using the **newgrp** command), this is rarely done.[6] Most sites put stars in the password field, but it is safe to leave the password field blank if you wish. The **newgrp** command will not change to a group without a password unless the user is already listed as being a member of that group. All our example distributions come configured with **/etc/gshadow** files, which are analogous in concept to **/etc/shadow** but of considerably less importance (group passwords are rarely used).

As with usernames and UIDs, group names and GIDs should be kept consistent among machines that share files through a network filesystem. Consistency can be hard to maintain in a heterogeneous environment since different operating systems use different GIDs for the same group names. We've found that the best way to deal with this issue is to avoid using a system group as the default login group for a user.

If a user defaults to a particular group in **/etc/passwd** but does not appear to be in that group according to **/etc/group**, **/etc/passwd** wins the argument. The group memberships granted at login time are really the union of those found in the **passwd** and **group** files. However, it's a good idea to keep the two files consistent.

To minimize the potential for collisions with vendor-supplied GIDs, we suggest starting local groups at GID 500 or higher.

The UNIX tradition is to add new users to a group that represents their general category such as "students" or "finance." However, it's worth noting that this convention increases the likelihood that users will be able to read one another's files because of slipshod permission setting, even if that is not really the intention of the owner. To avoid this problem, we prefer to create a unique group for each user. You can use the same name for both the user and the group. You can also make the GID the same as the UID.

A user's personal group should contain only that user. If you want to let users share files by way of the group mechanism, create separate groups for that purpose. The idea behind personal groups is not to discourage the use of groups per se—it's simply to establish a more restrictive *default* group for each user so that files are not shared inadvertently.

 The **useradd** utilities on all of our example distributions except SUSE default to placing users in their own personal groups.

6.4 ADDING USERS

Before you create an account for a new user at a corporate, government, or educational site, it's *very* important that the user sign and date a copy of your local user agreement and policy statement. (What?! You don't have a user agreement and policy statement? See page 946 for more information about why you need one and what to put in it.)

---

6. The only reason we are aware of that someone might want to use the **newgrp** command under Linux is to set the default group of newly created files.

Users have no particular reason to want to sign a policy agreement, so it's to your advantage to secure their signatures while you still have some leverage. We find that it takes more effort to secure a signed agreement after an account has been released. If your process allows for it, have the paperwork precede the creation of the account.

Mechanically, the process of adding a new user consists of four steps required by the system, two steps that establish a useful environment for the new user, and several extra steps for your own convenience as an administrator.

Required:

- Edit the **passwd** and **shadow** files to define the user's account.
- Add the user to the **/etc/group** file.
- Set an initial password.
- Create, **chown**, and **chmod** the user's home directory.

For the user:

- Copy default startup files to the user's home directory.
- Set the user's mail home and establish mail aliases.

For you:

- Verify that the account is set up correctly.
- Add the user's contact information and account status to your database.

Starting on page 108, we discuss the **useradd** command and its brethren, which automate some of these steps. However, in the next few sections we go over the steps as you'd execute them by hand. This is mostly so that you can see what the supplied tools are doing. In real life, it's generally preferable (faster and less error prone) to run **useradd** or a similar home-grown script.

You must perform each step as root or use a program such as **sudo** that allows you to run commands as root. See page 41 for more information about **sudo**.

Editing the passwd and shadow files

To safely edit the **passwd** file, run **vipw** to invoke a text editor on a copy of it. The default editor is **vi**, but you can specify a different editor by setting the value of your EDITOR environment variable. The existence of the temporary edit file serves as a lock; **vipw** allows only one person to edit the **passwd** file at a time, and it prevents users from changing their passwords while the **passwd** file is checked out. When the editor terminates, **vipw** replaces the original **passwd** file with your edited copy.

On Fedora and RHEL systems, **vipw** automatically asks if you would like to edit the **shadow** file after you have edited the **passwd** file. SUSE, Debian, and Ubuntu systems use **vipw -s** for this function.

For example, adding the following line to **/etc/passwd** would define an account called "tyler":

```
tyler:x:2422:2422:Tyler Stevens, ECEE 3-27, x7919,:/home/tyler:/bin/sh
```

Adding New Users

We'd also add a matching entry to **/etc/shadow**:

```
tyler:*::::::14974:
```

This **shadow** line for tyler has no encrypted password or password aging, and it sets the account to expire on December 31, 2010.

Editing the /etc/group file

We should next create an entry in the **/etc/group** file for tyler's personal group, which we will also call "tyler". This group should have GID 2422 to match tyler's UID of 2422. This is the default GID we assigned to him in the **passwd** file.[7]

```
tyler::2422:tyler
```

Strictly speaking, tyler will be in group 2422 whether or not he is listed in **/etc/group**, because his **passwd** entry has already given him this membership. The kernel doesn't care about the contents of **/etc/passwd** and **/etc/group**; it only cares about UID and GID numbers. The main purpose of recording personal groups in the **group** file is to make sure that commands such as **ls** display the names of these groups correctly. Of course, it's always nice to have an authoritative list of the groups you have created and the users they include.

If we wanted to assign tyler to additional groups, we would simply add his login name to additional groups within the **/etc/group** file.

Setting an initial password

Root can change any user's password with the **passwd** command:

```
# passwd user
```

or

```
$ sudo passwd user
```

Rules for selecting good passwords are given on page 679.

passwd prompts you to enter a new password and asks you to repeat it. If you choose a short, all-lowercase, or otherwise obviously unsuitable password, **passwd** will complain and ask you to use something more complex. Most Linux systems also check prospective passwords against a dictionary for added security.

The **mkpasswd** utility that comes with Don Libes's **expect** package makes it easy to generate random passwords for new users. For better or worse, the assignment of a random password "forces" new users to change their passwords immediately, as the random ones are difficult to remember.[8] Don't confuse **expect**'s **mkpasswd** with the standard **mkpasswd** command, which simply encodes a given string as a password.

---

7. This naming and numbering is purely conventional; see page 102.

8. The passwords are not truly random, but rather pseudorandom. If one or more passwords in a pseudo-randomly generated sequence are cracked, it may be possible to reverse-engineer the sequence and discover additional passwords. Possible, but probably unlikely in the real world. We're relatively comfortable with this risk.

Never leave a new account—or any account that has access to a shell—without a password.

Creating the user's home directory

Any directory you create as root is initially owned by root, so you must change its owner and group with the **chown** and **chgrp** commands. The following sequence of commands would create a home directory appropriate for our example user:

```
# mkdir /home/tyler
# chown tyler:staff /home/tyler
# chmod 700 /home/tyler
```

Copying in the default startup files

You can customize some commands and utilities by placing configuration files in a user's home directory. Startup files traditionally begin with a dot and end with the letters **rc**, short for "run command," a relic of the CTSS operating system. The initial dot causes **ls** to elide these files from directory listings unless the **-a** option is used; the files are considered "uninteresting." Table 6.1 lists some common startup files.

Table 6.1   Common startup files and their uses

Command	Filename	Typical uses
csh/tcsh	**.login**	Sets the terminal type (if needed)
		Sets **biff** and **mesg** switches
	.cshrc	Sets up environment variables
		Sets command aliases
		Sets the search path
		Sets the **umask** value to control permissions
		Sets cdpath for filename searches
		Sets the prompt, history, and savehist variables
bash[a]	**.bashrc**	Similar to **.cshrc** for **bash**
	.bash_profile	Similar to **.login** for **bash**
vim	**.vimrc**	Sets **vim** editor options
emacs	**.emacs**	Sets **emacs** editor options
		Sets **emacs** key bindings
mail/mailx	**.mailrc**	Defines personal mail aliases
		Sets mail reader options
xrdb[b]	**.Xdefaults**	Specifies X11 configuration: fonts, color, etc.
startx[b]	**.xinitrc**	Specifies the initial X11 environment
	.Xclients	Specifies the initial X11 environment (RHEL, Fedora)
xdm[b]	**.xsession**	Specifies the initial X11 environment

a. **bash** will also read **.profile** or **/etc/profile** in emulation of **sh**.

b. Exact details of X Windows vary with the implementation and window manager in use; see Chapter 22 for more details.

Adding New Users

If you don't already have a set of good default startup files, **/usr/local/lib/skel** is a reasonable place to put them. Copy in some files to use as a starting point and modify them with a text editor. You may wish to start with vendor-supplied files from the **/etc/skel** directory, if your system provides them. Be sure to set a reasonable default value for **umask**; we suggest 077, 027, or 022, depending on the friendliness and size of your site.

Depending on the user's shell, **/etc** may contain system-wide startup files that are processed before the user's own startup files. For example, **bash** reads **/etc/profile** before processing **~/.bash_profile**. For other shells, see the man page for the shell in question for details.

It has become common for the system-wide startup files for shells to look in the **/etc/profile.d** directory for additional configuration snippets to execute. This convention provides a clean way for software packages to specify shell-level defaults. For example, the **/etc/profile.d/colorls.*** files on Fedora and RHEL are responsible for the technicolor **ls** output on those systems. (Yes, they can be safely deleted.)

The command sequence for installing startup files for the new user tyler would look something like this:

```
# cp /usr/local/lib/skel/.[a-zA-Z]* ~tyler
# chown tyler:staff ~tyler/.[a-zA-Z]*
# chmod 600 ~tyler/.[a-zA-Z]*
```

Note that we cannot use

```
# chown tyler:staff ~tyler/.*
```

because tyler would then own not only his own files but also the parent directory ".." (**/home**) as well. This is a very common and dangerous sysadmin mistake.

Setting the user's mail home

It is convenient for each user to receive email on only one machine. This scheme is often implemented with an entry in the global aliases file **/etc/mail/aliases** or the **sendmail** userDB on the central mail server. See Chapter 18 for general information about email; the various ways to implement mail homes are discussed starting on page 542.

Verifying the new login

To verify that a new account has been properly configured, first log out, then log in as the new user and execute the following commands:

```
$ pwd        /* To verify the home directory */
$ ls -la      /* Check owner/group of startup files */
```

You will need to notify new users of their login names and initial passwords. Many sites send this information by email, but for security reasons that's usually not a good idea. A new user's account can be compromised and back-doored before the user has even logged in. This is also a good time to point users toward additional documentation on local customs, if you have any.

See page 946 for more information about written user contracts.

If your site requires users to sign a written policy agreement or appropriate use policy, be sure this step has been completed before releasing the account. This check will prevent oversights and strengthen the legal basis of any sanctions you might later need to impose.Be sure to remind new users to change their passwords immediately. If you wish, you can enforce this by setting the password to expire within a short time. Another option is to have a script check up on new users and be sure their encrypted passwords in the **shadow** file have changed.[9]

Recording the user's status and contact information

In an environment in which you know all the users personally, it's relatively easy to keep track of who's using a system and why. But if you manage a large and changeable user base, you'll need a more formal way to keep track of accounts. Maintaining a database of contact information and account statuses will help you figure out who someone is and why they have an account, once the act of adding them has faded from memory. It's a good idea to keep complete contact information on hand so that you can reach users in the event of problems or misbehavior.

6.5 REMOVING USERS

When a user leaves your organization, that user's login account and files should be removed from the system. This procedure involves the removal of all references to the login name that were added by you or your **useradd** program. If you remove a user by hand, you may want to use the following checklist:

- Remove the user from any local user databases or phone lists.
- Remove the user from the **aliases** file or add a forwarding address.
- Remove the user's crontab file and any pending **at** jobs.
- Kill any of the user's processes that are still running.
- Remove the user from the **passwd**, **shadow**, **group**, and **gshadow** files.
- Remove the user's home directory.
- Remove the user's mail spool.

Before you remove a user's home directory, be sure to relocate any files that are needed by other users. Since you often can't be sure which files those might be, it's always a good idea to make an extra backup of the user's home directory and mail spool before deleting them.

Once you have removed a user, you may want to verify that the user's old UID owns no more files on the system. To find the paths of orphaned files, you can use the **find** command with the **-nouser** argument. Because **find** has a way of "escaping" onto

---

9. Because the same password can have many encrypted representations, this method verifies only that the user has reset the password, not that it has actually been changed to a different password. There is no practical way to force users to actually change their passwords except by maintaining a database of all prior values.

network servers if you're not careful, it's usually best to check filesystems individually with **-xdev**:

    # **find** *filesystem* **-xdev -nouser**

If your organization assigns individual workstations to users, it's generally simplest and most efficient to reinstall the entire system from a master template before turning the system over to a new user. Before you do the reinstallation, however, it's a good idea to back up any local files on the system's hard disk in case they are needed in the future.

6.6 DISABLING LOGINS

On occasion, a user's login must be temporarily disabled. A straightforward way to do this is to put a star or some other character in front of the user's encrypted password in the **/etc/shadow** file. This measure prevents most types of password-regulated access because the password no longer decrypts to anything sensible. Commands such as **ssh** that do not necessarily check the system password may continue to function, however.

 On all of our example distributions except SUSE, the **usermod -L** *user* and **usermod -U** *user* commands provide an easy way to lock and unlock passwords.

An alternative (and perhaps more secure) way to achieve a similar end is to replace the user's shell with a program that prints a message explaining why the login has been disabled and provides instructions for rectifying the situation. This pseudo-shell should not be listed in **/etc/shells**; many daemons that provide nonlogin access to the system (e.g., **ftpd**) check to see if a user's login shell is listed in **/etc/shells** and will deny access if it is not (which is the behavior you want). Unfortunately, this message may not be seen if the user tries to log in through a window system.

There is another problem with this method of disabling logins, however. By default, **sendmail** will not deliver mail to a user whose shell does not appear in **/etc/shells**. It's generally a bad idea to interfere with the flow of mail, even if the recipient is not able to read it immediately. You can defeat **sendmail**'s default behavior by adding a fake shell named **/SENDMAIL/ANY/SHELL/** to the **/etc/shells** file (although there may be unwanted side effects from doing so).

6.7 MANAGING ACCOUNTS

The **useradd** command adds users to the **passwd** file (and to the **shadow** file if applicable). It provides a command-line-driven interface that is easy to run by hand or to call from a home-grown **adduser** script. The **usermod** command changes the **passwd** entries of existing users. The **userdel** command removes a user from the system, optionally deleting the user's home directory. The **groupadd**, **groupmod**, and **groupdel** commands operate on the **/etc/group** file.

For example, to create a new user "hilbert" with **useradd** (using the system defaults), you could simply run:

```
# useradd hilbert
```

This command would create the following entry in **/etc/passwd**. Note that **useradd** puts a star in the password field, effectively disabling the account until you assign a real password.

```
hilbert:*:105:20::/home/hilbert:/bin/bash
```

 For some reason, SUSE uses a similar but independently developed set of user and group manipulation commands. The commands have the same names, but there are subtle differences in the meanings of some options and in the default behaviors. For example, most distributions create a dedicated personal group for new users if you do not specify otherwise on the command line. SUSE's **useradd** puts new users in group 100. (In the default configuration, it also adds them to the groups "video" and "dialout." Hmm.)

useradd is generally more useful when given additional arguments. In the next example, we specify that hilbert's primary group should be "faculty" and that he should also be added to the "famous" group. We also override the default home directory location and ask **useradd** to create the home directory if it does not already exist:

```
# useradd -c "David Hilbert" -d /home/math/hilbert -g faculty -G famous -m
    -s /bin/sh hilbert
```

This command creates the following **passwd** entry:

```
hilbert:x:1005:30:David Hilbert:/home/math/hilbert:/bin/sh
```

(the assigned UID is one higher than the highest UID on the system) and the corresponding **shadow** entry:

```
hilbert:!:11508:0:99999:7:0::
```

It also adds hilbert to the "faculty" and "famous" groups in **/etc/group**, creates the directory **/home/math/hilbert**, and populates it in accordance with the contents of the **/etc/skel** directory.

On all of our example distributions except SUSE, you can determine the default settings for **useradd** by running **useradd -D**. You can also use the **-D** flag in combination with other arguments to set those defaults.

Even on SUSE, the defaults are stored in **/etc/default/useradd** and can be edited directly if you prefer.

usermod modifies an account that already exists and takes many of the same flags as **useradd**. For example, we could use the following command to set an expiration date of July 4, 2007, on hilbert's account:

```
# usermod -e 2007-07-04 hilbert
```

Adding New Users

The **userdel** command deletes user accounts, effectively undoing all the changes made by **useradd**. To remove hilbert, we would use the following command:

> # userdel hilbert

This command removes references to hilbert in the **passwd**, **shadow**, and **group** files. By default, it would not remove hilbert's home directory.[10] The **-r** option makes **userdel** remove the user's home directory as well, but even at its most aggressive, **userdel** still performs only the last three tasks from the "user deletion chores" list.

Although the **useradd** and **userdel** commands are convenient, they are usually not sufficient to implement all of a site's local policies. Don't hesitate to write your own **adduser** and **rmuser** scripts; most larger sites do. (Perl is generally the appropriate tool for this task.) Your homebrew scripts can call the standard utilities to accomplish part of their work.

6.8 EXERCISES

E6.1   How is a user's default group determined? How would you change it?

E6.2   Explain the differences among the following umask values: 077, 027, 022, and 755. How would you implement one of these values as a site-wide default for new users? Can you impose a **umask** standard on your users?

E6.3   What is the purpose of the shadow password file?

★ **E6.4**   List the steps needed to add a user to a system without using the **useradd** program. What extra steps are needed for your local environment?

★ **E6.5**   Determine the naming convention for new users at your site. What are the rules? How is uniqueness preserved? Can you think of any drawbacks? How are users removed?

★★ **E6.6**   Find a list of names (from a local on-line telephone directory, perhaps) and use it as the input to a script that forms login names according to the naming convention at your site. How many users can you accommodate before you have a collision? How many collisions are there overall? Use the data to evaluate your site's naming convention, and suggest improvements.

★★ **E6.7**   Write a script to help monitor the health of your **/etc/passwd** file. (Parts b and e require root access unless you're clever.)

   a) Find any entries that have UID 0.
   b) Find any entries that have no password (needs **/etc/shadow**).
   c) Find any sets of entries that have duplicate UIDs.
   d) Find any entries that have duplicate login names.
   e) Find any entries that have no expiration date (needs **/etc/shadow**).

10. At our site, we generally preserve deleted users' home directories for a few weeks. This policy minimizes the need to restore data from backup tapes if a deleted user should return or if other users need access to the deleted user's work files.

7 *Adding a Disk*

It's hard to believe that with the last few decades' advances in chip, network, and software technology, we're still using essentially the same long-term data storage technology that was popular 40 years ago. Densities have increased (and prices decreased) by several orders of magnitude, but the basic idea remains unchanged.

Unfortunately, new uses for disk space have continued to appear, especially with the wide acceptance of the Internet. In many cases, disk space is still at a premium. MP3s, streaming video, and other multimedia content keep system administrators scrambling to keep up. Proper disk management is as important as ever.

Many server systems connect their disks through a standard peripheral bus called SCSI (the Small Computer Systems Interface, pronounced "scuzzy"). An alternative interface called Integrated Drive Electronics (IDE) is standard on desktop and laptop PCs. We begin this chapter with a general discussion of the SCSI and IDE standards and the structure of modern hard disks. We then discuss the general mechanisms for formatting and partitioning disks and the procedure for initializing filesystems. Finally, we discuss advanced features such as RAID and volume managers.

7.1 DISK INTERFACES

These days, only a few interface standards are in common use, although several new technologies are on the horizon. It's important to select disk drives that match the interfaces of the system on which they will be installed. If a system supports several different interfaces, use the one that best meets your requirements for speed, redundancy, mobility, and price.

- PATA (also known as IDE) was developed as a simple, low-cost interface for PCs. It was originally called Integrated Drive Electronics because it put the hardware controller in the same box as the disk platters and used a relatively high-level protocol for communication between the computer and the disks. This is now the standard architecture for modern disks, but the name lives on. IDE disks are medium to fast in speed, high in capacity, and unbelievably cheap. See the next section for more information about IDE.

- Serial ATA, SATA, is the successor to conventional IDE. In addition to supporting much higher transfer rates, SATA simplifies connectivity with tidier cabling and a longer maximum cable length. SATA has native support for hot-swapping and (optional) command queueing, two features that finally make IDE a viable alternative to SCSI in server environments.

- Though not as common as it once was, SCSI is one of the most widely supported disk interfaces. It comes in several flavors, all of which support multiple disks on a bus and various speeds and communication styles. SCSI is described in more detail on page 114.

- Fibre Channel is a serial interface that is gaining popularity in the enterprise environment thanks to its high bandwidth and to the large number of devices that can be attached to it at once. Fibre Channel devices connect with a fiber optic or twinaxial copper cable. Current speeds are 100 MB/s and up. Common topologies include loops, called Fibre Channel Arbitrated Loop (FC-AL), and fabrics, which are constructed with Fibre Channel switches. Fibre Channel can speak several different protocols, including SCSI and even IP. Fibre Channel devices are identified by a hard-wired ID number called a World Wide Name that's similar to an Ethernet MAC address.

- The Universal Serial Bus (USB) has become popular for connecting devices such as keyboards and mice, but current versions have enough bandwidth to support disk and CD-ROM drives. USB is common on PCs and enables you to easily move a disk among systems.

IDE and SCSI are by far the dominant players in the disk drive arena. They are the only interfaces we discuss in detail.

The PATA interface

PATA (Parallel Advanced Technology Attachment), also called IDE, was designed to be simple and inexpensive. It is most often found on PCs or low-cost workstations. IDE became popular in the late 1980s. Shortly thereafter, ATA-2 was developed to satisfy the increasing demands of consumers and hard drive vendors.

ATA-2 adds faster programmed I/O (PIO) and direct memory access (DMA) modes and extends the bus's Plug and Play features. It also adds a feature called logical block addressing (LBA), which (in combination with an enhanced PC BIOS) overcomes a problem that prevented BIOSes from accessing more than the first 1024 cylinders of a disk. This constraint formerly limited disk sizes to 504MB. Who would have thought a disk could get that big!

Since the BIOS manages part of the bootstrapping process, you formerly had to create a small bootable partition within the first 1024 cylinders to ensure that the kernel could be loaded by an old BIOS. Once the kernel was up and running, the BIOS was not needed and you could access the rest of your disk. This silly maneuver is unnecessary on modern hardware since LBA gets rid of cylinder-head-sector (CHS) addressing in favor of a linear addressing scheme.

ATA-3 adds extra reliability, more sophisticated power management, and self-monitoring capabilities. Ultra-ATA attempts to bridge the gap between ATA-3 and ATA-4, adding high-performance modes called Ultra DMA/33 and Ultra DMA/66 that extend the bus bandwidth from 16 MB/s to 33 MB/s and 66 MB/s, respectively. ATA-4 is also a much-needed attempt to merge ATA-3 with the ATA Packet Interface (ATAPI) protocol, which allows CD-ROM and tape drives to work on an IDE bus.

Newer additions to the family, ATA-5 and ATA-6, include enhanced performance management and error handling, both of which improve performance in a multiuser environment such as Linux. ATA-7 is expected to be the final update to parallel ATA. It supports data transfer rates as high as 133 MB/s.

IDE disks are almost always used internally (unless you consider a disk hanging out the side of the computer for testing purposes "external"). The maximum cable length for an ATA-2 bus is a mere 18 inches, which can make it difficult even to reach your system's top drive bay. In addition to the short cable length, an IDE bus can accommodate only two devices. To compensate for these shortcomings, most manufacturers put more than one IDE bus on their motherboards (typically two, referred to as a primary and secondary).

Older IDE devices were accessed in a connected manner, which meant that only one device could be active at a time. Performance on these legacy IDE drives was best if you spread these devices over multiple buses. The Extended IDE standard circumvents this limitation by simulating two IDE interfaces on a single interface, allowing two drives to be active at a time. Of course, the devices cannot simultaneously send data over the cable, but this applies to SCSI as well.

The IDE connector is a 40-pin header that connects the drive to the interface card with a ribbon cable. Newer IDE standards such as Ultra DMA/66 use a different cable with more ground pins and therefore less electrical noise. If a cable or drive is not keyed, be sure that pin 1 on the drive goes to pin 1 on the interface card. Pin 1 is usually marked with a small "1" on one side of the connector. If it is not marked, a rule of thumb is that pin 1 is usually the one closest to the power connector. Pin 1 on a ribbon cable is usually marked in red. If there is no red stripe on one edge of your cable, just make sure you have the cable oriented so that pin 1 is connected to pin 1, and mark it clearly for next time.

Adding a Disk

If you have more than one device on an IDE bus, you must designate one as the master and the other as the slave. A "cable select" jumper setting on modern drives (which is usually the default) lets the devices work out master vs. slave on their own. No performance advantage accrues from being the master. Some older IDE drives do not like to be slaves, so if you are having trouble getting one configuration to work, try reversing the disks' roles. If things are still not working out, try making each device the master of its own IDE bus.

When considering IDE hardware, keep the following points in mind:

- New IDE drives work on older cards, and old IDE drives work on newer cards. Naturally, only the features common to both devices are supported.

- At 18 inches, the cable length is exceedingly short, which can make adding an extra device to the bus a stretch. If you experience random flakiness, check the cable length.

- New cable design techniques use rounded cabling instead of the more common ribbon cable for IDE devices. The new cables effectively tidy up a chassis and improve airflow.

The SATA interface

As data transfer rates for PATA drives increased (especially with the advent of ATA-7), the standard's disadvantages started to become obvious. Electromagnetic interference and other electrical issues began to cause reliability concerns at high speeds. Serial ATA, SATA, was invented to address these problems. Although SATA has conceptually been around since 2000, it has only recently began to make an appearance on consumer workstations.

SATA smooths many of PATA's sharp edges. Although the initial SATA drives are only slightly faster than ATA-7 at 150 MB/s, SATA-2 will ultimately support 600 MB/s transfer rates by 2008.[1] Other notable changes include superior error checking, the ability to hot-swap drives, native command queuing, and sundry performance enhancements. Finally, SATA eliminates the need for master and slave designations because only a single device can be connected to each channel.

SATA overcomes the 18-inch cable limitation of PATA and introduces new cable and connector standards of 7 and 15 conductors, respectively.[2] These cables are infinitely more flexible and easier to work with than their ribbon cable predecessors—no more curving and twisting to fit drives on the same cable!

The SCSI interface

Several chipsets implement the SCSI standard, so vendors sometimes put SCSI support right on the motherboard. SCSI defines a generic data pipe that can be used by

1. Will we have disk drives that can actually read and write data at 600 MB/s? No, but even now, the bus is no longer a limiting factor.
2. That's right: for some reason, the power cable is more complicated than the data cable.

all kinds of peripherals. In the past it was used for disks, tape drives, scanners, and printers, but these days most peripherals have abandoned SCSI in favor of USB. The SCSI standard does not specify how a disk is constructed or laid out, only the manner in which it communicates with other devices.

The SCSI standard has been through several revisions, with SCSI-3 being the current version. SCSI-1 was developed in 1986 as an ANSI standard based on the Shugart Associates System Interface (SASI), which was a commercially available system bus. SCSI-2 was developed in 1990. It is backward compatible with SCSI-1 but adds several performance features. These features include command queuing, which allows devices to reorder I/O requests to optimize throughput, and scatter-gather I/O, which permits direct memory access (DMA) from discontiguous memory regions.

You might see the terms "fast" and "wide" applied to SCSI-2 devices; these terms mean that the bus speed is doubled or that the number of bits transferred simultaneously is larger, typically 16 or 32 bits instead of the usual 8.[3] Wide SCSI chains can also support up to 16 devices; narrow SCSI allows only 8. Fastness and wideness are separate features that are commonly used together for synergistic increases.

SCSI-3 is actually a family of standards. It includes specifications for various physical media, including the traditional parallel buses and high-speed serial media such as Fibre Channel and IEEE 1394 ("FireWire"). It also defines the SCSI command sets and introduces enhancements to support device autoconfiguration, multimedia applications, and new types of devices.

Although the SCSI-3 specification has been under development since 1993, it has still not been finalized. Many of its features, however, have already made their way to the marketplace, often under the name "Ultra SCSI." SCSI-3 encompasses SCSI-2, so a certain degree of backward compatibility is built in. Keep in mind, however, that putting an older device on a newer bus can slow down the entire bus. It will also affect the maximum cable length.

Table 7.1 on the next page summarizes the different SCSI versions and their associated bus bandwidths and cable lengths.

The maximum cable length for single-ended Ultra and wide Ultra SCSI depends on the number of devices in use. For eight devices, 1.5 meters is the maximum; if only four devices are used, the bus can be extended to 3 meters. Wide Ultra SCSI supports all sixteen devices only in differential mode.

Many types of connectors are used for SCSI devices. They vary, depending on the version of SCSI in use and type of connection: internal or external. Narrow SCSI devices have 50 pins, and wide SCSI devices have 68 pins. Internal devices typically accept a 50-pin header or a 68-pin male mini-micro connector attached to a ribbon cable. External drives usually connect to the computer with a high density 50- or 68-pin mini-micro connector.

---

3. 32-bit SCSI buses are not very common. Some may require multiple cables, referred to as the A cable and the B cable.

Table 7.1   **The evolution of SCSI**

Version	Freq.	Width	Speed	Length	Diff. length
SCSI-1	5 MHz	8 bits	5 MB/s	6m	25m
SCSI-2	5 MHz	8 bits	5 MB/s	6m	25m
Fast SCSI-2	10 MHz	8 bits	10 MB/s	3m	25m
Fast/wide SCSI-2	10 MHz	16 bits	20 MB/s	3m	25m
Ultra SCSI	20 MHz	8 bits	20 MB/s	1.5m[a]	25m
Wide Ultra SCSI[b]	20 MHz	16 bits	40 MB/s	1.5m[a]	25m
Wide Ultra2 SCSI[b]	40 MHz	16 bits	80 MB/s	–[c]	25m (HVD)[d] 12m (LVD)
Wide Ultra3 SCSI[e]	80 MHz	16 bits	160 MB/s	–[c]	12m (LVD)

a. Varies; see the comments in the text.

b. Wide Ultra SCSI and wide Ultra2 SCSI are sometimes called Fast-20 wide SCSI and Fast-40 wide SCSI, respectively.

c. These versions of SCSI use only differential signalling.

d. HVD is high voltage differential and LVD is low voltage differential. HVD is used for the earlier SCSI versions and is not defined above Ultra2 SCSI.

e. Wide Ultra3 SCSI is sometimes called Ultra-160. Similar standards that double and triple the data transfer rates are Ultra-320 and Ultra-640, respectively. Most new drives are Ultra-320.

An interesting variant that's especially useful for hot-swappable drive arrays is the single connector attachment (SCA) plug. It's an 80-pin connector that includes the bus connections, power, and SCSI configuration, allowing a single connector to meet all the drive's needs.

Exhibit A shows pictures of the most common connectors. Each connector is shown from the front, as if you were about to plug it into your forehead.

Exhibit A   **Common SCSI connectors (front view, male except where noted)**

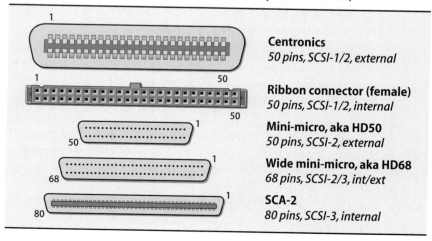

Centronics
50 pins, SCSI-1/2, external

Ribbon connector (female)
50 pins, SCSI-1/2, internal

Mini-micro, aka HD50
50 pins, SCSI-2, external

Wide mini-micro, aka HD68
68 pins, SCSI-2/3, int/ext

SCA-2
80 pins, SCSI-3, internal

SCSI buses use a daisy chain configuration, so most external devices have two SCSI ports. The ports are identical and interchangeable, so either one can be the input. For some reason, scanner vendors seem to consider themselves exempt from the normal laws of physics and sometimes provide only one SCSI port. If not internally terminated, these devices require a special type of terminator.

Internal SCSI devices are usually attached to a ribbon cable; only one port is needed on the actual SCSI device because connectors can be clamped onto the middle of the ribbon cable. When using a ribbon cable, make sure pin 1 on the SCSI bus is connected to pin 1 on the hard drive. (Pin 1 is usually marked with a red stripe.)

Each end of the SCSI bus must have a terminating resistor ("terminator"). These resistors absorb signals as they reach the end of the bus and prevent noise from reflecting back onto the bus. Terminators take several forms, from small external plugs that you snap onto a regular port to sets of tiny resistor packs that install onto a device's circuit boards. Most modern devices are autoterminating.

One end of the bus normally terminates inside the host computer, either on the SCSI controller or on an internal SCSI drive. The other end usually terminates on an external device or on the SCSI controller if there are no external devices. If you experience seemingly random hardware problems on your SCSI bus, first check that both ends of the bus are properly terminated. Improper termination is one of the most common SCSI configuration mistakes, and the errors it produces can be obscure and intermittent.

Each device has a SCSI address or "target number" that distinguishes it from the other devices on the bus. Target numbers start at 0 and go up to 7 or 15, depending on whether the bus is narrow or wide. The SCSI controller itself counts as a device and is usually target 7 (even on a wide bus, for backward compatibility). All other devices must have their target numbers set to unique values. It is a common error to forget that the SCSI controller has a target number and to set a device to the same target number as the controller.

A SCSI address is essentially arbitrary. Technically, it determines the device's priority on the bus, but in practice the exact priorities don't make much difference. Some systems pick the disk with the lowest target number to be the default boot disk, and some require the boot disk to be target 0.

If you're lucky, a device will have an external thumbwheel with which the target number can be set. Other common ways of setting the target number are DIP switches and jumpers. If it is not obvious how to set the target number on a device, consult the hardware manual. Most hardware specifications can be found on the manufacturer's web site these days; trying to set up a random disk formerly involved quite a lot of trial and error.

The SCSI standard supports a form of subaddressing called a "logical unit number." Each target can have several logical units inside it. A plausible example is a drive array with several disks but only one SCSI controller. However, logical units are seldom used in real life. When you hear "SCSI unit number," you should assume that it is really a target number that's being discussed until proven otherwise. If a SCSI device contains only one logical unit, the LUN usually defaults to 0.

SCSI buses are generally quite easy to configure, but a variety of things can go wrong:

- Many workstations have internal SCSI devices. Check the listing of current devices before you reboot to add a new device.

- After you have added a new SCSI device, check the listing of devices discovered by the kernel when it reboots to make sure that everything you expect is there. Most SCSI drivers do not detect multiple devices that have the same SCSI address—an illegal configuration. SCSI address conflicts can lead to very strange behavior.

- Some expansion boxes (enclosures with a power supply and one or more SCSI devices) terminate the bus inside the box. If devices are attached after the expansion box has been attached, you can have reliability problems with any of the devices on the SCSI chain. Always double-check that you have exactly two terminators and that they are both at the ends of the bus.

- The thumbwheel used to set a device's SCSI address is sometimes connected backwards. When this happens, the thumbwheel will change the SCSI address, but not to the displayed value.

- When figuring the length of your SCSI-2 bus, be sure to count the cables inside devices and expansion boxes. They can be quite long. Also remember that the permissible length is reduced if you are adding older SCSI devices to a newer SCSI bus.

- Never forget that your SCSI controller uses one of the SCSI addresses!

Which is better, SCSI or IDE?

In past editions of this book, SCSI has been the obvious winner for server applications. However, with the advent of SATA drives, SCSI simply does not deliver the bang for the buck that it used to. SATA drives compete with (and in some cases outperform) equivalent SCSI disks in almost every category. At the same time, the SATA devices are dramatically cheaper and far more widely available.

One advantage of SCSI drives is an integrated processor on the controller, which frees the system's CPU to focus on other things. On busy systems, this can mean big performance gains. Of course, it's up to you to decide whether the gain is worth the significant monetary cost.

In some situations SCSI is advisable or even mandatory:

- If you absolutely must have the best possible performance, go SCSI. Disk drive manufacturers use the IDE/SCSI divide to help them stratify the disk drive market. Some IDE drives may outperform SCSI on peak throughput, but SCSI almost always delivers better sustained throughput.

- Servers and multiuser systems require SCSI. The SCSI protocol is unparalleled in its ability to manage multiple simultaneous requests efficiently. On a busy system, you'll see a concrete and measurable improvement in performance.

- If you want to connect many devices, SCSI wins again. SCSI devices play well with others; IDE devices hog and fight over the bus.

7.2 DISK GEOMETRY

The geometry of a hard disk and the terminology used to refer to its various parts are shown in Exhibit B. This information is proffered mainly to improve your general knowledge. Modern disk drives are still based on this same basic design, but the software no longer knows (or needs to know) much about the physical construction of the drive.

A typical hard drive consists of spinning platters coated with a magnetic film. Data is read and written by a small head that changes the orientation of the magnetic particles on the surface of the platters. The data platters are completely sealed so that no dust or dirt can get in. This feature makes fixed hard disks far more reliable than removable media.

In the very early days of computer hardware, disk drives usually had one platter. Storage capacity was increased by an increase in the diameter of the platter. On the wall of one of our user areas, we used to display an ancient disk platter over four feet in diameter that held approximately 280K of data.

Today, hard disks usually have several small platters stacked on top of one another rather than having a single large platter. Both sides of the platters store data, although one side of one platter usually contains positioning information and cannot be used for storage. Single-platter densities are currently up around 130GB.

Exhibit B   Disk geometry lesson

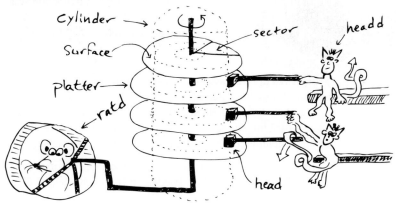

Platters rotate at a constant speed. They are read from and written to by little skating heads that move back and forth like the needle on a record player. The heads float very close to the surface of the platters but do not actually touch it. The distance between the head and the spinning platter can be compared to an F–16 fighter jet flying at full speed 10 feet above the ground. If a head does touch a platter, this event is called a head crash; it can be very destructive.

Rotational speeds have increased dramatically over time. Older disks ran at 3,600 RPM or 5,400 RPM. Currently, 7,200 RPM is the mass-market standard, and 10,000 RPM and 15,000 RPM drives are popular at the high end. Higher rotational speeds decrease latency and increase the bandwidth of data transfers but may potentially introduce thermal problems stemming from increased heat production. Be sure you have adequate air circulation if you plan to purchase a cutting-edge drive.

At least one head is required for each surface. The heads on early drives had to move huge distances, but the modern geometry of small, stacked platters is more efficient. The diameter of disks continues to decrease, from a standard of 14 inches 20 years ago, to 5¼ inches 10 years ago, to 3½ inches and smaller today.

Moving the head to the correct position to read a particular piece of data is called seeking. Each position that a head can occupy as the disk spins under it is called a track. Tracks are further divided into sectors, which are usually 512 bytes long.

A set of tracks on different platters that are the same distance from the spindle is called a cylinder. If all the heads move together, as is typical on most mass-market drives, the data stored in a single cylinder can be read without any additional move-ment. Although heads move amazingly fast, they still move much slower than the disks spin around. Therefore, any disk access that does not require the heads to seek to a new position will be faster.

7.3 LINUX FILESYSTEMS

Linux filesystem support has evolved rapidly as Linux has absorbed features from a variety of different operating systems. The kernel's Virtual File System (VFS) layer is particularly handy on PCs because it provides the framework needed to mount "native" filesystems such as the infamous Windows FAT filesystems.

Ext2fs and ext3fs

The second extended filesystem, known commonly as ext2fs, was for a long time the mainstream Linux filesystem. It was designed and implemented primarily by Rémy Card, Theodore Ts'o, and Stephen Tweedie. Although the code for ext2 was written specifically for Linux, it adopts many concepts from the BSD FFS filesystem de-signed and implemented by Kirk McKusick and team in 1984.

The third extended filesystem, ext3fs, is a remarkable extension to ext2fs that was originally developed by Stephen Tweedie. It is now the default filesystem used by most distributions. Ext3fs adds journaling capability to the existing ext2fs code, a conceptually simple modification that increases reliability enormously. Even more interestingly, the ext3fs extensions have been implemented without changing the fundamental structure of ext2fs. In fact, you can still mount an ext3fs filesystem as an ext2fs filesystem—it just won't have journaling enabled.

It's possible to convert an existing ext2fs filesystem to an ext3fs filesystem with **tune2fs**. For example, if you had an ext2fs filesytem on **/dev/hda4**, you could convert it with

```
# tune2fs -j /dev/hda4
```

You would then need to modify the corresponding entry in **/etc/fstab** to read ext3 rather than ext2 (see page 127 for more information on the **fstab** file).

Ext3fs sets aside an area of the disk for the journal file. When a filesystem operation occurs, the required modifications are first written to the journal file. When the journal update is complete, a "commit record" is written to mark the end of the entry. Only then is the normal filesystem modified. If a crash occurs during the update, you can use the journal log to reconstruct a perfectly consistent filesystem.

Journaling reduces the time needed to perform filesystem consistency checks (see the **fsck** section on page 131) to approximately one second per filesystem. Barring some type of hardware failure, the state of an ext3fs filesystem can almost instantly be assessed and restored.

Ext3fs is the only filesystem we describe in detail in this chapter.

ReiserFS

ReiserFS, written by Hans Reiser, is another up-and-coming filesystem for Linux and is the favorite filesystem for the SUSE distribution. Like ext3fs, it is also a journaling filesystem and hence can maintain filesystem consistency despite incidents such as system crashes and unplanned reboots (which may be common in a laptop or desktop workstation environment). ReiserFS version 4 was released in August 2004 and is included in the default installation of Ubuntu. Fedora and SUSE are still using an earlier release for now.

In addition to its journaling capabilities, Reiser4 provides a modular filesystem interface through which application developers and system administrators can specify how files should be handled (and secured) at a very granular level. This feature increases the security of files in specialized environments. ReiserFS is sponsored by DARPA[4] and is the only open source filesystem that claims to be architected for military grade security.

New algorithms in Reiser4 are more space-efficient than their predecessors. Other filesystems (as well as earlier versions of ReiserFS) use balanced tree algorithms to allocate blocks of disk space. Although this tried-and-true approach has proved

---

4. The Defense Advanced Research Projects Agency, the same entity that funded the creation of the Internet.

solid, there is typically a tradeoff between speed and disk usage. Reiser4's "dancing tree" algorithm doesn't force administrators to choose sides.

XFS and JFS

Two other contenders in the "modern, mainstream Linux filesystem" category are SGI's XFS and IBM's JFS. Both are supported natively by current kernels and distributions, and both are high-performance journaled filesystems. Both filesystems have proponents, but neither seems to be as widely used as ext3fs or ReiserFS.

It's difficult to explain with any degree of certainty why this is so, but the fundamental problem seems to be that these filesystems are rather poorly differentiated from ext3fs and ReiserFS. To be sure, the implementation details vary, and each filesystem has modest domains of superiority (e.g., XFS has superior fragmentation and extent management). Nevertheless, the performance of the major contenders is similar, and applications that allow any individual filesystem to really shine are rare.

If you would like to evaluate these filesystems in detail, you can find more information on the web. For JFS, see jfs.sourceforge.net. XFS is at oss.sgi.com/projects/xfs.

7.4 AN OVERVIEW OF THE DISK INSTALLATION PROCEDURE

The procedure for adding a new disk involves the following steps:

- Connecting the disk to the computer
- Formatting the disk if necessary (usually not)
- Labeling and partitioning the disk
- Creating filesystems within disk partitions
- Mounting the filesystems
- Setting up automatic mounting
- Setting up swapping on swap partitions

The following sections elaborate on these basic steps. Starting on page 133, we show the complete process from start to finish for an example disk drive.

Connecting the disk

The way a disk is attached to the system depends on the interface that is used. The rest is all mounting brackets and cabling. If the disk is IDE, try to configure the system with only one IDE disk per bus. Double-check your cable orientation and the master/slave settings on each disk. If the disk is SCSI, double-check that you have properly terminated both ends of the SCSI bus, that the cable length is less than the maximum appropriate for the SCSI variant you are using, and that the new SCSI target does not conflict with the controller or another device on the bus. For more details, see the system-specific sections toward the end of this chapter.

Before you can access a new disk, you need device files in **/dev** that point to it. Linux automatically creates files for most common disk devices. See page 79 for general information about device files.

It is possible to destroy a filesystem in seconds by writing randomly on the disk, so you should set the permissions on disk device files restrictively. Consider giving read access to the group owner ("operator" or "disk"); this setup allows operators without superuser privileges to run the **dump** command but prevents mere mortals from reading from the raw device.

Formatting the disk

Vendors quote disk capacities in terms of the number of unformatted bytes. About 10% of that capacity is typically used to mark the disk surfaces so that the hardware and software can find the data that is written there. When purchasing disks, always think in terms of formatted size and compare prices accordingly.

Disk sizes are specified in megabytes that are millions of bytes, as opposed to memory, which is specified in megabytes of 2^{20} (1,048,576) bytes. The difference is about 5%.[5] Be sure to check your units when estimating and comparing capacities.

The formatting process writes address information and timing marks on the platters to delineate each sector. It also identifies "bad blocks," imperfections in the media that result in areas that cannot be reliably read or written. Modern disks have bad block management built in, so neither you nor the driver need to worry about it.[6]

All hard disks come preformatted, and the factory formatting is usually more precise than any formatting you can do in the field. It is best to avoid doing a low-level format if it is not required. If you encounter read or write errors on a disk, first check for cabling, termination, and address problems, which can cause symptoms similar to those of a bad block. If after this procedure you are still convinced that the disk is bad, you might be better off replacing it with a new one rather than waiting long hours for a format to complete.

IDE disks are usually not designed to be formatted outside the factory. However, you may be able to get special formatting software from the manufacturer, usually for Windows. Make sure the software matches the drive you plan to format and follow the manufacturer's directions carefully.

SCSI disks format themselves in response to a command that you send from the host computer. The procedure for sending this command varies from system to system. On PCs, you can often send the command from the SCSI controller's BIOS.

Various utilities let you verify the integrity of a disk by writing random patterns onto it and then reading them back. Thorough tests take a long time (hours) and tend to be of little prognostic value. Unless you suspect that a disk is bad and are unable to simply replace it (or you bill by the hour), you should skip these tests. Barring that, let the tests run overnight. Don't be concerned about "wearing out" a disk with overuse or aggressive testing. Disks are designed to withstand constant activity.

---

5. Of course, the prefix "mega" really does mean "million," so the practice is not entirely indefensible.
6. However, any bad blocks that appear after a disk has been formatted will not be "handled"; they can manifest themselves in the form of read and write errors and lost data.

Labeling and partitioning the disk

After a disk has been formatted and its bad sectors remapped, it must be divided into chunks called *partitions*. Partitioning allows the disk to be treated as a group of independent data areas rather than as one vast expanse of blocks. Partitioning also allows "bonus" items such as the boot blocks and the partition table itself to be hidden from high-level software (e.g., the filesystem). The layout of the disk is simplified by the kernel; other software works with the cleaned-up abstraction of partitions.

Partitions make backups easier, prevent users from poaching each other's disk space, improve performance, and confine potential damage from runaway programs. The partition table is kept on the disk in a record called the label. The label usually occupies the first few blocks of the disk. Its exact contents vary, but it generally contains enough information to get the system booting.

Partitions are, in concept, distinct and separate from one another. However, the file **/dev/sda** is the disk's block device file, essentially an image of the entire disk. User-level commands can access the disk "directly" through this device file. For example, a user-level process can write the disk's label or duplicate its contents to a backup disk by using the **dd** command. Of course, this special file must be used carefully since it allows every partition on the disk to be screwed up at once.

Some systems go even farther down this treacherous path and allow you to define multiple overlapping sets of partitions. For example, partitions 1, 2, and 3 might divide up the disk one way, while partitions 4 and 5 do it another way. You're expected to use one set of self-consistent partitions and simply ignore the others. In real life, such overlapping partitions invite operator errors and are a potential cause of random data corruption.

Modern systems tend to use fewer partitions than their predecessors, but on most systems you will have at least two:

- **The root partition:** Everything needed to bring the system up to single-user mode is kept here. A replica of this partition stored on a different disk can be useful in emergencies.

- **The swap partition:** A swap area stores pages of virtual memory when not enough physical memory is available to hold them. Every system should have at least one swap partition.

Opinions differ on the best way to split disks into partitions. Here are some hints:

- If you have multiple disks, make a copy of the root filesystem on one of them and verify that you can boot from it.

- As you add memory to your machine, you should also add swap space. Allocate swap space as needed to accommodate the workload on your system. See page 809 for more information about virtual memory.

- Splitting swap space among several disks increases performance. This technique works for filesystems, too; put the busy ones on different disks. See page 814 for notes on this subject.

- If you intend to back up a partition, don't make it bigger than the capacity of your backup device. See page 161.

- Try to cluster information that changes quickly on a few partitions that are backed up frequently.

- Putting **/tmp** on a separate filesystem limits the files to a finite size and saves you from having to back them up.

- Since log files are kept in **/var**, it's a good idea for **/var** to be a separate disk partition. Leaving **/var** as part of a small root partition makes it easy to fill the root and bring the machine to a halt.

- It can be useful to define **/home** as a separate partition. Even if the root partition is corrupted or destroyed, user data has a good chance of remaining intact. Conversely, the system can continue to operate even after a user's misguided shell script fills up **/home**.

Creating filesystems within disk partitions

Even after a hard disk has been conceptually divided into partitions, it is still not ready to hold files. The filesystem needs to add a little of its own overhead before the disk is ready for use.

To install an ext3fs filesystem within a disk partition, use **mke2fs -j**. (There is no **mke3fs** command; the **-j** option tells **mke2fs** to create an ext3fs journal.) Unless you are doing something strange, you should be able to build the filesystem by specifying nothing but **mke2fs -j** and the partition name. Be careful with **mke2fs**; a mistake can destroy your system, rendering data recovery extremely difficult, if not impossible.

An ext3fs filesystem consists of five structural components:

- A set of inode storage cells
- A set of scattered "superblocks"
- A map of the disk blocks in the filesystem
- A block usage summary
- A set of data blocks

The journal is allocated as if it were a regular file in the root of the new filesystem, so it is not really a distinct structural component.

Each filesystem partition is divided into block groups. Structures such as inode tables are allocated among the block groups so that blocks that are accessed together can be stored close to each other on the disk. This grouping reduces the need to seek all over the disk when accessing blocks in the same file.

Adding a Disk

Inodes are fixed-length table entries that each hold information about one file. Since space for inodes is set aside when the filesystem is initially structured, you must decide in advance how many of them to create. It is impossible to predict exactly how many files (inodes) will someday be needed; filesystem building commands use an empirical formula to guesstimate an appropriate number, based on the size of the partition and an average file size.

You can adjust the number of inodes either up or down when you create the filesystem: more inodes for filesystems with lots of small files (such as source code repositories) and fewer inodes for filesystems with a few large files (such as a filesystem containing a database).

A superblock is a record that describes the characteristics of the filesystem. It contains information about the length of a disk block, the size and location of the inode tables, the disk block map and usage information, the size of the block groups, and a few other important parameters of the filesystem. Because damage to the superblock could erase some extremely crucial information, several copies of it are maintained in scattered locations (at the beginning of each block group).

For each mounted filesystem, the kernel keeps both an in-memory copy of the superblock and several on-disk copies. The **sync** system call flushes the cached superblocks to their permanent homes on disk, making the filesystem consistent for a split second. This periodic save minimizes the amount of damage that would occur if the machine were to crash when the filesystem had not updated the superblocks. **sync** also flushes modified inodes and cached data blocks. Syncs are traditionally done at intervals of 30 seconds, but ext3fs syncs every 5 seconds.

A filesystem's disk block map is a table of the free blocks it contains. When new files are written, this map is examined to devise an efficient layout scheme. The block usage summary records basic information about the blocks that are already in use.

Mounting the filesystems

A filesystem must be mounted before it becomes visible to processes. The mount point for a filesystem can be any directory, but the files and subdirectories beneath it are not accessible while a filesystem is mounted there. See page 73 for more information about mounting filesystems.

After installing a new disk, you should mount new filesystems by hand to be sure that everything is working correctly. For example, the command

```
# mount /dev/sda1 /mnt
```

would mount the filesystem in the partition represented by the device file **/dev/sda1** on the directory **/mnt**, which is a traditional path used for temporary mounts. If the filesystem is brand new, its contents should look something like this:

```
# ls /mnt
lost+found
```

The **lost+found** directory is automatically created when you build a filesystem. It is used by **fsck** in emergencies; do not delete it. The **lost+found** directory has some extra space preallocated so that **fsck** can store "unlinked" files there without having to allocate additional directory entries on an unstable filesystem.

You can verify the size of a filesystem with the **df** command. Here's an example:

```
$ df /home
Filesystem    1K-blocks    Used   Available   Use%   Mounted on
/dev/hda5     4128448    697968    3220768    18%    /home
```

The default units reported by **df** are 1K blocks, but you can use the **-h** option to request human-readable values (e.g., 2.4G).

Setting up automatic mounting

You will generally want to configure the system to mount local filesystems automatically at boot time. The file **/etc/fstab** contains a list of devices that correspond to filesystems.

An **fstab** file that included the filesystem above might look something like this:

```
LABEL=/        /              ext3      defaults            1  1
none           /dev/pts       devpts    gid=5,mode=620      0  0
/dev/hda5      /home          ext3      defaults            1  2
none           /proc          proc      defaults            0  0
none           /dev/shm       tmpfs     defaults            0  0
/dev/cdrom     /media/cdrom   iso9660   ro,noauto,owner     0  0
/dev/hda3      /usr           ext3      defaults            1  2
/dev/hda6      /var           ext3      defaults            1  2
/dev/hda2      swap           swap      defaults            0  0
```

There are six fields per line, separated by whitespace. Each line describes a single filesystem. The fields are traditionally aligned for readability, but alignment is not required.

See Chapter 16 for more information about NFS.

The first field gives the device name or the label that was associated with it by **e2label** (the LABEL= form). The **fstab** file can include mounts from remote systems, in which case the first field contains an NFS path. The notation *server:/export* indicates the */export* directory on the machine named *server*. Filesystems that have no actual backing store (such as **/proc** and **/dev/shm** above) have the placeholder none in the device field.

The second field specifies the mount point, and the third field names the type of filesystem. The exact type name used to identify local filesystems varies, depending on your system configuration. The names ext2 and ext3 are used for ext*fs, and reiserfs denotes ReiserFS.

The fourth field lists the mount options. The keyword defaults indicates a combination of the options rw, suid, dev, exec, auto, nouser, and async (see the man page for **mount** for details on each of these options). You may want to include acl to turn on access control lists as well; see page 88.

Adding a Disk

The ext3 journal management mode is set with the option data=*mode*, where *mode* is one of ordered, writeback, or journal. The mode is an operational choice, not a property of the filesystem itself; that's why it appears in **fstab** and not as an argument to **mke2fs**.

The options define three different tradeoffs between performance and reliability:

- The default mode, ordered, guarantees that the filesystem is always consistent and that as a result, files will never be corrupted by a crash. This is the best choice for most environments.

- The writeback mode can result in corrupted files after a crash but is faster in some cases. This is actually the way most journaling filesystems work, and it isn't substantially riskier than the default ext2fs behavior.

- The journal mode uses a larger journal file, which may slow down recovery on reboot but can be faster when used with a database application.

The fifth field in the **fstab** file specifies a "dump frequency" value that can theoretically be used by backup products but usually isn't.

fsck is described on page 131.

The sixth field specifies the pass in which **fsck** should check the filesystem. Filesystems with the same value in this field are checked concurrently if possible. This field was very important before the advent of journaling filesystems when **fsck** was a time-consuming process, but it is less so now. Do not set two non-journaled filesystems on the same disk to the same value or you will cause the disk head to seek back and forth so much that performance will be significantly degraded. Only filesystems on separate disks should be checked in parallel.

mount, **umount**, **swapon**, and **fsck** all read the **fstab** file, so it is important that the data presented there be correct and complete. **mount** and **umount** use the **fstab** file to figure out what you want done if you specify only a partition name or mount point on the command line. For example, using the **fstab** file just shown, the command

```
# mount /media/cdrom
```

would be the same as typing

```
# mount -t iso9660 -o ro,noauto,owner /dev/cdrom /media/cdrom
```

The command **mount -a** mounts all regular filesystems listed in the **fstab** file; it is usually executed from the startup scripts at boot time. The **-t** flag constrains the operation to filesystems of a certain type. For example,

```
# mount -at ext3
```

would mount all local ext3 disk filesystems. The **mount** command reads **fstab** sequentially. Therefore, filesystems that are mounted beneath other filesystems must follow their parent partitions in the **fstab** file. For example, the line for **/var/log** must follow the line for **/var** if **/var** is a separate filesystem.

The **umount** command for unmounting filesystems accepts a similar syntax. You cannot unmount a filesystem that a process is using as its current directory or on which files are open. There are ways of getting around this constraint; see page 73.

Enabling swapping

One of the early advantages of UNIX was its implementation of virtual memory. With this feature, the operating system can pretend that the machine has more memory than it actually does. If processes try to use this "extra" memory, the system's disks are brought into use as a kind of ultra-slow RAM. Juggling the contents of memory to and from disk is known as paging. Ideally, enough physical memory will be available to the system that this painfully slow activity never occurs.

Raw partitions, rather than structured filesystems, are normally used for swap space, making swapping more efficient. Instead of using a filesystem to keep track of the swap area's contents, the kernel maintains its own simplified mapping from memory blocks to disk blocks. It's also possible to swap to a file in a filesystem partition, but with older kernels this configuration is slower than using a dedicated partition.

See page 814 for more information about splitting swap areas. The more swap space you have, the more virtual memory your processes can allocate. The best virtual memory performance is achieved when the swap area is split among several drives (or better yet, among several SCSI buses).

You can manually enable swapping to a particular device, but you will generally want to have this function performed automatically at boot time. Swap areas can be listed in the **fstab** file, the same file that's used to enumerate mountable filesystems. A swap entry looks something like:

```
/dev/hda2      swap           swap     defaults         0  0
```

During startup, the **swapon** command is run to enable swapping on all swap partitions listed in the **fstab** file.

7.5   HDPARM: SET IDE INTERFACE PARAMETERS

The **hdparm** program interacts with the Linux IDE driver to obtain and alter disk parameters. Among other things, **hdparm** can set drive power options, enable or disable DMA, set the read-only flag, and print detailed drive information. You can realize significant performance gains by tuning a few of these disk parameters. This utility is IDE specific and does not work on SCSI or USB drives.

The syntax is

hdparm [*options*] [*device*]

Running **hdparm** with no options prints the current state of some of the more interesting settings.

```
$ sudo /sbin/hdparm -d /dev/hdb
```

```
/dev/hdb:
    multcount     =  0 (off)
    IO_support    =  0 (default 16-bit)
    unmaskirq     =  0 (off)
    using_dma     =  0 (off)
    keepsettings  =  0 (off)
    readahead     = 256 (on)
    geometry      = 36481/255/63, sectors = 300069052416, start = 0
```

From a disk performance perspective, these settings leave a lot to be desired.

- Direct memory access (DMA) is disabled. All modern disks can send data directly to memory, bypassing the CPU. It's almost always a good idea to enable DMA, but it does cause the occasional piece of poorly designed hardware to fail. Always test first on a system that isn't in production.

- 32-bit I/O support is disabled. Without 32-bit I/O, data transits the PCI bus in 16-bit chunks, potentially cutting performance in half.

- Interrupt unmasking is turned off. Turning on this (somewhat obscure) feature allows the disk driver to unmask pending interrupts while servicing a current disk interrupt.

hdparm includes a built-in drive performance test to help evaluate the impact of these settings. With these default values on an older IDE drive, our system produced the following results:

```
$ sudo /sbin/hdparm -Tt /dev/hdb
```

```
/dev/hdb:
    Timing cached reads:        228 MB in  2.41 seconds =  94.70 MB/sec
    Timing buffered disk reads: 6 MB in  4.62 seconds   =   1.30 MB/sec
```

Cached reads indicate the speed of data transfer on the IDE bus (independent of the throughput from the physical disk media), while buffered reads include the overhead of reading from the physical platters. As you might expect, the physical disk is a lot slower than the bus. Even so, 1.3 MB/s is pretty dismal.

Since DMA is such an important feature of modern hardware, it deserves immediate tuning attention. Newer drives support multiple DMA modes. Table 7.2 summarizes the speeds of the various DMA modes for each of the common DMA technologies.

Table 7.2   Maximum transfer rates (in MB/s) for various DMA modes

Mode	0	1	2	3	4	5	6
PIO	3.3	5.2	8.3	11.1	16.7		
SDMA	2.4	4.2	8.3				
MDMA	4.2	13.3	16.7				
UDMA	16.7	25.0	33.3	44.4	66.7	100.0	133.0

Using the table, we can easily identify the appropriate argument to pass to **hdparm**. We enable DMA using UDMA2 by entering the following **hdparm** command:

```
$ sudo /sbin/hdparm -d1 -Xudma2 /dev/hdb
```

```
/dev/hdb:
    setting using_dma to 1 (on)
    setting xfermode to 66 (UltraDMA mode2)
    using_dma = 1 (on)
```

We enable 32-bit I/O support:

```
$ sudo /sbin/hdparm -c1 /dev/hdb
```

```
/dev/hdb:
    setting 32-bit IO_support flag to 1
    IO_support = 1 (32-bit)
```

Finally, the interrupt-unmasking value is binary. We turn it on with

```
$ sudo /sbin/hdparm -u1 /dev/hdb
```

```
/dev/hdb:
    setting unmaskirq to 1 (on)
    unmaskirq = 1 (on)
```

We can determine the effect of these changes by rerunning **hdparm**'s benchmark:

```
$ sudo /sbin/hdparm -Tt /dev/hdb
```

```
/dev/hdb:
    Timing cached reads:       256 MB in  2.00 seconds = 127.83 MB/sec
    Timing buffered disk reads: 40 MB in  3.01 seconds  =  13.30 MB/sec
```

A few **hdparm** configuration tweaks resulted in significant increases in both values.

Experiment with different values on your drive to find the optimal settings. It's wise to run the benchmarks several times on each setting to get the most accurate data.

7.6 FSCK: CHECK AND REPAIR FILESYSTEMS

Modern filesystems are surprisingly reliable, and even the nonjournaling implementations seem to do a remarkable job of coping with unexpected system crashes and flaky hardware. However, filesystems can be damaged or become inconsistent in a number of ways.

Any time the kernel panics or the power fails, small inconsistencies may be introduced into the filesystems that were active immediately preceding the crash. Since the kernel buffers both data blocks and summary information, the most recent image of the filesystem is split between disk and memory. During a crash, the memory portion of the image is lost. The buffered blocks are effectively "overwritten" with the versions that were most recently saved to disk.

There are a couple of approaches to fixing this problem. Minor damage can usually be fixed with the **fsck** command ("filesystem consistency check," spelled aloud or pronounced "fs check" or "fisk"). This isn't a very architecturally elegant way of approaching the issue, but it works pretty well for all the common inconsistencies.

Journaling filesystems such as ReiserFS and ext3fs write metadata out to a sequential log file that is flushed to disk before each command returns. The metadata eventually migrates from the log to its permanent home within the filesystem. If the system crashes, the log can be rolled up to the most recent consistency point; a full filesystem cross-check is not required. **fsck** is still run at boot time to ensure that the filesystem is in a consistent state, but it runs much faster than when checking a traditional ext2 filesystem. This feature can save you many hours of boot time on a system with large filesystems.

If some form of journaling is not available, you must wait for **fsck** to work its magic. The five most common types of damage are

- Unreferenced inodes
- Inexplicably large link counts
- Unused data blocks not recorded in the block maps
- Data blocks listed as free that are also used in a file
- Incorrect summary information in the superblock

fsck can safely and automatically fix these five problems. If **fsck** makes corrections to a filesystem, you should rerun it until the filesystem comes up completely clean.

Disks are normally checked at boot time with **fsck -p**, which examines all local filesystems listed in **/etc/fstab** and corrects the five errors listed above. Linux keeps track of which filesystems were unmounted cleanly and checks only the "dirty" ones. If some form of journaling is enabled, **fsck** simply tells you that the filesystem is journaled and rolls up the log to the last consistent state.

You can also run **fsck -p** on a particular filesystem. For example:

```
# fsck -p /dev/sda5
```

When **fsck -p** reads the **fstab** file to find out which filesystems to check, it obeys the sequence indicated by the last field of each entry. Filesystems are checked in increasing numeric order. If two filesystems are on different disks, they can be given the same sequence number; this configuration makes **fsck** check them simultaneously, minimizing the time spent waiting for disk I/O. Always check the root partition first.

*See the **tune2fs** man page for a few (less useful) options.*

Linux can be set to force a filesystem check after it has mounted a filesystem a certain number of times even if all the unmounts were "clean." This precaution is good hygiene, and in most cases the default value (usually 20 mounts) is acceptable. However, on systems that mount filesystems frequently, such as desktop workstations, **fsck**s every 20 mounts may become tiresome. To increase the interval to 50 mounts, use the **tune2fs** command:

```
$ sudo /sbin/tune2fs -c 50 /dev/sda3
tune2fs 1.35 (28-Feb-2004)
Setting maximal mount count to 50
```

Errors that do not fall into one of the five categories above are potentially serious. They cause **fsck -p** to ask for help and then quit. In this case, run **fsck** without the **-p** option. When run in manual mode, **fsck** asks you to confirm each of the repairs that it wants to make. The following list shows some of the errors that **fsck** considers dangerous enough to warrant human intervention:

- Blocks claimed by more than one file
- Blocks claimed outside the range of the filesystem
- Link counts that are too small
- Blocks that are not accounted for
- Directories that refer to unallocated inodes
- Various format errors

Unfortunately, it is difficult to patch a disk by hand without extensive knowledge of the implementation of the filesystem. Never attempt to write directly to the filesystem through the device files.

In practice, this state of affairs means that you have little choice but to accept the fixes proposed by **fsck**. You can minimize problems by carefully recording the messages that **fsck** produces, since they can sometimes tip you off about the file or files that are causing problems. If **fsck** asks for permission to delete a file, you should try to copy it to a different filesystem before allowing **fsck** to proceed. Be aware that any time you attempt to access a damaged filesystem, you risk panicking the system.

See Chapter 9 for infor-
mation about backups.

If a damaged filesystem (one that **fsck** cannot repair automatically) contains valuable data, *do not* experiment with it before making an ironclad backup. You can try to **dump** the disk, but since **dump** expects to be reading an undamaged filesystem, the resulting image may be missing data (or the command may crash). The best insurance policy is to **dd** the entire disk to a backup file or backup disk.

If **fsck** finds a file whose parent directory cannot be determined, it puts the file in the **lost+found** directory in the top level of the filesystem. Since the name given to a file is recorded only in the file's parent directory, names for orphan files are not available and the files placed in **lost+found** are named with their inode numbers. The inode table does record the UID of the file's owner, so getting a file back to its original owner is relatively easy.

7.7   ADDING A DISK: A STEP-BY-STEP GUIDE

In this section we walk through the configuration of a new disk drive. We set up the drive with several partitions, including one for swap space. On the remaining partitions, we create ext3fs filesystems.

After you install a new disk, it's a good idea to make sure the system can see the new device before you boot up the kernel. If it's an IDE disk, check to be sure the disk is recognized in the BIOS setup display, which you usually access by typing a magic key sequence before the system boots. Consult the manuals that came with your computer or motherboard for specific information on BIOS configuration for IDE devices. In most cases, no special configuration is necessary.

Many SCSI cards also have a BIOS setup screen that you can invoke before the system boots. If this option is available, you scan the SCSI bus to make sure the new device appears. If this procedure hangs or produces a warning message, it's possible that you picked a SCSI ID that was already in use or that you did not install terminators in the right places.

You can also use the SCSI BIOS to do a low-level format of a disk. This operation takes a long time on some disks and cannot be interrupted, so plan ahead.

See page 878 for more information about installing device drivers. If your SCSI card does not have its own user interface, you can always just try to boot the system and note the messages displayed by the kernel. If you do not see any messages from a SCSI driver, you may need to install the driver before the disk can be recognized by the kernel.

In our case, we saw the following messages from our BusLogic SCSI host adaptor.

```
scsi0 : BusLogic BT-948
scsi : 1 host.
  Vendor: SEAGATE   Model: ST446452W      Rev: 0001
  Type:   Direct-Access              ANSI SCSI revision: 02
Detected scsi disk sda at scsi0, channel 0, id 3, lun 0
scsi0: Target 3: Queue Depth 28, Asynchronous
SCSI device sda: hdwr sector=512 bytes. Sectors=91923356 [44884 MB] [44.9 GB]
sda: unknown partition table
```

We ignore warnings about the partition table since this is the first time the disk has been used. Once the system has finished booting, we can move on to partitioning the disk.

Before partitioning, we must first check to see if device files for the disk already exist (they should). In Linux, the names for SCSI disk device files are of the form **/dev/sd**XN, where X is a lowercase letter that identifies the drive (**a** is the lowest-numbered SCSI disk, **b** is the second lowest, and so on[7]) and N is the partition number, starting at 1. When referring to the whole disk, simply omit the partition number. There are no character (raw) disk devices in Linux.

In this example, our disk is the first one on the SCSI chain. The first partition is therefore **/dev/sda1**, and the disk as a whole is referred to as **/dev/sda**. If these device files didn't exist, we could create them with **MAKEDEV** or **mknod**.

The disk is now ready to be partitioned. As in most PC operating systems, the tool used for partitioning under Linux is called **fdisk**. Though all versions of **fdisk** do approximately the same thing (they implement Microsoft's standard partitioning system), there are many variations among them. You would be wise to read the man page for your particular system to be sure it matches what we show here.

---

7. Note that this letter refers to the *order* of the target numbers of the SCSI devices, not to the target numbers themselves. If you add or remove a disk, all the drive letters change!

```
# fdisk /dev/sda
```
Device contains neither a valid DOS partition table, nor Sun, SGI or OSF disklabel
Building a new DOS disklabel. Changes will remain in memory only,
until you decide to write them. After that, of course, the previous
content won't be recoverable.

The number of cylinders for this disk is set to 5721.
There is nothing wrong with that, but this is larger than 1024,
and could in certain setups cause problems with:
1) software that runs at boot time (e.g., LILO)
2) booting and partitioning software from other OSs
   (e.g., DOS FDISK, OS/2 FDISK)

Since we are using this disk only on our Linux system, we can ignore the helpful warning. In the past, it has sometimes been important to make the first partition small to ensure that it will work with an old BIOS and will work with other operating systems that might be installed on the system.

The **fdisk** program is interactive; pressing **m** displays a list of all its commands. The ones we use here are:

- **n**, or **new**, to create a new partition
- **t**, or **type**, to change the type of a partition
- **p**, or **print**, to print the partition table
- **w**, or **write**, to write the partition table to disk

Since our disk does not yet have partitions, we start by creating a new one. If your disk has partitions defined from a former life, you may have to remove them with **fdisk**'s **delete** command before you can create new ones. The **fdisk** program does not change anything on disk until you tell it to write the partition table.

The partition table has room for four "primary" partitions that can hold data. Alternatively, you can create an "extended" partition, which is a primary partition that points to another partition table, giving you another four "logical" partitions. Although the use of extended partitions can overcome the normal four-partition restriction, it is simplest to stick with primary partitions if only a few will be needed, and that's what we do in this case:

```
Command (m for help): new
Command action
   e    extended
   p    primary partition (1-4): p
Partition number (1-4): 1
First cylinder (1-5721, default 1): 1
Last cylinder or +size or +sizeM or +sizeK (1-5721, default 5721): +2G

Command (m for help): print
Disk /dev/sda: 255 heads, 63 sectors, 5721 cylinders
Units = cylinders of 16065 * 512 bytes
   Device Boot  Start   End   Blocks    Id  System
/dev/sda1           1   255   2048256   83  Linux
```

We create a swap partition similarly, except that we change the type from "Linux" to "Linux swap." Although the kernel does not care about the partition type, some programs and scripts try to use the type to figure out what each partition is. We specify a size of 2GB, which is probably overkill for most applications, but since we have disk space to spare, we might as well be generous. **mkswap** will warn us if it cannot use all of the space we have allocated.

```
Command (m for help): new
   e   extended
   p   primary partition (1-4): p
Partition number (1-4): 2
First cylinder (256-5721, default 256): 256
Last cylinder or +size or +sizeM or +sizeK (256-1275, default 1275): 511
Command (m for help): type
Partition number (1-4): 2
Hex code (type L to list codes): 82
Changed system type of partition 2 to 82 (Linux swap)
```

The third partition, which contains the rest of the disk, is defined similarly. We review the partition table one last time before writing it.

```
Command (m for help): print
Disk /dev/sda: 255 heads, 63 sectors, 5721 cylinders
Units = cylinders of 16065 * 512 bytes
   Device  Boot  Start   End     Blocks    Id  System
/dev/sda1            1   255   2048256    83  Linux
/dev/sda2          256   511   2056320    82  Linux swap
/dev/sda3          512  5721  41849325    83  Linux
```

A star appears next to the number of blocks if the partition does not end on a cylinder boundary. We could either delete the partition and recreate it by entering a number of cylinders (as above) or live with the fact that a small bit of disk space may be unusable. We are happy with the new partition table, so we write the label out to disk:

```
Command (m for help): write
The partition table has been altered!
Calling ioctl() to re-read partition table.
Syncing disks.
```

We're now ready to create filesystems. To create a an ext3fs filesystem, we simply run **mke2fs -j** and specify the device name as an argument.

```
# mke2fs -j /dev/sda1
mke2fs 1.36 (05-Feb-2005)
Filesystem label=
OS type: Linux
Block size=4096 (log=2)
Fragment size=4096 (log=2)
245280 inodes, 489974 blocks
...
Superblock backups stored on blocks:
        32768, 98304, 163840, 229376, 294912
```

```
Writing inode tables: done
Creating journal (8192 blocks): done
Writing superblocks and filesystem accounting information: done
```

```
This filesystem will be automatically checked every 34 mounts or
180 days, whichever comes first.  Use tune2fs -c or -i to override.
done
```

In creating your filesystem, you could also use the **-J** option to explicitly specify either the size of the journal file that will reside on the new filesystem (**-J size**=x) or the identity of an external device that will contain the journal file (**-J device**=y). Typical installations locate the journal file (which must be between 1,024 and 102,400 filesystem blocks) inside the filesystem itself.

The process for creating the larger filesystem is the same, but it takes significantly longer. If you know that you will not need all of the inodes that **mke2fs** allocates by default, you can reduce the number of inodes per group, speeding up the **mke2fs** and giving you more space for real data. Likewise, you may wish to increase the number of inodes for filesystems that will house a large number of very small files. It's much better to have too many inodes than too few, since running out of inodes will prevent you from creating any more files. You cannot add more inodes after the filesystem has been created. If you run into this situation, you'll need to **dump** the data on the filesystem to tape or to a file on another partition, rerun **mke2fs** with a larger number of inodes (**-i**), and then **restore** the data to the partition. Days of fun!

We run **fsck** on our filesystems to make sure they were created properly. The **-f** flag forces **fsck** to check new filesystems rather than assuming that they are clean.

```
# fsck -f /dev/sda1
fsck 1.36 (05-Feb-2005)
e2fsck 1.36 (05-Feb-2005)
Pass 1: Checking inodes, blocks, and sizes
Pass 2: Checking directory structure
Pass 3: Checking directory connectivity
Pass 4: Checking reference counts
Pass 5: Checking group summary information
/dev/sda1: 11/245280 files (9.1% non-contiguous), 16629/489974 blocks
```

We can mount new filesystems as soon as their mount points are created:

```
# mkdir /bkroot
# mount /dev/sda1 /bkroot
# df /bkroot
Filesystem      1k-blocks    Used    Available   Use%   Mounted on
/dev/sda1       1981000        13    1878575     0%     /bkroot
```

To ensure that the system mounts the new filesystems at boot time, we add a line for each one to the **/etc/fstab** file. Each line lists, as required, the name of the device, the mount point, the filesystem type, the mount options, the backup frequency, and the pass number for **fsck**.

```
/dev/sda1          /bkroot        ext3      defaults      0  1
/dev/sda3          /new           ext3      defaults      0  2
```

A boot loader must be written to the disk device to make it bootable. Depending on the installation, either the **lilo** or the **grub** command does the actual installation. See page 26 for more information about configuring and installing a boot loader.

The final step is to create the swap space and add it to the system. We initialize swap partitions with **mkswap**, which takes the device name of the partition as an argument. It is no longer necessary to specify the size of the swap partition. With the swap area created, we enable it with the **swapon** command. **swapon** also verifies that the swap area was properly added.

```
# mkswap /dev/sda2
Setting up swapspace version 1, size = 2105667584 bytes
# swapon /dev/sda2
# swapon -s
Filename     Type        Size      Used   Priority
/dev/hda5    partition   133020    688    -1
/dev/sda2    partition   2056316   0      -2
```

As with regular filesystems, we must add the new swap partition to the **/etc/fstab** file so that the system remembers it the next time we reboot. The following entry is appropriate for our example disk:

```
/dev/sda2              swap              swap     defaults      0  0
```

Finally, we reboot to test the changes that were made to the **/etc/fstab** file and to make sure that the new filesystems and swap space come on-line correctly.

7.8 ADVANCED DISK MANAGEMENT: **RAID** AND **LVM**

The procedures we've discussed so far for adding new disks, filesystems, and swap areas are similar to those used on most UNIX systems. However, Linux has some additional tricks up its sleeve that many operating systems are still only dreaming about. Two distinct technologies, software RAID and logical volume management, give Linux disk management an additional layer of flexibility and reliability.

Hard disks fail frequently, and even with current backups, the consequences of a disk failure on a server can be disastrous. RAID, Redundant Array of Independent Disks, is a system that uses multiple hard drives to distribute or replicate data across several disks. RAID not only helps avoid data loss but also minimizes the downtime associated with a hardware failure (often to zero) and potentially increases performance as well. RAID systems can be implemented in hardware, but the Linux system implements all the necessary glue with software.

A second and equally useful tool called LVM (logical volume management) helps administrators efficiently allocate their available disk space among partitions. Imagine a world in which you don't know exactly how large a partition needs to be. Six months after creating a partition you discover that it is much too large, but a neighboring partition doesn't have enough space... Sound familiar? LVM allows space to be dynamically reallocated from the greedy partition to the needy partition.

Although these tools can be powerful when used individually, they are especially potent in combination. The sections below present a conceptual overview of both systems and an example that illustrates the detailed configuration.

Linux software RAID

We recently experienced a disk controller failure on an important production server. Although the data was replicated across several physical drives, a faulty hardware RAID controller destroyed the data on all disks. A lengthy and ugly tape restore process ensued, and it was more than two months before the server had completely recovered. The rebuilt server now relies on the kernel's software to manage its RAID environment, removing the possibility of another RAID controller failure.

RAID can do two basic things. First, it can improve performance by "striping" data across multiple drives, thus allowing several drives to work simultaneously to supply or absorb a single data stream. Second, it can duplicate or "mirror" data across multiple drives, decreasing the risk associated with a single failed disk. Linux RAID has some subtle differences from traditional RAID, but it is still logically divided into several levels:

- Linear mode provides no data redundancy or performance increases. It simply concatenates the block addresses of multiple drives to create a single (and larger) virtual drive.

- RAID level 0 is used strictly to increase performance. It uses two or more drives of equal size to decrease write and access times.

- RAID level 1 is the first level to offer redundancy. Data is duplicated on two or more drives simultaneously. This mode mirrors the data but harms performance because the information must be written more than once.

- RAID level 4 competes with (and consistently loses to) RAID level 5. It stripes data but dedicates a disk to parity information, thereby incurring wait times when writing to the parity disk. Unless you have a very good reason to use RAID 4, ignore it in preference to RAID 5.

- RAID level 5 is the Xanadu of RAID. By striping both data and parity information, it creates a redundant architecture while simultaneously improving read and write times. RAID 5 requires at least three disk drives.

Software RAID has been built into the Linux kernel since version 2.0, but early versions were buggy and incomplete. We recommend avoiding implementations older than those in the 2.4 kernel.

Logical volume management

LVM is an optional subsystem that defines a sort of supercharged version of disk partitioning. It allows you to group individual disks into "volume groups." The aggregate capacity of a volume group can then be allocated to logical volumes, which are accessed as regular block devices. Logical volume management lets you do the following:

- Use and allocate disk storage more efficiently
- Move logical volumes among different physical devices
- Grow and shrink logical volume sizes on the fly
- Take "snapshots" of whole filesystems
- Replace on-line drives without interrupting service

The components of a logical volume can be put together in various ways. Concatenation keeps each device's physical blocks together and lines the devices up one after another. Striping interleaves the components so that adjacent virtual blocks are actually spread over multiple physical disks. By reducing single-disk bottlenecks, striping can often provide higher bandwidth and lower latency.

An example configuration with LVM and RAID

Our previous example illustrated the configuration of a basic disk. In this section we walk through a setup procedure that includes both RAID and LVM. This kind of setup is especially useful for production servers.

Our objective is to create a RAID 5 array out of three empty disks. On top of this RAID array, we define two LVM partitions, web1 and web2. This structure gives us several advantages over a traditional system:

- RAID 5 confers redundancy; if one of the disks fails, our data remains intact. Unlike RAID 4, it doesn't matter which disk fails!

- Thanks to LVM, the partitions are resizable. When an enthusiastic webmaster fills up web2, we can easily steal some extra space from web1.

- More disk space could eventually be needed on both partitions. The design allows additional disks to be added to the RAID 5 array. Once this has been done, the existing LVM groups can be extended to include the additional space, all without recreating any partitions.

After showing the initial configuration, we describe how to handle a failed disk and show how to resize an LVM partition.

On our example system, we have four equally sized SCSI disks:

```
# fdisk -l

Disk /dev/sda: 18.2 GB, 18210036736 bytes
255 heads, 63 sectors/track, 2213 cylinders
Units = cylinders of 16065 * 512 = 8225280 bytes

   Device Boot    Start       End    Blocks   Id  System
/dev/sda1    *        1        13    104391   83  Linux
/dev/sda2            14       144  1052257+   82  Linux  swap
/dev/sda3           145      2213 16619242+   8e  Linux  LVM1G
```

```
Disk /dev/sdb: 18.2 GB, 18210036736 bytes
255 heads, 63 sectors/track, 2213 cylinders
Units = cylinders of 16065 * 512 = 8225280 bytes

   Device    Boot    Start         End     Blocks     Id        System

Disk /dev/sdc: 18.2 GB, 18210036736 bytes
255 heads, 63 sectors/track, 2213 cylinders
Units = cylinders of 16065 * 512 = 8225280 bytes

   Device    Boot    Start         End     Blocks     Id        System

Disk /dev/sdd: 18.2 GB, 18210036736 bytes
255 heads, 63 sectors/track, 2213 cylinders
Units = cylinders of 16065 * 512 = 8225280 bytes

   Device    Boot    Start         End     Blocks     Id        System
```

The first SCSI disk, **/dev/sda**, contains our system partitions. The other three (**sdb**, **sdc**, and **sdd**) have no partition tables.

To begin, we create the partitions on each of our SCSI disks. Since the disks are identical, we execute the same set of commands for each.

```
# fdisk /dev/sdb
...
Command (m for help): new
Command action
   e   extended
   p   primary partition (1-4): p
Partition number (1-4): 1
First cylinder (1-2213, default 1): <Enter>
Using default value 1
Last cylinder or +size or +sizeM or +sizeK (1-2213, default 2213): <Enter>
Using default value 2213

Command (m for help): type
Selected partition 1
Hex code (type L to list codes): fd
Changed system type of partition 1 to fd (Linux raid autodetect)

Command (m for help): write
The partition table has been altered!

Calling ioctl() to re-read partition table.
Syncing disks.
```

After writing the partition labels for the other two disks, it's time to get our hands dirty and build the RAID array. Most modern distributions use the single **mdadm** command for RAID management. Previous versions of RHEL used the **raidtools** suite, but since **mdadm** is both more powerful and easier to use than **raidtools**, that's what we demonstrate here.

Adding a Disk

The following command builds a RAID 5 array from our three SCSI partitions:

```
# mdadm --create /dev/md0 --level=5 --raid-devices=3 /dev/sdb1 /dev/sdc1
    /dev/sdd1
mdadm: array /dev/md0 started.
```

While the array is being built, the file **/proc/mdstat** shows progress information:

```
# cat /proc/mdstat
Personalities : [raid5]
md0 : active raid5 sdb1[3] sdc1[1] sdd1[2]
35566336 blocks level 5, 64k chunk, algorithm 2 [3/2] [_UU]
    [====>...............]  recovery = 22.4% (3999616/17783168) finish=5.1min
    speed=44800K/sec
unused devices: <none>
```

This file always reflects the current state of the kernel's RAID system. It is especially useful to keep an eye on this file after adding a new disk or replacing a faulty drive. (**watch cat /proc/mdstat** is a handy idiom.)

Once assembly of the array is complete, we see a notification message in the **/var/log/messages** file:

```
RAID5 conf printout:
--- rd:3 wd:3 fd:0
disk 0, o:1, dev:sdb1
disk 1, o:1, dev:sdc1
disk 2, o:1, dev:sdd1
```

The initial creation command also serves to "activate" the array (make it available for use), but on subsequent reboots we need to activate the array as a separate step, usually out of a startup script. RHEL, Fedora, and SUSE all include sample startup scripts for RAID.

mdadm does not technically require a configuration file, although it will use a configuration file if one is supplied (typically, **/etc/mdadm.conf**). We strongly recommend the use of a configuration file. It documents the RAID configuration in a standard way, thus giving administrators an obvious place to look for information when problems occur. The alternative to the use of a configuration file is to specify the configuration on the command line each time the array is activated.

mdadm --detail --scan dumps the current RAID setup into a configuration file. Unfortunately, the configuration it prints is not quite complete. The following commands build a complete configuration file for our example setup:

```
# echo DEVICE /dev/sdb1 /dev/sdc1 /dev/sdd1 > /etc/mdadm.conf
# mdadm --detail --scan >> /etc/mdadm.conf
# cat /etc/mdadm.conf
DEVICE /dev/sdb1 /dev/sdc1 /dev/sdd1
ARRAY /dev/md0 level=raid5 num-devices=3 UUID=21158de1:faaa0dfb:
    841d3b41:76e93a16
    devices=/dev/sdb1,/dev/sdc1,/dev/sdd1
```

mdadm can now read this file at startup or shutdown to easily manage the array. To enable the array at startup by using the freshly created **/etc/mdadm.conf**, we would execute

```
# mdadm -As /dev/md0
```

To stop the array manually, we would use the command

```
# mdadm -S /dev/md0
```

We've now assembled our three hard disks into a single logical RAID disk. Now it's time to define logical volume groups on which we can create expandable (and shrinkable) filesystems. LVM configuration proceeds in a few distinct phases:

- Creating (defining, really) and initializing physical volumes
- Adding the physical volumes to a volume group
- Creating logical volumes on the volume group

The LVM2 suite of tools addresses all of these tasks and facilitates later management of the volumes. **man lvm** is a good introduction to the system and its tools.

In LVM terminology, the physical volumes are the "things" that are aggregated to form storage pools ("volume groups"). "Physical volume" is a somewhat misleading term, however, because the physical volumes need not have a direct correspondence to physical devices. They *can* be disks, but they can also be disk partitions or (as in this example) high-level RAID objects that have their own underlying structure.

LVM commands start with letters that make it clear at which level of abstraction they operate: **pv** commands manipulate physical volumes, **vg** commands manipulate volume groups, and **lv** commands manipulate logical volumes.

Older versions of LVM required you to run the **vgscan** command as an initial step, but this is no longer necessary. Instead, you start by directly initializing each physical device with **pvcreate**. For this example, we use the **/dev/md0** RAID 5 device we just created.

```
# pvcreate /dev/md0
Physical volume "/dev/md0" successfully created
```

This operation destroys all data on the device or partition, so we were exceedingly careful! Although we're using only a single physical device in this example, LVM allows us to add multiple devices of different types to a single volume group.

Our physical device is now ready to be added to a volume group:

```
# vgcreate LVM1 /dev/md0
Volume group "LVM1" successfully created
```

To step back and examine our handiwork, we use the **vgdisplay** command:

```
# vgdisplay LVM1
--- Volume group ---
VG Name                LVM1
```

Adding a Disk

```
System ID
Format               lvm2
Metadata Areas       1
Metadata Sequence No 1
VG Access            read/write
VG Status            resizable
MAX LV               0
Cur LV               0
Open LV              0
Max PV               0
Cur PV               1
Act PV               1
VG Size              33.92 GB
PE Size              4.00 MB
Total PE             8683
Alloc PE / Size      0 / 0
Free                 PE / Size8683 / 33.92 GB
VG UUID              nhkzzN-KHmY-BfV5-6F6Y-3LF8-dpd5-JM5lMp
```

The last steps are to create logical volumes within the LVM1 volume group and make partitions on the volumes. We make both of the logical volumes 10GB in size:

```
# lvcreate -L 10G -n web1 LVM1
Logical volume "web1" created
```

```
# lvcreate -L 10G -n web2 LVM1
Logical volume "web2" created
```

Now that we've created two logical volumes, web1 and web2, in our LVM1 volume group, we can create and mount our filesystems.

```
# mke2fs -j /dev/LVM1/web1
...
```

```
# mke2fs -j /dev/LVM1/web2
...
```

```
# mkdir /web1 /web2
# mount /dev/LVM1/web1 /web1
# mount /dev/LVM1/web2 /web2
```

The filesystems are finally ready for use. We add the new filesystems to **/etc/fstab** and reboot the system to ensure that everything comes up successfully.

Dealing with a failed disk

Our nicely architected system looks pretty now, but because of the multiple layers at which the system is operating, things can get ugly in a hurry. When a hard drive fails or a partition is corrupted (or simply fills up), it's essential that you know how to repair it quickly and easily. You use the same tools as for the initial configuration above to maintain the system and recover from problems.

Consider the case of a failed hard disk. Because RAID 5 provides some data redundancy, the RAID 5 array we constructed in the previous sections will happily continue to function in the event of a disk crash; users will not necessarily be aware of any problems. You'll need to pay close attention to the system logs to catch the problem early (or have a program that does this for you; see page 220).

mdadm offers a handy option that simulates a failed disk:

```
# mdadm /dev/md0 -f /dev/sdc1
mdadm: set /dev/sdc1 faulty in /dev/md0
```

```
# tail /var/log/messages
May 30 16:14:55 harp kernel: raid5: Disk failure on sdc, disabling device.
    Operation continuing on 2 devices
kernel: RAID5 conf printout:
kernel:  --- rd:3 wd:2 fd:1
kernel:  disk 0, o:1, dev:sdb1
kernel:  disk 1, o:0, dev:sdc1
kernel:  disk 2, o:1, dev:sdd1
kernel: RAID5 conf printout:
kernel:  --- rd:3 wd:2 fd:1
kernel:  disk 0, o:1, dev:sdb1
kernel:  disk 2, o:1, dev:sdd1
```

As shown here, the system log **/var/log/messages** contains information about the (simulated) failure as soon as it occurs. Similar information is available from the RAID status file **/proc/mdstat**. At this point, the administrator should take the following actions:

- Remove the disk from the RAID array.
- Schedule downtime and shut down the computer (if necessary).
- Replace the physical drive.
- Add the new drive to the array.

To remove the drive from the RAID configuration, use **mdadm**:

```
# mdadm /dev/md0 -r /dev/sdc1
mdadm: hot removed /dev/sdc1
```

Once the disk has been logically removed, you can replace the drive. Hot-swappable drive hardware lets you make the change without turning off the system or rebooting.

If your RAID components are raw disks, you should replace them with an identical drive only. Partition-based components can be replaced with any partition of similar size, although for bandwidth matching it's best if the drive hardware is similar. (If your RAID configuration is built on top of partitions, you must run **fdisk** to define the partitions appropriately before adding the replacement disk to the array.)

In our example, the failure is just a simulation, so we can add the drive back to the array without replacing any hardware:

```
# mdadm /dev/md0 -a /dev/sdc1
mdadm: hot added /dev/sdc1
```

Linux rebuilds the array and reflects the progress, as always, in **/proc/mdstat**.

Reallocating storage space

Even more common than disk crashes are cases in which users or log files fill up partitions. We have experienced everything from servers used for personal MP3 storage to a department full of email packrats.

Suppose that in our example, **/web1** has grown more than we predicted and is in need of more space. Resizing LVM partitions involves just a few short steps. The exact commands depend on the filesystem in use. The steps in the following example are for an ext3 filesystem. The steps are:

- Examine the current LVM configuration
- Resize the partitions with **lvextend** and **ext2online**
- Verify the changes

Fortunately, we left some extra space in our volume group to grow **/web1** with, so we do not have to scavenge space from another volume. We use **vgdisplay** to see the space available on the volume group and **df** to determine how to reallocate it:

```
# vgdisplay LVM1
--- Volume group ---
VG Name               LVM1
System ID
Format                lvm2
Metadata Areas        1
Metadata Sequence No 3
VG Access             read/write
VG Status             resizable
MAX LV                0
Cur LV                2
Open LV               2
Max PV                0
Cur PV                1
Act PV                1
VG Size               33.92 GB
PE Size               4.00 MB
Total PE              8683
Alloc PE / Size       5120 / 20.00 GB
Free                  PE / Size3563 / 13.92 GB
VG UUID               nhkzzN-KHmY-BfV5-6F6Y-3LF8-dpd5-JM5lMp

# df -h /web1
Filesystem              Size   Used  Avail  Use%  Mounted on
/dev/mapper/LVM1-web1   9.9G   7.1G   2.3G   76%   /web1
```

These commands show 13.92GB free in the volume group and 76% usage of **/web1**. We'll add 10GB to **/web1**.

First we use **lvextend** to add space to the logical volume, then **ext2online** to resize the filesystem structures to encompass the additional space.

```
# lvextend -L+10G /dev/LVM1/web1
  Extending logical volume web1 to 20.00 GB
  Logical volume web1 successfully resized
# ext2online -d /dev/LVM1/web1
  ...
  ext2_close
```

That's it! Examining the output of **df** again shows the changes:

```
# df -h /web1
Filesystem              Size   Used   Avail   Use%   Mounted on
/dev/mapper/LVM1-web1   20G    7.1G   12G     38%    /web1
```

ReiserFS users must unmount the partition before running **lvextend**. Additionally, a tool creatively known as **resize_reiserfs** is used in place of **ext2online** to resize the filesystem.

7.9 MOUNTING USB DRIVES

Floppy disks have finally gone the way of the dodo, and good riddance. In their place are friendly, fast, and fun USB drives. These devices come in many flavors: personal "thumb" drives, digital cameras, iPods, and large external disks, to name a few. Recent Linux distributions include native kernel support for all these handy gizmos.

When connecting a USB drive, first make sure that Linux recognizes the device. The following command lists the USB devices the kernel has discovered:

```
$ sudo /sbin/lsusb
Bus 001 Device 003: ID 0781:7108 SanDisk Corp.
Bus 001 Device 001: ID 0000:0000
```

In this case, a SanDisk drive has been attached. If no devices are listed but the device is plugged in, the kernel may not have USB support and will need to be recompiled.

Next, find out how the kernel has identified the drive and what device file it is using to represent it. The kernel messages are recorded through syslog.

```
$ sudo tail -n 20 /var/log/messages | grep kernel[8]
Jul 27 20:52:13 harp kernel: USB Mass Storage support registered.
Jul 27 21:02:57 harp kernel: usb 1-2: USB disconnect, address 2
Jul 27 21:14:09 harp kernel: ohci_hcd 0000:00:0f.2: wakeup
Jul 27 21:14:09 harp kernel: usb 1-2: new full speed USB device using addr 3
Jul 27 21:14:09 harp kernel: scsi3 : SCSI emulation for USB Storage devices
Jul 27 21:14:09 harp kernel: Vendor: SanDisk Model: Cruzer Titanium Rev: 2000
Jul 27 21:14:09 harp kernel: Type: Direct-Access ANSI SCSI revision: 02
Jul 27 21:14:09 harp kernel: SCSI device sde: 512-byte hdwr sectors (520 MB)
Jul 27 21:14:09 harp kernel: sde: Write Protect is off
Jul 27 21:14:09 harp kernel: sde: assuming drive cache: write through
Jul 27 21:14:10 harp kernel: sde: sde1
Jul 27 21:14:10 harp kernel: Attached scsi removable disk sde at scsi3, channel
        0, id 0, lun 0
```

---
8. Look in **/var/log/kern.log** on Debian and Ubuntu systems.

Adding a Disk

The kernel messages indicate that this is a 520MB SanDisk Cruzer Titanium. (If you're in the market, this an excellent USB key!) The kernel has associated the device **/dev/sde** with the disk, and the disk contains only a single partition, **sde1**.

The drive needs to be mounted by Linux before it can be used. Create a mount point and mount the drive:

```
$ sudo mkdir /mnt/usb
$ sudo mount /dev/sde1 /mnt/usb
```

The drive is now mounted on **/mnt/usb** and is ready for use. To ease the process the next time you use the drive, you could add the following line to **/etc/fstab**:

```
/dev/sde1    /mnt/usb     auto    users,noauto,uid=ben,gid=users  0    0
```

The listed options autodetect the filesystem type and allow the user ben to mount and write to the drive.

7.10 EXERCISES

E7.1   Which SCSI connectors go with which variants of the specification? Ignoring the differences in connectors, what are the compatibility issues among the various SCSI versions?

E7.2   What's the difference between formatting a disk and partitioning a disk? What's the difference between partitioning and creating a filesystem?

E7.3   List the command and arguments you would use to create a filesystem on a disk in each of the following circumstances.

a) The disk will be used as storage for home directories.
b) The disk will be used as swap space.
c) The disk will store the mail queue at a large spam house.
d) The disk will hold a MySQL InnoDB database.

E7.4   The LVM tool suite is powerful but can be confusing if not well understood. Practice adding, removing, and resizing disks in a volume group. Show how you would successfully remove a device from one volume group and add it to another.

★ **E7.5**   Using printed or Internet resources, identify the best-performing SCSI and IDE drives. Do the benchmarks used to evaluate these drives reflect the way that a busy Linux server would use its boot disk? How much of a cost premium would you pay for SCSI, and how much of a performance improvement (if any) would you get for the extra money?

★ **E7.6**   Add a disk to your system. Make one partition on the new disk a backup root partition; install a kernel and boot from it. Keep a journal of all the steps required to complete this task. You may find the **script** command helpful. (Requires root access.)

★ **E7.7** What is a superblock and what is it used for? Look up the definition of the ext3fs superblock structure in the kernel header files and discuss what each of the fields in the structure represents.

★ **E7.8** Use **mdadm** and its **-f** option to simulate a failed disk in a RAID array. Remove the disk from the array and add it back. How does **/proc/md-stat** look at each step?

★★ **E7.9** What fields are stored in an inode on an ext3fs filesystem? List the contents of the inode that represents the **/etc/motd** file. Where is this file's filename stored? (Tools such as **hexdump** and **ls -i** might help.)

★★ **E7.10** Examine the contents of a directory file with a program such as **hexdump** or **od**. Each variable-length record represents a file in that directory. Look up the directory entry structure and explain each field, using an example from a real directory file. Next, look at the **lost+found** directory on any filesystem. Why are there so many names there when the **lost+found** directory appears to be empty?

★★★★★ **E7.11** Write a program that traverses the filesystem and prints the contents of the **/etc/motd** and **/etc/termcap** files. But don't open the files directly; open the raw device file for the root partition and use the **seek** and **read** system calls to decode the filesystem and find the appropriate data blocks. **/etc/motd** is usually short and will probably contain only direct blocks. **/etc/termcap** will probably require you to decode indirect blocks. Hint: when reading the system header files, be sure you have found the filesystem's on-disk inode structure, not the in-core inode structure. (Requires root access.)

Adding a Disk

8 *Periodic Processes*

The key to staying in control of your system is to automate as many tasks as possible. For example, an **adduser** program can add new users faster than you can, with a smaller chance of making mistakes. Almost any task can be encoded in a Perl, Python, shell, or **expect** script.

It's often useful to have a script or command executed without any human intervention. For example, you might want to have a script verify (say, every half-hour) that your network routers and bridges are working correctly and have it send you email when problems are discovered.[1]

8.1 CRON: SCHEDULE COMMANDS

Under Linux, periodic execution is normally handled by the **cron** daemon. **cron** starts when the system boots and remains running as long as the system is up. **cron** reads one or more configuration files containing lists of command lines and times at which they are to be invoked. The command lines are executed by **sh**, so almost anything you can do by hand from the shell can also be done with **cron**.[2]

cron originally appeared in the UNIX family tree in the 1970s. Linux distributions include a version known as ISC **cron** or "Vixie-**cron**," named after its author, Paul Vixie. It's is a modern rewrite that provides added functionality with less mess.

---

1. Many sites go further than this and send a text message to an administrator's pager as soon as a problem is detected.
2. **/bin/sh** under Linux is really a link to the **bash** shell, an enhanced (and reimplemented) version of the traditional Bourne shell found on UNIX systems. You can configure **cron** to use other shells as well.

A **cron** configuration file is called a "crontab," short for "cron table." **cron** looks for crontab files in three places: **/var/spool/cron** (**/var/spool/cron/tabs** on SUSE and **/var/spool/cron/crontabs** on Debian), **/etc/cron.d**, and **/etc/crontab**.

Crontab files for individual users are stored underneath **/var/spool/cron**. Typically, there is (at most) one crontab file per user: one for root, one for jsmith, and so on. Crontab files are named with the login names of the users they belong to, and **cron** uses these filenames to figure out which UID to use when running the commands that each file contains. The **crontab** command transfers crontab files to and from this directory.

Crontab files that schedule system maintenance tasks and other tasks defined by the system administrator are stored in the file **/etc/crontab** and in other files found in the **/etc/cron.d** directory. These files have a slightly different format from the per-user crontab files because they allow commands to be run as an arbitrary user. **cron** treats the **/etc/crontab** and **/etc/cron.d** entries in exactly the same way. In general, **/etc/crontab** is intended as a file for the system administrator to maintain by hand, whereas **/etc/cron.d** is provided as a place where software packages can install any crontab entries they might need.

When **cron** starts, it reads all of its config files, stores them in memory, and then goes to sleep. Once each minute, **cron** wakes up, checks the modification times on the crontab files, reloads any files that have changed, and then executes any tasks scheduled for that minute before returning to sleep.

For reasons that are unclear, **cron** has been renamed **crond** on Red Hat.

cron logs its activities through syslog, using the facility "cron," with most messages submitted at level "info." Default syslog configurations generally send **cron** log data to its own file.

8.2 THE FORMAT OF CRONTAB FILES

All the crontab files on a system share a similar format. Comments are introduced with a pound sign (#) in the first column of a line. Each noncomment line contains six or seven fields and represents one command:

minute hour day month weekday [username] command

The first six fields are separated by whitespace, but within the *command* field whitespace is taken literally. The *username* is found only in **/etc/crontab** and in files from the **/etc/cron.d** directory; it specifies on whose behalf the *command* should be run. This field is not present or necessary in the user-specific crontab files (those stored in **/var/spool/cron**) because the UID is implied by the filename.

The *minute, hour, day, month,* and *weekday* fields tell when to run the *command.* Their interpretations are shown in Table 8.1 on the next page.

Periodic Processes

Table 8.1   Crontab time specifications

Field	Description	Range
minute	Minute of the hour	0 to 59
hour	Hour of the day	0 to 23
day	Day of the month	1 to 31
month	Month of the year	1 to 12
weekday	Day of the week	0 to 6 (0 = Sunday)

Each of the time-related fields may contain

- A star, which matches everything
- A single integer, which matches exactly
- Two integers separated by a dash, matching a range of values
- A comma-separated series of integers or ranges, matching any listed value

Value ranges can include a step value. For example, the series 0,3,6,9,12,15,18 can be written more concisely as 0-18/3. You can also use text mnemonics for the names of months and days, but not in combination with ranges.

The time specification

```
45  10  *  *  1-5
```

means "10:45 a.m., Monday through Friday." A hint: never put a star in the first field unless you want the command to be run every minute.

There is a potential ambiguity to watch out for with the *weekday* and *day* fields. Every day is both a day of the week and a day of the month. If both *weekday* and *day* are specified, a day need satisfy only one of the two conditions in order to be selected. For example,

```
0,30  *  13  *  5
```

means "every half-hour on Friday, and every half-hour on the 13th of the month," not "every half-hour on Friday the 13th."

The *command* is the **sh** command line to be executed. It can be any valid shell command and should not be quoted. *command* is considered to continue to the end of the line and may contain blanks or tabs.

A percent sign (%) is used to indicate newlines within the *command* field. Only the text up to the first percent sign is included in the actual command; the remaining lines are given to the command as standard input.

Here are some examples of legal crontab commands:

```
echo The time is now `date` > /dev/console
mail -s Reminder evi@anchor % Don't forget to write your chapters.
cd /etc; /bin/mail -s "Password file" evi < passwd
```

And here are some complete examples of crontab entries:

```
30  2  *  *  1    (cd /users/joe/project; make)
```

This entry will be activated at 2:30 each Monday morning. It will run **make** in the directory **/users/joe/project**. An entry like this might be used to start a long compilation at a time when other users would not be using the system. Usually, any output produced by a **cron** command is mailed to the "owner" of the crontab.[3]

```
20  1  *  *  *      find /tmp -atime +3 -exec rm -f {} ';'
```

This command will run at 1:20 each morning. It removes all files in the **/tmp** directory that have not been accessed in 3 days.

```
55  23  *  *  0-3,6 /staff/trent/bin/checkservers
```

This line runs **checkservers** at 11:55 p.m. every day except Thursdays and Fridays.

It is also possible to specify environment variables and their values in a crontab file. See the **crontab**(5) man page for more details.

8.3 CRONTAB MANAGEMENT

crontab *filename* installs *filename* as your crontab, replacing any previous version. **crontab -e** checks out a copy of your crontab, invokes your editor on it (as specified by the EDITOR environment variable), and then resubmits it to the crontab directory. **crontab -l** lists the contents of your crontab to standard output, and **crontab -r** removes it, leaving you with no crontab file at all.

Root can supply a *username* argument to edit or view other users' crontabs. For example, **crontab -u jsmith -r** erases the crontab belonging to the user jsmith.

Without command-line arguments, most versions of **crontab** will try to read a crontab from standard input. If you enter this mode by accident, don't try to exit with <Control-D>; doing so will erase your entire crontab. Use <Control-C> instead. Some versions have been modified to require you to supply a dash as the *filename* argument to make **crontab** pay attention to its standard input.

Two config files, **/etc/cron.deny** and **/etc/cron.allow**, specify which users may submit crontab files. If the allow file exists, then it contains a list of all users that may submit crontabs, one per line. No unlisted person can invoke the **crontab** command. If the allow file doesn't exist, then the deny file is checked. It, too, is just a list of users, but the meaning is reversed: everyone except the listed users is allowed access. If neither the allow file nor the deny file exists, most systems allow only root to submit crontabs. (Debian and Ubuntu default to allowing submissions by all users.)

It's important to note that access control is implemented by **crontab**, not by **cron**. If a user sneaks a crontab file into the appropriate directory by other means, **cron** will blindly execute the commands that it contains.

Periodic Processes

---

3. That is, the user after whom the crontab file is named. On most (but not all) systems, the actual owner of crontab files is root.

8.4 SOME COMMON USES FOR CRON

A number of standard tasks are especially suited for invocation by **cron**, and these usually make up the bulk of the material in root's crontab. In this section we look at a variety of such tasks and the crontab lines used to implement them.

Linux systems often come with crontab entries preinstalled, mostly in **/etc/cron.d**. If you want to deactivate the standard entries, comment them out by inserting a pound sign (#) at the beginning of each line. Don't delete them; you might want to refer to them later.

In addition to the **/etc/cron.d** mechanism, Linux distributions also preinstall crontab entries that run the scripts in a set of well-known directories, thereby providing another way for software packages to install periodic jobs without any editing of a crontab file. For example, scripts in **/etc/cron.daily** are run once a day, and scripts in **/etc/cron.weekly** are run once a week.

Many sites have experienced subtle but recurrent network glitches that occur because administrators have configured **cron** to run the same command on hundreds of machines at exactly the same time. Clock synchronization with NTP exacerbates the problem. The problem is easy to fix with a random delay script or config file adjustment, but it can be tricky to diagnose because the symptoms resolve so quickly and completely.

Cleaning the filesystem

Some of the files on any Linux system are worthless junk (no, not the system files). For example, when a program crashes, the kernel may write out a file named **core** that contains an image of the program's address space.[4] Core files are useful for software developers, but for administrators they are usually a waste of space. Users often don't know about core files, so they tend not to delete them on their own.

NFS, the Network File System, is described in Chapter 16. NFS is another source of extra files. Because NFS servers are stateless, they have to use a special convention to preserve files that have been deleted locally but are still in use by a remote machine. Most implementations rename such files to **.nfs**xxx where xxx is a number. Various situations can result in these files being forgotten and left around after they are supposed to have been deleted.

Many programs create temporary files in **/tmp** or **/var/tmp** that aren't erased for one reason or another. Some programs, especially editors, like to make backup copies of each file they work with.

A partial solution to the junk file problem is to institute some sort of nightly disk space reclamation out of **cron**. Modern systems usually come with something of this sort set up for you, but it's a good idea to review your system's default behavior to make sure it's appropriate for your situation.

---

4. The word "core" means "memory." This term originated on early computer systems, which used as memory elements little ferrite donuts mounted on a woven mesh.

Below are several common idioms implemented with the **find** command.

```
find / -xdev -type f '(' -name core -o name 'core.[0-9]*' ')' -atime +7
    -exec rm -f {} ';'
```

This command removes core images that have not been accessed in a week. The **-xdev** argument makes sure that **find** won't cross over to filesystems other than the root; this restraint is important on networks where many filesystems may be cross-mounted. If you want to clean up more than one filesystem, use a separate command for each (note that **/var** is typically a separate filesystem).

The naming convention for core files can be set by the system administrator through the **/proc/sys/kernel/core_pattern** file. The **find** command above handles only the default names (**core** or **core.***PID*). The **-type f** argument is important because the Linux kernel source contains a directory called **core**, and you wouldn't want to be deleting that.

```
find / -xdev -atime +3 '(' -name '#*' -o -name '.#*' -o -name '*.CKP' -o
    -name '*~' -o -name '.nfs*' ')' -exec rm -f {} ';'
```

This command deletes files that have not been accessed in three days and that begin with # or **.#** or **.nfs** or end with ~ or **.CKP**. These patterns are typical of various sorts of temporary and editor backup files.

For performance reasons, some administrators use the noatime mount option to prevent the filesystem from maintaining access time stamps. That configuration will confuse both of the **find** commands shown above because the files will appear to have been unreferenced even if they were recently active. Unfortunately, the failure mode is to delete the files; be sure you are maintaining access times before using these commands as shown.

```
cd /tmp; find . ! -name . ! -name lost+found -type d -mtime +3
    -exec /bin/rm -rf {} ';'
```

This command recursively removes all subdirectories of **/tmp** not modified in 72 hours. Plain files in **/tmp** are removed at boot time by the system startup scripts, but some systems do not remove directories. If a directory named **lost+found** exists, it is treated specially and is not removed. This is important if **/tmp** is a separate filesystem. See page 133 for more information about **lost+found**.

If you use any of these commands, you should make sure that users are aware of your cleanup policies.

Network distribution of configuration files

See Chapter 17 for more information about sharing configuration files. If you are running a network of machines, it's often convenient to maintain a single, network-wide version of configuration files such as the mail aliases database (usually **/etc/mail/aliases**). Master versions of these files can be distributed every night with **rsync**, **rdist**, or an **expect** script.

Periodic Processes

Sometimes, postprocessing is required. For example, you might need to run the **newaliases** command to convert a text file of mail aliases to the hashed format used by **sendmail** if the AutoRebuildAliases option isn't set in your **sendmail.cf** file. You might also need to load files into an administrative database such as NIS.

Rotating log files

Linux does a good job of managing most of its log files, but some files grow without bound until they are manually reset. There are various ways to prevent logs from overflowing, the simplest being to simply truncate them at periodic intervals.

A more conservative strategy is to "rotate" log files by keeping several older versions of each one. This scheme prevents log files from getting out of control but never leaves you without any recent log information. Since log rotation is a recurrent and regularly scheduled event, it's an ideal task for **cron**. See *Rotating log files* on page 202 for more details.

8.5 OTHER SCHEDULERS: ANACRON AND FCRON

In general, **cron** does not compensate for commands that are missed while the system is down or for large discontinuities in the flow of time. However, Vixie-**cron** does make a good-faith effort to do the right thing for jobs that are scheduled on a less-frequently-than-hourly basis when the time changes by less than three hours. It does a good job at handling small adjustments such as those related to daylight saving time in the United States.

Laptops and other machines that are powered on sporadically have a more strained relationship with **cron** and can benefit from some backup. A nice complement to **cron** can be found in **anacron**, which is an interval-based scheduler. If **anacron** is not included in the default installation, you can install it through your system's default package management system.

Instead of specifying that a particular command be run at 2:00 a.m. on Monday mornings, in the **anacron** world you simply ask that it be run every week. Unlike **cron**, **anacron** maintains a record of each command's most recent execution time, so it can simply compare this time, the specified interval, and the current time to determine whether the command needs to be run again.

anacron provides several features that help prevent a newly booted machine from submerging under a wave of simultaneous maintenance tasks. Each task can have its own startup delay, and **anacron** can serialize the commands it runs so that only one command is active at a time.

Interval scheduling is probably more generally useful than fixed-time scheduling for administrative tasks. Unfortunately, **anacron** requires its intervals to be expressed in days, and this fact limits **anacron**'s utility as a first-line scheduling tool.

anacron itself must be run out of **cron**. Although **anacron**'s scheduling granularity is days, it makes sense to run **anacron** more frequently than once a day—if you knew **cron** would be able to consistently run **anacron** at the same time each day, you probably wouldn't be using **anacron** in the first place. Similarly, it makes sense to run **anacron** at system startup as well.

A more aggressive revamping of **cron** that includes **anacron**-like features can be found in **fcron**; see fcron.free.fr. Unlike **anacron**, **fcron** aims explicitly to replace Vixie-**cron**. It permits a number of sophisticated timing specifications that are not expressible in the **cron** and **anacron** configuration languages. Nevertheless, one has to wonder whether the practical value of these features justifies **fcron**'s added complexity and the hassle of using a nonstandard scheduler.

8.6 EXERCISES

E8.1 A local user on your system has been abusing his crontab privileges by running expensive tasks at regular intervals. After asking him to stop several times, you are forced to revoke his privileges. List the steps needed to delete his current crontab and make sure he can't add a new one.

E8.2 Think of three tasks (other than those mentioned in the chapter) that might need to be run periodically. Write crontab entries for each task and specify into which crontab files the entries should go.

E8.3 Choose three entries from your system's crontab files. Decode each one and describe when it runs, what it does, and why you think the entry is needed. (Requires root access.)

★ **E8.4** Write a script that keeps your startup files (~/.[a-z]*) synchronized among all the machines on which you have an account. Schedule this script to run regularly from **cron**. (Is it safe to blindly copy every file whose name starts with a dot? Should files being replaced on the destination machines be backed up before they are overwritten?)

★ **E8.5** Using the man pages for the **du**, **sort**, and **head** commands as references, write a script that determines which 10 home directories are the largest on the system. Schedule the script to run every Monday night at 12:00 a.m. and have it mail its output to you. Hint: you'll want to use a reverse numeric sort. (Requires root access.)

9 *Backups*

At most sites, the information stored on computers is worth more than the computers themselves. It is also much harder to replace. Protecting this information is one of the system administrator's most important (and, unfortunately, most tedious) tasks.

There are hundreds of creative and not-so-creative ways to lose data. Software bugs routinely corrupt data files. Users accidentally delete their life's work. Hackers and disgruntled employees erase disks. Hardware problems and natural disasters take out entire machine rooms.

If executed correctly, backups allow an administrator to restore a filesystem (or any portion of a filesystem) to the condition it was in at the time of the last backup. Backups must be done carefully and on a strict schedule. The backup system and backup media must also be tested regularly to verify that they are working correctly.

The integrity of backup media directly affects your company's bottom line. Senior management needs to understand what the backups are actually supposed to do, as opposed to what they *want* the backups to do. It may be okay to lose a day's work at a university computer science department, but it probably isn't okay at a commodity trading firm.

We begin this chapter with some general backup philosophy, followed by a discussion of the most commonly used backup devices and media (their strengths, weaknesses, and costs). Next, we discuss Linux backup and archiving commands and suggest which commands are best for which situations. We then talk about how to design a backup scheme and review the mechanics of the popular **dump** and **restore** utilities.

Finally, we take a look at Bacula, a free network backup package, and then offer some comments about commercial alternatives.

9.1   MOTHERHOOD AND APPLE PIE

Before we get into the meat and potatoes of backups, we want to pass on some general hints that we have learned over time (usually, the hard way). None of these suggestions is an absolute rule, but you will find that the more of them you follow, the smoother your dump process will be.

Perform all dumps from one machine

Many backup utilities allow you to perform dumps over the network. Although there is some performance penalty for doing dumps that way, the increase in ease of administration makes it worthwhile. We have found that the best method is to run a script from a central location that executes **rdump** (by way of **rsh** or **ssh**) on each machine that needs to be dumped; you can also use a software package (commercial, free, or shareware) to automate this process. All dumps should go to the same backup device (nonrewinding, of course).

If your systems are too large to be backed up by a single device, you should still try to keep your backup system as centralized as possible. Centralization facilitates administration and enables you to verify the integrity of the backup. Depending on the media you are using, you can often put more than one media device on a server without affecting performance.

Label your media

Label each piece of backup media clearly and completely—an unlabeled tape is a scratch tape. Directly label each piece of media to uniquely identify its contents. On the cases, write detailed information such as lists of filesystems and dump dates.

You must be able to restore critical servers' root and **/usr** filesystems without looking at dump scripts. Label the media accordingly, listing the filesystems they contain, the format of the backups, the exact syntax of the commands used to create them, and any other information you would need to restore the system without referring to on-line documentation.

Free and commercial labeling programs abound. Save yourself a major headache and invest in one. If you purchase labels for your laser printer, the label vendor can usually provide (Windows) software that generates labels. Better yet, buy a dedicated label printer for Windows. They are inexpensive and work well.

Pick a reasonable backup interval

The more often backups are done, the less data is lost in a crash. However, backups use system resources and an operator's time. You must provide adequate data integrity at a reasonable cost of time and materials.

On busy systems, it is generally appropriate to back up filesystems with home directories every workday. On systems that are used less heavily or on which the data is less volatile, you might decide that performing backups several times a week is sufficient. On a small system with only one user, performing backups once a week is probably adequate. How much data are your users willing to lose?

Choose filesystems carefully

Filesystems that are rarely modified do not need to be backed up as frequently as users' home directories. If only a few files change on an otherwise static filesystem (such as **/etc/passwd** in the root filesystem), you can copy these files every day to another partition that is backed up regularly.

If **/tmp** is a separate filesystem, it should not be backed up. The **/tmp** directory should not contain anything essential, so there is no reason to preserve it. In case this seems obvious, we know of one large site that does daily backups of **/tmp**.

Make daily dumps fit on one piece of media

*See Chapter 8 for more information about **cron**.*

In a perfect world, you could do daily dumps of all your user filesystems onto a single tape. High-density media such as DLT, AIT, and LTO make this goal practical for some sites. You can automate the process by mounting your backup media every day before leaving work and letting **cron** execute the backup for you. That way, dumps occur at a time when files are not likely to be changing, and the dumps have minimal impact on users.

As our work habits change and telecommuting becomes more popular, the range of "good" times to do backups is shrinking. From our logs, we see that between 3:00 a.m. and 6:00 a.m. is the best time. However, backing up 80TB of data in three hours isn't going to happen.

Another major problem is the rapid expansion of disk space that has resulted from reductions in the price of hard disks. You can no longer purchase a stock desktop machine with less than 100GB of disk space. Why clean up your disks and enforce quotas when you can just throw a little money at the problem and add more disk space? Unfortunately, it's all too easy for the amount of on-line storage to outstrip your ability to back it up.

If you can't fit your daily backups on one tape, you have several options:

- Buy a higher-capacity backup device.
- Buy a stacker or library and feed multiple pieces of media to one device.
- Change your dump sequence.
- Write a smarter script.
- Use multiple backup devices.

Your automated dump system should always record the name of each filesystem it has dumped. Good record keeping allows you to quickly skip forward to the correct filesystem when you want to restore a file. It is also a good idea to record the order of the filesystems on the outside of the tape. (We've said it before and we'll say it again: be sure to use the nonrewinding device to write to media with multiple dumps.)

Make filesystems smaller than your dump device

dump and other readily available utilities are perfectly capable of dumping filesystems to multiple pieces of media. However, if a dump spans multiple tapes, an operator or tape library robot must be present to change the media, and the media must be carefully labeled to allow restores to be performed easily. Unless you have a good reason to create a really large filesystem, don't do it.

Keep media off-site

Most organizations keep backups off-site so that a disaster such as a fire cannot destroy both the original data and the backups. "Off-site" can be anything from a safe deposit box at a bank to the President's or CEO's home. Companies that specialize in the secure storage of backup media guarantee a secure and climate-controlled environment for your archives. Always make sure your off-site storage provider is reputable, bonded, and insured. There are on-line (but off-site) businesses today that specialize in safeguarding your data.

The speed with which backup media are moved off-site should depend on how often you need to restore files and on how much latency you can accept. Some sites avoid making this decision by performing two dumps to different backup devices, one that stays on-site and one that is moved immediately.[1]

Protect your backups

Dan Geer, a security consultant, said, "What does a backup do? It reliably violates file permissions at a distance." Hmmm.

Secure your backup media. They contain all your organization's data and can be read by anyone who has physical access to them. Not only should you keep your media off-site, but you should also keep them under lock and key. If you use a commercial storage facility for this purpose, the company you deal with should guarantee the confidentiality of the tapes in their care.

Encryption of backup media is an option to consider. Many commercial backup utilities make encryption relatively painless. On the other hand, you must make sure that the encryption keys cannot be lost or destroyed and that they are available for use in an emergency.

Some companies feel so strongly about the importance of backups that they make duplicates, which is really not a bad idea at all.

---

1. A large financial institution located in the World Trade Center kept its "off-site" backups one or two floors below their offices. When the building was bombed (the first time), the backup tapes (as well as the computers) were destroyed. Make sure "off-site" really is.

Limit activity during dumps

Filesystem activity should be limited during dumps because changes can cause your backup utility to make mistakes. You can limit activity either by doing the dumps when few active users are around (in the middle of night or on weekends) or by making the filesystem accessible only to the backup utility. (This latter precaution sounds fine in theory, but it is rarely practiced. Users want 24/7 access to all filesystems. These days it is impossible to do a backup with no disk activity.)

See page 496 for more information about file servers.

Dedicated file servers such as those manufactured by Network Appliance provide on-line backups with snapshots of the filesystem at regular, tunable intervals. This feature enables safe backups to be made of an active filesystem and is one of the important advantages of using a dedicated file server.

Verify your media

We've heard many horror stories about system administrators who did not discover problems with their dump regime until after a serious system failure. It is essential that you continually monitor your backup procedure and verify that it is functioning correctly. Operator error ruins more dumps than any other problem.

The first check is to have your backup software attempt to reread tapes immediately after it has finished dumping.[2] Scanning a tape to verify that it contains the expected number of files is a good check. It's best if every tape is scanned, but this no longer seems practical for a large organization that uses hundreds of tapes a day. A random sample would be most prudent in this environment.

See page 173 for more information about restore.

It is often useful to generate a table of contents for each filesystem (**dump** users can use **restore -t**) and to store the results on disk. These catalogs should be named in a way that relates them to the appropriate tape; for example, **okra:usr.Jan.13**. A week's worth of these records makes it easy to discover what piece of media a lost file is on. You just **grep** for the filename and pick the newest instance.

In addition to providing a catalog of tapes, successfully reading the table of contents from the tape is a good indication that the dump is OK and that you will probably be able to read the media when you need to. A quick attempt to restore a random file gives you even more confidence in your ability to restore from that piece of media.[3]

You should periodically attempt to restore from random media to make sure that restoration is still possible. Every so often, try to restore from an old (months or years) piece of dump media. Tape drives have been known to wander out of alignment over time and become unable to read their old tapes. The media can be recovered by a company that specializes in this service, but it is expensive.

A related check is to verify that you can read the media on hardware other than your own. If your machine room burns, it does not do much good to know that the backup

---

2. You can use **restore -C** to verify a dump tape against a directory tree.
3. For example, **restore -t** reads only the table of contents for the dump, which is stored at the beginning of the tape. When you actually restore a file, you are testing a more extensive region of the media.

could have been read on a tape drive that has now been destroyed. DAT tapes have been particularly susceptible to this problem in the past but more recent versions of the technology have improved.

Develop a media life cycle

All media has a finite life. It's great to recycle your media, but be sure to abide by the manufacturer's recommendations regarding the life of the media. Most tape manufacturers quantify this life in terms of the number of passes that a tape can stand: a backup, a restore, and an **mt fsf** (file skip forward) each represent one pass. Nontape technologies have a much longer life that is sometimes expressed in mean-time-to-failure (MTTF).

Before you toss your old tapes in the trash, remember to erase or render them unreadable. A bulk tape eraser (a large electromagnet) can help with this, but be sure to keep it far, far away from computers and active media. Cutting or pulling out part of a backup tape does not really do much to protect your data, because tape is easy to splice or respool. Document-destruction companies shred tapes for a fee.

Design your data for backups

With disks so cheap and new storage architectures so reliable, it's tempting not to back up all your data. A sensible storage architecture—designed rather than grown willy nilly as disk needs increase—can do a lot to make backups more tractable. Start by taking an inventory of your storage needs:

- The various kinds of data your site deals with
- The expected volatility of each type of data
- The backup frequency you require to feel comfortable with potential losses
- The political boundaries over which the data are spread

Use this information to design your site's storage architecture with backups and potential growth in mind. Keeping project directories and users' home directories on a dedicated file server can make it easier to manage your data and ensure its safety.

Prepare for the worst

After you have established a backup procedure, explore the worst case scenario: your site is completely destroyed. Determine how much data would be lost and how long it would take to get your system back to life (include the time it would take to acquire new hardware). Then determine whether you can live with your answers.

9.2 BACKUP DEVICES AND MEDIA

Many failures can damage several pieces of hardware at once, so backups should be written to some sort of removable media. Backing up one hard disk to another on the same machine provides little protection against a controller failure, although it is certainly better than no backup at all. Companies that back up your data over the

Internet are becoming more popular for organizations that encrypt their data, but most backups are still stored locally.

Many kinds of media store data by using magnetic particles. These media are subject to damage by electrical and magnetic fields. You should beware of the following sources of magnetic fields: audio speakers, transformers and power supplies, unshielded electric motors, disk fans, CRT monitors, and even prolonged exposure to the Earth's background radiation. All magnetic tapes eventually become unreadable over a period of years. Most tape media will keep for three years, but if you plan to store data longer than that, you should either use another medium or rerecord the data onto tape.

The following sections describe some of the media that can be used for backups. The media are presented in rough order of increasing capacity.

Manufacturers like to specify their hardware capacities in terms of compressed data; they often optimistically assume a compression ratio of 2:1 or more. In the sections below, we ignore compression in favor of the actual number of bytes that can physically be stored on each piece of media.

The compression ratio also affects a drive's throughput rating. If a drive can physically write 1 MB/s to tape but the manufacturer assumes 2:1 compression, the throughput magically rises to 2 MB/s. As with capacity figures, we have ignored throughput inflation below.

Although cost and media capacity are both important considerations, it's important to consider throughput as well. Fast media are more pleasant to deal with, and they allow more flexibility in scheduling backups.

In the previous edition of this book we mentioned floppy disks, both traditional and supercapacity (e.g., Zip disks), as potential backup media. These media had their heyday, but since you can hardly buy a laptop with a floppy drive any longer, we now exclude these items from our list. Although floppies are useful for exchanging data, their high media cost make them a poor choice for backups.

Optical media: CD-R/RW, DVD±R/RW, and DVD-RAM

At a cost of about $0.40 each, CDs and DVDs are an attractive option for backups of small, isolated systems. CDs hold about 650MB and DVDs hold 4.7GB. Dual-layer DVDs, which are just becoming mainstream, clock in at about 8.5GB.

Drives that write these media are available for every common bus (SCSI, IDE, USB, etc.) and are in many cases are so inexpensive as to be essentially free. CD media used to be free as well, but the glut seems to be over. Now that CD and DVD prices have equilibrated, there's no reason to use CDs rather than DVDs except that CD readers are still more common in the world at large.

Optical media are written through a photochemical process that involves the use of a laser. Although hard data on longevity has been elusive, it is widely believed that optical media have a substantially longer shelf life than magnetic media. However, even the write-once versions (CD-R, DVD-R, and DVD+R) are not as durable as manufactured (stamped) CDs and DVDs.

CD-R is not a particularly good choice for normal backups, but it's good for archiving data you might want to recover a long time in the future. CD-RW works well for regularly archiving small amounts of personal data.

Today's fast DVD writers offer speeds as fast as—if not faster than—tape drives. The write-once versions are DVD-R (developed by Pioneer in 1997) and DVD+R (developed by a coalition in 2002). DVD-RW, DVD+RW, and DVD-RAM are rewritable. The DVD-RAM system has built-in defect management and is therefore more reliable than other optical media. On the other hand, it is much more expensive.

Manufacturers estimate a potential life span of hundreds of years for these media if they are properly stored. Their recommendations for proper storage include individual cases, storage at a constant temperature in the range 41°–68°F with relative humidity of 30%–50%, no exposure to direct sunlight, and marking only with water-soluble markers. Under average conditions, a reliable shelf life of 1–5 years is probably more realistic.

As borne out by numerous third-party evaluations, the reliability of optical media has proved to be exceptionally manufacturer dependent. This is one case in which it pays to spend money on premium quality media. Unfortunately, quality varies from product to product even within a manufacturer's line, so there is no safe-bet manufacturer. In recent years Taiyo Yuden has topped the reliability charts, but only with media manufactured in Japan; Taiyo Yuden media manufactured in other countries has a less consistent record.

A recent entry to the optical data storage market is the Blu-Ray disc, whose various flavors store from 25–100 GB of data. The high capacity is a result of the short wavelength (405 nm) of the laser used to read and write the disks (hence the "blue" in Blu-Ray). The first players were available in the United States in June 2006. This is a technology worth watching and promises to become a good solution for backups.

Removable hard disks (USB and FireWire)

External storage devices that connect through a USB or FireWire (IEEE1394) ports have become common. The underlying storage technology is usually some form of hard disk, but flash memory devices are common at the low end (the ubiquitous "jump drives"). Capacities range from less than 1MB to 600GB and up. The limit on flash memory devices is currently about 4GB.

The main limitation of these drives is the speed of the bus, but with the release of USB 2.0 and FireWire 800, both flavors have achieved respectable throughput in the 50–90 MB/s range.

The lifetime of flash memory devices is mostly a function of the number of write cycles. Midrange drives supposedly allow several million cycles.

Small tape drives: 8mm and DDS/DAT

Various flavors of 8mm and DDS/DAT tape drives compose the low end of the tape storage market. Exabyte 8mm tape drives were early favorites, but the drives tended to become misaligned every 6–12 months, requiring a trip to the repair depot. It was not uncommon for tapes to be stretched in the transport mechanism and become unreliable. The 2–7 GB capacity of these tapes makes them inefficient for backing up today's desktop systems, let alone servers.

DDS/DAT (Digital Audio Tape) drives are helical scan devices that use 4mm cartridges. Although these drives are usually referred to as DAT drives, they are really DDS (Digital Data Storage) drives; the exact distinction is unimportant. The original format held about 2GB, but successive generations have significantly improved DDS capacity. The current generation (DAT 72) holds up to 32GB of data at a transfer rate of 3.5 MB/s. The tapes should last for 100 backups and are reported to have a shelf life of 10 years.

DLT/S-DLT

Digital Linear Tape/Super Digital Linear Tape is a mainstream backup medium. These drives are reliable, affordable, and capacious. They evolved from DEC's TK-50 and TK-70 cartridge tape drives. DEC sold the technology to Quantum, which popularized the drives by increasing their speed and capacity and by dropping their price. In 2002, Quantum acquired Super DLT, a technology by Benchmark Storage Innovations that tilts the recording head back and forth to reduce crosstalk between adjacent tracks.

Quantum now offers two hardware lines: a performance line and a value line. You get what you pay for. The tape capacities vary from DLT-4 at 800GB to DLT-4 in the value line at 160GB, with transfer rates of 60 MB/s and 10 MB/s, respectively. Manufacturers boast that the tapes will last 20 to 30 years—that is, if the hardware to read them still exists. How many 9-track tape drives are still functioning and on-line these days?

The downside of S-DLT is the price of media, which runs about $30–45 per tape. A bit pricey for a university; perhaps not for a Wall Street investment firm.

AIT and SAIT

Advanced Intelligent Tape is Sony's own 8mm product on steroids. In 1996, Sony dissolved its relationship with Exabyte and introduced the AIT-1, an 8mm helical scan device with twice the capacity of 8mm drives from Exabyte. Today, Sony offers a higher-capacity version of AIT-1 and their follow-on technology AIT-4, which claims capacity of 200GB and a 24 MB/s maximum transfer rate.

SAIT is Sony's half-height offering, which uses larger media and has greater capacity than AIT. SAIT tapes holds up to 500GB of data and sport a transfer rate of 30 MB/s. This product is most popular in the form of tape library offerings.

The Advanced Metal Evaporated (AME) tapes used in AIT and SAIT drives have a long life cycle. They also contain a built-in EEPROM that gives the media itself some smarts. Software support is needed to make any actual use of the EEPROM, however. Drive and tape prices are both roughly on a par with DLT.

VXA/VXA-X

Exabyte's current offerings include VXA and VXA-X technologies. The VXA drives use what Exabyte describes as a packet technology for data transfer. The VXA-X products still rely on Sony for the AME media; the V series is upgradable as larger-capacity media becomes available. The VXA and X series claim capacities in the range of 33–160 GB, with a transfer rate of 24 MB/s.

LTO

Linear Tape-Open was developed by IBM, HP, and Quantum as an alternative to the proprietary format of DLT. LTO-3, the latest version, has a 400GB capacity at a speed of 80 MB/s. LTO media has an estimated storage life of 30 years but is susceptible to magnetic exposure. The cost of media is about $80 for the 400GB tapes.

Jukeboxes, stackers, and tape libraries

With the low cost of disks these days, most sites have so much disk space that a full backup requires many tapes, even at 100GB per tape. One possible solution for these sites is a stacker, jukebox, or tape library.

A stacker is a simple tape changer that is used with a standard tape drive. It has a hopper that you load with tapes; it unloads full tapes as they are ejected from the drive and replaces them with blank tapes from the hopper. Most stackers hold about ten tapes.

A jukebox is a hardware device that can automatically change removable media in a limited number of drives, much like an old-style music jukebox that changed records on a single turntable. Jukeboxes are available for all the media discussed here. They are often bundled with special backup software that understands how to manipulate the changer. Storage Technology (now Sun Microsystems) and Sony are two large manufacturers of these products.

Tape libraries are a hardware backup solution for large data sets—terabytes, usually. They are large-closet-sized mechanisms with multiple tape drives (or CDs) and a robotic arm that retrieves and files media on the library's many shelves. As you can imagine, they are quite expensive to purchase and maintain, and they have special power, space, and air conditioning requirements. Most purchasers of tape libraries also purchase an operations contract from the manufacturer to optimize and run the device. The libraries have a software component, of course, which is what really runs the device. Storage Technology (Sun Microsystems) is a leading manufacturer of tape libraries.

Backups

Hard disks

The decreasing cost of hard drives makes disk-to-disk backups an attractive option to consider. Although we suggest that you not duplicate one disk to another within the same physical machine, hard disks can be a good, low-cost solution for backups over a network.

One obvious problem is that hard disk storage space is finite and must eventually be reused. However, disk-to-disk backups are an excellent way to protect against the accidental deletion of files. If you maintain a day-old disk image in a well-known place that's shared over NFS or CIFS, users can recover from their own mistakes without involving an administrator. Other popular options are today's high-volume FireWire and USB disks for backing up individual desktops. The Cintre ZDisc 1-Button Instant Backup is a 3.5" external USB 2.0 hard drive, an attractive option at around $100.

Summary of media types

Whew! That's a lot of possibilities. Table 9.1 summarizes the characteristics of the media discussed in the previous sections.

Table 9.1   Backup media compared

Medium	Capacity[a]	Speed[a]	Drive	Media	Cost/GB	Reuse?	Random?[b]
CD-R	650MB	4MB/s	$15	20¢	32¢	No	Yes
CD-RW	650MB	4MB/s	$20	30¢	48¢	Yes	Yes
DVD±R	4.7GB	10MB/s	$50	40¢	9¢	No	Yes
DVD+R DL[c]	8.5GB	10MB/s	$50	$2	24¢	No	Yes
DVD±RW	4.7GB	10MB/s	$50	80¢	17¢	Yes	Yes
DDS-4 (4mm)	20GB	10MB/s	$300	$5	25¢	Yes	No
DLT/S-DLT	160GB	10MB/s	$1,000	$20	13¢	Yes	No
AIT-4 (8mm)	200GB	6MB/s	$2,500	$40	20¢	Yes	No
SAIT-1	500GB	30MB/s	$6,500	$126	25¢	Yes	No
VXA-172	86GB	12MB/s	$600	$30	35¢	Yes	No
VXA-320	160GB	12MB/s	$800	$60	35¢	Yes	No
LTO-3	400GB	30MB/s	$3,000	$65	16¢	Yes	No

a. Uncompressed capacity and speed
b. Allows random access to any part of the media?
c. Dual-layer

W. Curtis Preston has compiled an excellent reference list of backup devices by manufacturer. It's available from www.backupcentral.com/hardware-drives.html.

What to buy

When you buy a backup system, you pretty much get exactly what you see in Table 9.1. All the media work reasonably well, and among the technologies that are close in price, there generally isn't a compelling reason to prefer one over another. Buy a system that meets your specifications and your budget.

DDS, AIT, and LTO drives are excellent solutions for small workgroups and for individual machines with a lot of storage. The startup costs are relatively modest, the media are widely available, and several manufacturers are using each standard. All of these systems are fast enough to back up beaucoup data in a finite amount of time.

DLT, AIT, and LTO-3 are all roughly comparable. There isn't a clear winner among the three, and even if there were, the situation would no doubt change within a few months as new versions of the formats were deployed. All of these formats are well established and would be easy to integrate into your environment, be it a university or corporation.

In the following sections, we use the generic term "tape" to refer to the media chosen for backups. Examples of backup commands are phrased in terms of tape devices.

9.3   SETTING UP AN INCREMENTAL BACKUP REGIME WITH DUMP

The **dump** and **restore** commands are the most common way to create and restore from backups. These programs have been around for a very long time, and their behavior is well known. At most sites, **dump** and **restore** are the underlying commands used by automated backup software.

You may have to explicitly install **dump** and **restore** on your Linux systems, depending on the options you selected during the original installation. A package is available for easy installation on all our example systems. The current Red Hat and Fedora Core releases offer a system administration package at installation time that includes **dump**.

Under Linux, nothing is statically linked, so you need the shared libraries in **/lib** to do anything useful. Static linking makes it easier to recover from a disaster because **restore** is then completely self-contained.

Dumping filesystems

dump builds a list of files that have been modified since a previous dump, then packs those files into a single large file to archive to an external device. **dump** has several advantages over most of the other utilities described in this chapter:

- Backups can span multiple tapes.
- Files of any type (even devices) can be backed up and restored.
- Permissions, ownerships, and modification times are preserved.
- Files with holes are handled correctly.[4]
- Backups can be performed incrementally (with only recently modified files being written out to tape).

4. Holes are blocks that have never contained data. If you open a file, write one byte, seek 1MB into the file, then write another byte, the resulting "sparse" file takes up only two disk blocks even though its logical size is much bigger. Files created by Berkeley DB or **ndbm** contain many holes.

Backups

The GNU version of **tar** used in Linux provides all these features as well. However, **dump**'s handling of incremental backups (discussed later) is a bit more sophisticated than **tar**'s. You may find the extra horsepower useful if your needs are complex.

Actually, the most compelling reason to choose **dump** over **tar** in a Linux environment has nothing to do with Linux at all. Unfortunately, the version of **tar** shipped with most major UNIX distributions lacks many of GNU **tar**'s features. If you must support backups for both Linux and UNIX variants, **dump** is your best choice. It is the only command that handles these issues (fairly) consistently across platforms, so you can be an expert in one command rather than being familiar with two. If you are lucky enough to be in a completely homogeneous Linux environment, pick your favorite. **dump** is less filling, but **tar** tastes great!

The **dump** command understands the layout of raw filesystems, and it reads a filesystem's inode table directly to decide which files must be backed up. This knowledge of the filesystem makes **dump** very efficient, but it also imposes a few limitations.[5]

See Chapter 16 for more information about NFS.

The first limitation is that every filesystem must be dumped individually. If you have a disk that is partitioned, you must dump each partition separately. The other limitation is that only filesystems on the local machine can be dumped; you cannot dump an NFS filesystem mounted from a remote machine. However, you can dump a local filesystem to a remote tape drive with **dump**'s evil twin, **rdump**.

The most important feature of **dump** is its support for the concept of an "incremental" backup. Although you could back up the entire system each day, doing so is usually not practical. With incremental dumps, you can back up only files that have changed since the last backup.

When you do a dump, you assign it a backup level, which is an integer from 0 to 9. A level N dump backs up all files that have changed since the last dump of level less than N. A level 0 backup places the entire filesystem on the tape. With an incremental backup system, you may have to restore files from several sets of backup tapes to reset a filesystem to the state it was in during the last backup.[6]

Another nice feature of **dump** is that it does not care about the length of filenames. Hierarchies can be arbitrarily deep, and long names are handled correctly.

The first argument to **dump** must be the incremental dump level. **dump** uses the **/etc/dumpdates** file to determine how far back an incremental dump must go. The **-u** flag causes **dump** to automatically update **/etc/dumpdates** when the dump completes. The date, dump level, and filesystem name are recorded. If you never use the **-u** flag, all dumps become level 0s because no record of having previously dumped the filesystem is ever created. If you change a filesystem's name, you can edit the **/etc/dumpdates** file by hand.

---

5. **dump** requires access to raw disk partitions. Anyone allowed to do dumps can read all the files on the system with a little work.

6. Actually, **dump** does not keep track of files that have been deleted. If you restore from incremental backups, deleted files are recreated.

See page 870 for information about device numbers.

dump sends its output to some default device, usually the primary tape drive. To specify a different device, use the **-f** flag. If you are placing multiple dumps on a single tape, make sure you specify a nonrewinding tape device (a device file that does not cause the tape to be rewound when it is closed—most tape drives have both a standard and a nonrewinding device entry).[7] For the system's first SCSI tape drive, Linux uses **/dev/st0** for the rewinding device and **/dev/nst0** for the nonrewinding device.

If you choose the rewinding device by accident, you end up saving only the last filesystem dumped. Since **dump** does not have any idea where the tape is positioned, this mistake does not cause errors. The situation only becomes apparent when you try to restore files.

When you use **rdump** to dump to a remote system, you specify the identity of the remote tape drive as *hostname:device*; for example,

```
# rdump -0u -f anchor:/dev/nst0 /spare
```

Permission to access remote tape drives should be controlled through an SSH tunnel. See page 697 for more information.

In the past, you had to tell **dump** exactly how long your tapes were so that it could stop writing before it ran off the end of a tape. Modern tape drives can tell when they have reached the end of a tape and report that fact back to **dump**, which then rewinds and ejects the current tape and requests a new one. Since the variability of hardware compression makes the "virtual length" of each tape somewhat indeterminate, it's always best to rely on the end-of-tape indication if your hardware supports it. If not, you can specify the tape length in kilobytes with the **-B** option.

```
# dump -5u -B 2000000 -f /dev/nst0 /work
DUMP: Date of this level 5 dump: Wed May  8 16:59:45 2006
DUMP: Date of last level 0 dump: the epoch
DUMP: Dumping /dev/hda2 (/work) to /dev/nst0
DUMP: mapping (Pass I) [regular files]
DUMP: mapping (Pass II) [directories]
DUMP: estimated 18750003 tape blocks on .23 tape(s)
....
```

The flags **-5u** are followed by the flags **-B** (length of the tape: 20 GB) and **-f** (tape device: **/dev/nst0**). The last argument, which is mandatory, is the name of the filesystem to be dumped (**/work**).

Dump sequences

Because dump levels have meaning only in relation to other levels, dumps can be performed according to various schedules.

---

7. All the entries for a tape unit use the same major device number. The minor device number tells the tape device driver about special behaviors (rewinding, byte swapping, etc.).

Backups

The schedule that is right for you depends on:

- The activity of your filesystems
- The capacity of your dump device
- The amount of redundancy you want
- The number of tapes you want to buy

In the days when it took many tapes to back up a filesystem, complicated dump sequences were useful for minimizing the number of tapes consumed by each day's backups. As tape capacities have grown, it has become less useful to make fine distinctions among dump levels.

Because most files never change, even the simplest incremental schedule eliminates many files from the daily dumps. As you add additional levels to your dump schedule, you divide the relatively few active files into smaller and smaller segments.

A complex dump schedule provides the following three benefits:

- You can back up data more often, limiting your potential losses.
- You can use fewer daily tapes (or fit everything on one tape).
- You can keep multiple copies of each file, to protect against tape errors.

In general, the way to select a sequence is to determine your needs in each of these areas. Given these constraints, you can design a schedule at the appropriate level of sophistication. We describe a couple of possible sequences and the motivation behind them. One of them might be right for your site—or, your needs might dictate a completely different schedule.

A simple schedule

If your total amount of disk space is smaller than the capacity of your tape device, you can use a completely trivial dump schedule. Do level 0 dumps of every filesystem each day. Reuse a group of tapes, but every N days (where N is determined by your site's needs), keep the tape forever. This scheme costs you

$$(365/N) * (\text{price of tape})$$

per year. Don't reuse the exact same tape for every night's dump. It's better to rotate among a set of tapes so that even if one night's dump is blown, you can still fall back to the previous night.

This schedule guarantees massive redundancy and makes data recovery easy. It's a good solution for a site with lots of money but limited operator time (or skill). From a safety and convenience perspective, this schedule is the ideal. Don't stray from it without a specific reason (e.g., to conserve tapes or labor).

A moderate schedule

A more reasonable schedule for most sites is to assign a tape to each day of the week, each week of the month (you'll need 5), and each month of the year. Every day, do a level 9 dump to the daily tape. Every week, do a level 5 dump to the weekly tape. And every month, do a level 3 dump to the monthly tape. Do a level 0 dump whenever the incrementals get too big to fit on one tape, which is most likely to happen on a monthly tape. Do a level 0 dump at least once a year.

The choice of levels 3, 5, and 9 is arbitrary. You could use levels 1, 2, and 3 with the same effect. However, the gaps between dump levels give you some breathing room if you later decide you want to add another level of dumps.

This schedule requires 24 tapes plus however many tapes are needed for the level 0 dumps. Although it does not require too many tapes, it also does not afford much redundancy.

9.4 RESTORING FROM DUMPS WITH RESTORE

The program that extracts data from tapes written with **dump** is called **restore**. We first discuss restoring individual files (or a small set of files), then explain how to restore entire filesystems.

Restoring individual files

The first step to take when you are notified of a lost file is to determine which tapes contain versions of the file. Users often want the most recent version of a file, but that is not always the case. For example, a user who loses a file by inadvertently copying another file on top of it would want the version that existed before the incident occurred. It's helpful if you can browbeat users into telling you not only what files are missing but also when they were lost and when they were last modified. We find it helpful to structure users' responses with a request form.

If you do not keep on-line catalogs, you must mount tapes and repeatedly attempt to restore the missing files until you find the correct tape. If the user remembers when the files were last changed, you may be able to make an educated guess about which tapes the files might be on.

After determining which tapes you want to extract from, create and **cd** to a temporary directory such as **/var/restore** where a large directory hierarchy can be created; most versions of **restore** must create all the directories leading to a particular file before that file can be restored. Do not use **/tmp**—your work could be wiped out if the machine crashes and reboots before the restored data has been moved to its original location.

The **restore** command has many options. Most useful are -**i** for interactive restores of individual files and directories and -**r** for a complete restore of an entire filesystem. You might also need -**x**, which requests a noninteractive restore of specified files— be careful not to overwrite existing files.

restore -**i** reads the table of contents from the tape and then lets you navigate through it as you would a normal directory tree, using commands called **ls**, **cd**, and **pwd**. You mark the files that you want to restore with the **add** command. When you finish selecting, type **extract** to pull the files off the tape.

Backups

*See page 178 for a description of **mt**.*

If you placed multiple files on a single tape, you must use the **mt** command to position the tape at the correct dump file before running **restore**. Remember to use the nonrewinding device!

For example, to restore the file **/users/janet/iamlost** from a remote tape drive, you might issue the following commands. Let's assume that you have found the right tape, mounted it on **tapehost:/dev/nst0,** and determined that the filesystem containing janet's home directory is the fourth one on the tape.

```
# mkdir /var/restore
# cd /var/restore
# ssh tapehost mt -f /dev/nst0 fsf 3
# rrestore -i -f tapehost:/dev/nst0
restore> ls
.:
janet/  garth/  lost+found/  lynda/
restore> cd janet
restore> ls
afile bfile cfile iamlost
restore> add iamlost
restore> ls8
afile bfile cfile iamlost*
restore> extract
You have not read any volumes yet.
Unless you know which volume your files are on you should
start with the last volume and work towards the first.
Specify next volume #: 1
set owner/mode for '.'? [yn] n
```

Volumes (tapes) are enumerated starting at 1, not 0, so for a dump that fits on a single tape, you specify 1. When **restore** asks if you want to set the owner and mode for "·", it's asking whether it should set the current directory to match the root of the tape. Unless you are restoring an entire filesystem, you probably do not want to do this.

Once the **restore** has completed, you need to give the file to janet:

```
# cd /var/restore
# ls janet
iamlost
# ls ~janet
afile bfile cfile
# cp -p janet/iamlost ~janet/iamlost.restored
# chown janet ~janet/iamlost.restored
# rm -rf /var/restore
# mail janet
Your file iamlost has been restored as requested and has
been placed in /users/janet/iamlost.restored.

Your name, Humble System Administrator
```

---

8. The star next to **iamlost** indicates that it has been marked for extraction.

Some administrators prefer to restore files into a special directory, allowing users to copy their files out by hand. In that scheme, the administrator must protect the privacy of the restored files by verifying their ownership and permissions. If you choose to use such a system, remember to clean out the directory every so often.

If you created a backup with **rdump** and are unable to restore files from it with **restore**, try running **rrestore** instead. To minimize the chance of problems, use the same host that wrote the tape to read it.

restore -i is usually the easiest way to restore a few files or directories from a dump. However, it does not work if the tape device cannot be moved backwards a record at a time (a problem with some 8mm drives). If **restore -i** fails, try **restore -x** before jumping out the window. **restore -x** requires you to specify the complete path of the file you want to restore (relative to the root of the dump) on the command line. The following sequence of commands repeats the previous example, but with **-x**:

```
# mkdir /var/restore
# cd /var/restore
# ssh tapehost mt -f /dev/nst0 fsf 3
# rrestore -x -f tapehost:/dev/nst0 ./janet/iamlost
```

Restoring entire filesystems

With luck, you will never have to restore an entire filesystem after a system failure. However, the situation does occasionally arise. Before attempting to restore the filesystem, be absolutely sure that whatever problem caused the filesystem to be destroyed in the first place has been taken care of. It's pointless to spend numerous hours spinning tapes only to lose the filesystem once again.

Before you begin a full restore, create and mount the target filesystem. See Chapter 7, *Adding a Disk*, for more information about how to prepare the filesystem. To start the restore, **cd** to the mount point of the new filesystem, put the first tape of the most recent level 0 dump in the tape drive, and type **restore -r**.

restore prompts for each tape in the dump. After the level 0 dump has been restored, mount and restore the incremental dumps. Restore incremental dumps in the order in which they were created. Because of redundancy among dumps, it may not be necessary to restore every incremental. Here's the algorithm for determining which dumps to restore:

Step 1: Restore the most recent level 0 dump.

Step 2: Restore the lowest-level dump made after the dump you just restored. If multiple dumps were made at that level, restore the most recent one.

Step 3: If that was the last dump that was ever made, you are done.

Step 4: Otherwise, go back to step 2.

Backups

Here are some examples of dump sequences. You would need to restore only the levels shown in boldface.

0 0 0 0 0 **0**
0 **5** 5 5 **5**
0 **3** 2 5 4 **5**
0 **9**9599**3**99599
0 **3** 5 9 **3** 5 9

*See Chapter 7 for more information about **mke2fs** and **mount**.*

Let's take a look at a complete command sequence. If the most recent dump was the first monthly after the annual level 0 in the "moderate" schedule on page 172, the commands to restore **/home**, residing on the physical device **/dev/sda1**, would look like this (the device names are hardware dependent):

```
# /etc/mke2fs -j /dev/sda1 QUANTUM_PD1050S
# /etc/mount /dev/sda1 /home
# cd /home
/* Mount first tape of level 0 dump of /home. */
# restore -r
/* Mount the tapes requested by restore. */
/* Mount first tape of level 3 monthly dump. */
# restore -r
```

If you had multiple filesystems on one dump tape, use the **mt** command to skip forward to the correct filesystem before running each **restore**. See page 178 for a description of **mt**.

This sequence would restore the filesystem to the state it was in when the level 3 dump was done, except that all deleted files would be ghoulishly resurrected. This problem can be especially nasty when you are restoring an active filesystem or are restoring to a disk that is nearly full. It is quite possible for a **restore** to fail because the filesystem has been filled up with ghost files.

9.5 DUMPING AND RESTORING FOR UPGRADES

We recommend that when you perform a major OS upgrade, you back up all filesystems with a level 0 dump and, possibly, restore them. The restore is needed only if the new OS uses a different filesystem format or if you change the partitioning of your disks. However, you *must* do backups as insurance against any problems that might occur during the upgrade. A complete set of backups also gives you the option to reinstall the old OS if the new version does not prove satisfactory. Fortunately, with the progressive upgrade systems used by most distributions these days, you are unlikely to need these tapes.

Be sure to back up and restore any system-specific files that are in the root filesystem or in **/usr**, such as **/etc/passwd**, **/etc/shadow**, or **/usr/local**. Linux's directory organization mixes local files with vendor-distributed files, making it quite difficult to pick out your local customizations.

You should do a complete set of level 0 dumps immediately after an upgrade, too. Most vendors' upgrade procedures set the modification dates of system files to the time when they were mastered rather than to the current time. Ergo, incremental dumps made relative to the pre-upgrade level 0 are not sufficient to restore your system to its post-upgrade state in the event of a crash.

9.6   USING OTHER ARCHIVING PROGRAMS

dump is not the only program you can use to archive files to tapes; however, it is usually the most efficient way to back up an entire system. **tar**, **cpio**, and **dd** can also move files from one medium to another.

tar: package files

tar reads multiple files or directories and packages them into one file, often a tape file. **tar** is a useful way to back up any files whose near-term recovery you anticipate. For instance, if a user is leaving for six months and the system is short of disk space, you can use **tar** to put the user's files on a tape and then remove them from the disk.

tar is also useful for moving directory trees from place to place, especially if you are copying files as root. **tar** preserves ownership and time information, but only if you ask it to. For example,

```
tar -cf - fromdir | ( cd todir ; tar --atime-preserve -xpf - )
```

creates a copy of the directory tree *fromdir* in *todir*. Avoid using ".." in the *todir* argument, since symbolic links and automounters can make it mean something different from what you expect. We've been bitten several times.

tar does not follow symbolic links by default, but it can be told to follow them. **tar** can also be told to include only files that were modified since a given date, a useful option for creating your own incremental backup scheme. Consult the **tar** man page for this and other nifty features.

One problem with some non-Linux versions of **tar** is that pathnames are limited by default to 100 characters. This restriction prevents **tar** from archiving deep hierarchies. If you're creating **tar** archives on your Linux systems and exchanging them with others, remember that people with the standard **tar** may not be able to read the tapes or files you create.

tar's **-b** option lets you specify a "blocking factor" to use when writing a tape. The blocking factor is specified in 512-byte blocks; it determines how much data **tar** buffers internally before performing a write operation. Some DAT devices do not work correctly unless the blocking factor is set to a special value, but other drives do not require this setting.

On some systems, certain blocking factors may yield better performance than others. The optimal blocking factor varies widely, depending on the computer and tape drive

Backups

hardware. In many cases, you will not notice any difference in speed. When in doubt, try a blocking factor of 20.

Linux **tar** expands holes in files unless you use the **-S** option when creating the original archive. Linux **tar** is relatively intolerant of tape errors.

cpio: archiving utility from ancient times

cpio is similar to **tar** in functionality. It dates from the beginning of time and is not used much any longer.

Like **tar**, **cpio** can move directory trees. The command

    find *fromdir* **-depth -print | cpio -pdm** *todir*

makes a copy of the directory tree *fromdir* in *todir*. The GNU version of **cpio** used in Linux allows multiple tape volumes, but most versions do not. Only the superuser can copy special files. Even if you are familiar with **cpio** from another system, we recommend that you review the man page carefully because the options vary greatly among systems.

dd: twiddle bits

dd is a file copying and conversion program. Unless it is told to do some sort of conversion, **dd** just copies from its input file to its output file. If a user brings you a tape that was written on some non-Linux system, **dd** may be the only way to read it.

One historical use for **dd** was to create a copy of an entire filesystem. However, a better option these days is to **mke2fs** the destination filesystem and then run **dump** piped to **restore**. **dd** can sometimes clobber partitioning information if used incorrectly. It can only copy filesystems between partitions of exactly the same size.

dd can also be used to make a copy of a magnetic tape. With two tape drives, say, **/dev/st0** and **/dev/st1**, you'd use the command

```
$ dd if=/dev/st0 of=/dev/st1 cbs=16b
```

With one drive (**/dev/st0**), you'd use the following sequence:

```
$ dd if=/dev/st0 of=tfile cbs=16b
/* Change tapes. */
$ dd if=tfile of=/dev/st0 cbs=16b
$ rm tfile
```

Of course, if you have only one tape drive, you must have enough disk space to store an image of the entire tape.

9.7 USING MULTIPLE FILES ON A SINGLE TAPE

In reality, a magnetic tape contains one long string of data. However, it's often useful to store more than one "thing" on a tape, so tape drives and their Linux drivers conspire to provide you with a bit more structure. When **dump** or some other command writes a stream of bytes out to a tape device and then closes the device file, an end-of-file marker is automatically placed on the tape. This marker separates the stream from other streams that are written subsequently. When the stream is read back in, reading stops automatically at the EOF.

You can use the **mt** command to position a tape at a particular stream or "file set," as **mt** calls them. **mt** is especially useful if you put multiple files (for example, multiple dumps) on a single tape. It also has some of the most interesting error messages of any Linux utility. The basic format of the command is

> **mt** [**-f** *tapename*] *command* [*count*]

There are numerous choices for *command*. They vary from platform to platform, so we discuss only the ones that are essential for doing backups and restores:

rew	rewinds the tape to the beginning.
offl	puts the tape off-line. On most tape drives, this command causes the tape to rewind and pop out of the drive. Most scripts use this command to eject the tape when they are done, clearly indicating that everything finished correctly.
status	prints information about the current state of the tape drive (whether a tape is loaded, etc.).
fsf [*count*]	fast-forwards the tape. If no *count* is specified, **fsf** skips forward one file. With a numeric argument, it skips the specified number of files. Use this command to skip forward to the correct filesystem on a tape with multiple dumps.
bsf [*count*]	should backspace *count* files. The exact behavior of this directive depends on the tape drive hardware and its associated driver. In some situations, the current file is counted. In others, it is not. On some equipment, **bsf** does nothing silently. If you go too far forward on a tape, your best bet is to run **mt rew** on it and start again from the beginning.

Consult the **mt** man page for a list of all the supported commands.

If you're fortunate enough to have a robotic tape library, you may be able to control its tape changer by installing the **mtx** package, an enhanced version of the **mt** command. For example, we use it for unattended tape swapping with our groovy HP 6x24 DAT tape cartridge system. Look ma, no hands!

9.8 BACULA

Bacula is an enterprise level client/server backup solution that manages backup, recovery, and verification of files over a network. Bacula runs on a variety of UNIX and Linux systems, including all our example distributions. It also backs up data from multiple operating systems, including Microsoft Windows.

Backups

In the previous edition of this book, Amanda was our favorite noncommercial backup tool. If you need Amanda information, see the first edition of this book or www.amanda.org. The feature list below explains why Bacula is our new favorite.

- It has a modular design.
- It backs up UNIX, Linux, and Windows systems.
- It supports MySQL, PostgreSQL, or SQLite for its back-end database.
- It supports an easy-to-use, menu-driven command-line console.
- It's available under an open source license.
- Its backups can span multiple tape volumes.
- Its servers can run on multiple platforms.
- It creates SHA1 or MD5 signature files for each backed-up file.
- It verifies backup jobs.
- It supports tape libraries and autochangers.
- It can execute scripts or commands before and after backup jobs.
- It centralizes backup management for an entire network.

The Bacula model

To deploy Bacula, you should understand its major components. Exhibit A illustrates Bacula's general architecture.

Exhibit A   Bacula components and their relationships

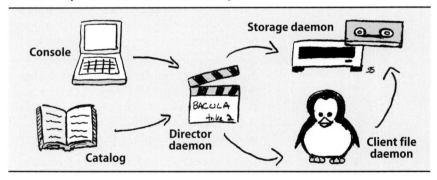

The Bacula director is the daemon that coordinates backup, restore, and verification operations. You can submit backup or restore jobs to the director daemon by using the Bacula console. You can also ask the director daemon to query the Bacula storage daemon or the file service daemons located on client computers.

You communicate with the director daemon through the Bacula console, which can be run either as a GNOME GUI or as a command-line tool. The console can run anywhere; it doesn't have to be located on the same computer as the director daemon.

A storage daemon is the Bacula component that reads and writes tapes or other backup media. This service must run on the machine that is connected to the tape drive or storage device used for backups, but it does not have to be installed on the same server as the director (although it can be).

A Bacula file daemon runs on each system that is to be backed up. File daemon implementations for each supported operating system send the appropriate file data and attributes to the storage daemon as backup jobs are executed.

The final Bacula component is the catalog, a relational database in which Bacula stores information about every file and volume that is backed up. The catalog makes Bacula fast and efficient during a restore because the entire backup history is available on-line; Bacula knows what storage volumes are needed to restore a particular file set before it reads a single tape. Bacula currently supports three different databases: MySQL, PostgreSQL, and SQLite. The catalog database need not reside on the same server as the director.

An additional, optional component is the Bacula Rescue CD-ROM. This component is a separately downloadable package that creates individualized, bootable rescue CDs for Linux systems to use during disaster recovery. The CDs contain a statically linked copy of the system's file daemon as well as customized shell scripts that incorporate configuration information about the system's disks, kernel, and network interfaces. If a Linux system has a catastrophic failure, you can use its rescue CD to boot the system, repartition the disk, and connect to the Bacula director to perform a full system restore over the network.

Setting up Bacula

Because of Bacula's complexity, advanced feature set, and modular design, there are many ways to set up a site-wide backup scheme. In this section we walk through a basic Bacula configuration.

In general, five steps get Bacula up and running:

- Install a supported third-party database and the Bacula daemons.
- Configure the Bacula daemons.
- Install and configure the client file daemons.
- Start the Bacula daemons.
- Add media to media pools with the Bacula console.

Our example setup consists of two machines, harp and bull. The machine harp is the client; it runs only a file daemon. The remaining four Bacula components (director daemon, storage daemon, catalog, and console) all run on the server bull. The storage device is a SureStore LTO1 tape library. Our backup schedule consists of weekly full backups followed by daily incremental backups. MySQL is used for the catalog.

Installing the database and Bacula daemons

Before we can install Bacula, we must first install the back-end database for its catalog. For easiest integration with Bacula, we recommend MySQL with its default configuration paths.

Stability and reliability are a must when dealing with a backup platform, so once you have installed the database, we recommend that you download and install the latest stable source code from the Bacula web site. Step-by-step installation documentation is included with the source code in the **docs** directory. The documentation is also on-line at www.bacula.org, where it is available in both HTML or PDF format. Helpful tutorials and developer guides can also be found there.

After unpacking the source code, we ran

> **./configure --with-mysql --prefix=/etc/bacula**

followed by **make** to compile the binaries, and finally **make install** to complete the installation.

Once Bacula has been installed, the next step is to create the actual MySQL database and the data tables inside it. We made sure MySQL was running, then **cd**'ed to the installation directory (**/etc/bacula**) and ran three shell scripts that were created as part of the **make install** procedure. The **grant_mysql_privileges** script grants the Bacula user access privileges to MySQL. The **create_mysql_database** script creates the Bacula database, and finally, the **make_mysql_tables** script populates the database with the required tables.

Configuring the Bacula daemons

Before we begin a more detailed discussion of our example setup, we first define some key Bacula terms:

- "Jobs" are the unit of Bacula activity. They come in two flavors: backup and restore.

- "Pools" are groups of physical media that store jobs. Our example configuration uses two pools, one for full backups and another for incrementals.

- "Filesets" are lists of partitions and files. Filesets can be explicitly included or excluded in backup or restore jobs.

- The "bootstrap" file is a special text file, created by Bacula, that contains information about files that should be restored. Bootstrap files are created during the restore command or during a backup if the Write Bootstrap parameter is defined for the backup job.

- "Messages" are inter-daemon communications (log entries, really) regarding the status of daemons and jobs. Messages can also be sent by email and written to log files.

The config files reside in the directory specified with the **--prefix** option during installation, typically **/etc/bacula**. In the next sections, we cover the options for the director daemon (**bacula-dir.conf**), the storage daemon (**bacula-sd.conf**), and the console (**bconsole.conf**).

We do not cover all the possible configuration parameters in our sample configuration files. Instead, we begin each section with a general overview and then point out some parameters that we think are either particularly useful or hard to grasp.

bacula-dir.conf: director configuration

The **bacula-dir.conf** file is the most complex of Bacula's configuration files. We look below at its ten logical sections: Director, Catalog, JobDefs, Job, FileSet, Schedule, Pool, Client, Storage, and Messages. More detailed information about each section and its parameters can be found in the on-line documentation.

Each resource section is enclosed in curly braces. Comments are introduced with a # sign in all Bacula configuration files.

```
# Sample Bacula director configuration file, /etc/bacula-dir.conf

Director {
    Name = bull-dir
    DIRport = 9101
    Query File = "/etc/bacula/query.sql"
    Working Directory = "/var/Bacula/working"
    Pid Directory = "/var/run"
    Maximum Concurrent Jobs = 1
    Password = "B@cu1@Lik3s,fRu17"
    Messages = Standard
}
```

The Director resource is more or less the mother ship of the Bacula sea. Its parameters define the name and basic behavior of the director. Options set the communication port through which the other daemons communicate with the director, the location in which the director stores its temporary files, and the number of concurrent jobs that the director can handle at once.

The Password parameter defines the password the console program uses to authenticate itself to the director. An identical password must be set in the Director resource of the console configuration file, **bconsole.conf**. Although the password appears in plaintext in the config files, it is never transmitted over the network.

In our example configuration, the director and console are hosted on the same machine. However, a password is still required in both configuration files.

```
# Generic catalog service

Catalog {
    Name = ATE
    DBName = bacula;
    user = bacula;
    password = "fRu17,B0wL"
}
```

The Catalog resource section identifies the database in which Bacula stores its operational records. For simplicity, we defined one catalog for all jobs. Bacula does support multiple catalogs, however, and this feature is useful if you prefer to maintain a separate database for each client group. Currently, all catalog databases must reside within the same physical database server.

The DBName parameter is the name of the catalog database. This database is set up during installation according to the database options passed to **configure**. Bacula's prebuilt database creation scripts can be found in the **src/cats** directory of the Bacula source code distribution.

```
# Job definitions

Job {
    Name = "harp"
    Level = Full
    Write Bootstrap = "/atrust/admin/backups/bootstraps/harp.bsr"
    Client = harp
    File Set = harp
    Storage = SureStore
    Pool = SSFullPool
    Incremental Backup Pool = SSIncrementalPool
    Schedule = Nightly
}
```

A Job resource defines the default parameters for a particular backup job. In general, there is one Job definition per client. Most of the parameters are self-explanatory, but a few merit additional discussion.

Write Bootstrap tells Bacula where to write bootstrap information about the backup for use during a restore. Bootstrap files list the files and volumes needed for a restore job. They are not mandatory but are highly recommended. Bootstrap files are overwritten during full backups and appended during incremental backups.

The Client, File Set, Storage, Pool, and Schedule parameters are all forward references to resources defined later in the **bacula-dir.conf** file.

```
# File set definitions

FileSet {
    Name = "harp"
    Include {
        Options {
            signature=MD5
            compression=GZIP
        }
        File = "/"
        File = "/boot"
        File = "/usr"
        File = "/usr/local"
        File = "/var"
    }
    Exclude = { /proc /tmp /.journal /.fsck }
}
```

A FileSet resource defines the files and directories to be included in or excluded from a backup job. Each file set can define multiple Include and Exclude parameters along with individual Options. By default, Bacula recursively backs up directories but does not span partitions. Take care to list all the partitions you want to back up in separate File parameters.

Many additional Options are supported, including regular expressions and wild card characters. Two noteworthy options are signature (set to SHA1 or MD5), which computes a hash value for each file backed up, and compression, which compresses data before writing it to tape. The signature option increases the CPU overhead for backups but may prove valuable during a suspected security incident.

```
Schedule {
    Name = "Nightly"
    Run = Level=Full Pool=SSFullPool 1st-5th tue at 20:10
    Run = Level=Incremental Pool=SSIncrementalPool wed-mon at 20:10
}
```

Schedule resources define timetables for backup jobs. The Name parameter and at least one Run parameter are needed for automatic backup jobs, but multiple Run parameters may be included in a single Schedule. Here, the full backups run on the first and fifth Tuesday of each month at 8:10 p.m., and the incremental backups run every week from Wednesday through Monday at 8:10 p.m.

The date and time specifications are the only required part of the Run parameter, but as you can see from this example, you can sneak in additional parameter values. These values then override the default parameters set in the Job specification. Here, we set the backup Level and media Pool to use for each backup.

Refer to the on-line Bacula documentation for a complete list of date/time specification keywords and job parameters.

```
# Pool definitions -- first pool is default

Pool {
    Name = SSFullPool
    Pool Type = Backup
    Recycle = yes
    Accept Any Volume = yes
}
Pool {
    Name = SSIncrementalPool
    Pool Type = Backup
    Recycle = yes
    Accept Any Volume = yes
}
```

The Pool resource groups backup media, typically tapes, into sets that are used by specific backup jobs. In this example we run weekly full backups and daily incrementals, so we created two Pool resources. Many options tweak the behavior of the Pool

Backups

resource; two particularly useful parameters are Recycle and Accept Any Volume. If the Recycle parameter is set to yes, Bacula automatically uses purged volumes whose recycle flag is set when it needs an appendable volume for a backup job. The Accept Any Volume parameter specifies whether Bacula can write to any appendable volume within the pool. If this option is set to no, Bacula fills volumes sequentially and does not accept an appendable volume out of sequence.

```
Client {
    Name = harp
    Address = 192.168.7.2
    FDPort = 9102
    Catalog = ATE
    Password = "Ch@ch1s@Fru17"
    File Retention = 3 months
    Job Retention = 36 months
    AutoPrune = yes
}
```

Client resources identify the computers to be backed up. One is required for each computer. The File Retention and Job Retention parameters specify how long file and job records for this client are kept in the catalog. If the AutoPrune parameter is set, then expired data is deleted from the catalog. Pruning affects only the catalog records and not the actual files stored on backup tapes.

```
# Definition of file storage devices

Storage {
    Name = SureStore
    Address = bull.atrust.com
    SDPort = 9103
    Password = "Fru1t&V3gg1es"
    Device = SureStoreDevice
    Autochanger = yes
    Media Type = LTO1
}
```

The Storage resource describes how to communicate with the storage daemon, which controls the backup devices. In our example, we have a SureStore LTO1 tape library connected to our primary Bacula server (bull.atrust.com). The storage daemon has its own configuration file that is reviewed below.

```
Messages {
    Name = Standard
    mailcommand = "/sbin/bsmtp -h localhost -f \"\(Bacula\)
        bacula@atrust.com\" -s \"Bacula: %t %e of %c %l\" %r"
    operatorcommand = "/sbin/bsmtp -h localhost -f \"\(Bacula\)
        bacula@atrust.com\" -s \"Bacula: Intervention needed for %j\" %r"
    mail = Bacula@atrust.com = all, !skipped
    operator = bacula-pager@atrust.com = mount
    console = all, !skipped, !saved
    append = "/var/log/bacula.log" = all, !skipped
}
```

The Messages resource tells Bacula how to handle specific message types generated by each Bacula daemon. Multiple Messages resources can be defined and then assigned to specific jobs in their Job resources.

This resource type is very configurable; a complete list of variables and commands can be found in the on-line documentation. The configuration above sends information about the status of daemons and jobs to the console and to a standard log file, as well as distributing it through email.

bacula-sd.conf: storage daemon configuration

Storage daemons accept data from file daemons and transfer it to the actual storage media (or vice versa, in the case of a restore). Four resources must be defined within the **bacula-sd.conf** file: Storage, Device, Messages, and Director. Here is a complete example configuration:

```
# Storage daemon configuration file, bacula-sd.conf

Storage {
    Name = bull-sd
    SDPort = 9103
    Working Directory = "/var/bacula/working"
    Pid Directory = "/var/run"
}

Device {
    Name = SureStoreDevice
    Media Type = LTO1
    Archive Device = /dev/nst0
    Autochanger = yes
    Changer Device = /dev/sg0
    Changer Command = "/etc/bacula/mtx-changer %c %o %S %a %d"
    AutomaticMount = yes;
    Always Open = yes;
    Removable Media = yes;
    Random Access = no;
}

Messages {
    Name = Standard
    director = bull-dir = all
}

Director {
    Name = bull-dir
    Password = "Fru1t&V3gg1es"
}
```

A storage daemon configuration file must contain only one Storage resource.

These resources are relatively straightforward. They define some basic working parameters, such as the daemon's network port and working directory, and identify the director daemon to which the storage daemon should send messages.

The Device resource characterizes the actual backup device. In our case, it is an LTO (Linear Tape-Open) drive with an automatic tape changer. You can define multiple Device resources. The Archive Device parameter names the device file for the tape drive; note that **/dev/nst0** is a nonrewinding device, which is almost invariably what you want. The automatic tape changer has its own device file; in addition to specifying that, we also set the Autochanger parameter. The Always Open parameter tells Bacula to keep the device open unless an administrator specifically requests an unmount. This option saves time and tape stress because it avoids rewinding and positioning commands between jobs.

bconsole.conf: console configuration

You use the console program to communicate with the director to schedule jobs, check the status of jobs, or restore data. You can start the console from the installation directory by typing **./bconsole**.

bconsole.conf tells the console how to communicate with the Bacula director daemon. The parameters in this file must correspond to those given in the Director resource in the director's configuration file (**bacula-dir.conf**), with the exception of the address parameter.

```
# Console configuration file, bconsole.conf

Director {
    Name = bull-dir
    DIRport = 9101
    address = bull.atrust.com
    Password = "B@cu1@Lik3s,fRu17"
}
```

Installing and configuring the client file daemon

The file daemon on backup clients communicates with the Bacula storage daemon as backups and restores are executed. This daemon must be installed and configured on every computer that is to be backed up with Bacula.

For Windows clients, prebuilt binaries can be downloaded from the Bacula web site. Bacula is great for backing up Windows data files, but it's not so good at creating a bomb-proof level 0 backup of a Windows system. Unfortunately, Bacula has no concept of Windows open file locks or of the Windows registry or system state, so additional steps must be taken to ensure that this data is saved before a Bacula dump is performed. The on-line documentation does a good job of addressing these issues.

On UNIX and Linux systems, you can install the daemon by copying the Bacula source tree to each client and running

./configure --enable-client-only --prefix=/etc/bacula

Then run **make** and **make install**.

After the binaries have been installed, configure the file daemon by editing the **/etc/bacula/bacula-fd.conf** file:

```
# File daemon configuration for harp, bacula-fd.conf

Director {
    Name = bull-dir
    Password = "Ch@ch1s@Fru17"
}

# "Global" file daemon configuration specifications

FileDaemon {
    Name = harp
    FDport = 9102
    Working Directory = /var/bacula/working
    Pid Directory = /var/run
}

# Send all messages except skipped files back to the director

Messages {
    Name = Standard
    director = bull-dir = all, !skipped
}
```

The config file is broken into three parts. The first part consists of the Director resource, which tells the file daemon which director can schedule backups from this client's file daemon. The Director resource also includes the Password parameter, which must be identical to the password listed in the Client resource within the director's own configuration file. The second part is the FileDaemon resource, which names the client and specifies the port on which the file daemon listens for commands from the director daemon. The final component is the Messages resource, which defines how local messages are to be handled.

Starting the Bacula daemons

Now that we have our server daemons installed and our client configured, the next step is to fire up the daemons by running the startup script in the server's installation directory (**./bacula start**). This same command is also used on each client to start the file daemon. This script should also be linked to the appropriate run-level startup scripts in the **rc** and **init.d** directories.

Once the Bacula daemons are running, you can use the console program (**bconsole** in the installation directory) to check their status, add media to pools, and execute backup and restore jobs. You can run **bconsole** from any computer as long as it has been properly installed and configured.

```
$ sudo ./bconsole
Password: <entered password>
Connecting to Director bull:9101
1000 OK: bull-dir Version: 1.38.11 (29 June 2006)
Enter a period to cancel a command.
```

Use the console's **help** command to see a complete list of the commands it supports.

Adding media to pools

Before you can run backup jobs, you need to label some tapes and assign them to media pools defined in the director configuration file. Use the console's **label** command to do this.

```
* label
Automatically selected Storage: SureStore
Enter new Volume name: 003061L1
Enter slot (0 for none): 14
Defined Pools:
    1: SSFullPool
    2: SSOneOffPool
...
Select the Pool (1-5): 1
Connecting to Storage daemon SureStore at bull.atrust.com:9103
...
Sending label command for Volume "003061L1" Slot 14 ...
...
3001 Mounted Volume: 003061L1
3001 Device /dev/nst0 is mounted with Volume "003061L1"
```

In this example, the tape in slot 14 of the automatic tape changer was named 003061L1 and was assigned to the SSFullPool pool. Use the **list media** command to verify that the tape has been added to the correct pool and marked as appendable.

Running a manual backup

Use the console's **run** command to perform a manual backup. No arguments are needed; the console displays all the backup jobs defined in the director's configuration file. You can modify any option within the **run** command by following the console's menu-driven prompts.

The following example shows a manual full backup of the server harp, using the defaults specified in our configuration files.

```
$ sudo ./bconsole
...
Connecting to Director bull:9101
1000 OK: bull-dir Version: 1.34.6 (28 July 2004)
Enter a period to cancel a command.
* run
A job name must be specified.
The defined Job resources are:
    1: harp
    2: RestoreFiles
Select Job resource (1-2): 1
Run Backup job
JobName:  harp
FileSet:  harp
```

```
Level:      Full
Client:     harp
Storage:    SureStore
Pool:       SSFullPool
When:       2006-07-08 13:14:24
Priority:   10
OK to run? (yes/mod/no): yes
Run command submitted.
```

After the backup job has been successfully submitted to the director, you can track its status with the console's **status** command. You can also use the **messages** command to obtain blow-by-blow updates as they arrive. Depending on how you have set up the system's Message resources, a detailed summary report may also be sent to the Bacula administrator. The output below was produced by the **messages** command after the backup job successfully completed. It includes a lot of useful summary information.

```
* messages
08-Jul-2006 14:21 bull-dir: Start Backup JobId 5216, Job=harp.2006-07-08_14.21.03
08-Jul-2006 14:23 bull-sd: 3301 Issuing autochanger "loaded drive 0" command.
08-Jul-2006 14:23 bull-sd: 3302 Autochanger "loaded drive 0", result is Slot 6.
08-Jul-2006 14:23 bull-sd: 3303 Issuing autochanger "unload slot 6, drive 0" command.
08-Jul-2006 14:24 bull-sd: 3304 Issuing autochanger "load slot 14, drive 0" command.
08-Jul-2006 14:25 bull-sd: 3305 Autochanger "load slot 14, drive 0", status is OK.
08-Jul-2006 14:25 bull-sd: Volume "003048L1" previously written, moving to end of data.
08-Jul-2006 14:25 bull-sd: Ready to append to end of Volume "003048L1" at file=7.
08-Jul-2006 14:54 bull-dir: Bacula 1.34.6 (28Jul04): 08-Jul-2006 14:54
JobId:                  5216
Job:                    harp.2006-07-08_14.21.03
Backup Level:           Full
Client:                 harp
FileSet:                "harp" 2006-01-06 20:37:06
Start time:             08-Jul-2006 14:21
End time:               08-Jul-2006 14:54
FD Files Written:       176,451
SD Files Written:       176,451
FD Bytes Written:       12,968,821,897
SD Bytes Written:       12,993,427,904
Rate:                   6379.2 KB/sSoftware Compression:None
Volume name(s):         003048L1
Volume Session Id:      263
Volume Session Time:    1149888981
Last Volume Bytes:      13,298,706,752
Non-fatal FD errors:    0
SD Errors:              0
FD termination status:  OK
SD termination status:  OK
Termination:            Backup OK
08-Jul-2006 14:54 bull-dir: Begin pruning Jobs.
08-Jul-2006 14:54 bull-dir: No Jobs found to prune.
08-Jul-2006 14:54 bull-dir: Begin pruning Files.
```

08-Jul-2006 14:55 bull-dir: Pruned 2,206 Files from 48 Jobs for client harp from catalog.
08-Jul-2006 14:55 bull-dir: End auto prune.

Running a restore job

To restore files, start up the console and run the **restore** command. Like **run**, **restore** is menu driven. It starts by helping you identify which jobs need to be read to restore the target files. **restore** presents you with several methods of specifying the relevant job IDs. Once you have selected a set of jobs, you can then select the files from those jobs to restore.

```
* restore
To select the JobIds, you have the following choices:
     1: List last 20 Jobs run
     2: List Jobs where a given File is saved
     3: Enter list of comma separated JobIds to select
     4: Enter SQL list command
     5: Select the most recent backup for a client
     6: Select backup for a client before a specified time
     7: Enter a list of files to restore
     8: Enter a list of files to restore before a specified time
     9: Cancel
Select item:  (1-9):
```

The two most useful queries are probably "Select the most recent backup for a client" (#5) and "List Jobs where a given File is saved" (#2). The latter option comes in handy for those pesky users that can never seem to remember exactly where the file they accidentally removed really lives. Another powerful command is option #4, "Enter SQL list command," which lets you enter any properly formatted SQL query.

Suppose that a user needs a copy of his **pw_expire.pl** script restored from around April 2006; however, he's not sure which machine he was using for development at that time. In addition, he would like the files restored to the **/tmp** directory of the original machine. A request like this would set many a system administrator to grumbling around the water cooler, but for the Bacula administrator it's a snap. (Unfortunately, Bacula's format for search results is so wide that we had to shrink it down to nearly invisible proportions below.)

```
* restore
To select the JobIds, you have the following choices:
     1: List last 20 Jobs run
     2: List Jobs where a given File is saved
     3: Enter list of comma separated JobIds to select
 ...
     9: Cancel
Select item:  (1-9): 2
Enter Filename: pw_expire.pl
```

JobId	Client	Name	StartTime	JobType	JobFiles	JobBytes
4,667	harp	/home/seidel/pw_expire.pl	2006-05-09 23:55:21	B	176,072	12,664,064,296
5,220	bull	/home/seidel/bin/pw_expire.pl	2006-07-08 20:15:49	B	14	248,386
5,216	harp	/home/seidel/pw_expire.pl	2006-07-08 14:21:05	B	176,451	12,968,821,897
4,523	harp	/home/seidel/pw_expire.pl	2006-04-25 23:43:56	B	167,435	12,539,537,882

Bacula's list of **pw_expire.pl** instances reveals that the April 2006 version lived on the client harp and was backed up as part of job 4,523. Bacula then returns us to the restore menu, where we can use option #3 ("Enter list of comma separated JobIds to select") to focus in on this specific job.

```
Select item:  (1-9): 3
Enter JobId(s), comma separated, to restore: 4523
You have selected the following JobId: 4523
Building directory tree for JobId 4523 ...
1 Job inserted into the tree.
You are now entering file selection mode, where you add and
remove files to be restored. All files are initially added.⁹
Enter "done" to leave this mode.

cwd is: /
$ cd /home/seidel
cwd is: /home/seidel
$ dir
...
-rwxr-xr-x  1 seidel  atrust      321 2005-10-27 11:25:24  /home/seidel/pw_expire.pl
$ mark pw_expire.pl
1 files marked.
$ done
```

Note that even though Bacula originally displayed the job ID with a comma (4,523), we have to omit the comma when we reenter the ID; otherwise, Bacula interprets 4,523 as the two job IDs 4 and 523.

After Bacula loads the specified job, it starts up an interactive restore mode in which you can browse to the file and use the **mark** command to select it. When you are finished marking files, the **done** command exits interactive mode.

```
Bootstrap records written to /var/bacula/working/restore.bsr
The restore job will require the following Volumes:

   003048L1

1 file selected to be restored.

Defined Clients:
     1: bull
     2: harp
Select the Client (1-2): 2
```

Bacula then writes a bootstrap file that it will use to perform the restore, displays the names of the tape volumes it requires, and prompts you to select a client to which it should restore the files. In this example, we restored back to the original host harp.

9. Liar, liar, pants on fire. If you proceed to the restore phase without selecting any files, Bacula tells you no files were selected.

```
Run Restore job
JobName:      RestoreFiles
Bootstrap:    /var/Bacula/working/restore.bsr
Where:        /scratch02/restore/
Replace:      always
FileSet:      BullHomes
Client:       harp
Storage:      SureStore
When:         2006-07-08 16:45:20
Priority:     10
OK to run? (yes/mod/no): mod
```

For this particular job, we modify the default settings. Specifically, the correct file set name is harp, which is the default file set configured in the director daemon configuration file. In addition, we change the location of this restore to **/tmp** in accordance with the user's request.

```
Select parameter to modify (1-11): 9
Please enter path prefix for restore (/ for none): /tmp
Run Restore job
JobName:      RestoreFiles
Bootstrap:    /var/Bacula/working/restore.bsr
Where:        /tmp
Replace:      never
FileSet:      harp
Client:       harp
Storage:      SureStore
When:         2006-07-08 16:45:20
Priority:     10
OK to run? (yes/mod/no): yes
Run command submitted.
Restore command done.
```

After making the changes, we submit the job to the director, which executes it. We then use the **messages** command to view the job's logging output.

```
* messages
08-Jul-2006 17:06 bull-dir: Start Restore Job RestoreFiles.2006-07-08_17.06.02
08-Jul-2006 17:06 bull-sd: Ready to read from volume "003048L1" on device /dev/nst0.
08-Jul-2006 17:06 bull-sd: Forward spacing to file:block 11:0.
08-Jul-2006 17:08 bull-sd: End of Volume at file 11 on device /dev/nst0, Volume
    "003048L1"
08-Jul-2006 17:08 bull-sd: End of all volumes.
08-Jul-2006 17:08 harp: -rwxr-xr-x   1 seidel   atrust      321 2005-10-27 11:25:24
    /tmp/home/seidel/pw_expire.pl
08-Jul-2006 17:08 bull-dir: Bacula 1.34.6 (28Jul04): 08-Jul-2006 17:08
JobId:                  5217
Job:                    RestoreFiles.2006-07-08_17.06.02
Client:                 harp
Start time:             08-Jul-2006 17:06
End time:               08-Jul-2006 17:08
```

```
Files Expected:              1
Files Restored:              1
Bytes Restored:              321
Rate:                        0.0 KB/s
FD Errors:                   0
FD termination status:       OK
SD termination status:       OK
Termination:                 Restore OK
```

```
08-Jul-2006 17:08 bull-dir: Begin pruning Jobs.
08-Jul-2006 17:08 bull-dir: No Jobs found to prune.
08-Jul-2006 17:08 bull-dir: Begin pruning Files.
08-Jul-2006 17:08 bull-dir: No Files found to prune.
08-Jul-2006 17:08 bull-dir: End auto prune.
```

Monitoring and debugging Bacula configurations

You can use the console's **status** command to query the various Bacula daemons for information. The following example displays information about the director daemon. The output includes information about upcoming jobs, currently running jobs, and jobs that were terminated.

```
* status dir
bull-dir Version: 1.34.6 (28 July 2004) i686-redhat-linux-gnu redhat Enterprise release
Daemon started 09-Jun-06 15:36, 269 Jobs run since started.

Scheduled Jobs:
Level          Type       Scheduled        Name     Volume
============================================================
Incremental    Backup     08-Jul-06 20:10  harp      003005L1

Running Jobs:
JobId    Level    Name                        Status
====================================================
5216     Full     harp.2006-07-08_14.21.03    is running

Terminated Jobs:
JobId   Level   Files   Bytes         Status   Finished         Name
====================================================================
5205    Incr    204     898,066,578   OK       06-Jul-06 20:36  harp
```

Bacula jobs produce a job report that is routed according to the job's Message resource in the director daemon's configuration file. The report includes basic information about the volumes used, the size and number of files backed up, and any errors that may have occurred. The report usually gives you enough information to troubleshoot any minor problems.

Two issues that seem to come up frequently are client file daemons that aren't running and storage daemons that cannot find any appendable tape volumes. In the example below, the director daemon reports that a backup job terminated with a fatal error because it could not communicate with the file daemon on host harp. This error can be seen repeatedly at the end of the summary report.

Backups

```
bull-dir: Start Backup JobId 5215, Job=harp.2006-07-08_13.19.49
bull-dir: harp.2006-07-08_13.19.49 Error: Bacula 1.34.6 (28Jul04): 08-Jul-2006 13:49
```

```
JobId:                  5215
Job:                    harp.2006-07-08_13.19.49
Backup Level:           Full
Client:                 harp
FileSet:                "harp" 2006-01-06 20:37:06
Start time:             08-Jul-2006 13:19
End time:               08-Jul-2006 13:49
FD Files Written:       0
SD Files Written:       0
FD Bytes Written:       0
SD Bytes Written:       0
Rate:                   0.0 KB/s
Software Compression:   None
Volume name(s):
Volume Session Id:      262
Volume Session Time:    1149888981
Last Volume Bytes:      0
Non-fatal FD errors:    0
SD Errors:              0
FD termination status:
SD termination status:  Waiting on FD
Termination:            *** Backup Error ***
```

```
bull-dir: harp.2006-07-08_13.19.49 Warning: bnet.c:666 Could not connect to
    File daemon on 192.168.7.2:9102. ERR=Connection refused Retrying ...
bull-dir: harp.2006-07-08_13.19.49 Fatal error: bnet.c:672 Unable to connect to
    File daemon on 192.168.7.2:9102. ERR=Connection refused
```

The example below shows the storage daemon reporting that no tape volumes from the appropriate pool are available to perform a requested backup. You can fix the problem either by adding a new volume to the pool or by purging and recycling an existing volume. There's no need to restart the job; Bacula should continue to execute it unless you cancel it explicitly.

```
bull-sd: Job baikal.2006-07-04_20.10.06 waiting. Cannot find any appendable volumes.
Please use the "label" command to create a new Volume for:
    Storage:    SureStoreDevice
    Media type: LTO1
    Pool:       SSFullPool
```

If you ever need to see more detailed information about what the daemons are doing, you can have them send a slew of debugging information to the console by appending the option **-d***nnn* to the startup command. For example,

```
$ sudo ./bacula start -d100
```

The *nnn* represents the debug level. Typical values range between 50 and 200. The higher the number, the more information is displayed. You can also enable debugging from within the console with the **setdebug** command.

Alternatives to Bacula

Several other free or shareware backup tools are available for download. The following packages are particularly noteworthy; all are still under active development.

- Amanda: a very popular and proven system that backs up UNIX and Linux systems to a single tape drive. See www.amanda.org.

- Mondo Rescue: a utility that backs up Linux systems to CD-R, DVD-R, tape, or hard disk. This tool is particularly useful for bare-metal recovery. Read more at www.mondorescue.org.

- **rsync**: a free tool that is part of many default Linux installations. It can synchronize files from one computer to another and can be run in conjunction with SSH to transfer data securely over the Internet. See page 508 for some additional discussion of **rsync**.

- **star**: a faster implementation of **tar**; **star** is included with all our example distributions.

9.9 COMMERCIAL BACKUP PRODUCTS

We would all like to think that Linux is the only OS in the world, but unfortunately, that is not the case. When looking at commercial backup solutions, you should consider whether they can handle any other operating systems that you are responsible for backing up. Most contemporary products address cross-platform issues and let you include UNIX, Windows, and Macintosh workstations in your Linux backup scheme. You must also consider non-Linux storage arrays and file servers.

Users' laptops and other machines that are not consistently connected to your network should also be protected from failure. When looking at commercial products, you may want to ask if each product is smart enough not to back up identical files from every laptop. How many copies of **command.com** do you really need?

Since we find that Bacula works well for us, we don't have much experience with commercial products. We asked some of our big-bucks buddies at commercial sites for quick impressions of the systems they use. Their comments are reproduced here.

ADSM/TSM

The ADSM product was developed by IBM and later purchased by Tivoli. It is marketed today as the Tivoli Storage Manager (TSM), although the product is once again owned by IBM. TSM is a data management tool that also handles backups. More information can be found at www-306.ibm.com/software/tivoli.

Pros:

- Owned by IBM; it's here to stay
- Attractive pricing and leasing options
- Very low failure rate

- Uses disk cache; useful for backing up slow clients
- Deals with Windows clients
- Excellent documentation (priced separately)

Cons:

- Poorly designed GUI interface
- Every 2 files =1K in the database.
- The design is incremental forever

Veritas

Veritas merged with Symantec in 2005. They sell backup solutions for a variety of systems. When you visit their web site (www.symantec.com), make sure you select the product that's appropriate for you.

Pros:

- Decent GUI interface
- Connects directly to Network Appliance filers
- Push install for Linux
- Can write tapes in GNU **tar** format
- Centralized database, but can support a distributed backup system

Cons:

- Some bugs
- Pricing is confusing and annoying

Other alternatives

W. Curtis Preston, author of the O'Reilly book *UNIX Backup and Recovery*, maintained a web page about backup-related topics (disk mirroring products, advanced filesystem products, remote system backup products, off-site data-vaulting products, etc.) at www.backupcentral.com. It's not clear whether any of this information is still being updated, but the existing material is still quite useful.

9.10 RECOMMENDED READING

PRESTON, W. CURTIS. *Backup & Recovery.* Sebastopol, CA: O'Reilly Media, 2006.

9.11 EXERCISES

E9.1   Investigate the backup procedure used at your site. Which machine(s) perform the backups? What type of storage devices are used? Where are tapes stored? Suggest improvements to the current system.

E9.2   What steps are needed to restore files on a system that uses Bacula? How do you find the right tape?

E9.3   Given the following output from **df** and **/etc/dumpdates**, identify the
steps needed to perform the three restores requested. Enumerate your
assumptions. Assume that the date of the restore request is January 18.

df output from the machine khaya.cs.colorado.edu:

/dev/hda8	256194	81103	161863	33%	/
/dev/hda1	21929	4918	15879	24%	/boot
/dev/hda6	3571696	24336	3365924	1%	/local
/dev/hda10	131734	5797	119135	5%	/tmp
/dev/hda5	1815580	1113348	610004	65%	/usr
/dev/hda7	256194	17013	225953	7%	/var

/etc/dumpdates from khaya.cs.colorado.edu:

/dev/hda8	2	Tue Jan	17	22:59:23 2006
/dev/hda6	3	Tue Jan	17	22:51:51 2006
/dev/hda7	3	Tue Jan	17	22:50:24 2006
/dev/hda5	9	Tue Jan	17	22:46:25 2006
/dev/hda5	1	Thu Jan	12	22:45:42 2006
/dev/hda7	0	Thu Jan	12	23:14:47 2006
/dev/hda6	1	Thu Jan	12	23:14:32 2006
/dev/hda8	1	Thu Jan	12	23:14:17 2006
/dev/hda6	0	Tue Jan	10	22:47:31 2006
/dev/hda1	1	Sun Jan	8	22:16:05 2006
/dev/hda7	1	Sat Jan	7	22:08:09 2006
/dev/hda1	4	Tue Jan	3	22:51:53 2006
/dev/hda7	2	Sat Dec	24	22:53:52 2005
/dev/hda5	0	Thu Nov	3	22:46:21 2005
/dev/hda1	0	Wed Sep	21	22:46:29 2005
/dev/hda8	0	Wed Aug	24	23:01:24 2005
/dev/hda1	3	Fri Jul	29	22:52:20 2005
/dev/hda6	2	Fri Jul	29	23:01:32 2005

a) "Please restore my entire home directory (**/usr/home/clements**)
from some time in the last few days. I seem to have lost the entire
code base for my senior project."

b) "Umm, I accidentally did a **sudo rm -rf /*** on my machine khaya.
Could you please restore all the filesystems from the latest backups?"

c) "All my MP3 files that I have been collecting from BitTorrent over the
last month are gone. They were stored in **/tmp/mp3/**. Could you
please restore them for me?"

Exercises are continued on the next page.

Backups

☆ **E9.4**   Design a backup plan for the following scenarios. Assume that each computer has a 100GB disk and that users' home directories are stored locally. Choose a backup device that balances cost vs. support needs and explain your reasoning. List any assumptions you make.

    a) A research facility has 50 machines. Each machine holds a lot of important data that changes often.

    b) A small software company has 10 machines. Source code is stored on a central server that has 500GB of disk space. The source code changes throughout the day. Individual users' home directories do not change very often. Cost is of little concern and security is of utmost importance.

    c) A home network has two machines. Cost is the most important issue.

☆ **E9.5**   Design a restore strategy for each of the three situations above.

☆ **E9.6**   Outline the steps you would take to perform a secure **rdump** through a secure SSH tunnel.

☆☆ **E9.7**   Write Bacula configuration statements that implement the backup plans you came up with for exercise 9.4.

10 Syslog and Log Files

The system daemons, the kernel, and various utilities all emit data that is logged and eventually ends up on your finite-sized disks. Most of that data has a limited useful life and needs to be summarized, compressed, archived, and eventually thrown away.

10.1 LOGGING POLICIES

Logging policies vary from site to site. Common schemes include the following:

- Throw away all data immediately.
- Reset log files at periodic intervals.
- Rotate log files, keeping data for a fixed time.
- Compress and archive logs to tape or other permanent media.

The correct choice for your site depends on how much disk space you have and how security conscious you are. Even sites with an abundance of disk space must deal with the cancerous growth of log files.

Whatever scheme you select, you should automate the maintenance of log files with **cron**. See Chapter 8, *Periodic Processes*, for more information about **cron**.

Throwing away log files

We do not recommend throwing away all logging information. Sites that are subject to security problems routinely find that log files provide important evidence of break-ins. Log files are also helpful for alerting you to hardware and software problems. In general, given a comfortable amount of disk space, you should keep data for at least a month. In the real world, it may take this long for you to realize that your site has been compromised by a hacker and that you need to review the logs. If you need to go back further into the past, you can recover older log files from your backup tapes.

Some administrators allow log files to grow to a size at which they become embarrassing, then restart them from zero. This plan is better than keeping no data at all, but it does not guarantee that log entries will be retained for any particular length of time. Average disk usage may also be higher than with other management schemes.

On rare occasions, a site may determine that certain log files are more likely to be subpoenaed than to serve any beneficial purpose. A site in this situation may keep several weeks of log data around, but it will probably ensure that the files are never archived to permanent media. A case in point: Microsoft has been accused in more than one recent lawsuit of unduly destructive management policies for log files and email. The plaintiffs allege that Microsoft's data retention policies constitute destruction of evidence, despite the fact that the deletions (or at least, the deletion policies) predate the particular legal actions. Unfortunately, it is too early to tell how the courts will ultimately respond to these claims.[1] In the United States, the Sarbanes-Oxley Act has recently instituted new recordkeeping requirements; see page 956.

Rotating log files

It's a common (but not universal) practice to store each week's or month's log information in a separate file. The periodic files are kept for a specific period of time and then deleted. We dedicate a disk partition (**/var/log**) on a central host to log files.

At the end of each rotation period, a script or utility program renames each file to push older data toward the end of the chain. For example, if a log is called **logfile**, the backup copies might be called **logfile.1**, **logfile.2**, and so on. If you rotate every week and keep eight weeks' worth of data, there will be a **logfile.8** but no **logfile.9**. Every week, the data in **logfile.8** is lost as **logfile.7** overwrites it.

You can use data compression to extend the retention time, at a slight cost in convenience. You can run **zgrep** to search the compressed files without permanently unpacking them.

Suppose a file needs weekly attention and you want to archive its contents for three weeks (to keep the example short). The following script would implement an appropriate rotation policy:

```
#!/bin/sh
cd /var/log
mv logfile.2 logfile.3
mv logfile.1 logfile.2
mv logfile logfile.1
cat /dev/null > logfile
chmod 600 logfile
```

---

1. It's worth noting that the deletion of relevant email or log files once a lawsuit appears imminent (or worse yet, during the course of a lawsuit) is decidedly improper. Only an explicit, ongoing nonretention policy has any prospect of legal protection.

Ownership information is important for some log files. You may need to run your rotation script from **cron** as the log files' owner rather than as root, or you may need to add a **chown** command to the sequence.

Most Linux distributions (including all our examples) supply a very nice log rotation utility called **logrotate**, which we describe starting on page 208. It's much easier (and more reliable) than writing your own scripts and is worth seeking out and installing if your distribution doesn't include it.

Some sites identify log files by date rather than by sequence number; for example, **logfile.tues** or **logfile.2005.04.01**. This system is a little harder to implement, but it can be worth the effort if you frequently refer to old log files. It's much easier to set up in Perl than in **sh**. One useful idiom that doesn't require any programming is

```
mv logfile logfile.`date +%Y.%m.%d`
```

This scheme also has the advantage of making **ls** sort the log files chronologically. (The **-t** option to **ls** makes it sort files chronologically by modification time in any directory, but it's nice if the files arrange themselves without being asked.)

Some daemons keep their log files open all the time. Because of the way the filesystem works, the simple script shown above cannot be used with such daemons. Instead of new log data being added to the recreated **logfile**, log data will continue to go to **logfile.1**; the active reference to the original file persists even after the file has been renamed. To install a new log file, you must either signal the daemon or kill and restart it. Each program behaves differently with respect to logging. Consult the appropriate chapter in this book (or your manuals) to determine what procedures are necessary in each case.

Here is a slightly more detailed example that uses both compression and signals:

```
#!/bin/sh
cd /var/log
mv logfile.2.gz logfile.3.gz
mv logfile.1.gz logfile.2.gz
mv logfile logfile.1
cat /dev/null > logfile
chmod 600 logfile
kill -signal pid
gzip logfile.1
```

signal represents the appropriate signal for the program writing the log file; *pid* is its process ID. The signal can be hardcoded into the script, but you must determine the PID of the daemon dynamically, either by reading a file that the daemon has left around for you (e.g., **/var/run/syslogd.pid**, described below) or by using the **killall** variant of **kill**, which can look up the PID in the process table for you.

For example, the command

```
killall -e -HUP syslogd
```

Syslog / Log Files

is equivalent to

kill -HUP `cat **/var/run/syslogd.pid`**

Archiving log files

See Chapter 9 for more
information about
backups.
Unless you explicitly wish to avoid leaving a paper trail, you should always include
log files in your regular backup sequence. Because they contain information that is
vital for investigating security incidents, log files should be backed up at the highest
frequency your dump schedule permits. Log files change frequently, so they can represent a significant portion of the system information that is stored on incremental
backups. Keep the interaction between your logging policy and your backup policy
in mind when designing both.

In addition to being stored as part of regular backups, logs can also be archived to a
separate tape series. Separate tapes are more cumbersome, but they impose less
documentation burden and won't interfere with your ability to recycle dump tapes.
If you use separate tapes, we suggest that you use **tar** format and write a script to
automate your log file backup scheme.

10.2 LINUX LOG FILES

Traditional UNIX systems are often criticized for their inconsistent and even somewhat bizarre approach to logging. Fortunately, Linux systems are generally a bit more
sane, although each distribution has its own way of naming and dividing up the log
files. For the most part, Linux packages send their logging information to files in the
/var/log directory. On some distributions, a few logs are also stored in **/var/adm**.

The format of the
syslog.conf *file is*
described on
page 210.
Most programs these days actually send their log entries to a central clearing system
called syslog, which is described later in this chapter. The default syslog configuration typically dumps most of these messages somewhere into **/var/log**. Check syslog's configuration file, **/etc/syslog.conf**, to find out the specific locations.

Table 10.1 compiles information about some of the more common log files on our
example distributions. Specifically, it lists

- The log files to archive, summarize, or truncate
- The program that creates each
- An indication of how each filename is specified
- The frequency of cleanup that we consider reasonable
- The distributions (among our examples) that use the log file
- A description of the file's contents

Filenames are relative to **/var/log** unless otherwise noted.

The character in the Where column tells how the log file is specified: S for programs
that use syslog, F for programs that use a configuration file, and H if the filename is
hardwired in code. The Freq column offers our suggested cleanup frequency. The
Distros column lists the distributions to which the entry applies.

Table 10.1   Log files on parade

File	Program	Where[a]	Freq[a]	Distros[a]	Contents
auth.log	**su**, etc.[b]	S	M	DU	Authorizations
apache2/*	**httpd** version 2	F	D	SDU	Apache HTTP server logs (v2)
boot.log	**rc** scripts	F[c]	M	RF	Output from system startup scripts
boot.msg	kernel	H	–	S	Dump of kernel message buffer
cron	**cron**	S	W	RF	**cron** executions and errors
cups/*	CUPS	C	W	all	Printing-related messages (CUPS)
daemon.log	various	S	W	DU	All daemon facility messages
debug	various	S	D	DU	Debugging output
dmesg	kernel	H	–	RFDU	Dump of kernel message buffer
dpkg.log	**dpkg**	F	M	DU	Package management log
faillog	**login**	H	W	SDU	Unsuccessful login attempts
httpd/logs/*	**httpd**	F	D	RF	Apache HTTP server logs (in **/etc**)
kern.log	kernel	S	W	DU	All kern facility messages
lastlog	**login**	H	–	all	Last login time per user (binary)
mail*	mail-related	S	W	all	All mail facility messages
messages	various	S	W	all	Often the main system log file
rpmpkgs	**cron.daily/rpm**	H	D	RF	List of installed RPM packages
samba/*	**smbd**, etc.	C	W	–	Samba (Windows/CIFS file sharing)
secure	**sshd**, **sudo**, etc.	S	M	RF	Private authorization messages
syslog	various	S	W	DU	Often the main system log file
warn	various	S	W	S	All warning/error level messages
wtmp	**login**	H	M	all	Login records (binary)
Xorg.*n*.log	**Xorg**	F	W	RFS	X Windows server errors
yum.log	**yum**	F	M	RF	Package management log

a. Where: S = Syslog, H = Hardwired, F = Configuration file
   Freq: D = Daily, W = Weekly, M = Monthly
   Distros: R = Red Hat Enterprise Linux, F = Fedora, D = Debian, S = SUSE, U = Ubuntu

b. **passwd**, **login**, and **shutdown** also write to the authorization log. It's in **/var/adm** on Red Hat and Fedora systems.

c. Actually logs through syslog, but the facility and level are configured in **/etc/initlog.conf**.

Log files are generally owned by root, although conventions for the ownership and mode of log files vary slightly among distributions. In our opinion, logs at most sites should be given mode 600 (read and write for the owner only) because their contents are potentially useful to hackers. If your users are relatively sophisticated, they can benefit from the ability to review the logs, and in this case it's reasonable to relax the permissions on a subset of the log files.

Another reasonable compromise is to set the group owner of log files to a group that you create for this purpose and to make the files group-readable. You can add your local sysadmins to this group, allowing them to review log files without having to use **sudo**. This setup is especially useful if your site has junior sysadmins who do not have full **sudo** privileges.

At the very least, the **secure**, **auth.log**, and **sudo.log** files should be off-limits to casual browsing. Never give write permission on any log file to anyone but the owner.

It's worth noting that many of the log files in Table 10.1 are maintained by syslog but that the default syslog configuration varies widely among systems. With a more consistent **/etc/syslog.conf** file, the log files would look more similar among Linux distributions.

Special log files

Most logs are text files to which lines are written as "interesting" events occur. A few of the logs listed in Table 10.1 have a rather different context, however.

/var/log/wtmp contains a record of users' logins and logouts as well as entries that record when the system was rebooted or shut down. It's a fairly generic log file in that new entries are simply added to the end of the file. However, the **wtmp** file is maintained in a binary format. Use the **last** command to decode the information. Despite its unusual format, the **wtmp** file should be rotated or truncated like any other log file because of its natural tendency to grow without limit.

See the footnote on page 169 for more info about sparse files.

/var/log/lastlog contains similar information to that in **/var/log/wtmp**, but it records only the time of last login for each user. It is a sparse, binary file that's indexed by UID. It will stay smaller if your UIDs are assigned in some kind of numeric sequence, although this is certainly nothing to lose sleep over in the real world. **lastlog** doesn't need to be rotated because its size stays constant unless new users log in.

Kernel and boot-time logging

The kernel and the system startup scripts present some special challenges in the domain of logging. In the case of the kernel, the problem is to create a permanent record of the boot process and the operation of the kernel without building in dependencies on any particular filesystem or filesystem organization. In the case of the startup scripts, the challenge is to capture a coherent narrative of the startup procedure without permanently tying any of the system daemons to a startup log file, interfering with any program's own logging, or gooping up the startup scripts with double entries or output redirections.

Kernel logging is dealt with by having the kernel store its log entries in an internal buffer of limited size. The buffer is large enough to accommodate messages about all the kernel's boot-time activities. Once the system has come all the way up, a user process accesses the kernel's log buffer and makes a final disposition of its contents. Distributions typically do this by running the **dmesg** command and redirecting its output to **/var/log/dmesg** (RHEL, Fedora, Debian, and Ubuntu) or **/var/log/boot.msg** (SUSE). This is the best place to look for details about the most recent boot cycle.

The kernel's ongoing logging is handled by a daemon called **klogd**. The functions of **klogd** are actually a superset of those of **dmesg**; in addition to dumping the kernel log and exiting, it can also read messages out of the kernel buffer as they are generated and pass them along to a file or to syslog. In normal operation, **klogd** runs in this latter mode. Syslog processes the messages according to the instructions for the "kern" facility (they are typically sent to **/var/log/messages**).

Our example distributions' startup scripts do not use **dmesg**'s **-c** flag when they make their initial dump of log messages, so the kernel's message buffer is read but not reset. When **klogd** starts up, it finds the same set of messages seen by **dmesg** in the buffer and submits them to syslog. For this reason, some entries appear in both the **dmesg** or **boot.msg** file and in another, syslog managed file such as **/var/log/messages**.

Another issue in kernel logging is the appropriate management of the system console. As the system is booting, it's important for all the output to come to the console. However, once the system is up and running, console messages may be more an annoyance than a help, particularly if the console is used for logins.

Both **dmesg** and **klogd** let you set the kernel's console logging level with a command-line flag. For example:

```
$ sudo dmesg -n 2
```

Level 7 is the most verbose and includes debugging information. Level 1 includes only panic messages (the lower-numbered levels are the most severe). All kernel messages continue to go to the central buffer (and to syslog) regardless of whether they are forwarded to the console.

The kernel provides some control files underneath the **/proc/sys** directory to allow floods of repeated log messages to be choked off at the source. See the section *Tuning Linux kernel parameters* starting on page 874 for more information about the general mechanism through which kernel parameters are set. The specific control files are **/proc/sys/kernel/printk_ratelimit**, which specifies the minimum number of seconds that must elapse between kernel messages once the choke has been activated (default 5), and **/proc/sys/kernel/printk_ratelimit_burst**, which specifies how many grouped messages to let through before activating the choke (default 10). These parameters are advisory, so they do not absolutely guarantee that a heavy flow of messages will be stanched.

 Logging for the system startup scripts is unfortunately not as well managed as kernel logging. Red Hat Enterprise Linux uses an **initlog** command to capture the output of startup commands and submit it to syslog. Unfortunately, **initlog** must be mentioned explicitly whenever a command is run, so the information comes at the cost of some complexity. Messages eventually make their way to **/var/log/boot.log**.

Our other example systems make no coherent effort to capture a history of the startup scripts' output. Some information is logged by individual commands and daemons, but much goes unrecorded.

Fedora formerly used the same **initlog** system as Red Hat, but the commands to submit log entries have been commented out of the startup files. Fortunately, there's a central library of utility functions, **/etc/init.d/functions**, where you can uncomment the **initlog** lines to reenable them.

10.3 LOGROTATE: MANAGE LOG FILES

Erik Troan's excellent **logrotate** utility implements a variety of log management policies and is standard on all our example distributions.

A **logrotate** configuration file consists of a series of specifications for groups of log files to be managed. Options that appear outside the context of a log file specification (such as errors, rotate, and weekly in the following example) apply to all following specifications; they can be overridden within the specification for a particular log file and can also be respecified later in the file to modify the defaults.

Here's a somewhat contrived example that handles several different log files:

```
# Global options
errors errors@book.admin.com
rotate 5
weekly

# Logfile rotation definitions and options
/var/log/messages {
      postrotate
            /bin/kill -HUP `cat /var/run/syslogd.pid`
      endscript
}

/var/log/samba/*.log {
      notifempty
      copytruncate
      sharedscripts
      postrotate
            /bin/kill -HUP `cat /var/lock/samba/*.pid`
      endscript
}
```

This configuration rotates **/var/log/messages** every week. It keeps five versions of the file and notifies **syslogd** each time the file is reset. The Samba log files (of which there may be several) are also rotated weekly, but instead of being moved aside and restarted, they are copied and then truncated. The Samba daemons are sent HUP signals only after all log files have been rotated.

Table 10.2 lists the most useful **logrotate.conf** options.

logrotate is normally run out of **cron** once a day. Its standard configuration file is **/etc/logrotate.conf**, but multiple configuration files (or directories containing configuration files) can appear on **logrotate**'s command line. This feature is used to great effect by our example distributions, which define the **/etc/logrotate.d** directory as a

Table 10.2 logrotate options

Option	Meaning
compress	Compresses all noncurrent versions of the log file
daily, weekly, monthly	Rotates log files on the specified schedule
delaycompress	Compresses all versions but current and next-most-recent
endscript	Marks the end of a prerotate or postrotate script
errors *emailaddr*	Emails error notifications to the specified *emailaddr*
missingok	Doesn't complain if the log file does not exist
notifempty	Doesn't rotate the log file if it is empty
olddir *dir*	Specifies that older versions of the log file be placed in *dir*
postrotate	Introduces a script to be run after the log has been rotated
prerotate	Introduces a script to be run before any changes are made
rotate *n*	Includes *n* versions of the log in the rotation scheme
sharedscripts	Runs scripts only once for the entire log group
size=*logsize*	Rotates if log file size > *logsize* (e.g., 100K, 4M)

standard place for **logrotate** config files. **logrotate**-aware software packages (of which there are many) can drop in log management instructions as part of their installation procedure, greatly simplifying administration.

In addition to **logrotate**, Debian and Ubuntu provide a simpler program called **savelog** that manages rotation for individual files. It's more straightforward than **logrotate** and doesn't use (or need) a config file. Some packages prefer to use their own **savelog** configurations rather than **logrotate**.

10.4 SYSLOG: THE SYSTEM EVENT LOGGER

Syslog, originally written by Eric Allman, is a comprehensive logging system. It has two important functions: to liberate programmers from the tedious mechanics of writing log files and to put administrators in control of logging. Before syslog, every program was free to make up its own logging policy. System administrators had no control over what information was kept or where it was stored.

Syslog is quite flexible. It allows messages to be sorted by their source and importance ("severity level") and routed to a variety of destinations: log files, users' terminals, or even other machines. Syslog's ability to centralize the logging for a network is one of its most valuable features.

Alternatives to syslog

Although syslog has long been the reigning logging system for UNIX and Linux, several alternatives have been developed in an attempt to address some of its shortcomings. One of these, syslog-ng (syslog, next generation), is now used on SUSE systems by default. From a configuration standpoint it is quite different from the standard syslog, and we will not describe it in detail in this book. It's available from www.balabit.com if you would like to try it on a non-SUSE system.

Syslog-ng adds additional configuration facilities, filtering based on message content, message integrity, and better support for firewall restrictions when messages are forwarded over the network.

SDSC Secure Syslog (from the San Diego Supercomupting Center) is also known as high-performance syslog. It provides a "forensically sound" auditing system by implementing the specifications of RFC3195. It was designed with high-traffic sites in mind and contains a number of performance optimizations. You can download the source code from sourceforge.net/projects/sdscsyslog.

Syslog architecture

Syslog consists of three parts:

- **syslogd**, the logging daemon (along with its config file, **/etc/syslog.conf**)
- **openlog** et al., library routines that submit messages to **syslogd**
- **logger**, a user-level command that submits log entries from the shell

In the following discussion, we first cover the configuration of **syslogd** and then briefly show how to use syslog from Perl scripts.

syslogd is started at boot time and runs continuously; it cannot be managed with **inetd**. Programs that are syslog aware write log entries (by using the **syslog** library routine) to the special file **/dev/log**, a UNIX domain socket. **syslogd** reads messages from this file, consults its configuration file, and dispatches each message to the appropriate destination.

A hangup signal (HUP, signal 1) causes **syslogd** to close its log files, reread its configuration file, and start logging again. If you modify **/etc/syslog.conf**, you must send a hangup signal to **syslogd** to make your changes take effect. A TERM signal causes **syslogd** to exit.

syslogd writes its process ID to the file **/var/run/syslogd.pid**. This convention makes it easy to send signals to **syslogd** from a script. For example, the following command sends a hangup signal:

```
# kill -HUP `/bin/cat /var/run/syslogd.pid`
```

Trying to compress or rotate a log file that **syslogd** has open for writing is not healthy and has unpredictable results. The proper procedure is to move the old log aside, recreate the log with the same ownerships and permissions, and then send a HUP signal to **syslogd**. This procedure is easily implemented with **logrotate**; see page 208 for an example.

Configuring syslogd

The configuration file **/etc/syslog.conf** controls **syslogd**'s behavior. It is a text file with a relatively simple format. Blank lines and lines with a pound sign (#) in column one are ignored. The basic format is:

selector <Tab> *action*

For example, the line

   mail.info   /var/log/maillog

would cause messages from the email system to be saved in the file **/var/log/maillog**.

Selectors identify the program ("facility") that is sending a log message and the message's severity level with the syntax

   facility.level

Both facility names and severity levels must be chosen from a short list of defined values; programs can't make up their own. Facilities are defined for the kernel, for common groups of utilities, and for locally written programs. Everything else is classified under the generic facility "user."

Selectors can contain the special keywords * and none, meaning all or nothing, respectively. A selector can include multiple facilities separated by commas. Multiple selectors can be combined with semicolons.

In general, selectors are ORed together: a message matching any selector will be subject to the line's *action*. However, a selector with a level of none excludes the listed facilities regardless of what other selectors on the same line may say.

Here are some examples of ways to format and combine selectors:

facility.level	*action*
facility1,facility2.level	*action*
facility1.level1;facility2.level2	*action*
.level	*action*
.level;badfacility.none	*action*

Table 10.3 (next page) lists the valid facility names. There are currently 21 facilities.

syslogd itself produces time stamp messages, which are logged if the "mark" facility appears in **syslog.conf** to specify a destination for them. Time stamps can help you figure out that your machine crashed between 3:00 and 3:20 a.m., not just "sometime last night." This information can be a big help when you are debugging problems that seem to occur regularly (e.g., the "mysterious crashes" that occur when the housekeeping staff plug in their vacuum cleaners late at night, tripping the circuit breakers).

If your system is quite busy, other log messages often provide adequate time stamp information. But in the wee hours of the morning, that is not always the case.

Table 10.4 (next page) lists syslog's severity levels in order of descending importance.

The severity level of a message specifies its importance. The distinctions between the various levels are sometimes fuzzy. There's a clear difference between notice and warning (and between warning and err), but the exact shade of meaning expressed by alert as opposed to crit is a matter of conjecture. Table 10.7 on page 218 lists the specific levels used by a variety of common software programs.

Table 10.3   Syslog facility names

Facility	Programs that use it
*	All facilities except "mark"
auth	Security and authorization-related commands
authpriv	Sensitive/private authorization messages [a]
cron	The **cron** daemon
daemon	System daemons
ftp	The FTP daemon, **ftpd**
kern	The kernel
local0-7	Eight flavors of local message
lpr	The line printer spooling system
mail	**sendmail** and other mail-related software
mark	Time stamps generated at regular intervals
news	The Usenet news system
syslog	**syslogd** internal messages
user	User processes (the default if not specified)
uucp	Obsolete, ignore

a. In reality, *all* authorization-related messages are sensitive. Neither authpriv messages nor auth messages should be world-readable.

Table 10.4   Syslog severity levels (descending severity)

Level	Approximate meaning
emerg	Panic situations
alert	Urgent situations
crit	Critical conditions
err	Other error conditions
warning	Warning messages
notice	Things that might merit investigation
info	Informational messages
debug	For debugging only

In the **syslog.conf** file, levels indicate the *minimum* importance that a message must have in order to be logged. For example, a message from the mail system at level warning would match the selector mail.warning as well as the selectors mail.info, mail.notice, mail.debug, *.warning, *.notice, *.info, and *.debug. If **syslog.conf** specifies that mail.info messages be logged to a file, then mail.warning messages will go there also.

As a refinement of the basic syntax, the Linux version of syslog also allows the characters = and ! to be prefixed to priority levels to indicate "this priority only" and "except this priority and higher," respectively. Table 10.5 shows some examples.

Table 10.5   Examples of Linux priority level qualifiers in syslog.conf

Selector	Meaning
mail.info	Mail-related messages of info priority and higher
mail.=info	Only messages at info priority
mail.info;mail.!err	Only priorities info, notice, and warning
mail.debug;mail.!=warning	All priorities except warning

The *action* field tells what to do with a message. The options are listed in Table 10.6.

Table 10.6   Syslog actions

Action	Meaning
filename	Appends the message to a file on the local machine
@*hostname*	Forwards the message to the **syslogd** on *hostname*
@*ipaddress*	Forwards the message to the **syslogd** on host *ipaddress*
|*fifoname*	Writes the message to the named pipe *fifoname* [a]
user1,user2,…	Writes the message to users' screens if they are logged in
*	Writes the message to all users who are currently logged in

a. See **info mkfifo** for more information.

If a *filename* (or *fifoname*) action is used, the name should be an absolute path. If you specify a nonexistent filename, **syslogd** will create the file when a message is first directed to it.[2] You can preface a *filename* action with a dash to indicate that the filesystem should not be **sync**ed after each log entry is written. **sync**ing helps preserve as much logging information as possible in the event of a crash, but for busy log files it can be costly in terms of system performance.

If a *hostname* is used in lieu of an IP address, it must be resolvable through a translation mechanism such as DNS or NIS.

Although multiple facilities and levels are allowed in a selector, there is no provision for multiple actions. To send a message to two places (such as to a local file and to a central logging host), you must include in the configuration file two lines with the same selectors.

Because syslog messages can be used to mount a denial of service attack, **syslogd** will not accept log messages from other machines unless it is started with the **-r** flag. By default, **syslogd** also refuses to act as a third-party message forwarder; messages that arrive from one network host cannot be sent on to another. Use the **-h** flag to override this behavior. (If you want these options turned on all the time, add the flags in **/etc/sysconfig/syslog** for RHEL and Fedora, or in **/etc/init.d/sysklogd** for Debian and Ubuntu.)

2. Note that this behavior is opposite to that of the original syslog implementation, which required log files to be created in advance.

Designing a logging scheme for your site

At a small site it is adequate to configure logging so that important system errors and warnings are kept in a file on each machine, much as was done before we had syslog. The **syslog.conf** file can be customized for each host.

On a large network, central logging is essential. It keeps the flood of information manageable and makes auditing data unavailable to a person who violates the security of a machine on the network. Hackers often edit system logs to cover their tracks; if log information is whisked away as soon as it is generated, it is much harder to destroy. Your site-wide firewall should not allow external sites to submit messages to your **syslogd**.

Be aware that anyone can call **syslog** and fake log entries from any daemon or utility. Syslog also uses the UDP protocol, which is not guaranteed to be reliable; messages can get lost.

See Chapter 17 for more information about distributing files on a network.

Choose a stable machine as your logging server, preferably one that is well secured and does not have many logins. Other machines can use a generic syslog configuration file that is maintained in a central place. Thus, only two versions of **syslog.conf** need be maintained. This approach allows logging to be complete but at the same time is not a nightmare to administer.

For maximum security, the syslog server should be firewalled off from the rest of the network, allowing connections only to the syslog port and only from hosts that are allowed to log to it, and nothing else. Depending on the ambient level of paranoia, SSH connections may be allowed from system administrators' workstations to make it easier for them to review the logs.

Some very large sites may want to add more levels to the logging hierarchy. Unfortunately, syslog retains the name of the originating host for only one hop. If host "client" sends some log entries to host "server," which sends them on to host "master," master will see the data as coming from server, not from client.

Config file examples

Syslog configuration is one area in which Linux distributions vary widely. Since it's relatively easy to read a **syslog.conf** file, we will not review our example distributions' config files in detail; they're all pretty straightforward. Instead, we'll look at some common ways that you might want to set up logging if you choose to depart from or expand on your system's default.

Below are three sample **syslog.conf** files that correspond to a stand-alone machine on a small network, a client machine on a larger network, and a central logging host on the same large network. The central logging host is called "netloghost."[3]

---

3. More accurately, it uses "netloghost" as one of its hostname aliases. This allows the identity of the log host to be modified with little reconfiguration. An alias can be added in **/etc/hosts** or set up with a CNAME record in DNS. See page 399 for more information about DNS CNAME records.

Stand-alone machine

A basic configuration for a stand-alone machine is shown below:

```
# syslog.conf file for small network or stand-alone machines

# emergencies: tell everyone who is logged on
*.emerg                              *
#  important messages
*.warning;daemon,auth.info;user.none /var/log/messages
#  printer errors
lpr.debug                           /var/log/lpd-errs
```

The first noncomment line writes emergency messages to the screens of all current users. An example of emergency-level messages are those generated by **shutdown** when the system is about to be turned off.

The second line writes important messages to **/var/log/messages**. The info level is below warning, so the daemon,auth.info clause includes additional logging from **passwd**, **su**, and daemon programs. The third line writes printer error messages to **/var/log/lpd-errs**.

Network client

A network client typically forwards serious messages to a central logging machine:

```
# syslog.conf file for nonmaster machines

# Emergencies: tell everyone who is logged on
*.emerg;user.none                    *

# Forward important messages to the central logger
*.warning;lpr,local1.none           @netloghost
daemon,auth.info                    @netloghost

# Send some local stuff to the central logger too
local2.info;local7.debug            @netloghost

# Keep printer errors local
lpr.debug                           /var/log/lpd-errs

# sudo logs to local2 - keep a copy here too
local2.info                         /var/log/sudo.log

# Keep kernel messages local
kern.info                           /var/log/kern.log
```

This configuration does not keep much log information locally. It's worth mentioning that if netloghost is down or unreachable, log messages will be irretrievably lost. You may want to keep local duplicates of important messages to guard against this possibility.

At a site with lots of local software installed, lots of messages can be logged inappropriately to facility user, level emerg. In this example, user/emerg has been specifically excluded with the user.none clause in the first line.

Syslog / Log Files

*See page 48 for more information about **sudo**.*

The second and third lines forward all important messages to the central logging host; messages from the printing system and the campus-wide card access system (local1) are explicitly excluded. The fourth line forwards a subset of local logging information to netloghost as well. The last three entries keep local copies of printer errors, **sudo** messages, and kernel messages.

Central logging host

This example is for netloghost, the central, secure logging host for a moderate-sized network of about 7,000 hosts.

```
# syslog.conf file for master logging host

# Emergencies to the console and log file, with timing marks
*.emerg                            /dev/console
*.err;kern,mark.debug;auth.notice  /dev/console
*.err;kern,mark.debug;user.none    /var/log/console.log
auth.notice                        /var/log/console.log

# Send non-emergency messages to the usual log files
*.err;user.none;kern.debug         /var/log/messages
daemon,auth.notice;mail.crit       /var/log/messages
lpr.debug                          /var/log/lpd-errs
mail.debug                         /var/log/mail.log

# Local authorization stuff like sudo and npasswd
local2.debug                       /var/log/sudo.log
local2.alert                       /var/log/sudo-errs.log
auth.info                          /var/log/auth.log

# Other local stuff

local4.notice                      /var/log/da.log
local7.debug                       /var/log/tcp.log

# User stuff (the default if no facility is specified)
user.info                          /var/log/user.log
```

Messages arriving from local programs and **syslogd**s on the network are written to log files. In some cases, the output from each facility is put into its own file.

The central logging host generates the time stamp for each message as it writes the message out. The time stamps do not reflect the time on the originating host. If you have machines in several time zones or your system clocks are not synchronized, the time stamps can be somewhat misleading.

Sample syslog output

Below is a snippet from one of the log files on the master syslog host at the University of Colorado's computer science department.

```
Dec 18 15:12:42 av18.cs.colorado.edu sbatchd[495]: sbatchd/main: ls_info()
    failed: LIM is down; try later; trying ...
```

```
Dec 18 15:14:28 proxy-1.cs.colorado.edu pop-proxy[27283]: Connection from
    128.138.198.84
Dec 18 15:14:30 mroe.cs.colorado.edu pingem[271]: maltese-
    office.cs.colorado.edu has not answered 42 times
Dec 18 15:15:05 schwarz.cs.colorado.edu vmunix: Multiple softerrors: Seen 100
    Corrected Softerrors from SIMM J0201
Dec 18 15:15:16 coyote.cs.colorado.edu PAM_unix[17405]: (sshd) session closed
    for user trent
Dec 18 15:15:48 proxy-1.cs.colorado.edu pop-proxy[27285]: Connection from
    12.2.209.183
Dec 18 15:15:50 av18.cs.colorado.edu last message repeated 100 times
```

This example contains entries from several different hosts (av18, proxy-1, schwarz, mroe, and coyote) and from several programs: **sbatchd**, **pop-proxy**, **pingem**, and the Pluggable Authentication Modules library.

Note the last line of the excerpt, which complains of a message being repeated 100 times. To help keep the logs shorter, syslog generally attempts to coalesce duplicate messages and replace them with this type of summary. However, the machine from which this example was drawn accepts log entries from many other hosts, so this particular message is a bit misleading, It actually refers to the previous log entry from av18, not the entry immediately preceding it in the composite log.

It's a good idea to peruse your log files regularly. Determine what is normal so that when an anomaly occurs, you can recognize it. Better yet, set up a log postprocessor such as **swatch** to trap these cases automatically; see *Condensing log files to useful information* on page 220.

Software that uses syslog

Table 10.7 on the next page lists some of the programs that use syslog, the facilities and levels they log to, and a brief description of each program.

With all this information, it should be perfectly clear which messages to keep and which to discard, right? Well, maybe not. In practice, you just have to learn what the useful logging levels are for your system. It's best to start with an excessive amount of logging and gradually winnow out the cases that you don't want. Stop winnowing when you feel comfortable with the average data rate.

Debugging syslog

The **logger** command is useful for submitting log entries from shell scripts. You can also use it to test changes in **syslogd**'s configuration file. For example, if you have just added the line

```
local5.warning          /tmp/evi.log
```

and want to verify that it is working, run

```
$ logger -p local5.warning "test message"
```

Syslog / Log Files

Table 10.7   Software that uses syslog

Program	Facility	Levels	Description
cron	cron, daemon	info	Task-scheduling daemon
cups	lpr	info–err	Common UNIX Printing System
ftpd	ftp	debug–crit	FTP daemon (**wu-ftpd**)
inetd	daemon	warning, err	Internet super-daemon (Debian)
imapd	mail	info–alert	IMAP mail server
login	authpriv	info–err	Login programs
lpd	lpr	info–err	BSD printing system
named	daemon	info–err	Name server (DNS)
ntpd	daemon, user	info–crit	Network time daemon
passwd	auth	notice, warning	Password-setting program
popper	local0	debug, notice	POP3 mail server
sendmail	mail	debug-alert	Mail transport system
ssh	auth	info	Secure shell (remote logins)
su	auth	notice, crit	Switches UIDs
sudo	local2	notice, alert	Limited **su** program
syslogd	syslog, mark	info-err	Internal errors, time stamps
tcpd	local7	debug-err	TCP wrapper for **inetd**
vmlinuz	kern	*all*	The kernel
xinetd	*configurable*	info (default)	Variant of **inetd** (Red Hat, SUSE)

A line containing "test message" should be written to **/tmp/evi.log**. If this doesn't happen, perhaps you forgot to send **syslogd** a hangup signal.

Be careful about logging to the console device, **/dev/console**, or to any pseudo-terminal or port that supports flow control. If someone has typed <Control-S> on the console, output to it will stop. Each call to **syslog** will block, and your system will slow to a crawl. A good way to check for this degenerate condition is to send a syslog message to the console with **logger**. If **logger** hangs, you need to find the offending port, type a <Control-Q>, and rethink your logging strategy.

Another drawback to logging on the console is that the flood of messages sparked by a major problem can make the console unusable at precisely the moment that it is most needed. On certain types of frame buffers with unoptimized console drivers, the flood of messages can actually make the whole *system* unusable.

Depending on how your console is set up and managed (e.g., through a console server), console logging may also have some security implications.

Using syslog from programs

The library routines **openlog**, **syslog**, and **closelog** allow programs to use the syslog system. Versions of these library routines are available for C, Perl, Python, and PHP; we describe only the Perl interface here.

To import the definitions of the library routines, include the line

```
use Sys::Syslog;
```

at the beginning of your Perl script.

The **openlog** routine initializes logging, using the specified facility name:

```
openlog(ident, logopt, facility);
```

Messages are logged with the options specified by *logopt* and begin with the identification string *ident*. If **openlog** is not used, *ident* defaults to the current username, *logopt* to an empty string, and *facility* to "user." The *logopt* string should contain a comma-separated list of options drawn from Table 10.8.

Table 10.8 Logging options for the openlog routine

Option	Meaning
pid	Include the current process's PID in each log message.
ndelay	Connect to **syslogd** immediately (don't wait until a message is submitted).
cons	Send messages to the system console if **syslogd** is unreachable.
nowait	Do not **wait**(3) for child processes forked to write console messages.

For example, a reasonable invocation of **openlog** might be

```
openlog("adminscript", "pid,cons", "local4");
```

The **syslog** routine sends a *message* to **syslogd**, which logs it at the specified *priority*:

```
syslog(priority, message, ...);
```

The date, time, hostname, and *ident* string from the **openlog** call are prepended to the message in the log file. *message* may be followed by various other parameters to form a **printf**-style output specification that can include text and the contents of other variables; for example,

```
syslog("info", "Delivery to '%s' failed after %d attempts.", $user, $nAttempts);
```

The special symbol %m expands to an error message derived from the current value of **errno** (the most recent error code).

A priority string of the form "*level|facility*" sets both the severity level and the facility name. If you did not call **openlog** and specify an *ident* string, the **syslog** routine also checks to see if your *message* has the form of a standard error message such as

```
adminscript: User "nobody" not found in /etc/passwd file.
```

If it does, the part before the colon is secretly adopted as your *ident* string. These helpful (but undocumented) features make it unnecessary to call **openlog** at all; however, it is still a good idea. It's better to specify the facility name in one place (the **openlog** call) than to repeat it throughout your code.

The **closelog** routine closes the logging channel:

```
closelog( );
```

You must call this routine if you want to reopen the logging channel with different options. It's good form to call **closelog** when your program exits, but doing so is not strictly necessary.

Here's a complete example:

```
use Sys::Syslog;

openlog("adminscript", "cons,pid", "user");
syslog("warning","Those whom the gods would destroy, they first teach Basic.");
closelog();
```

This scriptlet produces the following log entry (191 is **admincript**'s PID):

```
Dec 28 22:56:24 moet.colorado.edu adminscript[191]: Those whom the gods
    would destroy, they first teach Basic.
```

10.5 CONDENSING LOG FILES TO USEFUL INFORMATION

Syslog is great for sorting and routing log messages, but when all is said and done, its end product is still a bunch of log files. While they may contain all kinds of useful information, those files aren't going to come and find you when something goes wrong. Another layer of software is needed to analyze the logs and make sure that important messages don't get lost amid the chatter.

A variety of free tools are available to fill this niche, and most of them are pretty similar: they scan recent log entries, match them against a database of regular expressions, and process the important messages in some attention-getting way. Some tools mail you a report; others can be configured to make noise, print log entries in different colors, or page you. Tools differ primarily in their degree of flexibility and in the size of their off-the-shelf database of patterns.

Two of the more commonly used log postprocessors are Todd Atkins' **swatch** and Craig Rowland's **logcheck**. Both are available from sourceforge.net (**logcheck** comes with the sentrytools package: sourceforge.net/projects/sentrytools).

swatch is a Perl script that gets its marching orders from a configuration file. The configuration syntax is fairly flexible, and it also provides access to the full pattern-matching mojo of Perl. While **swatch** can process an entire file in a single bound, it's primarily intended to be left running so that it can review new messages as they arrive, a la **tail -f**. A disadvantage of **swatch** is that you must build your own configuration pretty much from scratch; it doesn't know about specific systems and the actual log messages they might generate.

logcheck is a more basic script written in **sh**. The distribution also includes a C program that **logcheck** uses to help it record its place within a log file. **logcheck** knows how far it has read in a log file, so there is perhaps less chance of a message slipping by at startup or shutdown time. In addition, **logcheck** can run at intervals from **cron** rather than running continuously.

logcheck comes with sample databases for several different versions of UNIX and Linux. Even if you don't want to use the actual script, it's worth looking over the patterns to see if there are any you might want to steal for your own use.

Both of these tools have the disadvantage of working on only a single log file at a time. If your syslog configuration sorts messages into many different files, you might want to duplicate some of the messages into a central file that is frequently truncated, then use that summary file to feed a postprocessing script. That's easier than setting up a complicated network of scripts to handle multiple files.

Another tool worth mentioning is Kirk Bauer's **logwatch**. It's more a log summarizer than an ongoing monitoring and alerting tool, but it has the advantages of being relatively simple, being installed by default on Fedora and Red Hat, and being available as both an RPM package and an APT package.

A different type of log management tool is SEC, the Simple Event Correlator. It's a Perl script that reads lines from files, named pipes, or standard input and converts them into various classes of "input events" by matching them to regular expressions. Configuration rules then specify how input events should be transmogrified into output events such as the execution of a particular script or the emission of a message to a specified pipe or file.

The SEC distribution is available from kodu.neti.ee/~risto/sec and contains an extensive man page with examples. Additional examples are available at the web site. SEC isn't as "off the shelf" as the other tools listed above, but it is a good base on which to build a custom log analysis tool.

No matter what system you use to scan log files, there are a couple of things you should be sure to look for and immediately bring to the attention of an administrator:

- Most security-related messages should receive a prompt review. It's often helpful to monitor failed login, **su**, and **sudo** attempts in order to catch potential break-ins before they happen. If someone has just forgotten his password (as is usually the case), a prompt and proactive offer of help will make a good impression and cement your reputation for clairvoyance.

- Messages about disks that have filled up should be flagged and acted on immediately. Full disks often bring useful work to a standstill.

- Messages that are repeated many times deserve attention, if only in the name of hygiene.

10.6 EXERCISES

E10.1   What are the main reasons for keeping old log files?

E10.2   What is the difference between **lastlog** and **wtmp**? What is a reasonable rotation policy for each?

E10.3   Dissect and understand the following **syslog.conf** line:

    *.notice;kern.debug;lpr.info;mail.crit;news.err /var/log/messages

Does it seem sensible?

E10.4   Look through your log files for entries from **named**, the DNS name server. Are any machines trying to update your domain files dynamically? Are they succeeding? (May require root access.)

★ **E10.5**   Where would you find the boot log for your machine? What are the issues that affect logging at boot time? How does **klogd** solve these issues?

★ **E10.6**   Investigate the logging policy in use at your site, including the log file rotation policy. How much disk space is dedicated to logging? How long are log files kept? Can you foresee circumstances in which your site's policy would not be adequate? What solution would you recommend? (Requires root access.)

★ **E10.7**   Some log messages are extremely important and should be reviewed by an administrator immediately. What system could you set up to make sure that this happens as quickly as possible?

★ **E10.8**   Write a program or script that submits messages to syslog with facility "user." (May require root access.)

11 *Software and Configuration Management*

Although Linux distributions are rapidly becoming more feature complete and user friendly, software configuration management is still a major element of the administrative landscape. In addition to performing off-the-shelf installations, you must implement any customizations that are appropriate for your site. Administrators must typically perform all the following tasks:

- Automating mass installations of the operating system
- Customizing systems for the local environment
- Keeping systems patched and up to date
- Managing add-on software packages

The process of configuring an off-the-shelf distribution or software package to conform to your needs (and to your local conventions for security, file placement, and network topology) is often referred to as "localization." This chapter explores some techniques and applications that help reduce the pain of software installation and make these tasks scale gracefully.

11.1 BASIC LINUX INSTALLATION

Current Linux distributions all provide straightforward procedures for basic installation. You boot a CD-ROM or floppy disk, answer a few questions, and tell the installer which software packages to copy onto your hard drive. Most distributions also have good installation guides.

Enterprise versions of Red Hat include a printed installation manual. These can also be found on-line (with other Red Hat manuals) at www.redhat.com/docs/manuals.

 Fedora has its own documentation project, but because the current releases of Fedora remain tightly coupled to Red Hat Enterprise Linux, Fedora volunteers do not seem to have been willing to spend time duplicating the content of existing Enterprise documentation. The Red Hat manuals are usually a good place to start when looking for answers to Fedora questions.

 The boxed SUSE Linux Enterprise set also includes installation manuals. These documents are available on-line from

> www.novell.com/documentation/suse.html

Analogous documentation for openSUSE can be found here:

> www.opensuse.org/Documentation

 You can find the Debian installation manual here:

> www.debian.org/releases/stable/installmanual

 Ubuntu nicely summarizes the installation options in wiki form here:

> https://wiki.ubuntu.com/Installation

If you have to install the operating system on more than one computer, you will quickly reach the limits of interactive installation. To begin with, it is not very reproducible. (Can you repeatedly select a consistent set of software packages from the hundreds offered to you at installation time?) You can minimize pilot errors with a localization checklist, but even this measure will not prevent all potential variations. Interactive installation also consumes time and effort.

The installers for our example distributions are all scriptable, so another option is to create a floppy or CD-ROM that contains the configuration you want. This solution solves the reproducibility problem, but it still doesn't scale very well. If you are installing hundreds of machines, building and deploying hundreds of configuration disks is the height of tedium.

It's also possible to perform automatic installation over a network, and this is usually the most convenient option for sites with hundreds or thousands of systems to upgrade. All of our example distributions can be installed this way, but the off-the-shelf systems do require some configuration before the process runs smoothly.

Also, several open source development projects are striving to produce third-party network installers; for example, SystemImager. These systems are discussed in more detail later in this chapter.

Netbooting PCs

Netbooting allows you to boot a computer completely over the net, instead of from a hard disk, floppy disk, or CD-ROM. It's convenient for software installation because it means that you can sit at your desk and netboot a machine somewhere else without having to walk to the machine and insert a physical piece of boot media.

Manufacturers of dedicated UNIX boxes have long supported netbooting, but only recently has this feature become standard on PCs. After years of hacks involving custom-made boot PROMs (see etherboot.sourceforge.net), Intel has done us all a favor by establishing the PXE (Pre-boot eXecution Environment) standard. Although PXE isn't perfect, an ugly standard is better than none. (Well, usually.)

PXE acts like a miniature OS sitting in a ROM on your network card. It exposes its network capabilities through a standardized API for the system BIOS to use. This cooperation makes it possible for a single boot loader to netboot Linux on any PXE-enabled PC without the need to supply special drivers for each network card.

See page 311 for more information about DHCP. The external (network) portion of the PXE protocol is straightforward and is similar to the netboot procedures used on other architectures. A host broadcasts a DHCP "discover" request with the PXE option set, and a DHCP server or proxy responds with a DHCP packet that includes PXE options (the name of a boot server and boot file). The client downloads its boot file by using TFTP (or, optionally, multicast TFTP) and then executes it.

Although the PXE spec is not totally backward compatible with generic DHCP, in practice all modern DHCP servers can provide PXE boot service.

The degree of PXE support built into installers varies among distributions. This is an area of active development, though, and functional PXE-based systems are becoming increasingly common.

Documents that describe PXE are available from a variety of sources. A good place to start is the *Remote Boot HOWTO* available from www.tdlp.org.

Setting up PXE for Linux

Several PXE-based netboot systems exist, but the one that works best at this time is H. Peter Anvin's PXELINUX, which is part of his SYSLINUX suite of boot loaders for every occasion. Check it out at syslinux.zytor.com.

PXELINUX provides a boot file that you install in your server's **tftpboot** directory and that is downloaded to the booting PC when PXE goes into action. The PC then executes the boot file and downloads its configuration from the server; the configuration specifies which kernel to use. This chain of events can occur without intervention, or you can create a custom boot menu if you choose.

PXELINUX uses the PXE API for its downloads and is therefore hardware independent all the way through the boot process. It is not limited to booting Linux—it can also boot other OSes and can even boot floppy images if you use the MEMDISK kernel, which is also part of the SYSLINUX package.

On the server side, make sure you are using the ISC (Internet Systems Consortium) DHCP server. If you're using a different server, you may have to either configure

Software Management

additional DHCP options or else use numerical representations in the server's configuration file.

 Chapter 14 of the *Red Hat Enterprise Linux 3 System Administration Guide* is all about PXE and netbooting. Find it at www.redhat.com/docs/manuals.

 RHEL's free cousin Fedora lets you access the graphical netboot configuration system by running the command **system-config-netboot**.

 SUSE doesn't ship with any PXE packages, but you can borrow the ones from Red Hat. YaST can easily be made to work with PXE, although this configuration isn't officially supported.

 The Debian installer can be netbooted without problems; just pick up the netboot kernel image from www.debian.org/devel/debian-installer. There is even a Wiki page that points to the available resources:

   wiki.debian.net/index.cgi?DebianInstallerNetbootPXE

 As of this writing, the formal Ubuntu installation guide for the 6.06 release has not been finalized. In the meantime, you can find a draft at doc.ubuntu.com. For a quick summary of options, see the Installation/Netboot and Installation/LocalNet topics available through the main installation wiki page:

   https://wiki.ubuntu.com/Installation/Netboot

Netbooting non-PCs

PXE is an Intel product and is limited to IA-32 and IA-64 hardware. Other architectures have their own methods of booting over the net, which are almost always more elegant than PXE. An interesting twist to the netboot story is that now that Linux has spread beyond the Intel architecture, many of these "dedicated" UNIX systems now have the option of netbooting Linux instead of their native operating systems.

Discussion of the many differences among architectures is really beyond the scope of this book, but a variety of resources on the web can help.

SPARC machines and most PowerPC boxes use Open Firmware, which is easy to netboot (type **boot net**). The UltraLinux FAQ (www.ultralinux.org) includes a useful guide to netbooting Linux on SPARC processors. Alpha boxes generally use the SRM console software to boot. The *SRM HOWTO* describes the use of this feature to start Linux. For Macs, RS/6000s, and other PowerPC-based machines, the netboot procedure is specific to both your hardware and the boot loader you are using, so check your boot loader's docs. AMD64 machines use PXE like their x86 PC siblings.

Kickstart: the automated installer for Enterprise Linux and Fedora

 Kickstart is Red Hat's tool for performing automated installations. It is really just a scripting interface to the standard Red Hat installer, Anaconda, and it is dependent on both the base distribution and RPM packages. Unlike SystemImager and other raw image copiers, Kickstart is flexible and quite smart about autodetecting the system's hardware.

See page 232 for more information about packages.

If your environment requires lots of localization, you can include a postinstall script that conforms the system to your local standards. Although this does work, we've found that the postinstall scripts tend to become large and unmaintainable over time. Another option is to create an RPM package that contains your local customizations. We recommend this route; it makes versioning easy, facilitates later upgrades, and gives you dependency support and all the other goodies that come with a packaging system.

Setting up a Kickstart configuration file

Kickstart's behavior is controlled by a single configuration file, generally called **ks.cfg**. The format of this file is straightforward. If you're visually inclined, Red Hat includes a handy GUI tool called **redhat-config-kickstart** in Enterprise Linux and **system-config-kickstart** in Fedora that lets you point and click your way to **ks.cfg** nirvana.[1]

The **ks.cfg** file is also quite easy to generate programmatically. For example, suppose that you wanted to install a different set of packages on servers and clients and that you also have two offices that require slightly different customizations. You could write a small Perl script that used a master set of parameters to generate a config file for the servers and clients in each office. Changing the complement of packages would become just a matter of changing this one Perl script rather than changing every config file. There may even be some cases in which you need to generate an individualized config file for each host. In this situation, you would certainly want the files to be automatically generated.

A nice manual for Kickstart (including a list of all the available options) can be found in Section II of *The Red Hat Enterprise Linux System Administration Guide*. It's available from www.redhat.com/docs/manuals.

One word of warning regarding the Kickstart config file: if you make an error, the diagnostics consist of an unintelligible Python traceback that may or may not contain a hidden message pointing you toward the mistake. One of the main advantages of using **redhat-config-kickstart** or **system-config-kickstart** to generate the config file is that it guarantees the resulting file to be at least syntactically valid.

A Kickstart config file consists of three ordered parts. The first part is the command section, which specifies options such as the language, keyboard, and time zone. This section also specifies the source of the distribution with the url option (in the following example, it's a host called installserver).

Software Management

---

1. Note that Fedora has renamed all the **redhat-config-*** tools to **system-config-***. The name change is part of the effort to distance Fedora from the Red Hat brand name and does not (yet) reflect underlying technical differences.

Here's an example of a complete command section:

```
text
lang en_US                          # lang is used during the installation...
langsupport en_US                   # ...and langsupport at run time.
keyboard us                         # Use an American keyboard.
timezone --utc America/EST          # --utc means hardware clock is on UTC (GMT)
mouse
rootpw whatever
reboot                              # Reboot after installation. Always a good idea.
bootloader --location=mbr           # Install default boot loader in the MBR.
install                             # Install a new system instead of upgrading.
url --url http://installserver/redhat
clearpart --all --initlabel         # Clear all existing partitions
part / --fstype ext3 --size 4096
part swap --size 1024
part /var --fstype ext3 -size 1 --grow
network --bootproto dhcp
auth --useshadow --enablemd5
firewall --disabled
xconfig --defaultdesktop=GNOME --startxonboot --resolution 1280x1024 --depth 24
```

Kickstart uses graphical mode by default, which defeats the goal of unattended installation. The text keyword at the top of the example fixes this.

The rootpw option sets the new machine's root password. The default is to specify the password in cleartext, which presents something of a security problem. You can use the --iscrypted flag to specify an already encrypted password; however, MD5 passwords are not supported.

The clearpart and part directives specify a list of disk partitions with sizes. You can use the --grow option to designate one of the partitions to expand to fill any remaining space on the disk. This feature makes it easy to accommodate systems that have different sizes of hard disk.

The second section is a list of packages to install, beginning with a %packages directive. The list can contain individual packages, collections such as @ GNOME, or the notation @ Everything to include the whole shebang. When selecting individual packages, specify only the package name, not the version or the **.rpm** extension. Here's an example:

```
%packages
@ Networked Workstation
@ X Window System
@ GNOME
mylocalpackage
```

In the third section of the Kickstart configuration file, you can specify arbitrary shell commands for Kickstart to execute. There are two possible sets of commands: one introduced with %pre that runs before installation, and one introduced with %post that runs afterward. Both sections have some restrictions on the ability of the system to resolve hostnames, so it's safest to use IP addresses if you want to access the network. In addition, the postinstall commands are run in a **chroot**ed environment, so they cannot access the installation media.

Building a Kickstart server

Kickstart expects its installation files to be laid out as they are on the distribution CD, with packages stored in a directory called **RedHat/RPMS** or **Fedora/RPMS** on the server. You can easily add your own packages to this directory. There are, however, a couple of issues to be aware of.

First, if you tell Kickstart to install all packages (with an @ Everything in the packages section of your **ks.cfg**), it installs the add-on packages in alphabetical order after the base packages have been laid down. If your package depends on other packages that are not in the base set, you may want to call your package something like **zzmypackage.rpm** to make sure that it gets installed last.

If you don't want to install all packages, either list your supplemental packages individually in the %packages section of the **ks.cfg** file or add your packages to one or more of the collection lists. Collection lists are specified by entries such as @ GNOME and stand for a predefined set of packages whose members are enumerated in the file **RedHat/base/comps** or **Fedora/base/comps** on the server. Unfortunately, the **comps** file format is not well documented. The collections are the lines that begin with 0 or 1; the number specifies whether the collection is selected by default. In general, it's not a good idea to tamper with the standard collections. We suggest that you leave them as Red Hat defined them and explicitly name all your supplemental packages in the **ks.cfg** file.

Pointing Kickstart at your config file

Once you've created a config file, you have a couple of ways to get Kickstart to use it. The officially sanctioned method is to boot with a floppy or CD-ROM and ask for a Kickstart installation by specifying **linux ks** at the initial boot: prompt. If you don't specify additional arguments, the system determines its network address by using DHCP. It then obtains the DHCP boot server and boot file options, attempts to mount the boot server with NFS, and uses the value of the boot file option as its Kickstart configuration file. If no boot file has been specified, the system looks for a file called **/kickstart/***hostipaddress***-kickstart**.

Alternatively, Kickstart can be told to get its configuration file in some other way by providing a path as an argument to the **ks** option. There are several possibilities. The instruction

    boot: **linux ks=http:***server***:/path**

tells Kickstart to use HTTP to download the file instead of NFS. Using **ks=floppy** tells Kickstart to look for **ks.cfg** on the local floppy drive.

To eliminate the use of boot media entirely, you'll need to graduate to PXE. See page 224 for more information about that.

Software Management

AutoYaST: SUSE's automated installation tool

YaST2 is SUSE's all-in-one installation and configuration tool. It comes with a nice GUI and is fun to use when installing a single system. Older SUSE releases allowed automation based on regular YaST, but the results were not to everyone's liking. SUSE 8 introduced a tool called AutoYaST that automates SUSE installations. It is the most powerful automated installation software of all the distributions described in this book. You can download detailed documentation from www.suse.com/~ug.

SUSE splits the autoinstallation process into three phases: preparation, installation, and configuration. Initial preparation is performed with the AutoYaST module:

```
$ /sbin/yast2 autoyast
```

This module helps you define the details of your desired setup. The result of running it is an XML control file that tells the installer how to configure a SUSE system; the structure of the file is described in the on-line documentation mentioned above.

A couple of shortcuts can speed the configuration process. The AutoYaST module can read in Red Hat Kickstart configuration files to help you upgrade from "legacy" systems. If you want to duplicate the configuration of the machine you are currently working on, an option automates this as well.

To perform an actual installation, you need three network services:

- A DHCP server on the same subnet as the machine you want to set up
- A SUSE install server or package repository
- A server that provides the configuration information for the installation

The last of these servers can supply the configuration files through your choice of HTTP, NFS, or TFTP.

In the most basic setup, you produce a control file for each machine you want to install. AutoYaST uses the IP address of the client to determine which control file to use. This approach is not all that efficient if you have to install a series of slightly different machines.

You can create more complex setups by using a rules system. Based on system properties such as disk size, host ID, or PCMCIA availability, different control files are matched to the target system. The contents of all selected control files are merged, with the last control file overriding earlier ones in the case of conflicts. (A control file does not have to specify all aspects of a system's configuration, so this merging does make sense.)

Control files can also define "classes" of machines based on hostnames or IP address ranges, and each class may have yet another subsidiary control file associated with it. Machines can belong to zero, one, or multiple classes, and their configurations will incorporate the contents of all the appropriate class control files.

Thanks to its ability to integrate the contents of multiple control files, the AutoYaST structure allows complex setups to be defined with minimal redundancy. The XML control files are somewhat cumbersome for humans to read, but the files are simple to process and edit with any of the commonly available XML processing tools.

The Debian and Ubuntu installer

The Debian installer (named, appropriately enough, **debian-installer**) was completely redone for the "sarge" release. It is now quite a fun tool to work with. It is used by Ubuntu as well, although Ubuntu (wisely, we think) preserves all the seemingly Debian-specific command names.

The new system has a modular design and is written in a combination of C and shell scripts. It can run off two floppies on machines with as little as 32MB of memory, and it can pull all the files required for installation directly off the net, including the list of files that it needs.

All the interactive parts of the Debian installer use the **cdebconf** utility for deciding which questions to ask and what default answers to use. By providing **cdebconf** with a database of preformulated answers, you can fully automate the installer. You can either generate the database by hand (it's just a text file), or you can perform an interactive installation on an example system and then dump out your **cdebconf** answers with the following commands:

```
# debconf-get-selections --installer > config.cfg
# debconf-get-selections >> config.cfg
```

Make the config file available on the net and then pass it into the kernel at installation time with the following kernel argument:

```
preseed/url=http://host/path/to/preseed
```

If you want to deploy Debian automatically, take a look at the **cdebootstrap** package as well. It is based on the same code as the Debian installer and allows you to create an installation image in a subdirectory of the local disk, pulling the required packages directly from a Debian repository. This facility can be very handy for use in automated setup scripts of your own devising.

In earlier Debian releases, the installer was the source of numerous complaints. Of necessity, many system administrators implemented their own installation and configuration systems, a variety of which have been catalogued here:

www.linuxmafia.com/faq/Debian/installers.html

Another alternative to the standard Debian tools is a package called FAI (for Fully Automatic Installation). The home site is www.informatik.uni-koeln.de/fai.

These alternative systems are needed less than in the past, but they are still worth reviewing if you decide to part ways with the standard installer.

Although it is a distribution outside the Red Hat lineage, Ubuntu has grafted compatibility with Kickstart control files onto its own underlying installer. It also includes the **system-config-kickstart** tool for creating these files. The Kickstart functionality in Ubuntu is not yet 100% solid, but it appears complete enough to use. Kickstart compatibility is not yet shared with Debian.

Installing from a master system

If you're forced to part ways from your distribution's standard installer, consider whether your site's hardware is uniform enough to allow you to simply duplicate the distribution from one machine to another. Duplication may be faster than traditional installation, and its guarantee of uniformity is slightly stronger.

You may find the following back-of-the envelope recipe helpful:

- Install and configure the master system, using either the distribution's normal installation process or a script such as Debian's **debootstrap**.

- Boot the machine onto which you want to duplicate the distribution, using either a bootable CD-ROM such as Knoppix[2] or a PXE-based method.

- Partition the disk by using **cfdisk** interactively or **sfdisk** from a script.

- Create filesystems, initialize swap space, and mount everything under **/mnt**.

- Duplicate the master installation to the newly partitioned disk by using **ssh** and **rsync** (see page 508). Make sure you exclude the **/tmp**, **/proc**, and **/sys** directories.

- Edit any files that require customization (e.g., **/etc/modules** or **/etc/fstab**), or better yet, automate this process.

- Make the new machine bootable by installing GRUB or LILO in the disk's master boot record. See page 26 for more information.

11.2 DISKLESS CLIENTS

In the 1980s, when hard disks were expensive, many sites deployed workstations that had no local hard disk. Instead, these computers, known as "diskless clients," mounted their filesystems from a network server. Today, disks are cheap, and almost nobody uses diskless clients anymore. The whole idea seems quaint, like nine-track tape or dot-matrix printers.

But wait! Diskless operation is still quite possible, and it's actually a reasonable option to consider for certain types of installations. Here are some of its advantages:

- In a diskless setup, all relevant data is kept on the server. Diskless clients never go off-line in the sense that their configuration information becomes inaccessible, so administrative procedures don't need to take account of inoperative machines as a potential special case.

---

2. Knoppix is a version of Debian that runs directly from a bootable CD/DVD-ROM; no hard disk installation is necessary. It's ideal for use during installation or rescue or when handling security incidents. See www.knoppix.org. Many other distributions (e.g., Ubuntu) are starting to become runnable from a live CD as well.

- The amount of truly local configuration information is kept to a minimum. Almost no administrative operation requires you to be physically present in front of a client machine.

- New clients can be set up on the server before they are running or even physically present. Clients behave much more like logical entities than physical entities.

- Major changes to a client's configuration can be executed in the time needed to reboot. An updated root tree can sit alongside the active one, waiting for the right moment to be activated. You can provide faster, more reliable service while using simpler software and update distribution concepts.

- For many applications, the expensive and complex RAID array you can afford to put on your server may be faster than cheap local disks, even after network latency is taken into account. The network server is also likely to be more reliable. Disks do fail, but a redundant server setup can protect an entire network of diskless clients.

- No rule mandates that diskless clients can't actually have disks. If you prefer, you can use local disks for swap space or cache. In the modern era, the point is not that the clients do not have physical disks; it is that they do not use these disks to store anything that requires administrative attention.

- Many applications are CPU-bound and have no particular dependency on disk speed. Others that are potentially heavy disk users can be converted to CPU-bound operation with the addition of memory. Web servers, database servers, and servers for network protocols all potentially fall into this category.

In a diskless environment, clients typically have small root filesystems dedicated to their exclusive use. Clients can share a common, read-only **/usr** directory because this directory contains no machine-specific information and is never written to in regular operation.

Red Hat Enterprise Linux is the only Linux distribution with a standardized system for setting up diskless clients out of the box. But even without elaborate vendor support, setting up is not rocket science and is not hard to do on your own. Many systems have a mechanism for netbooting X Windows terminals; you can use that as a starting point to netboot workstations.

If your distribution does not include instructions for setting up diskless clients, start by copying a freshly installed machine's root filesystem to your server as a basis for cloning new machines. Figure out how to boot your systems over the network with an NFS root directory. Share the read-only parts of a machine's filesystem tree (e.g., **/usr**) among all clients.

Software Management

When cloning a client root, you may have to customize the following:

- Mount table
- Hardware device support (if your network is not homogeneous)
- Network configuration (possibly)
- Startup scripts (possibly)

Commodity hardware is often shipped with cheap IDE disks. Use these for local swap space and scratch partitions.

See page 815 for more information about RAM disks.

Today's inexpensive RAM is a great boon for diskless nodes. Consider using a RAM-based filesystem as a backing store for the **/tmp** and **/dev** directories (or as a cache of frequently used files that you preload at boot time).[3] Keeping the **/dev** tree in RAM can boost performance considerably because programs that love to roam the **/dev** tree are not punished by NFS latency.

11.3 Package Management

Linux distributions all use some form of packaging system to facilitate the job of configuration management. Packages have traditionally been used to distribute software, but they can be used to wrap configuration files and administrative data as well. They have several advantages over the traditional unstructured **.tar.gz** archives. Perhaps most importantly, they try to make the installation process as atomic as possible. If an error occurs, the package can be backed out or reapplied.

UNIX vendors often have special procedures for distributing patches to their customers, but Linux distributors take advantage of their standard package management facilities. To issue a patch, the distributor simply releases an updated package. When installed by customers, the new version replaces the old.

Package installers are typically aware of configuration files and will not normally overwrite local customizations performed by a system administrator. They will either back up the existing config files that they change or provide example config files under a different name (e.g., **pkg.conf.rpmnew**). If you find that a newly installed package breaks something on your system, you can, at least in theory, back it out to restore your system to its original state. Of course theory != practice, so don't try this out on a production system without testing it first.

Packaging systems define a dependency model that allows package maintainers to ensure that all the libraries and support infrastructure on which their applications depend are properly installed. Packages can also run scripts at various points during the installation, so they can do much more than just disgorge new files. (This feature probably accounts for much of the observed failure of packages to restore the system to its original state after uninstallation.)

Packages are also a nice way to distribute your own localizations. You can easily create a package that, when installed, reads localization information about a machine

---

3. But note that **/dev** may already live in a kernel-based filesystem.

(or gets it from central database) and uses that information to set up local configuration files. You can also bundle up your local applications as packages, complete with dependencies, or make packages for third-party applications that aren't normally distributed in package format. You can versionize your packages and use the dependency mechanism to upgrade machines automatically when a new version of your localization package is installed.

You can also use the dependency mechanism to create groups of packages. For example, it's possible to create a package that installs nothing of its own but depends on many other patches. Installing the package with dependencies turned on results in all the patches being installed in a single step.

Available package management systems

Two package formats are in common use. Red Hat, Fedora, SUSE, and several other distributions use RPM, the Red Hat Package Manager. Debian and Ubuntu use a separate **.deb** format. The two formats are functionally similar.

It's easy to convert between the two package formats with a tool such as **alien** from kitenet.net/programs/alien. **alien** knows nothing about the software inside a package, so if the contents are not already compatible with your distribution, **alien** will not help. In general, it's best to stick with the native package mechanism used by your distribution.

Both the RPM and **.deb** packaging systems now function as dual-layer soup-to-nuts configuration management tools. At the lowest level are the tools that install, uninstall, and query packages: **rpm** for RPM and **dpkg** for **.deb**.

On top of these commands are systems that know how to find packages on the Internet, analyze interpackage dependencies, and upgrade all the packages on a system. The main contenders at this level are **yum**, which works with the RPM system, the Red Hat Network, which is specific to Red Hat Linux and uses RPM, and Debian's Advanced Package Tool (APT), which originated in the **.deb** universe but now works equally well with both **.deb** and RPM packages.

On the next couple of pages, we review the low-level commands **rpm** and **dpkg**. In the section *High-level package management systems* starting on page 237, we discuss the comprehensive update systems (e.g., APT and **yum**) that elaborate on these low-level facilities.

rpm: manage RPM packages

The **rpm** command installs, verifies, and queries the status of packages. It formerly built them as well, but this function has now been broken out into the **rpmbuild** command. However, **rpm** options still have complex interactions and can be used together only in certain combinations. It's most useful to think of **rpm** as if it were several different commands that happen to share the same name.

The mode you tell **rpm** to enter (such as **--install** or **--query**) specifies which of **rpm**'s multiple personalities you are hoping to access. **rpm --help** lists all the options broken down by mode, but it's worth your time to read the man page in some detail if you will frequently be dealing with RPM packages.

The bread-and-butter options are **--install**, **--upgrade**, **--erase**, and **--query**. The query option is a bit tricky in that it serves only to enable other options; you must supply an additional command-line flag to pose a specific question. For example, the command **rpm --query --all** lists the packages installed on the system.

Let's look at an example. Suppose you need to install a new version of OpenSSH because a security fix was recently published. Once you've downloaded the package to your local computer, run **rpm --upgrade** to replace the older version with the newer:

```
# rpm --upgrade openssh-2.9p2-12.i386.rpm
error: failed dependencies:
openssh = 2.9p2-7 is needed by openssh-askpass-2.9p2-7
openssh = 2.9p2-7 is needed by openssh-askpass-gnome-2.9p2-7
openssh = 2.9p2-7 is needed by openssh-clients-2.9p2-7
openssh = 2.9p2-7 is needed by openssh-server-2.9p2-7
```

D'oh! Perhaps it's not so simple after all. Here we see that the currently installed version of OpenSSH, 2.9p2-7, is required by a number of other packages. **rpm** won't let us upgrade OpenSSH because the change might affect the operation of these other packages. This type of conflict happens all the time, and it's a major motivation for the development of systems like APT and **yum**. In real life we wouldn't attempt to untangle the dependencies by hand, but let's continue with **rpm** alone for the purpose of this example.

We could force the upgrade with the **--force** option, but that's usually a bad idea. This isn't Windows; the dependency information is there to save you time and trouble, not just to get in your way. There's nothing like a broken SSH on a remote system to ruin a sysadmin's morning.

Instead, we'll grab updated versions of the dependent packages as well. If we were smart, we could have determined that other packages depended on OpenSSH before we even attempted the upgrade:

```
# rpm --query --whatrequires openssh
openssh-askpass-2.9p2-7
openssh-askpass-gnome-2.9p2-7
openssh-clients-2.9p2-7
openssh-server-2.9p2-7
```

Suppose that we've obtained updated copies of all the packages. We could install them one at a time, but **rpm** is smart enough to handle them all at once. If you list multiple RPMs on the command line, **rpm** sorts them by dependency before installation.

```
# rpm --upgrade openssh-*
```

Cool! Looks like it succeeded, and sure enough:

```
# rpm --query openssh
openssh-2.9p2-12
```

Note that **rpm** understands which package we are talking about even though we didn't specify the package's full name or version.

dpkg: manage Debian-style packages

Just as RPM packages have the all-in-one **rpm** command, Debian packages have the **dpkg** command. Useful options include **--install**, **--remove**, and **-l** to list the packages that have been installed on the system. Note that **dpkg --install** of a package that's already on the system removes the previous version before installing.

Suppose that the Debian security team recently released a fix to **nvi** to patch a potential security problem. After grabbing the patch, we run **dpkg** to install it. As you can see, it's much chattier than **rpm** and tells us exactly what it's doing:

```
# dpkg --install ./nvi_1.79-16a.1_i386.deb
(Reading database ... 24368 files and directories currently installed.)
Preparing to replace nvi 1.79-14 (using ./nvi_1.79-16a.1_i386.deb) ...
Unpacking replacement nvi ...
Setting up nvi (1.79-16a.1) ...
Checking available versions of ex, updating links in /etc/alternatives ...
(You may modify the symlinks there yourself if desired - see 'man ln'.)
Leaving ex (/usr/bin/ex) pointing to /usr/bin/nex.
Leaving ex.1.gz (/usr/share/man/man1/ex.1.gz) pointing to
    /usr/share/man/man1/nex.1.gz.
...
```

We can now use **dpkg -l** to verify that the installation worked. The **-l** flag accepts an optional search pattern, so we can just search for **nvi**:

```
$ dpkg -l nvi
Desired=Unknown/Install/Remove/Purge
| Status=Not/Installed/Config-files/Unpacked/Failed-config/Half-installed
|/ Err?=(none)/Hold/Reinst-required/X=both-problems (Status,Err: uppercase=bad)
||/ Name          Version          Description
+++-===========-==============-===============================
ii  nvi           1.79-16a.1       4.4BSD re-implementation of vi.
```

Our installation seems to have gone smoothly.

11.4 HIGH-LEVEL PACKAGE MANAGEMENT SYSTEMS

Meta-package-management systems such as APT, **yum**, and the Red Hat Network share several goals:

- To simplify the locating and downloading of packages
- To automate the process of updating or upgrading systems
- To facilitate the management of interpackage dependencies

Clearly, there is more to these systems than just client-side commands. They all require that distribution maintainers organize their offerings in an agreed-on way so that the software can be accessed and reasoned about by clients.

Software Management

Since no single supplier can encompass the entire "world of Linux software," the systems all allow for the existence of multiple software repositories. Repositories can be local to your network, so these systems make a dandy foundation for creating your own internal distribution system.

 The Red Hat Network is closely tied to Red Hat Enterprise Linux. It's a commercial service that costs money and offers more in terms of attractive GUIs and automation ability than do APT and **yum**. Unfortunately, it's something of a mysterious black box underneath the covers. The client side can reference **yum** and APT repositories, and this ability has allowed distributions such as CentOS to adapt the client GUI for nonproprietary use.

APT is better documented than the Red Hat Network, is significantly more portable, and is free. It's also more flexible in terms of what you can do with it. APT originated in the world of Debian and **dpkg**, but it has been extended to encompass RPMs, and versions that work with all of our example distributions are available. It's the closest thing we have at this point to a universal standard for software distribution.

yum is an RPM-specific analog of APT. It's the default package manager for Fedora, although it runs on any RPM-based system, provided that you can point it toward appropriately formatted repositories.

In head-to-head bakeoffs, **yum** has generally been preferred to the RPM version of APT, but it's not clear that there is a solid technical reason for this. **yum** has deeper roots in the RPM world, which gives it a presumptive lead. APT-RPM's future was clouded in early 2005 when the original developer, Gustavo Niemeyer, abandoned it to work on a more comprehensive system (the Smart Package Manager at labix.org; not yet mainstream but widely anticipated to be the next big thing). APT-RPM development was eventually resumed by Panu Matilainen, and the project is currently under active development once again.

We like APT and consider it a solid choice if you want to set up your own automated package distribution network, regardless of the distributions currently in use at your site. See the section *Setting up an internal APT server* on page 244 for more information.

 SUSE is something of a lame duck in the package management domain. It uses RPM packages, but previous releases supported only SUSE's own YaST Online Update tool for performing system updates. In a blaze of promiscuity, SUSE has recently added some degree of support for **yum**, APT-RPM, and Novell's own ZENworks Linux Management agent, with ZENworks being the primary update manager. (See **rug** for a command-line interface.)

ZENworks is part of a larger product line that embodies Novell's grab for dominance in the cross-platform configuration management space. Is it the best option for you? Well, maybe, if you're a Novell shop and are interested in paid support. Sites that want to keep their package management free and relatively apolitical might investigate the Smart Package Manager mentioned above.

Package repositories

Linux distributors maintain software repositories that work hand-in-hand with their chosen package management systems. The default configuration for the package management system usually points to one or more well-known web or FTP servers that are under the distributor's control.

However, it isn't immediately obvious what such repositories should contain. Should they include only the sets of packages blessed as formal, major releases? Formal releases plus current security updates? Up-to-date versions of all the packages that existed in the formal releases? Useful third-party software not officially supported by the distributor? Source code? Binaries for multiple hardware architectures? When you run **apt-get upgrade** or **yum upgrade** to bring the system up to date, what exactly should that mean?

In general, package management systems must answer all these questions and must make it easy for sites to select the specific cross-sections they want to define as their "software world." The following concepts help structure this process:

- A "release" is a self-consistent snapshot of the package universe. Before the Internet era, named OS releases were more or less immutable and were associated with one specific point in time; security patches were made available separately. These days, a release is a more nebulous concept. Releases evolve over time as packages are updated. Some releases, such as Red Hat Enterprise Linux, are specifically designed to evolve slowly; by default, only security updates are incorporated. Other releases, such as beta versions, change frequently and dramatically. But in all cases, the release is the baseline, the target, the "thing I want to update my system to look like."

- A "component" is a subset of the software within a release. Distributions partition themselves differently, but one common distinction is that between core software blessed by the distributor and extra software made available by the broader community. Another distinction that's common in the Linux world is the one between the free, open source portions of a release and the parts that are tainted by some kind of restrictive licensing agreement.

  Of particular note from an administrative standpoint are minimally active components that include only security fixes. Some releases allow you to combine a security component with an immutable baseline component to create a relatively stable version of the distribution.

- An "architecture" represents a specific class of hardware. The expectation is that machines within an architecture class will be similar enough that they can all run the same binaries. Architectures are specific instances of releases, for example, "Fedora Core 5 for the i386 architecture." Since components are subdivisions of releases, there's a corresponding architecture-specific instance for each of them as well.

Software Management

- Individual packages are the elements that make up components, and therefore, indirectly, releases. Packages are usually architecture-specific and are versioned independently of the main release and of other packages. The correspondence between packages and releases is implicit in the way the network repository is set up.

The existence of components that aren't maintained by the distributor (e.g., Debian's "contrib" or Fedora's "extras") raises the question of how these components relate to the core OS release. Can they really be said to be "a component" of the specific release, or are they some other kind of animal entirely? From a package management perspective, the answer is clear: extras are a true component. They are associated with a specific release, and they evolve in tandem with it. The separation of control is interesting from an administrative standpoint, but it doesn't affect the package distribution systems.

RHN: the Red Hat Network

With Red Hat having departed from the consumer Linux business, the Red Hat Network has become the system management platform for Red Hat Enterprise Linux. You purchase the right to access Red Hat Network by subscribing. At its simplest, you can use the Red Hat Network as a glorified web portal and mailing list. Used in this way, the Red Hat Network is not much different from the patch notification mailing lists that have been run by various UNIX vendors for years. But more features are available if you're willing to pay for them. See rhn.redhat.com for current rates and info.

The Red Hat Network provides a pretty GUI interface for downloading new packages and furnishes a command-line alternative. It even lets you download and install new packages without human intervention. Once you register, your machines get all the patches and bug fixes that they need without you ever having to leave your Quake session. The downside of automatic registration is that Red Hat decides what updates you need. You might consider how much you really trust Red Hat (and the software maintainers whose products they package) not to screw things up. Given some of the interesting choices Red Hat has made in the past when it comes to little things like which compiler to ship, some folks might remain skeptical.

A reasonable compromise might be to sign up one machine in your organization for automatic updates. You can take snapshots from that machine at periodic intervals to test as possible candidates for internal releases. Be sure that you review the terms of the Red Hat license agreement (available from www.redhat.com/licenses) before embarking on this path, however. You might be surprised to learn that Red Hat claims a proprietary interest in the open-source software distributed through the Red Hat Network, not to mention that you have agreed to allow Red Hat to audit your systems at will.

APT: the Advanced Package Tool

APT is one of the most mature package management systems. It's possible to upgrade an entire system full of software with a single **apt-get** command or even (as with the Red Hat Network) to have your boxes continuously keep themselves up to date without human intervention.

Because it originated in the Debian universe, the original APT supported only **.deb** packages. However, APT was later ported to the RPM package mechanism. This version, known as APT-RPM, is available from apt-rpm.org. The **yum** system, described starting on page 246, offers similar RPM-based functionality and is directly supported by the Fedora releases. When choosing between **yum** and APT-RPM, the heterogeneity of your site and your distributions' built-in preferences are more important than technical distinctions between the systems. Go with what's well supported and easy.

The first rule of using **apt-get** on Debian systems (and indeed all management of Debian packages) is to ignore the existence of **dselect**, which acts as a front end for the Debian package system. It's not a bad idea, but the user interface is poor. The Debian documentation will try to steer you toward **dselect**, but stay strong.

If you are using **apt-get** to manage a stock Debian or Ubuntu installation from a standard mirror, the easiest way to see the available packages is to visit the master list at packages.debian.org or packages.ubuntu.com. Both distributions include a nice search interface. If you set up your own **apt-get** server (see page 244), then of course you will know what packages you have made available and you can list them in whatever way you want.

Distributions commonly include dummy packages that exist only to claim other packages as prerequisites. **apt-get** downloads and upgrades prerequisite packages as needed, so the dummy packages make it easy to install or upgrade several packages as a block. For example, installing the **gnome-desktop-environment** package obtains and installs all the packages necessary to run the GNOME user interface.

Once you have set up your **sources.list** file and know the name of a package that you want, the only remaining task is to run **apt-get update** to refresh **apt-get**'s cache of package information. After that, just run **apt-get install** *package-name* to install the package. The same command updates a package that has already been installed.

Suppose we want to install a new version of the **sudo** package that fixes a security bug. First, it's always wise to do an **apt-get update**:

```
$ sudo apt-get update
Get:1 http://http.us.debian.org stable/main Packages [824kB]
Get:2 http://non-us.debian.org stable/non-US/main Release [102B]
...
```

Software Management

Now we can actually fetch the package. Note that we are using **sudo** as we fetch the new **sudo** package—**apt-get** can even upgrade packages that are in use!

```
$ sudo apt-get install sudo
Reading Package Lists... Done
Building Dependency Tree... Done
1 packages upgraded, 0 newly installed, 0 to remove and 191 not upgraded.
Need to get 0B/122kB of archives. After unpacking 131kB will be used.
(Reading database ... 24359 files and directories currently installed.)
Preparing to replace sudo 1.6.1-1 (using .../sudo_1.6.2p2-2_i386.deb) ...
Unpacking replacement sudo ...
Setting up sudo (1.6.2p2-2) ...
Installing new version of config file /etc/pam.d/sudo ...
```

Configuring apt-get

Configuring **apt-get** is straightforward; pretty much everything you need to know can be found in the *APT HOWTO:*

> www.debian.org/doc/manuals/apt-howto

The most important **apt-get** configuration file is **/etc/apt/sources.list**, which tells **apt-get** where to get its packages. Each line specifies the following:

- A type of package, currently deb or deb-src for Debian-style packages or rpm or rpm-src for RPMs
- A URL that points to a file, CD-ROM, HTTP server, or FTP server from which to fetch packages
- A "distribution" (really, a release name) that lets you deliver multiple versions of packages. Distributors use this for major releases, but you can use it however you want for internal distribution systems.
- A potential list of components (categories of packages within a release)

Unless you want to set up your own APT repository or cache, the default configuration generally works fine. If you have a reasonable network connection, you should comment out the lines for your distribution's CD-ROMs. If you want to download source code, uncomment the lines that specify deb-src or rpm-src.

As long as you're editing the file, you should change the identity of the mirror to one that is close to you; a full list of mirrors for Debian can be found here:

> www.debian.org/misc/README.mirrors

 Ubuntu maintains a similar list at wiki.ubuntu.com/Archive.

To make things even easier, a Debian tool called **netselect-apt** automatically generates a **sources.list** file for you; it selects the closest mirror it can find based on ping time. **netselect-apt** is part of the **netselect** package, which is available from your nearest mirror. (Off the shelf, **netselect-apt** is somewhat tied to the Debian mirror system, but most packages work fine with Ubuntu as well.)

Make sure that security.debian.org or security.ubuntu.com is listed as a source so that you have access to the latest security patches.

An example /etc/apt/sources.list file

The following example uses http.us.debian.org for the stable archive but also adds non-us.debian.org as a source for non-US packages (this was formerly important for cryptographic packages, but it is less so now). We've added security.debian.org, the source of all security patches, and our local APT server, local-debian-server. Finally, we've turned on downloading of source code.

```
# General format: type uri distribution [components]
deb http://ftp.us.debian.org/debian stable main contrib non-free
deb http://non-us.debian.org/debian-non-US stable/non-US main contrib non-free
deb http://security.debian.org stable/updates main contrib non-free
deb http://local-debian-server/mypackages/ ./
deb-src http://http.us.debian.org/debian stable main contrib non-free
deb-src http://non-us.debian.org/debian-non-US stable/non-US main contrib non-free
deb-src http://security.debian.org stable/updates main contrib non-free
```

The *distribution* and *components* fields help **apt-get** navigate the fileystem hierarchy of the Debian repository, which has a standardized layout. The root distribution can be stable for the most recent mainstream distribution, unstable (or testing) for the current work-in-progress distribution, or the name of a specific release such as etch. The available components are typically main, contrib, and non-free.

This example uses the stable repositories, which do not change as frequently as other sources. All the latest packages are included in Debian's bleeding-edge unstable distribution. "Unstable" does not (necessarily) mean that the packages themselves are unstable, but rather that the composition of the entire distribution is volatile. Weekly updates of more than 100MB are typical.

Lines in the **sources.list** file are consulted in order, so you can theoretically put the unstable and testing lines at the end of the file to give stable versions precedence. The problem with this approach is that because of APT's dependency tracking, one unstable package can drag in updated, unstable versions of all the packages it depends on. These packages in turn may pull in unstable versions of all their buddies, and so on. One bad apple spoils the whole barrel; don't play with unstable packages on your production systems.

If you must incorporate a package from the unstable world into your production environment, the right way to do it is to use a "backport" that has been recompiled on the stable release to get along with its stable libraries. To find these backports and other delicacies, check out the APT search engine hosted at www.apt-get.org. Many of the backported packages (as opposed to just pointers) can be found at Norbert Tretkowski's site www.backports.org. The backports in this repository are of excellent quality and have minimal external dependencies.

Using proxies to make apt-get scale

If you plan to use **apt-get** on a large number of machines, you will probably want to cache packages locally—downloading a copy of each package for every machine is not a sensible use of external bandwidth. You may also need to direct your **apt-get** through a proxy if your firewall requires this.

apt-get uses vanilla HTTP and FTP protocols, so you can use any existing web proxy that you might happen to have installed. **apt-get** honors the http_proxy environment variable, but you can also set an explicit proxy with a line in **/etc/apt/apt.conf**:

```
Acquire::http::Proxy "http://proxyserver:8080/
```

An alternative to a generic web proxy is a small application called **apt-proxy**. Despite the name, it is not a true proxy but rather an app that builds a cache of packages by **rsync**ing them from the real APT server. **apt-proxy** is available from

```
sourceforge.net/projects/apt-proxy
```

Setting up an internal APT server

Instead of using a proxy, you can also set up your own autonomous APT server and point your internal clients at it. This model lets you tweak the packages you offer to your clients, push out upgrades easily (just install new versions on the server), distribute your own applications as packages, and most importantly, provide your own versions of distributions.

Set page 724 for hints on setting up the Apache web server.

Because **apt-get** uses standard protocols (HTTP or FTP) to download its packages, setting up an APT server is simply a matter of establishing a web or FTP server that provides appropriate content.[4] Given the wide availability of HTTP-related servers and tools, HTTP is probably the most straightforward choice for use with APT.

The packages on the server can all be in one directory, or they can be arranged in a hierarchy as on the Debian and Ubuntu mirrors.

In addition to providing the package files, you must generate two summary files: **Packages.gz** and **Contents.gz**. **Packages.gz** must be a **gzip**ped list of the packages on the server and their dependencies. **apt-get update** uses this list to determine the available complement of packages. **Contents.gz** maps raw files to the packages that contain them; it is not actually used by **apt-get** itself. The **apt-ftparchive** command, which is included in the **apt-utils** package, automatically generates both of these summary files for you.

Once you have created the summary files, the rest is easy. A line such as

```
deb http://local-server/mypackages/ ./
```

in the **/etc/apt/sources.list** files of client machines connects **apt-get** to your local server. Run **apt-get update** on each client, then use **apt-get** normally.

---

4. There are other options as well. For example, you can set up an NFS server containing the update files or burn a DVD that you walk around to each system.

To distribute source code as well as binary packages, just put the source packages on the server. Unlike RPM, which has an SRPM equivalent for source packages, Debian distributes the source packages in three parts: the vanilla **.tar.gz** file, an optional **.diff.gz** file (used by packagers to show the changes they have made relative to the original code base), and a **.dsc** file that describes the package. The source code equivalent of **Packages.gz** is **Sources.gz**; it is also generated by **apt-ftparchive**.

The example **sources.list** line above does not specify a distribution parameter. If you like, you can use distribution names as a form of internal versioning. Just place each set of packages you want to define as a "release" in its own subdirectory and change the ./ in the **sources.list** file to the release name or number.

It's often useful to create generically named distributions such as "test" and "production" that are analogous to Debian's own "stable" and "testing" releases. Use symbolic links on the server to point these names at specific releases. You can later redefine the contents of the releases just by changing the targets of the links. For example, once you're confident that a test release is ready for deployment, you can point the production link at the same directory. Clients synchronizing themselves to the production release then automatically pick up the changes.

Automating apt-get

You can run **apt-get** on a regular schedule from **cron**. Even if you don't install packages automatically, you may want to run **apt-get update** regularly to keep your package summaries up to date.

apt-get dist-upgrade downloads and installs new versions of any packages that are currently installed on the local machine. **dist-upgrade** is similar to **upgrade** but has slightly more intelligent dependency handling. **dist-upgrade** may want to delete some packages that it views as irreconcilably incompatible with the upgraded system, so be prepared for potential surprises.

If you really want to play with fire, have machines perform the upgrade in an unattended fashion by using the **-yes** option. It answers any confirmation questions that **apt-get** might ask with an enthusiastic "Yes!"

It's probably not a good idea to perform automated upgrades directly from a distribution's mirror. However, in concert with your own APT servers, packages, and release control system, this is a perfect way to keep clients in sync. A quickie shell script like the following keeps a box up to date with its APT server:

```
#!/bin/sh
apt-get update
apt-get -yes dist-upgrade
```

Call this script from a **cron** job if you want to run it nightly. You can also refer to it from a system startup script to make the machine update at boot time. See Chapter 8, *Periodic Processes*, for more information about **cron**; see Chapter 2, *Booting and Shutting Down*, for more information about startup scripts.

Software Management

If you run updates out of **cron** on many machines, it's a good idea to use time randomization to make sure that everyone doesn't try to update at once. The short Perl script on page 511 can help with this task.

If you don't quite trust your source of packages, consider automatically downloading all changed packages without installing them. Use **apt-get**'s **--download-only** option to request this behavior, then review the packages by hand and install the ones you want to update. Downloaded packages are put in **/var/cache/apt**, and over time this directory can grow to be quite large. Clean out the unused files from this directory with **apt-get autoclean**.

If you use a formally designated stable Debian distribution, we can recommend automatic updates without much reservation. Changes in the stable distribution are generally limited to security updates, and integration is well tested. The only potential problem is that you may not want to upgrade automatically when a new major release occurs. To avoid this problem, specify an explicit distribution name rather than the keyword stable in **sources.list**.

yum: release management for RPM

yum, the Yellowdog Updater, Modified, is a metapackage manager based on RPM.[5] It may be a bit unfair to call **yum** an **apt-get** clone, but it's thematically and implementationally similar, although cleaner and slower in practice. **yum** is the official package management system for Fedora and comes preinstalled on many other distributions. If necessary, you can obtain the latest version from linux.duke.edu/yum.

As with **apt-get**, a server-side command (**yum-arch**) compiles a database of header information from a large set of packages (often an entire release). The header database is then shared along with the packages through HTTP or FTP. Clients use the **yum** command to fetch and install packages; **yum** figures out dependency constraints and does whatever additional work is needed to complete the installation of the requested packages. If a requested package depends on other packages, **yum** downloads and installs those packages as well.

The similarities between **apt-get** and **yum** extend to the command-line options they understand. For example, **yum install foo** downloads and installs the most recent version of the foo package (and its dependencies, if necessary). There is at least one treacherous difference, though: **apt-get update** refreshes **apt-get**'s package information cache, but **yum update** updates every package on the system (it's analogous to **apt-get upgrade**). To add to the confusion, there is also **yum upgrade**, which is the same as **yum update** but with obsolescence processing enabled.

yum does not match on partial package names unless you include shell globbing characters (such as * and ?) to explicitly request this behavior. For example, **yum update 'perl*'** refreshes all packages whose name starts with "perl". Remember to quote the globbing characters so the shell doesn't interfere with them.

---

5. Not to be confused with Yum Fish Bait with Live Prey Technology (LPT), yum3x.com.

Unlike **apt-get**, **yum** defaults to validating its package information cache against the contents of the network repository every time you run it. Use the **-C** option to prevent the validation and **yum makecache** to update the local cache (it takes awhile to run). Unfortunately, **-C** doesn't do much to improve **yum**'s sluggish performance.

yum's configuration file is **/etc/yum.conf**. It includes general options and pointers to package repositories. Multiple repositories can be active at once, and each repository can be associated with multiple URLs.

Fedora includes **yum**-format metadata in its standard distribution trees, so Fedora users can just point their **yum.conf** files at the closest mirror and update at will. RHEL does not follow suit in this regard, probably to encourage sales of subscriptions to the Red Hat Network.

11.5 REVISION CONTROL

Mistakes are a fact of life. Therefore, it's important to keep track of the changes you make so that when these changes cause problems, you can easily revert to a known-good configuration. Defining formal internal releases makes rollbacks easy, but it's a heavyweight solution that only works well at a coarse level of granularity. What if you just need to tweak one or two files?

In this section we discuss some common ways of managing changes at the level of individual files. These methods are complementary to the larger issues of internal release control and to each other—choose an assortment of tools that matches your local needs and the complexity of your site.

Backup file creation

Making backup copies of files you modify is a time-honored administrative tradition and one that can be adhered to by localization scripts as well as by individual administrators. Backup files let you revert configurations to an earlier state, but perhaps more importantly, they also allow you to **diff** the current and previous versions of a file to figure out what changes have been made.

You can best create backup files by moving (with **mv**) the original file aside to a new name such as **filename.old** or **filename.bak** and then copying it back to its original name. Use the **-p** option to **cp** to preserve the file's attribute settings. Once you update the active version of the file, its modification time reflects the most recent change, while the modification time of the backup file reflects the time of the previous modification. (If you just **cp**'ed, both files would have similar modtimes.) Moving the original file aside also handles the case in which an active process has an open reference to the file: changes that you make to the now-active copy are not seen until the file is closed and reopened.

Systems that are regularly backed up to tape can still benefit from the use of manually created backup files. Recovery from a backup file is faster and easier than recovery from a tape, and manual backups preserve an additional layer of history.

Formal revision control systems

Backup files are very useful, but they tend to be most practical at small sites. At the next level of complexity and robustness are formal revision control systems, which are software packages that track, archive, and provide access to multiple revisions of files. These packages originated in the world of software development, but they are quite useful for system administrators, too.

Revision control systems address several problems. First, they provide an organized way to trace the history of modifications to a file so that changes can be understood in context and so that earlier versions can be recovered. Second, they extend the concept of versioning beyond the level of individual files. Related groups of files can be versioned together in a manner that takes account of their interdependencies. Finally, revision control systems coordinate the activities of multiple editors so that race conditions cannot cause anyone's changes to be permanently lost[6] and so that incompatible changes from multiple editors do not become active simultaneously.

The simplest revision control system in common use is RCS, the appropriately named Revision Control System. It has been around for decades and comes preinstalled on many systems.

Another option is an open source system called CVS (Concurrent Versions System) which adds some functionality on top of RCS. It supports a distributed model (for use with a remote server) and better multideveloper support. A number of sites have been using CVS for sysadmin tasks; the client/server capability in particular can be quite useful. Unfortunately, CVS has some conceptual deficiencies that make it a mixed blessing.

A more recent (but still time-tested) entry into the open source arena is Subversion, a system that provides all the advantages of CVS but that seems to have much more sensible default behavior. Its main drawback for system administration is that the project model is rather directory-centric. However, it's still a very nice system and a reasonable choice for administrative use.

The last few years have witnessed a boom in open-source version control systems, and the available choices have expanded by almost an order of magnitude. Major contenders among the newer systems include Monotone, Darcs, Arch, and Bazaar-NG. These are all interesting systems, but they appear to share a bias toward decentralized work: multiple forks, multiple repositories, lots of parallel development. In our opinion, the traditional "central repository" model is more appropriate for version control in the context of system administration.

Several commercial revision control systems are also available. You may already have access to one them if you work in a development shop and might be tempted to adapt it for administrative data. Tread carefully, though; our experience has been that these commercial systems are usually overkill for sysadmin use.

---

6. For example, suppose that sysadmins Alice and Bob both edit the same file and that each makes some changes. Alice saves first. When Bob saves his copy of the file, it overwrites Alice's version. If Alice has quit from the editor, her changes are completely gone and unrecoverable.

If you are starting from scratch, we'd recommend beginning with RCS to get a feel for revision control in general. If you want to create a centralized repository for system administration information, then Subversion is your ticket.

RCS: the Revision Control System

RCS is one of the oldest UNIX applications around. It's actually a fairly simple system. It operates at the level of individual files and stores each file's revision history in a separate shadow file. The shadow file's name is the same as the original, but with the characters **,v** appended to it. For example, if you placed **/etc/syslog.conf** under RCS control, RCS would keep its revisions in **/etc/syslog.conf,v**.

To reduce clutter, RCS looks for a directory called **RCS** in the same directory as the original file. If it exists, RCS sequesters the **,v** file there instead of leaving it in plain view. Directory listings become much cleaner this way because many files can share an **RCS** directory. This is a terrific feature and one that we recommend highly.

The basic model used by RCS is that you "check out" files before modifying them. You then "check in" your changes to commit them. Accordingly, the only RCS commands you really need to know are **co** to check out files, **ci** to check them in, and **rcs**, which performs sundry housekeeping chores. If you use the **emacs** editor, you can avoid the command-line tools entirely because RCS support is built in.

To initiate RCS tracking of a file, you first check it in:

```
# ci -u syslog.conf
RCS/syslog.conf,v <-- syslog.conf
enter description, terminated with single '.' or end of file:
NOTE: This is NOT the log message!
>> This is the syslog configuration file.
```

The **-u** flag makes **ci** immediately check out the **syslog.conf** file in an unlocked (uneditable) state. If you were to omit this flag, **ci** would check in the file and delete the original copy, which is probably not what you want.

Every time you want to change an RCS-controlled file, you must check it out and lock it with **co -l**:

```
# co -l syslog.conf
RCS/syslog.conf,v --> syslog.conf revision 1.2 (locked)
done
```

This operation tells RCS that you are about to modify the file. RCS will not let anyone else check out the file until you have checked it back in.

RCS removes write permission on unlocked files as a reminder not to edit them until you have checked them out properly. A common error is to load a file into your editor, make changes, and not realize that you needed to check the file out until your editor refuses to save the changes. To fix, just pause the editor or bring up another shell window, run the appropriate **co -l**, and then retry the save operation. You could just **chmod** the file to be writable, but that would subvert and confuse RCS.

In theory, an RCS lock prevents two different people from modifying a file at the same time. In practice, you have to be root to modify system files, so anyone with **sudo** privileges can modify a file once it has been checked out as root. However, if a second administrator attempts another **co -l**, RCS will notice that a writable version already exists and print a warning. Sysadmins should get in the habit of always trying to check out the RCS-controlled files that they want to modify. The fact that a file is already writable means "Stop! Someone else already has this file checked out."

You may occasionally find that someone else has changed a file and left it locked—or even worse, overridden RCS and changed the file without locking it. You can review the changes made by the perpetrator with **rcsdiff**, which is an RCS-aware version of **diff**. For example:

```
# rcsdiff syslog.conf
===================================================================
RCS file: RCS/syslog.conf,v
retrieving revision 1.3
diff -r1.3 syslog.conf 4c4
< define(LOGHOST,moonbase)
---
> define(LOGHOST,spacelounge)
```

As a last resort, you can break the lock with the command **rcs -u** *filename*. This command prompts you to enter an explanation of your actions and sends mail to the user who had previously locked the file (usually root, unfortunately).

Once you are happy with your changes to a checked-out file, check it back in with **ci -u**. You will be asked to provide a comment that describes what you just did. Don't skip this step, but don't write a novel either. In a couple of years' time when you are trying to figure out why you made a particular change, useful comments can save your life.

```
# ci -u syslog.conf
RCS/syslog.conf,v <-- syslog.conf
new revision: 1.3; previous revision: 1.2
enter log message, terminated with single '.' or end of file:
>> Started logging debug messages to track down SSH problem
>> .
done
```

You can inspect a file's revision history with the **rlog** command:

```
# rlog syslog.conf
RCS file: RCS/syslog.conf,v
Working file: syslog.conf
head: 1.3
branch:
locks: strict
access list:
symbolic names:
keyword substitution: kv
```

```
total revisions: 3; selected revisions: 3
description:
----------------------------
revision 1.3
date: 2002/01/10 00:44:58; author: adam; state: Exp; lines: +1 -0
Started logging debug messages to track down problem
----------------------------
revision 1.2
date: 2000/07/19 08:23:10; author: evi; state: Exp; lines: +2 -0
Changed log destination to new logmaster
----------------------------
revision 1.1
date: 1998/03/14 11:13:00; author: matthew; state: Exp;
Initial revision
=================================================
```

If you want to see what the file looked like before you changed to the new logmaster, you could check out revision 1.2 of the file with **co**'s **-r** option:

```
# co -r1.2 syslog.conf
RCS/syslog.conf,v --> syslog.conf
revision 1.2
done
```

This command replaces the current **syslog.conf** file with the older version, so make sure you do a regular **co** when you are finished, or you (and **syslogd**) may become very confused. Another option would be **co -r1.2 -p syslog.conf**, which sends the contents of the requested version to standard output; unfortunately, there's no way to check out the file under a different filename. Never check out locked copies of older revisions (with **co -l**), since this operation creates branches in the version tree. Version branches are occasionally useful for source code but are almost never used for sysadmin work; to make your life simpler, just ignore all the RCS documentation that deals with them.

More information about RCS can be found at

www.cs.purdue.edu/homes/trinkle/RCS/

CVS: the Concurrent Versions System

RCS has some significant weaknesses. You have to be careful not to tread on your colleagues' feet when editing files. You have to adhere to a fairly specific set of procedures. You cannot safely modify several files at once without exposing the system to your unfinished modifications. These shortcomings (and others) motivated the design of the next-generation Concurrent Versions System, which is currently the most widely used revision control system on UNIX and Linux systems.

One of the main ideas behind CVS is that project files (and their historical versions) are all stored in a central location. As in RCS, you check out copies of files to work on them and then check the files back in when you're done. The nice thing about CVS is that it does not have the concept of "locked" and "unlocked" checkouts; several people can check out and modify the same files at the same time (hence "concurrent").

Since CVS does not prevent multiple people from modifying a file, it must provide a way for their changes to be integrated when the files are checked back in. This merging normally occurs automatically, but it works only for text files and only if the various changes are compatible. If not, CVS relies on the person running the checkin to resolve conflicts manually. In the case of incompatible changes to a text file, CVS inserts helpful comments that show where the conflict occurred.

So much for the theory. It sounds cool, and indeed it is—even the merging works well. But CVS still has some problems:

- It does not support "atomic commits." If two people both try to check in a big modification that affects multiple files, the two versions may both end up being halfway accepted, with each operator assigned a random selection of conflicts to resolve. Not pretty.

- To rename a file, you must copy it under the new name and delete the original file, thereby losing track of all the file's past history. Similarly, it is not possible to rename directories except by copying them and removing the original versions.

- File attributes are not under revision control. They remain fixed at whatever settings a file had when it was first checked in.

Nevertheless, CVS is used by many open source software projects. Not so much because it is boundlessly wonderful, but more because of a former lack of viable alternatives. This situation has changed, though, as many groups have been working on CVS replacements. Today the choices are numerous, and holy wars are likely to be fought over the issue of which revision control system should succeed CVS. Shlomi Fish's *Better SCM Initiative* web site (better-scm.berlios.de) introduces most of the candidates and presents a systematic comparison (albeit an undated one) of their features.

Following is a quick rundown of the most important CVS commands from a user's point of view. The first step in modifying a project is to log in to the server and check out the module you want to work on. Here we work on a module called **sort**.

```
$ cvs -d :pserver:username@servername:/path/to/repository login
CVS password: <password>
$ cvs -d :pserver:username@servername:/path/to/repository co sort
```

Here, **pserver** is the access method used to contact the repository, which in this case is a dedicated CVS password server. The **login** operation verifies the password with the server and makes a copy of it for use in later transactions. The **co** operation is directly analogous to that of RCS.

You can now enter your local copy of the **sort** directory and edit files. When you're ready to check files back in to the CVS repository, you need not use the **-d** switch,

because CVS has made a copy of all the necessary location information in the
sort/CVS subdirectory.

```
$ cd sort
$ vi foo.c
$ cvs commit foo.c -m "Added more efficient sort routine"
```

If you have been working on your copy of the module for a while and want to refresh
your local copies of files that other people have modified (and checked in) since
your checkout, you can use the **cvs update** command. The **-d** option means to include all subdirectories, and -**P** asks CVS to remove any empty directories:

```
$ cvs update -dP
```

Keep in mind that although you are not checking your files in to the central repository, this is a kind of integration. There's always the possibility that other users'
changes will conflict with yours. CVS will let you know if there are conflicts you need
to address.

Subversion: CVS done right

Although CVS is currently the predominant revision control system, we suggest that
administrators graduating from RCS leapfrog directly to Subversion. This package
was written by Karl Fogel and Jim Blandy, who started Cyclic Software in 1995 to sell
support contracts for CVS. In 2000, they were contracted by CollabNet to write an
open source replacement for CVS. Subversion is the result; after a long pregnancy,
version 1.0 was released in February, 2004.

Subversion has all the "missing" features mentioned above (and then some), but
doesn't sacrifice clarity and usability. As in CVS, a centralized repository stores all
version-controlled files. Subversion can handle binary files and is faster than CVS.

By default, the Subversion server is a module in the Apache 2.x web server. Great for
distributed software development, but maybe not so good for administrative uses.
Fortunately, the Subversion folks provide a second type of server in the form of a
daemon called **svnserve**. You can run **svnserve** from your home directory while
experimenting with Subversion, but in production use it should have its own user
account and be run from **inetd**.

The initial release of Subversion used the Berkeley DB database as the backing store
for its repository, but Subversion 1.1 adds support for an alternative system known
as FSFS. Both stores have advantages and disadvantages. One of the main distinctions is that Berkeley DB relies on memory-mapped I/O semantics and is therefore
NFS-phobic.[7] Subversion repositories that use Berkeley DB must be local to the machine on which the subversion server runs. FSFS repositories do not have this limitation. See subversion.tigris.org for more pros and cons.

_____

7. See www.sleepycat.com for more information about this issue.

Setting up the repository is easy. For example, the following steps create a new Subversion repository called **admin**:

```
# cd /home/svn
# mkdir repositories
# cd repositories
# svnadmin create admin
# chmod 700 admin
```

If you want to use the FSFS format for your repository instead of the default Berkeley DB, add a **--fs-type=fsfs** option to the **svnadmin create** command. Choose wisely, Luke; the repository format is difficult to change after the fact.

If you peek inside the **admin** directory, you will find a well-organized repository structure, including a **README** file. The configuration file **svnserve.conf** can be found in the **conf** subdirectory. This file tells the server daemon how to provide access to the new repository. Here's an example configuration appropriate for administrative files:

```
[general]
anon-access = none
auth-access = write
password-db = passwd
realm = The Sysadmin Repository
```

Because one of Subversion's design goals was to facilitate collaboration among people at different sites, it has an access control model that is separate from that of the operating system. The file **passwd** (in the same directory) contains a list of users and their plaintext (!) passwords. The plaintext bit is not nice, but the saving grace is that the passwords are never transmitted over the network. They are also never typed from memory by users, so you may as well assign passwords that are long enough and random enough to be secure. For example:

```
[users]
tobi = lkadslfkjasdljkhe8938uhau7623rhkdfndf
evi = 09uqalkhlkasdgfprghkjhsdfjj83yyouhfuhe
fritz = kd939hjahkjaj3hkuyasdfaadfk3ijdkjhf
```

Naturally, permissions on the **passwd** file should be set restrictively.

All that remains is to start the server on the new repository:

```
# svnserve --daemon --root /home/svn/repositories
```

As an unprivileged user, you can now check out the **admin** archive from anywhere on the network:

```
$ svn checkout --username tobi svn://server.atrust.com/admin checkout
```

```
Authentication realm: <svn://server.atrust.com:3690> The Sysadmin Repository
Password for 'tobi': <password>
```

When you enter the password for the first time, Subversion squirrels away a copy in a **.subversion** directory that it creates in your home. To add or move files within your local copy of the project, use the **svn** command:

```
$ cd checkout
$ vi foo.c
$ svn add foo.c
```

Once you are done, commit your changes to the repository:

```
$ svn commit -m "Initial checkin; added foo.c"
```

It is not necessary to list the changed files you want to commit, although you can do so if you wish; **svn** will figure it out on its own. If you omit the **-m** option, **svn** starts an editor for you so that you can edit the commit message.

To get the latest updates from the repository, run **svn update** within the project. As in CVS, Subversion performs a merge operation on any files that have been modified in both your local copy of the project and the master repository. Files with unresolvable conflicts are marked as "conflicted," and Subversion does not allow you to check them in until you have fixed the problems and told Subversion that the conflicts have been resolved:

```
$ svn resolved foo.c
```

If you want to know who has changed what lines with a file, you can ask Subversion to dish out the blame:

```
$ svn blame bar.c
```

This command prints an annotated version of the file that shows when and by whom each line was last modified. (Those of a more forgiving or optimistic nature can use the synonym **svn praise**.) It's also easy to get diffs relative to a particular date or version. For example, if you want to know what has changed in **foo.c** since June 2, 2006, the following command will tell you:

```
$ svn diff -r "{2006-06-02}" foo.c
```

You can download the latest version of Subversion from subversion.tigris.org. The standard documentation is the book *Version Control with Subversion*, published by O'Reilly. The full text is available on-line at svnbook.red-bean.com.

Subversion also has an outstanding Windows GUI; see tortoisesvn.tigris.org. We used it to manage the source files for this book.

11.6 LOCALIZATION AND CONFIGURATION

Adapting computers to your local environment is one of the prime battlegrounds of system administration: tell the system about all the printers available on the network, start the special licensing daemon, add the **cron** job that cleans the **/scratch** directory once a week, integrate support for that special scanner they use over in the graphics department, and on and on. Taking care of these issues in a structured and reproducible way is a central goal of architectural thinking.

Keep the following points in mind:

- Users do not have root privileges. Any need for root privileges in the course of normal operations is suspicious and probably indicates that something is fishy with your local configuration.

- Users do not wreck the system intentionally. Design internal security so that it guards against unintentional errors and the widespread dissemination of administrative privileges.

- Users that misbehave in minor ways should be interviewed before being chastised. Users frequently respond to inefficient administrative procedures by attempting to subvert them, so it's wise to consider the possibility that noncompliance is an indication of architectural problems.

- Be customer-centered. Talk to users and ask them which tasks they find difficult. Find ways to make these tasks simpler.

- Your personal preferences are yours. Let your users have their own. Offer choices wherever possible.

- When your administrative decisions affect users' experience of the system, be aware of the reasons for your decisions. Let your reasons be known.

- Keep your local documentation up to date and easily accessible. See page 930 for more information on this topic.

Organizing your localization

If your site has a thousand computers and each computer has its own configuration, you will spend a major portion of your working time figuring out why one box has a particular problem and another doesn't. Clearly, the solution is to make every computer the same, right? But real-world constraints and the varying needs of your users typically make this impossible.

There's a big difference in administrability between *multiple* configurations and *countless* configurations. The trick is to split your setup into manageable bits. You will find that some parts of the localization apply to all managed hosts, others apply to only a few, and still others are specific to individual boxes.

In addition to performing installations from scratch, you will also need to continually roll out updates. Keep in mind that individual hosts have different needs for currency, stability, and uptime.

A prudent system administrator should never roll out new software releases en masse. Instead, rollouts should be staged according to a gradual plan that accommodates other groups' needs and allows time for the discovery of problems while their potential to cause damage is still limited. Never update critical servers until you have some confidence in the changes you are contemplating.[8]

However you design your localization system, make sure that all original data is kept in a revision control system. This precaution allows you to keep track of which changes have been thoroughly tested and are ready for deployment. In addition, it lets you identify the originator of any problematic changes. The more people involved in the process, the more important this last consideration becomes.

It is advantageous to separate the base OS release from the localization release. Depending on the stability needs of your environment, you may use minor local releases only for bug fixing. However, we have found that adding new features in small doses yields a smoother operation than queuing up changes into "horse pill" releases that risk a major disruption of service.

It's often a good idea to specify a maximum number of "releases" you are willing to have in play at any given time. Some administrators believe that there is no reason to fix software that isn't broken. They point out that upgrading systems for gratuitous reasons costs time and money and that "cutting edge" all too often means "bleeding edge." Those who put these principles into practice must be willing to collect an extensive catalog of active releases.

By contrast, the "lean and mean" crowd point to the inherent complexity of releases and the difficulty of comprehending (let alone managing) a random collection of releases dating years into the past. Their trump cards are security patches, which must typically be applied universally and on a tight schedule. Patching outdated versions of the operating system is often infeasible, so administrators are faced with the choice of skipping updates on some computers or crash-upgrading these machines to a newer internal release. Not good.

Neither of these perspectives is provably correct, but we tend to side with those who favor a limited number of releases. Better to perform your upgrades on your own schedule rather than one dictated by an external emergency.

Testing

It's important to test changes before unleashing them on the world. At a minimum, this means that you need to test your own local configuration changes. However, you should really test the software that your distributor releases as well. A major UNIX vendor once released a patch that, when applied a certain way, performed an **rm -rf /**. Imagine installing this patch throughout your organization without testing it first.

Testing is an especially pertinent issue if you use a service such as **apt-get** or the Red Hat Network that offers an automatic patching capability. Mission-critical systems should never be directly connected to a vendor-sponsored update service. Identify a sacrificial machine to be connected to the service, and roll out the changes from this

---

8. Security patches are a possible exception to this rule. It's important to plug security holes as soon as they are found. On the other hand, security patches do sometimes introduce bugs.

box to other machines at your site only after appropriate testing. Disable updates during your testing phase; otherwise, while you test, changes may occur upstream and sneak their way prematurely onto your production systems.

See page 934 for more information about trouble tracking.

If you foresee the occurrence of any user-visible problems or changes in association with a planned update, notify users well in advance and give them a chance to communicate with you if they have concerns regarding your intended changes or timing. Make sure that users have an easy way to report bugs.

If your organization is geographically distributed, make sure that other offices help with testing. International participation is particularly valuable in multilingual environments. If no one in the U.S. office speaks Japanese, for example, you had better get the Tokyo office to test anything that might affect kanji support. A surprising number of system parameters vary with location. Does the U.S. office test changes to the printing infrastructure with A4 paper, or will the non-U.S. offices be in for a surprise?

Local compilation

In the old days of UNIX, when there were many different architectures, programs were generally distributed in the form of source archives, usually **.tar.Z** files that you would uncompress and then compile. Once the program was built, you would then install the software in a location such as **/usr/local**. Today, the use of package management systems means that fewer programs need to be installed this way. It also means that administrators make fewer decisions since packages specify where their contents are installed.

Even with easy package management, some people still prefer to compile their own software.[9] Running your own build gives you more control over the software's compiled-in options. It also lets you be more paranoid because you can inspect the source code you are compiling. Some people seem to think that this once-over is important, but unless you've got the time and skill to inspect every line of a 20,000-line software package, we suspect that the added security value is minimal.

Since not every piece of software in the world has been packaged for every Linux distribution, it's likely that you will run across at least a few programs that you need to install yourself, especially if your computers are not 32-bit Intel systems. What's more, if yours is a development site, you will have to consider where to put your site's own locally developed software.

Historically, the most common location for local software has been **/usr/local**, and this convention is still widely followed today. The UNIX/Linux Filesystem Hierarchy Standard (FHS) specifies that **/usr/local** be present and empty after the initial OS installation, and many packages expect to install themselves there.

A depressingly large number of other packages (particularly commercial applications) expect to be installed in **/usr**, which is generally a bad idea outside the context

---

9. Hard-core compile-it-yourselfers should check out the Gentoo Linux distribution, which is designed to be recompiled from scratch on the destination system.

of a package management system.[10] Our experience has been that although many applications try to be installed in **/usr**, they generally work without problems when installed somewhere else. In the rare case of a misbehaving package, you can often patch things up by adding symbolic links to **/usr** that point to an installation directory somewhere else. Another possible solution is to check whether the misbehaving application might refer to an environment variable to find its installation directory; such a feature is usually documented, but not always.

Although **/usr/local** is traditional, many sites find it to be an unmanageable dumping ground. The traditional way it's laid out (basically the same as **/usr**, with binaries in **/usr/local/bin**, man pages in **/usr/local/man**, and so on) creates a raft of problems in some environments: it's hard to have multiple versions of the same software installed, the directories can be large, it's a pain to manage multiple architectures, etc.

Distributing localizations

Your site's localization system must handle both initial installation and incremental updates. The updates can be especially tricky. Efficiency can be a major concern since you probably do not want to repeat the entire localization dance to update the permissions of a single file. Even though the process is automated, the rebuild-from-scratch model makes updates an expensive and time-consuming process.

A simple and scalable way to organize localizations is to maintain files in a tree structure that mimics the (skeletonized) filesystem of a production machine. A dedicated installation script can copy the tree to the destination machine and perform any additional editing that is required.

This type of setup has several advantages. You can maintain as many localization trees as are necessary to implement your local administrative scheme. Some of the trees will be alternatives, with each machine getting only one of the available choices. Other trees will be overlays that can be copied on top of the trees that came before them. Localization trees can overwrite files if necessary, or they can be completely disjoint. Each tree that is potentially installed independently should be represented by a separate revision control project.

The overlay-tree approach allows flexibility in implementation. If you use a packaging system to distribute your local customizations, the overlays can simply be rolled up into independent packages. The appropriate customization scripts can be included in the package and set to run as part of the installation process.

Another good implementation idea is to use **rsync** to bring destination machines into compliance with their overlay trees. **rsync** copies only files that are out of date, so it can be very efficient for distributing incremental changes. This behavior is hard to simulate with a packaging system alone. Refer to page 508 for more information about **rsync**.

---

10. The point of keeping random software out of **/usr** and other system directories is to segregate local customizations from system software. Under package management, the packages themselves provide an audit trail, so it is more reasonable for packages to modify system directories.

Software Management

Resolving scheduling issues

Some sites update all their systems on a regular schedule. This plan is potentially intrusive, but it has the advantage of defining an upper bound on the out-of-date-ness of client systems. Other sites update their systems at boot time. This is a relatively safe option, but it can mean that a long time passes between updates. Some sites with technically sophisticated users allow the users themselves to choose when to update their machines. This is a cooperative and friendly plan, but it tends to require one of the other schemes as an adjunct because some users will never update.

Updates can be pushed out from the update server (usually by way of **cron**), or they can be pulled in by individual clients. A pull system gives clients better control over their own update schedules. For example, an organization with world-wide operations may find it easier to implement nightly updates with a pull system; a midnight upgrade in the United States is a middle-of-the-workday upgrade in Asia.

Depending on how many machines you manage and how large a geographical area they span, you might set up either a single distribution server or a hierarchy of servers. For example, you could have one master server that distributes to a slave in each building, and that slave could in turn distribute directly to clients. For geographically dispersed sites, this arrangement can drastically reduce your consumption of WAN bandwidth.

11.7 CONFIGURATION MANAGEMENT TOOLS

Localization systems tend to be homegrown. Part of the reason for this is that all sites are different and every site has its own bizarre quirks. However, NIH ("not invented here") syndrome is also a significant contributor. Perhaps the lack of a dominant open source tool for performing configuration management has conditioned us to think of this problem as lying outside the domain of standardized tools.

Nevertheless, the tools exist and are worth your review, if only to give yourself some clarity about why you choose not to make use of them. The following sections outline the more popular systems in rough order of popularity and similarity.

cfengine: computer immune system

One of the best-known localization tools is Mark Burgess' **cfengine**. It was envisioned as a sort of "computer immune system" that bases its operation on a model of how the system should be configured. When it detects a discrepancy between the model and the reality, **cfengine** takes the appropriate steps to bring the system into compliance. Because of this underlying model, **cfengine** is really useful for ongoing configuration maintenance.

cfengine can make backup copies of the files it modifies and can keep a detailed log of its changes. It can also be run in a no-action mode in which it describes the changes it would make without actually implementing them.

You use **cfengine**'s own special language to describe how you want your computers to be configured. You can specify rules such as, "The file **xyz** must exist in **/etc**, have permissions 644, and belong to root." You can also write rules regarding the content of individual files. For example, you can specify that **/etc/hosts** must contain the line "router 192.168.0.1". **cfengine** then adds this line if it is missing.

cfengine's configuration language lets you turn on individual rules depending on factors such as the hostname, the OS, or the subnet. This feature makes it easy to write a single configuration file that covers the needs of all the machines in your administrative domain.

The following is a simple example from the UNIX world. It makes sure that **/bin** is a symlink to **/usr/bin** on Suns, does some additional link checking on legacy OSF boxes, and removes everything from **/var/scratch** that is older than seven days:

```
control:
actionsequence = ( links tidy )
links:
sun4::
/bin -> /usr/bin
# other links
osf::
# some osf specific links
tidy:
/var/scratch pattern=* age=7 recurse=inf
```

See the **cfengine** home page at www.iu.hio.no/cfengine for more information.

LCFG: a large-scale configuration system

LCFG was originally developed by Paul Anderson at Edinburgh University in 1993. In its latest incarnation it is known as LCFG(ng) and has gained a number of users outside the university. LCFG is primarily geared toward managing large Red Hat installations, but ports to Mac OS X and Solaris are underway. The LCFG web site is www.lcfg.org.

Like **cfengine**, LCFG defines a specialized configuration language. The configurations of all managed machines are stored on a central server in a set of master configuration files. From these, LCFG generates customized XML files that describe the configuration of each managed host. A daemon on the central server monitors the master configuration files for changes and regenerates the XML files as required.

The XML files are published on an internal web server from which clients can then pull their own configurations. The clients use a variety of component scripts to configure themselves according to the XML blueprints.

The Arusha Project (ARK)

The Arusha Project was founded by Will Parain of Glasgow University. The motivation behind Arusha is the insight that most sysadmins do essentially the same things, but not quite. Or as Will puts it, "I want my service to be the same as theirs, but with these slight differences..." The Arusha Project web site at ark.sf.net goes into more detail regarding the philosophical underpinnings of the system.

The Arusha Project is based on an object-oriented language called ARK. It is expressed in XML and allows the administrator to define objects such as hosts, licenses, web sites, mailing lists, etc. You can describe the dependencies among these objects with ARK and can supply methods and data that clarify their interrelationships. As in object-oriented software development, it is possible to reuse and subclass objects, overriding only the parts that must be changed to make them work in your local environment.

Template Tree 2: cfengine helper

Template Tree 2 was created at the Swiss Federal Institute of Technology by Tobias Oetiker. It is a component-based system driven by a central configuration. It reduces complexity by taking a two-level approach to defining a site's configuration and can deal with the relocated root directories of diskless machines.

On the lower level, the system consists of a number of "feature packs." A feature pack is a collection of files accompanied by a **META** file that describes how these files must be installed on the target system. A feature can be anything from a network configuration to the latest version of OpenSSH. Features can expose configurable parameters that can be set in the master configuration file.

The upper level of configuration is a master site configuration file in which you pull the features together and associate them to machines or groups of machines. At this level, you must specify values for the unbound configuration parameters exposed by each feature. For example, one of the parameters for a mail server feature might be the name of the mail domain.

Template Tree 2 combines the information from the master configuration file and the individual features' **META** files to generate a **cfengine** configuration file for the whole site. Because each feature must contain documentation about its purpose and usage, Template Tree 2 can also generate composite documentation.

DMTF/CIM: the Common Information Model

The Distributed Management Task Force (DMTF), a coalition of "more than 3,000 active participants," has been working since 1992 to develop its Common Information Model (CIM) in an attempt to create standards for an object-oriented, cross-platform management system.

In DMTF's own words, CIM is "a management schema...provided to establish a common conceptual framework at the level of a fundamental topology both with respect to classification and association, and with respect to the basic set of classes intended to establish a common framework for a description of the managed environment." Or whatever.

All major vendors from Microsoft to Sun are members of the DMTF. Unfortunately, the standards they have produced demonstrate an impressive mastery of the arts of obfuscation and buzzword husbandry. The companies involved seem eager to demonstrate their willingness to standardize no matter what. The standards center on XML and object orientation. However, we have yet to see a sensible product built on top of them.

Because the standardization effort is being pushed primarily by our old closed-source vendor friends, the results are about what one might expect. Sun, for example, shipped a system for managing diskless clients based on these technologies with Solaris 8. A closer look revealed a Java-based server that was triggered by a Java-based client to spit out a shell script which then did the actual work. When problems occurred, the handbook instructed users to review the log file, which was a binary structure accessible only through a Java-based log viewer application.

If there is an upside to this quagmire, it is that the DMTF efforts at least require vendors to provide programatically accessible configuration interfaces to their systems based on an open standard. For UNIX and Linux environments this is nothing new, but the DMTF is not a UNIX creature. It includes Cisco, Microsoft, Symantec, and many other companies with little history of providing sensible ways of scripting their systems. Giving these products a configuration API is a good thing, even if the implementations are still lacking.

11.8 SHARING SOFTWARE OVER NFS

Where should extra software actually be installed: on individual clients or on a central file server from which it can be shared over NFS? The standard Linux answer is "on the clients," but the NFS solution makes updates quicker (it's faster and more reliable to update ten NFS servers than 1,000 clients) and saves disk space on clients (not that this matters much in the world of 400GB disks).

The question really boils down to manageability versus reliability. Network filesystem-based access is centralized and easier to manage from day to day, and it makes bug fixes and new packages instantaneously available on all clients. However, running over the network may be a bit slower than accessing a local disk. In addition, the network server model adds dependencies on the network and the file server, not only because it adds potential points of failure but also because it requires that clients and servers agree on such things as the shared libraries that will be available and the version of those libraries that will be installed. The bottom line is that NFS software libraries are an advanced administrative technique and should only be attempted in environments that allow for a high degree of central coordination.

If you work in an environment with efficient networks and can afford a fast RAID array for the central server, you may find that the network server actually performs faster than a local IDE disk. Whether for better or worse, the performance impact is likely to be small; performance considerations should not dominate this particular architectural decision.

Software Management

In general, networks of heterogeneous systems derive the most benefit from shared software repositories. If your site has standardized on one operating system and that operating system provides reasonable package management facilities, you're likely to be better off sticking with the native system.

Package namespaces

Traditional UNIX sprays the contents of new packages across multiple directories. Libraries go to **/usr/lib**, binaries to **/usr/bin**, documentation to **/usr/share/docs**, and so on. Linux inherits more or less the same system, although the Filesystem Hierarchy Standard helps to make the locations somewhat more predictable. (See www.pathname.com/fhs for more information about the FHS.)

The advantage of this convention is that files show up in well-known places—as long your PATH environment variable to points to **/usr/bin** and the other standard binary directories, for example, newly installed programs will be readily available.

The downsides are that the origins of files must be explicitly tracked (by means of package management systems) and that the scattered files are difficult to share on a network. Fortunately, sysadmins willing to put in some extra work have a reasonable way out of this dilemma: package namespaces.

The gist of the scheme is to install every package into its own separate root directory. For example, you might install **gimp** into **/tools/graphics/gimp**, with the binary being located at **/tools/graphics/gimp/bin/gimp**. You can then recreate an aggregate binary directory for your collection of tools by placing symbolic links into a directory such as **/tools/bin**:

```
/tools/bin/gimp -> /tools/graphics/gimp/bin/gimp
```

Users could then add the directory **/tools/bin** to their PATH variables to be assured of picking up all the shared tools.

There are various options for structuring the **/tools** directory. A hierarchical approach (e.g., **/tools/graphics**, **/tools/editors**, etc.) facilitates browsing and speeds performance. You may want to include the software version, hardware architecture, operating system, or responsible person's initials in your naming conventions to allow the same collection of tools to be served to many types of clients. For example, Solaris users might include **/tools/sun4/bin** in their PATHs, and Fedora users include **/tools/fedora/bin**.

When you install a new version of a major tool, it's a good idea to keep older versions around indefinitely, particularly when users may have significant time and effort invested in projects that use the tool. Ideally, new versions of tools would be backward compatible with old data files and software, but in practice, disasters are common. It's fine to require users to go through some configuration trouble to access an older version of a package; it's not fine to just break their existing work and make them deal with the consequences.

Dependency management

Some packages depend on libraries or on other software packages. When you install software locally through a package-management system, you get lots of help with resolving these issues. However, when you build your own site-wide network software repository, you must address these issues explicitly.

If you manage libraries in the same way you manage applications, you can compile your tools to use libraries from within the shared **/tools** directory. This convention lets you can keep multiple versions of a library active simultaneously. Because dependent applications are linked against specific versions of the library, the setup remains stable even when new versions of the library are released. The downside is that this type of setup can be quite complicated to use and maintain over time.

Resist the temptation to link against a global **/tools/lib** directory that contains generically named links to common libraries. If you change the links, you may run into unexpected and difficult-to-diagnose problems. Shared library systems are designed to address some of the potential headbutts, but it makes sense to play it safe in a complicated setup.

The exact steps needed to make the linker use a specific version of a shared library vary from system to system. Under Linux, you can set the LD_LIBRARY_PATH environment variable or use the linker's **-R** option.

Wrapper scripts

Unfortunately, library-level compatibility is only half the story. The fact that tools invoke one another directly raises another opportunity for conflict. For example, suppose the utility named **foo** makes frequent use of the utility named **bar**. If you update the default version of **bar**, you may find that **foo** suddenly stops working. In this case, you can conclude that **foo** depended on some behavior of **bar** that is no longer supported (or at least is no longer the default).

If your software repository supports multiple versions (e.g., **/tools/util/bar-1.0** and **/tools/util/bar-2.0**), you can fix this problem by moving the original version of **foo** to **foo.real** and replacing it with a little wrapper script:

```
#!/bin/sh
# make sure the program finds any files co-packaged with it
# first even if it does not use an explicit path.
PATH=/tools/util/bar-1.0/bin:$PATH
export PATH
exec /tools/util/foo-1.0/bin/foo.real "$@"
```

Now **foo** will be launched with a customized PATH environment variable, and it will call the old version of **bar** in preference to the new one.

Wrappers are a powerful tool that can address not only package dependencies but also issues such as security, architecture- or OS-dependence, and usage tracking. Some sites wrap all shared binaries.

Software Management

Implementation tools

The maintenance of shared software repositories is a common problem in system administration, and admins have developed various software solutions to help facilitate the process. As with localization, homegrown solutions have tended to predominate, but as always, it's worth checking out the available systems to see if any of them meet your needs.

For some of the classics, google for CMU Depot, CERN ASIS, or CITES Encap. Some of these projects are still alive and kicking, while others have been abandoned under pressure from Windows boxes and the ubiquitous availability of RPM-packaged updates. There are also several relatively new projects:

- GNU Stow (www.gnu.org/software/stow) maintains links from a central binary directory to the real binaries sitting in package-specific directories.

- Swpkg by Chrisophe Kalt (web.taranis.org/swpkg) is a collection of tools that address most of the steps in the construction of a shared software repository.

- Peter Kristensen's Pack Management Project (pack.sunsite.dk) started out with the bold ambition to provide not only a system for installing software but also the prepackaged software itself (with a focus on Solaris). The prepackaging part has since been abandoned, but work continues on the software tools.

- The SEPP system, created at the Swiss Federal Institute of Technology (www.sepp.ee.ethz.ch), implements most of the ideas discussed above.

11.9 RECOMMENDED SOFTWARE

Some tools are so important that we consider them mandatory for all machines. Other packages that we like may be necessary or useful only on selected machines. However, the price of disk space these days almost makes it easier to install everything everywhere and maintain the consistency of the local software tree. Table 11.1 shows our list of must-haves.

Table 11.2 shows our picks of nice-but-not-essential programs; we've divided the table into a sysadmin section and a general user section.

All the programs listed in Tables 11.1 and 11.2 are free. Most of them are available on the web (try freshmeat.net), but a few are still distributed only through FTP. If they are not included in your distribution, use a search engine to locate them or see if a pointer is given elsewhere in this book (check the index to see if a command is discussed elsewhere).

Table 11.1 Essential software packages

Package	Description and comments
ssh/scp	Secure shell – uses cryptography, doesn't reveal passwords
sudo	**su** replacement – adds control and logging
sendmail or **postfix**	Choice of mail transport programs
traceroute	Network route tracing– needed to debug network problems
tcpdump or Wireshark	Choice of network sniffers – used to analyze network traffic
gzip	GNU data compressor – needed to unpack downloads
mozilla or **firefox**	Choice of web browsers – gotta have it
RCS/CVS/Subversion	Revision control systems – useful for both sysadmins and users
Perl	Scripting language – general-purpose problem solving

Table 11.2 Useful software packages

	Package	Description and comments
Tools for administrators	**gcc**	C/C++ compiler – a high-quality compiler from GNU
	BIND	Name service tools – get current version (for security reasons)[a]
	npasswd	**passwd** replacement – forces users to choose good passwords
	xntpd	Time daemon – keeps machines' clocks correct and synced
	Samba	Windows SMB – shares files/printers with Windows systems
	Apache	Web server
	Squid	Web proxy and caching software
	imapd/procmail	Mail tools – for accessing and filtering email
	mrtg, RRDtool	Monitoring tools – for network traffic and other data
Tools for users	Acrobat Reader	PDF file display, a nice (free) tool from Adobe[b]
	gimp	Bitmap image editor
	xfig	Simple X Windows drawing program
	GnuPG	Signs, verifies, and encrypts messages
	nvi/vim	**vi**-like text editors – recommended for sysadmins
	emacs	Text editor/operating system – good for power users
	pico, nedit	Text editors – very nice choice for beginners
	enscript, mpage	Printing utilities – pretty-printer and N-up formatter
	pine	Mail reader appropriate for beginners
	thunderbird	Mail reader for those who prefer a GUI
	mh/exmh	Mail reader for processing lots of mail (not well maintained)
	glimpse	Indexing tool – indexes your files and performs fast searches
	gs, **gv**, **ghostview**	Tools for previewing and printing PostScript documents

a. The BIND package includes **dig**, **host**, and **nslookup**.
b. The free package Evince is a reasonable replacement for Acrobat Reader under GNOME.

Software Management

11.10 RECOMMENDED READING

INTEL CORPORATION AND SYSTEMSOFT. *Preboot Execution Environment (PXE) Specification, Version 2.1*. 1999. www.pix.net/software/pxeboot/archive/pxespec.pdf

MINTHA, JIM, AND PIETER KRUL. *UltraLinux FAQ*. www.ultralinux.org/faq.html

PXELinux Questions. syslinux.zytor.com/pxe.php

RODIN, JOSIP. *Debian New Maintainers' Guide*. www.debian.org/doc/maint-guide
This document contains good information about **.deb** packages.

SILVA, GUSTAVO NORONHA. *APT HOWTO*. www.debian.org/doc/manuals/apt-howto

HOHNDEL, DIRK, AND FABIAN HERSCHEL. *Automated Installation of Linux Systems Using YaST*. www.usenix.org/events/lisa99/full_papers/hohndel/hohndel_html

STÜCKELBERG, MARC VUILLEUMIER, AND DAVID CLERC. *Linux Remote-Boot mini-HOWTO: Configuring Remote-Boot Workstations with Linux, DOS, Windows 95/98 and Windows NT*. 1999. tldp.org/HOWTO/Remote-Boot.html

The Red Hat Enterprise Linux System Administration Guide. www.redhat.com/docs

WACHSMANN, ALF. *How to Install Red Hat Linux via PXE and Kickstart*. www.stanford.edu/~alfw/PXE-Kickstart/PXE-Kickstart.html

BURGESS, MARK. *Cfengine: A Site Configuration Engine*. USENIX Computing Systems, Vol 8, No 3. 1995. www.cfengine.org

OETIKER, TOBIAS. *SEPP: Software Installation and Sharing System*. Boston: LISA 1998. people.ee.ethz.ch/oetiker/sepp

11.11 EXERCISES

E11.1 Outline the differences between Kickstart and AutoYaST. When would you look for an alternative to the distribution-specific installers?

E11.2 Install a copy of Subversion from subversion.tigris.org. Set up **svnserve** and create a repository. How can you make the repository usable from anywhere on the local network but still maintain reasonable security?

E11.3 Review the way that local software is organized at your site. Will the system scale? Is it easy to use? Discuss.

☆ **E11.4** Figure out the steps needed to create an RPM package. Use this procedure to package a software product of your choice.

☆ **E11.5** Repeat the previous exercise, but create a Debian-format **.deb** package.

☆☆ **E11.6** Set up the network installer of your choice and install a new machine by using your server. Outline all the steps needed to perform this task. What were some of the stumbling blocks? What are some of the scalability issues you discovered with the installer that you chose?

SECTION TWO

NETWORKING

12 *TCP/IP Networking*

there is no need
for Microsoft to
support TCP/IP.

GATES
1994

Microsoft has invented
a new protocol. We're
calling it TCP/IP.

GATES
1995

It would be hard to overstate the importance of networks to modern computing, although that doesn't seem to stop people from trying. At many sites, web and email access are now the main activities for which computers are used. As of early 2006, the Internet is estimated to have more than a billion users, a 55% increase over 2001's estimate. Maintenance of local networks, Internet connections, web sites, and network-related software is a bread-and-butter part of most sysadmins' jobs.

TCP/IP is the networking protocol suite most commonly used with Linux/UNIX, Mac OS, Windows, and most other operating systems. It is also the native language of the Internet. TCP stands for Transmission Control Protocol and IP stands for Internet Protocol.

Devices that speak the TCP/IP protocol can exchange data ("interoperate") despite their many differences. IP, the suite's underlying delivery protocol, is the workhorse of the Internet. TCP and UDP (the User Datagram Protocol) are transport protocols built on top of IP to deliver packets to specific applications.

TCP is a connection-oriented protocol that facilitates a conversation between two programs. It works a lot like a phone call: the words you speak are delivered to the person you called, and vice versa. The connection persists even when neither party is speaking. TCP provides reliable delivery, flow control, and congestion control.

UDP is a packet-oriented service. It's analogous to sending a letter through the post office. It is a connectionless protocol, does not have any form of congestion control, and does not guarantee that packets will be delivered in the same order in which they were sent (or even that they will be delivered at all).

TCP/IP

271

TCP is a polite protocol that forces competing users to share bandwidth and generally behave in ways that are good for the productivity of the overall network. UDP, on the other hand, blasts packets out as fast as it can.

As the Internet becomes more popular and more crowded, we need the traffic to be mostly TCP to avoid congestion and effectively share the available bandwidth. Today, TCP accounts for the vast majority of Internet traffic, with UDP and ICMP checking in at a distant second and third, respectively. UDP applications such as games, music, voice, and video are making their presence felt but are overwhelmed by the web and by programs such as BitTorrent that are popular bandwidth hogs but use TCP instead of UDP for transport.

This chapter introduces the TCP/IP protocols in the political and technical context of the Internet. Unfortunately, even basic networking is too big a topic to be covered in a single chapter. Other network-related chapters in this book include Chapter 13, *Routing*, Chapter 19, *Network Management and Debugging*, Chapter 15, *DNS: The Domain Name System*, and Chapter 20, *Security*.

The next few sections include background material on the protocols and politics of the Internet and are quite opinionated and fluffy. Skip ahead to page 282 to go directly to the gory details of IP, or to page 307 to jump to distribution-specific configuration information.

12.1 TCP/IP AND THE INTERNET

TCP/IP and the Internet share a history that goes back several decades. The technical success of the Internet is due largely to the elegant and flexible design of TCP/IP and to the fact that TCP/IP is an open and nonproprietary protocol suite. In turn, the leverage provided by the Internet has helped TCP/IP prevail over several competing protocol suites that were favored at one time or another for political or commercial reasons.

A brief history lesson

Contrary to popular belief, the Internet is not a Microsoft product that debuted in 1995, nor is it the creation of a former U.S. vice president. The progenitor of the modern Internet was a network called ARPANET that was established in 1969 by DARPA (Defense Advanced Research Project Agency), the R&D arm of the U.S. Department of Defense. The ARPANET eventually became the NSFNET backbone, which connected supercomputer sites and regional networks.

By the end of the 1980s, the network was no longer a research project and it was time for the National Science Foundation to extract itself from the networking business. We transitioned to the commercial Internet over a period of several years; the NSFNET was turned off in April of 1994. Today's backbone Internet is a collection of private networks owned by Internet service providers (ISPs) that interconnect at many so-called peering points.

In the mid-1980s, the Internet essentially consisted of the original ARPANET sites and a handful of universities with Digital Equipment Corporation's VAX computers running Berkeley UNIX on 10 Mb/s Ethernets connected by 56 Kb/s leased digital telephone lines. Every September, when students went back to school, the Internet would suffer what became known as congestion collapse. Van Jacobson, then a researcher in the Network Research Group at Lawrence Berkeley Labs, would look at the protocols' behavior under load and fix them. The algorithms we now know as *slow start*, *congestion avoidance*, *fast retransmit*, and *fast recovery* arose from this context.

Moore's law (the rule of thumb that hardware speeds double every 18 months) and market pressure have greatly accelerated the development of the Internet. Since the late 1980s when the current TCP algorithms were stabilized, the speed of network interfaces has increased by a factor of 1,000 (from 6% efficiency on early 10 Mb/s Ethernets to near 100% efficiency on 10 gigabit Ethernets), the speed of leased circuits by a factor of 12,000, and the total number of hosts by a factor of 80,000.

Anyone who has designed a software system and has seen it rendered obsolete by the next generation of hardware or the next release of an operating system knows how amazing it is that our Internet is still alive and kicking, running basically the same TCP/IP protocol suite that was designed 30 years ago for a very different Internet. Our hats are off to Bob Kahn, Vint Cerf, Jon Postel, Van Jacobson, and all the other people who made it happen.

How the Internet is managed today

The development of the Internet has always been a cooperative and open effort. Now that it is a driving force in the world economy, several sectors worry that the Internet seems to be in the hands of a bunch of computer geeks, with perhaps a little direction from the U.S. government. Like it or not, Internet governance is coming.

Several organizations are involved:

- ICANN, the Internet Corporation for Assigned Names and Numbers: if anyone can be said to be in charge of the Internet, this group is it. (www.icann.org)

- ISOC, the Internet Society: ISOC is a membership organization that represents Internet users. (www.isoc.org)

- IETF, the Internet Engineering Task Force: this group oversees the development and standardization of the technical aspects of the Internet. It is an open forum in which anyone can participate. (www.ietf.org)

Of these groups, ICANN has the toughest job: establishing itself as the authority in charge of the Internet, undoing the mistakes of the past, and foreseeing the future.

In addition to these organizations, an international group of academic researchers, government entities, and industry leaders has formed a networking consortium called Internet2. These organizations have banded together to contribute ideas and develop technologies that are critical to forward progress of the Internet. Contrary

TCP/IP

to regular media reports, Internet2 is not a distinct network from the Internet. Although it uses a private network backbone called Abilene for networking research, it will not replace the Internet as we know it today. Learn more about Internet2 at www.internet2.edu.

Network standards and documentation

The technical activities of the Internet community are summarized in documents known as RFCs; an RFC is a Request for Comments. Protocol standards, proposed changes, and informational bulletins all usually end up as RFCs. RFCs start their lives as Internet Drafts, and after lots of email wrangling and IETF meetings they either die or are promoted to the RFC series. Anyone who has comments on a draft or proposed RFC is encouraged to reply. In addition to standardizing the Internet protocols, the RFC mechanism sometimes just documents or explains aspects of existing practice.

RFCs are numbered sequentially; currently, there are about 4,000. RFCs also have descriptive titles (e.g., *Algorithms for Synchronizing Network Clocks*), but to forestall ambiguity they are usually cited by number. Once distributed, the contents of an RFC are never changed. Updates are distributed as new RFCs with their own reference numbers. By convention, updated RFCs contain all the material that remains relevant, so the new RFCs completely replace the old ones, at least in theory.

The process by which RFCs are published is itself documented in the RFC titled *Internet Official Protocol Standards*. This RFC also includes pointers to the most current RFCs for various protocol standards. Since the information changes frequently, this RFC is reissued every 100 RFCs. The Internet standards process itself is detailed in RFC2026. Another useful meta-RFC is RFC2555, *30 Years of RFCs*, which describes some of the cultural and technical context behind the RFC system.

Don't be scared away by the wealth of technical detail found in RFCs. Most contain introductions, summaries, and rationales that are useful for system administrators. Some are specifically written as overviews or general introductions. RFCs may not be the gentlest way to learn about a topic, but they are authoritative, concise, and free.

Not all RFCs are dry and full of boring technical details. Some of our favorites on the lighter side (often written on April 1st) are RFCs 1118, 1149, 1925, 2324, and 2795:

- RFC1118 – *The Hitchhiker's Guide to the Internet*
- RFC1149 – *A Standard for the Transmission of IP Datagrams on Avian Carriers*[1]
- RFC1925 – *The Twelve Networking Truths*
- RFC2324 – *Hyper Text Coffee Pot Control Protocol (HTCPCP/1.0)*
- RFC2795 – *The Infinite Monkey Protocol Suite (IMPS)*

---

1. A group of Linux enthusiasts from BLUG, the Bergen (Norway) Linux User Group, actually implemented the Carrier Pigeon Internet Protocol (CPIP) as specified in RFC1149. For details, see the web site www.blug.linux.no/rfc1149!

They are a good read and give a bit of insight into the people who are designing and building our Internet.

In addition to being assigned its own serial number, an RFC can also be assigned an FYI (For Your Information) number, a BCP (Best Current Practice) number, or a STD (Standard) number. FYIs, STDs, and BCPs are subseries of the RFCs that include documents of special interest or importance.

FYIs are introductory or informational documents intended for a broad audience. They are usually an excellent place to start research on an unfamiliar topic. STDs document Internet protocols that have completed the IETF's review and testing process and have been formally adopted as standards. BCPs document recommended procedures for Internet sites; they consist of administrative suggestions and for system administrators are often the most valuable of the RFC subseries.

RFCs, FYIs, STDs, and BCPs are numbered sequentially within their own series, so a document can bear several different identifying numbers. For example, RFC1635, *How to Use Anonymous FTP*, is also known as FYI0024.

RFCs are available from numerous sources. There's a list of actively maintained RFC mirrors at www.rfc-editor.org, which is dispatch central for RFC-related matters.

12.2 NETWORKING ROAD MAP

Now that we've provided a bit of context, let's take a look at the TCP/IP protocols themselves. TCP/IP is a "protocol suite," a set of network protocols designed to work smoothly together. It includes several components, each defined by a standards-track RFC or series of RFCs:

- IP, the Internet Protocol, which routes data packets from one machine to another (RFC791)

- ICMP, the Internet Control Message Protocol, which provides several kinds of low-level support for IP, including error messages, routing assistance, and debugging help (RFC792)

- ARP, the Address Resolution Protocol, which translates IP addresses to hardware addresses (RFC823)[2]

- UDP, the User Datagram Protocol, and TCP, the Transmission Control Protocol, which deliver data to specific applications on the destination machine. UDP provides unverified, "best effort" transport for individual messages, whereas TCP guarantees a reliable, full duplex, flow-controlled, error-corrected conversation between processes on two hosts. (RFCs 768 and 793)

TCP/IP

---

2. This is actually a little white lie. ARP is not really part of TCP/IP and can be used with other protocol suites. However, it's an integral part of the way TCP/IP works on most LAN media.

TCP/IP is designed around the layering scheme shown in Table 12.1.

Table 12.1   TCP/IP network model

Layer	Function
Application layer	End-user application programs
Transport layer	Delivery of data to applications[a]
Network layer	Basic communication, addressing, and routing
Link layer	Network hardware and device drivers
Physical layer	The cable or physical medium itself

a. Optionally addressing reliability and flow control issues

After TCP/IP had been implemented and deployed, the International Organization for Standardization came up with its own seven-layer protocol suite called OSI. It was a consummate design-by-committee white elephant, and it never really caught on because of its complexity and inefficiency. Some think a financial layer and a political layer should have been added to the original seven OSI layers.[3]

Exhibit A shows how the various components and clients of TCP/IP fit into its general architecture and layering scheme.

Exhibit A   One big happy TCP/IP family

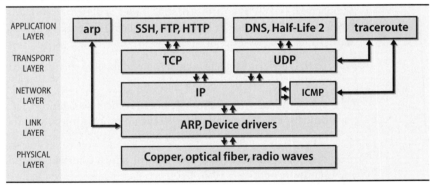

12.3 PACKETS AND ENCAPSULATION

UNIX Linux can support a variety of physical networks, including Ethernet, FDDI, token ring, ATM (Asynchronous Transfer Mode), wireless Ethernet, and serial-line-based systems. Hardware is managed within the link layer of the TCP/IP architecture, and higher-level protocols do not know or care about the specific hardware being used.

3. In fact, a T-shirt showing this extended nine-layer model is available from the Internet Systems Consortium web site, www.isc.org.

Data travels on a network in the form of *packets*, bursts of data with a maximum length imposed by the link layer. Each packet consists of a header and a payload. The header tells where the packet came from and where it's going. It can also include checksums, protocol-specific information, or other handling instructions. The payload is the data to be transferred.

The name of the primitive data unit depends on the layer of the protocol. At the link layer it is called a *frame*, at the IP layer a *packet*, and at the TCP layer a *segment*. Here, we use "packet" as a generic term that encompasses all these cases.

As a packet travels down the protocol stack (from TCP or UDP transport to IP to Ethernet to the physical wire) in preparation for being sent, each protocol adds its own header information. Each protocol's finished packet becomes the payload part of the packet generated by the next protocol. This nesting is known as encapsulation. On the receiving machine, the encapsulation is reversed as the packet travels back up the protocol stack.

For example, a UDP packet being transmitted over Ethernet contains three different wrappers or envelopes. On the Ethernet wire, it is "framed" with a simple header that lists the source and next-hop destination hardware addresses, the length of the frame, and the frame's checksum (CRC). The Ethernet frame's payload is an IP packet, the IP packet's payload is a UDP packet, and the UDP packet's payload is the actual data being transmitted. Exhibit B shows the components of such a frame.

Exhibit B   A typical network packet

Ethernet header	IP header	UDP header	Application data	Ethernet CRC
14 bytes	20 bytes	8 bytes	100 bytes	4 bytes

UDP packet (108 bytes)
IP packet (128 bytes)
Ethernet frame (146 bytes)

We use the term "byte" to refer to an 8-bit data unit. In days of yore, "byte" was a more general term, so you will often see the term "octet" used in RFCs instead.

The link layer

In this section, we cover several topics that bridge the gap between the lowest layers of the networking software and the network hardware itself.

Ethernet framing standards

One of the main chores of the link layer is to add headers to packets and to put separators between them. The headers contain the packets' link-layer addressing information and checksums, and the separators ensure that receivers can tell where one

TCP/IP

packet stops and the next one begins. The process of adding these extra bits is known generically as framing.

Today, a single standard for 10 Mb/s Ethernet framing is in common use: DIX Ethernet II.[4] Historically, another standard known as IEEE 802.2 LLC/SNAP was commonplace for Novell-based networks. Some administrators may find remnants of this flavor of framing on their network.

The framing that a machine uses is determined both by its interface card and by the interface card's driver. On PCs running Windows you can choose which style of framing you want, but on Linux you usually cannot. Both types of framing interoperate just fine from Linux's perspective. On the other hand, Windows machines that use different framing on the same network cannot talk to each other. As a sysadmin, you usually don't need to worry about framing mismatches unless you are performing low-level debugging of a mixed network.

Ethernet cabling and signalling standards

The cabling options for the various Ethernet speeds (10 Mb/s, 100 Mb/s, 1 Gb/s, and now 10 Gb/s) are usually specified as part of the IEEE's standardization efforts. Often, a single type of cable with short distance limits will be approved as a new technology emerges. Cheaper media types and more generous limits will be added later.

Refer to Chapter 14, *Network Hardware*, for more information about the various Ethernet standards. Another useful reference to the ins and outs of Ethernet is the web site www.ethermanage.com/ethernet/, which is maintained by Charles Spurgeon.

Wireless networking

The IEEE 802.11 standard attempts to define framing and signalling standards for wireless links. Unfortunately, it was originally rather vague and included several parameters and options that were not fully specified. One interoperability issue you may need to pay attention to is that of "translation" vs. "encapsulation."

Translation converts a packet from one format to another; encapsulation wraps the packet with the desired format. Windows systems tend to default to encapsulation, and Linux systems to translation; the wireless base stations must be explicitly configured. If you are deploying a wireless network, you must make sure that your base stations and the workstations they talk to are all operating in the same mode.

Maximum transfer unit

The size of packets on a network may be limited both by hardware specifications and by protocol conventions. For example, the payload of a standard Ethernet frame can be no longer than 1,500 bytes. The size limit is associated with the link-layer

---

4. The link layer is actually divided into two parts: MAC, the Media Access Control sublayer, and LLC, the Link Layer Control sublayer. The MAC layer deals with the media and transmits packets onto the wire. The LLC layer handles the framing.

protocol and is called the maximum transfer unit or MTU. Table 12.2 shows typical values for the MTU.

Table 12.2   MTUs for various types of network link layer

Network type	Maximum transfer unit
Ethernet	1,500 bytes (1,492 with 802.2 framing)
FDDI	4,470 bytes (4,352 for IP/FDDI)
Token ring	Configurable[a]
PPP modem link	Configurable, often 512 or 576 bytes
PC stacks	Configurable, usually defaults to 512
Point-to-point WAN links (T1, T3)	Configurable, often 1,500 or 4,500 bytes

a. Common values are 552; 1,064; 2,088; 4,508; and 8,232. Sometimes 1,500 to match Ethernet.

In the TCP/IP suite, the IP layer splits packets to conform to the MTU of a particular network link. If a packet is routed through several networks, one of the intermediate networks may have a smaller MTU than the network of origin. In this case, the router that forwards the packet onto the small-MTU network further subdivides the packet in a process called fragmentation. Fragmentation is an unwelcome chore for a busy router.

The TCP protocol can determine the smallest MTU along the path to the destination and use that size from the outset. UDP is not so nice and is happy to shunt extra work to the IP layer. In IPv6, a new protocol winding its way through the standards process, intermediate routers can no longer perform fragmentation; MTU discovery is required.

Fragmentation problems can be insidious. Although path MTU discovery should automatically resolve MTU conflicts, an administrator must occasionally intervene. If you are using a tunneled architecture for a virtual private network, for example, you should look at the size of the packets that are traversing the tunnel. They are often 1,500 bytes to start with, but once the tunneling header is added, they become 1,540 bytes or so and must be fragmented. Setting the MTU of the link to a smaller value averts fragmentation and increases the overall performance of the tunneled network. Consult the **ifconfig** man page to see how to set an interface's MTU.

Packet addressing

Like letters or email messages, network packets must be properly addressed in order to reach their destinations. Several addressing schemes are used in combination:

- MAC (medium access control) addresses for hardware
- IP addresses for software
- Hostnames for people

TCP/IP

A host's network interface usually has a link-layer MAC address that distinguishes it from other machines on the physical network, an IP address that identifies it on the global Internet, and a hostname that's used by humans.

The lowest level of addressing is dictated by network hardware. For example, Ethernet devices are assigned a unique 6-byte hardware address at the time of manufacture.[5] Token ring interfaces have a similar address that is also 6 bytes long. Some point-to-point networks (such as PPP, described on page 320) need no hardware addresses at all; the identity of the destination is specified as the link is established.

A 6-byte Ethernet address is divided into two parts: the first three bytes identify the manufacturer of the hardware, and the last three bytes are a unique serial number that the manufacturer assigns. Sysadmins can often identify at least the brand of machine that is trashing the network by looking up the 3-byte identifier in a table of vendor IDs. A current vendor table is available from

    www.iana.org/assignments/ethernet-numbers

This information used to be published regularly in the RFC series, but it is no longer distributed that way. RFC1700 (1994) was the last *Assigned Numbers* RFC. The official repository of all the Internet's magic numbers is www.iana.org/numbers.htm.

Ethernet hardware addresses should be permanently assigned and immutable; unfortunately, some network interface cards let you specify the hardware address. Wireless cards are especially bad in this respect. Don't assign values in the multicast address range (odd second digit) or use other special values.

Linux lets you change the hardware address of the Ethernet interface, but please don't do that; it can break firewalls and some DHCP implementations. However, this feature can be handy if you have to replace a broken machine or network card and for some reason must use the old MAC address (e.g., all your switches filter it or your DHCP server hands out addresses based on MAC addresses).

At the next level up from the hardware, Internet addressing (more commonly known as IP addressing) is used. Typically, one[6] 4-byte IP address is assigned to each network interface. IP addresses are globally unique[7] and hardware independent. We ramble on for pages about IP addresses in the next section.

---

5. Unique at least in theory. At one time, 3Com duplicated Ethernet numbers among cards with different types of network connector; they assumed that customers would order only a single type. This shortcut raised havoc at sites that were transitioning between media and even caused problems on 3Com's own internal network. MAC address conflicts are deadly on the same network but OK on networks that are separated by a router.

6. Network interfaces can actually have more than one IP address associated with them, but this is a specialized configuration that's used in only a few specific circumstances. See *Virtual interfaces* on page 727 for more information.

7. This is a small lie that's true in most situations. See the discussion of NAT starting on page 289 for the skinny on nonunique IP addresses.

See page 296 for more information about ARP.

The mapping between IP addresses and hardware addresses is implemented at the link layer of the TCP/IP model. On networks that support broadcasting (i.e., networks that allow packets to be addressed to "all hosts on this physical network"), the ARP protocol allows mappings to be discovered automatically, without assistance from a system administrator.

Since IP addresses are long, seemingly random numbers, they are hard for people to remember. Linux systems allow one or more hostnames to be associated with an IP address so that users can type yahoo.com instead of 216.115.108.245. This mapping can be set up in several ways, ranging from a static file (**/etc/hosts**) to the NIS database system to DNS, the world-wide Domain Name System. Keep in mind that hostnames are really just a convenient shorthand for IP addresses.

Ports

IP addresses identify machines, or more precisely, network interfaces on a machine. They are not specific enough to address particular processes or services. TCP and UDP extend IP addresses with a concept known as a "port." A port is 16-bit number that supplements an IP address to specify a particular communication channel. Standard services such as email, FTP, and the web all associate themselves with "well known" ports defined in **/etc/services**. To help prevent impersonation of these services, Linux systems restrict server programs from binding to port numbers under 1,024 unless they are run as root. (But anyone can communicate with a server running on a low port number; the restriction applies only to taking control of the port.)

Address types

Both the IP layer and the link layer define several different types of addresses:

- Unicast – addresses that refer to a single host (network interface, really)
- Multicast – addresses that identify a group of hosts
- Broadcast – addresses that include all hosts on the local network

Multicast addressing facilitates applications such as video conferencing in which the same set of packets must be sent to all participants. The Internet Group Management Protocol (IGMP) constructs and manages sets of hosts that are treated as one multicast destination. Multicast IP addresses begin with a byte in the range 224 to 239.

Broadcast addresses reach all hosts on the local network by using a special wild card form of address in which the binary representation of the host part (defined next) is all 1s.

Multicast is virtually unused on today's Internet, but several active research projects are underway. See Internet2.org for more information.

TCP/IP

12.4   IP ADDRESSES: THE GORY DETAILS

An IP or Internet address is four bytes long and is divided into a network portion and a host portion. The network portion identifies a logical network to which the address refers, and the host portion identifies a machine on that network.

By convention, IP addresses are written as decimal numbers, one for each byte, separated by periods. For example, the IP address for our machine "boulder" is written as 128.138.240.1. The leftmost byte is the most significant and is always part of the network portion.

When 127 is the first byte of an address, it denotes the "loopback network," a fictitious network that has no real hardware interface and only one host. The loopback address 127.0.0.1 always refers to the current host. Its symbolic name is "localhost".

An interface's IP address and other parameters are set with the **ifconfig** command. Jump ahead to page 299 for a detailed description of **ifconfig**.

IP address classes

Historically, IP addresses were grouped into "classes," depending on the first bits of the leftmost byte. The class determined which bytes of the address were in the network portion and which were in the host portion. Today, routing systems use an explicit mask to specify the network portion and can draw the line between any two bits, not just on byte boundaries. However, the traditional classes are still used as defaults when no explicit division is specified.

Classes A, B, and C denote regular IP addresses. Classes D and E are used for multicasting and research addresses. Table 12.3 describes the characteristics of each class. The network portion of an address is denoted by N, and the host portion by H.

Table 12.3   Historical Internet address classes

Class	1st byte[a]	Format	Comments
A	1-126	N.H.H.H	Very early networks, or reserved for DoD
B	128-191	N.N.H.H	Large sites, usually subnetted, were hard to get
C	192-223	N.N.N.H	Easy to get, often obtained in sets
D	224-239	–	Multicast addresses, not permanently assigned
E	240-255	–	Experimental addresses

a. The value 0 is special and is not used as the first byte of regular IP addresses. 127 is reserved for the loopback address.

Subnetting and netmasks

It is rare for a single physical network to have more than a hundred computers attached to it. Therefore, class A and class B addresses (which allow for 16,777,214 and 65,534 hosts per network, respectively) are really quite silly and wasteful. For example, the 126 class A networks use up half the available address space.

Sites that have these addresses use a refinement of the addressing scheme called subnetting, in which part of the host portion of an address is "borrowed" to extend the network portion. For example, the four bytes of a class B address would normally be interpreted as N.N.H.H. If subnetting is used to assign the third byte to the network number rather than the host number, the address would be interpreted as N.N.N.H. This use of subnetting turns a single class B network address into 256 distinct class-C-like networks, each capable of supporting 254 hosts.

*See page 299 for more information about **ifconfig**.*

This reassignment is effected by use of the **ifconfig** command to associate an explicit "subnet mask" with a network interface. Each bit of the netmask that corresponds to the network portion of an IP address is set to 1, and host bits are set to 0. For example, the netmask for the N.N.N.H configuration would be 255.255.255.0 in decimal or 0xFFFFFF00 in hex. **ifconfig** normally uses the inherent class of an address to figure out which bits are in the network part. When you set an explicit mask, you simply override this behavior.

The division between network portion and host portion need not fall on a byte boundary. However, the network bits must be contiguous and must appear at the high order end of the address.[8]

Netmasks that do not end at a byte boundary can be annoying to decode and are often written as /XX, where XX is the number of bits in the network portion of the address. This is sometimes called CIDR (Classless Inter-Domain Routing) notation. For example, the network address 128.138.243.0/26 refers to the first of four networks whose first bytes are 128.138.243. The other three networks have 64, 128, and 192 as their fourth bytes. The netmask associated with these networks is 255.255.255.192 or 0xFFFFFFC0; in binary, it's 26 ones followed by 6 zeros. Exhibit C shows the relationships among these numbers in a bit more detail.

Exhibit C   Subnet mask base conversion

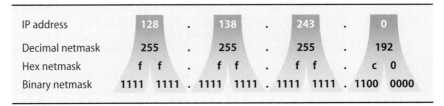

IP address	128 .	138 .	243 .	0
Decimal netmask	255 .	255 .	255 .	192
Hex netmask	f f .	f f .	f f .	c 0
Binary netmask	1111 1111 .	1111 1111 .	1111 1111 .	1100 0000

A /26 network has 6 bits left (32 − 26 = 6) to number hosts. 2^6 is 64, so the network has 64 potential host addresses. However, it can only accommodate 62 actual hosts because the all-0 and all-1 host addresses are reserved (they are the network and broadcast addresses, respectively).

8. Configurations such as N.N.H.N were once allowed but were uncommon; they are no longer permitted.

It's confusing to do all this bit twiddling in your head, but some tricks can make it simpler. The number of hosts per network and the value of the last byte in the netmask always add up to 256:

last netmask byte = 256 – net size

For example, 256 – 64 = 192, which is the final byte of the netmask in the preceding example. Another arithmetic fact is that the last byte of an actual network address (as opposed to a netmask) must be evenly divisible by the number of hosts per network. We see this fact in action in the current example, where the last bytes are 0, 64, 128, and 192—all evenly divisible by 64.

In our example, the extra two bits of network address obtained by subnetting can take on the values 00, 01, 10, and 11. The 128.138.243.0/24 network has thus been divided into four /26 networks.

- 128.138.243.0/26   (0 in decimal is **00**000000 in binary)
- 128.138.243.64/26   (64 in decimal is **01**000000 in binary)
- 128.138.243.128/26   (128 in decimal is **10**000000 in binary)
- 128.138.243.192/26   (192 in decimal is **11**000000 in binary)

The boldfaced bits of the last byte of each address are the bits that belong to the network portion of that byte.

Given an IP address (say, 128.138.243.100), we cannot tell without the associated netmask what the network address and broadcast address will be. Table 12.4 shows the possibilities for /16 (the default for a class B address), /24 (a sensible value), and /26 (a realistic value if address space is tight).

Table 12.4   Example IP address decodings

IP address	Netmask	Network	Broadcast
128.138.243.100/16	255.255.0.0	128.138.0.0	128.138.255.255
128.138.243.100/24	255.255.255.0	128.138.243.0	128.138.243.255
128.138.243.100/26	255.255.255.192	128.138.243.64	128.138.243.127

A handy online script called IP Calculator by Krischan Jodies (available at www.jodies.de/ipcalc) helps with binary/hex/mask arithmetic. **ipcalc** displays everything you might need to know about a network address and its netmask, broadcast address, hosts, etc. A tarball is available in addition to the online version; Debian and Ubuntu include the command-line **ipcalc** version by default.

Here's some sample IP Calculator output, munged a bit to help with formatting:

```
Address:   24.8.175.69         00011000.00001000.10101111 .01000101
Netmask:   255.255.255.0 = 24  11111111.11111111.11111111 .00000000
Wildcard:  0.0.0.255           00000000.00000000.00000000 .11111111
```

```
=>
Network:   24.8.175.0/24    00011000.00001000.10101111 .00000000 (Class A)
Broadcast: 24.8.175.255     00011000.00001000.10101111 .11111111
HostMin:   24.8.175.1       00011000.00001000.10101111 .00000001
HostMax:   24.8.175.254     00011000.00001000.10101111 .11111110
```

The output provides both easy-to-understand versions of the addresses and "cut and paste" versions. Cool.

 Red Hat includes a program, also called **ipcalc**, that is pretty lame and for most calculations assumes that IP addresses are in class A, B, or C.

The original RFC on IP subnetting (RFC950) did not permit the use of the first or last subnets (all 0s and all 1s). In our example with the /26 networks, this rule would eliminate half the subnets: the 0 subnet and the 192 subnet. Everyone ignored the RFC except Novell and Cisco. (In early versions of Cisco's IOS operating system, you had to explicitly enable subnet 0 with the ip subnet zero command. On versions 12.0 and later, subnet 0 is available by default.)

The RFC is wrong, although its intentions were fine. Subnet 0 was disallowed because the thinking was that confusion might arise if a subnet address was indistinguishable from an unsubnetted network address. The fear proved groundless, however, and all-0/all-1 subnets are in common use today. It is the host portion that should not be all 0s or all 1s.

The network address and broadcast address steal two hosts from each network, so it would seem that the smallest meaningful network would have four possible hosts: two real hosts—usually at either end of a point-to-point link—and the network and broadcast addresses. To have four values for hosts requires two bits in the host portion, so such a network would be a /30 network with netmask 255.255.255.252 or 0xFFFFFFFC. However, a /31 network is treated as a special case (see RFC3021) and has no network or broadcast address; both of its two addresses are used for hosts, and its netmask is 255.255.255.254.

Although the hosts on a network may agree that they are using subnetted addresses, the rest of the world doesn't know about this and continues to treat addresses according to their implicit class.[9] Rather than advertising every subnet to the outside world, in our 128.138.243.100 example you would need to advertise only a single class B network. Once a packet arrived within the subnetted area, its destination address would be reinterpreted with local netmasks, the real target network "discovered," and the packet routed to its exact destination.

The IP address crisis

The Internet community realized in about 1992 that the original address allocation scheme raised three fundamental problems.

---

9. Another lie in the name of a simple, as yet incomplete description; see the discussion of Classless Inter-Domain Routing (CIDR) on page 287 for the real scoop.

- First, we were going to run out of class B addresses—the most desirable ones for moderately large organizations—by mid-1995.

- Second, the routing tables of Internet backbone sites were growing so large that they would not fit in the memory of available routers.

- Finally, IP addresses were being allocated on a first-come, first-served basis with no locality of reference; that is, numerically adjacent addresses could be within the same organization or on different continents. Imagine the confusion that would result if postal codes were assigned in this haphazard fashion.

To solve the problem, two solutions were advanced in tandem: one for the immediate future and one for the long term.

The short-term solution, Classless Inter-Domain Routing (CIDR), is a different way of managing the existing 4-byte address space, namely, CIDR uses the available addresses more efficiently and simplifies routing tables by accounting for numerical adjacencies. We discuss CIDR in more detail in the next section.

The long-term solution, IPv6, is a revision of the IP protocol. IPv6 expands the address space to 16 bytes and incorporates several other lessons learned from the use of IP over the last 25 years. It removes several features of IP that experience has shown to be of little value, making the protocol potentially faster and easier to implement. IPv6 also integrates security and authentication into the basic protocol and eliminates fragmentation at intermediate routers.

IPv6 is still in the early stages of deployment, but CIDR has been fully operational for years. CIDR is supported and used by the Internet backbone and by the major manufacturers of routing equipment. Network Address Translation (NAT), a scheme for reusing IP addresses that's covered on page 289, also played a large role in reducing the demand for IP addresses.

The complexity of IPv6, the efficiency of CIDR and NAT, and the inertia of an Internet that already works pretty well all combine to suggest that it may be some time before we move to IPv6. Although many applications and operating systems already feature native support for IPv6, cost alone is prohibitive in the minds of many folks in the United States. Nevertheless, extensive efforts on the part of distributors and volunteer developers have ensured that when the network switches to IPv6, Linux will be ready.

The IPv4 address shortage is felt more acutely in the international theater, and so IPv6 has received a warmer welcome there. In the United States, it may take a killer application to boost IPv6 over the hill, for example, a new generation of cell phones that map an IPv6 address to a telephone number. (Voice-over-IP systems would also benefit from a closer correspondence between phone numbers and IPv6 addresses.)

Some additional details on IPv6 addressing are given on page 291.

CIDR: Classless Inter-Domain Routing

CIDR, defined in RFC1519 (September 1993), eliminates the class system that formerly determined the network portion of an IP address. Like subnetting, of which it is a direct extension, it relies on an explicit netmask to define the boundary between the network and host parts of an address. But unlike subnetting, it allows, for purposes of routing, the network portion to be made *smaller* than would be implied by an address's implicit class. Using a shorter netmask has the effect of aggregating several networks. Hence, CIDR is sometimes referred to as supernetting.

With CIDR, several class C networks can be allocated to a site such that the Internet need not have separate routing table entries for each one. The site could also be allocated a subspace of a class A or B address. For example, suppose a site has been given a block of eight class C addresses numbered 192.144.0.0 through 192.144.7.0 (in CIDR notation, 192.144.0.0/21). Internally, the site could use them as

- 1 network of length /21, 2,046 hosts,[10] netmask 255.255.248.0
- 8 networks of length /24, 254 hosts each, netmask 255.255.255.0
- 16 networks of length /25, 126 hosts each, netmask 255.255.255.128
- 32 networks of length /26, 62 hosts each, netmask 255.255.255.192

and so on. It's also possible to mix and match regions of different subnet lengths, as long as all the pieces fit together without overlaps. This is called variable length subnetting. For example, an ISP with the 192.144.0.0/21 allocation could define some /30 networks for PPP dial-up customers, some /24s for large customers, and some /27s for smaller folks.

When you mix and match like this, all the hosts on a particular network must be configured with the same netmask. You cannot tell one host on the network that it is a /24 and another host on that same network that it is a /25.

The beauty and value of CIDR is that from the perspective of the Internet, it's not necessary to have 256, 128, or even 32 routing table entries for these addresses. They all refer to the same organization, and all the packets are to go to the same place. A single routing entry for the address 192.144.0.0/21 suffices. In addition, CIDR makes it easy to allocate portions of class A and B addresses and thus increases the number of available addresses manyfold.

With the advent of CIDR, system administrators have gotten good at binary and hex arithmetic or have discovered that the Linux utility **bc** can do math in any base, using the **ibase** and **obase** directives.[11] You can use Table 12.5 (next page) as a cheat sheet.

When CIDR was introduced in 1993, the backbone tables contained approximately 20,000 routes. The slow but steady growth of the Internet since the dot com implosion has increased the size of the routing table to around 250,000 in 2006.[12]

10. The original Ethernet on RG-11 coaxial cable allowed at most 1,024 hosts on a single network; with today's switches, it's possible (but not very sensible) to build really huge networks.
11. But be careful not to back yourself into a corner… This puzzle is left as an exercise for the reader.
12. See bgp.potaroo.net for current information about the BGP routing table.

TCP/IP

Table 12.5   Network configurations for various lengths of netmask

Length[a]	Host bits	Hosts/net[b]	Decimal netmask	Hex netmask
/20	12	4094	255.255.240.0	0xFFFFF000
/21	11	2046	255.255.248.0	0xFFFFF800
/22	10	1022	255.255.252.0	0xFFFFFC00
/23	9	510	255.255.254.0	0xFFFFFE00
/24	8	254	255.255.255.0	0xFFFFFF00
/25	7	126	255.255.255.128	0xFFFFFF80
/26	6	62	255.255.255.192	0xFFFFFFC0
/27	5	30	255.255.255.224	0xFFFFFFE0
/28	4	14	255.255.255.240	0xFFFFFFF0
/29	3	6	255.255.255.248	0xFFFFFFF8
/30	2	2	255.255.255.252	0xFFFFFFFC

a. The network length + the number of host bits is always 32 since we are dividing up the fixed-size "pie" of a 32-bit IP address.

b. Mathy folks will notice that the number of hosts per net is 2^#hostbits – 2; the –2 reflects the fact that the all-0 and all-1 host addresses are special.

An unaggregated region of the address space, called the 192 swamp (and smaller swamps in the 199 and 205 ranges), consists of early class C addresses whose owners cannot aggregate them and do not want to turn them in and then have to renumber. The United States is particularly bad in this regard. Europe and Asia, which started a bit later, learned from our mistakes and did a much better job of allocating addresses. Sites with an unaggregated 192 network should return it to the American Registry for Internet Numbers (ARIN) and get a new block from their ISP. Unfortunately, the cost of renumbering (in IPv4 space at least) precludes most sites from doing this.

Although CIDR was only intended as an interim solution, it has proved to be strong enough to handle the Internet's growth problems for the foreseeable future. In fact, the combination of CIDR and NAT has worked so well that it is unclear if we really need a new IP protocol. An enormous amount of engineering work has gone into the IPv6 specification and the production implementations of IPv6. It would be a shame to waste this work, but wholesale deployment of IPv6 will probably require a new must-have application written only for IPv6, a yuppie toy that uses IPv6 addressing, or a decision by Microsoft to obsolete IPv4.

Address allocation

In the early days of the Internet, individual sites applied to the Internet Network Information Center (InterNIC) for address space. ARIN and LACNIC have now replaced the InterNIC in the Americas. Only ISPs who allocate significant amounts of address space per year are eligible to apply to ARIN for IP address space. All other sites must apply to their ISP.

Only network numbers are formally assigned; sites must define their own host numbers to form complete IP addresses. You can subdivide the address space given to you into subnets however you like.

Administratively, ICANN (the Internet Corporation for Assigned Names and Numbers) has delegated blocks of addresses to five regional Internet registries, and these regional authorities are responsible for doling out subblocks to ISPs within their regions (see Table 12.6). These ISPs in turn divide up their blocks and hand out pieces to individual clients. Only large ISPs should ever have to deal directly with one of the ICANN-sponsored address registries.

Table 12.6 Regional Internet Registries

Name	Web address	Region covered
ARIN	www.arin.net	North America, part of the Caribbean
APNIC	www.apnic.net	Asia/Pacific region
AfriNIC	www.afrinic.net	Africa
LACNIC	www.lacnic.net	Central and South America, part of the Caribbean
RIPE	www.ripe.net	Europe and surrounding areas

The delegation from ICANN to regional registries and then to national or regional ISPs has allowed for further aggregation in the backbone routing tables. ISP customers who have been allocated address space within the ISP's block do not need individual routing entries on the backbone. A single entry for the aggregated block that points to the ISP suffices.

Originally, address space was not very fairly allocated. The U.S. government reserved about half the address space for itself and gave relatively small blocks to Europe and Asia. But Europe and Asia managed their address space much more wisely than we did in the United States. The address space map at

www.caida.org/analysis/learn/ipv4space

illustrates this fact quite effectively. It shows the IP address space as a whole, the portions that have been allocated, the portions that are routed (and therefore reachable), and the addresses for which traffic has been observed at a couple of major exchange points in the U.S.

Private addresses and NAT

Another temporary solution to address space depletion is the use of private IP address spaces, described in RFC1918 (February 1996). In the CIDR era, sites normally obtain their IP addresses from their Internet service provider. If a site wants to change ISPs, it may be held for ransom by the cost of renumbering its networks. The ISP gave it the address space as long as it was a customer. If the site now wants to choose a different ISP, it has to convince the old ISP to let it have the addresses and also convince the new ISP to make the routing work correctly to the new location with the old addresses. Typically, ISPs don't want to bother with these issues and will require customers to renumber.

One alternative to using ISP-assigned addresses is to use private addresses that are never shown to your ISP. RFC1918 sets aside 1 class A network, 16 class B networks, and 256 class C networks that will never be globally allocated and can be used internally by any site. The catch is that packets bearing those addresses must never be allowed to sneak out onto the Internet. You should filter them at your border router just to make sure. If some packets slip by, you should track down the misconfigurations that allowed them to escape.

Table 12.7 shows the network numbers reserved for private addressing. (The "CIDR range" column shows the range for each class in the more compact CIDR notation; it does not add additional information.)

Table 12.7   IP addresses reserved for private use

IP class	From	To	CIDR range
Class A	10.0.0.0	10.255.255.255	10.0.0.0/8
Class B	172.16.0.0	172.31.255.255	172.16.0.0/12
Class C	192.168.0.0	192.168.255.255	192.168.0.0/16

Sites can choose from this set the size of network that best fits their organization.

To allow hosts that use these private addresses to talk to the Internet, the site's border router runs a system called NAT (Network Address Translation). NAT intercepts packets addressed with these internal-only addresses and rewrites their source addresses, using a real external IP address and perhaps a different source port number. It also maintains a table of the mappings it has made between internal and external address/source-port pairs so that the translation can be performed in reverse when answering packets arrive from the Internet.

NAT's use of port number mapping allows several conversations to be multiplexed onto the same IP address so that a single external address can be shared by many internal hosts. In some cases, a site can get by with only one "real" IP address.

A site that uses NAT must still request address space from its ISP, but most of the addresses thus obtained are used for NAT mappings and are not assigned to individual hosts. If the site later wants to choose another ISP, only the border router and its NAT configuration need to change, not the configurations of the individual hosts.

NAT is widely used in the consumer sector as well as in corporations. It is also possible to have a Linux box perform the NAT function, although many sites prefer to delegate that task to their routers or network connection devices. See the vendor-specific sections later in this chapter for details. For some reason, the Linux world used to call NAT "IP masquerading." However, after the introduction of the 2.4 kernel, the Linux folks began to call it NAT as well.

An incorrect NAT configuration can let private-address-space packets escape onto the Internet. The packets will get to their destinations, but answering packets won't be able to get back. CAIDA,[13] an organization that measures everything in sight about the backbone networks, finds that 0.1% to 0.2% of the packets on the backbone have either private addresses or bad checksums. This sounds like a tiny percentage, and it is, but it represents about 20,000 packets every 10 minutes on a busy circuit at MAE-West (one of the major public exchanges at which different ISPs exchange traffic). See www.caida.org for other interesting statistics and network measurement tools.

One disadvantage of NAT (or perhaps an advantage) is that an arbitrary host on the Internet cannot connect directly to your site's internal machines. Some implementations (e.g., Linux and Cisco PIX) let you configure "tunnels" that support direct connections for particular hosts.

Another problem is that some applications embed IP addresses in the data portion of packets; these applications are foiled or confused by NAT. Examples include some routing protocols, streaming programs such as RealVideo and SHOUTcast, some FTP commands such as PORT and PASV, ICQ instant messaging, and many games. NAT sometimes breaks VPNs (virtual private networks), too.

Large corporations that use NAT and RFC1918 addresses must institute some form of central coordination so that all hosts, independently of their department or administrative group, have unique IP addresses. The situation can become complicated when one company that uses RFC1918 address space acquires or merges with another company that's doing the same thing. Parts of the combined organization must often renumber.

NAT hides interior structure. This secrecy feels like a security win, but the security folks say NAT doesn't really help for security and certainly does not replace the need for a firewall. NAT also foils attempts to measure the size or topology of the Internet.

At least one tool has been developed in an attempt to identify NAT-using hosts. The utility's algorithm correlates well-known operating system TTL values with the expected TTL values on the network. When they don't match, the source IP address is identified as a NAT device. The idea is effective in theory but expensive and ungainly to implement in reality. Learn more about the method at www.sflow.org/detectNAT.

IPv6 addressing

An IPv6 address is 128 bits long. These long addresses were originally intended to solve the problem of IP address exhaustion. Now that they're here, however, they are being exploited to help with issues of routing, mobility, and locality of reference.

IP addresses have never been geographically clustered in the way that phone numbers or zip codes are. Now, with the proposed segmentation of the IPv6 address space, they will at least cluster to ISPs. The boundary between the network portion and the

---

13. CAIDA, pronounced "kay duh," is the Cooperative Association for Internet Data Analysis at the San Diego Supercomputer Center on the UCSD campus (www.caida.org).

host portion of an IPv6 address is fixed at /64; the boundary between public topology and a site's local topology is fixed at /48. Table 12.8 shows the various parts of an IPv6 address.

Table 12.8   The parts of an IPv6 address

	Complete IPv6 address (128 bits)		
ISP prefix		**Subnet**	**Host identifier**
45 bits		16 bits	64 bits

↳ **Address type** 3 bits

Bits	Acronym	Translation
1-3	FP	Format prefix; the type of address, e.g., unicast
4-16	TLA ID	Top-level aggregation ID, like backbone ISP
17-24	RES	Reserved for future use
25-48	NLA ID	Next-level aggregation ID, e.g., regional ISPs and site ID
49-64	SLA ID	Site-level aggregation ID, like local subnet
65-128	INTERFACE ID	Interface identifier (MAC address plus padding)

Of these pieces, only the SLA ID and the INTERFACE ID belong to the host and its site. The other parts are provided by the upstream ISP. The SLA specifies a local subnet. The 64-bit interface ID identifies the host network interface. It typically contains the 48-bit MAC address with the hex digits 0xFFFE in the middle. A special bit in the MAC address (bit 6 of the first byte, numbering bits from the left, starting at 0) called the universal/local bit must be complemented (see RFC2373). This scheme allows hosts to be automatically numbered, which is a nice feature for the sysadmin since only the subnet needs to be managed.

In IPv6, the MAC address is seen at the IP layer, a situation with both good and bad implications. The brand and model of interface card are encoded in the first half of the MAC address, so hackers with code for a particular architecture will be helped along. The visibility of this information has also worried some privacy advocates. The IPv6 folks have responded by pointing out that sites are not actually required to use MAC addresses; they're free to use whatever they want for the host address. A scheme to include a random token in the local part of the address has also been proposed. Too many bits to play with!

On the other hand, assigning IPv6 addresses should be easier than assigning IPv4 addresses since you only need to keep track of the subnet address. The hosts can configure themselves—or at least, that's the theory.

The format prefix identifies the type of IPv6 address: unicast, multicast, or anycast. Unicast addresses set FP to 001 (binary). The TLA and NLA IDs identify your top-level IP backbone carrier and the local ISPs up the chain to your backbone provider.

These days, most vendors are IPv6 ready. Almost all distributions come with native IPv6 support, and network hardware has had IPv6 support for nearly a decade.

ARIN generally allocates IPv6 space only to large ISPs or to local Internet registries that plan to dole out large chunks of address space in the near future. These organizations can then allocate subspaces to their downstream customers. The fee structure is a minimum charge of $1,250/year and a maximum of $36,000/year. ARIN has extended a fee waiver to members in good standing.

Here are some useful sources of IPv6 information:

- www.ipv6tf.net – An IPv6 information portal
- www.ipv6.org – FAQs and technical information
- www.ipv6forum.com – marketing folks and IPv6 propaganda

One major advantage of IPv6 is that it was designed to solve the renumbering issue. In the IPv4 world, ISPs allocate address space to customers, but the addresses are not portable; when customers leave an ISP, they must return their addresses and renumber with addresses from their new ISP. With IPv6, the new ISP gives you an address prefix that you simply prepend to the local parts of your addresses, probably at your border router. This scheme is similar to that of NAT for IPv4 addressing, but without any of NAT's little problems.

Various schemes have been proposed to ease the transition from IPv4 to IPv6, including the use of NAT to hide IPv6 addresses while packets are tunneled across the existing IPv4 infrastructure.

12.5 ROUTING

Routing is the process of directing a packet through the maze of networks that stand between its source and its destination. In the TCP/IP system, it is similar to asking for directions in an unfamiliar country. The first person you talk to might point you toward the right city. Once you were a bit closer to your destination, the next person might be able to tell you how to get to the right street. Eventually, you get close enough that someone can identify the building you're looking for.

TCP/IP routing information takes the form of rules ("routes") such as, "To reach network A, send packets through machine C." There can also be a default route that tells what to do with packets bound for a network to which there is no explicit route.

Routing information is stored in a table in the kernel. Each table entry has several parameters, including a netmask for each listed network (once optional but now required if the default netmask is not correct). To route a packet to a particular address, the kernel picks the most specific of the matching routes (that is, the one with the longest netmask). If the kernel finds no relevant route and no default route, then it returns a "network unreachable" ICMP error to the sender.

TCP/IP

The word "routing" is commonly used to mean two distinct things:

- Looking up a network address in the routing table to forward a packet toward its destination

- Building the routing table in the first place

In this section we examine the forwarding function and look at how routes can be manually added to or deleted from the routing table. We defer the more complicated topic of routing protocols that build and maintain the routing table until Chapter 13.

Routing tables

You can examine a machine's routing table with **netstat -r**. Use **netstat -rn** to avoid DNS lookups and to present all the information numerically. We discuss **netstat** in more detail starting on page 649, but here is a short example to give you a better idea of what routes look like. This host has two network interfaces: 132.236.227.93 (eth0) on the 132.236.227.0/24 net and 132.236.212.1 (eth1) on the 132.236.212.0/26 net.

```
$ netstat -rn
Kernel IP routing table
Destination     Genmask          Gateway         Fl   MSS   Iface
132.236.227.0   255.255.255.0    132.236.227.93  U    1500  eth0
default         0.0.0.0          132.236.227.1   UG   1500  eth0
132.236.212.0   255.255.255.192  132.236.212.1   U    1500  eth1
132.236.220.64  255.255.255.192  132.236.212.6   UG   1500  eth1
127.0.0.1       255.255.255.255  127.0.0.1       U    3584  lo
```

The destination field is usually a network address; the gateway must be a host address. For example, the fourth route says that to reach the network 132.236.220.64/26, packets must be sent to the gateway 132.236.212.6 through interface eth1. The second entry is a default route; packets not explicitly addressed to any of the three networks listed (or to the machine itself) are sent to the default gateway host, 132.236.227.1. Hosts can route packets only to gateway machines that are directly attached to their same network.

*See page 303 for more information about the **route** command.*

Routing tables can be configured statically, dynamically, or with a combination of the two approaches. A static route is one that you enter explicitly with the **route** command. Static routes should stay in the routing table as long as the system is up; they are often set up at boot time from one of the system startup scripts. For example, the Linux commands

```
route add -net 132.236.220.64 netmask 255.255.255.192 gw 132.236.212.6 eth1
route add default gw 132.236.227.1 eth0
```

add the fourth and second routes displayed by **netstat -rn** above. (The first and third routes in that display were added by **ifconfig** when the eth0 and eth1 interfaces were configured.)

The final route is also added at boot time. It configures a pseudo-device called the loopback interface. The loopback prevents packets sent from the host to itself from going out on the network; instead, they are transferred directly from the network output queue to the network input queue inside the kernel.

In a stable local network, static routing is an efficient solution. It is easy to manage and reliable. However, it requires that the system administrator know the topology of the network accurately at boot time and that the topology not change often.

Most machines on a local area network have only one way to get out to the rest of the network, so the routing problem is easy. A default route added at boot time suffices to point toward the way out. Hosts that use DHCP (see page 311) to get their IP addresses can also obtain a default route with DHCP.

For more complicated network topologies, dynamic routing is required. Dynamic routing is typically performed by a daemon process that maintains and modifies the routing table. Routing daemons on different hosts communicate to discover the topology of the network and to figure out how to reach distant destinations. Several routing daemons are available.

ICMP redirects

Although IP generally does not concern itself with the management of routing information, it does define a small damage control feature called an ICMP redirect. When a router forwards a packet to a machine on the same network from which the packet was originally received, something is clearly wrong. Since the sender, the router, and the next-hop router are all on the same network, the packet could have been forwarded in one hop rather than two. The router can conclude that the sender's routing tables are inaccurate or incomplete.

In this situation, the router can notify the sender of its problem by sending an ICMP redirect packet. In effect, a redirect says, "You should not be sending packets for host *xxx* to me; you should send them to host *yyy* instead." The ICMP protocol allows redirects to be sent for both individual host addresses and entire networks. However, many implementations generate only host redirects; network redirects are pretty much useless these days because they only apply to class A, B, or C networks.

Upon receiving a redirect, a naive sender updates its routing table so that future packets bound for that destination will take the more direct path. In the early days of multicasting, a few systems generated ICMP routing redirects in response to multicast packets. Modern systems do not have this problem.

The standard ICMP scenario contains no authentication step. Your router receives a redirect that claims to be from another, well-respected router and directs you to send traffic elsewhere. Should you listen? Paying attention to redirects actually creates something of a security problem. Redirects are generally ignored by Linux (for security reasons) and by Cisco routers (because they are routers). It's not a good idea to let untrusted hosts modify your routing tables.

Under Linux, the variable **accept_redirects** in the **/proc** hierarchy controls the acceptance of ICMP redirects. See page 314 for instructions on examining and resetting this variable.

TCP/IP

12.6 ARP: THE ADDRESS RESOLUTION PROTOCOL

Even though IP packets are usually thought of in terms of IP addresses, hardware addresses must be used to actually transport data across a network's link layer.[14] ARP, the Address Resolution Protocol, discovers the hardware address associated with a particular IP address. It can be used on any kind of network that supports broadcasting but is most commonly described in terms of Ethernet.

If host A wants to send a packet to host B on the same Ethernet, it uses ARP to discover B's hardware address. If B is not on the same network as A, host A uses the routing system to determine the next-hop router along the route to B and then uses ARP to find that router's hardware address. Since ARP uses broadcast packets, which cannot cross networks,[15] it can only be used to find the hardware addresses of machines directly connected to the sending host's local network.

Every machine maintains a table in memory called the ARP cache, which contains the results of recent ARP queries. Under normal circumstances, many of the addresses a host needs are discovered soon after booting, so ARP does not account for a lot of network traffic.

ARP functions by broadcasting[16] a packet of the form, "Does anyone know the hardware address for 128.138.116.4?" The machine being searched for recognizes its own IP address and sends back a reply, "Yes, that's the IP address assigned to one of my network interfaces, and the corresponding Ethernet address is 8:0:20:0:fb:6a."

The original query includes the IP and Ethernet addresses of the requestor so that the machine being sought can reply without issuing an ARP query of its own. Thus, the two machines learn each other's ARP mappings with only one exchange of packets. Other machines that overhear the requestor's initial broadcast can record its address mapping, too. This passive inspection of ARP traffic is sometimes called snooping.

The **arp** command examines and manipulates the kernel's ARP cache, adds or deletes entries, and flushes or shows the table. The command **arp -a** displays the contents of the ARP cache. For example:

```
redhat$ /sbin/arp -a
sprint-gw (192.168.1.254) at 00:02:4B:5B:26:45 [ether] on eth0
inura-local.toadranch.com (192.168.1.101) at 00:04:76:37:AE:7E [ether] on eth0
```

The **arp** command is generally useful only for debugging and for situations that involve special hardware. Some devices are not smart enough to speak ARP (for example, network-attached printers or special-purpose graphics displays). To support such devices, you might need to configure another machine as a proxy ARP server for your

---

14. Except on point-to-point links, on which the identity of the destination is sometimes implicit.
15. Routers can often be configured to flood broadcast packets to other networks; don't do this.
16. ARP uses the underlying link layer's broadcasting conventions, not IP broadcasting.

crippled hardware. That's normally done with the **arp** command as well (using the -**s** flag). For example:

```
# /sbin/arp -s printer.toadranch.com  00:50:04:ce:ef:38
```

Linux kernels 2.4 and later do not support proxy ARP service for a whole subnet but automatically act as a proxy ARP server when a route exists and the interface is configured to forward packets.

If two hosts on a network are using the same IP address, one has the right ARP table entry and one is wrong. You can use the **arp** command to track down the offending machine.

Sometimes, hardware addresses need to be translated into IP addresses. A lot of handicapped hardware (e.g., diskless workstations, network computers, printers) needs to perform this translation at boot time. Instead of having an IP address hardwired into a configuration file, a machine can query a central server to discover its own address.

This ends our coverage of networking background material. In the sections that follow, we address the issues involved in configuring Linux machines for a local network and the Internet.

12.7 ADDITION OF A MACHINE TO A NETWORK

Only a few steps are involved in adding a new machine to an existing local area network, but some vendors hide the files you must modify and generally make the chore difficult. Others provide a setup script that prompts for the networking parameters that are needed, which is fine until you need to undo something or move a machine. Before bringing up a new machine on a network that is connected to the Internet, you should secure it (Chapter 20, *Security*) so that you are not inadvertently inviting hackers onto your local network.

The basic steps to add a new machine to a local network are as follows:

- Assign a unique IP address and hostname.
- Set up the new host to configure its network interfaces at boot time.
- Set up a default route and perhaps fancier routing.
- Point to a DNS name server, to allow access to the rest of the Internet.

Of course, you could add a debugging step to this sequence as well. After any change that might affect booting, you should always reboot to verify that the machine comes up correctly. Six months later when the power has failed and the machine refuses to boot, it's hard to remember what change you made that might have caused the problem. (Refer also to Chapter 19, *Network Management and Debugging*.)

If your network uses DHCP, the Dynamic Host Configuration Protocol, the DHCP server will do these chores for you. Refer to the DHCP section starting on page 311 for general information about DHCP and the specifics of configuring our example distributions to use DHCP at boot time.

TCP/IP

We first cover the general outline of these steps, then return to the details for each distribution in a series of vendor-specific sections. The commands involve the Linux kernel's networking stack and are the same across different distributions. However, each distribution has established its own configuration files for automating network configuration at boot time, as summarized in Table 12.9.

Table 12.9   Network configuration files

System	File	What's set there
Red Hat, Fedora	**/etc/sysconfig/network** **network-scripts/ifcfg-***ifname*	Hostname, default route IP address, netmask, broadcast address
SUSE	**/etc/rc.config** **/etc/route.conf**	Hostname, IP address, netmask, and more Default route
Debian, Ubuntu	**/etc/hostname** **/etc/network/interfaces**	Hostname IP address, netmask, default route

The process of designing and installing a physical network is touched on in Chapter 14, *Network Hardware*. If you are dealing with an existing network and have a general idea of how it is set up, it may not be necessary for you to read too much more about the physical aspects of networking unless you plan to extend the existing network.

We describe the process of network configuration in terms of Ethernet; other technologies are essentially similar.

Hostname and IP address assignment

See Chapter 15 for more information about DNS.

Administrators have various theories about how the mapping from hostnames to IP addresses is best maintained at a local site: through the **hosts** file, NIS, the DNS system, or perhaps some combination of those sources. If you have multiple systems, you must also have a sensible plan for how they are to work together. The conflicting values are scalability and maintainability versus a system that is flexible enough to allow machines to boot when not all services are available (and flexible enough to handle the heterogeneity of your site).

Another longer-term issue that may be relevant is that of renumbering. If your site changes ISPs, you may have to return your old IP addresses and renumber with addresses assigned by the new ISP. That process becomes quite daunting if you must visit each host on the network to reconfigure it. To expedite such renumbering, use hostnames in configuration files and make the hostname-to-IP-address translation only in the DNS database files. On the other hand, using IP addresses in configuration files reduces dependencies during bootup, when not all services are available. Damned if you do, damned if you don't.

The **/etc/hosts** file is the oldest and simplest way to map names to IP addresses. Each line starts with an IP address and continues with the various symbolic names by which that address is known.

Here is a typical **/etc/hosts** file for the host lollipop:

```
127.0.0.1          localhost
192.108.21.48      lollipop.xor.com lollipop loghost
192.108.21.254     chimchim-gw.xor.com chimchim-gw
192.108.21.1       ns.xor.com ns
192.225.33.5       licenses.xor.com license-server
```

A minimalist version would contain only the first two lines. localhost is commonly the first entry in the **/etc/hosts** file.

Because **/etc/hosts** contains only local mappings, most modern systems use it only for mappings that are needed at boot time. DNS is then consulted to find mappings for the rest of the local network and the rest of the world. You can also use **/etc/hosts** to specify mappings that you do not want the rest of the world to know about and therefore do not publish in DNS.

/etc/hosts was once important during the boot process because DNS was not yet available and hostnames were sometimes used in config files instead of IP addresses. Modern Linux distributions don't really need the **/etc/hosts** file, but it should probably contain at least the mappings for the host itself and the loopback address. Mappings for the default gateway machine and a name server might also be helpful. Many sites put all their really important hosts, servers, and gateways in the **/etc/hosts** file. Others put only the host itself and the loopback interface; still others add in all local hosts and their off-site backup name servers.

Our example Linux systems install a mishmash of **/etc/hosts** files. Debian's and Ubuntu's contain localhost on 127.0.0.1, the system's hostname on 127.0.1.1, and some IPv6 information. Red Hat's and Fedora's define localhost and the machine itself. SUSE's contains localhost and IPv6 addresses for localhost and a few special IPv6 names.

The **hostname** command assigns a hostname to a machine. **hostname** is typically run at boot time from one of the startup scripts, which obtains the name to be assigned from a configuration file. Of course, each vendor names that configuration file differently. See the vendor-specific sections beginning on page 307 for information about your specific distribution. Most systems today assign a fully qualified name (that is, a name that includes both the hostname and the DNS domain name, such as anchor.cs.colorado.edu).

See page 520 for more information about LDAP. At a small site, you can easily dole out hostnames and IP addresses by hand. But when many networks and many different administrative groups are involved, it helps to have some central coordination to ensure uniqueness. For dynamically assigned networking parameters, DHCP takes care of the uniqueness issues. Some sites now use LDAP databases to manage their hostnames and IP addresses assignments.

ifconfig: configure network interfaces

ifconfig enables or disables a network interface, sets its IP address and subnet mask, and sets various other options and parameters. It is usually run at boot time (with command-line parameters taken from config files), but it can also make changes on the fly. Be careful if you are making **ifconfig** changes and are logged in remotely; many a sysadmin has been locked out this way and had to drive in to fix things.

An **ifconfig** command most commonly has the form

> **ifconfig** *interface address options* …

for example:

> ifconfig eth0 192.168.1.13 netmask 255.255.255.0 up

interface identifies the hardware interface to which the command applies. On UNIX systems this is usually a two- or three-character device name (derived from the chipset used on the interface card) followed by a number, but for Linux it is almost always something like eth0.[17] The hardware's true identity and the mapping to an appropriate device driver are stored in the **/etc/modprobe.conf** file on an alias line. The loopback interface is called lo.

ifconfig *interface* displays the current settings for *interface* without changing them. Many systems understand **-a** to mean "all interfaces," and **ifconfig -a** can therefore be used to find out what interfaces are present on the system. If your system does not understand **ifconfig -a**, try **netstat -i** to find the interface names.

The *address* parameter specifies the interface's IP address. Many versions of **ifconfig** also accept a hostname for the address parameter. We prefer to use the actual IP address; if **ifconfig** is given a hostname (or the output of the **hostname** command), the potential for boot-time problems is increased. If there's a problem resolving the hostname, the machine won't boot or it will boot into a state in which it cannot be accessed from the network, requiring you to physically go to the machine to debug the problem. DNS queries that cannot complete take a long while to time out, making it seem that the machine is hung. On the other hand, if you ever have to renumber your network, finding all those hidden hardwired IP addresses in configuration files can be a nightmare.

The keyword **up** turns the interface on; **down** turns it off. When an **ifconfig** command assigns an IP address to an interface, as in the example above, the **up** parameter is implicit and does not need to be mentioned by name.

ifconfig understands many other options. We cover only the most common ones; as always, consult your man pages for the final word on your particular system. **ifconfig** options all have symbolic names. Some options require an argument, which should be placed immediately after the option name.

The **netmask** option sets the subnet mask for the interface and is required if the network is not subnetted according to its address class (A, B, or C). The mask can be

---

17. You can assign more than one IP address to an interface by making use of the concept of "virtual network interfaces" or "IP aliases." Administrators often do this to allow one machine to host several web sites. On Linux systems, the virtual interfaces are named eth0:0, eth0:1, and so on. You don't need to declare the interfaces ahead of time, just **ifconfig** them to set them up. See page 727 for more information.

specified in dotted decimal notation or as a 4-byte hexadecimal number beginning with **0x**. In either case, bits set to 1 are part of the network number, and bits set to 0 are part of the host number.

The **broadcast** option specifies the IP broadcast address for the interface, expressed in either hex or dotted quad notation. The correct broadcast address is one in which the host part is set to all 1s, and most systems default to this value; they use the netmask and IP address to calculate the broadcast address.

On Linux, you can set the broadcast address to any IP address that's valid for the network to which the host is attached. Some sites have chosen weird values for the broadcast address in the hope of avoiding certain types of denial of service attacks that are based on broadcast pings. We dislike this approach for several reasons.

First, it requires you to reset the broadcast address on every host on the local network, a chore that can be time-consuming on a large net. Second, it requires you to be absolutely sure that you reconfigure every host; otherwise, broadcast storms, in which packets travel from machine to machine until their TTLs expire, can erupt.

Broadcast storms occur because the same link-layer broadcast address must be used to transport packets no matter what the IP broadcast address has been set to. For example, suppose that machine X thinks the broadcast address is A1 and machine Y thinks it is A2. If X sends a packet to address A1, Y will receive the packet (because the link-layer destination address is the broadcast address), will see that the packet is not for itself and also not for the broadcast address (because Y thinks the broadcast address is A2), and will then forward[18] the packet back to the net. If two machines are in Y's state, the packet circulates until its TTL expires. Broadcast storms can erode your bandwidth, especially on a large switched net.

A better way to avoid problems with broadcast pings is to prevent your border routers from forwarding them and to tell individual hosts not to respond to them. See page 316 for instructions on how to implement these constraints.

In the **ifconfig** example at the beginning of this section, the broadcast address is 192.168.1.255 because the network is a /24, as specified by the netmask value of 255.255.255.0.

Executing **ifconfig** shows the following output:

```
redhat$ /sbin/ifconfig eth0
eth0  Link encap:Ethernet  HWaddr 00:02:B3:19:C8:86
      inet addr:192.168.1.13  Bcast:192.168.1.255  Mask:255.255.255.0
      UP BROADCAST RUNNING MULTICAST  MTU:1500  Metric:1
      RX packets:206983 errors:0 dropped:0 overruns:0 frame:0
      TX packets:218292 errors:0 dropped:0 overruns:0 carrier:0
      collisions:0 txqueuelen:100
      Interrupt:7 Base address:0xef00
```

TCP/IP

_____

18. Machine Y must be configured with ip_forwarding turned on for this to happen.

The lack of collisions on the Ethernet interface in this example may indicate a very lightly loaded network or, more likely, a switched network. On a shared network (built with hubs instead of switches), you should check this number to ensure that it is below about 5% of the output packets. Lots of collisions indicate a loaded network that needs to be watched and possibly split into multiple subnets or migrated to a switched infrastructure.

Let's look at some complete examples.

```
# ifconfig lo 127.0.0.1 up
```

This command configures the loopback interface, which doesn't usually require any options to be set. You should never need to change your system's default configuration for this interface. The implied netmask of 255.0.0.0 is correct and does not need to be manually overridden.

```
# ifconfig eth0 128.138.243.151 netmask 255.255.255.192
    broadcast 128.138.243.191 up
```

This is a typical example for an Ethernet interface. The IP and broadcast addresses are set to 128.138.243.151 and 128.138.243.191, respectively. The network is class B (you can tell from the first byte of the address), but it has been subnetted by an additional 10 bits into a /26 network. The 192 in the netmask is 11000000 in binary and so adds 2 extra bits to the 24 contained in the three 255 octets. The 191 in the broadcast address is 10111111 in binary, which sets all 6 host bits to 1s and indicates that this interface is part of the 3rd network (first two bits 10) in the group of 4 carved out of the 4th octet. (This is the kind of situation in which an IP calculator comes in handy!)

Now that you know how to configure a network interface by hand, you need to figure out how the parameters to **ifconfig** are set when the machine boots, and you need to make sure that the new values are entered correctly. You normally do this by editing one or more configuration files; see the vendor-specific sections starting on page 307 for more information.

mii-tool: configure autonegotiation and other media-specific options

Occasionally, network hardware has configurable options that are specific to its media type. One extremely common example of this is modern-day Ethernet, wherein an interface card may support 10, 100, or even 1000 Mb/s in both half duplex and full duplex modes. Most equipment defaults to autonegotiation mode, in which both the card and its upstream connection (usually a switch port) try to guess what the other wants to use.

Historically, autonegotiation has worked about as well as a blindfolded cowpoke trying to rope a calf. More recently, vendor network devices play better together, but autonegotiation is still a common source of failure. High packet loss rates (especially for large packets) are a common artifact of failed autonegotiation.

The best way to avoid this pitfall is to lock the interface speed and duplex both on servers and on the switch ports to which they are connected. Autonegotiation is useful for ports in public areas where roving laptops may stop for a visit, but it serves no useful purpose for statically attached hosts. If you're having problems with mysterious packet loss, turn off autonegotiation everywhere as your first course of action.

Under Linux, the **mii-tool** command queries and sets media-specific parameters such as link speed and duplex. You can query the status of an interface with the **-v** flag. For example, this eth0 interface has autonegotiation enabled:

```
$ mii-tool -v eth0
eth0: negotiated 100baseTx-FD flow-control, link ok
  product info: vendor 00:10:5a, model 0 rev 0
  basic mode:   autonegotiation enabled
  basic status: autonegotiation complete, link ok
  capabilities: 100baseTx-FD 100baseTx-HD 10baseT-FD 10baseT-HD
  advertising:  100baseTx-FD 100baseTx-HD 10baseT-FD 10baseT-HD flow-control
  link partner: 100baseTx-FD 100baseTx-HD 10baseT-FD 10baseT-HD flow-control
```

To lock this interface to 100 Mb/s full duplex, use the command

```
# mii-tool -force=100BaseTx-FD eth0
```

Add this command to a system startup script to make it permanent. Afterward, the status query returns

```
$ mii-tool -v eth0
eth0: 100 Mbit, full duplex, link ok
  product info: vendor 00:10:5a, model 0 rev 0
  basic mode:   100 Mbit, full duplex
  basic status: link ok
  capabilities: 100baseTx-FD 100baseTx-HD 10baseT-FD 10baseT-HD
  advertising:  100baseTx-FD 100baseTx-HD 10baseT-FD 10baseT-HD flow-control
```

route: configure static routes

The **route** command defines static routes, explicit routing table entries that never change (you hope), even if you run a routing daemon. When you add a new machine to a local area network, you usually need to specify only a default route; see the next section for details.

This book's discussion of routing is split between this section and Chapter 13, *Routing*. Although most of the basic information about routing and the **route** command is here, you might find it helpful to read the first few sections of Chapter 13 if you need more information.

Routing is performed at the IP layer. When a packet bound for some other host arrives, the packet's destination IP address is compared with the routes in the kernel's routing table. If the address matches or partially matches a route in the table, the packet is forwarded to the "next-hop gateway" IP address associated with that route.

There are two special cases. First, a packet may be destined for some host on a directly connected network. In this case, the "next-hop gateway" address in the routing table is one of the local host's own interfaces, and the packet is sent directly to its

TCP/IP

destination. This type of route is added to the routing table for you by the **ifconfig** command when you configure an interface.

Second, it may be that no route matches the destination address. In this case, the default route is invoked if one exists. Otherwise, an ICMP "network unreachable" or "host unreachable" message is returned to the sender. Many local area networks have only one way out, and their default route points to it. On the Internet backbone, the routers do not have default routes—the buck stops there. If they do not have a routing entry for a destination, that destination cannot be reached.

Each **route** command adds or removes one route. The format is

> **route** [*op*] [*type*] *destination* **gw** *gateway* [*metric*] [**dev** *interface*]

The *op* argument should be **add** to add a route, **del** to remove one, and omitted to display the routing tables. *destination* can be a host address (type -**host**), a network address (type -**net**), or the keyword **default**. If *destination* is a network address, you should also specify a netmask.

The *gateway* is the machine to which packets should be forwarded. It *must* be on a directly connected network; forwarding can only be performed one hop at a time. Linux lets you specify an interface instead of (or along with) the *gateway*. The **dev** keyword in the interface specification is optional and can be omitted.

metric is the number of forwardings (the hop count) required to reach the destination. Linux does not require or use the hop count, but if you set it, Linux keeps the value in the routing tables so that routing protocols can use it.

The optional *type* argument supports host routes, which apply to a complete IP address (a specific host) rather than to a network address. The values -**net** and -**host** are accepted for the *type* parameter. If a *type* isn't specified, **route** checks the host part of the destination address to see if it's zero. If the host part is 0 or the address is a network defined in the **/etc/networks** file, then the route is assumed to be a normal network route.[19]

Since **route** cannot magically know which network numbers have been subnetted, you must frequently use the *type* field to install certain routes. For example, the address 128.138.243.0 refers to a subnetted class B network at our site, but to **route** it looks like a class B address of 128.138 with a host part of 243.0; you must specify the -**net** option to deconfuse **route**. In general, it's good hygiene to provide an explicit *type* for all routes that involve subnets.

route del *destination* removes a specific entry from the routing table. Other UNIX systems have an option to **route**, usually -**f** or -**flush**, that completely flushes the routing tables and starts over. Linux does not support this option, so you might be

---

19. **/etc/networks** can map names to network numbers, much like the **/etc/hosts** file maps hostnames to complete IP addresses. Many commands that expect a network number can accept a network name if it is listed in the **/etc/networks** file (or in DNS).

faced with many **route del**s to clean out a large routing table—be sure you are logged in locally or you may end up half done and disconnected!

To inspect existing routes, use the command **netstat -nr** or **netstat -r** if you want to see names instead of numbers. Numbers are often better if you are debugging, since the name lookup may be the thing that is broken.

```
redhat$ netstat -nr
Kernel IP routing table
Destination   Gateway        Genmask         Flags  MSS  Window  irtt  Iface
192.168.1.0   0.0.0.0        255.255.255.0   U        0  0          0  eth0
127.0.0.0     0.0.0.0        255.0.0.0       U        0  0          0  lo
0.0.0.0       192.168.1.254  0.0.0.0         UG       0  0          0  eth0

redhat$ netstat -r
Kernel IP routing table
Destination   Gateway        Genmask         Flags  MSS  Window  irtt  Iface
192.168.1.0   *              255.255.255.0   U        0  0          0  eth0
127.0.0.0     *              255.0.0.0       U        0  0          0  lo
default       sprint-gw      0.0.0.0         UG       0  0          0  eth0
```

The Genmask is the netmask associated with the destination. The Flags specify the status of the route, how it was learned, and other parameters. Finally, the Iface is the interface through which packets using that route are sent. These examples are from a Red Hat system, but SUSE and Debian are identical except that Debian doesn't show the loopback route by default.

Default routes

A default route causes all packets whose destination network is not found in the kernel's routing table to be sent to the indicated gateway. To set a default route, simply add the following line to your startup files:

route add default gw *gateway-IP-address*

Rather than hardcoding an explicit IP address into the startup files, most vendors have their systems get the gateway IP address from a configuration file. The way that local routing information is integrated into the startup sequence is unfortunately different for each of our Linux systems (hurry LSB, fix this not-invented-here syndrome!). Table 12.10 summarizes the necessary incantations.

Table 12.10 How to set the default route

System	File to change	Variable to change
Red Hat, Fedora	**/etc/sysconfig/network**	GATEWAY
SUSE	**/etc/route.conf**	add line: default *IP-addr mask interface*
Debian, Ubuntu	**/etc/network/interfaces**	gateway

DNS configuration

To configure a machine as a DNS client, you need to edit only one or two files: all systems require **/etc/resolv.conf** to be modified, and some require you to modify a "service switch" file as well.

The **/etc/resolv.conf** file lists the DNS domains that should be searched to resolve names that are incomplete (that is, not fully qualified, such as anchor instead of anchor.cs.colorado.edu) and the IP addresses of the name servers to contact for name lookups. A sample is shown here; for more details, see page 418.

```
search cs.colorado.edu colorado.edu
nameserver 128.138.242.1
nameserver 128.138.243.151
nameserver 192.108.21.1
```

/etc/resolv.conf should list the "closest" stable name server first because the server in the first position will be contacted first. You can have up to three nameserver entries. If possible, you should always have more than one. The timeout period for a DNS query to a particular name server seems quite long, so if the first name server does not respond, your users will notice.

You will sometimes see a domain line instead of a search line. Such a line indicates either an ancient **resolv.conf** file that has not been updated to use the search directive or an ancient resolver that doesn't understand search. domain defines only the current domain, whereas search accepts up to six different domains to query. Thus, search is preferred.

See Chapter 17 for more information about NIS.

Also, some ancient systems do not use DNS by default, even if a properly configured **resolv.conf** file exists. These systems have a "service switch" file that determines which mechanisms will be used to resolve hostname-to-IP-address mappings. Prioritization of information sources is covered in more detail starting on page 515, but we mention the topic here as well, since it sometimes foils your attempts to configure a legacy machine.

The service switch file lets you specify the order in which DNS, NIS, and **/etc/hosts** should be consulted. In most cases, you can also rule out certain sources of data entirely. Your choice of order impacts the machine's ability to boot and the way in which booting interacts with the contents of the **/etc/hosts** file.

If DNS is chosen as the first data source to consult, you may need to have a name server on the local network and have its hostname and IP address in the **hosts** file in order for everything to work at boot time.

Table 12.11 lists the location of the relevant config files and the default configuration for host lookups on each of our example systems.

Table 12.11 Service switch files by system

System	Switch file	Default for hostname lookups
Ubuntu	**/etc/nsswitch.conf** **/etc/host.conf**	files dns mdns[a] hosts, bind
Others	**/etc/nsswitch.conf** **/etc/host.conf**	files dns hosts, bind

a. mdns = multicast DNS, a somewhat uncommon protocol that allows DNS-like name resolution on a small network with no local DNS server.

The Linux networking stack

See page 727 for more information about virtual interfaces.

The networking stack in Linux kernels 2.2 and above supports virtual network interfaces and selective acknowledgements (or SACKs, as they are called). Kernels 2.4 and up implement explicit congestion notification (ECN).

ECN marks TCP packets to inform the remote peer of congestion problems instead of letting dropped packets serve as the only indication that something has gone wrong. ECN was originally specified in RFC2481 (January 1999) and is now a proposed standard documented in RFC3168. RFC2884 (July 2000) included an evaluation of ECN's performance. It found that ECN benefited a variety of network transactions.

Linux is always one of the first networking stacks to include new features. The Linux folks are sometimes so quick that the rest of the networking infrastructure cannot interoperate. For example, the Linux ECN feature (which is on by default) collided with incorrect default settings on an older Cisco firewall product, causing all packets with the ECN bit set to be dropped. Oops.

Linux developers love to tinker, and they often implement features and algorithms that aren't yet accepted standards. One example is the Linux 2.6.13 addition of pluggable congestion control algorithms. The several options include variations for lossy networks, high-speed WANs with lots of packet loss, satellite links, and more. The standard TCP "reno" mechanism (slow start, congestion avoidance, fast retransmit, and fast recovery) is still used by default, but a variant may be more appropriate for your environment.

12.8 DISTRIBUTION-SPECIFIC NETWORK CONFIGURATION

Chapter 2 describes the details of our example systems' booting procedures. In the next few sections, we simply summarize the chores that are related to configuring a network. Our example systems automatically configure the loopback interface; you should never need to modify that part of the configuration. Beyond that, each system is a bit different.

Four files are common to each of our example systems: **/etc/hosts**, **/etc/resolv.conf**, **/etc/nsswitch.conf**, and **/etc/host.conf**. These were covered in the generic network configuration sections above and, except for **resolv.conf** and possibly **hosts**, usually do not need to be modified when you add a machine to the network.

After any change to a file that controls network configuration at boot time, you may need to either reboot or bring the network interface down and then up again for your change to take effect. On all of our example distributions you can use the **ifup** and **ifdown** commands.

Network configuration for Red Hat and Fedora

Table 12.12 shows the Red Hat and Fedora network configuration files.

Table 12.12   Red Hat and Fedora network configuration files

File in /etc/sysconfig	What's set there
network	Hostname, default route
static-routes	Static routes
network-scripts/ifcfg-*ifname*	Per-interface parameters: IP address, netmask, etc.

You set the machine's hostname in **/etc/sysconfig/network**, which also contains lines that specify the machine's DNS domain and default gateway. For example, here is a **network** file for a host with a single Ethernet interface:

```
NETWORKING=yes
HOSTNAME=redhat.toadranch.com
DOMAINNAME=toadranch.com      ### optional
GATEWAY=192.168.1.254
```

Interface-specific data is stored in **/etc/sysconfig/network-scripts/ifcfg-***ifname*, where *ifname* is the name of the network interface. These configuration files let you set the IP address, netmask, network, and broadcast address for each interface. They also include a line that specifies whether the interface should be configured "up" at boot time.

Typically, files for an Ethernet interface (eth0) and for the loopback interface (lo) are present. For example,

```
DEVICE=eth0
IPADDR=192.168.1.13
NETMASK=255.255.255.0
NETWORK=192.168.1.0
BROADCAST=192.168.1.255
ONBOOT=yes
```

and

```
DEVICE=lo
IPADDR=127.0.0.1
NETMASK=255.0.0.0
NETWORK=127.0.0.0
BROADCAST=127.255.255.255
ONBOOT=yes
NAME=loopback
```

are the **ifcfg-eth0** and **ifcfg-lo** files for the machine redhat.toadranch.com described in the **network** file earlier in this section.

A couple of handy scripts facilitate interface management. **ifup** and **ifdown** accept the name of a network interface as an argument and bring the specified interface up or down. After changing network information in any of the **/etc/sysconfig** directories, be sure to run **ifdown** *ifname* followed by **ifup** *ifname*. Better yet, reboot the system to be sure your changes don't cause some kind of subtle problem. There are no man pages for **ifup** and **ifdown**, but they are shell scripts (kept in **/sbin**), so you can take a look and see what they do in detail.

If you need to manage all the interfaces at once, run the **/etc/rc.d/init.d/network** script, which accepts the arguments **start**, **stop**, **restart**, and **status**. This script is invoked at boot time with the **start** argument.

The startup scripts can also configure static routes. Any routes added to the file **/etc/sysconfig/static-routes** are entered into the routing table at boot time. The entries specify arguments to **route add**, although in mixed-up order (the interface is first instead of last):

```
eth0 net 130.225.204.48 netmask 255.255.255.248 gw 130.225.204.49
eth1 net 192.38.8.0 netmask 255.255.255.224 gw 192.38.8.129
```

The interface is specified first, followed by arguments to **route**: the route type (net or host), the target network, the netmask associated with that network, and finally, the next-hop gateway. The keyword gw is required. Current Linux kernels do not use the metric parameter to **route** but allow it to be entered and maintained in the routing table for routing daemons to use. The **static-routes** example above would produce the following **route** commands:

```
route add -net 130.225.204.48 netmask 255.255.255.248 gw 130.225.204.49 eth0
route add -net 192.38.8.0 netmask 255.255.255.224 gw 192.38.8.129 eth1
```

Network configuration for SUSE

Table 12.13 on the next page shows the network configuration files used by SUSE.

SUSE has a unique network configuration scheme. With the exceptions of DNS parameters and the system hostname, SUSE sets most networking configuration options in **ifcfg-**-*interface* files in the **/etc/sysconfig/network** directory. One file should be present for each interface on the system.

TCP/IP

Table 12.13   **SUSE network configuration files in /etc/sysconfig/network**

File	What's set there
ifcfg-_interface_	Hostname, IP address, netmask, and more
ifroute-_interface_	Interface-specific route definitions
routes	Default route and static routes for all interfaces
config	Lots of less commonly used network variables

For a real network interface (that is, not the loopback), the filename has the extended form **ifcfg-**_interface_**-id-**_MAC_, where _MAC_ is the hardware address of the network interface. (**ifcfg-eth-id-00:0c:29:d4:ea:26** is an example.)

In addition to specifying the IP address, gateway, and broadcast information for an interface, the **ifcfg-*** files can tune many other network dials; the **ifcfg.template** file is a well-commented rundown of the possible parameters.

SUSE's YaST tool includes a mother-in-law-ready interface for configuring the network. It works well, and we recommend it for managing the **ifcfg-*** files whenever possible. If you must configure the network manually, here's a simple template with our comments:

```
BOOTPROTO='static'        # Static is implied but it doesn't hurt to be verbose.
IPADDR='192.168.1.4/24'   # The /24 defines the NETWORK and NETMASK vars
NAME='AMD PCnet - Fast 79C971' # Used to start and stop the interface.
STARTMODE='auto'          # Start automatically at boot
USERCONTROL='no'          # Disable control through kinternet/cinternet GUI
```

Global static routing information for a SUSE system (including the default route) is stored in the **routes** file. Each line in this file is like a **route** command with the command name omitted: destination, gateway, netmask, interface, and optional extra parameters to be stored in the routing table for use by routing daemons. For the host configured above, which has only a default route, the **routes** file contains the line

```
default 192.168.1.1 - -
```

Routes unique to specific interfaces are kept in **ifroute-**_interface_ files, where the nomenclature of the _interface_ component is the same as for the **ifcfg-*** files. The contents have the same format as the **routes** file.

Network configuration for Debian and Ubuntu

As shown in Table 12.14, Debian and Ubuntu configure the network mostly in **/etc/hostname** and **/etc/network/interfaces**, with a bit of help from the file **/etc/network/options**.

The hostname is set in **/etc/hostname**. The name in this file should be fully qualified; its value is used in a variety of contexts, some of which require that. However, the standard Debian installation leaves a short name there.

Table 12.14   Debian and Ubuntu network configuration files

File	What's set there
/etc/hostname	Hostname
/etc/network/interfaces	IP address, netmask, default route
/etc/network/options	Low-level network options (IP forwarding, etc.)

The IP address, netmask, and default gateway are set in **/etc/network/interfaces**. A line starting with the iface keyword introduces each interface. The iface line can be followed by indented lines that specify additional parameters. For example:

```
iface lo inet loopback
iface eth0 inet static
      address 192.168.1.102
      netmask 255.255.255.0
      gateway 192.168.1.254
```

The **ifup** and **ifdown** commands read this file and bring the interfaces up or down by calling lower-level commands (such as **ifconfig**) with the appropriate parameters. The inet keyword in the iface line is the address family; this is always inet. The keyword static is called a "method" and specifies that the IP address and netmask for eth0 are directly assigned. The address and netmask lines are required for static configurations; earlier versions of the Linux kernel also required the network address to be specified, but now the kernel is smarter and can figure out the network address from the IP address and netmask. The gateway line specifies the address of the default network gateway and is used to install a default route.

The **options** file lets you set networking variables at boot time. By default, Debian turns IP forwarding off, spoof protection on, and syn cookies off.

12.9   DHCP: THE DYNAMIC HOST CONFIGURATION PROTOCOL

DHCP is defined in RFCs 2131 and 2132.

Linux hosts have historically required manual configuration to be added to a network. When you plug a Mac or PC into a network, it just works. Why can't Linux do that? The Dynamic Host Configuration Protocol (DHCP) brings this reasonable expectation several steps closer to reality.

The protocol enables a DHCP client to "lease" a variety of network and administrative parameters from a central server that is authorized to distribute them. The leasing paradigm is particularly convenient for PCs that are turned off when not in use and for ISPs that have intermittent dial-up customers.

Leasable parameters include

- IP addresses and netmasks
- Gateways (default routes)
- DNS name servers
- Syslog hosts

TCP/IP

- WINS servers, X font servers, proxy servers, NTP servers
- TFTP servers (for loading a boot image)

and dozens more (see RFC2132). Real-world use of the more exotic parameters is rare, however. In many cases, a DHCP server supplies only basic networking parameters such as IP addresses, netmasks, default gateways, and name servers.

Clients must report back to the DHCP server periodically to renew their leases. If a lease is not renewed, it eventually expires. The DHCP server is then free to assign the address (or whatever was being leased) to a different client. The lease period is configurable, but it's usually quite long (hours or days).

DHCP can save a formerly hapless sysadmin a lot of time and suffering. Once the server is up and running, clients can use it to automatically obtain their network configuration at boot time. No fuss, no mess.

DHCP software

Linux distributions historically shipped a variety of different DHCP servers and clients. These days, they have all more or less standardized on the reference implementation from the Internet Systems Consortium, ISC. The ISC server also speaks the BOOTP protocol, which is similar in concept to DHCP, but older and less sophisticated. The DHCP client software is installed by default on all modern distributions, but you must sometimes install additional packages to get the ISC server and relay agent up and running.

DHCP clients initiate conversations with the DHCP server by using the generic all-1s broadcast address—the clients don't yet know their subnet masks and therefore cannot use the subnet broadcast address.

ISC's DHCP server speaks the DNS dynamic update protocol. Not only does the server give your host its IP address and other networking parameters but it also updates the DNS database with the correct hostname-to-IP-address mapping. See page 448 for more information about dynamic DNS updates.

In the next few sections, we briefly discuss the DHCP protocol, explain how to set up the ISC server that implements it, and then discuss some client configuration issues.

How DHCP works

DHCP is a backward-compatible extension of BOOTP, a protocol that was originally devised to enable diskless UNIX workstations to boot. BOOTP supplies clients with their IP address, netmask, default gateway, and TFTP booting information. DHCP generalizes the parameters that can be supplied and adds the "lease" concept.

A DHCP client begins its interaction with a DHCP server by broadcasting a "Help! Who am I?" message. If a DHCP server is present on the local network, it negotiates with the client to lease it an IP address and provides other networking parameters (netmask, name server information and default gateway). If there is no DHCP server on the local net, servers on different subnets can also receive the initial broadcast message from a proxy called a "relay agent."

When the client's lease time is half over, it will renew the lease. The server is obliged to keep track of the addresses it has handed out, and this information must persist across reboots. Clients are supposed to keep their lease state across reboots too, although many do not. The goal is to maximize stability in network configuration.

Incidentally, DHCP is normally not used to configure dial-up PPP interfaces. PPP's own PPPCP (PPP Control Protocol) typically fills that role.

ISC's DHCP server

To configure the DHCP server, **dhcpd**, edit the sample **dhcpd.conf** file from the **server** directory and install it in **/etc/dhcpd.conf**.[20] You must also create an empty lease database file called **/var/db/dhcp.leases**; use the **touch** command. Make sure that **dhcpd** can write to this file. To set up the **dhcpd.conf** file, you need the following information:

- The subnets for which **dhcpd** should manage IP addresses, and the ranges of addresses to dole out

- The initial and maximum lease durations, in seconds

- Configurations for BOOTP clients if you have any (they have static IP addresses and must have their MAC-level hardware address listed as well)

- Any other options the server should pass to DHCP clients: netmask, default route, DNS domain, name servers, etc.

The **dhcpd** man page reviews the configuration process. The **dhcpd.conf** man page covers the exact syntax of the config file. Both are located in the distribution's **server** subdirectory. Some distributions include a sample **dhcpd.conf** file in the **/etc** directory; change it to match your local site's network configuration.

dhcpd should be started automatically at boot time. You may find it helpful to make the startup of the daemon conditional on the existence of **/etc/dhcpd.conf**.

Here's a sample **dhcpd.conf** file from a Linux box with two interfaces: one internal and one that connects to the Internet. This machine performs NAT translation for the internal network and leases out a range of 10 IP addresses on this network as well. The **dhcpd.conf** file contains a dummy entry for the external interface (required) and a host entry for one particular machine that needs a fixed address.

```
# dhcpd.conf
#
# global options
option domain-name "synack.net";
option domain-name-servers gw.synack.net;
```

---

20. Be careful: the **dhcpd.conf** file format is a bit fragile. Leave out a semicolon, and you'll receive an obscure, unhelpful error message.

```
option subnet-mask 255.255.255.0;
default-lease-time 600;
max-lease-time 7200;

subnet 192.168.1.0 netmask 255.255.255.0 {
    range 192.168.1.51 192.168.1.60;
    option broadcast-address 192.168.1.255;
    option routers gw.synack.net;
}

subnet 209.180.251.0 netmask 255.255.255.0 {
}

host gandalf {
    hardware ethernet 08:00:07:12:34:56;
    fixed-address gandalf.synack.net;
}
```

See Chapter 15 for more information about DNS.

Addresses assigned by DHCP might potentially be in conflict with the contents of the DNS database. Sites often assign a generic name to each dynamically leased address (e.g., dhcp1.synack.net) and allow the names of individual machines to "float" with their IP addresses. If you are running a recent version of BIND that supports dynamic updates, you can also configure **dhcpd** to update the DNS database as it hands out addresses. The dynamic update solution is more complicated, but it has the advantage of preserving each machine's hostname.

dhcpd records each lease transaction in the file **dhcp.leases**. It also periodically backs up this file by renaming it to **dhcpd.leases~** and recreating the **dhcp.leases** file from its in-memory database. If **dhcpd** were to crash during this operation, you might end up with only a **dhcp.leases~** file. In that case, **dhcpd** will refuse to start and you will have to rename the file before restarting it. *Do not* just create an empty **dhcp.leases** file, or chaos will ensue as clients end up with duplicate addresses.

The DHCP client does not really require configuration. It stores status files for each connection in the directory **/var/lib/dhcp** or **/var/lib/dhclient**. The files are named after the interfaces they describe. For example, **dhclient-eth0.leases** would contain all the networking parameters that **dhclient** had set for the eth0 interface.

12.10 DYNAMIC RECONFIGURATION AND TUNING

Linux has its own special way of tuning kernel and networking parameters. Instead of supplying a regular configuration file that is read to determine appropriate values, Linux puts a representation of each variable that can be tuned into the **/proc** virtual filesystem. The networking variables are in **/proc/sys/net/ipv4**:

```
$ cd /proc/sys/net/ipv4; ls -F
conf/                               ip_local_port_range      tcp_mem
icmp_echo_ignore_all                ip_nonlocal_bind         tcp_moderate_rcvbuf
icmp_echo_ignore_broadcasts         ip_no_pmtu_disc          tcp_no_metrics_save
icmp_errors_use_inbound_ifaddr      neigh/                   tcp_orphan_retries
icmp_ignore_bogus_error_responses   route/                   tcp_reordering
```

icmp_ratelimit	tcp_abc	tcp_retrans_collapse
icmp_ratemask	tcp_abort_on_overflow	tcp_retries1
igmp_max_memberships	tcp_adv_win_scale	tcp_retries2
igmp_max_msf	tcp_app_win	tcp_rfc1337
inet_peer_gc_maxtime	tcp_congestion_control	tcp_rmem
inet_peer_gc_mintime	tcp_dma_copybreak	tcp_sack
inet_peer_maxttl	tcp_dsack	tcp_stdurg
inet_peer_minttl	tcp_ecn	tcp_synack_retries
inet_peer_threshold	tcp_fack	tcp_syncookies
ip_autoconfig	tcp_fin_timeout	tcp_syn_retries
ip_default_ttl	tcp_frto	tcp_timestamps
ip_dynaddr	tcp_keepalive_intvl	tcp_tso_win_divisor
ip_forward	tcp_keepalive_probes	tcp_tw_recycle
ipfrag_high_thresh	tcp_keepalive_time	tcp_tw_reuse
ipfrag_low_thresh	tcp_low_latency	tcp_window_scaling
ipfrag_max_dist	tcp_max_orphans	tcp_wmem
ipfrag_secret_interval	tcp_max_syn_backlog	
ipfrag_time	tcp_max_tw_buckets	

Many of the variables with **rate** and **max** in their names are used to thwart denial of service attacks. The **conf** subdirectory contains variables that are set per interface. It contains subdirectories **all** and **default** and a subdirectory for each interface (including the loopback). Each subdirectory contains the same set of files.

```
$ cd conf/default; ls -F
```

accept_redirects	bootp_relay	log_martiansrp_filter
accept_source_route	disable_policy	mc_forwardingsecure_redirects
arp_announce	disable_xfrm	medium_idsend_redirects
arp_filter	force_igmp_version	promote_secondariesshared_media
arp_ignore	forwarding	proxy_arptag

If you change something in the **all** subdirectory, your change applies to all interfaces. If you change the same variable in, say, the **eth0** subdirectory, only that interface is affected. The **defaults** subdirectory contains the default values as shipped.

The **neigh** directory contains a subdirectory for each interface. The files in each subdirectory control ARP table management and IPv6 neighbor discovery for that interface. Here is the list of variables; the ones starting with **gc** (for garbage collection) determine how ARP table entries are timed out and discarded.

```
$ cd neigh/default; ls -F
```

anycast_delay	gc_interval	locktimeretrans_time_ms
app_solicit	gc_stale_time	mcast_solicitucast_solicit
base_reachable_time	gc_thresh1	proxy_delayunres_qlen
base_reachable_time_ms	gc_thresh2	proxy_qlen
delay_first_probe_time	gc_thresh3	retrans_time

To see the value of a variable, use **cat**; to set it, use **echo** redirected to the proper filename. For example, the command

```
$ cat icmp_echo_ignore_broadcasts
0
```

shows that this variable's value is 0, meaning that broadcast pings are not ignored. To set it to 1 (and avoid falling prey to smurf-type denial of service attacks), run

```
$ sudo sh -c "echo 1 > icmp_echo_ignore_broadcasts"²¹
```

from the **/proc/sys/net** directory. You are typically logged in over the same network you are tweaking as you adjust these variables, so be careful! You can mess things up badly enough to require a reboot from the console to recover, which might be inconvenient if the system happens to be in Point Barrow, Alaska, and it's January. Test-tune these variables on your desktop system before you even think of attacking a production machine.

To change any of these parameters permanently (or more accurately, to reset them every time the system boots), add the appropriate variables to **/etc/sysctl.conf**, which is read by the **sysctl** command at boot time. The format of the **sysctl.conf** file is *variable=value* rather than **echo value > variable** as you would run from the shell to change the variable by hand. Variable names are pathnames relative to **/proc/sys**; you can also use dots instead of slashes if you prefer. For example, either of the lines

```
net.ipv4.ip_forward=0
net/ipv4/ip_forward=0
```

in the **/etc/sysctl.conf** file would cause IP forwarding to be turned off (for this host).

The document **/usr/src/linux/Documentation/proc.txt**, written by the SUSE folks, is a nice primer on kernel tuning with **/proc**.²² It tells you what the variables really mean and sometimes provides suggested values. The **proc.txt** file is a bit out of date—the Linux coders seem to write faster than the documenters.

12.11 SECURITY ISSUES

We address the topic of security in a chapter of its own (Chapter 20), but several security issues relevant to IP networking merit discussion here. In this section, we briefly look at a few networking features that have acquired a reputation for causing security problems, and we recommend ways to minimize their impact. The details of our example Linux systems' default behavior on these issues (and appropriate methods for changing them) are covered later in this section.

IP forwarding

A Linux box that has IP forwarding enabled can act as a router. Unless your system has multiple network interfaces and is actually supposed to function as a router, it's advisable to turn this feature off. Hosts that forward packets can sometimes be coerced into compromising security by making external packets appear to have come

---

21. If you try this command in the form **sudo echo 1 > icmp_echo_ignore_broadcasts**, you just generate a "permission denied" message—your shell attempts to open the output file before it runs **sudo**. You want the **sudo** to apply to both the **echo** command and the redirection. Ergo, you must create a root subshell in which to execute the entire command.

22. To have a copy of **proc.txt** available, you must install the kernel source code.

from inside your network. This subterfuge can help naughty packets evade network scanners and packet filters.

ICMP redirects

ICMP redirects can be used maliciously to reroute traffic and mess with your routing tables. Most operating systems listen to them and follow their instructions by default. It would be bad if all your traffic were rerouted to a competitor's network for a few hours, especially while backups were running! We recommend that you configure your routers (and hosts acting as routers) to ignore and perhaps log ICMP redirects.

Source routing

IP's source routing mechanism lets you specify an explicit series of gateways for a packet to transit on the way to its destination. Source routing bypasses the next-hop routing algorithm that's normally run at each gateway to determine how a packet should be forwarded.

Source routing was part of the original IP specification; it was intended primarily to facilitate testing. It can create security problems because packets are often filtered according to their origin. If someone can cleverly route a packet to make it appear to have originated within your network instead of the Internet, it might slip through your firewall. We recommend that you neither accept nor forward source-routed packets.

Broadcast pings and other forms of directed broadcast

Ping packets addressed to a network's broadcast address (instead of to a particular host address) are typically delivered to every host on the network. Such packets have been used in denial of service attacks; for example, the so-called smurf attacks. Most hosts have a way to disable broadcast pings—that is, the host can be configured not to respond to or forward broadcast pings. Your Internet router can also filter out broadcast pings before they reach your internal network. It's a good idea to use both host and firewall-level security measures if you can.

Broadcast pings are a form of "directed broadcast" in that they are packets sent to the broadcast address of a distant network. The default handling of such packets has been gradually changing. For example, versions of Cisco's IOS up through 11.x forwarded directed broadcast packets by default, but IOS releases since 12.0 do not. It is usually possible to convince your TCP/IP stack to ignore broadcast packets that come from afar, but since this behavior must be set on each interface, this can be a nontrivial task at a large site.

IP spoofing

The source address on an IP packet is normally filled in by the kernel's TCP/IP implementation and is the IP address of the host from which the packet was sent. However, if the software creating the packet uses a raw socket, it can fill in any source address it likes. This is called IP spoofing and is usually associated with some kind of malicious network behavior. The machine identified by the spoofed source IP address (if it is a real address) is often the victim in the scheme. Error and return packets can disrupt or flood the victim's network connections.

You should deny IP spoofing at your border router by blocking outgoing packets whose source address is not within your address space. This precaution is especially important if your site is a university where students like to experiment and often feel vindictive toward "jerks" on their favorite chat channels.

At the same time, if you are using private address space internally, you can filter to catch any internal addresses escaping to the Internet. Such packets can never be answered (owing to the lack of a backbone route) and usually indicate that your site has an internal configuration error.

With Linux-based firewalls, described in the next section, you can implement such filtering per host. However, most sites prefer to implement this type of filtering at their border routers rather than at each host. This is the approach we recommend as well. We describe host-based firewalls only for completeness and for use in special situations.

You must also protect against a hacker forging the source address on external packets to fool your firewall into thinking that they originated on your internal network. The kernel parameter **rp_filter** (settable in the **/proc/sys/net/ipv4/conf/**ifname directory) can help you detect such packets; the **rp** stands for reverse path. If you set this variable to 1, the kernel discards packets that arrive on an interface that is different from the one on which they would leave if the source address were the destination. This behavior is turned on by default.

If your site has multiple connections to the Internet, it may be perfectly reasonable for inbound and outbound routes to be different. In this situation, set **rp_filter** to 0 to make your routing protocol work properly. If your site has only one way out to the Internet, then setting **rp_filter** to 1 is usually safe and appropriate.

Host-based firewalls

Linux includes packet filtering (aka "firewall") software. Although we describe this software later in this chapter (page 319) and also in the *Security* chapter (page 701), we don't really recommend using a workstation as a firewall. The security of Linux (especially as shipped by our friendly vendors) is weak, and security on Windows is even worse. We suggest that you buy a dedicated hardware solution to use as a firewall. Even a sophisticated software solution like Check Point's FireWall-1 product (which runs on a Solaris host) is not as good as a piece of dedicated hardware such as Cisco's PIX box—and it's almost the same price!

A more thorough discussion of firewall-related issues begins on page 701.

Virtual private networks

Many organizations that have offices in several parts of the world would like to have all those locations connected to one big private network. Unfortunately, the cost of leasing a transoceanic or even a transcontinental data line can be prohibitive. Such organizations can actually use the Internet as if it were a private data line by establishing a series of secure, encrypted "tunnels" among their various locations. A "private" network that includes such tunnels is known as a virtual private network or VPN.

See page 709 for more information about IPsec.

Some VPNs use the IPsec protocol, which was standardized by the IETF in 1998. Others use proprietary solutions that don't usually interoperate with each other. If you need VPN functionality, we suggest that you look at products like Cisco's 3660 router or the Watchguard Firebox, both of which can do tunneling and encryption. The Watchguard device uses PPP to a serial port for management. A sysadmin can dial into the box to configure it or to access the VPN for testing.

For a low-budget VPN solution, see the example on page 328 that uses PPP over an **ssh** connection to implement a virtual private network.

Security-related kernel variables

Table 12.15 shows Linux's default behavior with regard to various touchy network issues. For a brief description of the implications of these behaviors, see page 316. We recommend that you change the values of these variables so that you do not answer broadcast pings, do not listen to routing redirects, and do not accept source-routed packets.

Table 12.15 **Default security-related network behaviors in Linux**

Feature	Host	Gateway	Control file (in /proc/sys/net)
IP forwarding	off	on	**ipv4/ip_forward** for the whole system **ipv4/conf**/*interface*/**forwarding** per interface[a]
ICMP redirects	obeys	ignores	**ipv4/conf**/*interface*/**accept_redirects**
Source routing	ignores	obeys	**ipv4/conf**/*interface*/**accept_source_route**
Broadcast ping	answers	answers	**ipv4/icmp_echo_ignore_broadcasts**

a. The *interface* can be either a specific interface name or **all**.

12.12 LINUX NAT

Linux traditionally implements only a limited form of Network Address Translation (NAT) that is more properly called Port Address Translation, or PAT. Instead of using a range of IP addresses as a true NAT implementation would, PAT multiplexes all connections onto a single address. To add to the confusion, many Linux documents refer to the feature as neither NAT nor PAT but as "IP masquerading." The details and differences aren't of much practical importance, so we refer to the Linux implementation as NAT for the sake of consistency.

iptables implements not only NAT but also packet filtering. In earlier versions of Linux this was a bit of a mess, but **iptables** makes a much cleaner separation between the NAT and filtering features.

TCP/IP

Packet filtering features are covered in more detail in the *Security* chapter starting on page 701. If you use NAT to let local hosts access the Internet, you *must* use a full complement of firewall filters when running NAT. The fact that NAT "isn't really IP routing" doesn't make a Linux NAT gateway any more secure than a Linux router. For brevity, we describe only the actual NAT configuration here; however, this is only a small part of a full configuration.

To make NAT work, you must enable IP forwarding in the kernel by setting the **/proc/sys/net/ipv4/ip_forward** kernel variable to 1. Additionally, you must insert the appropriate kernel modules:

```
$ sudo /sbin/modprobe iptable_nat
$ sudo /sbin/modprobe ip_conntrack
$ sudo /sbin/modprobe ip_conntrack_ftp
```

The **iptables** command to route packets using NAT is of the form

```
$ sudo iptables -t nat -A POSTROUTING -o eth1 -j SNAT --to 63.173.189.1
```

In this example, eth0 is the interface connected to the Internet, and its IP address is the one that appears as the argument to **--to**. The eth1 interface is the one connected to the internal network.

To Internet hosts, it appears that all packets from hosts on the internal network have eth0's IP address. The host performing NAT receives incoming packets, looks up their true destinations, rewrites them with the appropriate internal network IP address, and sends them on their merry way.

12.13 PPP: THE POINT-TO-POINT PROTOCOL

PPP, the Point-to-Point Protocol, has the distinction of being used on both the slowest and fastest Internet links. In its synchronous form, it is the encapsulation protocol used on high-speed circuits that have fat routers at either end. In its asynchronous form, it is a serial line encapsulation protocol that specifies how IP packets must be encoded for transmission on a slow (and often unreliable) serial line. Serial lines simply transmit streams of bits and have no concept of the beginning or end of a packet. The PPP device driver takes care of encoding and decoding packets on the serial line; it adds a link-level header and markers that separate packets.

PPP is sometimes used with the newer home technologies such as DSL and cable modems, but this fact is usually hidden from you as an administrator. Encapsulation is typically performed by the interface device, and the traffic is bridged to Ethernet. You just see an Ethernet connection.

Designed by committee, PPP is the "everything *and* the kitchen sink" encapsulation protocol. It was inspired by the SLIP (Serial Line IP) and CSLIP (Compressed SLIP) protocols designed by Rick Adams and Van Jacobson, respectively. PPP differs from these systems in that it allows the transmission of multiple protocols over a single link. It is specified in RFC1331.

Addressing PPP performance issues

PPP provides all the functionality of Ethernet, but at *much* slower speeds. Normal office LANs operate at 100 Mb/s or 1 Gb/s—that's 100,000–1,000,000 Kb/s. A dial-up connection operates at about 28–56 Kb/s. To put these numbers in perspective, it takes about 5 minutes to transfer a one-megabyte file across a dial-up PPP line. The speed is OK for email or web browsing with images turned off, but glitzy web sites will drive you crazy. To improve interactive performance, you can set the MTU of the point-to-point link quite low. It usually defaults to 512 bytes; try 128 if you are doing a lot of interactive work. If you are using PPP over Ethernet, use **tcpdump** to see the sizes of the packets going over the network and set the MTU accordingly. Ethernet's MTU is 1500, but the PPP encapsulation makes slightly smaller values more efficient. For example, **pppoe** suggests 1412 bytes for hosts behind the PPP connection and 1492 on the PPP link. You certainly don't want each packet to be fragmented because you've set your default MTU too big.

See Chapter 16 for more information about NFS.

Running NFS over a PPP link can be painfully slow. You should consider it only if you can run NFS over TCP instead of UDP.

The X Window System protocol uses TCP, so it's possible to run X applications over a PPP link. Programs like **xterm** work fine, but avoid applications that use fancy fonts or bitmapped graphics.

Connecting to a network with PPP

To connect a host to a network with PPP, you must satisfy three prerequisites:

- Your host's kernel must be able to send IP packets across a serial line as specified by the PPP protocol standard.

- You must have a user-level program that allows you to establish and maintain PPP connections.

- A host on the other end of the serial line must understand the protocol you are using.

Making your host speak PPP

See page 299 for more information about ***ifconfig***.

For a PPP connection to be established, the host must be capable of sending and receiving PPP packets. On Linux systems, PPP is a loadable kernel module that places network packets in the serial device output queue, and vice versa. This module usually pretends to be just another network interface, so it can be manipulated with standard configuration tools such as **ifconfig**.

Controlling PPP links

The exact sequence of events involved in establishing a PPP connection depends on your OS and on the type of server you are dialing in to. Connections can be initiated either manually or dynamically.

TCP/IP

To establish a PPP connection manually, you run a command that dials a modem, logs in to a remote host, and starts the remote PPP protocol engine. If this procedure succeeds, the serial port is then configured as a network interface. This option normally leaves the link up for a long time, which makes it best suited for a phone line dedicated to IP connectivity.

In a dynamic configuration, a daemon watches your serial "network" interfaces to see when traffic has been queued for them. When someone tries to send a packet, the daemon automatically dials a modem to establish the connection, transmits the packet, and if the line goes back to being idle, disconnects the line after a reasonable amount of time. Dynamic dial-up is often used if a phone line carries both voice and data traffic or if the connection involves long distance or connect-time charges.

Software to implement both of these connection schemes is included with most versions of PPP.

Assigning an address

See page 298 for more information about assigning IP addresses.

Just as you must assign an IP address to a new host on your Ethernet, you need to assign an IP address to each PPP interface. There are a number of ways to assign addresses to these links (including assigning no addresses at all). We discuss only the simplest method here.

Think of a PPP link as a network of its own. That is, a network of exactly two hosts, often called a "point to point" network. You need to assign a network number to the link just as you would assign a network number to a new Ethernet segment, using whatever rules are in effect at your site. You can pick any two host addresses on that network and assign one to each end of the link. Follow other local customs, such as subnetting standards, as well. Each host then becomes a "gateway" to the point-to-point network as far as the rest of the world is concerned. (In the real world, you usually do not control both ends of the link; your ISP gives you the IP address you must use at your end.)

DHCP can also assign the IP address at the end of a PPP link. Some ISPs offer home service that uses DHCP and business service that is more expensive but includes a set of static addresses.

Routing

See Chapter 13 for more information about routing.

Since PPP requires the remote server to act as an IP router, you need to be as concerned with IP routing as you would be for a "real" gateway, such as a machine that connects two Ethernets. The purpose of routing is to direct packets through gateways so that they can reach their ultimate destinations. Routing can be configured in several different ways.

A run-of-the-mill PPP client host should have a default route that forwards packets to the PPP server. Likewise, the server needs to be known to the other hosts on its network as the gateway to the leaf machine.

Most PPP packages handle these routing chores automatically.

Ensuring security

See Chapter 20 for more information about security.

Security issues arise whenever you add a host to a network. Since a host connected via PPP is a bona fide member of the network, you need to treat it as such: verify that the system has no accounts without passwords or with insecure passwords, that all appropriate vendor security fixes have been installed, and so on. See the *Security issues* section on page 316 for some specifics on network security. PPP on Linux supports two authentication protocols: PAP, the Password Authentication Protocol, and CHAP, the Challenge Handshake Authentication Protocol.

Using chat scripts

The Linux serial line PPP implementation uses a "chat script" to talk to the modem and also to log in to the remote machine and start up a PPP server. A chat script consists of a sequence of strings to send and strings to expect in return, with a limited form of conditional statement that can express concepts such as "expect the string 'Login', but if you don't get it, send a carriage return and wait for it again."

The idea of a chat script originated with the UUCP store-and-forward system of days gone by. In the 1980s, machines would call each other up in the middle of the night, log in through chat scripts, and exchange files. Despite popular demand, UUCP is not quite completely dead yet: the user uucp is the group owner of serial device files on SUSE, and you must be a member of the uucp group to use a dial-out modem for PPP.

Most PPP implementations come with sample chat scripts that you can adapt to your own environment. You need to edit the scripts to set parameters such as the telephone number to call and the command to run after a successful login. Most chat scripts contain a cleartext password; set the permissions accordingly.

Configuring Linux PPP

Modems (along with printers) have always been a thorn in the side of system administrators. And it's no wonder, when the software to configure a PPP connection over a random modem has over 125 possible options—far too many to weigh and configure carefully.

All our distributions except Debian include Paul Mackerras's PPP package in the default installation. It uses a daemon called **pppd** and keeps most of its configuration files in **/etc/ppp**. Run the command **pppd --version** to see what version of the PPP package has been installed on your particular distribution. Use **apt-get install ppp** to install this package on Debian.

Our reference systems include a version of PPP from Roaring Penguin Software that's designed for use over Ethernet (for example, on a DSL connection to a local ISP). The reference systems also include PPP support for ISDN connections. The configuration files for these additional media are co-located with those for PPP over serial links in the directory **/etc/ppp**. Filenames are usually similar but with the addition of **oe** for "over Ethernet" or **i** for ISDN. Table 12.16 on the next page shows the locations of the relevant commands and config files.

TCP/IP

Table 12.16   PPP-related commands and config files by system

System	Commands or config files	Description
All	**/usr/sbin/pppd**	PPP daemon program
	/usr/sbin/chat	Talks to modem
	/usr/sbin/pppstats	Shows statistics of PPP link
	/usr/sbin/pppdump	Makes PPP packets readable ASCII
	/etc/ppp/options	Config file for **pppd**
Debian,	**/usr/bin/pon**	Starts up a PPP connection
Ubuntu	**/usr/bin/poff**	Shuts down a PPP connection
	/usr/bin/plog	Shows the tail end of **ppp.log**
	/usr/sbin/pppconfig	Configures **pppd**
	/etc/ppp/peers/provider	Options for **pon** to contact your ISP
	/etc/chatscripts/provider	Chat script for **pon** to talk to the ISP
Red Hat (DSL)	**/usr/sbin/pppoe**	PPP-over-Ethernet client
	/usr/sbin/pppoe-server	PPP-over-Ethernet server
	/usr/sbin/pppoe-sniff	Sniffer that debugs provider's quirks
	/usr/sbin/adsl-connect	Script that manages link
	/usr/sbin/adsl-setup	Script that configures **pppoe**
	/usr/sbin/adsl-start	Script that brings up **pppoe** link
	/usr/sbin/adsl-stop	Script that shuts down **pppoe** link
	/usr/sbin/adsl-status	Shows the status of **pppoe** link
	/etc/ppp/pppoe.conf	Config file used by **adsl-***
	/etc/ppp/pppoe-server-options	File for extra options to server
SUSE (DSL)	**/usr/sbin/pppoed**	PPP over Ethernet client
	/etc/pppoed.conf	Config file for **pppoed**
All (ISDN)	**/usr/sbin/ipppd**	PPP over ISDN daemon
	/usr/sbin/ipppstats	Shows ISDP PPP statistics
	/etc/ppp/ioptions	Options to **ipppd**

See page 853 for more information about the names of serial ports.
In our configuration file examples, **/dev/modem** is our name for the serial port that has a modem attached to it. Some distributions actually have a **/dev/modem** file that is a link to one of the system's serial ports (usually **/dev/ttyS0** or **/dev/ttyS1**), but this practice is now deprecated. Substitute the device file appropriate for your situation.

In addition to PPP software, each distribution includes the **wvdial** program to actually dial the telephone and establish a connection.

We talked above about the modem ports and dialer software; now we talk about how to set up **pppd** to use them. Global options are set in the file **/etc/ppp/options**, and options for particular connections can be stored in the directories **/etc/ppp/peers** and **/etc/chatscripts** (on Debian and Ubuntu). Red Hat, Fedora, and SUSE tend to put chat scripts in the **/etc/ppp** directory with names like **chat.***remotehost*. Alternatively, on Red Hat, the file **/etc/sysconfig/network-scripts/ifcfg-***ttyname* can include connection-specific options for a particular PPP interface.

By default, **pppd** consults the **options** file first, then the user's personal ~/**.ppprc** startup file, then the connection-specific **options.**_ttyname_ file (if one exists), and finally, its command-line arguments.

A handy trick suggested by Jonathan Corbet, a Linux old-timer, is to define more than one PPP interface: one for home, one for hotels while traveling, etc. This setup can make it easier to switch contexts.

wvdial is smarter than **chat** and has sensible default behavior if parameters are left unspecified. **wvdial** gets its configuration information from **/etc/wvdial.conf**: modem details, login name, password, telephone number, etc. You can provide information for multiple destinations in the single configuration file. Use the **wvdialconf** program to figure out your modem's characteristics and create an initial **wvdial.conf** file for it.

The configuration files below are drawn from several different PPP setups. The first file, **/etc/ppp/options**, sets global options for **pppd**. The active options for each distribution as shipped are shown below:

 Red Hat and Fedora **/etc/ppp/options**:

```
lock
```

 SUSE **/etc/ppp/options**:

```
noipdefault
noauth
crtscts
lock
modem
asyncmap 0
nodetach
lcp-echo-interval 30
lcp-echo-failure 4
lcp-max-configure 60
lcp-restart 2
idle 600
noipx
file /etc/ppp/filters
```

 Debian and Ubuntu **/etc/ppp/options**:

```
asyncmap 0
auth
crtscts
lock
hide-password
modem
proxyarp
lcp-echo-interval 30
lcp-echo-failure 4
noipx
```

TCP/IP

We like to use the following **options** file:

```
# Global PPP options
lock                    # Always lock the device you're using
asyncmap 0x00000000     # By default, don't escape anything
crtscts                 # Use hardware flow control
defaultroute            # Add default route thru the ppp interface
mru 552                 # MRU/MTU 512 (data) + 40 (header)
mtu 552
```

 The following **/etc/sysconfig/network-scripts/ifcgf-ppp0** file comes from a Red Hat system. This skeletal file was constructed by the **linuxconf** utility.

```
PERSIST=yes
DEFROUTE=yes
ONBOOT=no
INITSTRING=ATZ
MODEMPORT=/dev/modem
LINESPEED=115200
ESCAPECHARS=no
DEFABORT=yes
HARDFLOWCTL=yes
DEVICE=ppp0
PPPOPTIONS=
DEBUG=yes
PAPNAME=remote
REMIP=
IPADDR=
BOOTPROTO=none
MTU=
MRU=
DISCONNECTTIMEOUT=
RETRYTIMEOUT=
USERCTL=no
```

Here is a sample chat script (**chat-ppp0**) that corresponds to the **ifcfg-ppp0** file above (with all of its terse and slightly bizarre syntax):

```
'ABORT' 'BUSY'
'ABORT' 'ERROR'
'ABORT' 'NO CARRIER'
'ABORT' 'NO DIALTONE'
'ABORT' 'Invalid Login'
'ABORT' 'Login incorrect'
'' 'ATZ'
'OK' 'ATDT phone-number'
'CONNECT' ''
'TIMEOUT' '120'
'ogin:' 'account'
'ord:' 'password'
'TIMEOUT' '5'
'~--' ''
```

Several lines in this chat script contain a null parameter indicated by a pair of single quotes, which look similar to double quotes in this font.

You can usually adapt an existing chat script to your environment without worrying too much about exactly how it works. Here, the first few lines set up some general conditions on which the script should abort. The next lines initialize the modem and dial the phone, and the remaining lines wait for a connection and enter the appropriate username and password.

The timeout in the chat script sometimes needs to be adjusted to deal with complicated dialing situations such as those in hotels or businesses with local telephone switches, or to deal with the voice mail signal that some phone companies use before they give you a real dial tone. On most modems, a comma in the phone number indicates a pause in dialing. You may need several commas if you have to dial a particular digit and then wait for a second dial tone before continuing.

PPP logins at our site are just usernames with a P in front of them. This convention makes it easy to remember to whom a particular PPP machine belongs.

The association between **ifcfg-ppp0** and **chat.ppp0** is made by the **ifup** command, which runs automatically during startup since the **ifcfg** file exists. You can also call **pppd** explicitly with a connection-specific options file as an argument, provided that file contains a connect line that lists the corresponding chat filename.

 Our next dial-up example is from a Debian system. It uses the **peers** directory, puts its chat script in the **/etc/chatscripts** directory, and uses the PAP authentication mechanism instead of storing the password in the chat script. First, the options for this connection, **/etc/ppp/peers/my-isp**:

```
/dev/modem            ### fill in the serial port of your modem
debug
crtscts
name username         ### username at my-isp
remotename my-isp
noauth
noipdefault
defaultroute
connect '/usr/sbin/chat -v -f /etc/chatscripts/my-isp'
```

/etc/chatscripts/my-isp contains the following entries:

```
'ABORT' 'BUSY'
'ABORT' 'ERROR'
'ABORT' 'NO CARRIER'
'ABORT' 'NO DIALTONE'
'' 'ATZ'
'OK' 'ATDT phonenumber'
'CONNECT' ''
'TIMEOUT' 15
'~' ''
```

The authentication file used to connect to the ISP, **/etc/ppp/pap-secrets**, needs to contain the line:

```
login-name my-isp password
```

where *my-isp* is the value of the remotename variable in the options above. To bring up the connection in this scenario, use the command **pppd call my-isp**.

Here is an example that uses PPP over existing generic Internet connectivity but teams up with **ssh** to create a secure connection through a virtual private network (VPN). We show both the server and client configurations.

The server's **/etc/ppp/options** file:

```
noauth
logfile pppd.log
passive
silent
nodetach
```

Each connection also has an **/etc/ppp/options.***ttyname* file that contains the IP address assignments for the connection:

```
local-IPaddress:remote-IPaddress
```

The PPP user's shell is set to **/usr/sbin/pppd** on the server so that the server daemon is started automatically. All the authentication keys have to be set up in advance with **ssh-agent** so that no password is requested. On the client side, the configuration is done in the **/etc/ppp/peers** directory with a file named for the server—let's call the configuration "my-work". The client's **/etc/ppp/peers/my-work** file would contain

```
noauth
debug
logfile pppd.log
passive
silent
pty "ssh -t user@remotehost"
```

To log in to work from home on a secure PPP connection, the user would just type **pppd call my-work**.

Finally, we include an example that uses the **wvdial** command and its easy configuration to avoid all the chat script magic that seems to be necessary:

/etc/wvdial.conf:

```
[Dialer Defaults]
Phone = phonenumber
Username = login-name
Password = password
Modem = /dev/ttyS1

[Dialer creditcard]
Phone = long-distance-access-code,,,phone-number,,cc-number
```

If **wvdial** is invoked with no arguments, it uses the dialer defaults section of the **/etc/wvdial.conf** file or your **~/.wvdialrc** to make the call and start up PPP. If called with a parameter (e.g., **wvdial creditcard**) it uses the appropriate section of the config file to override any parameters specified in the defaults section.

To take a PPP connection down, you're better off using **ifdown** than just killing the **pppd** daemon. If you kill **pppd** directly, Linux will notice and restart it on you.

```
$ sudo ifdown ppp0
```

If your machine is portable and sometimes uses Ethernet instead of PPP, there may be a default route through the Ethernet interface before **pppd** starts up. Unfortunately, **pppd** is too polite to rip out that route and install its own, which is the behavior you'd actually want. To fix the problem, simply run **ifdown** on the appropriate interface to remove the route.

Here's what the PPP interface configuration and routing table look like after the PPP connection has been brought up:

```
$ ifconfig ppp0
ppp0   Link encap:Point-to-Point Protocol
       inet addr:10.0.0.56  P-t-P:10.0.0.55  Mask:255.255.255.255
       UP POINTOPOINT RUNNING NOARP MULTICAST  MTU:1500  Metric:1
       RX packets:125 errors:0 dropped:0 overruns:0 frame:0
       TX packets:214 errors:0 dropped:0 overruns:0 carrier:0
       collisions:0 txqueuelen:3
       RX bytes:11446 (11.1 Kb)  TX bytes:105586 (103.1 Kb)
```

```
$ netstat -nr
Kernel IP routing table
Destination  Gateway    Genmask          Flags MSS Window irtt Iface
10.0.0.55    0.0.0.0    255.255.255.255  UH    40  0         0 ppp0
0.0.0.0      10.0.0.55  0.0.0.0          UG    40  0         0 ppp0
```

You can obtain statistics about the PPP connection and the packets it has transferred with the **pppstats** command:

```
$ pppstats
    IN  PACK VJCOMP VJUNC VJERR |   OUT  PACK VJCOMP VJUNC NON-VJ
 11862   133      8    96     0 | 110446  226     27    89    110
```

The VJCOMP column counts packets that use Van Jacobson's TCP header compression, and the VJUNC column counts those that don't. See RFC1144 for details.

Debugging a PPP connection can be a real pain because so many players are involved. **pppd** submits log entries to the daemon facility through syslog on Red Hat and Debian systems and to facility local2 on SUSE. You can increase the logging level by using the **debug** flag on **pppd**'s command line or by requesting more logging in the options file. **pppd** also provides detailed exit codes on failure, so if you try to run **pppd** and it balks, run **echo $status** (before you do anything else) to recover the exit code and then look up this value in the **pppd** man page.

SUSE tends to include sample configuration files for each subsystem; the files are mostly comments that explain the format and the meaning of available options. The files in SUSE's **/etc/ppp** directory are no exception; they are well documented and contain sensible suggested values for many parameters.

 Debian also has well-documented sample configuration files for PPP. It has a subdirectory, **/etc/chatscripts**, devoted to chat scripts. To bring up an interface with PPP, you can include it in the **/etc/network/interfaces** file with the ppp method and the provider option to tie the name of your provider (in our case, my-isp) to a filename in the **/etc/peers** directory (**/etc/peers/my-isp**). For example:

```
iface eth0 inet ppp
    provider my-isp
```

In this case, the Debian-specific commands **pon** and **poff** manage the connection.

12.14 LINUX NETWORKING QUIRKS

Unlike most kernels, Linux pays attention to the type-of-service (TOS) bits in IP packets and gives faster service to packets that are labeled as being interactive (low latency). Cool! Unfortunately, brain damage on the part of Microsoft necessitates that you turn off this perfectly reasonable behavior.

All packets originating on older Windows systems are labeled as being interactive, no matter what their purpose. UNIX systems, on the other hand, usually do not mark any packets as being interactive. If your Linux gateway serves a mixed network of UNIX and Windows systems, the Windows packets will consistently get preferential treatment. If you work in an environment with some older technologies, the performance hit for UNIX can be quite noticeable.

You can turn off TOS-based packet sorting when you compile the Linux kernel. Just say no to the option "IP: use TOS value as routing key."

When IP masquerading (NAT) is enabled, it tells the kernel to reassemble packet fragments into a complete packet before forwarding them, even if the kernel must immediately refragment the packet to send it on its way. This reassembly can cost quite a few CPU cycles, but CPUs are fast enough now that it shouldn't really be an issue on modern machines.

Linux lets you change the MAC-level addresses of certain types of network interfaces:

```
redhat$ ifconfig eth1
eth1   Link encap:Ethernet  HWaddr 00:02:B3:19:C8:87
       BROADCAST MULTICAST  MTU:1500  Metric:1
       RX packets:0 errors:0 dropped:0 overruns:0 frame:0
       TX packets:0 errors:0 dropped:0 overruns:0 carrier:0
       collisions:0 txqueuelen:100
       Interrupt:7 Base address:0xee80

redhat$ sudo ifconfig eth1 hw ether 00:02:B3:19:C8:21
```

```
redhat$ ifconfig eth1
eth1   Link encap:Ethernet  HWaddr 00:02:B3:19:C8:21
       BROADCAST MULTICAST  MTU:1500  Metric:1
       RX packets:0 errors:0 dropped:0 overruns:0 frame:0
       TX packets:0 errors:0 dropped:0 overruns:0 carrier:0
       collisions:0 txqueuelen:100
       Interrupt:7 Base address:0xee80
```

This is a dangerous feature that tends to break things. It can be handy, but it use it only as a last resort.

12.15 RECOMMENDED READING

STEVENS, W. RICHARD. *TCP/IP Illustrated, Volume One: The Protocols.* Reading, MA: Addison-Wesley, 1994.

WRIGHT, GARY R., AND W. RICHARD STEVENS. *TCP/IP Illustrated, Volume Two: The Implementation.* Reading, MA: Addison-Wesley, 1995.

These two books are an excellent and thorough guide to the TCP/IP protocol stack. A bit dated, but still solid.

STEVENS, W. RICHARD. *UNIX Network Programming.* Upper Saddle River, NJ: Prentice Hall, 1990.

STEVENS, W. RICHARD, BILL FENNER, AND ANDREW M. RUDOFF. *UNIX Network Programming, Volume 1, The Sockets Networking API (3rd Edition).* Upper Saddle River, NJ: Prentice Hall PTR, 2003.

STEVENS, W. RICHARD. *UNIX Network Programming, Volume 2: Interprocess Communications (2nd Edition).* Upper Saddle River, NJ: Prentice Hall PTR, 1999.

These books are the student's bibles in networking classes that involve programming. If you need only the Berkeley sockets interface, the original edition is a fine reference. If you need the STREAMS interface too, then the third edition, which includes IPv6, is a good bet. All three are clearly written in typical Rich Stevens style.

TANENBAUM, ANDREW. *Computer Networks (4th Edition).* Upper Saddle River, NJ: Prentice Hall PTR, 2003.

This was the first networking text, and it is still a classic. It contains a thorough description of all the nitty-gritty details going on at the physical and link layers of the protocol stack. The latest edition includes coverage on wireless networks, gigabit Ethernet, peer-to-peer networks, voice over IP, and more.

SALUS, PETER H. *Casting the Net, From ARPANET to INTERNET and Beyond.* Reading, MA: Addison-Wesley Professional, 1995.

This is a lovely history of the ARPANET as it grew into the Internet, written by a historian who has been hanging out with UNIX people long enough to sound like one of them!

TCP/IP

COMER, DOUGLAS. *Internetworking with TCP/IP Volume 1: Principles, Protocols, and Architectures (5th Edition)*. Upper Saddle River, NJ: Pearson Prentice Hall, 2006.

Doug Comer's *Internetworking with TCP/IP* series was for a long time the standard reference for the TCP/IP protocols. The books are designed as undergraduate textbooks and are a good introductory source of background material.

HEDRICK, CHARLES. "Introduction to the Internet Protocols." Rutgers University, 1987.

This document is a gentle introduction to TCP/IP. It does not seem to have a permanent home, but it is widely distributed on the web; search for it.

HUNT, CRAIG. *TCP/IP Network Administration (3rd Edition)*. Sebastopol, CA: O'Reilly Media, 2002.

Like other books in the nutshell series, this book is directed at administrators of UNIX systems. Half the book is about TCP/IP, and the rest deals with higher-level UNIX facilities such as email and remote login.

An excellent collection of documents about the history of the Internet and its various technologies can be found at www.isoc.org/internet/history.

12.16 EXERCISES

E12.1 How could listening to (i.e., obeying) ICMP redirects allow an unauthorized user to compromise the network?

E12.2 What is the MTU of a network link? What happens if the MTU for a given link is set too high? Too low?

★ **E12.3** Explain the concept of subnetting and explain why it is useful. What are netmasks? How do netmasks relate to the split between the network and host sections of an IP address?

★ **E12.4** The network 134.122.0.0/16 has been subdivided into /19 networks.

a) How many /19 networks are there? List them. What is their netmask?
b) How many hosts could there be on each network?
c) Determine which network the IP address 134.122.67.124 belongs to.
d) What is the broadcast address for each network?

★ **E12.5**   Host 128.138.2.4 on network 128.138.2.0/24 wants to send a packet to host 128.138.129.12 on network 128.138.129.0/24. Assume the following:

- Host 128.138.2.4 has a default route through 128.138.2.1.
- Host 128.138.2.4 has just booted and has not sent or received any packets.
- All other machines on the network have been running for a long time.
- Router 128.138.2.1 has a direct link to 128.138.129.1, the gateway for the 128.138.129.0/24 subnet.

a) List all the steps that are needed to send the packet. Show the source and destination Ethernet and IP addresses of all packets transmitted.

b) If the network were 128.138.0.0/16, would your answer change? How or why not?

c) If the 128.138.2.0 network were a /26 network instead of a /24, would your answer change? How or why not?

★★ **E12.6**   After installing a new Linux system, how would you address the security issues mentioned in this chapter? Check to see if any of the security problems have been dealt with on the Linux systems in your lab. (May require root access.)

★★ **E12.7**   What steps are needed to add a new machine to the network in your lab environment? In answering, use parameters appropriate for your network and local situation. Assume that the new machine already runs Linux.

★★ **E12.8**   Show the configuration file needed to set up a DHCP server that assigns addresses in the range 128.138.192.[1-55]. Use a lease time of two hours and make sure that the host with Ethernet address 00:10:5A:C7:4B:89 always receives IP address 128.138.192.55.

TCP/IP

13 Routing

Keeping track of where network traffic should flow next is no easy task. Chapter 12 briefly introduced IP packet forwarding. In this chapter, we examine the forwarding process in more detail and investigate several network protocols that allow routers to automatically discover efficient routes. Routing protocols not only lessen the day-to-day administrative burden of maintaining routing information, but they also allow network traffic to be redirected quickly if a router or network should fail.

It's important to distinguish between the process of actually forwarding IP packets and the management of the routing table that drives this process, both of which are commonly called "routing." Packet forwarding is simple, whereas route computation is tricky; consequently, the second meaning is used more often in practice. This chapter describes only unicast routing; multicast routing involves an array of very different problems and is beyond the scope of this book.

For the vast majority of cases, the information covered in Chapter 12, *TCP/IP Networking*, is all that you need to know about routing. If the appropriate network infrastructure is already in place, you can set up a single static route (as described in the *Routing* section starting on page 293) and voilà, you have enough information to reach just about anywhere on the Internet. If you must survive within a complex network topology or if you are using a Linux system for part of the network infrastructure, then this chapter's information about dynamic routing protocols and tools can come in handy.

Conventional wisdom says that IP routing is exceptionally difficult, understood only by a few long-haired hippies living in the steam tunnels under the Lawrence Berkeley

Laboratories campus in California. In reality, this is not the case, as long as you understand the basic premise that IP routing is "next hop" routing. At any given point, you only need to determine the *next* host or router in a packet's journey to its final destination. This is a different approach from that of many legacy protocols that determine the exact path a packet will travel before it leaves its originating host, a scheme known as source routing.[1]

13.1 PACKET FORWARDING: A CLOSER LOOK

Before we jump into the management of routing tables, let's take a more detailed look at how the tables are used. Consider the network shown in Exhibit A.

Exhibit A   Example network

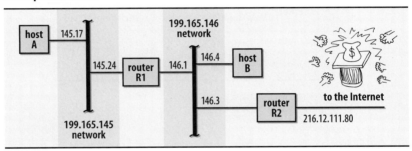

Router R1 connects the two networks, and router R2 connects one of the nets to the outside world. (For now, we assume that R1 and R2 are Linux computers rather than dedicated routers.) Let's look at some routing tables and some specific packet forwarding scenarios. First, host A's routing table:

```
A$ netstat -rn
Kernel IP routing table
Destination   Gateway         Genmask        Flags MSS Window irtt Iface
199.165.145.0 0.0.0.0         255.255.255.0  U       0 0         0 eth0
127.0.0.0     0.0.0.0         255.0.0.0      U       0 0         0 lo
0.0.0.0       199.165.145.24  0.0.0.0        UG      0 0         0 eth0
```

*See page 299 for more information about **ifconfig**.*

Host A has the simplest routing configuration of the four machines. The first two routes describe the machine's own network interfaces in standard routing terms. These entries exist so that forwarding to directly connected networks need not be handled as a special case. eth0 is host A's Ethernet interface, and lo is the loopback interface, a virtual network interface emulated in software. Entries such as these are normally added automatically by **ifconfig** when a network interface is configured.

Routing

---

1. IP packets can also be source-routed, but this is almost never done. The feature is not widely supported because of security considerations.

The default route on host A forwards all packets not addressed to the loopback address or to the 199.165.145 network to the router R1, whose address on this network is 199.165.145.24. The G flag indicates that this route goes to a gateway, not to one of A's local interfaces. Gateways must be only one hop away.

See page 279 for more information about addressing.

Suppose a process on A sends a packet to B, whose address is 199.165.146.4. The IP implementation looks for a route to the target network, 199.165.146, but none of the routes match. The default route is invoked and the packet is forwarded to R1. Exhibit B shows the packet that actually goes out on the Ethernet (the addresses in the Ethernet header are the MAC addresses of A's and R1's interfaces on the 145 net).

Exhibit B   Ethernet packet

Ethernet header	IP header	UDP header and data
From: A To: R1 Type: IP	From: 199.165.145.17 To: 199.165.146.4 Type: UDP	110010101101010111010101101101 011101101101110101000101001000 10 010111110110101010100111010000

UDP PACKET

IP PACKET

ETHERNET FRAME

The Ethernet destination hardware address is that of router R1, but the IP packet hidden within the Ethernet frame does not mention R1 at all. When R1 inspects the packet it has received, it will see from the IP destination address that it is not the ultimate destination of the packet. It then uses its own routing table to forward the packet to host B without rewriting the IP header so that it still shows the packet coming from A.

Here's the routing table for host R1:

```
R1$ netstat -rn
Kernel IP routing table
Destination    Gateway        Genmask        Flags MSS Window irtt Iface
127.0.0.0      0.0.0.0        255.0.0.0      U     0   0       0 lo
199.165.145.0  0.0.0.0        255.255.255.0  U     0   0       0 eth0
199.165.146.0  0.0.0.0        255.255.255.0  U     0   0       0 eth1
0.0.0.0        199.165.146.3  0.0.0.0        UG    0   0       0 eth1
```

This table is similar to that of host A, except that it shows two physical network interfaces. The default route in this case points to R2, since that's the gateway through which the Internet can be reached. Packets bound for either of the 199.165 networks can be delivered directly.

Like host A, host B has only one real network interface. However, B needs an additional route to function correctly because it has direct connections to two different routers. Traffic for the 199.165.145 net must travel through R1, while other traffic should go out to the Internet through R2.

```
B$ netstat -rn
Kernel IP routing table
Destination    Gateway        Genmask          Flags MSS Window irtt Iface
127.0.0.0      0.0.0.0        255.0.0.0        U     0   0         0 lo
199.165.145.0  199.165.146.1  255.255.255.0    U     0   0         0 eth0
199.165.146.0  0.0.0.0        255.255.255.0    U     0   0         0 eth0
0.0.0.0        199.165.146.3  0.0.0.0          UG    0   0         0 eth0
```

See page 295 for an explanation of ICMP redirects.

You can configure host B with initial knowledge of only one gateway, thus relying on the help of ICMP redirects to eliminate extra hops. For example, here is one possible initial configuration for host B:

```
B$ netstat -rn
Kernel IP routing table
Destination    Gateway        Genmask          Flags MSS Window irtt Iface
127.0.0.0      0.0.0.0        255.0.0.0        U     0   0         0 lo
199.165.146.0  0.0.0.0        255.255.255.0    U     0   0         0 eth0
0.0.0.0        199.165.146.3  0.0.0.0          UG    0   0         0 eth0
```

If B then sends a packet to host A (199.165.145.17), no route matches and the packet is forwarded to R2 for delivery. R2 (which, being a router, presumably has complete information about the network) sends the packet on to R1. Since R1 and B are on the same network, R2 also sends an ICMP redirect notice to B, and B enters a host route for A into its routing table:

```
199.165.145.17 199.165.146.1  255.255.255.255 UGHD 0  0          0  eth0
```

This route sends all future traffic for A directly through R1. However, it does not affect routing for other hosts on A's network, all of which have to be routed by separate redirects from R2.

Some sites have chosen ICMP redirects as their primary routing "protocol," thinking that this approach is dynamic. Unfortunately, once the kernel learns a route from a redirect, either the route must be manually deleted or the machine must be rebooted if that information changes. Because of this problem and several other disadvantages of redirects (increased network load, increased load on R2, routing table clutter, dependence on extra servers), we don't recommend the use of redirects for configurations such as this. In a properly configured network, redirects should never appear in the routing table.

13.2 ROUTING DAEMONS AND ROUTING PROTOCOLS

In simple networks such as the one shown in Exhibit A, it is perfectly reasonable to configure routing by hand. At some point, however, networks become too complicated to be managed this way (possibly because of their growth rate). Instead of

Routing

having to explicitly tell every computer on every network how to reach every other computer and network, it would be nice if the computers could just put their heads together and figure it all out. This is the job of routing protocols and the daemons that implement them.

Routing protocols have a major advantage over static routing systems in that they can react and adapt to changing network conditions. If a link goes down, the routing daemons can quickly discover and propagate alternative routes to the networks that link served, if any such routes exist.

Routing daemons collect information from three sources: configuration files, the existing routing tables, and routing daemons on other systems. This information is merged to compute an optimal set of routes, and the new routes are then fed back into the system routing table (and possibly fed to other systems through a routing protocol). Because network conditions change over time, routing daemons must periodically check in with one another for reassurance that their routing information is still current.

The exact way that routes are computed depends on the routing protocol. Two types of protocols are in common use: distance-vector protocols and link-state protocols.

Distance-vector protocols

Distance-vector (aka "gossipy") protocols are based on the general idea, "If router X is five hops away from network Y, and I'm adjacent to router X, then I must be six hops away from network Y." You announce how far you think you are from the networks you know about. If your neighbors don't know of a better way to get to each network, they mark you as being the best gateway. If they already know a shorter route, they ignore your advertisement.[2] Over time, everyone's routing tables are supposed to converge to a steady state.

This is really a very elegant idea. If it worked as advertised, routing would be relatively simple. Unfortunately, this type of algorithm does not deal well with changes in topology. In some cases, infinite loops (e.g., router X receives information from router Y and sends it on to router Z, which sends it back to router Y) can prevent routes from converging at all. Real-world distance-vector protocols must avoid such problems by introducing complex heuristics or by enforcing arbitrary restrictions such as the RIP (Routing Information Protocol) notion that any network more than 15 hops away is unreachable.

Even in nonpathological cases, it can take many update cycles for all routers to reach a steady state. Therefore, to guarantee that routing will not jam for an extended period, the cycle time must be made short, and for this reason distance-vector protocols as a class tend to be talkative. For example, RIP requires that routers broadcast

---

2. Actually, it is not quite this simple, since there are provisions for handling changes in topology that may lengthen existing routes. Some DV protocols such as EIGRP maintain information about multiple possible routes so that they always have a fallback plan. The exact details are not important.

all their routing information every 30 seconds. IGRP and EIGRP send updates every 90 seconds.

On the other hand, BGP, the Border Gateway Protocol, transmits the entire table once and then transmits changes as they occur. This optimization substantially reduces the potential for "chatty" (and mostly unnecessary) traffic.

Table 13.1 lists the distance-vector protocols that are in common use today.

Table 13.1   Common distance-vector routing protocols

Proto	Long name	Application
RIP	Routing Information Protocol	Internal LANs
IGRP	Interior Gateway Routing Protocol (deprecated)	Small WANs
EIGRP	Enhanced Interior Gateway Routing Protocol	WANs, corporate LANs
BGP	Border Gateway Protocol	Internet backbone routing

Link-state protocols

Link-state protocols distribute information in a relatively unprocessed form. The records traded among routers are of the form "Router X is adjacent to router Y, and the link is up." A complete set of such records forms a connectivity map of the network from which each router can compute its own routing table. The primary advantage that link-state protocols offer over distance-vector protocols is the ability to quickly converge on an operational routing solution after a catastrophe occurs. The tradeoff is that maintaining a complete "map" of the network at each node requires memory and CPU power that would not be needed by a distance-vector routing system.

Because the communications among routers in a link-state protocol are not part of the actual route-computation algorithm, they can be implemented in such a way that transmission loops do not occur. Updates to the topology database propagate across the network efficiently, at a lower cost in network bandwidth and CPU time.

Link-state protocols tend to be more complicated than distance-vector protocols, but this complexity can be explained in part by the fact that link-state protocols make it easier to implement advanced features such as type-of-service routing and multiple routes to the same destination. Neither of these features is supported on stock Linux systems; you must use dedicated routers to benefit from them.

The common link-state protocols are shown in Table 13.2.

Table 13.2   Common link-state routing protocols

Proto	Long name	Application
OSPF	Open Shortest Path First	Internal LANs, small WANs
IS-IS	Intermediate System to Intermediate System	Lab experiments, insane asylums

Routing

Cost metrics

For a routing protocol to determine which path to a network is shortest, it has to define what is meant by "shortest".[3] Is it the path involving the fewest number of hops? The path with the lowest latency? The largest minimal intermediate bandwidth? The lowest financial cost?

For routing, the quality of a link is represented by a number called the cost metric. A path cost is the sum of the costs of each link in the path. In the simplest systems, every link has a cost of 1, leading to hop counts as a path metric. But any of the considerations mentioned above can be converted to a numeric cost metric.

Networking mavens have labored long and hard to make the definition of cost metrics flexible, and some modern protocols even allow different metrics to be used for different kinds of network traffic. Nevertheless, in 99% of cases, all this hard work can be safely ignored. The default metrics for most systems work just fine.

You may encounter situations in which the actual shortest path to a destination may not be a good default route for political reasons. To handle these cases, you can artificially boost the cost of the critical links to make them seem less appealing. Leave the rest of the routing configuration alone.

Interior and exterior protocols

An "autonomous system" is a group of networks under the administrative and political control of a single entity. The definition is vague; real-world autonomous systems can be as large as a worldwide corporate network or as small as a building or a single academic department. It all depends on how you want to manage routing. The general tendency is to make autonomous systems as large as possible. This convention simplifies administration and makes routing as efficient as possible.

Routing within an autonomous system is somewhat different from routing between autonomous systems. Protocols for routing among ASes ("exterior" protocols) must often handle routes for many networks, and they must deal gracefully with the fact that neighboring routers are under other people's control. Exterior protocols do not reveal the topology inside an autonomous system, so in a sense they can be thought of as a second level of routing hierarchy that deals with collections of nets rather than individual hosts or cables.

In practice, small- and medium-sized sites rarely need to run an exterior protocol unless they are connected to more than one ISP. With multiple ISPs, the easy division of networks into local and Internet domains collapses, and routers must decide which route to the Internet is best for any particular address. (However, that is not to say that *every* router must know this information. Most hosts can stay stupid and route their default packets through an internal gateway that is better informed.)

While exterior protocols are not so different from their interior counterparts, this chapter concentrates on the interior protocols and the daemons that support them.

---

3. Fortunately, it does not have to define what the meaning of "is" is.

If your site must use an external protocol as well, see the recommended reading list on page 348 for some suggested references.

13.3 PROTOCOLS ON PARADE

Several interior routing protocols are in common use. In this section, we introduce the major players and summarize their main advantages and weaknesses.

RIP: Routing Information Protocol

RIP, defined in RFC1058, is an old Xerox protocol that has been adapted for IP networks. It is the protocol used by **routed**. RIP is a simple distance-vector protocol that uses hop counts as a cost metric. Because RIP was designed in an era when a single computer cost hundreds of thousands of dollars and networks were relatively small, RIP considers any host fifteen or more hops away to be unreachable. Therefore, large local networks that have more than fifteen routers along any single path cannot use the RIP protocol.

Although RIP is a resource hog because of its overuse of broadcasting, it does a good job when a network is changing often or when the topology of remote networks is not known. However, it can be slow to stabilize after a link goes down.

Many sites use **routed** in its **-q** ("quiet") mode, in which it manages the routing table and listens for routing updates on the network but does not broadcast any information of its own. At these sites, the actual route computations are usually performed with a more efficient protocol such as OSPF (see next section). The computed routes are converted to RIP updates for consumption by nonrouter machines. **routed** is lightweight (in **-q** mode) and universally supported, so most machines can enjoy the benefits of dynamic routing without any special configuration.

RIP is widely implemented on non-Linux platforms. A variety of common devices from printers to SNMP-manageable network components can listen to RIP advertisements to learn about possible gateways. In addition, **routed** is available for all versions of UNIX and Linux, so RIP is a de facto lowest common denominator routing protocol. Often, RIP is used for LAN routing, and a more featureful protocol is used for wide-area connectivity.

RIP-2: Routing Information Protocol, version 2

See page 287 for information about classless addressing, aka CIDR.

RIP-2 is a mild revision of RIP that adds support for a few features that were missing from the original protocol. The most important change is that RIP-2 distributes netmasks along with next-hop addresses, so its support for subnetted networks and CIDR is better than RIP's. A vague gesture towards increasing the security of RIP was also included, but the definition of a specific authentication system has been left for future development.

RIP-2 provides several features that seem targeted for this multiprotocol environment. "Next hop" updates allow broadcasters to advertise routes for which they are

Routing

not the actual gateway, and "route tags" allow externally discovered routes to be propagated through RIP.

RIP-2 can be run in a compatibility mode that preserves most of the new features of RIP-2 without entirely abandoning vanilla RIP receivers. In most respects, RIP-2 is identical to RIP and should be preferred over RIP if it is supported by the systems you are using. However, Linux distributions generally don't support it out of the box.

OSPF: Open Shortest Path First

OSPF is defined in RFC2328. It's a link-state protocol. "Shortest path first" refers to the mathematical algorithm used to calculate routes; "open" is used in the sense of "nonproprietary."

OSPF was the first link-state routing protocol to be broadly used, and it is still the most popular. Its widespread adoption was spurred in large part by its support in **gated**, a popular multiprotocol routing daemon of which we have more to say later. Unfortunately, the protocol itself is complex and hence only worthwhile at sites of significant size (where routing protocol behavior really makes a difference).

The OSPF protocol specification does not mandate any particular cost metric. Cisco's implementation uses hop counts by default and can also be configured to use network bandwidth as a cost metric.

OSPF is an industrial-strength protocol that works well for large, complicated topologies. It offers several advantages over RIP, including the ability to manage several paths to a single destination and the ability to partition the network into sections ("areas") that share only high-level routing information.

IGRP and EIGRP: Interior Gateway Routing Protocol

IGRP and its souped-up successor EIGRP are proprietary routing protocols that run only on Cisco routers. IGRP was created to address some of the shortcomings of RIP before robust standards like OSPF existed. It has now been deprecated in favor of EIGRP, although it is still in use at many sites. EIGRP is configured similarly to IGRP, though it is actually quite different in its underlying protocol design. IGRP handles only route announcements that respect traditional IP address class boundaries, whereas EIGRP understands arbitrary CIDR netmasks.

Both IGRP and EIGRP are distance-vector protocols, but they are designed to avoid the looping and convergence problems found in other DV systems. EIGRP in particular is widely regarded as the paragon of distance-vector routing. For most purposes, EIGRP and OSPF are equally functional.

In our opinion, it is best to stick with an established, nonproprietary, and multiply implemented routing protocol such as OSPF. More people are using and working on OSPF than EIGRP, and several implementations are available.

IS-IS: the ISO "standard"

IS-IS, the Intra-domain Intermediate System to Intermediate System Routeing Protocol, is the International Organization for Standardization's answer to OSPF. It was originally designed to manage "routeing" for the OSI network protocols and was later extended to handle IP routing.

Both IS-IS and OSPF were developed in the early 90s when ISO protocols were politically in vogue. Early attention from the IETF helped to lend IS-IS a veneer of legitimacy for IP, but it seems to be falling farther and farther behind OSPF in popularity. Today, IS-IS use is extremely rare outside of vendor certification test environments. The protocol itself is mired with lots of ISO baggage and generally should be avoided.

MOSPF, DVMRP, and PIM: multicast routing protocols

MOSPF (Multicast OSPF), DVMRP (Distance Vector Multicast Routing Protocol), and PIM (Protocol Independent Multicast) are protocols that support IP multicasting, a technology that is not yet widely deployed. You can find pointers to more information about these protocols at www.mbone.com.

Router Discovery Protocol

Router Discovery Protocol uses ICMP messages sent to the IP multicast address 224.0.0.1 to announce and learn about other routers on a network. Unfortunately, not all routers currently make these announcements, and not all hosts listen to them. The hope is that someday this protocol will become more popular.

13.4   ROUTED: **RIP** YOURSELF A NEW HOLE

You may not be rich. You may not be good looking. But you'll always have **routed**. **routed** was for a long time the standard UNIX routing daemon, and it's still supplied with most versions of UNIX, and Linux.

Linux's stock **routed** speaks only RIP. If you plan to use RIP-2, the Nexus Routing Daemon available from sourceforge.net/projects/nx-routed is an easy-to-configure choice. RIP-2 is essential only if you have subnets with masks not on a byte boundary.

routed can be run in server mode (**-s**) or in quiet mode (**-q**). Both modes listen for broadcasts, but only servers distribute their own information. Generally, only machines with multiple interfaces should be servers. If neither **-s** nor **-q** is specified, **routed** runs in quiet mode on hosts with one interface and in server mode on hosts with more that one interface.

*See page 303 for more about **route**.*

routed adds its discovered routes to the kernel's routing table. Routes must be re-heard at least every four minutes or they will be removed. However, **routed** knows which routes it has added and does not remove static routes that were installed with the **route** command.

routed -t can be used to debug routing. This option makes **routed** run in the foreground and print out all packets it sends or receives.

Routing

routed normally discovers routing information dynamically and does not require configuration. However, if your site contains gateways to the Internet or to other autonomous systems, you may have to take some additional steps to make these links work with **routed**.

If you have only a single outbound gateway, you can advertise it as a global default route by running its **routed** with the **-g** flag. This is analogous to setting the default route on a single machine, except that it is propagated throughout your network.

routed also supports a configuration file, **/etc/gateways**, which was designed to provide static information about gateways to "preload" into the **routed** routing table.

13.5 GATED: GONE TO THE DARK SIDE

gated was a fantastic and at one time freely available routing framework by which many different routing protocols could be used simultaneously. With **gated**, you could precisely control advertised routes, broadcast addresses, trust policies, and metrics. **gated** shared routes among several protocols, allowing routing gateways to be constructed between areas that had standardized on different routing systems. **gated** also had one of the nicest administrative interfaces and configuration file designs of any Linux administrative software.

gated started out as freely distributable software, but in 1992 it was privatized and turned over to the Merit GateD Consortium. Commercial versions of **gated** were available only to Consortium members. The Consortium was eventually disbanded, and the rights to **gated** were acquired by NextHop, an embedded network software developer. This transfer effectively ended **gated**'s life in the open source world, leaving a trail of bitter stories behind.

A promising new project, XORP (the eXtensible Open Router Platform), has sprung up to help fill the void created when **gated** was sucked under. Although XORP is just now in beta test, it's being readied for production use and we're hoping that it will grow to fill **gated**'s former niche. Check out the latest progress at www.xorp.org.

In the meantime, sites needing multiprotocol routing can consider using GNU Zebra (www.zebra.org), a nuts-and-bolts routing package that runs on most Linux platforms. Unfortunately, it lacks most of the features, creature comforts, and detailed documentation required to manage dynamic routing in a production environment. This may be one case in which buying a dedicated router (such as those made by Juniper or Cisco) is the best use of your resources.

13.6 ROUTING STRATEGY SELECTION CRITERIA

Routing for a network can be managed at essentially four levels of complexity:

- No routing
- Static routes only
- Mostly static routes, but clients listen for RIP updates
- Dynamic routing everywhere

The topology of the overall network has a dramatic effect on each individual segment's routing requirements. Different nets may need very different levels of routing support. The following rules of thumb can help you choose a strategy:

- A stand-alone network requires no routing.

- If a network has only one way out, clients (nongateway machines) on that network should have a static default route to the lone gateway. No other configuration is necessary, except on the gateway itself.

- A gateway with a small number of networks on one side and a gateway to "the world" on the other side can have explicit static routes pointing to the former and a default route to the latter. However, dynamic routing is advisable if both sides have more than one routing choice.

- If you use RIP and are concerned about the network and system load this entails, avoid using **routed** in active mode—it broadcasts everything it knows (correct or not) at short intervals. To have clients listen passively for routing updates without sending out their own information, use **routed -q**.

- Many people will tell you that RIP is a horrible, terrible protocol and that **routed** is the spawn of Satan. It isn't necessarily so. If it works for you and you are happy with the performance, go ahead and use it. You get no points for spending time on an overengineered routing strategy.

- **routed** listens to everyone and believes everything it hears. Even if your site uses RIP, you might want to manage the exchange of routing data with a dedicated router (such as a Cisco) and run **routed** only on client hosts.

- Use dynamic routing at points where networks cross political or administrative boundaries.

- On dynamically routed networks that contain loops or redundant paths, use OSPF if possible.

- Routers connected to the Internet through multiple upstream providers must use BGP. However, most routers connected to the Internet have only one upstream path and can therefore use a simple static default route.

A good routing strategy for a medium-sized site with a relatively stable local structure and a connection to someone else's net is to use a combination of static and dynamic routing. Machines within the local structure that do not have a gateway to external networks can use static routing, forwarding all unknown packets to a default machine that understands the outside world and does dynamic routing.

A network that is too complicated to be managed with this scheme should rely on dynamic routing. Default static routes can still be used on leaf networks, but machines on networks with more than one router should run **routed** in passive mode.

Routing

13.7 CISCO ROUTERS

Routers made by Cisco Systems, Inc., are the de facto standard for Internet routing today. Having captured over 70% of the router market, Cisco's products are well known, and staff that know how to operate them are relatively easy to find. Before Cisco, UNIX boxes with multiple network interfaces were often used as routers. Today, dedicated routers are the favored gear to put in datacom closets and above ceiling tiles where network cables come together. They're cheaper, faster, and more secure than their UNIX or Linux counterparts.

Most of Cisco's router products run an operating system called Cisco IOS, which is proprietary and unrelated to Linux. Its command set is rather large; the full documentation set fills up about 4.5 feet of shelf space. We could never fully cover Cisco IOS here, but knowing a few basics can get you a long way.

IOS defines two levels of access (user and privileged), both of which are password protected. By default, you can simply **telnet** to a Cisco router to enter user mode.[4] You are prompted for the user-level access password:

```
$ telnet acme-gw.acme.com
Connected to acme-gw.acme.com.
Escape character is '^]'.

User Access Verification
Password:
```

Upon entering the correct password, you receive a prompt from Cisco's EXEC command interpreter.

```
acme-gw.acme.com>
```

At this prompt, you can enter commands such as **show interfaces** to see the router's network interfaces or **show ?** to get help about the other things you can see.

To enter privileged mode, type **enable** and enter the privileged password when it is requested. Once you have reached the privileged level, your prompt ends in a #:

```
acme-gw.acme.com#
```

BE CAREFUL—you can do anything from this prompt, including erasing the router's configuration information and its operating system. When in doubt, consult Cisco's manuals or one of the comprehensive books published by Cisco Press.

You can type **show running** to see the current running configuration of the router and **show config** to see the current nonvolatile configuration. Most of the time, these are the same.

---

4. A variety of access methods can be configured. If your site already uses Cisco routers, contact your network administrator to find out which methods have been enabled.

Here's a typical configuration:

```
acme-gw.acme.com# show running
Current configuration:
version 12.1
hostname acme-gw
enable secret xxxxxxxx
ip subnet-zero

interface Ethernet0
description Acme internal network
ip address 192.108.21.254 255.255.255.0
no ip directed-broadcast
interface Ethernet1
description Acme backbone network
ip address 192.225.33.254 255.255.255.0
no ip directed-broadcast

ip classless
line con 0
transport input none

line aux 0
transport input telnet
line vty 0 4
password xxxxxxxx
login

end
```

The router configuration can be modified in a variety of ways. Cisco offers graphical tools that run under some versions of UNIX/Linux and Windows. Real network administrators never use these; the command prompt is always the "sure bet." It is also possible to **tftp** a config file to or from a router so that you can edit it with your favorite editor.[5]

To modify the configuration from the command prompt, type **config term**:

```
acme-gw.acme.com# config term
Enter configuration commands, one per line.  End with CNTL/Z.
acme-gw(config)#
```

You can then type new configuration commands exactly as you want them to appear in the **show running** output. For example, if we wanted to change the IP address of the Ethernet0 interface in the example above, we could enter

```
interface Ethernet0
ip address 192.225.40.253 255.255.255.0
```

---

5. Hot tip: Microsoft Word isn't the best choice for this application.

Routing

When you've finished entering configuration commands, press <Control-Z> to return to the regular command prompt. If you're happy with the new configuration, enter **write mem** to save the configuration to nonvolatile memory.

Here are some tips for a successful Cisco router experience:

- Name the router with the **hostname** command. This precaution helps prevent accidents caused by configuration changes to the wrong router. The hostname always appears in the command prompt.

- Always keep a backup router configuration on hand. You can write a short **expect** script that **tftp**s the running configuration over to a Linux box every night for safekeeping.

- Control access to the router command line by putting access lists on the router's VTYs (VTYs are like PTYs on a Linux box). This precaution prevents unwanted parties from trying to break into your router.[6]

- Control the traffic flowing among your networks (and possibly to the outside world) with access lists on each interface. See *Packet-filtering firewalls* on page 701 for more information about how to set up access lists.

- Keep routers physically secure. It's easy to reset the privileged password if you have physical access to a Cisco box.

13.8 RECOMMENDED READING

PERLMAN, RADIA. *Interconnections: Bridges, Routers, Switches, and Internetworking Protocols (2nd Edition)*. Reading, MA: Addison-Wesley, 2000.

This is the definitive work in this topic area. If you buy just one book about networking fundamentals, this should be it. Also, don't ever pass up a chance to hang out with Radia—she's a lot of fun and holds a shocking amount of knowledge in her brain.

HUITEMA, CHRISTIAN. *Routing in the Internet (2nd Edition)*. Upper Saddle River, NJ: Prentice Hall PTR, 2000.

This book is a clear and well-written introduction to routing from the ground up. It covers most of the protocols in common use and also some advanced topics such as multicasting.

MOY, JOHN T. *OSPF: Anatomy of an Internet Routing Protocol*. Reading, MA: Addison-Wesley, 1998.

A thorough exposition of OSPF by the author of the OSPF protocol standard.

STEWART, JOHN W. *BGP4 Inter-domain Routing in the Internet*. Reading, MA: Addison-Wesley, 1999.

There are many routing-related RFCs. The main ones are shown in Table 13.3.

---

6. Modern versions of IOS support the SSH protocol. You should use that instead of the standard TELNET interface if it's available in your environment.

Table 13.3   Routing-related RFCs

RFC	Title	Authors
2328	OSPF Version 2	John T. Moy
1058	Routing Information Protocol	C. Hedrick
2453	RIP Version 2	Gary Scott Malkin
1256	ICMP Router Discovery Messages	Stephen E. Deering
1142	OSI IS-IS Intra-domain Routing Protocol	David R. Oran
1075	Distance Vector Multicast Routing Protocol	D. Waitzman et al.
4632	CIDR: an Address Assignment and Aggregation Strategy	Vince Fuller et al.
4271	A Border Gateway Protocol 4 (BGP-4)	Yakov Rekhter et al.

13.9 EXERCISES

E13.1   Investigate the Linux **route** command and write a short description of what it does. Using **route**, how would you:

a) Add a default route to 128.138.129.1 using interface eth1?

b) Delete a route to 128.138.129.1?

c) Determine whether a route was added by a program such as **routed** or an ICMP redirect? (Note that this method works with the output of **netstat -rn** as well.)

E13.2   Compare static and dynamic routing, listing several advantages and disadvantages of each. Describe situations in which each would be appropriate and explain why.

★ **E13.3**   Consider the following **netstat -rn** output. Describe the routes and figure out the network setup. Which network, 10.0.0.0 or 10.1.1.0, is closer to the Internet? Which process added each route?

```
Destination   Gateway       Genmask         Flags MSS Window irtt Iface
10.0.0.0      0.0.0.0       255.255.255.0 U       40  0           0 eth1
10.1.1.0      0.0.0.0       255.255.255.0 U       40  0           0 eth0
0.0.0.0       10.0.0.1      0.0.0.0         UG    40  0           0 eth1
```

★★ **E13.4**   Figure out the routing scheme that is used at your site. What protocols are in use? Which machines directly connect to the Internet? You can use **tcpdump** to look for routing update packets on the local network and **traceroute** to explore beyond the local net. (Requires root access.)

★★ **E13.5**   If you were a medium-sized ISP that provided dial-in accounts and virtual hosting, what sort of routing setup up would you use? Make sure that you consider not only the gateway router(s) between the Internet backbone and your own network but also any interior routers that may be in use. Draw a network diagram that outlines your routing architecture.

Routing

14 *Network Hardware*

Whether it's video images from around the globe or the sound of your son's voice from down the hall, just about everything in the world we live in is handled in digital form. Moving data quickly from one place to another is on everyone's mind. Behind all this craziness is fancy network hardware and—you guessed it—a whole bunch of stuff that originated in the deep, dark caves of UNIX. If there's one area in which UNIX technology has touched human lives, it's the practical realization of large-scale packetized data transport.

Keeping up with all these fast-moving bits is a challenge. Of course the speed and reliability of your network has a direct effect on your organization's productivity, but today networking is so pervasive that the state of the network can affect our ability to perform many basic human interactions, such as placing a telephone call. A poorly designed network is a personal and professional embarrassment that can have catastrophic social effects. It can also be very expensive to fix.

At least four major factors contribute to a successful installation:

- Development of a reasonable network design
- Selection of high-quality hardware
- Proper installation and documentation
- Competent ongoing operations and maintenance

The first sections of this chapter discuss the media that are commonly used for local area and wide area networking, including Ethernet, ATM, frame relay, wireless, and DSL. We then cover design issues you are likely to face on any network, whether new or old.

14.1 LAN, WAN, OR MAN?

We're lucky, in a sense, that TCP/IP can easily be transported over a variety of media. In reality, however, the network hardware market is split into a variety of confusing classifications.

Networks that exist within a building or group of buildings are generally referred to as Local Area Networks or LANs. High-speed, low-cost connections prevail. Wide Area Networks—WANs—are networks in which the endpoints are geographically dispersed, perhaps separated by thousands of kilometers. In these networks, high speed usually comes at high cost, but there are virtually no bounds to the sites you can include on the network (Brugge, Belgium to Sitka, Alaska!). MAN is a telecom marketing term for Metropolitan Area Network, meaning a high-speed, moderate-cost access medium used within a city or cluster of cities. In this chapter, we explore some of the technologies used to implement these beasts.

14.2 ETHERNET: THE COMMON LAN

Having captured over 90% of the world-wide LAN market, Ethernet can be found just about everywhere in its many forms. It started as Bob Metcalfe's Ph.D. thesis at MIT. Bob graduated and went to Xerox PARC; together with DEC and Intel, Xerox eventually developed Ethernet into a product. It was one of the first instances in which competing computer companies joined forces on a technical project.[1]

Ethernet was originally specified at 3 Mb/s (mega*bits* per second), but it moved to 10 Mb/s almost immediately. In 1994, Ethernet caught attention as it was standardized at 100 Mb/s. Just after turning 19 years old in 1998, it was ready to fight a new war at 1 Gb/s. Now an adult in its late 20s, Ethernet is available over fiber at 10 Gb/s, having eclipsed all of its rivals. A 10 Gb/s standard for copper wire (802.3an) was approved by the IEEE in July 2006. Table 14.1 on the next page highlights the evolution of the various Ethernet standards.[2]

How Ethernet works

Ethernet can be described as a polite dinner party at which guests (computers) don't interrupt each other but rather wait for a lull in the conversation (no traffic on the network cable) before speaking. If two guests start to talk at once (a collision) they both stop, excuse themselves, wait a bit, and then one of them starts talking again.

The technical term for this scheme is CSMA/CD:

- Carrier Sense: you can tell whether anyone is talking.
- Multiple Access: everyone can talk.
- Collision Detection: you know when you interrupt someone else.

---

1. Bob Metcalfe also articulated "Metcalfe's Law," which states that the value of the network expands exponentially as the number of users increases.
2. We have omitted a few goofy Ethernet standards that have not proved popular, such as 100BaseT4 and 100BaseVG-AnyLAN.

Net Hardware

Table 14.1   The evolution of Ethernet

Year	Speed	Common name	IEEE#	Dist	Media[a]
1973	3 Mb/s	Xerox Ethernet	–	?	Coax
1976	10 Mb/s	Ethernet 1	–	500m	RG-11 coax
1982	10 Mb/s	DIX Ethernet (Ethernet II)	–	500m	RG-11 coax
1985	10 Mb/s	10Base5 ("Thicknet")	802.3	500m	RG-11 coax
1985	10 Mb/s	10Base2 ("Thinnet")	802.3	180m	RG-58 coax
1989	10 Mb/s	10BaseT	802.3	100m	Category 3 UTP copper
1993	10 Mb/s	10BaseF	802.3	2km / 25km	MM fiber / SM fiber
1994	100 Mb/s	100BaseTX ("100 meg")	802.3u	100m	Category 5 UTP copper
1994	100 Mb/s	100BaseFX	802.3u	2km / 20km	MM fiber / SM fiber
1998	1 Gb/s	1000BaseSX	802.3z	260m / 550m	62.5-μm MM fiber / 50-μm MM fiber
1998	1 Gb/s	1000BaseLX	802.3z	440m / 550m / 3km	62.5-μm MM fiber / 50-μm MM fiber / SM fiber
1998	1 Gb/s	1000BaseCX	802.3z	25m	Twinax
1999	1 Gb/s	1000BaseT ("Gigabit")	802.3ab	100m	Cat 5E and 6 UTP copper
2002	10 Gb/s	10GBase-SR / 10GBase-LR	802.3ae	300m / 10km	MM fiber / SM fiber
2006	10 Gb/s	10GBase-T	802.3an	100m	Category 7 UTP copper
2006[b]	100 Gb/s	TBD	TBD	TBD	Fiber
2008[b]	1 Tb/s	TBD	TBD	TBD	CWDM fiber
2010[b]	10 Tb/s	TBD	TBD	TBD	DWDM fiber

a. MM = Multimode, SM = Single-mode, UTP = Unshielded twisted pair,
   CWDM = Coarse wavelength division multiplexing, DWDM = Dense wavelength division multiplexing
b. Industry projection

The actual delay upon collision detection is somewhat random. This convention avoids the scenario in which two hosts simultaneously transmit to the network, detect the collision, wait the same amount of time, and then start transmitting again, thus flooding the network with collisions. This was not always true!

Ethernet topology

The Ethernet topology is a branching bus with no loops; there is only one way for a packet to travel between any two hosts on the same network. Three types of packets can be exchanged on a segment: unicast, multicast, and broadcast. Unicast packets are addressed to only one host. Multicast packets are addressed to a group of hosts. Broadcast packets are delivered to all hosts on a segment.

A "broadcast domain" is the set of hosts that receive packets destined for the hardware broadcast address, and there is exactly one broadcast domain for each logical Ethernet segment. Under the early Ethernet standards and media (such as 10Base5), physical segments and logical segments were exactly the same since all the packets traveled on one big cable with host interfaces strapped onto the side of it.[3]

Exhibit A   A polite Ethernet dinner party

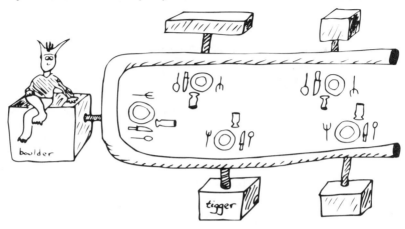

With the advent of switches, today's logical segments usually consist of many (possibly dozens or hundreds) physical segments (or, in some cases, wireless segments) to which only two devices are connected: the switch port and the host. The switches are responsible for escorting multicast and unicast packets to the physical (or wireless) segments on which the intended recipients reside; broadcast traffic is forwarded to all ports in a logical segment.

A single logical segment may consist of physical (or wireless) segments operating at different speeds (10 Mb/s, 100 Mb/s, 1 Gb/s, or 10 Gb/s); hence, switches must have buffering and timing capabilities to eliminate potential conflicts.

Unshielded twisted pair

Unshielded twisted pair (UTP) is the preferred cable medium for Ethernet. It is based on a star topology and has several advantages over other media:

- It uses inexpensive, readily available copper wire. (Sometimes, existing phone wiring can be used.)

- UTP wire is much easier to install and debug than coax or fiber. Custom lengths are easily made.

- UTP uses RJ-45 connectors, which are cheap, reliable, and easy to install.

- The link to each machine is independent (and private!), so a cabling problem on one link is unlikely to affect other hosts on the network.

---

3. No kidding! Attaching a new computer involved boring a hole into the outer sheath of the cable with a special drill to reach the center conductor. A "vampire tap" that bit into the outer conductor was then clamped on with screws.

The general "shape" of a UTP network is illustrated in Exhibit B.

Exhibit B   A UTP installation

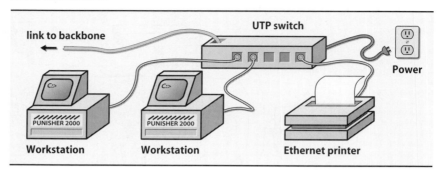

UTP wire suitable for use in modern LANs is commonly broken down into eight classifications. The performance rating system was first introduced by Anixter, a large cable supplier. These standards were formalized by the Telecommunications Industry Association (TIA) and are known today as Category 1 through Category 7, with a special Category 5E in the middle.

The International Organization for Standardization (ISO) has also jumped into the exciting and highly profitable world of cable classification and promotes standards that are exactly or approximately equivalent to the higher-numbered TIA categories. For example, TIA Category 5 cable is equivalent to ISO Class D cable. For the geeks in the audience, Table 14.2 illustrates the major differences among the various modern-day classifications. This is good information to memorize so you can impress your friends at parties.

Table 14.2   UTP cable characteristics

Parameter [a]	Category 5 Class D [b]	Category 5E	Category 6 Class E	Category 7 Class F
Frequency range	100 MHz	100 MHz	250 MHz	600 MHz
Attenuation	24 dB	24 dB	21.7 dB	20.8 dB
NEXT	27.1 dB	30.1 dB	39.9 dB	62.1 dB
ACR	3.1 dB	6.1 dB	18.2 dB	41.3 dB
ELFEXT	17 dB	17.4 dB	23.2 dB	? [c]
Return loss	8 dB	10 dB	12 dB	14.1 dB
Propagation delay	548 ns	548 ns	548 ns	504 ns

a. NEXT = Near-end crosstalk, ACR = Attenuation-to-crosstalk ratio, ELFEXT = Equal level far-end xtalk
b. Includes additional TIA and ISO requirements TSB95 and FDAM 2, respectively
c. Currently unspecified pending further study.

In practice, Category 1 and Category 2 cables are suitable only for voice applications (if that). Category 3 cable is as low as you can go for a LAN; it is the standard for 10 Mb/s 10BaseT. Category 4 cable is something of a orphan, not exactly suited for any particular application. It is occasionally used for 16 Mb/s UTP token ring or for fancy 10BaseT installations. Category 5 cable can support 100 Mb/s and is the most common standard currently in use for data cabling. Category 5E and Category 6 cabling support 1 Gb/s. Category 7 is intended for 10 Gb/s use once the 10 Gb/s Ethernet-over-copper standard is ready.

See page 366 for more information about wiring.

10BaseT connections require two pairs of Category 3 wire, and each link is limited to a length of 100 meters; 100BaseTX has the same length limitation but requires two pairs of Category 5 wire. Both PVC-coated and Teflon-coated wire are available. Your choice of jacketing should be based on the environment in which the cable will be installed. Enclosed areas that feed into the building's ventilation system ("return air plenums") typically require Teflon.[4] PVC is less expensive and easier to work with.

RJ-45 connectors wired with pins 1, 2, 3, and 6 are used to make the connections. Although only two pairs of wire are needed for a working 10 Mb/s or 100 Mb/s connection, we recommend that when installing a new network, you use four-pair Category 5E wire and connect all eight pins of the RJ-45 jack.

See page 844 for more information about the RS-232 standard.

For terminating the four-pair UTP cable at patch panels and RJ-45 wall jacks, we suggest that you use the TIA/EIA-568A RJ-45 wiring standard. This standard, which is compatible with other uses of RJ-45 (e.g., RS-232), is a convenient way to keep the wiring at both ends of the connection consistent, regardless of whether you can easily access the cable pairs themselves. The 568A standard is detailed in Table 14.3.

Table 14.3   TIA/EIA-568A standard for wiring four-pair UTP to an RJ-45 jack

Pair	Colors	Wired to	Pair	Colors	Wired to
1	White/Blue	Pins 5/4	3	White/Green	Pins 1/2
2	White/Orange	Pins 3/6	4	White/Brown	Pins 7/8

Existing building wiring may or may not be suitable for network use, depending on how and when it was installed. Many old buildings were retrofitted with new cable in the 1950s and 1960s. Unfortunately, this cable usually won't support even 10 Mb/s.

Connecting and expanding Ethernets

Ethernets can be logically connected at several points in the seven-layer ISO network model. At layer 1, the physical layer, you can use either hardware connectors or repeaters (commonly called hubs in modern times). They transfer the signal directly, much like two tin cans connected by string.

Net Hardware

---

4. Check with your fire marshall or local fire department to determine the requirements in your area.

At layer 2, the data link layer, switches are used. Switches transfer frames in accordance with the hardware source and destination addresses, much like delivering a message in a bottle by reading only the label on the outside of the bottle.

At layer 3, the network layer, routers are used. Routers transfer messages to the next hop according to the location of the final recipient, rather like looking at the message in a bottle to see who it's really addressed to.

Hubs

Hubs (which are also referred to as concentrators) are active devices that connect physical segments in UTP Ethernet networks. They require external power. Acting as a repeater, a hub retimes and reconstitutes Ethernet frames but does not interpret them; it has no idea where packets are going or what protocol they are using.

The two farthest points on the network must never be more than four hubs apart. Ethernet versions 1 and 2 specified at most two hubs in series per network. The IEEE 802.3 standard extended the limit to four for 10 Mb/s Ethernets. 100 Mb/s Ethernets allow two repeaters, 1000BaseT Ethernets allow only one, and 10 Gb/s networks do not allow them at all. Exhibit C shows both a legal and an illegal configuration for a 10 Mb/s network.

Exhibit C   **Count the hubs**

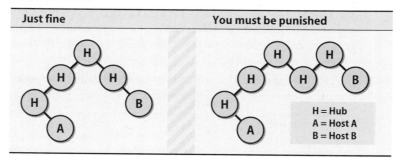

Hubs occasionally require attention from a system administrator, so they should not be kept in obscure or hard-to-reach locations. Power cycling usually allows them to recover from a wedged state.

Switches

Switches connect Ethernets at the data link layer (layer 2) of the ISO model. Their purpose is to join two physical networks in a way that makes them seem like one big physical network. Switches are the industry standard for connecting Ethernet devices today.

Switches receive, regenerate, and retransmit packets in hardware.[5] Most switches use a dynamic learning algorithm. They notice which source addresses come from one port and which from another. They forward packets between ports only when necessary. At first all packets are forwarded, but in a few seconds the switch has learned the locations of most hosts and can be more selective.

Since not all packets are forwarded between networks, each segment of cable is less saturated with traffic than it would be if all machines were on the same cable. Given that most communication tends to be localized, the increase in apparent bandwidth can be dramatic. And since the logical model of the network is not affected by the presence of a switch, few administrative consequences result from installing one.

Switches can sometimes become confused if your network contains loops. The confusion arises because packets from a single host appear to be on two (or more) ports of the switch. A single Ethernet cannot have loops, but as you connect several Ethernets with routers and switches, the topology can include multiple paths to a host. Some switches can handle this situation by holding alternative routes in reserve in case the primary route goes down. They perform a pruning operation on the network they see until the remaining sections present only one path to each node on the network. Some switches can also handle duplicate links between the same two networks and route traffic in a round robin fashion.

Switches keep getting smarter as more functionality is built into their firmware. Some can be used to monitor security on the network. They record any foreign Ethernet addresses they see, thereby detecting and reporting newly connected machines. Since they operate at the Ethernet layer, switches are protocol independent and can handle any mix of high-level packet types (for example, IP, AppleTalk, or NetBEUI).

Switches must scan every packet to determine if it should be forwarded. Their performance is usually measured by both the packet scanning rate and the packet forwarding rate. Many vendors do not mention packet sizes in the performance figures they quote; therefore, actual performance may be less than advertised.

Although Ethernet switching hardware is getting faster all the time, it is still not a reasonable technology for connecting more than a hundred hosts in a single logical segment. Problems such as "broadcast storms" often plague large switched networks since broadcast traffic must be forwarded to all ports in a switched segment. To solve this problem, use a router to isolate broadcast traffic between switched segments, thereby creating more than one logical Ethernet.

Large sites can benefit from switches that can partition their ports (through software configuration) into subgroups called Virtual Local Area Networks or VLANs. A VLAN is a group of ports that belong to the same logical segment, as if the ports were connected to their own dedicated switch. Such partitioning increases the ability

Net Hardware

---

5. Because packets are regenerated and retimed, fully switched networks do not suffer from the "repeater count" limitations shown in Exhibit C.

of the switch to isolate traffic, and that capability has beneficial effects on both security and performance.

Traffic between VLANs is handled by a router, or in some cases, by a routing module or routing software layer within the switch. An extension of this system known as "VLAN trunking" (such as is specified by the IEEE 802.1Q protocol) allows physically separate switches to service ports on the same logical VLAN.

Choosing a switch can be difficult. The switch market is a highly competitive segment of the computer industry, and it's plagued with marketing claims that aren't even partially true. When selecting a switch vendor, you should rely on independent evaluations ("bakeoffs" such as those that appear in magazine comparisons) rather than any data supplied by vendors themselves. In recent years, it has been common for one vendor to have the "best" product for a few months, but then completely destroy its performance or reliability when trying to make improvements, thus elevating another manufacturer to the top of the heap.

In all cases, make sure that the backplane speed of the switch is adequate—that's the number that really counts at the end of a very long day. A well-designed switch should have a backplane speed that exceeds the sum of the speeds of all its ports.

Routers

Routers are dedicated computers-in-a-box that contain two or more network interfaces; they direct traffic at layer 3 of the ISO protocol stack (the network layer). They shuttle packets to their final destinations in accordance with the information in the TCP/IP protocol headers. In addition to simply moving the packets from one place to another, routers can also perform other functions such as packet filtering (for security), prioritization (for quality of service), and big-picture network topology discovery. See all the gory details of how routing really works in Chapter 13.

Hardware interfaces of many different types (e.g., SONET, Ethernet, and ATM) can be found on a single router. On the software side, some routers can also handle non-IP traffic such as IPX or AppleTalk. In these configurations, the router and its interfaces must be configured for each protocol you want it to handle. These days, it's generally a good idea to migrate away from these legacy protocols and just support TCP/IP really well instead.

Routers take one of two forms: fixed configuration and modular. Fixed configuration routers have specific network interfaces permanently installed at the factory. They are usually suitable for small, specialized applications. For example, a router with a T1 interface and an Ethernet interface might be a good choice to connect a small company to the Internet.

Modular routers have a slot or bus architecture to which interfaces can be added by the end user. Although this approach is usually more expensive, it ensures greater flexibility down the road.

Depending on your reliability needs and expected traffic load, a dedicated router may or may not be cheaper than a Linux system configured to act as a router. However, the dedicated router usually results in superior performance and reliability. This is one area of network design in which it's usually advisable to spend the extra money up front to avoid headaches later.

14.3 WIRELESS: NOMAD'S LAN

Wireless networking is a hot growth area, and production-grade products are available at affordable prices. Given the recent advances in wired network technology, the speeds of wireless networks (usually ranging from 2 Mb/s to 54 Mb/s) may seem a bit inadequate for corporate use. In fact, these speeds are perfectly fine for many purposes. An 11 Mb/s wireless network in a home or small business environment can be a system administrator's dream. At 54 Mb/s, wireless can be acceptable in a corporate environment. In addition, wireless access for trade shows, coffee shops, marinas, airports, and other public places can really turn an out-of-touch day into a hyperconnected day for many people.

The most promising wireless standards today are the IEEE 802.11g and 802.11a specifications. 802.11g operates in the 2.4 GHz frequency band and provides LAN-like access at up to 54 Mb/s. Operating range varies from 100 meters to 40 kilometers, depending on equipment and terrain. 802.11a provides up to 54 Mb/s of bandwidth as well, but uses the 5.4 GHz frequency band. Some current equipment can aggregate two channels to provide 108 Mb/s of bandwidth. The up-and-coming 802.11n standard is expected to provide more than 200 Mb/s of bandwidth in late 2006.

Although both 802.11g and 802.11a are advertised to operate at 54 Mb/s, their intents and realized bandwidths can be quite different. 802.11g is primarily aimed at the consumer marketplace. It is typically less expensive than 802.11a and provides three nonoverlapping data channels versus 802.11a's twelve. Channels are much like the lanes on a highway: the more channels available, the greater the number of clients that can realize their full bandwidth potential.

For small sites, either standard is probably acceptable. Larger sites or campus-wide deployments may want to consider 802.11a because of its greater amount of spectrum. In reality, most current wireless radios can be used with either type of network.

Today, 802.11b (11 Mb/s), 802.11g, and 802.11a networks are all quite commonplace. The cards are inexpensive and available for (or built into) most laptop and desktop PCs. As with wired Ethernet, the most common architecture for an 802.11 network uses a hub (called an "access point" in wireless parlance) as the connection point for multiple clients. Access points can be connected to traditional wired networks or wirelessly connected to other access points, a configuration known as a "wireless mesh".

You can configure a Linux box to act as an 802.11a/b/g access point if you have the right hardware and driver. We are aware of at least one chipset that supports this configuration, the Intersil Prism II. An excellent standalone 802.11b/g wireless base station for the home or small office is Apple's AirPort Express, a wall-wart-like product that is inexpensive (around $150) and highly functional.[6] Buy one today!

Literally dozens of vendors are hawking wireless access points. You can buy them at Home Depot and even at the grocery store. Predictably, the adage that "you get what you pay for" applies. El cheapo access points (those in the $50 range) are likely to perform poorly when handling large file transfers or more than one active client.

Debugging a wireless network is something of a black art. You must consider a wide range of variables when dealing with problems. If you are deploying a wireless network at an enterprise scale, you'll probably need to invest in a wireless network analyzer. We highly recommend the analysis products made by AirMagnet.

Wireless security

The security of wireless networks has traditionally been very poor. Wired Equivalent Privacy (WEP) is a protocol used in conjunction with 802.11b networks to enable 40-bit, 104-bit, or 128-bit encryption for packets traveling over the airwaves. Unfortunately, this standard contains a fatal design flaw that renders it little more than a speed bump for snoopers. Someone sitting outside your building or house can access your network directly and undetectably.

More recently, the Wi-Fi Protected Access (WPA) security standards have engendered new confidence in wireless security. Today, WPA should be used instead of WEP in all new installations.Without WPA, wireless networks—both with and without WEP—should be considered completely insecure.

802.11i, aka WPA2, is a more recent alternative to WPA. It adds more authentication mechanisms for enterprise wireless networks.

Wireless switches

In much the same way that Ethernet hubs grew up to become Ethernet switches, wireless products are undergoing a gradual makeover for use in large enterprises. A number of vendors (such as Airespace) are now producing "wireless switches" that work in conjunction with a fleet of access points deployed throughout a campus. The theory is that hordes of inexpensive access points can be deployed and then centrally managed by an "intelligent" switch. The switch maintains the WAPs' configuration information and smoothly supports authentication and roaming.

If you need to provide ubiquitous wireless service throughout a medium-to-large-sized organization, it's definitely worth the time to evaluate this category of products. Not only do they decrease management time but most also include a means to monitor and manage the quality of service delivered to users.

---

6. In fact, it will also connect to your stereo to play music wirelessly from your PC or laptop.

One particularly neat trick is to deploy an 802.11a/b/g network throughout your facility and use it to support hand-held VoIP phones for staff. It's like a cellular network for free!

14.4 FDDI: THE DISAPPOINTING, EXPENSIVE, AND OUTDATED LAN

At 10 Mb/s, the Ethernet of the 1980s didn't offer enough bandwidth for some networking needs, such as connecting workgroups through a corporate (or campus) backbone. In an effort to offer higher-bandwidth options, the ANSI X3T9.5 committee produced the Fiber Distributed Data Interface (FDDI) standard as an alternative to Ethernet.[7] Designed and marketed as a 100 Mb/s token ring, FDDI once looked like it would be the easy solution to many organizations' bandwidth needs.

Unfortunately, FDDI has been a disappointment in absolutely every way, and at this time shouldn't be considered for any production use. We include information about FDDI here for historical perspective only (and in case you happen to find it still in use in some dark corner of your network).

See page 278 for more about MTUs. For good performance, FDDI needs a much higher MTU than the default, which is tuned for Ethernet. An MTU value of 4,352 (set with **ifconfig**) is about right.

The FDDI standard specifies a 100 Mb/s token-passing, dual-ring, all-singing, all-dancing LAN using a fiber optic transmission medium, as shown in Exhibit D. The dual-ring architecture includes a primary ring that's used for data transmission and a secondary ring that's used as a backup in the event the ring is cut (either physically or electronically).

Exhibit D FDDI dual token ring

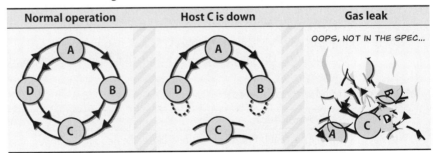

Hosts can be connected either to both rings (they are then referred to as class A or "dual attached" hosts) or to just the primary ring (class B or "single attached" hosts). Most commonly, backbone routers and concentrators are dual attached, and workstations are single attached, usually through a "concentrator," a sort of fiber hub.

7. FDDI has also been accepted as an ISO standard.

Net Hardware

One advantage of token ring systems is that access to the network is controlled by a deterministic protocol. There are no collisions, so the performance of the network does not degrade under high load, as it can with Ethernet. Many token ring systems can operate at 90% to 95% of their rated capacity when serving multiple clients.

For physical media, the FDDI standard suggests two types of fiber: single-mode and multimode. "Modes" are essentially bundles of light rays that enter the fiber at a particular angle. Single-mode fiber allows exactly one frequency of light to travel its path and thus requires a laser as an emitting source.[8] Multimode fiber allows for multiple paths and is usually driven by less expensive and less dangerous LEDs. Single-mode fiber can be used over much longer distances than multimode. In practice, 62.5 μm multimode fiber is most commonly used for FDDI.

Several fiber connector standards are used with FDDI, and they vary from vendor to vendor. Regardless of what connectors you use, keep in mind that a clean fiber connection is essential for reliable operation. Although self-service fiber termination kits are available, we suggest that whenever possible you have a professional wiring firm install the ends on fiber segments.

14.5 ATM: THE PROMISED (BUT SORELY DEFEATED) LAN

ATM stands for Asynchronous Transfer Mode, but some folks insist on Another Technical Mistake. One datacomm industry spokesman describes it as "an attempt by the phone company to turn your networking problem into something they know how to tariff."

ATM is technically "special" because it promotes the philosophy that small, fixed-size packets (called "cells") are the most efficient way to implement gigabit networks. ATM also promises capabilities that haven't traditionally been promised by other media, including bandwidth reservation and quality-of-service guarantees.

On top of ATM's 53-byte cells, five ATM Adaptation Layers (AALs) are described for cell transport. The purpose of each adaptation layer is summarized in Table 14.4.

Table 14.4   ATM adaptation layers

AAL	Application
1	Constant bit-rate applications, like voice (requires bounded delay)
2	Variable bit-rate applications requiring bounded delay
3	Connection-oriented data applications
4	Connectionless data applications
5	General data transport (especially IP traffic, replaces 3 and 4)

8. Most (but not all) lasers used in fiber optic networking are Class 1 devices, which can mean either "safe to shine in your eyes" or "not safe to shine in your eyes, but the device has been designed to prevent exposure during normal use." Unfortunately, "normal use" probably doesn't include messing around with severed cables, so there is really no guarantee of safety. Don't shine the laser in your eye, even if all the cool kids seem to be doing it.

It is unclear how AAL 2 would ever be used in real life. Currently, there is no defined standard for it. AALs 3 and 4 turned out to be very similar and were combined. A group of vendors that had to implement ATM were unhappy with AALs 3 and 4 because of their high overhead. They developed their own solution, the Simple and Efficient Adaptation Layer (SEAL), which soon became AAL 5.

ATM was widely marketed in the 1990s as an all-in-one switched network medium that could be used for LAN, WAN, and MAN needs. Today, ATM is mostly dead, preserved only in WAN environments in which large telco corporations are still trying to leverage their misguided investments in ATM hardware.

ATM switch vendors continue to aggressively market their products, and it is possible to order an ATM circuit in many locales. However, it is probably a good idea to consider technologies other than ATM for new network deployments.

14.6 FRAME RELAY: THE SACRIFICIAL WAN

Frame relay is a WAN technology that offers packet-switched data service, usually for a reasonable cost. Although the claim is not 100% accurate, frame relay is often said to be remarketed X.25, a scary packet-switched technology from the mid-1970s. Fortunately, it's in such widespread use that the equipment, software, and staff that support it have evolved to be robust and to perform well.

Traditionally, users who wished to connect to remote sites would purchase a dedicated circuit from the phone company, such as a 56 Kb/s DDS line or a T1 line. These are point-to-point data circuits that are connected 24 hours a day. Unfortunately, this type of connection is often expensive since it requires that the phone company dedicate equipment and bandwidth to the link.

In contrast, frame relay is an "economy of scale" approach. The phone company creates a network (often referred to as a "cloud"[9]) that connects its central offices. Users submit data in small packets for remote sites. The phone company switches the packets through the appropriate central offices, ultimately delivering them to their destinations. In this model, you and the phone company are gambling that at any given second, the total amount of traffic won't exceed the bandwidth of the network (a condition known euphemistically as "being oversubscribed").

A router encapsulates IP traffic over frame relay connections. Packets are switched over invisible "permanent virtual circuits" (PVCs), which allow your packets to travel only to the sites you've paid for them to reach. These PVCs afford some degree of privacy protection from the other sites connected to the frame relay network.

The biggest advantage of frame relay is that it is usually inexpensive. But in the world of "you get what you pay for," you may find that frame relay's performance is sometimes poor. Frame relay connections have some packet switching overhead, and link speed may degrade during periods of heavy use.

9. An all-too-appropriate name—it's never quite clear what the weather forecast will be in a frame relay network. Storm? Rain? Sleet? Hail?

14.7 **ISDN:** THE INDIGENOUS **WAN**

Integrated Services Digital Network (ISDN) is a phone company offering that takes many forms. In its most common and usable form, called Basic Rate Interface (BRI) ISDN, it is essentially an all-digital phone line that provides two dial-up 64 Kb/s "B" channels and a single 16 Kb/s signaling "D" channel. Each B channel can be used for either voice or data (a voice line can be carried on a single 64 Kb/s channel).

ISDN offers a relatively high-speed digital line at a reasonable cost ($30–$150 per month, depending on where you live). Devices called terminal adaptors convert the phone line into a more familiar interface such as RS-232. They are used (and priced) much like modems. Most adaptors can aggregate the two B channels, yielding a 128 Kb/s data channel.

ISDN can be used in place of normal dial-up networking and also as a wide-area technology that uses a router or bridge to connect remote sites across the line.

Although many U.S. phone companies have installed switches that are compatible with ISDN, they still haven't figured out how to market or support them.[10] Only in a few areas can you just call up the phone company and order an ISDN line. Some tips: make sure you deal with the branch of the phone company that handles business services, since that is how ISDN is usually classified. In many regions, you will have to argue your way past several waves of drones before you reach someone who has heard of ISDN before, even if the service really is available.

14.8 **DSL** AND CABLE MODEMS: THE PEOPLE'S **WAN**

It's easy to move large amounts of data among businesses and other large data facilities. Carrier-provided technologies such as T1, T3, SONET, ATM, and frame relay provide relatively simple conduits for moving bits from place to place. However, these technologies are not realistic options for connecting individual houses and home offices. They cost too much, and the infrastructure they require is not universally available.

Digital Subscriber Line (DSL) uses ordinary copper telephone wire to transmit data at speeds of up to 7 Mb/s (although typical DSL connections yield between 256 Kb/s and 3 Mb/s). Since most homes already have existing telephone wiring, DSL is a viable way to complete the "last mile" of connectivity from the telephone company to the home. DSL connections are usually terminated in a box that acts as a TCP/IP router and connects to other devices within the home over an Ethernet. DSL is typically both cheaper and faster than ISDN, so it is now the preferred technology for home users.

Unlike regular POTS (Plain Old Telephone Service) and ISDN connections, which require you to "dial up" an endpoint, most DSL implementations supply a dedicated

---

10. Hence the interpretation: It Still Does Nothing.

service that is always connected. This feature makes DSL even more attractive because there is no setup or connection delay when a user wants to transfer data.

DSL comes in several forms, and as a result it's often referred to as xDSL, with the x representing a specific subtechnology such as A for asymmetric, S for symmetric, H for high speed, RA for rate adaptive, and I for DSL-over-ISDN (useful for locations too far from the central office to support faster forms of DSL). The exact technology variants and data transfer speeds available in your area depend on the central office equipment that your telephone company or carrier has chosen to deploy.

The race for "last mile" connectivity to hundreds of millions of homes is a hot one. It's also highly politicized, well capitalized, and overpublicized. The DSL approach leverages the copper infrastructure that is common among the Incumbent Local Exchange Carriers (ILECs), who favored higher profit margins over investments in infrastructure as the networking revolution of the 1980s and 90s passed them by.

Cable television companies, which already have fiber infrastructure in most neighborhoods, are promoting their own "last mile" solutions, which yield similar (though asymmetric) high-bandwidth connections to the home. The cable modem industry has recently become enlightened about data standards and is currently promoting the Data Over Cable Service Interface Specification (DOCSIS) standard. This standard defines the technical specs for both the cable modems and the equipment used at the cable company, and it allows various brands of equipment to interoperate.

All in all, the fight between cable modem and DSL technologies largely boils down to "my marketing budget is bigger than yours." DSL has something of an inherent advantage in that, in most cases, each connection is private to the particular customer; cable modems in a neighborhood share bandwidth and can sometimes eavesdrop on each other's traffic.

14.9 WHERE IS THE NETWORK GOING?

When you look closely at the technologies described above, you'll see one thing in common: the simple, inexpensive ones are succeeding, whereas the complex and expensive ones are dying quickly. Where does this put us down the road?

Ethernet has pummeled its rivals because it is incredibly inexpensive. It's so simple to implement that today you can even buy microwave ovens with Ethernet interfaces. Ethernet has scaled well: in many organizations, 10 Mb/s Ethernet infrastructure from the early 1980s is still in production use, connected into 100 Mb/s and 1 Gb/s segments. 10 Gb/s Ethernet over fiber is already available and we'll soon see it in widespread use on copper cables. We expect to see this trend continue, with faster and faster switching hardware to connect it all.

On the "connectivity to the home" front, DSL offers new life to the tired old Ma Bell copper plant. The proliferation of cable modems has brought high-speed access (and real security problems) within reach of millions of homes.

Net Hardware

What's great about all of these new developments is that regardless of the medium or its speed, TCP/IP is compatible with it.

14.10 NETWORK TESTING AND DEBUGGING

One major advantage of the large-scale migration to Ethernet (and other UTP-based technologies) is the ease of network debugging. Since these networks can be analyzed link by link, hardware problems can often be isolated in seconds rather than days.

The key to debugging a network is to break it down into its component parts and test each piece until you've isolated the offending device or cable. The "idiot lights" on switches and hubs (such as "link status" and "packet traffic") often hold immediate clues to the source of the problem. Top-notch documentation of your wiring scheme is essential for making these indicator lights work in your favor.

As with most tasks, having the right tools for the job is a big part of being able to get the job done right and without delay. The market offers two major types of network debugging tools (although they are quickly growing together).

The first is the hand-held cable analyzer. This device can measure the electrical characteristics of a given cable, including its length (with a groovy technology called "time domain reflectrometry"). Usually, these analyzers can also point out simple faults such as a broken or miswired cable. Our favorite product for LAN cable analysis is the Fluke LanMeter. It's an all-in-one analyzer that can even perform IP pings across the network. High-end versions have their own web server that can show you historical statistics. For WAN (telco) circuits, the T-BERD line analyzer is the cat's meow. The T-BERD and its high-end LAN-testing companion, the FIREBERD series, are made by Acterna (www.acterna.com).

The second type of debugging tool is the network sniffer. This device disassembles network packets to look for protocol errors, misconfigurations, and general snafus. Commercial sniffers are available, but we find that the freely available program Wireshark (www.wireshark.org) running on a fat laptop is usually the best option.[11]

14.11 BUILDING WIRING

Whether you're running gigabit Ethernet or just serial cables, we recommend that you use the highest possible quality of wire. It will increase the chances that you can still use the same wire ten years down the road. It's cheapest to wire an entire building at once rather than to wire it one connection at a time.

UTP cabling options

Category 5E wire typically offers the best price vs. performance tradeoff in today's market. Its normal format is four pairs per sheath, which is just right for a variety of data connections from RS-232 to gigabit Ethernet.

11. Like so many popular programs, Wireshark is often the subject of attack by hackers. Make sure you stay up to date with the current version.

Category 5E specifications require that the twist be maintained to within half an inch of the connection to the punchdown block. This implies that any wire with more than four pairs per sheath will have to be taped or secured to maintain the twist, since it feeds more than one connection.

You must use Category 5E termination parts in addition to Category 5E wire. We've had the best luck using parts manufactured by Siemon.

Connections to offices

One connection per office is clearly not enough. But should you use two or four? We recommend four, for several reasons:

- They can be used for serial connections (modem, printer, etc.).
- They can be used with voice telephones.
- They can be used to accommodate visitors or demo machines.
- The cost of the materials is typically only 5%–10% of the total cost.
- Your best guess doubled is often a good estimate.
- It's much cheaper to do it once rather than adding wires later.
- When ports run low, people add 10 Mb/s hubs purchased from the nearest office supply store, then complain to the help desk about connection speed.

If you're in the process of wiring your entire building, you might consider installing a few outlets in the hallways, conference rooms, lunch rooms, bathrooms, and of course, ceilings for wireless access points. Don't forget to keep security in mind, however, and place publicly accessible ports on a "guest" VLAN that doesn't have access to your internal network resources.

Wiring standards

Modern buildings often require a large and complex wiring infrastructure to support all the various activities that take place inside. Walking into the average telecommunications closet is usually a shocking experience for the weak of stomach, as identically colored, unlabeled wires often cover the walls.

In an effort to increase traceability and standardize building wiring, the Telecommunications Industry Association released the TIA/EIA-606 Administration Standard for the telecommunication infrastructure of commercial buildings in February, 1993. EIA-606 specifies requirements and guidelines for the identification and documentation of telecommunications infrastructure.

Items covered by EIA-606 include

- Termination hardware
- Cables
- Cable pathways
- Equipment spaces
- Infrastructure color coding
- Symbols for standard components

Net Hardware

In particular, it specifies standard colors to be used for wiring. The occult details are revealed in Table 14.5.

Table 14.5   EIA-606 color chart

Termination type	Color	Code[a]	Comments
Demarcation point	Orange	150C	Central office terminations
Network connections	Green	353C	Also used for aux circuit terminations
Common equipment[b]	Purple	264C	Major switching/data eqpt. terminations
First-level backbone	White	–	Cable terminations
Second-level backbone	Gray	422C	Cable terminations
Station	Blue	291C	Horizontal cable terminations
Interbuilding backbone	Brown	465C	Campus cable terminations
Miscellaneous	Yellow	101C	Maintenance, alarms, etc.
Key telephone systems	Red	184C	–

a. According to the Pantone Matching System®
b. PBXes, hosts, LANs, muxes, etc.

Pantone now sells software to map between the Pantone systems for ink-on-paper, textile dyes, and colored plastic. Hey, you could color-coordinate the wiring, the uniforms of the installers, and the wiring documentation! On second thought…

14.12   NETWORK DESIGN ISSUES

This section addresses the logical and physical design of the network. It's targeted at medium-sized installations. The ideas presented here will scale up to a few hundred hosts but are overkill for three machines and inadequate for thousands. We also assume that you have an adequate budget and are starting from scratch, which is probably only partially true.

Most of network design consists of the specification of

- The types of media that will be used
- The topology and routing of cables
- The use of switches and routers

Another key issue in network design is congestion control. For example, file sharing protocols such as NFS and CIFS tax the network quite heavily, and so file serving on a backbone cable is undesirable.

The issues presented in the following sections are typical of those that must be considered in any network design.

Network architecture vs. building architecture

The network architecture is usually more flexible than the building architecture, but the two must coexist. If you are lucky enough to be able to specify the network before the building is constructed, be lavish. For most of us, both the building and a facilities management department already exist and are somewhat rigid.

In existing buildings, the network must use the building architecture, not fight it. Modern buildings often contain utility raceways for data and telephone cables in addition to high-voltage electrical wiring and water or gas pipes. They often use drop ceilings, a boon to network installers. Many campuses and organizations have underground utility tunnels that facilitate network installation.

The integrity of fire walls[12] must be maintained; if you route a cable through a fire wall, the hole must be snug and filled in with a noncombustible substance. Respect return air plenums in your choice of cable. If you are caught violating fire codes, you may be fined and will be required to fix the problems you have created, even if that means tearing down the entire network and rebuilding it correctly.

Your network's logical design must fit into the physical constraints of the buildings it serves. As you specify the network, keep in mind that it is easy to draw a logically good solution and then find that it is physically difficult or impossible to implement.

Existing networks

Computer networks are the focus of this discussion, but many organizations already have CATV networks and telephone networks capable of transmitting data. Often, these include fiber links. If your organization is ready to install a new telephone system, buy lots of extra fiber and have it installed at the same time.

We had that opportunity several years ago and asked the contractors if they would string some fiber for us. They said, "Sure, no charge" and were a bit miffed when we showed up with a truckload of fiber for them to install.

Expansion

It is very difficult to predict needs ten years into the future, especially in the computer and networking fields. It is important, therefore, to design the network with expansion and increased bandwidth in mind. As cable is being installed, especially in out-of-the-way, hard-to-reach places, pull three to four times the number of pairs you actually need. Remember: the majority of installation cost is labor, not materials.

Even if you have no plans to use fiber, it's wise to install some when wiring your building, especially if it is hard to install cables later. Run both multimode and single-mode fiber; the kind you need in the future is always the kind you didn't install.

Congestion

A network is like a chain: it is only as good as its weakest or slowest link. The performance of Ethernet, like that of many other network architectures, degrades nonlinearly as the network gets loaded.

---

12. This type of fire wall is a concrete, brick, or flame-retardant wall that prevents flames from spreading and burning down a building. While much different from a network security firewall, it's probably just as important.

Overtaxed switches, mismatched interfaces, and low-speed links can all lead to congestion. It is helpful to isolate local traffic by creating subnets and by using interconnection devices such as routers. Subnets can also be used to cordon off machines that are used for experimentation. It's difficult to run an experiment that involves several machines if there is no easy way to isolate those machines both physically and logically from the rest of the network.

Maintenance and documentation

We have found that the maintainability of a network correlates highly with the quality of its documentation. Accurate, complete, up-to-date documentation is absolutely indispensable.

Cables should be labeled at all termination points and also every few feet so that they can easily be identified when discovered in a ceiling or wall.[13] It's a good idea to post copies of local cable maps inside communications closets so that the maps can be updated on the spot when changes are made. Once every few weeks, someone should copy down the changes for entry into an wiring database.

Joints between major population centers in the form of switches or routers can facilitate debugging by allowing parts of the network to be isolated and debugged separately. It's also helpful to put joints between political and administrative domains.

14.13 MANAGEMENT ISSUES

If the network is to work correctly, some things need to be centralized, some distributed, and some local. Reasonable ground rules and "good citizen" guidelines need to be formulated and agreed on.

A typical environment includes

- A backbone network among buildings
- Departmental subnets connected to the backbone
- Group subnets within a department
- Connections to the outside world (e.g., Internet or field offices)

Several facets of network design and implementation must have site-wide control, responsibility, maintenance, and financing. Networks with charge-back algorithms for each connection grow in very bizarre but predictable ways as departments try to minimize their own local costs. Prime targets for central control are

- The network design, including the use of subnets, routers, switches, etc.
- The backbone network itself, including the connections to it
- Host IP addresses, hostnames, and subdomain names
- Protocols, mostly to ensure that they interoperate
- Routing policy to the Internet

---

13. Some cable manufacturers will prelabel spools of cable every few feet for you.

Domain names, IP addresses, and network names are in some sense already controlled centrally by authorities such as ARIN and ICANN. However, your site's use of these items must be coordinated locally as well.

A central authority has an overall view of the network: its design, capacity, and expected growth. It can afford to own monitoring equipment (and the staff to run it) and to keep the backbone network healthy. It can insist on correct network design, even when that means telling a department to buy a router and build a subnet to connect to the campus backbone network. Such a decision might be necessary so that a new connection does not adversely impact the existing network.

If a network serves many types of machines, operating systems, and protocols, it is almost essential to have a very smart router (e.g., Cisco) as a gateway between nets.

14.14 RECOMMENDED VENDORS

In the past 15+ years of installing networks around the world, we've gotten burned more than a few times by products that didn't quite meet specs or were misrepresented, overpriced, or otherwise failed to meet expectations. Below is a list of vendors in the United States that we still trust, recommend, and use ourselves today.

Cables and connectors

AMP (now part of Tyco)
(800) 522-6752
www.amp.com

Black Box Corporation
(724) 746-5500
www.blackbox.com

Anixter
(800) 264-9837
www.anixter.com

Newark Electronics
(800) 463-9275
www.newark.com

Belden Cable
(800) 235-3361
(765) 983-5200
www.belden.com

Siemon
(860) 945-4395
www.siemon.com

Test equipment

Fluke
(800) 443-5853
www.fluke.com

Acterna
(866) 228-3762
www.acterna.com

Siemon
(860) 945-4395
www.siemon.com

Net Hardware

Routers/switches

Cisco Systems
(415) 326-1941
www.cisco.com

14.15 RECOMMENDED READING

BARNETT, DAVID, DAVID GROTH, AND JIM MCBEE. *Cabling: The Complete Guide to Network Wiring (3rd Edition)*. San Francisco: Sybex, 2004.

SEIFERT, RICH. *Gigabit Ethernet: Technology and Applications for High Speed LANs.* Reading, MA: Addison-Wesley, 1998.

ANSI/TIA/EIA-568-A, *Commercial Building Telecommunications Cabling Standard*, and ANSI/TIA/EIA-606, *Administration Standard for the Telecommunications Infrastructure of Commercial Buildings*, are the telecommunication industry's standards for building wiring. Unfortunately, they are not free. See www.tiaonline.org.

SPURGEON, CHARLES. "Guide to Ethernet." www.ethermanage.com/ethernet

14.16 EXERCISES

E14.1 Today, most office buildings house computer networks and are wired with UTP Ethernet. Some combination of hubs and switches is needed to support these networks. In many cases, the two types of equipment are interchangeable. List the advantages and disadvantages of each.

★ **E14.2** Draw a simple, imaginary network diagram that connects a machine in your computer lab to Amazon.com. Include LAN, MAN, and WAN components. Show what technology is used for each component. Show some hubs, switches, and routers.

★ **E14.3** Research WPA's Temporal Key Integrity Protocol. Detail what advantages this has over WEP, and what types of attacks it prevents.

★★ **E14.4** TTCP is a tool that measures TCP and UDP performance (look for it at www.rpmfind.net). Install TTCP on two networked machines and measure the performance of the link between them. What happens to the bandwidth if you adjust buffer sizes up or down? How do your observed numbers compare with the theoretical capacity of the physical medium?

15 DNS: The Domain Name System

Zillions of hosts are connected to the Internet. How do we keep track of them all when they belong to so many different countries, networks, and administrative groups? Two key pieces of infrastructure hold everything together: the Domain Name System (DNS), which keeps track of who the hosts are, and the Internet routing system, which keeps track of how they are connected.

This chapter (mini-book, some would say) is about DNS. Although DNS has come to serve several different purposes, its primary job is to map between hostnames and IP addresses. Users and user-level programs like to refer to machines by name, but low-level network software understands only numbers. DNS provides the glue that keeps everyone happy. It has also come to play an important role in the routing of email, web server access, and many other services.

DNS is a distributed database. "Distributed" means that my site stores the data about my computers, your site stores the data about your computers, and somehow, our sites automatically cooperate and share data when one site needs to look up some of the other's data.

Our DNS coverage can be divided into three major sections:

- The DNS system in general: its history, data, and protocols

- BIND, a specific implementation of the DNS system

- The operation and maintenance of BIND servers, including related topics such as security

If you need to set up or maintain your site's DNS servers and already have a general idea how DNS works, feel free skip ahead.

Before we start in on the general background of DNS, let's first take a brief detour to address everyone's most frequently asked question: how do I add a new machine to a network that's already using BIND? What follows is a cookbook-style recipe that does not define or explain any terminology and that probably does not fit exactly with your local sysadmin policies and procedures. Use with caution.

15.1 DNS FOR THE IMPATIENT: ADDING A NEW MACHINE

If your network is set up to use the Dynamic Host Configuration Protocol (DHCP) you may not need to perform any manual configuration for DNS. When a new computer is connected, the DHCP server informs it of the DNS servers it should use for queries. Hostname-to-IP-address mappings for use by the outside world were most likely set up when the DHCP server was configured and are automatically entered through DNS's dynamic update facility.

For networks that do not use DHCP, the following recipe shows how to update the DNS configuration by copying and modifying the records for a similar computer.

Step 1: Choose a hostname and IP address for the new machine in conjunction with local sysadmins or your upstream ISP.

Step 2: Identify a similar machine on the same subnet. You'll use that machine's records as a model for the new ones. In this example, we'll use a machine called templatehost.my.domain as the model.

Step 3: Log in to the master name server machine.

Step 4: Look through the name server configuration file, usually **/etc/named.conf**:

- Within the options statement, find the directory line that tells where zone data files are kept at your site (see page 424). The zone files contain the actual host and IP address data.

- From the zone statements, find the filenames for the forward zone file and reverse zone file appropriate for your new IP address (page 432).

- Verify from the zone statements that this server is in fact the master server for the domain. The forward zone statement should look like this:

    ```
    zone "my.domain" {
        type master;
        ...
    ```

Step 5: Go to the zone file directory and edit the forward zone file. Find the records for the template host you identified earlier. They'll look something like this:

    ```
    templatehost    IN    A     128.138.243.100
                    IN    MX    10  mail-hub
                    IN    MX    20  templatehost
    ```

Your version might not include the MX lines, which are used for mail routing.

Step 6: Duplicate those records and change them appropriately for your new host. The zone file might be sorted by hostname; follow the existing convention. Be sure to also change the serial number in the SOA record at the beginning of the file (it's the first of the five numbers in the SOA record). The serial number should only increase; add 1 if your site uses an arbitrary serial number, or set the field to the current date if your site uses that convention.

Step 7: Edit the reverse zone file,[1] duplicate the record for the template host, and update it. It should look something like this:

```
100                 IN    PTR   templatehost.my.domain.
```

Note that there is a trailing dot after the hostname; don't omit it. You must also update the serial number in the SOA record of the reverse zone file.

If your reverse zone file shows more than just the last byte of each host's IP address, you must enter the bytes in reverse order. For example, the record

```
100.243             IN    PTR   templatehost.my.domain.
```

corresponds to the IP address 128.138.243.100 (here, the reverse zone is relative to 138.128.in-addr.arpa rather than 243.138.128.in-addr.arpa).

Step 8: While still logged in to the master name server machine, run **rndc reload**, or if it's a busy server, just reload the domains (or views) that you changed:

```
# rndc reload forward-zone-name
# rndc reload reverse-zone-name
```

Step 9: Check the configuration with **dig**; see page 473. You can also try to **ping** or **traceroute** to your new host's name, even if the new host has not yet been set up. A "host unknown" message means you goofed; "host not responding" means that everything is probably OK.

The most common errors are

- Forgetting to update the serial number and reload the name server, and
- Forgetting to add a dot at the end of the hostname in the PTR reverse entry.

15.2 THE HISTORY OF DNS

DNS was formally specified by Paul Mockapetris in RFCs 882 and 883 (1983) and updated in RFCs 1034 and 1035 (1987). It contained two key concepts: hierarchical hostnames and distributed responsibility.

---

1. The reverse zone might be maintained elsewhere (e.g., at your ISP's site). If so, the reverse entry will have to be entered there.

BIND implementations

The original UNIX implementation was done by four graduate students at Berkeley (Douglas Terry, Mark Painter, David Riggle, and Songnian Zhou) in 1984. It was then added to the Berkeley UNIX distribution by Kevin Dunlap in the mid-1980s and became known as BIND, the Berkeley Internet Name Domain system. Paul Vixie and ISC, the Internet Systems Consortium (www.isc.org, known as the Internet Software Consortium before 2004) currently maintain BIND. It is an open source project. In 2000 and 2001, ISC developed a totally new version of BIND—BIND 9— with funding from several vendors, government agencies, and other organizations.

ISC also provides various types of support for these products, including help with configuration, classes on BIND and DNS, and even custom programming. These services are a boon for sites that must have a support contract before they can use open source software. Several companies use service contracts as a way to contribute to the ISC—they buy expensive contracts but never call for help.

Thanks to a port by Nortel, BIND is available for Windows as well as UNIX/Linux. Since the DNS protocol is standardized, UNIX and non-UNIX DNS implementations can all interoperate and share data. Many sites run UNIX servers to provide DNS service to their Windows desktops; this combination works well.

RFCs 1034 and 1035 are still considered the baseline specification for DNS, but more than 40 other RFCs have superseded and elaborated on various aspects of the protocol and data records over the last decade (see the list at the end of this chapter). Currently, no single standard or RFC brings all the pieces together in one place. Historically, DNS has more or less been defined as "what BIND implements," although this is becoming less accurate as other DNS servers emerge.

Other implementations of DNS

In the beginning, BIND was the only DNS implementation in widespread use. Today there are several, both open source and commercial. Many do not implement all the specifications defined by the many DNS RFCs that are winding their way through the standardization process. Table 15.1 lists the more popular DNS implementations and shows where to go for more information.

Table 15.1   Some popular implementations of DNS

Name	Author	Source	Comments
BIND	ISC	isc.org	Authoritative or caching
NSD	NLnet Labs	www.nlnetlabs.nl	Authoritative only
PowerDNS	PowerDNS BV	www.powerdns.com	Authoritative only
djbdns[a]	Dan Bernstein	tinydns.org	Violates some RFCs
Microsoft DNS	Microsoft	microsoft.com	Guilty of a myriad of sins
ANS, CNS	Nominum	www.nominum.com	Authoritative or caching

a. Also known as tinydns, which is the server component of the djbdns package

ISC's ongoing domain survey keeps track of the various DNS implementations and the number of name servers using each. To see the current population demographics, go to www.isc.org, click ISC Internet Domain Survey, click Latest Survey Results, and finally click Domain Server Software Distribution. DNS appliances such as Infoblox (www.infoblox.com) are used by some large sites but do not yet show up in the survey's fingerprinting.

In this book we discuss only BIND, which is considered the reference implementation of DNS. It is by far the most widely used implementation and is an appropriate choice for most sites. BIND tracks all the standards and proposed standards of the IETF, often implementing features before their specifications are complete. This is good because some standards-track features turn out to be flawed—their inclusion in BIND allows problems to be recognized and fixed before being written into "law."

NSD, the name server daemon, was developed in 2003 by NLnet Labs in Amsterdam. It provides a fast, secure, authoritative name server appropriate for use by root and top-level domain servers. (An authoritative server is appropriate for providing the answers to queries about hosts in your domain, but it cannot answer users' queries about other domains.)

PowerDNS is an open source authoritative name server that provides a uniquely flexible back-end system. The DNS data can come from files or from a long list of other sources: MySQL, Oracle (8i and 9i), IBM's DB2, PostgreSQL, Microsoft's SQL Server, LDAP, ODBC, XDB, or even a UNIX pipe.

djbdns is an alternative name server package that consists of an authoritative server called tinydns and a caching server called dnscache. It claims to be secure and very fast, although some of the measurement data we are aware of is inconclusive. Its main drawback is that it violates the DNS standards frequently and intentionally, making interoperation with other DNS servers difficult.

Microsoft provides a DNS server for Windows, but the Microsoft implementation has its own special quirks and differences. It interoperates with BIND but also tends to clutter the net with unnecessary and malformed packets.

Nominum, the contractor that wrote the initial version of BIND 9 for ISC, sells its own name servers and network management tools. The Nominum servers are blindingly fast and include most of the currently proposed standards.

15.3   WHO NEEDS DNS?

DNS defines

- A hierarchical namespace for hosts and IP addresses
- A distributed database of hostname and address information
- A "resolver" to query this database
- Improved routing for email
- A mechanism for finding services on a network
- A protocol for exchanging naming information

To be full citizens of the Internet, sites need DNS. Maintaining a local **/etc/hosts** file with mappings for every host you might ever want to contact is not possible.

Each site maintains one or more pieces of the distributed database that makes up the world-wide DNS system. Your piece of the database consists of text files that contain records for each of your hosts. Each record is a single line consisting of a name (usually a hostname), a record type, and some data values. The name field can be omitted if its value is the same as that of the previous line.

For example, the lines

```
bark          IN   A    206.168.198.209
              IN   MX   10 mailserver.atrust.com.
```

in the "forward" file, and

```
 209          IN   PTR  bark.atrust.com.
```

in the "reverse" file associate "bark.atrust.com" with the IP address 206.168.198.209 and reroute email addressed to this machine to the host mailserver.atrust.com.

DNS is a client/server system. Servers ("name servers") load the data from your DNS files into memory and use it to answer queries both from internal clients and from clients and other servers out on the Internet. All of your hosts should be DNS clients, but relatively few need to be DNS servers.

If your organization is small (a few hosts on a single network), you can run a server on one host or ask your ISP to supply DNS service on your behalf. A medium-sized site with several subnets should run multiple DNS servers to reduce query latency and improve reliability. A very large site can divide its DNS domain into subdomains and run several servers for each subdomain.

15.4 THE DNS NAMESPACE

The DNS namespace is organized into what mathematicians call a tree; each domain name corresponds to a node in the tree. One branch of the DNS naming tree maps hostnames to IP addresses, and a second branch maps IP addresses back to hostnames. The former branch is called the "forward mapping," and the BIND data files associated with it are called "forward zone files." The address-to-hostname branch is the "reverse mapping," and its data files are called "reverse zone files." Sadly, many sites do not maintain their reverse mappings.

Each domain represents a distinct chunk of the namespace and is loosely managed by a single administrative entity. The root of the tree is called "." or dot, and beneath it are the top-level (or root-level) domains.

For historical reasons, two types of top-level domain names are in current use. In the United States, top-level domains originally described organizational and political structure and were given three-letter names such as com and edu. Some of these domains (primarily com, org, and net) are used outside the United States as well; they are called the generic top-level domains or gTLDs for short.

The top-level domains were relatively fixed in the past, but ICANN approved seven new ones in late 2000: biz, info, name, pro, museum, aero, and coop.[2] More recently, "jobs" was added to the gTLD list. These domains are now operational and available for use. The biz, info, and name domains are called "unsponsored" gTLDs and are open to anyone; museum, aero, jobs, pro, and coop are "sponsored" TLDs that are limited to specific types of registrants.

Table 15.2 lists the most important gTLDs along with their original purposes. When good names in the com domain became scarce, the registries began to offer names in org and net without regard to those domains' original restrictions. The domains in the left column of Table 15.2 are the originals, dating from about 1988; the right column includes the new domains added since 2001.

Table 15.2   Generic top-level domains

Domain	What it's for	Domain	What it's for
com	Commercial companies	aero	Air transport industry
edu	U.S. educational institutions	biz	Businesses
gov	U.S. Government agencies	coop	Cooperatives
mil	U.S. military agencies	info	Unrestricted use
net	Network providers	jobs	Human resources folks
org	Nonprofit organizations	museum	Museums
int	International organizations	name	Individuals
arpa	Anchor for IP address tree	pro	Accountants, lawyers, etc.

For most domains outside the United States, two-letter ISO country codes are used. These domains are known as ccTLDs, or "country code top-level domains." Both the geographical and the organizational TLDs coexist within the same global namespace. Table 15.3 shows some common country codes.

Table 15.3   Common country codes

Code	Country	Code	Country	Code	Country
au	Australia	fi	Finland	hk	Hong Kong
ca	Canada	fr	France	ch	Switzerland
br	Brazil	jp	Japan	mx	Mexico
de	Germany	se	Sweden	hu	Hungary

Some countries outside the United States build an organizational hierarchy with second-level domains. Naming conventions vary. For example, an academic institution might be in edu in the United States and in ac.jp in Japan.

---

2. ICANN is the Internet Corporation for Assigned Names and Numbers. See page 273 for more information about ICANN.

The top-level domain "us" is also sometimes used in the United States, primarily with locality domains; for example, bvsd.k12.co.us, the Boulder Valley School District in Colorado. The "us" domain is never combined with an organizational domain—there is no "edu.us" (yet). The advantage of "us" domain names is that they are inexpensive to register; see www.nic.us for more details. The restrictions on second-level domains beneath "us" (which were formerly limited to U.S. states) have been relaxed, and domain names like evi-nemeth.us are possible.

Domain mercenaries have in some cases bought an entire country's namespace. For example, the domain for Moldovia, "md", is now being marketed to doctors and residents of the state of Maryland (MD) in the United States. Another example is Tuvalu, for which the country code is "tv". The first such sale was Tonga ("to"), the most active is currently Niue ("nu"), and perhaps the most attractive is "tm" from Turkmenistan. These deals have sometimes been fair to the country with the desirable two-letter code and sometimes not.

Domain squatting is also widely practiced: folks register names they think will be requested in the future and then resell them to the businesses whose names they have snitched. Years ago, domain names for all the Colorado ski areas were registered to the same individual, who made quite a bit of money reselling them to individual ski areas as they became web-aware.

The going rate for a good name in the com domain is between several thousand and a few million dollars. We were offered $50,000 for the name admin.com, which we obtained years ago when sysadmin.com had already been taken by /Sys/Admin magazine. The highest price so far (or at least, the highest on public record) was the $7.5 million paid for business.com during the heyday of the tech stock boom. $20,000 to $100,000 is a more common range these days, but multimillion dollar sales are still occurring, an example being the July 2004 sale of CreditCards.com for $2.75 million.

Internet entrepreneur Dan Parisi was expected to receive several million dollars for former porn site whitehouse.com, which was placed on the block in early 2004. A series of different businesses have used the name since then, but the exact terms and financial details were never made public.

Currently, valid domain names consist only of letters, numbers, and dashes. Each component of a name can be no longer than 63 characters, and names must be shorter than 256 characters overall. Internationalization of the DNS system and support for non-ASCII character sets will eventually change all the naming rules, but for now names from other character sets are mapped back to ASCII; see page 388.

Domain names are case insensitive. "Colorado" is the same as "colorado", which is the same as "COLORADO" as far as DNS is concerned. Current DNS implementations must ignore case when making comparisons but propagate case when it is supplied. In the past it was common to use capital letters for top-level domains and an initial capital for second-level domains. These days, fingers are weary from typing and all-lowercase is the norm.[3]

An Internet host's fully qualified name is formed by appending its domain name to its hostname. For example, boulder.colorado.edu is the fully qualified name for the host boulder at the University of Colorado. Other sites can use the hostname boulder without colliding, because the fully qualified names will be different.

Within the DNS system, fully qualified names are terminated by a dot; for example, "boulder.colorado.edu.". The lack of a final dot may indicate a relative address. Depending on the context in which a relative address is used, additional components might be added. The final dot convention is generally hidden from everyday users of DNS. In fact, some systems (such as mail) will break if you supply the dot yourself.

It's common for a host to have more than one name. The host boulder.colorado.edu could also be known as www.colorado.edu or ftp.colorado.edu if we wanted to make its name reflect the services it provides. In fact, it's a good practice to make service hostnames such as www be "mobile," so that you can move servers from one machine to another without changing any machine's primary name. You can assign extra names by using the CNAME construct; see page 399.

When we were issued the name colorado.edu, we were guaranteed that colorado was unique within the edu domain. We have further divided that domain into subdomains along department lines. For example, the host anchor in the computer science department is called anchor.cs.colorado.edu on the Internet.

The creation of each new subdomain must be coordinated with the administrators of the domain above to guarantee uniqueness. Entries in the configuration files for the parent domain delegate authority for the namespace to the subdomain.

Masters of their domains

Management of the top-level domains com, org, net, and edu was formerly coordinated by Network Solutions, Inc., under contract with the National Science Foundation. This monopoly situation has now changed, and other organizations are allowed to register domain names in those gTLDs. Other top-level domains, such as those for individual countries, are maintained by regional organizations.

There have been various proposals to allow private companies to operate their own top-level domains, and it is likely that additional top-level domains will be available in the near future. Consult www.icann.org for up-to-date information.

Most ISPs offer fee-based domain name registration services. They deal with the top-level domain authority on your behalf and configure their DNS servers to handle name lookups within your domain. The disadvantage of relying on an ISP's servers is that you lose direct control over the administration of your domain.

---

3. BIND preserves case, but some implementations (e.g., Microsoft's and djbdns) change case according to their own preference. So much for tight standards.

*See page 287 for
more information
about CIDR.*

To manage your own DNS services, you must still coordinate with your ISP. Most ISPs supply reverse DNS mappings for IP addresses within their CIDR blocks. If you take over DNS management of your addresses, make sure that your ISP disables its service for those addresses and delegates that responsibility to you.

A domain's forward and reverse mappings should be managed in the same place whenever possible. Some ISPs are happy to let you manage the forward files but are reluctant to relinquish control of the reverse mappings. Such split management can lead to synchronization problems. See page 400 for an elegant (?) hack that makes delegation work even for tiny pieces of address space.

DNS domains should (must, in fact; see RFC1219) be served by at least two servers. One common arrangement is for a site to operate its own master server and to let the ISP's servers act as slaves. Once the system has been configured, the ISP's servers automatically download host data from the master server. Changes made to the DNS configuration are reflected on the slave servers without any explicit work on the part of either site's administrator.

Don't put all of your DNS servers on the same network. When DNS stops working, the network effectively stops for your users. Spread your DNS servers around so that you don't end up with a fragile system with a single point of failure. DNS is quite robust if configured carefully.

Selecting a domain name

Our advice used to be that names should be short and easy to type and that they should identify the organization that used them. These days, the reality is that all the good, short names have been taken, at least in the com domain. It's tempting to blame this state of affairs on squatters, but in fact most of the good names are in actual use. In 2004, over 60% of the registered names were in use; historically, less than half of registered names were actually used.

Domain bloat

DNS was designed to map an organization's domain name to a name server for that organization. In that mode it needs to scale to the number of organizations in the world. Now that the Internet has become a conduit of mass culture, however, domain names are being applied to every product, movie, sporting event, English noun, etc. Domain names such as twinkies.com are not (directly) related to the company that makes the product; they're simply being used as advertisements. It's not clear that DNS can continue to scale in this way. The real problem here is that the DNS naming tree is a more efficient data structure when it has some hierarchy and is not totally flat. With each organization naming hundreds or thousands of products at the top level of the tree, hierarchy is doomed.

What we really need is a directory service that maps brand and marketing names to organizations, leaving DNS free to deal with IP addresses. Another possible solution is to enforce hierarchy in the system; for example, twinkies.hostess-foods.com. But this will never happen—we've already gone too far down the marketing path.

Sony does things the right way from DNS's perspective—all of its products are sub-domains of sony.com. It might take an extra click or two to find the products you want, but DNS appreciates the hierarchy.

Registering a second-level domain name

To obtain a second-level domain name, you must apply to a registrar for the appropriate top-level domain. ICANN accredits various agencies to be part of its shared registry project for registering names in the gTLDs. As of this writing, you have something like 500 choices of registrar. Check www.icann.org for the definitive list.

To register for a ccTLD name in Europe, contact the Council of European National Top-level Domain Registries at www.centr.org to identify your local registry and apply for a domain name. For the Asia-Pacific region, the appropriate body is the Asia-Pacific Network Information Center, www.apnic.net.

To complete the domain registration forms, you must identify a technical contact person, an administrative contact person, and at least two hosts that will be servers for your domain.

Creating your own subdomains

The procedure for creating a subdomain is similar to that for creating a second-level domain, except that the central authority is now local (or more accurately, within your own organization). Specifically, the steps are as follows.

- Choose a name that is unique in the local context.
- Identify two or more hosts to be servers for your new domain.
- Coordinate with the administrator of the parent domain.

Parent domains should check to be sure that a child domain's name servers are up and running before performing the delegation. If the servers are not working, a "lame delegation" results, and you might receive nasty email asking you to clean up your DNS act. Page 475 covers lame delegations in more detail.

15.5 HOW DNS WORKS

Each host that uses DNS is either a client of the system or simultaneously a client and a server. If you do not plan to run any DNS servers, it's not essential that you read the next few sections (skip ahead to *Resolver configuration* on page 418), although they will help you develop a more solid understanding of the architecture of DNS.

Delegation

All name servers read the identities of the root servers from a local config file. The root servers in turn know about com, net, fi, de, and other top-level domains. Farther down the chain, edu knows about colorado.edu, com knows about admin.com, and so on. Each zone can delegate authority for its subdomains to other servers.

Let's inspect a real example. Suppose we want to look up the address for the machine vangogh.cs.berkeley.edu from the machine lair.cs.colorado.edu. The host lair asks its local name server, ns.cs.colorado.edu, to figure out the answer. Exhibit A illustrates the subsequent events.

Exhibit A   DNS query process for vangogh.cs.berkeley.edu

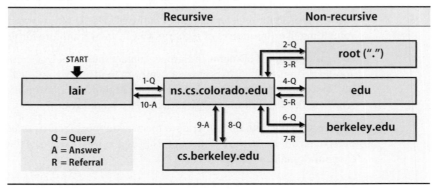

The numbers on the arrows between servers show the order of events, and a letter indicates the type of transaction (query, referral, or answer). We assume that none of the required information was cached before the query, except for the names and IP addresses of the servers of the root domain.

The local name server doesn't know the address; furthermore, it doesn't know anything about cs.berkeley.edu or berkeley.edu or even edu. It does know some servers for the root domain, however, and since it is a recursive server, it queries a root server about vangogh.cs.berkeley.edu and receives a referral to the servers for edu.

The local name server then sends its query to an edu server (asking, as always, about vangogh.cs.berkeley.edu) and gets back a referral to the servers for berkeley.edu. It then repeats the query in the berkeley.edu domain. If the Berkeley server doesn't have the answer cached, it returns a referral to cs.berkeley.edu. The cs.berkeley.edu server is authoritative for the requested information and returns vangogh's address.

When the dust settles, ns.cs.colorado.edu has cached vangogh's address. It has also cached data on the servers for edu, berkeley.edu, and cs.berkeley.edu.

Caching and efficiency

Caching increases the efficiency of lookups: a cached answer is almost free and is usually correct because hostname-to-address mappings typically change infrequently. An answer is saved for a period of time called the "time to live" (TTL), which is specified by the owner of the data record in question. Most queries are for local hosts and can be resolved quickly. Users also inadvertently help with efficiency because they repeat many queries; after the first instance of a query, the rest are "free."

DNS

For a long time, caching was only applied to positive answers. If a host's name or address could not be found, that fact was not saved. A scheme for negative DNS caching was described in RFC1034, but it was incomplete and was not widely implemented. A better scheme was outlined in RFC2308 in 1998. This scheme was implemented in BIND 8.2 as an optional feature and is now mandatory in BIND 9.

One measurement at the RIPE root server in Europe showed that 60% of DNS queries were for nonexistent data (many queries were for 127.in-addr.arpa or for Microsoft services as hostnames). Caching this information farther down the DNS tree should dramatically reduce the load on the root servers.

Negative caching saves answers of the following types:

- No host or domain matches the name queried.
- The type of data requested does not exist for this host.
- The server to ask is not responding.
- The server is unreachable because of network problems.

The first two types of negative data are cached for 10 minutes by default. You can increase this duration to three hours with a parameter in the SOA record discussed on page 392 and to one week with a BIND option.

Most implementations do not perform the last two types of negative caching. However, BIND does penalize unresponsive servers and will not query them as long as other choices are available. If all of a zone's servers fail to respond, BIND does not cache that fact.

Nonauthoritative answers *may* be cached; authoritative negative answers *must* be cached. BIND follows these guidelines from the RFCs, but Windows machines seem to implement the TTLs selectively, at least for negative caching. They use the correct default value (the minimum from the SOA record) the first time a query returns NXDOMAIN (no such domain), then reset the TTL to 15 minutes and let it time out normally from there.

A name server often receives multiple DNS records in response to a query. For example, a query for the name servers of the root domain would receive a response that listed all 13 root servers. Which one should your server query?

When the BIND name server must choose among several remote servers, all of which are authoritative for a domain, it first determines the network round trip time (RTT) to each server. It then sorts the servers into "buckets" according to their RTTs and selects a server from the fastest bucket. Servers within a bucket are treated as equals and are used in a round robin fashion.

You can achieve a primitive but effective form of load balancing by assigning a single hostname to several IP addresses (which in reality are different machines):

```
www          IN   A     192.168.0.1
             IN   A     192.168.0.2
             IN   A     192.168.0.3
```

Busy web servers such as Yahoo! or Google are not really a single machine; they're just a single name in the DNS.[4] A name server that has multiple records for the same name and record type returns all of them to the client, but in round robin order. For example, round robin order for the A records above would be 1, 2, 3 for the first query; 2, 3, 1 for the next; 3, 1, 2 for the third, and so on.

The extended DNS protocol

The original DNS protocol definition dates from the late 1980s and uses both UDP and TCP on port 53. UDP is typically used for queries and responses, and TCP for zone transfers between master servers and slave servers. Unfortunately, the maximum packet size that's guaranteed to work in all UDP implementations is 512 bytes, which is much too small for some of the new DNS features (e.g., DNSSEC) that must include digital signatures in each packet.

The 512-byte constraint also affects the number and names of the root servers. So that all root server data will fit in a 512-byte UDP packet, the number of root servers is limited to 13, and each server is named with a single letter of the alphabet.

Many resolvers issue a UDP query first; then, if they receive a truncated response, they reissue the query over TCP. This procedure gets around the 512-byte limit, but it is inefficient. You might think that DNS should just bail on UDP and use TCP all the time, but TCP connections are much more expensive. A UDP name server exchange can be as short as two packets: one query and one response. A TCP exchange involves at least seven packets: a three-way handshake to initiate the conversation, a query, a response, and a final handshake to close the connection.

15.6 WHAT'S NEW IN DNS

The latest developments on the DNS front fall in the political domain rather than the technical domain. VeriSign, the registry company that used to have a monopoly on registering domain names and that is currently responsible for the com and net zones, added a wild card address record to those zones. This caused every user who mistyped a domain name to be directed to a site maintained by one of VeriSign's advertisers. The service was known as Site Finder.

The Internet community screamed about the unfairness of it all, so ISC added a delegation-only option to BIND that recognized these wild card results and returned a more accurate "no such domain" response instead of the addresses blessed by VeriSign. This correction was fine for most top-level domains, but not all, so an exceptions clause was later added to provide finer control. We cover these new BIND options on page 429. After about a month of complaints, VeriSign removed the wild card record and turned off the service. After the lawyers sort things out, they will probably turn it back on again. The IETF may eventually tighten the specifications to allow no wild card records at all.

---

4. Last time we checked, Google was more than 400,000 Linux machines (they won't tell, but we googled for an estimate), and Yahoo! consisted of more than 100,000 FreeBSD machines.

Several significant technical changes have been made to DNS over the last few years. In particular, the DNS-related standards for IPv6 and DNS security have been radically altered by the IETF, rendering the coverage of these topics in earlier editions of this book totally wrong. Table 15.4 lists the major changes and provides a road map to the pages where they are covered in more detail.

Table 15.4   Recent developments in DNS and BIND

Page	RFCs	Description
388	3492	Internationalized domain names via Punycode
389	2671	EDNS0, protocol changes and extensions
394	1996	Asynchronous notification of zone changes
400	2317	Classless in-addr delegation (the CNAME hack)
402	2782, 3958	SRV records for the location of services
404	–	AAAA records for IPv6 addresses (A6 is obsolete)
405	2672–3	DNAME records abandoned
405	–	ip6.arpa for reverse IPv6 mappings; ip6.int abandoned
–	3596, 3646	IPv6 support
447	1995	Incremental zone transfers
448	2136	Dynamic update (for sites that use DHCP)
453	2845, 2930, 3645	TSIG/TKEY transaction signatures and key exchange
456	3225-6, 4033-5	DNSSEC, authentication, and security for zone data[a]

a. Totally redone in 2004

Some of these new features are enormous projects that the IETF has not yet finished standardizing. The working groups that are writing the standards have good writers but lack vigilant code warriors; some of the more recent specifications may be difficult or even impossible to implement. The current release of BIND (9.4) includes most of the new features.

IPv6 is described in more detail in Chapter 12.

Two massive new features, IPv6 support and DNSSEC, warrant a bit of commentary. IPv6 increases the length of IP addresses from 32 bits to 128 bits. If ever fully implemented, it will have an enormous impact on the Internet. BIND 9 supports the pieces of IPv6 that have been standardized so far, but it appears unlikely that IPv6 will be widely deployed during the lifetime of this book. Therefore, our coverage of BIND 9's IPv6 support is brief. There's enough in this chapter to give you the general flavor, but not enough to let you migrate your site to IPv6 and configure DNS for it.

The DNSSEC standard adds authentication data to the DNS database and its servers. It uses public key cryptography to verify the source and integrity of DNS data and uses DNS to distribute keys as well as host data.

Simpler authentication mechanisms have also been introduced, such as support for authentication through the use of a "shared secret." However, the shared secret must be distributed to each pair of servers that wants to perform mutual authentication.

Although that's fine for a local site with a handful of servers, it doesn't scale to the level of the Internet. BIND 9 implements both the DNSSEC public key system and the TSIG (transaction signatures) shared-secret system.

BIND releases starting with 9.3 have included the new specifications for DNSSEC. However, as people started to experiment with signed zones a couple of years ago, they realized that the original DNSSEC system was impractical. Under the original system, a parent zone signed the key of a child zone, and copies of the signed key were kept in both zones. If the child wanted to change its key, it had to negotiate with the parent and request that its new key be signed. Fine. However, if the parent wanted to change its key, it had to update all the child keys stored both within its own zone and in all its child zones. This operation proved to be unmanageable for large zones such as com because some child zones would invariably be unreachable during an update. Their keys would go out of sync and leave DNS unable to verify signatures.

The current solution is to have each child's signed key live only in the child zone, but to introduce a new resource record in the parent: DS, the delegation signer. We cover DNSSEC in detail beginning on page 456.

The introduction of internationalized domain names, which allow the use of non-English characters, is proceeding by way of a hack that maps Unicode characters back to ASCII. A system called Punycode performs the mapping uniquely and reversibly by using an algorithm known as Bootstring; see RFC3492 for details. As of 2005, registrars have begun publishing the Punycode names and most browsers have implemented some form of the system. Unfortunately, a few Punycode-related spoofing and security issues have also manifested themselves. In addition, internationalized domain names effectively reduce the maximum length (both per-component and total) allowed for DNS names.

The current internationalization scheme has skirted a key issue, antialiasing, because it is very difficult to address. Antialiasing involves resolving inconsistencies in the mapping between Asian language characters and the Punycode-encoded Unicode that represents them in the DNS. If a character can mean one of 3 or 4 or 10 different things in Unicode, then language experts must agree on translation standards, and characters displayed on a computer screen must be designed to differentiate among the various meanings.

Each of these three big issues (IPv6, DNSSEC, and internationalization) significantly increases the size of DNS data records, thereby making it more likely that DNS will bump into limits on UDP packet sizes.

In the mid-1990s, the DNS protocol was amended to include incremental zone transfers (like a **diff** between old and new zone files, inspired by Larry Wall's **patch** program), asynchronous notifications (to tell slaves when the master's data files have been updated), and dynamic updates (for DHCP hosts). These changes added features but did not really address the fundamental transport problem.

In the late 1990s, EDNS0 (Extended DNS, version 0) addressed some of the short-comings of the DNS protocol in today's Internet. It lets speakers advertise their reassembly buffer size, supported options, and protocol versions spoken. If the receiving name server responds with an error message, the sender drops back to the original DNS protocol. BIND 9 implements EDNS0 in both the server and the resolver.

15.7 THE DNS DATABASE

A domain's DNS database is a set of text files maintained by the system administrator on the domain's master name server. These text files are often called zone files. They contain two types of entries: parser commands (things like $ORIGIN and $TTL) and "resource records," or RRs as they are sometimes called. Only the resource records are really part of the database; the parser commands just provide some shorthand ways to enter records.

We start this section by describing the DNS resource records, which are defined in RFCs 1035, 1183, 1876, 2230, 2782, 2930, 3596, and 3658. We defer discussion of the parser commands until page 405.

Resource records

Each zone of the DNS hierarchy has a set of resource records associated with it. The basic format of a resource record is

```
[name] [ttl] [class] type data
```

Fields are separated by whitespace (tabs or spaces) and can contain the special characters shown in Table 15.5.

Table 15.5 Special characters used in RRs

Character	Meaning
;	Introduces a comment
@	The current zone name
( )	Allows data to span lines
*	Wild card[a] (*name* field only)

a. See page 399 for some cautionary statements.

The *name* field identifies the entity (usually a host or domain) that the record describes. If several consecutive records refer to the same entity, the name can be omitted after the first record as long as the subsequent records begin with whitespace. If it is present, the *name* field must begin in column one.

A name can be either relative or absolute. Absolute names end with a dot and are complete. Internally, the software deals only with absolute names; it appends the current domain and a dot to any name that does not already end in a dot. This feature allows names to be shorter, but it also invites mistakes.

For example, in the cs.colorado.edu domain, the name "anchor" would be interpreted as "anchor.cs.colorado.edu.". If the name were entered as "anchor.cs.colorado.edu", the lack of a final dot would still imply a relative name, and the default domain would be appended, resulting in the name "anchor.cs.colorado.edu.cs.colorado.edu.". This is a very common mistake.

The *ttl* (time to live) field specifies the length of time, in seconds, that the data item can be cached and still be considered valid. It is often omitted, except in the root server hints file. It defaults to the value set by the $TTL directive at the top of the data file for the zone. In BIND 9, the $TTL directive is required. If there is no $TTL directive in BIND 8, the *ttl* defaults to a per-zone value set in the zone's SOA record.

See Chapter 17 for more information about NIS.

Increasing the value of the *ttl* parameter to about a week substantially reduces network traffic and DNS load. However, once records have been cached outside your local network, you cannot force them to be discarded. If you plan a massive renumbering, set the $TTL value low (e.g., an hour) so that stale records that have been cached elsewhere on the Internet expire quickly.

Some sites set the TTL on the records for Internet-facing servers to a low value so that if a server experiences problems (network failure, hardware failure, denial of service attack, etc.), the administrators can respond by changing the server's name-to-IP-address mapping. Because the original TTLs were low, the new values will propagate quickly. For example, the name google.com has a five-minute TTL, but Google's name servers have a TTL of four days (345,600 seconds):

```
google.com.      300      IN  A   216.239.37.99
google.com.      345600   IN  NS  ns1.google.com.
ns1.google.com.  345600   IN  A   216.239.32.10
```

We used the **dig** command (**dig @ns1.google.com google.com**) to recover this data; the output is truncated here.

BIND 9 enforces a concept known as TTL harmonization, which forces all records in an RRset (that is, all records of the same type that pertain to a single node) to have the same TTL. The value that's actually used is that of the first resource record for the node/type pair.

The *class* specifies the network type. Three values are recognized:

- IN for the Internet
- HS for Hesiod
- CH for ChaosNet

The default value for the class is IN. It is often specified explicitly in zone data files even though it is the default. Hesiod, developed at MIT, is a database service built on top of BIND. ChaosNet is an obsolete network protocol formerly used by Symbolics Lisp machines.

Today, only two pieces of identification data are normally tucked away in the Chaos-Net class: the version number of the name server software and the name of the host on which the server is running. These data nuggets can be extracted with **dig** as shown on page 410. Administrators use the name server version number to identify servers in need of upgrades, and they use the host identification to debug name servers that are replicated through the use of anycast routing. Making this information available through the CH class was originally a feature (some might say "hack") of the BIND implementations, but it is now being standardized by the IETF as part of DNS proper.[5]

Many different types of DNS records are defined, but fewer than 10 are in common use; IPv6 adds a few more. We divide the resource records into four groups:

- Zone records – identify domains and their name servers
- Basic records – map names to addresses and route mail
- Security records – add authentication and signatures to zone files
- Optional records – provide extra information about hosts or domains

The contents of the *data* field depend on the record type. Table 15.6 lists the common record types.

Table 15.6 DNS record types

	Type	Name	Function
Zone	SOA	Start Of Authority	Defines a DNS zone
	NS	Name Server	Identifies zone servers, delegates subdomains
Basic	A	IPv4 Address	Name-to-address translation
	AAAA[a]	IPv6 Address	Name-to-IPv6-address translation
	PTR	Pointer	Address-to-name translation
	MX	Mail Exchanger	Controls email routing
Security	DS	Delegation Signer	Hash of signed child zone's key-signing key
	DNSKEY	Public Key	Public key for a DNS name
	NSEC	Next Secure	Used with DNSSEC for negative answers
	RRSIG	Signature	Signed, authenticated resource record set
Optional	CNAME	Canonical Name	Nicknames or aliases for a host
	LOC	Location	Geographic location and extent
	SRV	Services	Gives locations of well-known services
	TXT	Text	Comments or untyped information

a. The AAAA and A6 IPv6 address records have been sparring partners in the IETF for the past few years. AAAA eventually won and went from obsolete to standard. A6 is now labeled experimental.

Some record types are obsolete, experimental, or not widely used. See the BIND documentation for a complete list. Most records are maintained by hand (by editing text files), but the security resource records require cryptographic processing and so

5. Unfortunately, there is some dispute about the name under which this data should be filed. Should it be version.bind, hostname.bind, id-server, or…

must be managed with software tools. These records are described in the DNSSEC section beginning on page 456.

The order of resource records is almost arbitrary. The SOA record for a zone formerly had to be first, but that requirement has now been relaxed. The SOA is typically followed by the NS records. The records for each host are usually kept together. It's common practice to sort by the *name* field, although some sites sort by IP address so that it's easier to identify unused addresses.

As we describe each type of resource record in detail in the next sections, we will inspect some sample records from cs.colorado.edu's data files. The default domain in this context is "cs.colorado.edu.", so a host specified as "anchor" really means "anchor.cs.colorado.edu.".

The SOA record

An SOA record marks the beginning of a zone, a group of resource records located at the same place within the DNS namespace. This node of the DNS tree is also called a delegation point or zone cut. As we discuss in greater detail on page 396, the data for a DNS domain usually includes at least two zones: one for translating hostnames to IP addresses, and others that map in the reverse direction. The DNS tree has a forward branch organized by name and a reverse branch organized by IP address.

Each zone has exactly one SOA record. The SOA record includes the name of the zone, a technical contact, and various timeout values. An example:

```
; Start of authority record for cs.colorado.edu

@               IN  SOA  ns.cs.colorado.edu. hostmaster.cs.colorado.edu. (
                         2004111300    ; Serial number
                         7200          ; Refresh    (2 hours)
                         1800          ; Retry      (30 minutes)
                         604800        ; Expire     (1 week)
                         7200 )        ; Minimum    (2 hours)
```

Here, the *name* field contains the symbol @, which is shorthand for the name of the current zone. In this example, "cs.colorado.edu." could have been used instead. The value of @ is the domain name specified in the zone statement in the name server configuration file; it can be changed from within the zone file with the $ORIGIN parser directive (see page 405).

This example has no *ttl* field. The class is IN for Internet, the type is SOA, and the remaining items form the *data* field.

"ns.cs.colorado.edu." is the zone's master name server.

"hostmaster.cs.colorado.edu." is the email address of the technical contact in the format "*user.host.*" rather than the standard *user@host.* Just replace that first dot with an @ and remove the final dot if you need to send mail to a domain's administrator. Sites often use an alias such as admin or hostmaster in place of an actual login name. The sysadmin responsible for hostmaster duties may change, and it's easier to change one entry in the **aliases** file (see page 544) than to change all your zone files when you need to update the contact person.

The parentheses continue the SOA record over several lines. Their placement is not arbitrary in BIND 4 or 8—we tried to shorten the first line by splitting it before the contact address, but then BIND failed to recognize the SOA record. In some implementations, parentheses are only recognized in SOA and TXT records. BIND 9 has a better parser and parentheses can be used anywhere.

The first numeric parameter is the serial number of the zone's configuration data. The serial number is used by slave servers to determine when to get fresh data. It can be any 32-bit integer and should be incremented every time the data file for the zone is changed. Many sites encode the file's modification date in the serial number. For example, 2004111300 is the first change to the zone on November 13, 2004.

Serial numbers need not be continuous, but they must increase monotonically. If by accident you set a really large value on the master server and that value is transferred to the slaves, then correcting the serial number on the master will not work. The slaves request new data only if the master's serial number is larger than theirs.

There are three ways to fix this problem; only the first two work in BIND 9.

- One way to fix the problem is to exploit the properties of the sequence space in which the serial numbers live. This procedure involves adding a large value (2^{31}) to the bloated serial number, letting all the slave servers transfer the data, and then setting the serial number to just what you want. This weird arithmetic, with explicit examples, is covered in detail in the O'Reilly DNS book; RFC1982 describes the sequence space.

- A sneaky but more tedious way to fix the problem is to change the serial number on the master, kill the slave servers, remove the slaves' backup data files so they are forced to reload from the master, and restart the slaves. It does not work to just remove the files and reload; you must kill and restart the slave servers.

- BIND 4.9 and BIND 8 include a hack that lets you set the serial number to zero for one refresh interval and then restart the numbering. The zero always causes a reload, so don't forget to set it to a real value after each of the slaves has reloaded the zone with serial number 0.

It is a common mistake to change the data files but forget to update the serial number. Your name server will punish you by failing to propagate your changes to the slave servers.

The next four entries in the SOA record are timeout values, in seconds, that control how long data can be cached at various points throughout the world-wide DNS database. Times can also be expressed in units of minutes, hours, days, or weeks by addition of a suffix of m, h, d, or w, respectively. For example, 1h30m means 1 hour and 30 minutes. Timeout values represent a tradeoff between efficiency (it's cheaper to use an old value than to fetch a new one) and accuracy (new values should be more accurate).

Here's another copy of that same example SOA record, just so you don't have to keep turning back to the previous page:

```
; Start of authority record for cs.colorado.edu

@            IN  SOA  ns.cs.colorado.edu. hostmaster.cs.colorado.edu. (
                    2004111300    ; Serial number
                    7200          ; Refresh    (2 hours)
                    1800          ; Retry      (30 minutes)
                    604800        ; Expire     (1 week)
                    7200 )        ; Minimum    (2 hours)
```

The first timeout is the *refresh* timeout, which specifies how often slave servers should check with the master to see if the serial number of the zone's configuration has changed. Whenever the zone changes, slaves must update their copy of the zone's data. The slave compares the serial numbers; if the master's serial number is larger, the slave requests a zone transfer to update the data. Common values for the *refresh* timeout range from one to six hours (3,600 to 21,600 seconds).

Instead of just waiting passively for slave servers to time out, BIND servers now notify their slaves every time a zone changes, unless the notify parameter is specifically turned off in the configuration file. Slaves that understand the notification immediately refresh themselves. It's possible for an update notification to be lost due to network congestion, so the refresh timeout should always be set to a reasonable value.

If a slave server tries to check the master's serial number but the master does not respond, the slave tries again after the *retry* timeout period has elapsed. Our experience suggests that 20–60 minutes (1,200–3,600 seconds) is a good value.

If a master server is down for a long time, slaves will try to refresh their data many times but always fail. Each slave should eventually decide that the master is never coming back and that its data is surely out of date. The *expire* parameter determines how long the slaves will continue to serve the domain's data authoritatively in the absence of a master. The system should be able to survive if the master server is down for a few days, so this parameter should have a longish value. We recommend a week to a month.

The *minimum* parameter in the SOA record sets the time to live for negative answers that are cached.[6] The default for positive answers (i.e., actual records) is specified at the top of the zone file with the $TTL directive. Experience suggests values of several hours to a few days for $TTL and a couple of hours to a day for the *minimum*. The $TTL value must be larger than or equal to the *minimum*.

The $TTL, *expire*, and *minimum* parameters eventually force everyone that uses DNS to discard old data values. The initial design of DNS relied on the fact that host

---

6. Prior to BIND 8.2, the *minimum* parameter set the default time to live for resource records. It was included with each record and used to expire the cached records on nonauthoritative servers.

data was relatively stable and did not change often. However, DHCP and mobile hosts have changed the rules. BIND is desperately trying to cope by providing the dynamic update and incremental zone transfer mechanisms described starting on page 447. For more information about TTLs and a concept called TTL harmonization, see page 390.

NS records

NS (name server) records identify the servers that are authoritative for a zone (that is, all the master and slave servers) and delegate subdomains to other organizations. NS records usually follow the SOA record.

The format is

zone [*ttl*] IN NS *hostname*

For example:

```
cs.colorado.edu.   IN   NS    ns.cs.colorado.edu.
cs.colorado.edu.   IN   NS    anchor.cs.colorado.edu.
cs.colorado.edu.   IN   NS    ns.cs.utah.edu.
```

Since the zone name is the same as the *name* field of the SOA record that precedes these NS records, it can be left blank. Thus, the lines

```
                   IN   NS    ns.cs.colorado.edu.
                   IN   NS    anchor.cs.colorado.edu.
                   IN   NS    ns.cs.utah.edu.
```

immediately following the SOA record for cs.colorado.edu are equivalent.

To be visible to the outside world, an authoritative server of cs.colorado.edu should be listed both in the zone file for cs.colorado.edu and in the file for the parent zone, colorado.edu. Caching-only servers cannot be authoritative; do not list them. No parameter in the NS records specifies whether a server is a master or a slave. That information is specified in the name server configuration file.

BIND uses a zone's NS records to identify slave servers when it wants to send out notifications of changes to the zone. Those same NS records inside the parent zone (colorado.edu) define the cs subdomain and delegate authority for it to the appropriate name servers. If the list of name servers in the parent zone is not kept up to date with those in the zone itself, any new servers that are added become "stealth servers" and are not used to answer queries from the outside world. This configuration occurs sometimes through design and sometimes through forgetfulness. It is not seriously wrong as long as the parent has at least one valid NS record for the child zone.

See page 407 for more information about delegation. A quick look at our own delegations revealed a major server for colorado.edu that the edu domain knew nothing about. Do as we say and not as we do: check your delegations with **dig** to be sure they specify an appropriate set of servers (see page 473).

A records

A (address) records are the heart of the DNS database. They provide the mapping from hostnames to IP addresses that was formerly specified in the **/etc/hosts** file. A host usually has one A record for each of its network interfaces. The format is

```
hostname [ttl] IN A ipaddr
```

For example:

```
anchor        IN   A     128.138.243.100
```

A machine with multiple network interfaces can use a single hostname associated with all interfaces or can have separate hostnames for each interface.

PTR records

PTR (pointer) records perform the reverse mapping from IP addresses to hostnames. As with A records, a host must have one PTR record for each network interface. Before we describe PTR records, however, we need to digress and talk about a special top-level domain called in-addr.arpa.

Fully qualified hostnames can be viewed as a notation in which the "most significant part" is on the right. For example, in the name anchor.cs.colorado.edu, anchor is in cs, cs is in colorado, and colorado is in edu. IP addresses, on the other hand, have the "most significant part" on the left. In the address 128.138.243.100, host 100 is on subnet 243, which is part of network 128.138.

The in-addr.arpa domain was created to allow one set of software modules and one naming tree to map from IP addresses to hostnames as well as from hostnames to IP addresses. Domains under in-addr.arpa are named like IP addresses with their bytes reversed. For example, the zone for our 243 subnet is 243.138.128.in-addr.arpa.

The general format of a PTR record is

```
addr [ttl] IN PTR hostname
```

For example, the PTR record in the 243.138.128.in-addr.arpa zone that corresponds to anchor's A record above is

```
100           IN   PTR   anchor.cs.colorado.edu.
```

The name 100 does not end in a dot and therefore is relative. But relative to what? Not "cs.colorado.edu.". For this sample record to be accurate, the default domain has to be "243.138.128.in-addr.arpa.".

You can set the domain by putting the PTR records for each subnet in their own file, as in this example. The default domain associated with the file is set in the name server configuration file. Another way to do reverse mappings is to include records such as

```
100.243       IN   PTR   anchor.cs.colorado.edu.
```

with a default domain of 138.128.in-addr.arpa. Some sites put all reverse records in the same file and use $ORIGIN directives to specify the subnet. Note that the hostname anchor.cs.colorado.edu must end with a dot to prevent 138.128.in-addr.arpa from being appended to its name.

Since cs.colorado.edu and 243.138.128.in-addr.arpa are different regions of the DNS namespace, they constitute two separate zones. Each zone must have its own SOA record and resource records. In addition to defining an in-addr.arpa zone for each real network, you should also define one that takes care of the loopback network, 127.0.0.0.

This all works fine if the subnets are on byte boundaries. But how do you handle the reverse mappings for a subnet such as 128.138.243.0/26? An elegant hack defined in RFC2317 exploits CNAME resource records to accomplish this feat; see page 400.

The reverse mappings provided by PTR records are used by any program that authenticates inbound network traffic. For example, **sshd** may allow remote logins without a password if the machine of origin is listed, by name, in a user's ~/**.shosts** file. When the destination host receives a connection request, it knows the source machine only by IP address. It uses DNS to convert the IP address to a hostname, which is then compared to the appropriate file. **netstat**, **tcpd**, **sendmail**, **sshd**, X Windows, and **ftpd** all do reverse mappings to get hostnames from IP addresses.

It is important that A records match their corresponding PTR records. Mismatched and missing PTR records cause authentication failures that can slow your system to a crawl. This problem is annoying in itself; it can also facilitate denial of service attacks against any application that requires the reverse mapping to match the A record.

MX records

The mail system uses mail exchanger records to route mail more efficiently. An MX record preempts the destination of a message, in most cases directing it to a mail hub at the recipient's site rather than to the recipient's own workstation.

The format of an MX record is

name [ttl] IN MX *preference host ...*

Two examples are shown below, one for a host that receives its own mail unless it is down, and one for a host that can't receive mail at all:

```
piper      IN   MX    10 piper
           IN   MX    20 mailhub
           IN   MX    50 boulder.colorado.edu.
xterm1     IN   MX    10 mailhub
           IN   MX    20 anchor
           IN   MX    50 boulder.colorado.edu.
```

Hosts with low preference values are tried first: 0 is the most desirable, and 65,535 is as bad as it gets. In this example, mail addressed to bob@xterm1 would be sent to mailhub if it were accessible, to anchor as a second choice, and if both mailhub and anchor were down, to boulder. Note that boulder's name must be fully qualified since it is not a member of the default zone (here, "cs.colorado.edu.").

The list of preferences and hosts can all be on the same line, but separate lines are easier to read. Leave numeric "space" between preference values so you don't have to renumber if you need to squeeze in a new destination.

MX records are useful in many situations:

- When you have a central mail hub
- When the destination host is down
- When the destination host isn't directly reachable from the Internet
- When the destination host doesn't speak SMTP
- When the local sysadmin knows where mail should be sent better than your correspondents do

In the first of these situations, mail is routed to the mail hub, the machine where most users read mail. In the second case, mail is routed to a nearby host and forwarded when the destination comes back up.

Hosts that are not directly accessible from the (public) Internet can still have MX records. Such MX-only hosts might be machines behind a firewall, domain names hosted by an ISP or hosting service, or machines that are not turned on all the time. **sendmail** can't connect to the destination host, but it can get the mail closer by connecting to one of the destination's MX hosts.

The final and most important reason to use MX records is that the local sysadmins probably know the mail architecture much better than your correspondents. They need to have the final say on how your site channels its mail stream.

Every host that the outside world knows about should have MX records. For minor hosts, one or two alternates are enough. A major host should have several records. For example, the following set of records might be appropriate for a site at which each host sends and receives its own mail:

- One for the host itself, as first choice
- A departmental mail hub as second choice
- A central mail hub for the domain or parent domain as a backup

The domain itself should have an MX record to a mail hub machine so that mail to *user@domain* will work. Of course, this configuration does require that user names be unique across all machines in the domain. For example, to be able to send mail to evi@cs.colorado.edu, we need a machine called cs, MX records in cs.colorado.edu, or perhaps both.

```
cs          IN   MX   10 mailhub.cs.colorado.edu.
            IN   MX   20 anchor.cs.colorado.edu.
            IN   MX   50 boulder.colorado.edu.
```

A machine that accepts mail for another host must list that other host in its **sendmail** configuration files; see page 574 for a discussion of **sendmail**'s use_cw_file feature and the file **local-host-names**.

Wild card MX records are also sometimes seen in the DNS database:

```
*              IN   MX   10 mailhub.cs.colorado.edu.
```

At first glance, this record seems like it would save lots of typing and add a default MX record for all hosts. But wild card records don't quite work as you might expect. They match anything in the *name* field of a resource record that is *not* already listed as an explicit name in another resource record.

Thus, you *cannot* use a star to set a default value for all your hosts. But perversely, you can use it to set a default value for names that are not your hosts. This setup causes lots of mail to be sent to your hub only to be rejected because the hostname matching the star really does not belong to your domain. Ergo, avoid wild card MX records.

CNAME records

CNAME records assign additional names to a host. These nicknames are commonly used either to associate a function with a host or to shorten a long hostname. The real name is sometimes called the canonical name (hence, "CNAME").

Some examples:

```
ftp            IN   CNAME  anchor
kb             IN   CNAME  kibblesnbits
```

The format of a CNAME record is

nickname [ttl] IN CNAME *hostname*

When the DNS software encounters a CNAME record, it stops its query for the nickname and switches to the real name. If a host has a CNAME record, other records (A, MX, NS, etc.) for that host must refer to its real name, not its nickname.[7] For example, the following lines are OK:

```
colo-gw        IN   A      128.138.243.25
moogie         IN   CNAME  colo-gw
www            IN   CNAME  moogie
```

However, assigning an address or mail priority (with an A or MX record) to either www or moogie in this example would be wrong.

CNAME records can nest eight deep in BIND. That is, a CNAME record can point to another CNAME, and that CNAME can point to a third CNAME, and so on, up to seven times; the eighth target must be the real hostname with an A record.

Usually you can avoid CNAMEs altogether by just using A records for the host's real name and its nicknames.

---

7. This rule for CNAMEs was explicitly relaxed for DNSSEC, which adds digital signatures to each DNS resource record set. The RRSIG record for the CNAME refers to the nickname.

The CNAME hack

*See page 287 for
more information
about CIDR.*

CNAMEs are also used to torture the existing semantics of DNS into supporting reverse zones for networks that are not subnetted on a byte boundary. Before CIDR addressing was commonplace, most subnet assignments were on byte boundaries or within the same organization, and the reverse delegations were easy to manage. For example, if the class B network 128.138 was subnetted into a set of class C-like networks, each subnet would make a tidy package for the in-addr.arpa domain. The reverse zone for the 243 subnet would be 243.138.128.in-addr.arpa.

But what happens if the 243 subnet is further divided into, say, four pieces as a /26 network? If all four pieces are assigned to the same organization, there is actually no problem. The four subnets can still share a single file that contains all their PTR records. However, if the 243 subnet is assigned to an ISP that wants to delegate each /26 network to a different customer, a more complicated solution is necessary. The ISP must either maintain the reverse records on behalf of each client, or it must find a way to take the third octet of the IP address (243 in this case) and divide it into four different pieces that can be delegated independently.

When an administrative boundary falls in the middle of a byte, you have to be sneaky. You must also work closely with the domain above or below you. The trick is this: for each possible host address in the natural in-addr.arpa zone, add a CNAME that deflects the lookup to a zone controlled by the owner of the appropriate subnet. This scheme makes for messy zone files on the parent, but it does let you delegate authority to the actual users of each subnet.

Here is the scheme in gory detail. The parent organization (in our case, the ISP) creates CNAME records for each possible IP address with an extra fake component (dot-separated chunk) that represents the subnet. For example, in the /26 scenario just described, the first quarter of the addresses would have a "0-63" component, the second quarter would have a "64-127" component, and so on. Here's what it looks like:

```
$ORIGIN 243.138.128.in-addr.arpa.
1          IN   CNAME   1.0-63
2          IN   CNAME   2.0-63
...
63         IN   CNAME   63.0-63
64         IN   CNAME   64.64-127
65         IN   CNAME   65.64-127
...
```

To delegate the 0-63 piece of the reverse zone to the customer that has been assigned that subnet, we'd add the following NS records:

```
0-63       IN   NS      ns1.customer1.com.
0-63       IN   NS      ns2.customer1.com.
...
```

customer1.com's site would have a zone file that contained the reverse mappings for the 0-63.243.138.128.in-addr.arpa zone.

For example,

```
1              IN   PTR     host1.customer1.com.
2              IN   PTR     host2.customer1.com.
...
```

By adding this extra component, we create a new "cut" at which to perform delegation. When someone looks up the reverse mapping for 128.138.243.1, for example, the CNAME record at 1.243.138.128.in-addr.arpa refocuses the search to the name 1.0-63.243.138.128.in-addr.arpa, and that name is controlled by the customer.

The customer's files are clean; it's only the ISP that must deal with an inelegant configuration mess. But things can get even more complicated. Customer1 could itself be an ISP that wants to further subdivide its addresses. But that's OK: BIND supports CNAME chains up to 8 links long, and since a byte has only eight bits, we can never run out. CNAME chains are discouraged but not forbidden in the RFCs; they do slow down name resolution since each link in a CNAME chain causes the link to be followed and a new query for the target to be initiated.

Early in the life of the CNAME hack, the $GENERATE command (see page 405) was added to BIND's repertoire to facilitate the creation of resource records in the parent zone. For example, the following lines produce the records for the first subnet:

```
$ORIGIN 243.138.128.in-addr.arpa.
$GENERATE 0-63 $ CNAME $.0-63
0-63           NS  ns1.customer1.com.
0-63           NS  ns2.customer1.com.
```

The $ in the $GENERATE command iterates from 0 to 63 and creates 64 different CNAME records. The other three /26 networks would be handled similarly.

LOC records

LOC records are defined in RFC1819.

An LOC record describes the geographic location and, optionally, the physical size (diameter) of a DNS object. LOC records currently have no effect on the technical operation of the Internet, and no standard software looks for them. However, a number of interesting potential uses for the information have been suggested, including route tracing and optimization, automated mapping, and network research.

The format is

name [ttl] IN LOC lat lon [alt [size [hp [vp]]]]

The latitude and longitude are given as space-separated degrees, minutes, and seconds followed by N, S, E, or W. Seconds can be omitted; if they are, minutes can also be omitted.

The other fields are all specified in centimeters (no suffix) or meters (m). *alt* is the object's altitude, *size* is the diameter of the object's bounding sphere, *hp* is the horizontal precision of the measurement, and *vp* is the vertical precision. The default size is one meter, and the default horizontal and vertical precisions are 10 meters and 10 kilometers, respectively.

Here is an example for caida.org in San Diego, California:

```
caida.org.     IN   LOC   32 53 01 N 117 14 25 W 107m 30m 18m 15m
```

Many of the graphical visualization tools written by CAIDA (the Cooperative Association for Internet Data Analysis) require latitude and longitude data, and sites are encouraged to include it in their DNS. However, if you are paranoid and run a high-visibility server or ISP, you may not want the general public to know the exact location of your machines. In such situations, we recommend that you use inexact values with a large horizontal precision parameter. Imprecise LOC records are still of value to the network research folks but offer some anonymity.

SRV records

An SRV record specifies the location of services within a domain. For example, the SRV record allows you to query a remote domain directly and ask for the name of its FTP server. Until now, you mostly had to guess. To contact the FTP server for a remote domain, you had to hope that the remote sysadmins had followed the current custom and added a CNAME for "ftp" to their server's DNS records.

SRV records make more sense than CNAMEs for this application and are certainly a better way for sysadmins to move services around and control their use. However, SRV records must be explicitly sought and parsed by clients, so it will be a while before their effects are really felt. They are used extensively by Windows.

SRV records resemble generalized MX records with fields that let the local DNS administrator steer and load-balance connections from the outside world. The format is

```
service.proto.name [ttl] IN SRV pri wt port target
```

where *service* is a service defined in the IANA assigned numbers database (see www.iana.org/numbers.htm), *proto* is either tcp or udp, *name* is the domain to which the SRV record refers, *pri* is an MX-style priority, *wt* is a weight used for load balancing among several servers, *port* is the port on which the service runs, and *target* is the hostname of the server that provides this service. The A record of the target is usually returned automatically with the answer to a SRV query. A value of 0 for the *wt* parameter means that no special load balancing should be done. A value of "." for the target means that the service is not run at this site.

Here is an example snitched from RFCs 2052 and 2782 (in which SRV is defined) and adapted for the cs.colorado.edu domain:

```
_ftp._tcp          SRV  0  0  21  ftp-server.cs.colorado.edu.

; don't allow finger anymore (target = .)
_finger._tcp       SRV  0  0  79  .

; 1/4 of the connections to old box, 3/4 to the new one
_ssh._tcp          SRV  0  1  22  old-slow-box.cs.colorado.edu.
                   SRV  0  3  22  new-fast-box.cs.colorado.edu.

; main server on port 80, backup on new box, port 8000
```

```
_http._tcp        SRV  0  0  80  www-server.cs.colorado.edu.
                  SRV  10 0  8000 new-fast-box.cs.colorado.edu.

; so both http://www.cs.colo... and http://cs.colo... work
_http._tcp.www    SRV  0  0  80  www-server.cs.colorado.edu.
                  SRV  10 0  8000 new-fast-box.cs.colorado.edu.

; block all other services (target = .)
*._tcp            SRV  0  0  0  .
*._udp            SRV  0  0  0  .
```

This example illustrates the use of both the weight parameter (for SSH) and the priority parameter (HTTP). Both SSH servers will be used, with the work being split between them. The backup HTTP server will only be used when the principal server is unavailable. The **finger** service is not included, nor are other services that are not explicitly mentioned. The fact that the **finger** daemon does not appear in DNS does not mean that it is not running, just that you can't locate the server through DNS.

WKS (well-known services) was an earlier service-related DNS record that did not catch on. Instead of pointing you to the host that provided a particular service for a domain, it listed the services provided by a particular host. WKS seems sort of useless and was also deemed a security risk. It was not widely adopted.

TXT records

A TXT record adds arbitrary text to a host's DNS records. For example, we have a TXT record that identifies our site:

```
          IN   TXT  "University of CO, Boulder Campus, CS Dept"
```

This record directly follows the SOA and NS records for the "cs.colorado.edu." zone and so inherits the *name* field from them.

The format of a TXT record is

```
name [ttl] IN TXT info ...
```

All *info* items must be quoted. You can use a single quoted string or multiple strings that are individually quoted. Be sure the quotes are balanced—missing quotes wreak havoc with your DNS data because all the records between the missing quote and the next occurrence of a quote mysteriously disappear.

Many administrators use TXT records to publish the names of machines at their sites from which legitimate email originates. Other sites can use these so-called SPF (Sender Policy Framework) records to help identify and eliminate spam. The SPF information lives inside the *info* part of the TXT records; there is no separate DNS record type for SPF.

Here are a couple of examples:

```
sendmail.com.   IN  TXT  "v=spf1 ip4:209.246.26.40 ip4:63.211.143.38 ip4:
      209.246.26.36 ip4:209.246.26.12 ip4:209.246.26.18 ip4:209.246.26.10 ~all"
example.com.    IN  TXT  "v=spf1 MX PTR -all"
```

In the first line, the domain sendmail.com is listing the IP addresses of its mail servers. If mail claims to have originated from sendmail.com but is not being sent from a machine whose IP address is included in the SPF record list, then the mail is forged and should be dropped. The second line requires that the machine sending the email have a matching MX and PTR record in the DNS in order to be validated.

The clause v=spf1 refers to the version of the SPF protocol; only version 1 is currently defined or implemented. Several mail transport agents (including **sendmail**, Postfix, and **exim**) support SPF processing. There are many other bells and whistles that can be invoked through SPF records; see page 599 for a more complete discussion.

TXT records have no intrinsic order. If you use several of them to add a paragraph of information to your DNS, they may all be scrambled by the time **named** and UDP are done with them.

IPv6 resource records

See Chapter 12 for a more detailed discussion of IPv6.

IPv6 is a new version of the IP protocol. It has spent over 10 years in the specification process and still isn't done.[8] IPv6 was originally motivated by a perceived need for more IP network addresses. However, the stopgap solutions to this problem—CIDR, NAT, and stricter control of addresses—have been so successful that a mass migration to IPv6 has turned out to be not as essential as originally envisioned. The adoption of IPv6 is now being driven by Asia, where IPv4 addresses are spread more thinly. The next generation of cell phones, which may have IP addresses, might also help tip the scales in favor of IPv6.

Earlier proposals for IPv6 support in DNS went to great lengths to support shared ownership of IPv6 addresses with the A6 and DNAME resource records. Although these record types made address renumbering easier, they were so complicated that the IETF has now backed off from its original plan in favor of the much simpler AAAA records for forward mapping and the ip6.arpa domain for reverse mappings. We no longer describe A6 records, bitstrings, or DNAME records in this book. If you are curious, you can refer to previous editions or to the RFCs for details on how they were intended to work.

IPv6 forward records

The format of an AAAA record is

    hostname [*ttl*] IN AAAA *ipaddr*

For example:

    anchor   IN   AAAA   3ffe:8050:201:9:a00:20ff:fe81:2b32

Each colon-separated chunk is 4 hex digits, with leading zeros usually omitted. Two adjacent colons stand for "enough zeros to fill out the 128 bits for a complete IPv6 address." An address can contain at most one such double colon.

---

8. Tony Li, an active member of the IETF community, once described IPv6 as "too little, too soon."

IPv6 reverse records

*See page 396 for a
discussion of the IPv4
version of PTR records.*

In IPv4, reverse mappings live in the in-addr.arpa domain and forward mappings live in the other branches of the domain tree (under com or edu, for example). In IPv6, the reverse mapping information corresponding to an AAAA address record is a PTR record in the ip6.arpa[9] top-level domain.

The "nibble" format reverses an AAAA address record by expanding each colon-separated address chunk to the full 4 hex digits and then reversing the order of those digits and tacking on ip6.arpa at the end. For example, the PTR record that corresponds to our sample AAAA record for anchor would be

```
2.3.b.2.1.8.e.f.f.f.0.2.0.0.a.0.9.0.0.0.1.0.2.0.0.5.0.8.e.f.f.3.ip6.arpa PTR anchor.cs.colorado.edu.
```

It certainly doesn't look friendly for a sysadmin to have to type or debug or even read. Of course, in your actual DNS zone files, the $ORIGIN statement would hide some of the complexity.

IPv6 is still young, at least from the deployment point of view. The registries are starting to assign addresses, and the process will become smoother with experience. Some of the root name servers recently (2004) started advertising IPv6 addresses. Questions remain about default behavior. For example, if a name has an IPv4 address but no IPv6 address and is queried for an AAAA record, should it say "no such record" or should it return the IPv4 A record?

Security-related records

The DNSSEC-related resource records (DNSKEY, DS, RRSIG, and NSEC) comprise a major topic of their own. We discuss these records in the section on DNS security that begins on page 451. These records are fundamentally different from most in that they are typically generated with software tools rather than being typed in by hand.

Commands in zone files

Now that we have looked at all the basic resource records, let's look at the commands that can be embedded in a zone file. These commands are really just parser directives that help make zone files more readable and easier to maintain. The commands either influence the way that the parser interprets subsequent records or they expand into multiple DNS records themselves. Once a zone file has been read in and interpreted, none of these commands remain a part of the zone's data (at least, not in their original forms).

There are four commands:

```
$ORIGIN domain-name
$INCLUDE filename [origin]
$TTL default-ttl
$GENERATE lots-of-args
```

---

9. The IPv6 reverse branch of the naming tree was originally called ip6.int.

Commands must start in the first column and occur on a line by themselves. The $ORIGIN and $TTL commands are specified in the RFCs and should be understood by all name servers; $INCLUDE and $GENERATE were originally BIND specific but have been picked up by some of the other DNS implementations.

As the name server reads a zone file, it adds the default domain (or "origin") to any names that are not already fully qualified. The origin is initially set to the domain name specified in the corresponding zone statement in the name server configuration file. However, you can set the origin by hand within a zone file by using the $ORIGIN directive.

The use of relative names where fully qualified names are expected saves lots of typing and makes zone files much easier to read. For example, the reverse records for a subnetted class B site might all be in one zone file, with $ORIGIN statements setting the context for each subnet. A statement such as

    $ORIGIN 243.138.128.in-addr.arpa

could precede the records for the 243 subnet.

Many sites use the $INCLUDE directive in their zone database files to separate overhead records from data records, to separate logical pieces of a zone file, or to keep cryptographic keys in a file with restricted permissions. The syntax of the $INCLUDE directive is

    $INCLUDE *filename [origin]*

The specified file is read into the database at the point of the $INCLUDE directive; if an *origin* is specified, an $ORIGIN directive precedes the contents of the file being read. If *filename* is not an absolute path, it is interpreted relative to the home directory of the running name server.

The $TTL directive sets a default value for the time-to-live field of the records that follow it. It should precede the SOA record for the zone. The default units for the $TTL value are seconds, but you can also qualify numbers with h for hours, m for minutes, d for days, or w for weeks. For example, the lines

    $TTL 86400
    $TTL 24h
    $TTL 1d

all set the $TTL to one day.

$GENERATE, a relatively new construct, provides a simple way to generate a series of similar records. It serves mostly to help with generating RFC2317-style classless in-addr.arpa mappings (the CNAME hack for reverse zone files) for cases in which the boundaries of administrative authority do not match the boundaries of bytes in an IP address.

The format of the $GENERATE directive is

    $GENERATE *start-stop/[step] lhs type rhs [comment]*

and the generated lines are of the form

```
lhs type rhs
```

The *start* and *stop* fields specify the range of values for a single numeric iterator. One line is generated for each value in the interval. The iterator value is incorporated into *lhs* (left-hand side) and *rhs* (right-hand side) with the $ character. If you also specify a *step*, the iteration is by *step*-size increments. *type* is the record type. BIND 9 supports $GENERATE for the record types CNAME, PTR, NS, DNAME, A, and AAAA. See page 401 for an example.

Glue records: links between zones

Each zone stands alone with its own set of data files, name servers, and clients. But zones need to be connected to form a coherent hierarchy: cs.colorado.edu is a part of colorado.edu, and we need some kind of DNS linkage between them.

Since DNS referrals occur only from parent domains to child domains, it is not necessary for a name server to know anything about the domains (or more accurately, zones) above it in the DNS hierarchy. However, the servers of a parent domain must know the IP addresses of the name servers for all of its subdomains. In fact, *only* the name servers known to the parent zone can be returned as referrals in response to external queries.

In DNS terms, the parent zone needs to contain the NS records for each delegated zone. Since NS records are written in terms of hostnames rather than IP addresses, the parent server must also have a way to resolve the hostnames, either by making a normal DNS query (if this does not create a dependency loop) or by having copies of the appropriate A records.

There are two ways in which you can meet this requirement: by including the necessary records directly or by using stub zones.

With the first method, you simply include the necessary NS and A records in the parent zone. For example, the colorado.edu zone file could contain these records:

```
; subdomain information

cs            IN   NS    ns.cs.colorado.edu.
              IN   NS    piper.cs.colorado.edu.
              IN   NS    ns.atrust.com.
ee            IN   NS    ns.ee.colorado.edu.
              IN   NS    ns.cs.colorado.edu.

; glue records

ns.cs         IN   A     128.138.243.151
piper.cs      IN   A     128.138.204.4
ns.ee         IN   A     128.138.200.1
```

The "foreign" A records are called glue records because they don't really belong in this zone. They're only reproduced here to connect the new domain to the naming tree. Missing or incorrect glue records leave part of your namespace inaccessible, and users trying to reach it get "host unknown" errors.

It is a common error to include glue records for hostnames that don't need them. For example, ns.atrust.com in the example above can be resolved with a normal DNS query. An A record would initially just be unnecessary, but it could later become downright misleading if ns.atrust.com's address were to change. The rule of thumb is to include A records only for hosts that are within the current domain or any of its subdomains. Current versions of BIND ignore unnecessary glue records and log their presence as an error.

The scheme just described is the standard way of connecting zones, but it requires the child to keep in touch with the parent and tell the parent about any changes or additions to its name server fleet. Since parent and child zones are often run by different sites, updates are often a tedious manual task that requires coordination across administrative boundaries. A corollary is that in the real world, this type of configuration is often out of date.

The second way to maintain links is to use stub zones. A stub zone is essentially the same thing as a slave zone, but it includes only the zone's NS records. Automatically updating the stub zone eliminates the need for communication between parent and child. An important caveat is that stub zones must be configured identically on both the master and slave servers *of the parent zone*. It might just be easiest to keep in touch manually with your parent domain and to verify its configuration at least a couple of times a year (especially if it is local).

You can use the **dig** command to see which of your servers your parent domain is currently advertising. First run

```
$ dig parent-domain ns
```

to determine the name servers for your parent domain. Pick one and run

```
$ dig @name-server.parent-domain child-domain ns
```

to see your list of public name servers. Here is an actual example with some of **dig**'s wordiness deleted:

```
$ dig colorado.edu ns
;;      ...
;; ANSWER SECTION:
colorado.edu.          5h9m22s IN NS   ns1.westnet.net.
colorado.edu.          5h9m22s IN NS   boulder.colorado.edu.
colorado.edu.          5h9m22s IN NS   cujo.colorado.edu.

$ dig @boulder.colorado.edu cs.colorado.edu ns
;;; ANSWER SECTION:
cs.colorado.edu.       6H IN NS        cs.colorado.edu.
cs.colorado.edu.       6H IN NS        huizil.cs.colorado.edu.
cs.colorado.edu.       6H IN NS        anyns.pch.net.
cs.colorado.edu.       6H IN NS        pacifier.com.
```

Only four servers for the cs.colorado.edu domain are visible from the outside world. A **dig** from within the department yields a different list:

```
;; ANSWER SECTION:
cs.colorado.edu.        2H IN NS        cs.colorado.edu.
cs.colorado.edu.        2H IN NS        moet.cs.colorado.edu.
cs.colorado.edu.        2H IN NS        piper.cs.colorado.edu.
cs.colorado.edu.        2H IN NS        anchor.cs.colorado.edu.
cs.colorado.edu.        2H IN NS        vulture.cs.colorado.edu.
```

Note that the TTL values vary (2 hours vs. 6 hours) depending on whether a query comes from inside or outside the department. That's because BIND's view statement has been used to define internal and external views of the data; see page 438. (Both values are on the short side; a few days to a week would be a better choice.)

One situation in which stub zones are very useful is when your internal network uses RFC1918 private IP address space and you need to keep the RFC1918 delegations in sync. The example from isc.org starting on page 444 uses stub zones extensively.

A couple of stub zone subtleties (stubtleties?) are worth mentioning:

- Stub zones are not authoritative copies of the zone's data, and stub servers should not be listed among the zone's NS records.

- Since stub servers are not listed in NS records, they are not notified automatically when the zone's data changes. Stub servers simply wait for the zone to be updated at the end of the refresh interval specified in the zone's SOA record. If this interval is long, it can potentially result in transitory lame delegations (see page 475).

- Theoretically, it's of no use for a name server to have copies of a zone's NS records if it cannot also obtain the matching A records. However, the name server can bootstrap itself by using the master's IP address from its configuration file (the masters clause of the zone statement, see page 434).

- Why limit yourself to NS records? Why not just be a secondary server for the subdomains? This works, too. However, if every server of the parent domain is also a server of a child domain, then no referrals will ever be made to downstream servers. The parent domain's servers will be providing all the DNS service for the subdomain. Perhaps this is what you want, and perhaps not.

We have now covered most of the background information that applies to the Domain Name System generally and to its database. In the next section, we continue our coverage of DNS with configuration details specific to the BIND implementation.

15.8 THE BIND SOFTWARE

BIND, the Berkeley Internet Name Domain system, is an open source software package from ISC, the Internet Systems Consortium, which implements the DNS protocol for Linux, UNIX, Mac OS, and Windows systems.

Versions of BIND

There have been three main flavors of BIND: BIND 4, BIND 8, and BIND 9. BIND 4 has been around since the late 1980s (roughly corresponding to the release of RFCs 1034 and 1035). BIND 8 was released in 1997, and BIND 9 in mid-2000. There is no BIND 5, 6, or 7; BIND 8 was such a significant update that the authors felt it merited a version number twice as big as the old one.[10] Well, not really... BIND 8 was released with 4.4BSD (the Berkeley Software Distribution of UNIX), for which all version numbers were raised to 8. **sendmail** also skipped a few numbers and went to version 8 at the same time.

BIND 8 incorporated numerous technical advances that improved efficiency, robustness, and security. BIND 9 raises the ante even further with multiprocessor support, thread-safe operation, real security (public key cryptography), IPv6 support, incremental zone transfers, and a host of other features. A new data structure (at least, new to BIND), the red-black tree, stores zone data in memory. BIND 9 is a complete redesign and reimplementation. It isolates the OS-specific parts of the code, making it easier to port BIND to non-UNIX systems. The internals of BIND 9 are significantly different, but its configuration procedure remains the same. We cover only BIND 9 in this book.

Finding out what version you have

It often doesn't seem to occur to vendors to document which version of an external software package they have included with their systems, so you might have to do some sleuthing to find out exactly what software you are dealing with. In the case of BIND, you can sometimes determine the version number with a sneaky query from **dig**, a command that comes with BIND. The command

    $ dig @*server* **version.bind txt chaos**

returns the version number unless someone has decided to withhold that information by changing it in BIND's configuration file. For example, the command works on isc.org:

    $ dig @ns-ext.isc.org version.bind txt chaos
    version.bind.   0S CHAOS TXT   "9.4.0a0"

But it doesn't work on cs.colorado.edu:

    $ dig @mroe.cs.colorado.edu version.bind txt chaos
    version.bind.   0S CHAOS TXT "wouldn't you like to know..."

Some sites configure BIND to conceal its version number on the theory that this provides some degree of "security through obscurity." We don't really endorse this practice, but it might help fend off some of the script kiddies. See page 424 for a more detailed discussion of this topic.

---

10. Who says marketing and engineering can't get along?

The output from this query includes "0S". The 0 is the digit zero and represents the TTL. The S stands for seconds, but that is the default for TTLs and is not usually printed. Perhaps we should report this as a bug—at first glance it looks like OS for operating system.

The IETF is busy standardizing the data in this odd CHAOS-class zone and generalizing it so that other implementations can use this convention, too. Many already do so and let the variable name remain version.bind; others are offended that the name includes "bind." Since the IETF is still arguing about what the variable names should be, ISC has implemented all the candidates in their current release. For example, you can also query the CHAOS class for hostname.bind or the more generic id.server.

See Chapter 10 for more information about syslog.

You can also usually tell what BIND version you have by inspecting the log files in **/var/log**. The BIND server daemon, **named**, logs its version number to syslog (facility "daemon") as it starts up. **grep** for lines like this:

```
Feb 23 00:25:13 senna named[433]: starting BIND 9.4.0a0 -c
    /var/named/named.ns-ext.conf
```

If **named** is installed but your system does not normally start it at boot time, just run **named -v** and it will output its version number and exit.

Table 15.7 shows the versions of BIND that are included with our example distributions. On Debian and Ubuntu, you have your choice of a **bind** package that installs BIND 8 and a **bind9** package that installs BIND 9. Versions earlier than 9.3.1 or 8.4.6 have known security problems; forget BIND 4. Using the current releases is the safest.

Table 15.7   Versions of BIND on our example systems

System	OS vers	BIND vers
ISC	–	9.4.0b
RHEL	4.3	9.2.4 via rpm
Fedora	FC5	9.3.2
SUSE	10.2	9.3.2
Debian	3.2b	8.4.6 or 9.2.4
Ubuntu	6.06	8.4.6 or 9.3.2

Most Linux distributors back-port security fixes to older releases.

Components of BIND

The BIND system has three components:

- A name server daemon called **named** that answers queries
- Library routines that resolve host queries by contacting the servers of the DNS distributed database
- Command-line interfaces to DNS: **nslookup**, **dig**, and **host**

In DNS parlance, a daemon like **named** (or the machine on which it runs) is called a "name server," and the client code that contacts it is called a "resolver." We briefly discuss the function of each component below but postpone the actual configuration of BIND until page 420.

named: the BIND name server

named answers queries about hostnames and IP addresses. If **named** doesn't know the answer to a query, it asks other servers and caches their responses. **named** also performs "zone transfers" to copy data among the servers of a domain. (Recall that a "zone" is essentially a domain minus its subdomains. Name servers deal with zones, but "domain" is often used where "zone" is really meant.)

Name servers can operate in several different modes. The distinctions among them fall along several axes, so the final categorization is often not very tidy. To make things even more confusing, a single server can play different roles with respect to different zones. Table 15.8 lists some of the adjectives used to describe name servers. Indented entries are loosely classified under their unindented headings.

Table 15.8   A name server taxonomy

Type of server	Description
authoritative	An official representative of a zone
master	The primary server for a zone; gets data from a disk file
slave	Copies its data from the master (also called a secondary server)
stub	Similar to a slave, but copies only name server data (not host data)
distribution	A server that's visible[a] only inside a domain; (aka "stealth server")
nonauthoritative[b]	Answers a query from cache; doesn't know if the data is still valid
caching	Caches data from previous queries; usually has no local zones
forwarder	Performs queries on behalf of many clients; builds a large cache
recursive	Queries on your behalf until it returns either an answer or an error
nonrecursive	Refers you to another server if it can't answer a query

a. A distribution server can be visible to anyone who knows its IP address.
b. Strictly speaking, "nonauthoritative" is an attribute of a DNS query response, not a server.

These categorizations are based on a name server's source of data (authoritative, caching, master, slave), on the type of data saved (stub), on the query path (forwarder), on the completeness of answers handed out (recursive, nonrecursive), and finally, on the visibility of the server (distribution). The next few sections provide some additional details on the most important of these distinctions; the others are described elsewhere in this chapter.

Authoritative and caching-only servers

Master, slave, and caching-only servers are distinguished by two characteristics: where the data comes from and whether the server is authoritative for the domain.

Each zone has one master name server. The master server keeps the official copy of the zone's data on disk. The system administrator changes the zone's data by editing the master server's data files.

See page 447 for more information about zone transfers.

A slave server gets its data from the master server through a "zone transfer" operation. A zone can have several slave name servers and *must* have at least one. A stub server is a special kind of slave that loads only the NS (name server) records from the master. See page 434 for an explanation of why you might want this behavior. It's fine for the same machine to be both a master server for your zones and a slave server for other zones. Such cooperation usually makes for good DNS neighbors.

A caching-only name server loads the addresses of the servers for the root domain from a startup file and accumulates the rest of its data by caching answers to the queries it resolves. A caching-only name server has no data of its own and is not authoritative for any zone, except perhaps the localhost zone.

An authoritative answer from a name server is "guaranteed" to be accurate; a non-authoritative answer might be out of date. However, a very high percentage of non-authoritative answers are perfectly correct. Master and slave servers are authoritative for their own zones, but not for information they have cached about other domains. Truth be told, even authoritative answers can be inaccurate if a sysadmin changes the master server's data but forgets to propagate the changes (e.g., doesn't change the data's serial number).

A zone's master server should be located on a machine that is stable, does not have many users, is relatively secure, and is on an uninterruptible power supply. There should be at least two slaves, one of which is off-site. On-site slaves should live on different networks and different power circuits. When name service stops, all normal network access stops, too.

Although they are not authoritative, caching-only servers can reduce the latency seen by your users and the amount of DNS traffic on your internal networks. Consider putting a caching-only server on each subnet. At most sites, desktop machines typically go through a caching server to resolve queries about hosts on the Internet.

In BIND 4 and BIND 8, it wasn't a good idea to use a single name server as your authoritative server for your own zones and as a caching server for your users. Each **named** ran with a single in-memory database, and cross-contamination could occur if memory was tight and cached data mixed with authoritative data. BIND 9 has eliminated this problem, so mix away. However, security and general DNS hygiene still argue for separating the functions of serving your authoritative data to the world from serving the world's data to your users.

Recursive and nonrecursive servers

Name servers are either recursive or nonrecursive. If a nonrecursive server has the answer to a query cached from a previous transaction or is authoritative for the domain to which the query pertains, it provides an appropriate response. Otherwise, instead of returning a real answer, it returns a referral to the authoritative servers of another domain that are more likely to know the answer. A client of a nonrecursive server must be prepared to accept and act on referrals.

Although nonrecursive servers may seem lazy, they usually have good reason not to take on extra work. Root servers and top-level domain servers are all nonrecursive, but at over 10,000 queries per second we can excuse them for cutting corners.

A recursive server returns only real answers and error messages. It follows referrals itself, relieving clients of this responsibility. In other respects, the basic procedure for resolving a query is essentially the same. For security reasons, an organization's externally accessible name servers should always be nonrecursive.

Resolver libraries *do not* understand referrals; any local name server that clients point to must be recursive.

One side effect of having a name server follow referrals is that its cache acquires information about intermediate domains. On a local network, this caching is often the behavior you want since it allows subsequent lookups from any host on the network to benefit from the name server's previous work. On the other hand, the server for a high-level domain such as com or edu should not save up information requested by a host several domains below it.

Early versions of BIND required source code changes and recompilation to modify a server's recursiveness. This option then moved to a command-line flag (**-r**), and it is now a parameter in the configuration file. A server can even be configured to be recursive for its own clients and nonrecursive for outsiders.

Name servers generate referrals hierarchically. For example, if a server can't supply an address for the host lair.cs.colorado.edu, it refers to the servers for cs.colorado.edu, colorado.edu, edu, or the root domain. A referral must include addresses for the servers of the referred-to domain, so the choice is not arbitrary; the server must refer to a domain for which it already knows the servers.

The longest known domain is generally returned. If the address of lair was not known but the name servers for cs.colorado.edu were known, then those servers' address would be returned. If cs.colorado.edu was unknown but colorado.edu was known, then the addresses of name servers for colorado.edu would be returned, and so on.

Name servers preload their caches from a "hints" file that lists the servers for the root domain. Some referral can always be made, even if it's just "Go ask a root server."

The resolver library

Clients look up hostname mappings by calling the **gethostbyname** family of library routines. The original implementation of **gethostbyname** looked up names in the **/etc/hosts** file. For host mappings to be provided by DNS, these routines must use the resolver library, which knows how to locate and communicate with name servers. The resolver is usually integrated into the standard libraries against which applications are compiled.

Most systems' implementations of **gethostbyname** can draw upon information from several different sources: flat files (such as **/etc/hosts**), DNS, and perhaps a local administrative database system such as NIS. A switch file allows for detailed administrative control over which sources are searched and in what order. See page 479 or *Prioritizing sources of administrative information* on page 523 for specifics. The distribution-specific sections of our DNS coverage present bite-sized treatments of this topic as it pertains to host lookups; they start on page 478.

Applications that use the network are typically linked with a stub resolver library that sends DNS queries to a local caching name server. IPv6 support makes things more complicated, but BIND 9 provides a "lightweight resolver library" and resolver daemon, **lwresd**, for sites that do not need to speak IPv6. The term lightweight may sound like an oxymoron in the context of DNS, but in this instance, it refers to the protocol used between the resolver library and the resolver daemon. If the lwres statement is included in **named**'s configuration file, the name server itself also acts as a lightweight resolver. The resolver daemon currently does not use the name service switch file mentioned above: it looks only to DNS for name resolution.

Shell interfaces to DNS

The BIND software distribution includes the **dig**, **host**, and **nslookup** commands, which provide command-line interfaces for executing DNS queries. They are useful as debugging aids and as tools for extracting information from DNS. Although the commands are similar in function, they are somewhat different in design. See page 473 for more information.

15.9 DESIGNING YOUR DNS ENVIRONMENT

Many factors affect the design of a robust and efficient DNS system for your particular environment: the size of your organization, whether you use RFC1918 private IP addresses on your local network, whether you use DHCP, whether you use Microsoft's active directory, whether your internal network is routed or switched, and where your firewall is in relation to your DNS servers, to name a few. You may find it helpful to split the problem into three parts:

- Managing the namespace hierarchy: subdomains, multiple levels, etc.,
- Serving the authoritative data about your site to the outside world, and
- Providing name lookups for your users.

Namespace management

If your site is small and independent, the use of subdomains is neither necessary nor desirable unless your management requires them for some nontechnical reason. On the other hand, in a medium-sized organization with several independent sysadmin groups, subdomains can reduce the need for site-wide coordination. (Subdomains divided along geographic or departmental lines are most common.) A large organization has little hope of enforcing unique names throughout its site and therefore needs subdomains, perhaps at multiple levels.

The creation of subdomains requires communication and cooperation between the sysadmins responsible for the parent domain and those responsible for the subdomain. At the time the subdomain is delegated and set up, be sure to make a note of who to contact if you want to add, change, or delete servers. Make sure your firewall does not block access to the subdomain's servers if you want the subdomain to be accessible from outside your organization.

If you use subdomains to manage your namespace, run the **doc** (domain obscenity control) tool from **cron** once a week to be sure that your delegations stay synchronized and that you don't inadvertently create lame delegations. The DNS tools section (page 466) describes **doc** and several other tools that help keep DNS healthy.

Authoritative servers

The DNS specifications require at least two authoritative servers for each domain. Master and slave servers are authoritative; caching and stub servers are not. Ideally, a site has multiple authoritative servers, each on a separate network and power circuit. Many sites maintain an authoritative server off-site, often hosted by their ISP. If your ISP does not offer this service, you can purchase it from a DNS service provider or trade with a local firm (ideally, not a competitor) or university.

A few years ago, Microsoft got caught violating the rule of separate networks. They had all three of their authoritative servers on the same subnet, and when the router that connected that subnet to the Internet failed, the servers became unreachable. Two hours later, as cached records expired, microsoft.com and all their other domains dropped off the Internet. The number of queries for Microsoft-related names at the root servers increased to 25% of the total load (10,000 queries/second), up from its typical value of 0.000001%. Problems persisted for a couple of days. When the dust settled, Microsoft had fixed the router and outsourced their DNS service!

Authoritative servers keep their data synchronized by using zone transfers. Use TSIG keys to authenticate and control the zone transfers from your master server to your slave servers. See page 453 for TSIG configuration information.

You may want the query responses provided by your authoritative servers to depend to some extent on who is asking. A query from outside your network might receive one answer, while the same query originating inside your organization would receive a different (more complete) answer. This configuration is called "split DNS" and is implemented at the zone level, not the server level.

Each version of the zone is called a "view," after the view statement with which it is configured in the BIND configuration file. External folks see one view of the data, and internal folks see another. This feature is commonly used to conceal the existence of internal machines from prying eyes and to ensure that machines using RFC1918 private IP addresses do not leak them onto the Internet. Views are tricky to debug, but BIND's extensive logging capabilities, together with clever use of the **dig** command, can help; see page 466 for some hints.

Caching servers

Recursive caching servers answer local users' queries about sites on the Internet. Each computer at your site should have ready access to a local caching server, preferably one that is on the same subnet.

Organizations of a certain size should consider using a hierarchy in which one or more machines are designated as "forwarders" through which the local subnets' caching servers pass their queries. The forwarders thereby develop a cache that is common to multiple subnets.

Depending on the size of your site, forwarders can be independent or arranged in a hierarchy. For example, subnet servers might forward to a departmental server that in turn forwards to a site-wide gateway. The site-wide forwarder caches all names requested by users throughout the site. This configuration minimizes the external bandwidth used for name service and allows all local machines to share one large cache. Forwarders are covered in the configuration section starting on page 427.

If a caching server dies, the network essentially stops working for all the users that were clients of that server. (And your phone starts ringing.) Start your caching name servers with a script that restarts them after a few seconds if they die. Here is an example of a keep-running script from a machine that runs two separate instances of **named**. The script takes a single argument to identify the log file and name server configuration file to use:

```
#!/bin/sh

PATH=/usr/local/sbin:/usr/sbin:/sbin:$PATH
export PATH

trap "" 1
while :; do
    named -f -c /var/named/named.$1.conf >> /var/log/named.$1 2>&1 < /dev/null
    logger "named ($1) restart"
    sleep 15
done
exit
```

The script waits 15 seconds (an arbitrary value) before restarting **named** and runs the **logger** command to submit a syslog entry whenever it has to restart the server.

Security

DNS security is covered in a whole section of its own, starting on page 451. We won't duplicate that discussion here except to remind you that if you use a firewall, be sure that your DNS system does not emit queries to which your firewall blocks the answers. This means essentially that your DNS administrators should have ongoing communication with your security and network administrators. By default, DNS uses UDP with random unprivileged source ports (>1023) for queries; the answers are UDP packets addressed to those same ports.

Summing up

Exhibit B illustrates the design recommended in the previous paragraphs. It shows a two-level forwarding hierarchy, which is overkill for small sites. Adjust the balance between servers that handle outgoing queries and servers that handle incoming queries so that neither group is too loaded

Also note the use of the off-site slave server, which is highly recommended. Companies with multiple offices can designate one location as the master; this location becomes "off site" relative to the rest of the company.

Exhibit B   DNS server architecture

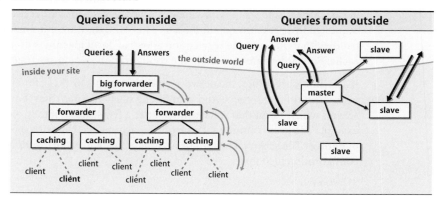

A taxonomy of DNS/BIND chores

See Chapter 17 for more information about distributing files on a network.

Table 15.9 summarizes what must be done, for whom, and how often when you use BIND and DNS. An entry in the "How often" column that includes the word "distribute" means that you do it once per subnet or architecture and then copy the result to the appropriate hosts with a tool such as **rdist** or **rsync**. Alternate rows are shaded to improve readability.

15.10   BIND CLIENT ISSUES

Since each host on the network must be a BIND client, we begin our detailed discussion with client-side chores.

Resolver configuration

Each Linux host on the network has a file called **/etc/resolv.conf** that lists the DNS servers the host should query. If your host gets its IP address and network parameters from a DHCP server, the **/etc/resolv.conf** file should be set up for you automatically. Otherwise, you must edit the file by hand. The format is

```
search domainname ...
nameserver ipaddr
```

Table 15.9   BIND installation and maintenance chores

Chore	For	How often
Obtain domain name	Site	Once
Choose name servers	Site	Once or more
Obtain BIND distribution	Site	Once, but keep current
Configure resolver	Client	Once and distribute
Configure efficient resolver	Client	Each subnet and distribute
Configure services switch	Client	Each architecture and distribute
Start **named** at boot time	Server	Each name server
Set up **named** config file	Server	Each type of server
Configure hints file	Server	Once[a] and distribute to servers
Configure zone files	Master	Once
Update zone files	Master	As needed
Review log files	Log host	At least weekly
Educate users	All hosts	Continuously and repeatedly

a. But must be redone if the root servers change.

Up to three name servers can be listed. Here's a complete example:

```
search cs.colorado.edu colorado.edu ee.colorado.edu
nameserver 128.138.243.151   ; ns
nameserver 128.138.204.4     ; piper
nameserver 128.138.240.1     ; anchor
```

Comments were never defined for the **resolv.conf** file. They are somewhat supported in that anything that is not recognized is ignored. It's safe to put comments at the end of nameserver lines because the parser just looks for an IP address and ignores the rest of the line. Because the search line can contain multiple arguments, comments there could cause problems.

The search line lists the domains to query if a hostname is not fully qualified. If a user issues the command **ssh foo**, for example, the resolver completes the name with the first domain in the search list (in the **resolv.conf** above, cs.colorado.edu) and looks for foo.cs.colorado.edu. If no such name can be found, the resolver also tries foo.colorado.edu and foo.ee.colorado.edu. The number of domains that can be specified in a search directive is resolver-specific; most allow between six and eight.

The servers listed in **resolv.conf** must be recursive since the resolver does not understand referrals. The servers in nameserver lines are contacted in order; as long as the first one continues to answer queries, the others are ignored. If a problem occurs, the query times out and the next name server is tried. Each server is tried in turn, up to four times. The timeout interval increases with every failure.

Most resolvers allow a maximum of three name servers to be listed. If more are provided, they are silently ignored. If a host is itself a name server, it should be listed first in its own **resolv.conf** file. If no name servers are listed, localhost is assumed.

Earlier versions of BIND used the domain directive in **resolv.conf** instead of the search directive. It specified a single domain to add to names that were not fully qualified. We recommend replacing domain directives with search directives. The directives are mutually exclusive, so only one should be present. If you have an older resolver and include both directives in the **resolv.conf** file, the last one listed is used.

Resolver testing

Most Linux distributions will attempt to look up hostnames in DNS by default as long as there is a nameserver line in **/etc/resolv.conf**. The ordering of various sources of hostname information, including DNS, is set in the **/etc/nsswitch.conf** file; see page 479.

After configuring **/etc/resolv.conf** (and assuming that your local network connection is up and running), you should be able to refer to other machines by name rather than by IP address. If you try to reach another local machine and the command just hangs, try referring to the machine by its IP address. If that works, then your DNS configuration is the problem. Verify that the name server IP addresses in **/etc/resolv.conf** are correct and that the servers you point to allow queries from your network (see page 428). **dig** from a working machine can answer these questions.

Impact on the rest of the system

The change from static host tables to DNS creates some potential dependencies in booting and configuration that you need to protect against.

As a host boots, references to hostnames in the startup files might be unresolvable if they are encountered before the network is up. The commands in the startup files will unsuccessfully try to contact DNS. Thanks to the resolver's robustness, they will try multiple times on multiple servers, increasing their timeout period with each attempt. A couple of minutes later, the command needing the hostname will finally fail.

To fix the problem, use only literal IP addresses in the early stages of the boot process. Or, since Linux systems support the simultaneous use of both DNS and **/etc/hosts** by way of the switch file, you can install a **hosts** file that contains the server addresses needed at boot time. Be sure the **hosts** file is checked before DNS so that you don't have to wait for DNS to time out.

15.11 BIND SERVER CONFIGURATION

In this section, we assume that your political chores have been completed. That is, we assume that you have a domain name (possibly a subdomain), have coordinated with the DNS administrator of the parent domain, and have been delegated your address space in the in-addr.arpa reverse tree. You have chosen your master name server and a couple of secondaries, and you have installed BIND.

Hardware requirements

BIND is a memory hog. Its database is kept in memory, so as the cache grows, so does the **named** process. Some of the new features of BIND 9 are also CPU intensive, most notably DNSSEC. To help reduce this burden, BIND 9 is multithreaded and can make full use of multiprocessor systems. BIND 9 also contains configuration options that control **named**'s use of resources.

The best way to determine if a name server machine has enough memory is to run it for a while and watch the size of the **named** process. It takes a week or two to converge on a stable size at which old cache records are expiring at about the same rate that new ones are being inserted. Once stable, the system should not be swapping, and its paging rates should be reasonable.

If your name server runs on a dedicated machine, a good rule of thumb is for the machine to have double the amount of memory consumed by **named** after it has been running for a week. The **top** and **vmstat** commands show memory usage; see *Analyzing memory usage* on page 811 for more details.

Configuration files

The complete configuration for **named** consists of the config file, the root name server hints file, and, for master servers, the zone data files that contain address mappings for each host. **named**'s config file has its own format; all the other files are collections of individual DNS data records that are formatted according to the DNS specification. We discuss the config file in the next two sections. The format of DNS data records is described beginning on page 389.

named's configuration file, **named.conf**, specifies the roles (master, slave, stub or caching-only) of this host and the manner in which it should obtain its copy of the data for each zone it serves. It's also the place where options are specified—both global options related to the overall operation of **named** and server- or zone-specific options that apply to only a portion of the DNS traffic.

The config file consists of a series of statements, each terminated by a semicolon. Tokens are separated by whitespace, which can include newlines. Curly braces are sometimes used for grouping, but only in specific contexts. The format is quite fragile, and a missing semicolon can wreak havoc.

Fortunately, BIND 9 includes a couple of handy tools to check the syntax of the config file (**named-checkconf**) and the zone data files (**named-checkzone**). They look for both errors and omissions. For example, **named-checkzone** will tell you if you've forgotten to include a $TTL directive. Unfortunately, it doesn't catch everything. For example, missing glue records (see page 407) are not reported and cause heavy loads on the root and gTLD servers.

Comments can appear anywhere that whitespace is appropriate. C, C++, and shell-style comments are all understood:

```
/* This is a comment and can span lines. */
// Everything to the end of the line is a comment.
# Everything to the end of the line is a comment.
```

Each statement begins with a keyword that identifies the type of statement. There can be more than one instance of each type of statement, except for options and logging. Statements and parts of statements can also be left out, invoking default behavior for the missing items. Table 15.10 lists the available statements; the Page column points to our discussion of each statement in the upcoming sections. Alternate rows have been shaded to improve readability.

Table 15.10   Statements used in named.conf

Statement	Page	Function
include	423	Interpolates a file (e.g., trusted keys readable only by **named**)
options	423	Sets global name server configuration options and defaults
acl	429	Defines access control lists
key	430	Defines authentication information
trusted-keys	430	Uses preconfigured keys
server	431	Specifies per-server options
masters	432	Defines a list of masters for inclusion in stub and slave zones
logging	432	Specifies logging categories and their destinations
zone	432	Defines a zone of resource records
controls	436	Defines channels used to control the name server with **rndc**
view	438	Defines a view of the zone data
lwres	–	Specifies that the name server should be a resolver too

Before describing these statements and the way they are used to configure **named**, we need to describe a data structure that is used in many of the statements: the address match list. An address match list is a generalization of an IP address that can include the following items:

- An IP address, either v4 or v6 (e.g., 199.165.145.4)
- An IP network specified with a CIDR[11] netmask (e.g., 199.165/16)
- The name of a previously defined access control list (see page 429)
- The name of a cryptographic authentication key
- The ! character to negate things

Address match lists are used as parameters to many statements and options. Some examples:

```
{ ! 1.2.3.13; 1.2.3/24; };
{ 128.138/16; 198.11.16/24; 204.228.69/24; 127.0.0.1; };
```

11. CIDR netmasks are described starting on page 287.

The first of these lists excludes the host 1.2.3.13 but includes the rest of the 1.2.3/24 network; the second defines the networks assigned to the University of Colorado. The braces and final semicolon are not really part of the address match lists but are included for illustration; they would be part of the enclosing statements of which the address match lists are a part.

When an IP address or network is compared to a match list, the list is searched in order until a match is found. This "first match" algorithm makes the ordering of entries important. For example, the first address match list above would not have the desired effect if the two entries were reversed, because 1.2.3.13 would succeed in matching 1.2.3/24 and the negated entry would never be encountered.

Now, on to the statements! Some are short and sweet; others almost warrant a chapter unto themselves.

The include statement

To break up or better organize a large configuration, you can put different portions of the configuration in separate files. Subsidiary files are brought into **named.conf** with an include statement:

```
include "path";
```

If the *path* is relative, then it is interpreted relative to the directory specified in the directory option. A common use of the include statement is to bring in cryptographic keys that should not be world-readable. Rather than closing read access to the whole **named.conf** file, some sites keep keys in files with restricted permissions that only **named** can read. Those files are then included into **named.conf**.

The options statement

The options statement specifies global options, some of which may later be overridden for particular zones or servers. The general format is

```
options {
    option;
    option;
    ...
};
```

If no options statement is present in **named.conf**, default values are used.

BIND 8 had about 50 options, and BIND 9 has over 100. For a complete list, refer to the BIND documentation[12] or to O'Reilly's *DNS and BIND* by Paul Albitz and Cricket Liu (the fourth edition covers both BIND 8 and 9). We have biased our coverage of these options and discuss only the ones whose use we recommend. (We also asked the BIND developers for their suggestions on which options to cover and took their advice.) The default values are listed in square brackets beside each option. For most sites the defaults are just fine. The options are listed in no particular order.

---

12. The file **doc/misc/options** in the distribution contains the syntax for the configuration language and includes all the options.

```
directory "path";                    [directory where the server was started]
```

The directory statement causes **named** to **cd** to the specified directory. Wherever relative pathnames appear in **named**'s configuration files, they are interpreted relative to this directory. The *path* should be an absolute path. Any output files (debugging, statistics, etc.) are also written in this directory.

We recommend putting all BIND-related configuration files (other than **named.conf** and **resolv.conf**) in a subdirectory beneath **/var** (or wherever you keep your configuration files for other programs). We use **/var/named**.

```
version "string";                    [real version number of the server]
hostname "string";                   [real hostname of the server]
server-id "string";                  [none]
```

The version string identifies the version of the name server software running on the server; the hostname string identifies the server itself, as does the server ID string. These options let you lie about the true values. Each puts data into CHAOS-class TXT records where curious onlookers will search for them.

There are two schools of thought on the issue of hiding the version number of the name server software. Some sites believe that their servers will be more vulnerable to attack if hackers can tell what version they are running. Others think that hiding the version information is counterproductive because hackers will try their luck anyway and most newly discovered bugs are present in all versions of the software.

We recommend that you not reset the version string. It is very handy to be able to query your name servers and find out what version they are running (e.g., if you want to know whether your vendor is shipping a current release, or if you need to verify that you have in fact upgraded all your servers to the latest revision).

The hostname and server ID parameters are recent additions motivated by the use of anycast routing to duplicate instances of the root and gTLD servers. For example, there are 20 instances of f.root-servers.net spread around the world, and as a user or sysadmin trying to debug things, you have no idea which of those 20 servers answered (or failed to answer) your query. Querying for hostname.bind in the CHAOS class would tell you which instance of the F root server was answering (as long as the routing had not changed in the meantime). "Server-id" is a politically correct name for hostname.bind, since not all name servers run BIND.

```
notify yes | no;                     [yes]
also-notify servers_ipaddrs;         [empty]
```

If notify is set to yes and this **named** is the master server for one or more zones, **named** automatically notifies those zones' slave servers whenever the corresponding zone database changes. The slave servers can then rendezvous with the master to update their copies of the zone data. You can use the notify option as both a global option and as a zone-specific option. It makes the zone files converge much more quickly after you make changes.

*See page 434 for
more information
about stub zones.*

named normally figures out which machines are slave servers of a zone by looking at
that zone's NS records. If also-notify is specified, a set of additional servers that are
not advertised with NS records can also be notified. This tweak is sometimes necessary when your site has internal servers. Don't also-notify stub servers; they are only
interested in the zone's NS records and can wait for the regular update cycle. The
target of an also-notify must be a list of IP addresses. The localhost reverse zone is a
good place to turn notification off.

```
recursion yes | no;                        [yes]
allow-recursion { address_match_list };    [all hosts]
```

The recursion option specifies whether **named** queries other name servers on behalf of clients, as described on page 413. It's fairly unusual to configure a name server
with recursion off. However, you might want to allow recursion for your own clients
but not for outside queries.

Recursion can be controlled at a finer granularity with the allow-recursion option
and an address list that includes the hosts and networks on whose behalf you are
willing to perform recursive queries.

```
transfer-format one-answer | many-answers;     [many-answers]
```

This option affects the way in which DNS data records are replicated from master
servers to their slaves. The actual transmission of data records used to take place one
record at a time, which is a recipe for sloth and inefficiency. An option to combine
many records into one packet (many-answers) was added in BIND 8.1; it is the
default in BIND 9. If you have a mixed environment, you can specify a transfer format in individual server statements to override the global option. Your mix of servers will dictate whether you choose many-answers globally and override it for specific servers, or vice versa.

```
transfers-in number;            [10]
transfers-out number;           [10 (V9 only)]
transfers-per-ns number;        [2]
transfer-source IP-address;     [system dependent]
```

A large site—one that serves a very large zone (such as com, which currently is over
two gigabytes) or one that serves thousands of zones—may need to tune some of
these zone transfer options.

The transfers-in and transfers-out options limit the number of inbound or outbound zone transfers that can happen concurrently.[13] The transfers-per-ns option
sets the maximum number of inbound zone transfers that can be running concurrently from the same remote server. Large sites may need to increase transfers-in or
transfers-out; be careful that you don't run out of file descriptors for the **named**
process. You should increase transfers-per-ns only if all remote master servers are
willing to handle more than two simultaneous zone transfers. Changing it per server

13. The BIND code enforces a hard-wired limit of 20 for the transfers-in parameter.

with the transfers clause of the server statement is a better way to fine-tune the convergence of slave zones.

The transfer-source option lets you specify the IP address of the interface you want to use for incoming transfers. It must match the address specified in the master's allow-transfer statement.

As with any parameter that you change drastically, you should watch things carefully after changing one of these throttle values to be sure the machine is not thrashing. The log files are your friends.

```
files number;                 [unlimited]
datasize number;              [OS default value, system dependent]
```

The files option sets the maximum number of files the server is allowed to have open concurrently. The default value is as close as possible to the number of open files the kernel can support. (To change the number of open files that the kernel can support, set the value of **/proc/sys/fs/file-max.** See page 874.)

The datasize option sets the maximum amount of data memory the server is allowed to use. The units are bytes, but **named** understands G for gigabytes, M for megabytes, etc. This option should not be used to try to control the cache size; it's a hard limit, and depending on where it is encountered in the code, may cause the name server to crash or hang. It is usually used to increase the operating system's default max-memory-per-process limit. To control the size of the cache, use the max-cache-size and recursive-clients options instead.

```
max-cache-size number;        [unlimited]
recursive-clients number;     [1000]
```

The max-cache-size option limits the amount of memory that the server may use for caching answers to queries. If the cache grows too large, records will be removed from the cache before their TTL expires to ensure that cache memory usage remains within the stated limit.

The recursive-clients option limits the number of simultaneous recursive queries that the server will process. Each recursive query consumes a chunk of memory in the server; servers that have limited memory may need to set this limit lower than the default value.

```
query-source address ip_addr port ip_port;   [random]
listen-on port ip_port address_match_list;    [53 any]
```

The query-source option specifies the interface and port that **named** uses to query other name servers. The listen-on option specifies the network interfaces and ports on which **named** listens for queries. The values of these options default to the standard **named** behavior: listening on port 53 on all interfaces and using a random, high-numbered UDP port and any interface for queries.

If your site has a firewall, you may want to use the query-source option to give external DNS queries a specific, recognizable profile. Some sites set **named** to use port

53 as the source port (as well as the listened-to port) so that the firewall can recognize outbound DNS traffic as being trustworthy packets from one of your name servers. However, this convention makes it hard for a packet filter to distinguish between inbound and outbound DNS traffic. You can use another port instead of 53 as long as the firewall knows which ports are which.

Don't set the source port to zero—that's an illegal port and **named** will log the query as an error and not answer it. One large ISP has a sysadmin who likes port 0 and has rendered many of their name servers ineffective through his use of the query-source clause. It's curious that their customers don't notice and complain.

```
avoid-v4-udp-ports { port_list };        [empty]
avoid-v6-udp-ports { port_list };        [empty]
```

If you don't use the query-source option, BIND 9 typically uses any outgoing interface and assigns the source port for a query randomly from the unprivileged port range (>1023). This is a problem if your site's firewall blocks certain ports in this range. For example, some firewalls incorrectly consider port 1024 to be part of the privileged port range or correctly block port 2049 (SunRPC) from the outside world. When your name server sends a query and uses one of the blocked ports as its source, the firewall blocks the answer, and the name server eventually gives up waiting and sends out the query again. Not fatal, but annoying to the user caught in the crossfire.

To avoid this problem, use the avoid-v4-udp-ports option to make BIND stay away from the blocked ports. Any high-numbered UDP ports blocked by your firewall should be included in the list.[14] If you update your firewall in response to some threatened attack, be sure to update the port list here, too.

```
forwarders { in_addr; in_addr; ... };    [empty list]
forward only | first;                    [first]
```

Instead of having every name server perform its own external queries, you can designate one or more servers as forwarders. A run-of-the-mill server can look in its cache and the records for which it is authoritative; if it doesn't find the answer it's looking for, it can then send the query on to a forwarder host. That way, the forwarders build up caches that benefit the entire site. The designation is implicit—there is nothing in the configuration file of the forwarder to say "Hey, you're a forwarder."

The forwarders option lists the IP addresses of the servers you want to use as forwarders. They are queried in turn. The use of a forwarder circumvents the normal DNS procedure of starting at a root server and following the chain of referrals. Be careful not to create forwarding loops.

A forward only server caches values and queries forwarders, but it never queries anyone else. If the forwarders do not respond, queries will fail. A forward first server prefers to deal with forwarders but will query directly if need be.

---

14. Some firewalls are stateful and may be smart enough to recognize the DNS answer as being paired with the corresponding query of a second ago. Such firewalls don't need help from this option.

Since the forwarders option has no default value, forwarding does not occur unless it has been specifically configured. You can turn on forwarding either globally or within individual zone statements.

```
allow-query { address_match_list };      [all hosts]
allow-transfer { address_match_list };   [all hosts]
blackhole { address_match_list };        [empty]
```

These options specify which hosts (or networks) can query your name server and request block transfers of your zone data. The blackhole address list identifies servers that you never want to talk to; **named** will not accept queries from these servers and will not ask them for answers.

```
sortlist { address_match_list };         [should die, don't use]
```

We mention the sortlist option only to warn you away from it. Its original purpose was to assist primitive resolvers that don't sort record sets properly. It lets you specify the order in which multiple answers are returned and works against current BINDs' internal smarts.

Other BIND options that meddle with the order of things are the rrset-order statement, which specifies whether to return multiple answers in cyclic (round robin), fixed, or random order, and the topology statement, which tries to second-guess BIND's system for selecting remote servers to query. In most cases there is no need to use these statements either.

```
lame-ttl number;         [600 (10 minutes)]
max-ncache-ttl number;   [10800 (3 hours)]
max-cache-ttl number;    [604800 (1 week)]
```

The TTL options set limits on the time-to-live values that control the caching of positive, negative, and no-response query results. All incoming resource records arrive with their own TTLs, but these options let the local server set its own limits in an effort to reduce the memory consumed by cached data. The max- options cap the TTL values and will never increase them. The DNS specifications require that the TTL for negative answers ("no such domain," for example) be smaller than the TTL for real data.

lame-ttl specifies the number of seconds to cache a lame server indication. The maximum value is 1800 seconds or 30 minutes. Most lame servers (see page 475) stay lame indefinitely because their owners don't know they are not in sync with their parent zone. Setting this parameter to the maximum value should be fine. max-ncache-ttl sets the TTL limit for negative caching. It defaults to three hours and has a maximum value of one week. max-cache-ttl sets the maximum TTL for a positive answer to a query.

```
enable-dnssec yes | no;      [no]
```

This option configures support for DNSSEC. The current default is no, but hopefully in a year or two it can be toggled to yes.

```
edns-udp-size number;              [4096]
```

The ancient default size for UDP packets is 512 bytes; all machines on the Internet are required to be able to reassemble a fragmented UDP packet of 512 bytes or less. Although this limit made sense in the 1980s, it no longer does. The limit now seriously affects programs such as name servers that use UDP for queries and responses.

BIND 9 sets the default UDP packet size to 4096 bytes (the maximum allowed) to accommodate new features such as DNSSEC, IPv6, and internationalized domain names. However, some (broken) firewalls will not allow UDP packets larger than 512 bytes; if you are behind one, you will need this option as a work-around until you fix your firewall. Legal values range from 512 to 4096 bytes.

```
ixfr-from-differences yes | no;       [no]
```

Incremental zone transfers (IXFRs) were previously supported only for zones that used dynamic updates (which are described starting on page 448). With this option, zones that are maintained by hand (i.e., with a text editor) can now take advantage of incremental zone transfers as well. IXFRs save network bandwidth at the expense of a bit of CPU and memory to sort the zone records and to calculate and apply the diffs. This option uses the same robust journaling employed by dynamic updates.

```
root-delegation-only exclude { namelist };[empty]
zone "name" { type delegation-only; };
```

See page 386 for more background regarding Site Finder.

VeriSign's Site Finder tool attempts to reroute everyone's typos to their own servers by using a wild card DNS record. Attempts are being made to address this form of hijacking through political means, but in the meantime BIND 9 has implemented a delegation-only zone type, a delegation-only zone option, and the global option root-delegation-only as stopgap measures. These options restrict root and TLD servers to providing delegation information (name server records and name servers' addresses) and forbids them to supply host data. With them enabled, your local caching servers will return "no such domain" as the answer to mistyped queries.

The exclude clause was added because not all TLDs are delegation-only zones. For example, museum, us, and de are not, but com, net, and org should be. The following excerpt from the cs.colorado.edu domain's zone files illustrates the use of this new zone type to neutralize Site Finder.

```
// to deal with VeriSign Site Finder crap
zone "com" { type delegation-only; };
zone "net" { type delegation-only; };
```

The acl statement

An access control list is just an address match list with a name:

```
acl acl_name {
     address_match_list
};
```

You can use an access control list anywhere that an address match list is called for.

An acl must be a top-level statement in **named.conf**, so don't try sneaking it in amid your other option declarations. **named.conf** is read in a single pass, so access control lists must be defined before they are used. Four lists are predefined:

- any – all hosts
- localnets – all hosts on the local network
- localhost – the machine itself
- none – nothing

The localnets list includes all of the networks to which the host is directly attached. In other words, it's a list of the machine's network addresses modulo their netmasks.

The key statement

The key statement defines a named encryption key to be used for authentication with a particular server. Background information about BIND's support for cryptographic authentication is given in the *Security issues* section starting on page 451. Here, we touch briefly on the mechanics of the process.

To build a key record, you specify both the cryptographic algorithm that you want to use and a "shared secret" (i.e., password) represented as a base-64-encoded string:

```
key key-id {
    algorithm string;
    secret string;
};
```

As with access control lists, the *key-id* must be defined with a key statement before it is used. To associate the key with a particular server, just include *key-id* in the keys clause of that server's server statement. The key is used both to verify requests from that server and to sign the responses to those requests.

The trusted-keys statement

The trusted-keys statement for DNSSEC security is specified in RFC2535. Each entry is a 5-tuple that identifies the domain name, flags, protocol, algorithm, and key that are needed to verify data in that domain. The format is:

```
trusted-keys {
    domain flags protocol algorithm key;
    domain flags protocol algorithm key;
    ...
}
```

Each line represents the trusted key for a particular domain. The *flags*, *protocol*, and *algorithm* are nonnegative integers. The *key* is a base-64-encoded string.

The trusted-keys construct is intended to be used when a zone is signed but its parent zone is not, so you cannot be sure that the public key for the zone that you get from DNS is really kosher. Entering a trusted key with a trusted-keys statement (using out-of-band methods) ensures that you really have the appropriate key for the domain in question.

DNSSEC is covered in more detail starting on page 456.

The server statement

named can potentially talk to many servers, not all of which are running the latest version of BIND, and not all of which are even nominally sane. The server statement tells **named** about the characteristics of its remote peers.

```
server ip_addr {
       bogus yes | no;                                          [no]
       provide-ixfr yes | no;                                   [yes]
       request-ixfr yes | no;                                   [yes]
       edns yes | no;                                           [yes]
       transfers number;                                        [2]
       transfer-format one-answer | many-answers;               [many-answers]
       keys { key-id; key-id; ... };
       transfer-source ip-address [port]
       transfer-source-v6 ipv6-address [port]
};
```

You can use a server statement to override the values of server-related configuration options. Just list the ones for which you want nondefault behavior.

If you mark a server as being bogus, **named** won't send any queries its way. This directive should be reserved for servers that really are bogus. bogus differs from the global option blackhole in that it suppresses only outbound queries. By contrast, the blackhole option completely eliminates all forms of communication with the listed servers.

A BIND 9 name server acting as master for a zone will perform incremental zone transfers if provide-ixfr is set to yes. Likewise, a server acting as a slave will request incremental zone transfers from the master if request-ixfr is set to yes.

The edns clause determines whether the local server will try to use the extended DNS protocol when contacting the remote server. Many of the newer features in BIND (IPv6 and DNSSEC, for example) generate packets bigger than 512 bytes and therefore require the use of the EDNS protocol to negotiate a larger UDP packet size.

Slave servers stay synchronized with their master server by receiving a zone transfer when data has changed (see page 447 for more information about zone transfers). The transfers clause limits the number of concurrent inbound zone transfers from the remote server. It is a server-specific version of transfers-in, but because it applies to only one server, it acts like a per-server override of the transfers-per-ns option. The name is different to preserve compatibility with BIND 8.

The transfer-format clauses are the server-specific forms of the options discussed on page 425. Use transfer-format if you talk to both BIND 8/9 and BIND 4 servers, or if you have old Microsoft name servers on your network. Windows NT cannot handle anything but the one-answer format; Windows 2000 and later are OK with either format, though early versions cannot cope with DNS messages larger than 16K.

The keys clause identifies a key ID that has been previously defined in a key statement for use with TSIG transaction signatures (see page 453). Any requests sent to the remote server are signed with this key. Requests originating at the remote server are not required to be signed, but if they are, the signature will be verified.

The transfer-source clauses give the IPv4 or IPv6 address of the interface (and optionally, the port) that should be used as a source address (port) for zone transfer requests. This clause is only needed when the system has multiple interfaces and the remote server has specified a specific IP address in its allow-transfer clause.

The masters statement

How can there be more than one master? See page 434.

The masters statement lets you name a set of one or more master servers by specifying their IP addresses and cryptographic keys. You can then use this name in the masters clause of zone statements instead of repeating the IP addresses and keys.

The masters facility can be helpful when multiple slave or stub zones get their data from the same remote servers. If the addresses or cryptographic keys of the remote servers change, you can update the masters statement that introduces them rather than changing many different zone statements.

The syntax is

```
masters name { ip_addr [port ip_port] [key key] ; ... } ;
```

The logging statement

named is the current holder of the "most configurable logging system on Earth" award. Syslog put the prioritization of log messages into the programmer's hands and the disposition of those messages into the sysadmin's hands. But for a given priority, the sysadmin had no way to say, "I care about this message but not about that message." BIND 8 added categories that classify log messages by type, and channels that broaden the choices for the disposition of messages. Categories are determined by the programmer, and channels by the sysadmin.

Since the issue of logging is somewhat tangential (especially given the amount of explanation required), we discuss it in the debugging section beginning on page 466.

The zone statement

zone statements are the heart of the **named.conf** file. They tell **named** about the zones for which it is authoritative and set the options that are appropriate for managing each zone. A zone statement is also used to preload the root server hints—the names and addresses of the root servers, which bootstrap the DNS lookup process.

The exact format of a zone statement varies, depending on the role that **named** is to play with respect to that zone. To be specific, the possible zone types are master, slave, hint, forward, stub, and delegation-only. We describe the delegation-only type on page 429. The others are described in the following brief sections.

Many of the global options covered earlier can become part of a zone statement and override the previously defined values. We have not repeated those options here, except to mention certain ones that are frequently used.

Configuring the master server for a zone

Here's the format you need for a zone of which this **named** is the master server:

```
zone "domain_name" {
    type master;
    file "path";
};
```

The *domain_name* in a zone specification must always appear in double quotes.

The zone's data is kept on disk in a human-readable (and human-editable) file. Since there is no default for the filename, you must provide a file statement when declaring a master zone. A zone file is just a collection of DNS resource records in the format described starting on page 389.

Other server-specific attributes are also frequently specified within the zone statement. For example:

```
allow-query { address_match_list };     [any]
allow-transfer { address_match_list };  [any]
allow-update { address_match_list };    [none]
zone-statistics yes | no                [no]
```

The access control options are not required, but it's a good idea to use them. If dynamic updates are used for this zone, the allow-update clause must be present with an address match list that limits the hosts from which updates can occur. Dynamic updates apply only to master zones; the allow-update clause cannot be used for a slave zone. Be sure that this clause includes just your local DHCP servers and not the whole Internet.[15]

The zone-statistics option makes **named** keep track of query/response statistics such as the number and percentage of responses that were referrals, that demanded recursion, or that resulted in errors. See the examples on page 473.

With all these zone-specific options (and about 30 more we have not covered), the configuration is starting to sound complicated. However, a master zone declaration consisting of nothing but a pathname to the zone file is perfectly reasonable. In BIND 4, that's all you could specify. Here is an example, which we have modified slightly, from the BIND documentation:

```
zone "example.com" {
    type master;
    file "forward/example.com";
    allow-query { any; };
    allow-transfer { my-slaves; };
}
```

---

15. You also need ingress filtering at your firewall; see page 701. Better yet, use TSIG for authentication.

Here, my-slaves would be an access control list you had previously defined.

Configuring a slave server for a zone

The zone statement for a slave is similar to that of a master:

```
zone "domain_name" {
    type slave | stub;
    file "path";
    masters { ip_addr [port ip_port] [key keyname]; ... };    [no default]
    allow-query { address_match_list };                        [any]
    allow-transfer { address_match_list };                     [any]
};
```

Slave servers normally maintain a complete copy of their zone's database. However, if the type is set to stub instead of slave, only NS (name server) records are transferred. Stub zones allow the **named**s for the parent zone to automatically discover which machines provide DNS service for their delegated child zones, just in case the administrator of the child zone is not conscientious about informing the parent of changes. The parent needs this information in order to make appropriate referrals or recursive queries.

The file statement specifies a local file in which the replicated database can be stored. Each time the server fetches a new copy of the zone, it saves the data in this file. If the server crashes and reboots, the file can then be reloaded from the local disk without being transferred across the network.

You shouldn't edit this cache file, since it's maintained by **named**. However, it can be interesting to look at if you suspect you have made an error in the master server's data file. The slave's disk file shows you how **named** has interpreted the original zone data; relative names and origin directives have all been expanded. If you see a name in the data file that looks like one of these

> 128.138.243.151.cs.colorado.edu.
> anchor.cs.colorado.edu.cs.colorado.edu.

you can be pretty sure that you forgot a trailing dot somewhere.

The masters clause lists the IP addresses of one or more machines from which the zone database can be obtained. It can also contain the name of a masters list defined with a previous masters statement.

We have said that only one machine can be the master for a zone, so why is it possible to list more than one address? Two reasons. First, the master machine might have more than one network interface and therefore more than one IP address. It's possible for one interface to become unreachable (because of network or routing problems) while others are still accessible. Therefore, it's a good practice to list all of the master server's topologically distinct addresses.

Second, **named** really doesn't care where the zone data comes from. It can pull the database just as easily from a slave server as from the master. You could use this feature to allow a well-connected slave server to serve as a sort of backup master, since the IP addresses will be tried in order until a working server is found. In theory, you can also set up a hierarchy of servers, with one master serving several second-level servers, which in turn serve many third-level servers.

Setting up the root server hints

Another form of zone statement points **named** toward a file from which it can preload its cache with the names and addresses of the root name servers:

```
zone "." {
    type hint;
    file "path";
};
```

The "hints" are a set of DNS records that list servers for the root domain. They're needed to give **named** a place to start searching for information about other sites' domains. Without them, **named** would only know about the domains it serves and their subdomains.

When **named** starts, it reloads the hints from one of the root servers. Ergo, you'll be fine as long as your hints file contains at least one valid, reachable root server.

BIND 9 has root server hints compiled into its code, so no configuration of the root zone is really needed. If you provide a hints file, however, BIND 9 will use it. We recommend that you do supply explicit hints; politics have entered the DNS arena, making root name servers and their IP addresses more volatile.

The hints file is often called **root.cache**. It contains the response you would get if you queried a root server for the name server records in the root domain. In fact, you can generate the hints file in exactly this way by running **dig**:

```
$ dig @f.root-servers.net . ns > root.cache
```

Mind the dot. If f.root-servers.net is not responding, you can run the query without specifying a particular server:

```
$ dig . ns > root.cache
```

The output will be similar; however, you will be obtaining the list of root servers from the cache of a local name server, not from an authoritative source. That should be just fine—even if you have not rebooted or restarted your name server for a year or two, it has been refreshing its root server records periodically as their TTLs expire.

Here's what the cache file looks like (abridged from **dig @f.root-servers.net . ns**):

```
; <<>> DiG 9.3.0rc1 <<>> @f.root-servers.net . ns
;; global options:  printcmd
;; Got answer:
;; ->>HEADER<<- opcode: QUERY, status: NOERROR, id: 28797
;; flags: qr aa rd; QUERY: 1, ANSWER: 13, AUTHORITY: 0, ADDITIONAL: 13
```

```
;; QUESTION SECTION:
;.                          IN     NS

;; ANSWER SECTION:
.                518400  IN     NS     I.ROOT-SERVERS.NET.
.                518400  IN     NS     J.ROOT-SERVERS.NET.
.                518400  IN     NS     K.ROOT-SERVERS.NET.
.                518400  IN     NS     L.ROOT-SERVERS.NET.
...
;; ADDITIONAL SECTION:
I.ROOT-SERVERS.NET. 3600000    IN     A     192.36.148.17
J.ROOT-SERVERS.NET. 3600000    IN     A     192.58.128.30
K.ROOT-SERVERS.NET. 3600000    IN     A     193.0.14.129
L.ROOT-SERVERS.NET. 3600000    IN     A     198.32.64.12
...
;; Query time: 3 msec
;; SERVER: 192.5.5.241#53(f.root-servers.net)
;; WHEN: Wed Jul  7 13:54:26 2004
;; MSG SIZE  rcvd: 436
```

Note the dots that begin the first set of records; they are not fly specks but rather they define the domain (the root) to which the NS records apply.

Setting up a forwarding zone

A zone of type forward overrides **named**'s global forwarding settings (described on page 427) for a particular domain:

```
zone "domain_name" {
    type forward;
    forward only | first;
    forwarders { ip_addr; ip_addr; ... };
};
```

You might use a forward zone if your organization had a strategic working relationship with some other group or company and you wanted to funnel traffic directly to that company's name servers, bypassing the standard query path.

The controls statement

The controls statement specifies how **rndc** controls a running **named** process. **rndc** can start and stop **named**, dump its state, put it in debug mode, etc. **rndc** is a network program, and with improper configuration it might let anyone on the Internet mess around with your name server. The syntax is

```
controls {
    inet ip_addr port ip-port allow { address_match_list } keys { key_list };
}
```

The port that **rndc** uses to talk to **named** defaults to port 953 if it is not specified with the port clause.

DNS

Allowing your name server to be controlled remotely is both handy and dangerous. Strong authentication through a key entry in the allow clause is required; keys in the address match list are ignored and must be explicitly stated in the keys clause of the controls statement.

In BIND 9, you can use the **rndc-confgen** command to generate an authentication key for use between **rndc** and **named**. There are essentially two ways to set this up: you can have both **named** and **rndc** consult the same configuration file to learn the key (**/etc/rndc.key**), or you can include the key in both the **rndc** and **named** configuration files (**/etc/rndc.conf** for **rndc** and **/etc/named.conf** for **named**). The latter option is more complicated, but it's necessary when **named** and **rndc** will be running on different computers.

When no controls statement is present, BIND 9 defaults to the loopback address for the address match list and looks for the key in **/etc/rndc.key**. Because strong authentication is mandatory in BIND 9, you cannot use the **rndc** command to control **named** if there is no key. This may seem a bit draconian, but consider: even if **rndc** worked only from (127.0.0.1) and this address was blocked from the outside world at your firewall, you would still be trusting all local users to not mess with your name server. Any user could **telnet** to the control port and type "stop"—quite an effective denial of service attack.

Here is an example of the output (to standard out) from **rndc-confgen** when a 256-bit key is requested. We chose 256 because it fits on the page. You would normally choose a longer key and redirect the output to **/etc/rndc.conf**. The comments at the bottom of the output show the lines that need to be added to **named.conf** to make **named** and **rndc** play together.

```
$ ./rndc-confgen -b 256
# Start of rndc.conf
key "rndc-key" {
    algorithm hmac-md5;
    secret "orZuz5amkUnEp52zlHxD6cd5hACldOGsG/elP/dv2IY=";
};

options {
    default-key "rndc-key";
    default-server 127.0.0.1;
    default-port 953;
};
# End of rndc.conf

# Use with the following in named.conf, adjusting the allow list as needed:
# key "rndc-key" {
#       algorithm hmac-md5;
#       secret "orZuz5amkUnEp52zlHxD6cd5hACldOGsG/elP/dv2IY=";
# };
#
```

```
# controls {
#        inet 127.0.0.1 port 953
#                allow { 127.0.0.1; } keys { "rndc-key"; };
# };
# End of named.conf
```

"Automatic" mode, used to generate a shared configuration file, is simpler. Run as root, **rndc-confgen -a -b 256** produces the file **/etc/rndc.key**, which contains

```
key "rndc-key" {
    algorithm hmac-md5;
    secret "laGbZj2Cobyc0m/jFVNCu8OJzsLKNH+CCb2JCWY6yJw=";
};
```

The file has mode 600 and should be owned by the **named** user or root. It can then be incorporated into the **named.conf** file with the include statement.

Split DNS and the view statement

Many sites want the internal view of their network to be different from the view seen from the Internet. For example, you might reveal all of a zone's hosts to internal users but restrict the external view to a few well-known servers. Or, you might expose the same set of hosts in both views but supply additional (or different) records to internal users. For example, the MX records for mail routing might point to a single mail hub machine from outside the domain but point to individual workstations from the perspective of internal users.

See page 289 for more information about private address spaces. A split DNS configuration is especially useful for sites that use RFC1918 private IP addresses on their internal networks. For example, a query for the hostname associated with IP address 10.0.0.1 can never be answered by the global DNS system, but it is meaningful within the context of the local network. Of the queries arriving at the root name servers, 4%-5% are either *from* an IP address in one of the private address ranges or *about* one of these addresses. Neither can be answered; both are the result of misconfiguration, either of BIND's split DNS or Microsoft's "domains."

The view statement packages up an access list that controls which clients see which view, some options that apply to all the zones in the view, and finally, the zones themselves. The syntax is

```
view view-name {
    match-clients { address_match_list } ;
    view_option; ...
    zone_statement; ...
} ;
```

The match-clients clause controls who can see the view. Views are processed in order, so put the most restrictive views first. Zones in different views can have the same names, but take their data from different files. Views are an all-or-nothing proposition; if you use them, all zone statements in your **named.conf** file must appear in the context of a view.

Here is an example from the BIND 9 documentation. The two views define the same zone, but with different data

```
view "internal" {
        match-clients { our_nets; };      // only internal networks
        recursion yes;                     // internal clients only
        zone "example.com" {               // complete view of zone
            type master;
            file "example-internal.db";
        };
};

view "external" {
        match-clients { any; };            // allow all queries
        recursion no;                      // but no recursion
        zone "example.com" {               // only "public" hosts
            type master;
            file "example-external.db";
        }
};
```

If the order of the views were reversed, no one would ever see the internal view. Internal hosts would match the any value in the match-clients clause of the external view before they reached the internal view.

Our second DNS configuration example starting on page 441 provides some additional examples of views.

15.12   BIND CONFIGURATION EXAMPLES

Now that we have explored the wonders of **named.conf**, let's look at some complete examples. In the following sections, we discuss several sample configurations:

- The localhost zone
- A small security company that uses split DNS
- The experts: isc.org, the Internet Systems Consortium

The localhost zone

The address 127.0.0.1 refers to a host itself and should be mapped to the name "localhost".[16] Some sites map the address to "localhost.*localdomain*." and some do both. The corresponding IPv6 address is ::1.

If you forget to configure the localhost zone, your site may end up querying the root servers for localhost information. The root servers receive so many of these queries that the operators are considering adding a generic mapping between localhost and 127.0.0.1 at the root level. In measurements at the root server named F in San Francisco in March, 2004, localhost was the third most popular domain queried, just behind arpa and com. That's a lot of useless queries for a busy name server.

16. Actually, the whole class A network 127/8 refers to localhost but most folks just use 127.0.0.1.

The forward mapping for the name localhost.*localdomain* can be defined in the forward zone file for the domain or in its own file. Each server, even a caching server, is usually the master for its own reverse localhost domain.

Here are the lines in **named.conf** that configure localhost:

```
zone "localhost" {// localhost forward zone
     type master;
     file "for/localhost";
     allow-update { none; };
};

zone "0.0.127.in-addr.arpa" {// localhost reverse zone
     type master;
     file "rev/127.0.0";
     allow-update { none; };
};
```

The corresponding forward zone file, **for/localhost**, contains

```
$TTL 30d
; localhost.
@          IN   SOA   localhost. postmaster.localhost. (
                      1998050801      ;serial
                      3600            ;refresh
                      1800            ;retry
                      604800          ;expiration
                      3600 )          ;minimum

           NS    localhost.
           A     127.0.0.1
```

and the reverse file, **rev/127.0.0**:

```
$TTL 30d
; 0.0.127.in-addr.arpa
@          IN   SOA   localhost. postmaster.localhost. (
                      1998050801      ;serial
                      3600            ;refresh
                      1800            ;retry
                      604800          ;expiration
                      3600 )          ;minimum

           NS    localhost.
1          PTR   localhost.
```

The mapping for the localhost address (127.0.0.1) never changes, so the timeouts can be large. Note the serial number, which encodes the date; the file was last changed in 1998. Also note that only the master name server is listed for the localhost domain. The meaning of @ here is "0.0.127.in-addr.arpa.".

A small security company

Our first real example is for a small company that specializes in security consulting.
They run BIND 9 on a recent version of Red Hat Enterprise Linux and use views to
implement a split DNS system in which internal and external users see different host
data. They also use private address space internally; queries about those addresses
should never escape to the Internet to clutter up the global DNS system. Here is their
named.conf file, reformatted and commented a bit:

```
options {
        directory "/var/domain";
        version "root@atrust.com";
        allow-transfer {82.165.230.84; 71.33.249.193; 127.0.0.1; };
        listen-on { 192.168.2.10; 192.168.2.1; 127.0.0.1; 192.168.2.12; };
};

include "atrust.key";                        // defn of atkey in mode 600 file

controls {
        inet 127.0.0.1 allow { 127.0.0.1; } keys { atkey; };
};

view "internal" {                            // internal view

        match-clients { 192.168.0.0/16; 206.168.198.192/28; 172.29.0.0/24; };
        recursion yes;

        zone "." IN {                        // root hints zone
            type hint;
            file "named.cache";
        };
        zone "localhost" IN {                // localhost forward zone
            type master;
            file "localhost.forw";
            allow-update { none; };
        };
        zone "0.0.127.in-addr.arpa" IN {     // localhost reverse zone
            type master;
            file "localhost.rev";
            allow-update { none; };
        };
        zone "atrust.com" IN {               // internal forward zone
            type master;
            file "internal/atrust.com";
        };
        zone "1.168.192.in-addr.arpa" IN {   // internal reverse zone
            type master;
            file "internal/192.168.1.rev";
            allow-update { none; };
        };                                   // lots more reverse zones omitted
```

```
        zone "atrust.us" {                      // slave in internal view
            type slave;
            file "internal-slave/atrust.us";
            masters { 127.0.0.1; };
        };
        zone "atrust.org" {
            type slave;
            file "internal-slave/atrust.org";
            masters { 127.0.0.1; };
        };                                       // lots more zones omitted
};          // end of internal view

view "world" {                                   // external view

        match-clients { any; };
        recursion no;

        // zone statements for dot and localhost as above, omitted for brevity

        zone "atrust.com" {                      // external forward zone
            type master;
            file "world/atrust.com";
            allow-update { none; };
        };
        zone "189.173.63.in-addr.arpa" {         // external reverse zone
            type master;
            file "world/63.173.189.rev";
            allow-update { none; };
        };
        zone "atrust.us" {                       // master in world view
            type master;
            file "world/appliedtrust.com-aggregate";
            allow-update { none; };
        };
        zone "atrust.org" {                      // note that the file is the same
            type master;
            file "world/appliedtrust.com-aggregate";
            allow-update { none; };
        };                                       // lots more atrusty zones omitted
        zone "admin.com" {                       // master zones only in world view
            type master;
            file "world/admin.com";
            allow-update { none; };
        };                                       // lots more master zones omitted
        zone "eldoraskipatrol.org" {             // slave zones only in world view
            type slave;
            file "world-slave/eldoraskipatrol.org";
            masters { 192.231.139.1; };
        };                                       // lots more slave zones omitted
}; // end of external view
```

The file **atrust.key** contains the definition of the key named "atkey".

```
key "atkey" {
    algorithm hmac-md5;
    secret "shared secret key goes here";
};
```

The zones are organized by their view and type (master/slave), and the naming convention for zone data files reflects this same scheme. This server is recursive for the internal view, which includes all the local hosts, including many that use private addressing. The server is not recursive for the external view, which contains only selected hosts at atrust.com and the external zones for which they provide either master or slave DNS service.

Snippets of the files **internal/atrust.com** and **world/atrust.com** are shown below. First, the internal file:

```
; atrust.com - internal file
$TTL 86400
$ORIGIN com.
atrust              3600   SOA   ns1.atrust.com. trent.atrust.com. (
                                  2004012900 10800 1200 3600000 3600 )
                    3600   NS    NS1.atrust.com.
                    3600   NS    NS2.atrust.com.
                    3600   MX    10 mailserver.atrust.com.
                    3600   A     66.77.122.161

$ORIGIN atrust.com.
ns1                        A     192.168.2.11
ns2                        A     66.77.122.161
www                        A     66.77.122.161
mailserver                 A     192.168.2.11
exchange                   A     192.168.2.100
secure                     A     66.77.122.161
bark                       A     192.168.2.10
superg                     A     192.168.1.249
at-dmz-gw                  A     192.168.1.254
at-external-gw             A     192.168.2.254
at-external-outside-gw     A     206.168.198.220
indras-gw                  A     206.168.198.222
; dhcp host range
dhcp-0-hardwire      IN    A     192.168.1.64
dhcp-1-hardwire      IN    A     192.168.1.65
; ...

; booklab "subdomain", note that this is a subdomain but not a subzone

redhat.booklab      IN    A     192.168.10.1
redhat-ent.booklab  IN    A     192.168.10.2
debian.booklab      IN    A     192.168.10.3
fedora.booklab      IN    A     192.168.10.4
freebsd.booklab     IN    A     192.168.10.5
suse.booklab        IN    A     192.168.10.6
macos.booklab       IN    A     192.168.10.7
solaris.booklab     IN    A     192.168.10.8
```

Here is the external view of that same domain from **world/atrust.com**:

```
; atrust.com - external file
$TTL 57600
$ORIGIN .
atrust.com                      SOA  ns1.atrust.com. trent.atrust.com. (
                                        2004020400 10800 1200 3600000 3600 )
                                NS   NS1.atrust.com.
                                NS   NS2.atrust.com.
                                MX   10 mailserver.atrust.com.
                                A    66.77.122.161
ns1.atrust.com.                 A    206.168.198.209
ns2.atrust.com.                 A    66.77.122.161

$ORIGIN atrust.com.
www                             A    66.77.122.161
mailserver                      A    206.168.198.209
bark                            A    206:168.198.209
secure                          A    66.77.122.161

; reverse maps
exterior1                       A    206.168.198.209
209.198.168.206                 PTR  exterior1.atrust.com.
exterior2                       A    206.168.198.213
213.198.168.206                 PTR  exterior2.atrust.com.
exterior3                       A    206.168.198.220
220.198.168.206                 PTR  exterior3.atrust.com.
exterior4                       A    206.168.198.210
210.198.168.206                 PTR  exterior4.atrust.com.
```

Notice that when multiple names for the same machine are needed, they are presented as additional A records rather than as CNAME records. Very few hosts are actually visible in the external world view.

The TTL in these zone files is set to 16 hours (57,600 seconds). For internal zones, the TTL is a day (86,400 seconds). Most individual records in zone files are not assigned an explicit TTL value. The TTL is optional; it can be added to any individual line in the zone file just before the record type.

The bizarre PTR records at the end of the external file allow atrust.com's ISP to delegate the reverse mapping of a very small piece of address space. CNAME records at the ISP's site make this variation of the CNAME hack work; see page 400 for more information.

The Internet Systems Consortium, isc.org

ISC are the author and maintainer of BIND as well as operator of the F root name server. They are also a TLD server that serves about 60 top-level domains. That's why we call them the experts!

Below are snippets from their configuration files. Notice that they are using both IPv4 and IPv6. They also use TSIG encryption to authenticate between master and slave servers for zone transfers. The transfer-source options ensure that the source IP addresses for outgoing zone transfer requests conform to the allow-transfers statements on the master servers.

The **named.conf** file:

```
// isc.org TLD name server

options {
    directory "/var/named";
    datasize 1000M;
    listen-on { 204.152.184.64; };
    listen-on-v6 { 2001:4f8:0:2::13; };
    recursion no;
    transfer-source 204.152.184.64;
    transfer-source-v6 2001:4f8:0:2::13;
};

// rndc key
key rndc_key {
    algorithm hmac-md5;
    secret "<secret>";
};

// TSIG key for name server ns-ext
key ns-ext {
    algorithm hmac-md5;
    secret "<secret>";
};

server 204.152.188.234 { keys { ns-ext; }; };

controls {
    inet 204.152.184.64 allow { any; } keys { rndc_key; };
};

include "inf/named.zones";        // root, localhost, 127.0.0.1, ::1
include "master.zones";           // zones we master
include "slave.zones";            // lots of slaves
```

These include statements keep the **named.conf** file short and tidy. If you serve lots of zones, consider breaking up your configuration into bite-sized pieces like this. More importantly, set up your filesystem hierarchy so that you don't have a directory with a thousand zone files in it. Modern Linux filesystems handle large directories efficiently, but they can be a management hassle.

Here's more from the file **master.zones**:

```
zone "isc.org" {                  // ISC
    type master;
    file "master/isc.org";
    allow-update { none; };
    allow-transfer { none; };
};
```

```
zone "sfo2.isc.org" {                  // ISC
    type master;
    file "master/sfo2.isc.org";
    allow-update { none; };
    allow-transfer { none; };
};

// lots of zones truncated
```

And from **slaves.zones**:

```
zone "vix.com" {
    type slave;
    file "secondary/vix.com";
    masters { 204.152.188.234; };
};

zone "cix.net" {
    type slave;
    file "secondary/cix.net";
    masters { 204.152.188.234; };
};
```

With DNS background and BIND configuration out of the way, we now turn to the more operational issues of running a name service at your site, including the maintenance of zone files, security issues, testing, and debugging.

15.13 STARTING NAMED

The existence of BIND on Linux distributions depends both on the distribution and on the options selected when the distribution was installed. If BIND does not seem to be installed, you will have to obtain and install the BIND package. The package also installs a startup script for **named** that's run through **init**: **/etc/init.d/named** for RHEL, Fedora, and SUSE, and **/etc/init.d/bind9** for Debian and Ubuntu.

named is started at boot time and runs continuously. To control a running copy of **named**, you use the command-line interface **rndc**, which is described in more detail starting on page 471.

Sometimes the **init** scripts that start **named** provide extra entry points (e.g., **reload**) that are intended for use by system administrators. However, the implementation on some distributions is questionable, and it's easier to use **rndc** anyway. We suggest that you leave the startup scripts to your operating system and **init** and use **rndc** for control after **named** has been started.

*See page 887 for more information about **inetd**.*

named uses syslog, and therefore **syslogd** should be started before **named**. Do not use **inetd** or **xinetd** to manage **named**; it will restart **named** every time it's needed, thereby slowing response times and preventing any useful cache from being developed. Some sites use a keep-running script that puts the **named** startup command in an infinite loop to protect against **named**'s death; see page 417 for an example. The BIND distribution includes a script called **nanny** that serves a similar purpose.

15.14 UPDATING ZONE FILES

When you make a change to a domain (such as adding or deleting a host), the data files on the master server must be updated. You must also increment the serial number in the SOA record for the zone and then run **rndc reload** to signal **named** to pick up the changes. You can also kill and restart **named**, but this operation causes cached data from other domains to be discarded.

Earlier versions of BIND used signals and the **kill** command to control **named**, but just as the developers started running out of signal numbers, **rndc** came along and fixed it all. The historical signal stuff has been removed from BIND 9 (except for the HUP signal to reread the configuration file, reload zones, and restart **named**, and the TERM and INT signals to kill **named**), so we recommend sticking with **rndc**.

Updated zone data is propagated to slave servers right away because the notify option is on by default. If you have inadvertently turned this option off, your slave servers will not pick up the changes until after *refresh* seconds, as set in the zone's SOA record (typically one to six hours later). If you want a more timely update when the notify option is turned off, **rndc reload** on a slave causes it to check with the master, see that the data has changed, and request a zone transfer.

Don't forget to modify both the forward and reverse zones when you change a hostname or IP address. Forgetting the reverse files leaves sneaky errors: some commands work and some won't.

Changing the data files but forgetting to change the serial number makes the changes take effect on the master server (after a reload) but not on the slaves.

It is improper to edit data files belonging to slave servers. These files are maintained by **named**; sysadmins should not meddle with them. It's fine to look at the data files as long as you don't make changes.

BIND allows zone changes to be made through a programmatic API, as specified in RFC2136. This feature, called dynamic updates, is necessary to support autoconfiguration protocols such as DHCP. The dynamic update mechanism is described on page 448.

Zone transfers

DNS servers are synchronized through a mechanism called a zone transfer. The original DNS specification (and BIND 4) required all zone data to be transferred at once. Incremental updates were eventually defined in RFC1995 and implemented in BIND 8.2. Original and incremental-style zone transfers are sometimes referred to as AXFR and IXFR, respectively. Once configured, they're supposed to be equivalent.

A slave that wants to refresh its data requests a zone transfer from the master server and makes a backup copy of the zone data on disk. If the data on the master has not changed, as determined by a comparison of the serial numbers (not the actual data), no update occurs and the backup files are just touched (that is, their modification time is set to the current time).

Zone transfers use the TCP protocol on port 53 and log information with category "transfer-*". IXFR as specified by the IETF can use either TCP or UDP, but BIND has only implemented it over TCP.

Both the sending and receiving servers remain available to answer queries during a zone transfer. Only after the transfer is complete does the slave begin to use the new data. BIND 8 actually calls a separate **named-xfer** program to perform the transfer, but BIND 9's **named** handles the transfers directly.

When zones are huge (like com) or dynamically updated (see the next section), changes are typically small relative to the size of the entire zone. With IXFR, only the changes are sent (unless they are larger than the complete zone, in which case a regular AXFR transfer is done). The IXFR mechanism is like the **patch** program in that it applies differences to an old database to synchronize it with a new database.

In BIND 9, IXFR is the default for any zones configured for dynamic update, and **named** always maintains a transaction log called *zonename*.**jnl**. You can set the options provide-ixfr and request-ixfr in the server statements for individual peers. provide-ixfr enables or disables IXFR service for zones for which this server is the master. request-ixfr requests IXFRs for zones for which this server is a slave.

```
provide-ixfr yes ;          # in BIND 9 server statement
request-ixfr yes ;          # in BIND 9 server statement
```

Starting with BIND 9.3, **named** can now provide IXFRs to slave servers to transfer edits that are made by hand. Use the zone option ixfr-from-differences to enable this behavior; see page 429.

IXFR requires the zone file to be sorted in a canonical order. **named** takes care of this chore for you, but the requirement makes IXFRs a tradeoff. More memory and CPU are used on the servers in exchange for reduced network traffic.

Much effort has been expended to ensure that a server crash during an IXFR does not leave zones with trashed data. An IXFR request to a server that does not support it automatically falls back to the standard AXFR zone transfer.

Dynamic updates

The DNS system is built on the premise that name-to-address mappings are relatively stable and do not change frequently. However, a site that uses DHCP to dynamically assign IP addresses as machines boot and join the network breaks this rule constantly. There are two classical solutions: add generic entries to the DNS database or continually edit the DNS files. For many sites, neither solution is satisfactory.

The first solution should be familiar to anyone who has used a dial-up ISP. The DNS configuration looks something like this:

```
dhcp-host1.domain.    IN    A    192.168.0.1
dhcp-host2.domain.    IN    A    192.168.0.2
    ...
```

Although this is a simple solution, it means that hostnames are permanently associated with particular IP addresses and that computers therefore change hostnames whenever they receive a new IP address. Hostname-based logging or security measures become very difficult in this environment.

The dynamic update feature in recent versions of BIND provides an alternative solution. It allows the DHCP daemon to notify BIND of the address assignments it makes, thus updating the contents of the DNS database on the fly. Dynamic updates can add, delete, or modify resource records. While dynamic updates are occurring, a journal file (*zonename*.**jnl**) is kept to protect against the occurrence of a server crash.

You cannot hand-edit a dynamically updated zone without first stopping the dynamic update stream. **rndc freeze** *zone* or **rndc freeze** *zone class view* will do the trick. These commands sync the journal file to the master zone file on disk and then delete the journal file. You can then edit the zone file by hand. Of course, the original formatting of the zone file will have been destroyed by **named**'s monkeying—the file will look like those maintained by **named** for slave servers.

Dynamic update attempts will be refused while the zone is frozen; use **rndc thaw** with the same arguments you froze with to reload the zone file from disk and reenable dynamic updates.

The **nsupdate** program supplied with BIND 9 provides a command-line interface for making dynamic updates. It runs in batch mode, taking commands from the keyboard or a file. A blank line or send signals the end of an update and sends the changes to the server. Two blank lines signify the end of input. The command language includes a primitive if statement to express constructs such as "if this hostname does not exist in DNS, add it." As predicates for an **nsupdate** action, you can require a name to exist or not exist, or require a resource record set to exist or not exist.

For example, here is a simple **nsupdate** script that adds a new host and also adds a nickname for an existing host if the nickname is not already in use. The angle bracket prompt is produced by **nsupdate** and is not part of the command script.

```
$ nsupdate
> update add newhost.cs.colorado.edu 86400 A 128.138.243.16
>
> prereq nxdomain gypsy.cs.colorado.edu
> update add gypsy.cs.colorado.edu CNAME evi-laptop.cs.colorado.edu
```

Dynamic updates to DNS are scary. They can potentially provide uncontrolled write access to your important system data. Don't try to use IP addresses for access control—they are too easily forged. TSIG authentication with a shared-secret key is better; it's available and is easy to configure. BIND 9 supports both:

```
$ nsupdate -k keydir:keyfile
```

or

```
$ nsupdate -y keyname:secretkey
```

Since the password goes on the command line, anyone running **w** or **ps** at the right moment can see it. For this reason, the **-k** form is preferred. For more details on TSIG, see the section starting on page 453.

Dynamic updates to a zone are enabled in **named.conf** with an allow-update or update-policy clause. allow-update grants permission to update any records in accordance with IP- or key-based authentication. update-policy is a BIND 9 extension that allows fine-grained control for updates according to the hostname or record type. It requires key-based authentication. Both are zone options.

Use update-policy to allow clients to update their A or PTR records but not to change the SOA record, NS records, or KEY records. You can also use update-policy to allow a host to update only its own records. The parameters let you express names explicitly, as a subdomain, as a wild card, or as the keyword self, which sets a general policy for machines' access to their own records. Resource records are identified by class and type. The syntax of an update-policy rule is

```
update-policy ( grant | deny ) identity nametype name [types] ;
```

identity is the name of the cryptographic key needed up authorize the update. *nametype* has one of four values: name, subdomain, wildcard, or self. *name* is the zone to be updated, and the *types* are the resource record types that can be updated. If no types are specified, all types except SOA, NS, RRSIG, and NSEC can be updated. Here's an example:

```
update-policy { grant dhcp-key subdomain dhcp.cs.colorado.edu A } ;
```

This configuration allows anyone who knows the key dhcp-key to update address records in the dhcp.cs.colorado.edu subdomain. This statement would appear in the master server's **named.conf** file under the zone statement for dhcp.cs.colorado.edu. There would have to be a key statement to define dhcp-key as well.

The snippet below from the **named.conf** file at the Computer Science Department at the University of Colorado uses the update-policy statement to allow students in a system administration class to update their own subdomains but not to mess with the rest of the DNS environment.

```
// saclass.net
zone "saclass.net" in {
    type master;
    file "saclass/saclass.net";
    update-policy {
        grant feanor_mroe. subdomain saclass.net.;
        grant mojo_mroe. subdomain saclass.net.;
        grant dawdle_mroe. subdomain saclass.net.;
        grant pirate_mroe. subdomain saclass.net.;
        // and lots more
    };
    ...
```

15.15 SECURITY ISSUES

In the good old days, the Internet was small, friendly, and useful mostly to geeks. Now it is a hostile environment as well as a crucial piece of infrastructure. In this section, we cover several security-related topics in a manner that may appear to be somewhat paranoid. Unfortunately, these topics and precautions are sadly necessary on today's Internet.

DNS started out as an inherently open system, but it has steadily grown more and more secure—or at least, securable. By default, anyone on the Internet can investigate your domain with individual queries from tools such as **dig**, **host**, or **nslookup**. In some cases, they can dump your entire DNS database.

To address such vulnerabilities, BIND now supports various types of access control based on host and network addresses or on cryptographic authentication. Table 15.11 summarizes the security features that are configured in **named.conf**. The Page column shows where in this book to look for more information.

Table 15.11 Security features in named.conf

Feature	Statements	Page	What it specifies
acl	various	429	Access control lists
allow-query	options, zone	428	Who can query a zone or server
allow-recursion	options	425	Who can make recursive queries
allow-transfer	options, zone	428	Who can request zone transfers
allow-update	zone	433	Who can make dynamic updates
blackhole	options	428	Which servers to completely ignore
bogus	server	431	Which servers should never be queried
update-policy	zone	449	What updates are allowed

named can run in a **chroot**ed environment under an unprivileged UID to minimize security risks. It can use transaction signatures to control dynamic updates or zone transfers, and of course, it also supports the whole DNSSEC hairball. These topics are taken up in the next few sections.

Access control lists revisited

ACLs are named address match lists that can appear as arguments to statements such as allow-query, allow-transfer, and blackhole. Their basic syntax was described on page 429. ACLs can help beef up DNS security in a variety of ways.

Every site should at least have one ACL for bogus addresses and one ACL for local addresses.

For example:

```
acl bogusnets {                  // ACL for bogus networks
      0.0.0.0/8 ;                // default, wild card addresses
      1.0.0.0/8 ;                // reserved addresses
      2.0.0.0/8 ;                // reserved addresses
      169.254.0.0/16 ;           // link-local delegated addresses
      192.0.2.0/24 ;             // sample addresses, like example.com
      224.0.0.0/3 ;              // multicast address space
      10.0.0.0/8 ;               // private address space (RFC1918)[17]
      172.16.0.0/12 ;            // private address space (RFC1918)
      192.168.0.0/16 ;           // private address space (RFC1918)
} ;

acl cunets {                     // ACL for University of Colorado networks
      128.138.0.0/16 ;           // main campus network
      198.11.16/24 ;
      204.228.69/24 ;
};
```

In the global options section of your config file, you could then include

```
allow-recursion { cunets; } ;
blackhole { bogusnets; } ;
```

It's also a good idea to restrict zone transfers to legitimate slave servers. An ACL makes things nice and tidy.

```
acl ourslaves {
      128.138.242.1 ;            // anchor
      ...
} ;
acl measurements {
      198.32.4.0/24 ;            // bill manning's measurements, v4 address
      2001:478:6:0::/48 ;        // bill manning's measurements, v6 address
} ;
```

The actual restriction is implemented with a line such as

```
allow-transfer { ourslaves; measurements; } ;
```

Here, transfers are limited to our own slave servers and to the machines of an Internet measurement project that walks the reverse DNS tree to determine the size of the Internet and the percentage of misconfigured servers. Limiting transfers in this way makes it impossible for other sites to dump your entire database with a tool such as **dig** (see page 473).

For example, caida.org uses an ACL to limit transfers to just their secondary servers; using **dig** @*server domain* **axfr** succeeds from the machine jungle.caida.org but fails from gypsy.cs.colorado.edu:

```
jungle$ dig @rommie.caida.org caida.org axfr
```

----

17. Don't make private addresses bogus if you use them and are configuring your internal DNS servers!

```
; <<>> DiG 8.3 <<>> @rommie.caida.org caida.org axfr
; (1 server found)
$ORIGIN caida.org.
@                        4H   IN   SOA    @ postmaster (
                                          200406300    ; serial
                                          1H           ; refresh
                                          30M          ; retry
                                          1W           ; expiry
                                          )
...
```

gypsy$ **dig @rommie.caida.org caida.org axfr**

```
; <<>> DiG 9.2.4 <<>> @rommie.caida.org caida.org axfr
;; global options:  printcmd
; Transfer failed.
```

Of course, you should still protect your network at a lower level through router access control lists and standard security hygiene on each host. If those measures are not possible, you can refuse DNS packets except to a gateway machine that you monitor closely.

Confining named

To confine the damage that someone could do if they compromised your server, you can run **named** in a **chroot**ed environment, run it as an unprivileged user, or both. The **-t** flag specifies the directory to **chroot** to, and the **-u** flag specifies the UID under which **named** should run. For example, the command

```
# named -u 53 -t /var/named
```

starts **named** with UID 53 and a root directory of **/var/named**.

If hackers compromise your **named**, they can potentially gain access to the system under the guise of the user as whom **named** runs. If this user is root and you do not use a **chroot**ed environment, such a breach can be quite destructive. Many sites don't bother to use the **-u** and **-t** flags, but when a new vulnerability is announced, they must be faster to upgrade than the hackers are to attack.

The **chroot** directory cannot be an empty directory since it must contain all the files **named** normally needs in order to run: **/dev/null**, the zone files, **named.conf**, syslog target files and the syslog UNIX domain socket, **/var**, etc. BIND 9's **named** performs the **chroot** system call after all libraries have been loaded, so it is no longer necessary to copy shared libraries into the **chroot** directory.

 Fedora installs a **chroot**ed **named** by default.

Secure server-to-server communication with TSIG and TKEY

While DNSSEC (covered in the next section) was being developed, the IETF developed a simpler mechanism, called TSIG (RFC2845), to allow secure communication among servers through the use of "transaction signatures." Access control based on transaction signatures is more secure than access control based on IP source addresses alone. TSIG can secure zone transfers between a master server and its slaves and can implement secure dynamic updates.

TSIG signatures sign messages and responses between servers, not between servers and resolvers. The transaction signature authenticates the peer and verifies that the data has not been tampered with. The signatures are checked at the time a packet is received and are then discarded; they are not cached and do not become part of the DNS data.

TSIG uses a symmetric encryption scheme. That is, the encryption key is the same as the decryption key. This single key is called a shared-secret key. Although the TSIG specification allows multiple encryption methods, BIND implements only one, the HMAC-MD5 algorithm.

You should use a different key for each pair of servers that want to communicate securely. TSIG is much less expensive computationally than public key cryptography, but it is only appropriate for a local network on which the number of pairs of communicating servers is small. It does not scale to the global Internet.

BIND's **dnssec-keygen**[18] utility generates a key for a pair of servers. For example, to generate a shared-secret host key for two servers, master and slave1, use

```
# dnssec-keygen -a HMAC-MD5 -b 128 -n HOST master-slave1
```

The **-b 128** flag tells **dnssec-keygen** to create a 128-bit key. Two files are produced: **Kmaster-slave1.+157+09068.private** and **Kmaster-slave1.+157+09068.key**. The 157 stands for the HMAC-MD5 algorithm, and the 09068 is a random[19] number used as a key identifier in case you have multiple keys for the same pair of servers. The **.private** file looks like this:

```
Private-key-format: v1.2
Algorithm: 157 (HMAC_MD5)
Key: jxopbeb+aPc71Mm2vc9R9g==
```

and the **.key** file like this:

```
master-slave1. IN KEY 512 3 157 jxopbeb+aPc71Mm2vc9R9g==
```

Both of these files should have mode 600 and should be owned by the **named** user.

Note the dot that has been added after the master-slave1 argument string in both the filenames and the contents of the **.key** file. The motivation for this convention is that in other contexts, key names must be fully qualified domain names and must therefore end in a dot.

You don't actually need the **.key** file at all—it's produced because the **dnssec-keygen** program also generates public key pairs in which the public key (**.key** file) is inserted

---

18. This command was called **dnskeygen** in BIND 8.
19. It's not actually random, or even pseudo-random; it's a hash of the DNSKEY resource record.

into the DNS zone file as a KEY resource record. The 512 in the KEY record is not the key length, but rather a flag bit that specifies that the record is a DNS key record.

After all this complication, you may be disappointed to learn that the generated key is really just a long random number. You could generate the key manually by writing down an ASCII string of the right length (divisible by 4) and pretending that it's a base-64 encoding of something or by using **mmencode** to encode a random string. The way you create the key is not important; it just has to exist on both machines.

scp is part of the SSH suite. See page 697 for details.

Copy the key to both master and slave1 with **scp**, or cut and paste it. *Do not* use **telnet** or **ftp** to copy the key; even internal networks may not be secure. The key must be included in both machines' **named.conf** files. Since **named.conf** is usually world-readable and keys should not be, put the key in a separate file that is included into **named.conf**. For example, you could put the snippet

```
key master-slave1. {
    algorithm hmac-md5 ;
    secret "shared-key-you-generated" ;
} ;
```

in the file **master-slave1.tsig**. The file should have mode 600, and its owner should be **named**'s UID. In the **named.conf** file, add the line

```
include "master-slave1.tsig" ;
```

near the top.

This part of the configuration simply defines the keys. For them to actually be used to sign and verify updates, the master needs to require the key for transfers and the slave needs to identify the master with a server statement and keys clause. For example, you might add the line

```
allow-transfer { key master-slave1. ;} ;
```

to the zone statement on the master server, and the line

```
server master's-IP-address { keys { master-slave1. ; } ; } ;
```

to the slave's **named.conf** file. If the master server allows dynamic updates, it can also use the key in its allow-update clause in the zone statement.

We have used the generic names master and slave1 to identify the servers and key. If you use TSIG keys for many zones, you should include the zone in your naming scheme as well, to help you keep everything straight.

To test your TSIG configuration, run **named-checkconf** to verify that you have the syntax right. Then use **dig** to attempt a zone transfer (**dig @***master* **axfr**) from both slave1 and from some other machine. The first should succeed and the second should fail with the diagnostic "Transfer failed." To be totally sure everything is right, remove the allow-transfer clause and try the **dig** commands again. This time, both should succeed. (Don't forget to put the allow-transfer back in!) As a final test, increase the serial number for the zone on the master server and watch the log file on the slave to see if it picks up the change and transfers the zone.

When you first start using transaction signatures, run **named** at debug level 1 (see page 466 for information about debug mode) for a while to see any error messages that are generated. Older versions of BIND do not understand signed messages and complain about them, sometimes to the point of refusing to load the zone.

TKEY is a BIND 9 mechanism that allows two hosts to generate a shared-secret key automatically without phone calls or secure copies to distribute the key. It uses an algorithm called the Diffie-Hellman key exchange in which each side makes up a random number, does some math on it, and sends the result to the other side. Each side then mathematically combines its own number with the transmission it received to arrive at the same key. An eavesdropper might overhear the transmission but will be unable to reverse the math.[20] Unfortunately, the code to make TKEY really useful and avoid storing the TSIG key in the configuration file has never been implemented; hopefully, it's on the to-do list.

See page 902 for more information about NTP.
When using TSIG keys and transaction signatures between master and slave servers, you should keep the clocks of the servers synchronized with NTP. If the clocks are too far apart (more than 5 minutes in BIND 9), signature verification will not work. This problem can be very hard to debug.

It is currently not possible to use TSIG keys to secure communications between BIND and Microsoft servers. Microsoft uses TSIG in a nonstandard way (GSS-TSIG) and won't share the details of its scheme outside the context of a nondisclosure agreement. Negotiations are under way to resolve this conflict.

SIG(0) is another mechanism for signing transactions between servers or between dynamic updaters and the master server. It uses public key cryptography; see RFCs 2535 and 2931 for details.

DNSSEC

DNSSEC is a set of DNS extensions that authenticate the origin of zone data and verify its integrity by using public key cryptography. That is, the extensions permit DNS clients to ask the questions "Did this DNS data really come from the zone's owner?" and "Is this really the data sent by that owner?"

DNSSEC relies on a cascading chain of trust: the root servers provide validation information for the top-level domains, the top-level domains provide validation information for the second-level domains, and so on. BIND's trusted-keys configuration option lets us bootstrap the process and secure parts of the DNS tree before the root and top-level domains are secured.

Public key cryptosystems use two keys: one to encrypt (sign) and a different one to decrypt (verify). Publishers sign their data with a secret "private" key. Anyone can

---

20. The math involved is called the discrete log problem and relies on the fact that for modular arithmetic, taking powers is easy but taking logs to undo the powers is close to impossible.

verify the validity of a signature with a matching "public" key that is widely distributed. If a public key correctly decrypts a zone file, then the zone must have been encrypted with the corresponding private key. The trick is to make sure that the public keys you use for verification are authentic. Public key systems allow one entity to sign the public key of another, thus vouching for the legitimacy of the key; hence the term "chain of trust."

The data in a DNS zone is too voluminous to be encrypted with public key cryptography—the encryption would be too slow. Instead, since the data is not secret, a secure hash (e.g., an MD5 checksum) is run on the data and the results of the hash are signed (encrypted) by the zone's private key. The results of the hash are like a fingerprint of the data and are called a digital signature. The signatures are appended to the data they authenticate as RRSIG records in the signed zone file.

To verify the signature, you decrypt it with the public key of the signer, run the data through the same secure hash algorithm, and compare the computed hash value with the decrypted hash value. If they match, you have authenticated the signer and verified the integrity of the data.

In the DNSSEC system, each zone has its own public and private keys. The private key signs each RRset (that is, each set of records of the same type for the same host). The public key verifies the signatures and is included in the zone's data in the form of a DNSKEY resource record.

Parent zones sign their child zones' public keys. **named** verifies the authenticity of a child zone's DNSKEY record by checking it against the parent zone's signature. To verify the authenticity of the parent zone's key, **named** can check the parent's parent, and so on back to the root. The public key for the root zone would be included in the root hints file.

Before we jump into the mechanics of generating keys and signing zones, we need to be honest about the current status of DNSSEC and its impact on sysadmins. Sysadmins may need to deal with DNSSEC in a year or two, but it is certainly not on the must-do-this-week list. Many applications are crying for a public key infrastructure ("PKI"), and DNS is a prime candidate for supplying it. However, we have a bit of a chicken and egg problem. We need to be sure that DNS is secure before we can trust it with our keys for other Internet transactions. But we need a public key infrastructure in order to secure DNS.

Recent changes to the DNSSEC specifications have made it much closer to being deployable than it was in the past. The original DNSSEC spec kept copies of the signed keys for child zones in both the parent and the child domains, so continual communication was required if either the child or the parent wanted to change its key. Since there were multiple copies of each key, it was not clear which copy you should believe when the two were out of sync.

RFC4034 has introduced a new resource record type (DS, the delegation signer), has separated keys into key-signing keys and zone-signing keys, and has changed the names of some resource records:

- KEY became DNSKEY, for cryptographic keys
- SIG became RRSIG, the signature for a resource record set
- NXT became NSEC, to identify the next secure entry in the delegation

KEY and SIG records are still used with SIG(0) and TSIG security. DNSKEY, RRSIG, and NSEC are used with DNSSEC, and NXT is obsolete. The changes from SIG to RRSIG and from NXT to NSEC are minor; the names have changed so as not to confuse old software with the new scheme.

Keys included in a DNSKEY resource record can be either key-signing keys (KSKs) or zone-signing keys (ZSKs). A new flag, called SEP for "secure entry point," distinguishes between them. Bit 15 of the flags field is set to 1 for KSKs and to 0 for ZSKs. This convention makes KSKs odd and ZSKs even when treated as decimal numbers.

The DS record appears only in the parent zone and indicates that a subzone is secure (signed). It also identifies the key used by the child to self-sign its own key RRset. The DS record includes a key identifier (a 5-digit number), cryptographic algorithm, digest type, and a digest of the public key record allowed (or used) to sign the child's key resource record.

The question of how to change existing keys in the parent and child zones has been a thorny one that seemed destined to require cooperation and communication between parent and child. The creation of the DS record, the use of separate key-signing and zone-signing keys, and the use of multiple key pairs have helped address the problem.

Multiple keys can be generated and signed so that a smooth transition from one key to the next is possible. The child may change its zone-signing keys without notifying the parent; it need only coordinate with the parent if it changes its key-signing key. As keys roll over, there is a period during which both the old key and the new key are valid; once cached values on the Internet have expired, the old key can be retired.

Current BIND releases have removed OpenSSL from the distribution, so if you want to use DNSSEC, you will have to get a package that includes DNSSEC support or obtain the SSL libraries from www.openssl.org and then recompile BIND with cryptographic support turned on (use the **--with-openssl** option to **./configure**). If you don't do this, **dnssec-keygen** will complain. However, it will still work for generating TSIG keys, since these don't require OpenSSL.

You perform several steps to create and use signed zones. First, you generate one or more key pairs for the zone. For example,

```
# dnssec-keygen -a DSA -b 768 -n ZONE mydomain.com
```

generates a 768-bit key pair using the DSA algorithm to be used for signing a zone called mydomain.com. Several encryption algorithms are available with a range of key lengths: RSAMD5 (512–4096), RSASHA1 (512–4096), DH (128–4096), and DSA

(512–1024 and divisible by 64). You can include the **-f KSK** flag (not used here) to identify the generated key as a key-signing key by setting its SEP bit.

dnssec-keygen prints the following to standard out:

```
Kmydomain.com.+003+50302
```

where Kmydomain.com is the name of the key, 003 is the DSA algorithm's identifier, and 50302 is the key identifier. **dnssec-keygen** creates files containing the public and private keys:

Kmydomain.com.+003+50302.key   # Public key
Kmydomain.com.+003+50302.private   # Private key

The private key is used to sign a zone's data records, and the public key is used to verify signatures. The public key is typically inserted in the zone file right after the SOA record.

Ideally, the private key portion of any key pair would be kept off-line, or at least on a machine that is not on the Internet. This precaution is impossible for dynamically updated zones and impractical for zone-signing keys, but it is perfectly reasonable for key-signing keys, which are presumably quite long-lived.

It's hard to get a sense of these files generated by **dnssec-keygen** without inspecting their contents, so let's take a quick peek:

Kmydomain.com.+003+50302.key

```
mydomain.com. IN DNSKEY 256 3 3
        BMORyx8sRz6EJ6ETfRj0Ph4uraB1tLZTYI1WU6D7O7/GiBXwxAsvpgH6
        sNXE3uwZVaQFxvDHfa6amy3JSSilcRNfiiOs3LfoyZzUWOceVo6zRBoO
        3GTYpZ6efrFUackXKr9WsadC+4W+2fGx4yL8N6B32akBTiIMLp01FOJe
        xqLe6QrJVE21eXzRqC58TC25R6TPMoOH6cuue5w8eNphcsOsGRfOf4hy
        lOwkb6T7etH//EQgfkLWqcwolVF9hjzskX64e0QeeENXRV8sFvTMVzTk
        qA4KJsBCclVzrDSLAsLZtYH4g6VvrMZHuQ5C/ArCIsdn0RO0mpH6ZUIl
        WaSIE1pAxaZ7ynD4hT1RB5br2KiyGTr27dHi7QS4vOW7oDDPI9+lwAcK
        g2A3LHpmg1S59utmpxJa
```

Kmydomain.com.+003+50302.private

```
Private-key-format: v1.2
Algorithm: 3 (DSA)
Prime(p): tLZTYI1WU6D7O7/GiBXwxAsvpgH6sNXE3uwZVaQFxvDHfa6amy3JSSilc
        RNfiiOs3LfoyZzUWOceVo6zRBoO3GTYpZ6efrFUackXKr9WsadC+4W+2fGx4y
        L8N6B32akB
Subprime(q): w5HLHyxHPoQnoRN9GPQ+Hi6toHU=
Base(g): TiIMLp01FOJexqLe6QrJVE21eXzRqC58TC25R6TPMoOH6cuue5w8eNphcs
        OsGRfOf4hylOwkb6T7etH//EQgfkLWqcwolVF9hjzskX64e0QeeENXRV8sFvTM
        VzTkqA4K
Private_value(x): GqcQz8K56CmUxgo6ERuyEWMLVME=
Public_value(y): JsBCclVzrDSLAsLZtYH4g6VvrMZHuQ5C/ArCIsdn0RO0mpH6ZUIl
        WaSIE1pAxaZ7ynD4hT1RB5br2KiyGTr27dHi7QS4vOW7oDDPI9+lwAcKg2A3L
        Hpmg1S59utmpxJa
```

To facilitate key rollover, you should make several KSK key pairs and get them all signed by your parent zone. Once you and your parent zone have an established trust relationship (a KSK signed by the parent and included in the DS record delegating your secure zone), you can use that relationship to bootstrap the key rollover process. Just send the parent that key to establish who you are along with additional KSKs that you would like signed and pointed to by DS records. After the new keys are signed, you can retire the original one.

Once the parent has signed your KSK and inserted it in your DS record, you are ready to sign your zone's actual data. The signing operation takes a normal zone data file as input and adds RRSIG and NSEC records immediately after every set of resource records. The RRSIG records are the actual signatures, and the NSEC records support signing of negative answers.

To sign a zone, use the **dnssec-signzone** command. For example, the command

```
# dnssec-signzone -o mydomain.com db.mydomain
    Kmydomain.com+003+50302
```

reads the zone file **db.mydomain** and produces a signed version of that zone file called **db.mydomain.signed**. It also creates two keyset files:

keyset-mydomain.com.	# Keyset
dsset-mydomain.com.	# Secure delegation keyset

These keyset files are used for signing zones and keys, respectively. They contain:

keyset-mydomain.com.

```
$ORIGIN .
mydomain.com    172800    IN    DNSKEY    256 3 3 (
                          BMORyx8sRz6EJ6ETfRj0Ph4uraB1tLZTYI1W
                          U6D7O7/GiBXwxAsvpgH6sNXE3uwZVaQFxvDH
                          fa6amy3JSSilcRNfiiOs3LfoyZzUWOceVo6z
                          RBoO3GTYpZ6efrFUackXKr9WsadC+4W+2fGx
                          4yL8N6B32akBTiIMLp01FOJexqLe6QrJVE21
                          eXzRqC58TC25R6TPMoOH6cuue5w8eNphcsOs
                          GRfOf4hylOwkb6T7etH//EQgfkLWqcwolVF9
                          hjzskX64e0QeeENXRV8sFvTMVzTkqA4KJsBC
                          clVzrDSLAsLZtYH4g6VvrMZHuQ5C/ArCIsdn
                          0ROOmpH6ZUIlWaSIE1pAxaZ7ynD4hT1RB5br
                          2KiyGTr27dHi7QS4vOW7oDDPI9+lwAcKg2A3
                          LHpmg1S59utmpxJa
                          ) ; key id = 50302
```

dsset-mydomain.com.

```
mydomain.com. IN DS 50302 3 1 1B44471AFD5B4F4463BB3A0D7B66B6ABC018DA96
```

Any keyset files for child zones in the current directory are also signed and incorporated into DS records, which delegate the secure subzones to the children's servers and authenticate them with the signed keys. It can take a long time to sign a zone.

If a signed zone is passed as the argument to **dnssec-signzone**, the signatures of any records that are close to expiring are renewed. "Close to expiring" is defined as being three-quarters of the way through the validity period. By default, signatures are valid for 30 days, but a different period can be specified on the **dnssec-signzone** command line. Re-signing typically results in changes but does not automatically change the serial number (yet), so sysadmins will need to update the serial number by hand. Slave servers of the zone will have to perform a zone transfer operation to resynchronize themselves.

The following example shows zone data before and after signing.[21] Here's the before:

```
$TTL 172800 ; 2 days
@              IN   SOA   ns.mydomain.com. hostmaster.mydomain.com. (
                         2006081200     ; serial
                         7200           ; refresh (2 hours)
                         3600           ; retry (1 hour)
                         1728000        ; expire (2 weeks 6 days)
                         172800         ; minimum (2 days)
                         )

               IN   NS    ns.cs.colorado.edu.

mydomain.com. IN   DNSKEY 256 3 3
               BMORyx8sRz6EJ6ETfRj0Ph4uraB1tLZTYI1WU6D7O7/GiBXwxAsvpgH6
               sNXE3uwZVaQFxvDHfa6amy3JSSilcRNfiiOs3LfoyZzUWOceVo6zRBoO
               3GTYpZ6efrFUackXKr9WsadC+4W+2fGx4yL8N6B32akBTiIMLp01FOJe
               lOwkb6T7etH//EQgfkLWqcwolVF9hjzskX64e0QeeENXRV8sFvTMVzTk
               qA4KJsBCclVzrDSLAsLZtYH4g6VvrMZHuQ5C/ArCIsdn0RO0mpH6ZUIl
               WaSIE1pAxaZ7ynD4hT1RB5br2KiyGTr27dHi7QS4vOW7oDDPI9+lwAcK
               g2A3LHpmg1S59utmpxJa

anchor         IN   A     128.138.242.1
               IN   A     128.138.243.140
               IN   MX    10 anchor
               IN   MX    99 @
awesome        IN   A     128.138.236.20
...
```

And the after:

```
; File written on Thu Nov 11 17:41:25 2006
; dnssec_signzone version 9.3.0
mydomain.com. 172800 IN SOA ns.mydomain.com. hostmaster.mydomain.com. (
                         2006081200  ; serial
                         7200        ; refresh (2 hours)
                         3600        ; retry (1 hour)
                         1728000     ; expire (2 weeks 6 days)
                         172800      ; minimum (2 days)
                         )
```

21. We tried to simplify the example by just using two hosts and their A and MX records, but dnssec-sign-zone requires a "real" zone and so the SOA, NS, and DNSKEY records had to be added for a minimal example. Sorry for the clutter.

```
        172800  RRSIG    SOA 3 2 172800 20061211164125 (
                            20061111164125 50302 mydomain.com.
                            BElneYxZ3g9JnKbXdnmPhKVWfd13JTU8ajOO
                            5dQta2WeBAatNuWt8dQ= )
        172800  NS       ns.cs.colorado.edu.
        172800  RRSIG    NS 3 2 172800 20061211164125 (
                            20061111164125 50302 mydomain.com.
                            BLG6LRrXtRHRdRFtTOmlQsadOIefqHAq5Rid
                            PHZ74vOl/UkEW6wY6VA= )
        172800  NSEC     anchor.mydomain.com. NS SOA RRSIG NSEC DNSKEY
        172800  RRSIG    NSEC 3 2 172800 20061211164125 (
                            20061111164125 50302 mydomain.com.
                            BCz31GPChdQrmNrZypv4xxmXDCThZ0IlkEGL
                            TSkf7Q+TmCDmAADxmBE= )
        172800  DNSKEY   256 3 3 (
                            BMORyx8sRz6EJ6ETfRj0Ph4uraB1tLZTYI1W
                            U6D7O7/GiBXwxAsvpgH6sNXE3uwZVaQFxvDH
                            fa6amy3JSSilcRNfiiOs3LfoyZzUWOceVo6z
                            RBoO3GTYpZ6efrFUackXKr9WsadC+4W+2fGx
                            4yL8N6B32akBTiIMLp01FOJexqLe6QrJVE21
                            eXzRqC58TC25R6TPMoOH6cuue5w8eNphcsOs
                            GRfOf4hylOwkb6T7etH//EQgfkLWqcwolVF9
                            hjzskX64e0QeeENXRV8sFvTMVzTkqA4KJsBC
                            clVzrDSLAsLZtYH4g6VvrMZHuQ5C/ArCIsdn
                            0ROOmpH6ZUIlWaSIE1pAxaZ7ynD4hT1RB5br
                            2KiyGTr27dHi7QS4vOW7oDDPI9+lwAcKg2A3
                            LHpmg1S59utmpxJa
                            ) ; key id = 50302
        172800  RRSIG    DNSKEY 3 2 172800 20061211164125 (
                            20061111164125 50302 mydomain.com.
                            BAgZDfk/YCOhVfuoyG5pgfyFCmsGqg4W7uuM
                            Rm5eNP9Bn0EbBnuT6X0= )
anchor.mydomain.com. 172800 IN A 128.138.242.1
        172800  IN A     128.138.243.140
        172800  RRSIG    A 3 3 172800 20061211164125 (
                            20061111164125 50302 mydomain.com.
                            BIRtKW0Um7ItfbPqRew+jKo152WJh+4nHkmK
                            1ePNxjsQWcgaKm5jiMU= )
        172800  MX       10 anchor.mydomain.com.
        172800  MX       99 mydomain.com.
        172800  RRSIG    MX 3 3 172800 20061211164125 (
                            20061111164125 50302 mydomain.com.
                            BGtmN2u30y1pMDzstWGgWZfXB3lDlmy5W6DP
                            t/8D31QpyYNBjJPb8J4= )
        172800  NSEC     awesome.mydomain.com. A MX RRSIG NSEC
        172800  RRSIG    NSEC 3 3 172800 20061211164125 (
                            20061111164125 50302 mydomain.com.
                            BArN6oES72gzFgQmBHL3NzlquMbDbLfpvj7J
                            3CSb/c8U/bciWGXsV3Q= )
```

DNS

```
awesome.mydomain.com. 172800 IN A 128.138.236.20
        172800  RRSIG    A 3 3 172800 20061211164125 (
                         20061111164125 50302 mydomain.com.
                         BJ/qWBgLgS/2N5CoXGnI4vs91SsyIBKKfoq9
                         R+VsMpRmnVrSi1DU1n8= )
        172800  NSEC     mydomain.com. A RRSIG NSEC
        172800  RRSIG    NSEC 3 3 172800 20061211164125 (
                         20061111164125 50302 mydomain.com.
                         BKoByqF5wUceb2vc8H2uealgKrejH4VZ0S5m
                         Q4KukWCUo2IAFX+msQ4= )
```

As you can see, signed zones are ugly. They are typically four to ten times larger than the original zone, and your nice logical ordering is lost. For all practical purposes, a signed zone file is no longer human-readable, and it cannot be edited by hand because of the RRSIG and NSEC records. No user-serviceable parts inside!

An RRSIG record contains a wealth of information:

- The type of record set being signed
- The signature algorithm used (in our case, it's 3, the DSA algorithm)
- The TTL of the record set that was signed
- The time the signature expires (as *yyyymmddhhssss*)
- The time the record set was signed (also *yyyymmddhhssss*)
- The key identifier (in our case, 50302)
- The signer's name (mydomain.com.)
- And finally, the digital signature itself

To use the signed zone, change the file parameter in the **named.conf** zone statement for mydomain.com to point at **db.mydomain.signed** instead of **db.mydomain**. Whew! That's it.

Negative answers

Digital signatures are fine for positive answers such as "Here is the IP address for the host anchor.cs.colorado.edu, along with a signature to prove that it really came from cs.colorado.edu and that the data is valid." But what about negative answers like "No such host?" Such responses typically do not return any signable records.

In DNSSEC, this problem is handled by NSEC records that list the next secure record in the zone in a canonical sorted order.[22] If the next record after anchor in cs.colorado.edu were awesome.cs.colorado.edu and a query for anthill.cs.colorado.edu arrived, the response would be a signed NSEC record such as

```
anchor.cs.colorado.edu.  IN  NSEC awesome.cs.colorado.edu A MX NSEC
```

This record says that the name immediately after anchor in the cs.colorado.edu zone is awesome.cs.colorado.edu and that anchor has at least one A record, MX record,

---

22. The ordering is sort of alphabetical, but with names higher up the DNS tree coming first. For example, in the cs.colorado.edu zone, cs.colorado.edu comes before any host.cs.colorado.edu. Within a level of the hierarchy, the ordering is alphabetical.

and NSEC record. NSEC records are also returned if the host exists but the record type queried for does not exist. For example, if the query was for an LOC record for anchor, anchor's same NSEC record would be returned and would show only A, MX, and NSEC records.

The last NSEC record in a zone wraps around to the first name in the zone. For example, the NSEC record for zamboni.cs.colorado.edu would point back to the first record, that for cs.colorado.edu itself:

```
zamboni.cs.colorado.edu.  IN   NSEC cs.colorado.edu A MX NSEC
```

NSEC records provide a way for a persistent querier to enumerate the contents of a zone one record at a time. Not good for security or privacy.

Microsoft and DNS

Windows uses SRV resource records to discover pretty much everything: name servers, printers, filesystems, and so forth. Microsoft has followed the IETF specifications in their implementation of SRV records, but the manner in which the records are inserted into DNS by means of a secure dynamic update is nonstandard. Microsoft uses a variation of transaction signatures called GSS-TSIG that uses a shared secret obtained from the Kerberos KDC (Key Distribution Center). At the moment, Microsoft's implementation uses the vendor extensions field and therefore is not compatible with the open source version of Kerberos 5.

If you want to run Windows and use SRV records, you'll have to eliminate your existing Kerberos realm and run a Windows Kerberos server on your networks. For some sites with a rich Kerberos infrastructure, this problem is a showstopper. Microsoft seems to be using open protocols just enough to sneak past companies' purchasing checklists, but not enough to allow anyone else to interoperate and sell into their market. Let's hope that Microsoft will document their extensions without the currently required nondisclosure agreement so that ISC can make its TSIG and Microsoft's GSS-TSIG interoperate.

About a week after Windows 2000 was released, the query load on the DNS root servers increased significantly. A bit of digging revealed that Windows 2000 machines were trying to dynamically update the root or top-level zones. The number of UDP queries to the A root server more than doubled as a result. To make matters worse, when their update requests were refused, the Win2K machines asked for a KEY record to try an authenticated update. This also failed, so they tried one final time by opening a TCP connection to attempt an authenticated dynamic update. A root server does not have time for the zillions of TCP connection requests that resulted.

Bugs that affect the Internet infrastructure are both serious and potentially embarrassing, so we assumed that Microsoft would have fixed this problem by now. We were looking forward to converting this section to a historical footnote, but just to be thorough, we reviewed the network traffic of a newly installed Windows XP system running Service Pack 2. Surprisingly, we found it to be as intransigent as ever.

The problem appears most commonly (but not exclusively) in the reverse zones for the private IP address spaces defined in RFC1918. Information about these addresses should never escape the local environment, but Windows machines try to update their enclosing domain, and if that fails, they continue up the DNS naming tree until they finally reach the root servers.

For example, if assigned the address 192.168.1.10 by a DHCP server, a Windows machine will try to dynamically update the domain 1.168.192.in-addr.arpa. If that fails, it will try to update 168.192.in-addr.arpa, then 192.in-addr.arpa, then in-addr.arpa, and finally arpa.

Windows systems that have not reset their DNS defaults are part of a continuous, massive, slow, unintentional, distributed denial of service attack on the root name servers. To stop Windows 2000 or XP systems from attempting to update the root zones and make them play more nicely with your UNIX or Linux name servers, try the following procedure.

- Right-click on My Network Places and select Properties, which displays a window labeled Network Connections.

- Right-click on each connection in turn and select Properties.

- Click on Internet Protocol (TCP/IP), then click the Properties button.

- Click the Advanced... button at the bottom of the properties page.

- Click the DNS tab at the top.

- Toward the bottom of the page remove the check from the "Register this connection's address in DNS" line.

- Click OK all the way out.

To buy time, the operators of the root zones have delegated the reverse zones for RFC1918 address space to the servers called prisoner.iana.org, blackhole1.iana.org, and blackhole2.iana.org. These servers are authoritative (prisoner the master, blackholes the slaves) for these zones and intercept the dynamic updates generated by Windows systems that want to tell the world that the name "mypc" should be associated with the address 10.0.0.1. These iana.org servers are anycast and have an instance at most large ISPs, so the bogus DNS update messages that escape the local site do not have to clutter the Internet all the way to the root servers.

But wait, that is not the end of Microsoft's DNS misbehavior. If their preferred DNS servers don't respond to a query within one second, Windows systems rapidly escalate to issuing multiple simultaneous queries to every DNS server they know about.[23] In other words, at the first sign of server overload or network congestion, Windows tries to generate as much network and server traffic as possible. You can turn off this

---

23. This behavior is apparently intentional. See the Microsoft DNS white paper referred to in Microsoft's knowledge base article 286834 (support.microsoft.com) for more information.

behavior by disabling the DNS Client service, but be warned that doing so disables each machine's local DNS cache as well. Here's how to disable the DNS Client service:

- Select Settings->Control Panel from the Start menu.
- In the control panel, double-click Administrative Tools.
- On the Administrative Tools page, double-click Computer Management.
- On the left side, click the "+" next to Services and Applications to expand it.
- Select Services on the left side and double-click DNS Client on the right.
- Click the pull-down menu beside "Startup type" and select Manual.
- Click the Stop button to halt the already running copy of the service.
- Click OK all the way out.

If you are not using Microsoft's Active Directory service, you are probably best off using UNIX/Linux servers for DNS and avoiding the Microsoft implementation. Unfortunately, Active Directory complicates things, but you can support Active Directory with BIND.

A final point: Microsoft servers raise a ruckus when they query a zone whose servers are all lame. If your site delegates to servers that appear to be lame, it's good practice to at least install an empty zone file that substitutes for the missing servers. This measure will prevent Microsoft servers that query for the lame name from becoming confused and pummeling the root and gTLD servers.

15.16 TESTING AND DEBUGGING

named provides several built-in debugging aids, foremost among which is its voluptuously configurable logging. You can specify debug levels on the command line or set them with **rndc**. You can also instruct **named** to dump its operating statistics to a file. You can verify name lookups with external tools such as **dig**.

Logging

See Chapter 10 for more information about syslog.

named's logging facilities are flexible enough to make your hair stand on end. BIND originally just used syslog to report error messages and anomalies. Recent versions generalize the syslog concepts by adding another layer of indirection and support for logging directly to files. Before we dive in, let's take a look at the mini-glossary of BIND logging terms shown in Table 15.12.

You configure BIND logging with a logging statement in **named.conf**. You first define channels, the possible destinations for messages. You then tell various categories of message to go to particular channels.

When a message is generated, it is assigned a category, a module, and a severity at its point of origin. It is then distributed to all the channels associated with its category and module. Each channel has a severity filter that tells what severity level a message must have in order to get through. Channels that lead to syslog are also filtered according to the rules in **/etc/syslog.conf**.

Table 15.12 A BIND logging lexicon

Term	What it means
channel	A place where messages can go: syslog, a file, or **/dev/null**[a]
category	A class of messages that **named** can generate; for example, messages about dynamic updates or messages about answering queries
module	The name of the source module that generates a message
facility	A syslog facility name. DNS does not have its own specific facility, but you have your pick of all the standard ones.
severity	The "badness" of an error message; what syslog refers to as a priority

a. **/dev/null** is a pseudo-device that throws all input away.

Here's the outline of a logging statement:

```
logging {
        channel_def;
        channel_def;
        ...
        category category_name {
                channel_name;
                channel_name;
                ...
        };
};
```

Channels

A *channel_def* looks slightly different depending on whether the channel is a file channel or a syslog channel. You must choose file or syslog for each channel; a channel can't be both at the same time.

```
channel channel_name {

        file path [versions numvers | unlimited] [size sizespec];
        syslog facility;
        severity severity;

        print-category yes | no;
        print-severity yes | no;
        print-time yes | no;
};
```

For a file channel, *numvers* tells how many backup versions of a file to keep, and *sizespec* specifies how large the file should be allowed to grow (examples: 2048, 100k, 20m, 15g, unlimited, default) before it is automatically rotated. If you name a file channel **mylog**, then the rotated versions will be **mylog.0**, **mylog.1**, and so on.

See page 212 for a list of syslog facility names. In the syslog case, *facility* specifies what syslog facility name is used to log the message. It can be any standard facility. In practice, only daemon and local0 through local7 are reasonable choices.

The rest of the statements in a *channel_def* are optional. *severity* can have the values (in descending order) critical, error, warning, notice, info, or debug (with an optional numeric level, e.g., severity debug 3). The value dynamic is also recognized and matches the server's current debug level.

The various print options add or suppress message prefixes. Syslog prepends the time and reporting host to each message logged, but not the severity or the category. The source filename (module) that generated the message is also available as a print option. It makes sense to enable print-time only for file channels; no need to duplicate syslog's time stamps.

The four channels listed in Table 15.13 are predefined by default. These defaults should be fine for most installations.

Table 15.13   Predefined logging channels in BIND

Channel name	What it does
default_syslog	Sends to syslog, facility daemon, severity info
default_debug	Logs to the file **named.run**, severity set to dynamic
default_stderr	Sends to standard error of the **named** process, severity info
null	Discards all messages

Categories

Categories are determined by the programmer at the time the code is written; they organize log messages by topic or functionality instead of just by severity. Table 15.14 shows the current list of message categories.

Log Messages

The default logging configuration is:

```
logging {
    category default { default_syslog; default_debug; };
};
```

You should watch the log files when you make major changes to BIND and perhaps increase the logging level. Later, reconfigure to preserve only serious messages once you have verified that **named** is stable

Query logging can be quite educational. You can verify that your allow clauses are working, see who is querying you, identify broken clients, etc. It's a good check to perform after major reconfigurations, especially if you have a good sense of what your query load looked like before the changes.

To start query logging, just direct the queries category to a channel. Writing to syslog is less efficient than writing directly to a file, so use a file channel on a local disk when you are logging every query. Have lots of disk space and be ready to turn query logging off once you obtain enough data. (**rndc querylog** toggles query logging on and off dynamically.)

Table 15.14   BIND logging categories

Category	What it includes
client	Client requests
config	Configuration file parsing and processing
database	Messages about database operations
default	Default for categories without specific logging options
delegation-only	Queries forced to NXDOMAIN by delegation-only zones
dispatch	Dispatching of incoming packets to server modules
dnssec	DNSSEC messages
general	Catchall for unclassified messages
lame-servers	Servers that are supposed to be serving a zone, but aren't [a]
network	Network operations
notify	Messages about the "zone changed" notification protocol
queries	A short log message for every query the server receives (!)
resolver	DNS resolution, e.g., recursive lookups for clients
security	Approved/unapproved requests
unmatched	Queries **named** cannot classify (bad class, no view)
update	Messages about dynamic updates
xfer-in	Zone transfers that the server is receiving
xfer-out	Zone transfers that the server is sending

a. Either the parent zone or the child zone could be at fault; impossible to tell without investigating.

Views can be pesky to debug, but fortunately, the view that matched a particular query is logged as well as the query.

Some common log messages are listed below:

- *Lame server.* If you get this message about one of your own zones, you have configured something incorrectly. The message is relatively harmless if it's about some zone out on the Internet; it's someone else's problem. A good one to throw away by directing it to the null channel.

- *Bad referral.* This message indicates a miscommunication among a zone's name servers.

- *Not authoritative for.* A slave server is unable to get authoritative data for a zone. Perhaps it's pointing to the wrong master, or perhaps the master had trouble loading the zone in question.

- *Rejected zone.* **named** rejected a zone file because it contained errors.

- *No NS RRs found.* A zone file did not include NS records after the SOA record. It could be that the records are missing, or it could be that they don't start with a tab or other whitespace. In the latter case, the records are not attached to the zone of the SOA record and are therefore misinterpreted.

- *No default TTL set.* The preferred way to set the default TTL for resource records is with a $TTL directive at the top of the zone file. This error message indicates that the $TTL is missing; it is required in BIND 9.

- *No root name server for class.* Your server is having trouble finding the root name servers. Check your hints file and the server's Internet connectivity.

- *Address already in use.* The port on which **named** wants to run is already being used by another process, probably another copy of **named**. If you don't see another **named** around, it might have crashed and left an **rndc** control socket open that you'll have to track down and remove.[24] A good way to fix it is to stop and restart the **named** process, for example:

    ```
    # /etc/init.d/named stop (or /sbin/service named stop in Red Hat)
    # /etc/init.d/named start (or /sbin/service named start in Red Hat)
    ```

- *Dropping source port zero packet from …* Recent versions of BIND let you set the query source port number, and sysadmins use this feature to add rules to their firewalls that can recognize their DNS packets by source port. However, 0 is an illegal value for a TCP/UDP port number. If the error message relates to one of your hosts, you should change the query-source directive in that host's **named.conf** file to fix this error.

- *Denied update from […] for …* A dynamic update for a zone was attempted and denied because of the allow-update or update-policy clause in **named.conf** for this zone.

Sample logging configuration

The following snippet from the ISC **named.conf** file for a busy TLD name server illustrates a comprehensive logging regimen.

```
logging {

        channel default_log {
                file "log/named.log" versions 3 size 10m;
                print-time yes;
                print-category yes;
                print-severity  yes;
                severity info;
        };

        category default { default_log; default_debug; };

        channel xfer-log {
                file "log/xfer.log" versions 3 size 10m;
                print-category yes;
                print-severity yes;
                print-time yes;
                severity info;
        };
```

---

24. On a gTLD server, this message probably means that com is still loading. :-)

```
channel db-log {
    file "log/db.log" versions 3 size 1M;
    severity debug 1;
    print-severity yes;
    print-time yes;
};

category database { db-log; };
category dnssec { xfer-log; };
category xfer-in { xfer-log; };
category xfer-out { xfer-log; };
category notify { xfer-log; };
};
```

Debug levels

named debug levels are indicated by integers from 0 to 100. The higher the number, the more verbose the output. Level 0 turns debugging off. Levels 1 and 2 are fine for debugging your configuration and database. Levels beyond about 4 are appropriate for the maintainers of the code.

You invoke debugging on the **named** command line with the **-d** flag. For example,

```
# named -d2
```

would start **named** at debug level 2. By default, debugging information is written to the file **named.run** in the current working directory from which **named** is started. The **named.run** file grows very fast, so don't go out for a beer while debugging or you will have bigger problems when you return.

You can also turn on debugging while **named** is running with **rndc trace**, which increments the debug level by 1, or with **rndc trace** *level*, which sets the debug level to the value specified. **rndc notrace** turns debugging off completely. You can also enable debugging by defining a logging channel that includes a severity specification such as

```
severity debug 3;
```

which sends all debugging messages up to level 3 to that particular channel. Other lines in the channel definition specify the destination of those debugging messages. The higher the severity level, the more information is logged.

Watching the logs or the debugging output illustrates how often DNS data is misconfigured in the real world. That pesky little dot at the end of names (or rather, the lack thereof) accounts for an alarming amount of DNS traffic. Theoretically, the dot is required at the end of each fully qualified domain name.

Debugging with rndc

Table 15.15 on the next page shows some of the options accepted by **rndc**. Typing **rndc** with no arguments gives a list of available commands. Commands that produce files put them in the directory specified as **named**'s home in **named.conf**.

Table 15.15   rndc commands[a]

Command	Function
dumpdb	Dumps the DNS database to **named_dump.db**
flush [*view*]	Flushes all caches or those for a specified *view*
flushname *name* [*view*]	Flushes the specified *name* from the server's cache
freeze *zone* [*class* [*view*]]	Suspends updates to a dynamic *zone*
thaw *zone* [*class* [*view*]]	Resumes updates to a dynamic *zone*
halt	Halts **named** without writing pending updates
querylog	Toggles tracing of incoming queries
notrace	Turns off debugging
reconfig	Reloads the config file and loads any new zones
refresh *zone* [*class* [*view*]]	Schedules maintenance for a *zone*
reload	Reloads **named.conf** and zone files
reload *zone* [*class* [*view*]]	Reloads only the specified *zone* or *view*
restart[b]	Restarts the server
retransfer *zone* [*class* [*view*]]	Recopies the data for *zone* from the master server
stats	Dumps statistics to **named.stats**
status	Displays the current status of the running **named**
stop	Saves pending updates and then stops **named**
trace	Increments the debug level by 1
trace *level*	Changes the debugging level

a. The *class* argument here is the same as for resource records, typically IN for Internet.
b. Not yet implemented in BIND 9 (9.3.0), but promised

rndc reload makes **named** reread its configuration file and reload zone files. The **reload** *zone* command is handy when only one zone has changed and you don't want to reload all the zones, especially on a busy server. You can also specify a class and view to reload only the selected view of the zone's data. **rndc reconfig** makes it easy to add new zones without doing a full reload; it rereads the configuration file and loads any new zones without disturbing existing zones.

rndc freeze *zone* stops dynamic updates and reconciles the journal file of pending updates to the data files. After freezing the zone, you can edit the zone data by hand. As long as the zone is frozen, dynamic updates will be refused. Once you've finished editing, use **rndc thaw** *zone* to start accepting dynamic updates again.

rndc dumpdb makes **named** dump its database to **named_dump.db**. The dump file is big and includes not only local data but also any cached data the name server has accumulated. A recent dump of the database cache on our primary name server was over 16MB, but the zone data loaded was less than 200K. Lots of caching there.

If you are running **named** in a **chroot**ed environment, you will have to give **rndc** the path to the **rndc** socket because it will not be in **/var/run** where **rndc** expects it.

Use something like:

```
$ sudo rndc -l /var/named/var/run/rndc
```

In BIND 9, it's important to make sure that the version of **named** and the version of **rndc** match lest you get an error message about a protocol version mismatch. Just install both when you upgrade.

BIND statistics

named maintains some summary information that can be dumped to the file **named.stats** in its working directory on receipt of a nudge from **rndc**:

```
$ sudo rndc stats
```

Here's an example of the output from a busy server at isc.org:

```
+++ Statistics Dump +++ (1088897026)
success 19917007
referral 981446459
nxrrset 9958824
nxdomain 199644113
recursion 0
failure 322556
--- Statistics Dump --- (1088897026)
```

The statistics show the success vs. failure of lookups and categorize the various kinds of errors. This server answered 19.9 million queries successfully, gave out 980 million referrals, answered "no such domain" (nxdomain) about 200 million times, answered "no such resource record set" (nxrrset) about 10 million times, and could not answer 320 thousand times.

The 200 million nxdomain errors (almost 20% of the total 1 billion queries) would be way too many if their primary source were user typos and spelling errors. In this case, most of the errors come from Windows misconfigurations and a bug in Microsoft's resolver[25] that sends out many queries for address records with the data field set to an IP address rather than a hostname as required by the DNS specification. These bizarre queries have an apparent top-level domain of something like 56 (or whatever the last byte of the IP address string was), so they send the local DNS server scurrying off to nag the root servers about this nonexistent domain, ultimately yielding an nxdomain error.

The failure entry counts the failures that are neither nxdomain nor nxrrset.

Debugging with dig

Three tools can be used from the shell to query the DNS database: **nslookup**, **dig**, and **host**. All are distributed with BIND. **nslookup** is the oldest of these tools and has always been part of the BIND distribution. **dig**, the domain information groper, was originally written by Steve Hotz; it has been rewritten for BIND 9 by Michael

---

25. Fixed in Windows 2000 Service Pack 2 and later versions of Windows

Sawyer and is now shipped with BIND 9 as well. **host**, by Eric Wassenaar, is another open source tool; it features user-friendly output and functions that check the syntax of your zone files.

We recommend **dig** over **nslookup**; **host** is OK too.We discuss only **dig** in detail here. You might sometimes get different results from these tools because of the different resolver libraries they use: **dig** and **host** use BIND's resolver, and **nslookup** has its own.

By default, **dig** uses the local name server and returns address information. The @*nameserver* argument makes it query a specific name server.[26] The ability to query a particular server lets you check to be sure any changes you make to a zone are propagated to secondary servers and to the outside world. This feature is especially useful if you use views and need to verify that they are configured correctly.

If you specify a record type, **dig** will query for that type only. The pseudo-type **ANY** returns all data associated with the specified name. Another useful flag is **-x**, which reverses the bytes of an IP address for you and does a reverse query. The **+trace** flag shows the iterative steps in the resolution process from the roots down.

Here's what **dig**'s output looks like:

```
$ dig yahoo.com

; <<>> DiG 9.3.0rc2 <<>> yahoo.com
;; global options:  printcmd
;; Got answer:
;; ->>HEADER<<- opcode: QUERY, status: NOERROR, id: 16507
;; flags: qr rd ra; QUERY: 1, ANSWER: 3, AUTHORITY: 5, ADDITIONAL: 5

;; QUESTION SECTION:
;yahoo.com.              IN     A

;; ANSWER SECTION:
yahoo.com.         300   IN     A    66.94.234.13
yahoo.com.         300   IN     A    216.109.127.28
yahoo.com.         300   IN     A    216.109.127.29

;; AUTHORITY SECTION:
yahoo.com.         74804 IN     NS   ns3.yahoo.com.
yahoo.com.         74804 IN     NS   ns4.yahoo.com.
yahoo.com.         74804 IN     NS   ns1.yahoo.com.
yahoo.com.         74804 IN     NS   ns2.yahoo.com.

;; ADDITIONAL SECTION:
ns1.yahoo.com.     72593 IN     A    66.218.71.63
ns2.yahoo.com.     72596 IN     A    66.163.169.170
ns3.yahoo.com.     72594 IN     A    217.12.4.104
ns4.yahoo.com.     72594 IN     A    63.250.206.138
```

---

26. If the server does not exist, older versions of **dig** will silently fall back to the local server, so read your output carefully to verify the source. Since BIND 9.2, **dig** returns an error and no answer in this situation.

```
;; Query time: 6 msec
;; SERVER: 204.152.184.109#53(204.152.184.109)
;; WHEN: Sun Jul  9 16:03:43 2006
;; MSG SIZE  rcvd: 245
```

dig includes the notation aa in its list of flags if the answer is authoritative. Here we are asking the local name server about yahoo.com, so the answer is not authoritative.

dig's output includes not only the domain information but also the number of queries sent and the answers' round trip time. The output is formatted correctly to be used in a zone file, which is particularly handy when you are querying for the root servers for your hints file. The semicolon is the comment character in a zone file and is used by **dig** to embed comments into its output.

When testing a new configuration, be sure that you look up data for both local and remote hosts. If you can access a host by IP address but not by name, DNS is probably the culprit.

Lame delegations

When you apply for a domain name, you are asking for a part of the DNS naming tree to be delegated to your primary name server and your DNS administrator. If you never use the domain or you change the name servers without updating the parent domain's glue records, a "lame delegation" results.

The effects of a lame delegation can be very bad. If a user tries to contact a host in your lame domain, your name server will refuse the query. DNS will retry the query several hundred times, pummeling both your master server and the root servers. BIND uses a lame server "penalty box" to help with the load created by lameness, but Microsoft servers do not implement it.

There are two ways to find lame delegations: by reviewing the log files or by using a tool called **doc**, short for "domain obscenity control." We look at some **doc** examples in the next section, but let's first review some log entries.

Many sites point the lame-servers logging channel to **/dev/null** and don't bother fretting about the lame delegations of other people. That's fine as long as your own domain is squeaky clean and is not itself a source or victim of lame delegations.

In one log file that was 3.5MB after about a week (at level "info"), over one-third of the log entries were for lame delegations. Of those, 16% involved queries to the root servers, presumably for nonexistent domains. One persistent user queried the root servers for tokyotopless.net hundreds of times. Sigh. Here is an example of a lame delegation log message:

```
Jan 29 05:34:52 ipn.caida.org named[223]: Lame server on 'www.games.net' (in
    'GAMES.net'?): [207.82.198.150].53 'NS2.EXODUS.net'
```

Here's how we'd track down the problem with **dig** (we truncated some of **dig**'s verbose output):

```
$ dig www.games.net.
;; ...
;; QUESTIONS:
;;      www.games.net, type = A, class = IN
;; ANSWERS:
www.games.net.    3600      A    209.1.23.92
;; AUTHORITY RECORDS:
games.net.        3600      NS   ns.exodus.net.
games.net.        3600      NS   ns2.exodus.net.
games.net.        3600      NS   ns.pcworld.com.
;; ADDITIONAL RECORDS: ...
```

The first query at the local server returns the address record for www.games.net and a list of authoritative servers. The server at ns.exodus.net worked fine when we queried it (not shown), but ns2.exodus.net is another story:

```
$ dig @ns2.exodus.net www.games.net.
;; QUESTIONS:
;;      www.games.net, type = A, class = IN
;; AUTHORITY RECORDS:
net.             244362   NS   F.GTLD-SERVERS.net.
net.             244362   NS   J.GTLD-SERVERS.net.
net.             244362   NS   K.GTLD-SERVERS.net.
net.             244362   NS   A.GTLD-SERVERS.net.
;; ...
```

ns2 is listed as being an authoritative server for www.games.net, but it returns no records and refers us to the servers for the net top-level domain. Therefore, we can conclude that ns2.exodus.net is configured incorrectly.

Sometimes when you **dig** at an authoritative server in an attempt to find lameness, **dig** returns no information. Try the query again with the **+norecurse** flag so you can see exactly what the server in question knows.

doc: domain obscenity control

doc is not a part of BIND. It's currently maintained by Brad Knowles, from whose web site it can be downloaded:

> www.shub-internet.org/brad/dns/   *(Note: "shub", not "shrub")*

doc is C shell script. If you plan to put it in your path or run it from **cron**, you must edit the script and set the auxd variable to point to the installation directory.

doc checks delegations by making repeated calls to **dig**. It reports on inconsistencies, errors, and other problems related to a particular domain name. Its screen output summarizes the issues that it finds; it also produces a verbose log file in the current directory with details.

Let's look at some examples. First, atrust.com, where everything seems to be OK:

```
$ doc atrust.com
Doc-2.2.3: doc atrust.com
Doc-2.2.3: Starting test of atrust.com.   parent is com.
Doc-2.2.3: Test date - Thu Jul  6 08:54:38 MDT 2006
Summary:
    No errors or warnings issued for atrust.com.
Done testing atrust.com.  Thu Jul  6 08:54:46 MDT 2006
```

The log file (**log.atrust.com.**) mentions that both com and atrust.com agree on the identities of the name servers for atrust.com and that those two servers have the same serial number in their SOA records. **doc** also checks the PTR records for each of the name servers. The actual **dig** queries that were performed by **doc** are listed at the end of the log file, along with the responses they provoked.

Our next example is for the domain cs.colorado.edu:

```
$ doc cs.colorado.edu
Doc-2.2.3: doc cs.colorado.edu
Doc-2.2.3: Starting test of cs.colorado.edu.   parent is colorado.edu.
Doc-2.2.3: Test date - Thu Jul  6 08:55:15 MDT 2006
dig: Couldn't find server 'rs0.netsol.com.': No address associated with hostname
DIGERR (NOT_ZONE): dig @rs0.netsol.com. for SOA of parent (colorado.edu.) failed
DIGERR (NOT_AUTHORIZED): dig @pacifier.com. for SOA of cs.colorado.edu. failed
dig: Couldn't find server 'xor.com.': No address associated with hostname
DIGERR (FORMAT_ERROR): dig @xor.com. for SOA of cs.colorado.edu. failed
Summary:
    ERRORS found for cs.colorado.edu. (count: 2)
    Incomplete test for cs.colorado.edu. (2)
Done testing cs.colorado.edu.  Thu Jul  6 08:55:26 MDT 2006
```

Here we can see several problems in the parent domain, colorado.edu. The parent's zone data incorrectly lists rs0.netsol.com as a server for colorado.edu, and xor.com and pacifier.com as servers for cs.colorado.edu. To see the whole story, we would have to run **doc** against the parent domain, colorado.edu, and review the detailed log file.

Finally, let's take a look at nsa.cctldmd.net:

```
$ doc nsa.cctldmd.net
Doc-2.2.3: doc nsa.cctldmd.net
Doc-2.2.3: Starting test of nsa.cctldmd.net.   parent is cctldmd.net.
Doc-2.2.3: Test date - Thu Jul  6 08:56:20 MDT 2006
SYSerr: No servers for nsa.cctldmd.net. returned SOAs ...
Summary:
    YIKES: doc aborted while testing nsa.cctldmd.net.  parent cctldmd.net.
    WARNINGS issued for nsa.cctldmd.net. (count: 2)
    Incomplete test for nsa.cctldmd.net. (1)
Done testing nsa.cctldmd.net.  Thu Jul  6 08:56:22 MDT 2006
```

The cctldmd.net domain has a lame delegation to nsa.cctldmd.net. The entry below from the **log.nsa.cctldmd.net.** file clarifies the problem:

```
WARNING: register.dns.md. claims to be authoritative for nsa.cctldmd.net.
    == but no NS record at parent zone
```

If you manage a domain that includes subdomains (or don't trust the managers of your parent domain), consider running **doc** from **cron** once a week to verify that all delegations relating to your domain are correct.

Other DNS sanity checking tools

There are several other tools that check various aspects of your DNS environment. **named-checkconf** and **named-checkzone** are shipped with BIND 9; they check the basic syntax (not semantics) of the **named.conf** file and your zone files. The original DNS checking tool is **nslint**, written by Craig Leres when he was at Lawrence Berkeley Labs. The tool **lamers** (from the same web site as **doc**) riffles through log files and sends email to the DNS administrators of offending sites telling them that they have a lame delegation and describing how to fix the problem. **DDT** by Jorge Frazao and Artur Romao debugs cached data.

dnswalk traverses your delegation tree and identifies inconsistencies between parent and child or between forward and reverse records. It also finds missing dots, unnecessary glue records, etc. It is a general DNS hygiene nag. **dnswalk** needs to be able to do zone transfers in order to work its magic.

Performance issues

BIND 9 currently has a few performance issues that are being addressed by ISC. Its performance is approaching that of BIND 8, but its efficiency on multiprocessor architectures has been disappointing so far. The f.root-servers.net machines use BIND 9 and happily handle about 5,000 queries/second; the performance is probably fine for most sites.

We've said it multiple times already, but it bears repeating: set your TTLs to reasonable values (weeks or days, not hours or minutes). The use of short TTLs punishes both you (because you must constantly re-serve the same records) and your web clients (because they must constantly fetch them).

Paging degrades server performance nonlinearly, so don't be stingy with memory on servers that run **named**. You'll need to wait about a week for **named**'s memory footprint to stabilize; see page 421.

Use forwarders. See page 427 for a discussion of forwarding architecture.

15.17 DISTRIBUTION SPECIFICS

This section describes the details of each distribution's **named** software and its default configuration. Linux distributions are pretty good about updating when new versions of the BIND software are released by ISC.

Each of our reference distributions uses BIND as its default name server, but only a subset of distributions include it in the default installation. The other distributions include the BIND utilities (**dig**, **nslookup**, **host**, etc.) but not the name server software itself. You either have to specify that you want BIND installed when you build the machine or install the BIND package separately.

A Linux BIND client specifies its default domain, the other domains to search when names are not fully qualified, and the IP addresses of its local name servers in the file **/etc/resolv.conf**. A Linux host that acts as a BIND server also uses the **named** files listed in Table 15.16.

Table 15.16   BIND files in Linux

File	Directory[a]	Description
resolv.conf	/etc	Resolver library configuration file
named, lwres	/usr/sbin	Name server daemon
named.conf	/etc	**named** config file (RHEL, Fedora, and SUSE)
	/etc/bind	**named** config file (Debian, Ubuntu)
named.pid	/var/run/named	PID of the running **named** (RHEL/Fedora)
	/var/run/bind/run	PID of the running **named** (Debian, Ubuntu)
	home/**var/run/named**	PID of the running **named** (SUSE)
named.run	*home*	Output from debug mode
named.stats	*home*	Statistics output
	home/**var/log**	Statistics output (SUSE)
named_dump.db	*home*	Dump of the entire database
	home/**var/log**	Dump of the entire database (SUSE)

a. By *home*, we mean the directory specified in **named.conf** as the home for BIND files.

Linux uses a switch file, **/etc/nsswitch.conf,** to specify how hostname-to-IP address mappings should be performed and whether DNS should be tried first, last, or not at all. If no switch file is present, the default behavior is

```
hosts: dns [!UNAVAIL=return] files
```

The !UNAVAIL clause means that if DNS is available but a name is not found there, the lookup attempt should fail rather than continuing to the next entry (in this case, the **/etc/hosts** file). If no name server were running (as might be the case during the boot process), the lookup process *would* consult the **hosts** file.

Our example distributions all provide the following default **nsswitch.conf** file:

```
hosts: files dns
```

There is really no "best" way to configure the lookups—it depends on how your site is managed. In general, we prefer to keep as much host information as possible in DNS rather than in NIS or flat files, but we also try to preserve the ability to fall back to the static **hosts** file during the boot process if necessary.

Installing the RHEL or Fedora BIND package (currently **bind-9.2.3-13.i386.rpm**) puts the binaries in **/usr/sbin**, puts the man pages in **/usr/share/man**, adds a user and group called "named," and creates directories for zone files. The "named" user has access to the data files through the group permissions.

Unless you change this in **/etc/sysconfig/named**, the configuration file **named.conf** goes in **/etc** (as Paul Vixie and God intended) and the zone files go in **/var/named**. No sample files are provided, but the **bindconf** package should have them.

Debian and Ubuntu give you a choice of BIND 8 or BIND 9 depending on which package you install (**bind** vs. **bind9**). The following details assume BIND 9.

Programs and files have owner root and group owner "bind" with permissions set to allow access if **named** is invoked as user "bind" instead of root.

Some useful sample files are stashed in **/etc/bind**. Included are a **named.conf** file and zone files for root hints, localhost, the broadcast addresses, and private address space. The supplied **named.conf** includes the files **named.conf.options** and **named.conf.local**. It sets BIND's default directory to **/var/cache/bind**; as shipped, the directory exists but is empty.

The logic behind the configuration info being in **/etc** and the zone info in **/var** is that if you are a secondary server for other sites, you do not control the size of the zone files that **named** will write and so you will probably want to keep the files on **/var**. Zones for which you are the primary server can live with the config files and use absolute paths in the **named.conf** file, or they can live in **/var/cache/bind** too.

Debian's sample **named.conf** file does not need to be modified if you want to run a caching-only server. You must add any zones for which you are authoritative, preferably to the supplied **named.conf.local** file.

The sample files provided by Debian make use of some new BIND features to help your servers be good DNS citizens on the network. For example, they configure the com and net zones as delegation-only zones to keep your users' typos from generating advertising revenue for VeriSign through its Site Finder tool. If you don't use private address space (RFC1918) internally, then the empty RFC1918 zone files prevent those addresses from escaping the local network. Go, Debian!

The directory **/usr/share/doc/bind9** contains several useful references. Check out the **README.Debian** file (even on Ubuntu) to understand Debian's strategy for configuring BIND.

Installing BIND from an **rpm** package on SUSE was frustrating because of missing dependencies, but once these were resolved the installation went fine. The installation says what it is doing and produces a reasonable, well-documented name server installation. A SUSE wizard later suggested using YaST instead of **rpm** as the true SUSE way to install things, and that's probably the right answer.

By default, **named** runs in a **chroot**ed environment beneath **/var/lib/named** as user and group "named." The installer creates the **chroot** jail directory and populates it with all the files needed to run **named**, even niceties such as the UNIX domain socket for syslog. Extra configuration files (not **named.conf**) and zone files live in **/etc/named.d** and are copied to the jail when **named** is started. If you do not want to run **named chroot**ed, modify the line that says

```
NAMED_RUN_CHROOTED="yes"
```

in **/etc/sysconfig/named**. That's all you have to change; the startup scripts in **/etc/init.d** refer to this information and are able to start **named** in either fashion.

SUSE provides a sample **/etc/named.conf** file with helpful comments that explain many of the options. SUSE's **/etc/named.conf** file is not world-readable as is typical. The default file imports a file called **named.conf.include**, which then imports the **rndc-access.conf** file from **/etc/named.d**, both of which are readable to the world. It's not entirely clear what SUSE has in mind here concerning security. **rndc** is pre-configured to accept control commands from the localhost address only.

SUSE's **named.conf** file can be used as-is to run a caching-only server. If you want to serve your own zones, put the zone files in the **/etc/named.d** directory and list the zones' names in the **/etc/named.conf.include** file.

The ISC BIND documentation lives in **/usr/share/doc/packages/bind9**.

15.18 RECOMMENDED READING

DNS and BIND are described by a variety of sources, including the documentation that comes with the distribution, chapters in several books on Internet topics, several books in the O'Reilly Nutshell series, and various on-line resources.

Mailing lists and newsgroups

The following mailing lists are associated with BIND:

- bind-announce – mail bind-announce-request@isc.org to join
- namedroppers – mail namedroppers-request@internic.net to join
- bind-users – mail bind-users-request@isc.org to join
- bind9-workers – mail bind9-workers-request@isc.org (for code warriors)

Send bug reports to bind9-bugs@isc.org.

Books and other documentation

THE NOMINUM AND ISC BIND DEVELOPMENT TEAMS. *BINDv9 Administrator Reference Manual.* Available in the BIND distribution (**doc/arm**) from www.isc.org.

This document outlines the administration and management of BIND 9. A new version of the BIND documentation, the *BIND Reference Manual* (probably **doc/brm**), is currently being developed by ISC but is not yet available for review. An earlier document, the *Bind Operations Guide* (or BOG, as it was called), described the operation and configuration of BIND 4. The BOG is included in BIND distributions up through version 8.

ALBITZ, PAUL, AND CRICKET LIU. *DNS and BIND (5th Edition).* Sebastopol, CA: O'Reilly Media, 2006.

This popular and well-respected book about BIND includes coverage of both BIND 8 and BIND 9. It is very complete.

On-line resources

The DNS Resources Directory, www.dns.net/dnsrd, is a useful collection of resources and pointers to resources maintained by András Salamon.

Google has indexed DNS resources at

directory.google.com/Top/Computers/Internet/Protocols/DNS

The comp.protocols.dns.bind newsgroup also contains good information.

The RFCs

The RFCs that define the DNS system are available from www.rfc-editor.org. Early and evolving ideas appear first in the Internet-Drafts series and later move into the RFC series. We used to list a page or so of the most important DNS-related RFCs, but there are now so many (more than 100, with another 50 Internet drafts) that you are better off searching the rfc-editor.org web page to access the entire archive. Refer to the **doc/rfc** and **doc/draft** directories of the current BIND distribution to see the whole fleet.

The original, definitive standards for DNS, vintage 1987, are

- 1034 – Domain Names: Concepts and Facilities
- 1035 – Domain Names: Implementation and Specification

15.19 EXERCISES

E15.1 Explain the function of each of the following DNS records: SOA, PTR, A, MX, and CNAME.

E15.2 What are glue records and why are they needed? Use **dig** to find the glue records that connect your local zone to its parent.

E15.3 What are the implications of negative caching? Why is it important?

E15.4 Create SPF pseudo-records for your site to help control spam.

★ **E15.5** What steps are needed to set up a new second-level domain? Include both technical and procedural factors.

⭐ **E15.6**   What is the difference between an authoritative and a nonauthoritative answer to a DNS query? How could you ensure that an answer was authoritative?

⭐ **E15.7**   What machine is your local name server? What steps must it take to resolve the name www.admin.com, assuming that no information about this domain is cached anywhere in DNS?

⭐ **E15.8**   Explain the significance for DNS of the 512-byte limit on UDP packets. What workarounds address potential problems?

16 *The Network File System*

The Network File System, commonly known as NFS, enables sharing of filesystems among computers. NFS is almost transparent to users and is "stateless," meaning that no information is lost when an NFS server crashes. Clients can simply wait until the server returns and then continue as if nothing had happened.

NFS was introduced by Sun Microsystems in 1985. It was originally implemented as a surrogate filesystem for diskless clients, but the protocol proved to be well designed and very useful as a general file-sharing solution. In fact, it's difficult to remember what life was like before NFS. All full-featured Linux distributions support NFS.

16.1 GENERAL INFORMATION ABOUT NFS

Today, NFS is used only to share files among Linux and UNIX boxes. Windows clients should use CIFS/Samba for file service. See page 828 for more information about Samba and CIFS.

NFS consists of several components, including a mounting protocol and mount server, daemons that coordinate basic file service, and several diagnostic utilities. A portion of both the server-side and client-side software resides in the kernel. However, these parts of NFS need no configuration and are largely transparent from an administrator's point of view.

NFS protocol versions

The NFS protocol has been remarkably stable over time. The original public release of NFS was version 2. In the early 1990s, a collection of changes was integrated into

NFS

the protocol to produce version 3, which increased performance and improved support for large files. Early implementations of version 4 are now available. Version 4 includes many new enhancements, which we describe below.

Since NFS version 2 clients cannot assume that a write operation is complete until they receive an acknowledgment from the server, version 2 servers must commit each modified block to disk before replying, to avoid discrepancies in the event of a crash. This constraint introduces a significant delay in NFS writes since modified blocks would normally be written only to the in-memory buffer cache.

NFS version 3 eliminates this bottleneck with a coherency scheme that permits asynchronous writes. It also updates several other aspects of the protocol that were found to have caused performance problems. The net result is that NFS version 3 is quite a bit faster than version 2. Version 3 software is always capable of interoperating with version 2, although it simply falls back to using the earlier protocol.

NFS version 4 is becoming more stable and is shipping with some versions of Linux. It requires a 2.6.1 kernel or greater and needs to be manually turned on in the kernel. Featured enhancements include

- Compatibility and cooperation with firewalls and NAT devices
- Integration of the lock and mount protocols into the core NFS protocol
- Stateful operation
- Strong, integrated security
- Support for replication and migration
- Support for both UNIX and Windows clients
- Access control lists (ACLs)
- Support for Unicode filenames
- Good performance even on low-bandwidth connections

See nfs.sourceforge.net for current information about the state of NFSv4 on Linux and pointers to the latest software releases.

Because NFSv4 is still in development, we don't discuss it in detail in this chapter. But keep your eye on it; many of the planned features address longstanding shortcomings of NFS. We hope that version 4 lives up to its very promising specifications.

Choice of transport

NFS runs on top of Sun's RPC (Remote Procedure Call) protocol, which defines a system-independent way for processes to communicate over a network. One advantageous side effect of this architecture is that it allows the use of either UDP or TCP as the underlying transport protocol.

NFS originally used UDP because that was what performed best on the LANs and computers of the 1980s. Although NFS does its own packet sequence reassembly and error checking, UDP and NFS both lack the congestion control algorithms that are essential for good performance on a large IP network.

To remedy these potential problems, all modern systems now let you use TCP instead of UDP as the transport for NFS. This option was first explored as a way to help NFS work through routers and over the Internet. However, the current consensus seems to be that TCP is usually the best option for local NFS traffic as well. Over time, most of the original reasons for preferring UDP over TCP have evaporated in the warm light of fast CPUs, cheap memory, and smarter network controllers. Linux has supported NFS service over TCP since the 2.4 kernel.

Most servers that support TCP generally accept connections on either transport, so the choice between TCP and UDP is made by the client. The client specifies its preference as an option to the **mount** command (for manual mounts) or in a config file such as **/etc/fstab**.

File locking

File locking (as implemented by the **flock**, **lockf** and/or **fcntl** systems calls) has been a sore point on UNIX systems for a long time. On local filesystems, it has been known to work less than perfectly. In the context of NFS, the ground is shakier still. By design, NFS servers are stateless: they have no idea which machines are using any given file. However, this information is needed to implement locking. What to do?

The traditional answer has been to implement file locking separately from NFS. Most systems provide two daemons, **lockd** and **statd**, that try to make a go of it. Unfortunately, the task is difficult for a variety of subtle reasons, and NFS file locking has generally tended to be flaky.

Disk quotas

Access to remote disk quota information can be provided by an out-of-band server, **rquotad**. NFS servers enforce disk quotas if they are enabled on the underlying filesystem, but users cannot view their quota information unless **rquotad** is running on the remote server.

We consider disk quotas to be largely obsolete; however, some organizations still depend on them to keep users from hogging all available disk space. If you're supporting one of these organizations, you can consult the quota documentation for the appropriate Linux distributions. We don't discuss **rquotad** further.

Cookies and stateless mounting

A client must explicitly mount an NFS filesystem before using it, just as a client must mount a filesystem stored on a local disk. However, because NFS is stateless, the server does not keep track of which clients have mounted each filesystem. Instead, the server simply discloses a secret "cookie" at the conclusion of a successful mount negotiation. The cookie identifies the mounted directory to the NFS server and so provides a way for the client to access its contents.

Unmounting and remounting a filesystem on the server normally changes its cookie. As a special case, cookies persist across a reboot so that a server that crashes can return to its previous state. But don't try to boot single-user, play with filesystems, then boot again; this procedure revokes cookies and makes clients unable to access the filesystems they have mounted until they either reboot or remount.

Once a client has a magic cookie, it uses the RPC protocol to request filesystem operations such as creating a file or reading a data block. Because NFS is a stateless protocol, the client is responsible for ensuring that the server acknowledges write requests before it deletes its own copy of the data to be written.

Naming conventions for shared filesystems

It is easier to manage NFS if your naming scheme for mounts includes the name of each remote server (e.g., **/anchor/tools** for a filesystem that lives on anchor). Such names are useful because they let users translate announcements such as "anchor will be down on Saturday for an upgrade" into useful information such as "I won't be able to use **/anchor/tools/TeX** on Saturday to finish my thesis, so I should go skiing instead."

Unfortunately, this scheme requires the directory **/anchor** to exist in the root directory of all client machines. If a client gets filesystems from several other hosts, the root can get cluttered. Consider providing a deeper hierarchy (e.g., **/home/anchor**, **/home/rastadon**, etc.). We recommend implementing such a scheme with an automounter daemon as described starting on page 497.

Security and NFS

NFS provides a convenient way to access files on a network, and thus it has great potential to cause security problems. In many ways, NFS version 3 is a poster child for everything that is or ever has been wrong with UNIX and Linux security. The protocol was originally designed with essentially no concern for security, and convenience has its price. Fortunately, Linux supports a number of features that reduce and isolate the security problems from which NFS has traditionally suffered.

See page 490 for more information about the exports file.

Access to NFS volumes is granted by a file called **/etc/exports** that enumerates the hostnames (or IP addresses) of systems that should have access to a server's filesystems. Unfortunately, this is a weak form of security because the server trusts the clients to tell it who they are. It's easy to make clients lie about their identities, so this mechanism cannot be fully trusted. Nevertheless, you should export filesystems only to clients that you trust, and you should always check that you have not accidentally exported filesystems to the whole world.

Access to NFS ports should always be tightly restricted. Fortunately, all versions of Linux include a firewall that can handle this task.

As on local filesystems, file-level access control on NFS filesystems is managed according to UID, GID, and file permissions. But once again, the NFS server trusts the client to tell it who is accessing files. If mary and bob share the same UID on two separate clients, they will have access to each other's NFS files. In addition, users that have root access on a system can change to whatever UID they want; the server will happily give them access to the corresponding files. For these reasons, we strongly recommend the use of globally unique UIDs and the root_squash option described in the next section.

A rather large educational institution that we know made the mistake of not using root_squash. As a result, 5 large servers and 60 desktops were compromised. It took a long holiday weekend to contain the incident and rebuild the machines.

See page 701 for more information about network firewalls. If your site has installed a network firewall, it's a good idea to block access to TCP and UDP ports 2049, which are used by NFS. You should also block access to the **portmap** daemon, which normally listens on TCP and UDP ports 111. It's implicit in these precautions but perhaps worth saying explicitly that NFS filesystems should not be exported to nonlocal machines or exported across the open Internet.

Root access and the nobody account

Although users should generally be given identical privileges wherever they go, it's traditional to prevent root from running rampant on NFS-mounted filesystems. By default, the Linux NFS server intercepts incoming requests made on behalf of UID 0 and changes them to look as if they came from some other user. This modification is called "squashing root." The root account is not entirely shut out, but it is limited to the abilities of a normal user.

A placeholder account named "nobody" is defined specifically to be the pseudo-user as whom a remote root masquerades on an NFS server. The traditional UID for nobody is 65534 (the twos-complement equivalent of UID -2).[1] You can change the default UID and GID mappings for root with the anonuid and anongid export options. You can use the all_squash option to map all client UIDs to the same UID on the server. This configuration eliminates all distinctions among users and creates a sort of public-access filesystem.

At the other end of the spectrum, the no_root_squash option turns off UID mapping for root. This option is sometimes needed to support diskless clients or software that requires root access to the filesystem. It's generally a bad idea to turn this feature on because it allows users with root privileges on a client to modify files that are normally protected. Nonetheless, the option is available.

The intent behind these precautions is good, but their ultimate value is not as great as it might seem. Remember that root on an NFS client can **su** to whatever UID it wants, so user files are never really protected. System logins such as "bin" and "sys" aren't UID-mapped, so any files they own, such as the occasional system binary or third-party application, may be vulnerable to attack. The only real effect of UID mapping is to prevent access to files that are owned by root and not readable or writable by the world.

---

1. Although the Red Hat NFS server defaults to UID -2, the nobody account in the **passwd** file uses UID 99. You can leave things as they are, add a **passwd** entry for UID -2, or change anonuid and anongid to 99 if you wish. The other distributions use UID -2 for the nobody and nogroup accounts in the **passwd** file, as expected.

16.2 SERVER-SIDE NFS

A server is said to "export" a directory when it makes the directory available for use by other machines.

In NFS version 3, the process used by clients to mount a filesystem (that is, to learn its secret cookie) is completely separate from the process used to access files. The operations use separate protocols, and the requests are served by different daemons: **mountd** for mount requests and **nfsd** for actual file service. These daemons are actually called **rpc.nfsd** and **rpc.mountd** as a reminder that they rely on RPC as an underlying protocol (and hence require **portmap** to be running; see page 893). We omit the **rpc** prefix for readability.

On an NFS server, both **mountd** and **nfsd** should start when the system boots, and both should remain running as long as the system is up. The system startup scripts typically run the daemons automatically if you have any exports configured. The names of the NFS server startup scripts for each distribution are shown in Table 16.1.

Table 16.1 NFS server startup scripts

Distribution	Paths to startup scripts
Red Hat Enterprise	**/etc/rc.d/init.d/nfs**
Fedora	**/etc/rc.d/init.d/nfs**
SUSE	**/etc/init.d/nfsboot**[a]
Debian	**/etc/init.d/nfs-kernel-server**
	/etc/init.d/nfs-common
Ubuntu	**/etc/init.d/nfs-kernel-server**
	/etc/init.d/nfs-common

a. **/etc/init.d/nfs** mounts the NFS client filesystems on SUSE.

mountd and **nfsd** share a single access control database that tells which filesystems should be exported and which clients may mount them. The operative copy of this database is usually kept in a file called **/usr/lib/nfs/xtab** in addition to tables internal to the kernel. Since **xtab** isn't meant to be human readable, you use a helper command—**exportfs**—to add and modify entries. To remove entries from the exports table, use **exportfs -u**.

On most systems, **/etc/exports** is the canonical human readable list of exported directories. By default, all filesystems in **/etc/exports** are exported at boot time. You can manually export all the filesystems listed in **/etc/exports** by using **exportfs -a**, which should be run after you make changes to the **exports** file. You can also export filesystems once by specifying the client, path, and options directly on the **exportfs** command line.

NFS deals with the logical layer of the filesystem. Any directory can be exported; it doesn't have to be a mount point or the root of a physical filesystem. However, for security, NFS does pay attention to the boundaries between filesystems and does require each device to be exported separately. For example, on a machine that has a **/users** partition, you could export the root directory without exporting **/users**.

Clients are usually allowed to mount subdirectories of an exported directory if they wish, although the protocol does not require this feature. For example, if a server exports **/chimchim/users**, a client could mount only **/chimchim/users/joe** and ignore the rest of the **users** directory. Most versions of UNIX don't let you export subdirectories of an exported directory with different options, but Linux does.

The exports file

The **/etc/exports** file enumerates the filesystems exported through NFS and the clients that may access each of them. Whitespace separates the filesystem from the list of clients, and each client is followed immediately by a parenthesized list of comma-separated options. Lines can be continued with a backslash.

Here's what the format looks like:

```
/home/boggs        inura(rw,no_root_squash) lappie(rw)
/usr/share/man     *.toadranch.com(ro)
```

There is no way to list multiple clients for a single set of options, although some client specifications actually refer to multiple hosts. Table 16.2 lists the four types of client specifications that can appear in the **exports** file.

Table 16.2   Client specifications in the /etc/exports file

Type	Syntax	Meaning
Hostname	*hostname*	Individual hosts
Netgroup	*@groupname*	NIS netgroups; see page 517 for details
Wild cards	* and ?	FQDNs[a] with wild cards. "*" will not match a dot.
IP networks	*ipaddr/mask*	CIDR-style specifications (e.g., 128.138.92.128/25)

a. Fully qualified domain names

Table 16.3 shows the most commonly used export options.

Linux's NFS server has the unusual feature of allowing subdirectories of exported directories to be exported with different options. Use the noaccess option to "unexport" subdirectories that you would rather not share.

For example, the configuration

```
/home              *.toadranch.com(rw)
/home/boggs        (noaccess)
```

allows hosts in the toadranch.com domain to access all the contents of **/home** through mounting except for **/home/boggs**. The absence of a client name on the

Table 16.3   Common export options

Option	Description
ro	Exports read-only
rw	Exports for reading and writing (the default).
rw=list	Exports read-mostly. *list* enumerates the hosts allowed to mount for writing; all others must mount read-only.
root_squash	Maps ("squashes") UID 0 and GID 0 to the values specified by anonuid and anongid. This is the default.
no_root_squash	Allows normal access by root. Dangerous.
all_squash	Maps all UIDs and GIDs to their anonymous versions. Useful for supporting PCs and untrusted single-user hosts.
anonuid=xxx	Specifies the UID to which remote roots should be squashed
anongid=xxx	Specifies the GID to which remote roots should be squashed
secure	Requires remote access to originate at a privileged port
insecure	Allows remote access from any port
noaccess	Prevents access to this dir and subdirs (used with nested exports)
wdelay	Delays writes in hopes of coalescing multiple updates
no_wdelay	Writes data to disk as soon as possible
async	Makes server reply to write requests before actual disk write
nohide	Reveals filesystems mounted within exported file trees
hide	Opposite of nohide
subtree_check	Verifies that each requested file is within an exported subtree
no_subtree_check	Verifies only that file requests refer to an exported filesystem
secure_locks	Requires authorization for all lock requests
insecure_locks	Specifies less stringent locking criteria (supports older clients)
auth_nlm	Synonym for secure_locks
no_auth_nlm	Synonym for insecure_locks

second line means that the option applies to all hosts; it's perhaps somewhat more secure this way.

The subtree_check option (the default) verifies that every file accessed by the client lies within an exported subdirectory. If you turn off this option, only the fact that the file is within an exported filesystem is verified. Subtree checking can occasionally cause problems when a requested file is renamed while the client has the file open. If you anticipate many such situations, consider setting no_subtree_check.

The secure_locks option requires authorization and authentication in order for files to be locked. Some NFS clients don't send credentials with lock requests and do not work with secure_locks. In this case, you would only be able to lock world-readable files. Replacing these clients with ones that support credentials correctly is the best solution. However, you can specify the insecure_locks option as a stopgap.

Don't forget to run **exportfs -a** after updating the **exports** file to effect your changes.

nfsd: serve files

Once a client's mount request has been validated by **mountd**, the client can request various filesystem operations. These requests are handled on the server side by **nfsd**, the NFS operations daemon.[2] **nfsd** need not be run on an NFS client machine unless the client exports filesystems of its own.

nfsd takes a numeric argument that specifies how many server threads to fork. Selecting the appropriate number of **nfsd**s is important and is unfortunately something of a black art. If the number is too low or too high, NFS performance can suffer.

Generally, 8 **nfsd** threads are adequate for a server that is used infrequently and are few enough that performance problems don't really arise. On a production server, somewhere between 12 and 20 is a good number. If you notice that **ps** shows the **nfsd**s in state D most of the time and some idle CPU is available, consider increasing the number of threads. If you find the load average (as reported by **uptime**) rising as you add **nfsd**s, you've gone too far; back off a bit from that threshold. You should also run **nfsstat** regularly to check for performance problems that might be associated with the number of **nfsd** threads. See page 495 for more information about **nfsstat**.

On a loaded NFS server with a lot of UDP clients, UDP sockets can overflow if requests arrive while all **nfsd** threads are already in use. You can monitor the number of overflows with **netstat -s**. Add more **nfsd**s until UDP socket overflows drop to zero. Overflows indicate a severe undersupply of server daemons, so you should probably add a few more than this metric would indicate.

You can change the number of **nfsd** processes by editing the appropriate startup script in **/etc/init.d** or by specifying the number on the command line when manually starting **nfsd**. See Table 16.1 on page 489 for the name of the script to edit.

16.3 CLIENT-SIDE NFS

NFS filesystems are mounted in much the same way as local disk filesystems. The **mount** command understands the notation *hostname:directory* to mean the path *directory* on the host *hostname*. As with local filesystems, **mount** maps the remote *directory* on the remote *host* into a directory within the local file tree. After mounting, an NFS-mounted filesystem is accessed in the same way as a local filesystem. The **mount** command and its associated NFS extensions represent the most significant concerns to a system administrator of an NFS client.

Before an NFS file system can be mounted, it must be properly exported (see *Server-side NFS* on page 489). To verify that a server has properly exported its filesystems from the client's perspective, you can use the client's **showmount** command:

```
$ showmount -e coyote
Export list for coyote:
/home/boggs inura.toadranch.com
```

2. In reality, **nfsd** simply makes a nonreturning system call to NFS server code embedded in the kernel.

This example reports that the directory **/home/boggs** on the server coyote has been exported to the client system inura.toadranch.com. **showmount** output should be the first thing you check if an NFS mount is not working and you have already verified that the filesystems have been properly exported on the server with **exportfs**. (You might have just forgotten to run **exportfs -a** after updating the **exports** file.)

If the directory is properly exported on the server but **showmount** returns an error or an empty list, you might double-check that all the necessary processes are running on the server (**portmap**, **mountd**, **nfsd**, **statd**, and **lockd**), that the **hosts.allow** and **hosts.deny** files allow access to those daemons, and that you are on the right client system.

To actually mount the filesystem, you would use a command such as this:

```
# mount -o rw,hard,intr,bg coyote:/home/boggs /coyote/home/boggs
```

The options after **-o** specify that the filesystem should be mounted read-write, that operations should be interruptible, and that retries should be done in the background. These flags are pretty standard; other common flags are listed in Table 16.4.

Table 16.4   NFS mount flags/options

Flag	Description
rw	Mounts the filesystem read-write (must be exported that way)
ro	Mounts the filesystem read-only
bg	If the mount fails (server doesn't respond), keeps trying it in the background and continues with other mount requests
hard	If a server goes down, causes operations that try to access it to block until the server comes back up
soft	If a server goes down, causes operations that try to access it to fail and return an error. This feature is useful to avoid processes "hanging" on inessential mounts.
intr	Allows users to interrupt blocked operations (and return an error)
nointr	Does not allow user interrupts
retrans=n	Specifies the number of times to repeat a request before returning an error on a soft-mounted filesystem
timeo=n	Sets the timeout period (in tenths of a second) for requests
rsize=n	Sets the read buffer size to n bytes
wsize=n	Sets the write buffer size to n bytes
nfsvers=n	Selects NFS protocol version 2 or 3 (normally automatic)
tcp	Selects transport via TCP. UDP is the default.
async	Makes server reply to write requests before actual disk write

Filesystems mounted hard (the default) cause processes to hang when their servers go down. This behavior is particularly bothersome when the processes in question are standard daemons, so we do not recommend serving critical system binaries over NFS. In general, the use of the soft and intr options reduces the number of

NFS-related headaches. However, these options can have their own undesirable side effects, such as aborting a 20-hour simulation after it has run for 18 hours just because of a transient network glitch.[3] Automount solutions such as autofs, discussed later in this chapter, also provide some remedies for mounting ailments.

The read and write buffer sizes apply to both UDP and TCP mounts, but the optimal values differ. Because you can trust TCP to transfer data efficiently, the values should be higher; 32K is a good value. For UDP, good values when server and client are on the same network is 8K.[4] The default is 1K, though even the man page recommends increasing it to 8K for better performance.

In the legacy kernels Linux 2.2 and 2.4, the default input queue size is 64K. With eight **nfsd** threads running on the NFS server, only one request can be outstanding on each instance of **nfsd** before requests begin to be dropped. Therefore, you might consider increasing the receive queue size for **nfsd** only, returning it to the default value after running **nfsd** so that other processes are not negatively affected by the change. You can change the input queue size in your system startup scripts by using **procfs**.

This example sets the queue size to 256K, which is a reasonable default:

```
rmem_default='cat /proc/sys/net/core/rmem_default'
rmem_max='cat /proc/sys/net/core/rmem_max'
echo 262144 > /proc/sys/net/core/rmem_default
echo 262144 > /proc/sys/net/core/rmem_max
```

Run or restart **rpc.nfsd**, then return the settings to their original values:

```
echo $rmem_default > /proc/sys/net/core/rmem_default
echo $rmem_max > /proc/sys/net/core/rmem_max
```

You can test the mount with **df** just as you would test a local filesystem:

```
$ df /coyote/home/boggs
Filesystem          1k-blocks    Used   Available  Use%  Mounted on
coyote:/home/boggs 17212156  1694128  14643692   11%  /coyote/home/boggs
```

You unmount NFS partitions with the **umount** command. If the NFS filesystem is in use when you try to unmount it, you will get an error such as

```
umount: /coyote/home/boggs: device is busy
```

Like any other filesystem, an NFS filesystem cannot be unmounted while it is in use. Use **lsof** to find processes with open files on the filesystem; kill them or, in the case of shells, change directories. If all else fails or your server is down, try **umount -f** to force the filesystem to be unmounted.

---

3. Jeff Forys, one of our technical reviewers, remarked, "Most mounts should use hard, intr, and bg, because these options best preserve NFS's original design goals (reliability and statelessness). soft is an abomination, an ugly Satanic hack! If the user wants to interrupt, cool. Otherwise, wait for the server and all will eventually be well again with no data lost."

4. If you use **iptables**, you might have to add a rule to accept fragments because 8K is above the MTU for Ethernet. Accepting fragments may make you more vulnerable to a denial of service attack.

Mounting remote filesystems at boot time

See page 497 for more information about autofs.

You can use the **mount** command to establish temporary network mounts, but you should list mounts that are part of a system's permanent configuration in **/etc/fstab** so that they are mounted automatically at boot time. Alternatively, mounts can be handled by an automatic mounting service such as autofs.

The following **fstab** entries mount the filesystems **/home** and **/usr/local** from the hosts coyote and inura:

```
# filesystem     mountpoint    fstype  flags                           dump  fsck
coyote:/home     /coyote/home  nfs     rw,bg,intr,hard,nodev,nosuid    0     0
inura:/usr/local /usr/local    nfs     ro,bg,intr,soft,nodev,nosuid    0     0
```

See page 127 for more information about the fstab file.

When you add entries to **fstab**, be sure to create the appropriate mount point directories with **mkdir**. You can make your changes take effect immediately (without rebooting) by running **mount -a -t nfs** to mount all file systems of type nfs in **fstab**.

The flags field of **/etc/fstab** specifies options for NFS mounts; these options are the same ones you would specify on the **mount** command line.

Restricting exports to insecure ports

NFS clients are free to use any TCP or UDP source port they like when connecting to an NFS server. However, Linux servers may insist that requests come from a privileged port (a port numbered lower than 1024) if the filesystem is exported with the secure export option, which is on by default. In the world of PCs and desktop Linux boxes, the use of privileged ports provides little actual security.

Linux NFS clients adopt the traditional (and still recommended) approach of defaulting to a privileged port, to avert the potential for conflict. To accept mounts from unprivileged source ports, export the filesystem with the insecure export option.

16.4 NFSSTAT: DUMP NFS STATISTICS

The **nfsstat** command displays various statistics kept by the NFS system. **nfsstat -s** displays statistics for NFS server processes, and **nfsstat -c** shows information related to client-side operations. For example:

```
$ nfsstat -s
Server rpc stats:
calls          badcalls      badauth       badclnt       xdrcall
24314112       311           9             302           0
Server nfs v2:
getattr        null          setattr       root          lookup        readlink
8470054 34%    58      0%    55199 0%      0       0%    1182897 4%    917      0%
read           wrcache       link          create        remove        rename
6602409 27%    0       0%    7452  0%      61544   0%    46712   0%    11537    0%
write          symlink       mkdir         rmdir         readdir       fsstat
7785789 32%    744     0%    3446  0%      2539    0%    13614   0%    69201    0%
```

This example is from a relatively healthy NFS server. If more than 3% of calls are bad, the problem is likely to lie with your NFS server or network. Check the output of **netstat -s** for general network statistics. It may reveal problems with dropped packets, fragment reassembly, or network queue overruns that will affect your NFS performance. See page 649 for more on debugging your network with **netstat**.

Running **nfsstat** and **netstat** occasionally and becoming familiar with their output will help you discover NFS problems before your users do.

16.5 DEDICATED NFS FILE SERVERS

Fast, reliable file service is one of the most important elements of any production computing environment. Although you can certainly roll your own file server from a Linux workstation and a handful of off-the-shelf hard disks, doing so is often not the best-performing or easiest-to-administer solution (though it is often the cheapest).

Dedicated NFS file servers have been around for more than a decade. They offer a host of potential advantages over the homebrew approach:

- They are optimized for file service and typically afford the best possible NFS performance.

- As storage requirements grow, they can scale smoothly to support terabytes of storage and hundreds of users.

- They are more reliable than Linux boxes thanks to their simplified software, redundant hardware, and use of disk mirroring.

- They usually provide file service for both Linux and Windows clients. Some even contain integral web and FTP servers.

- They are often easier to administer than Linux file servers.

- They often include backup and checkpoint facilities that are superior to those found on vanilla Linux systems.

Some of our favorite dedicated NFS servers are made by Network Appliance, Inc. (www.netapp.com). Their products run the gamut from very small to very large, and their pricing is OK. EMC is another player in the high-end server market. They make good products, but be prepared for sticker shock and build up your tolerance for marketing buzzwords.[5]

Storage area network (SAN) servers are also very popular now. They differ from dedicated NFS file servers in that they have no understanding of filesystems; they simply serve disk blocks. A SAN is therefore unencumbered by the overhead of an operating system and provides very fast read/write access. That said, in the real world we have found them to be not quite ready for production use. They can be

---

5. Speaking of buzzwords, one of the main ones you'll hear in this context is "network attached storage," also known as NAS. It's just a fancy way of saying "file service."

quite complex to integrate into an existing environment, and they seem to require a significant amount of support time.

16.6 AUTOMATIC MOUNTING

Mounting filesystems one at a time by listing them in **/etc/fstab** introduces a number of problems in large networks.

First, maintaining **/etc/fstab** on a few hundred machines can be tedious. Each one may be slightly different and thus require individual attention.

Second, if filesystems are mounted from many different hosts, chaos ensues when one of those servers crashes. Every command that accesses the mount points will hang.

Third, when an important server crashes, it may cripple users by making important partitions like **/usr/share/man** unavailable. In this situation, it's best if a copy of the partition can be mounted temporarily from a backup server.

An automount daemon mounts filesystems when they are referenced and unmounts them when they are no longer needed. This procedure minimizes the number of active mount points and is mostly transparent to users. Most automounters also work with a list you supply of "replicated" (identical) filesystems so that the network can continue to function when a primary server becomes unavailable.

To implement this behind-the-scenes mounting and unmounting, the automounter mounts a virtual filesystem driver on the directories you've designated as locations for automatic mounting to occur. In the past, the automounter did this by posing as an NFS server, but this scheme suffers from several significant limitations and is rarely found on contemporary systems. These days, a kernel-resident filesystem driver called autofs is used.

Instead of mirroring an actual filesystem, an automounter "makes up" a filesystem hierarchy according to the specifications you list in its configuration file. When a user references a directory within the automounter's virtual filesystem, the automounter intercepts the reference and mounts the actual filesystem the user is trying to reach.

automount: mount filesystems on demand

The idea of an automounter originally comes from Sun. The Linux automounter, called autofs, mimics Sun's automounter, although it is an independent implementation of the concept and is different in a number of ways.

automount is a background process that configures a single mount point for autofs, the kernel portion of the Linux automounter. The startup script **/etc/init.d/autofs** parses a "master" file (usually **/etc/auto.master**) and runs **automount** for each of the listed mount points. It's typical to see a running instance of **automount** for each automatic mount point that has been configured.

You rarely need to run the **automount** command directly, because almost all administration of the automounter is performed through the **/etc/init.d/autofs** script (or in the case of Red Hat and Fedora, **/etc/rc.d/init.d/autofs**).[6] As with most startup scripts, the **autofs** script accepts on the command line a single parameter that can be **start**, **stop**, **reload**, **restart**, or **status**. Whenever changes are made to the automounter configuration, you must run **autofs reload** to make the changes take effect. **autofs status** gives you the status of existing automounts.

The **auto.master** file associates a mount point with a "map." A map translates the directory name accessed—known as the "key"—into a command line that **mount** can use to perform the real mount. A map can be a text file, an executable program, or an NIS or LDAP database.

When a user references a directory that has been mounted with the autofs kernel filesystem module, the kernel module notifies the user-land **automount** process of the access. The **automount** process figures out which filesystem to mount by consulting the relevant map file or program. It then performs the mount before returning control to the user who triggered the lookup.

You can see the autofs filesystems and the **automount** processes they are attached to by running **mount** and **ps**:

```
$ mount
/dev/hda3 on / type ext2 (rw)
proc on /proc type proc (rw)
/dev/hda1 on /boot type ext2 (rw)
automount(pid8359) on /misc type autofs          // automounter filesystem
    (rw,fd=5,pgrp=8359,minproto=2,maxproto=4)
automount(pid8372) on /net type autofs           // automounter filesystem
    (rw,fd=5,pgrp=8372,minproto=2,maxproto=4)

$ ps auxw | grep automount
root     8359  0.0  1.0  1360  652 ?      S    Dec27   0:00
    /usr/sbin/automount /misc file /etc/auto.misc
root     8372  0.0  1.0  1360  652 ?      S    Dec27   0:00
    /usr/sbin/automount /net program /etc/auto.net
```

Here we can see two autofs filesystems mounted on **/misc** and **/net**. These virtual filesystems are attached to the **automount** processes with PIDs 8359 and 8372, respectively. The **automount** commands run by the **/etc/init.d/autofs** script can be seen in the **ps** output. **auto.misc** is a regular map file, and **auto.net** is an executable program. These maps are described in more detail below.

The master file

The **/etc/auto.master** file lists the directories that should have autofs filesystems mounted on them and associates a map with each directory. In addition to specifying the root directory for the map and the map name, you can also specify options in the

---

6. Don't confuse the **autofs** script with the autofs filesystem. The relationship between them is that the script tells the kernel how to configure the filesystem.

"**-o**" format used by the **mount** command. These options apply to each entry in the map. The Linux conventions vary from Sun's conventions in that the master file's options unite with those of the map; both sets of options are handed to **mount**.

A simple master file that makes use of the map file shown in the next section would look something like this:

```
# Directory    Map              Options
/chimchim      /etc/auto.chim   -secure,hard,bg,intr
```

The master file can be replaced or augmented by a version shared through NIS. The source of the system's automount information is specified by the automount field in **/etc/nsswitch.conf**. See *Prioritizing sources of administrative information* on page 515 for more information about the **nsswitch.conf** file.

Map files

Map files (known as "indirect maps" on other systems) automount several filesystems underneath a common directory. The path of the directory is specified in the master file, not in the map itself. For example, a map for filesystems mounted under **/chimchim** (corresponding to the example above) might look like this:

```
users   chimchim:/chimchim/users
devel   -soft,nfsproto=3 chimchim:/chimchim/devel
info    -ro chimchim:/chimchim/info
```

The first column names the subdirectory in which each automount should be installed, and subsequent items list the mount options and source path of the filesystem. This example (stored in **/etc/auto.chim**) tells **automount** that it can mount the directories **/chimchim/users**, **/chimchim/devel**, and **/chimchim/info** from the host chimchim, with **info** being mounted read-only and **devel** being mounted soft with NFS protocol version 3.

In this configuration the paths on chimchim and the local host are identical. However, this correspondence is not required.

Executable maps

If a map file is executable, it's assumed to be a script or program that dynamically generates automounting information. Instead of reading the map as a text file, the automounter executes it with an argument (the key) that indicates which subdirectory a user has attempted to access. The script is responsible for printing an appropriate map entry; if the specified key is not valid, the script can simply exit without printing anything.

This powerful feature makes up for many of the deficiencies in **automounter**'s rather strange configuration system. In effect, it allows you to easily define a site-wide automount configuration file in a format of your own choice. You can write a simple Perl script to decode the global configuration on each machine. Some systems are shipped with a handy **/etc/auto.net** executable map that takes a hostname as a key and mounts all exported file systems on that host.

The automounter does have one confusing characteristic that deserves mention here: when you list the contents of an automounted filesystem's parent directory, the directory appears empty no matter how many filesystems have been automounted there. You cannot browse the automounts in a GUI filesystem browser. An example:

```
$ ls /portal
$ ls /portal/photos
art_class_2004    florissant_1003          rmnp03
blizzard2003      frozen_dead_guy_Oct2004  rmnp_030806
boston021130      greenville.021129        steamboat2002
```

The **photos** filesystem is alive and well and is automounted under **/portal**. It's accessible through its full pathname. However, a review of the **/portal** directory does not reveal its existence. If you had mounted this filesystem through the **/etc/fstab** file or a manual **mount** command, it would behave like any other directory and would be visible as a member of the parent directory.

One way around the browsing problem is to create a shadow directory that contains symbolic links to the automount points. For example, if **/automounts/photos** is a symbolic link to **/portal/photos**, you can **ls /automounts** to discover that **photos** is an automounted directory. References to **/automounts/photos** are still routed through the automounter and work correctly. Unfortunately, these symbolic links require maintenance and can go out of sync with the actual automounts unless they are periodically reconstructed by a script.

16.7 RECOMMENDED READING

CALLAGHAN, BRENT. *NFS Illustrated*. Reading, MA: Addison-Wesley, 1999.

STERN, HAL, MIKE EISLER, AND RICARDO LABIAGA. *Managing NFS and NIS (2nd Edition)*. Sebastopol, CA: O'Reilly Media, 2001.

Table 16.5 lists the various RFCs for the NFS protocol.

Table 16.5   NFS-related RFCs

RFC	Title	Author	Date
1094	Network File System Protocol Specification	Sun Microsystems	Mar 1989
1813	NFS Version 3 Protocol Specification	B. Callaghan et al.	Jun 1995
2623	NFS Version 2 and Version 3 Security Issues	M. Eisler	Jun 1999
2624	NFS Version 4 Design Considerations	S. Shepler	Jun 1999
3530	NFS Version 4 Protocol	S. Shepler et al.	April 2003

16.8 EXERCISES

☆ **E16.1** Explore your local NFS setup. Is NFS used, or is a different solution in place? Is automounting used? What tradeoffs have been made?

☆ **E16.2** What is the relationship between **mountd**, **nfsd**, and **portmap**? What does NFS's dependency on **portmap** mean in terms of security?

☆☆ **E16.3** What are some of the design ramifications of NFS being a stateless protocol? In particular, discuss any effects statelessness has on file locking, access permissions, and security. How would a stateful network filesystem differ from NFS?

☆☆ **E16.4** Your employer needs you to export **/usr** and **/usr/local** through NFS. You have been given the following information and requests:

    a) Because of office politics, you want only your department (local subnet 192.168.123.0/24) to be able to use these exported filesystems. What lines must be added to what files to implement this configuration? Pay attention to the proper export options.

    b) List the steps needed to make **mountd** and **nfsd** recognize these new shared filesystems. How could you verify that the directories were being shared without mounting them?

    c) Outline a strategy that would make all machines on your local subnet automatically mount the exported directories on the mount points **/mnt/usr** and **/mnt/usr/local**.

17 *Sharing System Files*

A properly functioning system depends on tens, perhaps hundreds, of configuration files all containing the right pieces of information. When you multiply the number of configuration files on a host by the number of hosts on a network, the result can be thousands of files—too many to manage by hand.

In the real world, machines are often similar from an administrative point of view. Instead of editing text files on each machine, you can, for efficiency, combine machines into groups that share configuration information. You can combine machines in several different ways.

The simplest way is to keep a master copy of each configuration file in one place and distribute it to members of the group whenever the file changes. This solution has the advantages of being simple and working on every Linux (and UNIX) system.

Another approach is to eliminate text files altogether and have each machine obtain its configuration information from a central server. This solution is more complicated than file copying, but it solves some additional problems. For example, clients can't miss updates, even if they are down when a change is made. It may also be faster to obtain information from a server than from a file, depending on the speed of the local disk and the amount of caching performed by the server. On the other hand, the entire network can hang when the central server goes down.

To add to the challenge, most organizations today are faced with supporting a mix of platforms—some UNIX, some Linux, and some Windows—and users are increasingly annoyed when they have to deal with inconveniences such as having to remember (and change) a different password on each platform. Synchronizing configuration and user information across wildly different systems (such as Windows and Linux) was once just a pipe dream. Today, it is commonplace.

The history of attempts to develop distributed administrative databases for large networks stretches back several decades and has produced a number of interesting systems. However, none of the systems currently in general use seem exactly right in their approach. Some are simple but not secure and not scalable. Others are functional but unwieldy. All the systems seem to have limitations that can prevent you from setting up the network the way you want to, and none of them manage all the information you may want to share across your machines.

In this chapter we first discuss some basic techniques for keeping files synchronized on a network. We then describe NIS, a historically popular database system originally introduced for UNIX. Finally, we address LDAP, a more sophisticated, platform-independent system that is becoming the de facto standard. Most sites today are migrating toward LDAP, driven largely by Microsoft's adoption of (most of) the LDAP standard in their Active Directory product and the desire to better integrate Linux and Windows environments.

17.1 WHAT TO SHARE

Of the many configuration files on a Linux system, only a subset can be usefully shared among machines. The most commonly shared files are listed in Table 17.1.

Table 17.1 System files that are commonly shared

Filename	Function
/etc/passwd	User account information database
/etc/shadow[a]	Holds shadow passwords
/etc/group	Defines UNIX groups
/etc/hosts	Maps between hostnames and IP addresses
/etc/networks[b]	Associates text names with IP network numbers
/etc/services	Lists port numbers for well-known network services
/etc/protocols	Maps text names to protocol numbers
/etc/ethers[b]	Maps between hostnames and Ethernet addresses
/etc/mail/aliases	Holds electronic mail aliases
/etc/rpc	Lists ID numbers for RPC services
/etc/netgroup[b]	Defines collections of hosts, users, and networks
/etc/cups/printcap	Printer information database
/etc/printcap.cups	Printer information database (alternative path)
/etc/termcap	Terminal type information database

a. Not necessarily sharable with other flavors of UNIX since the encryption can vary; see page 96.
b. Not used on all systems

Many other configuration files can potentially be shared among systems, depending on how similar you want machines at your site to be. For the most part, these other configuration files are associated with specific applications (e.g., **/etc/sendmail.cf** for **sendmail**) and are not supported by administrative database systems such as NIS and LDAP; you must share the files by copying them.

See page 681 for more information about PAM.

Historically, many of the files in Table 17.1 have been accessed through routines in the standard C library. For example, the **/etc/passwd** file can be searched with the **getpwuid**, **getpwnam**, and **getpwent** routines. These routines take care of opening, reading, and parsing the **passwd** file so that user-level programs don't have to do it themselves. Modern Linux distributions also use pluggable authentication modules (PAM), which afford a standard programming interface for performing security-related lookups. PAM allows systems such as Kerberos and LDAP to be easily integrated into Linux.

Administrative database systems complicate matters by providing alternative sources for much of this information. The traditional C library routines (**getpwent**, etc.) are aware of the common database systems and can access them in addition to (or instead of) the standard flat files. The exact complement of data sources that are consulted is set by the system administrator; see *Prioritizing sources of administrative information* on page 515 for details.

17.2 NSCD: CACHE THE RESULTS OF LOOKUPS

On some distributions, another finger in the system file pie belongs to **nscd**, the somewhat misleadingly titled name service cache daemon. **nscd** works in conjunction with the C library to cache the results of library calls such as **getpwent**. **nscd** is simply a wrapper for these library routines; it knows nothing about the actual data sources being consulted. **nscd** should in theory improve the performance of lookups, but any improvement is largely unnoticeable from the user's subjective view.

See Chapter 15 for more information about DNS.

We say that "name service cache daemon" is misleading because the term "name service" usually refers to DNS, the distributed database system that maps between hostnames and Internet addresses. **nscd** does in fact cache the results of DNS lookups (because it wraps **gethostbyname**, etc.), but it also wraps the library routines that access information from the **passwd** and **group** files and their network database equivalents. (For security, lookups to **/etc/shadow** are not cached.)

In concept, **nscd** should have no effect on the operation of the system other than to speed up repeated lookups. In practice, it can cause unexpected behavior because it maintains its own copy of the lookup results. Lookups are stored in the cache for a fixed amount of time (set in **nscd**'s configuration file, **/etc/nscd.conf**), and there is always the possibility that recent changes will not be reflected in **nscd**'s cache until the previous data has timed out. **nscd** is smart enough to monitor local data sources (such as **/etc/passwd**) for changes, so local updates should propagate within 15 seconds. For remote entries, such as those retrieved through NIS, you may have to wait for the full timeout period before changes take effect.

Among our example distributions, only SUSE runs **nscd** by default. Fedora and RHEL install **nscd** but do not start it at boot time by default; to enable the use of **nscd**, just run **chkconfig nscd on**. Debian and Ubuntu are **nscd** compatible but do not include **nscd** in the default installation; run **apt-get install nscd** to download it.

nscd starts at boot time and runs continuously. The default **/etc/nscd.conf** specifies a timeout of 10 minutes for **passwd** data and an hour for **hosts** and **group**, with a 20-second negative timeout (the amount of time before an unsuccessful lookup is retried). In practice, these values rarely need changing. If a change you recently made doesn't seem to show up, **nscd** is probably the reason.

17.3 COPYING FILES AROUND

Brute-force file copying is not an elegant solution, but it works on every kind of machine and is easy to set up and maintain. It's also a reliable system because it minimizes the interdependencies among machines (although it may also make it easier for machines to fall out of sync). File copying also offers the most flexibility in terms of what can be distributed and how. Indeed, it is also often used to keep applications and data files up to date as well as system files.

Quite a few configuration files are not supported by any of the common database services. Some examples are **/etc/ntp.conf**, which determines how hosts keep their clocks synchronized, and **/etc/sendmail.cf**, which tells **sendmail** how to deliver mail. To keep such files in sync (which is usually wise), you really have no choice but to use some sort of file-copying system, even if you distribute other types of configuration information through NIS or LDAP.

File-copying systems can use either a "push" model or a "pull" model. With push, the master server periodically distributes the freshest files to each client, whether the client wants them or not. Files can be pushed explicitly whenever a change is made, or they can simply be distributed on a regular schedule (perhaps with some files being transferred more often than others).

The push model has the advantage of keeping the distribution system centralized on one machine. Files, lists of clients, update scripts, and timetables are all stored in one place, making the scheme easy to control. One disadvantage is that each client must allow the master to modify its system files, thereby creating a security hazard.

In a pull system, each client is responsible for updating itself from the server. This is a less centralized way of distributing files, but it is also more adaptable and more secure. When data is shared across administrative boundaries, a pull system is especially attractive because the master and client machines need not be run by the same administrative group or political faction.

rdist: push files

The **rdist** command is the easiest way to distribute files from a central server. It has something of the flavor of **make**: you use a text editor to create a specification of the files to be distributed, and then you use **rdist** to bring reality into line with your specification. **rdist** copies files only when they are out of date, so you can write your specification as if all files were to be copied and let **rdist** optimize out unnecessary work.

rdist preserves the owner, group, mode, and modification time of files. When **rdist** updates an existing file, it first deletes the old version before installing the new. This feature makes **rdist** suitable for transferring executables that might be in use during the update.[1]

rdist historically ran on top of **rsh** and used **rsh**-style authentication to gain access to remote systems. Unfortunately, this system is not secure and is disabled by default on modern operating systems. Even though the **rdist** documentation continues to talk about **rsh**, do not be fooled into thinking that **rsh** is a reasonable choice.

Current versions of **rdist** are better in that they allow any command that understands the same syntax to be substituted for **rsh**. In practice, the substitute is **ssh**, which uses cryptography to verify the identity of hosts and to prevent network eavesdroppers from obtaining copies of your data. The downside is that you must run remote **ssh** servers in a mode that does not require a password (but authenticates the client with a cryptographic key pair). This is a less secure configuration than we would normally recommend, but it is still a huge improvement over **rsh**. See page 697 for more information about **sshd** and its authentication modes.

Now that we've belabored the perils of **rdist**, let's look at how it actually works. Like **make**, **rdist** looks for a control file (**Distfile** or **distfile**) in the current directory. **rdist -f** *distfile* explicitly specifies the control file's pathname. Within the **Distfile**, tabs, spaces, and newlines are used interchangeably as separators. Comments are introduced with a pound sign (#).

The meat of a **Distfile** consists of statements of the form

```
label: pathnames -> destinations commands
```

The *label* field associates a name with the statement. From the shell, you can run **rdist** *label* to distribute only the files described in a particular statement.

The *pathnames* and *destinations* are lists of files to be copied and hosts to copy them to, respectively. If a list contains more than one entry, the list must be surrounded with parentheses and the elements separated with whitespace. The *pathnames* can include shell-style globbing characters (e.g., **/usr/man/man[123]** or **/usr/lib/***). The notation *~user* is also acceptable, but it is evaluated separately on the source and destination machines.

By default, **rdist** copies the files and directories listed in *pathnames* to the equivalent paths on each destination machine. You can modify this behavior by supplying a sequence of commands and terminating each with a semicolon.

---

1. Though the old version disappears from the filesystem namespace, it continues to exist until all references have been released. You must also be aware of this effect when managing log files. See page 203 for more information.

The following commands are understood:

```
install options [destdir];
notify namelist;
except pathlist;
except_pat patternlist;
special [pathlist] string;
cmdspecial [pathlist] string;
```

The install command sets options that affect the way **rdist** copies files. Options typically control the treatment of symbolic links, the correctness of **rdist**'s difference-checking algorithm, and the way that deletions are handled. The options, which must be preceded by -o, consist of a comma-separated list of option names. For example, the line

```
install -oremove,follow ;
```

makes **rdist** follow symbolic links (instead of just copying them as links) and removes existing files on the destination machine that have no counterpart on the source machine. See the **rdist** man page for a complete list of options. The defaults are almost always what you want.

The name "install" is somewhat misleading, since files are copied whether or not an install command is present. Options are specified as they would be on the **rdist** command line, but when included in the **Distfile**, they apply only to the set of files handled by that install command.

The optional *destdir* specifies an installation directory on the destination hosts. By default, **rdist** uses the original pathnames.

The notify command takes a list of email addresses as its argument. **rdist** sends mail to these addresses whenever a file is updated. Any addresses that do not contain an at sign (@) are suffixed with the name of the destination host. For example, **rdist** would expand "pete" to "pete@anchor" when reporting a list of files updated on host anchor.

The except and except_pat commands remove pathnames from the list of files to be copied. Arguments to except are matched literally, and those of except_pat are interpreted as regular expressions. These exception commands are useful because **rdist**, like **make**, allows macros to be defined at the beginning of its control file. You might want to use a similar list of files for several statements, specifying only the additions and deletions for each host.

The special command executes a shell command (the *string* argument, in quotation marks) on each remote host. If a *pathlist* is present, **rdist** executes the command once after copying each of the specified files. Without a *pathlist*, **rdist** executes the command after every file. cmdspecial is similar, but it executes the shell command once after copying is complete. (The contents of the *pathlist* are passed to the shell as an environment variable.)

Here's a simple example of a **Distfile**:

```
SYS_FILES = (/etc/passwd /etc/group /etc/mail/aliases)
GET_ALL   = (chimchim lollipop barkadon)
GET_SOME  = (whammo spiff)

all: ${SYS_FILES} -> ${GET_ALL}
    notify barb;
    special /etc/mail/aliases "/usr/bin/newaliases";

some: ${SYS_FILES} -> ${GET_SOME}
    except /etc/mail/aliases;
    notify eddie@spiff;
```

*See page 551 for more information about **newaliases**.*

This configuration replicates the three listed system files on chimchim, lollipop, and barkadon and sends mail to barb@*destination* describing any updates or errors that occur. After **/etc/mail/aliases** is copied, **rdist** runs **newaliases** on each destination. Only two files are copied to whammo and spiff. **newaliases** is not run, and a report is mailed to eddie@spiff.

To get **rdist** working among machines, you must also tell **sshd** on the recipient hosts to trust the host from which you are distributing files. To do this, you generate a plaintext key for the master host and store a copy of the public portion in the file **~root/.ssh/authorized_keys** on each recipient. It's probably also wise to restrict what this key can do and where it can log in from. See the description of "method B" on page 697 for more information.

rsync: transfer files more securely

rsync is available from rsync.samba.org.

rsync, written by Andrew Tridgell and Paul Mackerras, is similar in spirit to **rdist** but with a somewhat different focus. It does not use a file-copying control file in the manner of **rdist** (although the server side does have a configuration file). **rsync** is a bit like a souped-up version of **scp** that is scrupulous about preserving links, modification times, and permissions. It is more network efficient than **rdist** because it looks inside individual files and attempts to transmit only the differences between versions. Most Linux distributions provide a prepackaged version of **rsync**, although it may not be installed by default.

From our perspective, the main advantage of **rsync** is the fact that receiving machines can run the remote side as a server process out of **xinetd** or **inetd**. The server (actually just a different mode of **rsync**, which must be installed on both the master and the clients) is quite configurable: it can restrict remote access to a set of given directories and can require the master to prove its identity with a password. Since no **ssh** access is necessary, you can set up **rsync** to distribute system files without making too many security compromises. (However, if you prefer to use **ssh** instead of an **inetd**-based server process, **rsync** lets you do that too.) What's more, **rsync** can also run in pull mode (pulling files down from the **rsync** server rather than pushing them to it), which is even more secure (see the section on pulling files, page 510).

Unfortunately, **rsync** isn't nearly as flexible as **rdist**, and its configuration is less sophisticated than **rdist**'s **distfile**. You can't execute arbitrary commands on the clients, and you can't **rsync** to multiple hosts at once.

As an example, the command

```
# rsync -gopt --password-file=/etc/rsync.pwd /etc/passwd lollipop::sysfiles
```

transfers the **/etc/passwd** file to the machine lollipop. The **-gopt** options preserve the permissions, ownerships, and modification times of the file. The double colon in **lollipop::sysfiles** makes **rsync** contact the remote **rsync** directly on port 873 instead of using **ssh**. The password stored in **/etc/rsync.pwd** authenticates the connection.[2]

This example transfers only one file, but **rsync** is capable of handling multiple files at once. In addition, the **--include** and **--exclude** flags let you specify a list of regular expressions to match against filenames, so you can set up a fairly sophisticated set of transfer criteria. If the command line gets too unwieldy, you can also read the patterns from separate files with the **--include-file** and **--exclude-file** options.

 Once the **rsync** package has been installed, Red Hat, Fedora, and SUSE all provide **xinetd** configurations for **rsync**. However, you must edit **/etc/xinetd.d/rsync** and change disable = yes to disable = no to actually enable the server.

 The **rsync** package on Debian and Ubuntu requires an entry in **/etc/inetd.conf** to enable the server functionality. Assuming that you use TCP wrappers, the entry should look something like this:

```
rsync stream tcp nowait root /usr/sbin/tcpd /usr/bin/rsyncd --daemon
```

It's a good idea to configure **tcpd** to block access from all hosts except the one that will be distributing your system files. Host rejection can be specified in **rsyncd.conf** as well, but it never hurts to erect multiple barriers.

Once you have enabled **rsync**, you need to set up a couple of config files to tell the **rsync** server how to behave. The main file is **/etc/rsyncd.conf**, which contains both global configurations parameters and a set of "modules," each of which is a directory tree to export or import. A reasonable configuration for a module that you can push to (i.e., that will accept incoming file transfers initiated by the connecting client) looks something like this:

```
# sysfiles is just an arbitrary title for the particular module.
[sysfiles]
# This is the path you allow files to be pushed to. It could be just /.
path = /etc
# This is the file specifying the user/password pair to authenticate the module
secrets file = /etc/rsyncd.secrets
```

---

2. Although the password is not sent in plaintext across the network, the transferred files are not encrypted. If you use **ssh** as the transport (**rsync -gopt -e ssh /etc/passwd /etc/shadow lollipop:/etc** – note the single colon), the connection will be encrypted, but **sshd** will have to be configured not to require a password. Name your poison!

```
# Can be read only if you are pulling files
read only = false
# UID and GID under which the transfer will be done
uid = root
gid = root
# List of hosts that are allowed to connect
hosts allow = distribution_master_hostname
```

Many other options can be set, but the defaults are reasonable. This configuration limits operations to the **/etc** directory and allows access only by the listed host. From the user's or client's point of view, you can **rsync** files to the server with the destination *hostname***::sysfiles**, which maps to the module above. If you want to set up **rsync** in pull mode (pulling files from a central **rsync** server), the configuration above will still work, although you may want to tighten things up a bit, for example, by setting the transfer mode to read-only.

The last thing you need to do is set up an **rsyncd.secrets** file. It's generally kept in **/etc** (although you can put it elsewhere) and contains the passwords that clients can use to authenticate themselves. For example:

```
root:password
```

As a general rule, **rsync** passwords should be different from system passwords. Because the passwords are shown in plaintext, **rsyncd.secrets** must be readable only by root.

Pulling files

You can implement a pulling system in several ways. The most straightforward way is to make the files available on a central FTP or web server[3] and to have the clients automatically download them as needed. In historical times, administrators would roll their own utilities to do this (often scripting **ftp** with a system such as **expect**), but standard utilities can now do it for you.

One such utility that ships with most Linux distributions is the popular **wget**. It's a straightforward little program that fetches the contents of a URL (either FTP or HTTP). For example, to FTP a file with **wget**, just run

```
wget ftp://user:password@hostname/path/to/file
```

The specified *file* is deposited in the current directory.

An alternative option for FTP only is **ncftp**, which also ships with most distributions. It's really just an enhanced FTP client that allows for easy scripting.

Some sites distribute files by publishing them on a networked filesystem such as NFS. This is perhaps the simplest technique from an automation point of view—all you need is **cp**, at least in theory. In practice, you would probably want to be a little more sophisticated and check for signs of security problems and corrupted content

---

3. Keep in mind that both HTTP and FTP transport data in plaintext. You may want to consider HTTPS or SFTP, respectively, if security is a concern.

before blindly copying system files. Publishing sensitive system files over NFS has many disadvantages from a security point of view, but it's a simple and effective way of moving the bits. You can always encrypt the data to reduce the chance of interception by an intruder.

A final option is to use **rsync** as described in the previous section. If you run an **rsync** server on your central distribution host, clients can simply **rsync** the files down. Using this method is perhaps slightly more complex than using FTP, but you then have access to all of **rsync**'s features.

Whatever system you use, be careful not to overload your data server. If a lot of machines on the network try to access your server simultaneously (e.g., if everyone runs an update out of **cron** at the same time), you can cause an inadvertent denial of service attack. Large sites should keep this problem in mind and allow for time staggering or randomization. A simple way to do this is to wrap **cron** jobs in a Perl script such as this:

```
#!/usr/bin/perl
sleep rand() * 600; # sleep between 0 and 600 seconds (i.e., 10 minutes)
system(copy_files_down);
```

17.4 NIS: THE NETWORK INFORMATION SERVICE

NIS, released by Sun in the 1980s, was the first "prime time" administrative database. It was originally called the Sun Yellow Pages, but eventually had to be renamed for legal reasons. NIS commands still begin with the letters **yp**, so it's hard to forget the original name. NIS was widely adopted among UNIX vendors and is supported by every Linux distribution.

The unit of sharing in NIS is the record, not the file. A record usually corresponds to one line in a config file. A master server maintains the authoritative copies of system files, which are kept in their original locations and formats and are edited with a text editor just as before. A server process makes the contents of the files available over the network. A server and its clients constitute an NIS "domain."[4]

Data files are preprocessed into database files by the Berkeley DB hashing library to improve the efficiency of lookups. After editing files on the master server, you use **make** to tell NIS to convert them to their hashed format.

Only one key can be associated with each entry, so a system file may have to be translated into several NIS "maps." For example, the **/etc/passwd** file is translated into two different maps called **passwd.byname** and **passwd.byuid**. One map is used to look up entries by username and the other to look up entries by UID. Either map can be used to enumerate the entries in the **passwd** file. However, because hashing libraries do not preserve the order of records, there is no way to reconstruct an exact duplicate of the original file (unless it was sorted).

---

4. Do not confuse NIS domains with DNS domains. They are completely separate and have nothing to do with each other.

NIS allows you to replicate the network maps on a set of slave servers. Providing more than one server helps relieve the load on the master and helps keep clients working even when some servers become unavailable. Whenever a file is changed on the master server, the corresponding NIS map must be pushed out to the slaves so that all servers provide the same data. Clients do not distinguish between the master server and the slaves.

In the traditional NIS implementation, you must place at least one NIS server on every physical network. Clients use IP broadcasting to locate servers, and broadcast packets are not forwarded by routers and gateways. The **ypset** command can point a client at a particular server; however, at the first hint of trouble, the client attempts to locate a new server by broadcasting. Unless a server on the client's network responds, this sequence of events can cause the client to hang.

This system causes a lot of problems, not least of which is that it is extremely insecure. An intruder can set up a rogue NIS server that responds to broadcasts and either provides bogus data or delivers a denial of service attack by allowing binding and then blocking on actual requests. These days, the preferred management technique is to give each client an explicit list of its legitimate NIS servers. This system also has the advantage that the servers need not be on the local subnet.

Under Linux, servers are listed in **/etc/yp.conf**. Here's an example for the NIS domain atrustnis:

```
domain  atrustnis  server  10.2.2.3
domain  atrustnis  server  10.2.2.4
```

There is one line for each server; if one server goes down, NIS fails over to another. Note that the servers are given in the form of IP addresses. **yp.conf** accepts hostnames, but these hostnames must then be resolvable at boot time (i.e., enumerated in the **/etc/hosts** file or resolvable through DNS).

If you *must* use broadcast mode, the syntax is

```
domain  atrustnis  broadcast
```

Understanding how NIS works

NIS's data files are stored in the directory **/var/yp**. Each NIS map is stored in a hashed format in a subdirectory of the NIS directory named for the NIS domain. There is one map (file) for each key by which a file can be searched. For example, in the domain cssuns, the DB files for the **/etc/passwd** maps might be

```
/var/yp/cssuns/passwd.byname
/var/yp/cssuns/passwd.byuid
```

The **passwd** file is searchable by both name and UID, so two maps are derived from it.

The **makedbm** command generates NIS maps from flat files. However, you need not invoke this command directly; a **Makefile** in **/var/yp** generates all the common NIS maps. After you modify a system file, **cd** to **/var/yp** and run **make**. The **make** command checks the modification time of each file against the modification times of the maps derived from it and runs **makedbm** for each map that needs to be rebuilt.

Maps are copied from the master server to the slave servers by the **ypxfr** command. **ypxfr** is a pull command; it must be run on each slave server to make that server import the map. Slaves usually execute **ypxfr** every so often just to verify that they have the most recent maps; you can use **cron** to control how often this is done.

The default implementation of map copying is somewhat inefficient. Linux furnishes a daemon called **rpc.ypxfrd** that can be run on the master server to speed responses to **ypxfr** requests. **rpc.ypxfrd** sidesteps the normal NIS protocol and simply hands out copies of the map files.

yppush is a "push" command that's used on the master server. It actually does not transfer any data but rather instructs each slave to execute a **ypxfr**. The **yppush** command is used by the **Makefile** in the NIS directory to ensure that newly updated maps are propagated to slaves.

The special map called **ypservers** does not correspond to any flat file. This map contains a list of all the servers of the domain. It's automatically constructed when the domain is set up with **ypinit** (see *Configuring NIS servers* on page 518). Its contents are examined when the master server needs to distribute maps to slaves.

After initial configuration, the only active components of the NIS system are the **ypserv** and **ypbind** daemons. **ypserv** runs only on servers (both master and slave); it accepts queries from clients and answers them by looking up information in the hashed map files.

ypbind runs on every machine in the NIS domain, including servers. The C library contacts the local **ypbind** daemon when it needs to answer an administrative query (provided that **/etc/nsswitch.conf** says to do so). **ypbind** locates a **ypserv** in the appropriate domain and returns its identity to the C library, which then contacts the server directly. The query mechanism is illustrated in Exhibit A.

Exhibit A   NIS query procedure

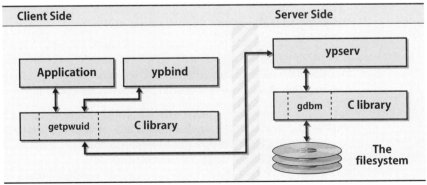

Current Linux versions of **ypbind** periodically check to be sure they are dealing with the most responsive server for an NIS domain. This is an improvement over the traditional implementation, which fixates on a particular server. Another feature unique to Linux is that clients can bind to different NIS domains for different maps.

NIS includes a number of minor commands that examine maps, find out which version of a map each server is using, and control the binding between clients and servers. A complete list of NIS commands and daemons is given in Table 17.2. (Rows are shaded to improve readability.)

Table 17.2   NIS commands and daemons

Program	Description
ypserv	Is the NIS server daemon, started at boot time
ypbind	Is the NIS client daemon, started at boot time
domainname	Sets the NIS domain a machine is in (run at boot time)
ypxfr	Downloads current version of a map from master server
ypxfrd	Serves requests from **ypxfr** (runs on master server)
yppush	Makes slave servers update their versions of a map
makedbm	Builds a hashed map from a flat file
ypmake	Rebuilds hashed maps from flat files that have changed
ypinit	Configures a host as a master or slave server
ypset	Makes **ypbind** connect to a particular server[a]
ypwhich	Finds out which server the current host is using
yppoll	Finds out what version of a map a server is using
ypcat	Prints the values contained in an NIS map
ypmatch	Prints map entries for a specified key
yppasswd	Changes a password on the NIS master server
ypchfn	Changes GECOS information on the NIS master server
ypchsh	Changes a login shell on NIS master server
yppasswdd	Is the server for **yppasswd**, **ypchsh**, and **ypchfn**

a. Must be specifically enabled with **ypbind -ypsetme** or **ypbind -ypset** (dangerous)

Weighing advantages and disadvantages of NIS

One nice feature of NIS is that it can be understood by mere mortals. NIS is analogous to copying files around; in most cases, it's unnecessary for administrators to be aware of NIS's internal data formats. Administration is done with the same old flat files, and only one or two new procedures need to be learned.

Since NIS domains cannot be linked, NIS is not suitable for managing a large network of machines unless a single configuration is to be applied to every machine. You can divide a large network into several NIS domains, but each domain must be administered separately. Even if a large network does use a single configuration, limitations on the scaling of slave servers mean that in practice these sites usually come up with some other mechanism to keep their NIS servers in sync. They often end up rolling their own back-end databases and making their NIS servers fetch their data from this central source.

*See Chapter 8 for more information about **cron**.*

If a slave server is down or inaccessible when a map is changed, the slave's copy will not be updated. Slaves must periodically poll the master to be sure that they have the most recent version of every map. Although basic tools for polling are provided with NIS, you must implement the polling scheme you want by using **cron**. Even so, two different versions of a map could possibly be served simultaneously for a while, with clients randomly seeing one or the other.

NIS is minimally secure. Broadcast mode is particularly bad; any host on a network can claim to serve a particular domain and feed bogus administrative data to NIS clients. You can avoid this problem by explicitly enumerating the permissible NIS servers for each client.

You can restrict the hosts that are able to read a server's maps by explicitly listing them in **/etc/ypserv.conf**; however, this technique is not 100% secure. You can also improve the security of your system by distributing your shadow password file with some other technique (such as **rdist** or **rsync**); we don't recommend using NIS to serve shadow passwords.

Older versions of Linux NIS contain known security holes. If you are running an older system, make sure you get the latest upgrades before starting NIS.

Prioritizing sources of administrative information

Configuration information can be distributed in several ways. Every system understands flat files and knows how to use DNS to look up hostnames and Internet addresses. Most also understand NIS. Since a given piece of information could come from several potential sources, Linux provides a way for you to specify the sources that are to be checked and the order in which the checks are made.

In the original (pre-Linux) implementation of NIS, some configuration files (the **/etc/passwd** and **/etc/group** files in particular) had to be configured to "invite in" the contents of the corresponding NIS maps. The invitation was extended by inclusion of special incantations in the files themselves. A lone "+" at the beginning of a line would include the entire NIS map, "+@*netgroup*" would include only entries relevant to a given netgroup, and "+*name*" would include a single entry.

This approach was never very well liked, and it has been superseded by a central config file, **/etc/nsswitch.conf**, that allows an explicit search path to be specified for each type of administrative information. The original behavior can be emulated by use of a compatibility mode, but it's unlikely you would want to use this feature on a newly configured network. (Unfortunately, emulation is most distributions' default.)

A typical **nsswitch.conf** file looks something like this:

```
passwd: files nis
hosts:  files dns
group:  files
...
```

Each line configures one type of information (usually, one flat-file equivalent). The common sources are nis, nisplus, files, dns, and compat; they refer to NIS, NIS+,[5] vanilla flat files (ignoring tokens such as "+"), DNS, and NISified flat files (honoring "+"), respectively. DNS is a valid data source only for host and network information.

Support for each source type comes from a shared library (**/lib/libnss***), so distributions vary slightly in the sources they support. Some distributions provide out-of-the-box support for LDAP (see page 520) and/or Hesiod, a directory service based on DNS. Another source commonly supported on Linux (and unfortunately not very well documented) is db, which reads a hashed version of the map from **/var/db** (for example, **/var/db/passwd.db**). If your flat files are large, the use of hashed versions can substantially increase lookup speed.

Sources are tried from left to right until one of them produces an answer for the query. In the example above, the **gethostbyname** routine would first check the **/etc/hosts** file, and if the host was not listed there, would then check DNS. Queries about UNIX groups, on the other hand, would check only the **/etc/group** file.

If necessary, you can define the "failure" of a source more specifically by putting bracketed expressions after it. For example, the line

```
hosts:   dns [NOTFOUND=return] nis
```

causes DNS to be used exclusively if it is available; a negative response from the name server makes queries return immediately (with a failure code) without checking NIS. However, NIS is used if no name server is available. The various types of failures are shown in Table 17.3; each can be set to return or continue, signifying whether the query should be aborted or forwarded to the next source.

Table 17.3   Failure modes recognized in /etc/nsswitch.conf

Condition	Meaning
UNAVAIL	The source doesn't exist or is down.
NOTFOUND	The source exists, but couldn't answer the query.
TRYAGAIN	The source exists but is busy.
SUCCESS	The source was able to answer the query.

By default, all Linux distributions ship with **nsswitch.conf** files that are reasonable for a stand-alone machine without NIS. All entries go to the flat files, with the exception of host lookups, which first consult flat files and then DNS. Most distributions default to compat mode for **passwd** and **group**, which is probably worth changing. If you really use NIS, just explicitly put it in the **nsswitch.conf** file.

---

5. An ill-starred successor to the original NIS now discontinued by Sun but still supported by some systems for historical reasons.

Debian and its kissing-cousin Ubuntu ship with protocols, services, ethers, and rpc going to db and then files. This is slightly odd, since Debian and Ubuntu don't, in fact, include **/var/db** or any mechanism to maintain it. Presumably it would be slightly more efficient to go directly to files; you can modify the settings to do that if you want.

Using netgroups

NIS introduced a popular abstraction known as netgroups. Netgroups name sets of users, machines, and nets for easy reference in other system files. They are defined in **/etc/netgroup** and are also shared as an NIS map.

The format of a **netgroup** entry is

groupname list-of-members

Members are separated by whitespace. A member is either a netgroup name or a triplet of the form

(hostname, username, nisdomainname)

Any empty field in a triplet is a wild card; thus the entry (boulder,,) refers to all users in all domains on the host boulder (or to the host boulder itself, depending on the context in which the netgroup is used). A dash in a field indicates negation, so the entry (boulder,-,) refers to the machine boulder and no users. Netgroup definitions can nest.

Here's a simple example of an **/etc/netgroup** file:

```
bobcats        (snake,,) (headrest,,)
servers        (anchor,,) (moet,,) (piper,,) (kirk,,)
anchorclients  (xx,,) (watneys,,) (molson,,)
beers          (anchor,,) (anchor-gateway,,) anchorclients
allhosts       beers bobcats servers
```

These netgroups are all defined in terms of hosts; that's typical for real-world use.

See Chapter 16 for more information about NFS. Netgroups can be used in several system files that define permissions. The most common application these days is for configuring NFS exports. Netgroups can be mentioned in the **/etc/exports** file to specify groups of hosts that are allowed to mount each filesystem. This feature is very handy when you are exporting to a lot of hosts, particularly on systems that require fully qualified domain names and that limit lines in the **exports** file to 1,024 characters.

Netgroups are a nice idea. They simplify system files, making them more understandable. They also add a layer of indirection that permits the status of a user or machine to be changed in one file rather than fifteen.

Setting up an NIS domain

You must initialize NIS on the master server, on the slave servers, and on each client. You do this in two steps. First, run **ypinit** on each server. Second, on every machine in the domain, set the domain name from **/etc/domainname** or one of the system startup files and configure **/etc/nsswitch.conf** to import NIS data.

Configuring NIS servers

The server side of NIS must usually be installed as a separate, optional package called **ypserv**. Debian and Ubuntu do things a little differently; their **nis** package includes both the client and server sides.

ypinit initializes both the master and slave servers for a domain. On the master, you use the following commands:

```
# cd /var/yp            /* The NIS directory, wherever it is */
# domainname foo        /* Name the new domain. */
# /usr/lib/yp/ypinit -m /* Initialize as master server. */
# ypserv                /* Start the NIS server. */
```

The **-m** flag tells **ypinit** that it's configuring a master server; it prompts you to enter a list of slave servers. Once the master is up and running, prime each slave server by running **ypinit** with the **-s** (slave) flag:

```
# cd /var/yp
# /usr/lib/yp/ypinit -s master /* Argument is  master's hostname. */
# ypserv
```

ypinit -s makes a local copy of the master's current data; the presence of the domain's data files is enough to let **ypserv** know that it should serve the domain.

*See Chapter 8 for more information about **cron**.*

On each slave, you should set up crontab entries to pull fresh copies of all maps from the master. The command **ypxfr** *map*, where *map* is a name such as **passwd.byuid**, transfers the specified map from the master server. You must run the command once for each map. Maps tend to change at different rates, so you may want to transfer some maps more often than others. In most circumstances, transferring all the maps once or twice a day (perhaps late at night) is good enough. The following script transfers every map:

```
#!/bin/sh
mydomain = `/bin/domainname`
cd /var/yp/$mydomain   # the NIS directory
for map in `/bin/ls`; do
    /usr/lib/yp/ypxfr $map
done
```

Additionally, prefabricated scripts in **/usr/lib/yp** transfer NIS maps at various frequencies (**ypxfr_1perday**, **ypxfr_2perday**, and **ypxfr_1perhour**).

If you want users to be able to change their passwords with **yppasswd**, you must run the **yppasswdd** daemon on the master NIS server. The Linux version of this server has been known to crash frequently, so be sure to verify that it is still running if the **yppasswd** command doesn't seem to be working.

Setting access control options in /etc/ypserv.conf

You can set options for the Linux version of the **ypserv** daemon in **/etc/ypserv.conf**; however, only a few options are defined, and most sites will not need to change their default values.

More importantly, **ypserv** looks to the **ypserv.conf** file for instructions about how to control access to NIS data. Rather than simply blurting out the answer to every incoming query as the traditional implementation does, the Linux **ypserv** checks incoming requests against an access list. Each control line is of the form

```
host:nisdomain:map:security
```

host, *nisdomain*, and *map* identify a particular subset of requests, and the *security* parameter tells how to handle it: deny to reject the request, port to allow the request as long as it originates at a privileged network port (< 1024), and none to always allow the request. Here is an example configuration:

```
128.138.24.0/255.255.252.0:atrustnis:*:none
*:*:passwd.byuid:deny
*:*:passwd.byname:deny
128.138.:atrustnis:*:port
*:*:*:deny
```

You can use a star in the *host*, *nisdomain*, and *map* fields to match any value, but partial matches are not allowed. (You can't, for example, use passwd.* to match all maps derived from the **/etc/passwd** file.) Control lines are checked in order until a matching line is found. If no lines match, the default is to answer the request.

See page 287 for a discussion of CIDR netmasks.

The *host* parameter can include a netmask, as on the first line, but **ypserv** does not understand the more common CIDR notation. As shown on the fourth line, you can also omit trailing components of an IP address to make **ypserv** fill it in with zeros and supply an analogous netmask.

The rules above allow access from any host on one of the 128.138.24/22 networks. Hosts within 128.138 can access all maps in atrustnis except those derived from the **/etc/passwd** file, as long as the request originates at a privileged port. All other access is denied.

Never forget that this type of access control is a stopgap measure at best. It may discourage casual browsing by people outside your organization, but it won't provide a very effective deterrent to a determined attacker.

An older security mechanism, the **/var/yp/securenets** file, is also supported for historical reasons. New configurations should use **ypserv.conf**.

Configuring NIS clients

After setting up servers, inform each client machine that it is a member of the new domain. The servers of a domain are generally clients as well.

See Chapter 2 for more information about the system startup scripts. The **domainname** command sets a machine's NIS domain. It's usually run at boot time from one of the startup scripts. The exact contortions necessary to configure this vary by distribution; details are given below.

Each client must have at least a minimal private version of the **passwd**, **group**, and **hosts** files. **passwd** and **group** are needed to allow root to log in when no NIS server is available. They should contain the standard system accounts and groups: root, bin, daemon, etc. The **hosts** file (or DNS) must be present to answer boot-time queries that occur before NIS is up and running.

NIS details by distribution

Under Fedora and RHEL, you set the NIS domain name in **/etc/sysconfig/network** by setting the variable NISDOMAIN. The server side of NIS is installed as a separate package called **ypserv**. The **ypbind**, **ypserv**, and **yppasswdd** daemons are enabled and disabled with **chkconfig**; for example,

```
# chkconfig ypbind on
```

SUSE sets the NIS domain name at boot time from the file **/etc/domainname**. The server side of NIS is installed as a separate package called **ypserv**. Use **chkconfig** to force the system to automatically start **ypserv** and/or **ypbind** at boot time. You can set command-line options for **ypbind** in **/etc/sysconfig/ypbind**. You must either set YPBIND_BROADCAST to yes in this file or install an **/etc/yp.conf** file; otherwise, the startup scripts will refuse to start **ypbind**.

Debian and Ubuntu keep the name of the NIS domain in **/etc/defaultdomain**. The startup scripts run **ypbind** automatically if this file is present. To run **ypserv**, edit the file **/etc/default/nis** and set the value of NISSERVER to slave or master.

17.5 LDAP: THE LIGHTWEIGHT DIRECTORY ACCESS PROTOCOL

UNIX and Linux sites need a good way to distribute their administrative configuration data; however, the problem is really more general than that. What about nonadministrative data such as telephone and email directories? What about information that you want to share with the outside world? What everyone really needs is a generalized directory service.

A directory service is just a database, but one that makes a few assumptions. Any data set that has characteristics matching the assumptions is a candidate for inclusion. The basic assumptions are as follows:

- Data objects are relatively small.
- The database will be widely replicated and cached.
- The information is attribute based.
- Data are read often but written infrequently.
- Searching is a common operation.

The current IETF standards-track system designed to fill this role is the Lightweight Directory Access Protocol (LDAP). The LDAP specifications don't really speak to the database itself, just the way that it's accessed through a network. But because they specify how the data is schematized and how searches are performed, they imply a fairly specific data model as well.

LDAP was originally designed as a gateway protocol that would allow TCP/IP clients to talk to an older directory service called X.500, which is now obsolete. Over time, it became apparent both that X.500 was going to die out and that UNIX really needed a standard directory of some sort. These factors have led to LDAP being developed as a full-fledged directory system in its own right (and perhaps to its no longer being quite so deserving of the L).[6]

At this point (in the year 2006), LDAP has become quite mainstream, spurred perhaps in part by Microsoft's adoption of LDAP as the basis for its Active Directory service. On the UNIX and Linux side, the OpenLDAP package (www.openldap.org) has become the standard implementation.

The structure of LDAP data

LDAP data takes the form of property lists, which are known in LDAP world as "entries." Each entry consists of a set of named attributes (such as "uid" or "description") along with those attributes' values. Windows users might recognize this structure as being similar to that of the Windows Registry. As in the Registry, an individual attribute can have several values.

As an example, here's a typical (but simplified) **/etc/passwd** line expressed as an LDAP entry:

```
uid: ghopper
cn: Grace Hopper
userPassword: {crypt}$1$pZaGA2RL$MPDJoc0afuhHY6yk8HQFp0
loginShell: /bin/bash
uidNumber: 1202
gidNumber: 1202
homeDirectory: /home/ghopper
```

This notation is a simple example of LDIF, the LDAP Data Interchange Format, which is used by most LDAP-related tools and server implementations. The fact that LDAP data can be easily converted back and forth from plain text is part of the reason for its success.

Entries are organized into a hierarchy through the use of "distinguished names" (attribute name: dn) that form a sort of search path. For example, the dn for the user above might be

```
dn: uid=ghopper,ou=People,dc=navy,dc=mil
```

---

6. Because of LDAP's tortured history, many sources tend to go into great detail about LDAP's X.500 and OSI connections. However, this history is not relevant to contemporary use of LDAP. Ignore it.

As in DNS, the "most significant bit" goes on the right. Here, the DNS name navy.mil has been used to structure the top levels of the LDAP hierarchy. It has been broken down into two domain components (dc's), "navy" and "mil," but this is only one of several common conventions.

Every entry has exactly one distinguished name. Therefore, the entry hierarchy looks like a simple branching tree with no loops. There are, however, provisions for symbolic links between entries and for referrals to other servers.

LDAP entries are typically schematized through the use of an objectClass attribute. Object classes specify the attributes that an entry can contain, some of which may be required for validity. The schema also assigns a data type to each attribute. Object classes nest and combine in the traditional object-oriented fashion. The top level of the object class tree is the class named "top", which specifies merely that an entry must have an objectClass attribute.

Table 17.4 shows some common LDAP attributes whose meaning might not be immediately apparent.

Table 17.4   **Some common attribute names found in LDAP hierarchies**

Attribute	Stands for	What it is
o	Organization	Often identifies a site's top-level entry
ou	Organizational unit	A logical subdivision, e.g., "marketing"
cn	Common name	The most natural name to represent the entry
dc	Domain component	Used at sites that model their LDAP hierarchy on DNS
objectClass	Object class	Schema to which this entry's attributes conform

The point of LDAP

Until you've had some experience with it, LDAP can be a slippery concept to grab hold of. Unlike NIS, LDAP by itself doesn't solve any specific administrative problem. There's no "primary task" that LDAP is tailor-made to handle, and sites diverge widely in their reasons for deploying LDAP servers. So before we move on to the specifics of installing and configuring OpenLDAP, it's probably worth reviewing some reasons why you might want to investigate LDAP for use at your site. Here are the big ones:

- You can use LDAP as a replacement for NIS. The advantages over NIS are numerous, but the main ones are better security, better tool support, and increased flexibility.

See page 555 for more information about using LDAP with sendmail.

- In a similar vein, you can use LDAP to distribute configuration information that lies outside the traditional domain of NIS. Most mail systems, including **sendmail** and Postfix, can draw a large part of their routing information from LDAP, and this is in fact one of LDAP's most popular applications. Tools as varied as the Apache web server and the autofs automounter can be configured to pay attention to LDAP, too. It's likely that LDAP support will become more and more common over time.

- It's easy to access LDAP data with command-line tools such as **ldapsearch**. In addition, LDAP is well supported by common scripting languages such as Perl and Python (through the use of libraries). Ergo, LDAP is a terrific way to distribute configuration information for locally-written scripts and administrative utilities.

- Excellent web-based tools are available for managing LDAP, for example, phpLDAPadmin (phpldapadmin.sourceforge.net) and Directory Admin-istrator (diradmin.open-it.org). These tools are so easy to use that you can just rip the box open and start playing without reading the manual.

- LDAP is well supported as a public directory service. Most major email clients, including those that run on PCs, support the use of LDAP to access user directories. Simple LDAP searches are also supported by many web browsers through the use of an LDAP URL type.

- Microsoft's Active Directory is based on LDAP, and the current release of Windows 2003 Server R2 includes extensions (originally called "Services for UNIX," now called "Windows Security and Directory Services for UNIX") that facilitate the mapping of Linux users and groups.

LDAP documentation and specifications

We are not aware of any really excellent source of introductory information on the general architecture of LDAP. The onetime FAQ is no longer maintained. The source that we recommended for LDAP version 2, *Understanding LDAP* by Johner et al, has unfortunately not been updated for version 3, and the differences in the protocol are significant enough that it's probably worthwhile to look elsewhere.

The current best places to start are with the documentation for the OpenLDAP package and the Linux *LDAP HOWTO*. Citations for a couple of reasonable LDAP books are also given at the end of this chapter.

The LDAP-related RFCs are numerous and varied. As a group, they tend to convey an impression of great complexity, which is somewhat unrepresentative of average use. Some of the high points are listed in Table 17.5 on the next page.

OpenLDAP: LDAP for Linux

OpenLDAP is an extension of work originally done at the University of Michigan and now continued as an open source project. It's shipped with most distributions, though it is not necessarily included in the default installation. The documentation is perhaps best described as "brisk."

In the OpenLDAP distribution, **slapd** is the standard server daemon and **slurpd** handles replication. A selection of command-line tools enable the querying and modification of LDAP data.

Table 17.5   Important LDAP-related RFCs

RFC	Title
4519	LDAP: Schema for User Applications
4517	LDAP: Syntaxes and Matching Rules
4516	LDAP: Uniform Resource Locator
4515	LDAP: String Representation of Search Filters
4514	LDAP: String Representation of Distinguished Names
4513	LDAP: Authentication Methods and Security Mechanisms
4512	LDAP: Directory Information Models
4511	LDAP: The Protocol
3672	Subentries in the Lightweight Directory Access Protocol (LDAP)
3112	LDAP Authentication Password Schema
2849	LDAP Data Interchange Format (LDIF)—Technical Specification
2820	Access Control Requirements for LDAP
2307	An Approach for Using LDAP as a Network Information Service

Setup is straightforward. First, create an **/etc/openldap/slapd.conf** file by copying the sample installed with the OpenLDAP server. These are the lines you need to pay attention to:

```
database bdb
suffix "dc=mydomain, dc=com"
rootdn "cn=admin, dc=mydomain, dc=com"
rootpw {crypt}abJnggxhB/yWI
directory /var/lib/ldap
```

The database format defaults to Berkeley DB, which is fine for data that will live within the OpenLDAP system. You can use a variety of other back ends, including ad hoc methods such as scripts that create the data on the fly.

The suffix is your "LDAP basename." It's the root of your portion of the LDAP namespace, similar in concept to your DNS domain name. This example illustrates a common practice: using your DNS domain name as your LDAP basename.

The rootdn is your administrator's name, and the rootpw is the administrator's UNIX-format (DES) password. Note that the domain components leading up to the administrator's name must also be specified. You can either copy and paste the password from **/etc/shadow** (if you don't use MD5 passwords) or generate it with a simple Perl one-liner

```
perl -e "print crypt('password','salt');"
```

where *password* is the desired password and *salt* is an arbitrary two-character string. Because of the presence of this password, make sure that the permissions on your **slapd.conf** file are 600 and that the file is owned by root.

You should edit **/etc/openldap/ldap.conf** to set the default server and basename for LDAP client requests. It's pretty straightforward—just set the argument of the host entry to your server and set the base to the same value as the suffix in **slapd.conf**. (Make sure both lines are uncommented.)

At this point, you should be able to start up **slapd** by simply running it with no arguments.

NIS replacement by LDAP

See page 681 for more information about pluggable authentication modules.

You needn't actually use NIS to "migrate" to LDAP, but because NIS defines a standard set of shared system files, it serves as a useful reference point.

The files distributable through NIS are already "virtualized" through the name service switch (the **/etc/nsswitch.conf** file), so client-side LDAP support is relatively easy to add. Some distributions install the necessary **nss_ldap** package by default, but if not, the package is usually provided as an option. This package includes a PAM module that lets you use LDAP with pluggable authentication modules in addition to the name service switch.

Client-side LDAP defaults for this package are set in **/etc/ldap.conf**, which shares its format with the **/etc/openldap/ldap.conf** file described in the previous section but which includes additional options specific to the name service and PAM contexts. You must also edit the **/etc/nsswitch.conf** file on each client to add ldap as a source for each type of data you want to LDAPify. (The **nsswitch.conf** changes make the C library pass requests to the **libnss_ldap** library, which then uses the **/etc/ldap.conf** information to figure out how to perform the LDAP queries.)

RFC2307 defines the standard mapping from traditional UNIX data sets, such as the **passwd** and **group** files, into the LDAP namespace. It's a useful reference document for sysadmins using LDAP as an NIS replacement, at least in theory. In practice, the specifications are a lot easier for computers to read than for humans; you're better off looking at examples.

Padl Software offers a free set of Perl scripts that migrate existing flat files or NIS maps to LDAP. It's available from www.padl.com/tools.html, and the scripts are straightforward to run. They can be used as filters to generate LDIF, or they can be run against a live server to upload the data directly. For example, the **migrate_group** script converts this line from **/etc/group**

```
csstaff:x:2033:evi,matthew,trent
```

to the following LDIF:

```
dn: cn=csstaff,ou=Group,dc=domainname,dc=com
cn: csstaff
objectClass: posixGroup
objectClass: top
userPassword: {crypt}x
```

```
gidNumber: 2033
memberuid: evi
memberuid: matthew
memberuid: trent
```

(Note the object class and distinguished name specifications, which were omitted from the **passwd** example on page 521.)

Once a database has been imported, you can verify that the transfer worked correctly by running the **slapcat** utility, which displays the entire database.

LDAP and security

Traditionally, LDAP was used more in the manner of a phone directory than anything else, and for that purpose, sending data without encrypting it was usually acceptable. As a result, the "standard" LDAP implementation grants unencrypted access through TCP port 389. However, we strongly advise against the use of unencrypted LDAP for the transmission of authentication information, even if passwords are individually hashed or encrypted.

As an alternative, LDAP-over-SSL (known as LDAPS, usually running on TCP port 686) is available in most situations (including the Microsoft world) on both the client and server. This access method is preferable because it protects the information contained in both the query and the response. Use LDAPS when possible.

A system with the complexity and with as many moving parts as LDAP inevitably has the potential to be misconfigured in a way that weakens security. Of course, it is likely to contain some plain, old-fashioned security holes, too. Caveat administrator.

17.6 RECOMMENDED READING

MALÈRE, LUIZ ERNESTO PINHEIRO. *LDAP Linux HOWTO.*

>   www.tldp.org/HOWTO/LDAP-HOWTO/

VOGLMAIER, REINHARD. *The ABCs of LDAP: How to Install, Run, and Administer LDAP Services.* Boca Raton, FL: Auerbach Publications, 2004.

CARTER, GERALD. *LDAP System Administration.* Sebastopol, CA: O'Reilly Media, 2003.

17.7 EXERCISES

E17.1 Why is a pull method of updating a local machine's files more secure than a push method?

E17.2 Explain the following excerpt from an **rdist** distfile:

```
LINUX_PASSWD = ( redhatbox debianbox susebox )

passwd:
    ( /etc/passwd ) -> ( ${LINUX_PASSWD} )
    install /etc/passwd.rdist;
    cmdspecial /etc/passwd.rdist "/usr/local/sbin/mkpasswd";
```

★ **E17.3** Explain the differences between **rdist** and **rsync**. In what situations would it be better to use one than the other?

★ **E17.4** Compare NIS and LDAP. When would you use one and not the other? Would you ever use both?

★ **E17.5** What method does your site use to share system files? What security issues are related to that method? Suggest an alternative way to share system files at your site, and detail the concerns that it addresses. What, if any, are the drawbacks?

★★★★★ **E17.6** Design an LDAP schema that stores user information such as login, password, shell, authorized machines, etc. Build a tool that enters new users into the database interactively or from a file containing a list of users. Build a tool that generates the **passwd**, **group**, and **shadow** files from the LDAP database for the machines in your lab. Allow users to have different passwords on each machine if they want. (Not all users are necessarily authorized to use each computer.) Your **adduser** system should be able to print lists of existing user login names and to print login/password pairs for new users.

18 *Electronic Mail*

It's hard to remember what the world was like without electronic mail. Everyone from school children to grandmas to the stodgiest of corporations now routinely uses email to communicate with family, co-workers, partners, customers, and even the government. It's a mad, mad, mad email-enabled world.[1]

Email is popular because the public can easily understand the concept of sending a message whose model closely parallels that of a traditional written letter. And email "just works"; if you know someone's email address, you type a message addressed to them and press Send. Voilà! Seconds later, the message is delivered to their electronic mailbox, whether they're next door or halfway around the world. From the user's perspective, nothing could be easier.

Unfortunately, it wasn't always this easy, and even today, the underlying infrastructure that makes electronic mail possible on such a large scale is rather onerous. There are several software packages you can run on your Linux system to transport and manage electronic mail (three of which are discussed later in this chapter), but they all require a certain degree of configuration and management. In addition, it's important that you understand the underlying concepts and protocols associated with email so that you don't spoil your users' illusion that cross-platform interorganizational email is a gift from the gods that magically works every time.

Today, there are alternatives to understanding and administering email infrastructure. A number of service providers now provide "managed" email service, where

1. Even as Evi is sailing in obscure, remote locations, she is almost always in email contact through her BlackBerry thanks to the ubiquity of the GPRS network. It works in 113 countries but not Vermont!

528

529

email is actually hosted on their servers in a data center far, far away, and you pay a monthly or annual fee (possibly per user) for access. Likewise, a number of "free" hosted services, such as Yahoo! Mail, MSN Hotmail, and Google's Gmail have become popular for individuals. If you're an individual looking for a personal email account or an account for a (very) small business, these may be viable options for you. These services offload a number of burdens, including storage, server management, software updates, configuration, spam filtering, and security vigilance, to name a few. In return for their "free" service, perhaps you'll see some advertising. It seems like a good deal in many cases; if that option works for you, you at least get the benefit of not needing to read the rest of this chapter.

However, hosted email isn't the solution for everyone. Businesses and other large organizations that depend on email service in order to operate often cannot take the risk of hosting email off-site. Such organizations may have a variety of reasons to host their own email systems, including security, performance, and availability. This chapter is for those people.

The sheer bulk of this chapter—more than 100 pages—attests to the complexity of email systems. The chapter contains both background information and details of software configuration, in roughly that order.

We tried to divide this chapter into five smaller ones (on mail systems, **sendmail** configuration, spam, Exim, and Postfix), but that left it confusing, full of chicken-and-egg problems, and, we think, less useful. Instead, we offer the annotated table of contents shown in Table 18.1.

Table 18.1 A road map for this chapter

	Section	Page	Contents
Background	1	530	Mail systems and their various pieces
	2	534	Addressing, address syntax, mail headers
	3	539	Philosophy, client/server design, mail homes
	4	544	Aliases, mail routing, LDAP
	5	551	Mailing list software,
sendmail configuration	6	557	**sendmail**: installation, startup, the mail queue
	7	565	Introduction to configuring **sendmail**, **m4** macros
	8	570	Basic **sendmail** configuration primitives
	9	574	Fancier **sendmail** configuration primitives
	10	588	Spam, **sendmail** access database
	11	599	Configuration case study
	12	603	Security
	13	611	Performance
	14	615	Collecting statistics, testing, and debugging
Other	15	621	Exim, an alternative to **sendmail**
	16	623	Postfix, another alternative to **sendmail**
	17	639	Additional sources of information

This organization makes the flow a bit smoother when the chapter is read straight through, but it sometimes separates the items relevant to a particular email-related task. The postmaster for a medium-sized organization might need to read the entire chapter, but a sysadmin setting up PC email support for a typical business client surely does not.

Table 18.2 presents a navigation guide for several common sysadmin chores.

Table 18.2 **Sections of this chapter relevant to various chores**

Chore	Sections
Upgrading **sendmail**	6, 7
Configuring **sendmail** for the first time	3, 6, 7, 8, 9, 10, 11, 12
Changing the config file	7
Designing a mail system for a site	3, 4, 5, 6, 7, 8, 9, 10, 11
Fighting spam	10
Auditing security	12
Setting up a PC to receive mail	1, 3
Setting up a mailing list	5
Performance tuning	3, 9, 13
Virtual hosting	9
Using Exim instead of **sendmail**	15
Using Postfix instead of **sendmail**	16

Most of this chapter deals with the configuration of **sendmail**, the standard program that parses and routes electronic mail. **sendmail** was originally written by Eric Allman at the University of California, Berkeley. There have been three major versions: version 5, IDA, and version 8. A completely redesigned version, Sendmail X, has recently been released in an early beta version but is not yet ready for production use. (According to insiders, it may never replace version 8.) Version 5 and IDA are no longer in common use; version 8 has replaced them. In this chapter we cover version 8 (8.13, to be precise).

sendmail is being developed commercially by Sendmail, Inc., which also maintains a free, open source version. The commercial versions feature a graphical configuration tool and centralized monitoring and reporting, features that are especially useful at high-volume mail sites.

18.1 MAIL SYSTEMS

In theory, a mail system consists of four distinct components:

- A "mail user agent" (MUA) that lets users read and compose mail
- A "mail transport agent" (MTA) that routes messages among machines

- A "delivery agent" that places messages in a local message store;[2] it is sometimes called a local delivery agent (LDA)
- An optional "access agent" (AA) that connects the user agent to the message store (e.g., through the IMAP or POP protocol)

Some sites also use a mail submission agent that speaks SMTP (the mail transport protocol) and does some of the work of the transport agent. Exhibit A shows the relationship of these components.

Exhibit A   Mail system components

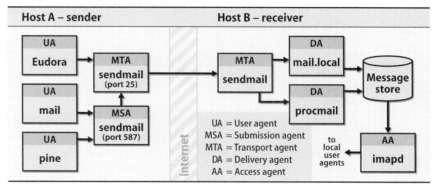

User agents

Email users employ a user agent to read and compose messages. Email messages originally consisted only of text, but a standard known as Multipurpose Internet Mail Extensions (MIME) is now used to encode text formats and attachments (including many viruses) into email. It is supported by most user agents. Since it does not affect the addressing or transport of mail, we do not discuss it further in this chapter.

One chore of user agents is to make sure that any text embedded in the contents of a mail message that might be misunderstood by the mail system gets protected. An example is the string "From " that serves as a record separator between messages.

/bin/mail was the original user agent, and remains the "good ol' standby" for reading text email messages at a shell prompt. For better or worse, email on the Internet has moved beyond the text era, so text-based user agents are no longer practical for most users. Graphical user interfaces allow point-and-click access to messages and deal appropriately with attachments such as images, Microsoft Word documents, and spreadsheets.

One of the elegant features illustrated in Exhibit A is that a user agent doesn't necessarily need to be running on the same system, or even on the same platform, as the rest of your mail system. Users might run one of the many user agents shipped with

---

2. The receiving users' mailboxes or, sometimes, a database.

Linux when logged into a Linux desktop, but they can also access their email through access agent (AA) protocols such as IMAP or POP from their Windows laptops. This is, by far, the most common configuration today. Who says Windows and Linux can't live happily together?

A sample of common user agents are listed below, along with their original sources.

- **/bin/mail** on Red Hat and Fedora is the BSD version of the original UNIX **mail** command; on SUSE, Debian and Ubuntu, this user agent is found in **/usr/bin/mail**.[3] This user agent is text-only and requires a local mail store.
- Thunderbird from Mozilla for Linux, Windows, and Mac OS
- Evolution (aka Novell Evolution, formerly Ximian Evolution) for Linux, Windows, and Mac OS
- **pine** from the University of Washington, www.washington.edu/pine
- Eudora from Qualcomm for Macs or PCs running Windows
- Outlook from Microsoft for Windows

Transport agents

A transport agent must accept mail from a user agent, understand the recipients' addresses, and somehow get the mail to the correct hosts for delivery. Most transport agents also act as message submission agents for the initial injection of new messages into the mail system. Transport agents speak the Simple Mail Transport Protocol (SMTP) defined in RFC2821 (originally defined in RFC821) or the Extended SMTP protocol (ESMTP) defined in RFCs 1869, 1870, 1891, and 1985.

Several transport agents are available for UNIX and Linux systems (PMDF, Postfix, **smail**, **qmail**, Exim, and **zmailer**, among others), but **sendmail** is the most comprehensive, most flexible, and most widely used. A 2001 survey[4] of mail systems reported that **sendmail** was used by 60% of the domains, Exim by 8%, Microsoft Exchange Server by 4%, and Postfix by 2%. Others (about 50 of them) were in the noise.

Red Hat, Fedora and SUSE ship with **sendmail** installed. Debian pretends to include **sendmail**, but if you look closely you'll find that **sendmail** is really a link to the Exim mail transport agent. Exim has been carefully crafted to understand **sendmail's** command-line flags. User agents that call "**sendmail**" explicitly to submit email should be none the wiser. Ubuntu ships Exim as the default.

Delivery agents

A delivery agent accepts mail from a transport agent and actually delivers it to the appropriate local recipients. Mail can be delivered to a person, to a mailing list, to a file, or even to a program.

Each type of recipient may require a different agent. **/bin/mail** is the delivery agent for local users. **/bin/sh** is the original delivery agent for mail going to a program;

---

3. This user agent is sometimes called **Mail** or **mailx** on other systems. Accordingly, Red Hat provides a link called **Mail**, and SUSE, Debian, and Ubuntu provide links called **Mail** and **mailx**.

4. Private study by Matrix.net for Sendmail, Inc.

delivery to a file is handled internally. Recent versions of **sendmail** ship with safer local delivery agents called **mail.local** and **smrsh** (pronounced "smursh"). **procmail** from www.procmail.org can also be used as a local delivery agent; see page 585. Likewise, if you run Cyrus **imapd** as your AA, it includes its own local delivery agent.

Message stores

The message store is the spot on the local machine where email is stored. It used to be the directory **/var/spool/mail** or **/var/mail**, with mail being stored in files named after users' login names. That's still the most common message store, but ISPs with thousands or millions of email clients are looking to other technologies for the message store (databases, usually).

On systems that use the **/var/spool/mail** or **/var/mail** store, the mail directory is created during the installation of the operating system. It should have permissions set to mode 775, with group owner mail,[5] unless you use **mail.local** as your local mailer, in which case the mode can be 755. Our Linux platforms vary a bit:

```
Red Hat: drwxrwxr-x  2  root  mail  1024 Dec  5 11:16  /var/spool/mail
Fedora:  drwxrwxr-x  2  root  mail  4096 Mar 17 08:42  /var/spool/mail
SUSE:    drwxrwxrwt  2  root  root  4096 Aug  2 23:25  /var/spool/mail
Debian:  drwxrwsr-x  2  root  mail  4096 Aug  3 16:17  /var/mail
Ubuntu:  drwxrwsr-x  2  root  mail  4096 Jan  8 03:22  /var/mail
```

See page 82 for more information about the sticky bit.

SUSE's permissions are a bit generous, but files inside the mail spool directory are mode 660 with group root. Directories with the sticky bit set (the t in the permissions) do not allow users to delete one another's files even though they have write permission on the directory. However, a malicious user could fill the mail spool, use it as a scratch partition, or create another user's mailbox.

Access agents

Programs such as **imapd** and **spop** are access agents for PC, Mac, or Linux users whose mail is delivered to a Linux server and then downloaded with the Internet Message Access Protocol (IMAP) or the Post Office Protocol (POP), respectively. IMAP and POP are covered starting on page 542.

Mail submission agents

Another newcomer to the mail arena that was necessitated by high-volume sites is the mail submission agent. The transport agent at a busy mail hub spends lots of time preprocessing mail messages: ensuring that all hostnames are fully qualified, modifying headers inherited from lame mail user agents, logging errors, rewriting headers, and so forth. RFC2476 introduced the idea of splitting the mail submission agent (MSA) from the mail transport agent (MTA) to spread out the workload and maximize performance.

---

5. Systems that deliver mail by giving away files with a nonroot **chown** need to have group write permission to the directory as well. In general, nonroot **chown** is a bad idea.

The idea is to use the MSA, which runs on a different port, as a sort of "receptionist" for new messages injected into the mail system by local user agents. The MSA does all the prep work and error checking that must be done before a message can be sent out by the transport agent. It's a bit like inserting a sanity checker between the MUA and the MTA.

In particular, the MSA ensures that all hostnames are fully qualified; it verifies that local hostnames are legitimate before adding the local domain portion. The MSA also fixes message headers if they are missing or nonconformant. Often, the MSA adds a From or Date header or adjusts the Message-Id header. One final chore that an MSA can do is to rewrite the sender's address from a login name to a preferred external form such as *First_Last*.

For this scheme to work, user agents must be configured to connect to the MSA on port 587 instead of to port 25, which is the traditional port for mail. If your user agents cannot be taught to use port 587, you can still run an MSA on port 25, but on a system other than the one that runs your MTA. You must also configure your transport agent so that it doesn't duplicate the work done by the MSA. Duplicate processing won't affect the correctness of mail handling, but it does represent useless extra work.

By default, **sendmail** acts as an MSA as well as an MTA. Starting with **sendmail** 8.10, a single instance of the program listens on both port 25 and port 587. User agents often call **sendmail** directly with flags that ask it to accept a mail message (**-bs** or **-bm**) or with no flags at all, in which case **sendmail**'s behavior defaults to **-bm**. The **sendmail** process keeps track of how it was called and becomes an MSA if called with flags **-bs** or **-bm** or an MTA if called with **-bd**.

User agents that directly open an SMTP connection must be modified to use port 587 to take advantage of an MSA.

18.2 THE ANATOMY OF A MAIL MESSAGE

A mail message has three distinct parts that we must understand before we become embroiled in **sendmail** configuration.

- The envelope
- The headers
- The body of the message

The envelope determines where the message will be delivered or, if the message can't be delivered, to whom it should be returned. The envelope addresses generally agree with the From and To lines of the header for an individual recipient but do not agree if the message is sent to a mailing list. The addresses are supplied separately to the MSA. The envelope is invisible to users and is not part of the message itself; it's used internally by **sendmail** to figure out where to send the message.

The headers are a collection of property/value pairs formatted according to RFC2822. They record all kinds of information about the message, such as the date and time it was sent and the transport agents through which it passed on its journey. The headers are a bona fide part of the mail message, although user agents often hide some of the less interesting ones when displaying messages for the user.

The body of the message is the actual content to be sent. It must consist of plain text, although that text often represents a mail-safe encoding of various binary content.

As we get into the configuration section, we sometimes speak of the envelope sender and recipients and sometimes speak of the header sender and recipients. We try to specify which addresses we are referring to if it's not clear from the context.

Mail addressing

Local addressing is simple because a user's login name is a unique identifier. An Internet address is also simple: *user@host.domain* or *user@domain*. In the deep dark past of email and the Internet, addresses such as those shown in Table 18.3 were common.

Table 18.3   Examples of obsolete address types

Address type	Example address	Modern form
UUCP	mcvax!uunet!ucbvax!hao!boulder!lair!evi	evi@lair
Route-based	<@site1,@site2,…,@siteN:user@final-site>	user@final.site
"Percent hack"	user%host1%host2@host3	user@host1

Much of the complexity of **sendmail** configuration stems from the early requirement to handle such addresses. Each of these forms of addressing relies on relaying, and thanks to spammers, sites are slowly turning relaying off. The percent hack (last line in Table 18.3) is a favorite tool of spammers who are trying to hide their identity or to relay mail through your machines. If you need to deal with any of these address forms, see the **sendmail** documentation or the O'Reilly **sendmail** book for help.

Mail header interpretation

Every mail message starts with several lines called headers that contain information about the message. Each header begins with a keyword such as To, From, or Subject, followed by a colon and the contents of the header. The format of the standard headers is defined in RFC2822; however, custom headers are allowed, too. Any header beginning with "X-" is ignored by the mail system but propagated along with the message. Ergo, you can add a header such as X-Joke-of-the-Day to your email messages without interfering with the mail system's ability to route them.[6]

---

6. Technically, you can add any header you like because mail routing uses only the envelope and ignores the headers.

Some headers are added by the user agent and some by the transport agent. Several headers trace the path of a message through the mail system. Many user agents hide these "uninteresting" headers from you, but an option is usually available to make the agent reveal them all. Reading headers is becoming an important skill as we are bombarded with spam and must sometimes try to trace a message back to its source. Here is the header block from a simple message:

```
From trent Fri, 30 Jun 2006 20:44:49 -0600
Received: from bull.atrust.com (bull.atrust.com [127.0.0.1]) by bull.atrust.com
    (8.13.1/8.13.1) with ESMTP id k612inkG001576 for <ned@bull.atrust.com>;
    Fri, 30 Jun 2006 20:44:49 -0600
Date: Fri, 30 Jun 2006 20:44:48 -0600
From: trent@atrust.com
Message-Id: <200607010244.k612im9h001575@bull.atrust.com>
To: ned@bull.atrust.com
Cc: steve@bull.atrust.com
Subject: Yonder Mountain

------ body of the message was here ---
```

This message stayed completely on the local machine; the sender was trent and the recipient was ned. The first From line was added by **mail.local**, which was the local delivery agent in this case. The Subject and Cc header lines were added by trent's mail user agent, which probably added the To, From, and Date headers as well. **sendmail**, the mail transport agent, adds To, From, and Date headers if they are not supplied by the MUA. Each machine (or more precisely, each MTA) that touches a message adds a Received header.

The headers on a mail message tell a lot about where the message has been, how long it stayed there, and when it was finally delivered to its destination. The following is a more complete dissection of a mail message sent across the Internet. It is interspersed with comments that describe the purpose of the various headers and identify the programs that added them. The line numbers at the left are for reference in the following discussion and are not part of the message. Some lines have been folded to allow the example to fit the page.

```
1: From eric@knecht.sendmail.org
```

Line 1 was added by **/bin/mail** or **mail.local** during final delivery to separate this message from others in the recipient user's mailbox. Some mail readers recognize message boundaries by looking for a blank line followed by the characters "From "; note the trailing space. This line does not exist until the message is delivered, and it is distinct from the "From:" header line. Many mail readers don't display this line, so you may not see it at all.

```
2: Return-Path: eric@knecht.Neophilic.COM
```

Line 2 specifies a return path, which may be a different address from that shown on the From: line later in the mail header. Error messages should be sent to the address in the Return-Path header line; it contains the envelope sender address.

```
3: Delivery-Date: Mon, 06 Aug 2001 14:31:07 -0600
```

Line 3 shows the date that the mail was delivered to evi's local mailbox. It includes the offset from UTC for the local time zone (MDT, mountain daylight time).

```
4: Received: from anchor.cs.colorado.edu (root@anchor.cs.colorado.edu
   [128.138.242.1]) by rupertsberg.cs.colorado.edu (8.10.1/8.10.1) with ESMTP
   id f76KV7J25997 for <evi@rupertsberg.cs.colorado.edu>; Mon, 6 Aug 2001
   14:31:07 -0600 (MDT)
5: Received: from mroe.cs.colorado.edu (IDENT:root@mroe.cs.colorado.edu
   [128.138.243.151]) by anchor.cs.colorado.edu (8.10.1/8.10.1) with ESMTP id
   f76KV6418006 for <evi@anchor.cs.colorado.edu>; Mon, 6 Aug 2001 14:31:06
   -0600 (MDT)
6: Received: from knecht.Neophilic.COM (knecht.sendmail.org [209.31.233.176])
   by mroe.cs.colorado.edu (8.10.1/8.10.1) with ESMTP id f76KV5Q17625 for
   <evi@anchor.cs.colorado.edu>; Mon, 6 Aug 2001 14:31:05 -0600 (MDT)
7: Received: from knecht.Neophilic.COM (localhost.Neophilic.COM [127.0.0.1])
   by knecht.Neophilic.COM (8.12.0.Beta16/8.12.0.Beta17) with ESMTP id
   f76KUufp084340 for <evi@anchor.cs.colorado.edu>; Mon, 6 Aug 2001 13:30:
   56 -0700 (PDT)
```

Lines 4–7 document the passage of the message through various systems en route to the user's mailbox. Each machine that handles a mail message adds a Received line to the message's header. New lines are added at the top, so in reading them you are tracing the message from the recipient back to the sender. If the message you are looking at is a piece of spam, the only Received line you can really believe is the one generated by your local machine.

Each Received line includes the name of the sending machine, the name of the receiving machine, the version of **sendmail** (or whatever transport agent was used) on the receiving machine, the message's unique identifier while on the receiving machine, the recipient (if there is only one), the date and time, and finally, the offset from Universal Coordinated Time (UTC, previously called GMT for Greenwich Mean Time) for the local time zone. This data is collected from **sendmail**'s internal macro variables. In the next few paragraphs, we trace the message from the sender to the recipient (backwards, from the point of view of header lines).

See page 397 for more information about MX records.

Line 7 shows that the message went from knecht's localhost interface (which Eric's particular mail user agent chose for its initial connection) to knecht's external interface via the kernel loopback pseudo-device. Line 6 documents that knecht then sent the message to mroe.cs.colorado.edu, even though the message was addressed to evi@anchor.cs.colorado.edu (see header line 9). A quick check with **dig** or **nslookup** shows that the host anchor has an MX record that points to mroe, causing the delivery to be diverted. The machine knecht was running **sendmail** version 8.12.0Beta16.

The machine mroe was running **sendmail** version 8.10.1, and it identified the message with queue ID f76KV5Q17625 while it was there. mroe then forwarded the message to anchor.cs.colorado.edu as addressed (line 5), which may seem strange given that the original transmission from knecht was diverted from anchor to mroe because of MX records. The reason for this apparent inconsistency is that the cs.colorado.edu domain uses a "split DNS" configuration. The MX record for anchor that is visible to the outside world points to the incoming master mail machine (mroe). However, a different record is seen within the cs.colorado.edu domain itself. The internal version of the record points first to anchor itself and then to mroe as a backup.

As soon as the mail arrived on anchor, it was immediately forwarded again, this time to rupertsberg. The cause of this hop was aliasing, a mail handling feature that is described in detail starting on page 544.

Aliases play an important role in the flow of mail. An alias maps a username to something else; for example, to the same user at a different machine, to a group of users, or even to an alternative spelling of the user's name. You cannot determine why the message was diverted by examining only the example headers. As with MX records, you must seek external sources of information.

Received lines 5 and 6 include the "for <evi@anchor.cs.colorado.edu>" phrase, which identifies how the mail was addressed when it arrived at the local site. This information helps when you are trying to unsubscribe from a mailing list that requires you to either send the unsubscribe message from the same host from which you subscribed (sometimes years earlier) or to know that address and use it as a parameter in your unsubscribe message.

The final Received line (line 4) shows "for <evi@rupertsberg.cs.colorado.edu>"; the value of **sendmail**'s destination address macro has been changed by the alias lookup on the machine anchor. The local mail delivery agent on rupertsberg put the mail in evi's mailbox.

```
8: Message-Id: <200108062030.f76KUufp084340@knecht.Neophilic.COM>
```

Line 8 contains the message ID, which is different from a queue ID and is unique within the world-wide mail system. It is added to the message when the message is initially submitted to the mail system.

```
9: To: evi@anchor.cs.colorado.edu
10: From: Eric Allman <eric@Sendmail.ORG>
11: X-URL: http://WWW.Sendmail.ORG/~eric
12: Subject: example message for Evi
13: Date: Mon, 06 Aug 2001 13:30:56 -0700
14: Sender: eric@knecht.Neophilic.COM
```

Lines 9, 10, 12, 13, and 14 are standard. Although a Subject header is not required, most user agents include it. The To line contains the address of the primary recipient or recipients. The From line lists the sender as eric@sendmail.org; however, the Received lines list the sending machine as being in the neophilic.com domain—Eric's machine knecht has several virtual domains tied to it in addition to sendmail.org.

The Date line shows the date and time the message was sent. In this case the send time matches the dates in the Received lines pretty closely, even though each was measured with a different clock.

Line 11 identifies the URL of Eric's home page. Notice that it begins with an X, making it an unofficial header. When mail was first specified, there was no such thing as the web or URLs.

The Received lines are usually added by the transport agent (unless they are forged), and the other headers are added by the user agent. Some user agents are lame and do not add proper headers; in this case, **sendmail** steps in to add the missing headers.

The first Received line that is added (usually on the sending machine, when the mail is transferred to the outgoing interface) sometimes includes an "ident" clause that gives the sender's login name. It should be the same as the name on the From line, but it won't be if the From line is forged. In our example, Eric's machine knecht was not running the daemon that implements this feature (**identd**), so there is no clause that lists the sender's login name.

Exhibit B illustrates this message's journey through the mail system. It shows what actions were taken, where they happened, and what programs performed them.

Exhibit B   **A message from Eric**

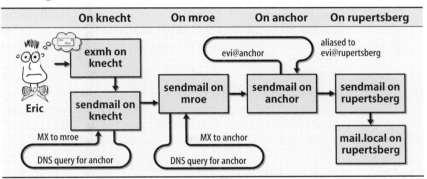

As you can see, **sendmail** is the workhorse in this process. It handles the message from the time it leaves **exmh** in Berkeley until it arrives on rupertsberg for delivery.

18.3 MAIL PHILOSOPHY

The mail philosophy we outline in this chapter is almost mandatory for keeping the administration of medium and large sites manageable. However, it is also appropriate for small sites. The main concepts that lead to easy administration are:

- Servers for incoming and outgoing mail; or for really large sites, a hierarchy
- A mail home for each user at a physical site
- IMAP or POP[7] to integrate PCs, Macs, and remote clients

---

7. IMAP is preferred over POP these days. If you support email access from outside your organization, make sure you use the SSL-encrypted versions of these protocols (IMAPS and POPS, respectively). See page 542 for more details.

See page 397 for
more information
about MX records.

We discuss each of these key issues below and then give a few examples. Other sub-systems must cooperate with the design of your mail system as well: DNS MX records must be set correctly, Internet firewalls must let mail in and out, the message store machine(s) must be identified, and so on.

Mail servers have four functions:

- To accept outgoing mail from user agents and inject it into the mail system
- To receive incoming mail from the outside world
- To deliver mail to end-users' mailboxes
- To allow users to access their mailboxes with IMAP or POP

At a small site, the servers that implement these functions might all be the same machine wearing different hats. At larger sites, they should be separate machines. It is much easier to configure your network firewall rules if incoming mail arrives at only one machine and outgoing mail appears to originate at only one machine.

Some sites use a proxy to receive mail from the outside world. The proxy doesn't really process mail; it just accepts and spools it. A separate process then forwards the spooled mail to **sendmail** for transport and processing. **smtpd** and **smtpfwdd** from www.obtuse.com are examples of such proxies for **sendmail**; **smtpd** can also filter incoming mail with access lists. Both are open source products. None of our Linux distributions include them in the standard installation package.

Using mail servers

Pick stable, reliable machines to use as your mail servers. Here, we outline a mail system design that seems to scale well and is relatively easy to manage and secure. It centralizes the handling of both incoming and outgoing mail on servers dedicated to those purposes. Exhibit C illustrates one form of this system.

Exhibit C   Mail system architecture

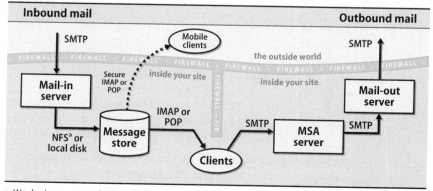

a. We don't recommend using NFS for the message store because of the potential for locking problems.

The mail system depicted in Exhibit C has a single point of exposure to the outside world: the mail server that receives messages from the Internet. The outgoing mail server is also directly connected to the Internet, but it is less exposed because it initiates connections rather than accepting connections from external sites. The incoming mail server should be carefully monitored, should be upgraded with security patches, and should run the latest version of **sendmail** with spam filters for incoming mail.

The server that handles outgoing mail must also be well maintained. It can include spam filters of its own to verify that no local user is contributing to the spam problem. If your site has concerns about the leakage of proprietary information, establishing a single server through which all outgoing mail must pass makes it easier to implement or enforce content policies. If your site manages large mailing lists, the outgoing mail server can be configured to take advantage of some of **sendmail**'s performance-oriented features; see page 611 for details.

Both the incoming and outgoing mail servers can be replicated if your mail load requires it. For example, multiple inbound mail servers can hide behind a load balancing box or use DNS MX records to crudely balance the load. Different client machines can route mail through different outbound servers. Don't pass any mail directly between the incoming servers and the outgoing servers, however; they should be separated from each other by an internal firewall.

At really large sites, incoming and outgoing mail servers would be replicated. An additional routing layer could be added to look up users' mailboxes (perhaps through LDAP) and route the mail to the appropriate message store. The routing layer could also do spam and virus filtering before delivering messages to users' mailboxes.

ISPs who are designing a mail system for customers should add another server that acts as the target of customers' backup MX records and handles mailing lists. This machine has to accept mail and relay it back out, but it must be heavily filtered to make sure that it only relays the mail of actual customers. It, too, should be separated from the incoming and outgoing mail servers by a firewall.

See page 505 for a discussion of file distribution issues. Garden-variety Linux hosts can be given a minimal **sendmail** configuration that forwards outgoing mail to the server for processing. They do not need to accept mail from the Internet. Some sites may want to relax this funneling model a bit and allow arbitrary hosts to send mail directly to the Internet. In either case, nonserver machines can all share the same **sendmail** configuration. You might want to distribute the configuration with a tool such as **rdist** or **rsync**.

Sites that use software such as Microsoft Exchange and Lotus Notes but are not comfortable directly exposing these applications to the Internet can use a design modeled on that shown in Exhibit D on the next page.

Whatever design you choose, make sure that your **sendmail** configuration, your DNS MX records, and your firewall rules are all implementing the same policy with respect to mail.

Exhibit D   Mail system architecture diagram #2

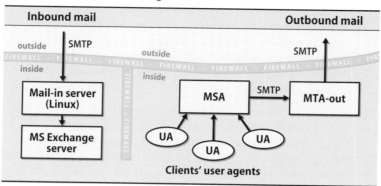

Using mail homes

It is convenient for users to receive and keep their mail on a single machine, even if they want to access that mail from several different systems. You can implement mail homes by using the **aliases** file or an LDAP database (see page 555). You can provide remote access to each user's mailbox with IMAP or POP.

The aliasing scheme we use lets the alias files be the same on all machines within an administrative domain. This uniformity is a big win from the administrator's point of view. (We assume that login names and UIDs are unique across all machines, a policy we recommend highly.)

Some sites centralize mail by exporting **/var/spool/mail** over NFS. Locking problems with NFS files can cause users to lose mail or to have their spool files garbled. Finger-pointing among NFS, **sendmail**, and the delivery agents with regard to proper locking does not help the poor user whose mailbox has been corrupted (however, **sendmail** is always innocent since it never actually delivers mail).

Some NFS implementations (such as those on dedicated NFS file servers) include a lock manager that works correctly. Most implementations either do not support locking or support it improperly. Some sites just ignore the locking problem and hope for the best, and others require users to read mail on the file server.

Our advice is to not use an NFS-shared **/var/spool/mail**.

Using IMAP or POP

IMAP and POP are protocols that download email to a user's desktop machine when it joins the network. This is the ideal way to manage mail, especially for hosts that are not always connected, either because they are turned off when not in use or because they are at home and share the phone line with teenagers. A password is required; be sure to use a version (IMAPS and POPS) that incorporates SSL encryption and hence does not transmit the password in cleartext over the Internet.

We like IMAP, the Internet Message Access Protocol, better than POP. It delivers your mail one message at a time rather than all at once, which is much kinder to the network (especially on a slow link) and better for someone traveling from location to location. It is especially nice for dealing with the giant attachments that some folks like to send: you can browse the headers of your mail messages and not download the attachments until you are ready to deal with them.

IMAP manages mail folders among multiple sites; for example, between your mail server and your PC. Mail that stays on the Linux server can be part of the normal backup schedule. www.imap.org contains lots of information about IMAP and a list of available implementations.

POP, the Post Office Protocol, is similar but assumes a model in which all the mail is downloaded from the server to the PC. It can be either deleted from the server (in which case it might not be backed up) or saved on the server (in which case your mail spool file grows larger and larger). The "whole mailbox at a time" paradigm is hard on the network and less flexible for the user. It can be really slow on dial-up lines if you are a pack rat and have a large mail spool file. Mail ends up getting scattered around with POP.

Both of these protocols can become resource hogs if users never delete any messages. In the case of IMAP, it takes forever to load the headers of all the mail messages; POP transmits the whole mailbox. Make sure your users understand the value of deleting messages or filing them in local folders.

A reasonable implementation of POP3, the current version of the protocol, is available from Qualcomm at www.eudora.com/products/unsupported/qpopper. The **qpopper** server includes TLS/SSL authentication between the server and client and encrypts messages.

You can find many other POP3 servers for Linux on the Internet; make sure you choose one that is being actively maintained.

IMAP server software is available from www.washington.edu/imap. No configuration is needed except to put the proper IMAP entries in the files **/etc/services** and **/etc/inetd.conf** and to make sure that your firewall (if any) doesn't prevent IMAP from working. IMAP has been guilty of security problems in the past; see the CERT advisories, and be sure to obtain the latest version of IMAP, especially if there are security bulletins that postdate your Linux distribution.

Carnegie Mellon University has developed an IMAP server called Cyrus IMAP that supports the POP protocol as well. We like it better than the UW IMAP implementation for its rich feature set and performance for high-end users.

Dovecot is a more recent package that implements both IMAP and POP service. It was written according to strict and explicit coding guidelines that increase its security, at least in theory. Dovecot also has some interesting features, such as the ability to store email in a SQL database rather than in the filesystem. Dovecot doesn't yet have the track record or installed base of Cyrus, but it's definitely a project to keep an eye on and evaluate.

All our example Linux distributions include an IMAP server called **imapd** and a client, **fetchmail**, that speaks both IMAP and POP. Red Hat's **imapd** is the Cyrus IMAP server from CMU; SUSE, Debian, and Ubuntu use the University of Washington version. Red Hat also includes **pop3d**, a POP server. Not to be outdone, SUSE includes three: **qpopper** (which SUSE renames **popper**), **pop2d**, and **pop3d**. Debian has several tools for managing mailboxes with IMAP; **man -k imap** tells you their names.

18.4 MAIL ALIASES

Aliases allow mail to be rerouted either by the system administrator or by individual users.[8] They can define mailing lists, forward mail among machines, or allow users to be referred to by more than one name. Alias processing is recursive, so it's legal for an alias to point to other destinations that are themselves aliases.

sendmail supports several aliasing mechanisms:

- A variety of flat file maps that users and system administrators can easily set up (such as **/etc/aliases**)
- Vendor-promoted legacy file distribution systems such as NIS and NIS+ from Sun[9] and NetInfo from Apple
- Various mail routing databases
- LDAP (the Lightweight Directory Access Protocol)

See page 555 for more information about LDAP.

Flat files such as the **/etc/aliases** file (discussed later in this section) are by far the most straightforward and easiest to set up for small- to mid-sized sites. If you want to use the mail homes concept and you have a large, complex site, we recommend that you implement mail homes by storing aliases in an LDAP server.

We cover LDAP in more detail in three places in this chapter, and we also mention it in Chapter 17, *Sharing System Files*. We introduce and explain LDAP on page 555. We then describe LDAP's interaction with **sendmail** and with **sendmail**'s configuration file on page 580. Before diving into LDAP, however, we first describe the traditional flat file aliasing mechanisms.

Aliases can traditionally be defined in the following three places (unfortunately, with three different syntaxes):

- In a user agent's configuration file (by the sending user)
- In the system-wide **/etc/mail/aliases** file (by the sysadmin)
- In a user's forwarding file, **~/.forward** (by the receiving user)[10]

---

8. Technically, aliases are configured only by sysadmins. The user's control of mail routing by use of a **.forward** file is not really aliasing, but we have lumped them together here.

9. Support for NIS+ was officially discontinued by Sun in 2005. LDAP is the designated replacement.

10. **~/.forward** is the default place that **sendmail** looks. However, you can override this path by setting **sendmail**'s ForwardPath option.

The user agent looks for aliases in the user's config files and expands them before injecting the message into the mail system. The transport agent, **sendmail**, looks for aliases in the global **aliases** file and then in the recipients' forwarding files. Aliasing is applied only to messages that **sendmail** considers to be local.[11]

Here are some examples of aliases in the **aliases** file format:

```
nemeth: evi
evi: evi@mailhub
authors: evi,garth,trent
```

The first line says that mail sent to "nemeth" should be delivered to the user evi on the local machine. The second line says that all mail to evi should be delivered on the machine mailhub, and the third line says that mail addressed to "authors" should be delivered to the users evi, garth, and trent. Recursion is supported, so mail sent to nemeth actually ends up going to evi@mailhub.

See Chapter 17 for more information about NIS.

The path to the global **aliases** file is specified in **sendmail**'s configuration file. It's **/etc/aliases** on Red Hat, SUSE, and Ubuntu. **/etc/mail/aliases** is actually the "standard" location. Sites can have multiple **aliases** files, and they can also use alternative ways of storing alias mappings such as NIS or database files.

The format of an entry in the **aliases** file is

```
local-name: recipient1,recipient2,…
```

where *local-name* is the original address to be matched against incoming messages and the recipient list contains either recipient addresses or the names of other aliases. Indented lines are considered continuations of the preceding lines.

From mail's point of view, the **aliases** file supersedes **/etc/passwd**, so the entry

```
david: david@somewhere-else.edu
```

would prevent the local user david from ever getting any mail. Therefore, administrators and **adduser** tools should check both the **passwd** file and the **aliases** file when selecting new user names.

The **/etc/mail/aliases** file should always contain an alias named "postmaster" that forwards mail to whoever maintains the mail system. Likewise, an alias for "abuse" is appropriate in case someone outside your organization needs to contact you regarding spam or suspicious network behavior that originates at your site. An alias for automatic messages from **sendmail** must also be present; it's usually called Mailer-Daemon and is often aliased to postmaster.

You should redirect root's mail to your site administrators or to someone who logs in every day. The bin, sys, daemon, nobody, and hostmaster accounts (and any other pseudo-user accounts you set up) should also have aliases that forward mail to a human. The file **sendmail/aliases** in the distribution is a good template for the

11. Actually, this statement is not completely true. If you add the F=A flag to the SMTP mailer, you can implement aliasing for remote addresses as well.

Electronic Mail

system-wide aliases that should be included. It also includes security suggestions and an example of how some common user requests are routed at Berkeley.

sendmail detects loops that would cause mail to be forwarded back and forth forever by counting the number of Received lines in a message's header and returning it to the sender when the count reaches a preset limit (usually 25).[12] Each visit to a new machine is called a "hop" in **sendmail** jargon; returning a message to the sender is known as "bouncing" it. The previous sentence, properly jargonized, would be, "Mail bounces after 25 hops."[13]

In addition to a list of users, aliases can refer to

- A file containing a list of addresses
- A file to which messages should be appended
- A command to which messages should be given as input

Since the sender of a message totally determines its content, these delivery targets were often abused by hackers. **sendmail** has become very fussy about the ownership and permissions on such files and commands. To override **sendmail**'s paranoia, you must set one of the DontBlameSendmail options, so named to discourage you from doing it. Unfortunately, the error messages that **sendmail** produces when it encounters unsafe permissions or ownerships are not always clear.

Getting mailing lists from files

The :include: directive is a great way to let users manage their own mailing lists. It allows the members of an alias to be taken from an external file rather than listed directly in the **aliases** file. The file can also be changed locally without intervention by the system administrator who is responsible for the global **aliases** file.

When setting up the list, the sysadmin must enter the alias into the global **aliases** file, create the included file, and **chown** the included file to the user maintaining the mailing list. For example, the **aliases** file might contain

```
sabook: :include:/usr/local/mail/lah.readers
```

The file **lah.readers** should be on a local filesystem, not on an NFS-mounted filesystem,[14] and should be writable only by its owner. To be really complete, we should also include aliases for the mailing list's owner so that errors (bounces) are sent to the owner of the list and not to the sender of a message addressed to the list:

```
owner-sabook: evi
```

---

12. The default hop limit is 25, but you can change it in the config file.

13. We have been inconsistent with terminology in this chapter, sometimes calling a returned message a "bounce" and sometimes calling it an "error." What we really mean is that a Delivery Status Notification (DSN) has been generated. Such a notification usually means that a message was undeliverable and is therefore being returned to the sender.

14. If the NFS filesystem is mounted "hard" and NFS fails, **sendmail** will block with several file handles open and several waiting processes. You may eventually run out of process IDs or file handles and have to reboot the machine to clear things.

See page 551 for more about mailing lists and their interaction with the **aliases** file.

Mailing to files

If the target of an alias is an absolute pathname (double-quoted if it includes special characters), messages are appended to the specified file. The file must already exist. For example:

```
complaints: /dev/null
```

It's useful to be able to send mail to files and programs, but this feature introduces security concerns and is therefore restricted. This syntax is only valid in the **aliases** file and in a user's **.forward** file (or in a file that's interpolated into one of these files with :include:). A filename is not understood as a normal address, so mail addressed to /etc/passwd@host.domain will bounce.

Some user agents let you save mail to a local file (such as an outbox folder). However, that copy of the message is saved by the user agent and is never really processed by the mail system.

If the destination file is referenced from the **aliases** file, it must be world-writable (not advisable), setuid but not executable, or owned by **sendmail**'s default user. The identity of the default user is set with the DefaultUser option. It is normally mailnull, sendmail, daemon, or UID 1, GID 1.

If the file is referenced in a **.forward** file, it must be owned and writable by the original message recipient, who must be a valid user with an entry in the **/etc/passwd** file and a valid shell that's listed in **/etc/shells**. For files owned by root, use mode 4644 or 4600, setuid but not executable.

Mailing to programs

An alias can also route mail to the standard input of a program. This behavior is specified with a line such as

```
autoftp: "|/usr/local/bin/ftpserver"
```

It's even easier to create security holes with this feature than with mailing to a file, so once again it is only permitted in **aliases**, **.forward**, or :include: files, and the default configuration of **sendmail** now requires use of the restricted shell **smrsh**.[15] In the **aliases** file, the program runs as **sendmail**'s default user; otherwise, the program runs as the owner of the **.forward** or :include: file. That user must be listed in the **/etc/passwd** file with a valid shell (one that is listed in **/etc/shells**).

The program mailer changes its working directory to the user's home directory (or, if that directory is inaccessible, to the root directory) before running the command that is to receive the mail. The default used to be **sendmail**'s queue directory, but some **csh**-based shells objected.

---

15. Mailing to programs is a major potential security hole. See *Security and sendmail* on page 603 for more information about **smrsh**.

Electronic Mail

Aliasing by example

Here are some typical aliases that a system administrator might use.

```
# Required aliases¹⁶
postmaster: trouble, evi
postmistress: postmaster
MAILER-DAEMON: postmaster
hostmaster: trent
abuse: postmaster
webmaster: trouble, trent
root: trouble, trent

# include for local trouble alias
trouble: :include:/usr/local/mail/trouble.alias
troubletrap: "/usr/local/mail/logs/troublemail"
tmr: troubletrap,:include:/usr/local/mail/tmr.alias

# sysadmin conveniences
diary: "/usr/local/admin/diary"
info: "|/usr/local/bin/sendinfo"

# class aliases that change every semester
sa-class: real-sa-class@nag
real-sa-class: :include:/usr/local/adm/sa-class.list
```

In this example, we would like users from all over campus to be able to send mail to a single alias "trouble" whenever problems occur. Problem reports should always be routed to an appropriate group of local system administrators. In particular, we'd like to set up the mail aliases so that

- Trouble mail always goes to an appropriate group.
- A single version of the aliases file is used on all hosts.
- Individual admin groups control their own distribution lists.
- A copy of all trouble mail goes to a local log file for each group.

The configuration above satisfies these goals by taking the definition of the trouble alias from a file on each machine. Mail sent to the addresses trouble@anchor and trouble@boulder would end up in different places even though anchor and boulder use the same **/etc/mail/aliases** file.

Trouble mail is usually handled on one particular machine in each locale. For example, the **trouble.alias** file on a slave machine could contain the address

    trouble@*master*

to make trouble mail go to the appropriate master machine.

When a trouble message is resolved, it is sent to the alias tmr, which stands for "trouble mail readers." The tmr alias archives the message to the troubletrap alias and also

---

16. A white lie. Only postmaster and MAILER-DAEMON are really required (by the RFCs), but it is conventional to include hostmaster, abuse, and webmaster as well.

sends it to a list of users taken from a file on the master machine. Adding novice administrators to the tmr list is a great way to let them see the support questions that arise, the administrators' replies, and the proper sycophantic tone that should be used with users (i.e., customers).

The sa-class alias has two levels so that the data file containing the list of students only needs to be maintained on a single machine, nag. The sabook alias example on page 546 should really have this same type of indirection so that the include file does not need to be replicated.

The diary alias is a nice convenience and works well as a documentation extraction technique for squirrelly student sysadmins who bristle at documenting what they do. Sysadmins can easily memorialize important events in the life of the machine (OS upgrades, hardware changes, crashes, etc.) by sending mail to the diary file. Don't put the file on a filesystem that contains your log files; that would allow hackers to fill up the filesystem and prevent syslog from writing log entries (thus covering their tracks).

Forwarding mail

The **aliases** file is a system-wide config file that should be maintained by an administrator. If users want to reroute their own mail (and your site doesn't use POP or IMAP to access mail), they can do so by creating **.forward** files in their home directories. **sendmail** always looks in a user's home directory for a **.forward** file unless the ForwardPath variable is set and overrides the default location. It's convenient to use a **.forward** file when a user wants to receive mail on a particular host or when someone leaves your site and wants to have mail forwarded to a new location.

A **.forward** file consists of a list of comma-separated addresses on a single line or several entries on separate lines. For example,

```
evi@ipn.caida.org
evi@atrust.com
```

or

```
\mcbryan, "/home/mcbryan/archive", mcbryan@f1supi1.gmd.de
```

In the first example, mail for evi is not delivered on the local machine, but is instead forwarded to the machine ipn at CAIDA in San Diego and to atrust.com. The second entry is from a user who does not trust mail systems and wants his mail replicated in three places: the regular mail spool on the local machine, a permanent archive of all incoming mail, and a temporary address in Germany where he is traveling at the moment. The backslash before his username says to deliver mail locally no matter what the aliases or forward files might say.

For temporary changes in mail routing, use of a **.forward** file is preferable to use of the global **aliases** file. The overhead (computer time and people time) required to change the system-wide aliases is quite high.

Electronic Mail

A user's **.forward** file must be owned by the user and must not be group- or world-writable. If **sendmail** thinks the directory path to the **.forward** file is safe (i.e., the permissions from the root all the way down are OK), it can be a link; otherwise, it cannot be a link. **sendmail** ignores forwarding files on which the permissions look suspicious; the permissions on the parent directory must also be safe (writable only by the user who owns the files).

Naturally, **sendmail** must be able to access a user's home directory on the machine where mail is delivered to determine whether it contains a **.forward** file. Permanent changes of address should be put in the **/etc/mail/aliases** file because a user's home directory and files will eventually be removed.

sendmail has a nifty feature, FEATURE(`redirect'), that helps with the management of permanent email changes. If an alias points to user@newsite.REDIRECT, mail will be returned to the sender with a notification of the new address. The message is not forwarded to the new address, so the sender must update his address book and re-send the message.

You can configure **sendmail** to support a central directory for **.forward** files, but users do not expect this configuration. The location of **.forward** files is controlled by the ForwardPath option, which usually points to that central directory and then to the user's home directory. The **generic.m4** domain file illustrated on page 572 contains an example of a central location for **.forward** files.

An entry in the global **aliases** file takes precedence over an entry in a **.forward** file. Since these files are maintained by different people, users must be careful not to inadvertently create mail loops. If a user on a network has a mail home (and therefore an entry in the global **aliases** file), that user cannot use a **.forward** file to reroute mail to another machine that shares the same aliases. For example, at the University of Colorado, where we use a site-wide **aliases** file, an entry such as

    evi: evi@boulder

and a **.forward** file on the machine boulder containing

    evi@anchor.cs

would create a loop. Mail addressed to evi would be forwarded to boulder, where the **.forward** file would cause it to be sent to anchor in the cs subdomain. The **aliases** file on anchor would cause it to be forwarded back to boulder, and so on. After 25 hops, the mail would be returned to the sender.

Notifying a user of a mail loop is challenging if your primary mode of communication is email. Mail to \user[17] delivers the message on the local machine, regardless of what the system-wide **aliases** file or the user's **.forward** file might say. If the local machine is where the user expects to read mail, fine; otherwise, send mail to the postmaster to report the loop or pick up the phone!

---

17. You may have to use two or more backslashes to get one of them past the shell and into **sendmail**.

The hashed alias database

Since entries in the **aliases** file are in no particular order, it would be inefficient for **sendmail** to search this file directly. Instead, a hashed version is constructed with the Berkeley DB database system. This hashing significantly speeds alias lookups, especially when the file gets big.

The file derived from **/etc/mail/aliases** is called **aliases.db**. Every time you change the **aliases** file, you must rebuild the hashed database with the **newaliases** command. **newaliases** is really just **sendmail** in disguise with command-line flags (**-bi**) that tell it to rebuild the database. Save the error output if you run **newaliases** automatically—you might have introduced formatting errors.

18.5 MAILING LISTS AND LIST WRANGLING SOFTWARE

A mailing list is a giant alias that sends a copy of each message posted to it to each person who has joined the list. It's like a Usenet newsgroup from the days of yore that is delivered by email. Some mailing lists have thousands of recipients.

Mailing lists are usually specified in the **aliases** file but maintained in an external file. Some standard naming conventions are understood by **sendmail** and most mailing list software. Experienced users have come to rely on them as well. Most common are the "-request" suffix and the "owner-" prefix, which are used to reach the maintainers of the list. The conventions are illustrated by the following aliases:

```
mylist: :include:/etc/mail/include/mylist
owner-mylist: mylist-request
mylist-request: evi
owner-owner: postmaster
```

In this example, mylist is the name of the mailing list. The members are read from the file **/etc/mail/include/mylist**. Bounces from mailing to the list are sent to its owner, evi, as are requests to join the list. The indirection from "owner" to "request" to evi is useful because the owner's address (in this case, mylist-request) becomes the Return-Path address on each message sent to the list. mylist-request is a bit better than the actual maintainer for this field. Errors in messages to the owner-mylist alias (evi, really) would be sent to owner-owner.

The case in which a message is undeliverable is called a bounce. The case in which the error message sent about the bounce cannot be delivered is a double bounce. So in our example, double bounces are sent to owner-owner or postmaster.

If you use a site-wide aliases file, you need to add an extra level of indirection pointing mylist to myreallist@master so that the data file containing the list of members only needs to exist in one place.

Software packages for maintaining mailing lists

Several software packages automate the maintenance of mailing lists. They typically allow users to add and remove themselves from the list, obtain information about the list, and obtain files through email. A few of the popular mailing list managers (and their download sources) are

- Majordomo, from www.greatcircle.com (included with SUSE)
- Mailman, the GNU mailing list processor, from www.list.org
- ListProc, from www.cren.net
- SmartList, derived from **procmail**
- **listmanager** from www.listmanager.org
- LISTSERV Lite, from www.lsoft.com (free version of the commercial LISTSERV)

In general, SmartList is small and simple, ListProc is large and complex, and the others are in between. They differ in their philosophies of list maintenance, with some leaning toward sysadmins as administrators (ListProc) and others leaning toward users as maintainers (Majordomo, Mailman, SmartList, LISTSERV Lite). Majordomo, Mailman, **listmanager**, and LISTSERV Lite support remote administration; the list maintainer does not even need to have a login on the machine where the list is located because all transactions take place through email. Most of the list packages allow information posted to the list to be assembled into digests, some automatically (ListProc, Mailman, **listmanager**, and LISTSERV Lite) and some through manual configuration (SmartList and Majordomo).

Mailman is our favorite list manager. It's a joy to administer and lets list maintainers tweak all the features of their own lists. ListProc and LISTSERV Lite are proprietary: the first expensive, the other binary-only and crippled. We have not tried SmartList, but we like **procmail**, on which it depends.

We describe each of these packages briefly below. For more detail, see the documentation with each package or the O'Reilly book *Managing Mailing Lists* by Alan Schwartz and Paula Ferguson.

Majordomo

Majordomo is a Perl/C package available from www.greatcircle.com. It was originally written by Brent Chapman. Development of Majordomo has ceased; Majordomo 2 is a total rewrite but seems to have fizzled in 2004, so we describe only the original version, which is still in common use. Among our example distributions, only SUSE ships Majordomo. Despite what the man page says (**/usr/lib/mail/majordomo**), it's hidden in the directory **/usr/lib/majordomo**.

See page 603 for more information about trusted users.

Majordomo runs as an unprivileged user, typically with username majordom or mdom and default group daemon. Since Linux supports long user names (more than 8 characters), you can also use majordomo as the login name. The user must be one that **sendmail** recognizes as "trusted" and so must be mentioned in your **sendmail** configuration, usually in a confTRUSTED_USERS declaration.[18]

Majordomo is configured through the **majordomo.cf** file, which consists of valid Perl commands that initialize variables, define the directories where things are (or

---

18. A "trusted" user is allowed to change the From header line of a message and to rebuild the **aliases** file.

where they should be put), specify the lists to be supported, and configure the handling of bounced mail. A helper program, **config-test**, tests your configuration file for missing variables or bad syntax. SUSE puts the config file in **/etc** and leaves **config-test** with the Majordomo distribution in **/usr/lib/majordomo**.

Majordomo requires special aliases to be installed in **sendmail**'s **aliases** file. The cleanest way to integrate these aliases is to create a separate alias file used just for Majordomo (recent versions of **sendmail** support multiple alias files). The file contains a set of aliases for Majordomo itself and a set for each mailing list that it manages. The distribution contains a sample aliases file, **majordomo.aliases**.

The most common user question about mailing lists is "How do I unsubscribe?" For lists managed by Majordomo, the answer for listname@host is to send mail to the address majordomo@host with the words "unsubscribe listname" or "unsubscribe listname email-address" in the body of the message (not on the subject line).

With the first form, you need to send the unsubscribe message from the same host that you used when you subscribed to the list; in the second form, that host is part of the email address. See page 535 for hints on how to glean this information from the mail headers so that you can unsubscribe properly, even if you have forgotten which machine you used when you joined the list. Some mailing lists also accept mail to listname-request@host with just the word "unsubscribe" in the body.

Never, ever, send an unsubscribe message to the list itself. If you do, your message announces to all the recipients of the list that you don't know what you're doing.

Mailman

Mailman, a fairly recent addition to the mailing list software fleet (version 2.1.8 released in April 2006), is available from www.list.org or the GNU archives. It was originally written by John Viega and is currently being developed in collaboration with Ken Manheimer, and Barry Warsaw. Like Majordomo, Mailman is primarily written in a scripting language with C wrappers, but in this case the language is Python (available from www.python.org).

Mailman was inspired by its authors' use of Majordomo and their frustration with bounce errors, tricky configuration of advanced features such as digests and moderated lists, and performance difficulties with bulk mailings. A Mailman script imports Majordomo lists. Mailman can also detect and control spam to some degree.

Mailman's big claim to fame is its web interface, which makes it easy for the moderator or postmaster to manage a list and also easy for users to subscribe, unsubscribe, and configure their options.

ListProc

ListProc is an old-timer in mailing list management software. It was written in 1991 by Anastasios Kotsikonas and maintained until about 1994. It then lay idle for a few years but was resurrected with a new beta release in 1998. It used to be available from the computer science department at Boston University for free, but with somewhat strange licensing rules. Now it is available from www.cren.net for a hefty licensing fee ($2,000 per copy, even for universities). Forget ListProc and go with one of the free, open source packages.

SmartList

SmartList was originally written by Stephen R. van den Berg, who is also the original author of **procmail**. It's available from www.procmail.org. SmartList uses **procmail**, so you will need to download both **procmail.tar.gz** and **SmartList.tar.gz**. It's probably easiest to just grab the Linux package appropriate to your system.

SmartList is small and simple. It's a combination of C code, **procmail** rules, and shell scripts. Bounces, the maintenance headache of mailing lists, are automatically dealt with by the software. Users are automatically removed from a list after a certain number of bounces to their address. SmartList requires a login entry in the **passwd** file ("smart" or perhaps "list") that is a trusted user in **sendmail**'s configuration file.

The installation includes **led**, a lock wrapper for editing that tries to protect Smart-List against being left with an incoherent, partially edited configuration file.

listmanager

listmanager by Murray Kucherawy is written in C and so is faster than the packages built on top of a scripting language such as Perl or Python. **listmanager** also improves speed by using the DB database package from sleepycat.com rather than flat files and the filesystem. Its feature list is about a page long and includes a web interface, digests, and several security enhancements.

listmanager really seems like a killer list manager—the only downside is that source code is not yet being distributed. According to the www.listmanager.org web page, the code is being withheld until the author finishes a cleanup pass to avoid possible embarrassment. A Linux binary is available.

LISTSERV Lite

LISTSERV Lite by Eric Thomas is a crippled version of LISTSERV, the commercial product from L-Soft International, Inc. Some of the features of the real version are missing, and the software is limited to managing 10 mailing lists of up to 500 people. LISTSERV Lite needs to run as the pseudo-user listserv, which must own its files. It also likes to have a listserv group. LISTSERV Lite provides a web interface both for subscribing to a list and for maintaining it.

The distribution is available from www.lsoft.com. Source code is not distributed, but precompiled binaries and stubs for many versions of UNIX and Linux are provided. If you already are familiar with LISTSERV and have lists that use it, you might be able to justify running a binary-only, crippled list manager. If you're starting from scratch, choose one of the open source, unrestricted alternatives mentioned above.

LDAP: the Lightweight Directory Access Protocol

LDAP is a protocol that provides access to a generic administrative directory service. It has been around for a few years, but it has just recently started to become popular.

Administrators are discovering that LDAP is good for lots of things:

- **sendmail** configuration: aliases, virtual domains, mail homes, the access database, and tables
- User management: login names, passwords, hosts (e.g., Stanford University)
- Administrative config files (e.g., SUSE)
- A replacement for NIS
- A calendar server
- Use with pluggable authentication modules (PAM)

It's envisioned that LDAP will eventually become a global directory system used for many different purposes. Unfortunately, tools for automating typical sysadmin tasks with LDAP are still missing.

LDAP grew out of the ISO protocols and the X.500 directory service. That heritage immediately suggests complex, bloated, verbose, bad, etc., but the L in LDAP is supposed to take care of all that. Protocol versions 1 and 2 have been standardized. Version 3 is close. Fortunately, all versions are backward compatible. Version 3 of the LDAP protocol supports hierarchical servers; querying one server for a piece of data can result in a referral to another server. Version 2 supported hierarchical *data*, but hierarchical *servers* are only in version 3.

Mail aliases are a particularly good match for LDAP, especially now that **sendmail** supports LDAP internally. **sendmail** can query the LDAP server for alias lookups instead of doing them directly. LDAP can also manage mail routing and virtual domains. LDAP support must be compiled into the **sendmail** binary.

If you are looking for an LDAP implementation, we recommend the server produced by the OpenLDAP group at www.openldap.org. This group took over and enhanced the code of an earlier server that was developed at the University of Michigan. For a bit more information about LDAP-related software, see page 520.

LDAP database entries resemble a termcap entry with longer variable names. The attributes (variable names) in the LDAP database are not yet fully standardized, and this fact can result in incompatibilities among different implementations.

The attributes on the first line of a database entry are defined by the LDAP configuration file. The examples in this section assume that the LDAP server daemon (**slapd**, in the OpenLDAP case) was configured with a root distinguished name (rootdn) of:

```
"cn=root, dc=synack, dc=net"
```

The dc attribute appears twice because the domain component values cannot contain a dot; to express the domain synack.net, two entries are necessary. Further attributes, or variable names, can be whatever you want. They are case insensitive.

sendmail (whose code looks for specific attribute names and assigns them predetermined interpretations), the LDAP server, and the builder of the LDAP database must all cooperate and use the same naming conventions.

Some possible attributes that can appear on the first line of a database entry (the database keys) are dn for a domain name, dc for a domain component, o for an organization name, c for a country name, and uid for a unique ID (e.g., a login name).

sendmail uses an LDAP server much like it uses the DNS name server. It calls on the DNS server to resolve names into IP addresses so that messages can be sent. It calls on the LDAP server to look up aliases so that messages can be routed to the right place. In both cases, the lookups have moved from flat files (**hosts** and **aliases**) to databases, with servers managing the queries.

By default, **sendmail** recognizes the following LDAP data tags:

```
mailLocalAddress
mailRoutingAddress
mailHost
```

Version 8.12 expanded this default set extensively (see **cf/sendmail.schema**) and also let you define your own schema to use any LDAP tags you like.

Here is an example of the OpenLDAP implementation's **slapd ldap.conf** file

```
# LDAP Defaults, ldap.conf file, should be world-readable.
#
BASE    dc=synack, dc=net
HOST    gw.synack.net
PORT    389
```

that supports database entries of the form

```
dn: uid=jon, dc=synack, dc=net
objectClass: inetLocalMailRecipient
mailLocalAddress: jon@synack.net
mailRoutingAddress: stabilej@cs.colorado.edu
uid:jon
```

When FEATURE(ldap_routing) has been specified in the **sendmail** configuration file, the incoming recipient is matched against the mailLocalAddress field. If it matches, the mail is redirected to the mailRoutingAddress. The objectClass line must be present—it comes from the draft RFC that defines the interaction of LDAP and mail systems.

On the host gw.synack.net, this database entry corresponds to the alias

```
jon: stabilej@cs.colorado.edu
```

A bit long-winded, isn't it? These database entries could replace the typical entries in the **aliases** file for defining a mail home for each user.

Some large organizations already store user provisioning information, such as each user's preferred mailbox, in another database. If that is the case at your site, you will probably want to write some short scripts to extract that information and shove it into LDAP. If yours is a small organization, you may want to stick with the traditional **/etc/mail/aliases** file or write a script to generate the correct LDAP entries from the command line.

The **aliases** file is also still the best way to define mailing lists (with the :include: directive). Mailing list software typically pipes the message to a wrapper script and resends it. An LDAP query can return aliases that point to :include: files or to programs such as **majordomo**, but it cannot directly call a program.

As of version 8.12, LDAP can also store the contents of some of **sendmail**'s other data (for example, tables and classes). See page 580 for more information about configuring **sendmail** to use LDAP.

18.6 SENDMAIL: RINGMASTER OF THE ELECTRONIC MAIL CIRCUS

All five of our Linux reference platforms ship a mail transport agent. Red Hat, Fedora, and SUSE ship with **sendmail**; Debian and Ubuntu include Exim by default. We describe Exim briefly starting on page 621. Many of the Exim constructs and configuration knobs have analogs within the **sendmail** world. Since this chapter is already far too long, we cover only **sendmail** in detail. We describe Exim in terms of the equivalent **sendmail** facilities.

sendmail can adapt to the whims of standards-makers thanks in part to the flexibility of its configuration file, which allows **sendmail** to meet the needs of a diverse community of users. The rest of this chapter is primarily devoted to the understanding and construction of this configuration file, the infamous **sendmail.cf**.

sendmail is a transport agent, a program that interfaces between user agents and delivery agents. It speaks the SMTP protocol and delivers messages to peers on remote machines through the Internet. **sendmail**'s list of chores includes

- Controlling messages as they leave the user's keyboard
- Understanding the recipients' addresses
- Choosing an appropriate delivery or transport agent
- Rewriting addresses to a form understood by the delivery agent
- Reformatting headers as required
- Passing the transformed message to the delivery agent

sendmail also generates error messages and returns undeliverable messages to the sender.

Versions of sendmail

As of this writing, our example distributions' versions of **sendmail** derive from V8. They are typically a release or two behind the master version from Sendmail, Inc., however. Vendors often customize a particular version of **sendmail** and are then reluctant to upgrade their base system to include current revisions.

We base our discussion of **sendmail** on V8.13 and totally ignore both V5 and IDA, which are obsolete. V8 uses the **m4** macro processor to allow easy configuration of the standard cases. This "config lite" is all that most sites need.

Unfortunately, if your configuration has a problem, you may have to base your debugging on an understanding of the raw config file, which we've heard described as unapproachable, daunting, picky, cryptic, onerous, infamous, boring, sadistic, confusing, tedious, ridiculous, obfuscated, and twisted. We talked quite a bit about the raw config file in older versions of this book, but since its relevance to modern administrators has waned, we now refer you to the O'Reilly **sendmail** book by Bryan Costales and Eric Allman (titled *sendmail*) or the *Sendmail Installation and Operations Guide* that is included in the **sendmail** distribution.

New releases of **sendmail** are sometimes issued to address security problems; we suggest that you check the release notes from www.sendmail.org and upgrade if you have missed any security-related patches. You can usually get updated **sendmail** packages directly from your Linux distributor, but make sure that the binary you receive corresponds to the current sendmail version. If you need to compile and install the source distribution directly from www.sendmail.org, you'll need a C compiler and the **m4** macro preprocessor (both of which are usually included in Linux distributions).

Sometimes it's difficult to determine the actual **sendmail** base release, but if the vendor hasn't meddled too much, you can run

```
$ /usr/sbin/sendmail -d0.1 -bt < /dev/null
```

to make **sendmail** disclose its version, the options that were compiled into it, and who it thinks it is after reading the config file. The **-d** flag sets a debug level (see page 616 for more info on debugging levels in **sendmail**), the **-bt** flag puts **sendmail** into address test mode, and the redirect from **/dev/null** gives it no addresses to test. Here is some sample output (slightly truncated) from a Red Hat system.

```
Version 8.11.6
 Compiled with: LDAPMAP MAP_REGEX LOG MATCHGECOS MIME7TO8
    MIME8TO7 NAMED_BIND NETINET NETINET6 NETUNIX NEWDB NIS
    QUEUE SASL SCANF SMTP TCPWRAPPERS USERDB
============ SYSTEM IDENTITY (after readcf) ============
      (short domain name) $w = coyote
   (canonical domain name) $j = coyote.toadranch.com
       (subdomain name) $m = toadranch.com
          (node name) $k = coyote.toadranch.com
========================================================
```

sendmail should always use DNS MX (mail exchanger) records and does so if compiled with the NAMED_BIND option (as in the preceding example). The one-letter variables such as $w are from the raw config file or determined at run time.

sendmail installation from sendmail.org

As of version 8.12, the installation environment for **sendmail** has changed a bit. It no longer runs setuid to root but instead is setgid to the sendmail group, smmsp. Before installing **sendmail**, you must create both the user smmsp and the group smmsp (the mysterious name stands for **s**end**m**ail **m**ail **s**ubmission **p**rogram). We use UID and GID 25 to match the SMTP mail protocol's well-known port number. The smmsp user should have smmsp as its default login group, which is typically set in the **/etc/passwd** file. The addition of a dedicated sendmail user and group lets **sendmail** run with reduced privileges and enhances security.

The second major change from a sysadmin's point of view is that **sendmail** now uses two configuration files: **submit.cf** and **sendmail.cf**. The file **submit.cf** controls the handling of mail that originates on the local machine (and is being initially submitted to the mail system), and **sendmail.cf** controls incoming mail and mail queued during the submission process. **submit.cf** is supplied with the distribution and is the same for all sites; there's usually no need to customize it.

This section briefly describes the installation process; refer to the installation notes in the **sendmail** distribution for the gory details and for issues related to particular architectures or operating systems. The next section describes **sendmail** installation on a Debian system with **apt-get**. If you are replacing your system's original version of **sendmail**, some of the configuration chores (such as installing help files) may already have been done for you.

The players:

- The **sendmail** binary, usually installed in **/usr/sbin**.

  ```
  -r-xr-sr-x    root     smmsp      /usr/sbin/sendmail
  ```

- The configuration files **/etc/mail/sendmail.cf** and (in versions 8.12 and later) **/etc/mail/submit.cf**, installed by the sysadmin:

  ```
  -rw-r--r--    root     bin        /etc/mail/sendmail.cf
  -rw-r--r--    root     bin        /etc/mail/submit.cf
  ```

- The mail queue directories, **/var/spool/mqueue** and (in versions 8.12 and later) **/var/spool/clientmqueue**, created by the sysadmin or the installation process:

  ```
  drwxrwx---  smmsp smmsp    /var/spool/clientmqueue
  drwx------  root  wheel    /var/spool/mqueue
  ```

- Various links to the **sendmail** binary (**newaliases**, **mailq**, **hoststat**, etc.)[19]

- **sendmail**'s safer local delivery agents, **smrsh** and **mail.local** (usually installed in **/usr/libexec**)

19. Be careful here. Some vendors use hard links, with the result that when you upgrade, you might end up with the version of **sendmail** not matching the version of **newaliases**, creating subtle and hard-to-find support headaches.

You can download the latest version of **sendmail** from www.sendmail.org. To compile and install the package, follow the directions in the top-level **INSTALL** file. Start by adding the smmsp user and group; do not give this user a real shell. Here is a typical **/etc/passwd** entry:

```
smmsp:x:25:25:Sendmail Mail Submission Prog:/nonexistent:/bin/false
```

And here is a typical **/etc/group** entry:

```
smmsp:*:25:smmsp
```

To compile the software, change to the distribution's **sendmail** directory, run the **Build** script and then run **Build install**. The file **devtools/OS/Linux** contains the assumptions used to build **sendmail** on Linux systems. Linux distributions have not standardized where things are, so **devtools/OS/Linux** contains best guesses and may not be exactly right for your distribution.

Before you start compiling, however, you must decide on a database format and a strategy for interfacing **sendmail** with administrative databases such as NIS. For on-disk databases, we recommend the Berkeley DB package specified in the **Makefile** as NEWDB (the default).

To customize the Makefile, don't edit it; create your own **site.config.m4** file and put it in the directory **devtools/Site** to tweak it for your operating system and local environment. For example, if you intend to use LDAP and the new mail filtering library for spam, create in that directory a **site.config.m4** file containing the lines

```
APPENDDEF(`confMAPDEF', `-DLDAPMAP')
APPENDDEF(`confLIBS', `-lldap -llber')
APPENDDEF(`conf_sendmail_ENVDEF', `-DMILTER')
```

A define replaces the current definition of an attribute; the APPENDDEF macro appends to the current definition.

Compiling **sendmail** with

```
$ sh ./Build
```

automatically includes the site-specific entries. To install **sendmail** in the proper place, run

```
$ sudo sh ./Build install
```

sendmail should *not* normally be set up to be controlled by **inetd/xinetd**, so it must be explicitly started in the **rc** files at boot time. A typical sequence is something like:

```
if [-f /usr/sbin/sendmail -a -f /etc/mail/sendmail.cf];
then
    (cd /var/spool/clientmqueue; rm -f [tTx]f*)
    (cd /var/spool/mqueue; rm -f [tTx]f*)
    /usr/sbin/sendmail -bd -q30m     ### queue runner for regular queue
    /usr/sbin/sendmail -Ac -q30m &  ### queue runner for client queue (8.12)
    echo -n ' sendmail' > /dev/console
fi
```

These lines check for the **sendmail** binary and its configuration file and then start the program in daemon mode. The **sendmail** package for your Linux distribution should provide a proper startup script that lives in **/etc/init.d**.

Several user agents explicitly run **sendmail** (sometimes with the **-bm** or **-bs** flags) when they submit a user's message to the mail system rather than directly speaking the SMTP protocol. In this situation, **sendmail** uses the config file **submit.cf** and puts messages in the **/var/spool/clientqueue** queue. Calling **sendmail** with the **-Am** or **-Ac** flags forces messages to the **mqueue** or **clientqueue**, respectively.

 Red Hat and Fedora have a **sendmail** startup script (**/etc/init.d/sendmail**) that does not clean cruft out of the **mqueue** directories (as shown in the example above). However, it does rebuild the database. With **sendmail** 8.12 and later, LDAP can be used for the database maps, and rebuilding the maps after changes is not necessary. Parameters defined in **/etc/sysconfig/sendmail** determine whether **sendmail** should start in daemon mode and how often it should run the queue, so that is where you should set the **sendmail** startup behavior for your site. Red Hat, as shipped, starts **sendmail** in daemon mode and runs the queue every 30 minutes.

 SUSE's startup script (**/etc/init.d/sendmail**) just checks for the binary and config file and then starts **sendmail** with the arguments defined in the SENDMAIL_ARGS environment variable; these are set in the file **/etc/rc.config.d/sendmail.rc.config**. SUSE also defaults to daemon mode and runs the queue every 30 minutes.

Add the **sh** fragment above (or one like it) to **/etc/init.d/sendmail** if your Linux distribution does not include a **sendmail** startup script. A fancier script in the installation guide tries to clean up previously interrupted queue runs. Mix and match as you like.

Historically, **sendmail**'s supporting files have wandered around the filesystem to glamorous destinations such as **/usr/lib**, **/etc**, **/usr/ucblib**, and **/usr/share**. With the 8.10 release of **sendmail**, all files (except the queue directories) are expected to be kept beneath the **/etc/mail** directory.[20] Let's hope that vendors take the hint and leave them together in one consistent place.

sendmail installation on Debian and Ubuntu systems

 You can use the **apt-get** program to install **sendmail**. The package installs **sendmail** and **m4** and also uninstalls Exim. After **apt-get** has downloaded and installed the **sendmail** package, it offers to configure it. Saying yes invokes a script that asks questions (20 or so) about the **sendmail** configuration you want. The defaults are generally reasonable. The only question that you really have to answer differently is "mail name"; the default answer is the unqualified hostname (e.g., lappie), but it needs to be the fully qualified name (e.g., lappie.toadranch.com).

---

20. Well, it's not quite totally true yet that all files are kept under **/etc/mail**. The **sendmail.pid** file and sometimes the statistics file are still kept elsewhere.

Answering the questions posed by the script will make more sense if you are familiar with **sendmail**'s various options and features, which are discussed in more detail later in this chapter. The configuration script does not take into account the contents of the generic domain file that it includes by default. As a result, you can decline a feature but end up with it turned on anyway (for example, the redirect feature).

The switch file

The service switch is covered in more detail in Chapter 17.

Linux systems have a "service switch" configuration file, **/etc/nsswitch.conf**, that enumerates the methods that can satisfy various standard queries such as user and host lookups. If more than one resolution method is listed for a given type of query, the service switch also determines the order in which methods are consulted.

The use of the service switch is normally transparent to software. However, **sendmail** likes to exert fine-grained control over its lookups, so it currently ignores the system switch file and uses its own internal one (**/etc/mail/service.switch**) instead.

Two fields in the switch file impact the mail system: aliases and hosts. The possible values for the hosts service are dns, nis, nisplus, and files. For aliases, the possible values are files, nis, nisplus, and ldap. Support for all the mechanisms you use (except files) must be compiled into **sendmail** before the service can be used.

sendmail's internal service switch contains

```
aliases    files nisplus nis      # if compiled with nis/nis+
hosts      dns nisplus nis files
```

Modes of operation

You can run **sendmail** in several modes, selected with the **-b** flag. **-b** stands for "be" or "become" and is always used with another flag that determines the role **sendmail** will play. Table 18.4 lists the legal values.

Table 18.4   Command-line flags for sendmail's major modes

Flag	Meaning
-bd	Run in daemon mode, listening for connections on port 25
-bD	Run in daemon mode, but in the foreground rather than the background[a]
-bh	View recent connection info (same as **hoststat**)
-bH	Purge disk copy of outdated connection info (same as **purgestat**)
-bi	Initialize hashed aliases (same as **newaliases**)
-bm	Run as a mailer, deliver mail in the usual way (default)
-bp	Print mail queue (same as **mailq**)
-bP	Print the number of entries in queues via shared memory (8.12 and later)
-bs	Enter SMTP server mode (on standard input, not port 25)
-bt	Enter address test mode
-bv	Verify mail addresses only; don't send mail

a. This mode is used for debugging so that you can see error and debugging messages.

If you expect incoming mail to arrive from the Internet, run **sendmail** in daemon mode (**-bd**). In this mode, **sendmail** listens on network port 25 and waits for work.[21] You will usually specify the **-q** flag, too—it sets the interval at which **sendmail** processes the mail queue. For example, **-q30m** runs the queue every thirty minutes, and **-q1h** runs it every hour.

sendmail normally tries to deliver messages immediately, saving them in the queue only momentarily to guarantee reliability. But if your host is too busy or the destination machine is unreachable, **sendmail** queues the message and tries to send it again later. **sendmail** used to fork a child process every time it processed the queue, but it now supports persistent queue runners that are usually started at boot time. RFC1123 recommends at least 30 minutes between runs. **sendmail** does locking, so multiple, simultaneous queue runs are safe.

sendmail 8.12 added a new feature to help with large mailing lists and queues: queue groups with envelope splitting. It is covered in more detail starting on page 611.

sendmail reads its configuration file, **sendmail.cf**, only when it starts up. Therefore, you must either kill and restart **sendmail** or send it a HUP signal when you change the config file. **sendmail** creates a **sendmail.pid** file that contains its process ID and the command that started it. You should start **sendmail** with an absolute path because it re**exec**s itself on receipt of the HUP signal. The **sendmail.pid** file allows the process to be HUPed with:

```
# kill -HUP `head -1 sendmail.pid`
```

The location of the PID file was formerly a compile-time parameter, but it can now be set in the **.mc** config file with the confPID_FILE option.

```
define(confPID_FILE, `/var/run/sendmail.pid')
```

The default value is OS dependent but is usually either **/var/run/sendmail.pid** or **/etc/mail/sendmail.pid**. The Red Hat, Fedora, Ubuntu, and Debian distributions use **/var/run/sendmail.pid**, and SUSE keeps it in the directory **/var/run/sendmail**.

The mail queue

Mail messages are stored in the queue directory when the machine is too busy to deliver them immediately or when a destination machine is unavailable. **sendmail** serves as a mail submission agent listening on port 587 as well as fulfilling its usual role as a daemon listening on port 25 and using the queue **/var/spool/mqueue**. Some user agents (**/bin/mail** for example) use port 587, the mail submission port, but others (Eudora, Outlook, etc.) speak SMTP directly to the **sendmail** running on port 25. Beginning with version 8.12, mail submission programs inject new messages into the mail system by using the queue directory **/var/spool/clientmqueue** and the configuration file **submit.cf**. All messages go into the queue briefly as they arrive.

---

21. The ports that **sendmail** listens on are determined by DAEMON_OPTIONS; port 25 is the default.

sendmail permits more than one mail queue and lets you identify subsets of the queues as belonging to a queue group. For example, if the **mqueue** directory contained the subdirectories **q1**, **q2**, and **q3** and you specified the queue directory as **/var/spool/mqueue/q***, then all three queues would be used. **sendmail**'s ability to handle multiple queues increases performance under high load.[22] If a site is running a large mailing list, **sendmail** splits the envelope recipient list into several smaller lists and assigns them to different queue groups. This trick can greatly enhance performance because the smaller recipient lists can be processed in parallel.

Queue groups were new in version 8.12 and give fine-grained control over individual types of messages. Any of the parameters associated with queues can also be set on a particular queue group, including execution priority (with the **nice** system call). Mail is submitted to a queue group according to the address of the first recipient of the message. The default queue group is called mqueue and is automatically defined and available for use without further configuration. Queue groups are covered in detail starting on page 611.

When a message is queued, it is saved in pieces in several different files. Each filename has a two-letter prefix that identifies the piece, followed by a random ID built from **sendmail**'s process ID. This ID is not fixed, because **sendmail** is constantly forking and each copy gets a new process ID. Table 18.5 shows the six possible pieces.

Table 18.5   Prefixes for files in the mail queue

Prefix	File contents
qf	The header of the message and control file
df	The body of the message
tf	A temporary version of the **qf** file while the **qf** file is being updated
Tf	Signifies that 32 or more failed locking attempts have occurred
Qf	Signifies that the message bounced and could not be returned
xf	Temporary transcript file of error messages from mailers

If subdirectories **qf**, **df**, or **xf** exist in a queue directory, then those pieces of the message are put in the proper subdirectory. The **qf** file contains not only the message header but also the envelope addresses, the date at which the message should be returned as undeliverable, the message's priority in the queue, and the reason the message is in the queue. Each line begins with a single-letter code that identifies the rest of the line.

Each message that is queued must have a **qf** and **df** file. All the other prefixes are used by **sendmail** during attempted delivery. When a machine crashes and reboots, the startup sequence for **sendmail** should delete the **tf**, **xf**, and **Tf** files from each queue

---

22. Directories are an efficient storage mechanism if they do not contain too many files. If you have a busy mail server with lots of mailing lists that get out of date, the queue directory can easily get so large that it cannot be dealt with efficiently.

directory. The sysadmin responsible for mail should check occasionally for **Qf** files in case local configuration is causing the bounces.

The mail queue opens up several opportunities for things to go wrong. For example, the filesystem can fill up (avoid putting **/var/spool/mqueue** and **/var/log** on the same partition), the queue can become clogged, and orphaned mail messages can get stuck in the queue.

sendmail has a configuration option (confMIN_FREE_BLOCKS) to help manage disk space. When the filesystem that contains the mail queue gets too full, mail is rejected with a "try again later" error until more space has been made available. This option leaves a bit of slop space so that mail starts being rejected before the filesystem is totally full and everything wedges.

See page 397 for more information about DNS MX records.
If a major mail hub goes down, its MX backup sites can become overloaded with thousands of messages. **sendmail** can fork too many copies of itself and thrash a machine to death. Several options help with performance on very busy machines; we have collected these in the performance section starting on page 611. To handle a temporarily clogged queue before version 8.12, move the clog aside, continue processing new mail as usual, and run a separate copy of **sendmail** on the clogged queue after things quiet down. For example, the procedure for handling a single queue directory would look like this:

```
# kill `head -1 sendmail.pid`
# mv mqueue cloggedqueue         /* To another FS if necessary */
# mkdir mqueue                   /* Set owner/perms, too */
# chown root mqueue
# chmod 700 mqueue
# /usr/sbin/sendmail -bd -q1h &
```

When things settle down, run **sendmail** with the following flags:

```
# /usr/sbin/sendmail -oQ/var/spool/cloggedqueue -q
```

These flags point **sendmail** at the clogged queue directory and specify that **sendmail** should process it immediately. Repeat this command until the queue empties. Starting with version 8.12, **sendmail** uses hard links in ways that will break if you move a queue. A better way to deal with clogged queues is to use a fallback machine and MX records; see the performance section for details.

The point at which the queue becomes clogged depends on the site and the hardware on which **sendmail** is running. Your system and the mail hub for aol.com, which processes millions of messages a day, have different definitions of a clogged queue. See page 615 for information about measuring your traffic levels.

18.7 SENDMAIL CONFIGURATION

Before version 8.12, **sendmail**'s actions were controlled by a single configuration file, **/etc/mail/sendmail.cf** (it was formerly found in **/etc** or **/usr/lib**). We call it the config file for short. Version 8.12 introduced a second instance of the configuration file called **submit.cf** (also in the **/etc/mail** directory). The flags with which **sendmail** is started determine which config file it uses: **-bm**, **-bs**, and **-bt** use **submit.cf** if it exists, and all other modes use **sendmail.cf**. Of course, some command-line flags and config file options change the names of the configuration files, but it is best to leave the names alone. The config file determines the following for **sendmail**:

- Choice of delivery agents
- Address rewriting rules
- Mail header formats
- Options
- Security precautions
- Spam resistance

The raw config file format was designed to be easy to parse. This focus has made it a bit lacking in warm, user-friendly features. Maintenance of the config file is the most significant administrative chore related to electronic mail and scares the pejeebers out of even seasoned sysadmins.

Every version of **sendmail** uses a config file, but modern versions make the configuration process easier through the use of **m4** macros, which disguise much of the underlying complexity. It might be said that the raw config file is at the level of assembly language, whereas **m4** configuration is more at the level of Perl.[23]

When the **m4** macros were first introduced, the hope was that they would handle 80%–90% of cases. In fact, the coverage rate turned out to be much higher, probably closer to 98%. In this book, we cover only the **m4**-based "config lite." You need delve into the low-level config file only if you are debugging a thorny problem, growing your mail site in bizarre ways, or running a very high volume mail hub.

Three key pieces of documentation are the O'Reilly book *sendmail* by Bryan Costales and Eric Allman, the paper *Sendmail Installation and Operations Guide* by Eric Allman (included in the **doc/op** directory of the **sendmail** distribution), and the file **README** (in the **cf** directory). We often refer to *sendmail* as a source for more information and refer to it as "the **sendmail** book." Likewise, we refer to the installation paper as "the installation guide" and the README file as **cf/README**.

Using the m4 preprocessor

We first describe a few **m4** features, show how to build a configuration file from an **m4** master file, and finally describe some of the important prepackaged **m4** macros that come with the **sendmail** distribution.

m4 was originally intended as a front end for programming languages that would let the user write more readable (or perhaps more cryptic) programs. **m4** is powerful enough to be useful in many input transformation situations, and it works nicely for **sendmail** configuration files.

---

23. The **sendmail** config language is "Turing complete," which means that it can be used to write any possible computer program. Readers who have experienced the raw config file will realize what a frightening concept this is …

m4 macros have the form

```
name(arg1, arg2, ..., argn)
```

There should be no space between the name and the opening parenthesis. Left and right single quotes designate strings as arguments. **m4**'s quote conventions are different from those of other languages you may have used, since the left and right quotes are different characters.[24] Quotes nest, too. With today's compiler building tools, one wonders how **m4** survived with such a rigid and exotic syntax.

m4 has some built-in macros, and users can also define their own. Table 18.6 lists the most common built-in macros used in **sendmail** configuration.

Table 18.6   m4 macros commonly used with sendmail

Macro	Function
define	Defines a macro named *arg1* with value *arg2*
undefine	Discards a previous definition of macro named *arg1*
include	Includes (interpolates) the file named *arg1*
dnl	Discards characters up to and including the next newline
divert	Manages output streams

Some sites add a dnl macro to the end of every line to keep the translated **.cf** file tidy; without dnl, **m4** adds extra blank lines to the configuration file. These blank lines don't affect **sendmail**'s behavior, but they make the config file hard to read. We have omitted the dnls from our examples. Other sites use dnl at the beginnings of lines that are intended as comments.

m4 does not really honor comments in files. A comment such as:

```
# And then define the ...
```

would not do what you expect because define is an **m4** keyword and would be expanded. Instead, use the m4 dnl keyword (for "delete to newline"). For example,

```
dnl # And then define the ...
```

would work. You must follow dnl with a space or punctuation mark for it to be recognized as an **m4** command.

The sendmail configuration pieces

The **sendmail** distribution includes a **cf** subdirectory that contains all the pieces necessary for **m4** configuration: a **README** file and several subdirectories, listed in Table 18.7 on the next page.

---

24. You could change the quote characters with the changequote macro, but doing so would totally break the use of **m4** in **sendmail** because various macros make assumptions about the quote characters.

Table 18.7   Configuration subdirectories

Directory	Contents
cf	Sample **.mc** (master configuration) files
domain	Sample **m4** files for various domains at Berkeley
feature	Fragments that implement various features
hack	Special features of dubious value or implementation
m4	The basic config file and other core files
ostype	OS-dependent file locations and quirks
mailer	**m4** files that describe common mailers (delivery agents)
sh	Shell scripts used by **m4**

The **cf/cf** directory contains examples of **.mc** files. In fact, it contains so many examples that yours will get lost in the clutter. We recommend that you keep your own **.mc** files separate from the distributed **cf** directory. Either create a new directory named for your site (**cf/**_sitename_) or move the **cf** directory aside to **cf.examples** and create a new **cf** directory. If you do this, copy the **Makefile** and **Build** script over to your new directory so the instructions in the **README** file still work. It's best to also copy all the configuration **.mc** files to a central location rather than leaving them inside the **sendmail** distribution. The **Build** script uses relative pathnames that will have to be changed if you try to build a **.cf** file from a **.mc** file and are not in the **sendmail** distribution hierarchy.

Building a configuration file from a sample .mc file

Before we dive into pages and pages of details about the various configuration macros, features, and options, we put the cart before the horse and create a "no frills" configuration to illustrate the process. Our example is for a leaf node, foo.com; the master configuration file is called **foo.mc**.

We put **foo.mc** in our shiny new **cf** directory. The translated (by **m4**) configuration file will be **foo.cf** in the same directory, and we ultimately install it as **sendmail.cf** in **/etc** or **/etc/mail**. **/etc/mail** is the **sendmail** standard for the location of the config file, but many distributions use **/etc**.

Some boilerplate should go in each new **.mc** file:

```
divert(-1)
#### basic .mc file for foo.com
divert(0)
VERSIONID(`$Id$')
```

If you want to put comments at the start of your file, use a divert statement on the first line to make **m4** discard the spurious material and obviate the need for dnl in #-style comments. The comments come next, followed by another divert.

A VERSIONID line (here, in RCS format) completes the boilerplate. It is described in detail in the next section.

In many cases, specifying an OSTYPE (see page 570) to bring in operating-system-dependent paths or parameters and also a set of MAILERs (see page 573) completes the configuration:

```
OSTYPE(`linux')
define(`confCOPY_ERRORS_TO', `postmaster')
MAILER(`local')
MAILER(`smtp')
```

Here, we also set an option (confCOPY_ERRORS_TO) that sends a copy of the headers of any bounced mail to the local postmaster. This notification allows the postmaster to intervene when the problem is at the local site.

To build the real configuration file, just run the **Build** command you copied over to the new **cf** directory:

```
# ./Build foo.cf
```

or

```
# make foo.cf
```

Finally, install **foo.cf** in the right spot—normally **/etc/mail/sendmail.cf**, but both Red Hat and SUSE stash it in **/etc/sendmail.cf**.

A larger site can create a separate **m4** file to hold site-wide defaults in the **cf/domain** directory; individual hosts can then include the contents of this file. Not every host needs a separate config file, but each group of similar hosts (same architecture and same role: server, client, etc.) will probably need its own configuration.

Changing the sendmail configuration

You will often find that your existing **sendmail** configuration is almost right, but that you just want to try out a new feature, add a new spam rule, or make a simple change. To do that:

- Edit the **.mc** file and enter your changes.
- Rebuild the config file with the **Build** script in the configuration directory.
- Install the resulting **cf** file as **sendmail.cf** in the right directory.
- Send **sendmail** a HUP signal to make it reread its config file.[25]

Even with **sendmail**'s easy new configuration system, you still have to make several configuration decisions for your site. As you read about the features described below, think about how they might fit into your site's organization. A small site will probably have only a hub node and leaf nodes and thus will need only two versions of the config file. A larger site may need separate hubs for incoming and outgoing mail and, perhaps, a separate POP/IMAP server.

---

25. Use the **kill** command to do this. The **sendmail.pid** file makes it easy to find **sendmail**'s process ID; unfortunately, its location is not consistent among distributions (try **/var/run/sendmail.pid**). See page 563 for an example of how to use it.

Whatever the complexity of your site and whatever face it shows to the outside world (exposed, behind a firewall, or on a virtual private network, for example), it's likely that the **cf** directory contains some appropriate ready-made configuration snippets just waiting to be customized and put to work.

18.8 BASIC SENDMAIL CONFIGURATION PRIMITIVES

sendmail configuration commands are case sensitive. By convention, the names of predefined macros are all caps (e.g., OSTYPE), **m4** commands are all lower case (e.g., define), and configurable variable names start with a lowercase conf and end with an all-caps variable name (e.g., confCOPY_ERRORS_TO). Macros usually refer to an **m4** file called **../**_macroname_**/**_arg1_**.m4**. For example, the macro OSTYPE(`linux') causes **../ostype/linux.m4** to be included.

In this section we cover the basic configuration commands and leave the fancier features for later.

The VERSIONID macro

You should maintain your config files with CVS or RCS, not only so that you can back out to an earlier config version if necessary but also so that you can identify the versions of the **m4** files that go into making up the config file. Use the VERSIONID macro to automatically embed version information. The syntax is

```
VERSIONID(`$Id$')
```

The actual version information is filled in by RCS as you check in the file. It appears in the final **sendmail.cf** file as a comment. This information can also be useful if you forget where you put the **sendmail** distribution; often, the location of files is dictated by available disk space and not by filesystem design logic.

The OSTYPE macro

Files in the **ostype** directory are named for the operating system whose default values they contain. An OSTYPE file packages up a variety of vendor-specific information, such as the expected locations of mail-related files, paths to commands that **sendmail** needs, flags to mailer programs, etc.

By convention, OS-specific information is interpolated into the config file with the OSTYPE macro.[26] Every config file must include an OSTYPE macro near the top, typically just after VERSIONID.

OSTYPE files do their work primarily by defining other **m4** variables. For example,

```
define(`ALIAS_FILE', `/etc/aliases')
```

specifies the location of the system-wide aliases file. You can override the default values for your OS later in the **.mc** file if you wish, but don't change the distributed

---

26. So where is the OSTYPE macro itself defined? In a file in the **cf/m4** directory, which is magically prepended to your config file when you run the **Build** script.

OSTYPE file unless it's actually wrong, in which case you should also submit a bug report to sendmail-bugs@sendmail.org. Some sites want a consistent location for the **aliases** file across platforms and so redefine its location in their DOMAIN file.

The **README** file in the **cf** directory lists all the variables that can be defined in an OSTYPE file. Some of the important ones are shown in Table 18.8, along with several that you may want to configure for spam abatement (but which are undefined by default). The default values are what you get if your OSTYPE file doesn't specify something else.

Table 18.8 Default values of some variables set in OSTYPE files

Variable	Default value
ALIAS_FILE	**/etc/mail/aliases**
HELP_FILE	**/etc/mail/helpfile**
STATUS_FILE	**/etc/mail/statistics**
QUEUE_DIR	**/var/spool/mqueue**
MSP_QUEUE_DIR	**/var/spool/clientmqueue**
LOCAL_MAILER_PATH	**/bin/mail**
LOCAL_SHELL_PATH	**/bin/sh**
LOCAL_MAILER_MAX	*undefined*
LOCAL_MAILER_MAXMSGS	*undefined*
SMTP_MAILER_MAX	*undefined*
SMTP_MAILER_MAXMSGS	*undefined*

If you install **sendmail** on a new OS release or architecture, be sure to create a corresponding OSTYPE file and give it to sendmail.org so that it can be included in the next release. Just model your new file after those already there and check it against the table of defaults in the **cf/README** file. If the value of a variable on your new system is the same as the default value, you don't need to include an entry for it (but it doesn't hurt to protect yourself in case the default changes).

Table 18.9 shows the OSTYPE files for our reference platforms.

Table 18.9 OSTYPE files for Linux systems

System	File	Directory	Usage
Red Hat	**linux.m4**	**/usr/share/sendmail-cf**	OSTYPE(`linux')
Fedora	**linux.m4**	**/usr/share/sendmail-cf**	OSTYPE(`linux')
SUSE	**suse-linux.m4**	**/usr/share/sendmail**	OSTYPE(`suse-linux')
Debian	**debian.m4**	**/usr/share/sendmail/sendmail.cf**	OSTYPE(`debian')
Ubuntu	**linux.m4**	**/usr/share/sendmail**	OSTYPE(`linux')

Electronic Mail

SUSE puts the **sendmail** distribution in **/usr/share/sendmail**. The **suse-linux.m4** OSTYPE file is in the **ostype** directory there and not part of the **sendmail** distribution from sendmail.org. That file is very long (over 80 lines) and contains numerous FEATUREs and other macros that are usually found in a site's master configuration file (the **.mc** file) and not in the OSTYPE file. This hides the real configuration from the sysadmin—a mixed blessing, perhaps, but *not* a practice we recommend.

Debian hides the config files beneath **/usr/share/sendmail/sendmail.cf/**. The directory **sendmail.cf** (confusing choice of names from the Debian folks) corresponds to the **cf** directory in the **sendmail** distribution and contains all the config pieces you need, including a Debian-specific OSTYPE file, **ostype/debian.m4**. The OSTYPE file is 50 lines long and consists mostly of pathnames and comments, as it should. Many are identical to the current defaults from sendmail.org and so don't really need to be explicitly restated. However, restating them protects Debian against changes in defaults that might otherwise introduce inconsistencies or errors. The only Debian sin in the **sendmail** OSTYPE style department is the inclusion of the generic DOMAIN file shipped with the **sendmail** distribution. A DOMAIN statement should appear early in the actual **.mc** file rather than being hidden in the OSTYPE file.

The DOMAIN macro

The DOMAIN directive lets you specify site-wide generic information in one place (**cf/domain/***filename***.m4**) and then refer to that place in each host's config file with

    DOMAIN(`filename')

Choose a filename that describes your site. For example, our file for the computer science department is called **cs.m4** and appears in our **.mc** files as:

    DOMAIN(`cs')

Like OSTYPE, DOMAIN is really just a nice way of doing an include. But it makes the structure of the config file clearer and provides a hook for future tweaks. It is most useful when you centralize and build all your site's **.cf** files from **.mc** files kept in a single location.

Small sites do not usually need a domain file, but larger sites often use them for references to relay machines, site-wide masquerading or privacy options, and references to tables for mailers, virtual domains, and spam databases.

The generic DOMAIN file included with the distribution shows the types of entries that are usually put in site-wide domain files. Its contents (with comments and dnls removed) is shown below.

    VERSIONID(`$Id: generic.m4,v 8.15 1999/04/04 00:51:09 ca Exp $')
    define(`confFORWARD_PATH', `$z/.forward.$w+$h:$z/.forward+$h:
        $z/.forward.$w:$z/.forward')
    define(`confMAX_HEADERS_LENGTH', `32768')
    FEATURE(`redirect')
    FEATURE(`use_cw_file')
    EXPOSED_USER(`root')

The file sets the path for the locations of users' forward files, limits header lengths,[27] includes the redirect feature for users who have left your organization, and turns on the use_cw_file feature for the handling of equivalent machine names. If your **.mc** file includes masquerading, the root user will not be masqueraded. Each of these constructs is described in more detail later in the chapter.

The MAILER macro

You must include a MAILER macro for every delivery agent you want to enable. You'll find a complete list of supported mailers in the directory **cf/mailers** in the **sendmail** distribution. Currently, the options are local, smtp, fax, usenet, procmail, qpage, cyrus, pop, phquery, and uucp. Typically, you need at least

```
MAILER(`local')
MAILER(`smtp')
```

The first line includes the local and prog mailers. The second line includes smtp, esmtp, dsmtp, smtp8, and relay. Support for *user+details@site.domain* email addresses was added to the local mailer starting with version 8.7.[28] The *user* defines the mailbox to which messages should be delivered, and the *details* add an extra parameter that a local mail program such as **procmail** can use to sort incoming mail.

If you plan to tune any mailer-related macros (such as USENET_MAILER_ARGS or FAX_MAILER_PATH), be sure that the lines that set these parameters *precede* the line that invokes the mailer itself; otherwise, the old values will be used. For this reason, MAILER declarations usually come toward the bottom of the config file.

The pop mailer interfaces to the **spop** program that is part of the **mh** mail handler package and implements the Post Office Protocol defined in RFC1460. It's used by PCs and Macs that need to access mail on a UNIX host. The cyrus mailer is for use with CMU's IMAP server and comes in two flavors: cyrus to deliver mail to users' mailboxes and cyrusbb to deliver mail to a central bulletin board. The cyrus mailer also understands the user+details syntax; its MAILER specification must come after that of the local mailer.

HylaFAX is available from www.hylafax.org. The fax mailer integrates Sam Leffler's HylaFAX package into the mail system. SUSE includes it as /usr/bin/faxmail; Red Hat, Fedora, Debian, and Ubuntu do not include HylaFAX by default. Mailing to *user@destination*.fax sends the body of the message as a fax document. The *destination* is typically a phone number. To allow symbolic names (rather than just phone numbers) as destinations, use a keyed database file.

ghostscript is available from www.gnu.org. You must glue HylaFAX and **sendmail** together by installing a script from the HylaFAX distribution in **/usr/local/bin**. You also might need to change the value of the macro FAX_MAILER_PATH. Human intervention is still needed to deliver incoming

---

27. Hackers have used very, very long headers as a way of causing a denial of service in older versions of **sendmail**. This line is there in case you are still running any of these vulnerable versions (pre-8.9.3).

28. The user+details syntax originated at Carnegie Mellon University, where it is used with local tools for routing and sorting mail.

faxes from the spool area to a user's mailbox. You can convert fax documents to Post-Script (with HylaFAX) and view them with the GNU package **ghostscript**.

The qpage mailer interfaces to QuickPage software to deliver email to your pager. See www.qpage.org for more information about QuickPage.

The macros VERSIONID, OSTYPE, and MAILER are all you need to build a basic *hostname*.**mc** file.

18.9 FANCIER SENDMAIL CONFIGURATION PRIMITIVES

In the next sections, we describe a few more macros and some of the most common FEATUREs that modify **sendmail**'s default behavior. We also discuss some policy issues in the context of **sendmail** configuration: security, privacy, spam, and the technique of hiding information by the use of masquerading and virtual domains.

The FEATURE macro

With the FEATURE macro you can enable several common options by including **m4** files from the **feature** directory. In the discussion below, we intermix our presentation of FEATUREs and some of **sendmail**'s other macros since they are occasionally intertwined. When **m4** configuration was first added to **sendmail**, describing the FEATURE macro became a big section of our mail chapter. Now, so many features have been added that the FEATURE macro almost needs its own chapter.

The syntax is

```
FEATURE(keyword, arg, arg, ...)
```

where *keyword* corresponds to a file *keyword*.**m4** in the **cf/feature** directory and the *args* are passed to it. See the directory itself or the **cf/README** file for a definitive list of features. A few commonly used ones are described below.

The use_cw_file feature

The **sendmail** internal class w (hence the name **cw**) contains the names of all local hosts for which this host accepts and delivers mail. A client machine might include its hostname, its nicknames, and localhost in this class. If the host being configured is your mail hub, then the w class should also include any local hosts and virtual domains for which you accept email.

The use_cw_file feature defines class w from the file **/etc/mail/local-host-names** (which used to be called **sendmail.cw**). The exact filename is configurable with the confCW_FILE option, discussed later. Without this feature, **sendmail** delivers mail locally only if it is addressed to the machine on which **sendmail** is running. An incoming mail server must list in the **local-host-names** file all the machines and domain names for which it will handle mail. If you change the file, you must send a HUP signal to **sendmail** to make your changes take effect because **sendmail** reads this file only when it starts.

```
FEATURE(`use_cw_file')
```

invokes the feature and uses the **local-host-names** file as the data source; here is an example **local-host-names** file:

```
# local-host-names - include all aliases for your machine here.
toadranch.com
coyote.toadranch.com
big-tr.com
yoherb.com
herbmorreale.com
appliedtrust.com
applied-trust.com
atrust.com
```

In this example, the entries are all virtual domains that are hosted locally.

The redirect feature

When people leave your organization, you usually either forward their mail or let mail to them bounce back to the sender with an error. The redirect feature provides support for a more elegant way of bouncing mail. If Joe Smith has graduated from oldsite.edu to newsite.com, then enabling redirect with

```
FEATURE(`redirect')
```

and adding the line

```
smithj: joe@newsite.com.REDIRECT
```

to the **aliases** file at oldsite.edu causes mail to smithj to be returned to the sender with an error message suggesting that the sender try the address joe@newsite.com instead. The message itself is not automatically forwarded.

The always_add_domain feature

This feature makes **sendmail** add the local hostname to local destination addresses that are not fully qualified. For example, suppose lynda@cs.colorado.edu sends a message to the local users barb and evi. Without always_add_domain, the mail headers would show sender and recipient addresses as simple login names. With always_add_domain turned on, all addresses would become fully qualified before the message left lynda's machine.

Use always_add_domain when you share spool directories among machines that do not share an alias file or that do not have the same **passwd** file (incidentally, you probably shouldn't do such sharing). Mail to an alias or user that is not known everywhere would be fully qualified on the originating machine and therefore could be replied to.

Another selling point for this feature is that unqualified names are often rejected as spam. We recommend that you always use it. (Unless you are sending spam!)

If you are using MASQUERADE_AS (see page 581), always_add_domain adds the name of the host you are masquerading as, not the local hostname. This convention can cause problems if the **aliases** file or **passwd** file on the local host is not a subset of the equivalent file on the MASQUERADE_AS host.

The nocanonify feature

sendmail typically verifies that the domain name portion of an address is fully qualified and not a DNS CNAME. If this is not so, **sendmail** rewrites the address. This process is called canonification and is usually done by a DNS lookup on the hostname. The nocanonify feature says not to do this rewriting, and the DNS lookup that is necessary to deliver a message is postponed. For example, at a site with a master mail hub and client machines that forward all their mail through the master, the clients might use

```
FEATURE(`nocanonify')
```

to avoid doing the DNS lookups locally. **sendmail** does not keep track of whether DNS lookups have been done as a message moves from machine to machine within a local site—it can't. The nocanonify feature lets you control the timing of these lookups. See our configuration case study (page 599) for an example.

nocanonify can also be used in an MSA/MTA scheme such as might be used at a very large mail site. In this scenario, the MSA does all the DNS lookups and the master machine running the MTA specifies nocanonify.

Sometimes you want to avoid DNS lookups that are potentially expensive but you are willing to do the lookups for the local domain. You can exempt specific domains from the nocanonify specification by including either the CANONIFY_DOMAIN or CANONIFY_DOMAIN_FILE macros, which take a list of domains or a filename as an argument, respectively. For example, the lines

```
FEATURE(`nocanonify')
CANONIFY_DOMAIN(`cs.colorado.edu cs')
```

would defer DNS lookups except for addresses of the form *user*@cs.colorado.edu or *user*@cs. These exception macros were first introduced in version 8.12.

Tables and databases

sendmail has several FEATUREs that use a construct called a "table" to figure out where mail should be routed. A table is usually a text file of routing, aliasing, policy, or other information that is converted to a database format externally with the **makemap** command and then used as an internal database for **sendmail**'s various lookups. Although the data usually starts as a text file, that is not required; data for **sendmail** tables can come from DNS, NIS, LDAP, or other sources. The use of a centralized IMAP or POP server relieves **sendmail** of the chore of chasing down users and obsoletes some of the tables discussed below. Table 18.10 on page 584 includes a summary of the available tables.

Two database libraries are supported: the **dbm/ndbm** library that is standard with most versions of Linux; and Berkeley DB, a more extensible library that supports multiple storage schemes. Your choice of database libraries must be specified at compile time. We recommend DB if you can install it; it's faster than **dbm** and creates smaller files. DB is available from sleepycat.com.

Three database map types are available:

- dbm – uses an extensible hashing algorithm (**dbm/ndbm**)
- hash – uses a standard hashing scheme (DB)
- btree – uses a B-tree data structure (DB)

For most table applications in **sendmail**, the hash database type—the default—is the best. Use the **makemap** command to build the database file from a text file; you specify the database type and the output file base name. The text version of the database should appear on **makemap**'s standard input, for example:

```
# makemap hash /etc/mail/access < /etc/mail/access
```

At first glance this command looks like a mistake that would cause the input file to be overwritten by an empty output file. However, **makemap** tacks on an appropriate suffix, so the actual output file is **/etc/mail/access.db** and in fact there is no conflict. Each time the text file is changed, the database file must be rebuilt with **makemap** (but **sendmail** need not be HUPed).

In most circumstances, the longest possible match is used for database keys. As with any hashed data structure, the order of entries in the input text file is not significant. FEATUREs that expect a database file as a parameter default to hash as the database type and **/etc/mail/**tablename**.db** as the filename for the database. To override this behavior, either specify the desired database type to both the **makemap** command and the FEATURE or reset the default by defining a different value for the variable DATABASE_MAP_TYPE. For example:

```
define(`DATABASE_MAP_TYPE', `dbm')
```

To use your new **access.db** database, you'd add the following line to your **.mc** file:

```
FEATURE(`access_db', `hash /etc/mail/access')
```

Since this line uses the default type and naming scheme, you could just write

```
FEATURE(`access_db')
```

You can specify the database filename either with or without the suffix (**.db**); without is preferred.

Don't forget to rebuild the database file with **makemap** every time you change the text file; otherwise, your changes will not take effect.

We cover the mailertable, genericstable, and virtusertable FEATUREs in the next few sections. access_db is covered later in the spam section. user_db is not covered at all because it has been deprecated and will eventually be removed.

Starting with version 8.12, all maps and classes can specify LDAP as the source of their data, so you can have **sendmail** contact the LDAP server to determine mail routing and header rewriting. Just specify LDAP as the second parameter:

```
FEATURE(`access_db', `LDAP')
```

This line causes the access_db to use the default LDAP schema that is defined in the file **cf/sendmail.schema** in the **sendmail** distribution. You can also define your own database schema with additional arguments to the FEATURE directive; see the **cf/README** file for details.

The mailertable feature

The mailertable feature redirects mail addressed to a particular host or domain to an alternate destination through a particular mailer. It is applied as the mail goes out from a site. The mailertable feature looks only at the host portion of the address, not the user portion. The header address is not rewritten, so the mail continues to be addressed to the same user but is sent to a different host through a different mailer. mailertable was originally designed to deal with other mail systems such as UUCP, DECnet, and BITNET, but today it is often used to redirect mail from a gateway machine to an internal server or to a server at a remote site that does not have direct Internet access.

To use a mailertable, include the following line in your **.mc** file.

```
FEATURE(`mailertable')
```

An entry in the mailertable has the form:

```
old_domain        mailer:destination
```

A leading dot in front of the key on the left side is a wild card that means any host in that domain. Only host and domain names are allowed as mailertable keys; usernames are not allowed. The *destination* value on the right side can be a domain, a user@domain clause, or even null, in which case the envelope is not changed. The *mailer* value must be the name of a mailer defined in a MAILER clause; see page 573.

As an example, suppose you used MS Exchange as your main internal mail server but were reluctant to have it facing the Internet. You could put a Linux box on the Internet as your mail gateway and then forward all mail to the Exchange server after virus scanning or whatever preprocessing you liked. Here is the mailertable entry that would do it, assuming that the Exchange server had the internal IP address shown:

```
my-domain        esmtp:[192.168.1.245]
```

However, this is a form of relaying, which, as we see on page 589, needs to be controlled. To complete this example, you would need to put the line

```
To: my-domain  RELAY
```

in your access database to allow relaying for all mail to any user at my-domain.

The genericstable feature

The genericstable feature ("generics table," not "generic stable") is like aliasing for outgoing mail. For example, it can map trent@atrust.com to trent.hein@atrust.com on outbound mail. It is the headers that are rewritten, not the envelope. Mail delivery is not affected, only replies.

Several mechanisms can map hostnames, but genericstable is the only one that includes both the username and the hostname as part of the mapping key. The masquerade_envelope and allmasquerade features discussed later in this section can also apply to addresses in the genericstable.

To use genericstable, make sure that your domain is in the generics class. To put a domain in the generics class, you can either list it in the GENERICS_DOMAIN macro or put it in the file specified by the GENERICS_DOMAIN_FILE macro.

For example, to use genericstable with the defaults for the database, add

```
GENERICS_DOMAIN_FILE(`/etc/mail/local-host-names')
FEATURE(`genericstable')
```

to your **.mc** configuration file. In this example, any host you accept mail for is included. Enabling the genericstable feature slows down **sendmail** slightly because every sender address must be looked up.

The virtusertable feature

The virtual user table supports domain aliasing for incoming mail. This feature allows multiple virtual domains to be hosted on one machine and is common at web hosting sites.

The key field of the table contains either an email address (*user@host.domain*) or a domain specification (*@domain*). The value field is a local email address or an external email address. If the key is a domain, the value can either pass the *user* field along as the variable %1 or route the mail to a different user. If the user specification has the form *user+details*, then the variable %2 contains the *details* and variable %3 contains *+details*; use whichever form you want.

Let's look at some examples (we added the comments):

```
info@foo.com    foo-info             # route to a local user
info@bar.com    bar-info             # another local user
joe@bar.com     error:No such user   # to return an error
@baz.org        jane@elsewhere.com   # all mail to jane
@zokni.org      %1@elsewhere.com     # to the same user, different domain
```

All the host keys on the left side of the data mappings must be listed in the **cw** file, **/etc/mail/local-host-names**, (or the VirtHost class); otherwise, **sendmail** tries to find the host on the Internet and to deliver the mail there. If DNS points **sendmail** back to this server, you get a "local configuration error" message in bounces. Unfortunately, **sendmail** cannot tell that the error message for this instance should really be "virtusertable key not in cw file."

Several pieces are actually involved here:

- DNS MX records must exist so that mail is routed to the right host in the first place; then

- **cw** entries must be present or VIRTUSER_DOMAIN specified (or equivalently, VIRTUSER_DOMAIN_FILE) to allow the local machine to accept the mail; and finally

- the virtual user table must tell **sendmail** what to do with the mail.

The feature is invoked with

```
FEATURE(`virtusertable')
```

The examples starting on page 599 use virtusertable to implement virtual hosting.

The ldap_routing feature

As a final chunk floating in this cesspool of aliasing, rewriting, and falsification, we have LDAP, the Lightweight Directory Access Protocol. LDAP (see page 555 for general information) can substitute for virtusertable with respect to routing email and accepting mail for virtual domains. It can also manage aliases, maps, and classes. And as of version 8.12, it can do a decent job with mailing lists.

To use LDAP in this way, you must include several statements in your config file, and you must have built **sendmail** to include LDAP support. In your **.mc** file you need the lines

```
define(`confLDAP_DEFAULT_SPEC', `-h server -b searchbase')
FEATURE(`ldap_routing')
LDAPROUTE_DOMAIN(`my_domain')
```

to tell **sendmail** that you want to use an LDAP database for routing incoming mail addressed to the specified domain. The LDAP_DEFAULT_SPEC option identifies the LDAP server and database search base name.

In the following example, the search base is o=sendmail.com, c=US. If you run LDAP on a custom port (not 389), add -p ldap_port# to the LDAP_DEFAULT_SPEC.

sendmail uses the values of two tags in the LDAP database:

- mailLocalAddress for the addressee on incoming mail
- mailRoutingAddress for the alias to send it to

sendmail also supports the tag mailHost, which if present routes mail to the MX records for the specified host, with mailRoutingAddress as recipient.

For example, the LDAP entry (for a server configured with a root distinguished name of cn=root, o=sendmail.com, c=US)

```
dn: uid=eric, o=sendmail.com, c=US
objectClass: inetLocalMailRecipient
mailLocalAddress: eric@sendmail.org
mailRoutingAddress: eric@eng.sendmail.com
```

would cause mail addressed to eric@sendmail.org (which DNS MX records caused to be delivered to sendmail.com) to be sent to eric@eng.sendmail.com. If the entry also contained the line

```
mailHost: mailserver.sendmail.com
```

then mail to eric@sendmail.org would be addressed to eric@eng.sendmail.com and sent to the host mailserver.sendmail.com after MX lookups.

LDAP database entries support a wild card entry, *@domain*, that reroutes mail addressed to anyone at the specified domain (as was done in the virtusertable).

In versions 8.12 and later, a bit more flexibility was added in the form of a configuration primitive, LDAPROUTE_EQUIVALENT (or LDAPROUTE_EQUIVALENT_FILE), with which you can define equivalent versions of the domain name you are rerouting with LDAP. For example, mail coming to user@host1.mydomain would normally be queried literally in the LDAP database and then queried as @host1.mydomain. Including the line

```
LDAPROUTE_EQUIVALENT(`host1.mydomain')
```

would also try the keys user@mydomain and @mydomain. This feature enables a single database to route mail at a complex site.

Additional arguments to the ldap_routing feature now enable you to specify more details about the LDAP schema to use and to specify the handling of user names that have a +detail part. As of sendmail version 8.13, a new ldap_routing argument (sendertoo) can reject SMTP mail from a sender that doesn't exist in LDAP. As always, see the **cf/README** file for exact details.

Masquerading and the MASQUERADE_AS macro

With the MASQUERADE_AS macro, you can specify a single identity that other machines hide behind. All mail appears to emanate from the designated machine or domain. The sender's address is rewritten to be *user@masquerading-name* instead of *user@original-host.domain*. Of course, those masqueraded addresses must be valid so that people can reply to the mail.

This configuration permits all users at a site to use a generic email address. For example, if all hosts at atrust.com masquerade behind the domain atrust.com, then mail from *user@host*.atrust.com is stamped as being from *user*@atrust.com, with no mention of the actual hostname from which the user sent the mail. The machine that represents atrust.com must know how to deliver all users' mail, even mail for users that do not have a login on the incoming mail server. Naturally, login names must be unique across the whole domain.

Some users and addresses (such as root, postmaster, hostmaster, trouble, operations, Mailer-Daemon, etc.) should be exempted from this behavior. They can be explicitly excluded with the EXPOSED_USER macro.

For example, the sequence

```
MASQUERADE_AS(`atrust.com')
EXPOSED_USER(`root')
EXPOSED_USER(`Mailer-Daemon')
```

would stamp mail as coming from user@atrust.com unless it was sent by root or the mail system; in these cases, the mail would carry the name of the originating host.

A feature introduced in 8.12 enables you to exempt mail for the local domain (or mail to specific hosts listed as exceptions) from the masquerading. For example, this feature might be handy for a site that uses an unregistered private domain name locally and wants masquerading only on messages bound for the Internet.

The syntax is

```
FEATURE(`local_no_masquerade')
MASQUERADE_EXCEPTION(`host.domain')
MASQUERADE_EXCEPTION_FILE(`filename')
```

The basic MASQUERADE_AS macro has several extensions, both through other macros and through FEATUREs:

- The MASQUERADE_DOMAIN macro
- The MASQUERADE_DOMAIN_FILE macro
- The MASQUERADE_EXCEPTION macro
- The MASQUERADE_EXCEPTION_FILE macro
- The limited_masquerade FEATURE
- The allmasquerade FEATURE
- The masquerade_envelope FEATURE
- The masquerade_entire_domain FEATURE

We recommend using the MASQUERADE_AS macro described above along with the allmasquerade and masquerade_envelope features. The limited_masquerade feature modifies the behavior of MASQUERADE_DOMAIN and is useful for virtual hosting environments. MASQUERADE_DOMAIN lets you list domains that you want to masquerade; the list is preloaded from the w class that is typically defined with the use_cw_file feature and lists the hosts in your domain. limited_masquerade does not preinitialize the list with class w. All those domains are hidden by the domain you are masquerading as.

The allmasquerade feature extends masquerading to the recipients of the message (as opposed to just the sender), and the masquerade_envelope feature extends it to the envelope as well as to the header addresses.[29] With these two extensions, all

---

29. The header addresses are the To, From, Cc, and Bcc addresses that appear in the header of a message. The envelope addresses are the addresses to which the mail is actually delivered. The envelope addresses are originally built from the header addresses by the user agent, but they are processed separately by **sendmail**. Many of **sendmail**'s masquerading and redirection features would be impossible to implement if the distinction between header and envelope addresses was not maintained.

addresses are hidden in a consistent fashion. The `masquerade_entire_domain` feature extends masquerading to all hosts in a specified list of other domains.

If you want to use other masquerading techniques, you can read about their behavior in the **cf/README** file or in the **sendmail** book. Read carefully; some of the masquerading primitives can hide too much.

The MAIL_HUB and SMART_HOST macros

Masquerading makes all mail appear to come from a single host or domain by rewriting the headers and, optionally, the envelope. Some sites may want all mail to really come from (or go to) a single machine. You can achieve this configuration with the macros MAIL_HUB for incoming mail and SMART_HOST for outgoing mail.

To route all incoming mail to a central server for delivery, set MAIL_HUB to the value *mailer:host*, where *mailer* is the agent to use to reach the designated *host*. If you don't specify a delivery agent, then relay is used. For example:

```
define(`MAIL_HUB', `smtp:mailhub.cs.colorado.edu')
```

The SMART_HOST designation causes a host to deliver local mail but to punt external mail to SMART_HOST. This feature is useful for machines that live behind a firewall and so cannot use DNS directly. Its syntax parallels that of MAIL_HUB; the default delivery agent is again relay. For example:

```
define(`SMART_HOST', `smtp:mailhub.cs.colorado.edu')
```

In these examples, the same machine acts as the server for both incoming and outgoing mail. A larger site might split these into separate machines. The SMART_HOST must allow relaying so that client machines can send mail through it. mailertable entries override the SMART_HOST designation.

Masquerading and routing

With all these features and macros ready and waiting to massage your email addresses, we thought it might be nice to try to compare the various mechanisms in terms of whether they change the headers, the envelope, or the delivery of a message, whether they apply to incoming or outgoing messages, sender or recipient addresses, etc. If the page were double or triple width, we might have succeeded in really illustrating the differences among the various constructs.

Instead, we give you just a hint in Table 18.10 (next page); you will have to look up the details in the **sendmail** documentation to get the nuances of the different variations.

Entries in Table 18.10 that are all capital letters are **m4** macros. Lowercase entries are the names of features that are invoked with the FEATURE macro. Indented items depend on the items above; for example, a feature that modifies the MASQUERADE_AS behavior does nothing unless MASQUERADE_AS has been turned on. In the table, the feature is indented to indicate this dependency. Masquerading affects the header addresses on outgoing mail and whether a message can be replied to; routing affects the actual delivery of the mail.

Table 18.10 **Comparison of masquerading and routing features**

	Construct	Dir	Affects[a]	Which piece
Masquerading	MASQUERADE_AS	out	SH	host.domain
	allmasquerade	out	RH[b]	host.domain
	MASQUERADE_DOMAIN[_FILE]	out	SH	host.domain
	masquerade_entire_domain	out	SH	host.sub.domain
	limited_masquerade	out	SH	host.domain
	masquerade_envelope	out	SE[c]	host.domain
	genericstable	out	SH	user@host.domain
Routing	mailertable	out	MAD	host.domain
	virtusertable	in	RD	user@host.domain
	ldap	in	RD	user@host.domain
	mailhub	in	RD	local mail
	smarthost	out	RD	remote mail

a. S = sender, R = recipient, D = delivery, H = header, E = envelope, M = mailer, A = address

b. Once recipient rewriting has been enabled with the allmasquerade feature, all other masquerading constructs rewrite not only the sender but also the recipient.

c. Once envelope rewriting has been enabled with the masquerade_envelope feature, all other masquerading constructs rewrite not only the header but the envelope as well.

The nullclient feature

nullclient is used for a host that should never receive mail directly and that sends all its mail to a central server. The **.mc** file for such a host has only two lines.

```
OSTYPE(`ostype')
FEATURE(`nullclient', `mail_server')
```

The nullclient feature overrides many other features. All mail, without exception, is delivered to *mail_server* for processing.[30] Note that the server must allow the client to relay through it if users regularly originate mail on the client and don't use a separate server for outgoing mail. Recent versions of **sendmail** have relaying turned off by default. See the spam section (page 588) for details on how to control relaying. A nullclient configuration masquerades as *mail_server*, so you might want to include an EXPOSED_USER clause for root.

The client that uses the nullclient feature must have an associated MX record that points to the server. It must also be included in the server's **cw** file, which is usually **/etc/mail/local-host-names**. These settings let the server accept mail for the client.

A host with a nullclient configuration should not accept incoming mail. If it did, it would just forward the mail to the server anyway. Starting **sendmail** without the **-bd** flag so that it doesn't listen for SMTP connections on port 25 is one way to avoid

30. If you configure a client this way and then test the configuration with **sendmail -bt**, the client appears to locally deliver local mail. The reason is that the nullclient directive is processed later, in ruleset 5 of the raw config file.

receiving mail. However, some user agents (MUAs) attempt the initial submission of a mail message through port 25 and so are foiled if your **sendmail** is not listening. A better way to disallow incoming mail is to run **sendmail** with the **-bd** flag but to use DAEMON_OPTIONS to listen only on the loopback interface. Either way, leave the **-q30m** flag on the command line so that if *mail_server* goes down, the client can queue outgoing mail and try to send it to *mail_server* later.

nullclient is appropriate for leaf nodes at sites that have a central mail machine. At larger sites, consider the mail load on the hub machine. You may want to separate the incoming and outgoing servers or to adopt a hierarchical approach.

 SUSE ships with a sample nullclient **mc** file in **/etc/mail/linux.nullclient.mc**. Just fill in the name of your *mail_server*, run **m4** on it to build the **sendmail.cf** file, and you are done.

The local_lmtp and smrsh features

By default, the local mailer uses **/bin/mail** as the local delivery agent for users and files and **/bin/sh** as the delivery agent for programs. **sendmail** now provides better alternatives, especially for delivery to programs. Both options are available through the FEATURE macro.

If the local_lmtp feature is specified, then its argument is a local mailer capable of speaking LMTP, the Local Mail Transport Protocol (see RFC2033). The default for delivery to users is the **mail.local** program from the **sendmail** distribution. Likewise, the smrsh feature specifies the path to the program to use for mail delivery to programs. See page 605 for a more detailed discussion of **mail.local** and **smrsh**.

The local_procmail feature

You can use Stephen van den Berg's **procmail** as your local mailer by enabling the local_procmail feature. It takes up to three arguments: the path to the **procmail** binary, the argument vector to call it with, and flags for the mailer. The default values are OK, but the default path (**/usr/local/bin/procmail**) conflicts with most distributions' usual **procmail** location (**/usr/bin**).

procmail can do fancier things for the user than plain **/bin/mail** or **mail.local** can. In addition to delivering mail to users' mailboxes, it can sort messages into folders, save them in files, run programs, and filter spam. Use of the local_procmail feature largely nullifies the security enhancements provided by **smrsh** (described on page 605). However, if you don't need to restrict the programs your users run (that is, if you trust *all* your users), **procmail** can be very handy. **procmail** is not distributed with **sendmail**; get it from www.procmail.org if it is not installed by your vendor.

You can use other mail processing programs in conjunction with this feature just by lying to **sendmail** and saying that you are just showing it the local copy of **procmail**:

```
FEATURE(`local_procmail', `/usr/local/bin/mymailer')
```

If you use **procmail**, check out **/usr/bin/mailstat** for some handy **procmail** statistics (not to be confused with **/usr/sbin/mailstats**, which shows **sendmail** statistics). It is installed on all of our example distributions and can be used to summarize **procmail** log files.

The LOCAL_* macros

If you really need to get your hands dirty and write some exotic new rules to deal with special local situations, you can use a set of macros prefaced by LOCAL_. The section on spam, later in this chapter, has some examples of this low-level construct.

Configuration options

Config file options and macros (the O and D commands in the raw config language) can be set with the define **m4** command. A complete list of options accessible as **m4** variables and their default values is given in the **cf/README** file. The default values are OK for most sites.

Some examples:

```
define(`confTO_QUEUERETURN', `7d')
define(`confTO_QUEUEWARN', `4h')
define(`confPRIVACY_FLAGS', `noexpn')
```

The queue return option determines how long a message will remain in the mail queue if it cannot be delivered. The queue warn option determines how long a message will sit before the sender is notified that there might be delivery problems. The first two lines set these to 7 days and 4 hours, respectively.

See page 606 for more information about privacy options.

The next line sets the privacy flags to disallow the SMTP EXPN (expand address) command. The confPRIVACY_FLAGS option takes a comma-separated list of values. Some versions of **m4** require two sets of quotes to protect the commas in a field with multiple entries, but the GNU **m4** shipped with Linux is smarter and doesn't require the extra quotes:

```
define(`confPRIVACY_FLAGS', ``noexpn, novrfy'')
```

The default values for most options are about right for a typical site that is not too paranoid about security or not too concerned with performance. In particular, the defaults try to protect you from spam by turning off relaying, requiring addresses to be fully qualified, and requiring that addresses resolve to an IP address. If your mail hub machine is very busy and services lots of mailing lists, you may need to tweak some of the performance values.

Table 18.11 lists some options that you might need to adjust (about 15% of the almost 175 configuration options), along with their default values. To save space, the option names are shown without their conf prefix; for example, the FALLBACK_MX option is really named confFALLBACK_MX. We divided the table into subsections that identify the kind of issue the variable addresses: generic, resources, performance, security and spam abatement, and miscellaneous. Some options clearly fit in more than one category, but we listed them only once.

Table 18.11 Basic configuration options

	Option name	Description and (default value)
Generic	COPY_ERRORS_TO	Addresses to Cc on error messages (none)
	DOUBLE_BOUNCE_ADDRESS	Catches a lot of spam; some sites use **/dev/null**, but that can hide serious problems (postmaster)
Resources	MIN_FREE_BLOCKS	Min filesystem space to accept mail (100)
	MAX_MESSAGE_SIZE	Max size in bytes of a single message (infinite)
	TO_*lots_of_stuff*	Timeouts for all kinds of things (various)
	TO_IDENT	Timeout for ident queries to check sender's identity; if 0, ident checks are not done (5s)
	MAX_DAEMON_CHILDREN	Max number of child processes[a] (no limit)
Performance	MCI_CACHE_SIZE	# of open outgoing TCP connections cached (2)
	MCI_CACHE_TIMEOUT	Time to keep cached connections open (5m)
	HOST_STATUS_DIRECTORY	See page 614 for description (no default)
	FALLBACK_MX	See page 613 for description (no default)
	FAST_SPLIT	Suppresses MX lookups as recipients are sorted and split across queues; see page 612 (1 = true)
	QUEUE_LA	Load average at which mail should be queued instead of delivered immediately (8 * #CPUs)
	REFUSE_LA	Load avg. at which to refuse mail (12 * #CPUs)
	DELAY_LA	Load avg. to slow down deliveries (0 = no limit)
	MIN_QUEUE_AGE	Minimum time jobs must stay in queue; makes a busy machine handle the queue better (0)
Security/spam	TRUSTED_USERS	For mailing list software owners; allows forging of the From line and rebuilding of the aliases database (root, daemon, uucp)
	PRIVACY_FLAGS	Limits info given out by SMTP (authwarnings)
	INPUT_MAIL_FILTERS	Lists filters for incoming mail (empty)
	MAX_MIME_HEADER_LENGTH	Sets max size of MIME headers (no limit)[b]
	CONNECTION_RATE_THROTTLE	Slows DOS attacks by limiting the rate at which mail connections are accepted (no limit)
	MAX_RCPTS_PER_MESSAGE	Slows spam delivery; defers extra recipients and sends a temporary error msg (infinite)
	DONT_BLAME_SENDMAIL	Overrides **sendmail**'s security and file checking; don't change casually! (safe)
	AUTH_MECHANISMS	SMTP auth mechanisms for Cyrus SASL[c]
Misc	LDAP_DEFAULT_SPEC	Map spec for LDAP database, including the host and port the server is running on (undefined)

a. More specifically, the maximum number of child processes that can run at once. When the limit is reached, **sendmail** refuses connections. This option can prevent (or create) denial of service (DOS) attacks.

b. This option can prevent user agent buffer overflows. "256/128" is a good value to use—it means 256 bytes per header and 128 bytes per parameter to that header.

c. The default value is EXTERNAL GSSAPI KERBEROS_V4 DIGEST-MD5 CRAM-MD5; don't add PLAIN LOGIN unless you want to reduce security.

Electronic Mail

18.10 SPAM-RELATED FEATURES IN SENDMAIL

Spam is the jargon word for junk mail, also known as unsolicited commercial email. It has become a serious problem, primarily because the senders typically do not pay by the byte but rather pay a flat rate for connectivity. Or if they do pay per byte, they send a single message with many thousands of recipients and relay it through another machine. The other machine pays the big per-byte cost and the spammer pays for only one copy. In many countries, end users pay for bytes received and get pretty angry at having to pay to receive spam.

From the marketing folks' point of view, spam works well. Response rates are high, costs are low, and delivery is instantaneous. A list of 30 million email addresses costs about $40.

Many spammers try to appear innocent by suggesting that you answer their email with a message that says "remove" if you want to be removed from their mailing list. Although they may remove you, you have just verified for them that they have a valid, current email address; this information can land you on other lists. Spammers also like to mess with their mail headers in an attempt to disguise who the mail is from and on which machine it originated.

Folks that sell email addresses to spammers have recently started to use a form of dictionary attack to ferret out unknown addresses. Starting with a list of common last names, the scanning software adds different first initials in hopes of hitting on a valid email address. To check the addresses, the software connects to the mail servers at, say, 50 large ISPs and does a VRFY or RCPT on each of zillions of addresses.

This probing has a huge impact on your mail server and its ability to deliver legitimate mail. **sendmail** can deal with this situation with the PrivacyOption goaway which is covered starting on page 606. But the smarter spam programs are very robust; if VRFY is blocked, they try EXPN, and if both are blocked they try RCPT. They can try millions of addresses that way and never send a single message—they sure keep your mail server busy, though.

sendmail has an option, BAD_RCPT_THROTTLE, to foil such behavior. If the number of rejected addresses in a message's envelope exceeds the value of this option, **sendmail** sleeps for one second after each rejected RCPT command.

sendmail has added some very nice features to help with spam control and also to help with the occasional mail-borne computer virus. Unfortunately, most ISPs must pass along all mail, so these features may be too draconian for customer policy (or then again, maybe they aren't). However, the features can be used to great effect at the end user's site.

Spam control features come in four flavors:

- Rules that control third-party or promiscuous relaying, which is the use of your mail server by one off-site user to send mail to another off-site user. Spammers often use relaying to mask the true source of their mail and thereby avoid detection by their ISPs. It also lets them use *your* cycles and save their own. That's the killer.

- The access database, by which mail is filtered by address, rather like a firewall for email.

- Blacklists containing open relays and known spam-friendly sites that **sendmail** can check against.

- Header checking and input mail filtering by means of a generic mail filtering interface called **libmilter**. It allows arbitrary scanning of message headers *and content* and lets you reject messages that match a particular profile.

We describe these new features here and then look at a couple of pieces of spam we received recently to see how we might have tuned our mail system to recognize and reject them automatically.

Relaying

sendmail and other mail transport agents accept incoming mail, look at the envelope addresses, decide where the mail should go, and then pass it along to an appropriate destination. That destination can be local or it can be another transport agent farther along in the delivery chain. When an incoming message has no local recipients, the transport agent that handles it is said to be acting as a relay.

Before **sendmail** version 8.9, promiscuous relaying (also called open relaying) was on by default. **sendmail** would accept any message presented to it on port 25 and try its best to make the delivery. It was the neighborly Internet thing to do.

Unfortunately, spammers started to abuse relaying; they exploited it to disguise their identities and, more importantly, to use your bandwidth and cycles instead of their own. It is now considered very bad to configure your mail server as an open relay. Nevertheless, many servers are still configured as open relays.

Only hosts that are tagged with RELAY in the access database (see page 591) or that are listed in **/etc/mail/relay-domains** are allowed to submit mail for relaying. In the next few years, the proportion of open relays should fall as a result of this change in default behavior, increasing public awareness, and proactive screening based on various black hole lists.

So, promiscuous relaying is bad. At the same time, some types of relaying are useful and legitimate. How can you tell which messages to relay and which to reject? Relaying is actually necessary in only two situations:

- *When the transport agent acts as a gateway for hosts that are not reachable any other way*; for example, hosts that are not always turned on (dial-up hosts, Windows PCs) and virtual hosts. In this situation, all the recipients for which you want to relay lie within the same domain.

- *When the transport agent is the outgoing mail server for other, not-so-smart hosts.* In this case, all the senders' hostnames or IP address will be local (or at least enumerable).

Any other situation that appears to require relaying is probably just an indication of bad design (with the possible exception of support for mobile users). You can obviate the first use of relaying (above) by designating a centralized server to receive mail (with POP or IMAP used for client access). The second case should always be allowed, but only for your own hosts. You can check IP addresses or hostnames; hostnames are easier to fake, but **sendmail** verifies that they are not forgeries.

Although **sendmail** comes with relaying turned off by default, several features have been added to turn it back on, either fully or in a limited and controlled way. These features are listed below for completeness, but our recommendation is that you be careful about opening things up too much. Most sites do not need any of the really dangerous features in the second bulleted list below. The access_db feature, covered in the next section, is the safest way to allow limited relaying.

- FEATURE(`relay_entire_domain`) – allows relaying for just your domain
- RELAY_DOMAIN(`domain, ...`)   – adds more domains to be relayed
- RELAY_DOMAIN_FILE(`filename`)   – same, but takes domain list from a file
- FEATURE(`relay_hosts_only`)   – affects RELAY_DOMAIN, accessdb

You will need to make an exception if you use the SMART_HOST or MAIL_HUB designations to route mail through a particular mail server machine. That server will have to be set up to relay mail from local hosts. Configure it with

```
FEATURE(`relay_entire_domain`)
```

Sites that do virtual hosting may also need RELAY_DOMAIN to allow relaying for their virtual names, although

```
FEATURE(`use_cw_file`)
```

effectively opens relays for those domains or hosts.

The few other possibilities are fraught with problems:

- FEATURE(`promiscuous_relay`) – allows all relaying; don't use
- FEATURE(`relay_based_on_MX`) – relays for anyone that MXes to you
- FEATURE(`loose_relay_check`) – allows "percent hack" addressing
- FEATURE(`relay_local_from`)   – bases relays on the From address

The promiscuous_relay feature relays from any site to any other site. Using it is a one-way ticket to the black hole lists. *Do not* use this feature on a machine reachable through the public Internet.

The relay_based_on_MX feature is bad because you do not control what sites are allowed to point their MX records at you. Typically, the only hosts that have an MX record pointing to your mail server are your own, but nothing prevents other sites from changing their MX records to point to you. Spammers usually cannot change MX records, but shady sites certainly could.

The `loose_relay_check` feature allows the "% hack" form of addressing (see page 535) that spammers love to use.

The `relay_local_from` feature trusts the sender address on the envelope of the message and relays messages that appear to be from a local address. Of course, both the envelope and the headers of mail messages are trivial to forge, and spammers are forgery experts.

If you consider turning on relaying in some form, consult the **sendmail** documentation in **cf/README** to be sure you don't inadvertently become a friend of spammers. When you are done, have one of the relay checking sites verify that you did not inadvertently create an open relay—try spam.abuse.net.

There are mismatched configurations in which your host might be convinced to relay weird addresses that misuse the UUCP addressing syntax. Just to be sure, if you have no UUCP connectivity, you can use

```
FEATURE(`nouucp', `reject')
```

to forestall this possibility. Current **sendmail** does not default to supporting any of the ancient networking technologies such as UUCP, BITNET, or DECnet.

Another common relay is the LUSER_RELAY for local users who do not exist. It is defined by default as

```
define(`LUSER_RELAY', `error:No such user')
```

A site with **sendmail** misconfigured sometimes leaks unqualified local user names to the Internet (usually on the Cc line). Someone who replies to the mail addresses the response to an apparently local user who does not exist. This relay is often called the "loser relay" and is directed to the error mailer.

You need not change this configuration unless you want to return a different message or implement some kind of special treatment. Some sites redirect "loser" mail to a person or program that does fuzzy matching in case the sender made a typo or just has the login name slightly wrong.

The access database

sendmail includes support for an access database that you can use to build a mail-specific firewall for your site. The access database checks mail coming in from the outside world and rejects it if it comes from specific users or domains. You can also use the access database to specify which domains a machine is willing to relay for.

The access database is enabled with the line

```
FEATURE(`access_db', `type filename')
```

If *type* and *filename* are not specified, the database defaults to type hash (if DB databases are used—depends on the DATABASE_MAP_TYPE setting) built from the file **/etc/mail/access**. DBM databases don't use the *type* field. As always, create the database with **makemap**:

```
# makemap hash /etc/mail/access < /etc/mail/access
```

The key field of the access file can contain email addresses, user names, domain names, or network numbers.

For example:

```
cyberspammer.com              550 Spam not accepted
okguy@cyberspammer.com  OK
badguy@aol.com                  REJECT
sendmail.org                       RELAY
128.32                                 RELAY
170.201.180.16                   REJECT
hotlivesex@                        550 Spam not accepted
friend@                              550 You are not my friend!
```

The value part must contain one of the items shown in Table 18.12. The value RELAY is the most permissive; it simply accepts the message and forwards it to its final destination. OK accepts the message but will not allow relaying. REJECT will not accept the message at all. SKIP allows you to make exceptions. For example, if you want to relay mail for all hosts except two in a certain domain, you could list the two hosts with the SKIP action and then list the domain with the RELAY action. The order does not matter.

Table 18.12   Things that can appear in the value field of the access database

Value	What it does
OK	Accepts mail and delivers it normally
RELAY	Accepts the mail as addressed and relays it to its destination; enables per-host relaying
SKIP	Allows for exceptions to more general rules
REJECT	Rejects the mail with a generic error message
DISCARD	Silently discards the message
FRIEND	For spam, used by delay-checks feature; if matched, skips other header checks
HATER	For spam, used by delay-checks feature; if matched, applies other header checks
xxx message	Returns an error; *xxx* must be an RFC821 numeric code[a]
ERROR:*xxx message*	Same as above, but clearly marked as an error message
ERROR:*x.x.x message*	*x.x.x* must be an RFC1893-compliant delivery status notification (a generalization of the 550 error code)

a. For example, 550 is the single-error code.

The database file above would allow messages from okguy@cyberspammer.com but would reject all other mail from cyberspammer.com with the indicated error message. Mail from either sendmail.org or 128.32.0.0/16 (UC Berkeley's network) would be relayed. Mail from badguy@aol.com and from hotlivesex or friend at any domain would also be rejected.

IPv6 addresses in their colon-separated form can be used on the left hand side as well, but they must be prefaced with "IPv6:". The @ after the usernames hotlivesex and friend is required; it differentiates usernames from domain names.

550 is an RFC821 error code. The RFC1893 error codes (or "delivery status notification messages," as they are called) are more extensive. First digit 4 signifies a temporary error; 5 means a permanent error. We've listed a few in Table 18.13.

Table 18.13   RFC1893 delivery status codes

Temporary	Permanent	Meaning
4.2.1	5.2.1	Mailbox is disabled
4.2.2	5.2.2	Mailbox is full
4.2.3	5.2.3	Message is too long
4.2.4	5.2.4	List expansion problem
4.3.1	5.3.1	Mail system is full
4.4.4	5.4.4	Unable to route
4.4.5	5.4.5	Mail congestion
4.7.*	5.7.*	Site policy violation

For even finer control, the key field (left side) can contain the tags Connect, To, From, and in 8.12 and later, Spam to control the way in which the filter is applied. Connect refers to connection information such as client IP address or client hostname. To and From refer to the envelope addresses, not the headers. The Spam tag allows exceptions to global rules through the "spam friend" and "spam hater" tests. It is enabled with the delay_checks feature:

```
FEATURE(`delay_checks', `friend')
FEATURE(`delay_checks', `hater')
```

The first feature skips other rulesets that might reject the message if there is a matching entry in the access_db with FRIEND as the right hand side of the mapping. The second applies the other rulesets if the access_db value is HATER. These four tags give you finer control over relaying and rejection of mail; they override other restrictions as well. Individual users who complain about your site-wide spam policy can be accommodated with the spam FRIEND or HATER tags.

If one of these tags is used, the lookup is tried first with the tag info and then without, to maintain backward compatibility with older access databases.

Here are some examples:

```
From:spammer@some.domain    REJECT
To:good.domain              RELAY
Connect:good.domain         OK
Spam:abuse@                 FRIEND
```

Mail from spammer@some.domain would be blocked, but you could still send mail to that address, even if it was blacklisted. Mail would be relayed to good.domain, but not from it (assuming that relaying has been disabled elsewhere). Connections from good.domain would be allowed even if the domain was in one of the DNS-based rejection lists. Mail to abuse@localdomain would get through, even from spammer@some.domain whose email would have been rejected by the first access database line.

Many sites use an access database to control spam or policy. The incoming master mail machine in the computer science department at the University of Colorado uses the access_db feature to reject mail from over 500 known spammers identified by addresses, domains, or IP networks.

User or site blacklisting

If you have local users or hosts to which you want to block mail, use

```
FEATURE(`blacklist_recipients')
```

which supports the following types of entries in your access file:

```
To:nobody@                  550 Mailbox disabled for this user
To:printer.mydomain.edu     550 This host does not accept mail
To:user@host.mydomain.edu   550 Mailbox disabled for this user
```

These lines block incoming mail to user nobody on any host, to host printer, and to a particular user's address on one machine. The use of the To: tag lets these users send messages, just not receive them; some printers have that capability.

Unfortunately, it's virtually impossible these days to manually maintain a blacklist like this. Fortunately, several community-maintained black hole lists are accessible through DNS, and some of these are provided at no charge.

To include a DNS-style black hole list, use the dnsbl feature:

```
FEATURE(`dnsbl', `sbl-xbl.spamhaus.org')
```

This feature makes **sendmail** reject mail from any site whose IP address is in the Spamhaus Block List of known spammers maintained at sbl-xbl.spamhaus.org. Other lists catalog sites that run open relays and known blocks of dial-up addresses that are likely to be a haven for spammers.

These blacklists are distributed through a clever tweak of the DNS system; hence the name dnsbl. For example, a special DNS resource record of the form

```
IP-address.sbl-xbl.spamhaus.org  IN  A  127.0.0.2
```

put into the DNS database of the sbl-xbl.spamhaus.org domain would block mail from that host if the dnsbl feature was enabled (because **sendmail** would check explicitly to see if such a record existed). The *IP-address* in this example is a host address in its dotted quad form with the order of the octets reversed.

You can include the dnsbl feature several times to check different lists of abusers: just add a second argument to specify the blacklist name server and a third argument with the error message that you would like returned. If the third argument is omitted, a fixed error message from the DNS database containing the records is returned.

Header checking

Spammers often try to hide their identities. Since **sendmail** 8.9, if the envelope From address is not of the form *user@valid.domain*, mail is rejected. You can waive this behavior with the following features:

```
FEATURE(`accept_unresolvable_domains')
FEATURE(`accept_unqualified_senders')
```

With the first feature, **sendmail** accepts mail from domains that do not exist or do not resolve in the DNS naming tree. With the second, **sendmail** accepts From addresses that contain only a user name with no host or domain portion. Don't use either of these features unless you are behind a firewall and have only local DNS data available there. If you find yourself wanting to turn these features on, you should probably think about redesigning your **sendmail** and DNS environments instead. Requiring a valid envelope sender address reduces spam significantly.

Detailed header checking is a powerful spam-fighting mechanism that makes use of the low-level **sendmail** configuration file syntax, which we do not cover here. By using header checking, **sendmail** can look for specified patterns in headers (e.g., "To: friend@public.com") and reject messages before they are delivered to your users' mailboxes.

Header checking can also recognize viruses carried by email if they have a distinctive header line. For example, the Melissa virus of 1999 contained the subject line "Important Message From …". Within hours of the Melissa virus being released and recognized, sendmail.com posted a local ruleset to identify it and discard it.

When the fingerprint of a virus is distinctive and easy to express in **sendmail** rules, sendmail.com will quickly post a fix for it at both sendmail.com and sendmail.org.

For a representative sample of filtering rules for spam and viruses, see the **sendmail** configuration for Eric Allman's home machine, knecht. This configuration is included in the **sendmail** distribution as **cf/cf/knecht.mc**. Steal the spam-filtering rules and add them to the end of your **.mc** file.

In looking at various examples, we have seen header checking rules for

- Mail addressed to any user in the domain public.com
- Mail addressed to "friend" or "you"

- Mail with the X-Spanska header, which indicates the Happy99 worm
- Mail with subject "Important Message From …" (the Melissa virus)
- Mail with subject "all.net and Fred Cohen …" (the Papa virus)
- Mail with subject "ILOVEYOU" (the iloveyou virus and variants)
- Zillions of marketing hype spam messages
- Mail with a broken Outlook Express header (the SirCam worm)

All the header checking rules go under LOCAL_CONFIG and LOCAL_RULESETS statements at the end of the **.mc** configuration file. With the help of **m4**'s divert command, **sendmail** just knows where to put them in the raw config file.

To some degree, any spam abatement that you implement blocks some spammers but raises the bar for the remaining ones. Use the error mailer with a "user unknown" error message instead of the discard mailer, because many spammers clean up their lists. Clean lists are more valuable, so you might get removed from some if you can intercept the spam, filter it, and respond with an error message.

Rate and connection limits

sendmail 8.13 added a ratecontrol feature that sets per-host or per-net limits on the rate at which incoming connections are accepted. This restriction can be particularly useful for slowing down spam from sources that can't be completely blocked without causing problems, such as large ISPs that have a high percentage of dial-up users. To enable rate controls, put a line like this one in the **.mc** file:

```
FEATURE(`ratecontrol', `nodelay',`terminate')
```

In addition, you must also list the hosts or nets to be controlled and their restriction thresholds in your **/etc/mail/access** file. For example, the lines

```
ClientRate:192.168.6.17  2
ClientRate:170.65.3.4    10
```

limit the hosts 192.168.6.17 and 170.65.3.4 to two new connections per minute and ten new connections per minute, respectively.

The conncontrol feature places similar restrictions on the number of simultaneous connections. You enable this feature in the **.mc** file with the following line:

```
FEATURE(`conncontrol', `no delay',`terminate')
```

As with ratecontrol, you specify which hosts and nets to limit in /etc/mail/access:

```
ClientConn:192.168.2.8 2
ClientConn:175.14.4.1  7
ClientConn:          10
```

This configuration results in limits of two simultaneous connections for 192.168.2.8, seven simultaneous connections for 175.14.4.1, and ten simultaneous connections for all other hosts.

Slamming

Another nifty feature introduced in 8.13 is greet_pause. When a remote MTA connects to your **sendmail** server, the SMTP protocol mandates that it wait for your server's welcome greeting before speaking. However, it's common for spam mailers (and worms/viruses) to blurt out an EHLO/HELO command immediately. This behavior is partially explainable as poor implementation of the SMTP protocol in spam-sending tools, but it may also be a feature that aims to save time on the spammer's behalf. Whatever the true cause, this behavior is suspicious and is known as "slamming."

The greet_pause feature makes **sendmail** wait for a specified period of time at the beginning of the connection before greeting its newfound friend. If the remote MTA does not wait to be properly greeted and proceeds with an EHLO or HELO command during the planned awkward moment, **sendmail** logs an error and refuses subsequent commands from the remote MTA.

You can enable greet pause with this entry in the **.mc** file:

```
FEATURE(`greet_pause', `700')
```

This line causes a 700 millisecond delay at the beginning of every new connection. It is possible to set per-host or per-net delays similar to conncontrol and ratecontrol, but most sites use a blanket value for this feature.

Miltering: mail filtering

sendmail version 8.12 introduced a generalization of header filtering that could develop into a most effective spam-fighting tool. It is a mail filtering API (application programming interface) that folks can use to develop their own mail filtering programs. These filtering programs sit between **sendmail** and incoming messages and can recognize the profile of a virus or spam message and discard or log it (or take whatever other action you feel is appropriate). Both metadata and message content can be targeted.

Miltering is potentially a powerful tool both for fighting spam and for violating users' privacy. Managers who want to know exactly what information is leaving the company by email may be early adopters. Miltering for outgoing mail is not available in 8.12, but it is on the to-do list.

The miltering library is called **libmilter. sendmail** invokes input filtering with the INPUT_MAIL_FILTER or MAIL_FILTER configuration directives and controls the miltering action with options named MILTER_MACROS_* that allow fine-grained control over the filters applied at each stage of the SMTP conversation.

For example, the line

```
INPUT_MAIL_FILTER(`filtername', `S=mailer:/var/run/filtername.socket')
```

passes each incoming message to the **/etc/mail/filtername** program through the socket specified in the second argument.

For more information, see **libmilter/README** or the HTML documentation in the **libmilter/docs** directory of the **sendmail** distribution. The **README** file gives an overview and simple example of a filter that logs messages to a file. The files in the **docs** describe the library interface and tell how to use the various calls to build your own mail filtering programs.

Spam handling

Fighting spam can be a difficult and frustrating job. Past a certain point, it's also quite futile. Don't be seduced into chasing down individual spammers, even though lots will get through your anti-spam shields. Time spent analyzing spam headers and fretting about spammers is wasted time. Yes, it's fighting the good fight, but time spent on these issues will probably not reduce the amount of spam coming into your site.

You can nail stationary spammers pretty quickly by ratting them out to their ISP, but hit-and-run spammers that use an ISP account once and then abandon it are hard to hold accountable. If they advertise a web site, then the web site is responsible; if it's a telephone number or postal address, it's harder to identify the perpetrator, but not impossible. Mobile spammers seem to be essentially immune from punishment.

The various black hole lists have been somewhat effective at blocking spam and have dramatically reduced the number of open relays. Being blacklisted can seriously impact business, so some ISPs and companies are careful to police their users.

Our main recommendation regarding spam is that you use the preventive measures and publicly maintained blacklists that are available. Another possibility is to redirect your incoming email to an outsourced spam fighting company such as Postini (www.postini.com). However, this option may entail some compromises in performance, privacy, or reliability.

Advise your users to simply delete the spam they receive. Many spam messages contain instructions on how recipients can be removed from the mailing list. If you follow those instructions, the spammers may remove you from the current list, but they immediately add you to several other lists with the annotation "reaches a real human who reads the message." Your email address is then worth even more.

If you'd like to take a seat on the spam-fighting bandwagon, some web sites can help. One good site is www.abuse.net. Two others of note are spamcop.net and cauce.org. SpamCop has tools that help parse mail headers and determine the real sender. The cauce.org site has good information on spam laws. In the United States you may be able to get the Federal Trade Commission to help. Visit them at www.ftc.gov/spam.

SpamAssassin

SpamAssassin is a filter (which can be invoked through a **sendmail** milter) that is very effective at identifying spam. It uses a point system for evaluating a message's sins. It catches essentially all the real spam and rarely has false positives. If a message accumulates too many points (configurable on both a site-wide and per-user basis), SpamAssassin tags the message. You can then refile suspicious messages in a spam folder, either by running a server-side filter such as Cyrus's **sieve** or by configuring your user agent. You can even teach SpamAssassin about good and bad messages. Be sure to scrutinize all the spam carefully as you are setting up SpamAssassin and tuning its parameters. Check it out at spamassassin.apache.org.

SPF and Sender ID

The best way to fight spam is to stop it at its source. This sounds simple and easy, but in reality it's almost an impossible challenge. The structure of the Internet makes it difficult to track the real source of a message and verify its authenticity. The community needs a sure-fire way to verify that the entity sending an email is really who or what it claims to be.

Many proposals have addressed this problem, but SPF and Sender ID have achieved the most traction. SPF or Sender Policy Framework is now standardized by the IETF (RFC4408). It defines a set of DNS TXT records (see page 403) by which an organization can identify its "official" outbound mail relays. MTAs can then refuse any email from that organization's domain if the email does not originate from these official sources. Of course, this only works well if the majority of organizations publish SPF records. Several milters available for download implement this functionality in **sendmail**.

Sender ID and SPF are virtually identical in form and function. However, key parts of Sender ID are patented by Microsoft, and hence it has been the subject of much controversy. As of this writing, Microsoft is still trying to strong-arm the industry into adopting its proprietary standards.

18.11 CONFIGURATION FILE CASE STUDY

As a case study of how **sendmail** is configured in the real world, this section reviews the config files for a small but **sendmail**-savvy company, Sendmail, Inc. Their mail design includes a master mail hub machine for both incoming mail and outgoing mail. All incoming mail is accepted and immediately routed to a set of internal IMAP servers that check each message for viruses before delivering it to a user's mailbox. The mail hub machine also checks each outgoing message for viruses so that Sendmail, Inc. is never responsible for spreading viruses by email. We look at the clients' configuration first, then inspect the more complicated master machines.

In the examples, we have modified the originals slightly, leaving out the copyright notices, adding occasional comments, and removing the **m4** dnl directive at the ends of lines. If you use any of these examples as a model for your **.mc** file, be sure to remove the comments from the ends of lines.

Client machines at sendmail.com

The **smi-client.mc** file for client machines is quite simple. It uses the master machine smtp.sendmail.com, which is really just another name for foon.sendmail.com. Using an MX record (or a CNAME[31]) to point to the mail server is a good idea; it's easy to change when you want to move your master mail machine.

Note that the date on this file is October 1998. **sendmail** has been upgraded many times since then, but the configuration file did not need to change.

```
divert(-1)
#####  This file contains definitions for a Sendmail,
#####  Inc. client machine's .mc file.
divert(0)
VERSIONID(`@(#)smi-client.mc 1.0 (Sendmail) 10/14/98')
OSTYPE(`bsd4.4')
FEATURE(`nocanonify')
undefine(`ALIAS_FILE')
define(`MAIL_HUB', `smtp.sendmail.com')
define(`SMART_HOST', `smtp.sendmail.com')
define(`confFORWARD_PATH', `')
MAILER(`local')
MAILER(`smtp')
```

The MAIL_HUB and SMART_HOST lines direct incoming and outgoing mail to the host smtp.sendmail.com. MX records in DNS should cooperate and list that host with higher priority (lower number in MX record) than the individual client machines. The path for **.forward** files is set to null, and the alias file is also set to null; all alias expansion occurs on the master machine. The nocanonify feature is specified here to save time, since DNS lookups are done on the master anyway.

Master machine at sendmail.com

The master machine at sendmail.com may be one of the most attacked **sendmail** installations around. It must be secure from all the twisty mailer attacks that people come up with and must protect the machines behind it. Here is its configuration file:

```
divert(-1)
# Created with Sendmail Switch, sendmail.com's commercial product.
divert(0)
ifdef(`COMMERCIAL_CONFIG', `INPUT_MAIL_FILTER(`mime-filter', `S=local:
    /var/run/mime-filter/mime-filter.sock')')
LDAPROUTE_DOMAIN(`sendmail.com sendmail.net sendmail.org')
MASQUERADE_AS(`sendmail.com')
MASQUERADE_DOMAIN(`sendmail.com')
RELAY_DOMAIN(`sendmail.com sendmail.net sendmail.org')
define(`MAIL_HUB', `internal-hub.sendmail.com')
define(`QUEUE_DIR', `/var/spool/mqueue/q*')
define(`SMART_HOST', `virus-scan.sendmail.com')
ifdef(`COMMERCIAL_CONFIG', `define(`confCACERT', `/local/certs/cacert.pem')')
ifdef(`COMMERCIAL_CONFIG', `define(`confCACERT_PATH', `/local/certs/trustedcerts')')
define(`confCHECK_ALIASES', `True')
ifdef(`COMMERCIAL_CONFIG', `define(`confCLIENT_CERT', `/local/certs/cert.pem')')
```

---

31. An MX record is actually more efficient than a CNAME; CNAMEs require a second lookup on the real name to get the IP address.

```
ifdef(`COMMERCIAL_CONFIG', `define(`confCLIENT_KEY', `/local/certs/key.pem')')
define(`confEIGHT_BIT_HANDLING', `mimify')
define(`confLDAP_DEFAULT_SPEC', ` -h "ldap.sendmail.com ldap2.sendmail.com"
    -b "dc=sendmail,dc=com" -p 1389')
define(`confREFUSE_LA', `99')
define(`confRUN_AS_USER', `mailnull')
ifdef(`COMMERCIAL_CONFIG', `define(`confSERVER_CERT', `/local/certs/cert.pem')')
ifdef(`COMMERCIAL_CONFIG', `define(`confSERVER_KEY', `/local/certs/key.pem')')
define(`confTO_IDENT', `0s')
define(`confTO_QUEUEWARN', `2d')
ifdef(`confPOP_TO', `', `define(`confPOP_TO', `900')')
FEATURE(`accept_unqualified_senders')
FEATURE(`accept_unresolvable_domains')
FEATURE(`allmasquerade')
FEATURE(`always_add_domain')
FEATURE(`domaintable')
FEATURE(`ldap_routing', `ldap -1 -v mailHost -k ldap -1 -v mailhost -k
    (&(objectclass=mailRecipient)(|(mail=%0)(|(mailAlternateAddress=%0))))',
    `ldap -1 -v mail -k
    (&(objectclass=mailRecipient)(|(mailalternateaddress=%0)))', `passthru')
FEATURE(`mailertable')
FEATURE(`masquerade_entire_domain')
FEATURE(`masquerade_envelope')
FEATURE(`relay_entire_domain')
FEATURE(`use_cw_file')
MAILER(`local')
MAILER(`smtp')

LOCAL_RULESETS
SLocal_check_rcpt
R$*     $: $&{verify}
ROK     $# OK
```

The master machine routes incoming mail to the correct internal server and serves as the smart relay host for outgoing mail. Because of the following two lines,

```
FEATURE(`accept_unqualified_senders')
FEATURE(`accept_unresolvable_domains')
```

all incoming mail is accepted, even mail from unqualified senders and unresolvable domains. This way, potential customers who have **sendmail** or DNS misconfigured can still get through. These rules undo the defaults that catch lots of spam with forged headers. Ident is turned off (timeout set to 0) to speed up delivery of incoming mail.

This master mail machine first checks incoming messages for certain types of MIME attachments that are frequently used by viruses (INPUT_MAIL_FILTER statement). The **mime-filter** called there contains lines such as

```
*:anniv.doc:* error:Your email was not accepted by Sendmail, it appears to be
    infected with the Melissa-X virus.
*:.vbs:*       error:For security and virus protection reasons, Sendmail does
    not accept messages with VBS files attached.  Please retransmit your
    message without the VBS file.
```

MIME attachments of type **.vba**, **.dot**, **.exe**, **.com**, **.reg**, and so on are rejected, but a full virus scan is not done here because it would slow the processing of incoming mail. The master uses LDAP (with a site-specific schema) to look up the recipient of each message and route it to the correct internal IMAP/POP server. If the recipient is not found in the LDAP database, the mail is sent to an internal master machine (the MAIL_HUB statement) for further processing. Both the IMAP/POP servers and the internal master machine do full virus scanning before delivering a message to a user's mailbox.

Outgoing mail is also routed through this master machine by SMART_HOST statements on the client machines. To send a message through the sendmail.com mail servers, hosts outside the sendmail.com domain must present a certificate signed by the sendmail.com certificate authority. Employees visiting a customer site can relay email to a third party through sendmail.com with this mechanism, but others cannot. This convention authenticates each user and prevents forged email from transiting sendmail.com.

After accepting email destined for the Internet, the master machine passes it to the SMART_HOST for virus scanning. The master mail machine is not too busy to do this virus scanning itself, but if the scanning were done there, users sending mail would have to wait for the scanning to complete before their message was really sent. Queueing it for the virus-scanning machine keeps the users happy—their messages seem to zip off instantaneously.

The LOCAL_CONFIG rules at the end of the config file are where header checking for various viruses and known spammers is usually put. Good examples can be found in the **knecht.mc** example file in the **sendmail** distribution. We have included a sample below.

*See page 597 for more details about **libmilter**.* During the summer of 2001, the destructive SirCam worm was circulating wildly. The following fragment from the **knecht.mc** file in the **sendmail** distribution catches it. SirCam is one of the first nastygrams to have random headers. The usual tools to catch it would have failed, except that its authors made an error that differentiates a SirCam message from a real Outlook Express message. The message's content is quite regular (it asks for your advice on the enclosed attachment) and would therefore be a candidate for the new **libmilter** filtering abilities in version 8.12. Without product liability guarantees in the software world, it seems the only solution to all these Microsoft viruses and worms is to dump Windows and install Linux everywhere!

```
LOCAL_RULESETS

KSirCamWormMarker regex -f -aSUSPECT multipart/mixed;boundary=----
    .+_Outlook_Express_message_boundary
HContent-Type: $>CheckContentType

SCheckContentType
R$+             $: $(SirCamWormMarker $1 $)
RSUSPECT        $#error $: "553 Possible virus, see http:
    //www.symantec.com/avcenter/venc/data/w32.sircam.worm@mm.html"
```

```
HContent-Disposition:$>CheckContentDisposition

SCheckContentDisposition
R$-                   $@ OK
R$- ; $+              $@ OK
R$*                   $#error $: "553 Illegal Content-Disposition"
```

Clients at sendmail.com have no spam control in their config files. The reason is that all mail coming into the site comes through the external mail hub and an internal hub and the spam is winnowed there. Some of the features and other constructs in this example are not covered in our configuration section, but you can find documentation on them in the **cf/README** file.

18.12 SECURITY AND SENDMAIL

With the explosive growth of the Internet, programs such as **sendmail** that accept arbitrary user-supplied input and deliver it to local users, files, or shells have frequently provided an avenue of attack for hackers. **sendmail**, along with DNS and even IP, is flirting with authentication and encryption as a built-in solution to some of these fundamental security issues.

Recent softening of the export laws of the United States regarding encryption freed **sendmail** to be shipped with built-in hooks for encryption. Versions 8.11 and later support both SMTP authentication and encryption with TLS, Transport Layer Security (previously known as SSL, the Secure Socket Layer). **sendmail** uses the term TLS in this context and has implemented it as an extension, STARTTLS, to the SMTP protocol. TLS brought with it six new configuration options for certificate files and key files. New actions for access database matches can require that authentication must have succeeded.

In this section, we describe the evolution of **sendmail**'s permissions model, ownerships, and privacy protection. We then briefly discuss TLS and SASL (the Simple Authentication and Security Layer) and their use with **sendmail**.

sendmail has gradually tightened up its security over time, and it is now very picky about file permissions before it believes the contents of, say, a **.forward** or **aliases** file. Although this tightening of security has generally been welcome, it's sometimes necessary to relax the tough new policies. To this end, **sendmail** introduced the DontBlameSendmail option, so named in hopes that the name will suggest to sysadmins that what they are doing is considered unsafe.

This option has many possible values—55 at last count. The default is safe. For a complete list of values, see **doc/op/op.ps** in the **sendmail** distribution. The values are not listed in the second edition of the O'Reilly **sendmail** book, but will surely be in the third. Or just leave the option set to safe.

Ownerships

Three user accounts are important in the **sendmail** universe: the DefaultUser, the TrustedUser, and the RunAsUser.

By default, all of **sendmail**'s mailers run as the DefaultUser unless the mailer's flags specify otherwise. If a user mailnull, sendmail, or daemon exists in the **/etc/passwd** file, DefaultUser will be that. Otherwise, it defaults to UID 1 and GID 1. We recommend the use of the mailnull account and a mailnull group. Add it to **/etc/passwd** with a star as the password, no valid shell, no home directory, and a default group of mailnull. You'll have to add the mailnull entry to the **/etc/group** file too. The mailnull account should not own any files. If **sendmail** is not running as root, the mailers must be setuid.

If RunAsUser is set, **sendmail** ignores the value of DefaultUser and does everything as RunAsUser. If you are running **sendmail** setgid (to smmsp), then the submission **sendmail** just passes messages to the real **sendmail** through SMTP. The real **sendmail** does not have its setuid bit set, but it runs as root from the startup files.

sendmail's TrustedUser can own maps and alias files. The TrustedUser is allowed to start the daemon or rebuild the **aliases** file. This facility exists mostly to support GUI interfaces to **sendmail** that need to provide limited administrative control to certain users. If you set TrustedUser, be sure to guard the account that it points to, because this account can easily be exploited to gain root access. The TrustedUser is different from the TRUSTED_USERS class, which determines who can rewrite the From line of messages.[32]

The RunAsUser is the UID that **sendmail** runs under after opening its socket connection to port 25. Ports numbered less than 1,024 can be opened only by the superuser; therefore, **sendmail** must initially run as root. However, after performing this operation, **sendmail** can switch to a different UID. Such a switch reduces the risk of damage or access if **sendmail** is tricked into doing something bad. Don't use the RunAsUser feature on machines that support user accounts or other services; it is meant for use on firewalls or bastion hosts only.

By default, **sendmail** does not switch identities and continues to run as root. If you change the RunAsUser to something other than root, you must change several other things as well. The RunAsUser must own the mail queue, be able to read all maps and include files, be able to run programs, etc. Expect to spend a few hours finding all the file and directory ownerships that must be changed.

Permissions

File and directory permissions are important to **sendmail** security. Use the settings listed in Table 18.14 to be safe.

sendmail does not read files that have lax permissions (for example, files that are group- or world-writable or that live in group- or world-writable directories). Some of **sendmail**'s rigor with regard to ownerships and permissions was motivated by

---

32. The TRUSTED_USERS feature is typically used to support mailing list software. For example, if you use Majordomo, you must add the "majordom" user to the TRUSTED_USERS class. The users root and daemon are the default members of the class.

Table 18.14   Owner and permissions for sendmail-related directories

Path	Owner	Mode	What it contains
/var/spool/clientmqueue	smmsp	770	Mail queue for initial submissions[a]
/var/spool/mqueue	RunAsUser	700	Mail queue directory
/, /var, /var/spool	root	755	Path to **mqueue**
/etc/mail/*	TrustedUser	644	Maps, the config file, aliases
/etc/mail	TrustedUser	755	Parent directory for maps
/etc	root	755	Path to **mail** directory

a. Version 8.12 and later

operating systems that let users give their files away with **chown** (those derived from System V, mostly).

Linux systems by default have a sane version of **chown** and do not allow file give-aways. However, an #ifdef in the code (CAP_CHOWN) can be set to give System V semantics to **chown**. You would then have to rebuild the kernel. But this behavior is evil; don't coerce your sensible Linux **chown** to behave in the broken System V way.

In particular, **sendmail** is *very* picky about the complete path to any alias file or forward file. This pickiness sometimes clashes with the way sites like to manage Majordomo mailing list aliases. If the Majordomo list is in **/usr/local**, for example, the entire path must be trusted; no component can have group write permission. This constraint makes it more difficult for the list owner to manage the alias file. To see where you stand with respect to **sendmail**'s ideas about permissions, run

```
# sendmail -v -bi
```

The **-bi** flag initializes the alias database and warns you of inappropriate permissions.

sendmail no longer reads a **.forward** file that has a link count greater than 1 if the directory path to it is unsafe (has lax permissions). This rule recently bit Evi when her **.forward** file, which was typically a hard link to either **.forward.to.boulder** or **.forward.to.sandiego**, silently failed to forward her mail from a small site at which she did not receive much mail. It was months before she realized that "I never got your mail" was her own fault and not a valid excuse.

You can turn off many of the restrictive file access policies mentioned above with the DontBlameSendmail option. But don't do that.

Safer mail to files and programs

We recommend that you use **smrsh** instead of **/bin/sh** as your program mailer and that you use **mail.local** instead of **/bin/mail** as your local mailer. Both programs are included in the **sendmail** distribution. To incorporate them into your configuration, add the lines

```
FEATURE(`smrsh', `path-to-smrsh')
FEATURE(`local_lmtp', `path-to-mail.local')
```

to your **.mc** file. If you omit the explicit paths, the commands are assumed to live in **/usr/libexec**. You can use **sendmail**'s confEBINDIR option to change the default location of the binaries to whatever you want. Red Hat's default installation does not include **mail.local** at all. SUSE puts it in **/usr/lib/sendmail.d/bin**, and Debian and Ubuntu put it in **/usr/lib/sm.bin**.

smrsh is a restricted shell that executes only the programs contained in one directory (**/usr/adm/sm.bin** by default). Red Hat and Fedora install the **smrsh** binary in **/usr/sbin**, SUSE puts it in **/usr/lib/sendmail.d/bin**, and Debian and Ubuntu put it in **/usr/lib/sm.bin**. smrsh ignores user-specified paths and tries to find any requested commands in its own known-safe directory. **smrsh** also blocks the use of certain shell metacharacters such as "<", the input redirection symbol. Symbolic links are allowed in **sm.bin**, so you don't need to make duplicate copies of the programs you allow.[33]

Here are some example shell commands and their possible **smrsh** interpretations:

```
vacation eric              # executes /usr/adm/sm.bin/vacation eric
cat /etc/passwd            # rejected, cat not in sm.bin
vacation eric < /etc/passwd  # rejected, no < allowed
```

sendmail's SafeFileEnvironment option controls where files can be written when email is redirected to a file by an **aliases** or a **.forward** file. It causes **sendmail** to execute a **chroot** system call, making the root of the filesystem no longer **/** but rather **/safe** or whatever path you specified in the SafeFileEnvironment option. An alias that directed mail into the **/etc/passwd** file, for example, would really be written to **/safe/etc/passwd**.

The SafeFileEnvironment option also protects device files, directories, and other special files by allowing writes only to regular files. Besides increasing security, this option ameliorates the effects of user mistakes. Some sites set the option to **/home** to allow access to home directories while keeping system files off-limits.

Mailers can also be run in a **chroot**ed directory. This option must be specified in the mailer definition at the moment, but it should soon be configurable with **m4**.

Privacy options

sendmail also has privacy options that control

- What external folks can determine about your site from SMTP
- What you require of the host on the other end of an SMTP connection
- Whether your users can see or run the mail queue

Table 18.15 lists the possible values for the privacy options as of this writing; see the file **doc/op/op.ps** in the distribution for current information.

---

33. Don't put programs such as **procmail** that can spawn a shell in **sm.bin**. And don't use **procmail** as the local mailer, because users can run any program they want from their ~/**.procmailrc** file. It's not secure.

Table 18.15 Values of the PrivacyOption variable

Value	Meaning
public	Does no privacy/security checking
needmailhelo	Requires SMTP HELO (identifies remote host)
noexpn	Disallows the SMTP EXPN command
novrfy	Disallows the SMTP VRFY command
needexpnhelo	Does not expand addresses (EXPN) without a HELO
needvrfyhelo	Does not verify addresses (VRFY) without a HELO
noverb[a]	Disallows verbose mode for EXPN
restrictmailq	Allows only **mqueue** directory's group to see the queue
restrictqrun	Allows only **mqueue** directory's owner to run the queue
restrictexpand	Restricts info displayed by the **-bv** and **-v** flags[b]
noetrn[c]	Disallows asynchronous queue runs
authwarnings	Adds Authentication-Warning header (this is the default)
noreceipts	Turns off delivery status notification for success return receipts
nobodyreturn	Does not return message body in a DSN
goaway	Disables all SMTP status queries (EXPN, VRFY, etc.)

a. Verbose mode follows **.forward** files when an EXPN command is given and reports more information on the whereabouts of a user's mail. Use noverb or, better yet, noexpn on any machine exposed to the outside world.

b. Unless executed by root or the TrustedUser.

c. ETRN is an ESMTP command for use by a dial-up host. It requests that the queue be run just for messages to that host.

We recommend conservatism; use

```
define(`confPRIVACY_OPTIONS', ``goaway, authwarnings, restrictmailq,
    restrictqrun")
```

in your **.mc** file. **sendmail**'s default value for the privacy options is authwarnings; the line above would reset that value. Notice the double sets of quotes; some versions of **m4** require them to protect the commas in the list of privacy option values. Red Hat and Fedora default to authwarnings, and SUSE, Debian, and Ubuntu default to authwarnings, needmailhelo, novrfy, noexpn, and noverb.

Running a chrooted sendmail (for the truly paranoid)

If you are worried about the access that **sendmail** has to your filesystem, you can start it in a **chroot**ed jail. Make a minimal filesystem in your jail, including things like **/dev/null**, **/etc** essentials (**passwd**, **group**, **resolv.conf**, **sendmail.cf**, any map files, **mail/***), the shared libraries that **sendmail** needs, the **sendmail** binary, the mail queue directory, and any log files. You will probably have to fiddle with the list to get it just right. Use the **chroot** command to start a jailed **sendmail**. For example:

```
# chroot /jail /usr/sbin/sendmail -bd -q30m
```

Denial of service attacks

Denial of service attacks are difficult to prevent because there is no a priori way to determine that a message is an attack rather than a valid piece of email. Attackers can try various nasty things, including flooding the SMTP port with bogus connections, filling disk partitions with giant messages, clogging outgoing connections, and mail bombing. **sendmail** has some configuration parameters that can help slow down or limit the impact of a denial of service attack, but these parameters can also interfere with legitimate mail. The mail filtering library (milter) may help sysadmins thwart a prolonged denial of service attack.

The MaxDaemonChildren option limits the number of **sendmail** processes. It prevents the system from being overwhelmed with **sendmail** work, but it also allows an attacker to easily shut down SMTP service. The MaxMessageSize option can help prevent the mail queue directory from filling, but if you set it too low, legitimate mail will bounce. (You might mention your limit to users so that they aren't surprised when their mail bounces. We recommend a fairly high limit anyway, since some legitimate mail is huge.) The ConnectionRateThrottle option, which limits the number of permitted connections per second, can slow things down a bit. And finally, setting MaxRcptsPerMessage, which controls the maximum number of recipients allowed on a single message, might help.

sendmail has always been able to refuse connections (option REFUSE_LA) or queue email (QUEUE_LA) according to the system load average. A variation, DELAY_LA, introduced in 8.12 keeps the mail flowing, but at a reduced rate. See page 613 in the performance section for details.

In spite of all these knobs to turn to protect your mail system, someone mail bombing you will still interfere with legitimate mail. Mail bombing can be quite nasty.

The University of Colorado gives each student (~25,000) an email account with **pine** as the default mail reader. A few years ago, a student with a new job at a local computer store was convinced to give his employer a copy of the password file. The company then sent an advertisement to everyone in the password file, in batches of about 1,000 recipients at a time (which made for a very long To: line).

pine had been compiled with the default reply mode set to reply to all recipients as well as the sender. Many students replied with questions such as, "Why did you send me this junk?", and of course it went to everyone else on the To: line. The result was total denial of service on the server—for email or any other use. **sendmail** took over all the CPU cycles, the mail queue was enormous, and all useful work ground to a halt. The only solution seemed to be to take the machine off-line, go into the mail queues and every user's mailbox, and remove the offending messages. (A header check on the Subject line could have been used as well.)

Forgeries

Forging email has in the past been trivial. In the old days, any user could forge mail to appear as though it came from someone else's domain. Starting with **sendmail**

8.10, SMTP authentication was instituted to verify the identity of the sending machine. Authentication checking must be turned on with the AuthMechanisms option. Unfortunately, **sendmail** authentication is not end-to-end but just between adjacent servers. If a message is handled by several servers, the authentication helps but cannot guarantee that the message was not forged.

Likewise, any user can be impersonated in mail messages. Be careful if mail messages are your organization's authorization vehicle for things like keys, access cards, and money. You should warn administrative users of this fact and suggest that if they see suspicious mail that appears to come from a person in authority, they should verify the validity of the message. This is doubly true if the message asks that unreasonable privileges be given to an unusual person. Mail authorizing a grand master key for an undergraduate student might be suspect!

The authwarnings privacy option flags local attempts at forgery by adding an Authentication-Warning header to outgoing mail that appears to be forged. However, many user agents hide this header by default.

If forged mail is coming from a machine that you control, you can actually do quite a bit to thwart it. You can use the **identd** daemon to verify a sender's real login name. **sendmail** does a callback to the sending host to ask the **identd** running there for the login name of the user sending the mail. If **identd** is not running on the remote host, **sendmail** learns nothing. If the remote machine is a single-user workstation, its owner could configure **identd** to return a bogus answer. But if the remote host is a multiuser machine such as that found at many university computing centers, **identd** returns the user's real login name for **sendmail** to put in the message's header.

Many sites do not run **identd**; it's often blocked by firewalls. **identd** is only really useful within a site, since machines you don't control can lie. At a large site with somewhat irresponsible users (e.g., a university), it's great—but also a performance hit for **sendmail**.

Several years ago, when we were first experimenting with **identd**, a student at our site became frustrated with the members of his senior project team. He tried to send mail to his teammates as his instructor, telling them he knew that they were not pulling their weight and that they should work harder. Unfortunately, he made a syntax error and the message bounced to the instructor. **sendmail**'s use of the IDENT protocol told us who he was. **sendmail** included the following lines in the bounced message:

    The original message was received at Wed, 9 Mar 1994 14:51 -0700 from
        student@benji.Colorado.EDU [128.138.126.10]

But the headers of the message itself told a different story:

    From: instructor@cs.Colorado.EDU

Moral: avoid syntax errors when sneaking around. Our policy on forging mail caused the student's login to be disabled for the rest of the semester, which actually accomplished exactly what the student wanted. He was unable to work on the project and his partners had to pick up the slack.

Message privacy

See page 696 for more information about PGP.

Message privacy basically does not exist unless you use an external encryption package such as Pretty Good Privacy (PGP) or S/MIME. By default, all mail is sent unencrypted. End-to-end encryption requires support from mail user agents.

Both S/MIME and PGP are documented in the RFC series, with S/MIME being on the standards track. However, we prefer PGP; it's more widely available and was designed by an excellent cryptographer, Phil Zimmermann, whom we trust. These emerging standards offer a basis for email confidentiality, authentication, message integrity assurance, and nonrepudiation of origin. Traffic analysis is still possible since the headers and envelope are sent as plaintext.

Tell your users that they must do their own encryption if they want their mail to be private.

SASL: the Simple Authentication and Security Layer

sendmail 8.10 and later support the SMTP authentication defined in RFC2554. It's based on SASL, the Simple Authentication and Security Layer (RFC2222). SASL is a shared secret system that is typically host-to-host; you must make explicit arrangements for each pair of servers that are to mutually authenticate.

SASL is a generic authentication mechanism that can be integrated into a variety of protocols. So far, **sendmail**, Cyrus's **imapd**, Outlook, Thunderbird, and some versions of Eudora use it. The SASL framework (it's a library) has two fundamental concepts: an authorization identifier and an authentication identifier. It can map these to permissions on files, account passwords, Kerberos tickets, etc. SASL contains both an authentication part and an encryption component. To use SASL with **sendmail**, get Cyrus SASL from asg.web.cmu.edu/sasl.

TLS, another encryption/authentication system, is specified in RFC2487. It is implemented in **sendmail** as an extension to SMTP called STARTTLS. You can even use both SASL and TLS.

TLS is a bit harder to set up and requires a certificate authority. You can pay VeriSign big bucks to issue you certificates (signed public keys identifying an entity) or set up your own certificate authority. Strong authentication is used in place of a hostname or IP address as the authorization token for relaying mail or for accepting a connection from a host in the first place. An entry such as

```
TLS_Srv:secure.example.com      ENCR:112
TLS_Clt:laptop.example.com      PERM+VERIFY:112
```

in the access_db indicates that STARTTLS is in use and that email to the domain secure.example.com must be encrypted with at least 112-bit encryption keys. Email from a host in the laptop.example.com domain should be accepted only if the client has authenticated itself.

Gregory Shapiro, also of Sendmail, Inc., has created some nifty tutorials about security and **sendmail**, available from www.sendmail.org/~gshapiro.

18.13 SENDMAIL PERFORMANCE

sendmail has several configuration options that improve performance. Although we have scattered them throughout the chapter, we try to expand on the most important ones in this section. These are options and features you should consider if you run a high-volume mail system (in either direction). Actually, if you really need to send 1,000,000 mail messages an hour and you aren't a spammer, your best bet might be to use the commercial side of **sendmail**, Sendmail, Inc.

Delivery modes

sendmail has four basic delivery modes: background, interactive, queue, and defer. Each represents a tradeoff between latency and throughput. Background mode delivers the mail immediately but requires **sendmail** to fork a new process to do it. Interactive mode also delivers immediately, but delivery is done by the same process and makes the remote side wait for the results. Queue mode queues incoming mail for delivery by a queue runner at some later time. Defer mode is similar to queue mode, but it also defers all map, DNS, alias, and forwarding lookups. Interactive mode is rarely used. Background mode favors lower latency, and defer or queueing mode favors higher throughput. The delivery mode is set with the option confDELIVERY_MODE and defaults to background.

Queue groups and envelope splitting

Queue groups are a new feature of **sendmail** 8.12; they enable you to create multiple queues for outgoing mail and to control the attributes of each queue group individually. Queue groups can contain a single queue directory or several directories. For example, if your Linux box is the mail hub for an ISP, you might define a queue group for your dial-up users and then permit them to initiate a queue run (using the SMTP command ETRN) when they connect to download their email. Queue groups are used with an envelope-splitting feature with which an envelope with many recipients can be split across queue groups. This feature and the use of multiple queue directories per queue group ameliorate performance problems caused by having too many files in a single filesystem directory.[34]

When a message enters the mail system, it is assigned to one or more queue groups. The queue group for each recipient is determined independently. Envelopes are rewritten to correspond to queue group assignments. If multiple queue directories are used, messages are assigned randomly to the queues in the correct queue group.

If a queue group has a limit on the maximum number of recipients per envelope, **sendmail** splits the envelope of the message into several smaller envelopes that fit within the queue group's parameters.

---

34. If you're using an ext3 filesystem with a 2.6 or later kernel, directory indexes may also help reduce the performance impact of large directories. You can modify an existing filesystem to use this feature with the command **tune2fs -O dir_index**.

Queue groups are declared with directives in the **.mc** file but are really configured in the raw config file language by LOCAL_RULESETS, which we don't describe at all in this book. The example below will get you started if you want to use queue groups to improve performance or to give different quality of service to different destinations.

Table 18.16 lists the attributes that can be specified for a queue group. Only the first letter of the attribute name need be specified when the queue group is defined.

Table 18.16   Queue group attributes

Attribute	Meaning
Flags	Mostly for future knobs; must set **f** flag to have multiple queue runners
Nice	Priority for this queue group; lowers priority a la the **nice** system call
Interval	Time to wait between queue runs
Path	Path to the queue directory associated with the queue group (required)
Runners	Number of **sendmail** processes to run concurrently on the queue group
recipients	Maximum number of recipients per envelope

Here is an example that has queue groups for local mail, for mail to aol.com, for mail to other remote sites, and a default queue for all the rest of the mail. The following lines go in the regular part of the **.mc** file:

```
dnl ##### -- queues
QUEUE_GROUP(`local', `P=/var/spool/mqueue/local')
QUEUE_GROUP(`aol', `P=/var/spool/mqueue/aol, F=f, r=100')
QUEUE_GROUP(`remote', `P=/var/spool/mqueue/remote, F=f')
```

And then at the end of the **.mc** file:

```
LOCAL_RULESETS
Squeuegroup
R<$+>                   $1
R$*@aol.com             $# aol
R$*@mydomain.com        $# local
R$*@$*                  $# remote
R$*                     $# mqueue
```

In this example, we specified a limit of 100 recipients per message when we defined the AOL queue group. If an outgoing message had 10,000 recipients, of whom 1,234 were at AOL, envelope splitting would put 13 messages in the aol queue group, 12 of 100 recipients each and 1 with the remaining 34 recipients.

To speed things up even more, try fast splitting, which defers MX lookups during the sorting process:

```
define(`confFAST_SPLIT', `1')
```

Queue runners

sendmail forks copies of itself to perform the actual transport of mail. You can control how many copies of **sendmail** are running at any given time and even how many are attached to each queue group. By using this feature, you can balance the activities of **sendmail** and the operating system on your busy mail hub machines.

Three **sendmail** options control the number of queue runner daemons processing each queue:

- The MAX_DAEMON_CHILDREN option specifies the total number of copies of the **sendmail** daemon that are allowed to run at any one time, including those running queues and those accepting incoming mail.

- The MAX_QUEUE_CHILDREN option sets the maximum number of queue runners allowed at one time.

- The MAX_RUNNERS_PER_QUEUE option sets the default runner limit per queue if no explicit value is set with the Runners= (or R=) parameter in the queue group definition.

If you set values that can conflict (for example, a maximum of 50 queue runners total, but 10 for the local queue, 30 for the mydomain queue, and 50 for the AOL queue), **sendmail** batches the queues into workgroups and round robin between workgroups. In this example, the local and mydomain queues would be one workgroup and the AOL queue would be a second workgroup. If you choose limits that must conflict (e.g., max=50 but AOL=100), **sendmail** uses MAX_QUEUE_CHILDREN as its absolute limit on the number of queue runners.

Load average controls

sendmail has always been able to refuse connections or queue messages instead of delivering them when the system load average goes too high. Unfortunately, the load average has only a one-minute granularity, so it's not a very finely honed tool for smoothing out the resources consumed by **sendmail**. The new DELAY_LA primitive lets you set a value of the load average at which **sendmail** should slow down; it will sleep for one second between SMTP commands for current connections and before accepting new connections. The default value is 0, which turns the mechanism off.

Undeliverable messages in the queue

Undeliverable messages in the mail queue can really kill performance on a busy mail server. **sendmail** has several features that help with the issue of undeliverable messages. The most effective is the FALLBACK_MX option, which hands a message off to another machine if it cannot be delivered on the first attempt. Your primary machine then cranks out the messages to good addresses and shunts the problem children to a secondary fallback machine. Another aid is the host status directory, which stores the status of remote hosts across queue runs.

The FALLBACK_MX option is a big performance win for a site with large mailing lists that invariably contain addresses that are temporarily or permanently undeliverable. To use it you must specify host to handle the deferred mail. For example,

```
define(`confFALLBACK_MX', `mailbackup.atrust.com')
```

forwards all messages that fail on their first delivery attempt to the central server mailbackup.atrust.com for further processing. As of 8.12, there can be multiple fallback machines if the designated hosts have multiple MX records in DNS.

On the fallback machines you can use the HOST_STATUS_DIRECTORY option to help with multiple failures. This option directs **sendmail** to maintain a status file for each host to which mail is sent and to use that status information to prioritize the hosts each time the queue is run. This status information effectively implements negative caching and allows information to be shared across queue runs. It's a performance win on servers that handle mailing lists with a lot of bad addresses, but it can be expensive in terms of file I/O.

Here is an example that uses the directory **/var/spool/mqueue/.hoststat** (create the directory first):

```
define(`confHOST_STATUS_DIRECTORY', `/var/spool/mqueue/.hoststat')
```

If the **.hoststat** directory is specified with a relative path, it is stored beneath the queue directory. **sendmail** creates its own internal hierarchy of subdirectories based on the destination hostname.

For example, if mail to evi@anchor.cs.colorado.edu were to fail, status information would go into the **/var/spool/mqueue/.hoststat/edu./colorado./cs./** directory in a file called **anchor** because the host anchor has an MX record with itself as highest priority. If the DNS MX records had directed anchor's email to host foo, then the filename would have been **foo**, not anchor.

A third performance enhancement for busy machines involves setting a minimum queue age so that any message that cannot be delivered on the initial try is queued and stays in the queue for a minimum time between tries. This technique is usually coupled with command-line flags that run the queue more often (e.g., **-q5m**). If a queue runner hangs on a bad message, another one starts in 5 minutes, improving performance for the messages that can be delivered. The entire queue is run in batches determined by which messages have been there for the required minimum time. Running **sendmail** with the flags **-bd -q5m** and including the option

```
define(`confMIN-QUEUE_AGE', `27m')
```

in the config file could result in a more responsive system.

Kernel tuning

If you plan to use a Linux box as a high-volume mail server, you should modify several of the kernel's networking configuration parameters and perhaps even build a custom kernel (depending on your hardware configuration and expected load).

Remove any unnecessary drivers so you start with a streamlined kernel that is just right for your hardware configuration.

The custom kernel should include support for multiple processors if the host machine has more than one processor (SMP). (We realize that for true Linux geeks, this comment is analogous to a reminder not to forget to breathe. But since Linux users' kernel-building skills vary, we have ignored reviewers' comments and have retained this reminder.)

To reset the parameters of the networking stack, use the shell's **echo** command redirected to the proper variable in the **/proc** filesystem. Chapter 12, *TCP/IP Networking*, contains a general description of this procedure starting on page 314. Table 18.17 shows the parameters to change on a high-volume mail server along with their suggested and default values. These changes should probably be put in a shell script that runs at boot time and performs the corresponding **echo**s.

Table 18.17   Kernel parameters to change on high-volume mail servers

Variable (relative to /proc/sys)	Default	Suggested
net/ipv4/tcp_fin_timeout	180	30
net/ipv4/tcp_keepalive_time	7200	1800
net/core/netdev_max_backlog	300	1024
fs/file_max	4096	16384
fs/inode_max	16384	65536

For example, you could use the command

```
echo 30 > /proc/sys/net/ipv4/tcp_fin_timeout
```

to change TCP's FIN timeout value.

18.14   SENDMAIL STATISTICS, TESTING, AND DEBUGGING

sendmail can collect statistics on the number and size of messages it has handled. You display this data with the **mailstats** command, which organizes the data by mailer. **sendmail**'s STATUS_FILE option (in the OSTYPE file) specifies the name of the file in which statistics should be kept. The existence of the specified file turns on the accounting function.

The default location for **sendmail**'s statistics file is **/etc/mail/statistics**, but some vendors call the file **sendmail.st** and put it in **/var/log**. The totals shown by **mailstats** are cumulative since the creation of the statistics file. If you want periodic statistics, you can rotate and reinitialize the file from **cron**.

Electronic Mail

Here is an example:

```
$ mailstats
Statistics from Tue Aug  1 02:13:30 2006
 M   msgsfr  bytes_from   msgsto   bytes_to   msgsrej   msgsdis   Mailer
 4       12         25K       63       455K         0         0   esmtp
 7        0          0K       18        25K         0         0   relay
 8       54        472K        0         0K         0         0   local
=====================================================================
 T       66        497K       81       480K         0         0
 C       66                   81                    0
```

If the mail statistics file is world-readable, you don't need to be root to run **mailstats**.

Six values are shown: messages and kilobytes received (msgsfr, bytes_from), messages and kilobytes sent (msgsto, bytes_to), messages rejected (msgsrej), and messages discarded (msgsdis). The first column is a number identifying the mailer, and the last column lists the name of the mailer. The T row is total messages and bytes, and the C row is connections. These values include both local and relayed mail.

Testing and debugging

m4-based configurations are to some extent pretested. You probably won't need to do low-level debugging if you use them. One thing the debugging flags cannot test is your design. While researching this chapter, we found errors in several of the configuration files and designs that we examined. The errors ranged from invoking a feature without the prerequisite macro (e.g., using masquerade_envelope without having turned on masquerading with MASQUERADE_AS) to total conflict between the design of the **sendmail** configuration and the firewall that controlled whether and under what conditions mail was allowed in.

You cannot design a mail system in a vacuum. You must be synchronized with (or at least not be in conflict with) your DNS MX records and your firewall policy.

sendmail provides one of the world's richest sets of debugging aids, with debug flags that are not simple Booleans or even integers but are two-dimensional quantities $x.y$, where x chooses the topic and y chooses the amount of information to display. A value of 0 gives no debugging, and 127 wastes many trees if you print the output. Topics range from 0 to 99; currently, about 80 are defined.

The file **sendmail/TRACEFLAGS** in the distribution lists the values in use and the files and functions in which they are used. All debugging support is at the level of the raw config file. In many cases, it's helpful to look at the **sendmail** source along with the debug output.

If **sendmail** is invoked with a **-d**$x.y$ flag, debugging output comes to the screen (standard error). Table 18.18 shows several important values of x and some suggested values for y. Be careful if you turn on debugging for a **sendmail** running as a daemon (**-bd**) because the debug output may end up interjected into the SMTP dialogue and cause odd failures when **sendmail** talks to remote hosts.

Table 18.18   Debugging topics

Topic	Meaning and suggestions
0	Shows compile flags and system identity (try y = 1 or 10)
8	Shows DNS name resolution (try y = 8)
11	Traces delivery (shows mailer invocations)
12	Shows local-to-remote name translation
17	Lists MX hosts
21	Traces rewriting rules (use y = 2 or y = 12 for more detail)
27	Shows aliasing and forwarding (try y = 4)
44	Shows file open attempts in case things are failing (y = 4)
60	Shows database map lookups

checksendmail is available from www.harker.com.

Gene Kim and Rob Kolstad have written a Perl script called **checksendmail** that invokes **sendmail** in address test mode on a file of test addresses that you supply. It compares the results to those expected. This script lets you test new versions of the configuration file against a test suite of your site's typical addresses to be sure you haven't inadvertently broken anything that used to work.

Verbose delivery

Many user agents that invoke **sendmail** on the command line accept a **-v** flag, which is passed to **sendmail** and makes it display the steps taken to deliver the message. The example below uses the **mail** command. The words in bold were typed as input to the user agent, and the rest is **sendmail**'s verbose output.

```
$ mail -v trent@toadranch.com
Subject: just testing, please ignore
hi
.
Cc:
trent@toadranch.com... Connecting to coyote.toadranch.com. via esmtp...
220 coyote.toadranch.com ESMTP Sendmail 8.11.0/8.11.0; Tue, 7 Aug 2001 20:
    08:51 -0600
>>> EHLO anchor.cs.colorado.edu
250-coyote.toadranch.com Hello anchor.cs.colorado.edu [128.138.242.1], pleased
    to meet you
250-ENHANCEDSTATUSCODES
250-EXPN
250-VERB
250-8BITMIME
250-SIZE
250-DSN
250-ONEX
250-ETRN
250-XUSR
250-AUTH DIGEST-MD5 CRAM-MD5
250 HELP
>>> MAIL From:<evi@anchor.cs.colorado.edu> SIZE=65
```

```
250 2.1.0 <evi@anchor.cs.colorado.edu>... Sender ok
>>> RCPT To:<trent@toadranch.com>
250 2.1.5 <trent@toadranch.com>... Recipient ok
>>> DATA
354 Enter mail, end with "." on a line by itself
>>> .
250 2.0.0 f7828pi03229 Message accepted for delivery
trent@toadranch.com... Sent (f7828pi03229 Message accepted for delivery)
Closing connection to coyote.toadranch.com.
>>> QUIT
221 2.0.0 coyote.toadranch.com closing connection
```

The **sendmail** on anchor connected to the **sendmail** on toadranch.com. Each machine used the ESMTP protocol to negotiate the exchange of the message.

Talking in SMTP

You can make direct use of SMTP when debugging the mail system. To initiate an SMTP session, use **sendmail -bs** or **telnet** to TCP port 25. By default, this is the port on which **sendmail** listens when run in daemon (**-bd**) mode; **sendmail** uses port 587 when running as the mail submission agent. Table 18.19 shows the most important SMTP commands.

Table 18.19   SMTP commands

Command	Function
HELO *hostname*	Identifies the connecting host if speaking SMTP
EHLO *hostname*	Identifies the connecting host if speaking ESMTP
MAIL From: *revpath*	Initiates a mail transaction (envelope sender)
RCPT To: *fwdpath*[a]	Identifies envelope recipient(s)
VRFY *address*	Verifies that *address* is valid (deliverable)
EXPN *address*	Shows expansion of aliases and **.forward** mappings
DATA	Begins the message body[b]
QUIT	Ends the exchange and closes the connection
RSET	Resets the state of the connection
HELP	Prints a summary of SMTP commands

a. There can be multiple RCPT commands for a message.
b. You terminate the body by entering a dot on its own line.

The whole language has only 14 commands, so it is quite easy to learn and use. It is not case sensitive. The specification for SMTP can be found in RFC2821.

Most transport agents, including **sendmail**, speak both SMTP and ESMTP; **smap** is the lone exception these days. Unfortunately, many firewalls boxes that provide active filtering do not speak ESMTP.

ESMTP speakers start conversations with the EHLO command instead of HELO. If the process at the other end understands and responds with an OK, then the participants negotiate supported extensions and arrive at a lowest common denominator for the exchange. If an error is returned, then the ESMTP speaker falls back to SMTP.

Queue monitoring

You can use the **mailq** command (which is equivalent to **sendmail -bp**) to view the status of queued messages. Messages are "queued" while they are being delivered or when delivery has been attempted but has failed.

mailq prints a human-readable summary of the files in **/var/spool/mqueue** at any given moment. The output is useful for determining why a message may have been delayed. If it appears that a mail backlog is developing, you can monitor the status of **sendmail**'s attempts to clear the jam.

Note that in **sendmail** version 8.12 and later, there are two default queues: one for messages received on port 25 and another for messages received on port 587 (the client submission queue). You can invoke **mailq -Ac** to see the client queue.

Here is some typical output from **mailq**. This case shows three messages that are waiting to be delivered:

```
$ sudo mailq
/var/spool/mqueue (3 requests)
-----Q-ID-----      --Size-- -----Q-Time-----  ------------Sender/Recipient-----------
k623gYYk008732   23217   Sat Jul 1 21:42   MAILER-DAEMON
     8BITMIME   (Deferred: Connection refused by agribusinessonline.com.)
                                     <Nimtz@agribusinessonline.com>
k5ULkAHB032374  279      Fri Jun 30 15:46  <randy@atrust.com>
            (Deferred: Name server: k2wireless.com.: host name lookup fa)
                                     <relder@k2wireless.com>
k5UJDm72023576  2485     Fri Jun 30 13:13  MAILER-DAEMON
            (reply: read error from mx4.level3.com.)
                                     <lfinist@bbnplanet.com>
```

If you think you understand the situation better than **sendmail** or you just want **sendmail** to try to redeliver the queued messages immediately, you can force a queue run with **sendmail -q**. If you use **sendmail -q -v**, **sendmail** shows the play-by-play results of each delivery attempt, which is often useful for debugging. Left to its own devices, **sendmail** retries delivery every queue run interval (typically 30 minutes).

Logging

See Chapter 10 for more information about syslog.

sendmail uses syslog to log error and status messages with syslog facility "mail" and levels "debug" through "crit"; messages are tagged with the string "sendmail." You can override the logging string "sendmail" with the **-L** command-line option, which is handy if you are debugging one copy of **sendmail** while other copies are doing regular email chores.

The confLOG_LEVEL option, specified on the command line or in the config file, determines the severity level that **sendmail** uses as a threshold for logging. High values of the log level imply low severity levels and cause more info to be logged.

Recall that a message logged to syslog at a particular level is reported to that level and all those above it. The **/etc/syslog.conf** file determines the eventual destination of each message.

On Red Hat and Fedora systems, the **sendmail** logs go to **/var/log/maillog** by default. For SUSE, it's **/var/log/mail**; for Debian and Ubuntu, it's **/var/log/mail.log**. Wouldn't it be nice if the standardization efforts could sort out some of these random and apparently meaningless differences so our scripts could be more portable?

Table 18.20 gives an approximate mapping between **sendmail** log levels and syslog severity levels.

Table 18.20   sendmail log levels vs. syslog levels

L	Levels	L	Levels
0	No logging	4	notice
1	alert or crit	5–11	info
2	crit	≥12	debug
3	err or warning		

A nice program called **mreport** by Jason Armstrong is available from

> ftp://ftp.riverdrums.com/pub/mreport

It summarizes log files written by **sendmail**. It builds out of the box with just **make** and then **make install**. Here is a sample of **mreport**'s output from a Red Hat system:

```
# mreport -f -i /var/log/maillog -o mreport.out
[redhat.toadranch.com] [/var/log/maillog]

* [  7]  592601  herb@yoherb.com                  trent@toadranch.com
* [  8]  505797  SNYDERGA@simon.rochester.edu  trent@toadranch.com
  [  1]  179386  steph@toadranch.com              bennettr@ci.boulder.co.us
  [  1]   65086  herb@yoherb.com                  ned@xor.co
  [  7]   19029  evi@anchor.cs.colorado.edu       trent@toadranch.com
  [ 11]   17677  lunch-request@moose.org          trent@toadranch.com
  [  2]   16178  trent@toadranch.com              ned@camelspit.org
  [  3]   15229  reminders@yahoo-inc.com          herb@toadranch.com
  [  2]    4653  trent@toadranch.com              garth@cs.colorado.edu
  [  2]    1816  UNKNOWN                          trent@toadranch.com

. . . many lines deleted . . .

=====================
Total Bytes        : 7876372
Number of Records  : 192
--------------------
User Unknown       : 125
--------------------
Host Name          : redhat.toadranch.com
```

```
Input File          : maillog
Output File         : mreport.out
First Record        : Aug  5 04:47:31
Last Record         : Aug  7 18:16:25
--------------------
Time Taken          : 24317 μs
======================
```

You must use **sudo** or be root to run **mreport** if your mail log files are only readable by root (as they should be). Flags and options are documented in the **mreport** man page. The **-f** flag in this instance says to aggregate and sort by sender; an analogous **-t** flag lets you sort by recipient. The **-i** argument is the input file, and **-o** the output file.

If you intend to run **mreport** regularly, you should inform your users. They might feel it was an invasion of their privacy for sysadmins to be browsing the mail logs with such a nice tool.

18.15   THE EXIM MAIL SYSTEM

The Debian and Ubuntu distributions ship with the Exim mail transport agent instead of **sendmail**. It's a simpler system with fewer bells and whistles, but it also features easier configuration for sites that don't bear a heavy mail load and don't have a bizarre mail system design. Exim's functionality maps to the most commonly used features of **sendmail**.

History

Exim was written in 1995 by Philip Hazel of the University of Cambridge and is distributed under the GNU General Public License. Exim version 4 (aka exim4) was released in 2002 and is currently the version distributed with Debian and Ubuntu. Philip Hazel has also written a book called *The Exim Smtp Mail Server: Official Guide for Release 4* which was published in 2003. We defer to that book and to the Exim documentation at www.exim.org for the details of Exim configuration and give only a brief description here.

Exim on Linux

As in the **sendmail** suite, some separate commands in Exim perform specific mail functions. These are implemented by a call to **exim** with certain command-line flags. Table 18.21 shows the behaviors and their equivalent flags.

Table 18.21   Exim utilities (with equivalent flags)

Command	Equiv	Function
mailq	exim -bp	Shows the mail queue
rsmtp	exim -bS	Batched SMTP connection
rmail	exim -i	For compatibility with **smail**[a]
runq	exim -q	Runs the mail queue

a. Accepts a message terminated by a dot on a line by itself

Electronic Mail

Exim configuration

Exim contains three logical pieces: directors, routers, and transports. Directors handle local addresses—that is, addresses inside the home domain. Routers handle remote addresses, and transports do the actual delivery.

Exim is configured much like **smail3** or Postfix, with the configuration language taking the form *keyword = value*. As of Exim 4, the system is configured through an elaborate collection of config files that live in **/etc/exim4/conf.d**. After you add or modify one of these files, you must run the **update-exim4.conf** script, which then creates **/var/lib/exim4/config.autogenerated**. The **config.autogenerated** file is used by Exim at run time.

Fortunately, the Exim configuration files are well documented, with comments preceding each variable to describe what the variable does, what the usual value is, and what (bad) things might happen if you fail to define it. The default configuration files have about 100 variables defined, but this is largely boilerplate that emulates much of the **sendmail** behavior documented in previous sections.

On our testbed system we had to set just four variables to get basic email working. Two of those variables related to privacy concerns and were not absolutely required. Here are the four variables, with our comments on the side:

```
qualify_domain = domain-name      ### by default set to unqualified hostname
local_domains = localhost:domain-name
smtp_verify = false               ### default is on, off disables SMTP VRFY
modemask = 002                    ### default 022 assumes a group for each user
```

In the next section, we describe a few of Exim's features in **sendmail** terms so that you can compare the two systems' functionality and decide if you want to install the real **sendmail** instead of Exim.

Exim/sendmail similarities

Some parts of Exim run setuid to root much like **sendmail** did before version 8.12. Therefore, it's particularly important to stay up to date on security patches. The Exim concept of trusted users matches that of **sendmail** and primarily helps facilitate the management of mailing lists, for which From lines are routinely rewritten. Exim also lets you define administrative users who are allowed to initiate queue runs. The SMTP verify command (VRFY) is allowed by default.

exim must be sent the SIGHUP signal with the **kill** command when its config file changes. It stores its process ID in **/var/spool/exim/exim-daemon.pid**. It typically logs to files in the **/var/log/exim** directory but can also use syslog. By default, **exim** logs to its own files and ignores syslog, yet **syslog.conf** is configured with several mail log files that are empty and are rotated and compressed every day. (Empty files are larger after compression than before!)

Exim permits forwarding of outgoing mail to a smart host and filtering of inbound mail at both the host and user levels. It supports virtual domains and has a retry database similar in functionality to **sendmail**'s host status directory for keeping track of difficult deliveries. A system-wide (not per-user) filtering mechanism can screen for Microsoft attachments, worms, or viruses.

Exim includes a nice feature that is not available in **sendmail**, namely, recognition of alias and forwarding loops and sensible handling of them.

Finally, **man -k exim** yields several useful tools to help keep the mail system tidy.

18.16 POSTFIX

Postfix is yet another alternative to **sendmail**. The Postfix project started when Wietse Venema spent a sabbatical year at IBM's T. J. Watson Research Center. Postfix's design goals included an open source distribution policy, speedy performance, robustness, flexibility, and security. It is a direct competitor to **qmail** by Dan Bernstein. All major Linux distributions include Postfix, and since version 10.3, Mac OS X has shipped it instead of **sendmail** as the default mail system.

The most important things about Postfix are, first, that it works almost out of the box (the simplest config files are only one or two lines long), and second, that it leverages regular expression maps to filter email effectively, especially in conjunction with the PCRE (Perl Compatible Regular Expression) library. Postfix is compatible with **sendmail** in the sense that Postfix's **aliases** and **.forward** files have the same format and semantics as those of **sendmail**.

Postfix speaks ESMTP. Virtual domains and spam filtering are both supported. Postfix does not use an address rewriting language as **sendmail** does; instead, it relies on table lookups from flat files, Berkeley DB, **dbm**, LDAP, NIS, NetInfo, or databases such as MySQL.

Postfix architecture

Postfix comprises several small, cooperating programs that send network messages, receive messages, deliver email locally, etc. Communication among the programs is performed through UNIX domain sockets or FIFOs. This architecture is quite different from that of **sendmail**, wherein a single large program does most of the work.

The **master** program starts and monitors all Postfix processes. Its configuration file, **master.cf**, lists the subsidiary programs along with information about how they should be started. The default values set in that file are right for all but very slow or very fast machines (or networks); in general, no tweaking is necessary. One common change is to comment out a program, for example, **smtpd**, when a client should not listen on the SMTP port.

The most important server programs involved in the delivery of email are shown in Exhibit E on the next page.

Electronic Mail

Exhibit E   **Postfix server programs**

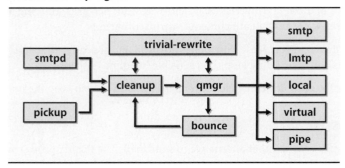

Receiving mail

Mail is received on the SMTP port by **smtpd**, which also checks that the connecting clients are authorized to send the mail they are trying to deliver. When email is sent locally through the **/usr/lib/sendmail** compatibility program, a file is written to the **/var/spool/postfix/maildrop** directory. That directory is periodically scanned by the **pickup** program, which processes any new files it finds.

All incoming email passes through **cleanup**, which adds missing headers and rewrites addresses according to the canonical and virtual maps. Before inserting it in the incoming queue, **cleanup** gives the email to **trivial-rewrite**, which does minor fixing of the addresses, such as appending a mail domain to addresses that are not fully qualified.

The queue manager

Mail waiting to be delivered is controlled by **qmgr**, the queue manager of five queues:

- incoming – mail that is arriving
- active   – mail that is being delivered
- deferred – mail for which delivery has failed in the past
- hold   – mail blocked in the queue by the administrator
- corrupt   – mail that can't be read or parsed

The queue manager generally selects the next message to process with a simple FIFO strategy, but it also supports a a complex preemption algorithm that prefers messages with few recipients over bulk mail.

In order not to overwhelm a receiving host, especially after it has been down, Postfix uses a slow start algorithm to control how fast it tries to deliver email. Deferred messages are given a try-again time stamp that exponentially backs off so as not to waste resources on undeliverable messages. A status cache of unreachable destinations avoids unnecessary delivery attempts.

Sending mail

qmgr decides with the help of **trivial-rewrite** where a message should be sent. The routing decision made by **trivial-rewrite** can be overridden by the transport map.

Delivery to remote hosts through the SMTP protocol is performed by the **smtp** program. **lmtp** delivers mail by using LMTP, the Local Mail Transfer Protocol defined in RFC2033. LMTP is based on SMTP, but the protocol has been modified so that the mail server is not required to manage a mail queue. This mailer is particularly useful for delivering email to mailbox servers such as the Cyrus IMAP suite.

local's job is to deliver email locally. It resolves addresses in the **aliases** table and follows instructions found in recipients' **.forward** files. Messages are either forwarded to another address, passed to an external program for processing, or stored in users' mail folders.

The **virtual** program delivers email to "virtual mailboxes"; that is, mailboxes that are not related to a local Linux account but that still represent valid email destinations. Finally, **pipe** implements delivery through external programs.

Security

Postfix implements security at several levels. Most of the Postfix server programs can run in a **chroot**ed environment. They are separate programs with no parent/child relationship. None of them are setuid. The mail drop directory is group-writable by the postdrop group, to which the **postdrop** program is setgid.

Impressively, no exploits other than denial of service attacks have yet been identified in any version of Postfix.

Postfix commands and documentation

Several command-line utilities permit user interaction with the mail system:

- **sendmail**, **mailq**, **newaliases** – are **sendmail**-compatible replacements
- **postfix** – starts and stops the mail system (must be run as root)
- **postalias** – builds, modifies, and queries alias tables
- **postcat** – prints the contents of queue files
- **postconf** – displays and edits the main configuration file, **main.cf**
- **postmap** – builds, modifies, or queries lookup tables
- **postsuper** – manages the mail queues

The Postfix distribution includes a set of man pages that describe all the programs and their options. Additionally, on-line documents at www.postfix.org explain how to configure and manage various aspects of Postfix. These same documents are included in the Postfix distribution, so you should find them installed on your system, usually in a directory called **README_FILES**.

Configuring Postfix

The **main.cf** file is Postfix's principal configuration file. The **master.cf** file configures the server programs. It also defines various lookup tables that are referenced from **main.cf** and that provide different types of service mappings.

The **postconf**(5) man page describes every parameter that can be set in the **main.cf** file. If you just type **man postconf**, you'll get the man page for the **postconf** program. Use **man -s 5 postconf** to get the version that describes **main.cf** options.

The Postfix configuration language looks a bit like a series of Bourne shell comments and assignment statements. Variables can be referenced in the definition of other variables by being prefixed with a $. Variable definitions are stored just as they appear in the config file; they are not expanded until they are used, and any substitutions occur at that time.

You can create new variables by assigning them values. Be careful to choose names that do not conflict with existing configuration variables.

All Postfix configuration files, including the lookup tables, consider lines starting with whitespace to be continuation lines. This convention results in very readable configuration files, but you must start new lines in column one.

What to put in main.cf

More than 300 parameters can be specified in the **main.cf** file. However, just a few of them need to be set at an average site, since the defaults are mostly good. The author of Postfix strongly recommends that only parameters with nondefault values be included in your configuration. That way, if the default value of a parameter changes in the future, your configuration will automatically adopt the new value.

The sample **main.cf** file that comes with the distribution includes many commented-out example parameters, along with some brief documentation. The original version is best left alone as a reference. Start with an empty file for your own configuration so that your settings are not lost in a sea of comments.

Basic settings

Let's start with as simple a configuration as possible: an empty file. Surprisingly, this is a perfectly reasonable Postfix configuration. It results in a mail server that delivers email locally within the same domain as the local hostname and that sends any messages directed to nonlocal addresses directly to the appropriate remote servers.

Another simple configuration is a "null client"; that is, a system that doesn't deliver any email locally but rather forwards outbound mail to a designated central server For this configuration, we define several parameters, starting with mydomain, which defines the domain part of the hostname, and myorigin, which is the mail domain appended to unqualified email addresses. If the mydomain and myorigin parameters are the same, we can write something like this:

```
mydomain = cs.colorado.edu
myorigin = $mydomain
```

Another parameter we should set is mydestination, which specifies the mail domains that are local. (These are also known as the "canonical" domains.) If the recipient address of a message has mydestination as its mail domain, the message is
delivered through the **local** program to the corresponding user (assuming that no
relevant alias or **.forward** file is found). If more than one mail domain is included in
mydestination, these domains are all considered aliases for the same domain.

We want no local delivery for our null client, so this parameter should be empty:

    mydestination =

Finally, the relayhost parameter tells Postfix to send all nonlocal messages to a
specified host instead of sending them directly to their apparent destinations:

    relayhost = [mail.cs.colorado.edu]

The square brackets tell Postfix to treat the specified string as a hostname (DNS A
record) instead of a mail domain name (DNS MX record).

Since null clients should not receive mail from other systems, the last thing to do in a
null client configuration is to comment out the **smtpd** line in the **master.cf** file. This
change prevents Postfix from running **smtpd** at all. With just these few lines, we've
defined a fully functional null client!

For a "real" mail server, you'll need a few more configuration options as well as some
mapping tables. We cover these in the next few sections.

Using postconf

postconf is a handy tool that helps you configure Postfix. When run without arguments, it prints all the parameters as they are currently configured. If you name a
specific parameter as argument, **postconf** prints the value of that parameter. The **-d**
option makes **postconf** print the defaults instead of the currently configured values.
For example:

    $ postconf mydestination
    mydestination =
    $ postconf -d mydestination
    mydestination = $myhostname, localhost.$mydomain, localhost

Another useful option is **-n**, which makes **postconf** print only the parameters that
differ from the default. If you ask for help on the Postfix mailing list, that's the configuration information you should put in your email.

Lookup tables

Many aspects of Postfix's behavior are shaped through the use of lookup tables,
which can map keys to values or implement simple lists. For example, the default
setting for the alias_maps table is

    alias_maps = dbm:/etc/mail/aliases, nis:mail.aliases

Data sources are specified with the notation *type:path*. Note that this particular table actually uses two distinct sources of information simultaneously: a **dbm** database and an NIS map. Multiple values can be separated by commas, spaces, or both. Table 18.22 lists the available data sources; **postconf -m** shows this information as well.

Table 18.22   **Information sources usable as Postfix lookup tables**

Type	Description
dbm / sdbm	Traditional **dbm** or **gdbm** database file
cidr	Network addresses in CIDR form
hash / btree	Berkeley DB hash table (replacement for **dbm**) or B-tree file
ldap	LDAP directory service
mysql	MySQL database
nis	NIS directory service
pcre	Perl-Compatible Regular Expressions
pgsql	PostgreSQL database
proxy	Access through **proxymap**, e.g., to escape a **chroot**
regexp	POSIX regular expressions
static	Returns the value specified as *path* regardless of the key
unix	Linux **/etc/passwd** and **/etc/group** files; uses NIS syntax[a]

a. unix:passwd.byname is the **passwd** file, and unix:group.byname is the **group** file.

Use the dbm and sdbm types only for compatibility with the traditional **sendmail** alias table. Berkeley DB (hash) is a more modern implementation; it's safer and faster. If compatibility is not a problem, use

```
alias_database = hash:/etc/mail/aliases
alias_maps = hash:/etc/mail/aliases
```

The alias_database specifies the table that is rebuilt by **newaliases** and should correspond to the table that you specify in alias_maps. The reason for having two parameters is that alias_maps might include non-DB sources such as mysql or nis that do not need to be rebuilt.

All DB-class tables (dbm, sdbm, hash, and btree) are based on a text file that is compiled to an efficiently searchable binary format. The syntax for these text files is similar to that of the configuration files with respect to comments and continuation lines. Entries are specified as simple key/value pairs separated by whitespace, except for alias tables, which must have a colon after the key to retain **sendmail** compatibility. For example, the following lines are appropriate for an alias table:

```
postmaster:     david, tobias
webmaster:      evi
```

As another example, here's an access table for relaying mail from any client with a hostname ending in cs.colorado.edu.

```
.cs.colorado.edu   OK
```

Text files are compiled to their binary formats with the **postmap** command for normal tables and the **postalias** command for alias tables. The table specification (including the type) must be given as the first argument. For example:

```
$ postmap hash:/etc/postfix/access
```

postmap can also query values in a lookup table:

```
$ postmap -q blabla hash:/etc/postfix/access
$ postmap -q .cs.colorado.edu hash:/etc/postfix/access
OK
```

Local delivery

The **local** program is responsible for the delivery of mail to the canonical domain. It also handles local aliasing. For example, if mydestination is set to cs.colorado.edu and an email for evi@cs.colorado.edu arrives, **local** first performs a lookup on the alias_maps tables and then substitutes any matching entries recursively.

If no aliases match, **local** looks for a **.forward** file in user evi's home directory and follows the instructions in the file if it exists. (The syntax is the same as the right side of an alias map.) Finally, if no **.forward** is found, the email is delivered to evi's local mailbox.

By default, **local** writes to standard mbox-format files under **/var/mail**. You can change that behavior with the parameters shown in Table 18.23.

Table 18.23 Parameters for local mailbox delivery (set in main.cf)

Parameter	Description
mail_spool_directory	Delivers mail to a central directory serving all users
home_mailbox	Delivers mail to ~*user* under the specified relative path
mailbox_command	Delivers mail with an external program, typically **procmail**
mailbox_transport	Delivers mail through a service as defined in **master.cf**[a]
recipient_delimiter	Allows extended usernames (see description below)

a. This option interfaces with mailbox servers such as the Cyrus **imapd**.

The mail_spool_directory and home_mailbox options normally generate mbox-format mailboxes, but they can also produce **Maildir** mailboxes in the style of **qmail**. To request this behavior, add a slash to the end of the pathname.

If recipient_delimiter is set to +, mail addressed to evi+whatever@cs.colorado.edu is accepted for delivery to the evi account. With this facility, users can create special-purpose addresses and sort their mail by destination address. Postfix first attempts lookups on the full address, and only if that fails does it strip the extended components and fall back to the base address. Postfix also looks for a corresponding forwarding file, **.forward+whatever**, for further aliasing.

Virtual domains

If you want to host a mail domain on your Postfix mail server, you have three choices:

- List the domain in mydestination. Delivery is performed as described above: aliases are expanded and mail delivered to the corresponding users.

- List the domain in the virtual_alias_domains parameter. This option gives the domain its own addressing namespace that is independent of the system's user accounts. All addresses within the domain must be resolvable (through mapping) to real addresses outside of it.

- List the domain in the virtual_mailbox_domains parameter. As with the virtual_alias_domains option, the domain has its own namespace. However, mail can be delivered to all mailboxes under a specified path, independently of user accounts.

List the domain in only one of these three places. Choose carefully, because many configuration elements depend on that choice. We have already reviewed the handling of the mydestination method. The other options are discussed below.

Virtual alias domains

If a domain is listed as a value of the virtual_alias_domains parameter, mail to that domain is accepted by Postfix and must be forwarded to an actual recipient either on the local machine or elsewhere.

The forwarding for addresses in the virtual domain must be defined in a lookup table included in the virtual_alias_maps parameter. Entries in the table have the address in the virtual domain on the left side and the actual destination address on the right.

An unqualified name on the right is interpreted as a username on the local machine.

Consider the following example from **main.cf**:

```
myorigin = cs.colorado.edu
mydestination = cs.colorado.edu
virtual_alias_domains = admin.com
virtual_alias_maps = hash:/etc/mail/admin.com/virtual
```

In **/etc/mail/admin.com/virtual** we could then have the lines:

```
postmaster@admin.com  evi, david@admin.com
abuse@admin.com       evi
david@admin.com       david@schweikert.ch
evi@admin.com         evi
```

Mail for evi@admin.com would be redirected to evi@cs.colorado.edu (myorigin is appended) and would ultimately be delivered to the mailbox of user evi because cs.colorado.edu is included in mydestination.

Definitions can be recursive: the right hand side can contain addresses that are further defined on the left hand side. Note that the right hand side can only be a list of addresses. If you need to execute an external program or to use :include: files, then redirect the email to an alias, which can then be expanded according to your needs.

To keep everything in one file, you can set virtual_alias_domains to the same lookup table as virtual_alias_maps and put a special entry in the table to mark it as a virtual alias domain. In **main.cf**:

```
virtual_alias_domains = $virtual_alias_maps
virtual_alias_maps = hash:/etc/mail/admin.com/virtual
```

In **/etc/mail/admin.com/virtual**:

```
admin.com                notused
postmaster@admin.com  evi, david@admin.com
...
```

The right hand side of the entry for the mail domain (admin.com) is never actually used; admin.com's existence in the table as an independent entry is enough to make Postfix consider it a virtual alias domain.

Virtual mailbox domains

Domains listed under virtual_mailbox_domains are similar to local (canonical) domains, but the list of users and their corresponding mailboxes must be managed independently of the system's user accounts.

The parameter virtual_mailbox_maps points to a table that lists all valid users in the domain. The map format is

```
user@domain        /path/to/mailbox
```

If the path ends with a slash, the mailboxes are stored in **Maildir** format. The value of virtual_mailbox_base is always prefixed to the specified paths.

You may often want to alias some of the addresses in the virtual_mailbox_domain. Use a virtual_alias_map to do this. Here is a complete example.

In **main.cf**:

```
virtual_mailbox_domains = admin.com
virtual_mailbox_base = /var/mail/virtual
virtual_mailbox_maps = hash:/etc/mail/admin.com/vmailboxes
virtual_alias_maps = hash:/etc/mail/admin.com/valiases
```

/etc/mail/admin.com/vmailboxes might contain entries like these:

```
evi@admin.com            nemeth/evi/
```

/etc/mail/admin.com/valiases might contain:

```
postmaster@admin.com  evi@admin.com
```

Electronic Mail

You can use virtual alias maps even on addresses that are not virtual alias domains. Virtual alias maps let you redirect any address from any domain, independently of the type of the domain (canonical, virtual alias, or virtual mailbox). Since mailbox paths can only be put on the right hand side of the virtual mailbox map, use of this mechanism is the only way to set up aliases in that domain.

Access control

Mail servers should relay mail for third parties only on behalf of trusted clients. If a mail server forwards mail from unknown clients to other servers, it is a so-called open relay, which is bad. See *Relaying* on page 589 for more details about this issue.

Fortunately, Postfix doesn't act as an open relay by default. In fact, its defaults are quite restrictive; you are more likely to need to liberalize the permissions than to tighten them. Access control for SMTP transactions is configured in Postfix through "access restriction lists." The parameters shown in Table 18.24 control what should be checked during the different phases of an SMTP session.

Table 18.24   Postfix parameters for SMTP access restriction

Parameter	When applied
smtpd_client_restrictions	On connection request
smtpd_helo_restrictions	On HELO/EHLO command (start of the session)
smtpd_sender_restrictions	On MAIL FROM command (sender specification)
smtpd_recipient_restrictions	On RCPT TO command (recipient specification)
smtpd_data_restrictions	On DATA command (mail body)
smtpd_etrn_restrictions	On ETRN command[a]

a. This is a special command used for resending messages in the queue.

The most important parameter is smtpd_recipient_restrictions, since access control is most easily performed when the recipient address is known and can be identified as being local or not. All the other parameters in Table 18.24 are empty in the default configuration. The default value is

```
smtpd_recipient_restrictions = permit_mynetworks, reject_unauth_destination
```

Each of the specified restrictions is tested in turn until a definitive decision about what to do with the mail is reached. Table 18.25 shows the most common restrictions.

Table 18.25   Common Postfix access restrictions

Restriction	Function
check_client_access	Checks the client host address by using a lookup table
check_recipient_access	Checks the recipient mail address by using a lookup table
permit_mynetworks	Grants access to addresses listed in mynetworks
reject_unauth_destination	Rejects mail for nonlocal recipients; no relaying

Everything can be tested in these restrictions, not just specific information like the sender address in the smtpd_sender_restrictions. Therefore, for simplicity, you might want to put all the restrictions under a single parameter, which should be smtpd_sender_restrictions since it is the only one that can test everything (except the DATA part).

smtpd_recipient_restriction is where mail relaying is tested. You should keep the reject_unauth_destination restriction, and carefully choose the "permit" restrictions before it.

Access tables

Each restriction returns one of the actions shown in Table 18.26. Access tables are used in restrictions such as check_client_access and check_recipient_access to select an action based on the client host address or recipient address, respectively.

Table 18.26 Actions for access tables

Action	Meaning
4nn text	Returns temporary error code *4nn* and message *text*
5nn text	Returns permanent error code *5nn* and message *text*
DEFER_IF_PERMIT	If restrictions result in PERMIT, changes it to a temp error
DEFER_IF_REJECT	If restrictions result in REJECT, changes it to a temp error
DISCARD	Accepts the message but silently discards it
DUNNO	Pretends the key was not found; tests further restrictions
FILTER transport:dest	Passes the mail through the filter *transport:dest*[a]
HOLD	Blocks the mail in the queue
OK	Accepts the mail
PREPEND header	Adds a header to the message
REDIRECT addr	Forwards this mail to a specified address
REJECT	Rejects the mail
WARN message	Enters the given warning *message* in the logs

a. See the section about spam and virus handling in Postfix starting on page 623.

As an example, suppose you wanted to allow relaying for all machines within the cs.colorado.edu domain and that you wanted to allow only trusted clients to post to the internal mailing list newsletter@cs.colorado.edu. You could implement these policies with the following lines in **main.cf**:

```
smtpd_recipient_restrictions =
        check_client_access hash:/etc/postfix/client_access
        check_recipient_access hash:/etc/postfix/recipient_access
        reject_unauth_destination
```

Note that commas are optional when the list of values for a parameter is specified.

In **/etc/postfix/client_access**:

```
.cs.colorado.edu     OK
```

In **/etc/postfix/recipient_access**:

```
newsletter@cs.colorado.edu REJECT Internal list
```

The text after REJECT is an optional string that is sent to the client along with the error code. It tells the sender why the mail was rejected.

Authentication of clients

For users sending mail from home, it is usually easiest to route outgoing mail through the home ISP's mail server, regardless of the sender address that appears on that mail. Most ISPs trust their direct clients and allow relaying. If this configuration isn't possible or if you are using a system such as Sender ID or SPF, ensure that mobile users outside your network can be authorized to submit messages to your **smtpd**.

One way to solve this problem is to piggyback on the authentication protocols used by POP or IMAP. Users that need to send mail also need to read their mail, so a single authentication step can serve to enable both processes.

The piggybacking system, called POP-before-SMTP or IMAP-before-SMTP, works like this: as soon as a user has been authenticated by the POP or IMAP daemon, the user's IP address is explicitly whitelisted for SMTP for 30 minutes or so. The database of whitelisted clients is maintained by a daemon dedicated to this task. The configuration in Postfix looks like the following:

```
smtpd_recipient_restrictions = permit_mynetworks
            check_client_access hash:/etc/postfix/pop-before-smtp
            reject_unauth_destination
```

A nicer solution to this problem is to use the SMTP AUTH mechanism to authenticate directly at the SMTP level. Postfix must be compiled with support for the SASL library to make this work. You can then configure the feature like this:

```
smtpd_sasl_auth_enable = yes
smtpd_recipient_restrictions = reject_non_fqdn_recipient
            permit_mynetworks
            permit_sasl_authenticated
```

You also need to support encrypted connections to avoid sending passwords in clear text. With Postfix versions before 2.2, patch the source with the Postfix/TLS patch. Add lines like the following to **main.cf**:

```
smtpd_use_tls = yes
smtpd_tls_auth_only = yes
smtpd_tls_cert_file = /etc/certs/smtp.pem
smtpd_tls_key_file = $smtpd_tls_cert_file
```

Fighting spam and viruses

Postfix has many features that can help block suspicious email.

One class of protection features calls for strict implementation of the SMTP protocol. Legitimate mail servers should respect the protocol, but spam and virus senders often play fast and loose with it, thus giving themselves away. Unfortunately, broken mailers handling legitimate mail are still out in the world, so this technique isn't quite foolproof. Choose restrictions carefully, and monitor the log files. Table 18.27 shows some of the features in this category.

Table 18.27 Parameters and restrictions for strict SMTP protocol checking

Option	Purpose
reject_non_fqdn_sender reject_non_fqdn_recipient reject_non_fqdn_hostname	Rejects messages without a fully qualified sender domain, recipient domain or HELO/EHLO hostname (restriction)
reject_unauth_pipelining	Aborts the current session if the client doesn't wait to see the status of a command before proceeding (restriction)
reject_unknown_sender_domain	Rejects messages that have an unresolvable sender domain (restriction)[a]
smtpd_helo_required	Requires HELO/EHLO at the start of the conversation (parameter, either yes or no)
strict_rfc821_envelopes	Requires correct syntax for email addresses in the MAIL FROM and RCPT TO commands (parameter, either yes or no)

a. Returns a temporary error message because the problem may result from a transient DNS glitch

To test a restriction before putting it in production (always a good idea), insert the restriction warn_if_reject in front of it to convert the effect from outright rejection to warning log messages.

Black hole lists

As with **sendmail**, you can instruct Postfix to check incoming email against a DNS-based black hole list; see *User or site blacklisting* on page 594 for more details. To enable this behavior, use the reject_rbl_client restriction followed by the address of the DNS server to be consulted. A similar feature is reject_rhsbl_sender, which checks the domain name of the sender's address rather than the client's hostname.

The following example represents a relatively complete spam-fighting configuration from the **main.cf** file:

```
strict_rfc821_envelopes = yes
smtpd_helo_required = yes
smtpd_recipient_restrictions =reject_unknown_sender_domain
          reject_non_fqdn_sender
          reject_non_fqdn_recipient
          permit_mynetworks
```

```
check_client_access hash:/etc/postfix/client_access
reject_unauth_destination
reject_unauth_pipelining
reject_rbl_client relays.ordb.org
reject_rhsbl_sender dsn.rfc-ignorant.org
```

Note that we put some restrictions in front of permit_mynetworks. That tweak lets us verify that our own clients are sending out correctly formatted mail. This is an easy way to find out about configuration errors.

SpamAssassin and procmail

Postfix supports SpamAssassin and other filters of that ilk. See *SpamAssassin* on page 598 and *The local_procmail feature* on page 585 for general information about these tools.

procmail can be started from users' **.forward** files, but that's complicated and error prone. A better solution is to put the following line in **main.cf**:

```
mailbox_command = /usr/bin/procmail -a "$EXTENSION"
```

Postfix then uses **procmail** to deliver mail instead of writing messages directly to the mail spool. The arguments given to **procmail** pass the address extension (the portion after the +); it can then be accessed in **procmail** as $1.

Policy daemons

Postfix version 2.1 introduced a mechanism for delegating access control to external programs. These programs, called policy daemons, receive all the information that Postfix has about an email message and must return one of the disposition actions listed in Table 18.26 on page 633.

Perhaps the most interesting feature that can be implemented with such a policy daemon is "greylisting." Greylisting classifies each incoming message by the triplet of client hostname, sender address, and recipient address. The first time a given triplet is seen, Postfix returns a temporary error message to the sender. Legitimate mail servers attempt redelivery after 10 minutes or so, at which time the message is allowed in. Because the first redelivery attempt is usually made in a matter of minutes, mail is not unduly delayed.

Greylisting is similar in spirit to the Postfix features that require strict compliance with the SMTP protocol. In the case of greylisting, the redelivery attempt itself constitutes evidence of legitimate-mail-serverness. Greylisting has proved to be quite effective at weeding out spam because many spam sources use unsophisticated software that does not attempt redelivery.

Content filtering

Postfix can use regular expressions to check the headers and bodies of email messages for contraband. It can also pass messages to other programs such as dedicated spam fighting tools or antivirus applications.

Header and body checks are performed in real time as messages are accepted through SMTP. Each regular expression that is checked invokes an action as specified in Table 18.26 on page 633 if the regex matches. For example, the line

```
header_checks = regexp:/etc/postfix/header_checks
```

in **main.cf** along with the following line in **/etc/postfix/header_checks**

```
/^Subject: reject-me/ REJECT You asked for it
```

would reject any message whose subject started with "reject-me". Though regular expression support is always nice, it provokes many caveats in the context of email processing. In particular, this is not an effective method of spam or virus filtering.

Industrial-strength virus filtering is usually implemented through Amavis, a Perl program that interfaces mail server software with one or more antivirus applications. Such filters are configured with Postfix's content_filter parameter, which instructs Postfix to pass every incoming message once through the specified service. In addition to setting the content_filter parameter, you must modify some existing entries in the **master.cf** file and add some new ones. Amavis comes with detailed instructions about how to do this. Many variants of Amavis are available: we recommend **amavisd-new** by Mark Martinec.

Debugging

When you have a problem with Postfix, first check the log files. The answers to your questions are most likely there; it's just a question of finding them. Every Postfix program normally issues a log entry for every message it processes. For example, the trail of an outbound message might look like this:

```
Aug 18 22:41:33 nova postfix/pickup: 0E4A93688: uid=506
    from=<dws@ee.ethz.ch>
Aug 18 22:41:33 nova postfix/cleanup: 0E4A93688: message-id=
    <20040818204132.GA11444@ee.ethz.ch>
Aug 18 22:41:33 nova postfix/qmgr: 0E4A93688: from=<dws@ee.ethz.ch>,
    size=577,nrcpt=1 (queue active)
Aug 18 22:41:33 nova postfix/smtp: 0E4A93688:
    to=<evi@ee.ethz.ch>,relay=tardis.ee.ethz.ch[129.132.2.217],delay=0,
    status=sent (250 Ok: queued as 154D4D930B)
Aug 18 22:41:33 nova postfix/qmgr: 0E4A93688: removed
```

As you can see, the interesting information is spread over many lines. Note that the identifier 0E4A93688 is common to every line: Postfix assigns a queue ID as soon as a message enters the mail system and never changes it. Therefore, when searching the logs for the history of a message, first concentrate on determining the message's queue ID. Once you know that, it's easy to **grep** the logs for all the relevant entries.

Postfix is good at logging helpful messages about problems that it notices. However, it's sometimes difficult to spot the important lines among the thousands of normal status messages. This is a good place to consider using some of the tools discussed in the section *Condensing log files to useful information*, which starts on page 220.

Looking at the queue

Another place to look for problems is the mail queue. As in the **sendmail** system, a **mailq** command prints the contents of a queue. You can use it to see if and why a message has become stuck.

Another helpful tool is the **qshape** script that's shipped with recent Postfix versions. It shows summary statistics about the contents of a queue. The output looks like this:

```
# qshape deferred
                  T   5  10  20  40  80  160  320  640  1280  1280+
        TOTAL  78   0   0   0   7   3    3    2   12     2     49
      expn.com  34   0   0   0   0   0    0    0    9     0     25
   chinabank.ph   5   0   0   0   1   1    1    2    0     0      0
  prob-helper.biz   3   0   0   0   0   0    0    0    0     0      3
```

qshape summarizes the given queue (here, the deferred queue) sorted by recipient domain. The columns report the number of minutes the relevant messages have been in the queue. For example, you can see that 49 messages bound for expn.com have been in the queue longer than 1280 minutes. All the destinations in this example are suggestive of messages having been sent from vacation scripts in response to spam.

qshape can also summarize by sender domain with the **-s** flag.

Soft-bouncing

If soft_bounce is set to yes, Postfix sends temporary error messages whenever it would normally send permanent error messages such as "user unknown" or "relaying denied." This is a great testing feature; it lets you monitor the disposition of messages after a configuration change without the risk of permanently losing legitimate email. Anything you reject will eventually come back for another try. Don't forget to turn off this feature when you are done testing, however. Otherwise, you will have to deal with every rejected message over and over again.

Testing access control

The easiest way to test access control restrictions is to try to send a message from an outside host and see what happens. This is a good basic test, but it doesn't cover special conditions such as mail from a specific domain in which you have no login.

Postfix 2.1 introduced an extension to the SMTP protocol called XCLIENT that simulates submissions from another place. This feature is disabled by default, but with the following configuration line in **main.cf**, you can enable it for connections originating from localhost :

```
smtpd_authorized_xclient_hosts = localhost
```

A testing session might look something like this:

```
$ telnet localhost 25
Trying 127.0.0.1...
Connected to localhost.
Escape character is '^]'.
```

```
220 tardis.ee.ethz.ch ESMTP Postfix
XCLIENT NAME=mail.cs.colorado.edu ADDR=192.168.1.1
250 Ok
HELO mail.cs.colorado.edu
250 tardis.ee.ethz.ch
MAIL FROM: <evi@colorado.edu>
250 Ok
RCPT TO: <david@colorado.edu>
554 <david@colorado.edu>: Relay access denied
```

18.17 RECOMMENDED READING

COSTALES, BRYAN, and ERIC ALLMAN. *sendmail (3rd Edition)*. Sebastopol, CA: O'Reilly Media, 2002.

This book is the definitive tome—1,200 pages' worth. It includes a tutorial as well as a complete reference section. The book reads well in the open-to-a-random-page mode, which we consider an important feature for a reference book. It has a good index too.

CLAYTON, RICHARD. "Good Practice for Combating Unsolicited Bulk Email." RIPE/Demon Internet. 2000, www.ripe.net/ripe/docs/ripe-206.html

This document is aimed at ISPs. It has lots of policy information and some good links to technical subjects.

SCHWARTZ, ALAN. *SpamAssassin*. Sebastopol, CA: O'Reilly Media, 2005.

SCHWARTZ, ALAN, AND PAULA FERGUSON. *Managing Mailing Lists*. Sebastopol, CA: O'Reilly Media, 1998.

HAZEL, PHILIP. *The Exim Smtp Mail Server: Official Guide for Release 4*. Cambridge, UK: User Interface Technologies, Ltd., 2003.

Exim documentation and information can also be found at www.exim.org.

The man page for **sendmail** describes its command-line arguments. See *Sendmail: An Internetwork Mail Router*, by Eric Allman, for an overview.

Installation instructions and a good description of the configuration file are covered in *Sendmail Installation and Operation Guide*, which can be found in the **doc/op** subdirectory of the **sendmail** distribution. This document is quite complete, and in conjunction with the **README** file in the **cf** directory, it gives a good nuts-and-bolts view of the **sendmail** system.

www.sendmail.org, www.sendmail.org/~ca, and www.sendmail.org/~gshapiro all contain **sendmail**-related documents, HOWTOs, and tutorials.

RFC2822, which supersedes RFC822, describes the syntax of messages and addresses in a networked mail system, and RFC1123 describes host requirements. These are, in a sense, the functional specifications to which **sendmail** was built.

RFC2821, which supersedes RFC821, defines the Simple Mail Transport Protocol (SMTP), and RFCs 1869, 1870, 1891, and 1985 extend it to ESMTP.

RFC974 describes MX records in the Domain Name System and their relationship to mail routing. Other mail-related RFCs include:

- RFC1731 – IMAP4 Authentication Mechanisms
- RFC1733 – Distributed Electronic Mail Models in IMAP4
- RFC2033 – Local Mail Transfer Protocol
- RFC2076 – Common Internet Message Headers
- RFC2142 – Mailbox Names for Common Services, Roles and Functions
- RFC2505 – Anti-Spam Recommendations for SMTP MTAs
- RFC2635 – DON'T SPEW: Guidelines for Mass Unsolicited Mailings[35]
- RFC2821 – Simple Mail Transfer Protocol
- RFC2822 – Internet Message Format
- RFC4405 – SMTP Service Extension for Indicating Message Submitters[35]
- RFC4406 – Sender ID: Authenticating E-Mail
- RFC4408 – SPF for Authorizing Use of Domains in E-Mail, Version 1
- RFC4409 – Message Submission for Mail

RFCs 2821 (SMTP) and 2822 (Internet Message Format) tidy up some of the most commonly referred-to email RFCs; they supersede RFCs 821, 822, 974, and 1869. RFCs 2821 and 2822 were first published in April 2001 and are proposed standards.

18.18 EXERCISES

E18.1   [**sendmail** specific] Briefly list the differences and similarities between genericstable and virtusertable. In what situations would you use each?

E18.2   [**sendmail** specific] Compare the use of **/etc/mail/aliases** with the use of an LDAP server to store mail aliases. What are the advantages and disadvantages of each?

E18.3   Briefly explain the difference between a mail user agent (MUA), a delivery agent (DA), and an access agent (AA). Then explain the difference between a mail transport agent (MTA) and a mail submission agent (MSA).

E18.4   [**sendmail** specific] What is **smrsh**, and why should you use it instead of **/bin/sh**? If **smrsh** is in use at your site, what programs are allowed to run as the program mailer? Are any of them dangerously insecure?

E18.5   [**sendmail** specific] Write a small **/etc/mail/aliases** file that demonstrates three different types of aliases. Talk briefly about what each line does and why it could be useful.

---

35. Title paraphrased

★ **E18.6** Write a brief description of the following email header. What path did the email take? To whom was it addressed, and to whom was it delivered? How long did it take the email to go from the sender to the destination?

> From clements@boulderlabs.com Fri Dec 28 17:06:57 2001
> Return-Path: <clements@mail.boulderlabs.com>
> Received: from boulder.Colorado.EDU (boulder.Colorado.EDU
>   [128.138.240.1]) by ucsub.colorado.edu (8.11.6/8.11.2/ITS-5.0/student)
>   with ESMTP idfBT06vF10618 for <hallcp@ucsub.Colorado.EDU>; Fri,
>   28 Dec 2001 17:06:57-0700 (MST)
> Received: from mail.boulderlabs.com (mail.boulderlabs.com
>   [206.168.112.48]) by boulder.Colorado.EDU
>   (8.10.1/8.10.1/UnixOps+Hesiod (Boulder)) with ESMTP id
>   fBT06uL13184; Fri, 28 Dec 2001 17:06:56 -0700 (MST)
> Received: from ath.boulderlabs.com (cpe-24-221-212-162.co.sprintbbd.net
>   [24.221.212.162]) by mail.boulderlabs.com (8.11.6/8.11.6) with ESMTP
>   id fBT06oQ29214 for <booklist@boulderlabs.com>; Fri, 28 Dec 2001
>   17:06:50 -0700 (MST) (envelope-from
>   clements@mail.boulderlabs.com)
> From: David Clements <clements@boulderlabs.com>
> Received: (from clements@localhost) by ath.boulderlabs.com
>   (8.11.6/8.11.4) id fBT06ma01470 for booklist@boulderlabs.com; Fri,
>   28 Dec 2001 17:06:48 -0700 (MST) (envelope-from clements)
> Date: Fri, 28 Dec 2001 17:06:48 -0700 (MST)
> Message-Id: <200112290006.fBT06ma01470@ath.boulderlabs.com>
> To: boolist@boulderlabs.com
> Subject: Book Questions

★ **E18.7** [**sendmail** specific] List the prefixes for files in the mail queue directory and explain what each one means. Why is it important to delete some queue files but very wrong to delete others? How can some of the prefixes be used to debug **sendmail** configuration mistakes?

E18.8 Look at the **mailq** on your campus mail server. Is there any cruft in the directory? Are there any messages with no control files or control files with no messages? What is the oldest message in the queue? (Requires root access.)

★ **E18.9** [**sendmail** specific] Explain the purpose of each of the following **m4** macros. If the macro includes a file, provide a short description of what the contents of the file should be.

    a) VERSIONID
    b) OSTYPE
    c) DOMAIN
    d) MAILER
    e) FEATURE

Exercises are continued on the next page.

Electronic Mail

⋆ **E18.10** Explain what an MX record is. Why are MX records important for mail delivery? Give an example in which a misconfigured MX record might make mail undeliverable.

⋆ **E18.11** What are the implications of being blacklisted on sbl-xbl.spamhaus.org or a similar spam black hole list? Outline some techniques used to stay off such lists.

⋆ **E18.12** If your site allows **procmail** and if you have permission from your local sysadmin group, set up your personal **procmail** configuration file to illustrate how **procmail** can compromise security.

⋆⋆ **E18.13** Explore the current MTA configuration at your site. What are some of the special features of the MTA that are in use? Can you find any problems with the configuration? In what ways could the configuration be made better?

⋆⋆ **E18.14** Find a piece of spam in your mailbox and inspect the headers. Report any signs that the mail has been forged. Then run some of the tools mentioned in this chapter, such as SpamCop or SpamAssassin, and report their findings. How did you do at recognizing faked headers? Submit the spam and your conclusions about the sender, the validity of the listed hosts, and anything else that looks out of place.

19 Network Management and Debugging

Because networks increase the number of interdependencies among machines, they tend to magnify problems. As the saying goes, "Networking is when you can't get any work done because of the failure of a machine you have never even heard of."

Network management is the art and science of keeping a network healthy. It generally includes the following tasks:

- Fault detection for networks, gateways, and critical servers
- Schemes for notifying an administrator of problems
- General monitoring, to balance load and plan expansion
- Documentation and visualization of the network
- Administration of network devices from a central site

On a single network segment, it is generally not worthwhile to establish formal procedures for network management. Just test the network thoroughly after installation, and check it occasionally to be sure that its load is not excessive. When it breaks, fix it.

As your network grows, management procedures should become more automated. On a network consisting of several different subnets joined with switches or routers, you may want to start automating management tasks with shell scripts and simple programs. If you have a WAN or a complex local network, consider installing a dedicated network management station.

In some cases, your organization's reliability needs dictate the sophistication of your network management system. A problem with the network can bring all work to a standstill. If your site cannot tolerate downtime, it may well be worthwhile to obtain and install a high-end enterprise network management system.

Unfortunately, even the best network management system cannot prevent all failures. It is critical to have a well-documented network and a high-quality staff available to handle the inevitable collapses.

19.1 NETWORK TROUBLESHOOTING

Several good tools are available for debugging a network at the TCP/IP layer. Most give low-level information, so you must understand the main ideas of TCP/IP and routing in order to use the debugging tools.

On the other hand, network issues can also stem from problems with higher-level protocols such as DNS, NFS, and HTTP. You might want to read through Chapter 12, *TCP/IP Networking*, and Chapter 13, *Routing*, before tackling this chapter.

In this section, we start with some general troubleshooting strategy. We then cover several essential tools, including **ping**, **traceroute**, **netstat**, **tcpdump**, and Wireshark. We don't discuss the **arp** command in this chapter, though it, too, is a useful debugging tool—see page 296 for more information.

Before you attack your network, consider these principles:

- Make one change at a time, and test each change to make sure that it had the effect you intended. Back out any changes that have an undesired effect.

- Document the situation as it was before you got involved, and document every change you make along the way.

- Start at one "end" of a system or network and work through the system's critical components until you reach the problem. For example, you might start by looking at the network configuration on a client, work your way up to the physical connections, investigate the network hardware, and finally, check the server's physical connections and software configuration.

- Communicate regularly. Most network problems involve or affect lots of different people: users, ISPs, system administrators, telco engineers, network administrators, etc. Clear, consistent communication prevents you from hindering one another's efforts to solve the problem.

- Work as a team. Years of experience show that people make fewer stupid mistakes if they have a peer helping out.

- Use the layers of the network to negotiate the problem. Start at the "top" or "bottom" and work your way through the protocol stack.

This last point deserves a bit more discussion. As described on page 275, the architecture of TCP/IP defines several layers of abstraction at which components of the network can function. For example, HTTP depends on TCP, TCP depends on IP, IP depends on the Ethernet protocol, and the Ethernet protocol depends on the integrity of the network cable. You can dramatically reduce the amount of time spent debugging a problem if you first figure out which layer is misbehaving.

Ask yourself questions like these as you work up (or down) the stack:

- Do you have physical connectivity and a link light?
- Is your interface configured properly?
- Do your ARP tables show other hosts?
- Can you ping the localhost address (127.0.0.1)?
- Can you ping other local hosts by IP address?
- Is DNS working properly?[1]
- Can you ping other local hosts by hostname?
- Can you ping hosts on another network?
- Do high-level services like web and SSH servers work?

Once you've identified where the problem lies, take a step back and consider the effect your subsequent tests and prospective fixes will have on other services and hosts.

19.2 PING: CHECK TO SEE IF A HOST IS ALIVE

The **ping** command is embarrassingly simple, but in many situations it is all you need. It sends an ICMP ECHO_REQUEST packet to a target host and waits to see if the host answers back. Despite its simplicity, **ping** is one of the workhorses of network debugging.

You can use **ping** to check the status of individual hosts and to test segments of the network. Routing tables, physical networks, and gateways are all involved in processing a ping, so the network must be more or less working for **ping** to succeed. If **ping** doesn't work, you can be pretty sure that nothing more sophisticated will work either. However, this rule does not apply to networks that block ICMP echo requests with a firewall. Make sure that a firewall isn't interfering with your debugging before you conclude that the target host is ignoring a **ping**. You might consider disabling a meddlesome firewall for a short period of time to facilitate debugging.

ping runs in an infinite loop unless you supply a packet count argument. Once you've had your fill of pinging, type the interrupt character (usually <Control-C>) to get out.

Here's an example:

```
$ ping beast
PING beast (10.1.1.46): 56 bytes of data.
64 bytes from beast (10.1.1.46): icmp_seq=0 ttl=54 time=48.3ms
64 bytes from beast (10.1.1.46): icmp_seq=1 ttl=54 time=46.4ms
64 bytes from beast (10.1.1.46): icmp_seq=2 ttl=54 time=88.7ms
^C
--- beast ping statistics ---
3 packets transmitted, 3 received, 0% packet loss, time 2026ms
rtt min/avg/max/mdev = 46.490/61.202/88.731/19.481 ms
```

---

1. If your machine hangs at boot time, boots very slowly, or hangs on inbound SSH connections, DNS should be your prime suspect.

Network Management

The output for beast shows the host's IP address, the ICMP sequence number of each response packet, and the round trip travel time. The most obvious thing that the output above tells you is that the server beast is alive and connected to the network.

On a healthy network, **ping** can allow you to determine if a host is down. Conversely, when a remote host is known to be up and in good working order, **ping** can give you useful information about the health of the network. Ping packets are routed by the usual IP mechanisms, and a successful round trip means that all networks and gateways lying between the source and destination are working correctly, at least to a first approximation.

The ICMP sequence number is a particularly valuable piece of information. Discontinuities in the sequence indicate dropped packets; they're normally accompanied by a message for each missing packet. Despite the fact that IP does not guarantee the delivery of packets, a healthy network should drop very few of them. Lost-packet problems are important to track down because they tend to be masked by higher-level protocols. The network may appear to function correctly, but it will be slower than it ought to be, not only because of the retransmitted packets but also because of the protocol overhead needed to detect and manage them.

To track down the cause of disappearing packets, first run **traceroute** (see the next section) to discover the route that packets are taking to the target host. Then ping the intermediate gateways in sequence to discover which link is dropping packets. To pin down the problem, you need to send a statistically significant number of packets. The network fault generally lies on the link between the last gateway that you can ping without significant loss of packets and the gateway beyond it.

The round trip time reported by **ping** gives you insight into the overall performance of a path through a network. Moderate variations in round trip time do not usually indicate problems. Packets may occasionally be delayed by tens or hundreds of milliseconds for no apparent reason; that's just the way IP works. You should expect to see a fairly consistent round trip time for the majority of packets, with occasional lapses. Many of today's routers implement rate-limited or lower-priority responses to ICMP packets, which means that a router may delay responding to your ping if it is already dealing with a lot of other traffic.

The **ping** program can send echo request packets of any size, so by using a packet larger than the MTU of the network (1,500 bytes for Ethernet), you can force fragmentation. This practice helps you identify media errors or other low-level issues such as problems with a congested network or VPN. To specify the desired packet size in bytes, use the **-s** flag.

```
$ ping -s 1500 cuinfo.cornell.edu
```

Use the **ping** command with the following caveats in mind.

First, it is hard to distinguish the failure of a network from the failure of a server with only the **ping** command. In an environment where ping tests normally work, a failed ping just tells you that *something* is wrong. (Network firewalls sometimes intentionally block ICMP packets.)

Second, a successful ping does not guarantee much about the target machine's state. Echo request packets are handled within the IP protocol stack and do not require a server process to be running on the probed host. A response guarantees only that a machine is powered on and has not experienced a kernel panic. You'll need higher-level methods to verify the availability of individual services such as HTTP and DNS.

19.3   TRACEROUTE: TRACE IP PACKETS

traceroute, originally written by Van Jacobson, uncovers the sequence of gateways through which an IP packet travels to reach its destination. All modern operating systems come with some version of **traceroute**. The syntax is simply

> **traceroute** *hostname*

There are a variety of options, most of which are not important in daily use. As usual, the *hostname* can be specified with either a DNS name or an IP address. The output is simply a list of hosts, starting with the first gateway and ending at the destination.

For example, a **traceroute** from the host jaguar to the host nubark produces the following output:

```
$ traceroute nubark
traceroute to nubark (192.168.2.10), 30 hops max, 38 byte packets
 1  lab-gw (172.16.8.254)  0.840 ms  0.693 ms  0.671 ms
 2  dmz-gw (192.168.1.254)  4.642 ms  4.582 ms  4.674 ms
 3  nubark (192.168.2.10)  7.959 ms  5.949 ms  5.908 ms
```

From this output we can tell that jaguar is exactly three hops away from nubark, and we can see which gateways are involved in the connection. The round trip time for each gateway is also shown—three samples for each hop are measured and displayed. A typical **traceroute** between Internet hosts often includes more than 15 hops.

traceroute works by setting the time-to-live field (TTL, actually "hop count to live") of an outbound packet to an artificially low number. As packets arrive at a gateway, their TTL is decreased. When a gateway decreases the TTL to 0, it discards the packet and sends an ICMP "time exceeded" message back to the originating host.

See page 396 for more information about reverse DNS lookups.

The first three **traceroute** packets have their TTL set to 1. The first gateway to see such a packet (lab-gw in this case) determines that the TTL has been exceeded and notifies jaguar of the dropped packet by sending back an ICMP message. The sender's IP address in the header of the error packet identifies the gateway; **traceroute** looks up this address in DNS to find the gateway's hostname.

To identify the second-hop gateway, **traceroute** sends out a second round of packets with TTL fields set to 2. The first gateway routes the packets and decreases their TTL by 1. At the second gateway, the packets are then dropped and ICMP error messages

Network Management

are generated as before. This process continues until the TTL is equal to the number of hops to the destination host and the packets reach their destination successfully.

Most routers send their ICMP messages from the interface "closest" to your host. If you run **traceroute** backwards from the destination host, you will probably see different IP addresses being used to identify the same set of routers. You might also see completely different paths; this configuration is known as "asymmetric routing."

Since **traceroute** sends three packets for each value of the TTL field, you may sometimes observe an interesting artifact. If an intervening gateway multiplexes traffic across several routes, the packets might be returned by different hosts; in this case, **traceroute** simply prints them all.

Let's look at a more interesting example from a host at colorado.edu to xor.com:

```
rupertsberg$ traceroute xor.com
traceroute to xor.com (192.225.33.1), 30 hops max, 38 byte packets
 1  cs-gw3-faculty.cs.colorado.edu (128.138.236.3)  1.362 ms  2.144 ms  2.76 ms
 2  cs-gw-dmz.cs.colorado.edu (128.138.243.193)  2.720 ms  4.378 ms  5.052 ms
 3  engr-cs.Colorado.EDU (128.138.80.141)  5.587 ms  2.454 ms  2.773 ms
 4  hut-engr.Colorado.EDU (128.138.80.201)  2.743 ms  5.643 ms  2.772 ms
 5  cuatm-gw.Colorado.EDU (128.138.80.2)  5.587 ms  2.784 ms  2.777 ms
 6  204.131.62.6 (204.131.62.6)  5.585 ms  3.464 ms  2.761 ms
 7  border-from-BRAN.coop.net (199.45.134.81)  5.593 ms  6.433 ms  5.521 ms
 8  core-gw-eth-2-5.coop.net (199.45.137.14)  53.806 ms  *  19.202 ms
 9  xor.com (192.225.33.1)  16.838 ms  15.972 ms  11.204 ms
```

This output shows that packets must traverse five internal gateways before leaving the colorado.edu network (cs-gw3-faculty to cuatm-gw). The next-hop gateway on the BRAN network (204.131.62.6) doesn't have a name in DNS. After two hops in coop.net, we arrive at xor.com.

At hop 8, we see a star in place of one of the round trip times. This notation means that no response (error packet) was received in response to the probe. In this case, the cause is probably congestion, but that is not the only possibility. **traceroute** relies on low-priority ICMP packets, which many routers are smart enough to drop in preference to "real" traffic. A few stars shouldn't send you into a panic.

If you see stars in all the round trip time fields for a given gateway, no "time exceeded" messages are arriving from that machine. Perhaps the gateway is simply down. Sometimes, a gateway or firewall is configured to silently discard packets with expired TTLs. In this case, you can still see through the silent host to the gateways beyond. Another possibility is that the gateway's error packets are slow to return and that **traceroute** has stopped waiting for them by the time they arrive.

Some firewalls block ICMP "time exceeded" messages entirely. If one such firewall lies along the path, you won't get information about any of the gateways beyond it. However, you can still determine the total number of hops to the destination because the probe packets eventually get all the way there. Also, some firewalls may block the outbound UDP datagrams that **traceroute** sends to trigger the ICMP responses. This problem causes **traceroute** to report no useful information at all.

A slow link does not necessarily indicate a malfunction. Some physical networks have a naturally high latency; 802.11 wireless networks are a good example. Sluggishness can also be a sign of congestion on the receiving network, especially if the network uses a CSMA/CD technology that makes repeated attempts to transmit a packet (Ethernet is one example). Inconsistent round trip times would support such a hypothesis, since collisions increase the randomness of the network's behavior.

Sometimes, you may see the notation !N instead of a star or round trip time. It indicates that the current gateway sent back a "network unreachable" error, meaning that it doesn't know how to route your packet. Other possibilities include !H for "host unreachable" and !P for "protocol unreachable." A gateway that returns any of these error messages is usually the last hop you can get to. That host usually has a routing problem (possibly caused by a broken link): either its static routes are wrong or dynamic protocols have failed to propagate a usable route to the destination.

If **traceroute** doesn't seem to be working for you (or is working noticeably slowly), it may be timing out while trying to resolve the hostnames of gateways by using DNS. If DNS is broken on the host you are tracing from, use **traceroute -n** to request numeric output. This option prevents the use of DNS; it may be the only way to get **traceroute** to function on a crippled network.

19.4 NETSTAT: GET NETWORK STATISTICS

netstat collects a wealth of information about the state of your computer's networking software, including interface statistics, routing information, and connection tables. There isn't really a unifying theme to the different sets of output, except that they all relate to the network. Think of **netstat** as the "kitchen sink" of network tools—it exposes a variety of network information that doesn't fit anywhere else. Here, we discuss the five most common uses of **netstat**:

- Inspecting interface configuration information
- Monitoring the status of network connections
- Identifying listening network services
- Examining the routing table
- Viewing operational statistics for various network protocols

Inspecting interface configuration information

netstat -i displays information about the configuration and state of each of the host's network interfaces. You can run **netstat -i** as a good way to familiarize yourself with a new machine's network setup. Add the **-e** option for additional details.

Network Management

For example:

```
$ netstat -i -e
Kernel Interface table
eth0      Link encap:Ethernet  HWaddr 00:02:B3:19:C8:82
          inet addr:192.168.2.1  Bcast:192.168.2.255  Mask:255.255.255.0
          UP BROADCAST RUNNING MULTICAST  MTU:1500  Metric:1
          RX packets:1121527 errors:0 dropped:0 overruns:0 frame:0
          TX packets:1138477 errors:0 dropped:0 overruns:0 carrier:0
          collisions:0 txqueuelen:100
          Interrupt:7 Base address:0xef00

eth1      Link encap:Ethernet  HWaddr 00:02:B3:19:C6:86
          inet addr:192.168.1.13  Bcast:192.168.1.255  Mask:255.255.255.0
          UP BROADCAST RUNNING MULTICAST  MTU:1500  Metric:1
          RX packets:67543 errors:0 dropped:0 overruns:0 frame:0
          TX packets:69652 errors:0 dropped:0 overruns:0 carrier:0
          collisions:0 txqueuelen:100
          Interrupt:5 Base address:0xed00

lo        Link encap:Local Loopback
          inet addr:127.0.0.1  Mask:255.0.0.0
          UP LOOPBACK RUNNING  MTU:3924  Metric:1
          RX packets:310572 errors:0 dropped:0 overruns:0 frame:0
          TX packets:310572 errors:0 dropped:0 overruns:0 carrier:0
          collisions:0 txqueuelen:0
```

This host has two network interfaces: one for regular traffic plus a second connection for system management named eth1. RX packets and TX packets report the number of packets that have been received and transmitted on each interface since the machine was booted. Many different types of errors are counted in the error buckets, and it is normal for a few to show up.

Errors should be less than 1% of the associated packets. If your error rate is high, compare the rates of several neighboring machines. A large number of errors on a single machine suggests a problem with that machine's interface or connection. A high error rate everywhere most likely indicates a media or network problem. One of the most common causes of a high error rate is an Ethernet speed or duplex mismatch caused by a failure of autosensing or autonegotiation.

Collisions suggest a loaded network; errors often indicate cabling problems. Although a collision is a type of error, it is counted separately by **netstat**. The field labeled Collisions reports the number of collisions that were experienced while packets were being sent.[2] Use this number to calculate the percentage of output packets (TX packets) that result in collisions. On a properly functioning network, collisions should be less than 3% of output packets, and anything over 10% indicates serious congestion problems. Collisions should never occur on a full-duplex link that is operating properly.

---

2. This field has meaning only on CSMA/CD-based networks such as Ethernet.

Monitoring the status of network connections

With no arguments, **netstat** displays the status of active TCP and UDP ports. Inactive ("listening") servers waiting for connections aren't normally shown; they can be seen with **netstat -a**.[3] The output looks like this:

```
$ netstat -a
Active Internet connections (servers and established)
Proto   Recv-Q  Send-Q  Local Address   ForeignAddress      State
tcp     0       0       *:ldap          *:*                 LISTEN
tcp     0       0       *:mysql         *:*                 LISTEN
tcp     0       0       *:imaps         *:*                 LISTEN
tcp     0       0       bull:ssh        dhcp-32hw:4208      ESTABLISHED
tcp     0       0       bull:imaps      nubark:54195        ESTABLISHED
tcp     0       0       bull:http       dhcp-30hw:2563      ESTABLISHED
tcp     0       0       bull:imaps      dhcp-18hw:2851      ESTABLISHED
tcp     0       0       *:http          *:*                 LISTEN
tcp     0       0       bull:37203      baikal:mysql        ESTABLISHED
tcp     0       0       *:ssh           *:*                 LISTEN...
...
```

This example is from the host otter, and it has been severely pruned; for example, UDP and UNIX socket connections are not displayed. The output above shows an inbound SSH connection, two inbound IMAPS connections, one inbound HTTP connection, an outbound MySQL connection, and a bunch of ports listening for other connections.

Addresses are shown as *hostname.service*, where the *service* is a port number. For well-known services, **netstat** shows the port symbolically, using the mapping defined in the **/etc/services** file. You can obtain numeric addresses and ports with the **-n** option. As with most network debugging tools, if your DNS is broken, **netstat** is painful to use without the **-n** flag.

Send-Q and Recv-Q show the sizes of the send and receive queues for the connection on the local host; the queue sizes on the other end of a TCP connection might be different. They should tend toward 0 and at least not be consistently nonzero. Of course, if you are running **netstat** over a network terminal, the send queue for your connection may never be 0.

The connection state has meaning only for TCP; UDP is a connectionless protocol. The most common states you'll see are ESTABLISHED for currently active connections, LISTEN for servers waiting for connections (not normally shown without **-a**), and TIME_WAIT for connections in the process of closing.

This display is primarily useful for debugging higher-level problems once you have determined that basic networking facilities are working correctly. It lets you verify that servers are set up correctly and facilitates the diagnosis of certain types of miscommunication, particularly with TCP. For example, a connection that stays in state

---

3. Connections for "UNIX domain sockets" are also shown, but since they aren't related to networking, we do not discuss them here.

SYN_SENT identifies a process that is trying to contact a nonexistent or inaccessible network server.

See Chapter 28 for more information about kernel tuning.

If **netstat** shows a lot of connections in the SYN_WAIT condition, your host probably cannot handle the number of connections being requested. This inadequacy may be due to kernel tuning limitations or even to malicious flooding.

Identifying listening network services

One common question in this security-conscious era is "What processes on this machine are listening on the network for incoming connections?" **netstat -a** shows all the ports that are actively listening (any TCP port in state LISTEN, and potentially any UDP port), but on a busy machine those lines can get lost in the noise of established TCP connections. Use **netstat -l** to see only the listening ports. The output format is the same as for **netstat -a**.

You can add the **-p** flag to make **netstat** identify the specific process associated with each listening port. The sample output below shows three common services (**sshd**, **sendmail**, and **named**), followed by an unusual one:

```
$ netstat -lp
...
tcp    0    0    0.0.0.0:22     0.0.0.0:*    LISTEN    23858/sshd
tcp    0    0    0.0.0.0:25     0.0.0.0:*    LISTEN    10342/sendmail
udp    0    0    0.0.0.0:53     0.0.0.0:*              30016/named
udp    0    0    0.0.0.0:962    0.0.0.0:*              38221/mudd
...
```

Here, **mudd** with PID 38221 is listening on UDP port 962. Depending on your site's policy regarding user-installed software, you might want to follow up on this one.

Examining the routing table

netstat -r displays the kernel's routing table. The following sample is from a Red Hat machine with two network interfaces. (The output varies slightly among Linux distributions.)

```
$ netstat -rn
Kernel IP routing table
Destination    Gateway        Genmask        Flags MSS Window  irtt  Iface
192.168.1.0    0.0.0.0        255.255.255.0  U       0  0         0  eth0
10.2.5.0       0.0.0.0        255.255.255.0  U       0  0         0  eth1
127.0.0.0      0.0.0.0        255.0.0.0      U       0  0         0  lo
0.0.0.0        192.168.1.254  0.0.0.0        UG      0  0        40  eth0
...
```

Destinations and gateways can be displayed either as hostnames or as IP addresses; the **-n** flag requests numeric output.

See page 294 for more information about the routing table.

The Flags characterize the route: U means up (active), G is a gateway, and H is a host route. U, G, and H together indicate a host route that passes through an intermediate gateway. The D flag (not shown) indicates a route resulting from an ICMP redirect.

The remaining fields give statistics on the route: the current number of TCP connections using the route, the number of packets sent, and the interface used.

Use this form of **netstat** to check the health of your system's routing table. It's particularly important to verify that the system has a default route and that this route is correct. The default route is represented by an all-0 destination address (0.0.0.0). It is possible not to have a default route entry, but such a configuration would be highly atypical.

Viewing operational statistics for network protocols

netstat -s dumps the contents of counters that are scattered throughout the network code. The output has separate sections for IP, ICMP, TCP, and UDP. Below are pieces of **netstat -s** output from a typical server; they have been edited to show only the tastiest pieces of information.

```
Ip:
    671349985 total packets received
    0 forwarded
    345 incoming packets discarded
    667912993 incoming packets delivered
    589623972 requests sent out
    60 dropped because of missing route
    203 fragments dropped after timeout
```

Be sure to check that packets are not being dropped or discarded. It is acceptable for a few incoming packets to be discarded, but a quick rise in this metric usually indicates a memory shortage or some other resource problem.

```
Icmp:
    242023 ICMP messages received
    912 input ICMP message failed.
    ICMP input histogram:
        destination unreachable: 72120
        timeout in transit: 573
        echo requests: 17135
        echo replies: 152195
    66049 ICMP messages sent
    0 ICMP messages failed
    ICMP output histogram:
        destination unreachable: 48914
        echo replies: 17135
```

In this example, the number of echo requests in the input section matches the number of echo replies in the output section. Note that "destination unreachable" messages can still be generated even when all packets are apparently forwardable. Bad packets eventually reach a gateway that rejects them, and error messages are then sent back along the gateway chain.

```
Tcp:
    4442780 active connections openings
    1023086 passive connection openings
    50399 failed connection attempts
    0 connection resets received
    44 connections established
    666674854 segments received
    585111784 segments send out
    107368 segments retransmited
    86 bad segments received.
    3047240 resets sent
Udp:
    4395827 packets received
    31586 packets to unknown port received.
    0 packet receive errors
    4289260 packets sent
```

It's a good idea to develop a feel for the normal ranges of these statistics so that you can recognize pathological states.

19.5 SAR: INSPECT LIVE INTERFACE ACTIVITY

One good way to identify network problems is to look at what's happening right now. How many packets were sent in the last five minutes on a given interface? How many bytes? Are collisions or other errors occurring? You can answer all these questions by watching live interface activity.

On traditional UNIX systems, **netstat -i** is the tool of choice for this role. Unfortunately, **netstat**'s ability to report on live interface activity is broken under Linux. We recommend a completely different tool: **sar**. (We discuss **sar** from the perspective of general system monitoring on page 816.) Most distributions don't install **sar** by default, but it's always available as an optional package.

To make **sar** report on interface activity every two seconds for a period of one minute (i.e., 30 reports), use the syntax **sar -n DEV 2 30**. The **DEV** argument is a literal keyword, not a placeholder for a device or interface name.

The output includes instantaneous and average readings of network interface utilization in terms of bytes and packets. The sample below is from a Red Hat machine with two physical interfaces. The second physical interface (eth1) is clearly not in use.

17:50:43	IFACE	rxpck/s	txpck/s	rxbyt/s	txbyt/s	rxcmp/s	txcmp/s	rxmcst/s
17:50:45	lo	3.61	3.61	263.40	263.40	0.00	0.00	0.00
17:50:45	eth0	18.56	11.86	1364.43	1494.33	0.00	0.00	0.52
17:50:45	eth1	0.00	0.00	0.00	0.00	0.00	0.00	0.00

The first two columns state the time at which the data was sampled and the names of the network interfaces. The next two columns show the number of packets received and transmitted, respectively. The rxbyt/s and txbyt/s columns are probably the most useful since they show the actual bandwidth in use. The final three columns give statistics on compressed (rxcmp/s, txcmp/s) and multicast (rxmcst/s) packets.

sar -n DEV is especially useful for tracking down the source of errors. **ifconfig** can alert you to the existence of problems, but it can't tell you whether the errors came from a continuous, low-level problem or from a brief but catastrophic event. Observe the network over time under a variety of load conditions to solidify your impression of what's going on. Try running **ping** with a large packet payload (size) while you watch the output of **sar -n DEV**.

19.6 PACKET SNIFFERS

tcpdump and Wireshark belong to a class of tools known as packet sniffers. They listen to the traffic on a network and record or print packets that meet certain criteria specified by the user. For example, all packets sent to or from a particular host or TCP packets related to one particular network connection could be inspected.

Packet sniffers are useful both for solving problems you know about and for discovering entirely new problems. It's a good idea to take an occasional sniff of your network to make sure the traffic is in order.

Packet sniffers need to be able to intercept traffic that the local machine would not normally receive (or at least, pay attention to), so the underlying network hardware must allow access to every packet. Broadcast technologies such as Ethernet work fine, as do most other modern local area networks.

See page 355 for more information about network switches. Since packet sniffers need to see as much of the raw network traffic as possible, they can be thwarted by network switches, which by design try to limit the propagation of "unnecessary" packets. However, it can still be informative to try out a sniffer on a switched network. You may discover problems related to broadcast or multicast packets. Depending on your switch vendor, you may be surprised at how much traffic you can see.

The interface hardware, in addition to having potential access to all network packets, must transport those packets up to the software layer. Packet addresses are normally checked in hardware, and only broadcast/multicast packets and those addressed to the local host are relayed to the kernel. In "promiscuous mode," an interface lets the kernel read all packets on the network, even the ones intended for other hosts.

Packet sniffers understand many of the packet formats used by standard network services, and they can often print these packets in a human-readable form. This capability makes it easier to track the flow of a conversation between two programs. Some sniffers print the ASCII contents of a packet in addition to the packet header and so are useful for investigating high-layer protocols. Since some of these protocols send information (and even passwords) across the network as cleartext, you must take care not to invade the privacy of your users.

Each of our example distributions comes with a packet sniffer. A sniffer must read data from a raw network device, so it must run as root. Although the root limitation serves to decrease the chance that normal users will listen in on your network traffic, it is really not much of a barrier. Some sites choose to remove sniffer programs from most hosts to reduce the chance of abuse. If nothing else, you should check your systems' interfaces to be sure they are not running in promiscuous mode without your knowledge or consent. On Linux systems, an interface in promiscuous mode shows the flag PROMISC in its **ifconfig** status output. You can also use tools such as PromiScan (available from www.securityfriday.com) to check your network for interfaces running in promiscuous mode.

tcpdump: king of sniffers

tcpdump, yet another amazing network tool by Van Jacobson, is included in most Linux distributions. **tcpdump** has long been the industry-standard sniffer; most other network analysis tools read and write trace files in "**tcpdump** format."

By default, **tcpdump** tunes in on the first network interface it comes across. If it chooses the wrong interface, you can force an interface with the **-i** flag. If DNS is broken or you just don't want **tcpdump** doing name lookups, use the **-n** option. This option is important because slow DNS service can cause the filter to start dropping packets before they can be dealt with by **tcpdump**. The **-v** flag increases the information you see about packets, and **-vv** gives you even more data. Finally, **tcpdump** can store packets to a file with the **-w** flag and can read them back in with the **-r** flag.

For example, the following truncated output comes from the machine named nubark. The filter specification **host bull** limits the display of packets to those that directly involve the machine bull, either as source or as destination.

```
# sudo tcpdump host bull
12:35:23.519339 bull.41537 > nubark.domain:  A? atrust.com. (28) (DF)
12:35:23.519961 nubark.domain > bull.41537:  A 66.77.122.161 (112) (DF)
```

The first packet shows the host bull sending a DNS lookup request about atrust.com to nubark. The response is the IP address of the machine associated with that name, which is 66.77.122.161. Note the time stamp on the left and **tcpdump**'s understanding of the application-layer protocol (in this case, DNS). The port number on bull is arbitrary and is shown numerically (41537), but since the server port number (53) is well known, **tcpdump** shows its symbolic name ("domain") instead.

Packet sniffers can produce an overwhelming amount of information—overwhelming not only for you but also for the underlying operating system. To avoid this problem on busy networks, **tcpdump** lets you specify fairly complex filters. For example, the following filter collects only incoming web traffic from a specific subnet:

```
# sudo tcpdump src net 192.168.1.0/24 and dst port 80
```

The **tcpdump** man page contains several good examples of advanced filtering along with a complete listing of primitives.[4]

---

4. If your filtering needs exceed **tcpdump**'s capabilities, consider **ngrep**, which can filter packets according to their contents.

Wireshark: visual sniffer

If you're more inclined to use a point-and-click program for packet sniffing, then Wireshark may be for you. Available under the GNU General Public License from www.wireshark.org, Wireshark is a GTK+ (GIMP tool kit)-based GUI packet sniffer that has more functionality than most commercial sniffing products. You can run Wireshark on your Linux desktop, or if your laptop is still painfully suffering in the dark ages of Windows, you can download binaries for that too.

In addition to sniffing packets, Wireshark has a couple of features that make it extra handy. One nice feature is that Wireshark can read and write a large number of other packet trace file formats, including (but not limited to):

- TCPDUMP
- NAI's Sniffer
- Sniffer Pro
- NetXray
- Snoop
- Shomiti Surveyor
- Microsoft's Network Monitor
- Novell's LANalyzer
- Cisco Secure IDS iplog

The second extra-handy feature is that you can click on one packet in a TCP stream and ask Wireshark to "reassemble" (splice together) the payload data of all the packets in the stream. This feature is useful if you want to quickly examine the data transferred during a complete TCP conversation, such as a connection carrying an email message across the network.[5]

Wireshark has capture filters, which function identically to **tcpdump**'s. Watch out, though—one important gotcha with Wireshark is the added feature of "display filters," which affect what you see rather than what's actually captured by the sniffer. Oddly, display filters use an entirely different syntax from capture filters.

Wireshark is an incredibly powerful analysis tool and is included in almost every networking expert's tool kit. Moreover, it's also an invaluable learning aid for those just beginning to explore packet networking. Wireshark's help menu provides many great examples to get you started. Don't be afraid to experiment!

19.7 NETWORK MANAGEMENT PROTOCOLS

Networks have grown rapidly in size and value over the last decade, and along with that growth has come the need for an efficient way to manage them. Commercial vendors and standards organizations have approached this challenge in many different ways. The most significant developments have been the introduction of several standard device management protocols and a glut of high-level products that exploit those protocols.

---

5. You can use the **tcpflow** utility to perform a similar feat on the command line from a **tcpdump** trace.

Network Management

Network management protocols standardize the method of probing a device to discover its configuration, health, and network connections. In addition, they allow some of this information to be modified so that network management can be standardized across different kinds of machinery and performed from a central location.

The most common management protocol used with TCP/IP is the Simple Network Management Protocol, SNMP. Despite its name, SNMP is actually quite complex. It defines a hierarchical namespace of management data and a way to read and write the data at each node. It also defines a way for managed servers and devices ("agents") to send event notification messages ("traps") to management stations.

The SNMP protocol itself is simple; most of SNMP's complexity lies above the protocol layer in the conventions for constructing the namespace and in the unnecessarily baroque vocabulary that surrounds SNMP like a protective shell. As long as you don't think too hard about its internal mechanics, SNMP is easy to use.

Several other standards are floating around out there. Many of them originate from the Distributed Management Task Force (DMTF), which is responsible for concepts such as WBEM (Web-Based Enterprise Management), DMI (Desktop Management Interface), and the CIM (Conceptual Interface Model). Some of these concepts, particularly DMI, have been embraced by several major vendors and may become a useful complement to (or even a replacement for) SNMP. Many proprietary management protocols are also afloat out there. For now, however, the vast majority of network and Linux system management takes place over SNMP.

Since SNMP is only an abstract protocol, you need both a server program ("agent") and a client ("manager") to make use of it. (Perhaps counterintuitively, the server side of SNMP represents the thing being managed, and the client side is the manager.) Clients range from simple command-line utilities to dedicated management stations that graphically display networks and faults in eye-popping color.

Dedicated network management stations are the primary reason for the existence of management protocols. Most products let you build a topographic model of the network as well as a logical model; the two are presented together on-screen, along with a continuous indication of the status of each component.

Just as a chart can reveal the hidden meaning in a page of numbers, a network management station can summarize the state of a large network in a way that's easily accepted by a human brain. This kind of executive summary is almost impossible to get any other way.

A major advantage of management-by-protocol is that it promotes all kinds of network hardware onto a level playing field. Linux systems are all basically similar, but routers, switches, and other low-level components are not. With SNMP, they all speak a common language and can be probed, reset, and configured from a central location. It's nice to have one consistent interface to all the network's hardware.

19.8   SNMP: THE SIMPLE NETWORK MANAGEMENT PROTOCOL

When SNMP first became widely used in the early 1990s, it started a mini gold rush. Hundreds of companies have come out with SNMP management packages. Also, many hardware and software vendors ship an SNMP agent as part of their product.

Before we dive into the gritty details of SNMP, we should note that the terminology associated with it is some of the most wretched technobabble to be found in the networking arena. The standard names for SNMP concepts and objects actively lead you away from an understanding of what's going on. The people responsible for this state of affairs should have their keyboards smashed.

SNMP organization

SNMP data is arranged in a standardized hierarchy. This enforced organization allows the data space to remain both universal and extensible, at least in theory. Large portions are set aside for future expansion, and vendor-specific additions are localized to prevent conflicts. The naming hierarchy is made up of "Management Information Bases" (MIBs), structured text files that describe the data accessible through SNMP. MIBs contain descriptions of specific data variables, which are referred to with names known as object identifiers, or OIDs.

Translated into English, this means that SNMP defines a hierarchical namespace of variables whose values are tied to "interesting" parameters of the system. An OID is just a fancy way of naming a specific managed piece of information.

The SNMP hierarchy is very much like a filesystem. However, a dot is used as the separator character, and each node is given a number rather than a name. By convention, nodes are also given text names for ease of reference, but this naming is really just a high-level convenience and not a feature of the hierarchy (it is similar in principle to the mapping of hostnames to IP addresses).

For example, the OID that refers to the uptime of the system is 1.3.6.1.2.1.1.3. This OID is also known by the human readable name

> iso.org.dod.internet.mgmt.mib-2.system.sysUpTime

The top levels of the SNMP hierarchy are political artifacts and generally do not contain useful data. In fact, useful data can currently be found only beneath the OID iso.org.dod.internet.mgmt (numerically, 1.3.6.1.2).

The basic SNMP MIB for TCP/IP (MIB-I) defines access to common management data: information about the system, its interfaces, address translation, and protocol operations (IP, ICMP, TCP, UDP, and others). A later and more complete reworking of this MIB (called MIB-II) is defined in RFC1213. Most vendors that provide an SNMP server support MIB-II. Table 19.1 on the next page presents a sampling of nodes from the MIB-II namespace.

Table 19.1   Selected OIDs from MIB-II

OID[a]	Type	Contents
system.sysDescr	string	System info: vendor, model, OS type, etc.
system.sysLocation	string	Physical location of the machine
system.sysContact	string	Contact info for the machine's owner
system.sysName	string	System name, usually the full DNS name
interfaces.ifNumber	int	Number of network interfaces present
interfaces.ifTable	table	Table of infobits about each interface
ip.ipForwarding	int	1 if system is a gateway; otherwise,2
ip.ipAddrTable	table	Table of IP addressing data (masks, etc.)
ip.ipRouteTable	table	The system's routing table
icmp.icmpInRedirects	int	Number of ICMP redirects received
icmp.icmpInEchos	int	Number of pings received
tcp.tcpConnTable	table	Table of current TCP connections
udp.udpTable	table	Table of UDP sockets with servers listening

a. Relative to iso.org.dod.internet.mgmt.mib-2.

In addition to the basic MIB, there are MIBs for various kinds of hardware interfaces and protocols, MIBs for individual vendors, and MIBs for particular hardware products. A MIB for you, a MIB for me, catch that MIB behind the tree.

A MIB is only a convention about the naming of management data. To be useful, a MIB must be backed up with agent-side code that maps between the SNMP namespace and the device's actual state. Code for the basic MIB (now MIB-II) comes with the standard Linux agent. Some agents are extensible to include supplemental MIBs, and some are not.

SNMP protocol operations

There are only four basic SNMP operations: get, get-next, set, and trap.

Get and set are the basic operations for reading and writing data to a node identified by a specific OID. Get-next steps through a MIB hierarchy and can read the contents of tables as well.

A trap is an unsolicited, asynchronous notification from server (agent) to client (manager) that reports the occurrence of an interesting event or condition. Several standard traps are defined, including "I've just come up" notifications, reports of failure or recovery of a network link, and announcements of various routing and authentication problems. Many other not-so-standard traps are in common use, including some that simply watch the values of other SNMP variables and fire off a message when a specified range is exceeded. The mechanism by which the destinations of trap messages are specified depends on the implementation of the agent.

Since SNMP messages can potentially modify configuration information, some security mechanism is needed. The simplest version of SNMP security is based on the concept of an SNMP "community string," which is really just a horribly obfuscated way of saying "password." There's usually one community name for read-only access and another that allows writing.

Although many organizations still use the original community-string-based authentication, version 3 of the SNMP standard introduced access control methods with higher security. Although configuring this more advanced security requires a little extra work, the risk reduction is well worth the effort. If for some reason you can't use version 3 SNMP security, at least be sure you've selected a hard-to-guess community string.

RMON: remote monitoring MIB

The RMON MIB permits the collection of generic network performance data (that is, data not tied to any one particular device). Network sniffers or "probes" can be deployed around the network to gather information about utilization and performance. Once a useful amount of data has been collected, statistics and interesting information about the data can be shipped back to a central management station for analysis and presentation. Many probes have a packet capture buffer and can provide a sort of remote **tcpdump** facility.

RMON is defined in RFC1757, which became a draft standard in 1995. The MIB is broken up into nine "RMON groups." Each group contains a different set of network statistics. If you have a large network with many WAN connections, consider buying probes to reduce the SNMP traffic across your WAN links. Once you have access to statistical summaries from the RMON probes, there's usually no need to gather raw data remotely. Many switches and routers support RMON and store at least some network statistics.

19.9 THE NET-SMNP AGENT

When SNMP was first standardized, Carnegie Mellon University and MIT both produced implementations. CMU's implementation was more complete and quickly became the de facto standard. When active development at CMU died down, researchers at UC Davis took over the software. After stabilizing the code, they transferred the ongoing maintenance to the SourceForge repository. The package is now known as NET-SNMP.

The NET-SNMP distribution is now the authoritative free SNMP implementation for Linux. In fact, many network device vendors have integrated NET-SNMP into their products. NET-SNMP includes an SNMP agent, some command-line tools, a server for receiving traps, and even a library for developing SNMP-aware applications. We discuss the agent in some detail here, and on page 663 we look at the command-line tools. The latest version is available from net-snmp.sourceforge.net.

As in other implementations, the agent collects information about the local host and serves it to SNMP managers across the network. The default installation includes MIBs for network interface, memory, disk, process, and CPU statistics. The agent is

Network Management

easily extensible since it can execute an arbitrary Linux command and return the command's output as an SNMP response. You can use this feature to monitor almost anything on your system with SNMP.

By default, the agent is installed as **/usr/sbin/snmpd**. It is usually started at boot time and reads its configuration information from files in the **/etc/snmp** directory. The most important of these files is **snmpd.conf**, which contains most of the configuration information and comes shipped with a bunch of sample data collection methods enabled. Although the intention of the NET-SNMP authors seems to have been for users to edit only the **snmpd.local.conf** file, you must edit **snmpd.conf** at least once to disable any default data collection methods that you don't plan to use.

The NET-SNMP **configure** script lets you specify a default log file and a couple of other local settings. You can use **snmpd -l** to specify an alternative log file or **-s** to direct log messages to syslog. Table 19.2 lists **snmpd**'s most important flags. We recommend that you always use the **-a** flag. For debugging, you should use the **-V**, **-d**, or **-D** flags, each of which gives progressively more information.

Table 19.2 Useful flags for NET-SNMP snmpd

Flag	Function
-l *logfile*	Logs information to *logfile*
-a	Logs the addresses of all SNMP connections
-d	Logs the contents of every SNMP packet
-V	Enables verbose logging
-D	Logs debugging information (lots of it)
-h	Displays all arguments to **snmpd**
-H	Displays all configuration file directives
-A	Appends to the log file instead of overwriting it
-s	Logs to syslog (uses the daemon facility)

It's worth mentioning that many useful SNMP-related Perl modules are available. Look on CPAN[6] for the latest information if you are interested in writing your own network management scripts.

19.10 NETWORK MANAGEMENT APPLICATIONS

We begin this section by exploring the simplest SNMP management tools: the commands provided with the NET-SNMP package. These commands can help you become familiar with SNMP, and they're also great for one-off checks of specific OIDs. Next, we look at Cacti, a program that generates beautiful historical graphs of SNMP values, and Nagios, an event-based monitoring system. We conclude with some recommendations of what to look for when purchasing a commercial system.

6. CPAN, the Comprehensive Perl Archive Network, is an amazing collection of useful Perl modules. Check it out at www.cpan.org.

The NET-SNMP tools

Even if your system comes with its own SNMP server, you may still want to compile and install the client-side tools from the NET-SNMP package. Table 19.3 lists the most commonly used tools.

Table 19.3 Command-line tools in the NET-SNMP package

Command	Function
snmpdelta	Monitors changes in SNMP variables over time
snmpdf	Monitors disk space on a remote host via SNMP
snmpget	Gets the value of an SNMP variable from an agent
snmpgetnext	Gets the next variable in sequence
snmpset	Sets an SNMP variable on an agent
snmptable	Gets a table of SNMP variables
snmptranslate	Searches for and describes OIDs in the MIB hierarchy
snmptrap	Generates a trap alert
snmpwalk	Traverses a MIB starting at a particular OID

In addition to their value on the command line, these programs are tremendously handy in simple scripts. It is often helpful to have **snmpget** save interesting data values to a text file every few minutes. (Use **cron** to implement the scheduling; see Chapter 8, *Periodic Processes*.)

snmpwalk is another useful tool. Starting at a specified OID (or at the beginning of the MIB, by default), this command repeatedly makes "get next" calls to an agent. This behavior results in a complete list of available OIDs and their associated values. **snmpwalk** is particularly handy when you are trying to identify new OIDs to monitor from your fancy enterprise management tool.

Here's a truncated sample **snmpwalk** of the host tuva. The community string is "secret813community", and **-v1** specifies simple authentication.

```
$ snmpwalk -c secret813community -v1 tuva
SNMPv2-MIB::sysDescr.0 = STRING: Linux tuva.atrust.com 2.6.9-11.ELsmp #1
SNMPv2-MIB::sysUpTime.0 = Timeticks: (1442) 0:00:14.42
SNMPv2-MIB::sysName.0 = STRING: tuva.atrust.com
IF-MIB::ifDescr.1 = STRING: lo
IF-MIB::ifDescr.2 = STRING: eth0
IF-MIB::ifDescr.3 = STRING: eth1
IF-MIB::ifType.1 = INTEGER: softwareLoopback(24)
IF-MIB::ifType.2 = INTEGER: ethernetCsmacd(6)
IF-MIB::ifType.3 = INTEGER: ethernetCsmacd(6)
IF-MIB::ifPhysAddress.1 = STRING:
IF-MIB::ifPhysAddress.2 = STRING: 0:11:43:d9:1e:f5
IF-MIB::ifPhysAddress.3 = STRING: 0:11:43:d9:1e:f6
IF-MIB::ifInOctets.1 = Counter32: 2605613514
IF-MIB::ifInOctets.2 = Counter32: 1543105654
```

Network Management

```
IF-MIB::ifInOctets.3 = Counter32: 46312345
IF-MIB::ifInUcastPkts.1 = Counter32: 389536156
IF-MIB::ifInUcastPkts.2 = Counter32: 892959265
IF-MIB::ifInUcastPkts.3 = Counter32: 7712325
...
```

In this example, we see some general information about the system, followed by statistics about the host's network interfaces, lo0, eth0, and eth1. Depending on the MIBs supported by the agent you are managing, a complete dump can run to hundreds of lines.

SNMP data collection and graphing

Network-related data is best appreciated in visual and historical context. It's important to have some way to track and graph performance metrics, but your exact choice of software for doing this is not critical.

One of the most popular early SNMP polling and graphing packages was MRTG, written by Tobi Oetiker at ETH in Zurich. MRTG is written mostly in Perl, runs regularly out of **cron**, and can collect data from any SNMP source. Each time the program runs, new data is stored and new graph images are created.

Recently, Tobi has focused his energy on RRDTool, an application tool kit for storing and graphing performance metrics. All the leading open source monitoring solutions are based on RRDTool, including our favorite, Cacti.

Cacti, available from www.cacti.net, offers several attractive features. First, it implements a zero-maintenance, statically sized database; the software stores only enough data to create the necessary graphs. For example, Cacti could store one sample every minute for a day, one sample every hour for a week, and one sample every week for a year. This consolidation scheme lets you maintain important historical information without having to store unimportant details or consume your time with database administration.

Second, Cacti can record and graph any SNMP variable, as well as many other performance metrics. You're free to collect whatever data you want. When combined with the NET-SNMP agent, Cacti generates a historical perspective on almost any system or network resource.

Exhibit A shows some examples of the graphs created by Cacti. These graphs show the load average on a server over a period of multiple weeks along with a day's traffic on a network interface.

Cacti sports easy web-based configuration as well as all the other built-in benefits of RRDTool, such as low maintenance and beautiful graphing. See Tobi Oetiker's RRDTool home page at www.rrdtool.org for links to the current versions of RRDtool and Cacti, as well as dozens of other monitoring tools.

Exhibit A   Examples of Cacti graphs

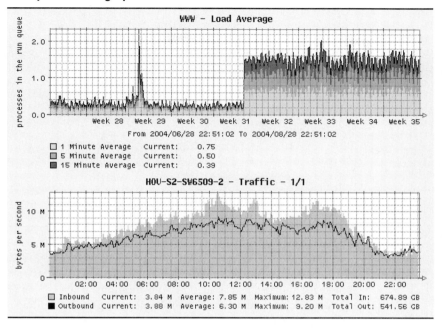

Nagios: event-based SNMP and service monitoring

Nagios specializes in real-time reporting of error conditions. It can poll any SNMP metric (as well as hundreds of other network services) and alert you to defined error conditions. Although Nagios does not help you determine how much your bandwidth utilization has increased over the last month, it can page you when your web server goes down.

The Nagios distribution includes plug-ins that supervise a variety of common points of failure. You can whip up new monitors in Perl, or even in C if you are feeling ambitious. For notification methods, the distribution can send email, generate web reports, and use a dial-up modem to page you. As with the monitoring plug-ins, it's easy to roll your own.

In addition to sending real-time notifications of service outages, Nagios keeps a historical archive of this data. It provides several powerful reporting interfaces that track availability and performance trends. Many organizations use Nagios to measure compliance with service level agreements; Exhibit B on the next page shows the availability of a DNS server.

Network Management

Exhibit B   Server availability as shown by Nagios

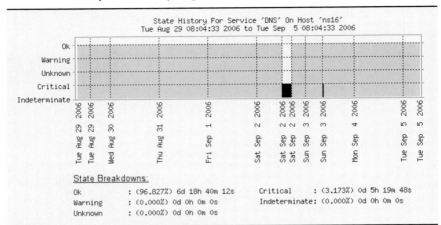

Nagios works very well for networks of fewer than a thousand hosts and devices. It is easy to customize and extend, and it includes powerful features such as redundancy, remote monitoring, and escalation of notifications. If you cannot afford a commercial network management tool, you should strongly consider Nagios. You can read more at www.nagios.org.

Commercial management platforms

Hundreds of companies sell network management software, and new competitors enter the market every week. Instead of recommending the hottest products of the moment (which may no longer exist by the time this book is printed), we identify the features you should look for in a network management system.

Data-gathering flexibility: Management tools must be able to collect data from sources other than SNMP. Many packages include ways to gather data from almost any network service. For example, some packages can make SQL database queries, check DNS records, and connect to web servers.

User interface quality: Expensive systems often offer a custom GUI or a web interface. Most well-marketed packages today tout their ability to understand XML templates for data presentation. A UI is not just more marketing hype—you need an interface that relays information clearly, simply, and comprehensibly.

Value: Some management packages come at a stiff price. HP's OpenView is both one of the most expensive and one of the most widely adopted network management systems. Many corporations find definite value in being able to say that their site is managed by a high-end commercial system. If that isn't so important to your organization, you should look at the other end of the spectrum for free tools like Cacti and Nagios.

Automated discovery: Many systems offer the ability to "discover" your network. Through a combination of broadcast pings, SNMP requests, ARP table lookups, and DNS queries, they identify all your local hosts and devices. All the discovery implementations we have seen work pretty well, but none are very accurate on a complex (or heavily firewalled) network.

Reporting features: Many products can send alert email, activate pagers, and automatically generate tickets for popular trouble-tracking systems. Make sure that the platform you choose accommodates flexible reporting; who knows what electronic devices you will be dealing with in a few years?

Configuration management: Some solutions step far beyond monitoring and alerting. They enable you to manage actual host and device configurations. For example, a CiscoWorks interface lets you change a router's configuration in addition to monitoring its state with SNMP. Because device configuration information deepens the analysis of network problems, we predict that many packages will develop along these lines in the future.

19.11 RECOMMENDED READING

CISCO ONLINE. *SNMP Overview.* 1996. www.cisco.com/warp/public/535/3.html

MAURO, DOUGLAS R. AND KEVIN J. SCHMIDT. *Essential SNMP (2nd Edition).* Sebastopol, CA: O'Reilly Media, 2005.

SIMPLEWEB. *SNMP and Internet Management Site.* www.simpleweb.org.

STALLINGS, WILLIAM. *Snmp, Snmpv2, Snmpv3, and Rmon 1 and 2 (3rd Edition).* Reading, MA: Addison-Wesley, 1999.

You may find the following RFCs to be useful as well. We replaced the actual titles of the RFCs with a description of the RFC contents because some of the actual titles are an unhelpful jumble of buzzwords and SNMP jargon.

- RFC1155 – Characteristics of the SNMP data space (data types, etc.)
- RFC1156 – MIB-I definitions (description of the actual OIDs)
- RFC1157 – Simple Network Management Protocol
- RFC1213 – MIB-II definitions (OIDs)
- RFC3414 – User-based Security Model for SNMPv3
- RFC3415 – View-based Access Control Model for SNMPv3
- RFC3512 – Configuring devices with SNMP (best general overview)
- RFC3584 – Practical coexistence between different SNMP versions

Exercises are presented on the next page.

19.12 EXERCISES

E19.1   You are troubleshooting a network problem and **netstat -rn** gives you the following output. What is the problem and what command would you use to fix it?

Destination	Gateway	Genmask	Flags	MSS	Window	irtt	Iface
128.138.202.0	0.0.0.0	255.255.255.0	U	40	0	0	eth0
127.0.0.0	0.0.0.0	255.0.0.0	U	40	0	0	lo

★ **E19.2**   Write a script that monitors a given set of machines and notifies an administrator by email if a machine becomes unresponsive to pings for some set amount of time. Don't hard-code the list of machines, the notification email address, or the amount of time to determine unresponsive behavior.

★ **E19.3**   Experiment with changing the netmask on a machine on your local network. Does it still work? Can you reach everything at your site? Can other machines reach you? Do broadcasts work (e.g., ARP requests or DHCP discover packets)? Explain your findings. (Requires root access.)

★ **E19.4**   Use the **traceroute** command to discover routing paths on your network.

   a) How many hops does it take to leave your facility?
   b) Are there any routers between machines on which you have accounts?
   c) Can you find any bottlenecks?
   d) Is your site multihomed?

★★ **E19.5**   Design a MIB that includes all the variables you as a Linux sysadmin might want to query or set. Leave ways for the MIB to be extended to include that important new sysadmin variable you forgot.

★★ **E19.6**   Use the **tcpdump** command to capture traffic that illustrates the following protocols. For TCP sessions, include and indicate the initial and final packets. Submit clean, well-formatted **tcpdump** output. (Requires root access.)

   a) ARP
   b) ICMP echo request and reply
   c) SMTP
   d) FTP and FTP-DATA
   e) DNS (called domain)
   f) NFS

★★ **E19.7**   Set up Cacti graphs that show the packets transmitted to and from a local router. This project requires an SNMP package to query the router, and you must know the read-only community string for the router.

20 *Security*

WarGames, a 1983 film starring Matthew Broderick, is a fascinating look at the early computer cracking subculture. In the movie, David Lightman employs several well-known attack techniques, including war dialing, social engineering, phone hacking (aka "phreaking"), and password guessing to start and then stop a nuclear attack. *WarGames* brought computer security into the limelight and, with it, the misnomer "hacker" as a label for troublesome teenage whiz kids. This early film was only the beginning of what has now become a global problem.

Five years later, the world of computer and network technology entered a new era when the Robert Morris, Jr., "Internet Worm" was unleashed on mankind. Before that event, the Internet lived in an age of innocence. Security was a topic that administrators thought about mostly in the "what if" sense. A big security incident usually consisted of something like a user gaining administrative access to read another user's mail, often just to prove that he could.

The Morris worm wasted thousands of administrator hours but greatly increased security awareness on the Internet. Once again, we were painfully reminded that good fences make good neighbors. A number of excellent tools for use by system administrators (as well as a formal organization for handling incidents of this nature) came into being as a result.

According to the 2006 CSI/FBI *Computer Crime and Security Survey,*[1] the majority of the organizations surveyed reported spending less than 5% of their IT budgets on

---

1. This survey is conducted yearly and can be found at www.gocsi.com.

security. As a result, a staggering $54,494,290 ($174,103 per organization) was lost to computer security breaches. These figures present a frightening picture of organizational security awareness. Of course, dollars spent does not necessarily equate to system security; a vigilant administrator can halt any attacker in his tracks.

In general, security is not something that you can buy in a box or as a service from some third party. Commercial products and services can be part of a solution for your site, but they are not a panacea.

Achieving an acceptable level of security requires an enormous amount of patience, vigilance, knowledge, and persistence—not just from you and other administrators, but from your entire user and management communities. As the system administrator, you must personally ensure that your systems are secure and that you and your users are properly educated. You should familiarize yourself with current security technology, actively monitor security mailing lists, and hire professional security experts to help with problems that exceed your knowledge.

20.1 IS LINUX SECURE?

No, Linux is not secure. Nor is any other operating system that communicates on a network. If you must have absolute, total, unbreachable security, then you need a measurable air gap[2] between your computer and any other device. Some people argue that you also need to enclose your computer in a special room that blocks electromagnetic radiation. (Google for "Faraday cage.") How fun is that?

You can work to make your system somewhat more resistant to attack. Even so, several fundamental flaws in the Linux model ensure that you will never reach security nirvana:

- Like UNIX, Linux is optimized for convenience and doesn't make security easy or natural. The Linux philosophy stresses easy manipulation of data in a networked, multiuser environment.

- Unless carefully implemented, Linux security is effectively binary: you are either a powerless user, or you're root. Linux facilities such as setuid execution tend to confer total power all at once. Thanks to Security-Enhanced Linux, a National Security Agency project, some progress has been made toward the implementation of more granular access controls. But in most cases, slight lapses in security can still compromise entire systems.

- Linux distributions are developed by a large community of programmers. They range in experience level, attention to detail, and knowledge of the Linux system and its interdependencies. As a result, even the most well-intended new features can introduce large security holes.

---

2. Of course, wireless networking technology introduces a whole new set of problems. Air gap in this context means "no networking whatsoever."

On the other hand, since Linux source code is available to everyone, thousands of people can (and do) scrutinize each line of code for possible security threats. This arrangement is widely believed to result in better security than that of closed operating systems, in which a limited number of people have the opportunity to examine the code for holes.

Many sites are a release or two behind, either because localization is too troublesome or because they do not subscribe to a distributor's software maintenance service. In any case, when security holes are patched, the window of opportunity for hackers often does not disappear overnight.

It might seem that Linux security should gradually improve over time as security problems are discovered and corrected, but unfortunately this does not seem to be the case. System software is growing ever more complicated, hackers are becoming better and better organized, and computers are connecting more and more intimately on the Internet. Security is an ongoing battle that can never really be won. (Of course, the Windows world is even worse…)

Remember, too, that

$$\text{Security} \;=\; \frac{1}{(1.072)(\text{Convenience})}$$

The more secure your system, the more constrained you and your users will be. Implement the security measures suggested in this chapter only after carefully considering the implications for your users.

20.2 HOW SECURITY IS COMPROMISED

This chapter discusses some common Linux security problems and their standard countermeasures. But before we leap into the details, we should take a more general look at how real-world security problems tend to occur. Most security lapses fit into the following taxonomy.

Social engineering

The human users (and administrators) of a computer system are often the weakest links in the chain of security. Even in today's world of heightened security awareness, unsuspecting users with good intentions are easily convinced to give away sensitive information.

This problem manifests itself in many forms. Attackers cold-call their victims and pose as legitimately confused users in an attempt to get help with accessing the system. Administrators unintentionally post sensitive information on public forums when troubleshooting problems. Physical compromises occur when seemingly legitimate maintenance personnel rewire the phone switch closet.

The term "phishing" describes attempts to collect information from users through deceptive email, instant messages, or even cell phone SMS messages. Phishing can be especially hard to defend against because the communications often include victim-specific information that lends them the appearance of authenticity.

Social engineering continues to be a powerful hacking technique and is one of the most difficult threats to neutralize. Your site security policy should include training for new employees. Regular organization-wide communications are an effective way to provide information about telephone dos and don'ts, physical security, email phishing, and password selection.

To gauge your organization's resistance to social engineering, you might find it informative to attempt some social engineering attacks of your own. Be sure you have explicit permission to do this from your own managers, however. Such exploits look very suspicious if they are performed without a clear mandate. They're also a form of internal spying, so they have the potential to generate resentment if they're not handled in an aboveboard manner.

Software vulnerabilities

Over the years, countless security-sapping bugs have been discovered in computer software (including software from third parties, both commercial and free). By exploiting subtle programming errors or context dependencies, hackers have been able to manipulate Linux into doing whatever they want.

Buffer overflows are a common programming error and one with complex implications. Developers often allocate a predetermined amount of temporary memory space, called a buffer, to store a particular piece of information. If the code isn't careful about checking the size of the data against the size of the container that's supposed to hold it, the memory adjacent to the allocated space is at risk of being overwritten. Crafty hackers can input carefully composed data that crashes the program or, in the worst case, executes arbitrary code.

Fortunately, the sheer number of buffer overflow exploits in recent years has raised the programming community's consciousness about this issue. Although buffer overflow problems are still occurring, they are often quickly discovered and corrected, especially in open source applications. Newer programming systems such as Java and .NET include mechanisms that automatically check data sizes and prevent buffer overflows.

Buffer overflows are a subcategory of a larger class of software security bugs known as input validation vulnerabilities. Nearly all programs accept some type of input from users (e.g., command-line arguments or HTML forms). If the code processes such data without rigorously checking it for appropriate format and content, bad things can happen. Consider the following simple example:

```
#!/usr/bin/perl
# Example user input validation error

open (HTMLFILE, "/var/www/html/$ARGV[0]") or die "trying\n";
while (<HTMLFILE>) { print; }
close HTMLFILE;
```

The intent of this code is probably to print the contents of some HTML file under **/var/www/html**, which is the default document root for Apache's httpd server on Red Hat servers. The code accepts a filename from the user and passes it as the argument to the open function. However, if a malicious user entered **../../../etc/shadow** as the argument, the contents of **/etc/shadow** would be echoed!

What can you as an administrator do to prevent this type of attack? Very little, at least until a bug has been identified and addressed in a patch. Keeping up with patches and security bulletins is an important part of most administrators' jobs. Most distributions included automated patching utilities, such as **yum** on Fedora and **apt-get** on Debian and Ubuntu. Take advantage of these utilities to keep your site safe from software vulnerabilities.

Configuration errors

Many pieces of software can be configured securely or not-so-securely. Unfortunately, because software is developed for convenience, not-so-securely is often the default. Hackers frequently gain access by exploiting software features that would be considered helpful and convenient in less treacherous circumstances: accounts without passwords, disks shared with the world, and unprotected databases, to name a few.

A typical example of a host configuration vulnerability is the standard practice of allowing Linux systems to boot without requiring a boot loader password. Both LILO and GRUB can be configured at install time to require a password, but administrators almost always decline the option. This omission leaves the system open to physical attack. However, it's also a perfect example of the need to balance security against usability. Requiring a password means that if the system were unintentionally rebooted (e.g., after a power outage), an administrator would have to be physically present to get the machine running again.

One of the most important steps in securing a system is simply making sure that you haven't inadvertently put out a welcome mat for hackers. Problems in this category are the easiest to find and fix, although there are potentially a lot of them and it's not always obvious what to check for. The port and vulnerability scanning tools covered later in this chapter can help a motivated administrator find and fix problems before they're exploited.

20.3 CERTIFICATIONS AND STANDARDS

If the subject matter of this chapter seems daunting to you, don't fret. Computer security is a complicated and vast topic, as countless books, web sites, and magazines can attest. Fortunately, much has been done to help quantify and organize the available information. Dozens of standards and certifications exist, and mindful Linux administrators should consider their guidance.

One of the most basic philosophical principles in information security is informally referred to as the "CIA triad."

The acronym stands for

- Confidentiality
- Integrity
- Availability

Data confidentiality concerns the privacy of data. In essence, access to information should be limited to those who are authorized to have it. Authentication, access control, and encryption are a few of the subcomponents of confidentiality. If a hacker breaks into a Linux system and steals a database containing customer contact information, a compromise of confidentiality has occurred.

Integrity relates to the authenticity of information. Data integrity technology ensures that information is valid and has not been altered in any unauthorized way. It also addresses the trustworthiness of information sources. When a secure web site presents a signed SSL certificate, it is proving to the user not only that the information it is sending is encrypted but also that a trusted certificate authority (such as VeriSign or Equifax) has verified the identity of the source. Technologies such as PGP and Kerberos also guarantee data integrity.

Information must be available to authorized users when they need it, or there is no purpose in having it. Outages not caused by intruders, such as those caused by administrative errors or power outages, also fall into the category of availability problems. Unfortunately, availability is often ignored until something goes wrong.

Consider the CIA principles whenever you design, implement, or maintain Linux systems. As the old security adage goes, "security is a process."

Certifications

This crash course in CIA is just a brief introduction to the larger information security field. Large corporations often employ many full-time employees whose job is guarding information. To gain credibility in the field and keep their knowledge current, these professionals attend training courses and obtain certifications. Prepare yourself for acronym-fu as we work through a few of the most popular certifications.

One of the most widely recognized security certifications is the CISSP, or Certified Information Systems Security Professional. It is administered by $(ISC)^2$, the International Information Systems Security Certification Consortium (say *that* ten times fast!). One of the primary draws of the CISSP is $(ISC)^2$'s notion of a "common body of knowledge" (CBK), essentially an industry-wide best practices guide for information security. The CBK covers law, cryptography, authentication, physical security, and much more. It's an incredible reference for security folks.

One criticism of the CISSP has been its concentration on breadth and consequent lack of depth. So many topics in the CBK, and so little time! To address this, $(ISC)^2$ has issued CISSP concentration programs that focus on architecture, engineering, and management. These specialized certifications add depth to the more general CISSP certification.

The System Administration, Networking, and Security (SANS) Institute created the Global Information Assurance Certification (GIAC) suite of certifications in 1999. Three dozen separate exams cover the realm of information security with tests divided into five categories. The certifications range in difficulty from the moderate two-exam GISF to the 23-hour expert level GSE. The GSE has the notorious reputation of being one of the most difficult certifications in the industry. Many of the exams focus on technical specifics and require quite a bit of experience.

Finally, the Certified Information Systems Auditor (CISA) credential is an audit and process certification. It focuses on business continuity, procedures, monitoring, and other management content. Some consider the CISA an intermediate certification that is appropriate for an organization's security officer role. One of its most attractive aspects is the fact that it involves only a single exam.

Although certifications are a personal endeavor, their application to business is undeniable. More and more companies now recognize certifications as the mark of an expert. Many businesses offer higher pay and promotions to certified employees. If you decide to pursue a certification, work closely with your organization to have it help pay for the associated costs.

Standards

Because of the ever-increasing reliance on data systems, laws and regulations have been created to govern the management of sensitive, business-critical information. Major U.S. legislation projects such as HIPAA, FISMA, and the Sarbanes-Oxley Act have all included sections on IT security. Although the requirements are sometimes expensive to implement, they have helped give the appropriate level of focus to a once-ignored aspect of technology.

Unfortunately, the regulations are filled with legalese and can be difficult to interpret. Most do not contain specifics on how to achieve their requirements. As a result, standards have been developed to help administrators reach the lofty legislative requirements. These standards are not regulation specific, but following them usually ensures compliance. It can be intimidating to confront the requirements of all the various standards at once, but these plans are a useful guideline.

The ISO/IEC 17799 standard is probably the most widely accepted in the world. First introduced in 1995 as a British standard, it is 34 pages long and is divided into 11 sections running the gamut from policy to physical security to access control. Objectives within each section define specific requirements, and controls under each objective describe the suggested "best practice" solutions.

The requirements are nontechnical and can be fulfilled by any organization in a way that best fits its needs. On the downside, the general wording of the standard leaves the reader with a sense of broad flexibility. Critics complain that the lack of specifics leaves organizations open to attack.

Nonetheless, this standard is one of the most valuable documents available to the information security industry. It bridges an often tangible gap between management and engineering and helps focus both parties on minimizing organizational risk.

The Payment Card Industry Data Security Standard (PCI DSS) is a different beast entirely. It arose out of the perceived need to improve security in the card processing industry following a series of dramatic exposures. For example, in June 2005, Card-Systems Services International revealed the "loss" of 40 million card numbers.

The U.S. Department of Homeland Security has estimated that $52.6 billion was lost to identity theft in 2004 alone. Not all of this can be linked directly to credit card exposure, of course, but increased vigilance by vendors would certainly have had a positive impact. The FBI has even connected credit card fraud to terrorist funding. Specific incidents include the bombings in Bali and the Madrid subway system.

The PCI DSS standard is the result of a joint effort between Visa and Mastercard, though it is currently maintained by Visa. Unlike ISO 17799, it is freely available for anyone to download. It focuses entirely on protecting cardholder data systems and has 12 sections defining requirements for protection.

Because PCI DSS is focused on card processors, it is not appropriate for businesses that don't deal with credit card data. However, for those that do, strict compliance is necessary to avoid hefty fines and possible criminal prosecution. You can find the document at the merchant security section of Visa's web site.

Many sites create custom software to fit a unique need, but haste often comes at the cost of security. Susceptibility to buffer overflows, SQL injections, and cross-site scripting attacks are a few examples of common flaws in homegrown software. Fortunately, the U.S. government has released a procedural document to help validate the security of such applications. The Department of Defense's *Application Security Checklist* is a thorough guide to testing an application for security weaknesses. The current version is available for download from

iase.disa.mil/stigs/checklist

Unlike the other standards discussed in this section, the *Application Security Checklist* delves deeply into technical specifics, at times touching on individual commands that should be run to conduct a particular test. The standard is not as readable and as formal as the other standards here, but it is immensely useful for sites that have in-house development needs.

20.4 SECURITY TIPS AND PHILOSOPHY

This chapter discusses a wide variety of security concerns. Ideally, you should address all of them within your environment. If you're short on time or patience, however, here are the six all-around most important security issues to consider, plus some bonus rules to live by. (Most administrators should really digest the contents of this entire chapter, probably more than once.)

Packet filtering

If you're connecting a Linux system to a network with Internet access, you *must* have a packet filtering router or firewall between the Linux system and the outside world. As an alternative, you can configure packet filtering by using **iptables** on the Linux system itself (discussed starting on page 704). Whatever the implementation, the packet filter should pass only traffic for services that you specifically want to provide or use from the Linux system.

Unnecessary services

Linux distributions differ widely regarding which network services are turned on as part of the default installation. Most include several that aren't needed. It's up to you to examine the services that are enabled on your system and to turn off any that aren't absolutely necessary. The **netstat** and **fuser** commands are a great way to get started. To really understand what services an attacker can see, scan your systems with a port scanner from a remote host. **nmap**, described starting on page 688, is a security practitioner's port-scanning dream come true.

Software patches

All major Linux distributors release a steady stream of security-related software patches, usually several every month. You *must* vigilantly watch for security patches relevant to your system software (and any software packages you're running) and install them immediately. Keep in mind that once a patch is available, the "bad guys" may have known about the security hole for weeks.

Backups

Put down that RAID array and back away from the data center, cowboy. You *must* perform regular backups of all your systems so that you can recover effectively from a security incident if one should occur. No amount of mirroring, RAID, or "hot standby" technology eliminates the need for backups. Information on performing backups is provided in Chapter 9.

Passwords

We're simple people with simple rules. Here's one: every account must have a password, and it needs to be something that can't easily be guessed. It's never a good idea to send plaintext reusable passwords across the Internet. If you allow remote logins to your system, you must use SSH or some other secure remote access system (discussed starting on page 697).

Vigilance

To ensure the security of your system, you must monitor its health, network connections, process table, and overall status regularly (usually, daily). Perform regular self-assessments using the power tools discussed later in this chapter. Security problems tend to start small and grow quickly, so the earlier you identify an anomaly, the better off you'll be.

General philosophy

Effective system security has its roots in common sense. Some rules of thumb:

- Don't put files on your system that are likely to be interesting to hackers or to nosy employees. Trade secrets, personnel files, payroll data, election results, etc., must be handled carefully if they're on-line. Securing such information cryptographically provides a far higher degree of security than simply trying to prevent unauthorized users from accessing the files that contain the juicy tidbits.

- Your site's security policy should specify how sensitive information is handled. See Chapter 30, *Management, Policy, and Politics*, and the security standards section in this chapter (page 675) for some suggestions.

- Don't provide places for hackers to build homes in your environment. Hackers often break into one system and then use it as a base of operations to get into others. Sometimes hackers may use your network to cover their tracks while they attack their real target. Publicly exposed services with vulnerabilities, world-writable anonymous FTP directories, shared accounts, and neglected systems all encourage nesting activity.

- Set traps to help detect intrusions and attempted intrusions. Tools such as samhain, **xinetd**, and John the Ripper (described starting on page 690) will keep you abreast of potential problems.

- Religiously monitor the reports generated by these security tools. A minor problem you ignore in one report may grow into a catastrophe by the time the next report is sent.

- Teach yourself about system security. Traditional know-how, user education, and common sense are the most important parts of a site security plan. Bring in outside experts to help fill in gaps, but only under your close supervision and approval.

- Prowl around looking for unusual activity. Investigate anything that seems unusual, such as odd log messages or changes in the activity of an account (more activity, activity at strange hours, or perhaps activity while the owner is on vacation).

20.5 Security problems in /etc/passwd and /etc/shadow

See page 93 for more information about the ***passwd*** *file.*

Poor password management is a common security weakness. The contents of the **/etc/passwd** and **/etc/shadow** files determines who can log in, so these files are the system's first line of defense against intruders. They must be scrupulously maintained and free of errors, security hazards, and historical baggage.

On legacy systems, the second field of **/etc/passwd** contained a string that represented the user's encrypted password. Since **/etc/passwd** must be world-readable for commands such as **ls** to work, the encrypted password string was available to all users on the system. Evildoers could encrypt entire dictionaries and compare the results with the strings in **/etc/passwd**. If the encrypted strings matched, a password had been found.

How much of a threat is this? In the 80s, there was at least one way to decrypt passwords posthaste,[3] but run-of-the-mill hackers had to be content with using the **crypt** library routine[4] to encrypt dictionary words for comparison. A "fast" machine in the 80s could do a few hundred encryptions a second. By contrast, brute force contests have now cracked 56-bit DES keys in under 24 hours. Thankfully, modern UNIX and Linux systems do not use **crypt** and are considerably more secure.

These results are frightening, and they suggest that user access to encrypted password strings really ought to be restricted. The standard way to impose restrictions is to put passwords in a separate file that is readable only by root, leaving the rest of **/etc/passwd** intact. The file that contains the actual password information is then called the shadow password file, **/etc/shadow**. All modern Linux distributions use shadow passwords.

Password checking and selection

Linux allows users to choose their own passwords, and although this is a great convenience, it leads to many security problems. When you give users their logins, you should also instruct them on how to choose a good password. Tell them not to use their name or initials, the name of a child or spouse, or any word that can be found in a dictionary. Passwords derived from personal data such as telephone numbers or addresses are also easily broken.

Passwords should be at least eight characters long and should include numbers, punctuation, and changes in case. Nonsense words, combinations of simple words, or the first letters of words in a memorable phrase make the best passwords. Of course, "memorable" is good but "traditional" is risky. Make up your own phrase. The comments in the section *Choosing a root password* on page 47 are equally applicable to user passwords.

It is important to continually verify (preferably daily) that every login has a password. Entries in the **/etc/shadow** file that describe pseudo-users such as "daemon" who own files but never log in should have a star (*) or an exclamation point (!) in their encrypted password field. These will not match any password and will thus prevent use of the account.

The **/etc/shadow** file is largely maintenance free. However, the following Perl one-liner checks for null passwords:

```
$ sudo perl -F: -ane 'print if not $F[1];' /etc/shadow
```

3. Evi Nemeth broke the Diffie-Hellman key exchange often used with DES in 1984, using a HEP supercomputer. Although DES is thought to be mathematically secure, the short key lengths in common use offer relatively little security.
4. Don't confuse the **crypt** library routine with the **crypt** command, which uses a different and less secure encryption scheme.

A script that performs this check and mails you the results can be run out of **cron**. To help verify that any account modifications are legitimate, you can write a script that **diff**s the **passwd** file against a version from the previous day and emails any differences to you.

Password aging

The Linux shadow password system can force users to change their passwords periodically through a facility known as password aging. This may seem like a good idea at first glance, but it has several problems. Users often resent having to change their passwords, and since they don't want to forget the new password, they choose something simple that is easy to type and remember. Many users switch between two passwords each time they are forced to change, defeating the purpose of password aging. PAM modules can help enforce strong passwords to avoid this pitfall.

See page 48 for more information about sudo.

Nevertheless, passwords should be changed regularly, especially the root password. A root password should roll easily off the fingers so that it can be typed quickly and cannot be guessed by someone watching the movement of fingers on the keyboard. At our site most people use **sudo** rather than the real root password, but we select the root password carefully all the same.

The **chage** program controls password aging. Using **chage**, administrators can enforce minimum and maximum times between password changes, password expiration dates, the number of days to warn users before expiring their passwords, the number of days of inactivity that are permissible before accounts are automatically locked, and more. The following command sets the minimum number of days between password changes to 2, the maximum number to 90, the expiration date to July 31, 2007, and warns the user for 14 days that the expiration date is approaching:

```
$ sudo chage -m 2 -M 90 -E 2007-07-31 -W 14 ben
```

Group logins and shared logins

Any login that is used by more than one person is bad news. Group logins (e.g., "guest" or "demo") are sure terrain for hackers to homestead and are prohibited in many contexts by federal regulations such as HIPAA. Don't allow them at your site.

Likewise, don't allow users to share logins with family or friends. If little Johnny needs a login to work on his science project, give him one with that stated purpose. It's much easier to take away Johnny's login when he abuses it than to get rid of Dad and his account, especially at government sites.

At some sites, "root" is a group login. Dangerous! We recommend using the **sudo** program to control access to rootly powers. See page 48.

User shells

Do not use a script as the shell for an unrestricted (passwordless) login. In fact, if you find yourself needing a passwordless login, you should probably consider a passphrase-less SSH keypair instead.

Rootly entries

The only distinguishing feature of the root login is its UID of zero. Since there can be more than one entry in the **/etc/passwd** file that uses this UID, there can be more than one way to log in as root.

A common way for hackers to install a back door once they have obtained a root shell is to edit new root logins into **/etc/passwd**. Programs like **who** and **w** refer to the name stored in **/var/run/utmp** rather than the UID that owns the login shell, so they cannot expose hackers that appear to be innocent users but are really logged in as UID 0.

The defense against this subterfuge is a mini-script similar to the one used for finding logins without passwords:

```
$ perl -F: -ane 'print if not $F[2];' /etc/passwd
```

This script prints out any lines in the **passwd** file that have null or 0 UIDs. You could easily adapt it to find entries with suspicious groups or UIDs that are the same as those of key people within your organization.

You should also check for **passwd** entries that have no username or that have punctuation as a username. These entries may seem nonsensical, but they often allow a hacker to log in.

PAM: cooking spray or authentication wonder?

The Pluggable Authentication Module API (aka PAM) was originally invented by Sun as a flexible way to authenticate users. For many years, authentication in the UNIX environment was as simple as associating users with their entry in the **/etc/passwd** file. The need for stronger security and support for a wider variety of authentication mechanisms (such as smart cards) has created a need for a more flexible approach. Certain PAM LDAP modules perform centralized authentication to global authentication directories.

Linux-PAM is shipped with all sane Linux distributions and is unrelated to Sun's current implementation of the PAM standard. The concept is simple: programs that require authentication only need to know that a module is available to perform the authentication for them. PAM is set up so that modules can be added, deleted, and reconfigured at any time— modules need not be linked in (or even exist) at the time a utility is compiled. As a result of this architecture, PAM has become an incredibly powerful tool for system administrators.

Dozens of PAM modules are available. You can download specialized modules and their documentation from www.kernel.org/pub/linux/libs/pam.

PAM modules are configured through files in the **/etc/pam.d** directory. Per-service files in this directory contain entries of the form

module-type control-flag module-path arguments

The *module-type* field can have the values auth, account, session, or password. An auth entry establishes who the user is and possibly grants group membership. The account tag performs non-authentication-based decisions, such as access based on time of day. Tasks that need to be performed before or after a user is given service are implemented with the session tag. Finally, the password tag is used when authentication information (such as a password) is requested from the user.

The *control-flag* field has four possible values: required, requisite, sufficient, and optional. required and optional are most commonly used, signifying that a module must succeed in order for execution to continue or that it doesn't matter whether the module succeeds, respectively.

The third and fourth fields are the pathname and the arguments for the dynamically loadable module object. If the first character of the path is /, the path is assumed to be an absolute path. Otherwise, the contents of the field are appended to the default path, **/lib/security**.

See page 690 for more information about John the Ripper.

PAM is one solution to the password complexity difficulties described above. The **pam_cracklib** module can force passwords to meet minimum requirements. Specifics vary widely, so use **grep** to find the proper configuration file. For example, to ensure that users passwords cannot be determined by John the Ripper, the file **/etc/pam.d/system-auth** on Fedora should contain

```
password required pam_cracklib.so retry=3 minlen=12 difok=4
```

With this line in place, PAM checks users' proposed new passwords against a password cracking dictionary and ruleset. (This setup requires the presence of the system library **libcrack** and also a system dictionary, **/usr/lib/cracklib_dict.***) An error message such as "The password is too simple" is printed on the screen if a user's password does not adhere to the **cracklib** requirements.

The **cracklib** argument rules are complicated, but here's the interpretation of the specific configuration shown above:

- The retry=3 argument specifies that the user be given three tries at entering a strong password.

- minlen=12 specifies a minimum password length. Uppercase letters, numbers, and punctuation get special treatment by the library and lower the minimum. With minlen=12, the shortest password a user can have is actually 8 characters, not 12, but the user must include all four available character types to set an 8-character password.

- difok=4 specifies that at least four characters of the new password must not be present in the old password.

Modern Linux distributions include and use the **pam_cracklib** module by default, but the password complexity rules are usually not enabled.

20.6 POSIX CAPABILITIES

Linux systems subdivide the powers of the root account according to the POSIX notion of "capabilities." For example, one capability allows a process to perform privileged operations on network sockets and network interfaces, while another allows a process to set hardware-related options. Capabilities are inherited, masked, and bestowed in a systematic manner by which programs can perform privileged tasks without accessing the full power of the root account. Because privileges can be doled out more stringently than in traditional UNIX, the likelihood of a security compromise leading to unrestricted root access is lower—at least in theory.

In practice, the capability system is of limited interest to system administrators. Software that is capability aware requires no special administrative attention; it simply sets itself to operate in a more restricted mode. But most UNIX and Linux software continues to assume the traditional all-powerful superuser model that really can't be disabled without significant trouble and sacrifice. Some of the accommodations the Linux kernel makes to maintain compatibility with traditional UNIX software make the capability system more "leaky" than it really should be.[5]

The upshot is that POSIX capabilities make good cocktail conversation but have limited real-world implications. For the most part they can be ignored, with one notable exception: the kernel applies a "global capability bounding set" (accessed and set through the file **/proc/sys/kernel/cap-bound**) every time a new program is executed. If you want to disable one or more capabilities throughout the entire system, you can add them to this global bounding set. See **man capabilities** for details.

20.7 SETUID PROGRAMS

Programs that run setuid, especially ones that run setuid to root, are prone to security problems. The setuid commands distributed with Linux are theoretically secure; however, security holes have been discovered in the past and will undoubtedly be discovered in the future.

The surest way to minimize the number of setuid *problems* is to minimize the number of setuid *programs*. Think twice before installing a software package that needs to run setuid, and avoid using the setuid facility in your own home-grown software. An average Linux distribution contains about 35 setuid programs, though this varies from distribution to distribution.

There's no rule that says setuid programs must run as root. If all you need to do is restrict access to a particular file or database, you can add to the **passwd** file a pseudo-user whose only reason for existence is to own the restricted resources. Follow the normal pseudo-user conventions: use a low UID, put a star in the password field, and make the pseudo-user's home directory be **/dev/null**.

---

5. One of our technical reviewers commented, "In fact, capability inheritance has never worked right in Linux; it's an ongoing embarrassment."

You can disable setuid and setgid execution on individual filesystems by specifying the **-o nosuid** option to **mount**. It's a good idea to use this option on filesystems that contain users' home directories or that are mounted from less trustworthy administrative domains.

It's useful to scan your disks periodically to look for new setuid programs. A hacker who has breached the security of your system sometimes creates a private setuid shell or utility to facilitate repeat visits. Some of the tools discussed starting on page 688 locate such files, but you can do just as well with **find**. For example,

```
/usr/bin/find / -user root -perm -4000 -print |
    /bin/mail -s "Setuid root files" netadmin
```

mails a list of all setuid root files to the "netadmin" user.

20.8 IMPORTANT FILE PERMISSIONS

Many files on a Linux system must have particular permissions if security problems are to be avoided. Some distributors ship software with permissions set for their own "friendly" development environment. These permissions may not be appropriate for you.

/etc/passwd and **/etc/group** should not be world-writable. They should have owner root and mode 644. **/etc/shadow** should have mode 600—no permissions for the group or world:

```
-rw-------   1 root     root         1835 May  8 08:07 /etc/shadow
```

The groups of all these files should be set to some system group, usually root. (The **passwd** command runs setuid to root so that users can change their passwords without having write permission on **/etc/passwd** or **/etc/shadow**.)

See page 734 for information about setting up an FTP server.
Historically, FTP programs have been riddled with security holes and insecure default configurations. FTP also transmits credentials in cleartext, an inherent problem in the protocol that makes it unacceptable on today's Internet.

New technologies such as SFTP have replaced FTP, and there are very few cases in which FTP should be allowed. In those rare cases, however, read the software documentation thoroughly to ensure proper configuration. If you must allow anonymous FTP access, either disable world-writable directories or scan them regularly for illegal or sensitive files.

Device files for hard disk partitions are another potential source of problems. Having read or write permission on a disk device file is essentially the same as having read or write permission on every file in the filesystem it represents. Only root should have both read and write permission. The group owner is sometimes given read permission to facilitate backups, but there should be no permissions for the world.

20.9 MISCELLANEOUS SECURITY ISSUES

The following sections present some miscellaneous security-related topics. Most are either features that are useful to you as an administrator or misfeatures that can provide nesting material for hackers if not kept in check.

Remote event logging

See Chapter 10 for more information about syslog.

The syslog facility allows log information for both the kernel and user processes to be forwarded to a file, a list of users, or another host on your network. Consider setting up a secure host that acts as a central logging machine, parses log files, and emails events of interest. This precaution prevents hackers from covering their tracks by rewriting or erasing log files.

Secure terminals

Linux can be configured to restrict root logins to specific "secure" terminals. It's a good idea to disable root logins on channels such as SSH, VPNs, or other remote links. Often, network pseudo-terminals are also set to disallow root logins.

The secure channels are specified as a list of TTY devices in the configuration file **/etc/securetty**. It's also possible to restrict nonroot logins to particular locations with entries in the file **/etc/security/access.conf** or to particular times with entries in the file **/etc/security/time.conf**.

Administrators can still log in normally and use **sudo** to access superuser powers.

/etc/hosts.equiv and ~/.rhosts

The **hosts.equiv** and **~/.rhosts** files define hosts as being administratively "equivalent" to one another, allowing users to log in (with **rlogin**) and copy files (with **rcp**) between machines without typing their passwords. Use of this facility was once common during the party days of UNIX, but everyone eventually woke up with a nasty headache and realized that it wasn't such a good idea.

Fortunately, the SSH protocol has virtually eliminated the use of insecure equivalents such as **telnet**, **rsh**, and **rlogin**. Its use is covered later in the chapter.

Some of the replacements for **rlogin** (including SSH!) pay attention to **.rhosts** and **/etc/hosts.equiv** if they are not configured properly. For added safety, you can create the **/etc/hosts.equiv** file and a **~/.rhosts** file for each user (including root) as an unwritable, zero-length file. It's easier to assess what the state of a file was at 3:00 a.m. if it exists and is untouched than to assess the state of a nonexistent file. This distinction can be crucial when you are tracking intruders and their attempts to compromise your system.

Security and NIS

See Chapter 17 for more information about NIS.

Other than in the title of this section, these words should never be used together. The Network Information Service (NIS, formerly the Yellow Pages) is a Sun database distribution tool that many sites use to maintain and distribute files such as

/etc/group, /etc/passwd, and /etc/hosts. Unfortunately, its very nature of "easy information access" makes it tasty hacker bait.

A more secure way to distribute these files is to create a service login such as "netadmin" and to place the most recent copies of these files in ~netadmin. You can then use cron to run a script on each client machine to scp, sanity check, and install the files. See page 697 for more information about SSH, of which scp is a component.

Security and NFS

NFSv4 is an IETF extension to Sun's earlier protocol that includes strong security and a number of other benefits over earlier implementations. Though the protocol is not yet complete, development is well underway, and NFSv4 is included in the Linux 2.6 kernel series.

Older versions of NFS use a weak security model. See page 487 for more information about NFS security. You can use **showmount -e** to see which filesystems are being exported and to whom. Every exported filesystem should have an access list, and all hostnames should be fully qualified.

Security and sendmail

See Chapter 18 for more information about sendmail.

sendmail is a huge program that runs as root, at least initially. As a result, it has often been subject to the attacks of hackers. Make sure that you're running the most up-to-date version of **sendmail** on all your systems. Since security problems are one of the most likely issues to spark new software releases, it's probable that all versions of **sendmail** but the most current have vulnerabilities.

Specific details about **sendmail** security are covered in the electronic mail chapter starting on page 603; www.sendmail.org has information about specific releases.

Security and backups

See Chapter 9 for more information about backups.

Regular system backups are an essential part of any site security plan. Make sure that all partitions are regularly dumped to tape and that you store some backups off-site. If a significant security incident occurs, you'll have an uncontaminated checkpoint from which to restore.

Backups can also be a security hazard. A stolen collection of tapes can circumvent the rest of the system's security. When storing tapes off-site, use a fireproof safe to avoid theft. Consider the use of encryption. If you are considering the use of a contract storage facility, ask for a physical tour.

Viruses and worms

Linux has been mostly immune from viruses. Only a handful exist (most of which are academic in nature), and none have done the costly damage that has become commonplace in the Windows world. Nonetheless, this hasn't stopped certain antivirus vendors from predicting the demise of the Linux platform from malware—unless you purchase their antivirus product at a special introductory price, of course.

The exact reason for the lack of malicious software is unclear. Some claim that Linux simply has less market share than its desktop competitors and is therefore not an interesting target for virus authors. Others insist that Linux's access controlled environment limits widespread damage from a self-propagating worm or virus.

The latter argument has some validity. Because Linux restricts write access to system executables at the filesystem level, unprivileged user accounts cannot infect the rest of the environment. Unless the virus code is being run by root, the scope of infection is significantly limited. The main moral, then, is not to use the root account for day-to-day activities.

Perhaps counterintuitively, one valid reason to run antivirus software on Linux servers is to protect your site's Windows systems from Windows-specific viruses. A mail server can scan incoming email attachments for viruses, and a file server can scan shared files for infection. However, this solution should supplement desktop antivirus protection rather than replace it.

ClamAV by Tomasz Kojm is a popular, free antivirus product for Linux. This widely used GPL tool is a complete antivirus toolkit with signatures for thousands of viruses. You can download the latest version from www.clamav.net.

Trojan horses

Trojan horses are programs that aren't what they seem to be. An example of a Trojan horse is a program called **turkey** that was distributed on Usenet a long time ago. The program said it would draw a picture of a turkey on your terminal screen, but it actually deleted files from your home directory.

A more controversial example of a Trojan horse was the copy protection software included on many Sony audio CDs in 2004 and 2005. In a misguided attempt to foil music sharers, Sony installed protection software on Windows systems without the listener's consent or knowledge. The software introduced vulnerabilities on the host computer that could be exploited by worms and viruses.

Trojan fragments appear in major Linux software packages now and then. **sendmail**, **tcpdump**, OpenSSH, and InterBase have all issued advisories regarding malicious software in their products. These Trojans typically embed malicious code that allows attackers to access the victim's systems at will. Fortunately, most vendors fix the software and issue an advisory in a week or two. Be sure to watch the security mailing lists for any network software packages you run on your Linux hosts.

Even given the number of security-related escapades the Linux community has seen over the last few years, it is remarkable how few Trojan horse incidents have occurred. Credit for this state of affairs is due largely to the speed of Internet communication. Obvious security problems tend to be discovered quickly and widely discussed. Malicious packages don't stay available for very long on well-known Internet servers.

You can be certain that any software that has been discovered to be malicious will cause a big stink on the Internet. If you want to do a quick check before installing something, type the name of the software package into your favorite search engine.

Rootkits

The craftiest hackers try to cover their tracks and avoid detection. Often, they hope to continue using your system to distribute software illegally, probe other networks, or launch attacks against other systems. They often use "rootkits" to help them remain undetected. Sony's Trojan horse employed rootkit-like capabilities to hide itself from the user.

Rootkits are programs and patches that hide important system information such as process, disk, or network activity. They come in many flavors and vary in sophistication from simple application replacements (such as hacked versions of **ls** and **ps**) to kernel modules that are nearly impossible to detect.

Host-based intrusion detection software such as samhain (described below) is an effective way to monitor systems for the presence of rootkits. Although programs are available to help administrators remove rootkits from a compromised system, the time it takes to perform a thorough cleaning would be better spent saving data, reformatting the disk, and starting from scratch. The most advanced rootkits are aware of common removal programs and try to subvert them.

20.10 SECURITY POWER TOOLS

Some of the time-consuming chores mentioned in the previous sections can be automated with freely available tools. Here are a few of the tools you'll want to look at.

Nmap: scan network ports

Nmap is a network port scanner. Its main function is to check a set of target hosts to see which TCP and UDP ports have servers listening on them.[6] Since most network services are associated with "well known" port numbers, this information tells you quite a lot about the software a machine is running.

Running Nmap is a great way to find out what a system looks like to someone who is trying to break in. For example, here's a report from a default installation of Red Hat Enterprise Linux:

```
$ nmap -sT rhel.booklab.example.com

Starting Nmap 4.00 ( http://www.insecure.org/nmap/ ) at 2006-05-15 23:48 EDT
Interesting ports on rhel.booklab.example.com (192.168.1.31):
(The 1668 ports scanned but not shown below are in state: closed)
PORT      STATE    SERVICE
22/tcp    open     ssh
25/tcp    open     smtp
111/tcp   open     rpcbind
631/tcp   open     ipp

Nmap run completed -- 1 IP address (1 host up) scanned in .158 second
```

6. As described in Chapter 12, a port is a numbered communication channel. An IP address identifies an entire machine, and an IP address + port number identifies a specific server or network conversation on that machine.

By default, **nmap** includes the **-sT** argument to try to connect to each TCP port on the target host in the normal way.[7] Once a connection has been established, **nmap** immediately disconnects, which is impolite but not harmful to a properly written network server.

From the example above, we can see that the host rhel is running several services that are likely to be unused and that have historically been associated with security problems: **portmap** (rpcbind), CUPS (ipp), and probably **sendmail** (smtp). Several potential lines of attack are now apparent.

The STATE column in **nmap**'s output shows open for ports with servers, unfiltered for ports in an unknown state, closed for ports with no server, and filtered for ports that cannot be probed because of an intervening packet filter. Unfiltered ports are the typical case and are normally not shown unless **nmap** is running an ACK scan. For example, here's a dump from a more secure server, secure.example.com:

```
$ nmap -sT secure.example.com

Starting Nmap 4.00 ( http://www.insecure.org/nmap/ ) at 2006-05-15 23:55 EDT
Interesting ports on secure.example.com (192.168.1.33):
(The 1670 ports scanned but not shown below are in state: closed)
PORT      STATE   SERVICE
22/tcp    open    ssh
1241/tcp  open    nessus

Nmap finished: 1 IP address (1 host up) scanned in 0.143 seconds
```

In this case, it's clear that the host is set up to allow SSH and the Nessus network scanner. A firewall blocks access to other ports.

In addition to straightforward TCP and UDP probes, **nmap** also has a repertoire of sneaky ways to probe ports without initiating an actual connection. In most cases, **nmap** probes with packets that look like they come from the middle of a TCP conversation (rather than the beginning) and waits for diagnostic packets to be sent back. These stealth probes may be effective at getting past a firewall or at avoiding detection by a network security monitor on the lookout for port scanners. If your site uses a firewall (see *Firewalls* on page 701), it's a good idea to probe it with these alternative scanning modes to see what they turn up.

nmap has the magical and useful ability to guess what operating system a remote system is running by looking at the particulars of its implementation of TCP/IP. It can sometimes even identify the software that's running on an open port. The **-O** and **-sV** options, respectively, turn on this behavior. For example:

```
$ nmap -O -sV secure.example.com

Starting Nmap 4.00 ( http://www.insecure.org/nmap/ ) at 2006-05-16 00:01 EDT
Interesting ports on secure.example.com (192.168.1.33):
(The 1670 ports scanned but not shown below are in state: closed)
```

---

7. Actually, only the privileged ports (those with port numbers under 1,024) and the well-known ports are checked by default. Use the **-p** option to explicitly specify the range of ports to scan.

```
PORT      STATE   SERVICE  VERSION
22/tcp    open    ssh      OpenSSH 3.6.1p2 (protocol 2.0)
1241/tcp  open    ssl      Nessus security scanner
Device type: general purpose
Running: Linux 2.4.X|2.5.X|2.6.X
OS details: Linux 2.4.0 - 2.5.20, Linux 2.5.25 - 2.6.8 or Gentoo 1.2 Linux 2.4.19
    rc1-rc7, Linux 2.6.3 - 2.6.10
Nmap finished: 1 IP address (1 host up) scanned in 8.095 seconds
```

This feature can be very useful for taking an inventory of a local network. Unfortunately, it is also very useful to hackers, who can base their attacks on known weaknesses of the target OS.

Keep in mind that most administrators don't appreciate your efforts to scan their network and point out its vulnerabilities, however well intended your motive. Do not run **nmap** on someone else's network without permission from one of that network's administrators.

Nessus: next generation network scanner

Nessus, originally released by Renaud Deraison in 1998, is a powerful and useful software vulnerability scanner. At the time of this writing, it uses more than 10,000 plug-ins to check for both local and remote security flaws. Although it is now a closed source, proprietary product, it is still freely available, and new plug-ins are released regularly. It is the most widely accepted and complete vulnerability scanner available.

Nessus prides itself on being the security scanner that takes nothing for granted. Instead of assuming that all web servers run on port 80, for instance, it scans for web servers running on any port and then checks them for vulnerabilities. Instead of relying on the version numbers reported by the service it has connected to, Nessus attempts to exploit known vulnerabilities to see if the service is susceptible.

Although a substantial amount of setup time is required to get Nessus running (it requires several packages that aren't installed on the typical default distribution), it's well worth the effort.

The Nessus system includes a client and a server. The server acts as a database and the client handles the GUI presentation. You must run the server on a UNIX or Linux system, but clients are available to control and display Nessus from a variety of other platforms.

One of the great advantages of Nessus is its modular design, which makes it easy for third parties to add new security checks. Thanks to an active user community (and despite recent licensing changes), Nessus is likely to be a useful tool for years to come.

John the Ripper: find insecure passwords

One way to thwart poor password choices is to try to break the passwords yourself and to force users to change passwords that you have broken. John the Ripper is a sophisticated tool by Solar Designer that implements various password-cracking algorithms in a single tool. It replaces the tool **crack**, which was covered in previous editions of this book.

Even though most systems use a shadow password file to hide encrypted passwords from public view, it's still wise to verify that your users' passwords are crack resistant. Knowledge of a user's password can be useful because people tend to use the same password over and over again. A single password might provide access to another system, decrypt files stored in a user's home directory, and allow access to financial accounts on the web. (Needless to say, it's not very security-smart to reuse a password this way. But nobody wants to remember ten passwords.)

Considering its internal complexity, John the Ripper is an extremely simple program to use. Direct **john** to the file to be cracked, most often **/etc/shadow**, and watch the magic happen:

```
$ sudo ./john /etc/shadow
Loaded 25 password hashes with 25 different salts (FreeBSD MD5 [32/32])
password  (bad2)
badpass   (bad1)
```

In this example, 25 unique passwords were read from the shadow file. As passwords are cracked, John prints them to the screen and saves them to a file called **john.pot**. The output contains the password in the left column with the login in parentheses in the right column. To reprint passwords after **john** has completed, run the same command with the **-show** argument.

As of this writing, the most recent stable version of John the Ripper is 1.7.0.2. It's available from www.openwall.com/john. Since John the Ripper's output contains the passwords it has broken, you should carefully protect the output and delete it as soon as you are done.

hosts_access: host access control

Network firewalls are a first line of defense against access by unauthorized hosts, but they shouldn't be the only barrier in place. Linux uses two files, **/etc/hosts.allow** and **/etc/hosts.deny**, to restrict access to services according to the origin of network requests. The **hosts.allow** file lists the hosts that are allowed to connect to a specific service, and the **hosts.deny** file restricts access. However, these files control access only for services that are **hosts_access** aware, such as those managed by **xinetd**, **sshd**, and some configurations of **sendmail**.

In most cases it is wise to be restrictive and permit access only to essential services from designated hosts. We suggest denying access by default in the **hosts.deny** file with the single line

```
ALL:ALL
```

You can then permit access on a case-by-case basis in **hosts.allow**. The following configuration allows access to SSH from hosts on the 192.168/16 networks and to **sendmail** from anywhere.

```
sshd: 192.168.0.0/255.255.0.0
sendmail: ALL
```

The format of an entry in either file is *service: host* or *service: network*. Failed connection attempts are noted in syslog. Connections from hosts that are not permitted to access to the service are immediately closed.

Most Linux distributions include **hosts.allow** and **hosts.deny** files by default, but they're usually empty.

Samhain: host-based intrusion detection

Samhain is a host intrusion detection system and file integrity monitor that is developed and maintained by Rainer Wichmann at Samhain Labs (la-samhna.de). Thanks to its modular interface, it can monitor the integrity of files, check mounted filesystems, search for rootkits, and more. For example, samhain makes it easy to determine that an intruder has replaced your copy of **/bin/login** with one that records passwords in a clandestine file.

Samhain's console-centric design keeps log data on a trusted host, which helps to maintain the integrity of the auditing data. Host change reports can be reviewed through a web interface or distributed via email. Samhain's logs can be useful as a forensic tool to help reconstruct the sequence of events in a security incident.

Samhain checks host characteristics against a database that contains file information and checksums known to be sane at the time the database was created. The general idea is to make a baseline database from a trusted state of the system and then regularly check for differences against the historical database. Files that are known to change under normal circumstances can be configured not to generate warnings. When a system's configuration changes or new software is installed, the database should be rebuilt so that real problems do not disappear among a flood of spurious warnings.

The full system includes three components. The **samhain** agent runs on clients and reports data to the log server. The log server daemon, called **yule**, accepts connections from **samhain** clients and adds data to the configured logging facilities, usually syslog or a database. A web-based management console called Beltane manages system baselines, edits configurations, and signs the configurations and baselines with a digital signature.

The system's component-based design offers several benefits over traditional file integrity scanners. The data that's collected lives on a trusted host, so attackers have a smaller chance of compromising the integrity of the database. Management is also easier because information is collected in one central location.

You can configure samhain to be incredibly paranoid. Samhain can do sneaky things like hide itself in the process list and append its database to a file that doesn't break with excess data such as a JPEG file, effectively hiding the database inside an image.

Cryptographic signatures of configuration files and databases can be created with
the web interface to help detect any unauthorized changes to those files.

Here's a simple example of a report from a samhain syslog entry:

```
# CRIT   : [2006-06-25T19:31:48-0600] msg=<POLICY [ReadOnly] --------T->,
          path=</bin/login>, ctime_old=<[2006-06-26T01:24:34]>, ctime_new=<[2006-
          06-26T01:31:47]>, mtime_old=<[2006-06-26T01:24:34]>, mtime_new=<[2006-
          06-26T01:31:47]>,
          48CA06CC50B857DE77C27956ADE7245B0DF63F6A8A42F5B7
```

It's a little cryptic, but this entry explains that a log message of severity CRITICAL
occurred, and that the **/bin/login** program's ctime and mtime attributes have
changed. Time to investigate.

Unfortunately, samhain requires a fair amount of maintenance overhead. Like any
system based on checks against a system baseline, it tends to generate a fair number
of false positive complaints caused by legitimate day-to-day activity. The samhain
configuration file helps weed out complaints about frequently changing files, but
administrators can't predict everything. Keep in mind that a fair amount of hand-
holding will be required, especially on a large-scale installation.

Security-Enhanced Linux (SELinux)

As we have seen, the Linux security model has its faults. Discretionary access controls (the concept of access to files being permitted at the discretion of an account
with appropriate permissions) is a convenient but insecure method of controlling
access to filesystem objects. It is inherently based on trust: trust that users with access are not malicious, trust that administrators know the proper permissions for
every file in a software package, and trust that third-party software packages install
themselves with strong controls in place. But even if all of these things were true, a
software vulnerability could still leave the system unprotected.

SELinux addresses this problem by using mandatory access controls, aka MAC. Under MAC, users do not have authoritative control over object access. Instead, an administrator defines system-wide access policies. A well-implemented MAC policy
relies on the principle of least privilege (allowing access only when necessary), much
as a properly designed firewall allows only specifically recognized services and clients to pass. MAC can prevent software with code execution vulnerabilities (e.g.,
buffer overflows) from compromising the system by limiting the scope of the breach
to the few specific resources required by that software.

SELinux is an NSA project that has been freely available since late 2000. It has been
integrated into the 2.6 series of the Linux kernel. Adoption of SELinux by individual
distributions has been relatively weak, however, with the notable exceptions of Red
Hat Enterprise Linux and Fedora.

Policy development is a complicated topic. At least one company offers a 3-day class
on SELinux policy. To protect a new daemon, for example, a policy must carefully
enumerate all the files, directories, and other objects to which the process needs

access. For complicated software like **sendmail** or the Apache **httpd**, this task can be quite complex.

Fortunately, many general policies are available online. These can easily be installed and configured for your particular environment. A full-blown policy editor that aims to ease policy application can be found at seedit.sourceforge.net.

 SELinux has been present in RHEL since version 4. Fedora incorporated the software in Core 2 and included additional support in Core 3. A default installation of Fedora or Red Hat Enterprise Linux actually includes some SELinux protections right out of the box.

The file **/etc/selinux/config** controls the SELinux configuration. The interesting lines are

```
SELINUX=enforcing
SELINUXTYPE=targeted
```

The first line has three possible values: enforcing, permissive, or disabled. The enforcing setting ensures that the loaded policy is applied and prohibits violations. permissive allows violations to occur but logs them through syslog. disabled turns off SELinux entirely.

SELINUXTYPE refers to the type of policy to be applied. Red Hat and Fedora have two policies: targeted, which defines additional security for daemons that Red Hat has protected,[8] and strict, which protects the entire system. Although the strict policy is available, it is not supported by Red Hat; the restrictions are so tight that the system is difficult to use. The targeted policy offers protection for important network daemons without affecting general system use, at least in theory. But even the targeted policy isn't perfect. If you're having problems with newly installed software, check **/var/log/messages** for SELinux errors.

 SUSE uses its own implementation of MAC called AppArmor and does not include SELinux.

 SELinux packages are maintained for Debian and Ubuntu by Russel Coker, the Red Hat bloke who generated the strict and targeted policies.

20.11 CRYPTOGRAPHIC SECURITY TOOLS

Many of the protocols in common use on Linux systems date from a time before the wide deployment of the Internet and modern cryptography. Security was simply not a factor in the design of many protocols; in others, security concerns were waved away with the transmission of a plaintext password or with a vague check to see if packets originated from a trusted host or port.

---

8. The protected daemons are **httpd, dhcpd, mailman, named, portmap, nscd, ntpd, mysqld, postgres, squid, winbindd,** and **ypbind.**

These protocols now find themselves operating in the shark-infested waters of large corporate LANs and the Internet, where, it must be assumed, all traffic is open to inspection. Not only that, but there is little to prevent anyone from actively interfering in network conversations. How can you be sure who you're really talking to?

Cryptography solves many of these problems. It has been possible for a long time to scramble messages so that an eavesdropper cannot decipher them, but this is just the beginning of the wonders of cryptography. Developments such as public key cryptography and secure hashing have promoted the design of cryptosystems that meet almost any conceivable need.[9]

Unfortunately, these mathematical developments have largely failed to translate into secure, usable software that is widely embraced and understood. The developers of cryptographic software systems tend to be very interested in provable correctness and absolute security and not so interested in whether a system makes practical sense for the real world. Most current software tends to be rather overengineered, and it's perhaps not surprising that users run away screaming when given half a chance. Today, the cryptography-using population consists largely of hobbyists interested in cryptography, black-helicopter conspiracy theorists, and those who have no choice because of administrative policy.

We may or may not see a saner approach to cryptography developing over the next few years. In the meantime, some current offerings discussed in the following sections may help out.

Kerberos: a unified approach to network security

The Kerberos system, designed at MIT, attempts to address some of the issues of network security in a consistent and extensible way. Kerberos is an authentication system, a facility that "guarantees" that users and services are in fact who they claim to be. It does not provide any additional security or encryption beyond that.

Kerberos uses DES to construct nested sets of credentials called "tickets." Tickets are passed around the network to certify your identity and to provide you with access to network services. Each Kerberos site must maintain at least one physically secure machine (called the authentication server) to run the Kerberos daemon. This daemon issues tickets to users or services that present credentials, such as passwords, when they request authentication.

In essence, Kerberos improves upon traditional Linux password security in only two ways: it never transmits unencrypted passwords on the network, and it relieves users from having to type passwords repeatedly, making password protection of network services somewhat more palatable.

---

9. An excellent resource for those interested in cryptography is "RSA Labs' Frequently Asked Questions about Today's Cryptography" at www.rsasecurity.com/rsalabs/faq. Additionally, Stephen Levy's book *Crypto* is a comprehensive guide to the history of cryptography.

Security

The Kerberos community boasts one of the most lucid and enjoyable documents ever written about a cryptosystem, Bill Bryant's "Designing an Authentication System: a Dialogue in Four Scenes." It's required reading for anyone interested in cryptography and is available at

> web.mit.edu/kerberos/www/dialogue.html

There's also a good FAQ:

> www.nrl.navy.mil/CCS/people/kenh/kerberos-faq.html

Kerberos offers a better network security model than the "ignoring network security entirely" model. However, it is neither perfectly secure nor painless to install and run. It does not supersede any of the other security measures described in this chapter. In our opinion, most sites are better off without it. Good system hygiene and a focused cryptographic solution for remote logins such as SSH (see page 697) should provide a more-than-adequate level of security for your users.

Unfortunately (and perhaps predictably), the Kerberos system distributed as part of Windows uses proprietary, undocumented extensions to the protocols. As a result, it does not interoperate well with distributions based on the MIT code.

PGP: Pretty Good Privacy

Philip Zimmermann's PGP package provides a tool chest of bread-and-butter cryptographic utilities focused primarily on email security. It can be used to encrypt data, to generate signatures, and to verify the origin of files and messages.

Attempts to regulate or stop the distribution of PGP have given it a rather checkered history. McAfee includes PGP in its E-Business server product, and the PGP corporation uses PGP for a variety of encryption products. The GNU project provides an excellent, free, and widely used implementation known as GnuPG at www.gnupg.org. A governmentally vetted version of PGP is available for use in the United States, and an international version with somewhat stronger and more varied encryption is available from www.pgpi.org. The international archive sites do not seem to screen out U.S. addresses, so American users must be very careful not to accidentally go to www.pgpi.org and download the full-featured version of PGP.

PGP is the most popular cryptographic software in common use. Unfortunately, the UNIX/Linux version is nuts-and-bolts enough that you have to understand a fair amount of cryptographic background in order to use it. Fortunately (?), PGP comes with an 88-page treatise on cryptography that can set the stage. Although you may find PGP useful in your own work, we don't recommend that you support it for users, because it has been known to spark many puzzled questions. We have found the Windows version of PGP to be considerably easier to use than the **pgp** command with its 38 different operating modes.

Software packages on the Internet are often distributed with a PGP signature file that purports to guarantee the origin and purity of the software. It is difficult for people who are not die-hard PGP users to validate these signatures—not because the validation process is complicated, but because true PGP security can only come from having collected a personal library of public keys from people whose identities you have directly verified. Downloading a single public key along with a signature file and software distribution is approximately as secure as downloading the distribution alone.

SSH: the secure shell

The SSH system, written by Tatu Ylönen, is a secure replacement for **rlogin**, **rcp**, and **telnet**. It uses cryptographic authentication to confirm a user's identity and encrypts all communications between the two hosts. The protocol used by SSH is designed to withstand a wide variety of potential attacks. The protocol is documented by RFCs 4250 through 4256 and is now a proposed standard to the IETF.

SSH has morphed from being a freely distributed open source project (SSH1) to being a commercial product that uses a slightly different (and more secure) protocol, SSH2. Fortunately, the open source community has responded by releasing the excellent OpenSSH package (maintained by OpenBSD), which now implements both protocols.

The main components of SSH are a server daemon, **sshd**, and two user-level commands: **ssh** for remote logins and **scp** for copying files. Other components are an **ssh-keygen** command that generates public key pairs and a couple of utilities that help to support secure X Windows.

sshd can authenticate user logins in several different ways. It's up to you as the administrator to decide which of these methods are acceptable:

- **Method A:** If the name of the remote host from which the user is logging in is listed in **~/.rhosts**, **~/.shosts**, **/etc/hosts.equiv**, or **/etc/shosts.equiv**, then the user is logged in automatically without a password check. This scheme mirrors that of the old **rlogin** daemon and in our opinion is *not* acceptable for normal use.

- **Method B:** As a refinement of method A, **sshd** can also use public key cryptography to verify the identity of the remote host. For that to happen, the remote host's public key (generated at install time) must be listed in the local host's **/etc/ssh_known_hosts** file or the user's **~/.ssh/known_hosts** file. If the remote host can prove that it knows the corresponding private key (normally stored in **/etc/ssh_host_key**, a world-unreadable file), then the user is logged in without being asked for a password. Method B is more restrictive than method A, but we think it's still not quite secure enough. If the security of the originating host is compromised, the local site will be compromised as well.

- **Method C:** **sshd** can use public key cryptography to establish the user's identity. At login time, the user must have access to a copy of his or her private key file and must supply a password to decrypt it. This method is the most secure, but it's annoying to set up. It also means that users cannot log in when traveling unless they bring along a copy of their private key file (perhaps on a USB key, hopefully encrypted). If you decide to use key pairs, make extensive use of **ssh -v** during the troubleshooting process.

- **Method D:** Finally, **sshd** can simply allow the user to enter his or her normal login password. This makes **ssh** behave very much like **telnet**, except that the password and session are both encrypted. The main drawbacks of this method are that system login passwords can be relatively weak if you have not beefed up their security, and that there are ready-made tools (such as John the Ripper) designed to break them. However, this method is probably the best choice for normal use.

Authentication policy is set in the **/etc/sshd_config** file. You will see at once that this file has been filled up with configuration garbage for you, but you can safely ignore most of it. The options relevant to authentication are shown in Table 20.1.

Table 20.1   Authentication-related options in /etc/sshd_config

Option	Meth[a]	Dflt	Meaning when turned on
RhostsAuthentication	A	no	Allows login via ~/.shosts, /etc/shosts.equiv, etc.
RhostsRSAAuthentication	B	yes	Allows ~/.shosts et al., but also requires host key
IgnoreRhosts	A,B	no	Ignores the ~/.rhosts and hosts.equiv files[b]
IgnoreRootRhosts	A,B	no[c]	Prevents rhosts/shosts authentication for root
RSAAuthentication	C	yes	Allows per-user public key crypto authentication
PasswordAuthentication	D	yes	Allows use of normal login password

a. The authentication methods to which this variable is relevant
b. But continues to honor ~/.shosts and shosts.equiv
c. Defaults to the value of IgnoreRhosts

Our suggested configuration, which allows methods C and D but not methods A or B, is as follows:

```
RhostsAuthentication no
RhostsRSAAuthentication no
RSAAuthentication yes
PasswordAuthentication yes
```

It is never wise to allow root to log in remotely. Superuser access should be achieved through the use of **sudo**. To encourage this behavior, use the option

```
PermitRootLogin no
```

One-time passwords

Brute force tools such as John the Ripper call attention to the insecurity of static passwords. Even when subjected to tools like PAM and password aging, users notoriously pick easy-to-remember but weak passwords, then write them down on sticky notes and share them with coworkers. One-time passwords confront this problem by enforcing a unique password at each login. Because the password is constantly changing, a brute force tool is worthless.

These days, the most common sightings of one-time passwords are in commercial security products. A number of vendors offer one-time password systems based on small "key chain"-sized (or credit card-sized) devices with LCD displays that generate passwords on the fly. At the very least, distributing and replacing the little hardware devices will keep your administrative assistant busy for a few hours a week.

Stunnel

Stunnel, created by Michal Trojnara, is an open source package that encrypts arbitrary TCP connections. It uses SSL, the Secure Sockets Layer, to create end-to-end "tunnels" through which it passes data to and from an unencrypted service. It is known to work well with insecure services such as Telnet, IMAP, and POP.

A **stunnel** daemon runs on both the client and server systems. The local **stunnel** usually accepts connections on the service's traditional port (e.g., port 25 for SMTP) and routes them through SSL to a **stunnel** on the remote host. The remote **stunnel** accepts the connection, decrypts the incoming data, and routes it to the remote port on which the server is listening. This system allows unencrypted services to take advantage of the confidentiality and integrity offered by encryption without requiring any software changes. Client software need only be configured to look for services on the local system rather than on the server that will ultimately provide them.

Telnet makes a good example because it consists of a simple daemon listening on a single port. To stunnelfy a Telnet link, the first step is to create an SSL certificate. Stunnel is SSL library independent, so any standards-based implementation will do; we like OpenSSL. To generate the certificate:

```
server# openssl req -new -x509 -days 365 -nodes -out stunnel.pem -keyout
    stunnel.pem
Generating a 1024 bit RSA private key
.++++++
................................++++++
writing new private key to 'stunnel.pem'
-----
You are about to be asked to enter information that will be incorporated
into your certificate request.
What you are about to enter is what is called a Distinguished Name or a DN.
There are quite a few fields but you can leave some blank
For some fields there will be a default value,
If you enter '.', the field will be left blank.
Country Name (2 letter code) [GB]:US
State or Province Name (full name) [Berkshire]:Colorado
Locality Name (eg, city) [Newbury]:Boulder
Organization Name (eg, company) [My Company Ltd]:Booklab, Inc.
Organizational Unit Name (eg, section) []:
Common Name (eg, your name or your server's hostname) []:
    server.example.com
Email Address []:
```

Security

This command creates a self-signed, passphrase-less certificate. Although not using a passphrase is a convenience (a real human doesn't have to be present to type a passphrase each time **stunnel** restarts), it also introduces a security risk. Be careful to protect the certificate file with strong permissions.

Next, define the configuration for both the server and client **stunnel**s. The standard configuration file is **/etc/stunnel/stunnel.conf**, but you can create several configurations if you want to run more than one tunnel.

```
cert = /etc/stunnel/stunnel.pem
chroot = /var/run/stunnel/
pid = /stunnel.pid
setuid = nobody
setgid = nobody
debug = 7
output = /var/log/stunnel.log
client = no

[telnets]
accept = 992
connect = 23
```

There are a couple of important points about the server configuration. First, note the **chroot** statement, which confines the **stunnel** process to the **/var/run/stunnel** directory. Paths for accessory files may need to be expressed in either the regular system namespace or the **chroot**ed namespace, depending on the point at which they are opened. Here, the **stunnel.pid** file is actually located in **/var/run/stunnel**.

The [telnetd] section has two statements: accept tells **stunnel** to accept connections on port 992, and connect passes those connections through to port 23, the actual Telnet service.

The client configuration is very similar:

```
cert = /etc/stunnel/stunnel.pem
chroot = /var/run/stunnel/
pid = /stunnel.pid
setuid = nobody
setgid = nobody
debug = 7
output = /var/log/stunnel.log
client = yes

[telnets]
accept = 23
connect = server.example.com:992
```

A couple of directives are reversed relative to the server configuration. The client = yes statement tells the program to initiate **stunnel** connections rather than accept them. The local **stunnel** listens for connections on port 23 and connects to the server on port 992. The hostname in the connect directive should match the entry specified when the certificate was created.

Both the client and the server **stunnel**s can be started with no command-line arguments. If you check with **netstat -an**, you should see the server **stunnel** waiting for connections on port 992 while the client **stunnel** waits on port 23.

To access the tunnel, a user simply **telnet**s to the local host:

```
client# telnet localhost 23
Trying 127.0.0.1...
Connected to localhost (127.0.0.1).
Escape character is '^]'.
Red Hat Enterprise Linux WS release 4 (Nahant Update 2)
Kernel 2.6.9-5.EL on an i686
login:
```

The user can now safely log in without fear of password thievery. A vigilant administrator would be careful to use TCP wrappers to restrict connections on the client to only the local interface—the intent is not to allow the world to **telnet** securely to the server! **stunnel** is one of several programs that have built-in wrapper support and do not require the use of **tcpd** to restrict access. Surf to www.stunnel.org for instructions.

20.12 FIREWALLS

In addition to protecting individual machines, you can also implement security precautions at the network level. The basic tool of network security is the "firewall." The three main categories of firewalls are packet-filtering, service proxy, and stateful inspection.

Packet-filtering firewalls

A packet-filtering firewall limits the types of traffic that can pass through your Internet gateway (or through an internal gateway that separates domains within your organization) on the basis of information in the packet header. It's much like driving your car through a customs checkpoint at an international border crossing. You specify which destination addresses, port numbers, and protocol types are acceptable, and the gateway simply discards (and in some cases, logs) packets that don't meet the profile.

Packet filtering is supported by dedicated routers such as those made by Cisco. It may also be available in software, depending on the machine you're using as a gateway and its configuration. In general, packet-filtering firewalls offer a significant increase in security with little cost in performance or complexity.

Linux includes packet filtering software (see the details beginning on 704 for more information). It's also possible to buy commercial software to perform this function. These packages all have entertainment value, and they can provide a reasonably secure firewall for a home or small office. However, you should refer to the comments at the beginning of this chapter before you consider a Linux system as a production grade corporate firewall.[10] This is one case in which you should really spend the money for a dedicated network appliance, such as Cisco's PIX firewall.

How services are filtered

Most well-known services are associated with a network port in the **/etc/services** file or its vendor-specific equivalent. The daemons that provide these services bind to the appropriate ports and wait for connections from remote sites.[11] Most of the well-known service ports are "privileged," meaning that their port numbers are in the range 1 to 1,023. These ports can only be used by a process running as root. Port numbers 1,024 and higher are referred to as nonprivileged ports.

Service-specific filtering is based on the assumption that the client (the machine that initiates a TCP or UDP conversation) uses a nonprivileged port to contact a privileged port on the server. For example, if you wanted to allow only inbound SMTP connections to a machine with the address 192.108.21.200, you would install a filter that allowed TCP packets destined for that address at port 25 and that permitted outbound TCP packets from that address to anywhere.[12] The exact way in which such a filter would be installed depends on the kind of router you are using.

See page 734 for more information about setting up an ftp server. Some services, such as FTP, add a twist to the puzzle. The FTP protocol actually uses two TCP connections when transferring a file: one for commands and the other for data. The client initiates the command connection, and the server initiates the data connection. Ergo, if you want to use FTP to retrieve files from the Internet, you must permit inbound access to all nonprivileged TCP ports since you have no idea what port might be used to form an incoming data connection.

This tweak largely defeats the purpose of packet filtering because some notoriously insecure services (for example, X11 at port 6000) naturally bind to nonprivileged ports. This configuration also creates an opportunity for curious users within your organization to start their own services (such as a **telnet** server at a nonstandard and nonprivileged port) that they or their friends can access from the Internet.

One common solution to the FTP problem is to use the SSH file transfer protocol. The protocol is currently an Internet draft but is widely used and mature. It is commonly used as a subcomponent of SSH, which provides its authentication and encryption. Unlike FTP, SFTP uses only a single port for both commands and data, handily solving the packet-filtering paradox. A number of SFTP implementations exist. We've had great luck with the command-line SFTP client supplied by OpenSSH.

If you must use FTP, a reasonable approach is to allow FTP to the outside world only from a single, isolated host. Users can log in to the FTP machine when they need to perform network operations that are forbidden from the inner net. Since replicating all user accounts on the FTP "server" would defeat the goal of administrative

---

10. We assume you already know not to consider something like Windows as a firewall platform. Does the name "Windows" evoke images of security? Silly rabbit, Windows is for desktops.

11. In many cases, **xinetd** does the actual waiting on their behalf. See page 887 for more information.

12. Port 25 is the SMTP port as defined in **/etc/services**.

separation, you may want to create FTP accounts by request only. Naturally, the FTP host should run a full complement of security-checking tools.

The most secure way to use a packet filter is to start with a configuration that allows nothing but inbound SMTP or SSH. You can then liberalize the filter bit by bit as you discover useful things that don't work.

Some security-conscious sites use two-stage filtering. In this scheme, one filter is a gateway to the Internet, and a second filter lies between the outer gateway and the rest of the local network. The idea is to leave the outer gateway relatively open and to make the inner gateway very conservative. If the machines in the middle are administratively separate from the rest of the network, they can provide a variety of services on the Internet with reduced risk. The partially secured network is usually called the "demilitarized zone" or "DMZ."

Service proxy firewalls

Service proxies intercept connections to and from the outside world and establish new connections on the opposite side of the firewall, acting as a sort of shuttle or chaperone between the two worlds. It's much like driving to the border of your country, walking across the border, and renting a sanitized, freshly washed car on the other side of the border to continue your journey.

Because of their design, service proxy firewalls are much less flexible (and much slower) than pure packet filters. Your proxy must have a module that decodes and conveys each protocol you want to let through the firewall. In the early 1990s this was relatively easy because only a few protocols were in common use. Today, Internauts might use several dozen protocols in an hour of web surfing. As a result, service proxies are relatively unpopular in organizations that use the Internet as a primary medium of communication.

Stateful inspection firewalls

The theory behind stateful inspection firewalls is that if you could carefully listen to and understand all the conversations (in all the languages) that were taking place in a crowded airport, you could make sure that someone wasn't planning to bomb a plane later that day. Stateful inspection firewalls are designed to inspect the traffic that flows through them and compare the actual network activity to what "should" be happening. For example, if the packets exchanged in an FTP command sequence name a port to be used later for a data connection, the firewall should expect a data connection to occur only on that port. Attempts by the remote site to connect to other ports are presumably bogus and should be dropped.

Unfortunately, reality usually kills the cat here. It's no more realistic to keep track of the "state" of the network connections of thousands of hosts using hundreds of protocols than it is to listen to every conversation in every language in a crowded airport. Someday, as processor and memory capacity increase, it may eventually be feasible.

So what are vendors really selling when they claim to provide stateful inspection? Their products either monitor a very limited number of connections or protocols or they search for a particular set of "bad" situations. Not that there's anything wrong with that; clearly, some benefit is derived from any technology that can detect traffic anomalies. In this particular case, however, it's important to remember that the claims are *mostly* marketing hype.

Firewalls: how safe are they?

A firewall should not be your primary means of defense against intruders. It's only appropriate as a supplemental security measure. The use of firewalls often provides a false sense of security. If it lulls you into relaxing other safeguards, it will have had a *negative* effect on the security of your site.

Every host within your organization should be individually secured and regularly monitored with tools such as **xinetd**, Nmap, Nessus, and samhain. Likewise, your entire user community needs to be educated about basic security hygiene. Otherwise, you are simply building a structure that has a hard crunchy outside and a soft chewy center.

Ideally, local users should be able to connect to any Internet service they want, but machines on the Internet should only be able to connect to a limited set of local services. For example, you may want to allow FTP access to a local archive server and allow SMTP (email) connections to your mail server.

For maximizing the value of your Internet connection, we recommend that you emphasize convenience and accessibility when deciding how to set up your network. At the end of the day, it's the system administrator's vigilance that makes a network secure, not a fancy piece of firewall hardware.

20.13 LINUX FIREWALL FEATURES: IP TABLES

We haven't traditionally recommended the use of Linux (or UNIX, or Windows) systems as firewalls because of the insecurity of running a full-fledged, general-purpose operating system. Embedded devices designed specifically for routing and packet filtering (such as a Cisco PIX box) make the best firewalls,[13] but a hardened Linux system is a great substitute for organizations that don't have the budget for a high-dollar firewall appliance.

If you are set on using a Linux machine as a firewall, please at least make sure that it's up to date with respect to security configuration and patches. A firewall machine is an excellent place to put into practice all of this chapter's recommendations. (The section that starts on page 701 discusses packet-filtering firewalls in general. If you are not familiar with the basic concept of a firewall, it would probably be wise to read that section before continuing.)

---

13. That said, many consumer-oriented networking devices, such as Linksys's router products, use Linux and **iptables** at their core.

Version 2.4 of the Linux kernel introduced an all-new packet handling engine called Netfilter. The tool used to control Netfilter, **iptables**, is the big brother of the older **ipchains** command used with Linux 2.2 kernels. **iptables** applies ordered "chains" of rules to network packets. Sets of chains make up "tables" and are used for handling specific kinds of traffic.

For example, the default **iptables** table is named "filter". Chains of rules in this table are used for packet-filtering network traffic. The filter table contains three default chains. Each packet that is handled by the kernel is passed through exactly one of these chains. Rules in the FORWARD chain are applied to all packets that arrive on one network interface and need to be forwarded to another. Rules in the INPUT and OUTPUT chains are applied to traffic addressed to or originating from the local host, respectively. These three standard chains are usually all you need for firewalling between two network interfaces. If necessary, you can define a custom configuration to support more complex accounting or routing scenarios.

In addition to the filter table, **iptables** includes the "nat" and "mangle" tables. The nat table contains chains of rules that control Network Address Translation (here, "nat" is the name of the **iptables** table and "NAT" is the name of the generic address translation scheme). The section *Private addresses and NAT* on page 289 discusses NAT, and an example of the nat table in action is shown on page 320. Later in this section, we use the nat table's PREROUTING chain for anti-spoofing packet filtering.

The mangle table contains chains that modify or alter the contents of network packets outside the context of NAT and packet filtering. Although the mangle table is handy for special packet handling, such as resetting IP time-to-live values, it is not typically used in most production environments. We discuss only the filter and nat tables in this section, leaving the mangle table to the adventurous.

Each rule that makes up a chain has a "target" clause that determines what to do with matching packets. When a packet matches a rule, its fate is in most cases sealed; no additional rules will be checked. Although many targets are defined internally to **iptables**, it is possible to specify another chain as a rule's target.

The targets available to rules in the filter table are ACCEPT, DROP, REJECT, LOG, MIRROR, QUEUE, REDIRECT, RETURN, and ULOG. When a rule results in an ACCEPT, matching packets are allowed to proceed on their way. DROP and REJECT both drop their packets. DROP is silent, and REJECT returns an ICMP error message. LOG gives you a simple way to track packets as they match rules, and ULOG provides extended logging.

REDIRECT shunts packets to a proxy instead of letting them go on their merry way. You might use this feature to force all your site's web traffic to go through a web cache such as Squid. RETURN terminates user-defined chains and is analogous to the return statement in a subroutine call. The MIRROR target swaps the IP source and destination address before sending the packet. Finally, QUEUE hands packets to local user programs through a kernel module.

A Linux firewall is usually implemented as a series of **iptables** commands contained in an **rc** startup script. Individual **iptables** commands usually take one of the following forms:

```
iptables -F chain-name
iptables -P chain-name target
iptables -A chain-name -i interface -j target
```

The first form (**-F**) flushes all prior rules from the chain. The second form (**-P**) sets a default policy (aka target) for the chain. We recommend that you use DROP for the default chain target. The third instance (**-A**) appends the current specification to the chain. Unless you specify a table with the **-t** argument, your commands apply to chains in the filter table. The **-i** parameter applies the rule to the named interface, and **-j** identifies the target. **iptables** accepts many other clauses, some of which are shown in Table 20.2.

Table 20.2   Command-line flags for iptables filters

Clause	Meaning or possible values
-p *proto*	Matches by protocol: **tcp**, **udp**, or **icmp**
-s *source-ip*	Matches host or network source IP address (CIDR notation is OK)
-d *dest-ip*	Matches host or network destination address
--sport *port#*	Matches by source port (note the double dashes)
--dport *port#*	Matches by destination port (note the double dashes)
--icmp-type *type*	Matches by ICMP type code (note the double dashes)
!	Negates a clause
-t *table*	Specifies the table to which a command applies (default is **filter**)

Below we break apart a complete example. We assume that the ppp0 interface goes to the Internet and that the eth0 interface goes to an internal network. The ppp0 IP address is 128.138.101.4, the eth0 IP address is 10.1.1.1, and both interfaces have a netmask of 255.255.255.0. This example uses stateless packet filtering to protect the web server with IP address 10.1.1.2, which is the standard method of protecting Internet servers. Later in the example, we show how to use stateful filtering to protect desktop users.

Before you can use **iptables** as a firewall, you must enable IP forwarding and make sure that various **iptables** modules have been loaded into the kernel. For more information on enabling IP forwarding, see *Tuning Linux kernel parameters on page 874* or *Security-related kernel variables* on page 319. Packages that install **iptables** generally include startup scripts to achieve this enabling and loading.

Our first set of rules initializes the filter table. First, all chains in the table are flushed, then the INPUT and FORWARD chains' default target is set to DROP. As with any other network firewall, the most secure strategy is to drop any packets that you have not explicitly allowed.

```
iptables -F
iptables -P INPUT DROP
iptables -P FORWARD DROP
```

Since rules are evaluated in the order in which they sit in a chain, we put our busiest rules at the front.[14] The first three rules in the FORWARD chain allow connections through the firewall to network services on 10.1.1.2. Specifically, we allow SSH (port 22), HTTP (port 80), and HTTPS (port 443) through to our web server. The first rule allows all connections through the firewall that originate from within the trusted net.

```
iptables -A FORWARD -i eth0 -p ANY -j ACCEPT
iptables -A FORWARD -d 10.1.1.2 -p tcp --dport 22 -j ACCEPT
iptables -A FORWARD -d 10.1.1.2 -p tcp --dport 80 -j ACCEPT
iptables -A FORWARD -d 10.1.1.2 -p tcp --dport 443 -j ACCEPT
```

The only TCP traffic we allow to our firewall host (10.1.1.1) is SSH, which is useful for managing the firewall. The second rule listed below allows loopback traffic, which stays local to our firewall host. Our administrators get nervous when they can't **ping** their default route, so the third rule here allows ICMP ECHO_REQUEST packets from internal IP addresses.

```
iptables -A INPUT -i eth0 -d 10.1.1.1 -p tcp --dport 22 -j ACCEPT
iptables -A INPUT -i lo -d 127.0.0.1 -p ANY -j ACCEPT
iptables -A INPUT -i eth0 -d 10.1.1.1 -p icmp --icmp-type 8 -j ACCEPT
```

For any TCP/IP host to work properly on the Internet, certain types of ICMP packets must be allowed through the firewall. The following eight rules allow a minimal set of ICMP packets to the firewall host, as well as to the network behind it.

```
iptables -A INPUT -p icmp --icmp-type 0 -j ACCEPT
iptables -A INPUT -p icmp --icmp-type 3 -j ACCEPT
iptables -A INPUT -p icmp --icmp-type 5 -j ACCEPT
iptables -A INPUT -p icmp --icmp-type 11 -j ACCEPT
iptables -A FORWARD -d 10.1.1.2 -p icmp --icmp-type 0 -j ACCEPT
iptables -A FORWARD -d 10.1.1.2 -p icmp --icmp-type 3 -j ACCEPT
iptables -A FORWARD -d 10.1.1.2 -p icmp --icmp-type 5 -j ACCEPT
iptables -A FORWARD -d 10.1.1.2 -p icmp --icmp-type 11 -j ACCEPT
```

We next add rules to the PREROUTING chain in the nat table. Although the nat table is not intended for packet filtering, its PREROUTING chain is particularly useful for anti-spoofing filtering. If we put DROP entries in the PREROUTING chain, they need not be present in the INPUT and FORWARD chains, since the PREROUTING chain is applied to all packets that enter the firewall host. It's cleaner to put the entries in a single place rather than duplicating them.

```
iptables -t nat -A PREROUTING -i ppp0 -s 10.0.0.0/8 -j DROP
iptables -t nat -A PREROUTING -i ppp0 -s 172.16.0.0/12 -j DROP
iptables -t nat -A PREROUTING -i ppp0 -s 192.168.0.0/16 -j DROP
iptables -t nat -A PREROUTING -i ppp0 -s 127.0.0.0/8 -j DROP
iptables -t nat -A PREROUTING -i ppp0 -s 224.0.0.0/4 -j DROP
```

14. However, you must be careful that reordering the rules for performance doesn't modify functionality.

Finally, we end both the INPUT and FORWARD chains with a rule that forbids all packets not explicitly permitted. Although we already enforced this behavior with the **iptables -P** commands, the LOG target lets us see who is knocking on our door from the Internet.

```
iptables -A INPUT -i ppp0 -j LOG
iptables -A FORWARD -i ppp0 -j LOG
```

Optionally, we could set up IP NAT to disguise the private address space used on the internal network. See *Linux NAT* on page 319 for more information about NAT.

One of the most powerful features that Netfilter brings to Linux firewalling is stateful packet filtering. Instead of allowing specific incoming services, a firewall for clients connecting to the Internet needs to allow incoming responses to the client's requests. The simple stateful FORWARD chain below allows all traffic to leave our network but only allows incoming traffic that's related to connections initiated by our hosts.

```
iptables -A FORWARD -i eth0 -p ANY -j ACCEPT
iptables -A FORWARD -m state --state ESTABLISHED,RELATED -j ACCEPT
```

Certain kernel modules must be loaded to enable **iptables** to track complex network sessions such as those of FTP and IRC. If these modules are not loaded, **iptables** simply disallows those connections. Although stateful packet filters can increase the security of your site, they also add to the complexity of the network. Be sure you need stateful functionality before implementing it in your firewall.

Perhaps the best way to debug your **iptables** rulesets is to use **iptables -L -v**. These options tell you how many times each rule in your chains has matched a packet. We often add temporary **iptables** rules with the LOG target when we want more information about the packets that get matched. You can often solve trickier problems by using a packet sniffer such as **tcpdump**.

20.14 Virtual private networks (VPNs)

One of the most interesting developments of the last few years has been the advent of the virtual private network or VPN. This technology has been made possible mostly by the increased processing power that is now available on a single chip (and on users' workstations). In its simplest form, a VPN is a connection that makes a remote network appear as if it is directly connected, even if it is physically thousands of miles and many router hops away. For increased security, the connection is not only authenticated in some way (usually with a "shared secret" such as a password), but the end-to-end traffic is also encrypted. Such an arrangement is usually referred to as a "secure tunnel."

Here's a good example of the kind of situation in which a VPN is handy: Suppose that a company has offices in Chicago, Boulder, and Miami. If each office has a connection to a local Internet service provider, the company can use VPNs to transparently (and, for the most part, securely) connect the offices across the untrusted Internet.

The company could achieve a similar result by leasing dedicated lines to connect the three offices, but that option would be considerably more expensive.

Another good example is a company whose employees telecommute from their homes. VPNs would allow those users to reap the benefits of their high-speed and inexpensive cable modem service while still making it appear that they are directly connected to the corporate network.

Because of the convenience and popularity of this functionality, everyone and his brother is offering some type of VPN solution. You can buy it from your router vendor, as a plug-in for your operating system, or even as a dedicated VPN device for your network. Depending on your budget and scalability needs, you may want to consider one of the many commercial VPN solutions in the marketplace.

If you're without a budget and looking for a quick fix, SSH will do secure tunneling for you. SSH normally provides one-port-at-a-time connectivity, but it can also supply pseudo-VPN functionality as shown in the example on page 328, which runs PPP through an SSH tunnel.

IPsec tunnels

If you're a fan of IETF standards (or of saving money) and need a real VPN solution, take a look at IPsec (Internet Protocol security). IPsec was originally developed for IPv6, but it has also been widely implemented for IPv4. IPsec is an IETF-approved, end-to-end authentication and encryption system. Almost all serious VPN vendors ship a product that has at least an IPsec compatibility mode.

IPsec uses strong cryptography to provide both authentication and encryption services. Authentication ensures that packets are from the right sender and have not been altered in transit, and encryption prevents the unauthorized examination of packet contents.

In its current form, IPsec encrypts the transport layer header, which includes the source and destination port numbers. Unfortunately, this scheme conflicts directly with the way that most firewalls work. A proposal to undo this feature is making its way through the IETF.

Linux kernels 2.5.47 and newer include a native IPsec implementation that is entirely different from the FreeS/WAN implementation commonly used with the 2.4 kernel series. Since IPsec is part of the kernel, it's included with all our distributions.

Note that there's a gotcha around IPsec tunnels and MTU size. It's important to ensure that once a packet has been encrypted by IPsec, nothing fragments it along the path the tunnel traverses. To achieve this feat, you may have to lower the MTU on the devices in front of the tunnel (in the real world, 1,400 bytes usually works). See page 278 in the TCP chapter for more information about MTU size.

Security

All I need is a VPN, right?

Sadly, there's a downside to VPNs. Although they do build a (mostly) secure tunnel across the untrusted network between the two endpoints, they don't usually address the security of the endpoints themselves. For example, if you set up a VPN between your corporate backbone and your CEO's home, you may be inadvertently creating a path for your CEO's 15-year-old daughter to have direct access to everything on your network. Hopefully, she only uses her newly acquired access to get a date with the shipping clerk.

Bottom line: you need to treat connections from VPN tunnels as external connections and grant them additional privileges only as absolutely necessary and after careful consideration. You may want to consider adding a special section to your site security policy that covers what rules apply to VPN connections.

20.15 HARDENED LINUX DISTRIBUTIONS

See page 693 for more information about SELinux.

Fortunately (?), we've been blessed with a variety of initiatives to produce "hardened" versions of Linux that offer a broader range of security features than are found in the mainstream releases. The hardening usually takes the form of special access controls and auditing capabilities. These features are probably particularly useful if you're planning to use Linux in some type of custom network appliance product. However, it's not clear that they afford substantial advantages to mainstream users. They still require good hygiene, a good packet filter, and all the other things discussed in this chapter. Perhaps they're good for added peace of mind.

Table 20.3 lists some of the better known hardening projects so that you can check out what they have to offer.

Table 20.3   Hardened Linux distributions

Project name	Web site
Bastille Linux	www.bastille-linux.org
Engarde Linux	www.engardelinux.com
Openwall GNU/*/Linux	www.openwall.com/Owl

20.16 WHAT TO DO WHEN YOUR SITE HAS BEEN ATTACKED

The key to handling an attack is simple: don't panic. It's very likely that by the time you discover the intrusion, most of the damage has already been done. In fact, it has probably been going on for weeks or months. The chance that you've discovered a break-in that just happened an hour ago is slim to none.

In that light, the wise owl says to take a deep breath and begin developing a carefully thought out strategy for dealing with the break-in. You need to avoid tipping off the intruder by announcing the break-in or performing any other activity that would seem abnormal to someone who may have been watching your site's operations for many weeks. Hint: performing a system backup is usually a good idea at this point and (hopefully!) will appear to be a normal activity to the intruder.[15]

This is also a good time to remind yourself that some studies have shown that 60% of security incidents involve an insider. Be very careful who you discuss the incident with until you're sure you have all the facts.

Here's a quick 9-step plan that may assist you in your time of crisis:

Step 1: Don't panic. In many cases, a problem isn't noticed until hours or days after it took place. Another few hours or days won't affect the outcome. The difference between a panicky response and a rational response will. Many recovery situations are exacerbated by the destruction of important log, state, and tracking information during an initial panic.

Step 2: Decide on an appropriate level of response. No one benefits from an over-hyped security incident. Proceed calmly. Identify the staff and resources that must participate and leave others to assist with the post-mortem after it's all over.

Step 3: Hoard all available tracking information. Check accounting files and logs. Try to determine where the original breach occurred. Back up all your systems. Make sure that you physically write-protect backup tapes if you put them in a drive to read them.

Step 4: Assess your degree of exposure. Determine what crucial information (if any) has "left" the company, and devise an appropriate mitigation strategy. Determine the level of future risk.

Step 5: Pull the plug. If necessary and appropriate, disconnect compromised machines from the network. Close known holes and stop the bleeding. CERT provides steps on analyzing an intrusion. The document can be found at

> www.cert.org/tech_tips/win-UNIX-system_compromise.html

Step 6: Devise a recovery plan. With a creative colleague, draw up a recovery plan on nearby whiteboard. This procedure is most effective when performed away from a keyboard. Focus on putting out the fire and minimizing the damage. Avoid assessing blame or creating excitement. In your plan, don't forget to address the psychological fallout your user community may experience. Users inherently trust others, and blatant violations of trust makes many folks uneasy.

Step 7: Communicate the recovery plan. Educate users and management about the effects of the break-in, the potential for future problems, and your preliminary recovery strategy. Be open and honest. Security incidents are part of life in a modern networked environment. They are not a reflection on your ability as a system administrator or on anything else worth being embarrassed about. Openly admitting that you have a problem is 90% of the battle, as long as you can demonstrate that you have a plan to remedy the situation.

---

15. If system backups are not a "normal" activity at your site, you have much bigger problems than the security intrusion.

Step 8: Implement the recovery plan. You know your systems and networks better than anyone. Follow your plan and your instincts. Speak with a colleague at a similar institution (preferably one who knows you well) to keep yourself on the right track.

Step 9: Report the incident to authorities. If the incident involved outside parties, you should report the matter to CERT. They have a hotline at (412) 268-7090 and can be reached by email at cert@cert.org. Provide as much information as you can.

A standard form is available from www.cert.org to help jog your memory. Here are some of the more useful pieces of information you might provide:

- The names, hardware types, and OS versions of the compromised machines
- The list of patches that had been applied at the time of the incident
- A list of accounts that are known to have been compromised
- The names and IP addresses of any remote hosts that were involved
- Contact information (if you know it) for the administrators of remote sites
- Relevant log entries or audit information

If you believe that a previously undocumented software problem may have been involved, you should report the incident to your Linux distributor as well.

20.17 SOURCES OF SECURITY INFORMATION

Half the battle of keeping your system secure consists of staying abreast of security-related developments in the world at large. If your site is broken into, the break-in probably won't be through the use of a novel technique. More likely, the chink in your armor is a known vulnerability that has been widely discussed in vendor knowledge bases, on security-related newsgroups, and on mailing lists.

CERT: a registered service mark of Carnegie Mellon University

In response to the uproar over the 1988 Internet worm, the Defense Advanced Research Projects Agency (DARPA) formed an organization called CERT, the Computer Emergency Response Team, to act as a clearing house for computer security information. CERT is still the best-known point of contact for security information, though it seems to have grown rather sluggish and bureaucratic of late. CERT also now insists that the name CERT does not stand for anything and is merely "a registered service mark of Carnegie Mellon University."

In mid-2003, CERT partnered with the Department of Homeland Security's National Cyber Security Division, NCSD. The merger has, for better or for worse, altered the previous mailing list structure. The combined organization, known as US-CERT, offers four announcement lists, the most useful of which is the "Technical Cyber Security Alerts." Subscribe to any of the four lists at forms.us-cert.gov/maillists.

SecurityFocus.com and the BugTraq mailing list

SecurityFocus.com is a site that specializes in security-related news and information. The news includes current articles on general issues and on specific problems; there's also an extensive technical library of useful papers, nicely sorted by topic.

SecurityFocus's archive of security tools includes software for a variety of operating systems, along with blurbs and user ratings. It is the most comprehensive and detailed source of tools that we are aware of.

The BugTraq list is a moderated forum for the discussion of security vulnerabilities and their fixes. To subscribe, visit www.securityfocus.com/archive. Traffic on this list can be fairly heavy, however, and the signal-to-noise ratio is fairly poor. A database of BugTraq vulnerability reports is also available from the web site.

Crypto-Gram newsletter

The monthly Crypto-Gram newsletter is a valuable and sometimes entertaining source of information regarding computer security and cryptography. It's produced by Bruce Schneier, author of the well-respected books *Applied Cryptography* and *Secrets and Lies*. Find current and back issues at this site:

> www.schneier.com/crypto-gram.html

You can also read Schneier's security blog at

> www.schneier.com/blog

SANS: the System Administration, Networking, and Security Institute

SANS is a professional organization that sponsors security-related conferences and training programs, as well as publishing a variety of security information. Their web site, www.sans.org, is a useful resource that occupies something of a middle ground between SecurityFocus and CERT: neither as frenetic as the former nor as stodgy as the latter.

SANS offers several weekly and monthly email bulletins that you can sign up for on their web site. The weekly NewsBites are nourishing, but the monthly summaries contain a lot of boilerplate. Neither is a great source of late-breaking security news.

Distribution-specific security resources

Because security problems have the potential to generate a lot of bad publicity, vendors are often eager to help customers keep their systems secure. Most large vendors have an official mailing list to which security-related bulletins are posted, and many maintain a web site about security issues as well. It's common for security-related software patches to be distributed for free, even by vendors that normally charge for software support.

Security portals on the web, such as www.securityfocus.com, contain vendor-specific information and links to the latest official vendor dogma.

 A list of Red Hat security advisories can be found at www.redhat.com/security. As of this writing, no official security mailing list is sponsored by Red Hat. However, there are a variety of Linux security resources on the net; most of the information applies directly to Red Hat.

 You can find SUSE security advisories at

> www.novell.com/linux/security/securitysupport.html

You can join the official SUSE security announcement mailing list by visiting

> www.suse.com/en/private/support/online_help/mailinglists/index.html

 Check out www.debian.org to view the latest in Debian security news, or join the mailing list at

> www.debian.org/MailingLists/subscribe#debian-security-announce

 Ubuntu has a security mailing list at

> https://lists.ubuntu.com/mailman/listinfo/ubuntu-security-announce

Security information about Cisco products is distributed in the form of field notices, a list of which can be found at

> www.cisco.com/public/support/tac/fn_index.html

along with a news aggregation feed. To subscribe to Cisco's security mailing list, send mail to majordomo@cisco.com with the line "subscribe cust-security-announce" in the message body.

Other mailing lists and web sites

The contacts listed above are just a few of the many security resources available on the net. Given the volume of info that's now available and the rapidity with which resources come and go, we thought it would be most helpful to point you toward some meta-resources.

One good starting point is the X-Force web site (xforce.iss.net) at Internet Security Systems, which maintains a variety of useful FAQs. One of these is a current list of security-related mailing lists. The vendor and security patch FAQs contain useful contact information for a variety of vendors.

www.yahoo.com has an extensive list of security links; look for the "Security and Encryption" section in the Yahoo! Directory. Another good source of links on the subject of network security can be found at www.wikipedia.org under the heading "computer security".

Linux Journal (www.linuxjournal.com) contains an excellent column called "Paranoid Penguin" that covers all aspects of Linux security. The magazine also occasionally includes various feature articles on security topics.

The Linux Weekly News is a tasty treat that includes regular updates on the kernel, security, distributions, and other topics. LWN's security section can be found at lwn.net/security.

20.18 RECOMMENDED READING

BRYANT, WILLIAM. "Designing an Authentication System: a Dialogue in Four Scenes." 1988. web.mit.edu/kerberos/www/dialogue.html

CERT COORDINATION CENTER. "Intruder Detection Checklist." 1999. www.cert.org/tech_tips/intruder_detection_checklist.html

CERT COORDINATION CENTER. "UNIX Configuration Guidelines." 1997. www.cert.org/tech_tips/unix_configuration_guidelines.html

CHESWICK, WILLIAM R., STEVEN M. BELLOVIN, AND AVIEL D. RUBIN. *Firewalls and Internet Security: Repelling the Wily Hacker (2nd Edition).* Reading, MA: Addison-Wesley, 2000.

CURTIN, MATT, MARCUS RANUM, AND PAUL D. ROBINSON. "Internet Firewalls: Frequently Asked Questions." 2004. www.interhack.net/pubs/fwfaq

FARMER, DAN, AND WIETSE VENEMA. "Improving the Security of Your Site by Breaking Into it." 1993. www.deter.com/unix/papers/improve_by_breakin.html

FARROW, RIK, AND RICHARD POWER. *Network Defense article series.* 1998-2004. www.spirit.com/Network

FRASER, B., EDITOR. *RFC2196: Site Security Handbook.* 1997. www.rfc-editor.org.

BAUER, MICHAEL D. *Linux Server Security (2nd Edition).* Sebastopol, CA: O'Reilly Media, 2005.

GARFINKEL, SIMSON, GENE SPAFFORD, AND ALAN SCHWARTZ. *Practical UNIX and Internet Security (3rd Edition).* Sebastopol, CA: O'Reilly Media, 2003.

BARRETT, DANIEL J., RICHARD E. SILVERMAN, AND ROBERT G. BYRNES. *Linux Security Cookbook.* Sebastopol, CA: O'Reilly Media, 2003.

KERBY, FRED, ET AL. "SANS Intrusion Detection and Response FAQ." SANS. 2003. www.sans.org/resources/idfaq/

MANN, SCOTT, AND ELLEN L. MITCHELL. *Linux System Security: The Administrator's Guide to Open Source Security Tools (2nd Edition).* Upper Saddle River, NJ: Prentice Hall PTR, 2002.

MORRIS, ROBERT, AND KEN THOMPSON. "Password Security: A Case History." Communications of the ACM, 22 (11): 594-597, November 1979. Reprinted in *UNIX Sys-*

tem Manager's Manual, 4.3 Berkeley Software Distribution. University of California, Berkeley, April 1986.

PICHNARCZYK, KARYN, STEVE WEEBER, AND RICHARD FEINGOLD. "UNIX Incident Guide: How to Detect an Intrusion." Computer Incident Advisory Capability, U.S. Department of Energy, 1994. www.ciac.org/cgi-bin/index/documents

RITCHIE, DENNIS M. "On the Security of UNIX." May 1975. Reprinted in *UNIX System Manager's Manual,* 4.3 Berkeley Software Distribution. University of California, Berkeley, April 1986.

SCHNEIER, BRUCE. *Applied Cryptography: Protocols, Algorithms, and Source Code in C.* New York, NY: Wiley, 1995.

THOMPSON, KEN. "Reflections on Trusting Trust." in *ACM Turing Award Lectures: The First Twenty Years 1966-1985.* Reading, MA: ACM Press (Addison-Wesley), 1987.

SONNENREICH, WES, AND TOM YATES. *Building Linux and OpenBSD Firewalls.* New York, NY: J.W. Wiley, 2000.

This is an awesome little book: it's easy to read, has good examples, shows a good sense of humor, and is just generally excellent. Our only gripe with this book is that it argues against the use of **sudo** for root access, claiming that it's too hard to use and not worth the trouble. We strongly disagree.

20.19 EXERCISES

E20.1   Discuss the strength of SSH authentication with Linux passwords vs. SSH authentication with a passphrase and key pair. If one is clearly more secure than the other, should you automatically require the more secure authentication method?

E20.2   Samhain identifies files that have changed.

   a) What is required to set up and use samhain on your machine?

   b) What recent Internet diseases would samhain be effective against?

   c) What recent Internet diseases would samhain be helpless against?

   d) Given physical access to a system, how could samhain be circumvented?

   e) What can you conclude if samhain says that **/bin/login** has changed, but it seems to have the same size and modification date as before? What if the **sum** program gives the same values for the old and new versions? How about **md5sum**?

★ **E20.3** SSH tunneling is often the only way to tunnel traffic to a remote machine on which you don't have administrator access. Read the **ssh** man page and provide a command line that tunnels traffic from localhost port 113 to mail.remotenetwork.org port 113. The forwarding point of your tunnel should also be the host mail.remotenetwork.org.

★ **E20.4** Pick a recent security incident and research it. Find the best sources of information about the incident and find patches or workarounds that are appropriate for the systems in your lab. List your sources and the actions you propose for protecting your lab.

★★ **E20.5** With permission from your local sysadmin group, install John the Ripper, the program that searches for logins with weak passwords.

   a) Modify the source code so that it outputs only the login names with which weak passwords are associated, not the passwords themselves.

   b) Run John the Ripper on your local lab's password file (you need access to **/etc/shadow**) and see how many breakable passwords you can find.

   c) Set your own password to a dictionary word and give **john** just your own entry in **/etc/shadow**. How long does **john** take to find it?

   d) Try other patterns (capital letter, number after dictionary word, single-letter password, etc.) to see exactly how smart **john** is.

★★ **E20.6** In the computer lab, set up two machines: a target and a prober.

   a) Install **nmap** and Nessus on the prober. Attack the target with these tools. How could you detect the attack on the target?

   b) Set up a firewall on the target using **iptables** to defend against the probes. Can you detect the attack now? If so, how? If not, why not?

   c) What other defenses can be set up against the attacks?

   (Requires root access.)

★★ **E20.7** A security team recently found a large hole in many current and older **sendmail** servers. Find a good source of information on the hole and discuss the issues and the best way to address them.

★★ **E20.8** Setuid programs are sometimes a necessary evil. However, setuid shell scripts should be avoided. Why?

★★ **E20.9** Use **tcpdump** to capture FTP traffic for both active and passive FTP sessions. How does the need to support an anonymous FTP server affect the site's firewall policy? What would the firewall rules need to allow? (Requires root access.)

Exercises are continued on the next page.

★★ **E20.10** What do the rules in the following **iptables** output allow and disallow? What would be some very easy additions that would enhance security and privacy? (Hint: the OUTPUT and FORWARD chains could use some more rules.)

```
Chain INPUT (policy ACCEPT)
target    prot opt  source     destination
block     all  --   anywhere   anywhere

Chain FORWARD (policy ACCEPT)
target    prot opt  source     destination
          all  --   anywhere   anywhere

Chain OUTPUT (policy ACCEPT)
target    prot opt  source     destination

Chain block (1 references)
target    prot opt  source        destination
ACCEPT    all  --   anywhere      anywhere      state RELATED,ESTABLISHED
ACCEPT    tcp  --   anywhere      anywhere      state NEW tcp dpt:www
ACCEPT    tcp  --   anywhere      anywhere      state NEW tcp dpt:ssh
ACCEPT    tcp  --   128.138.0.0/16 anywhere     state NEW tcp dpt:kerberos
ACCEPT    icmp --   anywhere      anywhere
DROP      all  --   anywhere      anywhere
```

★★ **E20.11** Inspect a local firewall's rulesets. Discuss what you find in terms of policies. Are there any glaring security holes? (This exercise is likely to require the cooperation of the administrators responsible for your local site's security.)

★★★★★ **E20.12** Write a tool that determines whether any network interfaces at your site are in promiscuous mode. Run it regularly on your networks to try to quickly spot such an intrusion. How much load does the tool generate? Do you have to run it on each machine, or can you run it from afar? Can you design a sneaky packet that would tell you if an interface was in promiscuous mode? (Requires root access.)

21 *Web Hosting and Internet Servers*

The complexity of web technology seems to be doubling every year. Fortunately, the vast majority of this technology lies in the domain of the web designer and programmer. Web hosting itself hasn't changed much over the past decade.

The kinks have been worked out of web server software, and as a result these servers are now quite secure and reliable—at least if they're configured correctly and your site has no rogue web programmers. Even with the advent of "Web 2.0," AJAX (Asynchronous JavaScript And XML), and dynamic HTML, the core web server software remains about the same.

These days we have a variety of web hosting platforms to choose from. Microsoft Windows has been widely marketed as a web hosting platform. The industry press has published countless articles that ask "Which web hosting platform is best?", usually positioning Windows and Linux at opposite corners of the ring. Although some of this brouhaha is akin to the "Less filling!" "Tastes great!" battle, Linux has become the most popular hosting platform because of its low cost, speed, reliability, and flexibility. The so-called LAMP platform (Linux, Apache, MySQL, and PHP/Perl/Python) is the dominant paradigm for today's web servers.

There are many different Internet-centric services that you might want to "host," either at your site or at one of the many co-location outsourcing providers. In this chapter, we address the two most common services: the web and FTP.

21.1 WEB HOSTING BASICS

Hosting a web site isn't substantially different from providing any other network service. The foundation of the World Wide Web is the Hyper-Text Transfer Protocol (HTTP), a simple TCP-based protocol for transmitting documents that contain a variety of media types, including text, pictures, sound, animation, and video. HTTP behaves much like other client/server protocols used on the Internet, for example, SMTP (for email) and FTP (for file transfer).

A web server is simply a system that's configured to answer HTTP requests. To convert your generic Linux system into a web hosting platform, you install a daemon that listens for connections on TCP port 80 (the HTTP standard), accepts requests for documents, and transmits them to the requesting user.

Web browsers such as Firefox, Opera, and Internet Explorer contact remote web servers and make requests on behalf of users. The documents thus obtained can contain hypertext pointers (links) to other documents, which may or may not live on the server that the user originally contacted. Since the HTTP protocol standard is well defined, clients running on any operating system or architecture can connect to any HTTP server. This platform independence, along with HTTP's ability to transparently pass a user from one server to another, has helped spark its amazing success.

There is life beyond straight HTTP, however. Many enhanced protocols have been defined for handling everything from encryption to streaming video. These additional services are often managed by separate daemons, even if they are provided by the same physical server.

Uniform resource locators

A uniform resource locator (URL) is a pointer to an object or service on the Internet. It describes how to access an object by means of five basic components:

- Protocol or application
- Hostname
- TCP/IP port (optional)
- Directory (optional)
- Filename (optional)

Table 21.1 shows some of the protocols that may be used in URLs.

How HTTP works

HTTP is the protocol that makes the World Wide Web really work, and to the amazement of many, it is an extremely basic, stateless, client/server protocol. In the HTTP paradigm, the initiator of a connection is always the client (usually a browser). The client asks the server for the "contents" of a specific URL. The server responds with either a spurt of data or with some type of error message. The client can then go on to request another object.

Table 21.1 URL protocols

Proto	What it does	Example
file	Accesses a local file	file://etc/syslog.conf
ftp	Accesses a remote file via FTP	ftp://ftp.admin.com/adduser.tar.gz
http	Accesses a remote file via HTTP	http://admin.com/index.html
https	Accesses a remote file via HTTP/SSL	https://admin.com/order.shtml
ldap	Accesses LDAP directory services	ldap://ldap.bigfoot.com:389/cn=Herb
mailto	Sends email to a designated address	mailto:linux@book.admin.com

Because HTTP is so simple, you can easily make yourself into a crude web browser by using **telnet**. Since the standard port for HTTP service is port 80, just **telnet** directly to that port on your web server of choice. Once you're connected, you can issue HTTP commands. The most common command is GET, which requests the contents of a document. Usually, GET / is what you want, since it requests the root document (usually, the home page) of whatever server you've connected to. HTTP is case sensitive, so make sure you type commands in capital letters.

```
$ telnet localhost 80
Trying 127.0.0.1...
Connected to localhost.atrust.com.
Escape character is '^]'.
GET /
<contents of your default file appear here>
Connection closed by foreign host.
```

A more "complete" HTTP request would include the HTTP protocol version, the host that the request is for (required to retrieve a file from a name-based virtual host), and other information. The response would then include informational headers as well as response data. For example:

```
$ telnet localhost 80
Trying 127.0.0.1...
Connected to localhost.atrust.com.
Escape character is '^]'.
GET / HTTP/1.1
Host: www.atrust.com

HTTP/1.1 200 OK
Date: Sun, 06 Aug 2006 18:25:03 GMT
Server: Apache/1.3.33 (Unix) PHP/4.4.0
Last-Modified: Sun, 06 Aug 2006 18:24:49 GMT
Content-Length: 7044
Content-Type: text/html

<contents of your default file appear here>
Connection closed by foreign host.
```

Web Hosting

In this case, we told the server we were going to speak HTTP protocol version 1.1 and named the virtual host from which we were requesting information. The server returned a status code (HTTP/1.1 200 OK), its idea of the current date and time, the name and version of the server software it was running, the date that the requested file was last modified, the length of the requested file, and the requested file's content type. The header information is separated from the content by a single blank line.

Content generation on the fly

In addition to serving up static documents, an HTTP server can provide the user with content that has been created on the fly. For example, if you wanted to provide the current time and temperature to users visiting your web site, you might have the HTTP server execute a script to obtain this information. This amaze-the-natives trick is often accomplished with the Common Gateway Interface, or CGI.

CGI is not a programming language, but rather a specification by which an HTTP server exchanges information with other programs. CGI scripts are most often written in Perl, Python, or PHP. But really, almost any programming language that can perform real-time I/O is acceptable. Just think of all those out-of-work COBOL programmers that can apply their skills to the Internet!

In addition to supporting external CGI scripts, many web servers define a plug-in architecture that allows script interpreters such as Perl and PHP to be embedded within the web server itself. This bundling significantly increases performance, since the web server no longer has to fork a separate process to deal with each script request. The architecture is largely invisible to script developers. Whenever the server sees a file ending in a specified extension (such as **.pl** or **.php**), it sends the content of the file to an embedded interpreter to be executed.

For the most part, CGI scripts and plug-ins are the concern of web developers and programmers. Unfortunately, they collide with the job of the system administrator in one important area: security. Because CGI scripts and plug-ins have access to files, network connections, and other methods of moving data from one place to another, their execution can potentially affect the security of the machine on which the HTTP server is running. Ultimately, a CGI script or plug-in gives anyone in the world the ability to run a program (the script) on your server. Therefore, CGI scripts and files processed by plug-ins must be just as secure as any other network-accessible program. A good source of information on the secure handling of CGI scripts is the page www.w3.org/Security/Faq. Although this page hasn't been updated in some time, all its information is still relevant.

Load balancing

It's difficult to predict how many hits (requests for objects, including images) or page views (requests for HTML pages) a server can handle per unit of time. A server's capacity depends on the system's hardware architecture (including subsystems), the operating system it is running, the extent and emphasis of any system tuning that has been performed, and perhaps most importantly, the construction of the sites being served. (Do they contain only static HTML pages, or must they make database calls and numeric calculations?)

Only direct benchmarking and measurement of your actual site running on your actual hardware can answer the "how many hits?" question. Sometimes, people who have built similar sites on similar hardware can give you information that is useful for planning. In no case should you believe the numbers quoted by system suppliers. Also remember that your bandwidth is a key consideration. A single machine serving static HTML files and images can easily serve enough data to saturate a T3 (45 Mb/s) link.

That said, instead of single-server hit counts, a better parameter to focus on is scalability; a web server typically becomes CPU- or IO-bound before saturating its Ethernet interface. Make sure that you and your web design team plan to spread the load of a heavily trafficked site across multiple servers.

Load balancing adds both performance and redundancy. Several different load balancing approaches are available: round robin DNS, load balancing hardware, and software-based load balancers.

See page 385 for more information about round robin DNS configuration.

Round robin DNS is the simplest and most primitive form of load balancing. In this system, multiple IP addresses are assigned to a single hostname. When a request for the web site's IP address arrives at the name server, the client receives one of the IP addresses in response. Addresses are handed out one after another, in a repeating "round robin" sequence.

The problem with round robin DNS is that if a server goes down, DNS data must be updated to remove the server from the response cycle. Remote caching of DNS data can make this operation tricky and unreliable. If you have a backup server available, it is often easier to reassign the disabled server's IP address to the backup server.

Load balancing hardware is a relatively easy alternative, but one that requires some spare cash. Commercial third-party load balancing hardware includes the Big-IP Controller from F5 Networks, Nortel's web switching products, and Cisco's Content Services Switches. These products distribute incoming work according to a variety of configurable parameters and can take the current response times of individual servers into account.

Software-based load balancers don't require specialized hardware; they can run on a Linux server. Both open source and commercial solutions are available. The open source category includes the Linux Virtual Server (www.linuxvirtualserver.org), Ultra Monkey (www.ultramonkey.org), and the **mod_backhand** module for Apache (www.backhand.org). An example of commercial offerings are those sold by Zeus, www.zeus.com.

You may wonder how a large site such as Google handles load balancing. Their system uses a combination of custom load-balancing DNS servers and load balancing hardware. See the Wikipedia article for "Google platform" for more details.

Web Hosting

Keep in mind that most sites these days are dynamically generated. This architecture puts a heavy load on database servers. If necessary, consult your database administrator to determine the best way to distribute load across multiple database servers.

21.2 HTTP SERVER INSTALLATION

Installing and maintaining a web server is easy. Web services rank far below email and DNS in complexity and difficulty of administration.

Choosing a server

Several HTTP servers are available, but you'll most likely want to start with the Apache server, which is well known in the industry for its flexibility and performance. As of September 2006, 63% of web servers on the Internet were running Apache. Microsoft accounts for most of the remainder at 30% of servers. This market share split between Apache and Microsoft has been relatively stable for the last five years. More detailed market share statistics over time are available here:

> news.netcraft.com/archives/web_server_survey.html

You can find a useful comparison of currently available HTTP servers at the site www.serverwatch.com/stypes/index.php (select "Web Servers"). Here are some of the factors you may want to consider in making your selection:

- Robustness
- Performance
- Timeliness of updates and bug fixes
- Availability of source code
- Level of commercial or community support
- Cost
- Access control and security
- Ability to act as a proxy
- Ability to handle encryption

The Apache HTTP server is "free to a good home," and full source code is available from the Apache Group site at www.apache.org. The less adventurous may want to install the binary-only Apache package that comes as part of your Linux distribution. (But chances are that it's already installed; try looking in **/etc/apache2**.)

Installing Apache

If you do decide to download the Apache source code and compile it yourself, start by executing the **configure** script included with the distribution. This script automatically detects the system type and sets up the appropriate makefiles. Use the **--prefix** option to specify where in your directory tree the Apache server should live. If you don't specify a prefix, the server is installed in **/usr/local/apache2** by default. For example:

```
$ ./configure --prefix=/etc/httpd/
```

You can use **configure --help** to see the entire list of possible options, most of which consist of --**enable**-*module* and --**disable**-*module* options that include or exclude various functional components that live within the web server.

You can also compile modules into dynamically shared objects files by specifying the option --**enable**-*module*=**shared** (or use --**enabled-mods-shared**=**all** to make all modules shared). That way, you can decide later which modules to include or exclude; only modules specified in your **httpd** configuration are loaded at run time. This is actually the default configuration for the binary-only Apache package—all the modules are compiled into shared objects and are dynamically loaded when Apache starts. The only disadvantages to using shared libraries are a slightly longer startup time and a very slight degradation in performance (typically less than 5%). For most sites, the benefit of being able to add new modules on the fly and turn existing modules off without having to recompile outweighs the slight performance hit.

For a complete list of standard modules, see httpd.apache.org/docs-2.0/mod.

Although the default set of modules is reasonable, you may also want to enable the modules shown in Table 21.2.

Table 21.2 Useful Apache modules that are not enabled by default

Module	Function
auth_dbm	Uses a DBM database to manage user/group access (recommended if you need per-user password-based access to areas of your web site)
rewrite	Rewrites URLs with regular expressions
expires	Lets you attach expiration dates to documents
proxy	Uses Apache as a proxy server (more on this later)
ssl	Enables support for the Secure Sockets Layer (SSL) (for HTTPS)

Likewise, you may want to disable the modules listed in Table 21.3. For security and performance, it's a good idea to disable modules that you know you will not be using.

Table 21.3 Apache modules we suggest removing

Module	Function
asis	Allows designated file types to be sent without HTTP headers
autoindex	Displays the contents of directories that don't have a default HTML file
env	Lets you set special environment variables for CGI scripts
include	Allows server-side includes, an on-the-fly content generation scheme
userdir	Allows users to have their own HTML directories

When **configure** has finished executing, run **make** and then run **make install** to actually compile and install the appropriate files.

Web Hosting

Configuring Apache

Once you've installed the server, configure it for your environment. The config files are kept in the **conf** subdirectory (e.g., **/usr/local/apache2/conf**). Examine and customize the **httpd.conf** file, which is divided into three sections.

The first section deals with global settings such as the server pool, the TCP port on which the HTTP server listens for queries (usually port 80, although you can choose another—and yes, you can run multiple HTTP servers on different ports on a single machine), and the settings for dynamic module loading.

The second section configures the "default" server, the server that handles any requests that aren't answered by VirtualHost definitions (see page 729). Configuration parameters in this section include the user and group as whom the server will run (something other than root!) and the all-important DocumentRoot statement, which defines the root of the directory tree from which documents are served. This section also addresses issues such as the handling of "special" URLs like those that include the ~*user* syntax to access a user's home directory.

You manage global security concerns in the second section of the configuration file as well. Directives control access on a per-file basis (the <File> directive) or on a per-directory basis (the <Directory> directive). These permission settings prevent access to sensitive files through **httpd**. You should specify at least two access controls: one that covers the entire filesystem and one that applies to the main document folder. The defaults that come with Apache are sufficient, although we recommend that you remove the AllowSymLinks option to prevent **httpd** from following symbolic links in your document tree. (We wouldn't want someone to accidentally create a symbolic link to **/etc**, now would we?) For more Apache security tips, see

>   httpd.apache.org/docs-2.0/misc/security_tips.html

The third and final section of the config file sets up virtual hosts. We discuss this topic in more detail on page 729.

Once you have made your configuration changes, check the syntax of the configuration file by running **httpd -t**. If Apache reports "Syntax OK," then you're good to go. If not, check the **httpd.conf** file for typos.

Running Apache

You can start **httpd** by hand or from your system's startup scripts. The latter is preferable, since this configuration ensures that the web server restarts whenever the machine reboots. To start the server by hand, type something like

> $ **/usr/local/apache2/bin/apachectl** start

*See Chapter 2 for more information about **rc** scripts.*

If you want to start **httpd** automatically at boot time, make a link in your **rc** directory that points to the **/etc/init.d/httpd** file (which is installed as part of the **httpd** package). It's best to start **httpd** late in the booting sequence, after daemons that manage functions such as routing and time synchronization have started.

Analyzing log files

With your web site in production, you're likely to want to gather statistics about the use of the site, such as the number of requests per page, the average number of requests per day, the percentage of failed requests, and the amount of data transferred. Make sure that you're using the "combined" log format (your CustomLog directives have the word combined at the end instead of common). The combined log format includes each request's referrer (the page from which the URL was linked) and user agent (the client's browser and operating system).

Your access and error logs appear in Apache's **logs** directory. The files are human readable, but they contain so much information that you really need a separate analysis program to extract useful data from them. There are literally hundreds of different log analyzers, both free and commercial.

Two free analyzers worth taking a look at are Analog (www.analog.cx) and AWStats (awstats.sourceforge.net). These both provide fairly basic information. If you want reports with a bit more pizazz, you may need a commercial package. A helpful list can be found at www.practicalapplications.net/kb/loganalysis.html.

Optimizing for high-performance hosting of static content

The hosting community has learned over the last few years that one of the easiest ways to create a high-performance hosting platform is to optimize some servers for hosting static content. Linux offers unique functionality in this arena through the TUX web server.

TUX is a kernel-based web server that runs in conjunction with a traditional web server such as Apache. Whenever possible, TUX serves up static pages without ever leaving kernel space, in much the same way that **rpc.nfsd** serves files. This architecture eliminates the need to copy data between kernel and user space and minimizes the number of context switches. TUX is not recommended for beginners, but it's an excellent choice for sites that must serve up static content with lightning speed.

Although TUX was developed by Red Hat (and is available from www.redhat.com), it's been released under the GPL and can be used with other Linux distributions. However, configuring TUX can be somewhat of a challenge. For details, see

> www.redhat.com/docs/manuals/tux

21.3 VIRTUAL INTERFACES

In the early days, a machine typically acted as the server for a single web site (e.g., www.acme.com). As the web's popularity grew, everybody wanted to have a web site, and overnight, thousands of companies became web hosting providers.

Providers quickly realized that they could achieve significant economies of scale if they were able to host more than one site on a single server. This trick would allow www.acme.com, www.ajax,com, www.toadranch.com, and many other sites to be

Web Hosting

transparently served by the same hardware. In response to this business need, virtual interfaces were born.

Virtual interfaces allow a daemon to identify connections based not only on the destination port number (e.g., port 80 for HTTP) but also on the connection's destination IP address. Today, virtual interfaces are in widespread use and have proved to be useful for applications other than web hosting.

The idea is simple: a single machine responds on the network to more IP addresses than it has physical network interfaces. Each of the resulting "virtual" network interfaces can be associated with a corresponding domain name that users on the Internet might want to connect to. Thus, a single machine can serve literally hundreds of web sites.

Using name-based virtual hosts

The HTTP 1.1 protocol also defines a form of virtual-interface-like functionality (officially called "name-based virtual hosts") that eliminates the need to assign unique IP addresses to web servers or to configure a special interface at the OS level. This approach conserves IP addresses and is useful for some sites, especially those at which a single server is home to hundreds or thousands of home pages (such as universities).

Unfortunately, the scheme isn't very practical for commercial sites. It reduces scalability (you must change the IP address of the site to move it to a different server) and may also have a negative impact on security (if you filter access to a site at your firewall according to IP addresses). Additionally, name-based virtual hosts cannot use SSL. It appears that true virtual interfaces will be around for a while.

Configuring virtual interfaces

Setting up a virtual interface involves two steps. First, you must create the virtual interface at the TCP/IP level. Second, you must tell the Apache server about the virtual interfaces you have installed. We cover this second step starting on page 729.

Linux virtual interfaces are named with an *interface:instance* notation. For example, if your Ethernet interface is eth0, then the virtual interfaces associated with it could be eth0:0, eth0:1, and so on. All interfaces are configured with the **ifconfig** command. For example, the command

    # ifconfig eth0:0 128.138.243.150 netmask 255.255.255.192 up

configures the interface eth0:0 and assigns it an address on the 128.138.243.128/26 network.

  To make virtual address assignments permanent on Red Hat and Fedora, you create a separate file for each virtual interface in **/etc/sysconfig/network-scripts**. For example, the file **ifcfg-eth0:0** corresponding to the **ifconfig** command shown above contains the following lines.

```
DEVICE=eth0:0
IPADDR=128.138.243.150
NETMASK=255.255.255.192
NETWORK=128.138.243.128
BROADCAST=128.138.243.191
ONBOOT=yes
```

 Debian's and Ubuntu's approaches are similar to Red Hat's, but the interface definitions must appear in the file **/etc/network/interfaces**. The entries corresponding to
the eth0:0 interface in our example above are

```
iface eth0:0 inet static
      address 128.138.243.150
      netmask 255.255.255.192
      broadcast 128.138.243.191
```

 On SUSE systems you can either create virtual interfaces with YaST or you can create
interface files manually.

Under SUSE, an interface's IP addresses are all configured within a single file. To
configure the files manually, look in the **/etc/sysconfig/network** directory for files
whose names start with **ifcfg-***ifname*. The filenames for real interfaces include a
hairy-looking 6-byte MAC address; those are the ones you want.

For example, one of the config files might contain the following entries to define two
virtual interfaces:

```
IPADDR_0=128.138.243.149
NETMASK_0=255.255.255.192
LABEL_0=0
IPADDR_1=128.138.243.150
NETMASK_1=255.255.255.192
LABEL_1=1
STARTMODE="onboot"
NETWORK=128.138.243.128
```

The suffixes that follow IPADDR and NETMASK (here, _0 and _1) don't have to be
numeric, but for consistency this is a reasonable convention.

Telling Apache about virtual interfaces

In addition to creating the virtual interfaces, you need to tell Apache what documents to serve when a client tries to connect to each interface (IP address). You do
this with a VirtualHost clause in the **httpd.conf** file. There is one VirtualHost
clause for each virtual interface that you've configured. Here's an example:

```
<VirtualHost 128.138.243.150>
      ServerName www.company.com
      ServerAdmin webmaster@www.company.com
      DocumentRoot /var/www/htdocs/company
      ErrorLog logs/www.company.com-error_log
      CustomLog logs/www.company.com-access_log combined
      ScriptAlias /cgi-bin/ /var/www/cgi-bin/company
</VirtualHost>
```

In this example, any client that connects to the virtual host 128.138.243.150 is served documents from the directory **/var/www/htdocs/company**. Nearly any Apache directive can go into a VirtualHost clause to define settings specific to that virtual host. Relative directory paths, including those for the DocumentRoot, ErrorLog, and CustomLog directives, are interpreted in the context of the ServerRoot.

With name-based virtual hosts, multiple DNS names all point to the same IP address. The Apache configuration is similar, but you specify the primary IP address on which Apache should listen for incoming named virtual host requests and omit the IP address in the VirtualHost clause:

```
NameVirtualHost 128.138.243.150

<VirtualHost *>
    ServerName www.company.com
    ServerAdmin webmaster@www.company.com
    DocumentRoot /var/www/htdocs/company
    ErrorLog logs/www.company.com-error_log
    CustomLog logs/www.company.com-access_log combined
    ScriptAlias /cgi-bin/ /var/www/cgi-bin/company
</VirtualHost>
```

In this configuration, Apache looks in the HTTP headers to determine the requested site. The server listens for requests for www.company.com on its main IP address, 128.138.243.150.

21.4 THE SECURE SOCKETS LAYER (SSL)

The SSL[1] protocol secures communications between a web site and a client browser. URLs that start with https:// use this technology. SSL uses cryptography to prevent eavesdropping, tampering, and message forgery.

The browser and server use a certificate-based authentication scheme to establish communications, after which they switch to a faster cipher-based encryption scheme to protect their actual conversation.

SSL runs as a separate layer underneath the HTTP application protocol. SSL simply supplies the security for the connection and does not involve itself in the HTTP transaction. Because of this hygienic architecture, SSL can secure not only HTTP but also protocols such as SMTP, NNTP, and FTP. For more details, see the Wikipedia entry for "Secure Sockets Layer."

See page 949 for more details on the legal issues surrounding cryptography.

In the "early days" of SSL use, most symmetric encryption keys were a relatively weak 40 bits because of U.S. government restrictions on the export of cryptographic technology. After years of controversy and lawsuits, the government relaxed some aspects of the export restrictions, allowing SSL implementations to use 128-bit keys for symmetric key ciphers.

---

1. Transport Layer Security (TLS) is the successor to SSL and is implemented in all modern browsers. However, the web community still refers to the overall protocol/concept as SSL.

Generating a certificate signing request

The owner of a web site that is to use SSL must generate a Certificate Signing Request (CSR), a digital file that contains a public key and a company name. The "certificate" must then be "signed" by a trusted source known as a Certificate Authority (CA). The signed certificate returned by the CA contains the site's public key and company name along with the CA's endorsement.

Web browsers have built-in lists of CAs whose signed certificates they will accept. A browser that knows of your site's CA can verify the signature on your certificate and obtain your public key, thus enabling it to send messages that only your site can decrypt. Although you can actually sign your own certificate, a certificate that does not come from a recognized CA prompts most browsers to notify the user that the certificate is potentially suspect. In a commercial setting, such behavior is obviously a problem. But if you want to set up your own certificate authority for internal use and testing, see

> httpd.apache.org/docs/2.0/ssl/ssl_faq.html#aboutcerts.

You can obtain a certificate signature from any one of a number of certificate authorities. Enter "SSL certificate" into Google and take your pick. The only real differences among CAs are the amount of work they do to verify your identity, the warranties they offer, and the number of browsers that support them out of the box (most CAs are supported by the vast majority of browsers).

Creating a certificate to send to a CA is relatively straightforward. OpenSSL must be installed, which it is by default on most distributions. Here is the procedure.

First, create a 1024-bit RSA private key for your Apache server:

```
$ openssl genrsa -des3 -out server.key 1024
```

You are prompted to enter and confirm a passphrase to encrypt the server key. Back up the **server.key** file to a secure location (readable only by root), and be sure to remember the passphrase you entered. The curious can view the numeric details of the key with this command:

```
$ openssl rsa -noout -text -in server.key
```

Next, create a Certificate Signing Request (CSR) that incorporates the server key you just generated:

```
$ openssl req -new -key server.key -out server.csr
```

Enter the fully qualified domain name of the server when you are prompted to enter a "common name." For example, if your site's URL is https://www.company.com, enter "www.company.com" as your common name. Note that you need a separate certificate for each hostname—even to the point that "company.com" is different from "www.company.com." Companies typically register only one common name; they make sure any SSL-based links point to that hostname.

Web Hosting

You can view the details of a generated CSR with the following command:

```
$ openssl req -noout -text -in server.csr
```

You can now send the **server.csr** file to the CA of your choice to be signed. It is not necessary to preserve your local copy. The signed CSR returned by the CA should have the extension **.crt**. Put the signed certificate in the same secure place as your private key.

Configuring Apache to use SSL

HTTP requests come in on port 80, and HTTPS requests use port 443. Both HTTPS and HTTP traffic can be served by the same Apache process. However, SSL does not work with name-based virtual hosts; each virtual host must have a specific IP address. (This limitation is a consequence of SSL's design.)

To set up Apache for use with SSL, first make sure that the SSL module is enabled within **httpd.conf** by locating or adding the line

```
LoadModule ssl_module        libexec/mod_ssl.so
```

Then add a VirtualHost directive for the SSL port:

```
<VirtualHost 128.138.243.150:443>
    ServerName www.company.com
    ServerAdmin webmaster@www.company.com
    DocumentRoot /var/www/htdocs/company
    ErrorLog logs/www.company.com-ssl-error_log
    CustomLog logs/www.company.com-ssl-access_log combined
    ScriptAlias /cgi-bin/ /var/www/cgi-bin/company
    SSLEngine on
    SSLCertificateFile /usr/local/apache2/conf/ssl.crt/server.crt
    SSLCertificateKeyFile /usr/local/apache2/conf/ssl.key/server.key
</VirtualHost>
```

Note the :443 after the IP address and the SSL directives that tell Apache where to find your private key and signed certificate.

When you restart Apache, you will be asked to enter the passphrase for your **server.key** file. Because of this interaction, **httpd** can no longer start up automatically when the machine is booted. If you want, you can remove the encryption from your private key to circumvent the need to enter a password:

```
$ cp server.key server.key.orig
$ openssl rsa -in server.key.orig -out server.key
$ chmod 400 server.key server.key.orig
```

Of course, anyone who obtains a copy of your unencrypted key can then impersonate your site.

For more information about SSL, see the following resources:

httpd.apache.org/docs-2.0/ssl/ssl_faq.html
httpd.apache.org/docs/2.0/mod/mod_ssl.html

21.5 CACHING AND PROXY SERVERS

The Internet and the information on it are growing rapidly. Ergo, the bandwidth and computing resources required to support it are growing rapidly as well. How can this state of affairs continue?

The only way to deal with this growth is to use replication. Whether it's on a national, regional, or site level, Internet content needs to be more readily available from a closer source as the Internet grows. It just doesn't make sense to transmit the same popular web page from Australia across a very expensive link to North America millions of times each day. There should be a way to store this information once it's been sent across the link once. Fortunately, there is.

The Squid cache and proxy server

One answer is the freely available Squid Internet Object Cache.[2] This package is both a caching and a proxy server that supports several protocols, including HTTP, FTP, and SSL.

Here's how it works. Client web browsers contact the Squid server to request an object from the Internet. The Squid server then makes a request on the client's behalf (or provides the object from its cache, as discussed in the following paragraph) and returns the result to the client. Proxy servers of this type are often used to enhance security or to filter content.

In a proxy-based system, only one machine needs direct access to the Internet through the organization's firewall. At organizations such as K–12 schools, a proxy server can also filter content so that inappropriate material doesn't fall into the wrong hands. Many commercial and freely available proxy servers (some based on Squid, some not) are available today. Some of these systems are purely software-based (like Squid), and others are embodied in a hardware appliance (e.g., BlueCoat; see www.cacheflow.com). An extensive list of proxy server technologies can be found at

www.web-caching.com/proxy-caches.html

Proxy service is nice, but it's the caching features of Squid that are really worth getting excited about. Squid not only caches information from local user requests but also allows construction of a hierarchy of Squid servers.[3] Groups of Squid servers use the Internet Cache Protocol (ICP) to communicate information about what's in their caches.

With this feature, administrators can build a system in which local users contact an on-site caching server to obtain content from the Internet. If another user at that site has already requested the same content, a copy can be returned at LAN speed (usually 100 Mb/s or greater). If the local Squid server doesn't have the object, perhaps the server contacts the regional caching server. As in the local case, if anyone in the

2. Why "Squid"? According to the FAQ, "all the good names were taken."

3. Unfortunately, some sites mark all their pages as being uncacheable, which prevents Squid from working its magic. In a similar vein, Squid isn't able to cache dynamically generated pages.

region has requested the object, it is served immediately. If not, perhaps the caching server for the country or continent can be contacted, and so on. Users perceive a performance improvement, so they are happy.

For many, Squid offers economic benefits. Because users tend to share web discoveries, significant duplication of external web requests can occur at a reasonably sized site. One study has shown that running a caching server can reduce external bandwidth requirements by up to 40%.

To make effective use of Squid, you'll likely want to force your users to use the cache. Either configure a default proxy through Active Directory (in a Windows-based environment) or configure your router to redirect all web-based traffic to the Squid cache by using the Web Cache Communication Protocol, WCCP.

Setting up Squid

Squid is easy to install and configure. Since Squid needs space to store its cache, you should run it on a dedicated machine that has a lot of free memory and disk space. A configuration for a relatively large cache would be a machine with 2GB of RAM and 200GB of disk.

You can grab the Squid package in RPM or **apt-get** format from your distribution vendor, or you can download a fresh copy of Squid from www.squid-cache.org. If you choose the compile-your-own path, run the **configure** script at the top of the source tree after you unpack the distribution. This script assumes that you want to install the package in **/usr/local/squid**. If you prefer some other location, use the **--prefix=***dir* option to **configure**. After **configure** has completed, run **make all** and then **make install**.

Once you've installed Squid, you must localize the **squid.conf** configuration file. See the **QUICKSTART** file in the distribution directory for a list of the changes you need to make to the sample **squid.conf** file.

You must also run **squid -z** by hand to build and zero out the directory structure in which cached web pages will be stored. Finally, you can start the server by hand with the **RunCache** script; you will eventually want to call this script from your system's **rc** files so that they start the Squid server when the machine boots.

To test Squid, configure your desktop web browser to use the Squid server as a proxy. This option is usually found in browser's preferences panel.

21.6 ANONYMOUS FTP SERVER SETUP

FTP is one of the oldest and most basic services on the Internet, yet it continues to be used today. Although FTP has a variety of internal uses, the most common application on the Internet continues to be "anonymous FTP," by which users that do not have accounts at your site can download files you have made available.

FTP is useful for distributing bug fixes, software, document drafts, and the like, but these days HTTP servers have all but replaced FTP servers. The arguments in favor of FTP are relatively weak: FTP can be a bit more reliable, and users don't need a web browser to access an FTP site (although of course, they need an FTP client).

Use vanilla FTP *only* when anonymous access is required. For nonanonymous applications, use the secure variant SFTP. FTP transmits passwords in plaintext and has a history of security incidents.

ftpd is managed by **inetd** and therefore has an entry in the **/etc/inetd.conf** and **/etc/services** files. (If your distribution uses **xinetd** instead of **inetd**, a file should exist in **/etc/xinetd.d** for **ftpd** instead.) When an FTP user logs in anonymously, **ftpd** executes a **chroot** (short for "change root") system call to make files outside the **~ftp** directory invisible and inaccessible. Because of the public nature of anonymous FTP, it is important that **ftpd** be configured correctly so that sensitive files are not accidentally made available to the whole world.

To allow anonymous **ftp** to your site, take the following steps in the sequence listed:

- Add the user "ftp" to your regular password and shadow password files (the ftp user should already exist on all distributions except for Debian). No one needs to log in to the ftp account, so use an "x" as ftp's password. It's also a good idea to specify **/sbin/nologin** or **/bin/false** as ftp's login shell.

- Create ftp's home directory if it doesn't already exist.

- Create subdirectories **bin**, **etc**, **lib**, and **pub** beneath ~ftp. Since an anonymous **ftp** session runs **chroot**ed to ~ftp, the subdirectories **bin** and **etc** must provide a copy of all the commands and configuration information needed by **ftpd**. After the **chroot**, ~**ftp/bin** and ~**ftp/etc** masquerade as **/bin** and **/etc**.

- Copy the **/bin/ls** program to the ~**ftp/bin** directory. For added security, make ~**ftp/bin/ls** execute-only by setting its mode to 111. This tweak prevents clients from copying the binary and studying it for weaknesses.

- Copy or hard-link the shared libraries needed by **ls** to ~**ftp/lib**. Check the documentation for your distribution to find out which files are necessary. Note that hard linking works only if the files live in the same disk partition.

- Copy **/etc/passwd** and **/etc/group** to ~**ftp/etc**.

- Edit the **passwd** and **group** files. **ftpd** uses only the **ls** command and skeletal copies of **/etc/passwd** and **/etc/group** from ~**ftp/etc**. The **passwd** and group files under ~**ftp** should contain only root, daemon, and ftp; and the password fields should contain "x".

- Set the proper permissions on files and directories under **~ftp**. We recommend that permissions be set as shown in Table 21.4.

Table 21.4   **Recommended permissions under ~ftp**

File/Dir	Owner	Mode	File/Dir	Owner	Mode
~ftp	root	555	**~ftp/etc/passwd**	root	444
~ftp/bin	root	555	**~ftp/etc/group**	root	444
~ftp/bin/ls	root	111	**~ftp/pub**	root	755
~ftp/etc	root	555	**~ftp/lib**	root	555

- Edit **/etc/ftpusers** and remove the entries for "ftp" and "anonymous" to enable anonymous users to log in.
- Put the files you want to make available in **~ftp/pub**.

One of the biggest security risks of anonymous FTP results from allowing users to deposit files in FTP directories. World-writable directories, no matter how obscure, quickly become "nests" where hackers and kids looking to trade warez can store files, sucking up all your bandwidth and putting you right in the middle of a chain of activities that's probably undesirable, if not downright illegal. Don't be part of the problem; never allow writable anonymous FTP directories on your system.

21.7 EXERCISES

★ **E21.1** Configure a virtual interface on your workstation. Run **ifconfig** before and after to see what changed. Can you ping the virtual interface from another machine on the same subnet? From a different network? Why or why not? (Requires root access.)

★ **E21.2** With a packet sniffer (**tcpdump**), capture a two-way HTTP conversation that uploads information (e.g., filling out a form or a search field). Annotate the session to show how your browser conveyed information to the web server. (Requires root access.)

★ **E21.3** Use a packet sniffer to capture the traffic when you open a busy web page such as the home page for amazon.com or cnn.com. How many separate TCP connections are opened? Who initiates them? Could the system be made more efficient? (Requires root access.)

★ **E21.4** Locate log files from an Internet-accessible web server, perhaps the main server for your site. Examine the log files. What can you say about the access patterns over a period of a few hours? What errors showed up during that period? What privacy concerns are illustrated by the contents of the log files? (May require root access.)

★★ **E21.5** Install Apache on your system and create a couple of content pages. From other machines, verify that your web server is operating. Find the Apache log files that let you see what browsers are hitting your server. Configure Apache to serve some of its content pages to the virtual interface created in E21.1. (Requires root access.)

SECTION THREE
BUNCH O' STUFF

22 *The X Window System*

The X Window System, also called X11 or simply X, is the foundation for most graphical user environments for UNIX and Linux. X is the natural successor to a window system called (believe it or not) W, which was developed as part of MIT's Project Athena in the early 1980s. Version 10 of the X Window System, released in 1985, was the first to achieve widespread deployment, and version 11 (X11) followed shortly thereafter. Thanks to the system's relatively liberal licensing terms, X spread quickly to other platforms, and multiple implementations emerged.

In 1988, the MIT X Consortium was founded to set the overall direction for the X protocol. Over the next decade, this group and its successors issued a steady stream of protocol updates. X11R7.1 is today's latest and greatest, with the trend apparently heading toward adding new numbers to the version designation instead of incrementing the existing ones.

XFree86 became the de facto X server implementation for Linux (and many other platforms) until a licensing change in 2004 motivated many distributions to switch to a fork of XFree86 that was unencumbered by the new licensing clause. That fork is maintained by the nonprofit X.Org Foundation and is the predominant Linux implementation today. In addition, the X.Org server has been ported to Windows for use in the Cygwin Linux compatibility environment. (Several commercial X servers for Windows are also available; see page 823 for more information.)

This chapter describes the X.Org version of X, which is used by all our example distributions. The implementations of X.Org and XFree86 have diverged architecturally, but most of the administrative details remain the same. It is often possible to substitute "xf86" for "xorg" in commands and filenames to guess at the appropriate XFree86 version. XFree86 is becoming obsolete by the day and will not be discussed further here.

The X Window System can be broken down into a few key components. First, it provides a *display manager* whose main job is to authenticate users, log them in, and start up an initial environment from startup scripts. The display manager also starts the *X server*, which defines an abstract interface to the system's bitmapped displays and input devices (e.g., keyboard and mouse). The startup scripts also run a *window manager*, which allows the user to move, resize, minimize, and maximize windows, as well as to manage separate virtual desktops. Finally, at the lowest level, applications are linked to a *widget library* that implements high-level user interface mechanisms such as buttons and menus. Exhibit A illustrates the relationship between the display manager, the X server, and client applications.

Exhibit A   The X client/server model

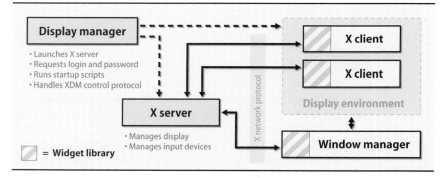

The X server understands only a very basic set of drawing primitives over a network API; it does not define a programming interface to high-level entities such as buttons, text boxes, menus, and sliders. This design achieves two important goals. First, it allows the X server to run on a completely separate computer from the client application. Second, it allows the server to support a variety of different window managers and widget sets.

Application developers have their choice of several common widget libraries and user interface standards. Unfortunately, the choice often depends more on religious affiliation than on any real design considerations. Although freedom of choice is good, X's user interface agnosticism has arguably resulted in many years of poor user interfaces.

In this chapter, we explain how to run programs on a remote display and how to enable authentication. We then discuss how to configure the X.Org server and how to troubleshoot configuration errors. Finally, we touch briefly on some of the available window managers and desktop environments.

22.1 THE X DISPLAY MANAGER

The display manager is the first thing a user usually sees when sitting down at the computer. It is not required; many users disable the display manager and start X from the text console or from their **.login** script by running **startx** (which itself is a wrapper for the **xinit** program, which starts the X server).

On the other hand, the display manager sports an attractive, user-friendly login screen and adds some extra configurability. The display manager can allow remote logins to other X servers through the XDMCP protocol. It can also handle display authentication (see *Client authentication* on page 745). The original display manager is called **xdm** (for X display manager), but modern replacements such as **gdm** (the GNOME display manager) and **kdm** (the KDE display manager) deliver more or less the same set of features and are much better looking.

In the typical scenario, the display manager launches the X server, authenticates the user, logs the user into the system, and executes the user's startup scripts. A set of configuration files, most often located in the **/etc/X11/xdm** directory, specifies how **xdm** will run. For example, you might want to edit the **Xservers** file to change the display number used for this server if multiple servers will be running on other virtual terminals. Or, you might alter the server layout with the **-layout** option if you have defined layouts to suit multiple systems.

See page 681 for more information about PAM.

After launching the X server, **xdm** prompts for a username and password. The user's password is authenticated according to the PAM modules (Pluggable Authentication Modules) specified in **/etc/pam.d/xdm** (or **kdm/gdm** if you are using the KDE or GNOME display managers). The login screen can also present the option to log in to several alternative desktop environments, including the important failsafe option discussed below.

The display manager's final duty is to execute the **Xsession** shell script, which sets up the user's desktop environment. The **Xsession** script, also most often found in **/etc/X11/xdm**, is a system-wide startup script. It sets application defaults, installs standard key bindings, and selects language settings. The **Xsession** script then executes the user's own personal startup script, usually called **~/.xsession**, to start up the window manager, task bar, helper applets, and possibly other programs. GNOME and KDE have their own startup scripts that configure the user's desktop in accordance with GNOME's and KDE's configuration tools; this scheme is less error-prone than users' editing of their own startup scripts.

When the execution of **~/.xsession** completes, the user is logged out of the system and the display manager goes back to prompting for a username and password. Therefore, **~/.xsession** must start all programs in the background (by appending an **&** to the end of each command) *except for the last one*, which is normally the window manager. (If all commands in **~/.xsession** are run in the background, the script terminates right away and the user is logged out immediately after logging in.) With the window manager as the final, foreground process, the user is logged out only after the window manager exits.

The failsafe login option lets users log in to fix their broken startup scripts. This option can usually be selected from the display manager's login screen. It opens only a simple terminal window; once the window closes, the system logs the user out. Every system should allow the failsafe login option; it helps users fix their own messes rather than having to page you in the middle of the night.

Forgetting to leave a process in the foreground is the most common startup problem, but it's hardly the only possibility. If the cause of problems is not obvious, you may have to refer to the ~/**.xsession-errors** file, which contains the output of the commands run from ~/**.xsession**. Look for errors or other unexpected behavior. In a pinch, move the ~/**.xsession** script aside completely and make sure you can log in without it. Then restore one or two lines at a time until you find the offending line.

22.2   RUNNING AN X APPLICATION

The process required to run an X application may at first seem overly complicated. However, you will soon discover the flexibility provided by the client/server display model. Because display updates are transmitted over the network, an application (the client) can run on a completely separate computer from the one that displays its graphical user interface (the server). An X server can have connections from many different applications, all of which run on separate computers.

To make this model work, clients must be told what display to connect to and what screen to inhabit on that display. Once connected, clients must authenticate themselves to the X server to ensure that the person sitting in front of the display has authorized the connection.

See page 697 for more information about SSH.

Even with authentication, X's intrinsic security is relatively weak. You can manage connections more securely by routing them through SSH (see *X connection forwarding with SSH* on page 747). We strongly recommend the use of SSH for X connections over the Internet. It's not unreasonable for local traffic, either.

The DISPLAY environment variable

X applications consult the DISPLAY environment variable to find out where to display themselves. The variable contains the hostname or IP address of the server, the display number (identifying the particular instance of an X server to connect to), and an optional screen number (for displays with multiple monitors). When applications run on the same computer that displays their interfaces, you can omit most of these parameters for simplicity.

The following example shows both the format of the display information and the **bash** syntax used to set the environment variable:

```
client$ DISPLAY=servername.domain.com:10.2; export DISPLAY
```

This setting points X applications at the machine servername.domain.com, display 10, screen 2. Applications establish a TCP connection to the server on port number

6000 plus the display number (in this example, port 6010), where the X server handling that display should be listening.

Keep in mind that every process has its own environment variables. When you set the DISPLAY variable for a shell, its value is inherited only by programs that you run from that shell. If you execute the commands above in one **xterm** and then try to run your favorite X application from another, the application won't have access to your carefully constructed DISPLAY variable.

Another point worth mentioning is that although X applications send their graphical output to the designated X server, they still have local stdout and stderr channels. Some error output may still come to the terminal window from which an X application was run.

See page 418 for more information about DNS resolver configuration.

If the client and server are both part of your local organization, you can usually omit the server's full domain name from the DISPLAY variable, depending on how your name server's resolver has been configured. Also, since most systems run only a single X server, the display is usually 0. The screen number can be omitted, in which case screen 0 is assumed. Ergo, most of the time it's fine to set the value of DISPLAY to servername:0.

If the client application happens to be running on the same machine as the X server, you can simplify the DISPLAY variable even further by omitting the hostname. This feature is more than just cosmetic: with a null hostname, the client libraries use a UNIX domain socket instead of a network socket to contact the X server. In addition to being faster and more efficient, this connection method bypasses any firewall restrictions on the local system that are trying to keep out external X connections. The simplest possible value for the DISPLAY environment variable, then, is simply ":0".

The same client libraries that read the DISPLAY environment variable usually accept this information in the form of a command-line argument as well. For example, the command

```
client$ xprogram -display servername:0
```

is equivalent to running the program with DISPLAY set to "servername:0". The command-line options override the environment variable settings. This feature is especially handy if you are running on the same machine several programs that are handled by different displays.

Client authentication

Although the X environment is generally thought to be relatively insecure, every precaution helps prevent unauthorized access. In the days before security was such a pressing concern, it was common for X servers to welcome connections from any client running on a host that had been marked as safe with the **xhost** command. But since any user on that host could then connect to your display and wreak havoc (either intentionally or out of confusion), the **xhost** method of granting access to clients was eventually deprecated. We do not discuss it further.

The most prevalent alternative to host-based security is called magic cookie authentication. While the thought of magic cookies might induce flashbacks in some of our readers, in this context they are used to authenticate X connections. The basic idea is that the X display manager generates a large random number, called a cookie, early in the login procedure. The cookie for the server is written to the ~/.**Xauthority** file in the user's home directory. Any clients that know the cookie are allowed to connect. Users can run the **xauth** command to view existing cookies and add new ones to this file.

The simplest way to show how this works is with an example. Suppose you have set your DISPLAY variable on the client system to display X applications on the machine at which you are sitting. However, when you run a program, you get an error that looks something like this:

```
client$ xprogram -display server:0
Xlib: connection to "server:0.0" refused by server
xprogram: unable to open display 'server:0'
```

This message tells you that the client does not have the right cookie, so the remote server refused the connection. To get the right cookie, log in to the server (which you have probably already done if you are trying to display on it) and list the server's cookies by running **xauth list**:

```
server$ xauth list
server:0   MIT-MAGIC-COOKIE-1   f9d888df6077819ef4d788fab778dc9f
server/unix:0   MIT-MAGIC-COOKIE-1   f9d888df6077819ef4d788fab778dc9f
localhost:0   MIT-MAGIC-COOKIE-1   cb6cbf9e5c24128749feddd47f0e0779
```

Each network interface on the server has an entry. In this example we have a cookie for the Ethernet, a cookie for the UNIX domain socket used for local connections, and a cookie for the localhost loopback network interface.

The easiest way to get the cookie onto the client (when not using SSH, which negotiates the cookie for you) is with good old cut-and-paste. Most terminal emulators (e.g., **xterm**) let you select text with the mouse and paste it into another window, usually by pressing the middle mouse button. Conveniently, the **xauth add** command accepts as input the same format that **xauth list** displays. You can add the cookie to the client like this:

```
client$ xauth add server:0   MIT-MAGIC-COOKIE-1
     9d888df6077819ef4d788fab778dc9f
```

You should verify that the cookie was added properly by running **xauth list** on the client. With the DISPLAY environment variable set and the correct magic cookie added to the client, applications should now display correctly on the server.

If you are having trouble getting cookies to work, you can drop back temporarily to **xhost** authentication just to verify that there are no other problems (for example, firewalls or local network restrictions that are preventing the client from accessing the server). Always run **xhost -** (that is, **xhost** with a dash as its only argument) to disable **xhost** authentication once your test is complete.

X connection forwarding with SSH

Magic cookies increase security, but they're hardly foolproof. Any user who can obtain your display's cookie can connect to the display and run programs that monitor your activities. Even without your cookie, the X protocol transfers data over the network without encryption, allowing it to be sniffed by virtually anyone.

See page 697 for more information about SSH.

You can boost security with SSH, the secure shell protocol. SSH provides an authenticated and encrypted terminal service. However, SSH can also forward arbitrary network data, including X protocol data, over a secure channel. X forwarding is similar to generic SSH port forwarding, but because SSH is X-aware, you gain some additional features, including a pseudo-display on the remote machine and the negotiated transfer of magic cookies.

You typically **ssh** from the machine running the X server to the machine on which you want to run X programs. This arrangement can be confusing to read about because the SSH *client* is run on the same machine as the X *server*, and it connects to an SSH *server* that is the same machine as the X *client* applications. To make it worse, the virtual display that SSH creates for your X server is local to the remote system. Exhibit B shows how X traffic flows through the SSH connection.

Exhibit B Using SSH with X

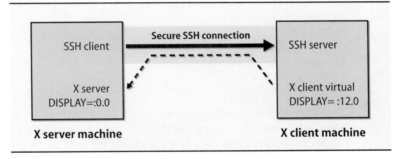

Your DISPLAY variable and authentication information are set up automatically by **ssh**. The display number starts at :10.0 and increments for each SSH connection that is forwarding X traffic.

An example might help show the sequence

```
x-server$ ssh -v -X x-client.mydomain.com
OpenSSH_3.9p1, OpenSSL 0.9.7a Feb 19 2003
debug1: Reading configuration data /home/boggs/.ssh/config
debug1: Reading configuration data /etc/ssh/ssh_config
debug1: Applying options for *
debug1: Connecting to x-client.mydomain.com [192.168.15.9] port 22.
debug1: Connection established.
Enter passphrase for key '/home/boggs/.ssh/id_rsa':
debug1: read PEM private key done: type RSA
```

```
debug1: Authentication succeeded (publickey).
debug1: Entering interactive session.
debug1: Requesting X11 forwarding with authentication spoofing.
debug1: Requesting authentication agent forwarding.
x-client$
```

You can see from the last two lines that the client is requesting forwarding for X11 applications. X forwarding must be enabled on both the SSH server and the SSH client, and the client must still have the correct cookie for the server. If things do not seem to be working right, try the **-X** and **-v** flags as shown above (for OpenSSH) to explicitly enable X forwarding and to request verbose output. Also check the global SSH configuration files in **/etc/ssh** to make sure that X11 forwarding has not been administratively disabled. Once logged in, you can check your display and magic cookies:

```
x-client$ echo $DISPLAY
localhost:12.0
x-client$ xauth list
x-client/unix:12   MIT-MAGIC-COOKIE-1   a54b67121eb94c8a807f3ab0a67a51f2
```

Notice that the DISPLAY points to a virtual display on the SSH server. Other SSH connections (both from you and from other users) are assigned different virtual display numbers. With the DISPLAY and cookie properly set, we can now run the client application.

```
x-client$ xeyes
debug1: client_input_channel_open: ctype x11 rchan 4 win 65536 max 16384
debug1: client_request_x11: request from 127.0.0.1 35411
debug1: channel 1: new [x11]
debug1: confirm x11
debug1: channel 1: FORCE input drain
```

With the debugging information enabled with **ssh -v**, you can see that **ssh** has received the X connection request and dutifully forwarded it to the X server. The forwarding can be a little slow on a distant link, but the application should eventually appear on your screen.

22.3 X SERVER CONFIGURATION

The X.Org server, **Xorg**, has a reputation for being notoriously difficult to configure for a given hardware environment. It is not undeserved. In part, the complexity of **Xorg**'s configuration is explained by the wide array of graphics hardware, input devices, video modes, resolutions, and color depths that it supports. In the early days of XFree86, a new user was often overwhelmed by a cryptic configuration file containing what appeared to be random numbers derived from obscure information in the back of the monitor's nonexistent manual. **Xorg**'s configuration file affords significantly more structure for some of these seemingly random numbers.

The **Xorg** configuration file is normally found in **/etc/X11/xorg.conf**, but the X server will search a whole slew of directories looking for it. The man page presents a complete list, but one point to note is that some of the paths **Xorg** searches contain the hostname and a global variable, making it easy for you to store configuration files for multiple systems in a central location.

Several programs can help you configure X (e.g., **xorgconfig**), but it's a good idea to understand how the configuration file is structured in case you need to view or edit the configuration directly. You can gather some useful starting information directly from the X server by running **Xorg -probeonly** and looking through the output for video chipset and other probed values. You can run **Xorg -configure** to have the X server create an initial configuration file that is based on the probed values. It's a good place to start if you have nothing else.

The **xorg.conf** file is organized into several sections, each starting with the Section keyword and ending with EndSection. The most common section types are listed in Table 22.1.

Table 22.1   Sections of the xorg.conf file

Section	Description
ServerFlags	Lists general X server configuration parameters
Module	Specifies dynamically loadable extensions for accelerated graphics, font renderers, and the like
Device	Configures the video card, driver, and hardware information
Monitor	Describes physical monitor parameters including timing and display resolutions
Screen	Associates a monitor with a video card (Device) and defines the resolutions and color depths available in that configuration
InputDevice	Specifies input devices such as keyboards and mice
ServerLayout	Bundles input devices with a set of screens and positions the screens relative to each other

It is often simplest to build a configuration file from the bottom up by first defining sections for the input and output devices and then combining them into various layouts. With this hierarchical approach, a single configuration file can be used for many X servers, each with different hardware. It's also a reasonable approach for a single system that has multiple video cards and monitors.

Exhibit C on the next page shows how some of these sections fit together into the X.Org configuration hierarchy. A physical display Monitor plus a video card Device form a Screen. A set of Screens plus InputDevices form a ServerLayout. Multiple server layouts can be defined in a configuration file, though only one is active for a given instance of the **Xorg** process.

Exhibit C   Relationship of xorg.conf configuration sections

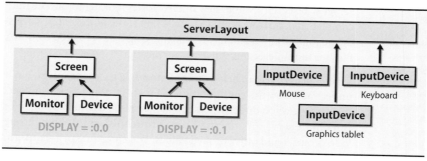

Some of the sections that make up the **xorg.conf** file are relatively fixed. The defaults can often be used straight from an existing or example configuration file. Others, such as the Device, Monitor, Screen, InputDevice, and ServerLayout sections, depend on the host's hardware setup. We discuss the most interesting of these sections in more detail in the following subsections.

Device sections

A Device section describes a particular video card. You must provide a string to identify the card and a driver appropriate for the device. The driver is loaded only if the device is referenced by a corresponding Screen section. A typical device section might look like this:

```
Section "Device"
        Identifier      "STBVirge3D"
        Driver          "s3virge"
        option          value
        ...
EndSection
```

The manual page for the driver, in this example s3virge, describes the hardware that's driven as well as the options the driver supports. If you are experiencing strange video artifacts, you might try setting options to turn off hardware acceleration (if supported), slowing down video memory access, or modifying PCI parameters. It is generally a good idea to check the web for others who might have experienced similar problems before you start randomly changing values.

Monitor sections

The Monitor section describes the displays attached to your computer. It can specify detailed timing values. The timing information is necessary for older hardware, but most modern monitors can be probed for it. Display specifications can usually be obtained from the manufacturer's web site, but nothing beats having the original manual that came with the monitor. Either way, you will want to know at least the horizontal sync and vertical refresh frequencies for your model.

A typical Monitor section looks like this:

```
Section "Monitor"
      Identifier      "ViewSonic"
      Option          "DPMS"
      HorizSync       30-65
      VertRefresh     50-120
EndSection
```

As with all of the sections, the Identifier line assigns a name by which you later refer to this monitor. Here we have turned on DPMS (Display Power Management Signaling) so that the X server powers down the monitor when we sneak away for a donut and some coffee.

The HorizSync and VertRefresh lines should be filled in with values appropriate for your monitor. They may be specified as a frequency range (as above) or as discrete values separated by commas. The driver can theoretically probe for supported modes, but specifying the parameters keeps the driver from attempting to use unsupported frequencies.

Horror stories abound of early CRTs being damaged by signals running at improper frequencies, but these days CRTs seem to be a bit more resilient. At worst, they are likely to emit a high-pitched squeal that is sure to get the dog's attention. Modern LCD monitors are even more tolerant of signal variations, but it is probably still wise to exercise caution when experimenting with monitor frequencies. Be prepared to turn off the monitor if it does not like the signal it is receiving.

Screen sections

A Screen section ties a device (video card) to a monitor at a specific color depth and set of display resolutions. Here's an example that uses the video card and monitor specified above.

```
Section "Screen"
      Identifier      "Screen 2"
      Device          "STBVirge3D"
      Monitor         "ViewSonic"
      DefaultDepth 24
      Subsection "Display"
            Depth    8
            Modes    "640x400"
      EndSubsection
      Subsection "Display"
            Depth    16
            Modes    "640x400" "640x480" "800x600" "1024x768"
      EndSubsection
      Subsection "Display"
            Depth    24
            Modes    "1280x1024" "1024x768" "800x600" "640x400" "640x480"
      EndSubsection
EndSection
```

X Windows

As you might expect, the screen is named with an Identifier, and the identifiers for the previously defined video device and monitor are mentioned. This is the first section we have introduced that has subsections. One subsection is defined for each color depth, with the default being specified by the DefaultDepth field.

A given instance of the X server can run at only one color depth. At startup, the server determines what resolutions are supported for that color depth. The possible resolutions generally depend on the amount of memory on the video card. On older cards with less memory, it's common for resolution to be limited at high color depths. *Special keyboard combinations for X* on page 754 describes how to cycle through the resolutions that are defined here.

Any decent modern video card should be able to drive your monitor at its full resolution in 24-bit or 32-bit color. If you want to run old programs that require a server running in 8-bit color, run a second X server on a separate virtual console. Use the **-depth 8** flag on the **Xorg** command line to override the DefaultDepth option.

InputDevice sections

An InputDevice section describes a source of input events such as a keyboard or mouse. Each device gets its own InputDevice section, and as with other sections, each is named with an Identifier field. If you are sharing a single configuration file among machines with different hardware, you can define all the input devices; only those referenced in the ServerLayout section are used. Here is a typical keyboard definition:

```
Section "InputDevice"
        Identifier      "Generic Keyboard"
        Driver          "Keyboard"
        Option          "AutoRepeat" "500 30"
        Option          "XkbModel" "pc104"
        Option          "XkbLayout" "us"
EndSection
```

You can set options in the keyboard definition to express your particular religion's stance on the proper position of the Control and Caps Lock keys, among other things. In this example, the AutoRepeat option specifies how long a key needs to be held down before it starts repeating and how fast it repeats.

The mouse is configured in a separate InputDevice section:

```
Section "InputDevice"
        Identifier      "Generic Mouse"
        Driver          "mouse"
        Option          "CorePointer"
        Option          "Device" "/dev/input/mice"
        Option          "Protocol" "IMPS/2"
        Option          "Emulate3Buttons" "off"
        Option          "ZAxisMapping" "4 5"
EndSection
```

The CorePointer option designates this mouse as the system's primary pointing device. The device file associated with the mouse is specified as an Option; it is typically set to **/dev/input/mice**, which is the mouse device multiplexer. The protocol depends on the particular brand of mouse that is used; you can set it to auto so that the server tries to figure it out for you. If your mouse wheel doesn't work, try setting the protocol to IMPS/2. If you have more than a few buttons, you might need to use the ExplorerPS/2 protocol.

If **/dev/input/mice** does not work for your mouse, then the configuration is slightly more complex. The **gpm** program implements X-like, mouse-controlled cut-and-paste facilities in text-mode virtual terminals. However, only one program can open a traditional mouse device at a time. To solve this problem, **gpm** replicates the mouse data to a FIFO file so that applications such as the X server can see it too (by using the FIFO as the mouse device).[1] This arrangement adds **gpm** functionality to the system while keeping it relatively transparent.

For example, the following command makes **gpm** get its input from **/dev/mouse** with the IMPS/2 protocol and forward it to the FIFO **/dev/gpmdata** (the name is not configurable) with no protocol translation.

```
$ gpm -m /dev/mouse -t imps2 -Rraw
```

You would then change the mouse device to **/dev/gpmdata** in the **xorg.conf** file. Since **gpm** must be run before the X server is started, this command must go in a system startup script such as **/etc/init.d/gpm**. See page 32 for more information about startup scripts.

The Emulate3Buttons option lets a two-button mouse emulate a three-button mouse by defining a click on both buttons to stand in for a middle button click. The ZAxisMapping option is sometimes needed to support a scroll wheel or joystick device by mapping the buttons appropriately. Most mice these days have at least three buttons, a scroll wheel, a built-in MP3 player, a foot massager, and a beer chiller.[2]

ServerLayout sections

The ServerLayout section is the top-level node of the configuration hierarchy. Each hardware configuration that the server will be run on should have its own instance of the ServerLayout section. The layout used by a particular X server is usually specified on the server's command line.

Here is an example of a complete ServerLayout section:

```
Section "ServerLayout"
     Identifier    "Simple Layout"
     Screen        "Screen 1" LeftOf "Screen 2"
     Screen        "Screen 2" RightOf "Screen 1"
     InputDevice   "Generic Mouse" "CorePointer"
     InputDevice   "Generic Keyboard" "CoreKeyboard"
```

---

1. FIFO files are created with the **mknod** command. For example, **mknod p /dev/gpmdata**.
2. Not all options are supported by **Xorg**. Some options sold separately.

```
        Option      "BlankTime"    "10"  # Blank the screen in 10 minutes
        Option      "StandbyTime" "20"  # Turn off screen in 20 minutes (DPMS)
        Option      "SuspendTime" "60"  # Full hibernation in 60 minutes (DPMS)
        Option      "OffTime"      "120"# Turn off DPMS monitor in 2 hours
    EndSection
```

This section ties together all the other sections to represent an X display. It starts with the requisite Identifier, which names this particular layout. It then associates a set of screens with the layout.[3] If multiple monitors are attached to separate video cards, each screen is specified along with optional directions to indicate how they are physically arranged. In this example, screen one is on the left and screen two is on the right.

Some video cards can drive multiple monitors at once. In this case, only a single Screen is specified in the ServerLayout section. For NVIDIA cards, currently the most common for this application under Linux, you set an option in the Driver section to signify support for TwinView. The details of this configuration are outside the scope of this book but can easily be found on various web forums.

Following the screen list is the set of input devices to associate with this layout. The CorePointer and CoreKeyboard options are passed to the InputDevice section to indicate that the devices are to be active for the configuration. Those options can also be set directly in the corresponding InputDevice sections, but it's cleaner to set them in the ServerLayout section.

The last few lines configure several layout-specific options. In the example above, these all relate to DPMS, which is the interface that tells Energy Star-compliant monitors when to power themselves down. The monitors must also have their DPMS options enabled in the corresponding Monitor sections.

22.4 TROUBLESHOOTING AND DEBUGGING

X server configuration has come a long way over the last decade, but it can still be difficult to get things working just the way you would like. You may need to experiment with monitor frequencies, driver options, proprietary drivers, or extensions for 3D rendering. Ironically, it is the times when the display is not working correctly that you are most interested in seeing the debugging output on your screen. Fortunately, the X.Org server gives you all the information you need (and a lot that you don't) to track down the problem.

Special keyboard combinations for X

Because the X server takes over your keyboard, display, mouse, and social life, you can imagine that it might leave you with little recourse but to power the system down if things are not working. However, there are a few things to try before it comes to that. If you hold down the Control and Alt keys and press a function key (F1-F6), the X server takes you to one of the text-based virtual terminals. From there you can log

---

3. Recall that screens identify a monitor/video card combination at a particular color depth.

in and debug the problem. To get back to the X server running on virtual terminal 7, press <Alt-F7>.[4] If you are on a network, you can also try logging in from another computer to kill the X server before resorting to the reset button.

If the monitor is not in sync with the card's video signal, try changing the screen resolution. The available resolutions are specified on a Modes line from the Screen section of the configuration file. The exact Modes line that is active depends on the color depth; see *Screen sections* on page 751 for details. The X server defaults to the first resolution shown on the active Modes line, but you can cycle through the different resolutions by holding down Control and Alt and pressing the plus (+) or minus (-) key on the numeric keypad.

Pressing <Control-Alt-Backspace> kills the X server immediately. If you ran the server from a console, you will find yourself back there when the server exits. If a display manager started the server, it usually respawns a new server and prompts again for a login and password. You have to kill the display manager (**xdm**, **gdm**, etc.) from a text console to stop it from respawning new X servers.

When good X servers go bad

Once you have regained control of the machine, you can begin to track down the problem. The simplest place to start is the output of the X server. This output is occasionally visible on virtual terminal one (<Control-Alt-F1>), which is where all the startup program output goes. Most often, the X server output goes to a log file such as **/var/log/Xorg.0.log**.

As seen below, each line is preceded by a symbol that categorizes it. You can use these symbols to spot errors (EE) and warnings (WW), as well as to determine how the server found out each piece of information: through default settings (==), in a config file (**), detected automatically (--), or specified on the X server command line (++).

Let's examine the following snippet:

```
X Window System Version 6.8.2
Release Date: 9 February 2005
X Protocol Version 11, Revision 0, Release 6.8.2
Build Operating System: Linux 2.4.21-23.ELsmp i686 [ELF]
Current Operating System: Linux chinook 2.6.12-1.1372_FC3 #1 Fri Jul 15 00:59:
    10 EDT 2005 i686
Markers: (--) probed, (**) from config file, (==) default setting,
        (++) from command line, (!!) notice, (II) informational,
        (WW) warning, (EE) error, (NI) not implemented, (??) unknown.
(==) Log file: "/var/log/Xorg.0.log", Time: Mon May  1 08:41:02 2006
(==) Using config file: "/etc/X11/xorg.conf"
(==) ServerLayout "Default Layout"
(**) |-->Screen "Screen0" (0)
(**) |   |-->Monitor "Monitor0"
(**) |   |-->Device "Videocard1"
```

---

4. The X server requires the <Control> key to be held down along with the <Alt-Fn> key combination to switch virtual terminals, but the text console does not.

```
(**) |-->Input Device "Mouse0"
(**) |-->Input Device "Keyboard0"
```

The first lines tell you the version number of the X server and the X11 protocol version that it implements. Subsequent lines tell you that the server is using default values for the log file location, the configuration file location, and the active server layout. The display and input devices from the config file are echoed in schematic form.

One common problem that shows up in the logs is difficulty with certain screen resolutions, usually evidenced by those resolutions not working or the X server bailing out with an error such as "Unable to validate any modes; falling back to the default mode." If you have not specified a list of frequencies for your monitor, the X server probes for them using Extended Display Identification Data (EDID). If your monitor does not support EDID or if your monitor is turned off when X is started, you need to put the frequency ranges for X to use in the Monitor section of the configuration file.

Rounding error in the results obtained from an EDID probe can cause some resolutions to be unavailable even though they should be supported by both your video card and monitor. Log entries such as "No valid modes for 1280x1024; removing" are evidence of this. The solution is to tell the X server to ignore EDID information and use the frequencies you specify with the following lines to the Device section:

```
Option   "IgnoreEDID" "true"
Option   "UseEdidFreqs" "false"
```

As another example, suppose you forgot to define the mouse section properly. The error would show up like this in the output:

```
(==) Using config file: "/etc/X11/xorg.conf"
Data incomplete in file /etc/X11/xorg.conf
        Undefined InputDevice "Mouse0" referenced by ServerLayout "Default
        Layout".
(EE) Problem parsing the config file
(EE) Error parsing the config file
Fatal server error:
no screens found
```

Once X is up and running and you have logged in, you can run the **xdpyinfo** command to get more information about the X server's configuration.[5] **xdpyinfo**'s output again tells you the name of the display and the X server version information. It also tells you the color depths that are available, the extensions that have been loaded, and the screens that have been defined, along with their dimensions and color configurations.

xdpyinfo's output can be parsed by a script (such as your ~/.xsession file) to determine the size of the active screen and to set up the desktop parameters appropriately.

5. We don't recommend logging into X as root because this operation may create a bunch of default startup files in root's home directory, which is usually /. It's also notably insecure. Instead, log in as a regular user and use **sudo**. Debian and Ubuntu enforce this discipline by default.

For debugging, **xdpyinfo** is most useful for determining that the X server is up and listening to network queries, that it has configured the correct screen and resolution, and that it is operating at the desired color bit depth. If this step works, you are ready to start running X applications.

22.5 A BRIEF NOTE ON DESKTOP ENVIRONMENTS

The flexibility and simplicity of the X client/server model has, over the years, led to an explosion of widget sets, window managers, file browsers, tool bar utilities, and utility programs. Out of Project Athena at MIT, where X has its roots, came the Athena widgets and **twm** (Tom's Window Manager, named for its creator Tom LaStrange; it's also called the Tab Window Manager). These rudimentary tools formed the de facto standard for early X applications.

OpenLook, developed by Sun Microsystems and AT&T, was an alternative tool kit that introduced oval buttons and pushpins to keep menus and dialog boxes visible. Around the same time, the Open Software Foundation introduced the competing Motif platform (later called CDE, or Common Desktop Environment), which was eventually adopted by Sun as well. These tool kits' three-dimensional chiseled look was elegant for the time, and the prevalence of advanced UI elements such as sliders and menus made them a reasonable choice for new software. However, both tool kits were highly proprietary, and licensing fees for the development libraries and window manager made them inaccessible to the general public.

Along with open source operating systems such as Linux came open source desktop environments. FVWM (the "F" Virtual Window Manager) was popular for Linux because of its high degree of configurability and support for "virtual desktops" that expanded the user's effective working area beyond the confines of the low-resolution displays available on most PCs at the time.[6] There was no associated widget set, however, so users were still faced with a multitude of programs, each with a rather different look and feel.

As applications became more advanced and required progressively more advanced user interface functionality, it became clear that a broader approach must be taken to unify the user experience and provide better support to application developers. From this need were born the two big players in modern Linux desktop environments: GNOME and KDE. Although some users have strong feelings regarding which is the One True Way, both are relatively complete desktop managers. In fact, just because you are running in one realm does not mean you cannot use applications from the other; just expect a different look and feel and a brief sense of discontinuity in the universe.

The freedesktop.org project is dedicated to creating an environment that will allow applications to be compatible with any desktop environment.

6. In fact, FVWM was so flexible that it could be configured to look like either **twm** or **mwm** (the Motif Window Manager).

KDE

KDE, which stands for the K Desktop Environment, is written in C++ and built on the Qt tool kit library. It is often preferred by users who enjoy eye candy, such as transparent windows, shadows, and animated cursors. It looks nice, but it can be slow on anything but a high-end PC. For users who spend a lot of time clicking around in the desktop rather than running applications, the tradeoff between look and feel may ultimately decide whether KDE is the appropriate choice.

KDE is often preferred by people transitioning from a Windows or Mac environment because of its pretty graphics. It's also a favorite of technophiles who love to be able to fully customize their environment. For others, KDE is simply too much to deal with and GNOME is the simpler choice.

Applications written for KDE almost always contain a K somewhere in the name, such as Konqueror (the web/file browser), Konsole (the terminal emulator), or KWord (a word processor). The default window manager, KWin, supports the freedesktop.org Window Manager Specification standard, configurable skins for changing the overall look and feel, and many other features. The KOffice application suite contains word processing, spreadsheet, and presentation utilities. KDE sports a comprehensive set of development tools, including an integrated development environment (IDE). With these foundations, KDE provides a powerful and consistent user interface experience.

GNOME

GNOME is another desktop environment written in C and based on the GTK+ widget set. Its underlying object communication model uses CORBA, the Common Object Request Broker Architecture. The name GNOME was originally an acronym for GNU Network Object Model Environment, but that derivation no longer really applies; these days, GNOME is just a name.

GNOME is less glitzy than KDE, is not as configurable, and is slightly less consistent overall. However, it is noticeably cleaner, faster, and simpler. Most Linux distributions use GNOME as the default desktop environment.

Like KDE, GNOME has a rich application set. GNOME applications are usually identifiable by the presence of a G in their names. One exception is the standard GNOME window manager, called Metacity (pronounced like "opacity"), which provides basic windowing functions and skins for a configurable look and feel. Following the GNOME model, Metacity is designed to be lean and mean. If you want some of the extra features you may be used to, like a virtual desktop or smart window placement, you need the support of external applications such as **brightside** or **devilspie**. (This is one area in which KDE has a leg up.)

Office applications include AbiWord for word processing, Gnumeric as a spreadsheet, and one of the more impressive projects to come out of GNOME, The GIMP for image processing. A file manager called Nautilus is also included, along with Epiphany for web browsing. Like KDE, GNOME provides an extensive infrastructure for application developers. Altogether, GNOME offers a powerful architecture for application development in an easy-to-use desktop environment.

Which is better, GNOME or KDE?

Ask this question on any public forum and you will see the definition of "flame war." Because of the tendency for people to turn desktop preference into a personal crusade, the following paragraphs may be some of the least opinionated in this book.

The best answer is to try both desktops and decide for yourself which best meets your needs. Keep in mind that your friends, your users, and your manager may all have different preferences for a desktop environment, and that is OK.

Now that freedesktop.org is creating standards to unify the desktop, the animosity that has developed between the KDE and GNOME camps is progressing into a healthy competition to create great software. Remember that your choice of desktop environment does not dictate which applications you can run. No matter which desktop you choose, you can select applications from the full complement of excellent software made available by both of these (and other) open source projects.

22.6 RECOMMENDED READING

The X.Org home page, x.org, includes information on upcoming releases as well as links to the X.Org wiki, mailing lists, and downloads.

The man pages for **Xserver** and **Xorg** cover generic X server options and **Xorg**-specific command-line options. They also include a general overview of X server operation. The **xorg.conf** man page covers the config file and describes its various sections in detail. This man page also lists video card drivers in its REFERENCES section. Look up your video card here to learn the name of the driver, then read the driver's own man page to learn about driver-specific options.

22.7 EXERCISES

E22.1   Use SSH to run an X program over the network. Use **ssh -v** to verify that X forwarding is set up correctly. What is the DISPLAY variable set to after you log in? List the cookies by running **xauth** and verify that magic cookie authentication is active for that display.

E22.2   Write a shell command line or script to parse the output of **xdpyinfo** and print the current screen resolution in the format XxY, e.g., 1024×768.

Exercises are continued on the next page.

E22.3   Examine the **Xorg** log file (**/var/log/Xorg.0.log**) and determine as many of the following items as possible:

a) What type of video card is present and which driver does it use?
b) How much video memory does the card have?
c) Was EDID used to probe monitor settings? How do you know?
d) What modes (resolutions) are supported?
e) Is DPMS enabled?
f) What does the server think the physical screen dimensions are?
g) What device file is used for the mouse?

E22.4   What flag disables nonlocal TCP connections to the server? Explain why this option is useful.

23 *Printing*

Printer configuration is annoying and difficult. Users take printing for granted, but the administrative contortions required for deliver of perfectly rendered pages to a printer a foot away from the user can be challenging.

Two decades ago, the most common printers were ASCII line printers. Laser printers were expensive and rare. High-resolution output devices required custom driver software and formatting programs.

Today, instead of connecting to a single computer through a serial or parallel port, laser printers often connect to a TCP/IP network over an Ethernet or wireless link. Laser printers have largely lost the low-end market to inkjet printers. Color printers used to be a luxury, but like color photography and color monitors, they have become common. Finding a black-and-white printer will soon be as hard as finding black-and-white film.

On the desktop and in the small office market, special-purpose printers, scanners, copiers, and fax machines are being pushed aside by multifunction devices that do all these jobs. Sometimes, these devices can even read files from your digital camera's memory card.

With so many changes in technology, you'd expect the Linux printing system to be flexible, and indeed it is. However, this flexibility is a relatively recent achievement. Until a few years ago, most Linux printing systems were based on software developed for the line printers of yore. These systems, hacked and overloaded in an attempt to keep up with evolving technologies, were never really up to the job of supporting modern printers on modern networks. Fortunately, CUPS, the Common UNIX

Printing System, has arrived on the scene to address many of the older systems' weaknesses.

You can find CUPS on most modern UNIX and Linux systems, including Mac OS X. A few older printing systems remain in use (such as PDQ, pdq.sourceforge.net, and LPRng, www.lprng.com), but early printing systems such as System V's printing system, Palladium, rlpr, PLP, GNUlpr, and PPR are all pretty much dead.

In this chapter, we focus on CUPS as the current de facto standard. We start with a general discussion of printers and printing terminology. We then describe Linux printing systems in general and outline the architecture of CUPS. We move on to the specifics of printer configuration and administration, then conclude with a brief guide to print-system debugging, a tour of optional printing-related software, and some general administration hints.

23.1 PRINTERS ARE COMPLICATED

Users lump printers in with other peripherals such as monitors and speakers, but that viewpoint doesn't give printers credit for their complexity. Once upon a time, the most powerful computer Apple made was the Apple LaserWriter. Today, your desktop machine is probably more powerful than your printer, but the printer is still a computer. It has a CPU, memory, an operating system, and perhaps even a disk. If it's a network printer, it has its own IP address and TCP/IP implementation.

If you have a modern network printer around, enter its network address into your web browser (e.g., 192.168.0.9). Chances are that the printer will return some web pages that let you administer the printer hardware; the printer is running its own web server.

Since system administrators are security minded, you may already be thinking, "Does that mean a printer could be compromised or hit by a denial of service attack?" You bet. See the section on security that starts on page 787.

What operating system is your printer running? What? You don't know? Not surprising. You probably can't find out, either, without some digging—and perhaps not even then. The operating system varies from vendor to vendor and sometimes even from model to model. Mid-range and higher-end printers may even run some derivative of UNIX or Linux.[1]

The OS confusion is just the beginning. Printers also handle a variety of network protocols and accept jobs in several different printer-specific page-description and document-description languages.

If you're administering a larger facility, you may need to support several models of printers from several different manufacturers. The printing software on your computers must be prepared to communicate with varied (and sometimes unknown) hardware and to use an array of protocols.

---

1. Hackers have ported Linux to iPods and Xboxes; we're waiting to see who's first to port it to an HP LaserJet.

23.2 PRINTER LANGUAGES

A print job is really a computer program written in a specialized programming language. These programming languages are known collectively as page description languages, or PDLs.

Pages encoded in a PDL can be much smaller and faster to transmit than the equivalent raw images. PDL descriptions can also be device- and resolution-independent.

The best-known PDLs today are PostScript, PCL5, PCL6 (also called PCL/XL or "pxl"), and PDF. Many printers can accept input in more than one language. We discuss each of these languages briefly in the sections below.

Printers have to interpret jobs in these languages and transform them into some form of bitmap representation that makes sense to the actual imaging hardware. Therefore, printers contain language interpreters. Just as with C or Java, these languages exist in multiple versions, and the versions make a difference. Most PostScript printers understand PostScript Level 3, but if you send a Level 3 program to a printer that only understands Level 2, the printer is likely to be confused. Would you try to compile a FORTRAN 90 program with a FORTRAN 77 compiler? Certainly not.

Rasterizing the PDL description (or anything else, such as image files) into bitmap page images is called "raster image processing," and a program that rasterizes is called a RIP. "To rip" is sometimes used informally as a verb.

It's possible to rip print jobs in your computer and view the images on your display. We discuss host-based interpreters that do this, such as Ghostscript, on page 785. You could in theory use your computer to rip jobs for printing and ship the completed (and much larger) bitmaps off to be printed by a not-very-smart print device. In fact, this is the way that many GDI (Windows) printers work, and it's somewhat supported under Linux as well.

PostScript

PostScript is the most common PDL found on Linux systems. It was originally developed by Adobe Systems, and many PostScript printers still use an interpreter licensed from Adobe. Almost all page layout programs can generate PostScript, and some work with PostScript exclusively.

PostScript is a full-fledged programming language. You can read most PostScript programs with a text editor or with **less**. The programs contain a multitude of parentheses, curly braces, and slashes and often start with the characters %!PS. Although these starting characters are not required by the language itself, PostScript interpreters and other printing software often look for them when trying to recognize and classify print jobs.

PCL

One alternative to PostScript is Hewlett-Packard's Printer Control Language. It's understood by HP printers as well as many others; some printers speak only PCL.

Unlike PostScript, which is a Turing-complete, generalized programming language, PCL just tells printers how to print pages. PCL jobs are binary, not human readable, and usually are much shorter than the equivalent PostScript. Linux applications seldom generate PCL directly, but filters can convert PostScript to PCL.

Unlike PostScript, every version of PCL is a little different. The differences are minor but significant enough to be annoying. Jobs that print correctly on a LaserJet 5si can print slightly wrong on a LaserJet 5500, and vice versa. It's not just this pair of models, either; every PCL printer has a PCL dialect with custom commands that take advantage of that printer's features.

For example, if you tell your computer you have a LaserJet 4500 when you actually have a LaserJet 4550, it may generate some PCL commands that the 4550 ignores or misinterprets. Also, if you have a stored PCL print job—say, a blank purchase request form—and you replace the printer for which it was generated with something newer, you may have to regenerate the job.

Worse still, HP has defined two almost completely unrelated language families called PCL: PCL5 (5C means color and 5E means black and white) and PCL6 (also called PCL/XL). Nowadays, it's normal for new HP printers to have language interpreters for both.

PCL4 is an archaic flavor of PCL5. Treat a PCL4 (or earlier) printer as you would a Perl 4 interpreter: replace it with something newer.

PDF

Adobe's Portable Document Format is produced by Adobe Acrobat and many other desktop publishing tools. OpenOffice, for example, can export documents as PDF.

PDF documents are platform independent, and PDF is routinely used to exchange documents electronically for both on-line and off-line (printed) use. The final text of this book was delivered to the book printer as a PDF file.

PDF is a document description language, not just a page description language. It describes not only individual pages, but also the overall structure of a document: which pages belong to which chapters, which text columns flow to other text columns, etc. It also accommodates a variety of multimedia features for on-screen use.

Some printers interpret PDF directly. If yours doesn't, a host of PDF viewers and translators (including Ghostview, **xpdf**, **kpdf**, Evince, and Acrobat Reader) can convert documents into something else (such as PostScript) that is more widely understood. Your print system may even hide the conversion requirement from you and automatically convert PDF documents before sending them to the printer.

XHTML

On the opposite end of the spectrum, looming just over the horizon, is XHTML-Print. A printer that receives an XHTML-Print data stream (describing, for example, a web page) produces a good-faith representation of the job, but different printers may produce different representations, just as different browsers may represent the same web page in different ways.

Why would users want that? Imagine that you're a VP of Marketing browsing the web on your cell phone and that you see a web page relevant to a presentation you're about to give. You walk over to a nearby Bluetooth-enabled printer and send it the URL from your phone. The printer does the rest: it downloads the page from the web, renders it, and prints copies. You take the copies from the output tray and head to your presentation.

PJL

PJL, Hewlett-Packard's Printer Job Language, is not really a PDL. It's a metalanguage that describes printer jobs. We describe it here because you'll see it mentioned in printer descriptions.

PJL is a job control language that specifies things such as a job's PDL, whether the job is duplex or simplex, what size paper to use, and so on. The PJL commands come at the start of the job, and the PJL statements all start with @PJL:

```
@PJL SET COPIES=3
@PJL COMMENT FOO BAR MUMBLE
@PJL SET DUPLEX=ON
@PJL SET PAGEPROTECT=OFF
@PJL ENTER LANGUAGE=PCL
```

PJL is widely understood (or deliberately ignored) by non-HP printers, but if you're having trouble printing something that contains PJL on a non-HP printer, try removing the PJL with a text editor and resubmitting the job.

Printer drivers and their handling of PDLs

The software that converts a file into something a particular printer understands is the "printer driver." To print PCL5 on a LaserJet 5500, you need a LaserJet 5500 PCL5 driver.

What if a printer supports only a subset of the languages you need to process? If you download a PostScript file from the web and your printer only understands PCL5E, what do you do? If your printer doesn't interpret PDF directly, how do you print a PDF file?

One option is to convert the file by hand. Linux boxes come with plenty of conversion utilities; there's almost always some way to turn what you have into something your printers can print. Browsers can transform HTML (or XHTML) pages into PostScript. OpenOffice can turn MS Word files into PDF. Ghostscript can turn PDF into PostScript and PostScript into almost anything, including PCL.

An easier approach is to let your printing system do the work for you. Many systems have some built-in knowledge about which conversions need to be done and can set up the conversions for you automatically.

Printing

If you need to determine what PDL a file uses and you can't tell from the filename (e.g., **foo.pdf**), the **file** command can tell you (unless the file starts with a chunk of PJL instructions, in which case **file** just says "HP Printer Job Language data").

Save a few print jobs to files instead of shipping them to a printer, and you can see what a program in one of these languages looks like. A minute or two perusing files of each of these types in your text editor will give you a good feel for how different they are. Don't **cat** them directly to your screen, since only PostScript is ASCII.

PostScript:

```
%!PS-Adobe-3.0
%%BoundingBox: 0 0 612 792
%%Pages: 1
% ...
% Draw a line around the polygons...
pop pop pop dup 0 setgray 0 0 moveto dup 0 lineto 0.707106781 mul dup
    lineto closepath stroke
```

PDF:

```
%PDF-1.3
%Ã¢Ã£ÃÃ"
 81 0 obj
<<
/Linearized 1
/O 83
/H [ 915 494 ]
/T 125075
>>
endobj
 xref
81 24
0000000016 00000 n
 Ãˆ<8f>
^P^@Ã¤Ã'<9e>
endstream
endobj
```

PCL5:

```
^[E^[&l1o0o1t0l6D^[&l1X^[*r0F^[*v0n1O^[*p4300X^[%1BDT~,1TR0TD1SP1FT10,50
CF3,1LB.~;^[%1A^[*c100G^[*v2T^[&a0P^[*p0X^[*p0Y^[(10U^[(s1p12vsb4148T^[&l0
E^[*p0Y^[*ct7920Y^[(10U^[(s1p12vsb4101T^[&a0P^[&l0o66f0E^[9^[&a0P^[*p0X^[*
p0Y^[*p474Y^[*p141X^[(10U^[(10U^[(s1p12vsb4101T^[*p402Y^[*p186X^[*v0O^[*c9
00a4b100g2P^[*v1O^[*p250Y^[*v0O^[*c900a4b100g2P^[*v1O^[*v0O^[*c4a156b100g2
P^[*v1O^[*p251Y^[*p187X^[*v0O^[*c899a154b10g2P^[*v1O^[*p346Y^[*p256X
```

PCL/XL:

```
Ã'X^BX^BÃ¸<89>Ã^@Ã¸<86>Ã^CÃ¸<8f>AÃ^@Ã¸<88>Ã^AÃ¸<82>HÃ^@Ã¸¡Ã^@Ã¸%Ã
Ã¸cÃˆÃ^P^@TimesNewRmnBdÃ¸Ã¨Ã...UUÃ©BÃ¸Â¡Ãu^BÃ¸Âªo<85>Ã"Ã¸^CA^BÃ¸Lk
Ãƒ^@^@Ã¸Â¡dÃˆÃ:^@
```

23.3 CUPS ARCHITECTURE

CUPS has a client/server architecture. A CUPS server is a spooler that maintains print queues for clients.

CUPS clients can be applications with command line interfaces such as **lpr** and **lpq**, or they can have graphical user interfaces such as **kprinter**. Other CUPS servers can also act as clients from the perspective of a given server.

Consider the simplest possible configuration: a CUPS server on a single machine, connected to a single printer, with a single print queue. The next few sections briefly survey the commands and processes involved in a few common printing tasks.

Document printing

Here's how you might print the files **foo.pdf** and **/tmp/testprint.pdf**:

```
$ lpr foo.pdf /tmp/testprint.ps
```

The client transmits copies of the files to the CUPS server, which stores them in the print queue. CUPS processes each file in turn as the printer becomes ready.

CUPS examines both the document and the printer's PostScript Printer Description (PPD) file to see what needs to be done to get the document to print properly. (As we explain later, PPDs are used even for non-PostScript printers.)

To prepare a job for printing on a specific printer, CUPS passes it through a pipeline of filters. These filters can perform a variety of functions. For example, a filter could reformat the job so that two reduced-size page images print on each physical page ("2-up") or transform the job from one PDL to another. A filter can also perform printer-specific processing such as printer initialization. A filter can even perform rasterization on behalf of printers that do not include their own RIPs.

The final stage of the print pipeline is a back end that sends the job from the host to the printer through an appropriate protocol such as USB. The back end also communicates status information back to the CUPS server. To see the available back ends, try the command

```
$ locate backend | grep -i cups
```

After transmitting the print job, the CUPS daemon goes back to processing its queues and handling requests from clients. The printer goes to work trying to print the job it was shipped.

Print queue viewing and manipulation

The **lpq** command requests job status information from the CUPS server and formats it for display.

lpstat -t reports a good summary of the print server's overall status.

Printing

CUPS clients can ask the server to suspend, cancel, or reprioritize jobs. They can also move jobs from one queue to another. Most changes require jobs to be identified by their job number, which is reported by **lpq**.

For example, to remove a print job, just run **lprm** *jobid*.

Multiple printers

If more than one printer is connected to a machine, CUPS maintains a separate queue for each printer.

Command-line clients accept an option (typically **-P** *printer* or **-p** *printer*) to specify the printer queue. You can also set a default printer for yourself by setting the PRINTER environment variable

```
$ export PRINTER=printer_name
```

or by telling CUPS to use a particular default for your account.

```
$ lpoptions -dprinter_name
```

lpoptions normally sets your personal defaults, which are stored in **~/.lpoptions**. When run as root, it sets system-wide defaults in **/etc/cups/lpoptions**. **lpoptions -l** lists the current options.

Printer instances

If you have only one printer but want to use it in several ways—say, both for quick drafts and for final production work—CUPS lets you set up different "printer instances" for these different uses.

For example, if you already have a printer named Phaser_6120, the command

```
$ lpoptions -p Phaser_6120/2up -o number-up=2 -o job-sheets=standard
```

creates an instance named Phaser_6120/2up that performs 2-up printing and adds banner pages. The command

```
$ lpr -P Phaser_6120/2up biglisting.ps
```

then prints the PostScript file **biglisting.ps** as a 2-up job with banners.

Network printing

From the CUPS perspective, a network of many machines isn't very different from an isolated machine. Every computer runs a CUPS daemon (**cupsd**), and all the CUPS daemons communicate with one another.

You configure a CUPS daemon to accept print jobs from remote systems by editing the **/etc/cups/cupsd.conf** file (see *Network print server setup* on page 773). CUPS servers that are set up this way broadcast information about the printers they serve every 30 seconds by default. As a result, computers on the local network automatically learn about the printers available to them.

Making printers available to multiple networks or subnets is a little trickier since broadcast packets do not cross subnet boundaries. The usual solution is to designate a slave server on each subnet that polls the other subnets' servers for information and then relays that information to machines on its local subnet.

For example, suppose the print servers allie (192.168.1.5) and jj (192.168.2.14) live on different subnets and that we want both of them to be accessible to users on a third subnet, 192.168.3. To make this work, we simply designate a slave server (say, copeland, 192.168.3.10) and add these lines to its **cupsd.conf** file:

```
BrowsePoll allie
BrowsePoll jj
BrowseRelay 127.0.0.1 192.168.3.255
```

The first two lines tell the slave's **cupsd** to poll the **cupsd**s on allie and jj for information about the printers they serve. The third line tells copeland to relay all the information it learns to its own subnet.

Need a more sophisticated setup? Multiple queues for one printer, each with different defaults? A single server performing load balancing by parceling out jobs to several printers? Multiple servers each handling interchangeable instances of the same kind of printer? LPD or Windows clients? There's too much variation to go through here, but CUPS handles all of these situations, and the CUPS documentation walks you through the details.

The CUPS underlying protocol: HTTP

HTTP is the underlying protocol for all interactions among CUPS servers and their clients. CUPS servers listen for connections on port 631. Clients submit jobs with the HTTP POST operation. Status requests are implemented through HTTP GET. The CUPS configuration files also look remarkably like Apache configuration files.

Some history may help you understand how this came about.

The earliest commercial UNIX application was document production. Key software included text editors, markup languages (**nroff/troff**), and printing software.

Printers were primitive, and so were the spoolers. This was true for non-UNIX systems, too, though the non-UNIX systems were proprietary: IBM systems knew how to drive IBM printers, Apple computers knew how to drive Apple printers, and so on. The computer you were working on was often assumed (correctly) to be connected directly to the printer. Printer configuration consisted of answering questions such as "Serial or parallel?"

When network printers became available, problems multiplied. Early network printing systems were idiosyncratic and used an assortment of protocols for printer-to-spooler communication, client-to-spooler communication, and network traffic negotiation.

As the complexity of the world increased, several attempts were made to create unified standards, but none achieved universal acceptance. The protocols in use got older and creakier. New printer features such as duplexing also spurred a lot of special-case hacking.

Gritting its teeth, the IETF's Printer Working Group created the Internet Printing Protocol (IPP), which is built on top of HTTP. Not only did this choice structure interactions in terms of simple GET and POST requests, but it also allowed printing to take advantage of standard, widely used technologies for authentication, access control, and encryption.

Michael Sweet and Andrew Senft of Easy Software Products (ESP) brought IPP to UNIX in the form of the CUPS implementation. Today, CUPS is the most complete implementation of IPP on the planet.

Although ESP has its own market niche and products, CUPS is an open source project and is freely redistributable. Most Linux and UNIX systems today use CUPS as their default printing system.

A CUPS server *is* a web server, albeit one that communicates on port 631 instead of port 80. You can verify this by contacting your local CUPS server through a web browser (localhost:631). You'll see that the CUPS server serves up a GUI interface to its full functionality. (You can also use SSL on port 433 for secure communication with printers.) CUPS speaks IPP to web browsers, printers, GUI and CLI tools, and other CUPS servers.

PPD files

When you invoke **kprinter** to print **book.ps** on the color printer Pollux, **kprinter** may come back and ask you what size paper you want to print on. But wait—how does CUPS know to tell its client, **kprinter**, that Pollux can print on A4 paper? How does CUPS know Pollux can handle PostScript, and what should CUPS do if it can't? Where does CUPS find the information that Pollux is a color printer?

All this information is kept in a PostScript Printer Description (PPD) file that describes the attributes and capabilities of a PostScript printer. The CUPS daemon reads the PPDs for its printers and passes information about them to clients and filters as needed.

PPDs were first developed for the Mac world, but they were quickly adopted by Windows software. Each new printer comes with a PPD from the vendor. Mac and Windows printer drivers use the PPD file to figure out how to send PostScript jobs to the printer. For example, it makes no sense to ask a single-sided black-and-white printer sold in America to print a duplex, color document on European B4-sized paper.

Older UNIX and Linux printing systems made no use of PPDs. Users either learned how to massage their PostScript, or they lived with what they got as default output. By contrast, CUPS was built from the ground up to take advantage of this rich source of information. In fact, CUPS depends on PPDs.

Finding PPD files can take a bit of sleuthing. If a PPD is on your machine, it's probably in **/etc/cups/ppd** or **/usr/share/cups/model**. The command **locate .ppd** helps track them down. For network printers, the PPDs are probably stored remotely; CUPS clients get the PPD information from the relevant CUPS server.

PPD files are just text files. It's informative to take a look at one and see the type of information that it contains.

PostScript printers all have vendor-supplied PPDs, which you can get from the installation disk or the vendor's web site. PPDs from the library distributed with CUPS are kept in **/usr/share/cups/model**; CUPS copies PPDs that are currently in use into **/etc/cups/ppd**.

CUPS also uses PPDs to describe printers that lack a PostScript interpreter. An extra field does the trick. Look:

```
$ grep cupsFilter /usr/share/cups/model/pxlmono.ppd
*cupsFilter: "application/vnd.cups-postscript 0 pstopxl"
```

You can **diff** a couple of closely related PPDs (try **pxlmono.ppd** and **pxlcolor.ppd**) to see exactly how two printer types differ.

If your printer vendor doesn't supply a PPD file—probably because the printer doesn't have a PostScript interpreter and the vendor doesn't care about anything but Windows—go to linuxprinting.org and hunt through the Foomatic database for more information. Your printer may also be supported by the Gutenprint project (gutenprint.sourceforge.net, formerly known as Gimp-Print). If you have a choice of PPDs from these sources and your users want every last drop of quality, try each option and see which output looks best.

If a PPD file is nowhere to be found, then

- You should have consulted linuxprinting.org before you got the printer.

- There may well be a generic PPD file that will let you print something, even if it doesn't take advantage of all your printer's features.

- If you enhance a generic PPD file to make it work better with your printer, you should contribute your new PPD to the Foomatic database.

Filters

Rather than using a specialized printing tool for every printer, CUPS uses a chain of filters to convert a file you print into something your printer understands.

The CUPS filter scheme is elegant. When you give CUPS a file to print, it figures out the file's MIME type, the MIME types understood by your printer, and the filters it needs to convert the former to one of the latter.

CUPS uses rules in **/etc/cups/mime.types** to suss out the incoming data type. For example, the rule

```
application/pdf        pdf string (0,%PDF)
```

means "If the file has a **.pdf** extension or starts with the string %PDF, then its MIME type is application/pdf."

CUPS figures out how to convert one data type to another by looking up rules in the file **/etc/cups/mime.convs**. For example,

```
application/pdf          application/postscript 33 pdftops
```

means "To convert an application/pdf file to an application/postscript file, run the filter **pdftops**." The number 33 is the cost of the conversion.

If you need to write your own filters (improbable), do not modify the distributed files. Create an additional set of files with its own basename and put it into **/etc/cups** where CUPS can find the files. CUPS reads all files with the suffixes **.types** and **.convs**, not just **mime.types** and **mime.convs**.

The last components in the CUPS pipeline are the filters that talk directly to the printer. In the PPD of a non-PostScript printer you may see lines such as

```
*cupsFilter: "application/vnd.cups-postscript 0 foomatic-rip"
```

or even

```
*cupsFilter: "application/vnd.cups-postscript foomatic-rip"
```

The quoted string has the same format as a line in **mime.convs**, but there's only one MIME type instead of two. This line advertises that the **foomatic-rip** filter converts data of type application/vnd.cups-postscript to the printer's native data format. The cost is zero (or omitted) because there's only one way to do this step, so why pretend there's a cost? (Gutenprint PPDs for non-PostScript printers are slightly different.)

Given a document and a target printer, CUPS uses the **types** files to figure out the document type. It then consults the PPD to figure out what data type the printer requires. It then uses the **.convs** files to deduce all the filter chains that could convert one to the other, and what each chain would cost. Finally, it picks the lowest-cost chain and passes the document through those filters.

The final filter in the chain passes the printable format to a back end, which communicates this data to the printer by using whatever protocol the printer understands.

To find the filters available on your system, try **locate pstops**. (**pstops** is a popular filter that massages PostScript jobs in various ways, such as adding PostScript commands to set the number of copies. The other filters won't be far away.)

You can ask CUPS for a list of the available back ends by running **lpinfo -v**. If your system lacks a back end for the network protocol you need, it may be available from the web or from the vendor.

23.4 CUPS SERVER ADMINISTRATION

cupsd starts at boot time and runs continuously. All our example Linux distributions are set up this way by default.

The CUPS configuration file is called **cupsd.conf**; it's usually found in **/etc/cups**. The file format is similar to that of the Apache configuration file. If you're comfortable with one of these files, you'll be comfortable with the other.

After you make changes to the config file, run **/etc/init.d/cups restart** to restart the daemon and make your changes take effect. (Debian and Ubuntu distributions use **/etc/init.d/cupsys restart** instead.)

The default config file is well commented. The comments and the **cupsd.conf** man page are good enough that we won't belabor the same information here.

You can edit the CUPS configuration file by hand, or if you have the KDE desktop environment installed, you configure the system through the KDE Print Manager, which is accessible through the KDE control center. The *KDEPrint Handbook* documents the process in detail (see the *Print Server Configuration* chapter) and is a good reference for CUPS variables, their meanings, and their default values.

You can directly run the CUPS-specific portion of the KDE print manager with the **cupsdconf** command. This command is included in most systems' **kdelibs** packages; it is not necessary to install all of KDE to use it.

We don't have production experience with the KDE GUI, but in our testing it complained about not understanding certain options found in the default **cupsd.conf** files on all of our reference systems. On SUSE it refused to run at all, apparently because the line

```
AuthType BasicDigest
```

in **cupsd.conf** caused it to look for the nonexistent file **/etc/passwd.md5**. (Other systems use AuthType Basic as a default.) Your mileage may vary.

Network print server setup

To make CUPS accept print jobs from the network, make two modifications to the **cupsd.conf** file. First, change

```
<Location />
Order Deny,Allow
Deny From All
Allow From 127.0.0.1
</Location>
```

to

```
<Location />
Order Deny,Allow
Deny From All
Allow From 127.0.0.1
Allow From netaddress
</Location>
```

Printing

Replace *netaddress* with the IP address of the network from which to accept print jobs (e.g., 192.168.0.0). Then look for the BrowseAddress keyword and set it to the broadcast address on that network plus the CUPS port:

```
BrowseAddress 192.168.0.255:631
```

These two steps tell the server to accept requests from any machine on the network and to broadcast what it knows about the printers it's serving to every CUPS daemon on the network.

That's it! Once you restart the CUPS daemon, it comes back as a server.

Printer autoconfiguration

You can actually use CUPS without a printer (for example, to convert files to PDF or fax format), but its typical role is to manage real printers. In this section we review the ways in which you can deal with the printers themselves.

In some cases, adding a printer is trivial. CUPS tries to autodetect USB printers when they're plugged in and to figure out what to do with them.

Printer manufacturers typically supply installation software that does most of the setup work for you on Windows and even Mac OS X (which also uses CUPS). However, you can't assume that vendors will handle installation for you on Linux.

Even if you have to do the work yourself, adding a printer often consists of nothing more than plugging in the hardware, connecting to the CUPS web interface at

> localhost:631/admin

and answering a few questions. KDE and GNOME come with their own printer configuration widgets, which you may prefer to the CUPS interface.

If someone else adds a printer and one or more CUPS servers running on the network know about it, your CUPS server will be notified of its existence. You don't need to explicitly add the printer to the local inventory or copy PPDs to your machine. It's all done with mirrors.

Network printer configuration

Network printers need some configuration of their own just to be citizens of the TCP/IP network. In particular, they need to know their IP address and netmask. That information is usually conveyed to them in one of two ways.

Most modern printers can get this information across the network from a BOOTP or DHCP server. This method works well in environments that have many homogeneous printers. See page 311 for more information about DHCP.

Alternatively, you can set a static IP address from the printer's console, which usually consists of a set of buttons on the printer's front panel and a one-line display. Fumble around with the menus until you discover where to set the IP address. (If there is a menu option to print the menus, use it and save the printed version.)

A few printers give you access to a virtual console through a serial port. It's a nice idea, but the total amount of work is probably similar to using the front-panel buttons. The principles are the same.

If all else fails, many printers come with manuals.

Once configured, network printers usually have a "web console" accessible from a browser. However, printers need to have an IP address before you can get to them this way, so there's a bootstrapping issue.

After your printer is on the network and you can ping it, make sure to secure it as described in the section *Secure your printers* on page 787.

Printer configuration examples

As examples, let's add the parallel printer groucho and the network printer fezmo from the command line.

```
# lpadmin -p groucho -E -v parallel:/dev/lp0 -m pxlcolor.ppd
# lpadmin -p fezmo -E -v socket://192.168.0.12 -m laserjet.ppd
```

As you can see, groucho is attached to port **/dev/lp0**, and fezmo is at IP address 192.168.0.12. We specify each device in the form of a universal resource indicator (URI), and choose a PPD from the ones in **/usr/share/cups/model**.

As long as the local **cupsd** has been configured as a network server, it immediately makes the new printers available to other clients on the network.

Instead of using the command-line interface, you can use the web-based configuration tools presented by the CUPS server if you prefer. That's true of all the administrative tasks in this section.

CUPS accepts a wide variety of URIs for printers. Here are a few more examples:

```
ipp://zoe.canary.com/ipp
lpd://riley.canary.com/ps
serial://dev/ttyS0?baud=9600+parity=even+bits=7
socket://gillian.canary.com:9100
usb://XEROX/Phaser%206120?serial=YGG210547
```

Some URIs take options (e.g., serial) and others don't. **lpinfo -v** lists the devices your system can see and the types of URIs that CUPS understands.

Printer class setup

A "class" is a set of printers that share a queue. Jobs in the queue can print on whichever printer becomes available first. The command below creates the class haemer and includes three printers in it: riley, gilly, and zoe.

```
# lpadmin -p riley -c haemer
# lpadmin -p gilly -c haemer
# lpadmin -p zoe -c haemer
```

Printing

Note that there is no explicit step to create the class; the class exists as long as printers are assigned to it. In fact, CUPS is even smarter than that: if multiple printers on a network are all given the same name, CUPS treats them as an implicit class and load-shares jobs among them automatically.

Service shutoff

If you want to remove a printer or class, that's easily done with **lpadmin -x**.

```
# lpadmin -x fezmo
# lpadmin -x haemer
```

But what if that you just want to disable a printer temporarily for service instead of removing it? You can block the print queue at either end. If you disable the tail (the exit or printer side) of the queue, users can still submit jobs, but the jobs will never print. If you disable the head (entrance) of the queue, jobs that are already in the queue will print, but the queue will reject attempts to submit additional jobs.

The **disable** and **enable** commands control the exit side of the queue, and the **reject** and **accept** commands control the submission side. For example:

```
# disable groucho
# reject corbet
```

Which to use? It's a bad idea to accept print jobs that have no hope of being printed in the foreseeable future, so use **reject** for extended downtime. For brief interruptions that should be invisible to users (e.g., clearing a paper jam), use **disable**.

Administrators occasionally ask for a mnemonic to help them remember which commands control which end of the queue. Consider: if CUPS "rejects" a job, that means you can't "inject" it. Another way to keep the commands straight is to remember that accepting and rejecting are things you can do to print jobs, whereas disabling and enabling are things you can do to printers. It doesn't make any sense to "accept" a printer or a print queue.

A word of warning: in addition to being a CUPS command, **enable** is also a **bash** built-in command. **bash** assumes you mean its own **enable** unless you specify the full pathname of the command, **/usr/bin/enable**. As it happens, **bash**'s version of **enable** enables and disables **bash** built-ins, so you can use it to disable itself:[2]

```
$ enable -n enable
```

CUPS itself sometimes temporarily disables a printer that it's having trouble with (e.g., if someone has dislodged a cable). Once you fix the problem, remember to reenable the queue. If you forget, **lpstat** will tell you. (For a more complete discussion of this issue and an alternative approach, see www.linuxprinting.org/beh.html).

---

2. For bonus points, figure out how to reenable **bash**'s built-in **enable** command now that you have blocked access to it. **enable enable** won't work!

Other configuration tasks

Today's printers are heavily configurable, and CUPS lets you tweak a wide variety of features through its web interface and through the **lpadmin** and **lpoptions** commands. As a rule of thumb, **lpadmin** is for system-wide tasks and **lpoptions** is for per-user tasks.

lpadmin lets you restrict access in more fine-grained ways than **disable** and **reject** do. For example, you can set up printing quotas and specify which users can print to which printers.

Paper sizes

In the United States and Canada, the most common paper size is called letter and is 8.5×11 inches. Some Linux distributions (e.g., Knoppix and SUSE) are produced in Europe, where they don't even know what inches are, or in England, where they do know but don't use them to measure paper. In these places, and in Japan, the common paper type is called A4, and printers all come with A4 trays. Ergo, some distributions' printing utilities produce A4 page images by default.

A4 paper makes sense because it's irrational—mathematically, that is. The ratio of length to width of A4 paper is $\sqrt{2}$. If you slice a piece of A4 paper in half horizontally, you get two half-size pieces of paper that have the same length-to-width ratio. This paper size is called A5. Cut A5 in half and you get two sheets of A6. In the other direction, A3 is twice the area of A4, but the same shape, and so on.

In other words, you can manufacture A0 paper, which has an area of 1 square meter, and use a paper cutter to create the other sizes you need. The only common U.S. paper size you can play this kind of game with is ledger (11×17 inches, also known as tabloid), which you can slice in half to get two sheets of letter.

There are also an ISO B series and C series that preserve the 1:$\sqrt{2}$ aspect ratio but have different base areas. B0 is 1 m in height and C0 paper has an area of $2^{1/4}$ m². Engineers will see immediately that the sides of Bn paper are the geometric means of An-1 and An sides, while Cn paper sides are the geometric means of An and Bn.

What does all this mean? Bn has the same look as An but is bigger, and Cn is intermediate between the two. A report on A4 paper fits beautifully in a C4 manila folder. Folding an A4 letter down the middle to make it A5 lets it slide into a C5 envelope. Fold it again and it slides just as nicely into a C6 envelope.

To confuse things slightly, Japan has its own B series that's slightly different. Although it has the same aspect ratio as the ISO papers, Japanese B4 paper size is the arithmetic mean of A3 and A4, which makes it slightly larger than ISO B4 paper. There is no Japanese C series.

Just as the ISO system makes it easy to copy two pages of a B5 textbook onto a single B4 handout, it makes all types of n-up printing (printing several reduced-sized page images on the same page) trivial. European copiers often have buttons that reduce or expand by a factor of $\sqrt{2}$.

If your system has the **paperconf** command installed, you can use the command to print the dimensions of various named papers in inches, centimeters, or printer's points (72nds of an inch). For the Americans, Table 23.1 lists some typical uses for common sizes to give a sense of their scale.

Table 23.1   Common uses for ISO paper sizes

Sizes	Common uses
A0, A1	Posters
A3, B4	Newspapers
A4	Generic "pieces of paper"
A5	Note pads (roughly 5×8 inches)
B5, B6	Books, postcards, German toilet paper
A7	"3×5" index cards
B7	Passports (even U.S. passports are B7)
A8	Business cards
B8	Playing cards

Unfortunately, A4 paper is slightly thinner and longer (8.3 x 11.7 inches) than American letter paper. Printing an A4 document on letter paper typically cuts off vital slivers such as headers, footers, and page numbers. Conversely, if you're in Europe or Japan and try to print American pages on A4 paper, you may have the sides of your documents chopped off (though the problem is less severe).

Individual software packages may have their own defaults regarding paper size. For example, GNU **enscript** is maintained in Finland by Markku Rossi and defaults to A4 paper. If you're American and your distribution hasn't compiled **enscript** with a different default, one option is to grab the source code and reconfigure it. Typically, however, it's easier to set the paper type on the command line or in a GUI configuration file. If your documents come out with the ends or sides cut off, paper size conflicts are a likely explanation.

You may also be able to adjust the default paper size for many printing tasks with the **paperconfig** command, the PAPERSIZE environment variable, or the contents of the **/etc/papersize** file. (Note: **paperconfig** != **paperconf**)

Compatibility commands

In the old days, there were two competing printing systems: one found on BSD UNIX systems, the other found on System V UNIX systems. The two systems each maintained relatively simple print queues and provided commands to create, delete, start, stop, and pause the queues and to queue or dequeue individual jobs.

You may ask, why were there two systems and was there any significant difference between them? Stand up in the middle of a Linux users group meeting and yell "Anyone who uses **vi** is an idiot!"—then come ask us again.

Wisely, CUPS provides compatibility commands that replace both systems. Part of the motivation is to grease the path for old-timers who are used to previous systems, but compatibility with existing software is also an important goal.

To be sure, these commands don't always do everything the originals did, and some less-used and vendor-specific commands aren't yet implemented. Still, many scripts that use these commands work just fine with CUPS. Think of what's missing as an opportunity: if you want to contribute to world peace and Pareto optimality, there's still code left for you to write.

Table 23.2 lists the CLI commands that come with CUPS and classifies them according to their origin.

Table 23.2   CUPS command-line utilities and their origins

	Command	Function
CUPS	**lpinfo**	Shows available devices or drivers
	lpoptions	Displays or sets printer options and defaults
	lppasswd	Adds, changes, or deletes digest passwords
	cupsdconf[a]	Is a CUPS configuration tool
	cups-config[a]	Prints cups API, compiler, directory, and link information
System V	**lp**	Prints files
	cancel	Cancels jobs
	accept, **reject**	Accepts or rejects queue submissions
	disable, **enable**	Stops or starts printers and classes
	lpstat	Prints CUPS status information
	lpadmin	Configures CUPS printers and classes
	lpmove	Moves a job to a new destination
BSD	**lpr**	Prints files
	lprm	Cancels print jobs
	lpq	Displays printer queue status
	lpc	Is a general printer control program

a. Don't confuse these similar names. **cupsdconf** is a GUI tool in KDEPrint, and **cups-config** is a CLI tool included with CUPS.

Common printing software

There's more to printing than just spooling and printing jobs. Even on a stock Ubuntu system, the command

```
$ man -k . | egrep -i 'ghostscript|cups|print(er|ing| *(job|queue|filter))'
```

lists more than 88 printing-related man pages—and that's just a quick and dirty search. (Speaking of printing-related commands, ponder the fact that the **print** command has nothing to do with printing.) Several of these commands and tools are worth knowing about.

pr is one of the oldest printing tools. It reformats text files for the printed page. It breaks its input into pagefuls of 66 lines, adds headers and footers, and can double-space text. It's perfect for minor massaging of text files on their way to the printer.

Adobe's **enscript** command performs similar conversions with quite a few more bells and whistles; it's output is also PostScript. GNU **enscript** is an open source version of this command that is backward compatible with Adobe's; however, GNU **enscript** offers a wealth of new features, including language-sensitive highlighting, support for various paper sizes, font downloading, and user-defined headers.

One of **enscript**'s main claims to fame was its implementation of 2-up printing. If you're still using **enscript** because of this feature, try CUPS's **-o number-up=2** option to **lpr**.

At the high end of the complexity spectrum is Ghostscript, originally written by L. Peter Deutsch so he could print PostScript documents on inexpensive PCL printers. Today, Ghostscript interprets both PostScript and PDF. CUPS uses it as a filter, but Ghostscript can also create page images for the screen, either on its own or with help from front ends such as **gv**, GNOME Ghostview (**ggv**), or KDE's KGhostView.

Linux distributions all come with a free version of Ghostscript; for more information, see www.ghostscript.com. A commercial version of Ghostscript with support is available from Artifex Software.

CUPS documentation

There's no shortage of CUPS documentation, but sometimes you have to hunt for it. Man pages, such as those for **lpr**, can be sketchy. If you don't find something in a man page, don't assume you can't do it; google it.

The CUPS installation comes with many manuals in PDF and HTML format. One place to see these is to connect to a CUPS server and click the link for on-line help. Unfortunately, this isn't any help if your problem is connecting to the CUPS server.

The same documentation can be found at www.cups.org. It should also be located under **/usr/share/doc/cups**. If your distribution doesn't have it installed there, try

```
$ locate doc | grep cups
```

Another option is to ask your distribution's package manager.

23.5 TROUBLESHOOTING TIPS

Always remember to restart **cupsd** after changing its configuration file. Your best bet for restarting is to run **/etc/init.d/cups restart** (**/etc/init.d/cupsys restart** on Debian and Ubuntu). You can also restart the daemon through the KDE Print Manager application. In theory you can also send **cupsd** a HUP signal, but this seems to just kill the daemon on SUSE systems.

CUPS logging

CUPS maintains three logs: a page log, an access log, and an error log. The page log is a list of pages printed. The other two are just like the access log and error log for Apache. Not surprising, since the CUPS server is a web server.

The **cupsd.conf** file specifies the logging level and the locations of the log files. They're all typically kept underneath **/var/log**.

Here's an excerpt from a log file that corresponds to a single print job:

```
I [26/Jul/2006:18:59:08 -0600] Adding start banner page "none" to job 24.
I [26/Jul/2006:18:59:08 -0600] Adding end banner page "none" to job 24.
I [26/Jul/2006:18:59:08 -0600] Job 24 queued on 'Phaser_6120' by 'jsh'.
I [26/Jul/2006:18:59:08 -0600] Started filter /usr/libexec/cups/filter/pstops (PID
    19985) for job 24.
I [26/Jul/2006:18:59:08 -0600] Started backend /usr/libexec/cups/backend/usb
    (PID 19986) for job 24.
```

Problems with direct printing

To verify the physical connection to a local printer, you can directly run the printer's back end. For example, here's what we get when we execute the back end for a USB-connected printer:

```
$ /usr/lib/cups/backend/usb
direct usb "Unknown" "USB Printer (usb)"
direct usb://XEROX/Phaser%206120?serial=YGG210547 "XEROX Phaser 6120"
    "Phaser 6120"
```

When the USB cable accidentally pulls out (or breaks), the line for that printer drops out of the back end's output:

```
$ /usr/lib/cups/backend/usb
direct usb "Unknown" "USB Printer (usb)"
```

Network printing problems

Before you start tracking down a network printing problem, make sure you can print from the machine that actually hosts the printer. Your "network printing problem" may just be a "printing problem." Also make sure that the network is up.

Next, try connecting to the hosting **cupsd** with a web browser (*hostname*:631) or the **telnet** command (**telnet** *hostname* **631**).

If you have problems debugging a network printer connection, keep in mind that there must be a queue for the job on some machine, a way to decide where to send the job, and a method of sending the job to the machine that hosts the print queue. On the print server, there must be a place to queue the job, sufficient permissions to allow the job to be printed, and a way to output to the device.

Printing

To track down these problems, you may have to look in several places:

- System log files on the sending machine, for name resolution and permission problems

- System log files on the print server, for permission problems

- CUPS log files on the sending machine, for missing filters, unknown printers, missing directories, etc.

- CUPS log files on the print server machine, for messages about bad device names, incorrect formats, etc.

The system log files' locations are specified in **/etc/syslog.conf**. The locations of CUPS log files are specified in **/etc/cups/cupsd.conf**.

Distribution-specific problems

CUPS is still evolving and bug fixes are released frequently. Some problems are worse than others, and some have security implications. On some older versions of Red Hat, CUPS is badly broken. The right solution for those systems is an OS upgrade. But if you can't install a newer release of Red Hat or Fedora, try getting the current release for CUPS.

Easy Software Products sells a commercial version of CUPS called ESP PrintPro that supports a much wider range of printers than the free version. If you have to support an unusual printer and you can't find the necessary drivers on the web, ESP may already have it running. They also sell support. Check them out at www.easysw.com.

23.6 PRINTER PRACTICALITIES

Dealing with printers can bring troubles and frustrations. Here are some general guidelines to help limit those. When all else fails, just be glad you're not still using a dot-matrix printer connected via an RS-232 serial port. Unless, of course, you are.

Printer selection

Before you buy a printer or accept a "free" printer that someone else is throwing away, go to the Foomatic database at linuxprinting.org and check to see how well the printer is supported under Linux. The database classifies printers into four categories ranging from Paperweight to Perfectly; you want Perfectly.

CUPS likes PostScript printers. Configuration of these printers is typically easy.

Non-PostScript printers are also supported, but not as well. To print to these, you need software that converts print jobs into the printer's preferred PDL or data format. Chances are, this software is available either from the CUPS distribution or from one of the other locations mentioned in this chapter.

GDI printers

Windows still holds an advantage in a couple of areas, one of which is its support for very low-end printers. The el cheapo printers used on Windows systems are known collectively as GDI printers or WinPrinters. These printers have very little built-in intelligence and lack interpreters for any real PDL. They expect rasterization to be performed by the host computer.

Some of the information needed to communicate with GDI printers is hidden in proprietary, Windows-specific code. Such secrecy hinders efforts to develop Linux support for these devices, but the open-source community has demonstrated a remarkable aptitude for reverse engineering. CUPS supports many WinPrinters.

A second area of strength for Windows is its support for brand-new printers. Just as with new video and audio cards, new printers are first released with Windows drivers, which fully support all the model's documented and undocumented features. Linux support generally lags. If you buy a fancy, just-released printer because you need its advanced features, you may have to resign yourself to driving it from Windows for a while.

Double-sided printing

A duplexer is a hardware component that lets a printer print on both sides of the page. Some printers include them by default, and others support them as an optional add-on.

If you don't have access to (or can't afford) a printer that duplexes, you can run paper through the printer once to print the odd pages, then flip the paper over and run it a second time for the even pages. Experiment with a two-page document to find out which way to flip the paper, then tape instructions to the printer.

A variety of printing software can help with this; for example, Ghostview (**gv**) has icons to let you mark either set and an option to print only marked pages. The CUPS versions of **lp** and **lpr** handle this task with the options **-o page-set=odd** and **-o page-set=even**. You can enshrine these options in a "printer instance" if you use them frequently; see page 768.

Some printers, particularly inexpensive laser printers, are not designed with double-sided printing in mind. Their manufacturers often warn of the irreparable damage that is sure to attend printing on both sides of the page. We have never actually seen a case of such damage, but surely the printer manufacturers wouldn't steer you wrong. Would they?

Other printer accessories

In addition to duplexers, many printers let you add memory, extra paper trays, hard disks, and other accessories. These upgrades can permit jobs to print that would be otherwise indigestible, or they can let jobs print more efficiently. If you have problems getting jobs to print, review the error logs to see if more printer memory might help resolve the problem. See *CUPS logging* on page 781.

Serial and parallel printers

If your printer is directly attached to your computer with a cable, it's using some form of serial or parallel connection.

Although the parallel standard has not aged gracefully, it does provide us with ports that require relatively little tinkering. If you have a parallel printer, it will probably be easy to set up—as long as your computer has a parallel port, too.

A serial connection on Mac hardware could be FireWire, but serial connections in the Linux world typically use USB. Check the database of supported USB devices at www.qbik.ch/usb/devices or www.linux-usb.org to see the status of your hardware.

You almost certainly do not have an old-fashioned RS-232 serial printer. If you do, it can require a mess of extra configuration. The spooler software has to know the appropriate values for the baud rate and other serial options so that it can communicate properly with the printer. You specify all these options in the URI for the device. See the on-line *CUPS Software Administrators Manual* for details. It may be faster to buy a different kind of printer than to figure out the exact combination of serial magic needed to get things working.

Network printers

Many printers contain full-fledged network interfaces that allow them to sit directly on a network and accept jobs through one or more network or printing protocols. Data can be sent to network-attached printers much faster than to printers connected to serial or parallel ports.

23.7 OTHER PRINTER ADVICE

Some administrative issues related to printing transcend the details of Linux and CUPS. For the most part, these issues arise because printers are temperamental mechanical devices that cost money every time they are used.

Use banner pages only if you have to

CUPS can print header and trailer pages for each job that show the title of the job and the user who submitted it. These banner pages are sometimes useful for separating jobs on printers used by many different people, but in most cases they're a waste of time, toner, and paper.

We suggest that you turn off banner pages globally in the CUPS GUI (or by running **lpadmin**), then turn them on for any individual jobs that might benefit from them:

```
$ lpr -o job-sheets=confidential gilly.ps
```

You can also turn on banners for individual users by using **lpoptions**. Another alternative to consider is a printer instance that adds banner pages to jobs (see *Printer instances* on page 768).

If needed, you can create custom banner pages by copying one of the existing ones from **/usr/share/cups/banners** and modifying it. Put the new page in with the others under a new name.

Provide recycling bins

All kinds of computer paper are recyclable. You can use the boxes that paper comes in as recycling bins; the paper fits in them perfectly. Post a sign asking that no foreign material (such as staples, paper clips, or newspaper) be discarded there.

Use previewers

Users often print a document, find a small error in the formatting, fix it, and then reprint the job. This waste of paper and time can easily be avoided with software that lets users see, on-screen, what the printed output will look like.

Having previewers isn't enough; your users have to know how to use them. They're usually happy to learn. One use of accounting records is to check for cases in which the same document has been printed repeatedly. That's sometimes a pointer to a user who doesn't know about previewers.

Previewing is built into many modern WYSIWYG editors, browsers, and print-job aggregators. For other types of documents, your options vary. Tools such as Ghostview (**gv**) preview random PostScript and PDF documents. For **roff**, pipe the output of **groff** into Ghostview; for TeX output, try **xdvi**, **kdvi**, or Evince.

Buy cheap printers

Printer hardware technology is mature. You don't need to spend a lot of money for good output and reliable mechanics.

Don't splurge on an expensive "workgroup" printer unless you need it. If you're only printing text, an inexpensive "personal" printer can produce good-quality output, be nearly as fast and reliable, and weigh tens of pounds less. A 10-page-a-minute printer can serve about five full-time writers. You may be better off buying five $250 printers for a group of 25 writers than one $1,250 printer.

In general, don't buy a printer (or a hard disk, or memory) from a computer manufacturer. Their printers are usually just rebranded commodity printers at twice the price. PostScript printers manufactured for the PC and Macintosh markets and sold independently are usually better deals. (Some companies, like HP, manufacture both computers and printers. They're fine.)

Even if you stick to mainstream brands, no individual manufacturer is a universally safe bet. We have had excellent experiences with HP laser printers. They are solid products, and HP has been very aggressive in supporting both Linux and CUPS. Even so, some of HP's printers have been complete disasters. Look for reviews on the Internet before buying.

Here, too, cheap is an advantage: a $250 mistake is easier to recover from than a $1,250 mistake.

Keep extra toner cartridges on hand

Laser printers occasionally need their toner cartridges replaced. Faded or blank areas on the page are hints that the printer is running out of toner. Buy replacement cartridges before you need them. In a pinch, remove the cartridge from the printer and gently rock it to redistribute the remaining toner particles. You can often get another hundred pages out of a cartridge this way.

Streaks and spots probably mean you should clean your printer. Look on the printer to see if there is a "clean" cycle. If not or if the cleaning cycle doesn't help, read the manufacturer's cleaning instructions carefully, or pay to have the printer serviced.

Printer manufacturers hate the use of recycled and aftermarket cartridges, and they go to great lengths to try to prevent it. Many devices use "keyed" consumables whose identities are detected—electronically or physically—by the printer. Even if two printers look identical (such as the Xerox Phaser 6120 and the Konica-Minolta Magicolor 2450), it doesn't necessarily mean you can use the same cartridges in both.

Sometimes you can do surgery to convert one vendor's cartridges for another's printer, but it helps to know what you're doing. Usually, you just make a mess. If you spill toner, vacuum up as much of the material as possible and wipe up the remainder with cold water. Contrary to common belief, laser printer toner is not a health or environmental hazard, although as with all fine powders, it's best to avoid breathing the toner dust.

When you replace a cartridge, save the box and baggie the new cartridge came in to use when recycling the spent one. Then look at the phone book or the web to find a company to take the old cartridge off your hands.

Keyed consumables have spurred the growth of companies ("punch and pours") that refill old cartridges for a fraction of the new-cartridge price. Cartridge recyclers are usually also punch-and-pours, so you can recycle your old cartridges and get replacements at the same time.

Opinions on the quality and lifespan of recycled cartridges vary. One punch-and-pour we know won't refill color toner cartridges or sell remanufactured ones because they believe the savings are less than the increased maintenance costs for the printers that use them.

Pay attention to the cost per page

Printer manufacturers use what MBAs call "metering" to make the total cost of the product scale as linearly as possible with the amount of use the customer gets out of it. That's why toner and ink are extortionately expensive and fancy printer hardware is sometimes sold below its manufacturing cost.

As of this writing, one manufacturer is selling a color laser printer for $299. A full set of replacement cartridges for it costs $278. You can buy an inkjet printer for less than $50 at Wal-Mart, but it won't be long before you need to buy a set of replacement ink cartridges that cost more than the printer.

You can feign outrage over this, but printer companies have to make their money on something. Cheaper cartridges would just mean pricier printers. A good rule of thumb is that inkjet printers are cheap as long as you don't print with them; laser printers have a higher initial cost, but the consumables are cheaper and last longer.

A full-color page from an inkjet printer can cost 20–50 times as much as an analogous print from a laser printer. It also requires special paper and prints more slowly. Inkjet cartridges empty quickly and frequently plug up or go bad. The ink runs when wet—don't use an inkjet to print out a recipe book for use in the kitchen. On the other hand, you can now get photo prints from an inkjet that look just as good as prints from a photo lab. Color laser photos? Not so nice.

All printers have failure-prone mechanical parts. Cheap printers break faster.

In other words, it's all tradeoffs. For low-volume, personal use—printing a web page or two a day or printing a couple of rolls of film a month—a low-cost, general-purpose inkjet is an excellent choice.

Next time you go printer shopping, estimate how long you want to keep your printer, how much printing you do, and what kind of printing you need before you buy. Assess quantitatively the long-term cost per page for each candidate printer. And ask your local punch-and-pour whether they remanufacture cartridges for the printer, and at what price.

Consider printer accounting

At medium-to-large installations, consider using printer accounting even if you don't plan to charge for printer use. The per-job overhead is unimportant, and you get to see who is using the printer. Demographic information about the sources of print jobs is valuable when you are planning deployment of new printers.

Several printer accounting packages (such as **accsnmp** and PyKota) have been developed for CUPS. ESP provides a central, searchable list of links to these and other CUPS-related products at www.easysw.com/~mike/cups/links.php

Secure your printers

Network printers typically support remote management. You can configure and monitor them over the net through IPP or SNMP, or from a web browser using HTTP. Through the remote interface, you can set parameters such as the printer's IP address, default gateway, syslog server, SNMP community name, protocol options, and administrative password.

By default, most remotely administrable printers are unprotected and must have a password (or perhaps an SNMP "community name") assigned as part of the installation process. The installation manuals from your printer manufacturer should explain how to do this on any particular printer, but GUI administration tools in CUPS and KDE Print Manager are increasingly able to hide vendor variations from you. Expect this trend to continue.

Printing

23.8 PRINTING UNDER KDE

We've mentioned KDE in passing several times in this chapter.[3] The KDE printing facilities are really pretty nice, however, and they deserve a bit more exposition. KDE has put a lot of effort into making its printing tools and interfaces independent of the underlying printing system. It was built after CUPS became popular, so it can handle all of CUPS's features. It works, however, with everything from LPRng to a generic external program.

GNOME's printing facilities have lagged KDE's, but the GNOME developers want users to have a good printing experience, too. Development is proceeding rapidly; by the time you read this, GNOME's printing features may rival KDE's. One reader of an early draft of this chapter noted the irony that CUPS replaced "warring print standards that had no reason to live but refused to die," only to pave the way for competition between suites of desktop printing utilities.

KDEPrint is the overarching framework for printing under KDE. KDEPrint provides tools for adding printers, administering print jobs, restarting print servers, and so on. Yes, CUPS lets you do all this too; the KDEPrint tools are there for two reasons.

First, they have a KDE look and feel, which offers consistency for KDE users. For example, the **kghostview** tool wraps Ghostview in a more KDE-appropriate skin. (You've probably noticed that even KDE utility *names* have a distinctive look and feel. Someone recently asked us if **ksh** was a KDE application.)

Second, KDEPrint is spooler-independent. If for some reason you don't run CUPS (or worse, you have to switch back and forth between print systems), you can still use KDEPrint to manage your printing. Be forewarned that CUPS is more capable than other printing systems, so if you have to downshift to an alternative printing system, some of KDEPrint's functionality may disappear.

Why should you worry about all these GUI interfaces if you do your printing work in the shell? Well, your users probably won't be using the shell interface, so you may end up having to know something about the KDE interface just to support them.

Here are the major components of KDEPrint that you should know about:

- **kprinter**, a GUI tool that submits print jobs

- The Add Printer wizard, which autodetects network printers (JetDirect, IPP, and SMB) and some locally connected printers. The Add Printer wizard also lets you add and configure printers that it doesn't autodetect.

- The Print Job Viewer, which moves and cancels print jobs and shows print job status information

---

3. KDE is a set of libraries and user interface standards for graphical interfaces running under the X Window System, the technology on which all Linux GUIs are based. It's an alternative to the GNOME system, which is most distributions' default. Despite appearances, it is not really necessary to choose between KDE and GNOME. For a more general description of GNOME and KDE, see page 757.

- The *KDEPrint Handbook,* which documents the system. It's available through the KDE Help Center but can be annoyingly hard to find. An easier route is to invoke something like **kprinter** and click on Help. Another alternative is to run **konqueror help:/kdeprint**. Another source of KDE-Print documentation is printing.kde.org.

- The Print Manager, which is the main GUI management tool for the printing system. It, too, can be a bit hard to find. You can poke around in your main desktop menu, although the location in the menu tree varies from distribution to distribution. Another option is to run **kcmshell printmgr** or **konqueror print:/manager**.

The Add Printer wizard and the Print Job Manager are accessible through either **kprinter** or the KDE Print Manager. (Not to mention the URLs **print:/manager** and **print:/printers** in Konqueror.)

Per-user information for KDEPrint is stored under **~/.kde**. The files are human-readable but designed to be changed through the Print Manager. Tinker with them at your peril.

kprinter: printing documents

kprinter is a GUI replacement for **lpr**. It can be used from the command line in similar ways. You can even suppress the GUI;

```
$ kprinter --nodialog -5 -P lj4600 riley.ps gillian.pdf zoe.prn
```

is equivalent to

```
$ lpr -5 -P lj4600 riley.ps gillian.pdf zoe.prn
```

Your users probably want a GUI. Show them how to drag files from a file manager or desktop into the **kprinter** dialog, then print the entire batch. Replace **lpr** with **kprinter** in their browser's print dialog, and they'll have a GUI print dialog. Teach them to click on their "Keep this dialog open after printing" check box, and they won't even have the delay of restarting the program every time they want to print.

Note the "Print system currently in use" menu, evidence of KDEPrint's system neutrality. Note also that **kprinter** offers print-to-PDF and print-to-fax functions even without an actual printer. The advanced options are also worth a look; you can queue your resume for printing and specify that it be printed after your boss goes home.

Konqueror and printing

Many web browsers recognize a set of special-purpose URIs that act as gateways to idiosyncratic functionality. You've probably at least tried about:config and about:mozilla in Firefox. Similarly, the print: family of URIs is Konqueror's gateway to KDEPrint.

The print:/ URL shows you all the possibilities. print:/jobs monitors print jobs, and print:/manager starts the Print Manager inside of Konqueror.

Printing

Note that you're not dealing with CUPS here, at least not directly. This is all part of the KDEPrint layer.

23.9 RECOMMENDED READING

Sweet, Michael. *CUPS: Common UNIX Printing System*. Indianapolis, Indiana: Sams Publishing, 2001. This is the CUPS bible, right from the horse's mouth.

We've mentioned linuxprinting.org several times in this chapter. It's a vast collection of Linux printing resources and a good place to start when answering questions. This site also has a nice CUPS tutorial that includes a troubleshooting section.

Wikipedia and SUSE both supply good CUPS overviews:

> en.opensuse.org/SDB:CUPS_in_a_Nutshell
> en.wikipedia.org/wiki/Common_Unix_Printing_System

You can find a collection of CUPS-related newsgroups at cups.org/newsgroups.php. This is a good place to ask questions, but do your homework first and ask politely.

KDE includes man pages for the KDEPrint commands and the *KDEPrint Handbook*. You can find additional information at printing.kde.org. All of these sources contain useful references to other documentation. (Even if you don't have KDE, the KDE documentation contains good, general information about CUPS.)

23.10 EXERCISES

E23.1 Using a web browser, visit a CUPS server on your network. What prevents you from making administrative changes to that server's printers?

E23.2 Find someone who isn't computer literate (an art student, your mother, or perhaps a Microsoft Certified Professional) and teach that person how to print a PDF document on a Linux system. Did your subject find any of the steps confusing? How could you make the process easier for other users?

E23.3 Visit a real or virtual big-box store such as Sam's Club or Amazon.com and list the printers you can buy for under $200. If you had to purchase one of these printers for your organization tomorrow, which one would it be and why? Justify your analysis with data from the linuxprinting.org database.

E23.4 You have been asked to design the system software for a Linux-based laser printer aimed at the corporate workgroup market. What Linux distribution will you start with? What additional software will you include, and what software will you have to write? How will you accommodate Windows and Mac OS clients? (Hint: check out Linux distributions designed for "embedded systems.")

24 *Maintenance and Environment*

With the influx of desktop workstations and the move away from big-iron comput-ing, it once appeared that the days of the central machine room (aka "data center") might be numbered. Never fear! Over the last decade, those desktop systems have become increasingly dependent on a nucleus of central servers running operating systems such as Linux. As a result, herds of servers can now be found roaming those once-abandoned machine rooms.

It's as important as ever to ensure a healthy, well-maintained environment for these servers. In fact, the power and air conditioning requirements of a rack of the latest 1U servers[1] often meet or exceed the demands of the mainframes they replace.

This chapter offers some hints on handling and maintaining hardware, as well as on giving it a good home.

24.1 HARDWARE MAINTENANCE BASICS

Hardware maintenance was traditionally covered by an expensive annual mainte-nance contract. Although such contracts are still readily available, today it is more common and cost effective to use the "fly by the seat of your pants" approach.

See page 926 for more information about retiring hardware.

If you keep a log book, a quick glance at the records for the last six to twelve months will give you an idea of your failure rates. It's a good idea to keep a careful record of failures and replacements so that you can accurately evaluate the different mainte-nance options available to you. Some parts fail more often than anticipated by the

---

1. One "U" is 1.75 vertical inches and is the standard unit of measurement for rack space.

manufacturer, so contracts are sometimes not only convenient but also financially advantageous. But remember, there comes a time when all hardware should be replaced, not maintained. Know your hardware and let it go gracefully when its time has finally come. You might even consider donating outdated equipment to your local university or school. For them, equipment is rarely too old to be useful.

When planning your maintenance strategy, consider which components are most likely to suffer from premature aging. Devices that include moving parts tend to be far less reliable than solid-state devices such as CPUs and memory. Here are some common candidates for the old folks farm:

- Tape drives
- Tape autoloaders and changers
- Hard disk drives
- Fans
- Keyboards
- Mice
- CRT monitors

24.2 MAINTENANCE CONTRACTS

Several major companies offer hardware maintenance on computer equipment that they do not sell. These vendors are often anxious to displace the original manufacturer and get their foot in the door, so to speak. You can sometimes negotiate attractive maintenance contracts by playing a manufacturer against a third-party provider. If possible, get references on all potential maintenance vendors, preferably from people you know and trust.

On-site maintenance

If you have an on-site maintenance contract, a service technician will bring spare parts directly to your machine. Guaranteed response time varies between 4 and 24 hours; it's usually spelled out in the contract. Response times during business hours may be shorter than at other times of the week.

If you are considering a quick-response maintenance contract, it's usually worth calculating the cost of keeping a couple of complete backup systems around that you can swap in to replace malfunctioning computers. A whole-system swap usually achieves faster repair than even the most deluxe maintenance contract can, and with today's low hardware prices, the investment is often minimal.

Board swap maintenance

A board swap program requires you and your staff to diagnose problems, perhaps with the help of hotline personnel at the manufacturer's site. After diagnosis, you call a maintenance number, describe the problem, and order the necessary replacement board. It is usually shipped immediately and arrives the next day. You then install the board, get the hardware back up and happy, and return the old board in the same box in which the new board arrived.

The manufacturer will usually want to assign a "return merchandise authorization" (RMA) number to the transaction. Be sure to write that number on the shipping documents when you return the bad board.

Warranties

The length of the manufacturer's warranty should play a significant role in your computation of a machine's lifetime cost of ownership. In most cases, the best maintenance scheme is probably the "selective warranty" strategy. Disk drive manufacturers offer warranties up to five years long, and some memory modules even come with a lifetime guarantee. A year's warranty is standard for computers, but warranties of several years or more are not uncommon. When purchasing new equipment, shop around for the best warranty—it will save you money in the long run.

In a many organizations, it seems to be easier to get funding for capital equipment than for support personnel or maintenance. We have occasionally paid for an "extended warranty" option on new hardware (which could also be described as prepaid maintenance) to convert equipment dollars to maintenance dollars.

With many pieces of hardware, the biggest maintenance and reliability problems occur soon after installation. Hardware failures that occur within a day or two of deployment are referred to as "infant mortality."

24.3 ELECTRONICS-HANDLING LORE

Circuit boards and other electronic devices should be handled gently, not dropped, not have coffee spilled on them, not have books piled on them, etc. Most customer engineers (those friendly repair people that come with your maintenance contract) are ten times rougher on equipment than seems reasonable.

Static electricity

Electronic parts are sensitive to static electricity. To handle components safely, you must ground yourself before and during installation. A ground strap worn on the wrist and attached to "earth ground" (usually available as the third prong of your power outlet) protects you appropriately.

Remember that you need to worry about static when you first open the package containing an electronic component and any time the component is handled—not just when you finally install it. Be especially careful if the office where you receive your mail (and where you might be tempted to open your packages) is carpeted; carpet generates more static electricity than does a hard floor.

One way to reduce static on carpeted floors is to purchase a spray bottle at your local Wal-Mart and fill it with one part Downy fabric softener to 30 parts water. Spray this on the carpet (but not on computing equipment) once every month to keep static

Maintenance

levels low. This procedure also leaves your office area with that all-important April-fresh scent.

Reseating boards

You can occasionally fix a hardware problem by simply powering down the equipment, cleaning the contacts on the edge connectors of the interface cards (SCSI, Ethernet, etc.), reseating the cards, and powering the system back up. If this works temporarily but the same problem comes back a week or a month later, the electrical contact between the card and the motherboard is probably poor.

You can clean contacts with a special cleaning solution and cleaning kit or with an ordinary pencil eraser. Don't use an eraser that is old and hard. If your eraser doesn't work well erasing pencil marks from paper, it won't work well on electrical contacts either. Try to keep your fingers off the contacts. Just "erase" them with the pencil eraser (a mild abrasive), brush off the eraser droppings, and reinstall the card.

24.4 MONITORS

Over the last few years, we've been fortunate to see the prices of LCD monitors decline to a level at which they can be widely deployed. Although the initial cost of LCDs is slightly higher than that of CRTs, these devices require less power, less maintenance, and typically cause less eye strain than their CRT-based predecessors. If you still have CRT monitors in your organization, a good maintenance plan is to simply replace them with LCD monitors.

If you are still forced to maintain CRT monitors, be aware that many of them have brightness and convergence adjustments that are accessible only from the circuit board. Unfortunately, CRT monitors often use internal charges of tens of thousands of volts that can persist long after the power has been disconnected. Because of the risk of electric shock, we recommend that you always have your monitors adjusted by a qualified technician. Do not attempt the job yourself.

24.5 MEMORY MODULES

Today's hardware accepts memory in the form of SIMMs (Single Inline Memory Modules), DIMMs (Dual Inline Memory Modules), or RIMMs (Rambus Inline Memory Modules) rather than individual chips. These modules range in size from 32MB to 4GB, all on one little stick.

If you need to add memory to a workstation or server, you can usually order it from a third-party vendor and install it yourself. Be cautious of buying memory from computer vendors; their prices are often quite imaginative.[2] When adding memory, think big. The price of memory is continually decreasing, but so is the standard allotment of expansion slots on a typical motherboard.

2. It's a different story if the memory is part of a package deal; some of these deals are pretty good.

It's worth double-checking your system documentation before ordering memory to make sure you have a clear idea of the types of memory modules that your systems will accept. You can often increase performance by installing memory that supports a higher bus rate or special features such as DDR (Double Data Rate). Make sure that you know how many memory slots each system has available and whether there are any restrictions on the addition of new modules. Some systems require modules to be added in pairs; others do not strictly require this but can yield higher performance when modules are paired.

Make sure that you understand how old and new memory modules will interact with each other. In most cases, only the features or speeds common to all modules can actually be used. It may sometimes be worthwhile to remove a system's original memory when upgrading.

If you install your own memory, keep in mind that memory is more sensitive than anything else to static electricity. Make sure you're well grounded before opening a baggie full of memory.

Memory modules are frequently a candidate for the pencil eraser cleaning technology described earlier in this chapter.

24.6 PREVENTIVE MAINTENANCE

It may sound primitive (and some of us thought we'd outgrow this affliction), but many pieces of hardware have air filters that must be regularly cleaned or changed. Clogged filters impede the flow of air and may result in overheating, a major cause of equipment failure. It's important to keep the air vents on all equipment open and unobstructed, but pay special attention to those servers that have been densely packed into small 1U or 2U enclosures. These systems depend on their ventilation to cool themselves. Without it, a core meltdown is assured.

Anything with moving parts may need regular lubrication, cleaning, and belt maintenance. Listen for squeaks from your older equipment and pamper it accordingly.

On server systems, the part that most frequently fails is the fan and power supply module—especially on PCs, where it is often a single field-replaceable unit (FRU). Periodically check your servers to make sure their main fans are spinning fast and strong. If not, you must usually replace the entire power supply assembly. Otherwise, you run the risk of overheating your equipment. Do not try to lubricate the fan itself; this procedure might postpone the inevitable breakdown, but it could also accelerate the problem or cause damage to other components.

Many PC cases provide a convenient mounting location for a second fan (and electrical connections to power it). If noise is not a consideration, it's always advisable to install the second fan.[3] In addition to lowering the operating temperature of the components, the extra fan acts as a backup if the primary fan fails. Extra fans are cheap; keep a couple around as spares.

3. Or learn about the latest in superquiet fans at www.silentpcreview.com.

Maintenance

A computer in a dusty environment will burn out components much more frequently than one whose environment is relatively clean. Dust clogs filters, dries out lubrication, jams moving parts (fans), and coats components with a layer of dusty "insulation" that reduces their ability to dissipate heat. All of these effects tend to increase operating temperatures. You may need to give your systems' innards an occasional housecleaning in bad environments. (Any environment that features carpeting is likely to be bad.)

Vacuuming is the best way to remove dust, but be sure to keep the motor at least five feet from system components and disks to minimize magnetic field interference. Your machine room should be vacuumed regularly, but make sure this task is performed by people who have been trained to respect proper distances and not harm equipment (office janitorial staff are usually not acceptable candidates for this task).

Tape drives usually require regular cleaning as well. You clean most drives by inserting a special cleaning cassette.

24.7 ENVIRONMENT

Just like humans, computers work better and longer if they're happy in their environment. Although they don't care much about having a window with a view, they do want you to pay attention to other aspects of their home.

Temperature

The ideal operating temperature for computer equipment is 64° to 68°F (17° to 20°C), with about 45% humidity. Unfortunately, this temperature does not coincide with the ideal operating temperature of a computer user. Ambient temperatures above 80°F (27°C) in the computer room imply about 120°F (49°C) inside machines. Commercial-grade chips have an operational range up to about 120°F, at which point they stop working; beyond about 160°F (71°C), they break. Inlet temperatures are critical; one machine's hot exhaust should never flow toward another machine's air intake.

Humidity

The ideal humidity for most computer hardware is in the range of 40% to 55%. If the humidity is too low, static electricity becomes a problem. If it is too high, condensation can form on the boards, causing shorting and oxidation.

Office cooling

These days, many computers live in people's offices and must survive on building air conditioning (often turned off at night and on weekends) and must overcome a healthy dose of papers and books resting on cooling vents. When you put a computer in an office, keep in mind that it will steal air conditioning that is intended for humans. If you are in a role in which you can influence cooling capacity, a good rule of thumb is that each human in the room produces 300 BTUH worth of heat, whereas your average office PC produces about 1,100 BTUH. Don't let the engineers forget to add in solar load for any windows that receive direct sunlight.

Machine room cooling

If you are "lucky" enough to be moving your servers into one of those fancy raised-floor machine rooms built in the 1980s that has enough capacity to cool all of your equipment *and* the state of Oklahoma, your biggest concern will likely be to find some remedial education in primitive cooling system maintenance. For the rest of us, correctly sizing the cooling system is what makes the difference in the long term. A well-cooled machine room is a happy machine room.

We have found that it's a good idea to double-check the cooling load estimated by the HVAC folks, especially when you're installing a system for a machine room. You'll definitely need an HVAC engineer to help you with calculations for the cooling load that your roof, walls, and windows (don't forget solar load) contribute to your environment. HVAC engineers usually have a lot of experience with those components and should be able to give you an accurate estimate. The part you need to check up on is the internal heat load for your machine room.

You will need to determine the heat load contributed by the following components:

- Roof, walls, and windows (see your HVAC engineer for this estimate)
- Electronic gear
- Light fixtures
- Operators (people)

Electronic gear

You can estimate the heat load produced by your servers (and other electronic gear) by determining their power consumption. Direct measurement of power consumption is by far the best method to obtain this information. Your friendly neighborhood electrician can often help, or you can purchase an inexpensive meter to do it yourself.[4] Most equipment is labeled with its maximum power consumption in watts, but typical consumption tends to be significantly less than the maximum. You can convert power consumption to the standard heat unit, BTUH, by multiplying by 3.413 BTUH/watt. For example, if you wanted to build a machine room that would house 25 servers rated at 450 watts each, the calculation would be

$$\left(25 \text{ servers}\right) \left(\frac{450 \text{ watts}}{\text{server}}\right) \left(\frac{3.412 \text{ BTUH}}{\text{watt}}\right) = 38,385 \text{ BTUH}$$

Light fixtures

As with electronic gear, you can estimate light fixture heat load based on power consumption. Typical office light fixtures contain four 40-watt fluorescent tubes. If your new machine room had six of these fixtures, the calculation would be

$$\left(6 \text{ fixtures}\right) \left(\frac{160 \text{ watts}}{\text{fixture}}\right) \left(\frac{3.412 \text{ BTUH}}{\text{watt}}\right) = 3,276 \text{ BTUH}$$

---

4. The KILL A WATT meter made by P3 is a popular choice at around $30.

Maintenance

Operators

At one time or another, humans will need to enter the machine room to service something. Allow 300 BTUH for each occupant. To allow for four humans in the machine room at the same time:

$$\left(4\,\text{humans}\right)\left(\frac{300\,\text{BTUH}}{\text{human}}\right) \;=\; 1{,}200\,\text{BTUH}$$

Total heat load

Once you have calculated the heat load for each component, add them up to determine your total heat load. For our example, we assume that our HVAC engineer estimated the load from the roof, walls, and windows to be 20,000 BTUH.

20,000	BTUH for roof, walls, and windows
38,385	BTUH for servers and other electronic gear
3,276	BTUH for light fixtures
1,200	BTUH for operators
62,861	BTUH total

Cooling system capacity is typically expressed in tons. You can convert BTUH to tons by dividing by 12,000 BTUH/ton. You should also allow at least a 50% slop factor to account for errors and future growth.

$$\left(62{,}681\,\text{BTUH}\right)\left(\frac{1\,\text{ton}}{12{,}000\,\text{BTUH}}\right)\left(1.5\right) \;=\; 7.86\,\text{tons of cooling required}$$

See how your estimate matches up with the one from your HVAC folks.

Temperature monitoring

If you are supporting a mission-critical computing environment, it's a good idea to monitor the temperature (and other environmental factors, such as noise and power) in the machine room even when you are not there. It can be very disappointing to arrive on Monday morning and find a pool of melted plastic on your machine room floor. Fortunately, automated machine room monitors can watch the goods while you are away. We use and recommend the Phonetics Sensaphone product family. These inexpensive boxes monitor environmental variables such as temperature, noise, and power, and they telephone you (or your pager) when a problem is detected. You can reach Phonetics in Aston, PA at (610) 558-2700 or visit them on the web at www.sensaphone.com.

24.8 POWER

Computer hardware would like to see nice, stable, clean power. In a machine room, this means a power conditioner, an expensive box that filters out spikes and can be adjusted to produce the correct voltage levels and phases. In offices, surge protectors placed between machines and the wall help insulate hardware from power spikes.

Servers and network infrastructure equipment should be placed on an Uninterruptible Power Supply (UPS). Good UPSes have an RS-232, Ethernet, or USB interface that can be attached to the machine to which they supply power. This connection enables the UPS to warn the computer that the power has failed and that it should shut itself down cleanly before the batteries run out.

See page 40 for more information about shutdown procedures.

One study has estimated that 13% of the electrical power consumed in the United States is used to run computers. Traditionally, UNIX boxes were based on hardware and software that expected the power to be on 24 hours a day. These days, only servers and network devices really need to be up all the time. Desktop machines can be powered down at night if there is an easy way for users to turn them off (and if you trust your users to do it correctly).

You may occasionally find yourself in a situation in which you have to regularly power-cycle a server because of a kernel or hardware glitch. Or, perhaps you have non-Linux servers in your machine room that are more prone to this type of problem. In either case, you may want to consider installing a system that will allow you to power-cycle problem servers by remote control.

A reasonable solution is manufactured by American Power Conversion (APC). Their MasterSwitch product is similar to a power strip, except that it can be controlled by a web browser through its built-in Ethernet port. You can reach APC at (401) 789-0204 or on the web at www.apcc.com.

24.9 RACKS

The days of the raised-floor machine room—in which power, cooling, network connections, and phone lines are all hidden underneath the floor—are over. Have you ever tried to trace a cable that runs under the floor of one of these labyrinths? Our experience is that while it looks nice through glass, a "classic" raised-floor room is a hidden rat's nest. Today, you should use a raised floor to hide electrical power feeds, distribute cooled air, and *nothing else*.

If your goal is to operate your computing equipment in a professional manner, a dedicated machine room for server-class machines is essential. A server room not only provides a cozy, temperature-controlled environment for your machines but also addresses their physical security needs.

In a dedicated machine room, storing equipment in racks (as opposed to, say, setting it on tables or on the floor) is the only maintainable, professional choice. The best storage schemes use racks that are interconnected with an overhead track system for routing cables. This approach confers that irresistible high-tech feel without sacrificing organization or maintainability.

The best overhead track system is manufactured by Chatsworth Products (Chatsworth, CA, (818) 882-8595). Using standard 19" single-rail telco racks, you can construct homes for both shelf-mounted and rack-mounted servers. Two back-to-back 19" telco racks make a high-tech-looking "traditional" rack (for cases in which

Maintenance

you need to attach rack hardware both in front of and in back of equipment). Chatsworth provides the racks, cable races, and cable management doodads, as well as all the hardware necessary to mount them in your building. Since the cables lie in visible tracks, they are easy to trace, and you will naturally be motivated to keep them tidy.

24.10 DATA CENTER STANDARDS

Server rooms have become so pervasive that a number of groups have produced standards for setting them up. These standards typically specify attributes such as the diversity of external network connectivity, the available cooling and power (along with backup plans for these resources), and the annual facility maintenance downtime. The Uptime Institute publishes one set of these standards; their categories are summarized in Table 24.1.

Table 24.1   Uptime Institute server standards

Tier	Uptime	Power/cooling	Redundancy
I	99.671%	Single path	No redundant components
II	99.741%	Single path	Some component redundancy
III	99.982%	Multipath, 1 active	Redundant components, concurrent maintenance
IV	99.995%	Multipath, >1 active	Redundant components, fully fault tolerant

In addition to providing an in-depth description of each of these tiers and describing how to achieve them, the Uptime Institute provides statistical and best-practice information on a variety of topics relevant to the infrastructure of fault-tolerant data centers. You can visit them on the web at www.upsite.com.

24.11 TOOLS

A well-outfitted system administrator is an effective system administrator. Having a dedicated tool box is an important key to minimizing downtime in an emergency. Table 24.2 lists some items to keep in your tool box, or at least within easy reach.

24.12 RECOMMENDED READING

The following sources present additional information about data center standards.

Telecommunications Infrastructure Standard for Data Centers. ANSI/TIA/EIA 942.

ASHRAE INC. *ASHRAE Thermal Guidelines for Data Processing Environments*. Atlanta, GA: ASHRAE, Inc., 2004.

EUBANK, HUSTON, JOEL SWISHER, CAMERON BURNS, JEN SEAL, AND BEN EMERSON. *Design Recommendations for High Performance Data Centers*. Snowmass, CO: Rocky Mountain Institute, 2003.

2

2

2

2

Table 24.2 A system administrator's tool box

General tools	
Phillips-head screwdrivers: #0, #1, and #2	Tweezers
Slot-head screwdrivers: 1/8", 3/16", and 5/16"	Scissors
Electrician's knife or Swiss army knife	Socket wrench kit
Pliers, both flat-needlenose and regular	Small LED flashlight
Teensy tiny jeweler's screwdrivers	Hex wrench kit
Ball-peen hammer, 4oz.	Torx wrench kit
Computer-related specialty items	
Wire stripper (with an integrated wire cutter)	Portable network analyzer
Cable ties (and their Velcro cousins)	Spare power cord
Spare Category 5 RJ-45 crossover cables	RJ-45 end crimper
Spare RJ-45 connectors (solid core and stranded)	SCSI terminators
Digital multimeter (DMM)	
Static grounding strap	
Miscellaneous	
List of emergency maintenance contacts[a]	Q-Tips
Home phone and pager #s of on-call support staff	Electrical tape
First-aid kit	Dentist's mirror
Six-pack of good microbrew beer[b]	Cellular telephone

a. And maintenance contract numbers if applicable
b. Recommended minimum

Exercises are presented on the next page.

24.13 EXERCISES

E24.1   Why would you want to mount your computers in a rack?

⭐ **E24.2**   Environmental factors affect both people and machines. Augment the factors listed in this book with some of your own (e.g., dust, noise, light, clutter, etc). Pick four factors and evaluate the suitability of your lab for man and machine.

⭐ **E24.3**   A workstation draws 0.8 A, and its monitor draws 0.7 A @ 120V.

    a) How much power does this system consume in watts? (Hint: P = EI)

    b) With electricity going for about $0.10/kWh, what does it cost to leave this system on year-round?

    c) How much money can you save annually by turning off the monitor for an average of 16 hours a day (either manually or by using Energy Star features such as Display Power Management Signaling)?

    d) What is the annual cost of cooling this system? (State your assumptions regarding cooling costs and show your calculations.)

⭐⭐ **E24.4**   Design a new computing lab for your site. State your assumptions regarding space, numbers of machines, and type and power load of each machine. Then compute the power and cooling requirements for the lab. Include both servers and client workstations. Include the layout of the room, the lighting, and the expected human load as well.

25 *Performance Analysis*

This chapter focuses on the performance of systems that are used as servers. Desktop systems typically do not experience the same types of performance issues that servers do, and the answer to the question of how to improve performance on a desktop machine is almost always "Upgrade the hardware." Users like this answer because it means they get fancy new systems on their desks more often.

One of the ways in which Linux differs from other mainstream operating systems is in the amount of data that it makes available about its own inner workings. Detailed information is available for every level of the system, and administrators control a variety of tunable parameters. If you still have trouble identifying the cause of a performance problem, the source code is always available for review. For these reasons, Linux is often the operating system of choice for performance-conscious consumers.

Unfortunately, Linux performance tuning isn't always easy. Users and administrators alike often think that if they only knew the right "magic," their systems would be twice as fast. One common fantasy involves tweaking the kernel variables that control the paging system and the buffer pools. These days, major distributions' kernels are pretuned to achieve reasonable (though admittedly, not optimal) performance under a variety of load conditions. If you try to optimize the system on the basis of one particular measure of performance (e.g., buffer utilization), the chances are high that you will distort the system's behavior relative to other performance metrics and load conditions.

The most serious performance issues often lie within applications and have little to do with the underlying operating system. Unless you've developed said applications in-house, you may be either out of luck or destined to spend a lot of time on the phone with the application vendor's support team. This chapter discusses system-level performance tuning and leaves application-level tuning to others.

In all cases, take everything you read on the web with a tablespoon of salt. In the area of system performance, you will see superficially convincing arguments on all sorts of topics. However, most of the proponents of these theories do not have the knowledge, discipline, and time required to design valid experiments. Popular support means very little; for every hare-brained proposal, you can expect to see a Greek chorus of "I increased the size of my buffer cache by a factor of ten just like Joe said, and my system feels MUCH, MUCH faster!!!" Right.

Performance tuning is hard work and requires patience, a methodical approach, and careful analysis. Here are some rules that you should keep in mind:

- Collect and review *historical* information about your system. If the system was performing fine a week ago, an examination of the aspects of the system that have changed is likely to lead you to a smoking gun. Keep regular baselines and trends in your hip pocket to pull out in an emergency. Review log files first to determine if a hardware problem has developed.

  Chapter 19, *Network Management and Debugging*, discusses some trend analysis tools that are also applicable to performance monitoring. The **sar** utility discussed on page 816 can also be used as a poor man's trend analysis tool.

- Always tune your system in a way that lets you compare the results to the system's previous baseline.

- Always make sure you have a rollback plan in case your magic fix actually makes things worse.

- Don't intentionally overload your systems or your network. Linux gives each process an illusion of infinite resources. But once 100% of the system's resources are in use, Linux has to work hard to maintain that illusion, delaying processes and often consuming a sizable fraction of the resources itself.

25.1 WHAT YOU CAN DO TO IMPROVE PERFORMANCE

Here are some specific things you can do to improve performance:

- Ensure that the system has enough memory. As we see in the next section, memory size has a major influence on performance. Memory is so inexpensive these days that you can usually afford to load every performance-sensitive machine to the gills.

- Double-check the configuration of the system and of individual applications. Many applications can be tuned in ways that yield tremendous performance improvements (e.g., by spreading data across disks, by not performing DNS lookups on the fly, or by running more instances of a popular server).

- Correct problems of usage, both those caused by users (too many jobs run at once, inefficient programming practices, jobs run at excessive priority, and large jobs run at inappropriate times of day) and those caused by the system (quotas, CPU accounting, unwanted daemons).

- If you are using Linux as a web server or as some other type of network application server, you may want to spread traffic among several systems with a commercial load balancing appliance such as Cisco's Content Services Switch (www.cisco.com), Foundry's ServerIron (www.foundry.com), or Nortel's Alteon Application Switch (www.nortel.com).[1] These boxes make several physical servers appear to be one logical server to the outside world. They balance the load according to one of several user-selectable algorithms such as "most responsive server" or "round robin."

- These load balancers also provide useful redundancy should a server go down. They're really quite necessary if your site must handle unexpected traffic spikes.

- Organize hard disks and filesystems so that load is evenly balanced, maximizing I/O throughput. Ensure that you've selected the appropriate Linux I/O scheduler for your disk (see page 815 for details). For specific applications such as databases, you can use a fancy multidisk technology such as striped RAID to optimize data transfers. Consult your database vendor for recommendations.

- It's important to note that different types of applications and databases respond differently to being spread across multiple disks. RAID comes in many forms; take time to determine which form (if any) is appropriate for your particular application.

- Monitor your network to be sure that it is not saturated with traffic and that the error rate is low. A wealth of network information is available from the **netstat** command, described on page 649. See also Chapter 19, *Network Management and Debugging*.

- Identify situations in which the system is fundamentally inadequate to satisfy the demands being made of it.

These steps are listed in rough order of effectiveness. Adding memory and balancing traffic across multiple servers can often make a huge difference in performance. The effectiveness of the other measures ranges from noticeable to none.

1. A free (though somewhat less stable) alternative is the Linux Virtual Server software available from linuxvirtualserver.org.

Analysis and optimization of software data structures and algorithms almost always lead to significant performance gains. But unless you have a substantial base of local software, this level of design is usually out of your control.

25.2 FACTORS THAT AFFECT PERFORMANCE

Perceived performance is determined by the efficiency with which the system's resources are allocated and shared. The exact definition of a "resource" is rather vague. It can include such items as cached contexts on the CPU chip and entries in the address table of the memory controller. However, to a first approximation, only the following four resources have much effect on performance:

- CPU time
- Memory
- Hard disk I/O
- Network I/O

All processes consume a portion of the system's resources. If resources are still left after active processes have taken what they want, the system's performance is about as good as it can be.

If there are not enough resources to go around, processes must take turns. A process that does not have immediate access to the resources it needs must wait around doing nothing. The amount of time spent waiting is one of the basic measures of performance degradation.

CPU time is one of the easiest resources to measure. A constant amount of processing power is always available. In theory, that amount is 100% of the CPU cycles, but overhead and various inefficiencies make the real-life number more like 95%. A process that's using more than 90% of the CPU is entirely CPU-bound and is consuming most of the system's available computing power.

Many people assume that the speed of the CPU is the most important factor affecting a system's overall performance. Given infinite amounts of all other resources or certain types of applications (e.g., numerical simulations), a faster CPU *does* make a dramatic difference. But in the everyday world, CPU speed is relatively unimportant.

A common performance bottleneck on Linux systems is disk bandwidth. Because hard disks are mechanical systems, it takes many milliseconds to locate a disk block, fetch its contents, and wake up the process that's waiting for it. Delays of this magnitude overshadow every other source of performance degradation. Each disk access causes a stall worth hundreds of millions of CPU instructions.

Because Linux provides virtual memory, disk bandwidth and memory are directly related. On a loaded system with a limited amount of RAM, you often have to write a page to disk to obtain a fresh page of virtual memory. Unfortunately, this means that using memory is often just as expensive as using the disk. Paging caused by bloated software is performance enemy #1 on most workstations.

Network bandwidth resembles disk bandwidth in many ways because of the latencies involved. However, networks are atypical in that they involve entire communities rather than individual computers. They are also susceptible to hardware problems and overloaded servers.

25.3 SYSTEM PERFORMANCE CHECKUP

Most performance analysis tools tell you what's going on at a particular point in time. However, the number and character of loads probably changes throughout the day. Be sure to gather a cross-section of data before taking action. The best information on system performance often becomes clear only after a long period (a month or more) of data collection. It is particularly important to collect data during periods of peak use. Resource limitations and system misconfigurations are often only visible when the machine is under heavy load.

Analyzing CPU usage

You will probably want to gather three kinds of CPU data: overall utilization, load averages, and per-process CPU consumption. Overall utilization can help identify systems on which the CPU's speed itself is the bottleneck. Load averages give you an impression of overall system performance. Per-process CPU consumption data can identify specific processes that are hogging resources.

You can obtain summary information with the **vmstat** command. **vmstat** takes two arguments: the number of seconds to monitor the system for each line of output and the number of reports to provide. If you don't specify the number of reports, **vmstat** runs until you press <Control-C>. The first line of data returned by **vmstat** reports averages since the system was booted. The subsequent lines are averages within the previous sample period, which defaults to five seconds. For example:

```
$ vmstat 5 5
procs    -----------memory---------- ---swap------io---- --system-- ----cpu----
 r  b   swpd    free   buff    cache  si so   bi bo    in    cs us sy id wa
 1  0    820 2606356 428776 487092   0  0  4741 65  1063 4857 25  1 73  0
 1  0    820 2570324 428812 510196   0  0  4613 11  1054 4732 25  1 74  0
 1  0    820 2539028 428852 535636   0  0  5099 13  1057 5219 90  1  9  0
 1  0    820 2472340 428920 581588   0  0  4536 10  1056 4686 87  3 10  0
 3  0    820 2440276 428960 605728   0  0  4818 21  1060 4943 20  3 77  0
```

User time, system (kernel) time, idle time, and time waiting for I/O are shown in the us, sy, id, and wa columns on the far right. CPU numbers that are heavy on user time generally indicate computation, and high system numbers indicate that processes are making a lot of system calls or performing I/O.

A rule of thumb for general purpose compute servers that has served us well over the years is that the system should spend approximately 50% of its nonidle time in user space and 50% in system space; the overall idle percentage should be nonzero. If you are dedicating a server to a single CPU-intensive application, the majority of time should be spent in user space.

The cs column shows context switches per interval, the number of times that the kernel changed which process was running. The number of interrupts per interval (usually generated by hardware devices or components of the kernel) is shown in the in column. Extremely high cs or in values typically indicate a misbehaving or misconfigured hardware device. The other columns are useful for memory and disk analysis, which we discuss later in this chapter.

Long-term averages of the CPU statistics allow you to determine whether there is fundamentally enough CPU power to go around. If the CPU usually spends part of its time in the idle state, there are cycles to spare. Upgrading to a faster CPU won't do much to improve the overall throughput of the system, though it may speed up individual operations.

As you can see from this example, the CPU generally flip-flops back and forth between heavy use and complete idleness. Therefore, it's important to observe these numbers as an average over time. The smaller the monitoring interval, the less consistent the results.

On multiprocessor machines, most Linux tools present an average of processor statistics across all processors. The **mpstat** command gives **vmstat**-like output for each individual processor. The -**P** flag lets you specify a specific processor to report on. **mpstat** is useful for debugging software that supports symmetric multiprocessing (SMP)—it's also enlightening to see how (in)efficiently your system uses multiple processors.

On a workstation with only one user, the CPU generally spends 99% of its time idle. Then, when you go to scroll one of the windows on your bitmap display, the CPU is floored for a short period. In this situation, information about long-term average CPU usage is not meaningful.

The second CPU statistic that's useful for characterizing the burden on your system is the "load average," which represents the average number of runnable processes. It gives you a good idea of how many pieces the CPU pie is being divided into. The load average is obtained with the **uptime** command:

```
$ uptime
11:10am  up 34 days, 18:42, 5 users, load average: 0.95, 0.38, 0.31
```

Three values are given, corresponding to the 5, 10, and 15-minute averages. In general, the higher the load average, the more important the system's aggregate performance becomes. If there is only one runnable process, that process is usually bound by a single resource (commonly disk bandwidth or CPU). The peak demand for that one resource becomes the determining factor in performance.

When more processes share the system, loads may or may not be more evenly distributed. If the processes on the system all consume a mixture of CPU, disk, and memory, the performance of the system is less likely to be dominated by constraints on a single resource. In this situation, it becomes most important to look at average measures of consumption, such as total CPU utilization.

See page 55 for
more information
about priorities.

Typically, Linux systems are busy with a load average of 3 and do not deal well with
load averages over about 8. A load average of this magnitude is a hint that you
should start to look for ways to artificially spread the load, such as using **nice** to set
process priorities.

The system load average is an excellent metric to track as part of a system baseline. If
you know your system's load average on a normal day and it is in that same range on
a bad day, this is a hint that you should look elsewhere (such as the network) for
performance problems. A load average above the expected norm suggests that you
should look at the processes running on the Linux system itself.

Another way to view CPU usage is to run the **ps** command with the **aux** arguments,
which show you how much of the CPU each process is using. On a busy system, at
least 70% of the CPU is often consumed by just one or two processes. (Remember
that **ps** consumes some CPU itself.) Deferring the execution of the CPU hogs or reducing their priority makes the CPU more available to other processes.

See page 65 for
more information
about **top**.

An excellent alternative to **ps** is a program called **top**. **top** presents about the same
information as **ps**, but in a "live" format that lets you watch the status of the system
change over time.[2]

How Linux manages memory

Before we jump into the specifics of Linux's memory management, it's worth mentioning once again that the Linux kernel evolves more rapidly than almost any other
operating system. The Linux memory management system has been in a period of
especially rapid flux, even by Linux standards, for many years.

The 2.6 kernel includes a vastly improved VM system.[3] However, at the level of our
discussion in this chapter, the exact kernel version does not really matter. These
concepts apply regardless of the exact kernel version you are using.

Like UNIX, Linux manages memory in units called pages. The size of a memory
page is currently 4KB[4] on PC hardware. The kernel allocates virtual pages to processes as they request memory. Each virtual page is mapped to real storage, either
RAM or "backing store" on disk. (Backing store is usually space in the swap area,
but for pages that contain executable program text, the backing store is the original
executable file.) Linux uses a "page table" to keep track of the mapping between
these made-up virtual pages and real pages of memory.

Linux can effectively allocate as much memory as processes ask for by augmenting
real RAM with swap space. Since processes expect their virtual pages to map to real

Performance Analysis

---

2. Refreshing **top**'s output too rapidly can itself be quite a CPU hog, so be judicious in your use of **top**.

3. The 2.6 kernel includes the option to run the system *without* virtual memory—an option that is partic-
    ularly useful for embedded systems. If you choose to run without virtual memory, you must ensure
    that enough physical memory is available to satisfy all possible demands.

4. You can also use 4MB pages by setting HPAGE_SIZE in the 2.6 kernel.

memory, Linux is constantly busy shuffling pages between RAM and swap. This activity is known as paging.[5]

Linux tries to manage the system's memory so that pages that have been recently accessed are kept in memory and less active pages are paged out to disk. This scheme is known as an LRU system since the least recently used pages are the ones that get bumped. It would be very inefficient for the kernel to actually keep track of all memory references, so Linux uses a page cache to decide which pages to move out. This system is much cheaper than a true LRU system but produces similar results.

Linux keeps track of an "age" for each page of virtual memory. Every time Linux examines a page and finds it to have been recently referenced, it increments the page's age. (The term "age" is somewhat misleading because the value really indicates frequency and recency of access. The higher the age, the fresher the page.) Meanwhile, Linux runs the **kswapd** process, which regularly decreases the ages of unreferenced pages.

The kernel maintains several lists of memory pages. Pages with an age greater than zero are marked as "active" and are contained in the page cache "active list." If a page's age reaches zero, **kswapd** swaps the page to the "inactive list." **kswapd** removes inactive pages from the page table and considers them eligible to be paged to disk. Although inactive pages are no longer immediately accessible through the page table, the kernel recovers them from memory or disk and sticks them back into the page table on demand.

When memory is low, the kernel tries to guess which pages on the inactive list were least recently used. If those pages have been modified by a process, Linux considers them "dirty" and must page them out to disk before the memory can be reused. Pages that have been laundered in this fashion or that were never dirty to begin with are "clean" and can be recycled by Linux for use elsewhere.

When a page on the inactive list is referenced by a process, the kernel returns its memory mapping to the page table, resets the page's age, and transfers it from the inactive list to the active list. Pages that have been written to disk must be paged in before they can be reactivated. A "soft fault" occurs when a process references an in-memory inactive page, and a "hard fault" results from a reference to a nonresident (paged-out) page. In other words, a hard fault requires a page to be read from disk and a soft fault does not.

Demand for memory varies, so the kernel can run **kswapd**'s page aging algorithm at different speeds. When the demand for memory is extreme, the algorithm is run more often and hence pages must be referenced more often to avoid being paged out because their age decreases to zero.

To sort active pages from inactive pages, the virtual memory (VM) system depends on the lag between the time a page is placed on the inactive list and the time it's actu-

---

5. Note that "paging" and "swapping" are implemented the same way and use the same "swap" area for storing pages when the pages are not in RAM.

ally paged out. Therefore, the VM system has to predict future paging activity to decide how often to run **kswapd**'s algorithm. If **kswapd's** algorithm doesn't run often enough, there might not be enough clean inactive pages to satisfy demand. If it runs too often, the kernel spends excessive time processing soft page faults.

Since the paging algorithm is predictive, there is not necessarily a one-to-one correspondence between page-out events and page allocations by running processes. The goal of the system is to keep enough free memory handy that processes don't have to actually wait for a page-out each time they make a new allocation. If paging increases dramatically when your system is busy, you will probably benefit from more RAM.

You can tune the kernel's "swappiness" parameter (**/proc/sys/vm/swappiness**) to give the kernel a hint about how quickly it should make physical pages eligible to be reclaimed from a process in the event of a memory shortage. By default, this parameter has a value of 60. If you set it to 0, the kernel resorts to reclaiming pages that have been assigned to a process only when it has exhausted all other possibilities. If it is set higher than 60 (the maximum value is 100), the kernel is more likely to reclaim pages from a process when starved for memory. In all cases, if you find yourself tempted to modify this parameter, it's probably time to buy more RAM for the system.

If the kernel fills up both RAM and swap, all VM has been exhausted. Linux uses an "out of memory killer" to handle this condition. This function selects and kills a process to free up memory. Although the kernel attempts to kill off the least important process on your system, running out of memory is always something to avoid. In this situation, it's likely that a substantial portion of the system's resources are being devoted to memory housekeeping rather than to useful work.

Even processes running at a low CPU priority can be sneaky page thieves. For example, suppose you're running a SETI[6] client at very low priority (high nice value) on your workstation while at the same time reading mail. As you pause to read a message, your CPU use falls to zero and the simulation is allowed to run. It brings in all of its pages, forcing out your shell, your window server, your mail reader, and your terminal emulator. When you go on to the next message, there is a delay as a large chunk of the system's memory is turned over. In real life, a high nice value is no guarantee that a process won't cause performance problems.

Analyzing memory usage

Three numbers quantify memory activity: the total amount of active virtual memory, and the swapping and paging rates. The first number tells you the total demand for memory, and the next two suggest the proportion of that memory that is actively used. The goal is to reduce activity or increase memory until paging remains at an acceptable level. Occasional paging is inevitable; don't try to eliminate it completely.

You can use the **free** command to determine the amount of memory and swap space that are currently in use. Use it with the **-t** flag to automatically calculate the total amount of virtual memory.

6. The Search for Extraterrestrial Intelligence; see www.seti.org/science/setiathome.html.

Performance Analysis

```
$ free -t
              total       used       free     shared    buffers     cached
Mem:         127884      96888      30996      46840      57860      10352
-/+ buffers/cache:        28676      99208
Swap:        265032       3576     261456
Total:       392916     100464     292452
```

The free column indicates the number of kilobytes on the system's free list; values lower than 3% of the system's total memory generally indicate problems. Use the **swapon** command to determine exactly what files and partitions are being used for swap space:

```
$ swapon -s
Filename                  Type       Size      Used    Priority
/dev/sdb7                 partition  265032    3576     -1
```

This system uses one disk partition, sdb7, for swap. Since paging activity can be a significant drain on disk bandwidth, it is almost always better to spread your swap space across multiple physical disks if possible. The use of multiple swap disks lowers the amount of time that any one disk has to spend dealing with swapped data and increases swap storage bandwidth.

On traditional UNIX systems, the **vmstat** command reveals information about paging and swapping. However, the **procinfo** command shipped with most Linux distributions is a better source of information. Although **procinfo** comes with all our example systems, it isn't necessarily included in the default installation, so you may need to add the **procinfo** package by hand.

See page 874 for more information about the /proc filesystem.

procinfo doesn't have a special way of getting information about your system; it simply formats the data from the files in your **/proc** filesystem. Without it, interpreting the **/proc** files can present a considerable challenge. For continuous updates every five seconds, run **procinfo -n5**.

```
$ procinfo
Linux 2.6.9-34.EL (root@bull) (gcc 3.4.3 20050227 ) #1 1CPU [main]

Memory:      Total       Used       Free      Shared     Buffers
Mem:        463728     371512      92216           0      144042
Swap:      1866470        218    1626252

Bootup: Sat Jul 29 08:47:20 2006   Load average: 0.08 0.06 0.00

user   :      1:20:32.12   1.3%     page in :     0
nice   :      0:02:36.30   0.0%    page out :     0
system :      3:06:46.90   0.8%     swap in :     0
idle   :  1d 7:23:49.50  97.9%    swap out :     0
steal  :      0:00:00.00   0.0%
uptime :  4d 1:51:43.64            context :  55465717

irq  0:  5748875398  timer         irq  8:           3  rtc
irq  1:           3                irq 11:    75300822  eth0
irq  2:           0  cascade [4]   irq 12:           3
irq  4:           4                irq 14:     7529735  ide0
```

Some of the information in **procinfo**'s output overlaps that of **free**, **uptime**, and **vmstat**. In addition, **procinfo** reports information about your kernel distribution, memory paging, disk access, and IRQ assignments. You can use **procinfo -a** to see even more information from your **/proc** filesystem, including kernel boot options, kernel loadable modules, character devices, and filesystems.

Any apparent inconsistencies among the memory-related columns are for the most part illusory. Some columns count pages and others count kilobytes. All values are rounded averages. Furthermore, some are averages of scalar quantities and others are average deltas. For example, you can't compute the next value of Free from the current Free and paging information, because the paging events that determine the next average value of Free have not yet occurred.

Use the page in/out and the swap in/out fields to evaluate the system's paging and swapping behavior. A page-in does not necessarily represent a page being recovered from the swap area. It could be executable code being paged in from a filesystem or a copy-on-write page being duplicated, both of which are normal occurrences that do not necessarily indicate a shortage of memory. On the other hand, page-outs always represent data written to disk after being forcibly ejected by the kernel.

If your system has a constant stream of page-outs, it's likely that you would benefit from more memory. But if paging happens only occasionally and does not produce annoying hiccups or user complaints, you can ignore it. If your system falls somewhere in the middle, further analysis should depend on whether you are trying to optimize for interactive performance (e.g., a workstation) or to configure a machine with many simultaneous users (e.g., a compute server).

If half the operations are page-outs, you can figure that every 100 page-outs cause about one second of latency. If 150 page-outs must occur to let you scroll a window, you will wait for about 1.5 seconds. A rule of thumb used by interface researchers is that an average user perceives the system to be "slow" when response times are longer than seven-tenths of a second.

It's also worth pointing out that **procinfo** provides some CPU information that is not visible with **vmstat** or **uptime**. In addition to reporting the load average over 5-, 10-, and 15-minute periods, **procinfo** lists the instantaneous number of running processes, the total number of processes, and the process ID of the last process that ran. For example, here's an excerpt from **procinfo**'s output on a busy server:

```
Load average:  2.37  0.71  0.29  3/67  26941
```

This server has 67 total processes, of which 3 were runnable. The last process to run had PID 26941 (in this case, it was the shell process from which **procinfo** was run).

Analyzing disk I/O

You can monitor disk performance with the **iostat** command. Like **vmstat**, it accepts optional arguments to specify an interval in seconds and a repetition count, and its first line of output is a summary since boot. Like **vmstat**, it also tells you how the CPU's time is being spent. Here is a quick example that omits some output not specific to disks:

```
$ iostat
...
Device:      tps   Blk_read/s   Blk_wrtn/s   Blk_read   Blk_wrtn
hdisk0      0.54         0.59         2.39     304483    1228123
hdisk1      0.34         0.27         0.42     140912     216218
hdisk2      0.01         0.02         0.05       5794      15320
hdisk3      0.00         0.00         0.00          0          0
```

iostat gathers information from the **/proc** filesystem to produce a row of output for each physical disk in your system. Unfortunately, Linux keeps only minimal disk statistics, and even the information that is kept is of limited use. Each hard disk has the columns tps, Blk_read/s, Blk_wrtn/s, Blk_read, and Blk_wrtn, indicating I/O transfers per second, blocks read per second, blocks written per second, total blocks read, and total blocks written. Rows of zeros are reported if the system has fewer than four disks.

Disk blocks are typically 1K in size, so you can readily determine the actual disk throughput in kilobytes. Transfers, on the other hand, are fairly nebulously defined. One transfer request can include several logical I/O requests over several sectors, so this data is also mostly useful for identifying trends or irregular behavior.

The cost of seeking is the most important factor affecting disk drive performance. To a first approximation, the rotational speed of the disk and the speed of the bus it's connected to have relatively little impact. Modern disks can transfer dozens of megabytes of data per second if they are read from contiguous sectors, but they can only perform about 100 to 300 seeks per second. If you transfer one sector per seek, you can easily realize less than 5% of the drive's peak throughput.

Seeks are more expensive when they make the heads travel a long distance. If you have a disk with several filesystem partitions and files are read from each partition in a random order, the heads must travel back and forth a long way to switch between partitions. On the other hand, files within a partition are relatively local to one another. When partitioning a new disk, you may want to consider the performance implications and put files that are accessed together in the same filesystem.

To really achieve maximum disk performance, you should put filesystems that are used together on different disks. Although the bus architecture and device drivers influence efficiency, most computers can manage multiple disks independently, thereby dramatically increasing throughput. For example, it is often worthwhile to split frequently accessed web server data and logs among multiple disks.

It's especially important to split the swap area among several disks if possible, since paging tends to slow down the entire system. This configuration is supported by the **swapon** command. The Linux kernel can use both dedicated swap partitions and swap files on a formatted filesystem.

Linux systems also allow you to set up multiple "memory-based filesystems," which are essentially the same thing as PC RAM disks. A special driver poses as a disk but actually stores data in high-speed memory. Many sites use a RAM disk for their **/tmp** filesystem or for other busy files such as web server logs or email spools. Using a RAM disk may reduce the memory available for general use, but it makes the reading and writing of temporary files blindingly fast. It's generally a good deal.

Most Linux kernels have been compiled with RAM disk support. On systems that support RAM disks, the **/dev** directory contains multiple RAM disk device files such as **/dev/ram0** and **/dev/ram1**. The number of devices may vary, but there are usually at least five.

To use a RAM disk, first format the filesystem on an unused RAM disk device, then mount it on an existing directory:

```
# mke2fs /dev/ram12
# mount /dev/ram12 /tmp/fastdisk
```

The default RAM disk size is only 4MB, which really isn't large enough for **/tmp**. Unfortunately, the procedure for changing the size is a bit painful because it is set as a kernel variable. You can either add a line such as ramdisk_size=100000 to your boot loader configuration to pass in the new value at boot time (the size is given in 1K blocks) or set up the RAM disk driver as a dynamically loadable module. In the latter case, you would add the necessary argument to the **/etc/modprobe.conf** file or pass it in as an argument to **insmod**.

Some packages degrade the system's performance by delaying basic operations. Two examples are disk quotas and CPU accounting. Quotas require a disk usage summary to be updated as files are written and deleted. CPU accounting writes a data record to an accounting file whenever a process completes. Disk caching helps to soften the impact of these features, but they may still have a slight effect on performance and should not be enabled unless you really use them.

Choosing an I/O scheduler

An I/O scheduling algorithm acts as a referee between processes competing for disk I/O. It optimizes the order and timing of requests to provide the best possible overall I/O performance.

Four different scheduling algorithms are built into the 2.6 kernel. You can take your pick. Unfortunately, the scheduling algorithm is set by the **elevator=***algorithm* kernel argument and so can only be set at boot time. If is usually set in the **grub.conf** file.

The available algorithms are:

- Completely Fair Queuing (**elevator=cfq**): This is the default algorithm and is usually the best choice for general-purpose servers. It tries to evenly distribute access to I/O bandwidth.

- Deadline (**elevator=deadline**): This algorithm tries to minimize latency for each request. The algorithm reorders requests to increase performance.

- NOOP (**elevator=noop**): This algorithm implements a simple FIFO queue. It assumes that I/O requests are optimized or reordered by the driver or device (such as might be done by an intelligent controller). This option may be the best choice in some SAN environments.

- Anticipatory (**elevator=as**): This algorithm delays I/O requests in the hope of ordering them for maximum efficiency. This might be a good choice for a desktop workstation, but it is rarely optimal for a server.

By determining which scheduling algorithm is most appropriate for your environment—and you may need to try all four—you may be able to directly affect disk I/O performance.

sar: Collect and report statistics over time

One performance monitoring tool that has become common on Linux systems is **sar**. This command has its roots in early AT&T UNIX, but it has been completely reincarnated for use under Linux.

At first glance **sar** seems to display much the same information as **procinfo**, **vmstat**, and **iostat**. However, there's one important difference: **sar** can report on historical as well as current data.

Without options, the **sar** command reports CPU utilization at 10-minute intervals for the day since midnight, as shown below. This historic data collection is made possible by the **sa1** script, which is part of the **sar** (sometimes called **sysstat**) package and must be set up to run from **cron** at periodic intervals. **sar** stores the data it collects in **/var/log/sa** in a binary format.

```
$ sar
Linux 2.6.9-11.ELsmp (bull.atrust.com)   08/04/2006

12:00:01 AM      CPU   %user   %nice   %system   %iowait    %idle
12:10:01 AM      all    0.10    0.00      0.04      0.06    99.81
12:20:01 AM      all    0.04    0.00      0.03      0.05    99.88
12:30:01 AM      all    0.04    0.00      0.03      0.04    99.89
12:40:01 AM      all    0.09    0.00      0.03      0.05    99.83
12:50:01 AM      all    0.04    0.00      0.03      0.04    99.88
01:00:01 AM      all    0.05    0.00      0.03      0.04    99.88
```

In addition to CPU information, **sar** can also report on metrics such as disk and network activity. Use **sar -d** for a summary of today's disk activity or **sar -n DEV** for network interface statistics. **sar -A** reports all available information.

See page 665 for a sample Cacti graph.

sar has some limitations, but it's a good bet for quick-and-dirty historical information. If you're serious about making a long-term commitment to performance monitoring, we suggest that you set up a data collection and graphing platform such as

Cacti. Cacti comes to us from the network management world, but it can actually graph arbitrary system metrics such as CPU and memory information.

oprofile: Comprehensive profiler

oprofile is an incredibly powerful integrated system profiler for Linux systems running the 2.6 kernel or later. All components of a Linux system can be profiled: hardware and software interrupt handlers, kernel modules, the kernel itself, shared libraries, and applications.

If you have a lot of extra time on your hands and want to know exactly how your system resources are being used (down to the smallest level of detail), consider running **oprofile**. This tool is particularly useful if you are developing your own in-house applications or kernel code.

Both a kernel module and a set of user-level tools are included in the **oprofile** distribution, which is available for download at oprofile.sourceforge.net.

 On Red Hat, you also need to install the **kernel-debuginfo** package to get the files you need to run **oprofile**.

25.4 HELP! MY SYSTEM JUST GOT REALLY SLOW!

In previous sections, we've talked mostly about issues that relate to the average performance of a system. Solutions to these long-term concerns generally take the form of configuration adjustments or upgrades.

However, you will find that even properly configured systems are sometimes more sluggish than usual. Luckily, transient problems are often easy to diagnose. Ninety percent of the time, they are caused by a greedy process that is simply consuming so much CPU power, disk, or network bandwidth that other processes have been stalled. On occasion, malicious processes hog available resources to intentionally slow a system or network, a scheme known as a "denial of service" or DOS attack.

You can often tell which resource is being hogged without even running a diagnostic command. If the system feels "sticky" or you hear the disk going crazy, the problem is most likely a disk bandwidth or memory shortfall.[7] If the system feels "sluggish" (everything takes a long time, and applications can't be "warmed up"), the problem may lie with the CPU load.

The first step in diagnosis is to run **ps auxww** or **top** to look for obvious runaway processes. Any process that's using more than 50% of the CPU is likely to be at fault. If no single process is getting an inordinate share of the CPU, check to see how many processes are getting at least 10%. If you snag more than two or three (don't count **ps** itself), the load average is likely to be quite high. This is, in itself, a cause of poor

---

7. That is, it takes a long time to switch between applications, but performance is acceptable when an application is repeating a simple task.

performance. Check the load average with **uptime**, and use **vmstat** or **top** to check whether the CPU is ever idle.

If no CPU contention is evident, run **vmstat** or **procinfo** to see how much paging is going on. All disk activity is interesting: a lot of page-outs may indicate contention for memory, and disk traffic in the absence of paging may mean that a process is monopolizing the disk by constantly reading or writing files.

There's no direct way to tie disk operations to processes, but **ps** can narrow down the possible suspects for you. Any process that is generating disk traffic must be using some amount of CPU time. You can usually make an educated guess about which of the active processes is the true culprit.[8] Use **kill -STOP** to suspend the process and test your theory.

Suppose you do find that a particular process is at fault—what should you do? Usually, nothing. Some operations just require a lot of resources and are bound to slow down the system. It doesn't necessarily mean that they're illegitimate. It is usually acceptable to **renice** an obtrusive process that is CPU-bound. But be sure to ask the owner to use the **nice** command in the future. Sometimes, application tuning can dramatically reduce a program's demand for CPU resources; this effect is especially visible with custom network server software such as web applications.

Processes that are disk or memory hogs can't be dealt with so easily. **renice** generally does not help. You do have the option of killing or stopping the process, but we recommend against this if the situation does not constitute an emergency. As with CPU pigs, you can use the low-tech solution of asking the owner to run the process later.

The kernel allows a process to restrict its own use of physical memory by calling the **setrlimit** system call. This facility is also available in the C shell through the built-in **limit** command. For example, the command

```
% limit memoryuse 32m
```

causes all subsequent commands that the user runs to have their use of physical memory limited to 32MB. This feature is roughly equivalent to **renice** for memory-bound processes. You might tactfully suggest that repeat offenders put such a line in their **.cshrc** files.

If a runaway process doesn't seem to be the source of poor performance, investigate two other possible causes. The first is an overloaded network. Many programs are so intimately bound up with the network that it's hard to tell where system performance ends and network performance begins. See Chapter 19 for more information about the tools used to monitor networks.

---

8. A large virtual address space or resident set used to be a suspicious sign, but shared libraries have made these numbers less useful. **ps** is not very smart about separating system-wide shared library overhead from the address spaces of individual processes. Many processes wrongly appear to have tens of megabytes of active memory.

Some network overloading problems are hard to diagnose because they come and go very quickly. For example, if every machine on the network runs a network-related program out of **cron** at a particular time each day, there will often be a brief but dramatic glitch. Every machine on the net will hang for five seconds, and then the problem will disappear as quickly as it came.

Server-related delays are another possible cause of performance crises. Linux systems are constantly consulting remote servers for NFS, NIS, DNS, and any of a dozen other facilities. If a server is dead or some other problem makes the server expensive to communicate with, the effects can ripple back through client systems.

For example, on a busy system, some process may use the **gethostent** library routine every few seconds or so. If a DNS glitch makes this routine take two seconds to complete, you will likely perceive a difference in overall performance. DNS forward and reverse lookup configuration problems are responsible for a surprising number of server performance issues.

25.5 RECOMMENDED READING

EZOLT, PHILLIP G. *Optimizing Linux Performance.* Upper Saddle River, NJ: Prentice Hall PTR, 2005.

JOHNSON, S., ET AL. *Performance Tuning for Linux Servers.* Indianapolis, IN: IBM Press, 2005.

LOUKIDES, MIKE, AND GIAN-PAOLO D. MUSUMECI. *System Performance Tuning (2nd Edition).* Sebastopol: O'Reilly & Associates, 2002.

25.6 EXERCISES

E25.1 Make an educated guess as to the problem in each of the following cases:

   a) When switching between applications, the disk thrashes and there is a noticeable lag.

   b) A numerical simulation program takes more time than normal, but system memory is mostly free.

   c) Users on a very busy LAN complain of slow NFS access, but the load average on the server is very low.

   d) Running a command (any command) often says "out of memory".

E25.2 Run **procinfo** on an available Linux machine and discuss the results. What, if any, resources appear to be in heavy use? What resources appear to be unused? Include the IRQ listing in your analysis.

Exercises are continued on the next page.

Performance Analysis

★ **E25.3** Load balancing can have a dramatic impact on server performance as seen from the outside world. Discuss several mechanisms that could be used to perform load balancing.

★ **E25.4** List the four main resources that can affect performance. For each resource, give an example of an application that could easily lead to the exhaustion of that resource. Discuss ways to alleviate some of the stress associated with each scenario.

★ **E25.5** Using the web and man pages, look into the command **hdparm**. What options does it provide to test disk access speeds? How can **hdparm** improve disk access speeds in some cases?

★★ **E25.6** Choose two programs that use a noticeable amount of system resources. Use **vmstat** and the other tools mentioned in the chapter to profile both applications. Make a claim as to what each program does that makes it a resource hog. Back up your claims with data.

26 *Cooperating with Windows*

windows   System administrator   Microsoft

Chances are high that your environment includes both Microsoft Windows and Linux systems. If so, there are many ways in which these operating systems can assist each other. Among other feats, Windows applications can run from a Linux desktop or access a Linux server's printers and files. Linux applications can display their user interfaces on a Windows desktop.

Both platforms have their strengths, and they can be made to work together. Windows is a popular and featureful desktop platform, capable of bridging the gap between the user and the network cable coming out of the wall. Linux, on the other hand, is a reliable and scalable infrastructure platform. So let's not fight, OK?

26.1 LOGGING IN TO A LINUX SYSTEM FROM WINDOWS

See page 697 for more information about SSH.

Users may often find themselves wanting to head for the snow-covered slopes of a good C shell or **bash** session without abandoning the Windows box on their desk. From the client's perspective, the easiest way to accomplish this is to use the **telnet** program that Microsoft ships with Windows. These days, though, most Linux systems have (wisely) disabled their **telnet** servers for security reasons. People who want to log in need a terminal emulator that understands SSH.

There are several SSH implementations for Windows. Our current favorite, the open source PuTTY, is simple and effective. It supports many of the features you have come to expect from a native terminal application such as **xterm**. The only complaint we have heard regarding PuTTY is that it does not handle multibyte characters correctly; Asian language users may be better off combining Tera Term Pro with the TTSSH plug-in, although this setup supports only version 1 of the SSH protocol. You can find PuTTY here:

www.chiark.greenend.org.uk/~sgtatham/putty

and Tera Term Pro here:

hp.vector.co.jp/authors/VA002416/teraterm.html

SSH also supports file transfer, and PuTTY includes two command-line clients for this purpose: **psftp** and **pscp**. Hard-core "never touch a command line" Windows users may prefer the graphical WinSCP client from winscp.sf.net.

Another plausible option is to install the more general UNIX-on-Windows Cygwin package and to run its SSH utilities from **rxvt**. There's more information about Cygwin starting on page 827.

A nifty zero-footprint Java implementation of SSH called MindTerm is available from AppGate (www.appgate.com). It's free for personal use. It runs on any system that supports Java and can be configured in a variety of ways.

An interesting feature of SSH is its ability to forward TCP ports back and forth between client and server. For example, this feature allows you to set up on the client a local port that forwards incoming connection to a different port on a machine that is only reachable from the server. Although this feature opens up a world of new possibilities, it is also potentially dangerous and is something you must be aware of when granting SSH access to your server. Fortunately, the port-forwarding feature can be disabled on the server side to limit SSH to terminal access and file transfer.

26.2 ACCESSING REMOTE DESKTOPS

Graphical desktops on Linux are tied to the free X Window System, which is in no way related to Microsoft Windows. X Windows was developed at MIT in the mid-1980s and has been adopted as a standard by all UNIX workstation manufacturers and Linux distributions. It has been through several major updates, but a stable base was finally reached with version 11, first published in the early 1990s. The version number of the protocol was appended to X to form X11, the name by which it is most commonly known. (The name "Windows" by itself always refers to Microsoft Windows, both in this chapter and in the real world.)

X11 is a client/server system. The X server is responsible for displaying data on the user's screen and for acquiring input from the user's mouse and keyboard. It communicates with client applications over the network. The server and clients need not be running on the same machine.

A more detailed discussion of the X Windows architecture can be found in Chapter Chapter 22, *The X Window System*, which starts on page 741.

Running an X server on a Windows computer

X11 is a rich protocol that has incorporated many extensions over the years. The implementation of an X server is, therefore, rather complex. Nevertheless, X server implementations now exist for almost every operating system. X Windows itself is OS-agnostic, so X11 clients running on a Linux box can display on an X server running under Microsoft Windows and allow a user to control them just as if that user were sitting at the system console.

Unfortunately, the original designers of the X protocols did not devote much thought to security. Every program that connects to your X server can read everything you type on the keyboard and see everything displayed on your screen. To make matters worse, remote programs do not even have to display a window when accessing your X server; they can simply lurk silently in the background.

Several methods of securing X11 have been proposed over time, but they have all tended to be somewhat complex. The bottom line is that you are best off preventing all remote connections to your X server unless you are absolutely sure what you are doing. Most X servers are configured to refuse remote connections by default, so you should be safe as long as you do not run the **xhosts** program (or its equivalent) to grant remote access.

See page 697 for more information about SSH.

Unfortunately, granting remote access is exactly what you need to do when you seek to run programs on Linux and display their interfaces on Windows. So, how to run a remote application without granting remote access to the X server? The most common method is to use a feature of the SSH protocol that is specifically designed to support X11. This scheme creates a secure tunnel between X clients running on the remote host and the local X server. Programs started on the remote host will display automatically on the local machine, but through the magic of SSH, the local X server will perceive them as having originated locally.

Note that X forwarding will only work if the X forwarding features have been enabled on both the SSH server and the SSH client. If you use the PuTTY SSH client on windows, simply activate the X11 forwarding feature in its setup screen. On the SSH server side (that is, the X11 client side; the Linux machine), make sure that the **/etc/ssh/sshd_config** file contains the line

```
X11Forwarding yes
```

If you modify the SSH server configuration, make sure you restart the **sshd** process to activate the new configuration.

Although Apple provides a free X server for Mac OS X, there is unfortunately no such offering from Microsoft. There is, however, a free X server available from the Cygwin project (cygwin.com) that works very well once it has been configured. Unfortunately, configuration may prove rather challenging for people who do not know how to configure an X server on Linux. Commercial X servers for windows include eXeed and X-Win32. These offer much simpler configuration at a rather steep price.

VNC: Virtual Network Computing

In the late 1990s, a few people at AT&T Labs in Cambridge, UK, developed a system for remote desktop access called VNC. Their idea was to marry the simplicity of a "dumb" terminal with the modern world of window systems. In contrast to X11, the VNC protocol does not deal with individual applications. Instead, it creates a complete virtual desktop (or provides remote access to an existing desktop) as a unit. Under VNC, a special X11 server runs on the central machine, and a viewer application is used to access that server.

AT&T published the VNC software under a liberal open source license. This allowed other folks to hop on the bandwagon and create additional server and viewer implementations, as well as protocol improvements for reduced bandwidth. Today, VNC viewers are available for most devices that provide some means for graphical display. VNC servers for UNIX/Linux and Windows are widely available.

The Linux VNC server implementation is essentially a graphics adaptor emulator that plugs into the X.Org X Windows server. Running a **vncserver** from your Linux account creates a new virtual desktop that runs in the self-contained world of the Linux machine. You can then use a VNC viewer to access that desktop remotely.

The VNC protocol is stateless and bitmap based. Therefore, viewers can freely connect and disconnect. It is even possible to have several viewers access the same VNC server at the same time. This last feature is especially useful for remote support and for training setups. It also facilitates shared console access for system administration.

VNC servers in the Windows world do not normally create an extra desktop; they simply export the standard Windows desktop as it is displayed on screen. The main application for this technology is remote support.

These days, the original authors of VNC are running their own company, RealVNC (realvnc.com). The Ultr@VNC project (ultravnc.sf.net) is concentrating on the Windows domain with a very fast and feature-rich Windows-based VNC server implementation, and TightVNC (tightvnc.com) is working on improved compression ratios. These groups do talk with each other, so features tend to cross-pollinate among the various implementations.

The VNC protocol has been designed with extensibility in mind. All combinations of viewers and servers can work together; they pick the best protocol variant that both sides understand. Implementation-specific features (such as file transfer) can usually only be accessed by running a server and client from the same project.

Windows RDP: Remote Desktop Protocol

Ever since Windows 2000 Server, every Windows box has the technical ability to provide graphical remote access to several users at the same time. The remote access component is called Remote Desktop, and it uses a protocol called the Remote Desktop Protocol (RDP) to communicate between client and server.

With decent PC hardware, you can easily run 50 concurrent Microsoft Office sessions on one Windows 2003 server. Due to licensing restrictions, this wonderful ability is only usable for a single session on Windows XP. If you log in from a remote machine, you will be logged out locally.

If you do have a Windows Server installation, you can enable the Terminal Server service and use the open source **rdesktop** program (www.rdesktop.org) to access a Windows desktop right from your Linux workstation. (Clients for Windows, Mac OS, and Windows CE are also available directly from Microsoft.) Like VNC, the RDP protocol is stateless. It is therefore possible to reconnect to a disconnected session or to perform remote support.

RDP even allows local printer and disk resources to be forwarded to the remote Windows session. Test the setup and have fun—just don't deploy it before you have the licensing sorted out. The Terminal Server will issue a 30-day test license to whoever connects to it, but after 30 days it will not allow any more connections from that client unless you have purchased a proper Terminal Server Client Access License.

The whole concept of remotely accessing a Windows box seems to confuse the licensing departments of both Microsoft and most other Windows software vendors. The license conditions keep changing as they try to nail down their approaches, so make sure you get the official word on current pricing before you whet your users' appetites. The one licensing scheme we would all love to see (license by number of concurrent users) does not seem to be on anybody's agenda. Currently, the choice is between buying licenses for every computer or for every individual user who is ever going to access the server.

26.3 RUNNING WINDOWS AND WINDOWS-LIKE APPLICATIONS

The commercial product VMware (vmware.com) lets you run multiple operating systems simultaneously on PC hardware. VMware emulates entire virtual "guest machines" on top of a host operating system, which must be either Linux or Windows. Regardless of the host operating system, you can install most Intel-compatible operating systems into one of VMware's virtual machines.

VMware is an ideal tool for development or testing environments. It even comes with a feature that networks your virtual operating systems so that they can communicate with one another and share the system's physical Ethernet connection.

A different approach is taken by the Wine system from winehq.org. Wine implements the Windows programming API in the Linux environment, allowing you to run Windows applications directly on top of Linux and X. This free software translates native Windows API calls to their Linux counterparts and can do so without using any Microsoft code. Wine provides support for TCP/IP networking, serial devices, and sound output.

The Wine project was started in 1993 by Bob Amstadt. Wine has come a very long way since then. A large number of Windows applications run without problems, and

Cooperating with Windows

others can be made to work with a few tricks; see the web site for details. Unfortunately, getting an application to run under Wine is often not so simple. The talented folks at codeweavers.com have written a commercial installer system that is able to make some of the balkier Windows apps work with correctly.

If your tool of choice is supported by CodeWeavers, great. But even if it is not, give the application a try—you might be pleasantly surprised. But if the application does not work on its own and you cannot find any prewritten hints, be prepared to spend some serious spare time whipping it into shape if you are determined to do it on your own. If you have the budget, you can consider contracting CodeWeavers to help you.

Win4Lin is a commercial alternative to Wine from NeTraverse. Win4Lin claims to be more stable than Wine and to support a few more Microsoft applications. However, it requires kernel modifications, which Wine does not. Win4Lin is available from netraverse.com.

Dual booting, or why you shouldn't

If you've ever installed Linux on a computer that had a former life as a Windows machine, you have doubtless been offered the option to set up a dual boot configuration. These days such configurations function pretty much as promised. It is even possible to mount Windows partitions under Linux and to access Linux filesystem under Windows. Read all about setting up a dual boot configuration on page 30.

But wait! If you are doing real work and need access to both Windows and Linux, be very skeptical of dual booting as a possible solution. Dual boot setups represent Murphy's Law at its worst: they always seem to be booted into the wrong OS, and the slightest chore usually requires multiple reboots. Computers are so cheap and remote access so easy that there's usually no reason to put yourself through this endless torture.

The OpenOffice.org alternative

A few years ago, Sun released an open source version of StarOffice, its Microsoft-Office-like application suite, under the name OpenOffice.org. OpenOffice.org includes a spreadsheet, a word processor, a presentation package, and a drawing application. These tools can read and write files generated by their Microsoft analogs. You can download the suite from openoffice.org.

OpenOffice.org is available on all major platforms, including Windows, Linux, Solaris, and most other versions of UNIX. There is also a version for Mac OS X. If you are looking for a package with a commercial support contract, you can also buy StarOffice from Sun, which is essentially OpenOffice.org in a box with better spell-checking and a database.

26.4 Using command-line tools with Windows

What many Linux people miss most when working on Windows systems is their beloved **xterm**. Not just any old terminal application or the abomination known as the DOS box, but a proper **xterm** with support for resizing, colors, mouse control, and all the fancy **xterm** escape sequences.

Although there is no stand-alone (i.e., without X) native port of **xterm** for Windows, a neat little program called **rxvt** comes awfully close. It is part of the Cygwin system, downloadable from cygwin.com. If you install Cygwin's X server, you can use the real **xterm**.

This system, which is distributed under the GNU General Public License, contains an extensive complement of common UNIX commands as well as a porting library that implements the POSIX APIs under Windows. Cygwin's way of reconciling the UNIX and Windows command-line and filesystem conventions is well thought out and manages to bring many of the creature comforts of a UNIX shell to native Windows commands. In addition to making UNIX users feel at home, Cygwin makes it easy to get UNIX software running under Windows. See cygwin.com for details.

The MKS Toolkit is a commercial alternative to Cygwin. See MKS's web site at mkssoftware.com for more information.

A growing list of UNIX software now also runs natively on Windows, including Apache, Perl, BIND, PHP, MySQL, Vim, Emacs, Gimp, Wireshark, and Python.

26.5   WINDOWS COMPLIANCE WITH EMAIL AND WEB STANDARDS

In an ideal world, everybody would use open standards to communicate, and happiness would abound. But this is not an ideal world, and many have accused Windows of being a mess of proprietary protocols and broken implementations of Internet standards. Partially true, perhaps, yet there are many areas in which Windows can play along nicely in the standards world. Two of these areas are email and web service.

In the wild history of the web, a number of corporations have tried to embrace and extend the web in ways that would allow them to lock out competition and give their own business a mighty boost. Microsoft is still engaged in this battle at the browser level with its numerous extensions peculiar to Internet Explorer. At the underlying level of the HTTP protocol, however, Windows and Windows browsers are relatively platform-agnostic.

Microsoft provides its own web server, IIS, but its performance has historically lagged that of Apache running on Linux by a significant margin. Unless you are locked into a server-side technology such as ASP, there's no compelling reason to use Windows machines as web servers. As web clients, however, they will happily lap up all the web content your UNIX and Linux servers can dish out.

For email, Microsoft touts its Exchange Server product as the preferred server-side technology. Truth be told, Exchange Server's capabilities do outshine those of Internet-standard mail systems, particularly when the mail clients consist of Windows boxes running Microsoft Outlook. But fear not: Exchange Server can also speak SMTP for inbound and outbound mail, and it can serve up mail to Linux clients,

Cooperating with Windows

using the standard IMAP and POP protocols. On the client side, both Outlook and its free younger sibling, Outlook Express, can connect to IMAP and POP servers. Mix and match in any combination you like. More information about POP and IMAP can be found starting on page 542.

26.6 SHARING FILES WITH SAMBA AND CIFS

In the early 1980s, IBM designed an API that allowed computers on the same network subnet to talk to one another by using names instead of cryptic numbers. The result was called the Network Basic/Input Output System, or NetBIOS. The combination of NetBIOS and its original underlying network transport protocol was called the NetBIOS Extended User Interface, or NetBEUI. The NetBIOS API became quite popular, and it was adapted for use on top of a variety of different network protocols such as IPX, DECNet, and TCP/IP.

Microsoft and Intel developed a file sharing protocol on top of NetBIOS and called it "the core protocol". Later, it was renamed the Server Message Block protocol or SMB for short. A later evolution of the SMB protocol known as the Common Internet File System (CIFS) is essentially a version of SMB that has been cleaned up and tuned for operation over wide area networks. CIFS is the current lingua franca of Windows file sharing.

In the Windows world, a filesystem or directory made available over the network is known as a "share." It sounds a bit strange to UNIX ears, but we follow this convention when referring to CIFS filesystems.

Samba: CIFS server for UNIX

Samba is an enormously popular software package, available under the GNU public license, that implements the server side of CIFS on Linux hosts. It was originally created by Andrew Tridgell, an Australian, who reverse-engineered the SMB protocol and published the resulting code in 1992.

Today, Samba is well supported and under active development to expand its functionality. It provides a stable, industrial-strength mechanism for integrating Windows machines into a Linux network. The real beauty of Samba is that you only need to install one package on the server; no special software is needed on the Windows side.[1]

CIFS provides five basic services:

- File sharing
- Network printing
- Authentication and authorization
- Name resolution
- Service announcement (file server and printer "browsing")

---

1. The Windows machine must have already been configured for "Microsoft networking."

Samba not only serves files through CIFS, but it can also perform the basic functions of a Windows primary domain controller.[2] Samba supports some advanced features, including Windows domain logins, roaming Windows user profiles, and CIFS print spooling.

Most of Samba's functionality is implemented by two daemons: **smbd** and **nmbd**. **smbd** implements file and print services, as well as authentication and authorization. **nmbd** provides the other major CIFS components: name resolution and service announcement.

Unlike NFS, which requires kernel-level support, Samba requires no driver and runs entirely as a user process. It binds to the sockets used for CIFS requests and waits for a client to request access to a resource. Once a request has been authenticated, **smbd** forks an instance of itself that runs as the user who is making the requests. As a result, all normal file access permissions (including group permissions) are obeyed. The only special functionality that **smbd** adds on top of this is a file locking service that provides client PCs with the locking semantics to which they are accustomed.

Samba installation

Samba is shipped with all the Linux distributions covered in this book. Patches, documentation, and other goodies are available from samba.org. Make sure you are using the most current Samba packages available for your system, since bugs might potentially cause data loss or security problems.

On all systems, you'll need to edit the **smb.conf** file (which is to be found in either **/etc/samba/smb.conf** or **/etc/smb.conf**) to tell Samba how it should behave. In this file, you specify the directories and printers that should be shared, their access rights, and Samba's general operational parameters. The Samba package comes with a well-commented sample **smb.conf** file that is a good starting place for new configurations. Note that once Samba is running, it checks its configuration file every few seconds and loads any changes you make.

It's important to be aware of the security implications of sharing files and other resources over a network. For a typical site, you need to do two things to ensure a basic level of security:

- Explicitly specify which clients can access the resources shared by Samba. This part of the configuration is controlled by the hosts allow clause in the **smb.conf** file. Make sure that it contains only the IP addresses (or address ranges) that it should.

- Block access to the server from outside your organization. Samba uses encryption only for password authentication. It does not use encryption for its data transport. Depending on the nature of the data stored on your

Cooperating with Windows

2. In combination with LDAP, Samba can also serve as a backup domain controller. See John H. Terpstra's *Samba-3 by Example* (citation on page 841) for an excellent discussion. Refer to Chapter 17 for more information about LDAP.

Samba server, you might want to block access to the server from outside your organization in order to prevent people from accidentally downloading files in the clear. This is typically done at the network firewall level; Samba uses UDP ports 137 through 139 and TCP ports 137, 139, and 445.

Since the release of Samba version 3, excellent documentation has been available online from samba.org.

Samba comes with sensible defaults for most of its configuration options, and most sites will need only a small configuration file. Use the command **testparm -v** to get a listing of all the Samba configuration options and the values to which they are currently set. This listing will include your settings from the **smb.conf** file as well as the default values.

Avoid setting options in the **smb.conf** file unless they are different from the default values and you are sure why you want to lock them down. The advantage of this approach is that your configuration will automatically adapt to the settings recommended by the Samba authors when you upgrade to a newer version of Samba.

That having been said, do make sure that password encryption is turned on:

```
encrypt passwords = true
```

This option encrypts the password exchange between Windows clients and the Samba server. It's currently the default, but there's no conceivable situation in which you would want to turn it off.

The encryption feature requires the Samba server to store a special Windows password hash for every user. Windows passwords work in a fundamentally different way from UNIX passwords, and therefore it is not possible to use the passwords from **/etc/shadow**.

Samba provides a special tool for setting up these passwords, **smbpasswd**. For example, let's add the user tobi and set a password for him:

```
$ sudo smbpasswd -a tobi
New SMB password: <password>
Retype new SMB password: <password>
```

Users can change their own Samba passwords with **smbpasswd** as well:

```
$ smbpasswd -r smbserver -U tobi
New SMB password: <password>
Retype new SMB password: <password>
```

This example changes the Samba password of user tobi on the server smbserver.

Filename encoding

Starting with version 3.0, Samba encodes all filenames in UTF-8. If your server runs with a UTF-8 locale, this a great match.[3] If you are in Europe and you are still using

---

3. Type **echo $LANG** to see if your system is running in UTF-8 mode.

one of the ISO 8859 locales on the server, you will find that filenames with special characters such as ä, ö, ü, é, or è will look rather odd when you type **ls** in a directory where such files have been created with Samba using UTF-8. The solution is to tell Samba to use the same character encoding as your server:

```
unix charset = ISO8859-15
display charset = ISO8859-15
```

It is important to make sure that the filename encoding is correct right from the start. Otherwise, files with oddly encoded filenames will accumulate, and fixing them can be quite a complex task later on.

Network Neighborhood browsing

Early Windows networking was very simple. One just plugged all the Windows boxes into an Ethernet segment, and the systems started seeing each other by name and were able to share resources. This feat was accomplished through a self-organizing system based on broadcasts and elections; one Windows box was selected to become the master, and this master then maintained a list of the available resources.

When Windows started to speak TCP/IP, this system was ported to use UDP broadcasts. The effect was much the same, but with the IP subnet being the operative unit rather than the Ethernet. The discovered hosts show up in the Windows desktop under Network Neighborhood or My Network Places, depending on the specific version of Windows. To structure the visibility a bit, every Windows box can also be assigned to a workgroup.

Samba participates in this system through the **nmdb** daemon. **nmbd** can even become the designated browse master and take on the role of organizing all the Windows systems on the local subnet. Unfortunately, as soon as the network starts to become more complex, with several subnets and servers, broadcasts will not be sufficient to allow the Windows boxes to see each other.

To fix this problem, set up one Samba server per subnet as a WINS (Windows Internet Naming Service) server by setting

```
wins support = yes
```

in **smb.conf** and then linking these servers with wins server options.

Our experience with Microsoft's browsing system has been mixed, even on pure Windows networks. We've often run into odd situations in which a host will not respond to its own name, or in which a nearby computer could not be found even though we were sure it was up and running. Problems are even more frequent on large networks with multiple subnets.

If you are serving modern Windows clients (Windows 2000 and up), have DNS entries for all your hosts, and do not require Network Neighborhood browsing, then you can drop NetBIOS support from your Samba server if you wish. It will be one less thing to worry about.

```
[global]
disable netbios = yes
name resolve order = host
```

Without NetBIOS, Windows will have to use DNS to figure out the IP address of a Samba server, just as with any other resource on the net. If you run Samba without NetBIOS support, there is no need to start **nmbd**. Remove it from the Samba startup script in **/etc/init.d**.

To connect a client to a Samba server that has disabled NetBIOS support, it is best to type the full DNS name of the server when connecting a share. For example:

```
\\server.example.com.\myshare
```

Note the dot at the end of the server name. It tells Windows not to bother trying to find the requested machine via NetBIOS, but rather to go directly to DNS.

User authentication

In the Windows authentication systems, the client does not trust the server; the user's password never travels across the net as plaintext. Instead, Windows uses a challenge/response method for authentication.

If you provide a username and password when logging in to a Windows system, Windows will try to use this information to authenticate whenever it is presented with an authentication request. Because of the challenge/response method, there is no danger in this behavior apart from the fact that the plaintext password is stored somewhere in RAM. The cool thing is that if a user has the same username and password combination on your Windows box as on your Samba server, Samba will grant seemingly passwordless access to the appropriate Samba shares. All the authentication happens transparently in the background.

The downside of the challenge/response approach is that the server has to store plaintext-equivalent passwords. In actual fact, the server's copies of the passwords are locally encrypted, but this is primarily a precaution against casual browsing. An intruder who gains access to the encrypted passwords can use them to access the associated accounts without the need for any further password cracking. Samba passwords must be protected even more vigorously than the **/etc/shadow** file.

In complex environments with multiple Samba servers, it makes sense to operate a centralized directory service that makes sure the same password is active on all servers. Samba supports NIS,[4] LDAP, and Windows as authentication services. NIS and LDAP are discussed in Chapter 17, *Sharing System Files*.

To merge the authentication systems of Windows and Linux, you have two basic options. First, you can configure a Samba server to act as a Windows NT4 Primary Domain Controller (not an Active Directory server, yet). Alternatively, you can install pGina (pgina.xpasystems.com) on your Windows clients. This clever application

---

4. Even though it is still listed in some of the documentation, there is no NIS+ support in Samba version 3. It seems that nobody was willing to maintain the code, so this feature was removed (at least for now).

replaces the standard Windows login system with a framework that supports all sorts of standard authentication services, including LDAP and NIS.

Basic file sharing

If each user has a home directory, the homes can be "bulk shared":

```
[homes]
comment = Home Directories
browseable = no
valid users = %S
writeable = yes
guest ok = no
```

This configuration will, for example, allow the user oetiker to access his home directory through the path \\sambaserver\oetiker from any Windows system.

At some sites, the default permissions on Linux home directories allow people to browse one another's files. Because Samba relies on UNIX file permissions to implement access restrictions, Windows users coming in through CIFS will be able to read one another's home directories as well. However, experience shows that this behavior tends to confuse Windows users and make them feel exposed. The valid users line in the configuration fragment above tells Samba to prevent connections to other people's home directories. Leave it out if this is not what you want.

Samba uses its magic [homes] section as a last resort. If there is an explicitly defined share in the configuration for a particular user's home directory, the parameters set there override the values set through [homes].

Group shares

Samba can map Windows access control lists (ACLs) to either file permissions or ACLs (if the underlying filesystem supports them). In practice, we find that the concept of ACLs tends to be too complex for most users. Therefore, we normally just set up a special share for each group of users that requires one and configure Samba to take care of setting the appropriate permissions. Whenever a user tries to mount this share, Samba checks to make sure the applicant is in the appropriate Linux group and then switches its effective UID to the designated owner of the group share (a pseudo-user created for this purpose). For example:

```
[eng]
comment = Group Share for engineering
; Everybody who is in the eng group may access this share.
; People will have to log in using their Samba account.
valid users = @eng
; We have created a special user account called "eng". All files
; written in this directory will belong to this account as
; well as to the eng group.
force user = eng
force group = eng
path = /home/eng
```

```
; Disable NT Acls as we do not use them here.
nt acl support = no

; Make sure that all files have sensible permissions.
create mask = 0660
force create mask = 0660
security mask = 0000
directory mask = 2770
force directory mask = 2770
directory security mask = 0000

; Normal share parameters
browseable = no
writeable = yes
guest ok = no
```

A similar effect can be achieved through Samba's inherit permissions option. If that option is enabled on a share, all new files and directories inherit their settings from their parent directory:

```
[eng]
comment = Group Share for engineering
path = /home/eng
nt acl support = no
browseable = no
writeable = yes
inherit permissions = yes
```

Because Samba will now propagate settings from the parent directory, it's important to set the permissions on the root of the share appropriately:

```
$ sudo chmod u=rw,g=rws,o= /home/eng
$ sudo chgrp eng /home/eng
$ sudo chown eng /home/eng
```

Note that this configuration still requires you to create an eng pseudo-user to act as the owner of the shared directory.

Transparent redirection with MS DFS

Microsoft's Distributed File System (MS DFS) allows directories within a share to trigger clients to transparently automount other shares as soon as they are accessed. For habitués of UNIX and Linux this does not sound like a big deal, but for Windows the whole concept is quite revolutionary and unexpected. That may be part of the reason why it is not widely used, even though DFS has been supported by every version of Windows since Windows 98.

Here is an example:

```
[global]
; Enable MS DFS support for this Samba server.
host msdfs = yes
...
```

```
[mydfs]
; This line tells Samba that it has to look out for
; DFS symlinks in the directory of this share.
msdfs root = yes
path = /home/dfs/mydfs
```

You create symbolic links in **/home/dfs/mydfs** to set up the actual automounts. For example, the following command makes the **jump** "directory" a link to one of two directories on other servers. (Note the single quotes. They are required to protect the backslashes.)

```
$ sudo ln -s 'msdfs:serverX\shareX,serverY\shareY' jump
```

If more than one source is provided (as here), Windows will fail over between them. Users who access **\\server\mydfs\jump** will now actually be reading files from shareX on serverX or shareY on serverY, depending on availability. If the filesystems are exported read/write, you must make sure you have some mechanism in place to synchronize the files. **rsync** can be helpful for this.

With Samba, it is also possible to redirect all clients that access a particular share to a different server. This is something a Windows server cannot do.

```
[myredirect]
msdfs root = yes
msdfs proxy = \\serverZ\shareZ
```

Note that DFS will only work for users who have the same username and password on all the servers involved.

smbclient: a simple CIFS client

In addition to its many server-side features, the Samba package includes a simple command-line file transfer program called **smbclient**. You can use this program to directly access any Windows or Samba server. For example:

```
$ smbclient //redmond/joes -U joe
Password: <password>
Doman=[REDMOND] OS=[Windows 5.0] Server=[Windows 2000 LAN Manager]
smb: \>
```

Once you have successfully logged in to the file server, you use standard **ftp**-style commands (such as **get**, **put**, **cd**, **lcd**, and **dir**) to navigate and transfer files.

The smbfs filesystem

Linux includes direct client-side support for the SMB/CIFS filesystem. You can mount a CIFS share into your filesystem tree much as you can with any other filesystem that is directly understood by the kernel. For example:

```
# mount -t smbfs -o username=joe //redmond/joes /home/joe/mnt
```

Although this feature is useful, keep in mind that Windows conceptualizes network mounts as being established by a particular user (hence the **username=joe** option

Cooperating with Windows

above), whereas Linux regards them as more typically belonging to the system as a whole. Windows servers generally cannot deal with the concept that several different people might be accessing a mounted Windows share.

From the perspective of the Linux client, all files in the mounted directory appear to belong to the user who mounted it. If you mount the share as root, then all files belong to root, and garden-variety users may not be able to write files on the Windows server.

The mount options **uid**, **gid**, **fmask**, and **dmask** let you tweak these settings so that ownership and permission bits are more in tune with the intended access policy for that share. Check the **mount.smbfs** manual page for more information about this behavior.

To allow users to mount a Windows share on their own, you can add a line in the following format to your **/etc/fstab** file:

```
//redmond/joes /home/joe/mnt smbfs
     username=joe,fmask=600,dmask=700,user,noauto 0 0
```

Because of the user option specified here, users can now mount the filesystem just by running the command

```
$ mount /home/joe/mnt
```

mount will prompt the user to supply a password before mounting the share.

See Chapter 16 for more information about NFS.

Although NFS is the UNIX standard for network file service, in some situations it may make more sense to use Samba and CIFS to share files among UNIX and Linux computers. For example, it is dangerous to allow users to perform NFS mounts of corporate filesystems from their personal laptops.[5] However, you can safely use CIFS to give these laptops access to their owner's home directories.

IBM has been investing resources in making CIFS access from Linux as seamless as possible, with the goal of establishing Samba as a robust alternative to NFS. An early result of this effort is that Samba 3.x can be configured to provide "UNIX extensions." With this feature turned on, you can see all UNIX file attributes, ownerships, and file types even when mounting a share by way of Samba.

Along with the server-side modifications, there is also a new client-side filesystem module being developed, called cifs. Current development is focused on the cifs module, which already has better debugging and configuration support than the traditional smbfs.

26.7 SHARING PRINTERS WITH SAMBA

The simple approach to printer sharing is to add a [printers] section to the **smb.conf** file; this makes Samba share all local printers. Samba uses the system printing com-

---

5. NFS security is based on the idea that the user has no root access on the client and that there are matching UIDs on the client and server. This is not normally the case for self-managed machines.

mands to do its work, but since Linux printing is not very standardized, you may have to tell Samba which particular printing system is in use on your server by setting the printing option to an appropriate value. Check the **smb.conf** man page for the list of printing systems that are currently supported.

```
[printers]
; Where to store print files before passing them to the printing system?
path = /var/tmp
; Everybody can use the printers.
guest ok = yes
; Let Samba know this share is a printer.
printable = yes
; Show the printers to everyone looking.
browseable = yes
; Tell samba what flavor of printing system the system is using.
printing = LPRNG
```

See Chapter 23 for more information about printing.

Windows clients can now use these printers as network printers, just as if they were hosted by a Windows server. There is one small problem, though. The Windows client will want know what kind of printer it is using, and it will ask the user to select an appropriate printer driver. This leads to quite a lot of support requests from users who do not know how to proceed in this situation. If the particular printer in question requires a driver that is not included with Windows, the situation will be even more support-intensive.

Fortunately, Samba can be configured to provide the necessary Windows printer drivers to the Windows clients. But to make this work, you must do some preparation. First, make sure that Samba behaves like a print server by adding appropriate entries to the [global] section of the **smb.conf** file:

```
[global]
; Who is our printer admin
printer admin = printadm
; The following have the right value by default.
disable spoolss = no
; Don't bother showing it; you cannot add printers anyway
show add printer wizard = no
; Assuming you want everybody to be able to print
guest ok = yes
browseable = no
```

Now Samba knows that it is a print server, and it will accept the user printadm as its printer administrator.

If you are going to provide printer drivers for your Windows clients, there has to be a place to store the drivers. This is done through a special share called [print$].

```
[print$]
comment = Printer Driver Area
; Place to store the printer drivers
path = /var/lib/samba/printers
```

```
browseable = yes
guest ok = yes
read only = yes
; Who can administer the printer driver repository
write list = printadm
```

Before you can start to upload printer drivers to the new print server, you must take care of a few more details at the system level. Make sure the printadm account exists and has permission to access Samba.

```
$ sudo useradd printadm
$ sudo smbpasswd -a printadm
```

Samba can only store printer drivers if the appropriate directory structure exists and is owned by printadm (as defined in the write list option):

```
$ sudo mkdir -p /var/lib/samba/printers
$ sudo cd /var/lib/samba/printers
$ sudo mkdir W32X86 WIN40
$ sudo chown -R printadm .
```

At this point there are two options: you can either walk to a Windows box and upload the printer drivers from there, or you can use Samba tools to do it all from the command line. Unfortunately, there is no simple way of knowing what exactly has to be installed for a particular driver, so we recommend the first approach in most circumstances. Only if you are faced with repeatedly installing a driver on multiple servers is it worthwhile to examine the installation and learn to replicate it with command-line tools.

Installing a printer driver from Windows

To install drivers from a Windows client, open a connection to the Samba server by typing \\samba-server.example.com in the Start -> Run dialog box. Windows will ask you to log on to the Samba server. Log in as the user printadm. If all goes well, a window pops up with a list of shares provided by the server.

Within the Printers subfolder you should see all the printers you have shared from your server. Right-click in the blank space around the printer icons to activate the Server Properties dialog, then add your favorite printer drivers via the Drivers tab.

The uploaded drivers end up in the directory specified for the [print$] share. At this point, you might want to take a quick peek at the properties of the driver you just uploaded. This list of files is what you will have to provide to the Samba command-line tool if you ever want to automate the uploading of the driver.

Once the proper drivers have been uploaded, you can now associate them with specific printers. Bring up the Properties panel of each printer in turn (by right-clicking and selecting Properties) and select the appropriate drivers in the Advanced tab. Then open the Printing Defaults dialog and modify the settings. Even if you are happy with the default settings, make at least one small change to force Windows to store the configuration data structures on the Samba server. Samba will then provide that data to clients that access the printer. If you miss this last step, you may end up with clients crashing because no valid default configuration can be found when they try to use the printer.

Installing a printer driver from the command line

As you may have guessed already, some of these steps are hard to replicate without using Windows, especially the setting of printer defaults. But if you want to set up hundreds of printers on a Samba server, you may want to try to do it from the command line all the same. Command-line configuration works particularly well for PostScript printers because the Windows PostScript printer driver works correctly without default configuration information.

If you have made a note of the files required by a particular driver, you can install the driver from the command line. First, copy the required files to the [print$] share:

```
$ cd ~/mydriver
$ smbclient -U printadm '//samba-server/print$' -c 'mput *.*'
```

Next, assign the driver to a particular printer. Let's assume you have a simple Post-Script printer with a custom PPD file:

```
$ rpcclient -U printadm -c "\
adddriver \"Windows NT x86\" \"Our Custom PS:\
PSCRIPT5.DLL:CUSTOM.PPD:PS5UI.DLL:PSCIPT.HLP:NULL:NULL:PSCRIPT.NTF\"" \
samba-server
```

The backslashes at the ends of lines allow the command to be split onto multiple lines for clarity; you can omit these and enter the command on one line if you prefer. The backslashes before double quotes distinguish the nested sets of quotes.

The long string in the example above contains the information listed in the property dialog of the printer driver that is seen when the printer driver is being installed from Windows:

- Long printer name
- Driver file name
- Data file name
- Configuration file name
- Help file name
- Language monitor name (set this to NULL if you have none)
- Default data type (set this to NULL if there is none)
- Comma-separated list of additional files

To configure a printer to use one of the uploaded drivers, run

```
$ rpcclient -U printadm -c "\
set driver \"myprinter\" \"Our Custom PS\"" samba-server
```

26.8 DEBUGGING SAMBA

Samba usually runs without requiring much attention. However, if you do have a problem, you can consult two primary sources of debugging information: the per-client log files and the **smbstatus** command. Make sure you have appropriate log file settings in your configuration file:

```
[global]
; The %m causes a separate file to be written for each client.
log file = /var/log/samba.log.%m
max log size = 1000
; How much info to log. You can also specify log levels for components
; of the system (here, 3 generally, but level 10 for authentication).
log level = 3 auth:10
```

Higher log levels produce more information. Logging takes time, so don't ask for too much detail unless you are debugging. Operation can be slowed considerably.

The following example shows the log entries generated by an unsuccessful connect attempt followed by a successful one.

```
[2004/09/05 16:29:45, 2] auth/auth.c:check_ntlm_password(312)
  check_ntlm_password: Authentication for user [oetiker] -> [oetiker] FAILED
     with error NT_STATUS_WRONG_PASSWORD
[2004/09/05 16:29:45, 2] smbd/server.c:exit_server(571)
  Closing connections
[2004/09/05 16:29:57, 2] auth/auth.c:check_ntlm_password(305)
  check_ntlm_password: authentication for user [oetiker] -> [oetiker] ->
     [oetiker] succeeded
[2004/09/05 16:29:57, 1] smbd/service.c:make_connection_snum(648)
  etsuko (127.0.0.1) connect to service oetiker initially as user oetiker
     (uid=1000, gid=1000) (pid 20492)
[2004/09/05 16:29:58, 1] smbd/service.c:close_cnum(837)
  etsuko (127.0.0.1) closed connection to service oetiker
[2004/09/05 16:29:58, 2] smbd/server.c:exit_server(571)
  Closing connections
```

The **smbcontrol** command is handy for altering the debug level on a running Samba server without altering the **smb.conf** file. For example,

```
$ sudo smbcontrol smbd debug "4 auth:10"
```

The example above would set the global debug level to 4 and set the debug level for authentication-related matters to 10. The **smbd** argument specifies that all **smbd** daemons on the system will have their debug levels set. To debug a specific established connection, you can use the **smbstatus** command to figure out which **smbd** daemon handles the connection and then pass its PID to **smbcontrol** to debug just this one connection. With log levels over 100 you will start seeing (encrypted) passwords in the logs.

smbstatus shows currently active connections and locked files. This information can be especially useful when you are tracking down locking problems (e.g., "Which user has file **xyz** open read/write exclusive?"). The first section of output lists the resources that a user has connected to. The second part lists any active file locks.[6]

```
Samba version 3.0.5

PID       Username   Group    Machine
-----------------------------------------------------------------
12636     zauck      ee       zhaka (192.168.1.228)
29857     milas      guests   beshil (192.168.1.123)

Service   pid        machine  Connected at
-----------------------------------------------------------------
milasa    29857      beshil   Fri Sep  3 17:07:39 2004
zaucker   12636      zhaka    Thu Sep  2 12:35:53 2004

Locked files:

Pid    DenyMode     Access   R/W    Oplock Name
-----------------------------------------------------------------
29857  DENY_NONE    0x3      RDWR   NONE   /home/milasa/hello.dba
12636  DENY_NONE    0x2019f  RDWR   NONE   /home/zaucker/aufbest.doc
```

If you kill the **smbd** associated with a certain user, all its locks will disappear. Some applications handle this gracefully and will just reacquire a lock if they need it. Others (such as MS Access) will freeze and die a horrible death with much clicking required on the Windows side just to be able to close the unhappy application. As dramatic as this may sound, we have yet to see any file corruption resulting from such a procedure. In any event, be careful when Windows claims that files have been locked by some other application. Often Windows is right and you should fix the problem on the client side by closing the application instead of brute-forcing it from the server.

26.9 RECOMMENDED READING

TERPSTRA, JOHN H. *Samba-3 by Example: Practical Exercises to Successful Deployment (2nd Edition).* Upper Saddle River, NJ: Prentice Hall PTR, 2006. (An online version of this book is available at samba.org.)

TERPSTRA, JOHN H., JELMER R. VERNOOIJ. *The Official Samba-3 HOWTO and Reference Guide (2nd Edition).* Upper Saddle River, NJ: Prentice Hall PTR, 2006. (An online version of this book is available at samba.org.)

Exercises are presented on the next page.

---

6. **smbstatus** output contains some very long lines; we have condensed it here for clarity.

26.10 EXERCISES

E26.1 Why would you want to block Internet access to ports 137–139 and 445 on a Samba server?

E26.2 Install the Cygwin software on a Windows machine and use **ssh** in **rxvt** to connect to a Linux machine. What differences to PuTTY do you find?

★★ **E26.3** In the lab, compare the performance of a client that accesses files through Samba with one that accesses files from a native CIFS server (i.e., a Windows machine). If your two test servers have different hardware, devise a way to adjust for the hardware variation so that the comparison is more indicative of the performance of the server software. (May require root access.)

★★ **E26.4** In the lab, using a packet sniffer such as **tcpdump** or Wireshark, monitor a **telnet** session between Windows and a Linux server. Obtain and install the PuTTY software and repeat the monitoring. In each case, what can you see with the packet sniffer? (Requires root access.)

★★ **E26.5** Set up a Samba print server that provides Windows printer drivers for all the printers it shares. Make sure the printers come with a sensible default configuration.

27 *Serial Devices*

Child left to its own serial devices

Since 1969, the RS-232C serial interface standard has provided a way for devices of many types and from many manufacturers to communicate. It is the one computer interface standard that has remained virtually untouched across its almost 40-year history, and it is still in use today.

Serial ports are used with a variety of devices, including printers, terminals, and other computers. They're also found on a lot of custom-made, hobbyist, and low-volume equipment (media changers, temperature sensors, GPS receivers, even sewing machines). A serial device can be attached to the system either directly (with a cable) or through a telephone line with modems at each end.

This chapter describes how to attach serial devices to your system and explains how to configure your software to take advantage of them. We use modems and printers as specific examples, but other devices are essentially similar.

The first few sections address serial hardware and cabling considerations. Then, starting on page 855, we talk about the software infrastructure that has historically been used to support hardware terminals. Terminals are rarely used anymore, but their ghosts live on in Linux's handling of pseudo-terminals and window systems. The rest of the chapter (starting on page 862) provides some general background on modems, serial debugging, and USB (the Universal Serial Bus).

Serial Devices

27.1 THE RS-232C STANDARD

Most serial ports conform to some variant of the RS-232C standard. This standard specifies the electrical characteristics and meaning of each signal wire, as well as pin assignments on the traditional 25-pin (DB-25) serial connector shown in Exhibit A.

Exhibit A   A male DB-25 connector

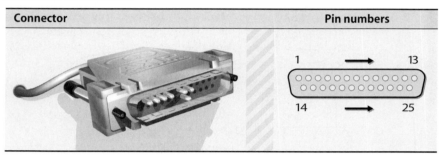

Full RS-232C[1] is overkill for all real-world situations since it defines numerous signals that are unnecessary for basic communication. DB-25 connectors are also inconveniently large. As a result, a number of alternative connectors have come into widespread use. These are described in the section titled *Alternative connectors* starting on page 847.

Traditional RS-232 used shielded twisted-pair cable (STP), usually stranded 22-gauge wire. In modern times, the same unshielded twisted pair (UTP) cable that is standard for Ethernet connections is used for serial cabling. This cable does not technically adhere to the RS-232 specification, but in practice it usually works OK.

The original RS-232 signal voltages were ±12 volts DC, but ±5 volts is more common these days. Sometimes, ±3 volts is used. Higher voltages are less susceptible to interference. All of these voltages comply with the RS-232 specification, so it's perfectly OK to connect devices that use different voltage standards.

RS-232 is not an electrically "balanced" system; it uses a single conductor for the data traveling in each direction. Ergo, the special electrical properties of twisted-pair cabling may be less significant for serial communication than they are for, say, Ethernet. In fact, twisted-pair cable can actually reduce the reliability and range of a serial connection if the two data lines (TD and RD) are placed together on a single pair. So don't do that.

There is no commonly agreed-on standard for which RS-232 signals should be run together on a twisted-pair cable. Some sources recommend pairing signal grounds with both TD and RD, but this pairing costs an extra conductor and provides multiple

---

1. To be technically correct, this standard should now be referred to as EIA-232-E. However, no one will have the slightest idea what you are talking about.

paths for the signal ground. As far as we know, there is no compelling reason to use this convention.

DB-25 connectors are either male (with pins sticking out, called DB25P) or female (with matching holes, DB25S). Tiny invisible numbers near the pins or holes label them from 1 to 25. You can see the numbers best by holding the connector up to the light and viewing it at an angle. Sometimes only pins 1, 13, 14, and 25 are numbered.

Exhibit A shows a male DB-25. As with all serial connectors, the pin numbers on a female connector are a mirror image of those on a male connector, so that like-numbered pins mate. The diagram is drawn from the orientation shown (as if you were facing the end of the cable, about to plug the connector into your forehead).

Note that in Exhibit A, only seven pins are actually installed. This is typical for the real world. The RS-232 signals and their pin assignments on a DB-25 connector are shown in Table 27.1. Only the shaded signals are ever used in practice (at least on generic computer systems); all others can be ignored.

Table 27.1   RS-232 signals and pin assignments on a DB-25

Pin	Name	Function	Pin	Name	Function
1	FG	Frame ground	14	STD	Secondary TD
2	TD	Transmitted data	15	TC	Transmit clock
3	RD	Received data	16	SRD	Secondary RD
4	RTS	Request to send	17	RC	Receive clock
5	CTS	Clear to send	18	–	Not assigned
6	DSR	Data set ready	19	SRTS	Secondary RTS
7	SG	Signal ground	20	DTR	Data terminal ready
8	DCD	Data carrier detect	21	SQ	Signal quality detector
9	–	Positive voltage	22	RI	Ring indicator
10	–	Negative voltage	23	DRS	Data rate selector
11	–	Not assigned	24	SCTE	Clock transmit external
12	SDCD	Secondary DCD	25	BUSY	Busy
13	SCTS	Secondary CTS			

The two interface configurations for serial equipment are DTE (Data Terminal Equipment) and DCE (Data Communications Equipment). DTE and DCE share the same pinouts, but they specify different interpretations of the RS-232 signals.

Every device is configured as either DTE or DCE; a few devices support both, but not simultaneously. Computers, terminals, and printers are generally DTE, and most modems are DCE. DTE and DCE serial ports can communicate with each other in any combination, but different combinations require different cabling.

There is no sensible reason for both DTE and DCE to exist; all equipment could use the same wiring scheme. The existence of two conventions is merely one of the many pointless historical legacies of RS-232.

Serial Devices

DTE and DCE can be quite confusing if you let yourself think about the implications too much. When that happens, just take a deep breath and reread these points:

- The RS-232 pinout for a given connector type is always the same, regardless of whether the connector is male or female (matching pin numbers always mate) and regardless of whether the connector is on a cable, a DTE device, or a DCE device.

- All RS-232 terminology is based on the model of a straight-through connection from a DTE device to a DCE device. (By "straight through," we mean that TD on the DTE end is connected to TD on the DCE end, and so on. Each pin connects to the same-numbered pin on the other end.)

- Signals are named relative to the perspective of the DTE device. For example, the name TD (transmitted data) really means "data transmitted from DTE to DCE." Despite the name, the TD pin is an *input* on a DCE device. Similarly, RD is an input for DTE and an output for DCE.

- When you wire DTE equipment to DTE equipment (computer-to-terminal or computer-to-computer), you must trick each device into thinking that the other is DCE. For example, both DTE devices will expect to transmit on TD and receive on RD; you must cross-connect the wires so that one device's transmit pin goes to the other's receive pin, and vice versa.

- Three sets of signals must be crossed in this fashion for DTE-to-DTE communication (if you choose to connect them at all). TD and RD must be crossed. RTS and CTS must be crossed. And each side's DTR pin must be connected to both the DCD and DSR pins of the peer.

- To add to the confusion, a cable crossed for DTE-to-DTE communication is often called a "null modem" cable. You might be tempted to use a null modem cable to hook up a modem, but since modems are DCE, that won't work! A cable for a modem is called a "modem cable" or a "straight cable."

Because the issue of DTE vs. DCE is so confusing, you may occasionally see well-intentioned but ill-advised attempts to bring some sanity to the nomenclature by defining DTE and DCE as if they had separate pinouts (e.g., renaming DCE's TD pin to be RD, and vice versa). In this alternate universe, pinouts vary but cable connections (by signal name) do not. We suggest that you ignore any material that talks about a "DTE pinout" or a "DCE pinout"; it is unlikely to be a reliable source of information.

Originally, DTE devices were supposed to have male connectors and DCE devices were supposed to have female ones. Eventually, hardware designers realized that male connectors are more fragile. Expensive computing hardware now usually has female connectors, and most cables are male on both ends.[2]

---

2. At Qwest, the terms "male" and "female" are considered inappropriate. Employees are encouraged to use the words "plug" and "receptacle." The standard connector names DB25P and DB25S actually derive from yet a third convention: "pin" and "socket."

Exhibit B shows pin assignments and connections for both null-modem and straight-through cables. Only signals used in the real world are shown.

Exhibit B   Pin assignments and connections for DB-25 cables

Legend		Straight	Null modem
Frame ground	FG	1 —— 1	1 ⤬ 1
Transmitted data	TD	2 —— 2	2 ⤬ 2
Received data	RD	3 —— 3	3 ⤬ 3
Request to send	RTS	4 —— 4	4 ⤬ 4
Clear to send	CTS	5 —— 5	5 ⤬ 5
Data set ready	DSR	6 —— 6	6 ⤬ 6
Signal ground	SG	7 —— 7	7 —— 7
Data carrier detect	DCD	8 —— 8	8 ⤬ 8
Data terminal ready	DTR	20 —— 20	20 ⤬ 20

27.2 ALTERNATIVE CONNECTORS

The following sections describe the most common alternative connector systems: mini DIN-8, DB-9, and RJ-45. Despite their physical differences, these connectors all provide access to the same electrical signals as a DB-25. Devices that use different connectors are always compatible if the right kind of converter cable is used.

The mini DIN-8 variant

Mini DIN-8s are found on many laptops and workstations. This almost circular and extremely compact connector provides connections for seven signals. It is illustrated in Exhibit C.

Exhibit C   A male mini DIN-8 connector

Connector	Pin numbers

Neighborhood computer dealers usually carry injection-molded DB-25 to mini DIN-8 converter cables. Don't try to make them yourself because a mini DIN-8 is so tiny that it defies attempts to secure connections with human fingers. Pin assignments are shown in Table 27.2 on the next page.

Table 27.2   Pins for a mini DIN-8 to DB-25 straight cable

DIN-8	DB-25	Signal	Function
3	2	TD	Transmitted data
5	3	RD	Received data
6	4	RTS	Request to send
2	5	CTS	Clear to send
4,8	7	SG	Signal ground
7	8	DCD	Data carrier detect
1	20	DTR	Data terminal ready

The DB-9 variant

Commonly found on PCs, this nine-pin connector (which looks like a DB-25 "junior") provides the eight most commonly used signals.

Exhibit D   A male DB-9 connector

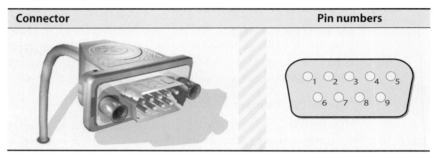

Connector	Pin numbers

PC dealers in your area should carry prefab DB-9 to DB-25 converter cables. Table 27.3 shows the pin assignments.

Table 27.3   Pins for a DB-9 to DB-25 straight cable

DB-9	DB-25	Signal	Function
3	2	TD	Transmitted data
2	3	RD	Received data
7	4	RTS	Request to send
8	5	CTS	Clear to send
6	6	DSR	Data set ready
5	7	SG	Signal ground
1	8	DCD	Data carrier detect
4	20	DTR	Data terminal ready

The RJ-45 variant

An RJ-45 is an 8-wire modular telephone connector. It's similar to the standard RJ-11 connector used for telephone wiring in the United States, but an RJ-45 has eight pins (an RJ-11 has only four).[3] In many situations, using RJ-45s makes it easier for you to run serial communications through your building's existing cable plant (which was probably installed with twisted-pair Ethernet in mind).

Exhibit E   **A male RJ-45 connector**

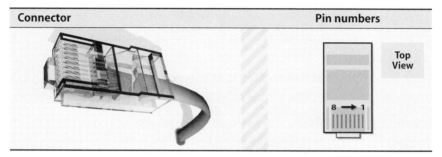

RJ-45 jacks for serial connections are usually not found on computers or garden-variety serial equipment, but they are often used as intermediate connectors for routing serial lines through patch panels. RJ-45s are sometimes used with flat telephone cable rather than twisted-pair. Either form of cable is acceptable for serial connections, although twisted pair cable generally yields better signal quality at a distance. Flat telephone cable is never acceptable for Ethernet connections, so many sites standardize on twisted pair cable to reduce the risk that a clueless user will accidentally grab the wrong type of cable.

RJ-45s are compact, self-securing, and cheap. They are crimped onto the cable with a special tool. It takes less than a minute to attach one. If you are designing a large cabling system from scratch, RJ-45s are a good choice for intermediate connectors.

Several systems map the pins on an RJ-45 connector to a DB-25. Table 27.4 on the next page shows the official RS-232D standard, which is used only haphazardly.

One alternative way of using RJ-45s is with Dave Yost's system, which adds an RJ-45 socket to every device and uses only a single type of RJ-45 connector cable regardless of whether the devices are DTE or DCE. Dave's system is more than just a pinout; it's a complete cabling system that addresses several different issues. With his kind permission, Dave's description of his standard is reproduced in the next section.

Serial Devices

---

3. Careful inspection will reveal that an RJ-11 plug actually has six slots where pins might go but that only four conductors are installed. A true four-conductor telephone connector is an RJ-10. An RJ-11 with all six pins installed is known as an RJ-12.

Table 27.4   Pins for an RJ-45 to DB-25 straight cable

RJ-45	DB-25	Signal	Function
1	6	DSR	Data set ready
2	8	DCD	Data carrier detect
3	20	DTR	Data terminal ready
4	7	SG	Signal ground
5	3	RD	Received data
6	2	TD	Transmitted data
7	5	CTS	Clear to send
8	4	RTS	Request to send

The Yost standard for RJ-45 wiring

This specification was written by Dave Yost (Dave@Yost.com).

Here is a scheme that offers solutions to several RS-232 hassles:

- All cable connectors are of the same sex and type (male RJ-45).
- There is no distinction between DTE and DCE.
- You need only one kind of connector cable.
- You can mass-produce cables quickly, using only a crimping tool.

Each serial port on every piece of equipment gets its own appropriately wired DB-25 or DB-9 to RJ-45 adaptor. This adaptor is permanently screwed onto the port. The port now presents the same connector interface, female RJ-45, regardless of whether its underlying connector is DB-25 or DB-9, DTE or DCE, male or female. Furthermore, every serial port now transmits and receives data on the same pins.

Once you have put these adaptors on your RS-232 ports, you can connect anything to anything without using null-modems or null-terminals, changing pins on cable connectors, or building special cables. You can connect modem to computer, modem to terminal, terminal to computer, terminal to terminal, computer to computer, etc., all with one kind of cable.

In Yost's original vision, the cables are jacketed, 8-wire ribbon cable. The connectors on each end are squeezed onto the cable with a crimping tool, so there is no soldering or messing with pins. Because of aversion to this type of cable, some organizations use the Yost standard with UTP cabling.

There are three signal wires (one data and two control) going in each direction, plus a pair of signal grounds. The cables are not wired normally (i.e., with each connector pin connected to the corresponding pin at the other end of the cable). They are wired "with a twist," or "mirror image," or "side-to-side reversed," or whatever you want to call it. That is, pin 1 at one end of the cable goes to pin 8 on the other end, etc. (This meaning of "twist" is distinct from its use in the term "twisted pair.") This scheme works because the layout of the signals on the ribbon cable is symmetrical. That is, each transmit pin has its corresponding receive pin at the mirror-image wire position across the flat cable.[4]

Ready-made RJ-45 cables are usually wired straight through. To use them with this system, you have to remove the connector from one end and crimp on a new one with the wires reversed. Female-to-female RJ-45 connectors ("butt blocks") are available for extending cable lengths, but remember: two twisted cables joined with such a coupler make a straight-through cable.

Many vendors make DB-25 to RJ-45 adaptors. Their internal color coding does not match the cable colors. The adaptors, wire connectors, and wire have become available at electronics stores, sadly without any help for using them for RS-232.

See page 353 for more information about Category 5 cable.

The Yost scheme was intended for use with jacketed ribbon cable, in which all the wires are side by side. Twisted-pair cable, by contrast, has four pairs of wire, each pair twisted against itself along the cable's length. If you use twisted-pair cable (such as Category 5 cable), you should not wire your cables as you normally would for RJ-45 (e.g., for 10BaseT, telephone, etc.). Rather, you should wire them so that wires 3:4 and wires 5:6 make pairs. Other pairings are susceptible to data signal crosstalk. The pairing of the remaining wires is not important, but 1:2 and 7:8 will be about as good as any.

Inside an adaptor is an RJ-45 socket with eight wires coming out of it. These wires have RS-232 pins (or pin sockets, as appropriate) crimped onto them. You simply push these pins into the proper holes in the RS-232 connector and then snap the adaptor housing on. Use the pinouts shown in Table 27.5.

Table 27.5   Wiring for a Yost RJ-45 to DB-25 or DB-9 adaptor

RJ-45 Cable			Adaptor	Connect to DCE pins			Connect to DTE pins		
				DB-25	DB-9	Signal	DB-25	DB-9	Signal
1	Brown	(to Gray)	Blue	4	7	RTS	5	8	CTS
2	Blue	(to Orange)	Orange	20	4	DTR	8	1	DCD
3	Yellow	(to Black)	Black	2	3	TD	3	2	RD
4	Green	(to Red)	Red	7	5	GND	7	5	GND
5	Red	(to Green)	Green	7	5	GND	7	5	GND
6	Black	(to Yellow)	Yellow	3	2	RD	2	3	TD
7	Orange	(to Blue)	Brown	8	1	DCD	20	4	DTR
8	Gray	(to Brown)	White	5	8	CTS	4	7	RTS

There is one problem, however: both ground pins have to go into the same DB-25 or DB-9 hole (pin 7 or 5, respectively). So that these wires come out to one pin, you can

Serial Devices

4. Dave doesn't say this explicitly, but if you are using flat ribbon cable, you must in fact wire the cable without a physical twist to achieve the "with a twist" effect. Because the connectors at the ends of a cable point away from each other, their pin numbering is automatically reversed.

crimp them with a tiny plastic thingy made by AMP and called a "Tel-splice connector ½ tap dry," part number 553017-4. So far, this part seems to be available only in quantity 1,000 for $80 or so. Believe me [Dave Yost], you want them if you're going to wire more than a few adaptors.

Some DTE devices require the DSR signal to be active before they will send data. This signal is usually provided by the DCE device, but you can fake it by wiring together pins 20 and 6 (4 and 6 on a DB-9 connector). This way, the DTE device receives the DSR signal from itself whenever it asserts DTR.

On some DCE printers, pin 7 of the RJ-45 adaptor (the brown wire) should be connected to the DSR line (pin 6 on both DB-25 and DB-9). Read your printer documentation to find out if your printer provides useful handshaking signals on DSR instead of DCD.

Dave Yost
Los Altos, CA
July 1999

Don't use either of these DSR hacks as a matter of course; add them only to specific devices that seem to need them (or that don't seem to work with the standard setup). Some "vanilla" devices tolerate the extra connections, but others become confused.

27.3 HARD AND SOFT CARRIER

Linux expects to see the DCD signal, carrier detect, go high (positive voltage) when a device is attached and turned on. This signal is carried on pin 8 of the standard DB-25 connector. If your serial cable has a DCD line and your computer really pays attention to it, you are using what is known as hard carrier. Most systems also allow soft carrier, that is, the computer pretends that DCD is always asserted.

For certain devices (particularly terminals), soft carrier is a great blessing. You can get away with using only three lines for each serial connection: transmit, receive, and signal ground. However, modem connections really need the DCD signal. If a terminal is connected through a modem and the carrier signal is lost, the modem should hang up (especially on a long distance call!).

You normally specify soft carrier for a serial port in the configuration file for whatever client software you are using in conjunction with the port (e.g., **/etc/gettydefs** or **/etc/inittab** for a login terminal or **/etc/cups/printcap** for a printer). You can also use **stty -clocal** to enable soft carrier on the fly. For example,

```
# stty -clocal < /dev/ttyS1
```

enables soft carrier for the port **ttyS1**.

27.4 HARDWARE FLOW CONTROL

The CTS and RTS signals make sure that a device does not send data faster than the receiver can process it. For example, if a modem is in danger of running out of buffer space (perhaps because the connection to the remote site is slower than the serial link between the local machine and the modem), it can tell the computer to shut up until more room becomes available in the buffer.

Flow control is essential for high-speed modems and is also very useful for printers. On systems that do not support hardware flow control (either because the serial ports do not understand it or because the serial cable leaves CTS and RTS disconnected), flow control can sometimes be simulated in software with the ASCII characters XON and XOFF. However, software flow control must be explicitly supported by high-level software, and even then it does not work very well.

XON and XOFF are <Control-Q> and <Control-S>, respectively. This is a problem for **emacs** users because <Control-S> is the default key binding for the **emacs** search command. To fix the problem, bind the search command to some other key or use **stty start** and **stty stop** to change the terminal driver's idea of XON and XOFF.

Most terminals ignore the CTS and RTS signals. By jumpering pins 4 and 5 together at the terminal end of the cable, you can fool the few terminals that require a handshake across these pins before they will communicate. When the terminal sends out a signal on pin 4 saying "I'm ready," it gets the same signal back on pin 5 saying "Go ahead." You can also jumper the DTR/DSR/DCD handshake in this way.

As with soft carrier, hardware flow control can be manipulated through configuration files or set with **stty**.

27.5 CABLE LENGTH

The RS-232 standard specifies a maximum cable length of 75 feet at 9,600 bps. Standards are usually conservative, and RS-232 is no exception. We have routinely run RS-232 cables much greater distances, up to about 1,000 feet. We have hit the limit somewhere between 800 and 1,000 feet but have found that the particular brand of devices on each end makes quite a difference.

Line drivers or repeaters are sometimes used with RS-232 to extend the maximum length of a connection. Unfortunately, these devices often boost only the RD and TD pins, so other signals may need to be jumpered.

27.6 SERIAL DEVICE FILES

Serial ports are represented by device files in or under **/dev**. Most computers have two serial ports built in: **/dev/ttyS0** and **/dev/ttyS1**. Linux distributions usually preinstall a full complement of device files (64 or more) for additional serial ports, but until you add more hardware to the system, the extra files are superfluous and should be ignored.

As always, the names of the device files do not really matter. Device mapping is determined by the major and minor device numbers, and the names of device files are merely a convenience for human users.

Serial Devices

27.7 SETSERIAL: SET SERIAL PORT PARAMETERS

The serial ports on a PC can be set to use several different I/O port addresses and interrupt levels (IRQs). These settings are normally accessed through the system's BIOS at power-on time. The most common reason to change them is to accommodate some cranky piece of hardware that is finicky about its own settings and only works correctly when it has co-opted the settings normally used by a serial port. Unfortunately, the serial driver may not be able to detect such configuration changes without your help.

The traditional UNIX response to such diversity is to allow the serial port parameters to be specified when the kernel is compiled. Fortunately, Linux lets you skip this tedious step and change the parameters on the fly with the **setserial** command.

setserial -g shows the current settings:

```
# setserial -g /dev/ttyS0
/dev/ttyS0, UART: 16550A, Port: 0x03f8, IRQ: 4
```

To set the parameters, you specify the device file and then a series of parameters and values. For example, the command

```
# setserial /dev/ttyS1 port 0x02f8 irq 3
```

sets the I/O port address and IRQ for **ttyS1**. It's important to keep in mind that this command does not change the hardware configuration in any way; it simply informs the Linux serial driver of the configuration. To change the actual settings of the hardware, consult your system's BIOS.

setserial changes only the current configuration, and the settings do not persist across reboots. Unfortunately, there isn't a standard way to make the changes permanent; each of our example distributions does it differently.

Red Hat and Fedora's **/etc/rc.d/rc.sysinit** script checks for the existence of **/etc/rc.serial** and executes it at startup time if it exists. No example file is provided, so you must create the file yourself if you want to make use of this feature. Just list the **setserial** commands you want to run, one per line. For completeness, it's probably a good idea to make the file executable and to put **#!/bin/sh** on the first line; however, these *touches d'élégance* aren't strictly required.

SUSE's **/etc/init.d/serial** script handles serial port initialization. Unfortunately, this script has no configuration file; you must edit it directly to reflect the commands you want to run. Bad SUSE! The script uses its own little metalanguage to construct the **setserial** command lines, but fortunately there are plenty of commented-out example lines to choose from.

Debian has a nicely commented configuration file, **/etc/serial.conf**, that is read by **/etc/init.d/setserial**. This file is also available for Ubuntu in the **setserial** package, but it is not installed by default. Its advanced features (such as persistent autoconfiguration) are probably only useful for the designers of the distribution. For simple cases, just uncomment the lines you want or add your own in **setserial** format (omit the command name).

27.8 SOFTWARE CONFIGURATION FOR SERIAL DEVICES

Once a device has been connected with the proper cable, software on the host machine must be configured to take advantage of it. The configuration chores for a new device depend on the type of device and the uses to which it will be put:

- For a hardwired terminal, you must tell the system to listen for logins on the terminal's port. You specify the speed and parameters of the serial connection. Configuration for terminals is described in the next section.

- Dial-in modems are configured similarly to hardwired terminals. However, the exact procedure may be slightly different on some systems.

- To see how to use a modem to connect to a remote network using PPP, refer to page 320.

- See Chapter 23, *Printing*, for information about how to set up a serial printer. Some printers only receive data; others are bidirectional and can return status information to the host computer.

- A custom serial device that you use only from your own software needs no special configuration. You can simply open the device file to access the device. Refer to the **termios** man page to learn how to set the speed, flag bits, and buffering mode of the serial port.

27.9 CONFIGURATION OF HARDWIRED TERMINALS

Over the last two decades, cheap computers have almost entirely replaced ASCII terminals. However, even the "terminal" windows on a graphical display use the same drivers and configuration files as real terminals, so system administrators still need to understand how this archaic technology works.

Terminal configuration involves two main tasks: making sure that a process is attached to a terminal to accept logins and making sure that information about the terminal is available once a user has logged in. Before we dive into the details of these tasks, however, let's take a look at the entire login process.

The login process

*See page 33 for more information about the **init** daemon.*

The login process involves several different programs, the most important of which is the **init** daemon. One of **init**'s jobs is to spawn a process, known generically as a **getty**, on each terminal port that is turned on in the **/etc/inittab** file. The **getty** sets the port's initial characteristics (such as speed and parity) and prints a login prompt.

The actual name of the **getty** program varies among Linux distributions, and some distributions include multiple implementations. Red Hat, Fedora, and SUSE use a simplified version called **mingetty** to handle logins on virtual consoles. To manage terminals and dial-in modems, they provide Gert Doering's **mgetty** implementation. Debian and Ubuntu use a single **getty** written by Wietse Venema et al.; this version is also available on SUSE systems under the name **agetty**. An older implementation called **uugetty** has largely been superseded by **mgetty**.

To distinguish among this plenitude of **getty**s, think of them in order of complexity. **mingetty** is the simplest and is essentially just a placeholder for a **getty**. It can only handle logins on Linux virtual consoles. **agetty** is a bit more well-rounded and handles both serial ports and modems. **mgetty** is the current king of the hill. It handles incoming faxes as well as logins and does proper locking and coordination so that the same modem can be used as both a dial-in and a dial-out line.

The sequence of events in a complete login is as follows:

- **getty** prints the contents of the **/etc/issue** file, along with a login prompt.
- A user enters a login name at **getty**'s prompt.
- **getty** executes the **login** program with the specified name as an argument.
- **login** requests a password and validates it against **/etc/shadow**.[5]
- **login** prints the message of the day from **/etc/motd** and runs a shell.
- The shell executes the appropriate startup files.[6]
- The shell prints a prompt and waits for input.

When the user logs out, control returns to **init**, which wakes up and spawns a new **getty** on the terminal port.

Most of the configurability in this chain of events is concentrated in **/etc/inittab**, where the system's normal complement of **getty**s is defined, and in **/etc/gettydefs**, where some versions of **getty** look for additional configuration information.

The /etc/inittab file

init supports various "run levels" that determine which system resources are enabled. There are seven run levels, numbered 0 to 6, with "s" recognized as a synonym for level 1 (single-user operation). When you leave single-user mode, **init** prompts you to enter a run level unless an initdefault field exists in **/etc/inittab** as described below. **init** then scans the **inittab** file for all lines that match the specified run level.

Run levels are usually set up so that you have one level in which only the console is enabled and another level that enables all **getty**s. You can define the run levels in whatever way is appropriate for your system; however, we recommend that you not stray too far from the defaults.

Entries in **inittab** are of the form

    id:run-levels:action:process

5. If shadow passwords are not in use, the password may come directly from **/etc/passwd**. In addition, **/etc/passwd** may be superseded or complemented by an administrative database system such as NIS. See Chapter 17 for more information.
6. **.profile** for **sh** and **ksh**; **.bash_profile** and **.bashrc** for **bash**; **.cshrc** and **.login** for **csh/tcsh**.

Here are some simple examples of **inittab** entries.

```
# Trap CTRL-ALT-DELETE
ca::ctrlaltdel:/sbin/shutdown -t3 -r now

# Run gettys in standard runlevels
1:2345:respawn:/sbin/mingetty tty1
2:2345:respawn:/sbin/mingetty tty2
```

In this format, *id* is a one- or two-character string that identifies the entry; it can be null. For terminal entries, it is customary to use the terminal number as the *id*.

run-levels enumerates the run levels to which the entry pertains. If no levels are specified (as in the first line), then the entry is valid for all run levels. The *action* tells how to handle the *process* field; Table 27.6 lists some of the more commonly used values.

Table 27.6 Common values for the /etc/inittab *action* field

Value	Wait?	Meaning
initdefault	–	Sets the initial run level
boot	No	Runs when **inittab** is read for the first time
bootwait	Yes	Runs when **inittab** is read for the first time
ctrlaltdel	No	Runs in response to a keyboard <Control-Alt-Delete>
once	No	Starts the process once
wait	Yes	Starts the process once
respawn	No	Always keeps the process running
powerfail	No	Runs when **init** receives a power-fail signal
powerwait	Yes	Runs when **init** receives a power-fail signal
sysinit	Yes	Runs before accessing the console

If one of the *run-levels* matches the current run level and the *action* field indicates that the entry is relevant, **init** uses **sh** to execute (or terminate) the command specified in the *process* field. The Wait? column in Table 27.6 tells whether **init** waits for the command to complete before continuing.

In the example **inittab** lines above, the last two lines spawn **mingetty** processes on the first two virtual consoles (accessed with <Alt-F1> and <Alt-F2>). If you add hardwired terminals or dial-in modems, the appropriate **inittab** lines will look similar to these. However, you must use **mgetty** or **getty** (**agetty** on SUSE) with such devices because **mingetty** is not sophisticated enough to handle them correctly. In general, respawn is the correct action and 2345 is an appropriate set of levels.

The command **telinit -q** makes **init** reread the **inittab** file.

Different **getty**s require different configuration procedures. The **getty/agetty** version found on SUSE, Debian and Ubuntu is generally a bit cleaner than the **mgetty** version because it accepts all of its configuration information on the command line (in **/etc/inittab**).

Serial Devices

The general model is

/sbin/getty *port speed termtype*

See page 858 for more information about the **terminfo** *database.*

where *port* is the device file of the serial port relative to **/dev**, *speed* is the baud rate (e.g., 38400), and *termtype* identifies the default terminal type for the port. The *termtype* refers to an entry in the **terminfo** database. Most emulators simulate a DEC VT100, denoted **vt100**. Most of the many other minor options relate to the handling of dial-in modems.

 mgetty, provided by Red Hat, Fedora, and SUSE, is a bit more sophisticated than **agetty** in its handling of modems and integrates both incoming and outgoing fax capability. Unfortunately, its configuration is a bit more diffuse. In addition to other command-line flags, **mgetty** can accept an optional reference to an entry in **/etc/gettydefs** that specifies configuration details for the serial driver. Unless you're setting up a sophisticated modem configuration, you can usually get away without a **gettydefs** entry.

 On Red Hat systems, use **man mgettydefs** to find the man page for the **gettydefs** file. It's named this way to avoid conflict with an older **gettydefs** man page that no longer exists on any Linux system.

A simple **mgetty** command line for a hardwired terminal looks something like this:

/sbin/mgetty -rs *speed device*

The *speed* is the baud rate (e.g., 38400), and the *device* is the device file for the serial port (use the full pathname).

If you want to specify a default terminal type for a port when using **mgetty**, you must do so in a separate file, **/etc/ttytype**, and not on the **mgetty** command line. The format of an entry in **ttytype** is

termtype device

device is the short name of the device file representing the port, and *termtype* is the name of the appropriate **terminfo** entry (see the next section). For example:

```
linux    tty1
linux    tty2
vt100    ttyS0
vt100    ttyS1
```

Terminal support: the termcap and terminfo databases

Linux supports many different terminal types aided by a database of terminal capabilities that specifies the features and programming quirks of each brand of terminal. There have historically been two competing database formats: **termcap** and **terminfo**. For maximum compatibility, Linux distributions generally provide both. The **termcap** database is contained in the file **/etc/termcap**, and the **terminfo** database is stored in **/usr/share/terminfo**. The two databases are similar and use the same name for each terminal type, so the distinction between them is unimportant.

As shipped, both databases contain entries for hundreds of different terminals. In this terminal-less era, most are completely irrelevant. A good rule of thumb is that everything emulates a DEC VT100 until proven otherwise. Many emulators also support "ansi"; "linux" and "xterm" are useful for Linux consoles and **xterm** (X Windows terminal) windows, respectively.

See page 861 for more information about configuring terminals at login time. Linux programs look at the TERM environment variable to determine what kind of terminal you are using. The terminal can then be looked up in **termcap** or **terminfo**. The system normally sets the TERM variable for you at login time, in accordance with the command-line arguments to **getty/agetty** or the contents of **/etc/ttytype**.

27.10 SPECIAL CHARACTERS AND THE TERMINAL DRIVER

The terminal driver supports several special functions that you access by typing particular keys (usually control keys) on the keyboard. The exact binding of functions to keys can be set with the **tset** and **stty** commands. Table 27.7 lists some of these functions, along with their default key bindings.

Table 27.7 Special characters for the terminal driver

Name	Default	Function
erase	<Control-?>	Erases one character of input
werase	<Control-W>	Erases one word of input
kill	<Control-U>	Erases the entire line of input
eof	<Control-D>	Sends an "end of file" indication
intr	<Control-C>	Interrupts the currently running process
quit	<Control-\>	Kills the current process with a core dump
stop	<Control-S>	Stops output to the screen
start	<Control-Q>	Restarts output to the screen
susp	<Control-Z>	Suspends the current process
lnext	<Control-V>	Interprets the next character literally

By default, PC versions of the Linux kernel generate a delete character (<Control-?>) when the backspace key is pressed. (This key may be labeled "backspace" or "delete," or it may show only a backarrow graphic. It depends on the keyboard.) In the past, many UNIX systems used the backspace character (<Control-H>) for this role. Unfortunately, the existence of two different standards for this function creates a multitude of problems.

You can use **stty erase** (see the next section) to tell the terminal driver which key code your setup is actually generating. However, some programs (such as text editors and shells with command-editing features) have their own idea of what the backspace character should be, and they don't always pay attention to the terminal driver's setting. In a helpful but confusing twist, some programs obey both the backspace and delete characters. You may also find that remote systems you log in to through the network make very different assumptions from those of your local system.

Solving these annoying little conflicts can be a Sunday project in itself. In general, there is no simple, universal solution. Each piece of software must be individually beaten into submission. Two useful resources to help with this task are the *Linux Backspace/Delete mini-HOWTO* from www.tldp.org and a nifty article by Anne Baretta at www.ibb.net/~anne/keyboard.html.

27.11 STTY: SET TERMINAL OPTIONS

stty lets you directly change and query the various settings of the terminal driver. There are about a zillion options, but most can be safely ignored. **stty** generally uses the same names for driver options as the **termios** man page does, but occasional discrepancies pop up.

stty's command-line options can appear in any order and in any combination. A dash before an option negates it. For example, to configure a terminal for 9,600 bps operation with even parity and without hardware tabs, use the command

```
$ stty 9600 even -tabs
```

A good combination of options to use for a plain-vanilla terminal is

```
$ stty intr ^C kill ^U erase ^? -tabs
```

Here, **-tabs** prevents the terminal driver from taking advantage of the terminal's built-in tabulation mechanism, a useful practice because many emulators are not very smart about tabs. The other options set the interrupt, kill, and erase characters to <Control-C>, <Control-U>, and <Control-?> (delete), respectively.

You can use **stty** to examine the current modes of the terminal driver as well as to set them. **stty** with no arguments produces output like this:

```
$ stty
speed 38400 baud; line = 0;
-brkint -imaxbel
```

For a more verbose status report, use the **-a** option:

```
$ stty -a
speed 38400 baud; rows 50; columns 80; line = 0;
intr = ^C; quit = ^\; erase = ^?; kill = ^U; eof = ^D; eol = <undef>;
eol2 = <undef>; start = ^Q; stop = ^S; susp = ^Z; rprnt = ^R; werase = ^W;
lnext = ^V; flush = ^O; min = 1; time = 0;
-parenb -parodd cs8 -hupcl -cstopb cread -clocal -crtscts
-ignbrk -brkint -ignpar -parmrk -inpck -istrip -inlcr -igncr icrnl ixon -ixoff
-iuclc -ixany -imaxbel
opost -olcuc -ocrnl onlcr -onocr -onlret -ofill -ofdel nl0 cr0 tab0 bs0 vt0 ff0
isig icanon iexten echo echoe echok -echonl -noflsh -xcase -tostop -echoprt
echoctl echoke
```

The format of the output is similar but lists more information. The meaning of the output should be intuitively obvious (if you've written a terminal driver recently).

stty operates on the file descriptor of its standard input, so you can set and query the modes of a terminal other than the current one by using the shell's input redirection character (<). You must be the superuser to change the modes on someone else's terminal.

27.12   TSET: SET OPTIONS AUTOMATICALLY

tset initializes the terminal driver to a mode appropriate for a given terminal type. The type can be specified on the command line; if the type is omitted, **tset** uses the value of the TERM environment variable.

tset supports a syntax for mapping certain values of the TERM environment variable into other values. This feature is useful if you often log in through a modem or data switch and would like to have the terminal driver configured correctly for the terminal you are really using on the other end of the connection rather than something generic and unhelpful such as "dialup."

For example, suppose that you use **xterm** at home and that the system you are dialing into is configured to think that the terminal type of a modem is "dialup." Putting the command

```
tset -m dialup:xterm
```

in your **.login** or **.profile** file sets the terminal driver appropriately for **xterm** whenever you dial in.

Unfortunately, the **tset** command is not really as simple as it pretends to be. To have **tset** adjust your environment variables in addition to setting your terminal modes, you need lines something like this:

```
set noglob
eval `tset -s -Q -m dialup:xterm`
unset noglob
```

This incantation suppresses the messages that **tset** normally prints (the **-Q** flag), and asks that shell commands to set the environment be output instead (the **-s** flag). The shell commands printed by **tset** are captured by the backquotes and fed to the shell as input with the built-in command **eval**, causing the commands to have the same effect as if they had been typed by the user.

set noglob prevents the shell from expanding any metacharacters such as "*" and "?" that are included in **tset**'s output. This command is not needed by **sh/ksh** users (nor is the **unset noglob** to undo it), since these shells do not normally expand special characters within backquotes. The **tset** command itself is the same no matter what shell you use; **tset** looks at the environment variable SHELL to determine what flavor of commands to print out.

27.13 TERMINAL UNWEDGING

Some programs (such as **vi**) make drastic changes to the state of the terminal driver while they are running. This meddling is normally invisible to the user, since the terminal state is carefully restored whenever the program exits or is suspended. However, a program could crash or be killed without performing this housekeeping step. When this happens, the terminal may behave very strangely: it might fail to handle newlines correctly, to echo typed characters, or to execute commands properly.

Another common way to confuse a terminal is to accidentally run **cat** or **more** on a binary file. Most binaries contain a delicious mix of special characters that is guaranteed to send some of the less-robust emulators into outer space.

To fix this situation, use **reset** or **stty sane**. **reset** is actually just a link to **tset**, and it can accept most of **tset**'s arguments. However, it is usually run without arguments. Both **reset** and **stty sane** restore the correctitude of the terminal driver and send out an appropriate reset code from **termcap/terminfo** if one is available.

In many cases for which a **reset** is appropriate, the terminal has been left in a mode in which no processing is done on the characters you type. Most terminals generate carriage returns rather than newlines when the Return or Enter key is pressed; without input processing, this key generates <Control-M> characters instead of sending off the current command to be executed. To enter newlines directly, use <Control-J> or the line feed key (if there is one) instead of the Return key.

27.14 MODEMS

A modem converts the digital serial signal produced by a computer into an analog signal suitable for transmission on a standard phone line. Fortunately, the advent of broadband Internet access has turned these once-essential devices into museum candidates at many locations.

External modems have an RJ-11 jack on the analog side and an RS-232 interface of some type on the digital side—usually a female DB-25. On the front they usually have a series of lights that display the modem's current state and level of activity. These lights are incredibly useful for debugging, so modems should generally be located somewhere in plain sight.

Internal modems are usually seen only on PCs. They plug into an ISA, PCI, or PCM-CIA slot and have an RJ-11 jack that sticks out the back of the computer's case once the modem has been installed. They are cheaper than external modems but more troublesome to configure, and they generally lack indicator lights.

If you are considering an internal modem, check to be sure it's supported by Linux. Fast CPUs have made it possible to simplify modem hardware by performing some signal processing tasks on the host processor. Unfortunately, modems that work this way (known generically as Winmodems) require sophisticated drivers and are not universally supported under Linux. See Sean Walbran and Marvin Stodolsky's

Linmodem HOWTO (available from www.tldp.org) for an overview of Winmodem support under Linux. (The *Modem HOWTO* is also very helpful for a broader perspective on the management of modems.)

Internal modems are usually made to appear as though they were connected through a phantom serial port from the perspective of user-level software. This convention helps insulate the logical function of the modem from its hardware implementation. Standard software packages can drive the modem without having to know anything about its peculiarities.

Modems vary somewhat in general robustness, but this characteristic is hard to judge without direct experience. In the past, we have found some modems to be significantly more tolerant of line noise than others. These days, most designs use a standard chipset from one of several large manufacturers, so it's likely that the variations among modems are not as great as they once were.

High-speed modems require complex firmware, and this firmware is occasionally buggy. Manufacturers share firmware among models when possible, so good or bad firmware tends to run in product lines. For this reason, we still recommend sticking with well-known brands.

Modulation, error correction, and data compression protocols

Long ago, it was important to check the exact protocols supported by a modem because standards were continually changing and modem manufacturers did not always implement a complete suite of protocols. These days, modems all support pretty much the same standards. The only real difference between them is the quality of the firmware, electronics, and support.

A protocol's baud rate is the rate at which the carrier signal is modulated. If there are more than two signal levels, then more than one bit of information can be sent per transition and the speed in bits per second will be higher than the baud rate. Historically, the data speed and signaling speed of modems were the same, leading to a casual confusion of the terms "baud" and "bps" (bits per second).

Most modems today use the "56K" V.90 standard, which doesn't actually provide 56 Kb/s of throughput. At best, it allows 33.6 Kb/s from computer to ISP and 53 Kb/s in the other direction. A recent update to the V.90 standard, V.92, sends 48 Kb/s rather than 33.6 Kb/s toward the ISP. V.90 and V.92 achieve speeds that are close to the theoretical and legal limits of signalling over ordinary voice telephone lines, and they're not expected to be superseded any time soon.

Line noise can introduce a significant number of errors into a modem connection. Various error correction protocols have been developed to packetize the transmitted data and provide checksum-based correction for errors, insulating the user or application from line faults. You once had to know something about this to configure your modem correctly, but these days it usually just works.

Serial Devices

Data compression algorithms can be used to shrink the number of bits that must be transmitted between analog endpoints. The amount of compression varies from worse than none (when transmitting data that has already been compressed) to at most about 4:1. A more typical value is 1.5:1. In general, the average configuration does better with one of these compression algorithms turned on.

minicom: dial out

The traditional UNIX dial-out programs **tip** and **cu** are relatively unpopular on Linux systems, although both have been ported (**cu** is usually packaged with UUCP, an obsolete telephone communication system). More common under Linux are all-in-one packages such as **kermit** and **minicom** that provide terminal emulation and support for data transfer protocols. For debugging and occasional use, we recommend **minicom**, mostly because it's the most likely to be preinstalled. Debian does not install it by default; run **apt-get install minicom** if it seems to be missing.

For better or for worse, **minicom** is a bit more PC-like than most Linux software. If your memories of 1986 include logging in at 1200 baud through an MS-DOS terminal emulator, **minicom** will make you feel right at home. To configure the software, run **minicom -s** as root and enter the "serial port setup" menu. Set the device file for the modem, turn on hardware flow control, set the coding to 8N1 (8 data bits, no parity, and 1 stop bit), and make sure the speed looks OK. Return to the main menu and choose "save settings as dfl" to write out your changes.

If you are familiar with the Hayes command language used by most modems, you can simply enter the commands directly (e.g., "ATDT5551212" to dial 555-1212). To have **minicom** do it for you, type <Control-A> and D to enter the dialing menu.

Bidirectional modems

It is often handy to use a single modem for both dial-in and dial-out services, particularly if you want to use fax support. This configuration requires **getty** to handle the serial port in an especially solicitous manner, since it can't just grab hold of the port and lock out all other processes. Port sharing is achieved through options to the **open** system call and involves features of both the serial driver and the kernel. All programs that share the port must obey the proper protocol.

In the past, configuring a modem for bidirectional use was a big huge deal that required many system-specific tweaks and often did not work very well. Fortunately, the major Linux software packages play pretty well with each other right out of the box as long as you use **mgetty** or its predecessor, **uugetty**. In general, **mgetty** is preferred; its default behavior is to share, so just plug and go.

27.15 DEBUGGING A SERIAL LINE

Debugging serial lines is not difficult. Some typical errors are

- Forgetting to tell **init** to reread its configuration files
- Forgetting to set soft carrier when using three-wire cables

- Using a cable with the wrong nullness
- Soldering or crimping DB-25 connectors upside down
- Connecting a device to the wrong wire because of bad or nonexistent wire maps
- Setting the terminal options incorrectly

A breakout box is an indispensable tool for debugging cabling problems. It is patched into the serial line and shows the signals on each pin as they pass through the cable. The better breakout boxes have both male and female connectors on each side and so are totally flexible and bisexual in their positioning. LEDs associated with each "interesting" pin (pins 2, 3, 4, 5, 6, 8, and 20) show when the pin is active.

Some breakout boxes are read-only and just let you monitor the signals; others let you rewire the connection and assert a voltage on a particular pin. For example, if you suspected that a cable needed to be nulled (crossed), you could use the breakout box to override the actual cable wiring and swap pins 2 and 3 and also pins 6 and 20.

See page 371 for more information about Black Box.

A bad breakout box can be worse than no breakout box at all. Our favorite implementation is the BOB-CAT-B made by Black Box. It is an easy-to-use box that costs around $250. You can reach Black Box at (724) 746-5500 or www.blackbox.com.

27.16 OTHER COMMON I/O PORTS

Serial ports were once the unchallenged standard for attaching low-speed peripherals to UNIX systems, but today most PC hardware ships with USB (Universal Serial Bus) ports that serve this function.

USB puts traditional serial (and parallel) ports to shame. It's fast (up to 480 Mb/s) and architecturally elegant, and it uses standardized cables that are both simple and cheap. USB has quickly become the standard for most external devices.

As an added twist, you can purchase adapters that have a USB port on one side and an RS-232C serial port on the other. These adapters allow newer PCs that don't have built-in serial ports to communicate with legacy serial devices. We've had good luck with the USB-to-RS-232C adapters sold by www.keyspan.com. Drivers for the Keyspan adapters are included in Linux kernel versions 2.4.22 and later.

Parallel ports were popular in the 1980s and are similar in concept to serial ports, but they transfer eight bits of data at once rather than just one bit. Parallel interfaces are traditionally found on printers, but in the Windows world they've also been historically used to connect Zip and tape drives. These bizarre uses have long been replaced by USB, and Linux support for parallel devices other than printers is scant.

USB: the Universal Serial Bus

For more information about USB, see the site www.usb.org.

USB is a generic peripheral interconnect system designed by Compaq, DEC, IBM, Intel, Microsoft, NEC, and Northern Telecom. The first USB standard was published in 1996. Acceptance of USB in the Windows world has snowballed rapidly over the last decade. All new PCs have USB ports, and most computer peripherals are available in USB versions.

Serial Devices

USB is a great system, and we think it's likely to stay in use for many years to come. It has almost all of the properties and features one could wish for in a utility communications bus.

- It's extremely cheap.
- Up to 127 devices can be connected.
- Cables have only four wires: power, ground, and two signal wires.
- Connectors and connector genders are standardized.
- The connectors are small, and the cables are thin and flexible.
- Devices can be connected and disconnected without power-down.
- Signalling speeds up to 480 Mb/s are possible (USB 2.0).
- Legacy serial and parallel devices can be connected with adaptors.

USB can even be used as a LAN technology, although it's really not designed for that.

Linux already has solid, broad support for USB devices. The USB standard defines standard interfaces for several classes of common equipment (such as mice, modems, and mass storage devices), so the use of these devices is often relatively straightforward. Devices such as cameras and scanners, on the other hand, can occasionally require chipset-specific drivers.

Information about available USB devices can be found in **/proc/bus/usb**. Numbered files (such as **001**, which represents the host's own USB controller) correspond to individual USB devices. The **/proc/bus/usb/devices** file provides detailed information about the current device census, and the **/proc/bus/usb/drivers** file contains the names of the currently registered USB drivers (whether or not they are being used). Both of these files can be inspected with **less** or your favorite text editor.

Although the **/proc/bus/usb** filesystem supports autoconfiguration and helps with debugging, it's generally not used directly by kernel-level drivers. Most USB devices are accessed through traditional UNIX-style device files under **/dev**.

USB is most commonly used with data storage devices such as flash memory drives. See page 147 for more specifics about how to mount USB drives. For up-to-date information about other types of devices, see the device list at www.linux-usb.org.

27.17 EXERCISES

E27.1 What is a null modem cable? How is it used to connect DCE and DTE serial devices?

E27.2 Can you use a 3-wire serial cable for a serial modem connection? For a serial printer? Why or why not?

E27.3 How does traditional serial hardware flow control work? What can be done if a system does not understand hardware flow control?

E27.4 What is a pseudo-terminal? What programs use pseudo-terminals?

E27.5 Devise **inittab** entries that

    a) Run a program called **server-fallback**, wait for it to finish, and then immediately halt the system if the power fails.

    b) Respawn a server called **unstable-srv** if it crashes.

    c) Run a script called **clean-temp** that removes all temporary files each time the system is rebooted.

E27.6 You've plugged a new USB device into your computer. How can you check to see that it's been recognized and is now accessible?

⭐ **E27.7** Compare the RS-232 and USB serial standards.

⭐ **E27.8** A friend of yours carelessly left himself logged in overnight in the Linux lab and is now experiencing strange problems when he runs shell applications. Programs quit or suspend, and previous input disappears, when certain commands and input are given; however, some things seem to work normally. What could an unfriendly user have done to cause such behavior? Explain how you could test your answer. How could the problem be fixed? Who would do such a mean thing?

Serial Devices

28 *Drivers and the Kernel*

The kernel is responsible for hiding the system's hardware underneath an abstract, high-level programming interface. It provides many of the facilities that users and user-level programs take for granted. For example, the kernel creates all the following concepts from lower-level hardware features:

- Processes (time sharing, protected address spaces)
- Signals and semaphores
- Virtual memory (swapping, paging, mapping)
- The filesystem (files, directories, namespace)
- General input/output (specialty hardware, keyboard, mouse)
- Interprocess communication (pipes and network connections)

The kernel contains device drivers that manage its interaction with specific pieces of hardware; the rest of the kernel is, to a large degree, device independent. The relationship between the kernel and its device drivers is similar to the relationship between user-level processes and the kernel. When a process asks the kernel to "Read the first 64 bytes of **/etc/passwd**," the kernel might translate this request into a device driver instruction such as "Fetch block 3,348 from device 3." The driver would further break this command down into sequences of bit patterns to be presented to the device's control registers.

The kernel is written mostly in C, with a sprinkling of assembly language to help it interface with hardware- or chip-specific functions that are not accessible through normal compiler directives.

One of the advantages of the Linux environment is that the availability of source code makes it relatively easy to roll your own device drivers and kernel modules from scratch. In the early days of Linux, having skills in this area was a necessity because it was difficult to effectively administer Linux systems without being able to "mold" the system to a specific environment.

Today, sysadmins can be perfectly effective without ever soiling their hands with gooey kernel code. In fact, one might argue that such activities are better left to programmers and that administrators should focus more on the overall needs of the user community. System administrators can tune the kernel or add preexisting modules as described in this chapter, but they don't need to take a crash course in C or assembly language programming to survive.

The bottom line is that you shouldn't confuse the administration of modern Linux environments with the frontier husbandry of just a few years back.

28.1 KERNEL ADAPTATION

Linux systems live in a world that could potentially include any of tens of thousands of different pieces of computer hardware. The kernel must adapt to whatever hardware is present in the machine on which it's running.

A kernel can learn about the system's hardware in a variety of ways. The most basic is for you to explicitly inform the kernel about the hardware it should expect to find (or pretend not to find, as the case may be). In addition, the kernel prospects for some devices on its own, either at boot time or dynamically (once the system is running). The latter method is the most common for modern-day devices such as those that reside on the Universal Serial Bus (USB), including memory sticks, modems, digital cameras, and printers. Fortunately, Linux has reasonable support for a wide array of these devices.

On the PC platform, where Linux is popular, the challenge of creating an accurate inventory of the system's hardware is particularly difficult (and sometimes impossible). PC hardware has followed an evolutionary path not unlike our own, in which early protozoa have now given rise to everything from dingos to killer bees. This diversity is compounded by the fact that PC manufacturers usually don't give you much technical information about the systems they sell, so you must often take your system apart and visually inspect the pieces to answer questions such as "What Ethernet chipset is on the motherboard?"

Modern Linux systems survive on a hybrid diet of static and dynamic kernel components, with the mix between the two being dictated primarily by the limitations of PC hardware. It's likely that at some point during your sysadmin career you'll need to lend a helping hand in the form of building a new kernel configuration.

Drivers / Kernel

28.2 DRIVERS AND DEVICE FILES

A device driver is a program that manages the system's interaction with a piece of hardware. The driver translates between the hardware commands understood by the device and the stylized programming interface used by the kernel. The driver layer helps keep Linux reasonably device independent.

Device drivers are part of the kernel; they are not user processes. However, a driver can be accessed both from within the kernel and from user space. User-level access to devices is usually through special device files that live in the **/dev** directory. The kernel transforms operations on these files into calls to the code of the driver.

The PC platform is a source of chaos in the system administrator's world. A dizzying array of hardware and "standards" with varying levels of operating system support are available. Behold:

- More than 30 different SCSI chipsets are currently available, and each is packaged and sold by at least twice that many vendors.

- Over 200 different network interfaces are out there, each being marketed by several different vendors under different names.

- Newer, better, and less expensive types of hardware are being developed all the time. Each requires a driver in order to work with your Linux of choice.

With the remarkable pace at which new hardware is being developed, it is practically impossible to keep mainline OS distributions up to date with the latest hardware. Occasionally, you will need to add a device driver to your kernel to support a new piece of hardware.[1]

Only device drivers designed for use with Linux (and usually, a specific version of the Linux kernel) can be successfully installed on a Linux system. Drivers for other operating systems (e.g., Windows) will not work, so when you purchase new hardware, keep this in mind. In addition, devices vary in their degree of compatibility and functionality when used with Linux, so it's wise to pay some attention to the results other sites have obtained with any hardware you are considering.

Vendors are becoming more aware of the UNIX and Linux markets, and they often provide Linux drivers with their products. In the optimal case, your vendor furnishes you with both drivers and installation instructions. Occasionally, you will only find the driver you need on some uncommented web page. In either case, this section shows you what is really going on when you add a device driver.

Device files and device numbers

Many devices have a corresponding file in **/dev**; notable exceptions on modern operating systems are network devices. Complex servers may support hundreds of devices.

---

1. On PC hardware, you can use the **lspci** command to view the devices that are currently attached to the PCI bus and recognized by the kernel.

By virtue of being device files, the files in **/dev** each have a major and minor device number associated with them. The kernel uses these numbers to map device-file references to the corresponding driver.

The major device number identifies the driver with which the file is associated (in other words, the type of device). The minor device number usually identifies which particular instance of a given device type is to be addressed. The minor device number is sometimes called the unit number.

You can see the major and minor number of a device file with **ls -l**:

```
$ ls -l /dev/sda
brw-rw---- 1 root    disk    8,   0 Jan 5 2005 /dev/sda
```

This example shows the first SCSI disk on a Linux system. It has a major number of 8 and a minor number of 0.

The minor device number is sometimes used by the driver to select the particular characteristic of a device. For example, a single tape drive can have several files in **/dev** representing it in various configurations of recording density and rewind characteristics. The driver is free to interpret the minor device number in whatever way it wants. Look up the man page for the driver to determine what convention it's using.

There are actually two types of device files: block device files and character device files. A block device is read or written one block (a group of bytes, usually a multiple of 512) at a time; a character device can be read or written one byte at a time.

It is sometimes convenient to implement an abstraction as a device driver even when it controls no actual device. Such phantom devices are known as pseudo-devices. For example, a user who logs in over the network is assigned a PTY (pseudo-TTY) that looks, feels, and smells like a serial port from the perspective of high-level software. This trick allows programs written in the days when everyone used a TTY to continue to function in the world of windows and networks.

When a program performs an operation on a device file, the kernel automatically catches the reference, looks up the appropriate function name in a table, and transfers control to it. To perform an unusual operation that doesn't have a direct analog in the filesystem model (for example, ejecting a floppy disk), a program can use the **ioctl** system call to pass a message directly from user space into the driver.

Creating device files

Device files can be created manually with the **mknod** command, with the syntax

> **mknod** *filename type major minor*

where *filename* is the device file to be created, *type* is **c** for a character device or **b** for a block device, and *major* and *minor* are the major and minor device numbers. If you are manually creating a device file that refers to a driver that's already present in your kernel, check the man page for the driver to find the appropriate major and minor device numbers.

Drivers / Kernel

Historically, device files in **/dev** were created manually by the system administrator. Most systems provided a script, called **MAKEDEV**, in the **/dev** directory to help with this task. **MAKEDEV** sometimes, but not always, knew how to create the correct device files for a particular component. It was a tedious process at best.

As of Linux kernel version 2.6,[2] the udev system dynamically manages the creation and removal of device files according to the actual presence (or absence) of devices. The **udevd** daemon listens for messages from the kernel regarding device status changes. Based on configuration information in **/etc/udev/udev.conf** and subdirectories, **udevd** can take a variety of actions when a device is discovered or disconnected. By default, **udevd** creates device files in **/dev**. It also attempts to run network configuration scripts when new network interfaces are detected.

sysfs: a window into the souls of devices

Another feature introduced in version 2.6 of the kernel is sysfs. This is a virtual filesystem that provides well-organized and very detailed information about available devices, their configurations, and their state. The information is accessible both from within the kernel and from user space.

You can explore the **/sys** directory, where sysfs is typically mounted, to find out everything from what IRQ a device is using to how many blocks have been queued for writing on a disk controller. One of the guiding principles of sysfs is that each file in **/sys** should represent only one attribute of the underlying device. This convention imposes a certain amount of structure on an otherwise chaotic data set.

Originally, information about device configuration was found in the **/proc** filesystem (procfs, discussed later in this chapter) if it was available at all. Although **/proc** will continue to hold run-time information about processes and the kernel, it is anticipated that device-specific information will be moved to **/sys** over time.

Because sysfs is relatively new, much of its potential is currently untapped. It may eventually be possible to configure devices in real time through sysfs. In the long term, it may even replace all or part of **/dev**. Only time will tell.

Naming conventions for devices

Naming conventions for devices are somewhat random. They are often holdovers from the way things were done under UNIX on a DEC PDP-11, as archaic as that may sound in this day and age.

See Chapter 27 for more information about serial ports.

Serial device files are named **ttyS** followed by a number that identifies the specific interface to which the port is attached. TTYs are sometimes represented by more than one device file; the extra files usually afford access to alternative flow control methods or locking protocols.

---

2. udev is a complete replacement for devfs, another recent attempt at similar functionality. udev does not implement all the features of devfs, but it's believed to be more architecturally pure. Didn't you know that all those extra, convenient features of devfs were just self-indulgent vices?

The names of tape devices often include not only a reference to the drive itself but also an indication of whether the device rewinds after the tape device is closed.

IDE hard disk devices are named **/dev/hd**LP, where L is a letter that identifies the unit (with **a** being the master on the first IDE interface, **b** being the slave on that interface, **c** being the master on the second IDE interface, etc.) and P is the partition number (starting with 1). For example, the first partition on the first IDE disk is typically **/dev/hda1**. SCSI disks are named similarly, but with the prefix **/dev/sd** instead of **/dev/hd**. You can drop the partition number on both types of devices to access the entire disk (e.g., **/dev/hda**).

SCSI CD-ROM drives are referred to by the files **/dev/scd**N, where N is a number that distinguishes multiple CD-ROM drives. Modern IDE (ATAPI) CD-ROM drives are referred to just like IDE hard disks (e.g., **/dev/hdc**).

28.3 WHY AND HOW TO CONFIGURE THE KERNEL

When the system is installed, it comes with a generic configuration that's designed to run almost any application on almost any hardware. The generic configuration includes many different device drivers and option packages, and it has tunable parameter values chosen for "general purpose" use. By carefully examining this configuration and adjusting it to your exact needs, you may be able to enhance your system's performance, security, or even reliability.

Modern Linux kernels are better than their ancestors at flushing unwanted drivers from memory, but compiled-in options will always be turned on. Although reconfiguring the kernel for efficiency is less important than it used to be, a good case can still be made for reconfiguration.

Instructions for adding a new driver start on page 878.

Another reason to reconfigure the kernel is to add support for new types of devices (i.e., to add new device drivers). The driver code can't just be mooshed onto the kernel like a gob of Play-Doh; it has to be integrated into the kernel's data structures and tables. On some systems, this procedure may require that you go back to the configuration files for the kernel and add in the new device, rebuilding the kernel from scratch. On other systems, you may only need to run a program designed to make these configuration changes for you.

The kernel is not difficult to configure; it's just difficult to fix once you break it.

You can use any one of four basic methods to configure a Linux kernel. Chances are you'll have the opportunity to try all of them eventually. The methods are

- Modifying tunable (dynamic) kernel configuration parameters

- Building a kernel from scratch (really, this means compiling it from the source code, possibly with modifications and additions)

- Loading new drivers and modules into an existing kernel on the fly

- Providing operational directives at boot time through the kernel loader, LILO, or GRUB. See page 26 for more information about these systems.

Drivers / Kernel

These methods are each applicable in slightly different situations. Modifying tunable parameters is the easiest and most common, whereas building a kernel from source files is the hardest and least often required. Fortunately, all these approaches become second nature with a little practice.

28.4 TUNING LINUX KERNEL PARAMETERS

Many modules and drivers in the kernel were designed with the knowledge that one size doesn't fit all. To increase flexibility, special hooks allow parameters such as an internal table's size or the kernel's behavior in a particular circumstance to be adjusted on the fly by the system administrator. These hooks are accessible through an extensive kernel-to-userland interface represented by files in the **/proc** filesystem (aka procfs). In many cases, a large user-level application (especially an "infrastructure" application such as a database) requires you to adjust parameters to accommodate its needs.

Special files in **/proc/sys** let you view and set kernel options at run time. These files mimic standard Linux files, but they are really back doors into the kernel. If one of these files has a value you would like to change, you can try writing to it. Unfortunately, not all files can be written to (regardless of their apparent permissions), and not much documentation is available. If you have the kernel source tree available, you may be able to read about some of the values and their meanings in the subdirectory **Documentation/syscnt**.

For example, to change the maximum number of files the system can have open at once, try something like

```
# echo 32768 > /proc/sys/fs/file-max
```

Once you get used to this unorthodox interface, you'll find it quite useful, especially for changing configuration options. A word of caution, however: changes are not remembered across reboots. Table 28.1 lists some commonly tuned parameters.

A more permanent way to modify these same parameters can be found on most systems in the form of the **sysctl** command. **sysctl** can set individual variables either from the command line or by reading a list of *variable=value* pairs from a file. By default, the file **/etc/sysctl.conf** is read at boot time and its contents are used to set initial (custom) parameter values.

For example, the command

```
# sysctl net.ipv4.ip_forward=0
```

turns off IP forwarding. Note that you form the variable names used by **sysctl** by replacing the slashes in the **/proc/sys** directory structure with dots.

Table 28.1 Files in /proc/sys for some tunable kernel parameters

Dir[a]	File	Default	Function and commentary
C	**autoeject**	0	Autoeject CD-ROM on dismount? Good for scaring machine room operators at 3:00 a.m.
F	**file-max**	4096	Sets the maximum number of open files. On a system that handles a large number of files, try increasing this to 16384.
F	**inode-max**	16384	Sets the maximum number of open inodes per process. This might be useful to tinker with if you're writing an app that opens tens of thousands of file handles.
K	**ctrl-alt-del**	0	Reboot on Ctrl-Alt-Delete sequence? This may be a matter of personal preference, or it may increase security on server consoles that aren't physically secured.
K	**printk_ratelimit**	5	Minimum seconds between kernel messages
K	**printk_ratelimit_burst**	10	Number of messages in succession before the **printk** rate limit is actually enforced.
K	**shmmax**	32M	Sets the maximum amount of shared memory. Tune if you have applications that require significant shared memory.
N	**conf/default/rp_filter**	0	Enables source route verification. This anti-spoofing mechanism makes the kernel drop packets received from "impossible" paths.
N	**icmp_echo_ignore_all**	0	Ignores ICMP pings when set to 1. Good if you want the system to be unpingable.
N	**icmp_echo_ignore_broadcasts**	0	Ignores broadcast pings when set to 1. Almost always a good idea to set this to 1.
N	**icmp_ignore_bogus_error_responses**	0	Ignores incorrectly formatted ICMP errors. Almost always a good idea to set this to 1.
N	**ip_forward**	0	Allows IP forwarding when set to 1. Improves security when set to 0; set it to 1 if you're using your Linux box as a router.
N	**ip_local_port_range**	32768 61000	Specifies local port range allocated during connection setup. For servers that initiate many outbound connections, enlarge this to 1024–65000 for improved performance.
N	**tcp_fin_timeout**	60	Specifies seconds to wait for a final FIN packet. Set to a lower value (~20) on high-traffic servers to increase peformance.
N	**tcp_syncookies**	0	Protects against SYN flood attacks. Turn on if you suspect denial of service (DOS) attacks.

a. F = **/proc/sys/fs**, N = **/proc/sys/net/ipv4**, K = **/proc/sys/kernel**, C = **/proc/sys/dev/cdrom**

Drivers / Kernel

28.5 BUILDING A LINUX KERNEL

Because Linux is evolving so rapidly, it is likely that you'll eventually be faced with the need to build a Linux kernel. Kernel patches, device drivers, and new functionality continually arrive on the scene. This is really something of a mixed blessing. On one hand, it's convenient to always support the "latest and greatest," but on the other hand it can become quite time consuming to keep up with the constant flow of new material. But after you successfully build a kernel once, you'll feel empowered and eager to do it again.

It's less likely that you'll need to build a kernel on your own if you're running a "stable" version. Originally, Linux adopted a versioning scheme in which the second part of the version number indicated whether the kernel is stable (even numbers) or in development (odd numbers). For example, kernel version 2.6.6 would be a "stable" kernel, whereas 2.7.4 would be a "development" kernel. Today, this scheme isn't religiously followed, so you'd best check the home page at kernel.org for the official word on this issue. The kernel.org site is also the best source for Linux kernel source code if you aren't relying on a particular distribution (or vendor) to provide you with a kernel.

If it ain't broke, don't fix it

With new Linux kernel versions arriving on the scene every few months and new drivers and patches being released every day, it's easy to become addicted to patching and upgrades. After all, what's more exciting than telling your user community that you just found a new kernel patch and that you'll be taking the mail server down for the afternoon to install it? Some administrators justify their existence this way; everybody likes to be the hero.

A good system administrator carefully weighs needs and risks when planning kernel upgrades and patches. Sure, the new release may be the latest and greatest, but is it as stable as the current version? Could the upgrade or patch be delayed and installed with another group of patches at the end of the month? It's important to resist the temptation to let "keeping up with the joneses" (in this case, the kernel hacking community) dominate the best interests of your user community.

A good rule of thumb is to upgrade or apply patches only when the productivity gains you expect to obtain (usually measured in terms of reliability and performance) will exceed the effort and lost time required to perform the installation. If you're having trouble quantifying the specific gain, that's a good sign that the patch can wait for another day.

Configuring kernel options

Linux kernel configuration has come a long way, but it still feels primitive compared to the procedures used on some other systems. Historically, Linux kernel source was stored in **/usr/src/linux** and root privileges were required to build a kernel. Kernel versions 2.4, 2.6, and later can be built as an unprivileged user, and hence it's now more politically correct to store the kernel source in a site-specific directory such as **/usr/local/src/kernel** or ~*username*/**kernel**.

In this chapter we use *path_to_kernel_src* as a placeholder for whichever directory you choose for kernel source code. In all cases, you need to install the kernel source package before you can build a kernel on your system; see page 232 for tips on package installation.

The kernel configuration process revolves around the **.config** file at the root of the kernel source directory. All the kernel configuration information is specified in this file, but its format is somewhat cryptic. Use the decoding guide in

> *path_to_kernel_src*/**Documentation/Configure.help**

to find out what the various options mean.

To save folks from having to edit the **.config** file directly, Linux has several **make** targets that let you configure the kernel with different interfaces. If you are running KDE, the prettiest configuration interface is provided by **make xconfig**. Likewise, if you're running GNOME, **make gconfig** is probably the best option. These commands bring up a graphical configuration screen on which you can pick the devices to add to your kernel (or compile as loadable modules).

If you are not running KDE or GNOME, you can use a **curses**-based[3] alternative invoked with **make menuconfig**. Finally, the older-style **make config** prompts you to respond to every single configuration option available without letting you later go back and change your mind. We recommend **make xconfig** or **make gconfig** if your environment supports them; otherwise, use **make menuconfig**. Avoid **make config**.

If you're migrating an existing kernel configuration to a new kernel version (or tree), you can use the **make oldconfig** command to read in the previous config file and to ask only the questions that are new.

These tools are straightforward as far as the options you can turn on, but unfortunately they are painful to use if you want to maintain several versions of the kernel for multiple architectures or hardware configurations.

The various configuration interfaces described above all generate a **.config** file that looks something like this:

```
# Automatically generated make config: don't edit
# Code maturity level options

CONFIG_EXPERIMENTAL=y
#
# Processor type and features
#
# CONFIG_M386 is not set
# CONFIG_M486 is not set
# CONFIG_M586 is not set
```

3. **curses** is a library from the days of yore used to create text-based GUIs that run in a terminal window.

Drivers / Kernel

```
# CONFIG_M586TSC is not set
CONFIG_M686=y
CONFIG_X86_WP_WORKS_OK=y
CONFIG_X86_INVLPG=y
CONFIG_X86_BSWAP=y
CONFIG_X86_POPAD_OK=y
CONFIG_X86_TSC=y
CONFIG_X86_GOOD_APIC=y
...
```

As you can see, the contents are rather cryptic and do not describe what the CONFIG tags mean. Sometimes you can figure out the meaning. Basically, each CONFIG line refers to a specific kernel configuration option. The value **y** compiles the option into the kernel; **m** enables it, but as a loadable module.

Some things can be configured as modules and some can't. You just have to know which is which; it's not clear from the **.config** file. Nor are the CONFIG tags easily mapped to meaningful information.

Building the kernel binary

Setting up an appropriate **.config** file is the most important part of the Linux kernel configuration process, but you must jump through several more hoops to turn that file into a finished kernel.

Here's an outline of the entire process:

- **cd** to the top level of the kernel source directory.
- Run **make xconfig**, **make gconfig**, or **make menuconfig**.
- Run **make dep** (not required for kernels 2.6.x and later).
- Run **make clean**.
- Run **make**.
- Run **make modules_install**.
- Copy **arch/i386/boot/bzImage** to **/boot/vmlinuz**.
- Copy **arch/i386/boot/System.map** to **/boot/System.map**.
- Edit **/etc/lilo.conf** (LILO) or **/boot/grub/grub.conf** (GRUB) to add a configuration line for the new kernel.
- If you're using LILO, run **/sbin/lilo** to install the reconfigured boot loader.

The **make clean** step is not always strictly necessary, but it is generally a good idea to start with a clean build environment. In practice, many problems can be traced back to this step having been skipped.

28.6 ADDING A LINUX DEVICE DRIVER

On Linux systems, device drivers are typically distributed in one of three forms:

- A patch against a specific kernel version
- A loadable module
- An installation script or package that installs appropriate patches

The most common form is the installation script or package. If you're lucky enough to have one of these for your new device, you should be able to follow the instructions to execute the script or install the package and your new device will be recognized by the kernel.

In situations in which you have a patch against a specific kernel version you can in most cases install the patch with the following procedure:[4]

> # **cd** *path_to_kernel_src* ; **patch -p1** < *patch_file*

Diffs made against a different minor version of the kernel may fail, but the driver should still work.

If not, you are likely in a situation where you must manually integrate the new device driver into the kernel source tree. With luck, this is because you are writing your own device driver, rather than because you have fallen victim to a commercial device vendor that has failed to provide appropriate installation scripts. In the following pages, we demonstrate how to manually add a hypothetical network "snarf" driver to the kernel. Linux actually makes this a rather tedious process, especially when compared to some other versions of UNIX.

Within the **drivers** subdirectory of the kernel source tree, you can find the subdirectory that corresponds to the type of device you have. A directory listing of **drivers** looks like this:

```
$ ls -F path_to_kernel_src/drivers
acorn/      char/      i2c/         Makefile    net/       s390/      telephony/
acpi/       dio/       ide/         md/         nubus/     sbus/      usb/
atm/        fc4/       ieee1394/    media/      parport/   scsi/      video/
block/      gsc/       input/       message/    pci/       sgi/       zorro/
bluetooth/  hil/       isdn/        misc/       pcmcia/    sound/
cdrom/      hotplug/   macintosh/   mtd/        pnp/       tc/
```

The most common directories to which drivers are added are **block**, **char**, **net**, **scsi**, **sound**, and **usb**. These directories contain drivers for block devices (such as IDE disk drives), character devices (such as serial ports), network devices, SCSI cards, sound cards, and USB devices, respectively. Some of the other directories contain drivers for the buses themselves (e.g., **pci**, **nubus**, and **zorro**); it's unlikely that you will need to add drivers to these directories. Some directories contain platform-specific drivers, such as **macintosh**, **s390**, and **acorn**. Some directories contain specialty devices such as **atm**, **isdn**, and **telephony**.

Since our example device is a network-related device, we add the driver to the directory **drivers/net**. We modify the following files:

- **drivers/net/Makefile** so that our driver will be compiled
- **drivers/net/Kconfig** so that our device will appear in the config options

---

4. Of course, the kernel source package must be installed before you can modify the kernel tree.

After putting the **.c** and **.h** files for the driver in **drivers/net/snarf**, we add the driver to **drivers/net/Makefile**. The line we add (near the end of the file) is

```
obj-$(CONFIG_SNARF_DEV) += snarf/
```

This configuration adds the snarf driver (stored in the **snarf/** directory) to the build process.

After adding the device to the **Makefile**, we have to make sure we can configure the device when we configure the kernel. All network devices must be listed in the file **drivers/net/Kconfig**. To add the device so that it can be built either as a module or as part of the kernel (consistent with what we claimed in the **Makefile**), we add the following line:

```
config SNARF_DEV
tristate 'Snarf device support'
```

The first token after `config` is the configuration macro, which must match the token following `CONFIG_` in the **Makefile**. The `tristate` keyword means that we can build the device as a module. If the device cannot be built as a module, we would use the keyword `bool` instead of `tristate`. The next token is the string to display on the configuration screen. It can be any arbitrary text, but it should identify the device that is being configured.

Device awareness

Having managed to link a new device driver into the kernel, how do you tell the kernel it needs to use the new driver? In kernel versions before 2.6, this was a tedious task that required programming knowledge. As part of the recent architectural changes made to the device driver model, there is now a standard way for drivers to associate themselves with the kernel.

It's beyond the scope of this chapter to explain how that happens in detail, but the result is that device drivers written for version 2.6 (and later) register themselves with the macro `MODULE_DEVICE_TABLE`. This macro makes the appropriate behind-the-scenes connections so that other utilities such as **modprobe** (discussed below) can enable new devices in the kernel.

28.7 LOADABLE KERNEL MODULES

Loadable kernel module (LKM) support allows a device driver—or any other kernel service—to be linked into and removed from the kernel while it is running. This facility makes the installation of drivers much easier since the kernel binary does not need to be changed. It also allows the kernel to be smaller because drivers are not loaded unless they are needed.

Loadable modules are implemented by means of one or more documented "hooks" into the kernel that additional device drivers can grab onto. The user-level command **insmod** communicates with the kernel and tells it to load new modules into memory. The **rmmod** command unloads drivers.

Although loadable drivers are convenient, they are not 100% safe. Any time you load or unload a module, you risk causing a kernel panic.[5] We don't recommend loading or unloading an untested module when you are not willing to crash the machine.

Under Linux, almost anything can be built as a loadable kernel module. The exceptions are the root filesystem type, the device on which the root filesystem resides, and the PS/2 mouse driver.

Loadable kernel modules are conventionally stored under **/lib/modules/***version*, where *version* is the version of your Linux kernel as returned by **uname -r**. You can inspect the currently loaded modules with the **lsmod** command:

```
# lsmod
Module          Size    Used by
ppp             21452   0
slhc            4236    0 [ppp]
ds              6344    1
i82365          26648   1
pcmcia_core     37024   0 [ds  i82365]
```

Loaded on this machine are the PCMCIA controller modules, the PPP driver, and the PPP header compression modules.

As an example of manually loading a kernel module, here's how we would insert the snarf module that we set up in the previous section:

```
# insmod /path/to/snarf.ko
```

We can also pass parameters to loadable kernel modules; for example,

```
# insmod /path/to/snarf.ko io=0xXXX irq=X
```

Once a loadable kernel module has been manually inserted into the kernel, it can only be removed if you explicitly request its removal or if the system is rebooted. We could use **rmmod snarf** to remove our snarf module.

You can use **rmmod** at any time, but it works only if the number of current references to the module (listed in the Used by column of **lsmod**'s output) is 0.

You can also load Linux LKMs semiautomatically with **modprobe**, a wrapper for **insmod** that understands dependencies, options, and installation and removal procedures. **modprobe** uses the **/etc/modprobe.conf** file to figure out how to handle each individual module.

You can dynamically generate an **/etc/modprobe.conf** file that corresponds to all your currently installed modules by running **modprobe -c**. This command generates a long file that looks like this:

```
#This file was generated by: modprobe -c
path[pcmcia]=/lib/modules/preferred
path[pcmcia]=/lib/modules/default
```

---

5. This risk is very small. It *may* be so small as to be considered insignificant in your environment.

Drivers / Kernel

```
path[pcmcia]=/lib/modules/2.6.6
path[misc]=/lib/modules/2.6.6
...
# Aliases
alias block-major-1 rd
alias block-major-2 floppy
...
alias char-major-4 serial
alias char-major-5 serial
alias char-major-6 lp
...
alias dos msdos
alias plip0 plip
alias ppp0 ppp
options ne io=x0340 irq=9
```

The path statements tell where a particular module can be found. You can modify or add entries of this type if you want to keep your modules in a nonstandard location.

The alias statement maps between block major device numbers, character major device numbers, filesystems, network devices, and network protocols and their corresponding module names.

The options lines are not dynamically generated. They specify options that should be passed to a module when it is loaded. For example, we could use the following line to tell the snarf module its proper I/O address and interrupt vector:[6]

```
options snarf io=0xXXX irq=X
```

modprobe also understands the statements install and remove. These statements allow commands to be executed when a specific module is inserted into or removed from the running kernel.

28.8 HOT-PLUGGING

Whereas loadable kernel modules address the need for the kernel to add and remove device drivers dynamically, the Linux hot-plugging features export information about device availability into user space. This facility lets user processes respond to events such as the connection of a USB-enabled digital camera or PDA. For example, you might want to automatically copy images to a local drive or hot-sync your PDA's calendar. The philosophy of the hot-plugging project is that no additional user input should be required beyond the plugging in of the device.

Beginning with kernel version 2.6, hot-plugging is available on buses and drivers that have been designed to use sysfs. Hot-plugging, sysfs, and the registration of device drivers discussed earlier are closely linked.

---

6. If you're using really oddball PC hardware, it can be a challenge to create a configuration in which device interrupt request vectors (IRQs) and I/O ports do not overlap. You can view the current assignments on your system by examining the contents of **/proc/interrupts** and **/proc/ioports**, respectively. The overlap isn't typically an issue with current mainstream PC hardware.

In the current implementation of hot-plugging, the kernel executes the user process specified by the parameter **/proc/sys/kernel/hotplug** (usually **/sbin/hotplug**) whenever it detects that a device has been added or removed. **/sbin/hotplug** is a shell script that calls a device-type-specific agent from the **/etc/hotplug/** directory to act on the event. For example, if the event was the addition of a network interface, the **/etc/hotplug/net.agent** script would be executed to bring the interface on-line. You can add or edit scripts in the **/etc/hotplug** directory to customize your system's hot-plugging behavior.

For security and other reasons, you may not want the hot-plugging system to act upon an event. In these instances, you can add devices to the **/etc/hotplug/blacklist** file to prevent their events from triggering actions.

Conversely, you can force hot-plug actions by creating "handmap" files, such as **/etc/hotplug/**_type_**.handmap**. (Make sure that _type_ doesn't conflict with an existing name if you're creating something new.)

28.9 SETTING BOOTSTRAP OPTIONS

Once you have a working, running kernel, you may need to pass special configuration options to it at boot time, such as the root device it should use or an instruction to probe for multiple Ethernet cards. The boot loader (LILO or GRUB) is responsible for transferring these options to the kernel.

To specify options that should be used every time the system boots, you can add static configurations to **/etc/lilo.conf** or **/boot/grub/grub.conf**, depending on which boot loader you use. See page 26 for more information.

If it's not possible to edit the boot loader configuration file (perhaps you broke something and the machine can't boot), you can pass the options in by hand. For example, at a LILO boot prompt you could type

    LILO: **linux root=/dev/hda1 ether=0,0,eth0 ether=0,0,eth1**

to tell LILO to load the kernel specified by the "linux" tag, to use the root device **/dev/hda1**, and to probe for two Ethernet cards.

A similar example using GRUB would look like this:

    grub> **kernel /vmlinuz root=/dev/hda1 ether=0,0,eth0 ether=0,0,eth1**
    grub> **boot**

Another common situation in which it's helpful to use boot-time options is when probing logical unit numbers (LUNs) on a storage area network (SAN). By default, the Linux kernel probes for LUN 0 only, which may not be adequate if your environment presents logical storage areas as different LUNs. (Contact your SAN administrator or vendor to determine if this is the case.) In this situation, you need to tell the kernel how many LUNs to probe since the probing occurs during bootstrapping.

Drivers / Kernel

For example, if you wanted a 2.4.x kernel to probe the first 8 LUNs, you might use a boot line like this:

```
grub> kernel /vmlinuz root=/dev/hda1 max_scsi_luns=8
grub> boot
```

In kernels 2.6.x and later, the parameter name has changed:

```
grub> kernel /vmlinuz root=/dev/hda1 max_luns=8
grub> boot
```

28.10 RECOMMENDED READING

BOVET, DANIEL P., AND MARCO CESATI. *Understanding the Linux Kernel (3rd Edition)*. Sebastopol, CA: O'Reilly Media, 2006.

CORBET, JONATHAN, ET AL. *Linux Device Drivers (3rd Edition)*. Sebastopol, CA: O'Reilly Media, 2005. This book is also available online at lwn.net/Kernel/LDD3.

LOVE, ROBERT. *Linux Kernel Development (2nd Edition)*. Indianapolis, IN: Novell Press, 2005.

28.11 EXERCISES

E28.1   Describe what the kernel does. Explain the difference between loading a driver as a module and linking it statically into the kernel.

★ **E28.2**   Examine the values of several parameters from Table 28.1 on page 875, using both the **/proc** method and the **sysctl** method. Change two of the values with one method and then read them back with the other method. Verify that the system's behavior has actually changed in response to your tuning. Turn in a typescript of your experiment. (Requires root access.)

★ **E28.3**   At a local flea market, you get a great deal on a laptop card that gives you Ethernet connectivity through the parallel port. What steps would you need to perform to make Linux recognize this new card? Should you compile support directly into the kernel or add it as a module? Why? (Bonus question: if your hourly consulting fee is $80, estimate the value of the labor needed to get this cheapie Ethernet interface working.)

★ **E28.4**   A new release of the Linux kernel just came out, and you want to upgrade all the machines in the local lab (about 50 machines, not all identical). What issues should you consider? What procedure should you follow? What problems might occur, and how would you deal with them?

★★ **E28.5**   In the lab, configure a kernel with **xconfig** or **menuconfig** and build a kernel binary. Install and run the new system. Turn in **dmesg** output from the old and new kernels and highlight the differences. (Requires root access.)

29 Daemons

A daemon is a background process that performs a specific function or system task. In keeping with the UNIX and Linux philosophy of modularity, daemons are programs rather than parts of the kernel. Many daemons start at boot time and continue to run as long as the system is up. Other daemons are started when needed and run only as long as they are useful.

"Daemon" was first used as a computer term by Mick Bailey, a British gentleman who was working on the CTSS programming staff at MIT during the early 1960s.[1] Mick quoted the Oxford English Dictionary in support of both the meaning and the spelling of the word. The words "daemon" and "demon" both come from the same root, but "daemon" is an older form and its meaning is somewhat different. A daemon is an attendant spirit that influences one's character or personality. Daemons are not minions of evil *or* good; they're creatures of independent thought and will. Daemons made their way from CTSS to Multics to UNIX to Linux, where they are so popular that they need a superdaemon (**xinetd** or **inetd**) to manage them.

This chapter presents a brief overview of the most common Linux daemons. Not all the daemons listed here are supplied with all Linux distributions, and not every daemon supplied with some Linux distribution is listed here. Besides making you more aware of how Linux works, a knowledge of what all the various daemons do will make you look really smart when one of your users asks, "What does **klogd** do?"

Before **inetd** was written, all daemons started at boot time and ran continuously (or more accurately, they blocked waiting for work to do). Over time, more and more

---

1. This bit of history comes from Jerry Saltzer at MIT, via Dennis Ritchie.

daemons were added to the system. The daemon population became so large that it began to cause performance problems. In response, the Berkeley gurus developed **inetd**, a daemon that starts other daemons as they are needed. **inetd** successfully popularized this superdaemon model, which remains a common way to minimize the number of processes running on a server. Most versions of UNIX and Linux now use a combination of **inetd** and always-running daemons.

There are many daemons that system administrators should be intimately familiar with, either because they require a lot of administration or because they play a large role in the day-to-day operation of the system. Some daemons that are described here in one or two lines have an entire chapter devoted to them elsewhere in this book. We provide cross-references where appropriate.

We start this chapter by introducing a couple of very important system daemons (**init** and **cron**) and then move on to a discussion of **xinetd** and **inetd**. Finally, we briefly describe most of the daemons a system administrator is likely to wrestle with on our four example distributions.

29.1 INIT: THE PRIMORDIAL PROCESS

init is the first process to run after the system boots, and in many ways it is the most important daemon. It always has a PID of 1 and is an ancestor of all user processes and all but a few system processes.

At startup, **init** either places the system in single-user mode or begins to execute the scripts needed to bring the system to multiuser mode. When you boot the system into single-user mode, **init** runs the startup scripts after you terminate the single-user shell by typing **exit** or <Control-D>.

In multiuser mode, **init** is responsible for making sure that processes are available to handle logins on every login-enabled device. Logins on serial ports are generally handled by some variant of **getty** (e.g., **agetty**, **mgetty**, or **mingetty**; see page 857 for details). **init** also supervises a graphical login procedure that allows users to log directly in to X Windows.

In addition to its login management duties, **init** also has the responsibility to exorcise undead zombie processes that would otherwise accumulate on the system. **init**'s role in this process is described on page 56.

*See page 856 for more information about the **inittab** file.*

init defines several "run levels" that determine what set of system resources should be enabled. There are seven levels, numbered 0 to 6. The name "s" is recognized as a synonym for level 1 (single-user mode). The characteristics of each run level are defined in the **/etc/inittab** file.

init usually reads its initial run level from the **/etc/inittab** file, but the run level can also be passed in as an argument from the boot loader. If "s" is specified, **init** enters single-user mode. Otherwise, it scans **/etc/inittab** for entries that apply to the requested run level and executes their corresponding commands.

The **telinit** command changes **init**'s run level once the system is up. For example, **telinit 4** forces **init** to go to run level 4 (which is unused on our example systems). **telinit**'s most useful argument is **q**, which causes **init** to reread the **/etc/inittab** file.

Linux distributions generally implement an additional layer of abstraction on top of the basic run-level mechanism provided by **init**. The extra layer allows individual software packages to install their own startup scripts without modifying the system's generic **inittab** file. Bringing **init** to a new run level causes the appropriate scripts to be executed with the arguments **start** or **stop**.

A more complete discussion of **init** and startup scripts begins on page 33.

29.2 CRON AND ATD: SCHEDULE COMMANDS

The **cron** daemon (known as **crond** on Red Hat) is responsible for running commands at preset times. It accepts schedule files ("crontabs") from both users and administrators.

cron is frequently employed for administrative purposes, including management of log files and daily cleanup of the filesystem. In fact, **cron** is so important to system administrators that we have devoted an entire chapter to it. That chapter, *Periodic Processes*, begins on page 150.

The **atd** daemon runs commands scheduled with the **at** command. Most versions of Linux also include the **anacron** scheduler, which executes jobs at time intervals rather than at specific times. **anacron** is particularly useful on systems that are not always turned on, such as laptops.

29.3 XINETD AND INETD: MANAGE DAEMONS

xinetd and **inetd** are daemons that manage other daemons. They start up their client daemons when there is work for them to do and allow the clients to die gracefully once their tasks have been completed.

The traditional version of **inetd** comes to us from the UNIX world, but most Linux distributions have migrated to Panos Tsirigotis's **xinetd**, a souped-up alternative that incorporates security features similar to those formerly achieved through the use of **tcpd**, the "TCP wrappers" package. **xinetd** also provides better protection against denial of service attacks, better log management features, and a more flexible configuration language.

Unfortunately, **inetd**'s configuration file is not forward-compatible with that of **xinetd**. We first discuss the more common **xinetd** and then take a look at **inetd** in a separate section.

Among our example distributions, only Debian and Ubuntu use the standard **inetd**; RHEL, Fedora, and SUSE all default to **xinetd**. You can convert any system to use the nondefault daemon manager, but there's no compelling reason to do so.

xinetd and **inetd** only work with daemons that provide services over the network. To find out when someone is trying to access one of their clients, **xinetd** and **inetd** attach themselves to the network ports that would normally be managed by the quiescent daemons. When a connection occurs, **xinetd/inetd** starts up the appropriate daemon and connects its standard I/O channels to the network port. Daemons must be written with this convention in mind if they are to be compatible.

Some daemons (such as those associated with NIS and NFS) rely on a further layer of indirection known as the Remote Procedure Call (RPC) system. RPC was originally designed and implemented by Sun as a way of promoting the sharing of information in a heterogeneous networked environment. Port assignments for daemons that use RPC are managed by the **portmap** daemon, which is discussed later in this chapter.

Some daemons can be run in either the traditional fashion (in which they are started once and continue to run until the system shuts down) or through **xinetd/inetd**. Daemons discussed in this chapter are marked with an Ⓣ if they are **xinetd/inetd**-compatible.

Because **xinetd/inetd** is responsible for managing many common network-based services, it plays an important role in securing your system. It's important to verify that only services you need and trust have been enabled. On a new system, you will almost certainly need to modify your default configuration to disable services that are unnecessary or undesirable in your environment.

Configuring xinetd

xinetd's main configuration file is traditionally **/etc/xinetd.conf**, although distributions commonly supply an **/etc/xinetd.d** configuration directory as well. Individual packages can drop their config files into this directory without worrying about overriding the configurations of other packages.

The example below shows the setting of default parameters and the configuration of an FTP service on a Red Hat Enterprise system.

```
defaults
{
    instances       = 60
    log_type        = SYSLOG authpriv
    log_on_success  = HOST PID
    log_on_failure  = HOST
    cps             = 25 30
}

service ftp
{
    # Unlimited instances because wu.ftpd does its own load management
    socket_type     = stream
    protocol        = tcp
    wait            = no
```

```
        user              = root
        server            = /usr/sbin/wu.ftpd
        server_args       = -a
        instances         = UNLIMITED
        only_from         = 128.138.0.0/16
        log_on_success   += DURATION
}

includedir /etc/xinetd.d
...
```

Table 29.1 provides a mini-glossary of parameters.

Table 29.1   xinetd configuration parameters (not an exhaustive list)

Parameter	Value	Meaning
bind	*ipaddr/host*	Interface on which to make this service available
cps	*num waittime*	Limits overall connections per second
disable	yes/no	Disables service; easier than commenting it out
include	*path*	Reads listed path as a supplemental config file
includedir	*path*	Reads all files in the specified directory
instances	*num* or UNLIMITED	Maximum number of simultaneous instances of a given service
log_on_failure	*special*[a]	Information to log for failures or access denials[b]
log_on_success	*special*[a]	Information to log for successful connections[b]
log_type	*special*[a]	Configures log file or syslog parameters
max_load	*num*	Disables service if load average > threshold
nice	*num*	Nice value of spawned server processes
no_access	*matchlist*	Denies service to specified IP addresses
only_from	*matchlist*	Accepts requests only from specified addresses
per_source	*num*	Limits number of instances per remote peer
protocol	tcp/udp	Service protocol
server	*path*	Path to server binary
server_args	*string*	Command-line arguments for server[c]
socket_type	stream/dgram	Uses stream for TCP services, dgram for UDP
user	*username*	User (UID) as whom the service should run
wait	yes/no	Should **xinetd** butt out until the daemon quits?

a. One or more values from a defined list too long to be worth reproducing in this table.

b. Note that the USERID directive used with these parameters causes **xinetd** to perform IDENT queries on connections, often resulting in significant delays.

c. Unlike **inetd**, **xinetd** does not require the server command to be the first argument.

Some **xinetd** parameters can accept assignments of the form += or -= (as seen in the log_on_success value for the FTP server) to modify the default values rather than replacing them outright. Only a few parameters are really required for each service.

Address match lists for the only_from and no_access parameters can be specified in several formats. Most useful are CIDR-format IP addresses with an explicit mask (as shown in the example) and host or domain names such as boulder.colorado.edu and .colorado.edu—note the preceding dot. Multiple specifications can be separated with a space (as in all **xinetd** lists).

xinetd can either log directly to a file or submit log entries to syslog. Since the volume of log information can potentially be quite high on a busy server, it may make sense to use direct-to-file logging for performance reasons. Keep in mind that logging to a file is less secure than logging to a remote server through syslog because a hacker that gains access to the local system can doctor the log files.

xinetd can provide some interesting services such as forwarding of requests to an internal host that is not visible to the outside world. It's worth reviewing **xinetd**'s man page to get an idea of its capabilities.

Configuring inetd

Debian and Ubuntu are the only major Linux distributions that still use the traditional **inetd**. This version of **inetd** consults **/etc/inetd.conf** to determine on which network ports it should listen. The config file includes much the same information as **xinetd.conf**, but it uses a tabular (rather than attribute/value list) format. Here's a (pared-down) example from a Debian system:

```
# Example /etc/inetd.conf - from a Debian system

#:INTERNAL: Internal services
#echo      stream  tcp      nowait     root     internal
#echo      dgram   udp      wait       root     internal
...
#time      stream  tcp      nowait     root     internal
#time      dgram   udp      wait       root     internal

#:STANDARD: These are standard services.
#:BSD: Shell, login, exec and talk are BSD protocols.

#:MAIL: Mail, news and uucp services.
imap2      stream  tcp      nowait     root     /usr/sbin/tcpd /usr/sbin/imapd
imaps      stream  tcp      nowait     root     /usr/sbin/tcpd /usr/sbin/imapd

#:INFO: Info services
ident      stream  tcp      wait       identd   /usr/sbin/identd identd
...
#:OTHER: Other services
swat       stream  tcp      nowait.400 root     /usr/sbin/swat swat
# finger   stream  tcp      nowait     nobody   /usr/sbin/tcpd in.fingerd -w
391002/1-2 stream  rpc/tcp  wait       root     /usr/sbin/famd fam
...
```

The first column contains the service name. **inetd** maps service names to port numbers by consulting either the **/etc/services** file (for TCP and UDP services) or the **/etc/rpc** file and **portmap** daemon (for RPC services). RPC services are identified by names of the form *name/num* and the designation rpc in column three. In the example above, the last line is an RPC service.

The only other RPC service that is commonly managed by **inetd** is **mountd**, the NFS mount daemon. Linux distributions seem to run this daemon the old-fashioned way (by starting it at boot time), so you may have no RPC services at all in your **inetd.conf** file.

On a host with more than one network interface, you can preface the service name with a list of comma-separated IP addresses or symbolic hostnames to specify the interfaces on which **inetd** should listen for service requests. For example, the line

```
inura:time    stream   tcp   nowait   root   internal
```

provides the time service only on the interface associated with the name inura in DNS, NIS, or the **/etc/hosts** file.

The second column determines the type of socket that the service will use and is invariably stream or dgram. stream is used with TCP (connection-oriented) services, and dgram is used with UDP; however, some services use both, e.g., **bind**.

The third column identifies the communication protocol used by the service. The allowable types are listed in the **protocols** file (usually in **/etc**). The protocol is almost always tcp or udp. RPC services prepend rpc/ to the protocol type, as with rpc/tcp in the preceding example.

If the service being described can process multiple requests at one time (rather than processing one request and exiting), column four should be set to wait. This option allows the spawned daemon to take over management of the port as long as it is running; **inetd** waits for the daemon to exit before resuming its monitoring of the port. The opposite of wait is nowait; it makes **inetd** monitor continuously and fork a new copy of the daemon each time it receives a request. The selection of wait or nowait must correspond to the daemon's actual behavior and should not be set arbitrarily. When configuring a new daemon, check the **inetd.conf** file for an example configuration line or consult the man page for the daemon in question.

The form nowait.400, used in the configuration line for **swat**, indicates that **inetd** should spawn at most 400 instances of the server daemon per minute. The default is more conservative, 40 instances per minute. Given the nature of this service (a web administration tool for Samba), it's not clear why the throttle threshold was raised.

The fifth column gives the username under which the daemon should run. It's always more secure to run a daemon as a user other than root if that is possible. In the example above, **in.fingerd** would run as the user nobody (if the line were not commented out).

The remaining fields give the fully qualified pathname of the daemon and its command-line arguments. The keyword internal indicates services whose implementations are provided by **inetd** itself.

Many of the service entries in this example run their daemons by way of **tcpd** rather than executing them directly. **tcpd** logs connection attempts and implements access control according to the source of the connection attempt. In general, all services should be protected with **tcpd**. This example configuration presents a potential security problem because **swat**, a file sharing configuration utility, is not protected.[2]

In the default **inetd.conf** shipped with Debian, the servers for **rlogin**, **telnet**, **finger**, and **rexec** are no longer even listed. See the section *Miscellaneous security issues* on page 685 for more security-related information.

See Chapter 10 for more information about syslog.

After you edit **/etc/inetd.conf**, send **inetd** a HUP signal to tell it to reread its configuration file and implement any changes you made. After signalling, wait a moment and then check the log files for error messages related to your changes (**inetd** logs errors to syslog under the "daemon" facility). Test any new services you have added to be sure they work correctly.

The services file

After adding a new service to **inetd.conf** or **xinetd.conf**, you may also need to make an entry for it in the **/etc/services** file. This file is used by several standard library routines that map between service names and port numbers. **xinetd** actually allows you to specify the port number directly, but it's always a good idea to maintain a master list of ports in the **services** file.

For example, when you type the command

```
$ telnet anchor smtp
```

telnet looks up the port number for the smtp service in the **services** file. Most systems ship with all the common services already configured; you need only edit the **services** file if you add something new.

The **services** file is used only for bona fide TCP/IP services; similar information for RPC services is stored in **/etc/rpc**.

Here are some selected lines from a **services** file (the original is ~570 lines long):

```
tcpmux      1/tcp                      # TCP port multiplexer
echo        7/tcp
echo        7/udp
...
ssh         22/tcp                     #SSH Remote Login Protocol
ssh         22/udp                     #SSH Remote Login Protocol
smtp        25/tcp      mail
rlp         39/udp      resource       # resource location
name        42/tcp                     # IEN 116
domain      53/tcp                     # name-domain server
domain      53/udp
...
```

2. If you are not using **tcpd** to protect a service, the daemon's first command-line argument should always be the short name of the daemon itself. This requirement is not a peculiarity of **inetd** but a traditional UNIX convention that is normally hidden by the shell.

The format of a line is

```
name        port/proto  aliases        # comment
```

Services are generally listed in numerical order, although this order is not required. *name* is the symbolic name of the service (the name you use in the **inetd.conf** or **xinetd.conf** file). The *port* is the port number at which the service normally listens; if the service is managed by **inetd**, it is the port that **inetd** will listen on.[3]

The *proto* stipulates the protocol used by the service; in practice, it is always tcp or udp. If a service can use either UDP or TCP, a line for each must be included (as with the ssh service above). The *alias* field contains additional names for the service (e.g., whois can also be looked up as nicname).

portmap: map RPC services to TCP and UDP ports

portmap maps RPC service numbers to the TCP/IP ports on which their servers are listening. When an RPC server starts up, it registers itself with **portmap**, listing the services it supports and the port at which it can be contacted. Clients query **portmap** to find out how to get in touch with an appropriate server.

This system allows a port to be mapped to a symbolic service name. It's basically another level of abstraction above the **services** file, albeit one that introduces additional complexity (and security issues) without solving any real-world problems.

If the **portmap** daemon dies, all the services that rely on it (including **inetd** and NFS) must be restarted. In practical terms, this means that it's time to reboot the system. **portmap** must be started before **inetd** for **inetd** to handle RPC services correctly.

29.4 KERNEL DAEMONS

For architectural reasons, a few parts of the Linux kernel are managed as if they were user processes. On older kernels, these processes could be identified by their low PIDs and names that start with **k**, such as **kupdate**, **kswapd**, **keventd**, and **kapm**. The naming is less consistent under the 2.6 kernels, but **ps** always shows the names of kernel threads in square brackets.

For the most part, these processes deal with various aspects of I/O, memory management, and synchronization of the disk cache. They cannot be manipulated by the system administrator and should be left alone.[4]

Table 29.2 on the next page briefly summarizes the functions of the major daemons in the current complement. Daemons that include an N parameter in their names

---

3. Port numbers are not arbitrary. All machines must agree about which services go with which ports; otherwise, requests will constantly be directed to the wrong port. If you are creating a site-specific service, pick a high port number (greater than 1023) that is not already listed in the **services** file.

4. If you are familiar with the implementation of the kernel, it is occasionally useful to change these processes' execution priorities. However, this is not a standard administrative task.

(as shown by **ps**) run separately on each CPU of a multi-CPU system; the N tells you which copy goes with which CPU.

Table 29.2   Major kernel daemons (2.6 kernels)

Daemon	Function
ksoftirqd/*N*	Handles software interrupts when the load is high
kacpid	Deals with the ACPI subsystem
kblockd/*N*	Blocks subsystem work
aio/*N*	Retries asynchronous I/Os
kswapd*N*	Moves pages to swap
ata/*N*	Does processing for serial ATA support
scsi_eh_*N*	Performs SCSI error handling
kjournald	Supports journaling filesystems
events/*N*	Does generic work queue processing

Another system daemon in this category, albeit one with a nonstandard name, is **mdrecoveryd**. It's part of the "multiple devices," implementation, more commonly known as RAID.

klogd: read kernel messages

klogd is responsible for reading log entries from the kernel's message buffer and forwarding them to syslog so that they can be routed to their final destination. It can also process messages itself if configured to do so. See *Kernel and boot-time logging* on page 206 for more information.

29.5 PRINTING DAEMONS

Several printing systems are in common use, and each has its own family of commands and daemons that provide printing-related services. In some cases the families have been hybridized; in others cases, multiple variants run on a single system.

cupsd: scheduler for the Common UNIX Printing System

See Chapter 23 for more information about CUPS.

CUPS provides a portable printing facility by implementing version 1.1 of the Internet Printing Protocol. It allows remote users to print to their offices (or vice versa) by using a web interface. CUPS has become quite popular and is most systems' default printing manager. It is flexible enough to allow for remote authentication.

lpd: manage printing

lpd is responsible for the old-style BSD print spooling system. It accepts jobs from users and forks processes that perform the actual printing. **lpd** is also responsible for transferring print jobs to and from remote systems. **lpd** can sometimes hang and then must be manually restarted.

Your system might have either the original flavor of **lpd** or the extra-crispy version
that's part of the LPRng package. See Chapter 23, *Printing*, for more information
about these alternatives.

29.6 FILE SERVICE DAEMONS

The following daemons are part of the NFS or Samba file sharing systems. We give
only a brief description of their functions here. NFS is described in detail in Chapter
16, and Samba is covered starting on page 828.

rpc.nfsd: serve files

rpc.nfsd runs on file servers and handles requests from NFS clients. In most NFS
implementations, **nfsd** is really just a part of the kernel that has been dressed up as a
process for scheduling reasons. Linux actually sports two different implementations,
one of which follows this convention and one of which runs in user space. The kernel implementation is more popular and is most distributions' default.

rpc.nfsd accepts a single argument that specifies how many copies of itself to fork.
Some voodoo is involved in picking the correct number of copies; see page 492.

rpc.mountd: respond to mount requests

rpc.mountd accepts filesystem mount requests from potential NFS clients. It verifies that each client has permission to mount the requested directories. **rpc.mountd**
consults the **/var/state/nfs/xtab** file to determine which applicants are legitimate.

amd and automount: mount filesystems on demand

amd and **automount** are NFS automounters, daemons that wait until a process attempts to use a filesystem before they actually mount it. The automounters later unmount the filesystems if they have not been accessed in a specified period of time.

The use of automounters is very helpful in large environments where dozens or hundreds of filesystems are shared on the network. Automounters increase the stability
of the network and reduce configuration complexity since all systems on the network
can share the same **amd** or **automountd** configuration. We cover the use of the
standard Linux automounter in detail starting on page 497.

rpc.lockd and rpc.statd: manage NFS locks

Although **rpc.lockd** and **rpc.statd** are distinct daemons, they always run as a team.
rpc.lockd maintains advisory locks (a la **flock** and **lockf**) on NFS files. **rpc.statd**
allows processes to monitor the status of other machines that are running NFS.
rpc.lockd uses **rpc.statd** to decide when to attempt to communicate with a remote
machine.

rpciod: cache NFS blocks

rpciod caches read and write requests on NFS clients. It performs both read-ahead and write-behind buffering and greatly improves the performance of NFS. This daemon is analogous to the **biod** and **nfsiod** daemons found on other systems, although it is structurally somewhat different.

rpc.rquotad: serve remote quotas

rpc.rquotad lets remote users check their quotas on filesystems they have mounted with NFS. The actual implementation of quota restrictions is still performed on the server; **rpc.rquotad** just makes the **quota** command work correctly.

smbd: provide file and printing service to Windows clients

smbd is the file and printer server in the Samba suite. It provides file and printer sharing service through the Windows protocol known variously as SMB or CIFS. See page 828 for more details.

nmbd: NetBIOS name server

nmbd is another component of Samba. It replies to NetBIOS name service requests generated by Windows machines. It also implements the browsing protocol that Windows machines use to populate the My Network Places folder and makes disks shared from the local host visible there. **nmbd** can also be used as a WINS server.

29.7 ADMINISTRATIVE DATABASE DAEMONS

Several daemons are associated with Sun's NIS administrative database system, which is described in Chapter 17, *Sharing System Files*. Although NIS originated at Sun, it is now used on many other vendors' systems as well, including Linux.

ypbind: locate NIS servers

The **ypbind** daemon runs on all NIS clients and servers. It locates an NIS server to which queries can be directed. **ypbind** does not actually process requests itself; it just tells client programs which server to use.

ypserv: NIS server

ypserv runs on all NIS servers. **ypserv** accepts queries from clients and responds with the requested information. See page 517 for information on how to configure the machines that run **ypserv**.

rpc.ypxfrd: transfer NIS databases

rpc.ypxfrd efficiently transfers NIS databases to slave servers. A slave initiates a transfer with the **ypxfr** command. Whenever a database is changed on the master, it should immediately be pushed out to all the slaves so that the NIS servers remain consistent with one another.

lwresd: lightweight resolver library server

lwresd provides a quick method of caching address-to-hostname and hostname-to-address lookups. It's contacted by a stub resolver that is part of the system's standard libraries and is called directly by many programs. The library and daemon communicate through a simple UDP protocol.

nscd: name service cache daemon

nscd caches the results of calls to the standard C library routines in the **getpw***, **getgr***, and **gethost*** families, which look up data that was traditionally stored in the **passwd**, **group**, and **hosts** files. These days, the range of potential sources is larger and includes options such as NIS and DNS. **nscd** does not actually know where the data comes from; it simply caches results and uses them to short-circuit subsequent library calls. Caching policy is set in the **/etc/nscd.conf** file.

29.8 ELECTRONIC MAIL DAEMONS

In addition to the core **sendmail** and Postfix mail delivery systems, which are both in widespread use, several daemons facilitate remote access to mailboxes.

ⓘ sendmail: transport electronic mail

sendmail's tasks include accepting messages from users and remote sites, rewriting addresses, expanding aliases, and transferring mail across the Internet. **sendmail** is an important and very complex daemon. Refer to Chapter 18, *Electronic Mail*, for the complete scoop.

ⓘ smtpd: Simple Mail Transport Protocol daemon

smtpd listens on port 25 for incoming email messages and forwards them to your back-end transport system for further processing. See pages 540 and 624 for more information about the use of **smtpd** in the **sendmail** and Postfix systems.

ⓘ popd: basic mailbox server

The **popd** daemon implements the Post Office Protocol (POP). This protocol is commonly used by non-Linux systems to receive electronic mail.

ⓘ imapd: deluxe mailbox server

The **imapd** daemon implements the Internet Message Access Protocol, IMAP, which is a more festive and featureful alternative to POP. It allows PC-based users (or Linux users with IMAP-enabled mail readers) to access their email from a variety of locations, with mail folders being stored on the Linux server. Check out www.imap.org for more information about IMAP.

29.9 REMOTE LOGIN AND COMMAND EXECUTION DAEMONS

The ability to log in and execute commands over the net was one of the earliest motivations for the development of UNIX networking, and this facility is still a bread-and-butter component of system administration today. Unfortunately, it took the UNIX community several decades to achieve a mature appreciation of the security implications of this technology. Modern production systems should be using SSH (**sshd**) and virtually nothing else.

ⓘ sshd: secure remote login server

sshd provides services that are similar to **in.rlogind**, but its sessions are transported (and authenticated) across an encrypted pipeline. A variety of encryption algorithms are available. Because of the harsh environment of the Internet today, you must allow shell access from the Internet *only* through a daemon such as this—*not* **in.rlogind** or **in.telnetd**. You can find more information about **sshd** starting on page 697.

ⓘ in.rlogind: obsolete remote login server

in.rlogind was the long-ago standard for handling remote logins. When invoked by **inetd**, it tries to automatically authenticate the remote user by examining the local user's **~/.rhosts** file and the system-wide **/etc/hosts.equiv**. If automatic authentication is successful, the user is logged in directly. Otherwise, **in.rlogind** executes the **login** program to prompt the user for a password. Because of its cheap 'n' easy authentication, **in.rlogind** is a major security hazard. See page 685 for more comments on this subject.

ⓘ in.telnetd: yet another remote login server

in.telnetd is similar to **in.rlogind**, except that it uses the TELNET protocol. This protocol allows the two sides (client and server) to negotiate flow control and duplex settings, making it a better choice than **in.rlogind** for links that are slow or unreliable. Like **rlogin**, **telnet** transmits plaintext passwords across the network. Its use is therefore discouraged in modern networks. However, many non-Linux systems support **telnet**.

ⓘ in.rshd: remote command execution server

in.rshd handles remote command execution requests from **rsh** and **rcmd**. The authentication process enforced by **in.rshd** is similar to that of **in.rlogind**, except that if automatic authentication does not work, **in.rshd** denies the request without allowing the user to supply a password. **in.rshd** is also the server for **rcp** (remote copy). Like **in.rlogind**, **in.rshd** has become something of a security albatross and is invariably disabled. See page 685 for more information.

29.10 BOOTING AND CONFIGURATION DAEMONS

In the 1980s, the UNIX world was swept by a wave of diskless workstation mania. These machines booted entirely over the network and performed all their disk I/O through a remote filesystem technology such as NFS. As disk prices dropped and speeds increased, interest in diskless workstations quickly faded. They could come back into fashion at any moment, however, like the platform shoes of the 1970s. The two main remnants of the diskless era are a plethora of daemons designed to support diskless systems and the bizarre organization of most vendors' filesystems.

For the curious, we discuss diskless systems themselves in some additional detail starting on page 232.

Although diskless workstations are not common anymore, their booting protocols have been usurped by other devices. Most manageable network hubs and network printers boot by using some combination of the services listed in this section.

dhcpd: dynamic address assignment

The Dynamic Host Configuration Protocol (DHCP) provides PCs, laptops, and other "mobile" platforms with information about their IP addresses, default gateways, and name servers at boot time. **dhcpd** is the daemon that implements this service under Linux. You can find more information about DHCP on page 311. A fancier elaboration of DHCP called PXE (Pre-boot eXecution Environment) helps compatible machines boot from the network without the need for a local boot device; see page 224 for more details.

in.tftpd: trivial file transfer server

in.tftpd implements a file transfer protocol similar to that of **ftpd**, but much, much simpler. Many diskless systems use TFTP to download their kernels from a server. **in.tftpd** does not perform authentication, but it is normally restricted to serving the files in a single directory (usually **/tftpboot**). Since anything placed in the TFTP directory is accessible to the entire network, the directory should contain only boot files and should not be publicly writable.

rpc.bootparamd: advanced diskless life support

rpc.bootparamd uses the **/etc/bootparams** file to tell diskless clients where to find their filesystems. **rpc.bootparamd** service is often used by machines that get their IP addresses by using RARP and that use NFS to mount their filesystems.

hald: hardware abstraction layer (HAL) daemon

hald collects information about the system's hardware from several sources. It provides a live device list through D-BUS.

udevd: serialize device connection notices

udevd is a minor part of the **udev** dynamic device-naming system. It allows for the proper serialization of hot-plug events, which the kernel can sometimes communicate out of order to user space.

29.11 OTHER NETWORK DAEMONS

The following daemons all use Internet protocols to handle requests. However, many of these "Internet" daemons actually spend the majority of their time servicing local requests.

talkd: network chat service

Connection requests from the **talk** program are handled by **talkd**. When it receives a request, **talkd** negotiates with the other machine to set up a network connection between the two users who have executed **talk**.

snmpd: provide remote network management service

snmpd responds to requests that use the Simple Network Management Protocol (SNMP) protocol. SNMP standardizes some common network management operations. See page 659 for more information about SNMP.

ftpd: file transfer server

See page 734 for more information about ftpd.

ftpd is the daemon that handles requests from **ftp**, the Internet file transfer program. Many sites disable it, usually because they are worried about security. **ftpd** can be set up to allow anyone to transfer files to and from your machine.

A variety of **ftpd** implementations are available for Linux systems. If you plan to run a high-traffic server or need advanced features such as load management, it might be wise to investigate the alternatives to your distribution's default **ftpd**.

WU-FTPD, developed at Washington University, is one of the most popular alternatives to the standard **ftpd**. See www.wu-ftpd.org for more information.

rsyncd: synchronize files among multiple hosts

rsyncd is really just a link to the **rsync** command; the **--daemon** option turns it into a server process. **rsyncd** facilitates the synchronization of files among hosts. It's essentially an efficient and security-aware version of **rcp**. **rsync** is a real treasure trove for system administrators, and in this book we've described its use in a couple of different contexts. See page 508 for general information and some tips on using **rsync** to share system files. **rsync** is also a large part of many sites' internal installation processes.

routed: maintain routing tables

routed maintains the routing information used by TCP/IP to send and forward packets on a network. **routed** deals only with dynamic routing; routes that are statically defined (that is, wired into the system's routing table with the **route** command) are never modified by **routed**. **routed** is relatively stupid and inefficient, and we recommend its use in only a few specific situations. See page 343 for a more detailed discussion of **routed**.

gated: maintain complicated routing tables

gated understands several routing protocols, including RIP, the protocol used by **routed**. **gated** translates routing information among various protocols and is very configurable. It can also be much kinder to your network than **routed**. See page 344 for more information about **gated**.

named: DNS server

named is the most popular server for the Domain Name System. It maps hostnames into network addresses and performs many other feats and tricks, all using a distributed database maintained by **named**s everywhere. Chapter 15, *DNS: The Domain Name System*, describes the care and feeding of **named**.

syslogd: process log messages

See page 209 for more information about syslog.

syslogd acts as a clearing house for status information and error messages produced by system software and daemons. Before **syslogd** was written, daemons either wrote their error messages directly to the system console or maintained their own private log files. Now they use the **syslog** library routine to transfer the messages to **syslogd**, which sorts them according to rules established by the system administrator.

ⓘ in.fingerd: look up users

in.fingerd provides information about the users that are logged in to the system. If asked, it can also provide a bit more detail about individual users. **in.fingerd** does not really do much work itself: it simply accepts lines of input and passes them to the local **finger** program.

finger can return quite a bit of information about a user, including the user's login status, the contents of the user's GECOS field in **/etc/passwd**, and the contents of the user's ~**/.plan** and ~**/.project** files.

If you are connected to the Internet and are running **in.fingerd**, anyone in the world can obtain this information. **in.fingerd** has enabled some really neat services (such as the Internet white pages), but it has also enabled people to run a variety of scams, such as finding people to cold-call and prospecting for spammable addresses. Some sites have responded to this invasion by turning off **in.fingerd**, while others just restrict the amount of information it returns. Don't assume that because **in.fingerd** is simple, it is necessarily secure—a buffer overflow attack against this daemon was exploited by the original Internet worm of 1988.

ⓘ httpd: World Wide Web server

httpd lets your site become a web server. **httpd** can send text, pictures, and sound to its clients. See Chapter 21, *Web Hosting and Internet Servers*, for more information about serving up web pages.

29.12   NTPD: TIME SYNCHRONIZATION DAEMON

As computers have grown increasingly interdependent, it has become more and more important for them to share a consistent idea of time. Synchronized clocks are essential for correlating log file entries in the event of a security breach, and they're also important for a variety of end-user applications, from joint development of software projects to the processing of financial transactions.

ntpd[5] implements the Network Time Protocol, which allows computers to synchronize their clocks to within milliseconds of each other. The first NTP implementation started around 1980 with an accuracy of only several hundred milliseconds. Today, a new kernel clock model can keep time with a precision of up to one nanosecond. The latest version of the protocol (version 4, documented in RFC2783) maintains compatibility with the previous versions and adds easy configuration and some security features.

NTP servers are arranged in a hierarchy, each level of which is called a "stratum." The time on stratum 1 servers is typically slaved to an external reference clock such as a radio receiver or atomic clock. Stratum 2 servers set their clocks from Stratum 1 servers and act as time distribution centers. Up to 16 strata are provided for. To determine its own stratum, a time server simply adds 1 to the stratum of the highest-numbered server to which it synchronizes. A 1999 survey of the NTP network by Nelson Minar indicated that there were (at that time) 300 servers in stratum 1; 20,000 servers in stratum 2; and more than 80,000 servers in stratum 3.[6]

Today, NTP clients can access a number of reference time standards, such as those provided by WWV and GPS. A list of authoritative U.S. Internet time servers maintained by the National Institute of Standards and Technology can be found at

www.boulder.nist.gov/timefreq/service/time-servers.html

Most ISPs maintain their own set of time servers, which should be closer in network terms for their downstream clients (and if NTP works correctly, just as accurate).

ntpd implements both the client and server sides of the NTP protocol. It reads **/etc/ntp.conf** at startup. In the config file you can specify access, client networks, time servers, multicast clients, general configuration, and authentication; but don't be scared off—it's all pretty self-explanatory.

Debian and Ubuntu don't seem to include **ntpd** by default, but it's readily available through **apt-get**. You can also obtain the current software from ntp.isc.org.

You can also use the quick and dirty **ntpdate** utility to set the system's clock from an NTP server. This is a less desirable solution than **ntpd** because it can make the flow of time appear discontinuous. It is especially harmful to set the clock back suddenly, since programs sometimes assume that time is a monotonically increasing function.

5. This daemon was also known as **xntpd** in earlier incarnations.
6. See www.media.mit.edu/~nelson/research/ntp-survey99

ntpd uses the gentler **adjtimex** system call to smooth the adjustment of the system's clock and prevent large jumps backward or forward. **adjtimex** biases the speed of the system's clock so that it gradually falls into correct alignment. When the system time matches the current objective time, the bias is cancelled and the clock runs normally.

29.13 EXERCISES

E29.1 Using **ps**, determine which daemons are running on your system. Also determine which daemons are available to run through **inetd.conf** or **xinetd.conf**. Combine the lists and describe what each daemon does, where it is started, whether multiple copies can (or do) run at the same time, and any other attributes you can glean.

E29.2 In the lab, install and set up the network time daemon, **ntpd**.

a) How do you tell if your system has the correct time?

b) Using the **date** command, manually set your system time to be 15 seconds slow. How long does it (or will it) take for the time become correct?

c) Manually set your system time a month ahead. How does **ntpd** respond to this situation?

(Requires root access.)

E29.3 In the lab, use a tool such as **netstat** to determine what ports are in a "listening" state on your machine.

a) How can you reconcile the **netstat** information with what is found in **inetd.conf** or **xinetd.conf**? If there is a discrepancy, what is going on?

b) Install the **nmap** tool on a different machine. Run a port scan targeting your system to verify what you learned in part a. What (if any) additional information did you learn from **nmap** that wasn't obvious from **netstat**? (See page 688 for more information about **nmap**.)

30 Management, Policy, and Politics

You may run the smartest team of administrators ever, but if your technical management is inadequate, you will hate life and so will your users. In this chapter we discuss the nontechnical aspects of running a successful information technology (IT) support organization, along with a few technical tidbits (infrastructure design, trouble ticketing systems, etc.) that help shore up the managerial end of system administration.

Most of the topics and ideas presented in this chapter are not specific to a particular environment. They apply equally to a part-time system administrator and to a large group of full-time professionals in charge of a major IT installation. Like green vegetables, they're good for you no matter what sized meal you're preparing. (For really huge sites with hundreds of IT employees, we also briefly describe the Information Technology Interface Library, a process-focused IT management architecture that's appropriate mostly for large sites. See page 960.)

In addition to management hints, we also include sections on documentation (page 930), trouble ticket systems (page 934), disaster recovery (page 938), policy development (page 943), legal issues (page 949), software patents (page 957), standardization efforts (page 958), Linux culture (page 961), and Linux-related professional organizations, conferences, and training opportunities for sysadmins (page 964).

30.1 MAKE EVERYONE HAPPY

System administration is a service industry, and both people and computers are the recipients of that service. Some more technically focused administrators seem to be under the impression that the users of their systems are little more than nuisances who get in the way of real work. That's an unhelpful and inaccurate viewpoint; our job is to provide users with the IT infrastructure they need to do their work efficiently and reliably.

We've all been on the other side of the help desk at some point in our career. So put yourself in your customers' shoes: what was the experience like, and what would you have changed?

Users are happy when

- Their computers are up and running and they can log in.
- Their data files stay as they left them.
- Their application software is installed and works as it's supposed to.
- Friendly, knowledgeable help is available when needed.

Users want these things 24 hours a day, 7 days a week. Preferably for free. Users hate

- Downtime, whether scheduled or unscheduled
- Upgrades that introduce sudden, incompatible changes
- Incomprehensible messages from the system or from administrators
- Long explanations of why things aren't working

When something is broken, users want to know when it's going to be fixed. That's it. They don't really care which hard disk or generator broke, or why; leave that information for your managerial reports.

From a user's perspective, no news is good news. The system either works or it doesn't, and if the latter, it doesn't matter why. Our customers are happiest when they don't even notice that we exist! Sad, but true.

Users are our primary customers, but it's equally important to keep your staff happy. Good administrators are hard to find, and their needs must be considered when your site's administrative systems are designed.

System administrators and other technical staff are happy when

- Their computers and support systems are up and running.
- They have the resources necessary to do their jobs.
- They have the latest and greatest software and hardware tools.
- They can work without being constantly interrupted.
- They can be creative without the boss meddling and micromanaging.
- Their work hours and stress level are within reason.

Technical people need more than just a paycheck at the end of the month to keep them going. They need to feel that they have a degree of creative control over their work and that they are appreciated by their peers, their boss, and their users.

The requirements for happy customers and happy IT staff have some factors in common. However, a few things seem to be orthogonal or even in direct conflict. The boss must make sure that all these differing expectations can be made compatible and attainable.

In some organizations, the boss interfaces with customers to protect the technical staff from front-line interruptions and free them to do their "real" work. Our experience is that this arrangement is usually a bad idea. It isolates the technical staff from direct exposure to customers' needs and often results in the boss making promises that the staff cannot fulfill.

30.2 COMPONENTS OF A FUNCTIONAL IT ORGANIZATION

As a sysadmin support organization starts to grow, it becomes obvious that not everybody in the group can or should know everything about the entire infrastructure. It's also impractical (impossible, really) for one person to make all the daily decisions. With growth, the following organizational subdivisions tend to evolve:

- *Management*: defines the overall strategy and leads the organization

- *Administration*: talks to customers about their needs, negotiates contracts, sends invoices, places purchase orders, pays vendors, deals with the administrative processes involved in hiring and firing staff

- *Development*: designs, implements, and tests new products and services before they are deployed to customers

- *Production*: provides direct services to customers, both system management and end-user support and training. We subdivide this area into *operations* (dealing with machines) and *support* (dealing with people).

These functional divisions don't necessarily have to map to individual people. Even at a small operation with a single system administrator, the four task areas are just different hats that the sysadmin must wear.

The relative size of each division reflects the type of organization that the administrative group serves. A research university has a different mix from a software development company or a manufacturing firm. Our experience at a research university suggests that management is about 5% of the work, administration is about 10%, development is 10%-20%, and production accounts for the remainder (65%-75%).

We suggest that in small- to medium-sized organizations, all employees work at least part time in the support division. This convention gives technical personnel first-hand exposure to the problems, frustrations, and desires of customers. Customer feedback can then be used to improve the current environment or to design future systems and services. As a side effect, it also makes some of the more knowledgeable employees accessible to customers. (Ever been stuck in tier-one technical support?)

Twenty percent may sound high for development, but without it your solutions will not scale as the number and complexity of supported systems increases. Your original management concepts will stagnate and eventually become outdated beyond hope of repair.

The ideal number of people for one person to directly manage seems to be between 5 and 10. Beyond that, consider adding more hierarchy.

We discuss all five task divisions in the following sections.

30.3 THE ROLE OF MANAGEMENT

The manager's overall goal is to facilitate the work of the technical staff, who are the experts regarding the organization's "real" work. Several tasks and responsibilities fall on the manager's shoulders:

- Leading the group, bringing vision, and providing necessary resources
- Hiring, firing, staff assessment, and skill development
- Assigning tasks to the staff and tracking progress
- Managing management
- Handling problems: staff conflicts, rogue users, ancient hardware, etc.
- Acting as a "higher authority" to whom users can escalate problems
- Overseeing the development of a scalable infrastructure
- Planning for disasters and emergencies
- Extracting documentation from squirrely sysadmin's heads

It might seem that the task of interfacing with customers is missing from this list. However, we believe that this role is actually best filled by members of the technical staff. Managers do not usually have the technical background to evaluate the difficulty and feasibility of customers' requirements. There are likely to be fewer surprises on both sides of the table when those doing the actual work have input into the deliverables and schedules that are promised to customers.

Below, we discuss some of these managerial functions in more detail. A few of them span the boundaries of multiple functional areas and are included elsewhere. For example, the development of scalable infrastructure is a joint project of the management and development functions; see page 919 for our comments. Similarly, disaster recovery is both a managerial and an operational issue; we discuss it starting on page 938. Documentation is so important and so thorny that it has a section of its own beginning on page 930.

Leadership

Leadership is hard to describe. But when lacking or poorly executed, its absence is all too readily apparent. In a way, leadership is the "system administration" of organizations; it sets the direction, makes sure the components work together, and keeps the whole system running with as few error messages as possible.

Unfortunately, the technical chops that make someone a great computer system administrator don't necessarily translate to the leadership role, which requires a more people-centered skill set. People are a lot harder to master than Perl.

For new managers with strong technical backgrounds, it can be particularly hard to focus on the job of management and avoid the temptation to do engineering work. It's more comfortable and more fun to dive into solving a technical problem than to have a long-overdue conversation with a "difficult" staff member. But which is more valuable for the organization?

A simple (and perhaps eye-opening) check on your level of leadership is the following. Make a list of the tasks your organization is working on. Use one color to mark the areas in which you are steering the boat, and a different color to mark the areas in which you are rowing or pulling the boat. Which color dominates the picture?

Hiring, firing, and personnel management

Personnel management can be particularly challenging. As part of your oversight function, you deal both with your employees' technical and personal sides. True to the stereotype, technically brilliant sysadmins are often poor communicators, and they sometimes tend to get along better with machines than with people. As their manager, you need to keep them on the growth curve in both dimensions.

Technical growth is relatively easy to promote and quantify, but personal growth is just as important. Below are some important questions to ask when assessing an employee's user interface:

- Is this person's behavior suitable for our work environment?
- How does this person interact with authorities, customers, and suppliers?
- Does this person get along with other members of the team?
- Does this person have leadership skills that should be developed?
- How does this person respond to criticism and technical disputes?
- Does this person actively work to address gaps in his or her knowledge?
- How are this person's communication skills?
- Can this person plan, implement, and demonstrate a customer's project?

Hiring

It's important to make these assessments for potential new hires as well as for existing employees. The personal qualities of job applicants are often overlooked or underweighted. Don't take shortcuts in this area—you'll surely regret it later!

A personal interview might answer some of these questions. A telephone conversation with references usually tells you more. Listen very carefully; many people do not like to say anything bad about a former employee or co-worker, so they find clever ways to tell you (if you are listening carefully) that a potential employee has problems. Be very suspicious if the applicant does not include recent employers as references.

There are two approaches to building a staff of system administrators:

- Hire experienced people.
- Grow your own.

Experienced people usually come up to speed faster, but you always want them to unlearn certain things. To do their job, they need root access. But you do not know them and may not be willing to put your company's data in their hands immediately. Breaking them in may require a bit of espionage and auditing as you expand your trust in them.

It takes quite a bit of time and effort to train a sysadmin, and production networks are not an ideal training ground. But given the right person (smart, interested, curious, careful, etc.), the end result is often better.

Some of the qualities of a good system administrator are contradictory. A sysadmin must be brash enough to try innovative solutions when stuck on a problem but must also be careful enough not to try anything truly destructive. Interpersonal skills and problem-solving skills are both important, yet they seem to lie on orthogonal axes among many of the sysadmins we have known. One of our reviewers suggested that a "personable sysadmin" was an oxymoron.

We have developed two evaluation tools for experienced applicants. We used to call them "tests," but we found that some institutions (like state universities in the United States) are not allowed to test applicants. We no longer test; we evaluate and assess.

The first written evaluation asks applicants to rate their experience and knowledge of various system and networking tasks. The scale of familiarity is 0 to 4:

- Never heard of it (0)
- Heard of it, never did it (1)
- Have done it, could do it with supervision (2)
- Could do it without supervision (3)
- Know it well, could teach someone else to do it (4)

Embedded among the questions are several ringers. For example, in the hardware section right after a question about RJ-45 connectors is one about "MX connectors" (MX refers to a mail exchanger record in DNS, not to a network or serial connector). These bogus questions let you measure the BS factor in an applicant's answers. A 3 on the MX connectors would be suspect. In the interview after the written evaluation, you might ask innocently, "So, what do *you* use MX connectors for?"

The second evaluation is designed for use during a telephone interview. Questions are set up to elicit quick answers from applicants who know their stuff. We score +1 for a right answer, 0 for an "I don't know," and -1 for obvious BS or typing **man xxx** in the background. You could also score +1 for a reasonable answer of the form "I don't know, but here's how I would find out." Often, knowing where to look something up is just as good as knowing the details by heart.

These two schemes have been quite good metrics for us. The percentage of bogus questions we use is determined by our HR folks; one or two questions aren't enough to disqualify someone.

910 Chapter 30 – Management, Policy, and Politics

Firing

If you make a hiring mistake, fire early. You may miss a few late bloomers, but keeping people who are not pulling their own weight will alienate your other staff members as they take up the slack and clean up after the losers. Your customers will also realize that so-and-so doesn't get things done and start demanding a particular sysadmin for their jobs. You don't want your customers interfering with management decisions in your daily business.

In many organizations it is very hard to fire someone, especially after the initial evaluation period is over. Make sure that initial evaluations are taken seriously. Later, you may have to collect data showing incompetence, give formal warnings, set performance goals, and so on. In extreme cases, the only way to fire an incompetent but savvy employee may be to eliminate his job.

Testing thoroughly and ensuring quality control

The manager sets the tone for what a completed task means. An inexperienced sysadmin will often think that a problem has been fixed, only to receive several more trouble reports as the task slowly gets done completely and correctly. This scenario can occur because the user who first reported the problem did not describe it clearly, or perhaps because the user suggested an inadequate (or incorrect) solution that the sysadmin accepted without bothering to make an independent diagnosis. Equally often, it can happen because the sysadmin did not test the solution carefully.

Some common mistakes include

- Man pages and documentation not installed for new software
- Software not installed everywhere
- Software that turns out to be owned by the sysadmin or installed with permissions that are wrong

Testing is boring, but a busy sysadmin can cut productivity in half by skipping it. Every trouble report costs time and effort, both for users and for the sysadmin.[1] The job is not done until all operational glitches have surfaced and been taken care of and the customer is satisfied.

Often a user reports that "X doesn't work on machine Y" and the sysadmin goes to machine Y and tries command X and it works fine. The trouble report answer comes back "works for me" with a bit of attitude attached.

If the sysadmin actually tried the command as the user who submitted the report (e.g., by executing **sudo su - username** in front of the command), the problem might have been nailed on the first try. The "-" argument to **su** causes the resulting shell to use the environment of the user being **su**'d to. Ergo, you can really reproduce the environment that was reported not to be working.

---

1. Sometimes there is a hard dollar cost associated with a trouble ticket or call to the help desk. For example, outsourced support currently seems to run about $75 for each call or new ticket.

Sometimes it's useful to schematize your testing. For example, if you suspect that problem P is caused by agent X, remove agent X and check to see that problem P goes away. Then reintroduce X and make sure that P comes back. Finally, remove X and verify that P resolves. This sequence gives you two chances to notice if P and X are in fact not related.

Users can become upset when a problem is not completely solved on the first attempt. Try to set their expectations appropriately. It is often useful to persuade the user who reported a problem to work with you in solving it, especially if the problem relates to an unfamiliar software package. You will obtain additional information, and the user will be less likely to think of your relationship as adversarial.

Managing, not meddling

As a technically competent manager, you will be constantly tempted to advise employees how to do their jobs. But if you do so, you may be denying them the chance to grow and to become fully become responsible for their work. It's even worse if you not only advise but also decide how chores should be done. Such micromanagement leads to frustrated staff who are not able to use their own expertise and creativity.

If you really know everything better than your staff, there is either something wrong with your organization (you are in charge of too narrow a field), or you have the wrong job or the wrong staff. Or you might just be a control freak.

Awarding time off for good behavior

University faculty enjoy leaves known as sabbaticals—a year or six months during which they have no teaching duties and can go to another university to conduct research or work on new projects of personal interest. The idea is that to do their best teaching and research, faculty need exposure to other people and institutions.

System administrators need sabbaticals too, but they are often thought of as being so indispensable that they cannot be spared for so long a time. That is, until they burn out and ultimately leave. Trading sysadmins with another organization for a summer (or even longer) can help reward valuable employees and release some of the pressure of uninterrupted front-line service. Loaner sysadmins may take a bit of time to come up to speed in your local infrastructure, but they bring with them ideas and procedures from their home environments that can improve your local sysadmin practices.

If an exchange crosses international borders, creative financing may be necessary to get around the red tape needed for official work visas. We have done a few swaps in which the exchange sysadmins were paid by their home institutions. In one case, they traded apartments, cars, pets, plants, etc.—everything but girlfriends!

Assigning and tracking tasks

One of the most critical aspects of project oversight is to ensure that every task has a clearly defined owner.

The twin perils to avoid are

- Tasks falling through the cracks because everyone thinks they are being taken care of by somebody else

- Resources wasted through duplication of effort when multiple people or groups work on the same problem without coordination

Work can be shared, but in our experience, responsibility is less amenable to diffusion; every task should have a single, clearly defined go-to person. That person need not be a supervisor or manager—just someone willing to act as a coordinator or project manager.

An important side effect of this approach is that it is implicitly clear who implemented what or who made which changes. This transparency becomes important if you want to figure out why something was done in a certain way or why something is suddenly working differently or not working anymore.

To be "responsible" for a task does not necessarily mean "to be a scapegoat" if problems arise. If your organization defines it that way, you may find that the number of available project owners quickly dwindles. The goal is simply to remove ambiguity about who should be addressing any given problem or issue.

From a customer's point of view, a good assignment system is one that routes problems to a person who is knowledgeable and can solve the problems quickly and completely. But from a managerial perspective, assignments need to occasionally be challenging and over the head of the assignee, so that the staff continue to grow and learn in the course of their jobs. Your job is to balance the need to play to employees' strengths with the need to keep employees challenged, all while keeping both customers and employees happy.

For day-to-day administrative tasks, the key to task assignments is a trouble ticketing system. Such systems ensure that trouble reports don't go unanswered and that they are efficiently routed to the person who can best address them. Trouble ticketing systems are a topic unto themselves; see page 934 for a more detailed discussion.

Larger tasks can be anything up to and including full-blown software engineering projects. These tasks may require the use of formal project management tools and industrial-strength software engineering principles. We don't describe these tools here; nevertheless, they're important and should not be overlooked.

Sometimes sysadmins know that a particular task needs to be done, but they don't do it because the task is unpleasant. An employee who points out a neglected, unassigned, or unpopular task is likely to receive that task as an assignment. This situation creates a conflict of interest because it motivates employees to remain quiet about such situations. Don't let that happen at your site.

Managing upper management

To effectively discharge your management duties (particularly those in the "leadership" arena), you need the respect and support of your own management. You need the ability to define your group's structure and staffing, including decision authority over hiring and firing. You need control over task assignments, including the authority to decide when goals have been achieved and staff can be reassigned. Finally, you need to be responsible for representing your group both within your larger organization and to the world at large.

Upper management often has no idea what system administrators do. Use your trouble ticketing system to provide this information; it can help when your boss campaigns for additional staff or equipment.

It may be wise to keep good records even in the absence of a particular goal. Managers, especially nontechnical managers, are often way off in their estimates of the difficulty of a task or the amount of time it will take to complete. This inaccuracy is especially noticeable for troubleshooting tasks.

Try to set expectations realistically. If you don't have much experience in planning your work, double or triple your time estimates for large or crucial tasks. If an upgrade is done in two days instead of three, most users will thank you instead of cursing you as they might have if your estimate had been one day.

Software licensing terms often do not quite match a company's actual use of the licensed software; upper management tends to turn a blind eye. See page 955 for suggestions on handling such discrepancies between policy and practice.

Management support for tough security policies is always hard to get. Tightening security invariably means inconveniencing users, and the users usually outweigh you both in number and in whining ability. Increased security may reduce users' productivity; before implementing a proposed security change, do a risk analysis to be sure management and users understand why you are suggesting it.

Make sure that any security change that impacts users (e.g., converting from passwords to RSA/DSA keys for remote logins) is announced well in advance, is well documented, and is well supported at changeover time. Documentation should be easy to understand and should provide cookbook-type recipes for dealing with the new system. Allow for extra staffing hours when you first cut over to the new system so that you can deal with the panicked users who didn't read their email.

Conflict resolution

Several chores that fall on the manager's plate have the general flavor of getting along with people (usually customers or staff) in sticky situations. We first look at the general approach and then talk about the special case of dealing with "rogue" customers, sometimes known as cowboys.

Conflicts in the system administration world often occur between system administrators and their customers, colleagues, or suppliers. For example, a customer is not happy with the services rendered to them, a vendor didn't deliver promised materials on time, a colleague didn't do what you expected, or an engineering department insists that it needs control over the OS configurations installed on its desktops.

Mediation

Most people don't like to talk about conflicts or even admit that they exist. When emotions flare, it's generally because conflict is addressed much too late, after an unsatisfactory situation has been endured for an extended period of time. During this buildup phase, the parties have the opportunity to develop a healthy burden of resentment and to ruminate on each other's villainous motives.

A face-to-face meeting with a neutral mediator in attendance can sometimes defuse the situation. Try to constrain the session to a single topic and limit the time allocated to half an hour. These measures lower the chance of the meeting degenerating into an endless gripe session.

Once the problem has been defined and each party's wishes have been stated, try to reach an agreement on ways to prevent a recurrence of the problem. After the solution has been implemented, review the situation to make sure that the solution is effective and practical for the long run.

Rogue users and departments

The process of introducing tightly managed systems often causes conflict. Technically inclined users (and sometimes entire departments) may feel that centralized system administration cannot adequately accommodate their configuration needs or their need for autonomous control over the computers they use.

Your first impulse may be to try and strong-arm such rogue users into accepting standard configurations in order to minimize the cost and time required to support them. However, such an iron-fist approach usually ends up creating both unhappy users and unhappy sysadmins. Keep in mind that rogue users' desires are often perfectly legitimate and that it is the sysadmins' job to support them or, at least, to refrain from making their lives more difficult.

The most desirable solution to this problem is to identify the underlying reasons for the rogues' reluctance to accept managed systems. In many cases, you can address their needs and bring the rogues back into the fold.

An alternative to the integration strategy is to trade support for autonomy. Allow rogue users or groups to do whatever they want, with the explicit understanding that they must also take on responsibility for keeping the customized systems running. Install a firewall to protect the systems you control from any break-ins or viruses that might originate on the rogues' network. And don't clean up the rogues' messes.

Be sure to have all residents of the rogues' network sign a written policy document that sets some security guidelines. For example, if their systems interfere with the rest of the organization, their network connection can be turned off until they are patched and no longer impacting the production network.

Creative system administration is needed to deal with the increasing number of laptops being brought to work. You must find ways of providing service for these (nontrustable) devices without endangering the integrity of your systems. A separate network might be a good idea.

All sites have their "bleeding edgers," users who are hooked on getting the latest stuff immediately. Such users are prepared to live with the inconvenience of beta versions and unstable prereleases as long as their software is up to date. Find ways to deal with these people as useful resources rather than thorns in your side. They are ideal candidates for testing new software and are often willing to feed bug reports back to you so that problems can be fixed.

30.4 THE ROLE OF ADMINISTRATION

In this context, "administration" includes all the tasks that don't contribute directly to the organization's output, such as accounting, human resources, secretarial work, sales, purchasing, and other logistical processes. It's also quite separate from the "administration" in "system administration."

Depending on your organization, administrative tasks may be totally your responsibility, totally performed by your parent organization, or somewhere in between. But they must all be done somehow.

In small, autonomous groups, these tasks tend to be distributed among the various staff members. However, this is probably not an efficient use of your highly skilled and hard-to-find IT experts. In addition, many people hate administrative work. Legal and organizational requirements impose strict rules that don't always sit well with creative professionals. An important chore for the boss is to make sure that administrative chores are kicked upstairs, performed by dedicated personnel, outsourced, or at least equitably distributed among the sysadmin staff.

We touch on only a few common administrative chores here because most are dictated by the parent organization and are not negotiable.

Sales

If you contemplate taking on a project for a new or an existing customer, you need the equivalent of a technical sales staff that understands the needs of potential customers, knows what services and products your group can provide, and is aware of the group's capacity (busyness). Nothing is worse than making promises that cannot be fulfilled. If the boss participates in the negotiations, the boss should be properly briefed by the technical staff. Even better, let the technical staff do the negotiating while the boss observes.

Management

Purchasing

At many sites, the system administration team and the purchasing team are totally separate. This is bad if the purchasing team makes decisions without consulting the sysadmins. It is even worse if purchasing decisions are made by upper management on the golf course or in vendor-supplied box seats at the opening game of their favorite football team.

A typical tale: The VP of IT at a tape storage company thought he knew what disk storage hardware was needed for a big server project. On the golf course one Sunday, he signed a contract with IBM without consulting his system administration staff. The IBM disk arrays were to be connected to a Sun server, and the IBM sales guy swore it would just work. It turned out that the device drivers consisted of barely functional, alpha-quality code. The company's mission-critical server was down more than it was up for the next three months while IBM worked on the drivers. Critical project deadlines were missed, and the IT department looked like idiots to the rest of the company. The storage debacle impacted the company's bottom line, too—they moved from being one of the largest in their market sector to one of the smallest because they were late to market with critical products.

Sysadmins can provide good information about compatibility in the local environment, the competence of vendors (especially third-party resellers), and the reliability of certain types of equipment. Reliability information is especially critical in the PC world, where pricing is so competitive that quality is often totally ignored.

Sysadmins need to know about any new hardware that's being ordered so that they can determine how to integrate it into the current infrastructure and predict what projects and resources are needed to support it.

Note that it is not the job of system administrators to decide *whether* a system can be supported. You can make recommendations to your customers, but if they need a particular piece of equipment to get their job done, it's your job to make it work. You might have to hire additional staff or neglect other systems. Give your boss the choices and let the folks upstairs decide what compromises they prefer.

A system administrator's participation in the specification of systems being purchased is especially valuable in organizations that by default must buy from the lowest bidder (e.g., government institutions and state universities). Most purchasing systems allow you to specify evaluation criteria. Be sure to include escape clauses such as "must be compatible with existing environment" or "must be able to run XYZ software package well."

The incremental impact and cost of an additional piece of hardware (or software, sometimes) is not constant. Is it the 60th of that architecture or the first? Does it have enough local disk space for the system files? Does it have enough memory to run today's bloated applications? Is there a spare network port to plug it into? Is it a completely new OS?

Questions like these tend to emphasize a more fundamental question: Do you stay stagnant and buy equipment from your current vendor, or do you try the latest whizzy toy from a startup that might shake the world or might be out of business in a year? The nature of your organization may answer this one. It's not a simple yes or no; you must often make a complex tradeoff between the latest and greatest equipment and the machines that you are comfortable with and understand. These are business decisions, and they should be addressed in a structured and impartial manner.

If you are allowed to negotiate with vendors (officially or otherwise), you can often do much better than your purchasing department. Don't be shy about quoting prices from other vendors for comparable equipment, and be optimistic about the size of expected purchases for the coming year. After all, the sales people have been optimistic about the value of their product.

Buying at the end of a quarter or just before or after a vendor's product line change can net you some good discounts. Sellers often need to improve the quarter's sales numbers or reduce their inventory of about-to-be-old models.

In our experience, it is difficult to find vendors with technically qualified personnel that are available to you for support and consultation. If you find one, make sure you keep each other happy.

Once items have been purchased, the person who specified the original order should review the final order, the packing list, and perhaps even the invoice submitted by the supplier to confirm that the right equipment was delivered and billed for. At most organizations, the items must also be entered into a local inventory control system in accordance with the organization's policy.

Accounting

Keeping your finances in order is another important administrative chore. However, this task is so site-specific that we cannot cover it in detail. It is imperative that you know what your legal and organizational requirements are and that you keep your records up to date. Audits are painful.

Personnel

We have already covered issues of hiring and firing (see page 908), but there is more to integrating a new employee into your infrastructure than just writing an offer letter. You must know about and honor your organization's rules regarding advertising for positions, trial periods, reviews, etc. Another set of chores comprises the mechanics of getting a new person settled with a desk, computer, keys, accounts, **sudo** access, and so on.

Perhaps more importantly, when an employee gives notice of intent to leave, you must undo all these processes. In the United States, it's common to give two weeks' notice before quitting. Some sites (e.g., security companies) forego the two-week period and walk the employee to the door, immediately revoking all physical and network access. This might be a good time for a quick internal check to verify that the quitting employee has not left any back doors into your servers. Some commercial software packages (e.g., Novell's directory product) tout their ability to delete former employees in a flash.

The system administration staff is not usually consulted when a company is planning massive layoffs, but they should be. Layoff day arrives, and management screams to get the former employees' machines backed up, their access revoked, etc. Hardware disappears because of disgruntled employees and bad planning.

Marketing

System administration is a funny business. If you do your job well, users take your seamless computing environment for granted and nobody notices what you do. But in today's world of viruses, spam, bloated applications, and total dependence on the Internet, the IT staff is an indispensable part of the organization.

Your satisfied customers are your best marketing device. However, there are other ways to gain visibility within your organization and within the broader community. Based on our experience with tooting our own horn, we suggest the following methods as being particularly effective.

- Hold town hall meetings where users can express their concerns and ask questions about the computing infrastructure. You might prepare for such a meeting by analyzing users' support requests and open the meeting with a short presentation on the most troublesome topics you've identified. Provide refreshments to ensure a good turnout.

- Leave plenty of time for questions and make sure you have knowledgeable staff available to answer them. Don't try to bluff your way out of unexpected questions, though. If you don't know the answer off-hand, it's best to admit this and follow up later.

- Design a seminar series directed at either your peers in the system administration community or the end users within your organization. Schedule meetings at two- or three-month intervals and publish the topics to be presented well in advance.[2]

- Attend conferences on system administration and give talks or write papers about the tools you develop. Such presentations not only give you feedback from your peers, but they also show your customers (and your boss) that you do your job well.

Although we have listed these marketing techniques in the administration section, clearly the whole team must be involved in the marketing effort.

System administration is ultimately about dealing with people and their needs. Personal relationships are just as important as they are in any business. Talk to your customers and colleagues, and make time for personal discussions and exchanges.

---

2. You can invite colleagues in the sysadmin community to give guest presentations at your seminar series. Make sure their presentations demonstrate the same high quality as your internal speakers.

Management

If you support multiple customers, consider assigning a specific person to each customer to act as an account manager. This liaison should take on responsibility for the general happiness of the customer and should speak regularly with the customer's end users. Channel news and information about changes in the computing environment through the liaison to create additional opportunities for contact.

Miscellaneous administrative chores

The administration group gets stuck with lots of little logistic items:

- Keeping inventory

- Acquiring furniture and other office equipment

- Maintaining the coffee machine and organizing the supply of coffee, sugar, and milk. Coffee supplies should be paid for out of the group's budget to ensure that every employee performs at their caffeine-fueled best. Some companies also stock snacks and drinks.

- Watering plants and flowers

- Interfacing with the building maintenance department (or outside contractors) to arrange cleaning, HVAC maintenance, etc.

- Organizing keys or other means of access control

30.5 THE ROLE OF DEVELOPMENT

Large sites need a robust, scalable computing infrastructure so that sysadmins do not spend all their time fighting an inflexible, poorly designed, labor-intensive system. In practical terms, this means that you need custom software, architectural structure, and staff who are formally charged with designing and maintaining them.

As your site grows and accumulates computers, you will either become increasingly frantic or you will start to devise ways to optimize and systematize the administration process. The most common (and most powerful) optimization tool is automation. It reduces manual labor and ensures that tasks are performed consistently.

Unfortunately, such automation often occurs in an unstructured fashion, with the sorry consequence that the site slowly accumulates a large and random assemblage of quick fixes and script fragments. This body of software eventually becomes an undocumented maintenance nightmare in its own right.

Controversy persists regarding the number of machines a site must have before it makes sense to start thinking in terms of a global game plan. Our sense is that it is not really a matter of head count so much as a question of professionalism and job satisfaction. A life of constant fire fighting and drama is no fun, and it invariably correlates with poor quality of service. Requirements also vary widely; what's appropriate for an installation that supports financial traders is unsuitable for a student lab at a university, and vice versa. Your solutions must be appropriate for the needs of your users.

The awkward term "infrastructure architecture" is sometimes used to describe the high-level conceptual work of system administration, as opposed to the day-to-day chores. The "infrastructure" part is a reference to IT's having become a commodity or utility. Like the phone system or the water faucets, it's supposed to just work. When the infrastructure breaks, it should be easy to locate and replace the failing component. The "architecture" part means that an infrastructure is designed for a specific purpose and is tailored to fit the needs of its customers.

In this section we outline some of the features of a functional infrastructure architecture. For deeper coverage of this topic, check out the references at the end of the chapter. Helpful pointers on implementation can be found in Chapter 11, *Software and Configuration Management*.

Architectural principles

The following sections present a selection of architectural "best practices" to consider when planning your site's IT design. These principles are particularly important when the configuration you will be supporting is new or unusual, since these situations can be difficult to benchmark against real-world peers. Well-designed processes incorporate or foster adherence to these principles.

Make processes reproducible

System administration is not one of the performing arts. Whatever is done should be done consistently and repeatably. Usually, this means that the lowest level of changes should be made by scripts or configuration programs rather than by system administrators. Variations in configuration should be captured in config files for your administrative software.

For example, a script that sets up a new machine should not be asking questions about IP numbers and packages to install. Instead, it should check a system configuration directory to determine what to do. It can present this information for confirmation, but the choices should be preordained. The less user interaction, the smaller the chance for human error.

But let us be clear: we are not describing a site at which high-level administrative priests make policy decisions to be carried out by mindless drones. Reproducibility is just as relevant if you are the only administrator at your site. It's generally not a good idea to make off-the-cuff configuration decisions that leave no audit trail. If something needs to be changed, change the central configuration information and propagate outward from there.

Leave a trail of bread crumbs

Who did what, and for what purpose? If there are problems with your system, fixing is much quicker when you can go back to the last working state, or at least figure out what has changed since then. Apart from the "what," it is also important to know the "who" and "why." Speaking with the person who implemented a troublesome change often leads to important insight. You may be able to quickly undo the change, but sometimes the change was made for a good reason and undoing it will only make things worse.

Revision control systems provide one useful way to keep track of changes; they are discussed in detail starting on page 247. They provide both a historical record of the actual data over time and information about which sysadmin performed the change. If used correctly, each modification is accompanied by a comment that explains the reasoning behind it. Automated tools can check in the config files they modify and identify themselves in the comment. That way, it's easy to identify a malfunctioning script and back out the changes it made.

Another useful facility is some form of email diary. This can be either a permanent record of messages sent to an actual administrative mailing list at your site or a mail drop that exists only to record diary updates. The diary provides a well-known place for information about configuration changes to be recorded, and the fact that it is implemented through email means that updates are not burdensome to system administrators. The drawback of an email diary is that the information has no structure other than chronology.

Recognize the criticality of documentation

In fact, documentation is so important to a scalable infrastructure that we made it a major section of its own, starting on page 930.

Customize and write code

Using existing tools is a virtue, and you should use them whenever possible. But no site in the world is exactly like yours, and your organization is certain to have some unique requirements. An IT infrastructure that precisely fills the organization's needs provides a competitive edge and increases everyone's productivity.

With its excellent scriptability and cornucopia of open source tools, Linux is the ideal basis for a well-tuned infrastructure. In our view, a system administration group without a software development function is hobbled.

Keep the system clean

System management is not only about installing and adding and configuring; it's also about knowing what to keep, what to throw out, and what to refurbish. We call this concept "sustainable management". It's wonderful to be able to add a new computer to your environment in 5 minutes, and it is great to be able to create a new user account in 10 seconds. But if you look ahead, it is equally important to be able to find and remove old accounts and computers in an organized way. Sustainability in system management means that you have the tools and concepts needed to run your operation over the long haul in an organized fashion.

Anatomy of a management system

Your management system should contain the following major elements:

- **Automated setup of new machines**. This is not just OS installation; it also includes the additional software and local configuration necessary to allow a machine to enter production use. It's inevitable that your site will need to support more than one type of configuration, so you should include multiple machine types in your plans from the beginning. *Basic Linux installation*, starting on page 223, discusses several systems that help with setup.

- **Systematic patching and updating of existing machines**. When you identify a problem with your setup, you need a standardized and easy way to deploy updates to all affected machines. Note that because computers are not turned on all the time (even if they are supposed to be), your update scheme must correctly handle machines that are not on-line when the update is initiated. You can check for updates at boot time or update on a regular schedule; see page 260 for more information.

- **A monitoring system**. Your users should not have to call you to tell you that the server is down. Not only is it unprofessional, but you have no idea how long the system has been down. The first person to call you is probably not the first person to have experienced problems. You need some kind of monitoring system that raises an alarm as soon as problems are evident. But alarms are tricky. If there are too many, sysadmins start to ignore them; if too few, important problems go unnoticed.

- **A communication system**. Don't forget to keep in touch with the needs of your users; supporting them is the ultimate goal of everything you do as a system administrator. A request-tracking system is a necessity (see page 934). A central location where users can find system status and contact information (typically on the web) is also helpful.

The system administrator's tool box

Good sysadmins are lazy (smart) and usually try to automate their work. A successful sysadmin shop writes scripts to fill the gaps between the tools inherited from vendors and the tools downloaded from the net, then makes sure these scripts are available wherever they are needed.

Most places have their own **adduser** script and probably an **rmuser** script as well. If you are a lone sysadmin, you probably save these little gems in your own ~/**bin** directory and live happily ever after. If you are part of a team of two or more people, life becomes more complex. Stopgap measures such as copying tools from one another or modifying search paths to point to other people's ~/**bin** directories will help for a little while. However, you will eventually need to find some kind of sustainable solution.

Our solution to this problem is the "sysadmin tool box." The tool box contains all the locally developed system administration software and lives in its own special directory tree (e.g., **/usr/satools**). Most importantly, we have a policy document that describes how to write tools for the tool box. One of the sysadmins "owns" the tool box and makes any policy decisions that are not covered by the policy document.

When creating a policy like this, it's important to make sure that each element of the policy has a clear reason for being there. Only if people understand the motivation for the rules are they able follow the spirit of the policy and not just its literal rules.

Some sample policy entries are listed below.

- Published tools are available under **/usr/satools/bin**. Configuration information is stored in **/usr/satools/etc**. Log files and any other data files that the tools create while running go into **/usr/satools/var**. Static data files are in **/usr/satools/share**. Reason: standardization.

- Tools should be written in Perl or Python. Reason: standardization; facilitates handoffs and code reuse among administrators.

- Each tool must have its own man page. Reason: if a tool has no documentation, only its author knows how it works.

- When developing a tool, write the documentation first and have the toolmaster review it before coding. Reason: catches redundancy and policy conformance issues before any work is done.

- Every tool must accept a **--no-action** option that makes it show what it would do without actually doing anything. If such an option cannot be implemented, the tool must at least fail with an appropriate message. Reason: helps prevent catastrophes, especially with more drastic tools such as **rmuser** or **mvhomedir**.

- All tools must be under revision control in **svn://server/satools** (a Subversion repository; see page 253). Reason: several people can work on the tools, and clear revision control simplifies source management and bug handling.

A real-world policy document might be a few pages long.

You may want to write a little tool box management tool that installs new tools from the Subversion repository into your **/usr/satools** tree. For quality control, the management tool can attempt to do some policy compliance testing as well. For example, it can verify that every tool installs documentation.

Software engineering principles

Because administrative scripts don't always seem like "real" software, you might be tempted to think that they don't need the degree of forethought and formalism that are found in typical software engineering projects. That may or may not be true. At some level of complexity and mission criticality, you need to really start treating these projects like the beasts that they are.

Frederick P. Brooks, Jr.'s classic book on software engineering, *The Mythical Man-Month: Essays on Software Engineering*, is an easy read and a good reference. It's interesting to see that the problems of software engineering that he discusses from the 1960s and 70s are still with us today. Here is a checklist of software project principles and pitfalls (in no particular order):

- Projects should have a clearly defined scope and a well-defined time frame for completion.

- Responsibilities should be clearly defined. The administrator working on the project, the sysadmin manager, and the ultimate customer must all agree on goals, scope, and potential risks.

- Preliminary documentation should be written before coding begins.

- Interfaces between various components of the software should be well defined and documented in advance.

- Critical pieces of code should be prototyped and tested first. It's important to get feedback from the people who will use the software at the earliest possible stage of development.

- Status information should be communicated honestly. No one likes surprises, and bad news always comes out in the end.

- Incorporate a postmortem analysis into every project. Learn from mistakes and successes.

The optimal management of software projects has always been hotly debated. Over the last decade, "agile" methods that stress rapid prototyping, early deployment, incremental addition of functionality, and the elimination of overhead work have received significant attention from developers. Their value is still far from universally agreed on, but many of the ideas seem like common sense, and the lightweight approach is well suited to the smaller projects found in the domain of system administration. Read more at en.wikipedia.org/wiki/Agile_methods.

30.6 THE ROLE OF OPERATIONS

The operations division is responsible for the installation and maintenance of the IT infrastructure. Along with the support division, it's a component of the "production" function described on page 906. As a rule of thumb, operations deals with computers and wires, and support deals with people.

Operations includes only existing services; all "new things" should be designed, implemented, and tested by the development division before they are placed into a production environment.

Operations focuses on creating a stable and dependable environment for customers. Availability and reliability are its key concerns. Operations staff should not perform experiments or make quick fixes or improvements on a Friday afternoon. The chance of failure (and of nobody but customers noticing the problems over the weekend) is just too high.

Aim for minimal downtime

Many people depend on the computing infrastructure we provide. A university department can probably live for a while without its web site, but an Internet mail order company such as Amazon.com cannot. Some folks won't notice if your print server is down, but a student or a professor with a hard deadline for submitting a research paper or proposal will be very unhappy indeed. Even in a university environment, losing access to email usually makes everybody crabby. Central file servers are another potential source of disaster.[3]

At some sites you will need to provide emergency service. In a commercial environment, this might mean 24/7 on-site coverage by experienced sysadmin staff. But even in a noncommercial environment such as a university department, it looks bad to have a major system failure over a long weekend.

Even if you don't have the budget to explicitly provide 24/7 coverage, you should be prepared to take advantage of any administrators that happen to be around late at night or on weekends. A rotating pager or other notification system can often afford "good enough" emergency coverage. Make sure that users can access this coverage in some easy and well-known way; for example, an email alias called support-pager that relays to the floating pager.

Document dependencies

To make accurate claims regarding availability or uptime, you must not only know your own strengths and weaknesses (including the reliability of the hardware you deploy) but also the dependencies of the IT systems on other hardware, software, and personnel. For example:

- Power: independent power sources and circuits, surge and short protection, backup power systems such as generators and UPSes, building power wiring, maps of power supplied to specific pieces of equipment

- Network: building wiring, backup lines, customer service for ISPs, network topology, contact information for other groups within the organization with their own network management function

- Hardware: high-availability systems and procedures for using them, hot/cold standbys, spare parts, hardware maintenance contracts

---

3. If a file server fails for an extended period of time, disgruntled users may insist on using their own personal hard disks instead of the file server for storage (at least until they get burned by the failure of the local disk, with no backup).

Repurpose or eliminate older hardware

To maintain your infrastructure, you must buy new machines, repurpose older ones, and throw out ancient ones. We covered procurement in the administration section starting on page 915, but getting rid of old favorites always seems to be more of an operations issue.

Every time hardware performance increases, software drags it back down, usually by getting bigger and more complex. For example, Windows 95 and 98 survived just fine with 32MB of memory. Windows 2000 ran poorly unless you had at least 128MB, and a laptop running Windows XP now seems to need more than 256MB just to run the task manager. Of course, this bloat is not only a problem with Windows; current Linux desktop environments need tons of memory as well.

Because users and management are often reluctant to upgrade obsolete equipment, you sometimes have to take the initiative. Financial information is the most persuasive evidence. If you can demonstrate on paper that the cost of maintaining old equipment exceeds the cost of replacement, you can remove many of the intellectual objections to upgrading. Sometimes it's also useful to replace heterogeneous hardware just to save the time and effort needed to keep all the different OS and software versions up to date.

Inexpensive Intel/PC hardware is the standard architecture base on the desktop, especially now that Apple ships on Intel hardware. The prevalence of PCs has over the years shifted the expense of computing from the hardware side to the software and support sides.

You can ease the transition for the users of old systems by keeping them available. Leave the old systems powered on, but step down the level of support that your administrative group provides. Discontinue hardware maintenance on old machines and allow them to limp along until they die of their own accord.

You can use older machines for dedicated services that don't require a lot of hardware resources (e.g., print, DHCP, or license servers). Just make sure you have a plan drawn up for fixing or replacing the machines or for moving services to another server in the event of problems.

Universities often receive donations of old computer gear from businesses that want the tax deduction. Often, the right answer is, "No thanks, we don't need 2,000 nine-track tapes and racks to put them in." One university in Budapest was given an IBM mainframe several years ago. Instead of saying no and buying fast PCs, they dedicated their whole budget to shipping and electrical wiring in the first year and maintenance in following years. Status just isn't worth it. On the other hand, many universities establish strong relationships with their local computer industry and get lots of valuable hardware donated—it's just last year's model. Consider total cost of ownership and know when to say "No, thanks."

If you are a company and have surplus computer gear, consider donating it to your local schools or colleges; they often do not have the budget to keep their labs current and may welcome your older PCs.

Obsolete computers that cannot be fobbed off on a charitable organization must be properly recycled; they contain hazardous materials (e.g., lead) and cannot go in regular trash. If your organization does not have a facilities department that can deal with old equipment, you may have to take the equipment to a local recycling center for disposal. The going rate for disposal in the United States is about $10 per system.

30.7 THE WORK OF SUPPORT

The task of the support division is to deal with the human beings who use and depend on the computer systems you maintain. In addition to offering the usual help desk or hotline support, this division can also offer consulting services to customers or produce training seminars on specific topics. Ideally, these ancillary services increase customers' self-sufficiency and reduce the number of support requests.

Availability

Good IT support means that qualified staff are available to help whenever a customer needs them.

Most problems are minor and can safely enter a service queue. Others are work-stoppers that merit immediate attention. Automated responses from a request-tracking system and recorded telephone messages announcing regular office hours just cause annoyance. Make sure that users can always access a path of last resort if the need arises. A cell phone that rotates among sysadmin staff outside of business hours is usually sufficient.

Unfortunately, excellent support breeds dependence. It's easy for users to get in the habit of consulting the help desk even when that isn't appropriate. If you recognize that someone is using the support system for answers they could get just as easily from the man pages or from Google, start answering their questions by quoting the relevant man page or URL. This tactic works well for students; it's probably less effective for executives.

Scope of service

You must clearly define the services your support group will supply; otherwise, users' expectations will not match reality. Here are some issues to consider:

- Response time
- Service during weekends and off-hours
- House calls (support for machines at home)
- Weird (one of a kind) hardware
- Ancient hardware
- Supported operating systems
- Standard configurations
- Expiration of backup tapes
- Special-purpose software
- Janitorial chores (cleaning screens and keyboards)

In a Linux shop, every user has access to the source code and could easily build a custom kernel for his or her own machine. You must consider this in your corporate policy and should probably try to standardize on a few specific kernel configurations. Otherwise, your goal of easy maintenance and scaling to grow with the organization will meet some serious impediments. Encourage your creative, OS-hacking employees to suggest kernel modifications that they need for their work. Make them a part of the standardization process so that you don't have to maintain separate kernels for each engineer.

In addition to knowing what services are provided, users must also know about the priority scheme used to manage the work queue. Priority schemes always have wiggle room, but try to design one that covers most situations with few or no exceptions. Some priority-related variables are listed below:

- The service level the customer has paid for/contracted for

- The number of users affected

- The importance of the affected users (this is a tricky one, but in general you don't want to annoy the person who signs your paycheck)

- The loudness of the affected users (squeaky wheels)

- The importance of the deadline (late homework vs. research grant proposal or contract)

Although all these factors will influence your rankings, we recommend a simple set of rules together with some common sense to deal with the exceptions. Basically, we use the following priorities:

- Many people cannot work
- One person cannot work
- Requests for improvement

If two or more requests have top priority and the requests cannot be worked on in parallel, we base our decision about which problem to tackle first on the severity of the issues (e.g., email not working makes almost everybody unhappy, whereas the temporary unavailability of some web service might hinder only a few people). Queues at the lower priorities are usually handled in a first-in, first-out manner.

You might want to calibrate your support staff's common sense. We usually ask them questions like, "What are you going to do if Ms. Big Boss walks into your office, you are working on a priority 1 issue, and she wants you to fix her printer because she needs to print some slides she is going to present at a meeting. The taxi to the airport leaves in 15 minutes, and of course, everybody on the IT staff except you is out to lunch." Any reasonable support person will realize (at least on second thought), that there is just no point in arguing with this person who is already under a lot of pressure. To provide some butt-coverage, it's reasonable to ask if it's okay to leave the broken central file server alone. If the answer is yes, it's appropriate to just drop everything and get the slides out.

Then we ask, "What are you going to do when Ms. Big Boss gets you into a similar situation a few weeks later?" Once again there's no point in arguing, but this time it's probably a good idea to schedule an appointment with her after she returns to discuss her support needs. Perhaps she really does need a person assigned to her personal support, and if she is willing to pay for that, what's the harm. Just don't try to have this discussion while she is worrying about missing her plane.

Users generally assume that all their important data is stored on backup tapes that will be archived forever. But backup tapes don't last indefinitely; magnetic media have a finite lifetime after which reading data becomes difficult. (You must periodically rewrite your data, possibly to newer media, if you want to keep it for a long time.) Backup tapes can also be subpoenaed; your organization may not want old data to be available forever. It's best to work with the people in charge of such decisions to draw up a written agreement that specifies how long backups must be kept, whether multiple copies are to be made (required? permissible? never?), and whether those copies must be stored at different locations.

You should make this information available to the users of your systems because it promotes realistic expectations regarding backups. It also puts users on notice that they should take precautions of their own if they feel they need better protection of their data.

Skill sets

There is nothing more annoying to an experienced user than a support contact who asks, "Have you plugged in the power cable?" while frantically searching a customer service database in the background. On the other hand, it's a waste of resources to have your most experienced administrator explain to a novice user how to find the delete key in some word processing system.

In our environment, each staff member is assigned a certain number of support hours per week.[4] Support staff reserve this time in their weekly planning and draw from it whenever a support request is assigned. Assignments are made according to the skills required to fix the problem and the time remaining in everybody's weekly support budget.

For this scheme to work successfully, make sure your skill list is balanced. Over the long term, everybody on the support staff must be able to fulfill their allocated support time. In general, a staff member with many entries in the skill list is more "valuable." However, there is nothing wrong with having staff with fewer skills, as long as you have enough work for them to do.

An accurate skill list helps you verify that you have sufficient skill-specific manpower to deal with vacations and illnesses. You can build the skill list as problems

---

4. By default, each sysadmin is assigned 25% time in support. When a project requires the full-time attention of a particular sysadmin, we deviate from the default scheme by removing that person from the support pool for the duration of the project.

arise and are solved by members of the staff. Include the task, the staff member's name, and the demonstrated level of expertise.

Skills should be defined at an appropriate level of abstraction, neither too specific nor too general. The following list of sample skills demonstrates the appropriate level of granularity:

- Create users, remove users, set passwords, change quotas
- Create CVS or SVN accounts
- Restore files from backups
- Integrate new hardware drivers into RIS (Windows)
- Package a Windows application in MSI Format
- Create and install software application packages on Linux
- Analyze log files
- Debug mail server issues
- Debug printing problems
- Debug general hardware problems
- Make DNS entries
- Manage software licenses
- Answer Windows security questions
- Answer UNIX security questions
- Resolve Samba-related requests
- Configure DHCP
- Configure an LDAP server
- Add or remove web sites (configure Apache)

Time management

System administration involves more context switches in a day than most jobs have in a year, and user support personnel bear the brunt of this chaos. Every administrator needs good time-management skills. Without them, you won't be able to keep up with your day-to-day responsibilities and you will become frustrated and depressed. (Or, if already frustrated and depressed, you will become more so.)

Sysadmin burnout is rampant. Most administrators last only a few years. No one wants to be constantly on call and continually yelled at. Finding ways to manage your time efficiently and keep your customers happy is a win/win situation.

In his recently published book *Time Management for System Administrators,* Tom Limoncelli suggests ways of avoiding these pitfalls. A complete reference is given at the end of this chapter.

30.8 DOCUMENTATION

Just as most people accept the health benefits of exercise and leafy green vegetables, everyone appreciates good documentation and has a vague idea that it's important.

Unfortunately, that doesn't necessarily mean that they'll write or update documentation without prodding.

Why should we care, really?

- Documentation reduces the likelihood of a single point of failure. It's wonderful to have tools that deploy workstations in no time and distribute patches with a single command, but these tools are nearly worthless if no documentation exists and the expert is on vacation or has quit.

- Documentation aids reproducibility. When practices and procedures aren't stored in institutional memory, they are unlikely to be followed consistently. When administrators can't find information about how to do something, they have to extemporize.

- Documentation saves time. It doesn't feel like you're saving time as you write it, but after spending a few days re-solving a problem that has been tackled before but whose solution has been forgotten, most administrators are convinced that the time is well spent.

- Finally, and most importantly, documentation enhances the intelligibility of a system and allows subsequent modifications to be made in a manner that's consistent with the way the system is supposed to work. When modifications are made on the basis of only partial understanding, they often don't quite conform to the architecture. Entropy increases over time, and even the administrators that work on the system come to see it as a disorderly collection of hacks. The end result is often the desire to scrap everything and start again from scratch.

Local documentation serves many purposes. Have you ever walked into a machine room needing to reboot one server, only to face racks and racks of hardware, all alike, all different, and all unlabeled? Or had to install a piece of hardware that you've handled before, but all you can remember about the chore was that it was hard to figure out?

Local documentation should be kept in a well-defined spot. Depending on the size of your operation, this might be a directory on a file server that is mounted on all your machines, or perhaps even in the home directory of a special system user account.

Standardized documentation

Our experience suggests that the easiest and most effective way to maintain documentation is to standardize on short, lightweight documents. Instead of writing a system management handbook for your organization, write many one-page documents, each of which covers a single topic. Start with the big picture and then break it down into pieces that contain additional information. If you have to go into more detail somewhere, write an additional one-page document that focuses on steps that are particularly difficult or complicated.

This approach has several advantages:

- Your boss is probably only interested in the general setup of your environment. That is all that's needed to answer questions from above or to conduct a managerial discussion. Don't pour on too many details or you will just tempt your boss to interfere in them.

- The same holds true for customers.

- A new employee or someone taking on new duties within your organization needs an overview of the infrastructure to become productive. It's not helpful to bury such people in information.

- It's more efficient to use the right document than to browse through a large document.

- It's easier to keep documentation current when you can do that by updating a single page.

This last point is particularly important. Keeping documentation up to date is a huge challenge; it's often is the first thing to be dropped when time is short. We have found that a couple of specific approaches keep the documentation flowing.

First, set the expectation that documentation be concise, relevant, and unpolished. Cut to the chase; the important thing is to get the information down. Nothing makes the documentation sphincter snap shut faster than the prospect of writing a mil-spec dissertation on design theory. Ask for too much documentation and you may not get any.

Second, integrate documentation into processes. Comments in configuration files are some of the best documentation of all. They're always right where you need them, and maintaining them takes virtually no time at all. Most standard configuration files allow comments, and even those that aren't particularly comment friendly can often have some extra information snuck into them. For example, the standard contents of the GECOS field of the **passwd** file (office, telephone number, etc.) are often not the most useful information you could put there. Feel free to define your own site-wide conventions. (But in this specific case, remember that users can change the contents of this field, so you cannot always believe the information stored there.)

Locally built tools can require documentation as part of their standard configuration information. For example, a tool that sets up a new computer can require information about the computer's owner, location, support status, and billing information even if these facts don't directly affect the machine's software configuration.

Documentation should not create information redundancies. For example, if you maintain a site-wide master configuration file that lists machines and their IP addresses, there should be no other place where this information is updated by hand. Not only is it a waste of your time to make updates in multiple locations, but inconsistencies are also certain to creep in over time. When this information is required in other contexts and configuration files, write a script that obtains it from (or updates)

Management

the master configuration. If you cannot completely eliminate redundancies, at least be clear about which source is authoritative. And write tools to catch inconsistencies, perhaps run regularly from **cron**.

Hardware labeling

Some documentation is most appropriate when written out on a piece of paper or taped to a piece of hardware. For example, emergency procedures for a complete system or network failure are not particularly useful if they are stored on a dead or unreachable machine.

Every computer should be identifiable without someone's switching it on and logging in, because those activities will not always be possible. Uniquely label each workstation (hostname, IP address) and put a sticker on it that includes contact information for the help desk.

In a server room, all systems and their external devices must be labeled with a hostname (fully qualified if machines from different domains are located there). It is useful to have these labels on both the front and the back of the machines (especially in cramped racks) so that you can easily find the power switch of the machine you want to power-cycle.

If your environment includes many different types of systems, it may be useful to add additional information such as architecture, boot instructions, special key sequences, pointers to additional documentation, the vendor's hotline, or the phone number of the person in charge. Recording key sequences may seem a bit silly, but servers are often connected to an aging terminal or console server rather than a dedicated monitor.

Be sure your central records or inventory data contain a copy of the information on all these little sticky labels. It will come in handy if you manage your machines through a TCP/IP connection to your console server instead of spending your workday in a noisy machine room.

Also tape the hostname to other pieces of hardware that are associated with each machine: disk drives, modems, printers, tape drives, etc. If several identical external subsystems are attached to the same host, make sure that the labels are unique.[5] In our installation, even the SCSI and Fibre Channel cables are labeled (and of course, the various ports on the server) so that we really know which device is connected to which interface.

If a host is an important citizen (for example, a major server or a crucial router), include the location of its circuit breaker. If a floppy disk or flash memory card is required for booting, point to its location. Major file servers should have information about disk device names, partition tables, mount points, and the locations of

---

5. One of our co-workers replaced the write-cache backup battery of the wrong RAID array recently. Fortunately, only degraded performance resulted from this particular mistake. But imagine if you replaced the wrong disk in a RAID5 array, didn't notice it, and then had a second disk fail.

backup superblocks readily available. Tape the information to the disk subsystems themselves or store it in a well-known location, perhaps in the machine room.

Tape drives should be labeled with the device files and commands needed to access them. It's also a good idea to list the type of tapes the drive requires, the nearest place to buy them, and even the approximate price.

Printers should be labeled with their names, brief printing instructions, and the hosts on which they depend. Printers often come with network interfaces and are full citizens of the network, but they still depend on a Linux host for spooling and configuration.

Network wiring must be scrupulously documented. Label all cables, identify patch panels and wall outlets, and mark network devices. Always make it easy for your wiring technician to keep the documentation up to date; keep a pencil and forms hanging on the wall of the wiring closet so that it's painless to note that a cable moved from one device to another. Later, you should transfer this data to on-line storage.

Yet another level of complexity is added if your network devices (e.g., routers and switches) can be reconfigured over the network. Although you can now move machines among subnets from your cozy office, documentation becomes even more important. Be even more careful, because you can screw up a much bigger part of your infrastructure more quickly and more thoroughly.

User documentation

It's a good idea to prepare a printed document that you can give to new users. It should document local customs, procedures for reporting problems, the names and locations of printers, your backup and downtime schedules, and so on. This type of document can save an enormous amount of sysadmin or user services time. You should also make the information available on the web. A printed document is more likely to be read by new users, but a web page is easier to refer to at the time questions arise. Do both and keep them updated regularly. There is nothing more annoying than outdated on-line documentation or FAQs.

In addition to documenting your local computing environment, you may want to prepare some introductory material about Linux. Such material is essential in a university environment in which the user community is transient and often Linux illiterate. We provide printed one-page crib sheets that list the commands and applications commonly needed by our user community.

30.9 REQUEST-TRACKING AND TROUBLE-REPORTING SYSTEMS

If you have a large staff, you will find it helpful to impose some formal structure on your work queue with a request-tracking system. Even if your IT organization is a one-person shop, such a system can be very helpful for tracking all the pending problems and requests. Request trackers are also a great source of historical information about the work your group has done, and they're an easy way to track your internal to-do lists and projects. Managers always want to know what you're doing; most systems can produce reports that show your workload, your resources, and your righteous need for more staff and a larger budget.

These system go by various names; most common are "request tracking systems," "trouble ticket systems," or "bug trackers." These are all names for the same kind of beast. The web site linas.org/linux/pm.html lists and categorizes a variety of open source implementations.

Common functions of trouble ticket systems

A trouble ticket system accepts requests through various interfaces (email, web forms, and command lines being the most common) and tracks them from submission to solution. Managers can assign tickets to staff groups or to individual staff members. Staff can query the system to see the queue of pending tickets and perhaps resolve some of them. Users can find out the status of a request and see who is working on it. Managers can extract high-level information such as

- The number of open tickets
- The average time to close a ticket
- The productivity of sysadmins
- The percentage of unresolved (rotting) tickets
- Workload distribution by time to solution

The request history stored in the ticket system becomes a history of the problems with your IT infrastructure and the solutions to these problems. If that history is easily searchable, it becomes an invaluable resource for the sysadmin staff.

Resolved trouble messages can be sent to novice sysadmins and trainees, inserted into a FAQ system, or just logged. It can be very helpful for new staff members to see the closed tickets because those tickets include not only technical information but also examples of the tone and communication style that are appropriate for use with customers.

Like all documents, your ticketing system's historical data can potentially be used against your organization in court. Follow the document retention guidelines set up by your legal department.

Most request-tracking systems automatically confirm new requests and assign them a tracking number that submitters can use to follow up or inquire about the request's status. The automated response message should clearly state that it is just a confirmation. It should be followed promptly by a message from a real person that explains the plan for dealing with the problem or request.

User acceptance of ticketing systems

Receiving a prompt response from a real person is a critical determinant of customer satisfaction, even if the personal response contains no more information than the automated response. For most problems, it is far more important to let the submitter know that the ticket has been reviewed by a real person than it is to fix the problem immediately. Users understand that administrators receive many requests, and they're willing to wait a fair and reasonable time for your attention. But they're not willing to be ignored.

Our trouble-reporting system uses an email alias called "support". At one time we were bombarded with trouble reports that were either incomplete or incomprehensible. We wrote a script that asked the user specific questions, such as

- On what host does the problem occur?
- Is the problem repeatable?
- How important is it that the problem be fixed immediately?

The user rebellion started about an hour later, and within a day we had backed the system out. Its only value seemed to be that with the furor over the script, many users actually read the questions it was asking, and the quality of our free-form trouble reports improved.

Another site dealt with this problem by sending out a message that explained what information is important in a trouble report and showed examples of useless reports. When a useless report was received, it was answered with an apology ("Sorry, I don't have enough information to…") and a copy of the explanatory message. The users caught on quickly.

In our experience, forms only work for tasks that are highly standardized, such as account creation or deletion requests. In these contexts, your customers understand that the requested information is necessary for you to do your job. Some tasks can be totally automated once the form is filled out, such as setting up a vacation message for a user. Others, such as account creation, may be partially automatable but require authorization or other staff processing.

Ticketing systems

Tables 30.1 and 30.2 below summarize the characteristics of several well-known trouble ticketing systems. Table 30.1 shows open source systems, and Table 30.2 shows commercial systems.

Table 30.1   Open source trouble ticket systems

Name	In[a]	Lang	Back[b]	URL
Mantis	WE	PHP	M	www.mantisbt.org
RT: Request Tracker	W	Perl	M	www.bestpractical.com
Scarab	W	Java	M	scarab.tigris.org
Double Choco Latte	W	PHP	PM	dcl.sourceforge.net
OTRS	WE	Perl	PMOD	www.otrs.org
JitterBug[c]	WE	C	F	www.samba.org/jitterbug
WREQ[c]	WE	Perl	G	math.duke.edu/~yu/wreq

a. Input types: W = web, E = email
b. Back end: M = MySQL, P = PostgreSQL, O = Oracle, D = DB2, F = flat files, G = **gdbm**
c. No longer maintained

We like Mantis a lot. It was originally developed to track bugs in the software for a video game. It runs on Linux, Solaris, Windows, Mac OS, and even OS/2. It's lightweight, simple, easily modifiable, and customizable. It requires PHP, MySQL, and a web server. But its most important feature is good documentation!

Another nice system is OTRS, the Open Ticket Request System. OTRS features web interfaces for both customers and sysadmins, as well as an email interface. OTRS is highly customizable (e.g., greeting messages configurable by queue) and can even log the time spent on a ticket. Packages for each of our example Linux platforms are available from the OTRS web site.

RT: Request Tracker release 3 has a rich set of features, including highly configurable web interfaces for both users and system administrators. Because it uses a myriad of Perl modules, it can be a bit of a pain to install. Its command line interface is also basic at best. Some sites use a patched version of release 1 (see ee.ethz.ch/tools) that fixes some of RT's more annoying shortcomings without adding the complexity of the more recent releases.

Table 30.2 shows some of the commercial alternatives for request management. Since the web sites for commercial offerings are mostly marketing hype, details such as the implementation language and back end are not listed.

Table 30.2 Commercial trouble ticket systems

Name	Scale	URL
Remedy (now BMC)	Huge	www.bmc.com/remedy
ServiceDesk	Huge	manageengine.adventnet.com
HEAT	Medium	www.frontrange.com
Track-It!	Medium	www.numarasoftware.com

Some of the commercial offerings are so complex that they need a person or two dedicated to maintaining, configuring, and keeping them running (you know who you are, Remedy and ServiceDesk). These systems are appropriate for a site with a huge IT staff but are a waste for the typical small, overworked IT staff.

Ticket dispatching

In a large group, even one with an awesome ticketing system, one problem still remains to be solved. It is inefficient for several people to divide their attention between the task they are working on right now and the request queue, especially if requests come in by email to a personal mailbox. We have experimented with two solutions to this problem.

Our first try was to assign half-day shifts of trouble queue duty to staff members in our sysadmin group. The person on duty would try to answer as many of the incoming queries as possible during their shift. The problem with this approach was that not everybody had the skills to answer all questions and fix all problems. Answers were sometimes inappropriate because the person on duty was new and was not really familiar with the customers, their environments, or the specific support contracts they were covered by. The result was that the more senior people had to keep an eye on things and so were not really able to concentrate on their own work. In the end, the quality of service was worse and nothing was really gained.

After this experience, we created a "dispatcher" role that rotates monthly among a group of senior administrators. The dispatcher is responsible for checking the ticketing system for new entries and farming tasks out to specific staff members. If necessary, the dispatcher contacts users to extract any additional information that is necessary to prioritize requests. The dispatcher uses a home-grown staff-skills database to decide who on the support team has the appropriate skills and time. The dispatcher also makes sure that requests are resolved in a timely manner.

30.10 DISASTER RECOVERY

Your organization depends on a working IT environment. Not only are you responsible for day-to-day operations, but you must also have plans in place to deal with any reasonably foreseeable eventuality. Preparation for such large-scale problems influences both your overall game plan and the way that you define daily operations.

In this section, we look at various kinds of disasters, the data you need to gracefully recover, and the important elements of a disaster plan.

We suggest that you make an explicit, written catalog of the potential disasters that you want to protect against. Disasters are not all the same, and you may need several different plans to cover the full range of possibilities. Consider the following threats:

- Security breaches: before the year 2000, about 60% originated from within the organization. By 2001, the sheer number of external attacks had driven the percentage down to more like 30%. In 2005, internally based attacks were back up to 47%.[6]

- Environmental problems: power spikes and outages, cooling failures, floods, hurricanes, earthquakes, meteors, terrorist or alien invasions

- Human error: deleted or damaged files and databases, lost configuration information

- Spontaneous hardware meltdowns: dead servers, fried hard disks, malfunctioning networks

Ask yourself, what benefits do my users get from the IT environment? Which of these are most important? What endangers these benefits? How can we protect against these threats? Getting the problem definition right is not a trivial task, and it is critical that your entire organization be involved, not just the system administration group.

---

6. This data comes from the FBI and the Computer Security Institute.

Backups and off-line information

For obvious reasons, data backups are a crucial part of disaster planning, and one that is covered in more detail in Chapter 9, *Backups*. But creating reliable off-site backups is only part of the story. How quickly can you access these backups? How will you bring together replacement hardware, manpower, and backup data to replace a server that has failed?

We are accustomed to using the network to communicate and to access documents. However, these facilities may be unavailable or compromised after an incident. Store all relevant contacts and procedures off-line. Know where to get recent dump tapes and what **restore** command to use without looking at **/etc/dumpdates**.

In all disaster scenarios, you will need access to both on-line and off-line copies of essential information. The on-line copies should, if possible, be kept on a self-sufficient machine: one that has a rich complement of tools, has key sysadmins' environments, runs its own name server, has a complete local **/etc/hosts** file, has no file sharing dependencies, has a printer attached, and so on. Don't use an old junker that's no good for anything else; the disaster recovery machine should be fast and should have plenty of memory and scratch disk space you can use for restores and compares during recovery. The machine needs a complete development environment so that it can patch and recompile any compromised software. It helps if the machine also has interfaces for all the types of disk drives used at your site (IDE, SATA, SCSI, FC-AL, etc.).

Here's a list of handy data to keep on the backup machine and in printed form:

- Outline of the disaster procedure: people to call, when to call, what to say
- Service contract phone numbers and customer numbers
- Key local phone numbers: staff, police, fire, boss, employment agency
- Data on hardware and software configurations: OS version, patch levels, partition tables, PC hardware settings, IRQs, DMAs, and the like[7]
- Backup tapes and the backup schedule that produced them
- Network maps
- Software serial numbers, licensing data, and passwords
- Vendor contact info for that emergency disk you need immediately

Staffing your disaster

Decide ahead of time who will be in charge in the event of a catastrophic incident. Set up a chain of command and keep the names and phone numbers of the principals off-line. It may be that the best person to put in charge is a sysadmin from the trenches, not the IT director (who is usually a poor choice for this role).

The person in charge must be somebody who has the authority and decisiveness to make tough decisions based on minimal information (e.g., a decision to disconnect

---

7. Network discovery and inventory tools can compile much of this data automatically. Two candidates to consider are H-Inventory (sourceforge.net/projects/h-inventory) and LANsurveyor (www.neon.com).

an entire department from the network). The ability to make such decisions, communicate them in a sensible way, and actually lead the staff through the crisis are probably more important than having theoretical insight into system and network management. We keep a little laminated card with important names and phone numbers printed in microscopic type. Very handy—and it fits in your wallet.

An important but sometimes unspoken assumption made in most disaster plans is that sysadmin staff will be available to deal with the situation. Unfortunately, people get sick, graduate, go on vacation, leave for other jobs, and in stressful times may even turn hostile. It's worth considering what you'd do if you needed extra emergency help. (Not having enough sysadmins around can sometimes constitute an emergency in its own right if your systems are fragile or your users unsophisticated.)

You might try forming a sort of NATO pact with a local consulting company or university that has sharable system administration talent. Of course, you must be willing to share back when your buddies have a problem. Most importantly, don't operate close to the wire in your daily routine. Hire enough system administrators and don't expect them to work 12-hour days.

Power and HVAC

Test your disaster recovery plan before you need to use it. Test your generators and UPSes on a monthly or quarterly schedule, depending on how much risk your management is willing to accept. Verify that everything you care about is plugged into a UPS, that the UPS batteries are healthy, and that the failover mechanism works. To test an individual UPS, just unplug it from the wall. To make sure that critical equipment is properly UPSified, you may have to throw the circuit breakers. Know your power system's dependencies and points of failure.

UPSes need maintenance, too. This function is probably outside the scope of your sysadmin duties, but you are responsible for ensuring that it is performed.

Most power hits are of short duration, but plan for two hours of battery life so that you have time to shut down machines properly in the event of a longer outage. Some UPSes have a serial port or Ethernet interface that you can use to initiate a graceful shutdown of noncritical machines after 5 minutes (configurable) of power outage.

Take advantage of power outages to do any 5-minute upgrades that you have already tested but have not yet deployed. You're down anyway, so people expect to be inconvenienced. In some shops, an extra 5 minutes during a power outage is easier to accept than a scheduled downtime with a week's notice. If you have old machines that you suspect are not in use anymore, leave them turned off until someone complains. It might not be until weeks later—or never—that the "missing" machine is noticed.

See page 776 for more information about environment issues.

Cooling systems often have a notification system that can call you if the temperature gets too high. Tune the value of "too high" so that after the cooling system pages you, you have time to get in before machines start to fry; we use 76 degrees instead of 90, but live in the mountains 45 minutes away (in summer, indeterminate in winter). Keep a couple of mechanical or battery-operated thermometers in the machine room—losing power means that you lose all those nifty electronic indicators that normally tell you the temperature.

A large U.S. government lab recently built a fancy new machine room and filled it with a 256-node Linux Alpha cluster for running large scientific models. Everything was plugged into a UPS, and all the facilities were state of the art. Unfortunately, a minor power outage brought the center down for four hours. Why? The PC that controlled the HVAC (air conditioner) was not on the UPS. It failed and messed up the air conditioning system. Test carefully.

If you co-locate equipment at a remote site, ask to see the hosting site's backup power facilities before you sign a contract. Verify that the generator is real and is tested regularly. Ask to be present at the next generator test; whether or not you get to see an actual test, you're likely to get useful information.

Network redundancy

ISPs are occasionally swallowed as part of a merger. Such mergers have demolished many companies' carefully laid plans for maintaining redundant connections to the Internet. A post-merger ISP often consolidates circuits that belonged to the independent companies. Customers that formerly had independent paths to the Internet may then have both connections running through a single conduit and once again be at the mercy of a single backhoe fiber cut.

ISPs have also been known to advertise "redundant circuits" or "backup connections" of questionable value. On closer inspection you may find that yes, there are two fibers, but both are in the same conduit, or the backup connection transits an already saturated ATM cloud. Hold a yearly review with your ISPs to verify that you still have genuine redundancy.

Security incidents

System security is covered in detail in Chapter 20, *Security*. However, it's worth mentioning here as well because security considerations impact the vast majority of administrative tasks. There is no aspect of your site's management strategy that can be designed without due regard for security. For the most part, Chapter 20 concentrates on ways of preventing security incidents from occurring. However, thinking about how you might recover from a security-related incident is an equally important part of security planning.

Having your web site hijacked is a particularly embarrassing type of break-in. For the sysadmin at a web hosting company, a hijacking can be a calamitous event, especially at sites that handle credit card data. Phone calls stream in from customers, from the media, from the company VIPs who just saw the news of the hijacking on CNN. Who will take the calls? What should that person say? Who is in charge? What role does each person play? If you are in a high-visibility business, it's definitely worth thinking through this type of scenario, coming up with some preplanned answers, and perhaps even having a practice session to work out the details.

Sites that accept credit card data have legal requirements to deal with after a hijacking. Make sure your organization's legal department is involved in security incident planning, and make sure you have relevant contact names and phone numbers to call in a time of crisis.

When CNN or Slashdot announces that your web site is down, the same effect that makes highway traffic slow down to look at an accident on the side of the road causes your Internet traffic to increase enormously, often to the point of breaking whatever it was that you just fixed. If your web site cannot handle an increase in traffic of 25% or more, consider having your load balancing device route excess connections to a server that presents a page that simply says "Sorry, we are too busy to handle your request right now."

Second-hand stories from the World Trade Center

We've heard some instructive stories that relate to the September 11, 2001, attack on the World Trade Center in New York City. Unfortunately, the sysadmins that "owned" these stories were unable to obtain their management's permission to share them. Rather than give up, we here include some second- and third-hand stories of unverified authenticity. They are certainly not the last word on disaster management, but they are interesting nonetheless.

One ISP routed all their calls and network traffic through a facility located in one of the smaller buildings of the World Trade Center complex. The ISP's building survived the attack, and the facility continued to operate under power from emergency generators, although it had trouble dissipating heat once the building's air conditioning had been disabled. Unfortunately, the ISP's staff were unable to enter the site to refill the generators' fuel tanks. Moral: make sure you have at least a few days' worth of generating capacity available for sustained emergency situations.

Another organization located in one of the WTC towers once maintained its disaster recovery facility in the other tower. Fortunately, the company rethought its definition of "off-site" before the attack. A third organization was able to recover because all of its critical data was replicated to multiple devices in multiple locations, mirrored synchronously over Fibre Channel. However, this particular organization lost a lot of paper documents—not everything was computerized.

One financial business located in the towers was outsourcing the storage of its off-site backups. However, the business didn't know that the storage facility was also in one of the towers. It can be important to know where your off-site materials are kept.

CNN's web site experienced traffic on September 11th that defied measurement. The telephone system in New York City was overloaded, and TV stations that had broadcast from antennas atop the WTC were knocked out. Everyone turned to the Internet and pummeled cnn.com. At first, the site was overwhelmed by the load. After trying to cope for a while by moving servers around, CNN eventually reduced the complexity of its home page to a single image and plain text with no links. After a couple of hours, the site was up again and handling the load.

The experience of this massive spike in web traffic resulted in policy changes at CNN regarding when the complexity of the home page can be reduced and who can decide on such a change. The power and responsibility moved down the management hierarchy toward the sysadmin trenches.

30.11   WRITTEN POLICY

While researching this chapter, we talked to bigshots in the system administration world, in computer security, in the standards community, and in computer law. We were surprised that they all mentioned "signed, written policy" as being essential to a healthy organization.

Several different policy documents should exist:

- Administrative service policies
- Rights and responsibilities of users
- Policies regarding sysadmins (users with special privileges)
- Guest account policy

Procedures in the form of checklists or recipes can be used to codify existing practice. They are useful both for new sysadmins and for old hands. Better yet are procedures in the form of executable scripts. Several benefits of standard procedures are:

- The chores are always done in the same way.
- Checklists reduce the likelihood of errors or forgotten steps.
- It's faster for the sysadmin to work from a recipe.
- The changes are self-documenting.
- Written procedures provide a measurable standard of correctness.

Today, Linux is replacing the big mainframes of the past and is performing mission-critical functions in the corporate world. In big shops, checklists, often called "run books," serve as the documentation for common tasks. They're usually kept on-line and also in the form of printed manuals. The sysadmins that write and maintain the run books are often a layer away from the support crew that uses them, but such organization and standardization pays off in the long run.

Here are some common tasks for which you might want to set up procedures:

- Adding a host
- Adding a user
- Localizing a machine
- Setting up backups for a new machine
- Securing a new machine
- Restarting a complicated piece of software
- Reviving a web site that is not responding or not serving data
- Unjamming and restarting a printer
- Upgrading the operating system
- Patching software

Management

- Installing a software package
- Installing software from the net
- Upgrading critical software (**sendmail**, **gcc**, **named**, etc.)
- Backing up and restoring files
- Expiring backup tapes
- Performing emergency shutdowns (all hosts, all but important hosts, etc.)

Many issues sit squarely between policy and procedure. For example:

- Who can have an account?
- What happens when they leave?

The resolutions of such issues need to be written down so that you can stay consistent and avoid falling prey to the well-known, four-year-old's ploy of "Mommy said no, let's go ask Daddy!" Often, the "if" portion is the policy and the "how" portion is the procedure

Some policy decisions will be dictated by the software you are running or by the policies of external groups, such as ISPs. Some policies are mandatory if the privacy of your users' data is to be protected. We call these topics "nonnegotiable policy."

In particular, we believe that IP addresses, hostnames, UIDs, GIDs, and usernames should all be managed site-wide. Some sites (multinational corporations, for example) are clearly too large to implement this policy, but if you can swing it, site-wide management makes things a lot simpler. We know of a company that enforces site-wide management for 35,000 users and 100,000 machines, so the threshold at which an organization becomes too big for site-wide management must be pretty high.

Other important issues may have a larger scope than just your local sysadmin group:

- Handling of security break-ins
- Filesystem export controls
- Password selection criteria
- Removal of logins for cause
- Copyrighted material (e.g., MP3s and DVDs)
- Software piracy

Maintaining good channels of communication among administrative groups at a large site can prevent problems and help develop trust and cooperation. Consider throwing a party as a communication vehicle. Some sysadmin groups use an IRC-like MUD or MOO or other chat system as a communication vehicle. It can get very chatty, but if used properly can make your organization run more smoothly, especially if some staff work off-site or from home. Chats can be snooped, so be careful not to send sensitive information about your network and organization over a third-party network.

Security policies

What do you want to protect? Your data? Your hardware? Your ability to recover quickly after a disaster? You must consider several tradeoffs when designing a security policy for your site:

- Services offered vs. security provided (more services = less secure)
- Ease of use and convenience vs. security (security = 1/convenience)
- Cost of security vs. risk (cost) of loss

RFC2196, the *Site Security Handbook*, is a 75-page document written in 1997 by a subgroup of the Internet Engineering Task Force (IETF). It advises sysadmins on various security issues, user policies, and procedures. It does not include a recipe for securing an Internet site, but it does contain some valuable information. The last 15 pages are a wonderful collection of both on-line and published references.

RFC2196 suggests that your policy documents include the following points:

- *Purchasing guidelines* for hardware and software. It can be a big win to involve sysadmins in the procurement process because they often know about hardware quirks, software limitations, and support issues that are not advertised by the vendors' marketing teams.

- A *privacy policy* that sets expectations regarding the monitoring of users' email and keystrokes and sets policies for dealing with user files

- An *access policy*: who can have access, what they can do with their access, what hardware and software they can install, etc. This document should include the same warnings about authorized use and line monitoring that are included in the privacy policy.

- An *accountability policy* that spells out the responsibilities of both users and sysadmins. The policy should explicitly say who can snoop network traffic, read users' email, and investigate other similarly sensitive areas. It should also outline the circumstances in which such investigations might take place.

- An *authentication policy* that sets guidelines for passwords and remote access

- An *availability policy* that describes when the system is supposed to be up, lists scheduled maintenance times, gives instructions for reporting problems, and sets expectations regarding response times

- A *maintenance policy* that includes rules about outsourcing and specifies procedures for giving access to third-party maintenance personnel

Noticeably missing from the RFC2196 list is an authorization policy that specifies who can authorize new accounts and extended privileges. The original *Site Security Handbook*, RFC1244, contained lists of concrete issues rather than types of policies, which might be a bit more useful from the sysadmin's point of view. The newer RFC includes recommendations for each type of service a machine might run and describes the problems of the services and potential solutions.

ISO 117999 is a more up-to-date reference and is seeing widespread use in the industry. COBIT is another popular standard (and one that covers more than just security).

Whatever policies you adopt, they must be explicit, written down, understood, and signed by all users and sysadmins. Enforcement must be consistent, even when users are customers who are paying for computing services. Failure to apply policies uniformly weakens their legal and perceived validity.

User policy agreements

At the University of Colorado's computer science department, user policy is delivered in the form of an initial shell that prints the policy and requires users to agree to and "sign" it before they can get a real shell and use their accounts. This scheme saves time and hassle, but check with *your own* lawyers before implementing it at your site.

Here are some explicit issues that should be addressed in a user policy agreement:

- Sharing accounts with friends and relatives (we suggest: never)
- Running password crackers on the local system's passwords
- Running password crackers on other sites' passwords
- Disrupting service
- Breaking into other accounts
- Misusing or forging electronic mail
- General use of email and electronic media
- Looking at other users' files (if readable? writable? invited?)
- Importing software from the net (never? always? if the user checks?)
- Mandatory use of firewall and antivirus software on Windows hosts
- Using system resources (printers, disk space, modems, CPU)
- Duplicating copyrighted material (software, music, movies, etc.)
- Allowing others to duplicate copyrighted material
- Using resources for private or commercial activities
- Practicing illegal activities (fraud, libel, etc.)
- Pursuing activities that are legal in some places but not others (e.g., porn, political activity)

You should realize, however, that no policy agreement can prevent somebody from violating it. You can use it as a weapon to hit the culprit on the head, have his or her account terminated, have him fired or expelled, or whatever seems appropriate in your environment.

Here is an example of a short and simple policy agreement that the computer science department at the University of Melbourne requires students to sign in order to use the university's computers:

I, the undersigned, HEREBY DECLARE that I will abide by the rules set out below:

- *I will use the Department's computing and network facilities solely for academic purposes directly related to my study of Computer Science subjects.*

- *I understand that the Department grants computer accounts for the exclusive use of the recipient. Therefore, I will not authorise or facilitate the use of my account or files by any other person, nor will I divulge my password to any other person.*

- *I will not access, or attempt to gain access to any computer, computer account, network or files without proper and explicit authorisation. Such access is illegal under State and Federal laws, and is contrary to University regulations. I will inform the Computer Science Office immediately should I become aware that such access has taken place.*

- *I understand that some software and data that reside on file systems that I may access are protected by copyright and other laws, and also by licenses and other contractual agreements; therefore, I will not breach these restrictions.*

- *I will not use University facilities for obtaining, making, running or distributing unauthorised copies of software.*

- *I will undertake to keep confidential any disclosure to me by the University of software (including methods or concepts used therein) licensed to the University for use on its computers and I hereby indemnify and hold harmless the University against claims of any nature arising from any disclosure on my part to another of the said software in breach of this undertaking.*

- *I undertake to maintain the highest standard of honesty and personal integrity in relation to my usage of the Department's computing and network facilities. I further warrant that I will avoid any actions in relation to my usage of the Department's computing or network facilities that may bring any disrepute upon the Department or the University.*

I understand that I am bound by Regulation 8.1.R7 of the University of Melbourne (set out in the Student Diary), which also governs and regulates my use of University computing and network facilities.

I understand that acting in breach of any of the principles set out above will incur severe penalties including failure in an assignment or a subject, the suspension or withdrawal of access to University computing facilities, suspension or expulsion from the University, imposition of fines, and/or legal action taken under the Crimes (Computer) Act 1988.[8]

---

8. Keep in mind that this is an Australian law, although similar computer- and software-related legislation has been passed in the United States.

Take special note of the weasel words about honesty, personal integrity, and not bringing the University into disrepute. Vague requirements such as these are meant to give some room for later maneuvering and to cover any specifics that may have been inadvertently left out of the policy. Although their true legal weight is probably negligible, it might be a good idea to include such requirements in your policy agreements.

Sysadmin policy agreements

The sysadmin policy agreement must set guidelines for using root privileges and for honoring users' privacy. IT managers must make sure that the sysadmin staff understand and uphold the implications of such a document. At the same time, it is hard to respond to a user's complaint that mail is broken without looking at the messages that have bounced. (However, a copy of the headers is often sufficient to characterize and fix the problem.)

*See page 48 for more information about **sudo** and page 690 for more about John the Ripper.*

If your site uses a tool such as **sudo** for root access, it is essential that your sysadmins use good passwords and not share their logins with *anyone*. Consider running John the Ripper on sysadmins' passwords regularly. It's also essential that admins not execute **sudo sh** or use a shell escape after **sudo**-ing their favorite text editor; these are just token usages of **sudo** and defeat **sudo**'s logging feature. The log is not there to spy on administrators; it's there to help reconstruct the sequence of events when something goes wrong.

For some sysadmins, the urge to show off rootly powers overcomes common sense. Gently but firmly suggest other career alternatives.

At some sites, having the root password is a status symbol, perhaps more valuable than a key to the executive washroom or access to the close-in parking lot. Often, the people having the password are engineers who don't need it or shouldn't have it. One site we know offered engineers the root password, but stipulated that any takers would have to wear a beeper and help others when necessary. Requests plummeted.

Another technique we have used with good success is to seal the root password in an envelope and hide it in a spot accessible to the sysadmin staff. Sysadmins generally use **sudo** to do their work; if they actually need the root password for some reason, they open the envelope. They must then change the root password and stash a new envelope. The procedure is straightforward while still being painful enough to motivate the use of **sudo**. It's important to keep the old passwords around for a while for those machines that were down or off-line when the new password was pushed out.

If your staff knows the root password, you must change it whenever a staff member leaves. There may be multiple administrative passwords at your site: for computers, printers, network hardware, PROMs or BIOSes, databases, etc. Write down all the things that must be changed (and how to do it) if a staff member leaves.

30.12 LEGAL ISSUES

The U.S. federal government and several states have laws regarding computer crime. At the federal level, there are two from the early 1990s and two more recent ones:

- The Federal Communications Privacy Act
- The Computer Fraud and Abuse Act
- The No Electronic Theft Act
- The Digital Millennium Copyright Act

Some big issues in the legal arena are the liability of sysadmins, network operators, and web hosting sites; strong cryptography for electronic commerce; peer to peer networks and their threat to the entertainment industry; copyright issues; and privacy issues. The topics in this section comment on these issues and a variety of other legal debacles related to system administration.

Encryption

The need for encryption in electronic commerce and communication is clear. However, encryption is against the law in some countries. Law enforcement agencies do not want citizens to be able to store data that they (the police) cannot decrypt.

In the United States, the laws regarding encryption are changing. In the past, it was illegal to export any form of strong encryption technology. Companies had to create two versions of software that incorporated encryption: one for sale in the domestic market and a crippled version for export. One side effect of this policy was that many encryption-related software projects came to be based in other countries. The policy's patent absurdity (the rest of the world has had cryptographic technology for a long time) and the needs of electronic commerce eventually motivated the government to change its stance.

Although the export restrictions are not yet completely gone, changes introduced in 2004 make the situation in the United States better than it used to be. To see how you might be effected, refer to www.bis.doc.gov/Encryption.

The IETF has worked on standards in the area of end-to-end secure communications at the protocol level—the IPsec effort—and vendors are beginning to ship systems that include it. The authentication part is typically bundled, but the encryption part is often installed separately. This architecture preserves flexibility for countries in which encryption cannot be used.

In a recent (2006) U.S. court decision, software code was likened to free speech and was judged to be protected under the first amendment to the Constitution of the United States. In 1990, Dan Bernstein developed a new cryptographic algorithm while a graduate student at U.C. Berkeley. However, he was denied permission to discuss the algorithm in public by the U.S. State Department, which classified the technology as a "munition." The Electronic Frontier Foundation (eff.org) pursued the case and eventually won. It only took 16 years!

Management

Copyright

The music and movie industries have noticed with some consternation that home computers are capable of playing music from CDs and displaying movies on DVD. It is both an opportunity and a threat for them. The ultimate outcome will depend on whether these industries respond in a proactive or reactive way; unfortunately, they seem to be headed down the reactive path.

The DVD format uses an encryption key to scramble the contents of a disk with an algorithm called CSS, the Content Scrambling System. The idea was to limit the ability to play DVDs to licensed and approved players. Consumer DVD players include the appropriate decoding key, as do the software players that come with most DVD computer drives.

A student from Norway reverse-engineered the CSS encryption process and posted a program called DeCSS to the web. The program did not bypass the DVD encryption scheme; it simply used the decryption key from a legitimate Windows player to decode the DVD data stream and save it to disk so he could play it on Linux instead of having to use Windows.

The Motion Picture Association of America and the DVD Copy Control Association both filed lawsuits against numerous "distributors" of the DeCSS software; everyone whose web site linked to a copy of DeCSS was considered a distributor. The lawsuits alleged that the defendants were engaged not in the theft of copyrighted materials but in the distribution of trade secrets and the "circumvention of copy protection."[9] In the United States, the latter activity was redefined as a form of copyright infringement by the Digital Millennium Copyright Act (DMCA) of 1998. The MPAA won this case; DeCSS was found to be in violation of the DMCA. Currently (2006), no open source DVD players are legal for use in the United States.

In two recent cases, companies have tried to use the copyright and anti-reverse-engineering aspects of the DMCA law to stifle their competition: Sears tried to prohibit third-party garage door openers from being used to operate Sears-branded garage doors, and Lexmark tried to use the law to ban companies from refilling Lexmark's empty laser printer cartridges and selling them more cheaply than new ones. In both cases, the EFF represented the little guy and won.

Another DMCA case, MGM vs. Grokster and Streamcast, made it to the U.S. Supreme Court. Previous decisions (e.g., the precedent-setting Sony Betamax case from the 1970s) had said that selling technology capable of infringing on someone's copyrighted material was not illegal; you had to use it to actually infringe to be guilty. In the Grokster case, Streamcast made money by advertising their software as being capable of duplicating copyrighted music and movies. This inducement to infringe was judged to be in violation of the DMCA, and the court ruled 9-0 against Grokster and for MGM.

9. The DMCA prohibits the "circumvention" of measures intended to keep digital content secure, even if the reason for circumvention falls under the "fair use" exemptions of traditional copyright law. Needless to say, this change represents a significant abridgement of the fair use exemptions.

Peer-to-peer networks such as BitTorrent may be safe from this "inducement" argument since many applications of file sharing do not involve copyrighted material. However, the details are still quite murky.

SCO has been shaking down Linux providers for using copyrighted bits of UNIX code in their distributions. They filed thousands of lawsuits against individuals and one against IBM. ODSL, the Open Source Development Labs, has set up a $10 million legal fund to protect Linux users. Some of the companies supporting ODSL include Cisco, Dell, Ericsson, Fujitsu, Hitachi, HP, IBM, Intel, Nokia, Red Hat, Sun, and Toshiba. A recent (July 2006) court decision supported IBM's contention that most of SCO's 250+ claims were too general and should be thrown out; see groklaw.net for additional details. The language of the decision discouraged an appeal, so perhaps the SCO lawsuits have hit a roadblock and the silliness will stop.

Privacy

Privacy has always been difficult to safeguard, but with the rise of the Internet, it is in more danger than ever. The medical records of patients in the University of Michigan health care system were inadvertently published on the Internet. The data was freely available for months until a student noticed the oversight. Databases full of credit card numbers have been compromised. Fake email arrives almost daily that appears to be from your bank and alleges that problems with your account require you to verify your account data. A closer glance at the email as text instead of letting it be interpreted as a web page shows that the data would go to a hacker in eastern Europe or Asia and not to your bank.

DoubleClick

Another big privacy scandal, this one intentional, has involved DoubleClick.net, an advertising agency that provides many of the banner ads shown on web pages. DoubleClick promised for years that users in their system were never tracked or identified. Recently, however, they purchased a company that does data mining and began gathering data from each user that visited a web page containing a DoubleClick ad. The furor that ensued caused DoubleClick to withdraw the project for now and to hire two high-powered lawyers into "privacy" positions to find a way for DoubleClick to legally stalk the users who are subjected to their ads.

Sony's rootkits

Sony included a program called XCP (for eXtended Copy Protection) on several dozen music CD products. The software installed itself on the owner's computer, hid its own files so the user wouldn't notice, and reported back to Sony about the music that was being listened to. Since XCP is a form of rootkit, the files installed could expose the machine to hackers; see page 688.

Mark Russinovich bought a Sony CD with DRM (Digital Rights Management) from amazon.com and installed it on his Windows system. Later, he discovered the Sony rootkit and analyzed its impact and extent.

> "Not only had Sony put software on my system that uses techniques commonly used by malware to mask its presence, the software is poorly written and provides no means for uninstall. Worse, most users that stumble across the cloaked files with a rootkit scan will cripple their computer if they attempt the obvious step of deleting the cloaked files.

> "While I believe in the media industry's right to use copy protection mechanisms to prevent illegal copying, I don't think that we've found the right balance of fair use and copy protection, yet. This is a clear case of Sony taking DRM too far."

The fact that the rootkit is there and cannot be uninstalled is not mentioned in the EULA license that users must sign to install the CD on their computers.[10] In the United Kingdom, this is in clear violation of their Computer Misuse Act. It's also illegal in California under the California Business & Protections Code and is punishable by a fine of $1,000 per infected computer. The EFF has filed a class action suit against Sony; to claim damages, go to www.sonybmgcdtechsettlement.com.

Why should sysadmins care? Well, if your desktop PCs have Sony's rootkit installed, your entire site is potentially vulnerable to exploitation.

Call records and web logs

Three of the largest American telephone companies have been accused of giving the phone and Internet records of their 200 million customers to the National Security Agency. Qwest, another large American telephone company, had refused to cooperate with the NSA because of privacy concerns. They even held out when the NSA strongly hinted that Qwest might not receive any more classified government contracts. Good for Qwest; the EFF is suing the other three telephone companies.

History illustrates the potential abuse that can be made of call records. In 2002, a Colombian drug cartel's computer was seized by police.[11] When the data contained on the computer's hard disks was analyzed, it revealed that in 1994, call records from phone switches had been used to determine the "distance" of cartel employees from law enforcement officials. Several employees who were "too close" were eliminated. Traffic analysis is a powerful tool, and it is being used.

Several of the large search engines and portal web sites (e.g., Yahoo!) were providing the U.S. government with data from users' web searches. Google is the only one that didn't cave in to government demands. However, Google did provide a crippled search engine to the Chinese government, which wanted to censor web search results throughout China. Google is reported to be rethinking that decision.

The U.S. cell phone network is also ruffling some privacy feathers. As you move around the country with a cell phone in your pocket, the phone automatically checks

---

10. EULA stands for End-User License Agreement.
11. See amsterdam.nettime.org/Lists-Archives/nettime-l-0207/msg00015.html.

in with local cells so that calls can be routed to you. Unfortunately, the government does not need a warrant or even probable cause to track your cell phone's location.

The underlying legal issue is the definition of so-called pen-register data. In the context of telephones, it is the information about who called whom and when, independent of the actual contents of the conversation. In 1984, the Electronic Privacy Communications Act distinguished pen-register data from content (both of which were formerly protected) and said it was OK for phone companies to disclose pen-register data based on an easy-to-obtain court order. In 2001, the Patriot Act extended the definition of "phone numbers" to include software programs and Internet-related information such as IP addresses and URLs.

Hence, the URLs that you visit and the web searches you perform are now classified as pen-register data. They are explicitly not protected as private information. A warrant is required before a sysadmin must turn over email or user files, but the contents of most log files require only a court order.

Another feature of pen-register data is that it can be used in court proceedings even if obtained illegally by law enforcement officers. Scary times.

Click-through EULAs

EULA is the acronym for the End User License Agreements that you are asked to accept when you install a piece of software you have purchased. Most folks don't read them carefully, or if they do read them, they click Yes anyway since they have already paid for the software, opened the CD, and started the installation process—it's too late to return the software and request your money back. Some EULAs are downright evil; here are some of the things you may be asked to agree to:

- Allow the vendor to monitor or audit your computer (Red Hat!)
- Not criticize the product or the vendor (Microsoft)
- Not benchmark the product or communicate the results (McAfee)
- Waive the right to enforce the company's stated privacy policy (McAfee)
- Refrain from customizing or repairing your computer
- Allow automatic software updates
- Not reverse-engineer the product
- Not remove the product from your computer
- Not use the product in conjunction with a competitor's product

Rather a long list, and we have surely missed many...

Policy enforcement

Log files may prove to you beyond a shadow of a doubt that person X did bad thing Y, but to a court it is all just hearsay evidence. Protect yourself with written policies. Log files sometimes include time stamps, which are useful but not necessarily admissible as evidence unless your computer is running the Network Time Protocol (NTP) to keep its clock synced to a reference standard.

You may need a security policy in order to prosecute someone for misuse. It should include a statement such as this: *Unauthorized use of University computing systems may involve not only transgression of University policy but also a violation of state and federal laws. Unauthorized use is a crime and may involve criminal and civil penalties; it will be prosecuted to the full extent of the law.*

We advise you to put a warning in **/etc/motd** (the message of the day file) that advises users of your snooping policy. Ours reads:

```
Your keyboard input may be monitored in the event of a real or
perceived security incident.
```

You may want to ensure that users see the notification at least once by including it in the startup files you give to new users. If you require the use of **ssh** to log in (and you should), then configure **sshd.config** to always show the **motd** file.

Be sure to specify that by the act of using their accounts, users acknowledge your written policy. Explain where users can get additional copies of policy documents and post key documents on an appropriate bulletin board. Also include the specific penalty for noncompliance (deletion of the account, etc.).

Control = liability

ISPs typically have an appropriate use policy (AUP) dictated by their upstream providers and required of their downstream customers. This "flow down" of liability assigns responsibility for users' actions to the users themselves, not to the ISP or the ISP's upstream provider. These policies have been used to attempt to control spam (unsolicited commercial email) and to protect ISPs in cases of customers' storing illegal or copyrighted material in their accounts. Check the laws in your area; your mileage may vary.

Suppose something naughty is emailed or posted to the web from your site. If you are CompuServe (now part of AOL), this is a problem. In a case called *Cubby v. CompuServe*, something libelous was posted. The judge ruled that CompuServe was not guilty, but found the moderator of the newsgroup to which it was posted negligent. The more you try to control information, the more liable you become.

This principle is beautifully illustrated by the story of a Texas business founded by an enterprising computer science student of ours, Cheeser. He wrote Perl scripts to mine the Usenet news groups, collect naughty pictures, and build a subscription web site based on that content. He charged $12/month to subscribers and was raking in money hand over fist.

Cheeser tried to be a responsible pornographer and did not subscribe to newsgroups known to carry child pornography. He also monitored several newsgroups that were on the edge, sometimes with illegal content, sometimes not. This minimal oversight and his choice of a conservative county in Texas in which to locate his business were his downfall.

Acting on an anonymous tip (perhaps from a competitor), the local police confiscated his computers. Sure enough, they found an instance of child pornography that had been posted to one of the "safer" newsgroups. The criminal case never went to trial, but during the plea bargaining it became clear that the judge thought Cheeser was guilty—not because he had created the content, but because he was not a good enough censor. The implication was that if Cheeser had done no censoring at all, he would have been legally OK. Never censor your porn!

This principle also applies to other interactions with the outside world. From a legal standpoint, the more you monitor your users' use of the Internet, the more you may be liable for their actions or postings. If you are aware of an illegal or actionable activity, you have a legal duty to investigate it and to report your findings to Big Brother.

For this reason, some sites limit the data that they log, the length of time for which log files are kept, and the amount of log file history kept on backup tapes. Some software packages (e.g., the Squid web cache) help with the implementation of this policy by including levels of logging that help the sysadmin debug problems but that do not violate users' privacy. But be aware of what kind of logging might be required by your local laws.

System administrators should be familiar with all relevant corporate or university policies and should make sure the policies are followed. Unenforced or inconsistent policies are worse than none, from both a practical and legal point of view.

Software licenses

Many sites have paid for K copies of a software package and have N copies in daily use, where $K << N$. Getting caught in this situation could be damaging to the company, probably more damaging than the cost of those N-minus-K other licenses. Other sites have received a demo copy of an expensive software package and hacked it (reset the date on the machine, found the license key, etc.) to make it continue working after the expiration of the demo period. How do you as a sysadmin deal with requests to violate license agreements and make copies of software on unlicensed machines? What do you do when you find that machines for which you are responsible are running pirated software? What about shareware that was never paid for?

It's a very tough call. Management will often not back you up in your requests that unlicensed copies of software be either removed or paid for. Often, it is a sysadmin who signs the agreement to remove the demo copies after a certain date, but a manager who makes the decision not to remove them.

Even if the job is the best one you've ever had, your personal and professional integrity are on the line. Fortunately, even in today's job market, quality sysadmins are in high demand and your job search will be short. We are aware of several cases in which a sysadmin's immediate manager would not deal with the situation and told the sysadmin not to rock the boat. The sysadmin then wrote a memo to the boss asking to correct the situation and documenting the number of copies of the software that were licensed and the number that were in use. The admin quoted a few phrases from the license agreement and cc'ed the president of the company and his boss' managers. In one case, this procedure worked and the sysadmin's manager was let go. In another case, the sysadmin quit when even higher management refused to do the right thing. Whatever you do in such a situation, get things in writing. Ask for a written reply, or if all you get is spoken words, write a short memo documenting your understanding of your instructions and send it to the person in charge.

Regulatory compliance

A rash of high-profile accounting scandals at companies such as Enron and World-Com (MCI) prompted the passage of a 2002 U.S. law called the Sarbanes-Oxley Act, known colloquially as SOX. SOX sets accountability rules for publicly traded companies in the United States and holds corporate officers personally responsible for the validity of their financial data.

Since computers keep track of most companies' records, SOX affects system administration. Some of the measures mandated by SOX are easy (email logs, audit trails, internal controls), but some are a bit harder. For example, SOX requires you to determine a baseline of normal activity for a data repository (e.g., database) and create tools to detect anomalous behavior or access. You must also document everything and prove that you make regular use of the controls you implemented. Compliance extracts a sizable toll on productivity and sysadmin morale.

On the other hand, Sarbanes-Oxley is a big win if you sell storage devices or accounting services. For large companies, the average cost of compliance was $4 million last year, and this is an ongoing expense. Now that executives are directly accountable for violations and can go to jail, they have sometimes demanded bizarre new system administration procedures in the name of SOX compliance.

SOX affects private and nonprofit companies, too. Written policy agreements that document how long data is kept and when scheduled purges will occur have become important for both printed and electronic documents.

A sysadmin was doing some penetration testing for a large computer company under the direction of an international accounting firm. He proved that almost anyone could get into a company's Oracle Financials database as root and mess with the company's books without being detected—exactly the sort of thing that SOX compliance is supposed to guarantee is impossible. The accounting firm wanted him to prove his claims by altering the customer's financial data. He refused, they persisted, and after much soul searching he decided to report the accounting firm to the customer's business conduct office. In the end the accounting firm was fired, and the sysadmin lost his job soon after.

IT auditing and governance are big issues today. Regulations and quasi-standards for specifying, measuring, and certifying compliance have spawned myriad acronyms: SOX, ITIL, COBIT, and ISO 17799, to name a few. Unfortunately, this alphabet soup is leaving something of a a bad taste in system administrators' mouths, and software to implement all the controls deemed necessary by recent legislation is currently lacking.

30.13 SOFTWARE PATENTS

In the beginning, the patent office ruled that you could not patent a mathematical theorem. Then the theorem became an algorithm, and it still could not be patented. Then the algorithm was implemented in hardware, and that could certainly be patented. Firmware, maybe. Software, still no. But patents can be appealed, and one of the lower courts liked software patents. Against its will, the patent office started issuing them, in some cases for applications that were filed 10 to 15 years earlier.

Unfortunately, the patent office has historically had scant comprehension of the state of the art in software and has issued many inappropriate (some would say, stupid) patents. Five different patents exist for the Lempel-Ziv data compression algorithm. That algorithm was published in a mathematical journal and was implemented and distributed in Berkeley UNIX. The concept of an include file is patented. The concept of a cursor is patented. Subtraction was patented as a measure to fix software that was not Y2K compliant. The process of copying an image from memory to an on-screen window is patented, as is the use of the XOR operation to handle overlapping windows. Several data encryption standards are patented. The concept of embedding advertising material in a user interface is patented.

According to U.S. patent law, if a certain invention is patentable, so is every minor improvement upon that invention. In the case of software, just about everything can be viewed as a step forward in the patent sense. The U.S. Patent and Trademark Office's naivete with respect to software, and their persistent inability to judge what constitutes prior art or obviousness, have caused them to issue thousands of shaky software patents every year.

In the United States, an even bigger threat has emerged: the business method software patent. Companies have persuaded the patent office that virtually any method of computerizing a standard business procedure is a patentable invention. Patents have been issued for mundane activities such as pulling up a customer's account from a computer database when the customer calls in to a help desk. Amazon.com obtained a business practice patent on "1-click technology"; they obtained an injunction requiring Barnes and Noble to make their customers perform at least two mouse clicks to purchase books.[12]

By contrast, the European Union ruled in July 2005 that anything that consists of "schemes, rules and methods for performing mental acts, playing games or doing business, and programs for computers" is not an invention and is therefore not patentable. The vote was a resounding 648 to 14.

The U.S. patent office is attempting to clean up its act, but the damage seems to have already been done in many cases. A major milestone was the 1994 recall of a patent

---

12. Perhaps DoubleClick.net could beat them to the punch by patenting double-clicking…

belonging to Compton's New Media which involved retrieval systems for data stored on CD-ROM. Some analysts considered it broad enough to cover 80% of all existing CD-ROM products, although that is probably an exaggeration. In the end, each of 41 claims was invalidated through an expensive and time-consuming campaign on the part of software vendors to demonstrate the existence of prior art.

The discovery of prior art is the real weakness in the patent office's process. Patent applications are kept secret, and with very little software expertise in the patent office, it is difficult for them to know which applications really represent new technology. Lawsuits will eventually decide, with the lawyers being the ultimate winners of every case.

In the U.S. system, even the patent office's failure to grant a patent to a proposed invention does not stop patent-related shenanigans from coming to court. NTP, Inc. applied for five patents in the broad area of wireless email. The patent office rejected them all; two of the five were final rejections without possibility of appeal. Yet based on these five bogus and rejected patents, NTP sued the Canadian company Research in Motion, makers of the email-receiving BlackBerry cell phone.

RIM was clearly in a strong position. They had done all their own research and development, and the NTP patent applications had been rejected by the patent office. Nevertheless, the judge hearing the case seemed inclined to award NTP an injunction that would have made it illegal for RIM to sell new BlackBerrys in the United States. More importantly, the injunction would have made it impossible for existing customers to continue to use their Blackberries for email.

RIM judged the risk of an injunction to be too great; they settled the lawsuit with a one-time payment of $612,500,000 in exchange for a permanent license to use the technology covered by NTP's five rejected patent applications. A happy day for BlackBerry users like us, but a sad day for small companies with good ideas and good products.

Check out the Electronic Frontier Foundation's archives at www.eff.org for more specifics. A good source of breaking news is slashdot.org's patent area.

30.14 STANDARDS

The standardization process helps us in some cases (Wi-Fi interfaces from different manufacturers can talk to each other) and hurts us in others (OSI network protocols, millions of dollars worth of software engineering down the drain). Standards committees should codify and formalize existing practice, not invent.

Standards are intended to level the playing field and make it possible for customers to buy compatible products from competing vendors. Some of the parties involved in the standardization process really do just want to codify existing practice. Others have a more political purpose: to delay a competitor or to reduce the amount of work required to bring their own company's products into conformance.

Government organizations are often the biggest procurers of standards-based systems and applications. The use of standards allows them to buy competitively without favoring a particular brand. However, some cynics have called standards a non-monetary trade barrier—companies slow down the standards process until their products catch up.

There are several standards bodies, both formal and informal. Each has different rules for membership, voting, and clout. From a system or network administrator's perspective, the most important bodies are the Free Standards Group's LSB (Linux Standard Base), POSIX (pronounced PAHZ-icks, Portable Operating System Interfaces) and the IETF (the Internet Engineering Task Force, described on page 273).

LSB: the Linux Standard Base

The Free Standards Group is a nonprofit organization that promotes open source standards—in particular, the Linux standardization effort. Currently, about 20 corporations contribute to the effort, including major manufacturers such as HP, IBM, and Silicon Graphics. Major Linux distributors such as Red Hat, Novell (SUSE), Debian, Mandriva, and Turbolinux also participate. The goal is to make it easier for third-party software developers to build a software product for Linux and have that be one product, not 20 or 50 slightly different variations of the same product.

The list of items being threaded through the standards process includes

- Library interfaces, including common shared libraries
- Configuration files
- System commands
- A common package format and installation guidelines
- An API for system interfaces
- Filesystem hierarchy standards

As of this writing, LSB 3.1, released in mid-2006, incorporates the ISO standard LSB core (ISO/IEC 23360) and for the first time also includes desktop functionality which standardizes the Gtk and Qt GUI toolkits. The Chinese government, which is creating a national standard for Linux in China, has signed an agreement to base their standard Linux on the LSB.

Sadly, no vendor has released an LSB-compliant application—not one. It's a great idea with good industry support that has gone nowhere.

POSIX

POSIX, an offshoot of the IEEE that charges for copies of their standards, has engaged itself for the last several years in defining a general standard for UNIX. Their major effort in the past has been focused on the commands and system call or library interfaces. Linux is POSIX compliant and tracks the POSIX standards.

ITIL: the Information Technology Interface Library

This is a procedural standard rather than a technical standard for Linux, but it's one that is relevant to larger IT shops.

Back in the 1980s, the ITIL system was developed in England to help manage mainframe computers and software development at large sites. The focus was on processes rather than people so that tasks within the organization could be executed consistently no matter who quit or went on vacation. Twelve functional areas were identified that mapped pretty well to the high-level IT needs of most European companies (disaster recovery, change control, capacity planning, etc.).

ITIL lay dormant until the Internet sparked the birth of information technology as a mandatory component of most organizations. Large organizations need some structure in their IT processes, and ITIL is no worse than any other structure. Industry best practices were defined for each of the ITIL areas.

To tame the chaos, ITIL classifies every operational IT event or activity as a "change," an "incident" (some kind of unexpected event), or a "problem" (something to be fixed in the long term).

There is now an ISO standard (ISO 20000) that is similar to ITIL, so you will occasionally see sites advertising themselves as being ITIL or ISO compliant. Typically, the ITIL/ISO model isn't quite right for your organization and you hire a consulting house to customize it. Several of the commercial trouble ticketing systems mentioned on page 937 claim partial ITIL compliance.

Many large corporations operating in the U.S. are looking to ITIL to help them solve their database and system administration problems related to the Sarbanes-Oxley Act. See page 956 for more information about SOX.

COBIT: Control Objectives for Information and related Technology

Like ITIL, COBIT is a framework for information management and is based on industry best practices. COBIT's mission is "to research, develop, publicize, and promote an authoritative, up-to-date, international set of generally accepted information technology control objectives for day-to-day use by business managers and auditors."

COBIT is a child of the Information Systems Audit and Control Association (ISACA) and the IT Governance Institute (ITGI). See www.isaca.org/cobit for details.

The first edition of the framework was published in 1996, and we are now at version 4.0, published in 2005. This latest iteration was strongly influenced by the requirements of the Sarbanes-Oxley Act. It includes 34 high-level objectives that cover 215 "control objectives" categorized into four domains: Plan and Organize, Acquire and Implement, Deliver and Support, and Monitor and Evaluate. (Hey wait, isn't that eight domains?)

30.15 LINUX CULTURE

In the 1980s and 90s you could differentiate PC users from Mac users by their level of intensity. PC users found their computers a useful tool, but Mac users loved theirs. A Mac user's computer was a member of the family, like a favorite pet.

The same intensity that pervaded the Mac world is now very strong in the Linux community. Linux users don't just like their systems—they are ready to do battle to defend them, fix them, and make them better and faster and more secure than a Windows box ever dreamed of being. Energy is pouring into Linux at an amazing rate, and Linux culture has its own ethics, myths, gods, and heroes.

A group of Linux enthusiasts from the Bergen Linux User Group in Bergen, Norway, were intrigued by one of the April Fools' Day RFCs from the IETF: RFC1149, *A Standard for the Transmission of IP Datagrams on Avian Carriers*. This RFC defines the Carrier Pigeon Internet Protocol (CPIP), which the team implemented with a neighbor's flock of pigeons. Here is a test of their implementation (taken from the project site at blug.linux.no/rfc1149):

```
Script started on Sat Apr 28 11:24:09 2001
vegard@gyversalen:~$ /sbin/ifconfig tun0
tun0     Link encap:Point-to-Point Protocol
         inet addr:10.0.3.2  P-t-P:10.0.3.1  Mask:255.255.255.255
         UP POINTOPOINT RUNNING NOARP MULTICAST  MTU:150  Metric:1
         RX packets:1 errors:0 dropped:0 overruns:0 frame:0
         TX packets:2 errors:0 dropped:0 overruns:0 carrier:0
         collisions:0
         RX bytes:88 (88.0 b)  TX bytes:168 (168.0 b)

vegard@gyversalen:~$ ping -i 900 10.0.3.1 [13]
PING 10.0.3.1 (10.0.3.1): 56 data bytes
64 bytes from 10.0.3.1: icmp_seq=0 ttl=255 time=6165731.1 ms
64 bytes from 10.0.3.1: icmp_seq=4 ttl=255 time=3211900.8 ms
64 bytes from 10.0.3.1: icmp_seq=2 ttl=255 time=5124922.8 ms
64 bytes from 10.0.3.1: icmp_seq=1 ttl=255 time=6388671.9 ms

--- 10.0.3.1 ping statistics ---
9 packets transmitted, 4 packets received, 55% packet loss
round-trip min/avg/max = 3211900.8/5222806.6/6388671.9 ms
vegard@gyversalen:~$ exit

Script done on Sat Apr 28 14:14:28 2001
```

One might say that these folks had too much time on their hands, but it's exactly this kind of creativity and enthusiasm that make the open source movement (and Linux's part in it) so powerful and so much fun. Linux rocks.

---

13. Note the appropriate use of RFC1918 private address space. Clearly, a pigeon-based NAT implementation would be needed to connect the test network to the outside world.

30.16 MAINSTREAM LINUX

Linux is currently the fastest -growing operating system, and it runs on everything from mainframes to wristwatches. However, it's beginning to suffer a bit from the incompatibilities and minor differences that hampered UNIX in its heyday.

It used to be common to hear statements such as "Oh, we can't use Linux—it's not supported!" in corporate circles. But the world has been changing fast enough to worry Microsoft. Linux is sneaking its way into the business world. It often arrives first with newly hired students who have used Linux in college and who run it either openly or surreptitiously on their desktop machines. After establishing a beachhead, Linux often becomes the preferred platform for mail or web servers, where its security, performance, and scalability make it preferable to proprietary solutions from Microsoft. Cost of ownership is also a big plus on the Linux side.

The "free" in free software has two meanings: free as in free beer—you don't have to pay for it—and free as in having relatively few limits on what you are allowed to do with it. The GNU Public License enforces both of these meanings, and this fact scares some corporate IT departments. Derivatives of GPL-licensed works inherit the GPL stipulations if you distribute them. Some managers view Linux developers as long-haired hippies and greet the GPL with fear, uncertainty, and doubt. But Linux seems to be winning them over, slowly but surely.

For the last few years, www.distrowatch.com has ranked the top 100 Linux distributions based on visitors to their web site. There is quite a bit of churn in the relative positions of our five example distributions. Table 30.3 shows some of the numbers.

Table 30.3   Distrowatch.com popularity rankings over time (as of 9/06)

Distro	past 6 mo	past 12 mo	2005	2004	2003
Ubuntu	1	1	1	13	–
SUSE	2	2	3	4	7
Fedora	3	4	4	2	–
Debian	7	7	6	5	5
Red Hat	29	24	23	12	2

The actual number of hits per day typically ranges from less than 100 to more than 3,000. More than anything, these rankings clearly show the rise of Ubuntu and the split between Red Hat Enterprise Linux and Fedora.

Major corporate players are now shipping and supporting the development of Linux: IBM, Hewlett-Packard, Silicon Graphics, and Sun, to name a few. It has been interesting to observe the marriage between these huge, sluggish software shops and a Linux culture driven by young, inexperienced software engineers whose energy often more than makes up for their rough edges. IBM has had to undergo a major paradigm shift to adapt to life in the anarchistic open source world of Linux. It has contributed by porting its extensive libraries of well-tested code. See ibm.com/linux and ibm.com/developerworks/opensource for more information.

SGI started the Linux Test Project, a series of test suites and stress testing methods that validate the reliability, robustness, and stability of Linux. IBM now maintains it. The latest release (June 2006 at the time of this writing) includes over 2,900 tests, plus documentation and testing tools.

The Linux Documentation Project (www.tldp.org) provides documentation at many levels of technical expertise, including longish introductory booklets, FAQs, HOW-TOs for various common chores, and man pages for all the Linux core commands and packages.[14] The LDP also supports two online magazines, *Linux Gazette* and *Linux Focus*. All the documentation is available without charge over the Internet.

At least one provider of computer intrusion insurance recognizes Linux's robustness in its pricing and charges 5% to 15% less to insure Linux web servers than to insure equivalent Microsoft systems. An August, 2001, ZDNet article made the following comments.[15]

> "Insurance broker J.S. Wurzler Underwriting Managers has started charging up to 15 percent more in premiums to clients that use Microsoft's Internet Information Server software, which the Code Red worm feasted on... Wurzler, who has been selling hacker insurance since 1998, based his decision on more than 400 security analyses done by his firm over the past three years. Wurzler found that system administrators working on open source systems tend to be better trained and stay with their employers longer than those at firms using Windows software."

Of our five example distributions, two are supported by large commercial organizations: Red Hat by itself and SUSE by Novell; Ubuntu is supported by a small company founded by South African Mark Shuttleworth called Canonical Ltd. Debian and Fedora are the little guys for now.

Within the Linux community, something of a schism has developed between Debian and the more enterprise-targeted distributions such as Red Hat and SUSE. Debian folks have had trouble having their good ideas taken seriously and incorporated into the standardization efforts of the LSB. We hope that the recent popularity of Ubuntu will help to integrate Debian a bit more solidly into the Linux mainstream.

The CentOS (Community ENTerprise Operating System) distribution, based in England, is gaining popularity in environments that want a stable Linux system without Red Hat's involvement. It's essentially a clone of Red Hat Enterprise Linux. The GPL requires Red Hat to make its software patches available to the public. The CentOS folks patch the source trees, remove Red Hat logos and trademarks, and

---

14. The web site used to be linuxdoc.org, but an internal scandal involving a forgetful or malicious webmaster, disputes over the ownership of the name, and a copycat commercial web site called linuxdoc.com all motivated the project to change its domain.

15. www.zdnet.com/zdnn/stories/news/0,4586,2805929,00.html

rebuild the distribution from scratch, yielding something similar to RHEL without cost or support contracts. Of course, support is nothing to sneeze at, and RHEL is guaranteed to be supported for 7 years—close to an eternity in the Linux world.

For most companies, total cost of ownership is important, too. Most distributions are free to start with, and they're also cheaper to maintain thanks to their inherent manageability over the network. Windows XP Professional currently costs about $250/seat just for the OS. Once applications have been added on, the price tag for a large company can be daunting. Google.com currently runs on hundreds of thousands of Linux boxes; imagine buying a Windows license for each of those machines.

Software piracy is rampant in the Far East. In an effort to "clean up their act," the Chinese government has endorsed Linux over Windows because it is open source and therefore not piratable. There are several Linux distributions with Chinese language capabilities. Red Flag Linux is one of the best known and boasts over 200 million users.

Linux is used by many branches of the U.S. government, including NASA, NERSC, NIH, NOAA, and USGS. It's also used at the Fermilab, Los Alamos, Oak Ridge, and Sandia National Laboratories. Many of the most powerful computers today are still big-iron systems, but Beowulf clusters (see www.beowulf.org) of Linux machines are catching up. In September 2004, IBM announced that it had produced the world's then fastest supercomputer, a cluster of 16,250 CPUs in only eight racks of space, running under Linux at a sustained performance of 36 teraflops.[16]

30.17 ORGANIZATIONS, CONFERENCES, AND OTHER RESOURCES

Many UNIX and Linux support groups—both general and vendor specific—help you network with other people that are using the same software. Table 30.4 presents a brief list of organizations. Plenty of national and regional groups exist that are not listed in this table.

Some of the organizations hold conferences dedicated to Linux-related topics, although most conferences are broader than just Linux or UNIX and include tracks and events for Windows, too.

Linux International and the Linux Professional Institute promote Linux in various ways—LI through marketing efforts to bring Linux into the business community (and to fund some of the open source development efforts) and LPI through its Linux system administrator certification program, discussed in the next section.

LI's web site has some good fodder for managers who are reluctant to use open source operating systems. They sponsor a Linux booth at several trade shows, including LinuxWorld, Linux Expo, and CeBit. LI is also leading an internationalization project to bring all the world's character sets to Linux. Their summer internship program matches students with Linux developers to give the students hands-on experience writing production-quality code.

---

16. A teraflop is one trillion floating-point calculations per second.

Table 30.4   Linux and UNIX organizations

Name	URL	What it is
LPI	www.lpi.org	Linux Professional Institute
LI	www.li.org	Linux International, may become a user group
FSF	www.fsf.org	Free Software Foundation, sponsor of the GNU project
OSDL	www. osdl.org	Open Source Development Lab, for developers
USENIX	www.usenix.org	UNIX users group, quite technical
SAGE	www.sage.org	The System Administrators Guild associated with USENIX; holds the LISA conference each year
LOPSA	www.lopsa.org	League of Professional System Administrators, a spinoff from USENIX/SAGE
SANS	www.sans.org	Runs sysadmin and security conferences; less technical than SAGE with a focus on tutorials
EUROPEN	www.europen.org	Used to be the United Nations of national user groups, but now largely defunct; remnants remain in NLUUG, DUUG, UKUUG, GUUG and others
AUUG	www.auug.org.au	Australian UNIX Users Group, covers both technical and managerial aspects of computing
SAGE-AU	www.sage-au.org.au	Australian SAGE, holds yearly conferences in Oz
SANE	www.sane.nl	System Administration and Network Engineering group holds yearly conferences in northern Europe

Linux International is winding down now that its objective of bringing Linux into the corporate world has been accomplished. LI may turn into a Linux user group of some sort in the near future.

FSF, the Free Software Foundation, is the sponsor of the GNU ("GNU's Not Unix," a recursive acronym) project. The "free" in the FSF's name is the "free" of free speech and not that of free beer. The FSF is also the origin of the GNU Public License, which covers the majority of Linux software. GPLv3 is now under development and drafts are available for public comment.

OSDL, the Open Source Development Lab, is a nonprofit group whose goal is to accelerate the deployment of Linux in the corporate enterprise arena. OSDL is supported by the major Linux customers and provides testing and technical support for the Linux development community.

Conferences and trade shows

Table 30.5 lists details for the three yearly Linux development conferences.

Table 30.5   Linux development conferences

Conference	URL	Length	Where
Linux Symposium	www.linuxsymposium.org	4 days	Ottawa, Canada
linux.conf.au	linux.conf.au	5 days	Australia
Linux Kongress	www.linux-kongress.org	4 days	Germany

The Ottawa conference, usually held in August, includes three tracks of papers and a parallel tutorial track. The Australian development conference offers tutorials, seminars, keynotes, and mini-conferences, one of which is dedicated to system administration. The conference is held in various Australian cities, usually in January. The German conference, Linux Kongress, includes two days of tutorials and two days of technical presentations, mostly in English. It moves around Germany and is most often held in September.

Linux Weekly News, lwn.net, is an online magazine devoted to Linux. It was started by Elizabeth Coolbaugh and Jonathan Corbet in 1997. It is supported by subscriptions, with members getting immediate access to all articles and nonmembers having to wait a week or so. The subscription rate varies depending on your category. "Starving hacker" is cheapest at $2.50/month, followed by "professional hacker" at $5/month and "project leader" at $10/month.

USENIX, an organization of users of Linux, UNIX, and other open source operating systems, holds one general conference and several specialized (smaller) conferences or workshops each year. The general conference has a parallel track devoted to open systems that features ongoing OS development in the Linux and BSD communities.

The big event for sysadmins is the USENIX LISA (Large Installation System Administration) conference held in late fall. Trade shows are often associated with these conferences.

For the last several years, USENIX has also dedicated one of its workshops to Linux kernel development as a service to the Linux community. Access to this two-day event is by invitation only.

SAGE, USENIX's System Administrators Guild, is the first international organization for system administrators. It promotes system administration as a profession by sponsoring conferences and informal programs. See www.sage.org for all the details.

In 2005, a falling out between USENIX and SAGE left the future of SAGE in doubt. The result was that some of the old-timers in the SAGE organization formed a separate organization called LOPSA, the League of Professional System Administrators, www.lopsa.org. They don't yet hold conferences but might start soon. SAGE had a sysadmin certification program, but has given it up; hopefully, LOPSA will pick it up.

Many local areas have regional UNIX, Linux, or open systems user groups. Some of these are affiliated with USENIX and some are not. The local groups usually have regular meetings, workshops with local or visiting speakers, and often dinner together before or after the meetings. They're a good way to network with other sysadmins in your area.

The biggest Linux trade show is the LinuxWorld Expo conference and exposition, which is now held once a year in the United States, usually in San Francisco in the fall. It is also repeated in Europe and Asia throughout the year; coming up are events in Beijing, Moscow, and Singapore.

The premier trade show for the networking industry is Interop; its tutorial series is also of high quality. Interop used to be an annual event that was eagerly awaited by techies and vendors alike. Interops now happens several times a year—a traveling network circus, so to speak. The salaries of tutorial speakers have been cut in half, but the quality of the tutorials seems to have survived.

LPI: the Linux Professional Institute

The LPI certifies Linux system administrators. That is, it administers tests that measure a sysadmin's competence and knowledge of various Linux tasks. Three levels of certification are available, each of which consists of a two-part test. The tests so far (Levels 1 and 2) are in a multiple-choice or short-answer format and are administered over the web by Vue Electronic Testing Service (www.vue.com/lpi).

Level 1 seems to cover Linux power-user commands and very basic sysadmin tasks. Level 2 is more in-depth and includes networking. Level 3 is defined but has not yet been fully developed. Sadly, the status of Level 3 has not changed since the last edition of this book five years ago. The LPI web site (www.lpi.org) outlines the kinds of knowledge expected at each level of certification and provides sample questions from each of the tests.

Certification is important and hard to do well. System administration is a hands-on type of science (or is it an art?). A multiple-choice test, while easy to administer and grade, is not very good at measuring the problem-solving skills that are the hallmark of a good sysadmin. We hope that Level 3 of the LPI suite will involve a hands-on lab component, more like the Cisco CCIE certification than the Microsoft MCSE exam.

Red Hat and SUSE have their own certification programs. Ubuntu's certification is currently piggybacking on top of the LPI certification.

Mailing lists and web resources

Sysadmins have access to a huge variety of mailing lists and web search engines. We list some of our favorites in Chapter 1, *Where to Start*. In addition, an extensive list of Linux-related mailing lists is available from www.linux.org/docs/lists.html.

For Linux-specific issues, a Linux-specific Google search can be quite effective. Go to www.google.com/linux and see how well it works.

There are also mailing lists that focus on particular distributions; Table 30.6 shows some specifics for our example distributions.

Table 30.6 Distribution-specific mailing lists

Distro	URL
Red Hat	www.redhat.com/mailing-lists
Fedora	www.redhat.com/mailing-lists
SUSE	www.suse.com/us/support/online_help/mailinglists/
Debian	www.debian.org/MailingLists/
Ubuntu	lists.ubuntu.com

Red Hat hosts a zillion mailing lists that cover both the Enterprise Linux and Fedora distributions; www.redhat.com/mailing-lists includes the list name and a brief summary of each. In addition to the URL shown in the table, SUSE also has mailing list info at www.suse.com/us/business/mailinglists.html. Archives of these lists can be found at lists.suse.com/archives.

Sysadmin surveys

SAGE, the System Administrators Guild associated with the USENIX Association, and SANS, the System Administration, Networking, and Security Institute, perform annual surveys focused mainly on the compensation of system administrators, but including other topics as well. The surveys are available from www.sage.org/salsurv and www.sans.org/salary2005. Recent SAGE surveys (50–60 pages) are available only to members; old ones can be downloaded by anyone. The SANS URL yields only a five-page PDF summary of the results of their most recent survey.

Some of the statistics gathered are

- Salary data: median salary, raise history, bonuses, and overtime pay
- Platform mix
- Hours worked per week
- Market demand for system administrators
- Experience level, education level, years on the job
- Geographic, sex, and age distribution of administrators
- Most bothersome and most appreciated parts of the job

It's interesting to see how your organization compares to the industry as portrayed by these results. However, the survey data must be interpreted carefully. The results are influenced by local conditions and the state of the economy. Salaries, costs of living, and tax rates can vary widely among countries or even regions.

30.18 RECOMMENDED READING

Infrastructure

TRAUGOTT, STEVE. "Bootstrapping and Infrastructure." Boston: LISA 1998. www.infrastructures.org/papers/bootstrap/bootstrap.html

SCHWEIKERT, DAVID. "ISGTC: an alternative to ~bofh/bin." Amsterdam, Netherlands: SANE 2004. isg.ee.ethz.ch/publications/papers/isgtc-sane.pdf

OETIKER, TOBIAS. "TemplateTree II: The Post-Installation Setup Tool." San Diego, CA: LISA 2001. isg.ee.ethz.ch/tools/tetre2/pub/tetre-lisa.pdf

BURGESS, MARK S. *Principles of Network and System Administration (2nd Edition).* Hoboken, NJ: Wiley, 2003.

Many of the tools and concepts described in the management section of this chapter can be found at isg.ee.ethz.ch/tools.

Management

Management

LIMONCELLI, THOMAS A., AND CHRISTINE HOGAN. *The Practice of System and Network Administration.* Boston, MA: Addison-Wesley, 2001.

This book has an associated web site, www.everythingsysadmin.com, that is also interesting. A new edition is due in 2007.

MACHIAVELLI, NICCOLÒ. *The Prince.* 1513. Available on-line from www.gutenberg.org/etext/1232

LIMONCELLI, THOMAS A. *Time Management for System Administrators.* Sebastopol, CA: O'Reilly Media, 2005.

BROOKS, FREDERICK P., JR. *The Mythical Man-Month: Essays on Software Engineering.* Reading, MA: Addison-Wesley, 1995.

A wonderful little book, originally published in the 1975 and still mostly true.

McCONNELL, STEVE. *Software Project Survival Guide: How to Be Sure Your First Important Project Isn't Your Last.* Redmond, WA: Microsoft Press, 1998.

This book is written in a lively manner and has good content throughout.

Pressman, Roger S. *Software Engineering: A Practitioner's Approach (6th Edition).* Boston, MA: McGraw-Hill, 2005.

SOMMERVILLE, IAN. *Software Engineering (8th Edition).* New York, NY: Addison-Wesley, 2006.

The site www.itil-toolkit.com is a good place to start if you seek to understand the mountains of jargon and management-speak associated with ITIL processes and standards.

Policy and security

RFC2196, *Site Security Handbook,* and its predecessor, RFC1244. The contents are rather different, so it's worth reviewing both versions.

Local policies, standards, and procedures for the San Diego Supercomputer Center are available from security.sdsc.edu/help/SGs.shtml. This is a great collection of policy documents, but it has gone a couple of years without an update.

Legal issues, patents, and privacy

The web site of the Electronic Frontier Foundation, eff.org, is a great place to find commentary on the latest issues in privacy, cryptography, and legislation. Always interesting reading.

www.groklaw.net is a great site for news of legal issues related to information technology. Issues are described and summarized in English rather than lawyer-speak.

General industry news

slashdot.org is a good source for technology news but is often a day or two behind sources like the security mailing lists.

HARROW, JEFFREY R. *The Harrow Technology Report*. www.theharrowgroup.com

This site hosts some interesting articles about technology-related issues. It's a combination of news and editorial content. J. R. Harrow is the author of the defunct periodical *The Rapidly Changing Face of Computing* that was formerly published by Compaq. The web site was maintained until the end of 2005.

www.heise.de is a great site for news. It's in German, but www.heise.de/english provides an English translation.

www.theregister.co.uk or www.theregister.com is a good IT news site.

30.19 EXERCISES

E30.1   What are your organization's recurring procedures? Which ones are infrequently performed and reinvented each time? Which ones are risky?

E30.2   What are your dependencies on external providers? Do you need and have a plan B? Explain why or why not. Describe plan B if it exists.

E30.3   Briefly interview several internal customers to determine their expectations with respect to the availability of the computing infrastructure. Are the expectations consistent? Are they reasonable? Are they consistent with the system administration group's stated goals?

E30.4   What organized infrastructure for system management is already established at your site? Identify the pieces that are still missing.

E30.5   One of your co-workers is going to leave for lunch tomorrow and never return, but you don't yet know which one. What critical procedures might be affected, and how prepared is your organization to cover for the missing staff member? What documentation would have to exist in order to avoid a service disruption?

E30.6   What would happen if *you* didn't come in for the next three months? How much would your colleagues hate you when you finally came back, and why? What can you do in the next two weeks to reduce the trauma of such an event?

E30.7   Your boss orders you to cut the system administration budget by 30% by the end of the current year. Can you quantify the consequences of this cut? Present a summary that will allow the boss to make an informed decision regarding which services to reduce or discontinue.

⋆ **E30.8**   Who are some of the current major corporate supporters of Linux? What are their interests and motivations? What sort of contributions are they making?

⋆ **E30.9**   You are cleaning up after a disk crash and notice files in the **lost+found** directory. When you investigate further, you find that some of the files are mail messages that were sent between two students who are setting up a back door around the department firewall to archive MP3 files on a remote file server. What should you do? Are there policies or regulations in place that cover such incidents?

⋆⋆ **E30.10** Evaluate your site's local documentation for new users, sysadmins, standard procedures, and emergencies.

⋆⋆ **E30.11** Forecast the future of the various commercial and free UNIX and Linux variants over the next five years. How will the current development and distribution models hold up over time? What will be the long-term impact of the adoption of Linux by hardware vendors? Differentiate between the server and desktop markets.

Management

Index

We have alphabetized files under their last components. And in most cases, *only* the last component is listed. For example, to find index entries relating to the **/etc/passwd** file, look under **passwd**. Our friendly Linux distributors have forced our hand by hiding standard files in new and inventive directories on each system.

A

A DNS records 396, 407
A6 DNS records 404
AAAA DNS records 404
Abell, Vic 74
access agents, email 533
access control lists *see* ACLs
access database, **sendmail** 589, 591–594
accounts *see* user accounts
ACLs, DNS 429–430, 451–453
ACLs, filesystem 88–92, 833
ACLs, firewall 701–708
Adams, Rick 320
address match lists, BIND 422
Address Resolution Protocol (ARP) 275, 296–297, 315
addresses, email 95, 535
addresses, Ethernet (aka MAC) 280, 292
addresses, IP *see* IP addresses
addresses, SCSI 117
adjtimex system call 903
ADSM/TSM backup system 197
agetty process 855–858
aio daemon 894
air conditioning 796–798
AirPort 360
AIT backup tapes 166
Albitz, Paul 423

aliases file 106, 545–551
aliases, email 544–551
   see also email
   see also **sendmail**
   abuse 548, 594
   distribution 156
   examples 548
   file format 545
   global 95
   hashed database 551
   loops 546, 550
   and mailing lists 551–554
   for new users 95
   postmaster 545
   root 548
aliases.db file 551
alien 235
Allman, Eric 209, 530, 558, 566, 595
allow-recursion option, DNS 425
allow-update clause, DNS 433, 450
always_add_domain feature, **sendmail** 575
Amanda backup system 197
amavisd email virus filter 637
amd 895
American Power Conversion (APC) 799
American Registry for Internet Numbers (ARIN) 288–289, 293, 371
Amstadt, Bob 825
Anaconda 226

anacron 156, 887
Analog Apache log analyzer 727
Anderson, Paul 261
anonymous FTP *see* FTP
Anvin, H. Peter 225
Apache *see* web hosting
Apache Software Foundation 12, 724
/etc/apache2 directory 724
APC (American Power Conversion) 799
APNIC (Asia-Pacific Network Information Center) 383
appropriate use policies (AUPs) 954
APT, software tool 241–246
apt-ftparchive 244
apt-get 241–246
apt-proxy 244
ARIN (American Registry for Internet Numbers) 288–289, 293, 371
ARK language 262
Armstrong, Jason 620
ARP (Address Resolution Protocol) 275, 296–297, 315
arp command 296
ARPANET 272
Arusha Project 261
Asia-Pacific Network Information Center (APNIC) 383
at 887
AT&T Bell Labs 5
ata daemon 894

ATA/ATAPI interface *see* IDE
ATAPI CD-ROM device names 873
atd 887
Athena, Project 741
Atkins, Todd 220
ATM networks 362–363
auth.log file 206
authors, contacting xxxvi
/etc/auto.master file 497–498
autofs script 497
automount daemon 497–499, 895
automounters
    amd 895
    automount 497–499, 895
    configuration 498–500
    NFS and 497–500
    Windows 834
autonomous systems 340
AutoYaST 230
AUUG group 965
avoid-v4-udp-ports option, DNS 427
AWStats Apache log analyzer 727

B

backspace vs. delete keys 859
backup software and systems
  see also backups
  see also Bacula
  ADSM/TSM 197
  Amanda 197
  Bacula 179–196
  commercial systems 197–198
  cpio 178
  dd 178
  dump/restore 169–176
  tar 177–178
  Veritas 198
backups 158–198
  see also backup software and systems
  see also Bacula
  see also media, backup
  compression 164
  of a damaged disk 133
  designing data for 163
  disaster planning 939
  filesystem size 161
  fitting on media 160
  full restore 175–176
  hints 159–163

backups *continued*
  incremental 170
  interval between 159
  off-site storage 161
  programs 177–197
  to removable disks 165
  restoring 173–177, 939
  schedules 171–173
  security 161, 686
  setting up 169–176
  for ugrades 176–177
  when to make 162
  for Windows 197
Bacula 179–196
  see also Bacula configuration files
  architecture 180
  client file daemon 188
  daemons, starting 189
  installation 181–182
  manual backup 190–192
  media pools 190
  restoring files 192–195
  troubleshooting 195–196
Bacula configuration files 182–189
  see also Bacula
  /etc/bacula directory 182
  /etc/bacula-dir.conf file 183–187
  /etc/bacula/bacula-fd.conf file 189
  bacula-sd.conf file 187
  bconsole.conf file 188
bad blocks, disk 123
Bailey, Mick 885
Baretta, Anne 860
bash shell 4, 32, 98
.bash_profile file 105
.bashrc file 105
Bastille Linux 710
baud rate 863
BCP documents 275
Beowulf clusters 964
Bergen Linux User Group 961
Berkeley DB library 169, 253–254, 551, 560, 577, 628
Berkeley Internet Name Domain system *see* BIND
Berkeley UNIX 5
BGP routing protocol 339
bidirectional modems 864
/bin directory 75

BIND
  see also DNS
  see also name servers
  see also **named**
  ACLs 451–453
  address match lists 422
  client configuration 418–420
  components 411
  configuration 420–446
  configuration examples 439–446
  configuration files 421–423
  debugging 466–478
  distribution-specific information 478–481
  DNSSEC 387, 456–463
  .key DNSSEC key file 454
  dnssec-keygen 454, 458
  dnssec-signzone 460–461
  doc (domain obscenity control) 476–478
  documentation 481–482
  forwarding zone, configuring 436
  hardware requirements 421
  incremental zone transfers 388, 429, 447
  ISC configuration example 444
  keys, generating 458
  KSK (key signing key) 458, 460
  localhost zone configuration example 439
  logging 411, 432, 446, 466–471
  loopback address 437
  master server, configuring 433
  /etc/named directory 424
  /etc/named.conf file 421–446, 450–451, 470, 480–481
  named-checkconf 421, 455, 478
  named-checkzone 421, 478
  nanny script 446
  notification options 424
  nsupdate 449
  performance 478
  .private DNSSEC key file 454
  query forwarding 427
  /etc/resolv.conf file 418–420
  resolver testing 420
  rndc 436–438, 447, 471–473
  /etc/rndc.conf file 437
  /etc/rndc.key file 437
  rndc-confgen 437
  root server hints 435
  root.cache file 435

BIND *continued*
  security 417, 424, 451–464
  shell interfaces *see* **dig** and
    nslookup
  signed zones, creating 458
  slave server, configuring 434
  split DNS 438–439, 441–444
  statistics 473
  stub zones, configuring 434
  /etc/syslog.conf file 466
  updating zone files 447–450
  versions 410–411
  zone transfers 413, 425, 447–448
BIOSes 25–26
  bootstrapping and IDE 113
  on SCSI cards 134
black hole lists, spam 598, 635
blackhole option, DNS 428
Blandy, Jim 253
block device files 77, 79, 871
blocking factor, tape 177
bogus directive, DNS 431
/boot directory 75
boot loaders 23, 26–31, 124, 138
  GRUB 26–28, 30, 32
  LILO 28–29, 31–32
  multibooting 30
boot.log file 207
boot.msg file 206
BOOTP protocol 312
/etc/bootparams file 899
bootstrapping 21–25
  automatic vs. manual 22
  device probing 23
  directly to **bash** 37
  filesystem checking 132
  fsck and 25
  kernel initialization 23
  kernel options 29
  kernel threads 23
  mounting NFS filesystems 495
  multibooting 30–31
  options 883
  PC-specific issues 25
  single-user mode 22, 24–25, 31–
    33
  startup scripts 32–40
  /etc/sysconfig directory 37–38
breakout boxes 865
broadcast addresses 281
broadcast domain 352
broadcast storms 301, 357
browsers, web 720
BSD (Berkeley UNIX) 6

BSD FFS filesystem 120
BugTraq 713
Burgess, Mark 260
bus errors 58
BUS signal 58
butt blocks (RJ-45 connectors) 851
byte swapping 178

C

CA (Certificate Authority) 731
cable modems 365
cables
  see also connectors
  10*Base* 352–355
  Category * 352–355, 366
  DB-9 to DB-25 848
  Ethernet 278, 353–355
  IDE 114
  labeling 370, 934
  mini DIN-8 to DB-25 848
  modem 846
  null modem 846–847
  RJ-45 to DB-25 850
  SATA 114
  SCSI 115–117
  serial, length limits 853
  STP 844
  straight-through 846
  UTP 844
  Yost RJ-45 standard 850–852
Cacti performance monitoring tool
  664
CAIDA (Cooperative Association
  for Internet Data Analysis) 291,
  402
Card, Rémy 120
ccTLDs 379
cdebconf 231
cdebootstrap 231
CentOS 7
Cerf, Vint 273
CERT 712
Certificate Authority (CA) 731
Certificate Signing Request (CSR)
  731
Certified Information Systems Au-
  ditor (CISA) 675
cf/cf directory, **sendmail** 568
cfengine 260
CGI scripting 722
chage password aging program 680
ChaosNet 390

Chapman, Brent 552
character device files 77, 79, 871
chat 325
chat scripts, PPP 323, 326–328
Chatsworth Products 799
chattr 87
checklists, system administration
  943
checksendmail 617
chfn 98
chgrp 86
chkconfig 36, 39, 520
chmod 81, 84–86, 89
chown 86
chroot
  for FTP 735
  for **named** 451, 453
  for Postfix 625
  for **sendmail** 607
chsh 98–99
ci, RCS check in 249–250
CIA triad 673
CIDR (Classless Inter-Domain
  Routing) 283, 286–288
CIFS *see* Samba
CIM (Common Information Module) system configuration 262
CISA (Certified Information Systems Auditor) 675
Cisco routers 346–348, 701, 714
CiscoWorks 667
CISSP (Certified Information Systems Security Professional) 674
clocks, synchronization 902
clone system call 56
closelog routine 218–220
CNAME DNS records 399
co, RCS check out 249, 251
COBIT (Control Objectives for Information and related Technology) 960
commands, finding 15
commands, scheduling 150–157
Computer Systems Research Group
  (CSRG) 5
concentrators *see* Ethernet, hubs
confCOPY_ERRORS_TO option,
  sendmail 569
.config file for kernel 877–878
configuration files
  copying 505–511
  pulling 510
  pushing 505–510
  sharing 502–526

ConnectionRateThrottle option,
   sendmail 608
connectors
   see also cables 843
   DB-25 844–847
   DB-9 848
   IDE 113
   mini DIN-8 847
   RJ-45 849
   RS-232 to USB adapters 865
   SCSI 115–117
console emulators 859
/dev/console file 218
console, logging to 218
CONT signal 58, 61, 68
contacting the authors xxxvi
control characters
   in filenames 77
   and the terminal driver 859–861
control terminal 56
controls statement, DNS 436–438
conventions used in this book 9–10
cookies, NFS 486
cooling systems 940
Cooper, Mendel 11
Cooperative Association for Internet Data Analysis (CAIDA) 402
copyright issues 950
Corbet, Jonathan 325
core files 154
Council of European National Top-
   level Domain Registries 383
country code top-level domains 379
cpio 178
CPIP 961
CPU
   load averages 808
   statistics 808
   usage, analyzing 806–809, 813
cracklib 682
cron daemon 150–156, 887
   common uses 154–156
   configuration (crontab) files
      151–153, 887
   logs 151
   management 153
   skipped commands 156
   to automate logging 201
/etc/cron.allow file 153
/etc/cron.deny file 153
crond *see* **cron** daemon
crontab command 153
crontab files 151–153, 887
crypt library routine 679

Crypto-Gram newsletter 713
cryptography
   DES algorithm 679
   Diffie-Hellman key exchange
      456, 679
   in DNS 387, 453–463
   IPsec 709
   in LDAP 526
   legal issues 949
   MD5 algorithm 96, 454
   password encryption 94, 96,
      542, 830
   public key 456
   in **sendmail** 603–610
   SSL 730
.cshrc file 105
CSLIP protocol 320
CSMA/CD (Ethernet) 351
CSR (Certificate Signing Request)
   731
CSRG (Computer Systems Research
   Group) 5
ctime file attribute 83
CTS (clear to send) signal 853
cu 864
CUPS 767–790, 894
   administration 772–780
   architecture 767–772
   command line utilities 779
   comparison to ATT/BSD print-
      ing 779
   compatibility commands 778
   configuration examples 775
   documentation 780
   filters 771–772
   HTTP and 769
   logging 781
   network printing 768
   PPD printer description files
      770–771
   print queues 767
   printer autoconfiguration 774
   printer classes 775
   printing a document 767
   removing a printer 776
   startup scripts 773, 780
   troubleshooting 780–782
/etc/cups directory 772
cupsd daemon 768, 780
/etc/cups/cupsd.conf file 768, 773,
   781
cupsdconf 773
CVS 251–253
Cygwin X server tools 823, 827

cylinders, disk 120
cyrus mailer 573

D

daemons
   see also individual daemon
     names
   booting 898
   configuration 898
   email 897
   kernel 893
   network 900–901
   NFS 895–896
   printing 894
   remote command execution 898
   remote login 898
   Samba 895–896
   sendmail queue runner 613
damaged filesystems 133
DARPA (Defense Advanced Research Project Agency) 272, 712
data center
   cooling 797
   power 798
   racks 799
   standards 800
   temperature monitoring 798
   tool box 800
   wiring tracks 799
data compression, modems 864
databases
   see also MySQL
   administrative 504, 511
   DNS 378, 389–409
   Foomatic printer database 771,
     782
   NIS 511–512
   sendmail 577–578, 591–594
   of supported USB devices 784
datasize option, DNS 426
date 203
Dawson, Terry 12
DB-25 connectors 844–847
DB-9 connectors 848
dbm/ndbm library 577
DCD (data carrier detect) signal
   852–853
DCE (Data Communications Equipment) interface 845–847
dd 133, 178
DDS/DAT tapes 166
.deb software package format 235

Debian network configuration 310
debian-installer 231
debugging *see* troubleshooting
DEC VT100 terminal 858
DeCSS 950
default route 305, 329, 336
DEFAULT_HOME variable in **log-in.defs** 98
DefaultUser option, **sendmail** 547, 603
DELAY_LA option, **sendmail** 608, 613
delegation-only option, DNS 429
delete vs. backspace keys 859
delivery agents, email 532
denial of service (DOS) attacks 213, 397, 511, 608, 817
Deraison, Renaud 690
DES encryption 679
desktop environments 757–759
/dev directory 75, 79, 870–872
device drivers 79, 868–870
 adding to kernel 878–880
 device awareness 880
 device numbers 870–872
 hot-plugging 882–883
 loadable modules 880–882
 MODULE_DEVICE_TABLE macro 880
 for PC hardware 870
 printer 765
 serial 872
 terminal and control characters 859–861
 Windows printer 838–839
device files 79
 attributes 84
 block vs. character 871
 creating 871
 for disks 122
 major/minor device numbers 870–872
 MAKEDEV script 79, 872
 names 872–873
 security 684
 for serial ports 853–855, 872
 for tape drives 171, 873
 udev 79
devices, pseudo 871
df 127, 494
DFS (Distributed File System, Windows) 834

DHCP (Dynamic Host Configuration Protocol) 311–314
 backward compatibility 312
 BIND and 449
 client configuration 314
 daemon 899
 duplicate addresses 314
 server configuration 313–314
dhcp.leases file 313–314
dhcpcd daemon 313–314
dhcpd daemon 899
/etc/dhcpd.conf file 313–314
dial-in modems 855
dial-out programs 864
dial-up networks *see* PPP protocol
Diffie-Hellman key exchange 456, 679
dig 408, 410, 435, 452, 473–476
Digital Millennium Copyright Act (DMCA) 950
directed broadcasts, network 317
directories 76–78
directories, copying 177
directory indexes 611
directory statement, DNS 424
disaster
 planning for 163, 939
 power supplies 940
 recovery 710–712, 938–943
diskless clients 232–234, 898
disks
 see also LVM, RAID, SATA, IDE, and SCSI
 as backup media 168
 boot loaders 124
 checking 131–133
 connecting 122
 device files for 122
 displaying free space 127
 failure and RAID 139
 Fibre Channel 112
 formatting 123
 geometry 119–120
 hot-swappable 112, 116, 145
 I/O analysis 813–815
 IDE 112–114, 118, 130
 installing 122–129, 133–138
 interfaces 111–119
 labels 124–125
 LBA (Logical Block Addressing) 112
 load balancing 805, 814

disks *continued*
 partitions 124–125, 134–136
 PATA *see* IDE
 performance 806–816
 performance tuning 130
 quotas 486
 RAID 805
 RAM 815
 reallocating storage space 146
 removable 165
 SCSI 112, 114–118
 Serial ATA *see* SATA
 swap space 812, 814
 testing 123
 tracks and sectors 120
 USB 112, 147–148, 165
DISPLAY variable 744, 748
displays (monitors) 794
distance-vector routing protocols 338
Distfile 506–508
Distributed Management Task Force (DMTF) 262
distributions, Linux 6–9, 962
 logos 10
 popularity 962
DIX Ethernet II 278
DMA, tuning 130
DMCA (Digital Millennium Copyright Act) 950
dmesg command 206
dmesg file 206
DMTF (Distributed Management Task Force) 262
DNAME DNS records 404
DNS 377–386
 see also BIND
 see also domain names, DNS
 see also name servers
 see also resource records, DNS
 see also zones, DNS
 adding a new machine 374–375
 anycast routing 424
 architecture 415–418
 asynchronous notification of zone changes 388
 authoritative servers 413, 416
 caching 384–386
 caching servers 413, 417
 use with CIDR 400–401
 client configuration 306
 CNAME hack 400–401

DNS *continued*
country code top-level domains 379
cryptography in 387, 453–463
database 378, 389–409
delegation 383
denial of service (DOS) attacks 397
design 415–418
doc (domain obscenity control) 476–478
domain names *see* domain names, DNS
dynamic updates 312, 448–450
EDNS0 protocol 389
efficiency 384–386
forward mapping 378, 382
forward zone files 378
fully qualified domain names 381
gTLDs (generic top-level domains) 378–379
history 375
implementations 376–377
in-addr.arpa domain 396
internationalization 388
IP addresses 374–375, 396–397
ip6.arpa for reverse IPv6 mappings 404
IPv6 support 404–405
ISP domain resgistration 381
lame delegations 469, 475–476
load balancing 385
lookups, **sendmail** 576
master name server 413
Microsoft and 464–466
namespace 378, 381, 415
negative answers 463
negative caching 385
nonauthoritative servers 413
nonrecursive servers 413
protocol 376, 386
public key cryptography 456
Punycode 388
query recursion 425
record types 391
recursive servers 413
referrals 414
resolver configuration 418–420
resolver library 414
resolver testing 420
resource records *see* resource records, DNS

DNS *continued*
reverse mapping 378, 382, 396–397, 405, 444
reverse zone files 378
RFCs 375–376, 482
root servers configuration file 383
round-robin 723
security 417, 424, 451–464
server architecture 418
server hints 414
service switch file 306–307
setup 415–418
slave server 413
SOA record serial number 393
SOA record shell interfaces 415
SOA record timeout values 393
spam, eliminating 403
SPF (Sender Policy Framework) pseudo-records 403
split DNS 438
stub servers 413
stub zones 408–409
subdomains 383
TKEY 453–456
top-level domains 378–379, 381
traceroute and 649
TSIG (transaction signatures) 444, 453–456
TTL harmonization 390
us domain 380
VeriSign Site Finder tool 429
ZSK (zone-signing keys) 458
DNSKEY DNS records 457–458
DNSSEC 387, 456–463
dnssec-keygen 454, 458
dnssec-signzone 460–461
doc (domain obscenity control), DNS 476–478
documentation
Linux 11–14
local 17, 930–934
sources 11–13
user 934
Doering, Gert 856
domain directive, DNS 420
DOMAIN macro, **sendmail** 572
domain names, DNS 378–383
case sensitivity 380
fully qualified 381
hierarchy 378
in-addr.arpa domain 396
internationalization 388
registration 371, 383

domain names, DNS *continued*
rules 378–383
second-level 383
selecting 382
squatting 380
subdomains 383
syntax 380
top-level 378, 381
trailing dot in 381
domainname 520
domains, setting up NIS 517–520
DontBlameSendmail option 603, 605
DOS (denial of service) attacks 397, 511, 608, 817
dot files 105–106
DoubleClick.net 951
dpkg 237
drivers directory, kernel source tree 879
drivers *see* device drivers
DS DNS records 458, 460
DSL networks 364–365
DSR (data set ready) signal 852–853
DTE (Data Terminal Equipment) interface 845–847
DTR (data terminal ready) signal 853
dual booting 30–31, 826
dump 123, 169–173
/etc/dumpdates file 170
dumps *see* backups
duplex, setting interface *see* **miitool**
DVD Copy Control Association 950
DVMRP protocol 343

E

e2label 127
ECN TCP option 307
EDITOR environment variable 103
EFF (Electronic Frontier Foundation) 958, 969
effective user IDs (EUIDs) 55
EIGRP protocol 339, 342
.emacs file 105
email
see also MX DNS records
see also Postfix
see also **sendmail**
access agents 533
addresses 95, 535

email *continued*
    aliases *see* aliases, email
    architecture 539–544
    backup servers, ISP 541
    blacklists 594–595
    bounced messages 569
    clients 532
    components 530–534
    daemons 897
    delivery agents 532
    delivery status codes 593
    denial of service (DOS) attacks
        608
    envelope 534
    Exim 621–623
    fallback MX 614
    forgery 608–609
    forwarding 549–550
    headers 535–539
    home mailbox 106, 542
    IMAP protocol 533, 543
    loops 546, 550
    mailing lists 551–554
    message stores 533
    message structure 534–535
    POP protocol 533, 543
    privacy 610
    proxies 540
    queue directory 563–565
    relaying 589–591
    SASL 610
    security 547, 603–610
    server setup 540–541, 614
    spam *see* spam
    submission agents (MSA) 533–
        534
    system administration tasks 530
    system components 530–534
    system design 539–544
    to a disabled account 108
    to files 547
    to programs 547
    transport agents 532
    undeliverable messages 613
    user agents 531
emergency *see* disaster
encryption *see* cryptography
Engarde Linux 710
enscript 778, 780
environmental monitoring 798
equipment racks 799
error correction protocols 863–864
ESMTP protocol 532
/etc directory 75

Ethernet 351–359
    addresses 280
    autonegotiation 302
    broadcast domain 352
    cables 278, 353–355
    collisions 352, 649–650
    congestion 356–357, 369
    design issues 368–370
    DIX II 278
    evolution 352
    frames *see* packets
    framing standards 277
    hardware addresses 280, 292
    hubs/concentrators 356
    packet encapsulation 276–277
    routers 358–359
    speed 352
    speed, setting 303
    switches 353, 356–358
    topology 352
    troubleshooting 366
    UTP cables 353–355, 366
EUIDs (effective user IDs) 55
EULAs (End User License Agree-
    ments) 953
EUROPEN 965
event correlation 221
events daemon 894
exec system call 56
executable maps, NFS automounter
    499
Exim mail system 621–623
expect 104, 348
EXPN command 588
exportfs 52, 491
/etc/exports file 489–491
EXPOSED_USER macro, **sendmail**
    581, 584
ext2fs filesystems 87, 120
ext3fs filesystems 87, 120, 125

F

FAI 231
fallback MX, email 614
FAT filesystems 120
fax mailer 573
FC-AL (Fibre Channel Arbitrated
    Loop) 112
fcntl system call 486
fcron 157
FDDI networks 361–362
fdisk 134–136, 140–141

FEATURE macro, **sendmail** 574–
    585
Fedora network configuration 308
FHS (Filesystem Hierarchy Stan-
    dard) 75
Fibre Channel 112
file attributes 81–88
    ACLs 88–92
    change time 83
    changing 81, 84–86
    chattr 87
    on device files 84
    directory search bit 82
    displaying using **ls** 81–84
    group ID number 83
    inode number 84
    link count 83
    lsattr 87
    permission bits 81, 684
    setuid/setgid bits 45, 82–83
    sticky bit 82–83
    supplemental 87
    symbolic links 80
    user ID number 83
file statement, DNS 434
filenames
    control characters in 77
    encoding under Samba 830
    length restrictions 72
    pattern matching 10, 77
    quoting 72
    removing sneaky 77–78
    shell globbing 10, 77
    spaces in 72
files
    see also configuration files
    see also device files
    see also file attributes
    see also filenames
    block device 77
    character device 77
    deleting 77
    device 122
    directory 77–78
    hard links 78
    links vs. original files 78
    local domain sockets 77, 80
    modes *see* file attributes
    named pipes 77, 80
    NFS locking 486
    ownership of 44–46
    permissions 81, 684
    regular 77–78
    removing temporary 154

files *continued*
    servers, dedicated NFS 496
    servers, system files 510
    sharing with Samba 833
    symbolic links 77, 80
    types of 76–81
Filesystem Hierarchy Standard
    (FHS) 75
filesystems 70–71
    see also partitions
    automatic mounting 127
    backing up 160
    BSD FFS 120
    checking and repairing 25, 128,
        131–133, 137
    cleaning using **cron** 154–155
    converting ext2fs to ext3fs 121
    copying 178
    creating 125–126, 136–138
    damaged 131–133
    disabling setuid execution 684
    enabling ACLs 88
    exporting NFS 489–492
    ext2fs 87, 120, 125
    ext3fs 87, 120
    FAT 120
    fuser 74
    inodes 126
    journaling 121
    labels 127
    Linux 120–122
    load balancing 805, 814
    loopback 73
    lost+found directories 127, 133
    lsof 74
    mounting 73–74, 126–129, 835
    mounting at boot time, NFS 495
    naming conventions, NFS 487
    organization 75
    patching 133
    quotas 486
    reinitializing 69
    ReiserFS 121
    root 24, 32, 75, 124
    sizing for backups 161
    smbfs 835
    superblocks 126
    sysfs 872, 882
    unmounting 73
filters, CUPS 771–772
find 72, 155
finger 98
FireWall-1 318

firewalls 701–708
    host-based 318
    ICMP blocking 645, 647–648
    Linux IP tables 704–708
    Netfilter 704–708
    packet-filtering 701–702
    proxy 703
    stateful 703–704
    traceroute and 648
flock system call 486
flow control, serial line 852–853
Fogel, Karl 253
Foomatic database 771, 782
fork system call 56
formatting disks 123
.forward file, email 549–550, 605
forward mapping, DNS 382
forwarders option, DNS 427
ForwardPath variable, **sendmail**
    549
fragmentation, IP 279
frame relay networks 363
frames *see* packets
framing standards, Ethernet 277
Frampton, Steve 12
free 811
Free Software Foundation (FSF) 965
free space, displaying 127
Free Standards Group 959
fsck 25, 128, 131–133, 137
/etc/fstab file 127–129, 132, 137,
    495, 497, 836
FSUID process parameter 55
FTP
    chrooted 735
    through firewalls 702–703
    and HTTP, compared 735
    permissions 736
    security 684, 736
    server setup 734–736
ftp 900
ftpd daemon 735, 900
/etc/ftpusers file 736
fully qualified hostnames 381, 396
functions script 208
fuser 74
FYI documents 275

G

gated routing daemon 344, 901
/etc/gateways file 344
GDI printers 783

gdm 743
GECOS information 98
Geer, Dan 161
$GENERATE directive, DNS 401,
    406
generic top-level domains 379
genericstable feature, **sendmail**
    579
getfacl 89
gethostbyname routine 414, 516
gethostent routine 819
getty process 25, 855–858
gettydefs file 858
Ghostscript 780
Ghostview 785
GIAC (Global Information Assur-
    ance Certification) 675
GIDs *see* group IDs
globbing, shell 10, 77
GNOME 758–759
    see also X Window System
GNU
    Free Software Foundation (FSF)
        965
    Openwall GNU/*/Linux (Owl)
        710
    Public License (GPL) 962
    Stow 266
    Zebra routing package 344
greet_pause feature, **sendmail** 597
greylisting for spam 636
/etc/group file 101–102
    defining groups 45, 97
    editing 104
    for FTP servers 735
    permissions 684
group IDs
    see also **/etc/group** file
    globally unique 102
    kernel and 104
    in **ls** output 83
    mapping to names 45
    numbers 45
    real, effective, and saved 45
    saved 55
groups
    see also **/etc/group** file
    default 97
    effective 55
    file attribute 83
    numbers (GIDs) 45
    passwords for 101
    of a process 55
grub 138

GRUB boot loader 26–28
    multiboot configuration 30
    options 883
    single-user mode 32
grub.conf file 27, 30, 883
grub-install 27
/etc/gshadow file 102
guest user accounts 944
Gutenprint project 771
gv 785

H

hald 899
halt 42
halting the system 40–42
Hamilton, Bruce 14
hard carrier 852
hard disks *see* disks
hard links 78
hardened Linux 710
hardware
    see also disks
    see also Ethernet
    see also maintenance
    see also networks
    see also PC hardware
    air conditioning 796–798
    BIND requirements 421
    computer displays 794
    cooling systems 940
    decommissioning 791
    environment 796–798
    equipment racks 799
    hubs 356
    kernel adaptation 869
    labeling 933
    logs 791
    memory 23, 794–795, 804
    power supplies 798
    probing 23
    purchasing 782–787, 916–917
    routers 358–359
    static electricity 793
    switches 353, 356–358, 360
    temperature monitoring 798
    tools 800
    USB *see* USB
    warranties 793
    wiring 366–368, 934
Hayes command language 864
Hazel, Philip 621
hdparm 129–131

header checking, **sendmail** 595–596
Hesiod 390
home directories 75
    creating 105
    location 75
    logging in to 98
    missing 98
    removing 107
/home partition 125
host 474
/etc/host.conf file 307
hostname command 299
/etc/hostname file 310
hostnames
    fully qualified 396
    mapping to IP addresses 281, 298
/etc/hosts file 281, 298–299, 420
/etc/hosts.allow file 691–692
/etc/hosts.deny file 691–692
/etc/hosts.equiv file 685, 898
hot-plugging kernel modules 882–883
hot-swappable drives 112, 116, 145
Hotz, Steve 473
HPAGE_SIZE kernel parameter 809
HTTP
    CUPS and 769
    protocol 720–722
    server *see* web hosting
httpd *see* web hosting
httpd.conf file 726–732
hubs, Ethernet 356
HUP signal 58–59
hwconf file 37
HylaFAX 573

I

I/O schedulers 815–816
ICANN (Internet Corporation for Assigned Names and Numbers) 273, 289, 371, 383
ICMP 275
    firewall blocking 645, 647–648
    netstat output 653
    packets 707
    ping and 645
    redirects 295, 317
    sequence numbers 646
    tracroute and 648
    TTL and 647

IDE 112–114
    accessing more than 1024 cylinders 112
    altering disk parameters 129–131
    device names 873
    DMA, tuning 130
    history 112–113
    performance tuning 130
    vs. SCSI 118
IDENT protocol 609
IEEE 802.* standards 278, 352, 356, 358–359
IETF (Internet Engineering Task Force) 273
ifconfig 299–302
    adding routes using 304, 335
    PPP and 321
    subnet masks and 283
    virtual addresses and 728
ifdown 309, 311
ifup 40, 309, 311, 327
IGMP (Internet Group Management Protocol) 281
IGRP (Interior Gateway Routing Protocol) 339, 342
IIS web server 827
IMAP (Internet Message Access Protocol) 533, 543, 897
imapd 897
in.fingerd 901
in.rlogind 898
in.rshd 898
in.telnetd 898
in.tftpd 899
in-addr.arpa domain 396
$INCLUDE directive, DNS 406
:include: directive, for email aliases 546
include statement, DNS 423
incremental backups 170
indirect maps, NFS automounter 499
inetd 885, 887–888, 890–893
/etc/inetd.conf file 890–892
init process 22–23, 56, 855–857, 886–887
    bootstrapping and 25
    logins and 886
    run levels and 33–36, 42, 886
    startup scripts and 32, 38, 40
    zombie processes and 56, 61
/etc/init.d directory 34–35, 38, 40
initlog 207

/etc/inittab file 34, 855–857, 886
inodes 84, 126
insmod 880–882
installation, Linux *see* Linux instal-
    lation
INT signal 58–59
integrity monitoring 692
/etc/interfaces file 311
interfaces, network *see* networks
International Organization for Stan-
    dardization (ISO) 354
Internet
    dial-up connections *see* PPP
        protocol
    Cache Protocol (ICP) 733
    Control Message Protocol *see*
        ICMP
    Corporation for Assigned
        Names and Numbers
        (ICANN) 289
    Engineering Task Force (IETF)
        273
    governance 273–275
    history 272–274
    Network Information Center
        (InterNIC) 288
    Official Protocol Standards 274
    protocol security (IPsec) 709
    protocol *see* IP
    registries 289
    RFC series 274–275
    Society (ISOC) 273
    standards and documentation
        274–275
    system administration resources
        13
    Systems Consortium (ISC) 12,
        312
    Worm 669
InterNIC (Internet Network Infor-
    mation Center) 288
intrusion detection, **samhain** 692–
    693
IOS (Cisco router OS) 346–348
iostat 813
IP 275
    see also IP addresses
    see also IPv6
    see also routing
    directed broadcast 317
    fragmentation 279
    masquerading *see* NAT

IP *continued*
    packet forwarding 303, 316
    source routing 317
    spoofing 317–318
    TOS (type-of-service) bits 330
IP addresses 279–293
    see also IPv6
    allocation 288–289
    broadcast 281
    CIDR (Classless Inter-Domain
        Routing) 283, 286–288
    classes 282
    hostnames and 281, 298
    loopback interface 282, 294,
        302, 397
    multicast 281–282
    netmasks 282–285
    ports 281
    PPP 322
    private 289–291, 409, 416, 438,
        465
    shortage of 285–286
    subnetting 282–285
    unicast 292
ipcalc 284
IPsec (Internet Protocol security)
    709, 949
iptables 319, 704–708
IPv6 286, 291–293
    DNS support 387, 404–405
    vs. CIDR 286
ISC (Internet Systems Consortium)
    312, 376
ISDN networks 364
IS-IS protocol 339, 343
ISO (International Organization for
    Standardization) 354
ISO/IEC 17799 standard 675
ISOC (Internet Society) 273
ISPs
    AOL 954
    domain registration 381
    IP address allocation 289–293
/etc/issue file 856
ITIL (Information Technology In-
    terface Library) 960

J

Jacobson, Van 273, 320, 329, 647,
    656
JFS filesystem 122

jobs, scheduling 887
John the Ripper 690
journaling filesystems 121
jukeboxes, tape media 167

K

kacpid daemon 894
Kahn, Bob 273
Kalt, Chrisophe 266
kblockd daemon 894
KDE 758–759
    see also X Window System
    Konqueror 789
    Print Manager 773
    printing under 788–790
kdm 743
Kerberos 464, 695–696
kermit 864
kernel 868–869
    ARP cache 296
    boot time options 29, 883
    building 876–878
    .config file, customizing 877–
        878
    configuration 873–874
    daemons 893
    device drivers 79, 868–870
    hot-plug blacklist 883
    hot-plugging modules 882–883
    HPAGE_SIZE 809
    initialization 23
    loadable modules 880–882
    location 75
    logging 206–208, 894
    network security variables 319
    options 874, 876–878
    panics 131, 133
    saved group IDs 55
    source tree 876–877, 879
    swappiness parameter 811
    threads 23
    TOS-based packet sorting 330
    tuning 314–316, 614, 874
kernel directory 877
KEY DNS records 455, 458
.key DNSSEC key file, DNS 454
key statement, DNS 430
keymap file, corrupted 37
keys, generating BIND 458
keys, SSH 697

kghostview 788
Kickstart 226–229
kill 60, 818
KILL signal 58–60
killall 60, 203
Kim, Gene 617
Kirch, Olaf 12
kjournald daemon 894
klogd daemon 207, 894
Knoppix 6, 232
Kolstad, Rob 617
Konqueror 789
Kotsikonas, Anastasios 553
kprinter 788–789
Kristensen, Peter 266
ks.cfg file 227–229
ksoftirqd daemon 894
kswapd daemon 810, 894
Kudzu 37

L

lame delegations, DNS 469, 475–476
LAMP platform 719
LANs 351
  ATM 362
  Ethernet 351–359
  FDDI 361–362
lastlog file 206
LBA (Logical Block Addressing) 112
LCFG (large-scale configuration system) 261
LDAP (Lightweight Directory Access Protocol) 520–526
  attribute names 522
  documentation 523–524
  OpenLDAP 523
  security 526
  setup 524–525
  structure of data 521
  use with **sendmail** 547, 555–557, 580–581
  user IDs and 97
  uses of 522–523
ldap_routing feature, **sendmail** 556, 580–581
LDP (Linux Documentation Project) 11
leadership 907
Leffler, Sam 573

legal issues 949–958
  appropriate use policies (AUPs) 954
  call records and web logs 952
  copyrights 950
  cryptography 949
  EULAs (End User License Agreements) 953
  liability for data 954
  pornography 954
  privacy 951
  software licenses 955
Libes, Don 104
licenses, software 955
lilo 28–29, 31, 138
LILO boot loader 28–29
  configuring 883
  multiboot configuration 31
  single-user mode 32
/etc/lilo.conf file 28, 31, 883
limit shell builtin 818
link layer, networks 277–279
links, hard 78–80, 83
link-state routing protocols 339
Linux
  culture 961, 963
  distributions 6–9, 962
  documentation 11–14
  Documentation Project (LDP) 11
  history 5
  installation see Linux installation
  International (LI) 964
  mailing lists 967
  popularity 962
  Professional Institute (LPI) 964, 967
  resources 964–968
  security flaws 670
  standards 958–960
  Test Project 963
  vendor logos 10
  vs. UNIX 4
/usr/src/linux directory 876
Linux installation 224–232
  see also system administration
  see also system configuration
  automating from a master system 232
  automating with AutoYaST 230–231
  automating with **cdebconf** 231

Linux installation continued
  automating with **cdebootstrap** 231
  automating with **debian-installer** 231
  automating with FAI 231
  automating with Kickstart 226–229
  automating with **system-config-kickstart** 231
  ks.cfg file 227–229
  netbooting 224–226
  PXE protocol 225–226
  PXELINUX 225
  system-config-netboot 226
  TFTP protocol 225
LinuxWorld conference 966
listen-on option, DNS 426
listmanager 554
ListProc 553
LISTSERV Lite 554
Liu, Cricket 423
LMTP protocol 625
ln 78, 80
load average, **sendmail** 613
load averages 808
load balancing
  disks and filesystems 805, 814
  DNS 385
  servers 805
  web server 722–724
loadable modules 880–882
LOC DNS records 401
local delivery agents, **sendmail** 533
local domain sockets 77, 80
/usr/local hierarchy 255–260
  compilation 258–259
  distribution 259
  organizing 256–257
  testing 257–258
LOCAL_* macros, **sendmail** 586
local_lmtp feature, **sendmail** 585
local_procmail feature, **sendmail** 585
localhost 282
localhost zone configuration example, BIND 439
local-host-names file 574
locate 15, 771
lockd daemon 486
lockf system call 486
/var/log directory 204

log files 209–220
 see also logging
 see also syslog
 analyzing and searching 220–
  221
 for Apache 727
 archiving 204
 lists of 205, 218
 for logins and logouts 206
 monitoring 220–221
 replacing while in use 203
 rotating 156, 202, 208–209
 to system console 218
 web hosting 727
/dev/log socket 210
logcheck 220
logger 217–218
logging
 see also log files
 see also syslog
 for BIND 411, 432, 446, 466–471
 boot-time 206–208
 to central server 214, 216
 for **cron** 151
 for CUPS 781
 hardware failures 791
 kernel 206–208
 for **sendmail** 619–621
 for **sudo** 49
 through syslog 218–220
 to system console 218
logging in from Windows 821–822
logging statement, DNS 432, 466
logical unit numbers, SCSI 117
logical volume managment *see* LVM
login command 46, 856
.login file 105
login process 855
login *see* user accounts
/etc/login.defs file 98, 100
logos, vendor 10
logrotate 208–209
/etc/logrotate.conf file 208
/etc/logrotate.d directory 208
logwatch 221
loopback
 address, BIND 437
 filesystem 73
 interface 282, 294, 302, 397
LOPSA 965
lost+found directories 127, 133
low-level formatting, disks 123
lpd daemon 894
lpd-errs file 215

lpinfo 772
ls 45, 77, 81–84
lsattr 87
lsmod 881
lsof 74, 494
LTO backup tapes 167
lvcreate 144
lvextend 146
LVM 139, 143–147
 creating 143–144
 resizing 146–147
lwresd 897

M

m4 566–570, 586
MAC addresses 280, 292
Mackerras, Paul 508
macros, **sendmail** 570–574
magic cookies, NFS 486
magic cookies, X Windows 746
mail *see* email
mail.local delivery agent 533, 585,
 605
MAIL_HUB macro, **sendmail** 583,
 600
MAILER macro, **sendmail** 573–574
mailers 573
 cyrus 573
 discard 596
 error 591, 596
 fax 573
 local 573
 pop 573
 qpage 574
mailertable feature, **sendmail** 578
mailing list software 551–554
 listmanager 554
 ListProc 553
 LISTSERV Lite 554
 Mailman 553
 Majordomo 552
 SmartList 554
mailing lists 546, 551–554, 967
mailq 619
.mailrc file 105
mailstats 615
main.cf file 626
maintenance 791–800
 see also hardware
 contracts 792–793
 environment 796–798
 equipment racks 799

maintenance *continued*
 power 798
 preventive 795–796
 Uninterruptible Power Supply
  (UPS) 799
major device numbers 79, 870–872
Majordomo 552–553, 605
makedbm 512
MAKEDEV script 79, 872
makemap 576–577
man pages 11–13
management 907–915
management standards, networks
 658
Manheimer, Ken 553
MANs 351
many-answers option, DNS 425
map files, NFS automounter 499–
 500
masks in ACLs 90
MASQUERADE_AS macro, **sendmail** 581–583, 616
masquerading, **sendmail** 581–583
master boot record (MBR) 26
master name server, DNS 413
master server, NIS 511–513, 517–
 518
master.cf file 623
masters statement, DNS 432, 434
match-clients clause, DNS 438
max-cache-size option, DNS 426
MaxDaemonChildren option,
 sendmail 608
MaxMessageSize option, **sendmail**
 608
MaxRcptsPerMessage option,
 sendmail 608
MBR (master boot record) 26
McKusick, Kirk 120
MDA (mail delivery agent) 532
mdadm RAID management utility
 141–143, 145
mdrecoveryd daemon 894
/proc/mdstat file 142, 145
media, backup 163–169
 see also tapes
 CD and DVD 164
 jukeboxes 167
 labeling 159
 life of 163
 magnetic 164
 optical 164
 summary of types 168
 verifying 162

memory
    buffering 40
    effect on performance 804, 806
    kernel initialization and 23
    management 809–811
    modules 794–795
    paging 809–814, 818
    RAM disks 815
    usage, analyzing 811–813
    virtual (VM) 810–811
message of the day 856, 954
message stores 533
/var/log/messages file 207, 215
Metcalfe, Bob 351
mgetty process 855–858
Microsoft Windows *see* Windows
mii-tool 303
Miller, Todd 49
miltering, **sendmail** 597
MIME (Multipurpose Internet Mail Extensions) 531, 601
/etc/cups/mime.convs file 772
/etc/cups/mime.types file 771
Minar, Nelson 902
mingetty process 855–858
mini DIN-8 connectors 847
minicom 864
minor device numbers 79, 870–872
mkdir 78
mke2fs 125, 136–137
mkfs 69
mknod 79–80, 871
mkpasswd 104
MKS Toolkit 827
mkswap 138
Mockapetris, Paul 375
model file 771
modems 852, 862–864
modprobe 881
/etc/modprobe.conf file 881
MODULE_DEVICE_TABLE macro 880
Mondo Rescue 197
monitoring log files 220–221
monitors 794
Moore's Law 273
Morris, Robert, Jr. 669
MOSPF protocol 343
/etc/motd file 856, 954
Motion Picture Association of America 950

mount 73, 126–128
    enabling filesystem ACLs 88
    NFS filesystems 492–495
mount point, filesystem 73
mount.smbfs 836
mountd daemon 489
mounting filesystems *see* filesystems, mounting
mpstat 808
/var/spool/mqueue directory 563, 619
mreport program 620
MRTG (Multi-Router Traffic Grapher) 664
MSA (mail submission agent) 533
mt 178
MTA (mail transport agent) 532
MTU (maximum transfer unit) 278–279, 361
mtx 179
MUA (mail user agent) 531
multibooting 30–31
multicast addresses 281–282
multiprocessor machines, analyzing performance 808
Multipurpose Internet Mail Extensions (MIME) 531, 601
multiuser mode 25
MX DNS records 397–399
MySQL 180–182, 377, 719, 936

N

Nagios SNMP monitoring tool 665
name servers
    see also DNS
    see also BIND
    see also **named**
    authoritative 413, 416
    caching 384–386, 417
    caching-only 413
    delegation 383
    dynamic updates 448–450
    forwarding 427
    hints 414
    keep-running script 417
    lame delegations 469, 475–476
    master 413
    negative caching 385
    nonauthoritative 413

name servers *continued*
    recursion 413, 425
    resolver 414, 418–420
    slave 413
    stub 413
    switch file 479
    zone delegation 407–409
    zone serial numbers 447
named 412, 446
    see also BIND
    see also DNS
    see also name servers
    acl statement 430
    ACLs 429, 451–453
    allow-recursion option 425
    allow-update clause 433, 450
    avoid-v4-udp-ports option 427
    blackhole option 428
    bogus directive 431
    chrooted 451, 453
    command-line interface *see* **named**, **rndc**
    compiling with OpenSSL 458
    configuration 420–446
    configuration examples 439–446
    confining with **chroot** 453
    controls statement 436–438
    datasize option 426
    debugging 466–478
    delegation-only option 386, 429
    directory statement 424
    domain directive 420
    error messages 469
    file statement 434
    forwarders option 427
    forwarding zone, configuring 436
    $GENERATE directive 401, 406
    hardware requirements 421
    $INCLUDE directive 406
    include statement 423
    init scripts 446
    ISC configuration example 444
    keep-running script 417
    key statement 430
    listen-on option 426
    localhost zone configuration example 439
    logging 411, 446, 466–471

named *continued*
    logging statement 432, 466
    many-answers option 425
    master server, configuring 433
    masters statement 432, 434
    match-clients clause 438
    max-cache-size option 426
    /etc/named.conf file 421–446,
        450–451, 470, 480–481
    named.run file 471
    named-checkconf 421, 455, 478
    named-checkzone 421, 478
    notify option 424
    options statement 423–429
    $ORIGIN directive 406
    provide-ixfr option 448
    query-source option 426
    recursion option 425
    recursive-clients option 426
    request-ixfr option 448
    rndc 436–438, 447, 471–473
    root server hints 435
    root.cache file 435
    rrset-order statement 428
    search directive 419
    server statement 431, 448
    slave server, configuring 434
    sortlist option 428
    starting 448
    statements, list of 422
    stub zones, configuring 434
    testing 466–478
    topology statement 428
    transfers-in option 425
    transfer-source option 426,
        445
    transfers-out option 425
    transfers-per-ns option 425
    trusted-keys statement 430
    $TTL directive 390, 394, 406
    TTL options 428
    update-policy clause 450
    updating zone files 447–450
    versions 411, 424
    view statement 438
    zone commands 405–407
    zone serial numbers 447
    zone statement 432–436
    zone-statistics option 433
named pipes 77, 80
/etc/named.conf file 421–446, 450–
    451, 470, 480–481
named.run file 471

named_dump.db file 472
named-checkconf 421, 455, 478
named-checkzone 421, 478
namespace, DNS 378
naming conventions
    device files 872
    shared filesystems 487
nanny script 446
NAT 290–291, 319
National Science Foundation (NSF)
    381
ncftp 510
ndbm library 169
neigh directory 315
Nemeth, Evi 679
Nessus 690
NetBIOS 828, 896
netbooting 224–226
Netfilter 704–708
/etc/netgroup file 517
netgroups, NIS 517
netmasks 282–285
NeTraverse 826
NET-SNMP 661–664
netstat 649–654
    displaying interface names 300
    examining the routing table 294
    examples 335–337
    interfaces 649
    monitoring connections 651
    network statistics 649–654
    and NFS UDP overflows 492
    open ports 652
    routing table 652
Network Appliance, Inc. 496
network configuration 298, 307–
    311
    Debian and Ubuntu 310
    Red Hat and Fedora 308
    SUSE 309
Network Information Service *see*
    NIS
Network Solutions, Inc. 381
Network Time Protocol (NTP) 902
network unreachable error 304
network wiring 934
    building 366–368
    cable analyzer 366
    cable choices 352–355, 366
    for offices 367
    maintenance and documenta-
        tion 370
    Wireshark network sniffer 366

networks
    see also Ethernet
    see also IP addresses
    see also network configuration
    see also network wiring
    see also routing
    see also TCP/IP
    adding a machine to a LAN 297–
        307
    address translation *see* NAT
    addresses 279–293
    administrative databases 504,
        511
    ARP (Address Resolution Proto-
        col) 296–297
    ATM 362–363
    broadcast storms 301, 357
    CIDR (Classless Inter-Domain
        Routing) 286–287
    connecting and expanding 355–
        359
    connecting with PPP 321
    daemons 900–901
    debugging with **mii-tool** 302–
        303
    default route 293–294, 305, 329,
        336
    design issues 368–370
    DHCP (Dynamic Host Configu-
        ration Protocol) 311–314
    firewalls 318, 701–708
    interface activity reports 654
    interface configuration 299–302
    load balancing 385, 805
    loopback 282, 294, 302, 397
    management issues 370–371,
        643
    management protocols 657–661
    management standards 658
    monitoring 650–651
    MTUs 278–279, 361
    NAT 290–291, 319
    netmasks 282–285
    packets *see* packets
    PAT 319
    ping and 645–647
    port scanning 688–690
    ports 281
    PPP 320–330
    redundancy 941
    routing tables 652
    scanner, Nessus 690
    security *see* security

networks *continued*
  statistics 649–654
  subnetting 282–285
  troubleshooting 366, 644–654
  tuning 314–316
  virtual private networks *see*
    VPNs
  VLANs 357
  wireless 278, 359–361
network-scripts directory 38
newaliases 551
newgrp 102
NFS (Network File System) 484–500
  all_squash option 488, 491
  anongid option 488, 491
  anonuid option 488, 491
  buffer sizes 494
  client 492–495
  common options 491
  configuration, server 489–492
  cookies 486
  daemons 895–896
  dedicated file servers 496
  disk quotas 486
  and **dump** 170
  exporting filesystems 489–492
  file locking 486
  firewalls and 488
  and the **fstab** file 127
  hard vs. soft mounts 493
  insecure option 491, 495
  mount 492–495
  mounting filesystems at boot
    time 495
  naming conventions 487
  no_root_squash option 488,
    491
  nobody account 51, 488
  protocol versions 484
  root access 488
  RPC and 485
  secure option 491, 495
  secure_locks option 491
  security 487–489, 495, 686
  statistics 495
  subtree_check option 491
  TCP vs. UDP 485
  tuning 494
  using to export email 542
nfsd daemon 489, 492, 494
nfsstat 495
nice 61–62, 818
nice value 55

NIS (Network Information Service)
511–520
  architecture 512–514
  commands 514
  configuring clients 519
  configuring servers 518
  database files 511–512
  files to share 503
  LDAP vs. 525
  map files 512
  master server 511–513, 517–518
  netgroups 517
  query procedure 513
  security 685–686
  setting access control options
    519
  setting up a domain 517–520
  slave servers 512–514, 517
nmap 688–690
nmbd 829, 896
nocanonify feature, **sendmail** 576
nohup 59
notify option, DNS 424
NS DNS records 395, 407
nscd daemon 504, 897
/etc/nscd.conf file 505, 897
NSEC DNS records 463
NSF (National Science Foundation)
381
NSFNET 272
/etc/nsswitch.conf file 307, 515,
562
nsupdate 449
NTP (Network Time Protocol) 902
/etc/ntp.conf file 902
ntpd 902–903
ntpdate 902
null modem serial cable 846–847
nullclient feature, **sendmail** 584–
585
NXT DNS records 458

O

Oetiker, Tobias 262, 664
office wiring 367
off-site backup storage 161
Oja, Joanna 11
one-time passwords 698
open relaying, email 589
OpenLDAP 523, 555
openlog routine 218–220
OpenOffice.org 826

Openwall GNU/*/Linux (Owl) 710
operating system installation *see*
  Linux installation
oprofile 817
options statement, DNS 423–429
$ORIGIN directive, DNS 406
orphaned processes 56, 61, 63
OSI layers 276
OSPF protocol 339, 342–343
OSTYPE macro, **sendmail** 570–572

P

Pack Management Project 266
package management 234–247
  alien conversion tool 235
  automating 244–246
  .deb format 235
  dpkg/APT 235, 237, 241–246
  Red Hat Network 240
  repositories 239–240
  RPM format 235
  rpm/**yum** 235–238, 246–247
packages *see* software packages
packets
  see also networks
  dropped 646
  encapsulation 276–277
  filtering 677, 701
  forwarding 335–337
  handling with Netfilter 704–708
  ICMP 707
  round trip time 646
  sniffers 366, 655–657
  tracing 647–649
pages, memory 809–811
paging 129, 809–814, 818
Painter, Mark 376
PAM (Pluggable Authentication
  Modules) 681–682
paper sizes for printers 777–778
paperconfig 778
PAPERSIZE environment variable
  778
/etc/papersize file 778
Parain, Will 261
partitions 124–125, 134–138
  see also filesystems
  load balancing 814
  resizing with LVM 146–147
  root 124
  setting up 134–136
  swap 124, 129, 138

passwd command 46, 96, 104
/etc/passwd file 93–99
  editing 96, 103
  for FTP servers 735
  group ID numbers 83
  permissions 684
  security 678–681, 684
  user ID numbers 45, 83
passwords
  aging 680
  boot loader 673
  cracking 690
  encryption 94, 96, 830
  FTP 735
  group 101
  initial 104
  one-time 698
  root 47
  Samba 830
  security 47, 678–681
  selection 47, 104, 679–680
  shadow 94, 99–100, 678
  strength 682, 690
PAT (Port Address Translation) 319
PATA *see* IDE
patches, software 677
patents
  EU patent policy 957
  software 957–958
  U.S. patent office 957
pathnames 48, 72
PC hardware
  see also hardware
  BIOSes 25
  boot device priority 26
  bootstrapping 25
  delete character 859
  device drivers 870
  multibooting 30–31
  vs. UNIX hardware 25
PCL printer language 763, 766
PDF 764, 766
pdftops 772
performance 803–819
  BIND 478
  CPU 806–809, 813
  disk 806, 813–815
  factors affecting 806–807
  improving 803–806
  kernel tuning for email 614
  load averages 808

performance *continued*
  measuring and monitoring 664, 807
  memory 68, 804, 806, 811–813
  network, TOS bits 330
  NFS 494
  nice 61
  partitioning disks to improve 124
  PPP 321
  using RAID to improve 139
  SDSC Secure Syslog 210
  sendmail 611–615
  Squid web cache 733–734
  st_atime flag 87
  syncing log files 213
  troubleshooting 817–819
  tuning IDE drives 130
  web server 722–724, 727
performance analysis tools
  free 811
  iostat 813
  mpstat 808
  oprofile 817
  procinfo 812
  sar 816
  top 809
  uptime 808
  vmstat 807
Perl 14, 150, 719, 722, 827, 923
  in administrative scripts 4
  example scripts 525
  generating passwords 524
  insecure example 672
  module sources 662
  null password check 679
  and **swatch** 220
  and syslog 219
  user ID check 681
  wrapping **cron** jobs 511
permissions
  chmod and 84
  file 81, 684
  important 684
  sendmail 604–605
  umask and 86
personnel management 908–910
PGP (Pretty Good Privacy) 610, 696
Phonetics Sensaphone 798
PIDs 54
PIM protocol 343
ping 317, 645–647

pipes, named 77, 80
piracy 955
PIX firewall box 318
PJL printer language 765
.plan file 901
platters, disks 119
Pluggable Authentication Modules (PAM) 681–682
poff command 330
policy
  agreements 107, 946–948
  backups 939
  documents 943–948
  enforcement 953
  logging 201
  Postfix policy daemons 636
  security 945–946
pon command 330
POP (Post Office Protocol) 533, 543, 828, 897
pop mailer 573
popd 897
pornography 954
portmap daemon 488, 888, 893
ports, network 281
  numbers 893
  privileged 281, 689, 702
  scanning 688–690
  well known 688, 702
ports, serial 844–847
POSIX 683, 959
  APIs under Windows 827
  root account capabilities 46
Post Office Protocol (POP) 533, 543, 828, 897
postconf Postfix configuration tool 627
Postel, Jon 273
Postfix 623–638
  access control 632–634, 638
  amavisd virus filter 637
  architecture 623
  authentication 634
  black hole lists 635
  chrooted 625
  command-line utilities 625
  configuring 626–634
  content filtering 636
  debugging 637–639
  greylisting 636
  local delivery 629
  lookup tables 627

Postfix *continued*
  policy daemons 636
  queue manager 624
  receiving email 624
  security 625
  sending email 625
  spam control 634–637
  virtual domains 630–632
  virus filtering 637
PostScript 763, 766
power management 798
power supplies, emergency 940
poweroff 42
/etc/cups/ppd file 771
PPD printer description files 770–771
PPIDs 54
/etc/ppp directory 323
PPP protocol 320–330
  commands, list of 324
  configuration 323–330
pppd daemon 323, 325, 327, 329
pppstats 329
pr 780
Practical Extraction and Report Language *see* Perl
Pre-boot eXecution Environment (PXE) 225–226, 899
Preston, W. Curtis 198
Pretty Good Privacy (PGP) 610, 696–697
printers
  see also printing
  accounting 787
  cartridges 786
  drivers 765
  languages 763–766
  network 773, 784
  PPD printer description files 770–771
  purchasing 782–787
  security 787
  selection 782–785
  serial and parallel 784
  USB 774, 781
  WinPrinters 783
printing
  see also CUPS
  see also printers
  banner pages 784–785
  daemons 894
  Foomatic database 771, 782
  Gutenprint project 771
  history 761–762

printing *continued*
  KDE Print Manager 773
  Konqueror and 789
  paper sizes 777–778
  PPD printer description files 770–771
  previewers 785
  sharing printers using Samba 836–839
  software 779
  under KDE 788–790
  using **kprinter** 789
  Windows driver installation 838–839
  XHTML 764
priority, processes 55, 61–62
privacy 951
.private DNSSEC key file 454
private IP addresses 289–291, 409, 416, 438, 465
privileged ports 281, 689, 702
/proc filesystem 65–66, 314–316, 872, 874
processes 53
  changing ownership credentials 45
  changing user and group IDs 46
  control terminal 56
  EGID (effective group ID) 55
  EUID (effective user ID) 55
  execution states 60–61
  FSUID parameter 55
  GID (group ID) 55
  identities: real, effective, and saved 45
  IDs 54
  monitoring 62–65
  orphaned 56, 61, 63
  owner 45, 54
  PPID (parent PID) 54
  priority 55, 61–62
  runaway 67–69
  scheduling 45
  sending signals to 60
  spontaneous 23
  standard I/O channels 56
  stopping and starting 61
  UID (user ID) 54
  zombie 56, 61, 63, 886
procinfo 812–813, 818
procmail 533, 585, 636
/etc/profile file 106
/etc/profile.d directory 106
profiler, system 817

programs, finding 15
Project Athena 741
.project file 901
promiscuous relaying, **sendmail** 589
provide-ixfr option, DNS 448
proxies, service 703
proxies, web servers 733
ps 62–64, 809, 817
pseudo-devices 871
pseudo-users 97
PTR DNS records 396, 444
/dev/pts directory 75
public key cryptography 456, 697
Punycode 388
purchasing hardware 782–787, 916–917
PuTTY 821
pvcreate LVM utility 143
PXE (Pre-boot eXecution Environment) 225–226, 899
PXELINUX 225
Python 4, 15–16, 523, 923

Q

qmgr 625
qpage mailer 574
qpopper email server 543
qshape 638
quad A DNS records 404
query-source option, DNS 426
queue groups, **sendmail** 611–612
queue runners, **sendmail** 613
QUIT signal 58–59
quotas, disk 486

R

racks, equipment 799
RAID 139–147, 805, 894
raidtools 141
RAM disks 815
/dev/ram0 and **/dev/ram1** files 815
rc scripts *see* startup scripts
rc.local script 36
rcmd 898
rcp 685, 898
RCPT command, SMTP 588
RCS 249–251
rcsdiff 250

rdesktop 825
rdist 505–508
RDP (Remote Desktop Protocol) 824
rdump 171
real-time scheduling 56
RealVNC 824
reboot 42
rebooting 40–41
recursion option, DNS 425
recursive-clients option, DNS 426
Red Hat network configuration 308
Red Hat Network, software repository 240
redirect feature, **sendmail** 575
REFUSE_LA option, **sendmail** 608
registration of domain names *see* domain names, registration
regular files 77–78
Reiser, Hans 121
ReiserFS filesystem 121
/etc/mail/relay-domains file 589
Remote Desktop Protocol (RDP) 824
Remote Procedure Call *see* RPC
renice 61–62, 818
repositories, software 239, 266
request-ixfr option, DNS 448
reset 862
resize_reiserfs 147
resizing disk partitions 146–147
/etc/resolv.conf file 418–420
resolver library, DNS 414
resource records, DNS 389–405
    A 396, 407
    A6 404
    AAAA 404
    CNAME 399
    DNAME 404
    DNSKEY 457–458
    DS 458, 460
    format 389
    glue 407–409
    KEY 455, 458
    LOC 401
    MX 397–399
    NS 407
    NSEC 458, 460, 463
    NXT 458
    PTR 396, 444
    quad A 404
    RRSIG 457–458, 460, 463
    SIG 458
    SOA 392–395, 447

resource records, DNS *continued*
    special characters in 389
    SRV 402–403, 464
    time to live 390
    trailing dot in names 389
    TXT 403, 424
    WKS 403
restore 173–176, 939
reverse mapping, DNS 382, 396–397, 405, 444
revision control 248–255
    CVS 251–253
    RCS 249–251
    Subversion 253–255
RFCs
    BCP documents 275
    DNS-related 375–376, 482
    email-related 532, 640
    FYI documents 275
    LDAP-related 523
    NFS-related 500
    overview 274–275
    private address space 289–291
    SNMP-related 667
    STD documents 275
    subnetting 285
RHN, repository package 240
.rhosts file 685, 898
Riggle, David 376
RIP protocol 339, 341–344
RIP-2 protocol 341
RJ-11 connectors 862
RJ-45 connectors 355, 849
rlog 250
rlogin 685
rm 77, 79
rmdir 78
rmmod 881
rndc 436–438, 447, 471–473
/etc/rndc.conf file 437
/etc/rndc.key file 437
rndc-confgen 437
root account 44, 46, 681
    accessing 48–51
    accessing via NFS 488
    operations 46
    passwords 47
    POSIX capabilities 46
    restricting access 685
    squashing, NFS 488
    /etc/sudoers file 49–50
    user ID 46
root filesystem 24, 32, 75
rootkits 688, 951

Rossi, Markku 778
rotating log files 156, 202, 208–209
route command 294, 303–305, 309, 900
routed daemon 341, 343–344, 900
Router Discovery Protocol 343
routers 358–359
routing 293–295, 334–348
    autonomous systems 340
    BGP protocol 339
    CIDR (Classless Inter-Domain Routing) 283–288
    Cisco routers 346–348
    cost metrics 340
    daemons and protocols 337–344
    default route 293–294, 305, 329, 336
    distance-vector protocols 338, 342
    EIGRP protocol 342
    exterior gateway protocols 340
    ICMP redirects 295, 317, 337
    IGRP protocol 342
    interior gateway protocols 341–343
    IS-IS protocol 343
    link-state protocols 339
    netmasks 282–285
    OSPF protocol 339, 342–343
    packet forwarding 303, 316, 335–337
    PPP 322
    protocols 341–343
    RIP protocol 339, 341–344
    sendmail 583
    static routes 294, 303–305
    static vs. dynamic routing 344–345
    strategy 344–345
    subnetting 282–285
    tables 293–295, 335–337, 652
    unreachable networks 304
    with multiple ISPs 340
    XORP (eXtensible Open Router Platform) 344
    Zebra package 344
Rowland, Craig 220
RPC (Remote Procedure Call)
    managing port assignments 888
    mapping service numbers to ports 893
    NFS and 485
    portmap and 893

rpc.bootparamd daemon 899
rpc.lockd daemon 895
rpc.mountd daemon 489, 895
rpc.nfsd daemon 489, 895
rpc.rquotad daemon 896
rpc.statd daemon 895
rpc.ypxfrd daemon 896
rpciod daemon 896
rpm 235–237
RPM software package format 235
rquotad daemon 486
RRDTool graphing tool 664
rrestore 175
rrset-order statement, DNS 428
RRSIG DNS records 457–458, 460,
    463
RS-232 standard 844–847, 853
RS-232 to USB adapters 865
rsh 898
rsync 197, 508–511, 900
rsyncd daemon 900
rsyncd.secrets file 510
RTS (request to send) signal 853
run levels 856
    changing 887
    init and 33–36, 42, 856, 886
RunAsUser **sendmail** user account
    603
runaway processes 67–69
running Linux programs from Win-
    dows 822–823
Russinovich, Mark 951
rxvt 827

S

S/MIME 610
SafeFileEnvironment option,
    sendmail 606
SAGE guild 965–966, 968
SAIT tapes 166
Samba 828–841
    see also Windows
    CIFS 828
    command-line file transfer pro-
        gam 835
    configuration 829
    daemons 829, 895–896
    debugging 840–841
    display active connections and
        locked files 840
    file and printer server daemon
        896

Samba *continued*
    file sharing 833
    filename encoding 830
    group shares 833
    installation 829–830
    listing configuration options
        830
    log files 840
    Network Neighborhood brows-
        ing 831
    password encryption 830
    printer sharing 836–839
    security 829
    setting up passwords 830
    sharing files 828
    user authentication 832
    UTF-8 encoding 830
    WINS server 831
samhain 692–693
SAN (Storage Area Network) serv-
    ers 496
SANE 965
SANS Institute 675, 713, 965, 968
sar 654, 816
Sarbanes-Oxley Act (SOX) 675, 956,
    960
SASL (Simple Authentication and
    Security Layer) 610
SATA (Serial ATA) 112, 114
savelog 209
Sawyer, Michael 473
/sbin directory 75
SCA (Single Connector Attachment)
    plug 116
schedulers, I/O 815–816
scheduling classes 56
scheduling commands 150–157
SCO 951
scp 697
SCSI 112, 114–118
    BIOS 134
    connectors 115–117
    device names 873
    fast and wide 115
    installing 134
    troubleshooting 118
    vs. IDE 118
scsi_eh_*N* daemon 894
SDSC Secure Syslog 210
search directive, DNS 419
search path 15
SEC (Simple Event Correlator) 221
sectors and tracks, disks 120
secure file 206

secure terminals 685
/etc/securetty file 685
security
    account hygiene 93
    Application Security Checklist
        676
    auth.log file 206
    backups 161, 686
    BIND 417, 424, 451–464
    certifications 673–675
    CISA (Certified Information
        Systems Auditor) 675
    CISSP (Certified Information
        Systems Security Professional)
        674
    vs. convenience 673
    denial of service (DOS) attacks
        397, 511, 608, 817
    device files 684
    directed broadcast 317
    DNS 417, 424, 451–464
    DNSSEC 387, 456–463
    DOS attack via syslog 213
    email 588
    email to programs 547, 605–606
    file permissions 684
    firewalls 701–708
    firewalls, host-based 318
    flaws in Linux 670
    FTP 684, 736
    GIAC (Global Information As-
        surance Certification) 675
    of **group** file 684
    handling attacks 710–712
    hardened Linux 710
    hints 678
    hot-plug blacklist 883
    ICMP redirects 295, 317
    identifying open ports 652
    information sources 712–715
    intrusion detection 692–693
    IP forwarding 316
    IP spoofing 317–318
    iptables 704–708
    Kerberos 695–696
    kernel network variables 319
    LDAP and 526
    log files 201, 214
    login names, uniqueness 95
    monitoring 17, 677–678, 688,
        692, 704
    of **named** 451, 453
    network 316–319
    NFS 487–489, 495, 686

security *continued*
 NIS 519, 685–686
 overview 669–670
 packet sniffers 655–657
 PAM (Pluggable Authentication
  Modules) 681–682
 of **passwd** file 678–681, 684
 of passwords 47, 94, 96, 679–
  680, 690
 policy 945–946
 port scanning 688–690
 of Postfix 625
 of PPP 323
 of printers 787
 remote event logging 685
 reporting break-ins 712
 restricting root access 685
 .rhosts file 685
 root account 48, 681
 rootkits 688, 951
 running **su** 48
 Samba 829
 SDSC Secure Syslog 210
 search path 48
 secure file 206
 /etc/securetty file 685
 SELinux 693–694
 of **sendmail** 558, 588–598, 603–
  610, 686
 setuid programs 683–684
 /etc/shadow file 678–681
 shadow passwords 94, 99–100,
  678
 SNMP 660
 social engineering 671
 software patches 677
 source routing 317
 SSH 685, 697–698
 SSL 730–732
 standards 675–676
 stunnel 699–701
 syslog 214
 terminals 685
 tools 688–701
 Trojan horses 687
 TSIG (transaction signatures)
  444, 453–456
 viruses 686–687
 of VPNs (virtual private networks) 318, 708–710
 of wireless networks 360
 X Window System 744–748, 823
SecurityFocus.com 713
segmentation violations 58

SEGV signal 58
SELinux 693–694
Sender ID 599
Sender Policy Framework (SPF)
 403, 599
sendmail 530, 897
 see also email
 see also spam
 access database 591–594
 acting as MSA/MTA 534
 aliases *see* aliases, email
 authentication and encryption
  603–610
 chrooted 607
 command line flags 562
 configuration 559–561, 565–
  587, 590–598
 configuration examples 599–
  603
 configuration options 586–587
 controlling forgery 609
 debugging 558, 566, 615–621
 delivery agents 533
 delivery modes 611
 documentation 566
 email to a disabled account 108
 envelope splitting 611–612
 headers 535–539, 595–596
 history 557
 *Installation and Operation
  Guide* 639
 installing 559–562
 logging 619–621
 m4 and 566–570, 586
 masquerading 581–583
 miltering 597
 MX backup sites 565
 ownership, files 603–604
 performance 611–615
 permissions 604–605
 privacy options 606–607
 queue groups 611–612
 queue runners 613
 queues 563–565, 611–613, 619
 rate and connection limits 596
 relaying 589–591
 security 558, 588–598, 603–610,
  686
 and the service switch file 562
 slamming 597
 using SMTP to debug 618
 spam control features 588–598
 startup script 38
 statistics 615

sendmail *continued*
 tables and databases 576–580
 verbose delivery 617–618
 versions 557
 virtusertable feature 579–580
Sendmail, Inc. 530, 610
sendmail.cf file 559, 563, 565
sendmail.cw file 574
sendmail.st file 615
SEPP 266
serial
 breakout boxes 865
 cables *see* serial cables
 connectors *see* serial connectors
 device drivers 872
 device files 853–855
 devices, software configuration
  855
 drivers, special characters 859–
  862
 interface, DCE vs. DTE 845–847
 line, debugging 864
 line, flow control 852–853
 ports *see* serial ports
 terminals, configuring 855–859
Serial ATA (SATA) 112, 114
serial cables
 length limits 853
 null modem 846–847
 straight-through 846–847
 Yost RJ-45 standard 850–852
serial connectors
 DB-25 844–847
 DB-9 848
 mini DIN-8 847
 RJ-11 862
 RJ-45 849
serial ports 844–847
 flow control 852–853
 hard/soft carrier 852
 parameters, setting 854–855
 resetting 862
 setting options 860–862
server statement, DNS 431, 448
servers
 Apache *see* web hosting
 DNS/BIND 412–414
 email backup 541
 FTP 734–736
 HTTP 724
 Kerberos Windows and DNS
  464
 load balancing 385, 805
 master NIS 511–513, 517–518

servers *continued*
   name *see* BIND, DNS, and
      named
   network printer 773
   NFS 489–492, 496
   NIS slave 512–514, 517
   Squid 733–734
   Storage Area Network (SAN)
      496
   system files 510
   TUX 727
   VNC 824
   web proxy 733
   web *see* web hosting
   WINS 831
   X Window System for Windows
      823, 827
service proxy firewalls 703
service switch file 306–307, 562
service.switch file 562
/etc/services file 281, 702, 892–893
setfacl 89, 91
setrlimit system call 818
setserial 854
setuid/setgid file attribute 45, 82–
   83, 683–684
/etc/shadow file 99–100, 678–681,
   856
shadow passwords 94, 99–100, 678
Shapiro, Gregory 610
share (Samba) 828
shell
   filename globbing 10, 77
   login 98
   search path 48
   startup files 105
SHELL variable 861
/etc/shells file 98, 108
showmount 492
shutdown 41–42, 215
shutting the system down 40–42
SIG DNS records 458
signals 57–60
   see also individual signal names
   caught, blocked, or ignored 57
   CONT 61, 68
   KILL 59–60
   list of important 58
   sending to a process 60
   STOP 61, 68
   TERM 59–60
   tracing 66
   TSTP 61

Simple Network Management Protocol *see* SNMP
single-user mode
   booting to 24, 32
   bypassing 24
   entering 31
   manual booting 22, 24
   remounting the root filesystem
      24, 32
size, file attribute 84
skel directory 106
slamming, controlling in **sendmail**
   597
slapd daemon 523, 555
slave servers, NIS 512–514, 517
SLIP 320
slurpd daemon 523
SMART_HOST macro, **sendmail**
   583, 600
SmartList 554
SMB protocol *see* Samba
smb.conf file 829–831, 836, 840
smbclient 835
smbcontrol 840
smbd daemon 829, 896
smbfs filesystem 835
smbpasswd 830
smbstatus 840
SMP (symmetric multiprocessing)
   808
smrsh email delivery agent 533,
   585, 605–606
SMTP protocol 532, 618, 625, 827
smtpd 897
smtpd/smtpfwdd 540
smurf attacks 317
SNMP 658–667, 900
   agents 661–662
   using Cacti 664
   CiscoWorks and 667
   community string 660
   data collection 664
   data organization 659–660
   MIBs (Management Informa-
      tion Bases) 659–660
   using Nagios 665
   NET-SNMP 661–664
   OIDs (object identifiers) 659–
      660
   RMON MIB 661
   tools 663–666
   traps 660
snmpd daemon 662, 900
snmpd.conf file 662

snmpwalk 663
SOA DNS records 392–395, 447
socket system call 80
sockets, local domain 80
soft carrier 852
soft links 80
software
   see also software package tools
   see also software packages
   configuration errors 673
   development 919–924
   engineering principles 923–924
   licenses 955
   management tools 266
   patches 677
   patents 957–958
   piracy 955
   printing 779
   recommended 266
   sharing over NFS 263
   vulnerabilities 672
software package tools
   see also package management
   see also software
   see also software packages
   alien 235
   APT 241–246
   apt-ftparchive 244
   apt-get 241–246
   apt-proxy 244
   dpkg 237
   high level 237–247
   RHN (Red Hat Network) 240
   rpm 235–237
   /etc/apt/sources.list file 242–
      243
   yum 246
software packages
   see also software
   see also software package tools
   dependencies 265
   installers 234
   list of 267
   localizations 255–260
   management 234–247
   namespaces 264
   repositories 239
   revision control 248–255
   RPM format 235
software RAID 139
Sony rootkits 951
sortlist option, DNS 428
source routing 317
/etc/apt/sources.list file 242–243

SOX (Sarbanes-Oxley Act) 675, 956, 960
spam
  amavisd virus filter 637
  blacklists 594–595, 598
  danger of replying to 588, 598
  eliminating using DNS 403
  email header checking 595–596
  fighting 598–599
  greylisting 636
  mobile spammers 598
  Postfix 634–637
  relaying 589–591
  Sender ID 599
  sendmail control features 588–598
  Spam Cop 598
  SpamAssassin 598
  SPF 403, 599
  web resources for fighting 598
Spam Cop 598
SpamAssassin 598
speed, setting for a network interface *see* **mii-tool**
SPF (Sender Policy Framework) 403, 599
split DNS 438–439, 441–444
squatting, domain 380
Squid web cache 733–734, 955
SRV DNS records 402–403, 464
SSH 697–698
  forwarding for X 747–748
  security 685
  Windows clients 821
  X forwarding 823
ssh 697
sshd daemon 697, 898
/etc/sshd_config file 698, 823
SSL 730–732
stackers, tape media 167
Stafford, Stephen 11
standards 958–960
  COBIT (Control Objectives for Information and related Technology) 960
  data center 800
  Ethernet 277, 352
  FHS (Filesystem Hierarchy Standard) 75
  IEEE 802.* 278, 352, 356, 358–359
  Internet 274–275
  ISO/IEC 27001 675

standards *continued*
  ITIL (Information Technology Interface Library) 960
  Linux 958–960
  LSB (Linux Standard Base) 959
  network management 658
  POSIX 959
  security 675–676
  Windows email and web compliance 827
star 197
StarOffice 826
startup files 105–106
startup scripts 32–40
  bootstrapping 32–40
  CUPS 773, 780
  examples 34, 38
  init and 22, 32, 38, 40
  /etc/init.d directory 34–35, 38, 40
  NFS server 489
  sendmail 38
startx 743
statd daemon 486
stateful inspection firewalls 703
static electricity 793
static routes 294, 303–305
statistics
  BIND 473
  CPU 808
  network 649–654
  NFS 495
  performance 816
  reporting 816
  sendmail 615
STD documents 275
sticky bit 82–83
STOP signal 58, 61, 68
Stow, GNU 266
STP cables 844
strace 66
straight-through serial cables 846–847
stty 852, 860–862
stunnel 699–701
su 48
subdomains, DNS 383
submission agents, email (MSA) 533
submit.cf file 559, 566
subnet masks *see* networks, netmasks
subnetting 282–285
Subversion 253–255

sudo 48–51, 97, 206
sudo.log file 206
/etc/sudoers file 49–50
superblocks 126
superuser *see* root account
SUSE network configuration 309
svn 254
svnserve daemon, Subversion 253
svnserve.conf file 254
swap space 124, 129, 138, 812, 814
swapon 128, 138, 812, 814
swatch 220
switch file 420, 479
switches 353, 356–358, 360
Swpkg 266
symbolic links 77, 80
symmetric multiprocessing (SMP) 808
sync command 42
sync system call 42, 126
synchronization of clocks 902
synchronizing files
  copying 505
  rdist 505–508
  rsync 508–510
  wget/ftp/expect 510–511
/proc/sys directory 874
/sys directory 872
/etc/sysconfig directory 37–38, 309
sysctl 874
/etc/sysctl.conf file 316, 874
sysfs virtual filesystem 872, 882
syslog 209–220
  see also log files
  see also logging
  actions 213
  alternatives 209
  architecture 210
  central server 214, 216
  configuration examples 214–217
  configuring 210–213
  debugging 217–218
  and DNS logging 466–471
  DOS attack via 213
  example using Perl 220
  facility names 212
  libraries 218–220
  output 216
  programming interface 218–220
  remote logging 685
  restarting 210
  security 214

syslog *continued*
  setup 214
  severity levels 212
  software that uses 218
  /etc/syslog.conf file 204, 210–
    216
  syslogd daemon 203, 210–213,
    901
  time stamps 211
syslog routine 210, 218
/etc/syslog.conf file 204, 210–216,
  620
syslogd daemon 203, 210–213, 901
syslog-ng 209
system administration 18
  see also hardware
  see also security
  see also system administration
    group responsibilities
  automation 922–924
  checklists 943
  configuring multiple machines
    502
  development 919–924
  disaster recovery 163, 938–943
  documentation 930–934
  emergency power supplies 940
  essential tasks 16–18
  Internet resources 13
  keeping users happy 904–906
  legal issues 949–958
  list of email tasks 530
  local scripts 922–924
  management 907–915
  operations 924–926
  orgs and conferences 964–967
  personality syndrome 18
  policy agreements 948
  purchasing hardware 782–787,
    916–917
  role of 915–919
  SOX (Sarbanes-Oxley Act) 956
  support 927–930
  survey results 968
  testing solutions 910
  toolbox 800, 922–923
  trouble ticketing and tracking
    935–938
system administration roles
  administration 915–919
  development 919–924
  management 906–915
  operations 924–927
  support 927–930

system configuration 255–263
  see also hardware
  see also Linux installation
  see also system administration
  Arusha Project 261
  cfengine 260
  CIM (Common Information
    Model) 262
  LCFG (large-scale configuration
    system) 261
  management 260–263
  Template Tree 2 262
system-config-kickstart 231
system-config-netboot 226

T

talk 900
talkd daemon 900
Tanenbaum, Andrew S. 5
tape drives, device names 873
tapes, backup
  see also media, backup
  4mm 166
  8mm 166
  AIT 166
  blocking factor 177
  copying 178
  DDS/DAT 166
  device files 171
  DLT/S-DLT 166
  library, robotic 179
  LTO 167
  positioning 178
  SAIT 166
  stackers 167
  VXA/VXA-X 167
tar 177–178
target number, SCSI 117
TCP
  connection states 651
  vs. UDP for NFS 485
  wrappers 887
TCP/IP 271, 275–281
  CIDR (Classless Inter-Domain
    Routing) 283, 286–288
  fancy options (SACK, ECN) 307
  fragmentation 279, 646
  history 272
  IPsec 949
  IPv6 286, 291–293
  loopback interface 282, 294,
    302, 397

TCP/IP *continued*
  NAT 290–291, 319
  netmasks 282–285
  network model 276
  packet encapsulation 276–277
  ports 281
  protocol suite 275–276
  subnetting 282–285
  TOS bits 330
tcpd daemon 887
tcpdump 656
tcpflow 657
telinit 32, 42, 857, 887
telnet 346
TELNET protocol 898
Tel-splice connector 852
Template Tree 2, system configuration 262
temporary files, removing 154
Tera Term Pro 821
TERM environment variable 859,
  861
TERM signal 58–60
/etc/termcap file 858–859
Terminal Server service, Windows
  825
terminals 855–859
  capability databases 858–859
  control 56
  secure 685
  setting options 860–862
  special characters 859–862
  unwedging 862
terminators, SCSI 117
/etc/terminfo file 858
Terry, Douglas 376
testing, system 257
testparm 830
Texinfo 11
TFTP 312, 899
tftp 347
Thomas, Eric 554
threads, kernel 23
TIA (Telecommunications Industry
  Association) 354
TightVNC 824
time synchronization 902–903
tip 864
TLS *see* SSL
TLT/S-DLT tapes 166
/tmp directory 75
/tmp partition 125
tools, hardware 800
top 65, 809, 817

top-level domains 379, 381
topology statement, DNS 428
Torvalds, Linus 5
traceroute 647–649
tracks and sectors, disks 120
transfers-in option, DNS 425
transfer-source option, DNS 426, 445
transfers-out option, DNS 425
transfers-per-ns option, DNS 425
transport agents, email 532
Tridgell, Andrew 508, 828
Troan, Erik 208
Trojan horses 687
Trojnara, Michal 699
trouble ticketing and tracking 935–938
troubleshooting
    Bacula 195–196
    BIND 466–478
    CUPS 780–782
    named 466–478
    network hardware, cable analyzers 366
    network hardware, sniffers 366
    network hardware, T-BERD line analyzer 366
    network printing 781
    networks 366, 644–654
    networks with **mii-tool** 302–303
    Postfix 637–639
    printers 780–782
    RAID 144–145
    runaway processes 67–69
    Samba 840–841
    SCSI 118
    sendmail 615–621
    serial line 864–865
    sluggish system 817–819
    syslog 217–218
    wedged terminal 862
    X Window System 754–757
    Xorg X server 754–757
trusted-keys statement, DNS 430
TrustedUser **sendmail** user account 603
Ts'o, Theodore 120
tset 861–862
TSIG (transaction signatures) 444, 453–456
Tsirigotis, Panos 887

TSM (Tivoli Storage Manager) 197
TSTP signal 58, 61
TTL (time to live), packets 647
$TTL directive, DNS 390, 394, 406
TTL for DNS resource records 390
tune2fs 121, 132
tuning
    IDE disks 130
    the kernel 314–316, 874
    network parameters 314–316
    NFS 494
TUX server 727
Tweedie, Stephen 120
TXT DNS records 403, 424
typographic conventions 9–10

U

U (rack unit) 791
Ubuntu network configuration 310
udev 79
udev system 872
udev.conf directory 872
udevd 872, 899
UDP (User Datagram Protocol) 271, 275, 485
UIDs see user IDs
Ultr@VNC project 824
Ultra SCSI see SCSI
umask 86, 105
umount 73, 129, 494
uname 881
undeliverable messages, **sendmail** 613
unicast addresses 292
Uninterruptible Power Supply (UPS) 799
UNIX vs. Linux 4
unlink system call 80
unshielded twisted pair see UTP cables
unsolicited commercial email see spam
update-policy clause, DNS 450
update-rc.d 40
updating zone files, DNS 447–450
upgrades 176–177
uptime 808, 818
URLs 720–721
us domain 380

USB 865–866
    device identification 869
    disks 112, 147–148, 165
    printers 774, 781
    RS-232 adapters 865
    in place of SCSI 115
    supported devices 784
use_cw_file feature, **sendmail** 574
USENIX association 965–966, 968
user accounts
    adding 102–107, 109
    aliases, global (email) 95
    authentication under Samba 832
    bin 51
    daemon 51
    deleting 110
    disabling 108
    email home machine 106
    ftp 735
    GECOS information 98
    guest 944
    home directories 75, 98, 105
    hygiene 93
    ID number see user IDs
    login process 46
    login shell 98
    modifying 109
    names 94–95
    nobody (NFS) 51, 488
    passwords 104
    pseudo-users 51
    removing 107
    root see root account
    sendmail use of 603
    shared 680
    site-wide management 944
    startup files 105
    superuser see root account
user agents, email 531
User Datagram Protocol see UDP
user IDs 45, 54–55, 96–97, 104
useradd 102, 109
userdel 110
usermod 99, 109
usernames see user accounts, names
users
    see also user accounts
    documentation 934
    keeping them happy 904–906
    policy agreements 946–948
/usr directory 75
UTP cables 353–355, 366, 844

V

V.90 modem standard 863
van den Berg, Stephen R. 554, 585
/var filesystem 75, 125
variables, initializing in startup files 105
vendor logos 10
vendors we like 371–372
Venema, Wietse 623, 856
VeriSign Site Finder tool 429
Veritas, backup tool 198
VERSIONID macro, **sendmail** 570
VFS (Virtual File System) 120
vgcreate LVM utility 143
vgdisplay LVM utility 143, 146
vgscan LVM utility 143
Viega, John 553
view statement, DNS 438
.vimrc file 105
vipw 103
virtual domains, Postfix 630–632
Virtual File System (VFS) 120
virtual hosts, web 727–730
virtual memory (VM) 124, 129, 810–811
Virtual Network Computing see VNC protocol
virtual network interfaces 300
virtual private networks see VPNs
virtual terminals and X 754–755
VirtualHost clause, Apache 729
virtusertable feature, **sendmail** 579–580
viruses 686–687
visudo 50
Vixie, Paul 150, 376
Vixie-**cron** see **cron** daemon
VLANs 357
vmlinuz file 29, 75
vmstat 807–808, 818
VMware 825
VNC protocol 824
vncserver 824
VPNs (virtual private networks) 318, 328, 708–710
    IPsec tunnels 709
    SSH tunnels 709
VRFY command 588
VT100 terminal 858
VXA/VXA-X backup tapes 167

W

wait system call 57
Wall, Larry 388
WANs 351
Ward, Grady 47
WarGames 669
warranties 793
Warsaw, Barry 553
Wassenaar, Eric 474
Watchguard Firebox 319
WBEM (Web-Based Enterprise Management) standard 658
web see World Wide Web
Web 2.0 719
web hosting 719–734
    Apache 724–732
    Apache configuration 726–732
    Apache installation 724–726
    caching server 733–734
    certificates 731–732
    CGI scripting 722
    httpd 901
    IIS (Windows) 827
    load balancing 385, 722–724
    log files 727
    performance 722–724
    proxy server 733–734
    Squid cache 733–734
    SSL 730–732
    static content 727
    TUX 727
    virtual interfaces 727–730
Weeks, Alex 11
well-known ports 688, 702
Wheeler, David A. 55
whereis 15
which 15
white pages 901
Win4Lin 826
WINCH signal 58–59
Windows
    see also Samba
    accessing remote desktops 822–825
    ACLs 833
    automounter 834
    backups 197
    DFS (Distributed File System) 834
    dual booting 826
    email and web standards compliance 827

Windows *continued*
    FAT filesystems 120
    IMAP 828
    Kerberos server and DNS 464
    logging in from 821–822
    mounting Windows filesystems 835
    multibooting with LINUX 30–31
    Network Neighborhood browsing using Samba 831
    POP (Post Office Protocol) 828
    printing 838–839
    RDP (Remote Desktop Protocol) 824
    running Linux programs from 822–823
    running under VMware 825
    running Windows programs under Linux 825
    sharing files 828
    SMTP 827
    SSH clients 821
    Terminal Server service 825
    UNIX software running on 827
    VNC servers 824
    Wine project 825
    X forwarding 823
    X Window System servers 823, 827
    xterm for 827
Wine project 825
Winmodems 863
WinPrinters 783
WINS server, Samba 831
WinSCP 822
wireless networks see networks, wireless
wiring see network wiring
Wireshark packet sniffer 366, 657
Wirzenius, Lars 11
WKS DNS records 403
workstations, diskless 898
World Wide Web
    see also web hosting
    browsers 720
    HTTP protocol 720–722
    URLs 720
wrapper scripts for localization 265
wtmp file 206
WU-FTPD 900
wvdial 325
WWW see World Wide Web

X

X display manager 743–744
X Window System
  see also **Xorg** X server
  architechture 742
  client authentication 745–746
  desktop environments 757–759
  DISPLAY environment variable
    744, 748
  display manager 743–744
  history 741–742
  killing the X server 755
  magic cookies 746
  running an application 744–748
  security 744–748
  security under Windows 823
  SSH and 747–748
  startup files 105
  terminal window 859
  troubleshooting 754–757
  virtual terminals 754–755
  Windows servers 823, 827
  X forwarding 823
  X server output 755–756
/etc/X11 directory 743
X11 *see* X Window System
xargs 72
xauth 746
.Xclients file 105
.Xdefaults file 105
xdm directory 743
xdm program 743
xdpyinfo 756
xdvi 785
XFS filesystem 122
xhost 745–746
XHTML 764
xinetd 887–890
  configuring 888–890
  ftpd and 735
  /etc/services file 892–893
  /etc/xinetd.conf file 888–890
/etc/xinetd.conf file 888
/etc/xinetd.d directory 888
xinit 743
.xinitrc file 105
xntpd 62
XON/XOFF 852–853
Xorg X server 748–754
  configuring 748–754
  debugging 754–757
  logging 755–757

xdpyinfo 756
/etc/X11/xorg.conf file 749–754
  xorgconfig 749
/etc/X11/xorg.conf file 749–754
xorgconfig 749
XORP (eXtensible Open Router
  Platform) 344
Xsession 743
~/.xsession file 105, 743
xtab file 489, 895
xterm console emulator 827

Y

Yellow Pages *see* NIS
Ylönen, Tatu 697
Yost serial wiring system 850–852
Yost, Dave 850
/var/yp file 512
yp* commands 513–518
/etc/yp.conf file 512
ypbind daemon 896
ypserv daemon 896
ypxfr 896
yum 246

Z

Zebra routing package 344
Zhou, Songnian 376
Zimmermann, Philip 696
zombie processes 56, 61, 63, 886
zone statement, DNS 432–436
zones, DNS 388, 412
  commands 405–407
  files 389
  incremental transfers 388, 429
  IXFRs 447
  linkage 407–409
  signed, creating 458
  transfers 413, 425, 447–448
  updating files 447–450
zone-statistics option, DNS 433

About the Contributors

Lynda McGinley has been doing system and network administration for 20 years in an educational environment and was a contributor to the third edition of the *UNIX System Administration Handbook*. She currently works at the University Corporation for Atmospheric Research as a system security engineer. Lynda believes she will be best remembered for being Evi's sysadmin for a number of years at the University of Colorado. :-)

Ben Whaley is a senior engineer at Applied Trust Engineering. He holds a degree in computer science from the University of Colorado and is a Red Hat Certified Engineer. In addition to dirtying his hands with Perl and PHP programming, Ben is a mentor in the Big Brother Big Sister program.

Adam Boggs was a student administrator in the trenches at the University of Colorado's undergraduate lab through the late 1990s. He has spent the past several years as a kernel developer working on filesystems and storage for Solaris and Linux. He is currently working as a network, storage, and cluster administrator for supercomputers used in atmospheric modeling.

Jeffrey S. Haemer (jsh@usenix.org) has been doing commercial UNIX and Linux work since 1983 and has still never used Microsoft Word. Eleven of those years were at various incarnations of the printer manufacturer QMS. Evi taught Jeff to drive. His favorite palindrome is, "A man, a plan, a canal, Suez."

Tobi Oetiker (tobi@oetiker.ch) is an electrical engineer by education and a system administrator by vocation. He has been working in system administration since 1994. After furnishing a deluxe computing environment to the students and staff of ETH Zurich for years and writing a few popular open source applications such as MRTG, RRDtool, and SmokePing, he is now working at Oetiker+Partner AG, a provider of IT and consulting services. He is married and lives in Switzerland. More information about Tobi can be found at tobi.oetiker.ch.

Fritz Zaucker is a physicist by training. After a few years of climate change research, he spent the last 10 years leading the IT Support Group (ISG.EE) at the Department of Information Technology and Electrical Engineering at ETH Zurich. Together with a group of dedicated coworkers, he transformed ISG.EE into a professional organization focused on efficient system administration, reliable IT infrastructure, and customer satisfaction. He has now joined some of his friends and colleagues at Oetiker+Partner AG, an IT and management consulting firm and provider of IT services. Please visit Fritz at www.zaucker.ch. Fritz sailed with Evi and her nieces in the Mediterranean and wholeheartedly recommends your joining her on *Wonderland*.

Scott Seidel is a senior engineer at Applied Trust Engineering, where he specializes in enterprise security and performance management. He holds a degree in business administration with areas of emphasis in information systems and in finance from the University of Colorado at Boulder. Scott's research interests include system monitoring and server virtualization. When not administering Linux systems, Scott can be found in the kitchen perfecting a new homebrew.

Bryan Buus is the vice president of engineering at Adeptive Software, a custom software development company. Before the dot-com bust, Bryan was vice president of development at XOR, leading the firm's web and Internet services division. Bryan holds a bachelors and masters degree in computer science from Boston University.

Ned McClain (ned@atrust.com) is co-founder and CTO of Applied Trust Engineering. He lectures about various system administration and security topics at technical conferences such as USENIX in the United States and APRICOT in Asia. Ned has a degree in computer science from Cornell University's College of Engineering and is CISSP #39389.

David Schweikert works as system administrator at ETH Zurich in Switzerland, where he is, among others, responsible for the email system for the Department for Electrical Engineering. He is the developer of the open source projects Mailgraph (a tool that plots mail statistics) and Postgrey (a greylisting implementation for Postfix). David is also interested in databases and large-site system administration.